Frontiers of Infant Psychiatry

VOLUME II

FRONTIERS OF INFANT PSYCHIATRY

VOLUME II

Justin D. Call, M.D.

Eleanor Galenson, M.D.

Robert L. Tyson, M.D.

EDITORS

Basic Books, Inc., Publishers

NEW YORK

1984

Library of Congress Cataloging in Publication Data
(Revised for volume 2)
Main entry under title:

Frontiers of infant psychiatry.

　Includes bibliographies and indexes.
　Vol. 2 contains papers presented at the First World
Congress on Infant Psychiatry, Cascais, Portugal, 1980,
and v. 2 contains papers presented at the Second World
Congress on Infant Psychiatry, Cannes, France, 1983.
　　1.　Infant psychiatry — Congresses.　2.　Child development
— Congresses.　I.　Call, Justin D.　II.　Galenson, Eleanor,
1916-　　　　　III.　Tyson, Robert L.　IV.　World Congress on
Infant Psychiatry (1st : 1980 : Cascais, Portugal)
V.　World Congress on Infant Psychiatry (2nd : 1983 :
Cannes, France) [DNLM: 1. Child psychiatry — Congresses.
2.　Child development — Congresses.　3.　Infant — Congresses
WS 350 F935 1980]
RJ502.5.F76　1983　　　618.92'89　　　81-68792
ISBN　0-465-02585-4　(v. I)
ISBN　0-465-02586-2　(v. II)

CONTENTS

PART I

Developmental Issues in Infancy

PART II

Perinatal Research and Clinical Applications

PART III

Clinical and Research Aspects of the Infant-Caregiver Relationship

PART IV

The Infant-Caregiver Relationship: Fathers and Infancy

PART V

Psychopathological Issues

EDITORS

Justin D. Call, M.D., Professor and Chief of Child and Adolescent Psychiatry, Professor of Pediatrics, College of Medicine, University of California, Irvine; Training and Supervising Analyst, San Diego Psychoanalytic Institute, San Diego, California.

Eleanor Galenson, M.D., Clinical Professor of Psychiatry, Mount Sinai School of Medicine, New York City; New York Psychoanalytic Institute and Society. Faculty, Columbia University Center for Psychoanalytic Training and Research.

Robert L. Tyson, M.D., F.R.C.Psych., Clinical Professor of Psychiatry, College of Medicine, University of California, Irvine; Training and Supervising Analyst (adult and child), San Diego Psychoanalytic Institute, San Diego, California; Senior Faculty, Los Angeles Psychoanalytic Society and Institute, Los Angeles, California.

ASSOCIATE EDITORS

EDITORIAL BOARD

FRENCH EDITORIAL COMMITTEE

CONTRIBUTORS

Thomas Achenbach, Ph.D., Professor of Child Psychiatry and Psychology, Department of Psychiatry, University of Vermont, College of Medicine, Burlington, Vermont.

Heidelise Als, Ph.D., Assistant Professor of Pediatrics (Psychology), Harvard Medical School; Director of Clinical Research, Child Development Unit, Children's Hospital Medical Center, Boston, Massachusetts.

Thomas F. Anders, M.D., Professor of Psychiatry and Pediatrics; Head, Division of Child Psychiatry and Child Development, Stanford University Medical Center, Stanford, California.

E. James Anthony, M.D., Blanche F. Ittleson Professor of Child Psychiatry; Director of the Edison Child Development Research Center, Washington University School of Medicine, St. Louis, Missouri; Training Analyst, St. Louis Psychoanalytic Institute.

Peter Barglow, M.D., Clinical Director, Department of Psychiatry, Institute for Psychosomatic and Psychiatric Research and Training, Michael Reese Hospital and Medical Center; Associate Professor, Department of Psychiatry, Pritzker School of Medicine, University of Chicago, Chicago, Illinois.

Marthe Barracco, Psychologist, Unité de Soins Spécialisés à Domicile pour Jeunes Enfants, Paris XIII, France

M. Patricia Boyle, Ph.D., Associate Director of Child Psychiatry, Cambridge Hospital, Cambridge, Massachusetts; Instructor in Psychology, Harvard Medical School, Boston, Massachusetts.

T. Berry Brazelton, M.D., Chief, Child Development Unit, Children's Hospital Medical Center; Associate Professor of Pediatrics, Harvard Medical School, Boston, Massachusetts.

John Brennan, M.B.B.S., M.R.A.N.Z.C.P., 1981–82 Visiting Research Fellow in Child Psychiatry of the New South Wales Institute of Psychiatry.

Maddy Brenot, M.D., Ancien Chef de Clinique de Psychiatrie, Responsable de l'Unité de Pédo-Psychiatrie de l'Hôpital d'Enfants, Dijon, France.

Jean-Louis Brenot, M.D., Ancien Chef de Clinique de Psychiatrie, Directeur du Centre Psycho-Médico-Pédagogique de l'Académie de Dijon, France.

Elsie R. Broussard, M.D., Dr. P.H., Director, Pittsburgh First-Born Project; Professor of Public Health Psychiatry, Department of Health Services Administration, Graduate School of Public Health; Associate Professor of Child Psychiatry, Department of Psychiatry, School of Medicine, University of Pittsburgh, Pittsburgh, Pennsylvania.

Lisbeth F. Brudal, dr. philos., Assistant Professor, Institute of Psychology, University of Oslo, Norway.

Yannick Buffet, M.D., Pédiatre, Psychiatre, Ancien Intern des Hôpitaux Psychiatriques de la Seine, Attaché de Consultation à la Clinique de Psychiatrie de l'Enfant et de l'Adolescent, Hôpital de la Salpêtrière, Paris, France.

Justin D. Call, M.D., Professor and Chief of Child and Adolescent Psychiatry, Professor of Pediatrics, College of Medicine, University of California, Irvine; Training and Supervising Analyst, Los Angeles Psychoanalytic Society and Institute, Los Angeles, California.

Olivia Capers, M.D., Clinical Assistant Professor, Department of Mental Health Sciences, Hahnemann Medical College, Philadelphia, Pennsylvania.

Jude Cassidy, M.A., Department of Psychology, University of Virginia, Charlottesville, Virginia.

Marie Choquet, Ph.D., Psychologue, Chargé

de Récherche à l'Institut National de la Santé et de la Récherche Médicale, Paris, France.

Barbro Cornut-Zimmer, Ph.D., FNRS Researcher, Centre d'Étude de la Famille, Clinique Psychiatrique Universitaire, Hôpital de Cery, Prilly, Switzerland.

Carl Corter, Ph.D., Professor of Psychology, University of Toronto.

Eugene J. D'Angelo, Ph.D., Staff Psychologist, Children's Hospital Medical Center/Judge Baker Guidance Center; Instructor in Psychology, Harvard Medical School, Boston, Massachusetts.

Myriam David, M.D., Directeur, Centre Familial d'Action Thérapeutique, Soisy sur Seine, France; Directeur, Unité de Soins Spécialisés à Domicile pour Jeunes Enfants, Paris, France.

Françoise Davidson, M.D., Maître de Récherche, Directeur de l'Unité de Récherche sur les Sociopathies, Institut National de la Santé et de la Récherche Medicale, Paris, France.

Peter de Château, M.D., Associate Professor, Department of Pediatrics and Child Psychiatry, Karolinska Hospital and Karolinska Institute, Stockholm, Sweden.

Didier-Jacques Duche, M.D., Professeur de Psychiatrie de l'Enfant et de l'Adolescent, Université Paris VI, Médecin des Hôpitaux de Paris, Hôpital de la Salpêtrière, Paris, France; Ancien Secrétaire Général de l'International Association for Child Psychiatry and Allied Professions.

Madame Georgina Dufoix, Secrétaire d'État Chargée de la Famille de la Population, et des Travailleurs Immigrés, Ministère des Affaires Sociales et de la Solidarité Nationale, Government of France.

Robert N. Emde, M.D., Professor of Psychiatry, University of Colorado Medical School, Denver, Colorado; Adjunct Professor, University of Denver.

Tiffany Field, Ph.D., Associate Professor of Pediatrics and Psychology, Mailman Center for Child Development, University of Miami Medical School, Miami, Florida.

Loretta P. Finnegan, M.D., Director of Family Center; Associate Professor of Pediatrics, and of Psychiatry and Human Behavior, Thomas Jefferson University Hospital, Philadelphia, Pennsylvania.

Elisabeth Fivaz, Ph.D., Teaching and Research Coordinator, Centre d'Étude de la Famille, Clinique Psychiatrique Universitaire, Hôpital de Cery, Prilly, Switzerland.

Judy Florsheim, M.S., Research Psychologist, Henry Ittleson Center for Child Research, New York City.

Juarlyn L. Gaiter, Ph.D., Departments of Neonatology and Pediatric Psychology, Children's Hospital National Medical Center, Director of Pediatric Psychology Research Laboratory; Assistant Professor of Child Health and Development, School of Medicine and Health Sciences, George Washington University School of Medicine and Health Sciences, Washington, D.C.

Richard Galdston, M.D., Assistant Clinical Professor of Psychiatry, Harvard Medical School; Faculty, Boston Psychoanalytic Society and Institute, Boston, Massachusetts.

Eleanor Galenson, M.D., Clinical Professor of Psychiatry, Mount Sinai School of Medicine, New York City; New York Psychoanalytic Institute and Society; Faculty, Columbia University Center for Psychoanalytic Training and Research.

Margaret P. Gean, M.D., Director, Infant/Toddler Program, New England Medical Center; Assistant Professor of Psychiatry, Division of Child Psychiatry, Tufts University School of Medicine, Boston, Massachusetts.

Françoise Gerstle, M.D., Psychiatrie Assistant, Clinique de Psychiatrie de l'Enfant et de l'Adolescent, Hôpital de la Salpêtrière, Paris, France.

Susan Goldberg, Ph.D. Research Scientist, The Hospital for Sick Children; Associate Professor of Psychology and Psychiatry, University of Toronto, Toronto, Canada.

Nathan Goldfarb, Ph.D., Statistical Consultant, Henry Ittleson Center for Child Research; Director of Quality Assurance, Rockland Children's Psychiatric Center, Orangeburg, New York.

William Goldfarb, M.D., Ph.D., Director, Henry Ittleson Center for Child Research; Clinical Professor Emeritus of Psychiatry, College of Physicians and Surgeons, Columbia University, New York City.

Peter A. Gorski, M.D., Director, Developmental and Behavioral Pediatrics, Mount Zion Hospital and Medical Center, San Francisco, California.

Stanley Grand, Ph.D., Clinical Associate Professor; Associate Program Director, Program of Research and Training in Psychiatry and Clinical Behavior, Department of Psychiatry, Downstate Medical Center, State University of New York, Brooklyn, New York.

Leonard Graziani, M.D., Professor of Pediatrics and Neurology, Thomas Jefferson University Hospital, Philadelphia, Pennsylvania.

Roger Hatcher, Ph.D., Assistant Professor, Departments of Pediatrics and Psychiatry, Northwestern University Medical School, Evanston, Illinois.

James M. Herzog, M.D., Director of Training and Child Psychiatry, Children's Hospital Medical Center and Judge Baker Guidance Center; Assistant Professor of Psychiatry, Harvard Medical School, Boston, Massachusetts.

Robert A. Hinde, Sc.D., F.R.S., Royal Society Research Professor at the University of Cambridge; Honorary Director of the Medical Research Council Unit on the Development and Integration of Behavior, Fellow of St. John's College, Cambridge, England.

David C. Howell, Ph.D., Professor of Psychology, Department of Psychology, University of Vermont, Burlington, Vermont.

Helga Huth, Ph.D., Research Assistant, Children's Hospital, Free University of Berlin, Berlin, West Germany.

Catherine D. Isserlis, Medical Assistant, Joint Mother-Child Hospitalization, Creteil, France.

Françoise Jardin, M.D., Unité de Soins Spécialisés à Domicile pour Jeunes Enfants, Paris XIII, France.

Lyle Joffe, Ph.D., Staff Psychologist, Pritzker Children's Psychiatric Unit, Department of Psychiatry, Michael Reese Hospital and Medical Center; Clinical Associate, University of Illinois, Chicago, Illinois.

Alix A. S. Johnson, Ph.D., Consulting Psychologist, Children's Hospital National Medical Center, Department of Psychiatry, Washington, D.C.

Karol A. Kaltenbach, Ph.D., Developmental Psychologist, Family Center, Department of Pediatrics, Thomas Jefferson University Hospital, Philadelphia, Pennsylvania.

Kirk A. Keegan, Jr., M.D., Assistant Professor, Associate Director, Division of Maternal-Fetal Medicine at the University of California Irvine Medical Center, Orange, California.

John H. Kennell, M.D., Professor of Pediatrics, Rainbow Babies' and Children's Hospital, Case Western Reserve University School of Medicine, Cleveland, Ohio.

Paulina F. Kernberg, M.D., Associate Professor of Psychiatry, Cornell University Medical College, New York, New York; Director, Child and Adolescent Psychiatry Service, The New York Hospital-Cornell Medical Center, Westchester Division, White Plains, New York; Training and Supervising Analyst, Columbia University Center for Psychoanalytic Training and Research, New York City.

Marshall H. Klaus, M.D., Professor and Chairman of Pediatrics, Michigan State University, East Lansing, Michigan.

Sabine Koch, M.D., Research Assistant, Children's Hospital, Free University of Berlin, Berlin, West Germany.

Arthur Kornhaber, M.D., Founder and Director, Foundation for Grandparenting, Mount Kisco, New York.

Léon Kreisler, M.D., Head of the Child Department, Psychosomatic Institute Hospital, Paris, France.

Lisa A. Krock, Ed.D., Staff Psychologist, South Shore Counselling Associates, Hanover, Massachusetts.

Michael E. Lamb, Ph.D., Professor of Psychology, Psychiatry, and Pediatrics, University of Utah; Director, Training Program in Developmental Psychology, University of Utah, Salt Lake City, Utah.

Serge Lebovici, M.D., Professor of Child Psychiatry, University of Paris XIII; Directeur de l'Institut Universitaire des Sciences Psychosociales et Neurobiologiques de la Faculté de Médecine de Bobigny, Bobigny, France.

Eve-Marie Léger, Psychologist, Centre Familial d'Action Thérapeutique, Soisy sur Seine, France.

Lewis P. Lipsitt, Ph.D., Professor of Psychology and Medical Science; Director, Child Study Center, Brown University, Providence, Rhode Island; Editor of *Monographs on Infancy* and *Advances in Infancy*.

Mary Main, Ph.D., Associate Professor of Psychology, University of California at Berkeley, Berkeley, California.

Emanuella Malaguzzi-Valeri, M.D., Centre Familial D'Action Thérapeutique, Soisy-sur-Seine, France.

Daniel Martin, Ph.D., FNRS Researcher, Centre d'Étude de la Famille, Clinique Psychiatrique Universitaire, Hôpital de Cery, Prilly, Switzerland.

Jay Martin, Ph.D., Research Psychoanalyst and Faculty, California Psychoanalytic Institute; Lecturer, Department of Psychiatry and Human Behavior, California College of Medicine, University of California, Irvine; Leo S. Bing Professor of Literature, University of Southern California.

Philippe Mazet, M.D., Maître de Conférence Agrégé, Université Paris VI; Médecin des Hôpitaux de Paris, Clinique de Psychiatrie de l'Enfant et de l'Adolescent, Hôpital de la Salpêtrière, Paris; Secrétaire, Société Française de Psychiatrie de l'Enfant et de l'Adolescent, France.

Anne-Marie Merlet, Educator, Centre Familial D'Action Thérapeutique, Soisy-sur-Seine, France.

Donald I. Meyers, M.D., Director of Experimental Psychiatry, Henry Ittleson Center for Child Research; Associate Clinical Professor of Psychiatry, College of Physicians and Surgeons, Columbia University, New York City.

Klaus K. Minde, M.D., F.R.C.P.(C), Professor of Research and Pediatrics, University of Toronto, Director of Psychiatric Research, The Hospital for Sick Children, Toronto, Canada.

Martine M. Morales, Psychologue Clinicienne, D.E.S.S. de Psychologie Clinique, Université de Paris-Nord, Faculté de Médecine Experimentale, Bobigny, France.

Barbara Murphy, M.S., University of Vermont, Department of Psychiatry, College of Medicine, Burlington, Vermont.

Patricia A. Nachman, Ph.D., Research Associate, Cornell University Medical College, New York Hospital; Margaret S. Mahler Assistant Professor of Psychology, New School for Social Research, New York City.

Barry Nurcombe, M.D., F.R.A.C.P., Associate Chairman, Professor and Director of Child Psychiatry, Department of Psychiatry, University of Vermont, College of Medicine, Burlington, Vermont.

Linda D. O'Neill, M.A., M.P.H., Staff Associate, Columbia University; Nurse Practitioner, Columbia-Presbyterian Hospital, New York City.

Joy D. Osofsky, Ph.D., Research and Staff Psychologist, The Menninger Foundation, Topeka, Kansas.

Marie-Françoise Pain, Psychiatric Nurse, Unité de Soins Spécialisés à Domicile pour Jeunes Enfants, Paris XIII, France.

Hanuš Papoušek, M.D., Sc.D., Professor of Developmental Psychobiology, Max Planck Institute for Psychiatry, Munich, West Germany.

Mechthild Papoušek, M.D., Research Psychiatrist, Max Planck Institute for Psychiatry, Munich, West Germany.

Matthew Pasto, M.D., Assistant Professor of Radiology, Thomas Jefferson University Hospital, Philadelphia, Pennsylvania.

Jeree H. Pawl, Ph.D., Associate Clinical Professor of Psychiatry, University of California, San Francisco; Acting Director, Infant-Parent Program, San Francisco General Hospital; Member, Board of Directors, National Center for Clinical Infant Programs.

Fiffi S. Piene, Ph.D., Chief Psychologist Nic Waals Institute for Child Psychiatry, Training and Research, Oslo, Norway; Specialist in Clinical Psychology and Psychotherapy, Norwegian Psychological Association; Training Analyst, Norwegian Psychoanalytic Institute; Member, International Psychoanalytic Association; Member, The Association for Child Psychoanalysis.

Kyle D. Pruett, M.D., Associate Clinical Professor of Psychiatry, Yale Child Study Center, New Haven, Connecticut.

Edward J. Quilligan, M.D., Professor and Chairman of Obstetrics and Gynecology, University of Wisconsin, School of Medicine, Madison, Wisconsin; Editor of *American Journal of Obstetrics and Gynecology*.

Didier Rabain, M.D., Psychiatrie Assistant, Clinique de Psychiatrie de l'Enfant et de l'Adolescent, Hôpital de la Salpêtrière, Paris, France.

Jacqueline Rabain-Jamin, Researcher at the Centre National de la Récherche Scientifique, Laboratoire de Psychologie Sociale, Université de Paris VIII, Paris, France.

Leo Rangell, M.D., Past President, American Psychoanalytic Association; Past President, International Psychoanalytic Association; Clinical Professor of Psychiatry, University of California at Los Angeles; Clinical Professor of Psychiatry (Psychoanalysis), University of California at San Francisco, California.

Shirley R. Rashkis, M.D., Clinical Assistant Professor, Department of Mental Health Sciences, Hahnemann Medical College, Philadelphia, Pennsylvania; Attending Psychiatrist, Institute of Pennsylvania Hospital.

Virginia Rauh, Sc.D., A.C.S.W., Assistant Professor of Child Psychiatry, University of Vermont, College of Medicine, Department of Psychiatry, Burlington, Vermont.

Margaret Redshaw, Research Officer/Lecturer, Perinatal Research Unit, St. Mary's Hospital, and Bedford College, University of London, London, England.

Dianne O'Malley Regan, R.N., M.S.W., Clinical Coordinator of Family Center, Department of Pediatrics, Thomas Jefferson University Hospital, Philadelphia, Pennsylvania.

Marianne Reigner, Psychologue Clinicienne, D.E.S.S. de Psychologie Clinique, Université de Paris-Nord, Faculté de Médecine Expérimentale, Bobigny, France.

Ruth Codier Resch, Ph.D., Adjunct Attending Psychologist, Memorial Sloan-Kettering Cancer Center, Cornell Medical Center, New York City.

Herman Roiphe, M.D., Associate Clinical Professor of Psychiatry, Mount Sinai College of Medicine, New York City.

Deborah Rosenblatt, Research Officer/Lecturer, Perinatal Research Unit, St. Mary's Hospital, and Bedford College, University of London, London, England.

Hano Rottman, M.D., Centre Familial D'Action Thérapeutique, Soisy-sur-Seine, France.

Paul Ruoff, M.D., Assistant Professor of Child Psychiatry, Department of Psychiatry, College of Medicine, University of Vermont, Burlington, Vermont.

Louis W. Sander, M.D., Professor of Psychiatry, University of Colorado School of Medicine, Denver, Colorado.

Janile A. R. Sanders-Woudstra, M.D., Ph.D., Professor of Child and Adolescent Psychiatry, Sophia Children's Hospital, Rotterdam; Member, International Psychoanalytic Association.

Victor D. Sanua, Ph.D., Professor, Department of Psychology, St. John's University, Jamaica, New York.

Stephen P. Seligman, D.M.H., Assistant Clinical Professor, Department of Psychiatry, University of California, San Francisco; Staff Doctor of Mental Health, Infant-Parent Program, San Francisco General Hospital; Fellow, National Center for Clinical Infant Programs.

Harriet Simonsen, M.D., Specialist in Child Psychiatry, Norwegian Medical Association; Assistant Head of Child Psychiatric Division, Buskerud Central Hospital, Norway.

Michel Soulé, M.D., Médecin-Chef du Centre de Guidance Infantile, Paris; Directeur d'Enseignement de Psychiatrie Infantile, Université de Paris V, France.

Hans-Christoph Steinhausen, M.D., Ph.D., Professor of Child and Adolescent Psychiatry and Neurology, Department of Child and Adolescent Psychiatry and Neurology, Free University of Berlin, Berlin, West Germany.

Daniel N. Stern, M.D., Professor, Department of Psychiatry; Chief, Laboratory of Developmental Processes, Cornell University Medical Center, New York Hospital, New York City.

Serge G. Stoleru, M.D., Chef de Clinique, Assistant des Hôpitaux, Université de Paris-Nord, Faculté de Médecine Expérimentale, Bobigny, France.

Lenore C. Terr, M.D., Associate Clinical Professor of Psychiatry, School of Medicine, University of California, San Francisco; Lecturer in Law and Psychiatry, The Law

Schools of the University of California at Berkeley and at Davis.

Douglas Teti, M.D., Department of Psychology, University of Vermont, Burlington, Vermont.

Sandra L. Tunis, Ph.D., Research Analyst, Thomas Jefferson University Hospital, Philadelphia, Pennsylvania.

Phyllis Tyson, Ph.D., Clinical Instructor, Department of Psychiatry, University of California at San Diego; Clinical Associate and Child Psychoanalysis Faculty, San Diego Psychoanalytic Institute, San Diego, California.

Robert L. Tyson, M.D., F.R.C.Psych., Clinical Professor of Psychiatry, College of Medicine, University of California, Irvine; Training and Supervising Analyst (adult and child), San Diego Psychoanalytic Institute, San Diego; Senior Faculty, Los Angeles Psychoanalytic Society and Institute, Los Angeles, California.

Marijke Uleman-Vleeschdrager, Ph.D., Child Psychologist, Department of Child and Ad-

olescent Psychiatry, Sophia Children's Hospital, Rotterdam, Netherlands.

Hedy Westerborg-van Loon, M.D., Trainee in Pediatrics under Professor Doctor H.K.A. Visser, Sophia Children's Hospital, Rotterdam, Netherlands.

Feizal Waffarn, M.D., Assistant Professor, Director of Neonatal Intensive Care Unit, Department of Pediatrics, University of California, Irvine, Medical Center, Orange, California.

Britt Wiberg, Psychologist, Department of Child and Youth Psychiatry, University Hospital, Umea, Sweden.

Michael W. Yogman, M.D., M.Sc., Assistant Professor of Pediatrics, Harvard Medical School; Associate Chief, Division of Child Development, The Children's Hospital, Boston, Massachusetts

Charles H. Zeanah, M.D., Chief Resident and Research Fellow in Child Psychiatry, Division of Child Psychiatry and Child Development, Stanford University School of Medicine, Stanford, California.

FOREWORD

Infant Psychiatry in a Changing World: Optimism and Paradox

The contributions of this volume, like those of its predecessor, give ample evidence that infant psychiatry is an emerging area of vital importance. The topic of infancy captures our imagination, and, increasingly, it also demands our clinical attention. Infants represent our "new beginning," they are inherently attractive to us, and they can be a source of enormous pleasure as they respond to our caregiving, as we play with them, and as we participate in the experience of their growth. But infants are also vulnerable, subject to parental abuse and neglect, to "turning off" and what appears to be depression, as well as to a variety of adaptive difficulties involving feeding, sleeping, and behavioral regulation. Adaptive difficulties are especially apt to involve physically and mentally handicapped infants, infants born prematurely, and infants with particular temperaments. Still other adaptive difficulties occur in infants born to parents with certain diseases, infants born into particular family constellations, and infants in disadvantaged environments. Conditions such as these interfere with the new beginning. Consequently, in this changing world we are becoming more appreciative that infants need our professional help.

Those diverse professionals who identify themselves with the area of infant psychiatry share a concern both with mental health and with the special problems of adaptation in infancy. There is a shared sense of uncertainty, but there is also optimism. Though there are

many unanswered questions about development and many puzzles for our clinical science, these papers document new knowledge and an exciting sense that important answers will soon inform our clinical judgments.

Orientation in a New Discipline

In orienting oneself to infant psychiatry, one encounters a number of apparent contradictions or paradoxes. The first has to do with the name itself, both in terms of "infant" and "psychiatry." Clearly, the commitment that joins the professionals in this volume is one involving more than infants. It includes a concern for mother, father, and family, as well. Further, the commitment to infancy goes beyond psychiatry. It involves a variety of other disciplines concerned with understanding and bettering conditions related to problems of adaptation and of psychopathology in infancy. These include health-related disciplines, such as pediatrics, psychoanalysis, clinical psychology, social work, and special education, as well as more basic scientific disciplines, such as developmental psychology, psychobiology, basic education, and family studies. At our first Congress, at which the problems of professional identity were discussed, including the common commitment of those from so many disciplines, Lebovici (1980) aptly commented that this new area is "transdisciplinary" rather than "interdisciplinary." The common commitment of those from multiple disciplines provides a tension and an air of excitement—the dynamics, if you will, for change and progress.

Another paradox in our orientation concerns our dual focus on illness and, more optimistically, on health and development. It is through immersion in the troubles and disorders of infancy that we gain a sense of how much can be done. Because of the potentialities of development and because infants reach to our core for nurturing, empathy, and a sense of "a new beginning," we recurrently have a feeling of optimism about our work in this area. Adding to that feeling is the enormous developmental thrust in infancy which often seems to carry us along. Research shows there are strong self-righting tendencies for important developmental functions in infancy; even in the face of severe handicaps (for example, congenital blindness, deafness, cerebral palsy, infant physical trauma or deprivation) infants can achieve self-awareness, object permanence, and major social emotional milestones in an adequate environment. The infant's adaptability is truly inspiring. Given half a chance by the social surround, an infant will show us (and involve us in) major developmental gains. Selma Fraiberg (1980) wrote about this compellingly in her book, *Clinical Studies in Infant Mental Health.* Commenting on the possible therapeutic gains in both troubled parents and their infants, she said, "It's a little bit like having God on your side," as a way of expressing the gratifying nature of this work. Even in the midst of poverty, helplessness, and despair, and in the face of major handicap, there is much that can be done.

Another paradox emerges from the findings of our science. The contributions in this volume summarize a great deal of our newly won knowledge about complex organizational capacities in early infancy. The newborn demonstrates much that is prepatterned and innate and, in that sense, "competent." But the more we discover about this, the more we appreciate the incompleteness of our knowledge about what is yet to develop, and the more we appreciate the importance of the caregiving environment for prevention of pathology and for buf-

fering against disorder in infancy. The paradox is that even though there is more social interconnectedness in the young infant than we had thought, there is also more vulnerability and more need for guiding and caregiving than is apparent to many.

To me it is also paradoxical that the more we appreciate "resiliency," the more we also appreciate the importance of a "good start" in infancy. Because of our expectations about the indelible effects of early experience, well-documented instances of resiliency after infantile deprivation and trauma have received considerable scientific and clinical attention. Resiliency can occur when, at some point, there is restoration of an enduring and adequate environment. But we have also become aware that this is not the whole story. An adequate sustaining environment is not always so easy to find, and there may be subtle or "sleeper" effects from untoward early experience on later emotional and social development. In general, the later development of both child and family is likely to be affected by a poor start. The more we understand about mutual or reciprocal influences between infants and their parents, the more we realize from a standpoint that is at once logical, scientific, and clinical that a good start with positive, mutually rewarding factors is a compelling rationale for early intervention (when there are signs of troubles in infancy), as well as for prevention (so that development is advantaged and buffered against later stress).

Still another paradox emerges from our recent clinical and scientific discoveries. The more we learn about infant cognitive and perceptual competence, the more we learn about the corresponding importance of ongoing emotional availability. Much of our emotional life may be built into our biology, but it cannot be taken for granted. I have elsewhere (Emde, 1980) argued that it is important for us to consider the natural rewards of infancy and what interferes with them. Just as there is a biology of pleasure for sexuality (to ensure reproduction of the species), there is also a biology of pleasure for parenting amid work, toil, and tribulations. There is much in the appearance and activity of the young infant that gives pleasure, and there are particular pleasures in parental interaction, but these can be inter-fered with. Interference can occur not only be-cause of an infant's physical handicap, but also because of specific parental fantasies, parental grief or other states of stress, and environmen-tal factors. Many of the contributions to this volume illustrate the sensitivity of the parent's emotional availability, with particular empha-sis placed on affect attunement, empathy, plea-surable exchanges, resonance, contingency ex-periences, and their variations. Emotional availability can be thought of as a barometer of developmental functioning, especially when the infant is observed with another in the fam-ily with whom there is a relationship.

This brings me back to the paradox I men-tioned earlier regarding the term *infant psychia-try*. In this volume, Robert Tyson and others allude to the arresting statement Winnicott made years ago to the effect that there is no such thing as a baby. By this Winnicott meant that the baby cannot be viewed in isolation. In his view, the baby always had to be assessed with the mother; today, most professionals would broaden this statement to emphasize that assessment must include the father and other members of the family. Perhaps the para-dox is stated most broadly of all by Madame Dufoix in her introduction: ". . . the infant is indeed within the world; this world is a world in change; and the infant himself is a maker of change." We can say that we are working in infant psychiatry, but this psychiatry *must* in-volve more than the infant for it to be in any way effective.

Our Clinical Science

The matter of mutual change and how it occurs brings us to the question of our clinical science in this area. I think it is important that we remind ourselves about the dialectical na-ture of scientific progress. Progress does not occur in a linear fashion. Typically, fortunate investigators may encounter some germs of truth; they make a discovery about certain re-lationships, and they compose a general state-ment. With time, it is then found that the gen-eral statement does not apply as simply or as

widely as was at first believed. The original statement is discovered to pertain to a more limited context. Eventually, with more re-search, the original statement may require so many exceptions that it is subsumed by a larger principle or is discarded altogether.

Three examples of this process are instruc-tive for infant psychiatry. The first concerns maternal deprivation of infants. Spitz (1946) originally stated that the relationship between infantile depression and retarded behavioral development was consequent upon maternal deprivation. Initially, it was thought that the deprivation was of *the mother;* later Spitz and others realized that the deprivation was not of *mother* but of *mothering.* A more general principle replaced the earlier, more limited one. Simi-larly, the importance of early experience was at first stated in terms that are now regarded as much too simplistic and broad. As noted above, early experience is important, but it is not generally true that the first year of life is critical or irreversible in decreeing later devel-opment, whether for strengths or psychopa-thology. In the midst of a considerable amount of longitudinal research, we are setting about to understand the particular contexts that will generate sustaining effects from particular early experiences. Now that we know more about resiliency and about mutual influences, much more can be understood about the im-portance of early experience. A new set of gen-eral statements has yet to emerge.

More can now be understood about the place of another discovery in today's changing world. In a series of extraordinary intervention studies, Klaus and Kennell and their colleagues (see review in Klaus and Kennell, 1982) have shown the salutary effects of added early to-getherness time for mothers and their new-borns. The statement of relationship was com-posed in terms of "maternal bonding," and initially it was thought that a "sensitive pe-riod" for early contact between a mother and her newborn infant was causally linked to the development of a loving parental relationship. It soon became apparent, however, that this causal link did not apply to all mothers. A cru-cial role for early contact was seen to apply only in certain limited contexts. For example, the original effects were seen in grossly disadvantaged populations, and such effects were not generally seen in advantaged populations. The hospital birthing environment, which this work helped to improve, was important in other ways. Further, as fathers were also seen as important, the original investigators came to speak of "parental bonding" instead of "maternal bonding." It may be that the concept of "maternal bonding" or "parental bonding" will soon be replaced or discarded as being more misleading than helpful in most contexts. This is the way our dialectical science works; it illustrates progress and should not be taken as a commentary on poor methods in our work or on the fragility of infancy findings.

Areas of Research Opportunity

The contributions to this volume not only provide new information. They also pose new questions for thinking about research. This situation reflects both the optimism and paradox inherent in the scientific process: as we understand more, more questions arise. Rather than listing the kinds of new questions raised by these contributions, I prefer to comment on two sets of cross-cutting issues that reflect both need and opportunity. One set has to do with nosology and the other with meaning, continuities, and the life cycle.

Although it is perhaps a less "romantic" area for research, I highlight nosology as the first research opportunity because, in order to advance knowledge in a clinical science, especially a new one, it is essential to have an adequate description of all relevant disorders. For any given disorder, a description should include not only signs and symptoms, but also their typical onset, course, and outcome. Such a nosology can then form the basis for research directed at understanding etiological factors and at developing a rational treatment. In infant psychiatry, nosology is virtually undeveloped, and establishing a nosology is no easy task. As many of the contributions in this volume illustrate, infancy presents major dilemmas for diagnosis, and it often seems difficult if not impossible to apply our traditional medical model. A discussion of some of

these issues might illuminate a research strategy for approaching nosology. Let me elaborate.

Prognosis has from Hippocratic times been a core activity in medical diagnosis and judgment. Yet, because of the plasticity of the infant, prediction is most uncertain, particularly when it involves behavioral development. Our poor predictive abilities in regard to infancy are of special concern because of the hazards of "labeling"; simply designating an early infant "problem" can play a role in the promulgation of that problem by parents and others in the environment. Usually when there are parenting difficulties we would rather emphasize strengths than weaknesses as a way of bolstering confidence, competence, and self-esteem. But whatever our strategy, we are aware of the special importance of appreciating the thrust of development in infancy; any attempt at diagnostic assessment must occur in the context of a developmental assessment. Otherwise it is uninterpretable.

One might say that the first issue is on the dimension of time—how long must a problem continue or how much do we have to predict in order for it to be called a disorder? A second diagnostic issue has to do with identification—who should get the diagnosis? This is a "systems" issue for nosology. There are strong mutual influences between infant and family members which are important in sustaining development and its disorders. Crying and difficulty sleeping in an infant, however they got started, may contribute to a distressed family and then be perpetuated. Very often attention to a parenting difficulty or a problem in the marriage leads to a disappearance of the infant problem. Who, then, should carry the diagnosis?

A third issue relevant for an infant nosology concerns the intensified influence of our social values. This affects what is considered salient (what is going well or not going well in infancy), as well as what is complained about. Not only is there a special drawing power or attractiveness about the physical appearance of the young infant, but infancy itself is colored with our high hopes and a sense of a "new beginning." This is true both in individual families, who see the infant as potentially overcoming their disappointments and fulfilling their dreams, and in a larger social sense: social injustice, it is widely thought, can be corrected by intervention in infancy. As has frequently been pointed out, there is a strong tendency to see the infant's experience as reflecting adult experience. This assumption may take several forms. We may make assumptions about particular fantasies in the infant. We may see the normal infant in terms of what we imagine we once had and lost. Or we may see the infant in terms of a valued scientific theory. Very often we also tend to see the infant as a diminished or opposite version of what we value as an ideal in an adult (Kagan et al., 1978). Indeed, our psychology and what we see as problems in infancy will be affected by our social values and our vision of developmental goals. Today, in the midst of goals for social cooperation and democratic social ideals more than authoritarian ideals, our psychology of development is action-oriented and participatory; we acknowledge sexual differences and strengths, and encourage a variety of sex roles and options for a parenting environment. We also look to biological models that point to multiple pathways in development, to "compensatory factors" in the development of the physically and mentally handicapped (Sameroff and Harris, 1979).

These problems, constituting diagnostic dilemmas for infancy, all point to the desirability of a multiaxial scheme (Call, 1983). A multiaxial diagnostic scheme can take into account different dimensions of the pathological syndrome in relation to crucial contexts which will affect the onset, course, and outcome of that syndrome. As I see it, there are at least three axes that have broad agreement for infant psychiatry. A primary axis consists of the descriptive syndromes, a secondary axis, of developmental assessment (cognitive, socioemotional, and sensorimotor), and a tertiary axis, of medical disorders (as described in the World Health Organization's 1977 classification of diseases, ICD-9). In addition, we propose a fourth essential axis: an assessment of family interactions.

One virtue of such a multiaxial scheme is that it points to directions for needed clinical research. For the first axis, we need to describe and catalogue the "common problems" in infant psychiatry as they emerge in different settings and in different parts of the world. In addition to individual descriptions, we need reliable research instruments for collecting such data. There are already such instruments in the form of symptom checklists for child behavior; these may be useful if they are extended to the first two years of life. In the second axis, that of developmental assessment, we are further ahead in having a variety of assessment techniques available to us, but there is still room for research: in combining ordinal, Piagetian approaches with normative test approaches for cognitive assessment and in developing standardized instruments for emotional and socioemotional assessment. In the third axis, we are learning more every day from technological advances which allow for earlier medical diagnoses; how medical disorders will affect mental health will be a continuing topic for research. Finally, there is a major need for research in family assessment. Currently there are only a few approaches for categorizing and assessing families in a way that is useful for diagnosis and prognosis. Research in this area is an urgent matter for infant psychiatry, with much remaining to be discovered.

MEANING, CONTINUITIES AND THE LIFE CYCLE

Other areas of research opportunity are suggested by this volume. One such area has to do with psychological meaning. The recent progress of infancy research has taken place by means of an insistence on objective behavioral measures and observations. The climate for this insistence arose, in part, as a reaction to earlier approaches to infancy in which speculative and abstract statements about the infant's experience were based on histories and reconstructions from older children and adults. This approach to knowledge about infants seemed to lead nowhere because there was no method with publicly verifiable ways of collecting evidence to choose between diverse or opposing views. But now things are different. We sense a renewed interest in the world of meaning for both infant and caregiver and predict that this will be a vigorous and productive area of research activity during the coming years. This impression comes from several directions. Infancy researchers are now increasingly beginning once again to make inferences about the infant's inner world. Even though the infant cannot tell us directly about that world, as a result of data collected directly in cognitive and socioemotional investigations, convergent operations are being used to make such inferences. An interesting time of advancing knowledge is forecast by these contributions. Appropriately, there is also a renewed interest in testing earlier clinical-intuitive theories such as those dealing with the emergence of self, with separation-individuation, and with the origins of empathy and moral sensibility.

But the renewed interest in meaning goes beyond the infant. There are promising investigations of the psychological world of the caregiver, including the role of particular caregiver experiences and unconscious fantasies in the pathogenesis and amelioration of infancy disorders. It seems important to emphasize that today's approach is direct rather than reconstructive: in assessment and intervention research, the independent variable is that of the caregiver's world of psychological meaning; and effects of change (for example, through intervention) are seen with respect to both the caregiver's behavior and the amelioration of disordered infant behavior. Still another aspect of this renewed interest in the world of meaning is perhaps the most innovative of all. I refer to investigation of the intersubjective world, that of the shared affective and cognitive meaning between infant and caregiver. That this is also susceptible to the methods of verifiable observation and scientific inference is illustrated by the research on "affect attunement" in this volume. One realizes that there is probably more in the domain of shared experience, intentions, and communications in infancy than we had imagined. With newer methods and ways of thinking about this, there is considerable research opportunity, and the likelihood of significant new knowledge in the near future seems strong.

Another area of research opportunity has to do with developmental continuities in relationship to discontinuities. In the past decade's research, investigators were disappointed at not finding more evidence of continuities from early psychological development to later ages. Most of this research was done with normal populations and not in defined clinical populations, and it yielded clear evidence of times of normative discontinuity or qualitative transformation in early development. But now it seems we may be at the dawn of a new era in the search for developmental continuities. As some of the contributions in this volume illustrate, it seems likely that the next wave of studies will search for continuities in the midst of definable discontinuities, using a newer generation of methods for longitudinal study that may tap subtler aspects of temperament and personality development. In addition, infant psychiatry carries the promise that longitudinal investigations will be carried out on a variety of at-risk populations as well as on populations with defined clinical disorders.

Another research opportunity is in the area of adult development and family development in relation to infant development and its disorders. We now appreciate that psychological development continues in a dynamic and active way throughout the life span. Further, families develop in terms of changing role structures and boundaries to the outside social world. A new discipline of "lifespan psychology" has brought forth methods of investigation which can be used for asking questions about adult development in relation to infancy. Does the meaning of parenting an infant change as a reflection of one's position in the life cycle (for example, parenting in adolescence or in midlife as opposed to the normative time of young adulthood)? One anticipates that research will show important features of synchronous and dissynchronous patterns. Similarly, experience may show more continuity for the infant with parenting at certain phases of adult and family development than at other phases.

The Importance of an International Forum

International collaboration in infant psychiatry holds particular promise for advancing the mental health of infants. From the point of view of basic knowledge, one cannot emphasize strongly enough the advantages of cross-national and cross-cultural work. We need to know all we can about infant development and its variations in different settings. We also need to know about methods of intervention and opportunities for helping in different settings, and there is much information that can be shared. Recently, the World Association for Infant Psychiatry and Allied Disciplines has taken shape as an organization for furthering research, clinical knowledge, and other related efforts in an area of common commitment and concern. This new organization has promising beginnings in joining professionals from Europe and North America. I look to this international forum growing to include the interesting work on behalf of infant development taking place in Latin American countries, in non-Western countries, and especially in developing countries.

In thinking about an international forum, I cannot help but think of a sea metaphor. It seems apt in many ways. Our forum has emerged in spanning the Atlantic, and now we anticipate going beyond this. The sea also reminds us of our common evolutionary past, and in its breadth, immensity, and depth it is surely humbling. The playwright, Arthur Miller (see Levinson, 1978) put it this way:

> . . . society is inside of man and man is inside society, and you cannot even create a truthfully drawn psychological entity on the stage until you understand his social relations and their power to make him what he is and to prevent him from being what he is not. The fish is in the water and the water is in the fish.

So it is with infants developing in different places. So it is with infant psychiatry in a changing world.

Robert N. Emde, M.D.

REFERENCES

Call, J. D. (1983). Toward a nosology of psychiatric disorders in infancy. In *Frontiers of Infant Psychiatry*, ed. J. D. Call, E. Galenson, and R. L. Tyson. New York: Basic Books.

Emde, R. N. (1980). Emotional availability: A reciprocal reward system for infants and parents with implications for prevention on psychosocial disorders. In *Parent-Infant Relationships*, ed. P. M. Taylor. Orlando: Grune & Stratton.

Fraiberg, S. (1980). *Clinical Studies in Infant Mental Health: The First Year of Life*. New York: Basic Books.

Kagan, J., Kearsley, R., and Zelaso, P. (1978). *Infancy, Its Place in Human Development*. Cambridge: Harvard University Press.

Klaus, M. H. and Kennell, J. H. (1982). *Parent-Infant Bonding*, 2nd ed. St. Louis: C. V. Mosby.

Lebovici, S. (1980). Presentation at First World Congress of Infant Psychiatry. Cascals, Portugal.

Levinson, D. (1978). *The Seasons of a Man's Life*. New York: Ballantine Books.

Sameroff, A. J. and Harris, A. E. (1979). Dialectical approaches to early thought and language. In *Psychological Development from Infancy: Image to Intention*, ed. M. Bornstein and W. Keesen. Hillsdale, New Jersey: Lawrence Erlbaum Associates.

Spitz, R. (1946). Anaclitic depression. In *The Psychoanalytic Study of the Child*, 2: 313–342. New York: International Universities Press.

World Health Organization (1977). *The Manual of the International Statistical Classification of Diseases, Injuries, and Causes of Death (ICD-9)*, 9th revision. Geneva: World Health Organization.

EDITORS' PREFACE

In the three years between the First World Congress on Infant Psychiatry in Cascais, Portugal, and the Second Congress in Cannes, France, infant psychiatry has become firmly established as a special area within the larger field of child psychiatry and the allied professions. Yet infant psychiatry remains unique by virtue of the intimacy of the relationship between the infant and his parents, the dependence of the infant upon this relationship, and the important role played by physiological and biological aspects in the infant's psychological development.

This book is an extension of the first volume entitled *Frontiers of Infant Psychiatry* and will be followed by additional volumes appearing at regular intervals reporting the progress of this field. The papers included were selected by the editors on the basis of scientific originality, analysis of data, and quality of interpretation of data. Stringent requirements were imposed in making this selection.

It is interesting to compare the contents of the two volumes of *Frontiers of Infant Psychiatry*, particularly in view of these special features of infancy. Volume II contains far more studies of the various aspects of the mother-infant interrelationship, particularly the role of affect interchange. Research and clinical work with premature infants and their caregivers have also increased to an astonishing degree, in keeping with the medical, psychological, and social problems encountered in dealing with this group of at-risk infants. More has been written about various types of psychopathology in infancy, particularly types involving pathological parenting, such as child abuse, and those accompanying or consequent to medical disorders such as epilepsy and hypothyroidism. There is greater emphasis in this volume on early intervention and prevention of psychological disorders in infancy, in keep-

ing with advances in our understanding of the causes of early psychopathology. There is also greater attention to the role of such infant caregivers as fathers and grandparents, paralleling societal shifts in infant care, especially in the United States.

But despite the large number of subjects included in this volume, it is not intended as a textbook of infant psychiatry or a guide for research methodology in infant psychiatry. Here, as in the first volume, the variety of concepts, methods, aims, and topics currently utilized in the different disciplines is impressive. Although this variety does not make for neatly organized sections, the contributions offer a full overview of what is currently in the forefront of this field.

Frontiers II, while rich in so many areas, does not include a specific section devoted to assessment as such, although many aspects of assessment in infancy are addressed in different ways throughout the book. Evaluation of assessment tools and methods will undoubtedly command increasing attention in the future from those carrying out research in infant psychiatry. Some assessment methods have been devised *de novo* to meet needs peculiar to the work in this field, as exemplified by the Brazelton Neonatal Assessment Inventory. Other methods are based on techniques first employed with older groups, now applied to infants, such as the Bayley Test. But the many quantitative scales being devised for application to work with infants tend by their very nature to be narrowly focused, so that one of their virtues becomes a handicap as a consequence of the things such methods do *not* take into account. This is an old problem being confronted anew: whether all important information is quantifiable and whether nonquantifiable information is therefore not important. In the clinical framework, a great deal of information can be assessed without formal quantification methods, though many such tools can be usefully applied; and it is in the clinical framework that such tools will have to prove their value and demonstrate their limitations, including the extent to which they have any predictive value. Our hope is that this book will provide a context within which this problem and others like it can be examined from a number of different viewpoints, that it will facilitate an open and ongoing assessment of the field in general and further continued debate on the issues, a hallmark of the scientific attitude.

As in volume I, space restrictions have precluded publishing many of the fine papers presented at the Cannes Congress. The French Organizing Committee, under the leadership of Professor Serge Lebovici, deserves much credit for its splendid work in organizing this large, multidisciplined, multinational representation of colleagues. The American Program Committee and the European consultants were responsible for the scientific richness of the program and for its excellent format. A host of consultants too numerous to mention individually have contributed invaluable critical opinions and other forms of assistance, both to the Congress and to the preparation of this book. Financial assistance from the Thrasher Research Fund of Salt Lake City, Utah supported the Thrasher Lecture given by Thomas F. Anders, included in this volume.

Finally, we wish to acknowledge the untiring assistance of Loretta Kramer and of Mrs. Bea Noble in preparing this book in its earlier stages, and we express our deep gratitude to Mrs. Natalie Altman for the technically difficult and masterful task she accomplished in editing this book.

Introduction

The Infant in a Changing World

Madame Georgina Dufoix, Secrétaire d'Etat Chargée de la Famille,
de la Population, et des Travailleurs Immigrés
Ministère des Affaires Sociales et de la Solidarité Nationale,
Government of France

I wish to thank you for having invited me to your Congress. Its theme is both exciting and of great interest, because the infant of today is the man or woman of tomorrow. "The Infant in a Changing World" is a beautiful title which can serve as the thread running through my discussion; I will tell you some of the associations which it evoked in me, in regard to the fact that the infant is indeed *within* the world; this world is a world in change; and the infant himself is a maker of change.

The Infant Is Within the World

Your title implies that you place the infant squarely in the world. The infant is from birth on, indeed before birth, in relation to the world. The infant *exists* in the literal sense of the word. He can no longer be considered a simple piece of protoplasm devoid of exchange with the external world, indifferent, deaf, blind, and mute. We can no longer refer to the infant as a digestive tube, a fragile little animal, a small being still on the periphery—a kind of nursing and screaming machine. You yourself state—and that is very much the contribution of two of your disciplines, psychoanalysis and psychiatry—that *man is from the beginning a social being.*

The importance you attach to the mother-father-infant interaction, to the creative anticipations of the mother, to the early competencies of the newborn is particularly impressive. We have a major duty in increasing the common awareness of these discoveries about the relationship *in utero,* the awakening of the senses, the readiness of the capabilities of the newborn, the awakening of the infant to all the stimuli from the external world, such as odors, light, sounds, and the voice of the mother.

All these studies are particularly fruitful because they increase our understanding of how we adults are constructed and how we function. This approach has proven of value for therapeutic work with adults, with children, and now more and more also with infants themselves. This is of special interest to me, as Secretary for the Family, because it gives us keys of enormous importance to prevent not only handicaps or individual difficulties—psychosomatic or psychological—but also to combat great sociocultural inequalities. Your concept of the infant as a whole person, still dependent but already in search of autonomy, corresponds to the concept we have in mind—as can be seen in the measures I am promoting in France. For instance, infants must not simply be protected but must be received with open arms by those people who are in charge of helping them develop. There are traditional barriers between what is sanitary, what promotes social development, and what is educational—a threefold approach that leads to separate compartments and, sometimes, diverging formations. This approach must be replaced by a much more integrated one. In France, we are rethinking the entire policy of social help for children so as to include the preventive approach and to avoid separating the newborn from their parents, especially from the mothers. We have published regulations with the Ministry of Health to encourage hospitals to maintain to a maximum degree the ties between parents and children, not just to facilitate visiting and conjoint hospitalization, but to keep newborns as much as possible on the services where their mothers are hospitalized.

A last example, which shows the degree of interest which I attach to the very first moments of life, is the Forum organized at my request in December, 1983, in Paris, on the conditions surrounding delivery and birth itself. In spite of the considerable progress realized in the area of the management of pregnancy and delivery, numerous women still have unsatisfactory deliveries, which can have disastrous consequences for the quality of the mother-child relationship. This is why we have thought it useful to open the debate on birth and delivery before a large audience.

The World in Change

The world is indeed in change, and we at the Secretariat, with responsibility for the nation's families, are particularly concerned by the changes. We are concerned by the changes resulting from several trends, such as the increasing frequency of mothers going to work, making it necessary to protect their children in a satisfactory way, both quantitatively and qualitatively; and the development of contraceptive devices which permit more and more— and you know how much this matters—that infants who are born are actually wanted. And we also want to make it possible that all the children who are wanted *can* be born; that is why the conditions and existence of family

life, notably housing conditions and working hours, have a high priority in my work. In order to permit local elected officials to take into account the dimension of the family in their planning, I have instituted what we call Family Contracts, which give financial help to communities interested in promoting better living conditions for children. The increase both of births outside marriage and of the divorce rate changes the place of the child within the family and within society. Does this result in new responsibilities for the government? This is another major issue. We are concerned about the infants who are abandoned at birth (there are about one thousand of these each year in France). One of our objectives is to switch to some extent from outright and irreversible adoption, "abandonment" legally speaking, to "placing for adoption." This is not just a nicety of language: we aim to bring about a change of mental attitude as well. Our policy is to that extent to promote simple adoptions and foster-parenthood.

We are deeply preoccupied with mistreatment in the family or in institutions and with the child abuse of which numerous children become victims. Because these conditions prevent the establishment of a good mother-child relationship, your studies can help us combat this scourge.

A world in change also confronts us with a mandate to establish an equilibrium among, first, our desire that each child will be born under optimal conditions and safety and well-being; second, the ethical problems which are raised by the development of new medical techniques; and third, the financial investments involved, as well as the management which these developments have brought with them. Our family and housing allowances have in this respect been significantly increased since May 1981.

The Infant as a Maker of Change

Nothing changes faster than "the art of raising infants." In fact, the infant destroys the barriers between the medical profession, the mental health profession, educators, and others. To be multidisciplinary becomes a necessity. Similarly, it is no longer possible to think of, or to take care of, the child as separate from the family; the infant challenges his parents.

The infant has also made it an order of the day for us to look at the problem of how institutions function: can the hospital and the nursery function as before? Isn't one of the gifts that the young child has given us the task of explaining the nature of the family to the family itself? Speaking at our Conference on Research and the Family, President Mitterrand spoke of "Hidden Knowledge Within the Family." I firmly believe that parents *are* competent, that it is possible for them to act responsibly. Is not your work here, and our work too, aimed at helping them to recognize this competency, whereas now they feel more and more dispossessed of it and too often deficient and inefficient?

Finally, I would like to tell you again that, as French Secretary of the Family, I welcome your studies and propositions because the management of the very small child in a changing world is a challenge for society. Of course, it is also a matter of love and tenderness on the part of individuals: in this field, political decisions are not enough. The government has its responsibilities; it can be a motivating force, but it must remain limited. However, it can foster change in mental attitudes, help children to live, teach them to make discoveries, and give them the place they deserve; these are also the objectives of a Congress such as yours, and I thank you for that.

In Memoriam–Selma Fraiberg

(1918–1981)

In her lifetime, Selma Fraiberg was referred to as "one of the world's leading authorities on how to read and respond to messages of need in those too young to speak for themselves." She referred to herself and her team of colleagues as "intermediaries" with respect to the baby, but her life work from the beginning of her professional career was always in the area of intermediation: as an analyst between the young patient and his or her disturbing inner world, as a developmental guide for the bewildered, immature mother and her infant, as a pair of understanding eyes between the blind and the outer environment, and as a rescuing intervener between children and the perils to which they are exposed.

Our common interests brought us together on a variety of panels devoted at times to child psychoanalysis, at times to vicissitudes of parenthood, at times to the vulnerabilities and resiliencies involved in preventative work. When I introduced her as the speaker for the first academic lecture of the Association for Child Psychoanalysis, she reviewed for us the work in progress at her new center in San Francisco. It always seemed to me that wherever she spoke and wherever she went she generated enthusiasm for her work and a dedication to the special vision of the infantile predicament that made her known throughout the world. After listening to her, one had the impulse to go and carry out this very important and necessary work, and it came as no surprise that her cardinal role in the field of infant mental health was recognized, in the year of her death, by the Dolly Madison Award. The citation recognized that her work was "unique in this century," and that "her insights into the needs and functioning of the very young, the handicapped, and their parents crossed the disciplinary lines of the helping professions," and that through her publications, she had accomplished "the rare feat of communicating directly, clearly, and understandably, yet without oversimplification." Her prose was indeed so clear that it seemed deceptively easy to grasp her ideas and become wise like her without prodigious effort. Two of her greatest communicative talents, in fact, lay in making the unconscious conscious, in the classic psychoanalytic sense, and in making the obscurities and complexities of the human condition clear, concise, and comprehensible to the majority of readers and listeners.

If we take a look at what she did for infant psychiatry alone, it appears to represent a number of professional lifetimes. She was able to accomplish so much only because she built up and maintained and encouraged interdiciplinary teams. In summary, it is an impressive record.

In her work with blind infants, apart from

elucidating the psychological lags in their development, she was able to help the parents to understand their babies better, to compensate for the sensory modality that was missing, and to enhance the relationship. This work culminated in her book *Insights from the Blind*.

She confronted the crucial problems that day care entailed for the mothers of today when the best interests of the developing infant are often overlooked in the welter of imperatives that dictate controversial compromises. Based on her long experience of infant management and mismanagement, she wrote uncompromisingly on behalf of motherhood. Her forthright views were published in *Every Child's Birthright: In Defense of Mothering*, which created a certain amount of pandemonium among those who misunderstood her primary intention of ensuring that every human baby have an adequate supply of devoted care that could only come, in all its essence, from the mother. How to implement this as a goal is one of the major dilemmas confronting the infant psychiatrist at the present time.

One of Professor Fraiberg's more startling insights, which was almost self-evident once it had been expressed, was that the baby became the "transference object" for parents who transposed their earliest disturbances into the current situation, with the infant as a "ghost in the nursery." When these transference contaminations were clarified within the context of "infant-parent psychotherapy" (a fascinating combination of developmental guidance and psychoanalytically oriented psychotherapy), a more rewarding relationship was fostered between infants and parents. A description of this work appeared in *Clinical Studies in Infant Mental Health: The First Year of Life*.

These three books rank with *Infants Without Families* by Anna Freud, *The First Year of Life* by René Spitz, *The Psychological Birth of the Human Infant* by Margaret Mahler, and sections of *Childhood and Society* by Erik Erikson as cornerstones to the new discipline of infant psychiatry. It is particularly sad to think that Professor Fraiberg will not be able to take us any further along her seminal pathway.

When I try to understand the strong sense of affinity I have always had for the products of her mind, I am reduced to the concept of magic.

It is not surprising that her best-known book, translated into more than a dozen languages, was called *The Magic Years*. In this book the magically transforming vision of the little child is exquisitely demonstrated. Both of us, throughout our therapeutic and research careers, returned over and over again to that "spooky world" populated by the dangerous creatures of the young imagination. Both of us had been well schooled by Piaget's surprising discoveries of the phenomenology of early childhood that is structured by imagination. As she put it so clearly and succinctly, imagination is the solution for many of the developmental problems of childhood, and children make use of imaginary companions, transitional objects, and magical thinking to overcome their common fears and difficulties creatively. The emphasis is on the last word because this was how she approached children and, interestingly enough, how children approached her.

Selma was so effective as a practitioner that we may sometimes overlook her considerable theoretical abilities. The concept of the mechanism, identification with the aggressor, first formulated by Anna Freud, was largely taken for granted as a dynamic event. Two questions regarding it remained unanswered: why did it appear in some cases and not others and why was it selected in preference to other defenses? On the basis of her research, Fraiberg came up with a possible answer to the first. Some parents who were abused as children in turn abused their children. It was a transference effect that stemmed from the repression of the associated affective experience of the childhood abuse endured by the parent, and this provided the energy and motion for repetition. Where the effects were remembered, the "fateful alliance with the aggressor" did not ensue. The second question, regarding the choice of defense, she left for the future research, so tragically cut short, and it is up to us, her scientific legatees, to pursue it further.

What, finally, can one say about her gift for language (which was undoubtedly enhanced by her husband's abiding influence)? We were all entranced many decades ago when Piaget first began to talk to children about how they saw themselves in relation to the world and the kinds of naive epistemologies for coping and mastering their problems they invented to make sense of what they experienced. At a different level, Selma Fraiberg had this same multilingual talent on both verbal and nonverbal levels, and this enabled her to communicate comfortably with children at all stages of development and to open up their minds to self-knowledge. We have lost a great "intermediary" who will not be easily replaced. It is our duty to cultivate younger infant psychopathologists who will carry on the great tradition.

E. JAMES ANTHONY, M.D.
President, World Association for Infant Psychiatry and Allied Disciplines

PART I

Developmental Issues in Infancy

1

Affect Attunement

Daniel N. Stern, M.D.

One of the most mysterious aspects of the parent-infant (or any human) relationship is how one knows what another is experiencing subjectively. Yet this very ability underlies what we mean by empathy. It also underlies the phenomena in which the parent's fantasies about the infant come to influence the infant's behavior and ultimately shape his fantasies. (It is largely the result of the conference leading to this book that I have become aware of the wealth of work in Europe, particularly in France, on this issue of reciprocal fantasy interaction [Cramer, 1982; Kreisler, 1981; Kreisler et al., 1974; Lebovici, 1982, 1983; Pinol-Douriez, 1983].) The ability I have in mind also underlies aspects of what we mean by the quality of a relationship—in particular, what Hinde (1976) has described as the penetration or degree of mutual disclosure, openness, or intimacy.

Whether one is considering empathy, reciprocal fantasy interactions, mutual intimacy, or any other manner in which the inner mental life of one person ends up penetrating and influencing another, there must be some general ways that mental states within one person are knowable to another. (And the ways must be nonverbal, because one partner is an infant.) The mental state must first become manifest as overt behavior—and that overt behavior must be translatable—so that a partner can sense the inner state lying behind another's overt behavior.

The phenomenon of affect attunement is one

such general way. Accordingly, we believe it occupies a place of importance in understanding the mechanisms behind crucial clinical issues such as empathy, "interactions fatasmatique," and intimacy, as well as "mirroring" and its related processes. In this essay I explore the nature, mechanism, and role of affect attunement in the sharing of affective mental states.

Some of the kernel ideas presented here are treated elsewhere in greater depth and related to other aspects of the growth of the infant's interpersonal world (Stern, in press).

Description of Affect Attunement

Affect attunement can so permeate other behaviors that they are difficult to find in pure form (the following examples are taken from Stern, 1984). Occasionally, a very unemcumbered example appears, such as:

EXAMPLE 1

A nine-month-old girl becomes very excited about a toy and reaches for it. As she grabs it, she lets out an exuberant "aaaah!" and looks at her mother. Her mother looks back, squinches up her shoulders, and performs a terrific shimmy of her upper body—like a go-go dancer. The shimmy lasts only about as long as her daughter's "aaaah!" but is equally excited, joyful, and intense.

EXAMPLE 2

Or, more commonly, the infant's behavior is nonvocal and the parent's is vocal. A nine-month-old boy bangs his hand on a soft toy, at first in some anger, but gradually with pleasure, exuberance, and humor. He sets up a steady rhythm. Mother falls into his rhythm and says, "kaaaaaaa-bam, kaaaaaaa-bam," the "bam" falling on the stroke and the "kaaaa" riding with the prepatory upswing and the suspenseful holding of his arm aloft before it falls.

EXAMPLE 3

An eight-and-one-half-month-old boy reaches for a toy just beyond reach. Silently he stretches toward it, leaning and extending arms and fingers fully out. Still short of the toy, he tenses his body to squeeze out the needed extra inch of reach. At that moment, his mother says, "uuuuuh . . . uuuuuh!" with a crescendo of vocal effort, the expiration of air pushing against her tensed vocal chords. The mother's accelerating vocal-respiratory effort matched the infant's accelerating physical effort.

EXAMPLE 4

A ten-month-old girl accomplishes an amusing routine between herself and mother and upon doing so looks at mother. The girl "opens up" her face (mouth opens, eyes widen, eyebrows raise) and then closes it back in a smooth arch. Mother responds with saying, "yeah." However, she intones it so that its pitch line is "y^{ea}h." The mother's prosodic contour has matched the child's facial-kinetic contour.

EXAMPLE 5

A nine-month-old boy is sitting facing his mother. He is shaking a rattle in his hand up and down with a display of interest and mild amusement. As mother watches, she begins to nod her head up and down, keeping tight beat with her son's arm motions.

These examples are very clear. More often, however, the attunement is partially masked. For example:

EXAMPLE 6

A ten-month-old girl finally places a piece in a jigsaw puzzle. She looks toward mother, throws her head up in the air with an arm flap, raising herself partly off the ground in a flurry of exuberance. The mother says, "YES, that a girl." The "YES" is intoned intensely with an explosive rise that echoes the girl's fling of gesture and posture. One could easily argue that the "YES, that a girl" functions as a routine response in the form of a positive reinforcer. And it certainly does do so. But, why does not the mother just say, "Yes, that a girl."? Why does she need to add the highly pitched "YES, . . ." that vocally matches the child's gestures? The "YES" is an attunement embedded within a routine response.

This is so common, and some of the embedded attunements are so subtle, that unless one is looking for them or asking why any behavior is being performed exactly the way it is they will pass unnoticed (except, of course, that we will gather from them—often unconsciously—what we imagine to be "really" going on). It is the embedded attunements that give one the impression of whether the mother is getting "inside of" the infant's behavior.

Characteristic Features of Affect Attunements

What are the characteristics of these attunements? We have the impression that a kind of imitation has occurred, yet there is no faithful rendering of the infant's overt behavior at all. Nonetheless, some form of matching is going on. The matching is largely crossmodal or intermodal; that is, the channel or modality of expression used by the mother to match is different from the channel or modality used by the infant to express. In the first example the child's voice is matched by the mother's body movements. In the second example the boy's arm movements are matched by the mother's voice.

What is being matched is not the other person's behavior per se but rather, it seems, some aspect of an internal feeling state. The reference for the match appears to be the internal state (inferred or directly apprehended), not the external behavioral event.

The match appears to occur between the expressions of inner state. These expressions can take forms that differ externally but that have some substitutability as corresponding manifestations of a single recognizable internal state. We appear to be dealing with behavior as expressionism rather than as sign or symbol.

A Name for the Phenomenon

There are many candidates contesting for the name of this phenomenon, which we call affect attunement. Imitation would have a large following. The problems with imitation are several. The first is faithfulness. Imitation implies a reasonably faithful copy or reproduction of the original behavior as performed. The mother's matches are often not even reasonably faithful. The value of a loose definition of imitation can be argued, and Kaye (1979) has pointed out that "modifying imitations" just miss the mark in order to maximize or minimize aspects of the original behavior. Nonetheless, fidelity of reproduction of all or even part of the original overt form of the behavior is necessary for any meaningful use of the term imitation. A second problem is with the referent: What is the original that is to be reproduced in the imitation? Imitation assumes that it is the observable behavior itself. We are suggesting that the referent is the internal state. How does one imitate an internal feeling state? A third problem is that of representations for imitation. Deferred imitation, as meant by Piaget (1924) requires the capacity for acting on the basis of an internal representation of the original. The reproduction (imita-

tion) is guided by the blueprint provided by the internal representation. Piaget had in mind the observed behaviors as the referent that was represented. The nature of such representations is well conceptualized. But, if the referent is the internal feeling state, how do we conceptualize its representation so that it can act as a blueprint? We require a different concept of the nature of the representation in operation, namely, one of the internal feeling state, not its exact behavioral manifestation. How much such representations must differ from representations of external behaviors remains to be seen. But for all of the reasons stated, imitation as both a term and concept is found lacking when applied to our phenomenon. This is not to deny that an enormous amount of true imitation occurs between mother and infant (Field, 1977; Francis et al., 1981; Malatesta and Haviland, 1983; Moss, 1967; Trevarthan and Hubley, 1978). Imitation and our phenomenon are both crucial processes but with different forms, functions, and mechanisms.

Mirroring, echoing, and identification, taken together, represent a second candidate both as terms and concepts. Mirroring and echoing, as terms, run into the faithfulness problem. Mirroring has the disadvantage of literally suggesting complete temporal synchrony. Echoing, taken literally, at least avoids the temporal constraint. In spite of these literal limitations, these terms have been used in attempts to grapple with the issue of one person "reflecting" another's inner state. In this important respect, these terms, unlike imitation, are appropriately concerned mainly with the subjective state rather than the manifest behavior as the central referent.

This meaning of reflecting inner state has been used mostly in clinical theories (Kohut, 1977; Lacan, 1977; Mahler et al., 1975), all of which have stressed the importance of "reflecting" back an infant's feeling state for the infant's gradual knowledge of his own affectivity and sense of self.

The problem with these concepts as articulated by clinical theorists is the inconsistency and over inclusiveness of usage. In these writings, mirroring, echoing, and identification sometimes refer to the behavior itself—to true imitation, a literal reflecting back—and at other times, to the reflecting or alignment of internal states. The names and concepts do not maintain this crucial distinction, and there is also inconsistency about which subjective states are includable by these terms—affects? intentions? motives? beliefs? ego functions? The result is that when using these terms one is unable to focus upon the distinctions between imitation and the phenomenon of concern to us, or between reflecting or sharing, affective versus motivational or cognitive states. This indeterminacy has prevented the careful pursuit of phenomena that appear to be truly different. Differences in mechanism, form, and function have not been adequately clarifiable. Thus, clinical theory has at least focused upon the essence of the problem, but has been unable to push further our understanding of its process of operation.

Intersubjectivity as articulated by Trevarthan (1977, 1980; Trevarthan and Hubley, 1978) approaches the essence of the problem, though arriving from a different direction. It touches the heart of the matter because it concerns the mutual sharing of psychic states. However, it refers mainly, though not exclusively, to the mental states of intentions and motives rather than those of qualities of feeling or affects. Its major concern is interintentionality not interaffectivity. Nonetheless, intersubjectivity is an entirely adequate term and concept. It is, however, too inclusive. Affect attunement is a particular form of intersubjectivity.

The last candidate is affect matching or affect contagion. This process refers to the automatic induction of a similar affect in another on the basis of seeing or hearing someone's affect display. This process may well be a basic biological tendency among highly evolved social species, which becomes more perfected in man (Malatesta and Izard, 1982). Affect contagion has best and earliest been demonstrated with the human distress cry. Wolff (1966) found that two-month-old infants showed "infectious crying" when they heard a tape recording of their own distress cries. Simner (1971) and Sagi and Hoffman (1976) showed that contagious crying occurred in newborns. Furthermore, newborns cried more to sounds of their own cry than to those of other infants

and cried far more to infant cries in general than to equally loud, artificially produced sounds. The contagious "properties" of the smile have been well documented in infancy, even though mechanisms for them may shift during development.

Affect matching or contagion with its probable basis in "motor mimicry" (Lipps, 1906) cannot alone explain affect attunement, though it may well provide one of the core mechanisms on which that phenomenon is founded. By itself, affect matching or contagion, like imitation, will only explain a reproduction of the original. It cannot account for the phenomenon of responding in different modes or with different forms of behavior with the internal state as the referent.

By affect attunement we mean the performance of behaviors that express the quality of feeling of a shared affect state, but without imitating the exact behavioral expression of the inner state. A sharp distinction between imitation of external behavior and affect attunement with internal state must be maintained to do justice to observable events. To put the situation most simply, if the mother wishes to attune with the infant or to show attunement for the infant's sake, why does she not simply imitate the infant? When the mother (or anyone else) is experiencing the sharing of an affect state, we do not see flurries of rampant imitation. Rather we see attunement behaviors, that is, behaviors that refer to the internal state but bypass true imitation by skirting any true reproduction of external behaviors. If we could demonstrate subjective affect-sharing only by true imitation we would be enormously limited. The idea of such a limitation being placed upon us is amusing to imagine.

The reason attunement behaviors may be so important as separate phenomena is that imitation does not permit the partners to "speak to" the internal state. Imitation maintains the focus of attention upon the forms of the external behaviors. Attunement behaviors are needed to shift the focus of attention to the inside, to the quality of feeling that is being shared. It is for the same reasons that imitation is the preferred way to teach the external forms and attunement the preferred way to commune with or indicate sharing of the internal states. Imitation renders form. Attunement renders feeling. So it seemed from these examples. However, in real life there does not appear to be a true dichotomy between attunement and imitation, rather they occupy two ends of a spectrum.

The Nature of the Match in Affect Attunement

Although the mother does not formally imitate the baby, she does match certain aspects of his behavior. It is these "matchings" that indicate attunements. The question is, what aspects of another person's behavior can be matched without formally imitating them? We came up with the following list: intensity, timing, and shape. We determined that there were two aspects of intensity that could be matched, absolute intensity (the intensity level of the mother's behavior appears to match that of the infant, regardless of what modality the behaviors are performed in) and intensity contour (the change in intensity over time, such as rapid acceleration or deceleration).

There were three features of timing that could be matched: beat, rhythm (a beat with unequal stress), and duration.

By shape we do not mean the same form. That would be imitation. We mean that only some feature of the criterion form is abstracted and rendered in a different act, such as "up and down" which can be rendered with the head, limbs, voice, or body (see example 5 described earlier).

To examine these features of matching we asked mothers to play with their infants as they normally do. This interaction was videotaped. Immediately afterward, the experimenters and each mother watched a replay of the interaction. The entry criteria for asking the mother questions were: (1) the baby makes some affective expression; (2) the mother responds along with or after (< three seconds) the infant's expression; and (3) the infant attends to the mother's response. Once the entry criteria are met, the mother is asked why she did what she did the way she did it and when

she did it? What did she think the baby felt at the moment that . . . ? Was she aware of her own behavior when she . . . ? and so on in a semistructured interview format.

Details of the methodology and the results of these experiments with ten dyads are reported elsewhere (Stern et al., 1984).

In summary, the major findings of relevence here are:

1. In response to an infant expression of affect, attunements were the most common maternal response (48 percent), followed by comments (33 percent), and imitations (19 percent). During play interactions attunements occurred at an average rate of one every sixty-five seconds.

2. Most attunements occurred across sensory modes. If the baby's expression was vocal the mother was likely to attune gesturally or facially or vice versa. In 39 percent of instances, the mother accomplished her attunement using entirely different modalities from those used by the infant (crossmodal). In 48 percent of the cases, the mother accomplished her attunement using some modalities that were the same and some that were different from those used by the infant (mixed modal). In only 13 percent of cases did the mother accomplish her attunement using the exact same modality as the infant (intramodal). Accordingly, 87 percent of the time the mothers responded partially, if not wholly, crossmodally.

3. Of the three aspects of behavior, intensity, timing, and shape, that a mother can match to accomplish an attunement, intensity matches were the most common, followed by timing matches and least by shape matches. In the majority of cases, more than one aspect of behavior is simultaneously matched. The percentage of all attunements that are matched by the different aspects are: absolute level of intensity, 61 percent; intensity contour, 81 percent; beat, 13 percent; rhythm, 11 percent; duration, 69 percent; shape, 47 percent.

4. The largest single reason that mothers gave (and we inferred) for performing an attunement was "to be with" the infant, "to share," "to participate in," "to join in." We have called these functions *interpersonal communion.* This group of reasons stand in contrast to the other reasons given: to respond, to tune the

baby up or down, to restructure the interaction, to reinforce, to engage in a standard game. This later group can be lumped together as serving the function of communication rather than communion. Communication generally means to exchange or transmit information, usually with propositional content, or to attempt to alter another's belief or action system. During many of these attunements, the mother is doing none of these things. Communion, on the other hand, means to participate together or to share in another's experience. This captures far better the mother's behavior as seen by experimenters and by mothers themselves.

It is clear that interpersonal communion, as created by attunement, will play an important role in the infant's coming to recognize that internal feeling states are forms of human experience that are sharable. The converse is also true. Feeling states that are never attuned to will remain as forms of experience that are only experienced alone, isolated from interpersonal context.

5. When mothers were shown the TV replay of their attunements, mothers judged themselves to be at the time of occurence entirely unaware of their behavior in 24 percent of cases; only particularly or slightly aware of their behavior in 43 percent of cases; and fully aware of their behavior in 32 percent of cases. The attunement process occurs largely unawares. (Even in the 32 percent of cases where the mothers said they were fully aware of their behavior, they were often referring to the desired consequences of their behavior more than to exactly what they did).

Does Maternal Attunement Influence the Baby?

It is easy enough to determine that misattunements (intentional and unintentional) influence the infant. They usually result in some alteration or interruption of ongoing infant behavior. That is their purpose, and it can be readily gauged. The situation with communing attunements is different. Most often, after the mother has made a communing attunement, the infant acts as if nothing special happened,

and we are left with no evidence, only speculation, that the fact of attunement has "got in," taken hold, and had some psychic consequence. To get beneath this still surface we chose the method of perturbing ongoing interactions and seeing what happens.

The approach of creating defined perturbations in naturalistic or seminaturalistic interaction is well established in infancy research. The "still face" procedure (Tronic et al., 1978) asks a mother or father to remove all facial expression in the middle of an interaction, creating a perturbation in the expected flow. Infants by three months react with mild upset and social withdrawal, alternating with attempts to reengage the impassive partner. Similarly, Travarthan (1977) has perturbed the flow of natural behaviors by showing infant TV recordings of mother in which her speech has been desynchronized from her facial movement and delayed slightly. This causes upset and avoidance in the infant. These two perturbations are applicable to any and all parent-infant pairs. Our perturbations had to be uniquely dyad-specific, tailored and aimed at an attunement episode already identified and likely to reoccur and characteristic of a particular mother-infant pair. No two pairs presented the same opportunity.

The specific attunement episode chosen for perturbation was identified while watching the replay of the TV recording with the mother. After discussing the structure of behaviors that made up the attunement episode, the mothers were instructed in how to perturb the structure. They then returned to the observation room and when the appropriate context for the expectable attunement behavior arose, they performed the planned perturbation. An example serves to clarify.

THE CHARACTERISTIC EPISODE

Baby A, a nine-month-old crawler crawls away from Mom and over to a new toy. While on his stomach he grabs the toy and begins to play with it. His play is animated, as judged by his movements, breathing, and vocalizations. Mother then approaches him from behind and puts her hand on his bottom and gives it an animated jiggle side to side. The speed and intensity of her jiggle appear to match well these aspects of the infant's behavior, qualifying this as an attunement. The infant's response to her attunement is nothing! He simply continues his play without dropping a stitch. Her jiggle left no overt trace, as if she had never acted. This attunement episode was fairly characteristic. The infant again wandered from her and became involved in a toy; she leaned over and jiggled his bottom or leg or foot. And the sequence would be repeated again.

To create the first perturbation, the mother was instructed to do exactly the same as always, except to purposely "misjudge" her baby's level of joyful animation, to pretend that the baby is somewhat less excited than he appears to be, and to jiggle accordingly. When the mother did jiggle somewhat more slowly and less intensely than she judged would make a good match, the baby quickly stopped playing and looked around at her, as if to say, "What's going on?" This perturbation was repeated twice with the same results. The second perturbation was in the opposite direction. The mother was to pretend that her baby was at a higher level of joyful animation and jiggle accordingly. The results were the same: the baby stopped and looked around. The mother was then asked to jiggle appropriately as she originally did, and again the infant did not respond.

Many such individualized perturbations have been performed, all indicating that the infant does, indeed, have some sense of the extent of matching, and that goodness of match, in itself, is an expectation under some circumstances, and its violation meaningful (Stern, 1985).

Underlying Mechanisms for Attunement

How can different behavioral expressions in different forms and different sensory channels be interchangeable? They must share some common currency that permits them to be transferred from one mode to another. There are some attributes or qualities of perception that are held in common by most or all the modalities of perception, such as intensity, shape, time, motion, number. These qualities of perception can be abstracted by any sensory mode from the invariant properties of the stimulus world and then translated into other modalities of perception. For this to occur, the perceptual quality must at some point exist in the mind in a form that is not inextricably bound to one particular way of perceiving it but is sufficiently abstract to be transposable across modalities. The abstract amodal form of any of these qualities must exist as abstract mental representations of the quality. It is the existence of these abstract representations of amodal qualities that permits us to experience a world that is perceptually unified.

I am arguing that the infant experiences a world of perceptual unity, in which amodal qualities can be perceived in any modality from any form of human expressive behavior, represented abstractly, and then transposed to other modalities. This position has been strongly put forth by developmentalists such as Bower (1974) and Meltzoff (1981), who posit that the infant, from the earliest days of life, forms and acts upon abstract representations of qualities of perception, and that the need and ability to form abstract representations of primary qualities of perception is one of the first orders of business at the start of mental life, and not the final product or a developmental landmark to be reached in the second year of life or later.

This view of the infant as an amodal perceiver has been suggested for a long time. The pioneering work of Werner and Kaplan (1963) in particular attests to this. But it is only in the past few years that we have had experimental evidence of the infant's ability to transfer information across modalities so that the structure of what is seen will inform what will be heard or felt and vice versa. Meltzoff and Borton's experiment (1979) led the way in this area of research. They showed that an infant two to three weeks old could tell, by looking, which object he had previously mouthed but never seen: In other words, the information gathered by the haptic sense (mouthing-touching) was "translated" into visual terms so that the same object would be recognized when seen for the first time.

Since then it has been shown (Kuhl and Meltzoff, 1982; MacKain et al., 1983) that infants can make similar transformations between the visual mode and the auditory mode (in the case of speech sounds). Similarly, the recent experiments of Meltzoff and Moore (1977) and Field (1983) on early imitation in the first days of life widen the modalities to include the visual and propioceptive, across which equivalence has been demonstrated. (Others have described very early imitation before, but not under rigorous experimental conditions.)

In all of these examples, the structure or form of an event as perceived in one modality was transferred to a different modality. Lewkowicz and Turkewitz (1983) demonstrated that instead of structure or form, the absolute level of intensity of an event can be transferred. When infants were asked to "judge" what level of brightness of white light matched what level of loudness of white noise, they made the same choices as adults. Intensity can thus be perceived amodally, as can form.

Finally, temporal pattern can also be perceived amodally (Wagner and Sakowits, 1983). Periodicity or continuousness was displayed to infants in one mode (auditory or visual) and was then recognized by the infant when shown in the other mode for the first time.

It thus appears that form or shape, intensity, and timing can all be perceived amodally. And, indeed, there is a long history in philosophy and psychology that has designated form, time, and intensity to be supramodal (which amounts to amodal) qualities of experience in psychological terms, or primary qualities of experience in philosophical terms (Marks, 1978). In point of fact, when we chose intensity, timing, and shape as the dimensions of matchings to score for attunements, we did not do so on the basis of the historical position of these qualities, or on the basis of the fact that there was experimental evidence that infants treat these qualities amodally. The relevance of these facts became apparent later. Our choice was on clinical-descriptive grounds; those qualities seemed to be the best descriptors, and thus definers, of what intuitively felt like at-

tunement. Thus, the choice was not lucky, and it could be interpreted as lending some added weight of convergent validity to the importance of the amodal perception of these qualities of experience.

The Role of Vitality Contours in Attunement

We do not truly experience another person's inner state in terms of intensity, timing, and shape—that is, perceptual qualities. Rather, these perceptual qualities transmute our experience so that we end up experiencing the other person's vitality, degree of pleasure, level of activation, and the discrete category of their affective sensation. We tend to transpose perceptual qualities into feeling qualities. For example, we may gather from the properties of someone's arm gesture the perceptual qualities of rapid acceleration, speed, fullness of display, and rapid deceleration. But, we will *not* experience their gesture in terms of these perceptual qualities of temporal relations, intensity, and size. We will experience it directly as "forceful," in terms of a quality of feeling or a form of vitality.

There is a problem here. "Forcefulness" is not an affect, or a level of pleasure, or (as it stands) a level of activation, or a motive per se. Yet most of the attunements occur with feeling qualities of this sort—explosions, fadings, rushings, and the like. Such qualities are more commonly the subject of attunements than are discrete affects proper. In fact, during an average mother-infant interaction, discrete affect displays occur only occasionally—perhaps every thirty to ninety seconds. Since this is so, how can the affective tracking or attuning with another occur as a continuous process? One cannot wait around for a discrete categorical affect display (such as a surprise expression) to occur to reestablish attunement. Attunement feels more like an unbroken process. It cannot await discrete affect eruptions; it must be able to work with virtually all behavior.

We need a new category or property or feeling quality that is manifest in all behavior and can thus be an almost omnipresent subject of attunement. A quality that concerns *how* a behavior, any behavior, all behavior, is performed, not *what* behavior is performed. I am calling this needed quality of feeling *vitality*, of which there are many distinct forms. By vitality, I mean those dynamic, kinetic qualities of feeling that distinguish animate from inanimate and that correspond to the momentary changes in feeling states involved in the organic processes of being alive. Vitality is captured in such terms as exploding, surging, fading, fleeting, persistent, drawn-out, decrescendo. Forms of vitality are not the same as discrete conventionalized affects. A smile can be "explosive" or "fading." And the way a parent reaches for the bottle can reveal multiple forms of vitality to the infant, but usually no single affect. (Most abstract art concerns vitality form not affects [Langer, 1967]). Forms of vitality are also not the same as the activation (or arousal or excitation) dimension of behavior. In most accounts of affects, what we are calling vitality forms would be subsumed under the all-purpose unswerving dimension of level of activation or arousal. Activation and arousal certainly occur, but we do not simply experience a feeling somewhere "along" or at some point "on" this dimension. We experience them rather as dynamic shifts or patterned changes within ourselves. I am urging that we need to add the new categorization of the dimension of activation, namely, forms of vitality that correspond to characteristic patterned changes in the activation dimension of experience. We must reconceptualize the dimension of activation into separate and discrete configurations of activation as contoured in time, and think in terms of *activation contours*. And activation contours are, no surprise at this point, a combination of the supramodal qualities of intensity and time that infants are so good at transposing across modalities.

It is interesting to recall here that the vast majority of attunements occurred with the dimensions of intensity (90 percent) and timing (71 percent) and that shape or form came in a poor third (17 percent).

The issue of vitality as a distinct form of feeling to be considered alongside of affect categories (happy, sad, and so forth) is an important issue in and of itself, which I treat in greater detail and depth elsewhere (Stern, in press). The idea, in one guise or another, of forms of vitality as a separate part of the subjective world of feeling is well prepared for in the work of Schneirla (1965) and Tompkins (1962). It is also very close in concept to the notions behind Effort-Shape analysis (Lamb, 1965) and other forms of dance or movement notation that have been applied to human social behavior, including that of mothers and infants (Kestenberg, 1923).

For our purposes here, forms of vitality must be added to affect categories as one of the subjective inner states that can be referenced in acts of attunement. Vitality is ideally suited as the inner feeling that is the subject of attunements because of its being composed of the amodal qualities of intensity and time and because it resides in virtually any behavior one can perform and thus provides a continuously present (though changing) subject for attunement. This means that attunements can be made with the inner quality of feeling of how an infant reaches for a toy, holds a block, kicks his foot, listens to a sound. The tracking of and attuning with vitality forms permits one human to "be with" another in the sense of sharing likely inner experiences on an almost continuous basis. But this is exactly our experience of feeling-connectedness—being in attunement with another. It feels like an unbroken process. It seeks out the form of vitality momentarily ongoing in any and every behavior and uses that to keep the thread of communion unbroken.

The Developmental Context of Attunement

Attuning behaviors begin as soon as social interaction begins. During the first half year of life it is our impression (as yet untested) that imitations predominate over attunements (the reverse is true after nine months). The role of both in initiating, maintaining, regulating, and terminating infants' social behaviors in the first six months of life has been richly commented on (Beebe et al., 1963; Kronin, 1982; Papoušek and Papoušek, 1979). During this earlier period, however, infants have less capacity to sense that they are being attuned with or imitated. These maternal behaviors simply have a direct effect on the infants' state and behavior. Beginning at around nine months, however, infants cross an interpersonal threshhold that makes of attunement an entirely different experience.

At this time infants come to the momentous but gradual discovery that they have a mind and that other people have separate minds. Intersubjectivity is now possible (Trevarthan and Hubley, 1978). It is at this point in development that infants begin to sense that they can "have," so to speak, or "occupy" a mental state. And they now begin to impute mental states to others. Further, they come to sense and even expect that their mental state and that of another can be interfaced. They are arriving at a "theory of interfaceable minds" (Bretherton and Bates, 1979). This conclusion seems inescapable when developmental evidence about infants' pointing gestures, language acquisition, and intentions to communicate all converge to indicate that the infant acts as if focus of attention and intentions were now parts of the sharable world (Bates, 1979; Bates et al., 1976; Bloom, 1983; Bower, 1974; Bruner, 1975a, 1975b; Collis and Schaffer, 1975; Dore, 1975; Greenfield and Smith, 1976; Halliday, 1975; Murphy and Messer, 1977; Shields, 1978; Trevarthan and Hubley, 1978).

This ushers in a new level of interpersonal relatedness, which we call *intersubjective relatedness* (Stern, in press), in which the sense of self

now includes a mental self (in addition to the physical core-self) and the sense of other also includes a mental other. A mental self and a mental other that can be "interfaced," can also be aligned or misaligned. And mental alignment in the domain of feeling is attunement.

Attunement, then, at the interpersonal level of subjective relatedness becomes a powerful tool in social development, especially as it relates to clinical matters. The clinical implications of attunements, misattunements and nonattunements are beyond our present scope and are treated elsewhere (Stern, 1984). Suffice it to say that what is at stake for the infant are issues such as the following. The extent and the specific segments of the subjective world of feeling that are attuned to will be considered sharable and become the stuff of intimacy. That which is not attuned to will remain private and may be experienced as idiosyncratic. The complexion of the infant's growing internal representations or object world will be largely determined by which self-experiences are communed with and thus supported, and which are under parental pressure to be altered in one way or another. Also, the infant's sense of self as "reflected" by the parents will be shaped by the history of past and present attunements and misattunements. Finally, the notion of attunement as conceptualized and operationalized may prove helpful as a theraputic tool, particularly as it depends upon the mother becoming a collaborator in discoveries about her own fantasies and how they are actualized in overt behavior.

REFERENCES

Bates, E., Camai, I. L., and Valterra, V. (1975). The acquisition of performatives prior to speech. *Merrill-Palmer Quarterly,* 21:205–226.

Bates, E. (1979). Insertions, conventions and symbols. In *The Emergence of Symbols: Cognition and Communication in Infancy,* ed. E. Bates et al. New York: Academic Press.

Beebe, B., Kronen, J., and Gerstman, L. (1983). Simultaneous directional tracking in mother-infant play. Paper presented at the Society for Research in Child Development, Detroit, Michigan.

Bloom, L. (1973). *One Word at a Time.* The Hague: Mouton.

Bower, T. G. R. (1974). *Development in Infancy* San Francisco: W. H. Freeman.

Bretherton, I. and Bates, E. (1979). The emergence of intentional communication. In *New Directions for Child Development,* vol. 4, ed. I. Uzzises. San Francisco: Jossey-Bass.

Bruner, J. S. (1977). Early social interaction and language acquisition. In *Studies in Mother-Infant Interaction,* ed. H. R. Schaffer. New York/London: Academic Press.

Bruner, J. S. (1975a). From communication to language —a psychological perspective. *Cognition,* 3:255–287.

Bruner, J. S. (1975b). The ontogenesis of speech acts. *Journal of Child Language,* 2:1–19.

Collis, G. M. and Schaffer, H. R. (1975). Synchronization of visual attention in mother-infant pairs. *Journal of Child Psychiatry and Psychology,* 16:315–320.

Cramer, B. (1982). La psychiatrie du bébé. In *La Dynamique du Nourrisson,* ed. L. Kreisler, R. Schappi, and M. Soulé. Paris: Editions ESF.

Dore, J. (1975). Holophases, speech acts and language universals. *Journal of Child Language,* 2:21–40.

Field, T. M. (1982). Discrimination and imitation of facial expressions by neonates. *Science,* 218:179–181.

Field, T. M. (1977). Effects of early separation, interactive deficits and experimental manipulations on infant-mother face-to-face interaction. *Child Development,* 48:763–771.

Francis, P. L., Self, P. A., and Noble, C. A. (1981). Imitation within the context of mother-newborn interaction. Presented at the New York City Meeting of the Eastern Psychological Association.

Greenfield, P. and Smith, J. H. (1976). *Language Beyond Syntax: The Development of Semantic Structure.* New York/London: Academic Press.

Halliday, M. A. (1975). *Learning How to Mean: Explorations in the Development of Language.* London: Edward Arnold.

Haviland, J. M. and Malatesta, C. Z. (1981). Fallacies, facts and fantasies: A description of the development of sex differences in nonverbal signals. In *Gender and Nonverbal Behavior,* ed. C. Mayo and N. Henley. New York: Springer.

Hinde, R. A. (1976). On describing relationships. *Journal of Child Psychology and Psychiatry,* 17:1–19.

Kaye, K. (1979). Thickening this data: The maternal role in developing communication and language. In *Before Speech,* ed. M. Bullowa. Cambridge, England: Cambridge University Press.

Kestenberg, J. (1975). *Children and Parents: Psychoanalytic Studies in Development.* New York: Jason Aronson.

Kreisler, L. (1981). *L'enfant du Désordre Psychosomatique.* Toulouse: Privat.

Kreisler, L., Fain, M., and Soulé, M. (1974). *L'Enfant et son Corps.* Paris: Presses Universitaires de France.

Kronen, J. (1982). Maternal facial responsibility to infant affective expressivity. Doctoral Dissertation, Ferkauf Graduate School, Yesheva University.

Kuhl, P. and Meltzoff, A. N. (1982). The bimodal perception of speech in infancy. *Science,* 218:1138–1141.

Lacan, J. (1977). The mirror stage as a formative of the function of the I revealed in psychoanalytic experience. In Lacan, J. *Ecrits: A Selection,* trans. A. Sheridan. New York: W. W. Norton.

Lamb, W. (1965). *Posture and Gesture.* London: Trinity Press.

Langer, S. K. (1967). *Mind; an Essay on Human Feeling,* vol. I. Baltimore: Johns Hopkins Press.

Lebovici, S. (1983). *Le Nourrisson, La Mère et le Psychanalyste. Les Interactions Précoces.* Paris: Editions du Centurion.

Lewkowicz, D. J. and Turkewitz, G. (1983). Cross-modal equivalence in early infancy. *Developmental Psychology,* 16:597–607.

Lipps, T. (1906). Das Wissen von Fremden Ichen. *Psychologische Untersuchung,* 1:694–722.

MacKain, K., Studdert-Kennedy, M., Spieker, S., and Stern, D. N. (1983). Infant intermodal speech perception is a left hemisphere function. *Science,* 219:1347–1349.

Mahler, M. S., Pine, F., and Bergman, A. (1975). *The Psychological Birth of the Human Infant.* New York: Basic Books.

Malatesta, C. Z. and Haviland, J. M. (1982). Learning display rules: The socialization of emotion expression in infancy. *Child Development,* 53:991–1003.

Malatesta, C. Z. and Izard, C. E. (1982). The ontogenesis of human social signals: From biological imperative to symbol utilization. In *Affective Development: A Psychobiological Perspective.* Hillsdale, New Jersey: Lawrence Erlbaum Associates.

Marks, L. F. (1978). *The Unity of the Senses: Interrelations Among the Modalities.* New York/London: Academic Press.

Meltzoff, A. N. (1981). Imitation, intermodal coordination, and representation in early infancy. In *Infancy and Epistomology,* ed. G. Butterworth. London: Harvester Press.

Meltzoff, A. N. and Borton, R. (1979). Intermodal matching by human neonates. *Nature,* 282:403–404.

Meltzoff, A. N. and Moore, M. K. (1977). Imitation of facial and manual gestures by human neonates. *Science,* 198:75–78.

Moss, H. A. (1967). Sex, age and state as determinant of mother-infant interaction. *Merrill-Palmer Quarterly,* 13:19–36.

Murphy, C. M. and Messer, K. J. (1977). Mothers, infants and pointing: A study of a gesture. In *Studies in Mother-Infant Interaction,* ed. H. R. Schaffer. New York/London: Academic Press.

Papoušek, H. and Papoušek M. (1979). Early ontogeny of human social interaction: Its biological roots and social dimensions. In *Human Ethology: Claims and Limits of a New Discipline,* ed. M. von Cranach, K. Foppa, W. Lepenies, and D. Ploog. Cambridge, England: Cambridge University Press.

Piaget, J. (1924). *The Construction of Reality in the Child.* New York: Basic Books, 1954.

Pinol-Douriez, M. (1983). Fantasy interactions or "proto representations"? The cognitive value of affect-sharing in early interactions. Paper presented at the World Association of Infant Psychiatry, Cannes, France.

Sagi, A. and Hoffman, M. L. (1976). Empathic distress in the newborn. *Developmental Psychology,* 12:175–176.

Scaife, M. and Bruner, J. S. (1975). The capacity for joint visual attention in the infant. *Nature,* 253:265–266.

Schaffer, H. R. (1977). Early interactive development. In *Studies in Mother-Infant Interaction,* ed. H. R. Schaffer. New York/London: Academic Press.

Schneirla, T. C. (1965). Aspects of stimulation and organization in approach/withdrawal processes underlying vertebrate behavioral development. In *Advances in the Study of Behavior,* vol. I, ed. D. S. Lehrman, R. A. Hinde, and E. Shaw. New York/London: Academic Press.

Sheilds, M. M. (1978). The child as psychologist: Construing the social world. In *Action, Gesture, and symbol,* ed. A. Lock. New York/London: Academic Press.

Simner, M. (1971). Newborns response to the cry of another infant. *Developmental Psychology,* 5:136–150.

Soulé, M. and Kreisler, L. (1983). *Les bons enfants.* Paris: Editions ESF.

Stern, D. N. (in press). *The Interpersonal Worlds of the Infant.* New York: Basic Books.

Stern, D. N., Hofer, L., Haft, W., and Dore, J. (1984). Affect attunement: A descriptive account of the intermodal communication of affective states between mothers and infants. In *Social Perception in Infants,* ed. T. Field and N. Fox. Norwood New Jersey; Ablex.

Tomkins, S. S. (1962). *Affect, Imagery, Consciousness, the Positive Affects.* New York: Springer.

Trevarthan, C. (1980). The foundations of intersubjectivity: Development of interpersonal and cooperative understanding in infants. In *The Social Foundation of Language and Thought, Essays in Honor of Jerome S. Bruner,* ed. D. R. Olson. New York: W. W. Norton.

Trevarthan, C. (1977). Descriptive analysis of infant communicative behavior. In *Studies in Mother-Infant Interaction,* ed. H. R. Schaffer. New York/London: Academic Press.

Trevarthan, C. and Hubley, P. (1978). Secondary intersubjectivity: Confidence, confiding and acts of meaning in the first year. In *Action, Gesture and Symbol: The Emergence of Language,* ed. A. Lock. New York/London: Academic Press.

Tronick, E. et al. (1978). The infant's response to entrapment between contradictory messages in face-to-face interaction. *Journal of the American Academy of Child Psychiatry,* 17:1–13.

Wagner, S. and Sakowits, L. (1983). Intersensory and intrasensory recognition: A quantitative and developmental evaluation. Paper presented at the Society for Research in Child Development, Detroit, Michigan.

Werner, H. and Kaplan, B. (1963). *Symbol Formation.* New York: John Wiley.

Wolff, P. (1966). The causes, controls, and organization of behavior in the neonate. *Psychological Issues.* Monograph 17. New York: International Universities Press.

2

From Early Patterns of Communication to the Grammar of Experience and Syntax in Infancy

Justin D. Call, M.D.

Order is entirely natural. Grammatical man inhabits a grammatical universe. —Claude Shannon

Language, like nature, is a metapsychological abstraction which defies definition. The use of speech and of the written word is not equivalent to language. Such communicative expressions are but one outward manifestation of linguistic performance, which, as Chomsky has shown, cannot be equated with the group of coordinated mental operations that determine linguistic competence. No definition of language has, in fact, yet been achieved. Many phenomena often called languages in nature, such as the language of bees and the genetic code, have been discovered. Humans have created other nonverbal communicative devices, such as the neurotic symptoms described by Anna Freud (1936), the dramatic action sequences described by Greenacre (1966), the creatively organized visual and auditory configurations seen in art and music, and the mathe-

matical symbol systems utilized in algebraic equations. It would seem, then, that new languages emerge as new symbols for meaning and their syntatic relations are either discovered in nature or created by humans consciously or unconsciously. The idea that languages exist in nature awaiting our discovery is a provocative assertion that graphically illustrates the problem of defining language. An essential feature of all scientific discovery is making the unknown puzzles of nature knowable through interpretation, which can only be achieved by utilizing man's linguistic competence. Such is also the task of the mother and the infant observer in coming to understand "infantese," that is, what is meant by the preverbal coordination of the infant's spontaneous physical reactions, vocalization, affective expressions, and intersensory responsiveness and the integration of these with the infant's communicating partners.

The phylogenetically derived semiotic or communicating function plays a central role in our capacity for social adaptation and technicalogical advance. A better understanding of what we ordinarily call language can, I believe,

I am grateful to Nadine Levinson for her suggestions in the preparation of this manuscript.

emerge from tracing all modes of human communication to their earliest roots and showing how these communicating functions are intertwined and integrated as the infant makes use of them in conversations with others and self-communing. I do not mean to imply that *all* linguistic competence can be traced to infantile origins (before age three). Language, like character, has important roots at all stages of development.

In this paper I continue themes of an earlier one (Call, 1981) which delineated patterns of mother-infant affective communication in the first year of life. Those observations will be extended into the second year of life when affects, gestures, symptoms, transitional phenomena, idiosyncratic utterance, and patterns of dramatic action become further elaborated and integrated. It is these experiences that provide the basis by which the infant begins to organize sequentially his or her own experience, that is, how a grammar of experience develops and functions. It is, I believe, from this grammar of experience that the infant is able to intuit the syntactic rules that underlie spoken utterance at the two- and three-word stage. In offering clinical examples of language development in normal and psychopathological development, I hope to demonstrate how language acquisition is codetermined by ongoing relations with people, places, and things, and how it cannot be understood through a single conceptual window, whether such a window provides the biological, the cognitive, the affective, or the social viewpoint.

Reciprocity, A Prelude to Language

A variety of studies (Anders, 1978; Brazelton et al., 1974; Condon and Sander, 1974; Emde, [chapter 4, herein]; Klaus and Kennell, 1976; Sander, 1978; Spitz, 1964; Stern et al., 1983; Wolff, 1959) demonstrate that the human infant is preadapted to participating with the mother in establishing a coordinated reciprocal pattern of sensorimotor interaction. Such reciprocity involves many physiological systems in both the mother and infant. States of psychophysiological arousal, sucking rhythms in the infant interacting with the psychophysiology of let-down reflex in the breast-feeding mother (Call, 1964), the visual system, the auditory system, kinesthetic modes of interaction are components of the reciprocal physiological patterns. Manifestations of the coordination between these interacting systems are demonstrated by the discovery (Call, 1964) of the infant's anticipatory approach behavior at feeding in the newborn and by Stern's work on gaze behavior (1977). These systems of reciprocity are temporally organized on a second-to-second, minute-to-minute level as in visual reciprocity, on the larger time scale of feeding intervals, or on a twenty-four-hour day-night cycle. This early biologically based temporal organization sets the stage for later language functioning as seen in the development of intermodal aspects of experience—the infant moving in response to the mother's voice, and the mother moving in response to the infant's voice. Sander (1978) has conceptualized this reciprocity as part of the infant's biologically derived preadapted behavior leading to the *process* of adaptation between the infant and the caregivers. Erikson's (1950) propositions regarding mutuality of mother and infant are illustrated by this reciprocity.

At birth, reciprocal communication may be initiated either by the infant or by the mother. The term *mother* is used generically here to refer to any mothering figure and is preferred over *caregiver* because it includes rather than excludes the mother's subjective experience with the infant. A private exclusive form of communication is developed with the mother, the primary purpose of which is mutual holding, maintenance, and enrichment of the duality. When Spitz (1964) referred to "the dialogue," he was referring to the nonverbal, affective reciprocity of responses between mother and infant before the establishment of self and object differentiation and before language functioning proper. Reciprocity with the caregiving and libidinally invested mother thus becomes the organizing principle for all forms of communication, including affects, gesture, and the acquisition of phonemes and morphemes.

Origins of Affects, Affect Differentiation, and Affective Communication

The cry of the newborn not only signals need states in the infant and elicits attentive responses from the mother, it also serves to consolidate the mother's healthy narcissistic identification with her infant. Soon after birth the mother slowly develops the capacity to make specific inferences about the internal state of the infant from specific kinds of crying she hears from the infant (Wolff, 1959). These inferences are derived not only from objective external data (what the mother sees, hears, and derives from touch and movement), but from the arousal of her internal feeling states by these perceptions. The meaning of such states to the mother is derived from a lifetime of previous experience and from her most recent experience (minutes, hours, days) with her infant. She thus responds not to what she hears, but to what she thinks and feels about what she hears (or touches, or sees). The mother's responses are in turn perceived by the infant in the context of the infant's own need states, wishes, and bodily experience and consequently are incorporated into the infant's own subjective bodily experience. Affect signals reflecting bodily states are modified by subjective experience with the mother to become affects, which in turn come to serve as signals (Call, 1981, 1982). Affective states are differentiated as the synchrony in affective states between mother and infant becomes more refined and the infant builds up differentiated affective expressions which operate as a communication system with others. It should be emphasized that biologically built-in need-state expressions such as crying and smiling rapidly become modified by experience with communicating partners whose subjective responses to the infant's cries and smiles are reflected back in modified form, which includes this subjective experience representation. Such representation, in turn, becomes further modified by the infant's internal states and desires. What then gains mental representation for the infant and mother includes the subjective experience of the other. It is in this way that the two communicating partners come to know the subjective feeling states of each other, upon which so much depends. Physiological sounds other than crying made by the infant, such as breathing, coughing, cooing, sucking, yawning, screaming, humming, and various nasal sounds, together with states of illness, discomfort, and pleasure as defined in affectomotor patterns are attended to and responded to by the mother similarly, that is, through her narcissistic investment in the infant.

As these differentiated affect expressions are responded to by the mother, the infant develops an illusion of omnipotence within what Winnicott (1953) has described as the infant's intermediate area of experience with the mother. This illusion of omnipotence is supported in the infant to the extent that the infant's own needs, wishes, and bodily states generate affect expressions which are responded to by the mother. Playful interactions and games occurring within the mother-infant dyad help consolidate this reciprocal experience through the mother's clueing in to the infant's responses (Call, 1968). The first phase of the game—responding to the infant's starting and stopping—provides for the ordering of utterance and action in the dyad. Such ordering provides an early model for the emergence of syntax in later language development within the context of libidinal and narcissistic investments of both mother and infant.

Smiling and Facial-Vocal Configurations

Smiling operates as an organizer of vocalization in relation to other intermodal cognitive and affective experience. Concurrent with the appearance of more subtle aspects of facial expression and vocalization during the last half of the first year of life, phonemetization of affective utterance occurs and is endowed with meaning. Following this achievement, oral sound-making becomes linguistically relevant, not only because the infant can produce some of the phonemes of what is to become his native tongue, but also because he is capable of silence; that is, he becomes an active listener, increasingly involved in deciphering and decoding the meaning of and responding in a timely way to the messages contained in the mother's facial-vocal configuration. The capacity to inhibit responses to stimuli and thus remain silent is based upon the maturation of the central nervous system and the parallel ego growth emerging from ongoing object relations. The infant's capacity for deciphering the meaning of the mother's utterance while remaining silent in active listening reflects a high level of ego organization, memory, and integrative functioning. The child's subjective experience with dynamically integrated facial-vocal configurations in relation to the mother provides a context for being able to attribute affective meaning to vocal utterance. Stern and his group (1983) have demonstrated that an intense face-to-face interaction associated with equally intense and variable sound-making engagement is present at four months. Kuhl and Meltzoff (1982) have shown that infants eighteen to twenty weeks of age can detect the correspondence between auditorily and visually perceived speech (seeing but not hearing the speaker). Recent work with infant rats has shown that visual and auditory stimuli are integrated at the level of the superior colliculus, and that a visual stimulus stimulates auditory projections to cortex and vice versa. This finding provides a neurophysiological model for intermodal learning.

Various kinds of imitative capacities develop slowly over time and emerge only in the context of a relatively positive conflict-free relationship of infant and mother. These capacities are easily subject to conflict, fixation, and regression. When all goes well, a clear progression of imitative capacity, from manual and vocal forms of imitation occurring in the first six months to facial imitation occurring thereafter, can be demonstrated (Meltzoff and Moore, 1983).

The Evolution of the Pointing Gesture as a Protosyntactic Device

One of the first and most easily recognized bridges between patterns of early communication and later syntactic functioning is found in the development and use of the pointing gesture by the infant. The pointing gesture can be defined as a purposeful extension of the index finger directed toward an object in the environment and is usually associated with the infant's looking at the object. The extended exploring index finger may be likened to what Greenacre (1966) calls the prehensile eye, an extension of vision to locate the object. The pointing gesture evolves maturationally through the first year of life; during what I call Stage 1 (see Call, 1981), the unintentional endogenous stage (birth to nine months), the index finger (and/or great toe) becomes extended during states of awake attentiveness and excitement. During Stage 2, the intentional exogenous phase (nine months to twelve months), pointing is utilized in association with looking at an object and as a homing device for reaching and grasping the object looked at. Sometimes pointing will actually occur before the infant reaches out to touch or pick up the object. At the same time, pointing becomes a means of directing maternal attention, that is, as a referencing device, described by Bruner and Sherwood (1983). Finally, during Stage 3 (after twelve months), pointing is utilized as an intentional specific communicative gesture. Intentional exogenous pointing comes quickly on the heels of pincer grasp and often in association with idiosyncratic utterances such as "ush," "da," "unh," "ah," "unhuh," "oh ho," "see see," and "mine" or "me." In such instances, pointing functions as a protosyntactic device, a gesture serving to articulate nouns and verbs together as in two- and three-word syntactically organized speech. For example, pointing may be used to designate either an object or an action in an object-action phrase. As the infant points toward an object and says, "Mine," the pointing gesture is used to designate the object, while the word *mine* can be translated (from context) into "it is" or "give me." In this case, pointing represents the object part of the object-action phrase. When the infant points toward an object and says, "Me," looking at the mother, pointing is used to designate the action component of the object-action phrase, that is, "get." Fully translated, the object-action phrase would be "You get it for me." Such a translation by the mother requires a translation from infantese at the gesture level to conventional language and depends upon the mother's understanding of context derived from her own previous experience with the infant. The infant's capacity to evaluate the context of utterance in relation to reciprocity with the mother depends in turn upon the mother's capacity to create meaningful situations—affective expressions and gestures with the infant. It can be said for emphasis that language emerges from the end of the index finger before meaningful vocal utterance is achieved.

Pointing may be accompanied by a variety of other gestures, attitudes, and behavior. All of these taken together may provide clues to the level of separation-individuation the child has achieved (Call, 1981).

Omnipotence during the Second Year of Life

The psychological significance of standing and walking during the practicing subphase (Mahler et al., 1975) cannot be overestimated. Self-motivated movement in the upright position beginning at about one year of age brings about a new orientation not only in the outside world, but also to the inside. New relations with people, places, and things emerge as the child's relative helplessness and dependency give way to the anxiety of separation (Freud, 1926), which, according to studies by Benjamin (1963) and Ainsworth (1964), reaches its peak in most infants at about fifteen months of age. The child's sensorimotor experience changes dramatically as walking begins and for the first time the child experiences what must be something like a kinetic art gallery. The world changes as the child moves in the world.

With falling, gravity makes its insulting impact upon the child's sense of omnipotence. The normal child, however, seems enthralled by the new experience and is usually free to both regress and progress with the expansion of courage, interests, and resourcefulness. The child can hold on, and the usually cooperative mother allows herself to be used in restoring the child's sense of omnipotence. Both the external and the internal landscape are fluid and changing, fluctuating with the vicissitudes of the child's instinctual demands and the facilitating or nonfacilitating relations with the parents and siblings. The tie to the mother can no longer be taken for granted, and the psychological significance of the mother becomes more obvious, both to the infant and to the observer. As the child's anxiety of separation occurs in regularly recurring fashion, the illusions of the first year of life slowly give way to vulnerability and disillusionment during the second year of life and to the trials and tribulations of an environment that does not yield to infantile omnipotence. Primary infantile omnipotence is slowly and reluctantly replaced by shared omnipotence with the mother; this sharing is achieved through unconscious identificatory processes that result in an enriched, sustaining internal world of subjectively shared experience, an internal point of reference for future communication.

Transitional Phenomena and Language Development during the Second Year

Prelinguistic forms of communication, including "motherese-infantese" (Call, 1981), pointing and other gestures (waving bye-bye), support the illusion of omnipotence in the first year of life. There are a number of factors that lead to stabilization of functioning in the second year of life. The child creates a personal moritorium on separation (Roiphe, 1979) by utilizing secondary transitional objects and phenomena (Busch et al., 1973). Let us now examine the ways that "words" and word sounds are used by the infant before conversational language is established.

Whereas first words usually occur at about ten or eleven months of age, the child's "vocabulary" increases dramatically from one or two words at age one to 200 words by age two (Moskowitz, 1978). The meanings of words change, and a great number of single and multisyllabic, rhythmically-organized sounds emerge and are used by the child both in solitary play and in activities with parents. Moskowitz has described these sentence-length utterances of the late babbling stage as sentence units with distinctive intonation contour. Since the child utilizes a repertory of sounds, songs, and words in going to sleep, Winnicott (1953) has included these utterances as transitional phenomena. Weich (1978) has recently summarized the literature in this area and added some clinical illustrations of his own to show that language as a transitional phenomenon unfolds ontogenetically during the second year of life and prepares the way for further stages of language development. Most interesting and illuminating is Weich's review of videotapes of Lois Bloom's child, Allison, (Bloom, 1973) who at sixteen months, one week, invented the word *weda* and associated words and ideas. This was the most used "word" in Allison's vocabulary for three weeks and then suddenly disappeared. It was possible for Weich, on viewing the tapes, to intuit the meaning and use of "weda" from context. Allison used "weda" or "weda" words as she made excursions away from the mother to other rooms carrying her Teddy bear. As she returned to the mother, she again used "weda" groups of words. Through such use, it appeared that "weda" was her companion (an object as well as a word) which she carried about with her as she did the Teddy bear. Bloom (1973) observed that at sixteen months, three weeks, Allison used 272 single-word utterances and 78 utterances longer than a single word, 65 of which included "weda." Allison's use of "weda," like her use of the Teddy bear, would suggest that she had some awareness of words as things and symbols of things, and the idea that two separate symbols of objects or experiences might be joined and separated. "Weda" was a word symbolizing her conception of syntax and preceded by one month her use of two-word speech, thus providing an il-

lustration of how words function as transitional phenomena. Echolalia, delayed echolalia, and negative echolalia (Griffith and Ritvo, 1967) have been described as further illustrations of language as a transitional phenomenon. Ekstein and Carruth (1969) stated that the schizophrenic child fails to internalize the symbiotic merger with the mother and hence does not develop transitional phenomena or transitional object relations, including the use of words as a transitional phenomenon. Language in the schizophrenic child is thus acquired only by imitation. Neologisms represent regression, disruption, fragmentation, and lack of differentiation of language, whereas language in the normal child becomes creative, constructive, and adaptive and furthers the process of separation-individuation. In traversing the phases of separation-individuation, the child invents a grammar of experience, utilizing transitional objects and phenomena, including words and groups of words in various ways, to safeguard the journey from psychological fusion with the mother to a state of separateness. It can be inferred from such illustrations that the use of language as a transitional phenomenon provides the child a way of maintaining a personal subjective experience while at the same time sharing that experience with others. The child utilizes an idiosyncratic symbol system while inventing or discovering syntax, one of the most central and most formal requirements of language. In this connection, syntax serves to articulate aspects of subjective experience in relation to separation-individuation, as well as to establish rules for grammatical constructions used in sharing that experience with others. Syntax thus also serves as a form of self-regulation.

Clinical Example

NATHAN

An illustration of how transitional and language phenomena operate in this manner was provided by observation of Nathan. We had seen Nathan in our Longitudinal Case Study Seminar since age three weeks. He was considered an extremely difficult child to care for in the early months; he did not sleep well and could not be soothed easily. When seen at eighteen months, the mother reported that Nathan was still sleeping poorly and making unusually strong demands upon her attention. She was in a power struggle with him regarding eating and sleeping, and Nathan was not using language. His mother was also worried about family money problems and was uncertain about future moving and job plans. Both she and her husband were working.

Nathan's family was very musically oriented. Music was introduced to Nathan at an early age to encourage both his ability and appreciation. When seen at nineteen months, the mother looked more relaxed. She said Nathan's irritability and the power struggle between them were now resolved and proudly announced that she had discovered how to soothe Nathan by placing a steamer in his bedroom, noting that Nathan had become upset when the steamer, used for mild night croup, was removed. So she kept it in his room as a method of soothing him at night. Most importantly, she also had begun playing musical games with him—she would point to the notes and sing them out as he sat on her lap while she was singing a song. She emphasized the rhythmic aspect of music by pointing to the notes as they were sung and demonstrated this to us. She noted that Nathan's language development had accelerated but still was not as clear as a girl of equal age in the neighborhood.

Nathan was now a babbler. He would produce an extended series of vowels and consonants in rhythmic fashion, imitating speech without content, but he also utilized these rhythmic exchanges in a reciprocal fashion as if answering questions and commenting on the verbal utterances of others. His vocabulary at nineteen months included "I see you. . . . where daddy go? . . . I see worm." Thus, he was now quite advanced for a nineteen-month-old and was producing two-word speech. In our session at nineteen months we asked the mother to leave the room, as we do on a regular basis to observe the child's separation distress and reunion responses. Nathan waved bye-bye to his mother, he was watchful of the door, only slightly subdued, and not openly distressed in

her absence. When the mother returned three minutes later, Nathan greeted her affectionately and babbled in his rhythmic, chatty way while looking into her face.

Comment. Nathan's improved self-soothing, utilizing the rhythmically-organized auditory stimulation produced by the croup steamer to smooth the pathway toward singing and rhythmic babbling with the mother coincided with an acceleration in Nathan's use of syntactically-organized two- and three-word speech and improved relations with his mother; it was correlated with a major step toward his mastery of separation anxiety. The sudden resolution of the behavioral discord between Nathan and his mother with the onset of two-word speech is very similar to what I have described (Call, 1975) as typical for two-year-olds and is referred to by Gesell (1940) as "The Terrible Twos." Nathan's use of the steamer and his rhythmic use of sounds, together with the mother's well-timed introduction of singing while pointing at words, demonstrated the way in which rhythmic sound games can establish the foundation for syntax and how transitional phenomena can stabilize the child's separation-individuation experience with the mother during this crucial time. These transitional phenomena operating as an organizing grammar for the experience of separation provide a model for the emergence of syntactic functioning. This is in agreement with Weich's (1978) statement, "The maturation of transitional language occurs approximately between sixteen and eighteen months, somewhere between the stages of the one-word and the two-word utterance. It prepares the way for a major leap in language function—the full-fledged articulation of experience with the aid of words in sentence form" (p. 417). Nathan's mother correctly picked up the attempt on Nathan's part to simulate language by organizing it rhythmically as a sequence of variable vowels and consonants during the babbling stage. Thus he had the idea of a sentence as a holophrase before he could organize a sentence by syntactic rules.

Slowly the child reorders his own experience, utilizing transitional phenomena, thus stabilizing the sense of self during separation from the mother. This reordering of internal and external experience leads to a grammar of experience which helps restore the infant's omnipotence without exclusive reliance upon the mother. Let us step back and summarize in some detail the development of syntax as the infant progresses from symbiosis to separation.

From the Grammar of Experience to the Grammar of Language

Before stable self and object representations are established, the infant participates as a member of a duality, symbiotically fused with libidinally and narcissistically invested caregivers in responding to the world and in communicating needs, wishes, and other aspects of experience in the world to others. Single thoughts, affects, and images are unattached, unsequential, but drive-organized. Two or more sequentially organized thoughts, affects, and images are relatively more stable and become a nucleus of structure and thought (Call, 1964), that is, ego nuclei (Glover, 1943). Such nuclei bind affects, images, and thoughts to each other. Without and prior to such binding, individual affects, images, and urges are free to unite in a loosely associated way according to the urgencies of instincts and under the sway of the pleasure principle as reflected in primary-process thought. We are justified in using the term *grammar* referring to experience because the sequences are organized in an orderly, predictable fashion just as word sequences are in linguistic form.

As the capacity for relative object constancy is developed, the child is able to maintain stable representations of experience even in the presence of conflict, powerful affects, and other drive derivatives. Thus, a clear approximation of actual experience with the mental representation of experience is possible, and mental life as a result becomes less fluid and more stable. Thinking about various experiences (reflection) is then possible because the connections between fragments of experience can be established and can become organized coherently into wholes and in rela-

tion to ongoing experience. Sequences can be established and resequenced mentally. The reorganization of experience through thought thereby establishes a grammar of experience. This makes possible the mental rearrangement of experiential events, with reversals, expansions, substitutions, conditions, and qualifications. Under the sway of the reality principle experience becomes predictable and secondary-thought processes emerge more fully.

Once the child is able to establish relatively good object constancy, each new situation after the age of two—for example, entry into nursery school, change of primary caregiver, regression with illness, trauma—results in a recapitulation of earlier stages of development, including internalization of experience, mobilization of affects, and use of language as a means of mastery.

Parents play a major role in providing a secure platform during this fluid time, giving life and meaning to such experience and providing a forum for open communication with the child about it. The father usually plays a significant role in facilitating this individuation largely by helping the child find words and phrases that redefine experience in objective rather than subjective terms *away* from the mother-infant unit. The use of words as symbols for experience and of grammar in sequencing events facilitates the differentiation of persons, place, time, and casuality at the end of the second year of life. This grammar of experience becomes the deep grammar of conversational language.

Thus, in conjunction with a facilitating environment, the infant's experience becomes meaningful and comes to have enduring mental representation as it is organized into sequences. Once such experience becomes structuralized, a grammar of experience can be recognized. Language proper can then be used as a tool in reconstructing earlier experience. However, when prelinguistic experience is being reconstructed in linguistic form, the transition between the two grammars, the grammar of experience and that of language, may become interchangeable. Some additional clinical vignettes will further illustrate what has been stated.

Further Clinical Examples

VANESSA

Nineteen-month-old Vanessa had a forty-word vocabulary but was not yet able to put words together. Vanessa was the fourth child in the family and was, according to her mother, the most meticulous. She had special routines around eating, toileting, and telephone play. At meal time she would sit quietly in the highchair until her mother placed a napkin neatly around her clothes, leaving her arms free. She fed herself carefully, usually finishing one dish before going on to the next. When she was satisfied, she began playing with whatever remained, using her spoon and sometimes her fingers, spreading food on her tray. When she was finished with this, she participated actively in cleaning it up, using a dishrag or tissue. She then removed the napkin, got down from the chair, and left the scene. She also developed a steady routine around toileting. When she felt the urge, she used the potty about half the time and deposited her bowel movements in her pants the other half. When she did use the potty, she immediately dumped her "pooh" into the toilet and flushed it away. She did the same with her bowel movements when deposited in her diaper. When she was undiapered, she insisted on dumping feces into the toilet and flushing the toilet. She made an extensive ritual out of being wiped and participated in wiping herself. As she finished with this, she put her pants back on, washed her hands and face, and left the bathroom. She referred to both urine and bowel movements as "pooh," clearly demonstrating a high level of mastery of the genital schema (Galenson and Roiphe, 1974). Her word for the breast was "boo-boo." Her word for the telephone was "phone." She would pick up the receiver, say, "Hello," listen, and speak, utilizing rhythmically organized gibberish interspersed with recognizable single words. These imaginary conversations could go on for as long as ten minutes. She would at times hand the receiver to her mother or father or to a sister or brother, then take the receiver back and continue talking. When she was finished, she would say, "Good-bye."

Comment. In each of these routines there is a clear beginning, as shown by Vanessa's waiting to be properly attired with a napkin in place before eating, by searching for the potty before producing the bowel movement, and by saying hello on the telephone to begin the conversation. A middle phase of elaboration in each of these sequences is shown in the complex ritual of eating and cleaning up after eating, by doing her "pooh" in the toilet, and in the extended conversation on the telephone during telephone play. Each of these sequences is specifically ended: by getting down from the chair when the cleaning is completed in the eating sequence, flushing the toilet in the toileting sequence, and saying good-bye on the telephone. Single words are used, but most of the meaning of the experience is clearly decipherable by the mother who knows her role and can easily participate with Vanessa in all three routines. Each of these activities, eating, toileting, and telephone play, denotes a clearly defined sequence of action language which provides an opportunity for Vanessa to organize her experience as well as to reflect her wishes, moods, and feelings and to involve others in participating with her. Each of these activities reflects a well-organized grammar of experience. In fact, Vanessa introduces words into these action sequences at the appropriate places. Her mother responds as participating partner to these actions just as she does to her older children's word sequences. It is reasonable to suggest, in fact, that the organization of these routines was, in fact, created jointly by mother and infant and can be utilized as a "format" for joint communication as described by Bruner (1974). The three sequentially-organized phases of these routines share a common syntactic structure in that there is a beginning, a doing phase, and an end phase, which correspond with the syntactic rules that govern the production and organization of later expressive phraseology where there is also a three-part structure—a noun, a verb, and an object either expressed or understood at the stage of pivotal grammar.

PAUL

Paul had been progressing uneventfully until at age two years he manifested a marked change in his behavior that lasted two weeks. He frequently became irritable, was easily frustrated, and had bad dreams and temper tantrums. He had not been ill, there were no significant upsets in his family, and his irritable behavior was difficult for his parents to understand. His language development at that point was still at the one-word level. Suddenly his behavior improved, and he returned to the cheerful little boy he had been before this period of irritability set in. What happened? Paul developed two- and three-word speech. He could now clearly designate his wishes and needs, and he could successfully manipulate the environment, utilizing expressive speech which was temporarily withheld just at the time he was withholding his bowel movements. His use of two- and three-word speech and his successful toilet training emerged simultaneously.

Comment. This syndrome of irritability associated with transitory difficulties in toilet training is often seen in children late in the second year or early in the third year of life, and its resolution is often correlated with the onset of two- and three-word speech. If toilet training is pressed during this period of cognitive struggle before the child has achieved two- and three-word speech, it may unfortunately become the focus of a power struggle or a sadomasochistic conflict between child and parent. It is noteworthy that toileting and two- and three-word speech occur almost simultaneously, which suggests that language and experience are codetermined, thus supporting the main thesis of this paper—that syntax, an indispensable ingredient of linguistic functioning, has its origins in the child's experience prior to the onset of two- and three-word speech. Paul showed a developmental conflict which was resolved by the acquisition of expressive speech at the two- and three-word phase. An example of how language orders experience is seen in many small children with behavior problems who are unable to express

themselves. Verbal expression carries with it the capacity for secondary-thought processes, the ordering of drives, and mastery of self and others. Language becomes a powerful organizing force in the child's own internal life as well as in relations with others. "Acting out" can be understood, as Greenacre (1966) has suggested, as the representation in action of experience not previously verbalized. Treatment of such individuals is centered around providing linguistic codes in place of actions; these provide an opportunity for anticipation and organization of experience.

MARTHA

Martha was brought for consultation by her well-educated parents at the age of two and a half because she was not speaking. They feared mental retardation, organic brain damage, or "some kind of aphasia." Her hearing was normal. In clinical interviews with her parents, it was soon discovered that Martha was involved in a desperate struggle for control with her mother through her clinging behavior and her refusal to do anything for herself. She did not speak but appeared to have a normal level of receptive language. She was quite willing to play but only when she could control the play scene either with her mother or with the examiner. The mother was very angry about Martha's controlling behavior and resented having to stay at home with her. This resentment seemed to increase Martha's determination to control her mother, especially her mother's leaving. Martha was much freer and easier with her father, but she did not speak to him either. Joint family interviews were begun with Martha and her parents and a new seven-month-old baby once each week for one and a half hours. During these visits, Martha engaged the author in playful activities similar to those she had done at home. She then became interested in some of the unfamiliar toys and puzzles in the examiner's office, objects that were not available elsewhere. Slowly she showed increasing interest in the examiner as he engaged her in a wide variety of affective exchanges and gestural language, as well as simplified English. It was within this arena of "total communication" that Martha began using a few words, first with the examiner and then with the mother as the mother became more relaxed with Martha following her decision not to go back to work for another year. Martha became increasingly more relaxed with both parents and began to speak quite clearly. Within a few weeks her language had developed very impressively and she clearly spoke three- and four-words together. This once-a-week treatment lasted sixteen weeks, was reduced to once in two weeks for the next two months, and then once a month for the following three months. Regular visits were discontinued nine months after the start of treatment. Yearly follow-up information has been available for four years since termination of treatment and shows that Martha has pursued a normal developmental course, is considered an outstanding student, has mastered use of symbols in language and mathematics, and to some teachers appears gifted in her capacities for self-expression.

Comment. Martha clearly demonstrated "Attachment Disorder, Symbiotic Type" (Call, 1982). Her delayed expressive language was associated with her failure adequately to traverse the rapprochement subphase of separation-individuation (Mahler et al., 1975) with her mother. As her separation anxiety diminished during treatment, she began to traverse this phase in development successfully with concurrent acceleration in language functioning and subsequent normal development. This case study suggests that an early critical period for language development coincides with the rapprochement subphase crisis in separation-individuation. The treatment was designed to deal with the underlying rapprochement crisis and was specifically tailored to deal with the externally manifest conflict between the child and the angry mother who wanted to go back to work. Martha's failure to separate from the mother was correlated with her failure to speak. Her mother, because of her own conflicts, was unable to provide a meaningful, nonconflictual context in which Martha could articulate a grammar of leave-taking and reunion experiences. Therapy provided sufficient conflict resolution for the mother to allow her to participate with the therapist and the father in creating a play situation free of conflict, which allowed Martha to restructure her leave-taking and reunion experience with the mother. Leave-taking, remembering, and reunion sequences were built into play sequences with the therapist; these were observed by the mother and were utilized by her in facilitating Martha's communication around these issues. Martha's use of a favorite transitional object was also revived in this context. The child's ready response to treatment shows that the conflict was an external one, not yet structuralized within the child's psyche, and thus amenable to supportive intervention and manipulation. One wonders what the outcome would have been had the child been referred for speech therapy, nursery school placement, and selection of a substitute mother at home, liberating the mother to return to work, thus bypassing working through the child's rapprochement crisis with the mother.

GEORGE

The pregnancy with George was unplanned. Delivery occurred at term after a prolonged labor. George was "slow to breathe" at the time of birth. His mother was depressed and preoccupied with marital problems and did not (in retrospect) feel that she was able to give him proper attention. He was a "stiff, colicky baby who cried a great deal and slept poorly throughout infancy." During the second year of life, he became aggressive, uncooperative, very stubborn, and showed frequent temper tantrums. He did not speak clearly until the age of four. He received a great deal of corporal punishment and regimentation by the father beginning in the second year of life. At the age of seven, George was having serious difficulty in school, centering mostly around his "aphasia." He was also diagnosed as a hyperactive child with behavior problems. Medications did not help. An underlying developmental problem in central nervous system functioning was suspected. George's language difficulties were now complicated by learning difficulties in all areas. When George moved from grade school to junior high school at the age of thirteen, he faced serious problems in his social functioning. He was a strong boy and utilized his physical strength and his capacity to intimidate teachers and children as a way of problem-solving; he became provocatively aggressive. He refused to expose himself to any possibility of failure in school, consequently shielding himself from new learning experience. He fought and challenged everyone, ran away, and was finally hospitalized for seven weeks at the age of thirteen. He was found to have extremely low feelings of self-esteem and felt guilty and unworthy of the attention he received. He provoked punishment, restriction, and regimentation. His written and spoken languages were very immature, and he was unable to read, although he showed normal intelligence. He presented many borderline and paranoid features. Following discharge, George became an unpredictable tyrant at home and began experimenting with drugs. He finally stole his father's gun, the police were called, and he was placed in Juvenile Hall and then returned home on probation.

Comment. Stubborn, provocative, aggressive behavior was for George a dramatic reenactment of traumatic experience. Experience here refers to a fateful combination of biological vulnerability, environmental insufficiency, and overwhelming physically and mentally punitive encounters with his father utilizing corporal punishment. Syntactic utterance was late in coming and remained flawed throughout childhood; it did not lead to a resolution of his severe behavior problems as it did in the case of Paul, cited earlier. George's dramatic reenactment of earlier traumatic experience led to new trauma and a persistent power struggle with his father. His mother was frightened and estranged.

Both parents were quite articulate in describing their problems with George, but this linguistic competence was not shared with George. Needless to say, George could not talk about his problems or, for that matter, very much else. He was embarrassed by his speech and writing. His feelings of self-esteem were low. George's compounded biological vulnerability together with his linguistic incompetence set him up for the serious psychosocial

crisis he encountered in early adolescence when his only area of competence was as a fighter. While in the hospital, he felt that his case was hopeless and we were wasting our time. Simultaneously, he repeated his aggressive, provocative, dramatic encounters with all of us.

What light does this problem shed upon the development of syntax in the second and third year of life? During the second year of life George was already channeled into a very narrow range of conflictual behavior with his father. This deprived George of a free exploration of other developmental possibilities. His horizon of personal experience was very limited. Internal syntactic rules were not required for stereotyped dramatic reenactment of traumatic events. Such reenactment was simply a repetitive response pattern to any frustrating experience in the environment that elicited the trauma. Eventually his entire personality crystalized around this mode of reaction. Syntactic functions were not developed during the prelinguistic phase and were poorly developed during the linguistic phase. Hence, language was of no use to him in social problem-solving. Further, there was no smooth transition from prelinguistic to linguistic modes of thought and no clear transition from primary-process to secondary-process thinking. This narrowed horizon of concerns persisted throughout the remainder of his development. Aggressive, provocative dramatization of action became his principal mode of communication.

Conclusion

I have outlined the psychobiological underpinnings of reciprocity, affective development, and multimodal patterns of communication during the prelinguistic phase of language development and have suggested that pointing marks the transition between this phase and the development of language proper. My special focus has been to define the prelinguistic underpinnings of syntax that occur during the complex psychological struggles of separation-individuation dominating the second year of life. Other areas, such as semantic functioning, the evolution of symbolic functioning as it eventually takes form in language, and pragmatics, have for the time being been left to the side not because they are unimportant but because they are beyond the scope of the present inquiry.

In the pursuit of semantic functioning, the search for meaning is as much a search for engagement, sharing, pleasure, and instinctual gratification as it is a search for mastery and understanding. The semantic aspect of language encompasses this very broad territory, including instinctually organized affective communication. It is for precisely this reason that an exclusive pursuit of the developmental aspects of semantic functioning in language will *not* lead us to an understanding of how language organizes logical thought. Drive-derivitive behavior follows the route of instinctual gratification, which is seldom logical. An understanding of semantics can lead us to a better understanding of object relations, problem-solving, and mastery of the environment, formidable and important problems, but it does not help us understand the transition from primary-process thought under the sway of the pleasure principle to secondary-process thought organized by the reality principle. Conversely, the evolution of syntactically organized experience and of language does parallel the development of secondary-process thought. Syntactic rules for language establish logical sequences in relation to time, stabilize causality, and increase the capacity for self-observation—that is, objectivity—independently from instinctual drives, affects, and the vicissitudes of object relations. It can be said that syntax and secondary process are codetermined by the structuralization of these functions in the ego.

It is important to note in this connection that syntactic functioning, a progression toward object constancy, two- and three-word speech, bowel control, microcosmic play, symbolic functioning, the resolution of the rapprochement subphase of separation-individuation, the role of the father in facilitating the child's separation from the mother, the resolution of early-genital-phase anxiety, and the emergence of operational thought all occur during the second year of life. Physiologically, the two

hemispheres of the brain begin to function more independently *and* in concert as specialized sequencing operations center predominantly in the left temporal lobe. I have emphasized earlier the significance of sequencing operations in organizing both experience and the syntactic functions of language.

Evidence points strongly to the emergence of syntactic functions from transitional phenomena, which in turn leads to the establishment of a grammar of experience. The transition from the grammar of experience to the grammar of language proper becomes then the launching point for the achievement of the capacity for syntactically organized two- and three-word speech, which so revolutionizes the child's development.

Five different case studies of very young children have been provided to illustrate these developmental processes: Nathan, whose linguistic syntax led to a resolution of a two-week period of behavior disorder; Vanessa, who clearly collaborated with her mother in utilizing a grammar of experience in the highchair, in the bathroom, and in her telephone play; Paul, who, like Nathan, reorganized his life when syntax arrived; Martha, who showed serious interrelated problems in both language development and separation-individuation late in the second year of life and who was helped in conjoint psychotherapy with her parents to establish a grammar of experience leading to a successful resolution of both her language delay and her separation problems; and finally George, who was vulnerable biologically and whose early patterns of communication crystalized into a pattern of dramatic reenactment of trauma leaving no room for the development of syntactic functions, with the result that language was not available to him either for learning or for negotiating difficult social relationships.

It has been said that sentences leave traces in the mind which are easier for thought to follow (Panel, 1978). I would like to conclude with the comment that such traces may become as much a prison as an adaptation. The outcome will depend upon the extent to which the child, after the age of two, and the child's speaking partners can integrate the grammar and vocabulary of conventional language with prelinguistic forms of expression and with the language of experience during the second year of life. The freely communicating child continues to utilize a wide range of prelinguistic modes of communication long after two- and three-word speech is acquired. The poet uses language and words to explore the area of subjective experience beyond language and before experience was subject to the constraints of grammar. Freely communicating children are like poets. We have much to learn from them.

REFERENCES

Ainsworth, M.D. (1964). Patterns of attachment behavior shown by the infant in interaction with his mother, *Merrill-Palmer Quarterly,* 10:51–58.

Anders, T. (1978). State and rhythmic processor, *Journal of the American Academy of Child Psychiatry,* 17:401–420.

Benjamin, J. (1963). Further comments on some developmental aspects of anxiety. In: *Counterpoint: Libidinal Object and Subject,* ed. H. S. Gaskill. New York: International Universities Press.

Bloom, L. (1973). *One Word at a Time.* The Hague: Moulton.

Brazelton, T. B., Koslowski, B., and Main, M. (1974). The origins of reciprocity: The early mother-infant interaction. In: *The Effect of the Infant on Its Caregiver,* ed. M. Lewis and L. Rosenblum. New York: Wiley-Interscience.

Bruner, J. S. (1974). From communication to language: A psychological perspective, *Cognition,* 3:255–287.

Bruner, J. and Sherwood, V. (1983). Thought, language, and interaction in infancy. In: *Frontiers of Infant Psychiatry,* ed. J. D. Call, E. Galenson, and R. L. Tyson. New York: Basic Books.

Busch, F., Nagera, H., McKnight, J., and Pizzarossi, G. (1973). Primary transitional objects, *Journal of the American Academy of Child Psychiatry,* 12:193–214.

Call, J. D. (1964). Newborn approach behavior and early ego development, *International Journal of Psycho-Analysis,* 45:286–294.

Call, J. D. (1968). Lap and finger play in infancy, implications for ego development, *International Journal of Psycho-Analysis,* 49:373–378.

Call, J. D. (1975). Psychoanalytically based conjoint therapy for children and their parents. In: *American Handbook of Psychiatry,* vol. V, 2nd ed, ed. D. X. Freedman and J. Dyrud. New York: Basic Books.

Call, J. D. (1981). Some prelinguistic aspects of language development, *Journal of the American Psychoanalytic Association,* 28:259–289.

Call, J. D. (1982). Attachment disorders of infancy. In: *Comprehensive Textbook of Psychiatry,* vol. III, ed. H. I. Kaplan, A. M. Freedman, and B. J. Sadock. Baltimore/London: Williams and Wilkins.

Condon, W. S. and Sander, L. W. (1974). Neonate movement is synchronized with adult speech: Interactional participation and language acquisition, *Science,* 183:99–101.

Ekstein, R. and Caruth, E. (1969). Levels of verbal communication in the schizophrenic child's struggle against, for, and with the world of objects. *The Psychoanalytic Study of the Child,* 24:115–137. New York: International Universities Press.

Erikson, E. (1950). *Childhood and Society.* New York: W. W. Norton, 1963.

Freud, A. (1936). *The Ego and the Mechanisms of Defense.* New York: International Universities Press, 1966.

Freud, S. (1926). Inhibitions, symptoms and anxiety, In: *Standard Edition,* ed. J. Strachey, vol. 23, pp. 211–253. London: Hogarth Press, 1955.

Galenson, E. and Roiphe, H. (1974). The emergence of genital awareness during the second year of life. In: *Sex Differences in Behavior,* ed. R. C. Friedman, R. M. Richart, and R. L. Van de Wiele. New York: John Wiley.

Gesell, A. (1940). *The First Five Years of Life.* New York: Harper and Row.

Glover, E. (1943). The concept of dissociation. In: *On the Early Development of Mind.* New York: International Universities Press, 1956.

Greenacre, P. (1966). Problems of acting out in the transference relationship. In: *The Developmental Approach to Problems of Acting Out, A Symposium,* ed. E. Rexford. New York: International Universities Press.

Griffith, R. and Ritvo, E. (1967). Echolalia, concerning the dynamics of the syndrome, *Journal of the American Academy of Child Psychiatry,* 6:184–193.

Klaus, M. and Kennell, J. H. (1976). *Maternal-Infant Bonding.* St. Louis: Mosby.

Kuhl, P. and Meltzoff, A. N. (1982). The biomodal perception of speech in infancy, *Science,* 218:1138–1141.

Mahler, M. Pine F., and Bergman, A. (1975). *The Psychological Birth of the Human Infant.* New York: Basic Books.

Meltzoff, A. N. and Moore, K. M. (1983). The origins of imitation in infancy: Paradigm, phenomena, and theories. In: *Advances in Infancy Research,* vol. III. Norwood: Ablex Publications.

Moskowitz, B. A. (1978). The acquisition of language. *Scientific American,* 239:92–108.

Panel (1978). Language and Psychoanalysis. reporter, S. Leavey. *Journal of the American Psychoanalytic Association,* 26:633–639.

Roiphe, H. (1979). A theoretical overview of preoedipal development during the first four years of life. In: *Basic Handbook of Child Psychiatry,* vol. I, ed. J. D. Noshpitz, J. D. Call, R. L. Cohen, and I. N. Berlin. New York: Basic Books.

Sander, L. W. (1978) Infant state regulation and the integration of action in early development. Presented at the First Infant Psychiatry Institute, Costa Mesa, California.

Shannon, C. E. (1948). A mathematical theory of information, *Bell System Technical Journal,* 27:379–423, 623–656.

Spitz, R. (1964). The derailment of dialogue: Stimulus overload, action cycles, and the completion gradient, *Journal of the American Psychoanalytic Association,* 12:752–775.

Stern, D. N. (1977). *The First Relationship, Infant and Mother.* Cambridge: Harvard University Press.

Stern, D. N., Spieker, S., Barnett, R. K., and MacKain, K. (1983). The prosody of maternal speech: Infant age and content related changes, *Journal of Child Language,* 10:1–15.

Weich, M. J. (1978). Transitional language. In: *Between Reality and Phantasy, Transitional Objects and Phenomena,* ed. S. Grolnich, L. Baskin, and W. Muensterberger. New York: Jason Aronson.

Winnicott, D. W. (1953). Transitional objects and transitional phenomena. In: *Collected Papers.* New York: Basic Books.

Wolff, P. (1959). Observations on newborn infants, *Psychosomatic Medicine,* 21:110–118.

3

Influences on the Development of the Symbolic Function

Eleanor Galenson, M.D.

Why are some people capable of expressing themselves in complex and richly varied language, others able to use highly sophisticated forms of nonverbal symbolic systems, as in the arts, while still others are confined to "direct action" as their major vehicle of expression? I argue that the roots of both the verbal and nonverbal symbolic systems lie in the infant's earliest experiences of the infant-mother relationship. I believe that the quality of infant play is an important indicator of the quality of the mother-infant relationship, and that the nonverbal symbolic systems we later employ emerge out of some forms of play and are facilitated by the joint use of inanimate objects by mother and infant. I shall present data to show that the predominant affect of the mother-infant relation exerts an overriding influence on the infant's ability to transfer from the nonverbal to the verbal mode, as well as to expand the symbolic range within each of these symbolic spheres—verbal and nonverbal.

In a previous publication (Galenson, 1971), I examined the inherent mental organization or structure of children's play, especially for the light it shed on the nature and genesis of thought, on understanding the development of various aspects of the symbolic function, and as a precursor of the process of sublimation. In this presentation, I continue to explore the relationship of play to the development of thinking. My particular focus here is on symbolization as a basic aspect of the thought process.

Even if language remains the primary mode of human intellectual interaction, other levels of human interaction continue to be mediated throughout life by nonverbal symbolic modes of communication (Langer, 1942). And although the existence of these different modalities in adults has long been accepted, their genetic roots have not been sufficiently explored.

The earliest forms of play during the first six or so months of life probably serve primarily the function of discharge of energy, although the presence of some underlying imagery cannot be definitely ruled out. Animals play, although they do not talk. In them, as in humans, play does not appear to have a deliberate goal for the sake of which it is engaged in, nor is play necessarily social or competitive in nature. The primary trait of play in both humans and animals appears to be some preparation and anticipation of modes of activity characteristic of adult life. While play appears to have some maturational pressure behind it, it also involves responses that arise in the infant or animal in reaction to the environment, and it is therefore likely that there is some biological advantage for some animals and for humans in play behavior.

Because play is spontaneous and not immediately goal-directed, it allows for testing new variations of experience and idiosyncratic experimentation which is partly imitative but serves primarily as an open-ended preparation for activities to come. I believe that play is indirectly related to the beginning of thought and fantasy and that it is possible to understand certain aspects of the behavioral repertoire of young infants which sometimes appear to be pointless unless we regard play in this context.

When I speak of play as related to thought, I am thinking of a particular attribute of thought—the ability to retain and utilize inner images that have arisen from either sensorimotor or other types of experience that are similar to one another in configuration and have occurred at different times and under different conditions. This capacity to evoke mental images of experiences in the absence of a direct and immediate external stimulus is the unique quality that distinguishes humans from animals (Beres, 1965). Whereas both animals and humans can and do habitually respond to an immediate stimulus, only humans are able to retain and build upon the image of this stimulus. Babies show this capacity as early as the first year of life, according to Piaget; various types of imitative behavior—facial expressions and vocalization—demonstrate this in that the infant can evoke and discharge such imitations at a time removed from the original registration of the experience. Although the capacity to evoke a past experience is in part maturationally determined, it also depends for its development upon those experiences through which the infant gradually learns to recognize that the original object, usually the primary caregiver, has been replaced by a substitute. Animals do not learn this. If we can trace the steps infants normally traverse as they achieve this capacity, we can identify those factors which either enhance or distort the development of this capacity.

The beginnings of thought are the primitive forerunners of the symbolic capacity. As each object which substitutes for another begins to constitute a primitive symbol, these symbols become a component of a system in which other components become linked together, and eventually come to have a meaningful and systematic relationship to one another for that individual as a symbolic system. Psychoanalysts and linguists define symbols differently. For psychoanalysts, symbols are the manifest expression of ideas which are more or less hidden from the subject's conscious awareness, the connection between the signifier and that which it signifies being an unconscious one. In contrast to this definition of symbols, linguists consider signifiers symbols only if they share some attribute of that which they signify, regardless of whether the connection between the two is a conscious or unconscious one. This distinction between the two definitions is probably not merely a semantic one but may indicate that there is a fundamental contradiction between the psychoanalytic and linguistic views of the genesis of the symbolic function. I adhere to the psychoanalytic definition of a symbol in regard to adults, since I regard the presence of unconscious mentation as a *sine qua non* of adult human mental activity.

Piaget (1937, 1945) describes two developmental symbolic lines, one for the symbolic system of language and another separate and distinct one for the symbolic system of play. In the symbolic system of language each word is assigned an arbitrary and conventional socially agreed-upon meaning that evolves for the child from his environment. In contrast to this, the play symbol may be and in fact usually is an individual and egocentric one, which continues to hold its idiosyncratic meaning for the child long after language has developed, according to Piaget. Not until the eighth or ninth year does play become accommodated to reality, or a reproduction of it, rather than performing its earlier function as an expression of the child's inner fantasy life.

While these two symbolic systems appear to differ in their later developmental lines, their earlier pathways share some features. Piaget describes the beginning of play symbolism as it takes the form of imitation in the presence of the model: soon the uniquely human capacity for deferred imitation appears, in that the model is no longer present when the infant performs an imitative act. The most complex form of recalling the absent object is demonstrated in some of the test items Piaget formulated in relation to his sixth-stage of sensorimotor intelligence. These items demonstrate that the hidden inanimate object has achieved permanence for the infant because he or she reaches for the hidden object at the site from which the examiner's hand last emerged after hiding the object. With the achievement of the more advanced capacity for internal imaging, which is demonstrated by this level of functioning, children's play becomes less and less dependent upon the external presence of concrete objects. Objects and experiences not actually present may be introduced in fantasy, enriching the quality of make-believe play. Piaget's ludic or play symbolic system continues to develop in complexity, apart from the language symbolic system, until the eighth or ninth year. I suggest that aspects of the nonverbal system described by Piaget continue to exist, to become the "presentational symbolism" described by Langer (1942) in the artistic forms of music and the visual arts. I also suggest that the early ludic or play forms of symbolism find expression not only in the symbolism of dreams but also in much of the unconscious fantasy life of adults.

Although dream symbolism, like play symbolism, is partially idiosyncratic in that it creates forms that appear to express the individual's personal experience, both of these symbolic forms contain many features that are common to other individuals, if not universal. These common features of symbolism may be sensorimotor, olfactory, tactile, visual, or auditory in nature. What is the source of these shared elements, elements that may then be utilized in an idiosyncratic manner? It seems likely that the experiences of every infant in the bodily exchanges with the mother during the earliest months before separation and individuation, and those subsequent experiences with the caregiver which lead to the sense of self as separate from object, form the basis for the common symbolic forms during infancy and for their later expansion as development proceeds.

It was Ferenczi (1916) who first suggested that the precursors of the symbolic function consisted of the equation of one part of the body with another, and the eventual replacement of the first part by the second. Greenacre, in a series of papers (1953, 1954, 1955, 1958, 1960) in which she described somatic configurations or patterns of behavior coming into existence because of particularly intense or repetitive stimulation sustained by the very young child, expanded on the idea of bodily experiences as the primitive source of all symbolic equations. Such somatic patterns are then evoked interchangeably under subsequent conditions of stress, particularly because of the greater plasticity of the body image in the child, so that one part of the infant's body could easily come to stand for another. However, under certain circumstances that tended to lead to a greater than optimal degree of body-image instability, this line of development might be distorted, and Greenacre enumerated special situations that interfered with the development of a stable sense of self: premature birth, congenital defects, physical illness, and environmental conditions, such as serious emotional disturbance in the mother or any other factor interfering with the developing mother-infant relationship.

Greenacre also pointed out that the basic maternal body gestalt offers a constant framework for the mother-infant interchange. While gross or sudden changes in the maternal gestalt cause stress or withdrawal in the infant, lesser changes would tend to stimulate responses over and above what is necessary for purely maturational progression. Greenacre thought that these smaller maternal/infant shifts are the earliest forerunners of play, allowing for testing new activities without pressure for immediate struggle for survival. She designated this nearly automatic reflection of maternal expressions and body tension as the mirroring reaction of the infant.

I agree with Greenacre in that the strength of the introjective-projective mechanism in infancy would argue for the fact that the infant experiences the maternal stimuli as belonging to him- or herself, so that what goes on in the mother would constitute part of the basic core of the infant's sense of self, rather than an imitation of the mother. In a short time, however, the infant reacts to the more externally experienced maternal activities, activities that may be similar but not identical to one another or to other environmental stimuli; or reactions may be stimulated by a memory of the maternal activity or gestalt. Toward the end of the first year, babies appear to be quite aware of likenesses and differences and are busily exploring them. For example, babies are commonly observed fingering their own bodies and faces and then in turn fingering the faces and bodies of their caregivers, as if comparing the self-image with that of the mother. Furthermore, inanimate objects are mouthed and fingered as babies explore their configurations and properties.

By the end of the first year, a new type of play activity appears; this seems to represent an externalization or projection of body sensations and body functions onto inanimate objects. These play sequences emerge in a systematic fashion and are correlated with the period during which behavioral derivatives of the psychosexual phases also appear (Galenson and Roiphe, 1982). For example, anal-zone experience is represented from about twelve months on by play sequences which involve filling and emptying, smearing, piling objects, and various olfactory behaviors. Urethral-zone experiences are reflected beginning at about fourteen months by play consisting of pouring, squirting, spitting, and the use of hoses and faucets or other containers, including the mouth. Beginning at sixteen to nineteen months, both boys and girls engage in a variety of play activities that indicate awareness of the contours and sensations of their own genitals and awareness of urinary functioning and genital contours of the opposite sex. For example, girls uniformly place phallic-shaped inanimate objects in their pubic areas, simulating a penis; they also build nestlike structures (externalization of inner genital sensations) and engage in a nurturing type of doll play that appears to reflect their underlying fantasy of feeding as they themselves were fed. By this time the stool appears to be equated with both phallus and baby, as reflected in play reminiscent of the anal withholding which often actually takes place during anal-phase development.

During the same chronological period, the play of boys is characterized by a phallic, thrusting quality, and there are many indica-tions of their awareness, similar to that observed in the girls, of the genital difference. The boys test objects for their intactness or lack of it; they are concerned with imperfections in their own bodies, in inanimate objects, and in other people's physical intactness as well. This period of endogenous genital sensations in both sexes, the consequent concern about the genital difference and the genital loss, and the preoedipal castration anxiety reactions have been described by Roiphe and Galenson (1981). We believe these developmental events shape much of the play behavior in this age group.

The influence of object relations on the onset, nature, configuration, and structure of symbolic nonverbal play is comingled with the influence of the unfolding psychosexual organization just described. Such social games as various forms of peek-a-boo and bye-bye are intimately tied to the anxiety of repeated minimal threats of object loss as they are utilized in the task of achieving a sense of separateness from the caregiving object.

The Effect of Disturbed Object Relations on the Symbolic Function

The early work of Spitz and Wolf (1949) and Provence and Lipton (1962) demonstrated that deficits in object relations exert a profound effect upon the infant's investment in toys and play of all kinds. It has remained to be demonstrated how inanimate object play is influenced by less extreme conditions of maternal deprivation, as well as by differences in maternal style. One of the few longitudinal studies of play was carried out by Shotwell and colleagues (1980). They reported their observations of eight children studied from about their twelfth to fourteenth month of life until their thirtieth to thirty-sixth month with regard to their use of two play media—symbolic play and three-dimensional construction. By their fourteenth month, these children had gradually divided themselves into two groups, one group showing strong interest and skill in the configurational use of materials, using them primarily for design and the mechanical possibilities of the material rather than for communication or for the re-creation of personal experience. The other group began with a strong interest in the world of persons and feelings, and they either invested play material within interpersonal exchanges or utilized the feature of representationality in the service of sharing experience and communicating with others. The two groups began to blend by about two and a half years of age, but those children who at an early age had become more interested in the concrete properties of inanimate objects remained interested in play that involved configurational possibilities of various other symbolic systems: they built with blocks or other materials and were interested in puzzles, painting, and design, in contrast to the group of children who had stressed social interaction. The second group remained fascinated with the world of people and were interested primarily in communicating with them.

The drawback of this study is that it fails to describe differences in parental attitudes and other environmental factors that may have influenced the choice of play, as well as genetic features and early bodily experiences, which might also have influenced their choice of symbolic forms. Nonetheless, the consistency and the continuity in the type of symbolism and the use to which they are put is striking.

Our own clinical experience with infants and their parents has been an extremely rich source of data regarding factors that affect the infant's choice of symbols. We have observed, for example, that many caregivers do not use toys or any other inanimate objects in their interchange with their infants (Galenson et al., 1983). These parents described having had a similar experience with their own parents. This deficit in the parent-infant interaction seems to have important consequences for development in that the infants of such parents do not use the inanimate world of toys or other objects as an intermediary area between themselves and their parents. If and when these infants go on to develop the capacity to communicate through language, their language is often delayed in its appearance and characterized by an impressive paucity in the capacity to express feelings and ideation verbally. Insofar as

language remains the primary everyday functional mode of human intellectual interaction, as I stated at the outset, these infants' difficulty in verbal expression of feeling and ideation represents a fundamental handicap.

How does the normal infant learn to transpose nonverbal thoughts and fantasies into the verbal mode? Which factors might enhance or interfere with this process? It appears that play which involves maternal use of inanimate objects in interchange with the infant is an important facilitator, and we suspect that parental failure to use inanimate objects in this way to play with their infants impedes the infant's capacity to transpose meaning from the nonverbal to the verbal mode of symbolism.

Once language has been established, a primary means of expanding it is through the use of metaphor. Metaphors allow the individual to express his experiences and memories in extended descriptions, substitutions, and other forms of expanded verbal forms. How much more is conveyed to us when we hear not only that a room is painted yellow, but that the yellow is like that of early morning sunlight! We think the capacity to utilize such metaphoric devices has a genetic history in its own right. We suspect that again it is precisely those experiences whereby the inanimate world is consistently and collaboratively used by parents in their reciprocal communication with their infants that support the growth of the infant's capacity to effect a transfer from his inner private symbolic system into the common symbolic system of their shared use of the inanimate toy. The inanimate object shared in playful interchange is experienced by both members of the dyad almost simultaneously. The mother who engages in rolling a ball playfully to and fro with her child not only may use the word for ball, but she also acts upon the ball and acknowledges through her actions such "ball" features or properties as its roundness, rollability, and consistency, properties the mother and child experience together. In summary, the mother normally acts as a facilitator, helping the child bridge the presymbolic and symbolic states of mental functioning and then to transpose from nonverbal to verbal symbolism.

The Transitional Object and Anal-Phase Development

An early behavioral landmark of the developing symbolic process is the emergence of the special attachment to inanimate objects described by Winnicott (1953) as transitional-object attachment. While Winnicott described these objects as falling in the developmental line toward object relatedness, they clearly have additional roles in other developmental lines as well. In the developmental process from simple mental registration to the symbolic capacity, the transitional object may constitute for many infants their first personally created symbol. This early symbol depends on but also furthers many aspects of ego development, particularly in relation to reality testing and the sense of self and of others.

The influence of the caregiver on the emergence of the transitional object has been widely studied in a variety of situations and under varying circumstances. Roiphe and Galenson (1981) have identified a number of special factors that influenced transitional-object development in a group of seventy normal boys and girls coming from middle-class homes, averaging twelve months of age at the beginning of the study and twenty-two months at its close. We found that 80 percent of the boys and 86 percent of the girls had developed an attachment to an inanimate object which endured for at least a period of months; these were not part of the mother's own body and were used in a freely created way for self-soothing. Eight children developed attachments to nonsucking objects (excluding dolls) during their first year, and an additional eight infants developed attachments to blankets during their second year; twenty infants developed an attachment to animals or dolls, also during the second year. Breast-feeding did not preclude the development of transitional-object attachments, although some infants who were breast-fed did not develop such an attachment.

An important finding in our study was the fact that the few infants who did not experience separation from the mother at bedtime, who were rocked to sleep consistently in the mother's arms or in a crib, failed to develop a transitional-object attachment during the period of observation and remained dependent upon the mother's actual presence at bedtime. In these instances the mother's own fear of separation interfered with the development of the infant's early sense of separateness and with his capacity for self-soothing and his control and modulation of anxiety. These infants were not supported in their bedtime separation by the mental imagery that we assume accompanies the attachment to these special types of inanimate transitional objects; their mothers had not facilitated this basic step in symbolic development in which the transitional object is presumed to stand in part for the mother and in part for the child.

During the era when transitional-object attachment is emerging, anal-phase development is proceeding actively, and the stool comes to have a complex meaning for all infants, with more or less symbolic significance, depending upon the individual circumstances. For all the infants in our study the stool clearly had significance in that they reacted in a variety of ways to its loss; their behavior indicated interest and involvement in the appearance, smell, consistency, and other aspects of the stool. But for some of the infants in our study the stool appeared to represent a particularly important aspect of themselves or their caregiver, a meaning reflected in their refusal to part with the stool and their enormous anxiety when forced to do so. This reaction contrasted to the only moderate degree of interest in the stool shown by the majority of other infants. This excessively intense attachment to the stool was observed in those infants whose relationship to the mother was of a highly ambivalent nature, where hostile aggression predominated. We think that their hostile aggressive feelings had become excessively attached to their stool and to bowel functioning as a whole, and that defecation was then experienced psychologically as a discharge of hostile aggression toward the mother, as well as a loss of body part. Roiphe (1983) has postulated that the child is able to preserve an attachment to the mother by investing the stool with a greater degree of hostile aggression and thereby protecting her from the inroads of the child's excessive hostile aggression. Early excessive ambivalent attachment to the stool is of particular interest in that our clinical data indicate that the symbolic functioning of these infants is adversely affected by such investment in the anal product and its function. We have concluded that wherever intense and highly ambivalent anal involvement is present, it is likely to be correlated with delay in the emergence of symbolic functioning in general and of language in particular (Galenson et al., 1983).

Genital Psychosexual Development and the Mother's Facilitating Role

Other evidence of the facilitating role played by the mother in the symbolic development of her infant comes from our study of infants' reaction to the discovery of the genital difference, a normal developmental sequence observed in seventy boys and girls, sometimes between sixteen and nineteen months of age (Roiphe and Galenson, 1981). Several children had experiences during their first year of life that had made them particularly vulnerable to developmental disturbances when they reached the period of genital discovery. Among these disturbances was a variety of distortions in symbolic functioning. For example, several severely stressed girls lost their recently acquired verbal labels for boys and all male attributes, and they also regressed in their play with dolls during this period. In contrast, those who had not been particularly stressed during their first year of life showed an advance in the level and complexity of their semisymbolic play, an important aspect of the developing symbolic function. We surmise that the quality of the earlier object relationship affected the infants' later reaction to the discovery of the genital difference, including their symbolic development.

Deprived Infants

We have subsequently studied a group of infants from a lower socioeconomic level. A feature common to most of these infants was a marked delay in almost all areas of symbolic development, including language (Galenson et al., 1983). Another common feature was the unpredictability of the affective interchange between infant and caregiver and the unusual predominance of negative maternal affect toward the infant, present in many instances from the earliest months on. Mutually provocative interactions between mother and child often emerged in this group during the infant's first year of life, interchanges initiated by the mother.

In the course of therapeutic intervention with these infants and mothers, symbolic function in the infants improved along with the improvement in the quality of the infant-mother relationship; semisymbolic play, gestures, and then language itself appeared. However, their play has remained impoverished, and the transition from nonverbal symbolic behavior into language itself has remained far less than optimal in these infants. Since our longitudinal study is still limited in its duration, we do not yet know whether there will be a resolution of this early serious deviation in symbolic development observed.

In summary, the general quality of maternal responsiveness to the infant has long been identified as facilitating or inhibiting psychological development. But it is particularly in relation to affect, the mother's capacity to both correctly acknowledge and validate the nature of her infant's affective state and act contingently with it that the mother's bridging function is especially important. This is how the infant is gradually helped to sort out affective states. I believe that this constant reciprocal interaction not only facilitates the emergence of various aspects of affective development, but also plays a vital role in the development of thought and the symbolic function. Furthermore, failure in maternal recognition and maternal contingent unresponsiveness to the infant's emerging thought capacities and primitive symbolic steps may lead to a disturbance in the capacity to transform mental representations into the various symbolic systems that require ideas and conceptual organization for their development.

These normal symbolic stages include the emergence of the first symbol, the combination of a number of symbolic elements into a symbolic system, the elaboration of a variety of nonverbal symbolic systems, the transformation or transposition from nonverbal to verbal symbolic systems, and the elaboration of language by means of metaphor. Although we cannot yet identify the landmarks for each of these steps in symbolic development, I believe it is most useful to have in mind the systematic developmental sequence of the symbolic function. Only then can we identify deviations from this sequence, and the factors that may contribute to its advance or its delay.

Our therapeutic efforts in the area of symbolic usage will succeed only if they are firmly grounded in systematic infant research and the data derived from direct observation of both normal and deviant infants and their caregivers.

REFERENCES

Beres, D. (1965). Symbol and object. *Bulletin of the Menninger Clinic,* 29:2–23.

Ferenczi, S. (1916). On eye symbolism. In *Sex and Psychoanalysis: Contributions to Psychoanalysis.* Boston: Badger, 1922.

Galenson, E. (1971). A consideration of the nature of thought in childhood play. In *Separation-Individuation: Essays in Honor of Margaret S. Mahler,* ed. J. B. McDevitt and C. F. Settlage. New York: International Universities Press.

Galenson, E. and Roiphe, H. (1982). The emergence of transitional-object attachment during the second year in normal infants. (Unpublished.)

Galenson, E., Roiphe, H., and Zeifman, I. (1983). Infant psychiatry and pediatric ambulatory care. (Unpublished).

Gardner, H. and Wolf, D. (1980). *Symbol as Sense.* New York: Academic Press.

Greenacre, P. (1953). Certain relationships between fetishism and the faulty development of the body image. In *Emotional Growth.* New York: International Universities Press, 1971.

Greenacre, P. (1954). Problems of infantile neurosis. In *Emotional Growth.* New York: International Universities Press, 1971.

Greenacre, P. (1955). Further considerations regarding fetishism. In *Emotional Growth.* New York: International Universities Press, 1971.

Greenacre, P. (1958). Early physical determinants in the development of the sense of identity. In *Emotional Growth.* New York: International Universities Press, 1971.

Greenacre, P. (1960). Further notes on fetishism. In *Emotional Growth.* New York: International Universities Press, 1971.

Jones, E. (1916). The theory of symbolism. In *Papers on Psychoanalysis.* Baltimore: Williams & Wilkins, 1948.

Langer, S.K. (1942). *Philosophy in a New Key.* New York: Mentor Books, 1949.

Piaget, J. (1937). *The Construction of Reality in the Child.* New York: Basic Books, 1954.

Piaget, J. (1945). *Play, Dreams and Imitation in Childhood.* New York: E.P. Dutton, 1951.

Provence, S.A. and Lipton, R. C. (1962). *Infants in Institutions.* New York: International Universities Press.

Roiphe, H. (1983). Precocious anal zone arousal: A developmental variant in the differentiation process. In *Frontiers of Infant Psychiatry,* ed. J. Call, E. Galenson, and R. Tyson. New York: Basic Books.

Roiphe, H. and Galenson, E. (1981). *Infantile Origins of Sexual Identity.* New York: International Universities Press.

Shotwell, J., Wolf, D., and Gardner, H. (1980). Styles of achievement in early symbol use. In *Universals and Constraints in Symbolization,* ed. M. Foster and S. Brandes. New York: Academic Press.

Spitz, R.A. and Wolf, K.M. (1949). Autoerotism: Some empirical findings and hypotheses on three of its manifestations in the first year of life, *The Psychoanalytic Study of the Child,* 3/4:85–119. New York: International Universities Press,

Winnicott, D.W. (1953). Transitional objects and transitional phenomena. In *Collected Papers.* New York: Basic Books, 1958.

4

The Affective Self: Continuities and Transformations from Infancy

Robert N. Emde, M.D.

It is widely acknowledged that we are in a new era concerning the psychology of emotions (Campos et al., in press). Instead of being regarded as reactive, intermittent, and disruptive states, emotions are now regarded as active, ongoing, and adaptive processes. Emotions serve evaluation; they provide signals and incentives for new plans, new thoughts, and new actions. At any given time they allow us to monitor *ourselves,* our states of being and engagement with the world; they also allow us to monitor *others,* their intentions, their needs, and their states of well-being and engagement. Recently I proposed another adaptive function of our emotions (Emde, in press),[1] resting on research that has shown that emotions are biologically patterned with a similar organization throughout the life span. The proposal is as follows: our emotions provide us with a core of continuity for our self experience, an "affective self" throughout development. An affective self is adaptive in two ways.

First, because we can get in touch with our own consistent feelings, we know we are the same in spite of the many ways we change. Second, because of the biological consistency of our human "affective core," we can also get in touch with the feelings of others and be empathic.

Recent infancy research has contributed in a major way to this picture. It highlights the existence of a definitely patterned emotional signaling system between infant and caregiver, and it highlights the fact that emotional availability of both is essential for development. In this presentation a review of the recently proposed theory of a prerepresentational self and its affective core is followed by a review of the issue of continuities, with some new data concerning emotions. I then discuss *transformations in infancy,* times of biobehavioral shift, and some new research incentives for studying these. Finally, in a crucial addition for a theory of the affective self, I propose that affect has a transformational role in our self experience.

---

[1] In this presentation I use the term *affect* in a more abstract sense than the term *emotion.* Affect refers to the general category of psychological functioning that is theoretically separable from cognition, perception, and volition. Emotion refers to one or more specific patterns of expression, state, or feelings. These include joy, surprise, interest, anger, distress, sadness, fear, and disgust as well as more complex emotions such as shame, guilt, anxiety, and depression.

The Prerepresentational Self and Its Affective Core

A theory of the affective self must begin by acknowledging the recent empirical advances in our documentation of the developmental emergence of self-awareness. A variety of recognition studies (Amsterdam, 1972; Lewis and Brooks-Gunn, 1979; Schulman and Kaplowitz, 1977) have indicated that, during the age period bracketed by fifteen to twenty months, the infant emerges with a concept of self that includes a sense of continuity over time and space. Careful experimental studies have demonstrated clear self-recognition of the face by use of the mirror, and by use of videotape and photographic images. Taken together, the capacity to identify one's own image and respond differentially to it clearly shows that there is some kind of preexisting identity on the part of the one-and-a-half-year-old making such an inference (see discussion in Gallup, 1979). Recent studies using cognitive tasks instead of self-recognition tasks (Kagan, 1981) have reached the same conclusions: self-awareness emerges during the last six months of the second year, as indicated by self-descriptive utterances, by a variety of gestural directives, and by emotional reactions to success or failure. By twenty months, personal pronouns are being used when infants look at their own images in mirrors or pictures.

These studies add to what has become, over the years, a rich treasury of psychoanalytic observations concerning related phenomena. This is an age when there are corresponding developments concerning willfulness (Freud, 1905), autonomy (Erikson, 1950), the semantic no (Spitz, 1957), the beginnings of the representational world of self and objects (Sandler and Rosenblatt, 1962) and, most poignantly, the awareness of separateness, which inaugurates the subphase of rapprochement for separation-individuation (Mahler et al., 1975).

SELF AS PROCESS

The convergence of evidence is remarkable. It is also true, however, that one could be mis-led by thinking of a sharply focused age when self-awareness emerges, as if self were some sort of fixed attainment. Rather, self is more usefully regarded as a continuing developmental *process,* as a vital set of synthetic functions increasing in complexity and depth throughout the life span. Important later developments in the second and third years include gender identity (Galenson, 1982; Galenson and Roiphe, 1971; Jacklin and Maccoby, 1978; Money and Ehrhardt, 1972) and emotional object constancy (Mahler et al., 1975); in the fourth through sixth years, oedipal identifications (now documented by nearly four generations of analysts); in adolescence, another enhancement of self sense (Erikson, 1968); in midlife, still another new integration of self experience (Jung, 1939; Levinson, 1978); and then again in later life, a final integration of another sort (Erikson, 1959; Kohut, 1977).

Considering the self as a developmental process not only allows us to think of self-awareness as beginning in the second year and evolving to higher levels of organization throughout the life span, it also enables us to explore an aspect of self-process earlier than fifteen months, even before representation is possible.

BIOLOGICAL AND DEVELOPMENTAL PRINCIPLES

In thinking about a "prerepresentational self," I encountered three biological principles. The first concerns *self-regulation,* a principle that is basic for all living systems. But beyond self-regulation in physiological systems, there is self-regulation in behavioral systems. This is true not only for the short-term sense for arousal regulation, for attentiveness and sleep/wakefulness cycles, but in a more profound, longer-term sense for growth and vital developmental functions. The developing individual maintains an integrity during major environmental changes and sometimes in spite of considerable handicap. From a biological point of view, development is goal-oriented and there are multiple ways of reaching species-important developmental goals (Bertalanffy, 1968). Thus, children who are congenitally blind (Fraiberg, 1977), who are congenitally deaf (Freedman et al., 1971), who are born without limbs (DeCarie, 1969), or who have cerebral palsy (Sameroff, personal communication, 1981) have different sensorimotor experiences in infancy, but develop object permanence, representational intelligence, and self-awareness in early childhood. Another aspect of this form of self-regulation is evidenced by self-righting tendencies in development. For important biological functions, there is a strong tendency to get back on a developmental pathway after deficit or perturbation (Sackett et al., 1981; Sameroff and Chandler, 1976; Waddington, 1962). Recent observations of developmental resiliency—of infant deprivation syndromes corrected by later environmental change—are illustrations of this aspect of self-regulation (Clarke & Clarke, 1976).

Social fittedness is a second biological principle underlying the prerepresentational self. The human infant is preadapted for participating in human interaction, with biological adaptation ensuring organized capacities for initiating, maintaining, and terminating such interactions with other humans. These remarkable capacities have been elucidated not only in the infant, but also in the parent of the young infant where recent research has revealed a variety of species-wide nurturing behaviors that are performed automatically, beyond awareness, and do not seem the product of individual experience (Papoušek and Papoušek, 1982). Current research on behavioral synchrony also illustrates this point. There seems to be a biological predisposition of parent and infant to mesh their behaviors in timed mutual interchange during social interaction (Brazelton and Als, 1979; Butterworth and Jarrett, 1980; Sander, 1975; Stern, 1977; Tronick, 1980).

Affective monitoring is a third biological principle. In terms of the first two principles, this indicates that the self-regulating, social being in infancy monitors experience according to what is pleasurable and unpleasurable (Emde, 1981); in other words, there is a preadapted organized basis in the central nervous system for guiding behavior. In early infancy such monitoring is preeminently social in that infant affective expressions are used to guide caregiving. The mother hears a cry and acts to relieve the presumed cause of distress. She sees a smile and hears cooing and cannot resist maintaining a playful interaction. Later the infant makes use of the affective monitoring system for guiding his or her own behavior, whether mother intervenes or not.

Besides these biological principles, the prerepresentational self has a basis in several developmental principles. These reflect today's scientific appreciation of the fundamental activity of the infant who moves toward increasing psychological complexity: the infant constructs reality rather than having it as a "given." Further, these principles reflect an appreciation of human experience as organized according to polar opposites, which must be continually integrated by the developing individual (Erikson, 1950; Freud, 1905, 1915; Sander, 1962, 1964, 1983). These developmental principles include (1) the development of a sense of others and of self; (2) the development of a sense of the past and of the future; (3) the development of a sense of causality and noncontingency; and (4) the development of a sense of communicative competence prior to language (affective signaling).[2]

THE AFFECTIVE CORE OF CONTINUITY:
SUPPORTING EVIDENCE

The above principles, biological and developmental, provide a framework for the theory of an affective self. Its main thesis is the following: *our affective life gives continuity to our experience in spite of the many ways we change.* This is so because its central organization is biological and its vital relations are unchanging (Izard, 1977). Further, not only is the continuity of experience across development guaranteed, but what we may call our "affective core" ensures that we are able to understand others who are human. Finally, because our affective core touches upon those aspects of experience which are most important to us as individuals, it also allows us to get in touch with the uniqueness of our own (and others') experience.

---

[2]For an argument concerning the coherence of these principles, as well as the research which they summarize, the reader may wish to consult Emde (1983).

Several arguments support this thesis. The first is from *clinical practice and everyday experience.* We are aware of how much we rely upon knowing other people by means of understanding their feelings. Once we are in touch with another's emotional life, we are in touch with his or her humanity; this then becomes a basis for going further and appreciating that individual as a unique human being.

The second argument for affective continuity concerns a similar *organization of emotional expression in infants, children, and adults.* Our infancy studies have revealed a striking consistency concerning the organization of infant facial expression of emotions. Using a multidimensional approach for analyzing adult judgments, we sampled photographs of infant facial expressions in a variety of ways and at four different ages. We found that after three months, three-dimensional scaling solutions are typical. In these, hedonic tone is consistently predominant, with activation the second most prominent dimension, and an internally oriented/externally oriented dimension is third and least prominent. These results show striking consistency with research on adult emotional expression, which includes not only the earlier thinking of Spencer (1890), Wundt (1896), and Freud (1915) but also a host of experimental investigations (Abelson and Sermat, 1962; Frijda, 1970; Frijda and Phillipszoon, 1963; Gladstone, 1962; Osgood, 1966; Woodworth and Schlosberg, 1954). Recently a similar organization has been found in a series of studies of school children from grades three through seven (Russell and Ridgeway, 1983).[3]

The third argument for affective continuity concerns *cross-cultural evidence for discrete emotions.* Although Darwin (1877) had long ago postulated the species-wide existence of discrete emotional expressions, this idea was not systematically tested until a hundred years later by means of programatic cross-cultural research. Two separate teams of investigators

(Ekman et al., 1972; Izard, 1971), using photographs of adults who posed peak expressions, found remarkable agreement concerning specific facial expressions of emotion. Agreement was found among adults in nonwestern as well as western cultures and in nonliterate as well as literate cultures. Agreement was found for the emotions of joy, surprise, anger, fear, sadness, disgust and, to a lesser extent, for interest. This agreement seemed to imply a universal human basis not only for the expression of particular emotions but also for their recognition; furthermore, the specific facial movements involved in each of these patterns of emotion have now been specified. For recent reviews of measurement and coding schemes see Izard (1982) and Ekman (1982). Since the implication from this work is that we are born with a pre-adapted readiness to express and recognize these patterned emotions, a natural question arises: Are discrete emotional expressions present in infancy?

The fourth argument concerns just that, the *presence of discrete patterns of emotional expression in infancy.* Although research is in its early phases, there are already consistent conclusions. Infant facial expressions of emotion can be judged reliably by those who know nothing about eliciting circumstance or context; furthermore, such expressions fit the patterning suggested from research on adult discrete emotions (Ekman and Friesen, 1975; Izard, 1971; Plutchik, 1980; Tomkins, 1962/1963). Thus far this is true for happiness, fear, sadness, surprise, anger, disgust, and pain (Emde et al., 1978; Hiatt et al., 1979; Izard et al., 1980; Stenberg, 1982; Stenberg et al., 1983). Agreement is also possible among groups of judges looking at emotions expressed in still photographs of infants; such studies have been replicated both within and across laboratories (Emde et al., in preparation).

Research on vocal expressions of emotion, although relatively recent, is now becoming a lively area, with clear evidence for discrete vocalic expressions of emotion in adults (Scherer, 1979) but with work in infancy just beginning.

The final argument for the continuity in our affective life, for its human patterning, and for its significance in self-development concerns the *importance of emotional availability and emotional*

---

[3]The third dimension in this organizational structure typically accounts for little variance in scaling studies and is often difficult to interpret. It is probable that this third dimension is not a central aspect of emotional organization and probably represents a related subsystem of mental functioning; some studies only reveal the first two dimensions.

referencing. The importance of the emotional availability of the caregiver in infancy has been implicit in investigations of attachment (Bowlby, 1973; Matas et al., 1978) and has been explicitly stated by Mahler and her colleagues (1975). In a recent experimental study of fifteen-month-olds, we found striking effects of mother's emotional availability on infant exploration and play, depending upon whether mother was reading a newspaper (Sorce and Emde, 1981). But most recently, we have been absorbed in researching a phenomenon which we and others have termed "social referencing" (Campos and Stenberg, 1981; Feinman and Lewis, 1981; Klinnert et al., 1982; Sorce et al., in preparation). This is an aspect of emotional signaling that begins toward the end of the first year and continues to have major importance during the second year. Social referencing is a general process whereby a person of any age seeks out emotional information from a significant other in order to make sense of an event that is otherwise ambiguous or beyond the person's own intrinsic appraisal capabilities.[4]

It is already apparent that social referencing may be especially important at the dawn of self-awareness. Infants then regularly experience more uncertainty about the impact of environmental events in terms of their own safety or in terms of the consequences of their own actions. Also, at the beginning of intentional action, as infants are becoming aware of "rules," they check to see if the ongoing action is approved, disapproved, or ignored by adults.

Continuities from Infancy

A major challenge now presents itself to the theory of an affective self; namely, finding continuities from infancy to early childhood. The supporting evidence I have cited for the thesis of an affective core of connectedness throughout the life span has come from many

areas except one—longitudinal study. But before discussing the search for longitudinal affective continuities, I would like to review a bit about our search for developmental continuities in general. After all, without continuities there can be no self.

A RESEARCH PERSPECTIVE: DISAPPOINTMENTS AND NEW OPPORTUNITIES

In the past two decades, developmental investigators engaged in longitudinal study have been disappointed in finding little predictability from infancy to later ages. This has been true for behavior related to cognition as well as behavior presumed to be related to temperament (see Kagan, in press; McCall, 1979; Plomin, 1983). At the same time, clinicians who had assumed indelible effects from early experience have repeatedly been surprised by well-documented instances of resiliency following major infantile deficit or trauma (for reviews see Clarke and Clarke, 1976; Emde, 1981; Kagan et al., 1978). Thus, in spite of our expectations for continuity and connectivity, research evidence supporting such expectations has been meager. How do we understand this? As clinicians and as human beings we have an undeniable, intuitive sense that there are important continuities from infancy.

As a start, it is helpful to realize that recent developmental research has not simply been negative. We have learned a lot about early developmental processes, and, related to this, we may have become wiser about how to look for meaningful continuities. I believe, in fact, that some new strategies have emerged that are likely to generate major discoveries in the next decade. Let me enumerate a few.

One strategy will be to search for continuities in the second and third years when internalized sets of intentions and rule structures begin to appear and when the representational self becomes consolidated. We will return to this theme prior to concluding.

Other strategies concern a newer wave of methods in longitudinal research. In part these result from our hard-won knowledge about developmental processes and a change in thinking. Before turning to some new data

---

[4]Social referencing could be considered a type of secondary appraisal along the lines of the theories of Arnold (1960), Bowlby (1969), and Lazarus (1968). This is so because it is evoked when prior appraisal processes fail to predict the impact of an event or person.

from our laboratories relevant to infant affective continuities, I will discuss four of these newer approaches.

First are methods that look for developmental continuities within an individual. Up to now, developmental studies have used a correlative approach in which an individual's relative position in a group at one time is assessed in relation to that individual's relative position in the same group later. This is a rank order form of continuity search, one that describes an individual's position over time within an arbitrary group distribution. Although this has been the predominant way of searching for longitudinal continuities, this method is minimally relevant to a clinician's interest. The clinician is interested in meaningful continuities *within an individual* over time. Furthermore, the developmentalist has now learned that times of major transformation, or developmental reorganization, are frequent in infancy. Therefore, ways of typifying continuities within individuals as they pass through such transformations have assumed more importance. Newer methods seek *ipsative* continuities over time; these characterize meaningful constant relationships among intraindividual variables of behavioral organization. Block (1971) pioneered such an approach (using the "Q-sort") and found major ipsative continuities in adolescence. More recently, Martin found ipsative continuities in preschool children (as cited in Moss, 1983). This approach has yet to be applied directly to infancy, although a similar way of thinking has been used by Sroufe and his colleagues (Arend et al., 1979) in finding continuities in the organization of attachment from the beginning of the second year into preschool times.

A second, newer wave of thinking has to do with the appreciation of subgrouping. In any sample under longitudinal study, some groups are more likely to show stability than others. It is often possible to specify "moderating variables," which are the basis for subgrouping. Thus, in the Fels' (Kagan and Moss, 1962) longitudinal study, continuities were found through childhood according to gender subgroups (with aggressiveness for males and dependency for females) and in the Berkeley growth study (Block, 1971), important differences were found for adolescents who showed stability in personality variables over time as compared with those who showed instability. Closer to our age of interest, Moss, in preliminary data from a NIMH study, has found evidence for biological characteristics being more predictive for the behavior of males and environmental characteristics more predictive for that of females across the first seven postnatal years. Perhaps most dramatic of all, however, are data from two longitudinal studies from infancy into the preschool years; one conducted in Boston and the other in Sapporo (Japan). Both Kagan (in press) and Miyake (personal communication, 1983) have found a subgroup of "shy" infants who remain shy in early childhood, showing a remarkable continuity in their behavior in social situations. Perhaps even more striking is the fact that this subgrouping is based on those shy infants who have a physiological pattern of high, unvarying heart rate when processing information during a cognitive task. Thus, the moderating variable for this subgrouping appears to be a psychophysiological-temperamental one.

A third new approach for studying continuities takes account of the fact that we are not merely interested in stability of behavior over time, we are interested in antecedent-consequent relations. Thus, any given behavior of interest may appear different at a later age, particularly if the infant passes through a time of developmental transformation. Furthermore, related to this, it is increasingly appreciated that we must sample enough behavior at any given point of time to allow for a meaningful test of this kind of continuity; sampling for an hour or even a day may not be enough to be representative of the individual. Working from this framework, Bretherton and Bates (in press) have recently shown continuities in communication and language competence from one year through three years.

Finally, we have learned about the importance of infant transactions with the environment in early development. We must therefore find ways of searching for continuities in the relationship of the developing infant with that environment, in the "match" between the infant's characteristics and the characteristics of the caregiving environment. Thus the active field of temperament research is now at a crossroads in which methods are being sought to characterize the matches and mismatches that contribute to goodness-of-fit between temperament and environment and in searching for continuities that have not heretofore been found (Plomin, 1983; Thomas and Chess, 1977).

THE ROLE OF EMOTIONS: SOME NEW DATA

We have just completed two studies in our laboratory which suggest significant continuities in the affective life of early infancy, continuities that, although we have not yet typified "matches" between individual infants and caregivers, do suggest the importance of the social interactional level.

The story of this research began when we turned to the systematic study of mothers' perceptions of their own infants' emotions. Our view that emotions are highly adaptive and prepatterned in infancy did not specify how separate, discrete emotions appeared.

Are emotions present at birth or do they "unfold" postnatally in some way that is prescribed by maturational timing to be in accordance with adaptive coordinations relative to new emerging capacities? From our research experience, and that of many others, we knew that many emotional expressions become apparent considerably after the newborn period —for example, smiling and joyful expressiveness become prominent at two months, fear expressiveness at seven to nine months. But we also became aware that mothers of young infants report that their infants show a wider range of complex emotions than we had presumed possible. Further, recent data also indicated patterned facial expressions for a variety of emotions, although some were not seen very often (Gaensbauer and Hiatt, 1983; Izard, 1978; Izard et al., 1980; Oster and Ekman, 1977). We reasoned that prolonged observation was needed. Mothers spend more time with their infants than researchers and have more opportunities for seeing rare but salient expressions.

In a cross-sectional study of 611 mothers of infants ranging in age from birth to eighteen months, we asked mothers about emotions perceived in their own infants. One of the most striking findings concerned the perception of several discrete emotions seen by three months. Almost all mothers described interest, enjoyment, and distress in their infants at this early age. But a majority of mothers also reported seeing surprise (69 percent), anger (86 percent), and fear (69 percent) in their infants by three months of age. The reports of fear, anger, and surprise contrasted with previous findings in the literature, which suggested their onset several months later (see Bridges, 1933; Sroufe, 1979).

We therefore carried out a second longitudinal study to see if these results regarding early onset of emotions would be replicated and to learn about their developmental course. Thirty-four mothers were recruited to collect detailed information from their own infants at the ages of three, six, nine, twelve, fifteen, and eighteen months. At each age we asked whether a list of emotions was present and, for each emotion considered to be present, we asked (1) what caused the emotion, (2) what baby behaviors indicated the emotion was present, and (3) what response the baby's emotion typically elicited from them.

The results of our first study were replicated. Interest and enjoyment were reported present in 100 percent of infants from three months onward, and distress was reported to be high in the longitudinal study for all ages. For surprise and anger, 91 percent of the mothers reported both of the emotions present at three months, and between 91 percent and 100 percent of mothers reported these emotions from six through eighteen months. For fear, 65 percent of mothers reported the emotion present at three months and the proportion rose to 97 percent by eighteen months.

Surprise, on the basis of three-month reports as well as those through eighteen months, was most commonly described in terms of infant facial expressions, usually wide open eyes or mouth opened into an "O." Infant motor reactions, such as jumps, were also frequently cited. For maternal responses, a pattern was also consistent across age. Mothers indicated that at the moment of surprise, when they were unclear about whether the baby would react positively or negatively they tried to influence things to go the right way. Most often this would be by talking in a pleasant voice in order to prevent a negative reaction. Across age, the most frequently mentioned cause for surprise was sudden or unexpected events. But at three months these were more often reported to be sudden sounds, while at later infant ages unexpected events were more complex.

For fear, we also found an emotional communication system was present by three months, and was consistent across the age period studied. At all ages, the behavior most frequently reported was the infant's cry. Crying was described as screaming, piercing, or frantic. Although facial expressions were not salient in mothers' descriptions, information from at least one other area of infant behavior was usually noted. Early behaviors tended to be motoric, such as startles or jumps. Later, "increased tension" became prominent, and from nine to eighteen months, purposeful behaviors such as making contact with mother and avoidance replaced generalized motor reactions as the second most salient indicator of fear. Earlier, loud sounds were prominent as elicitors of fear, but beginning at nine months, strangers became increasingly mentioned. Again, despite age-related qualitative changes in infant behavior, the mother-infant signaling system appeared relatively constant. Whether infants were three or eighteen months, all mothers who perceived fear reported that their response was to comfort. Early maternal responses involved physical touching more than they did later (although infants were then contacting mother). Thus, from three through eighteen months the signaling system involved a cry. The mother soothed, and the goal seemed to be the achievement of physical proximity between the two.

For anger, mothers identified a unique group of behaviors. Crying was one element of this group, with a quality described as "hard," "loud," or "forceful." Mothers typically noted at least one other behavior besides crying. About one half of the mothers of three-month-olds described facial expression (usually red-faced) as signaling anger. Equally

prominent were more generalized responses such as kicking and back-arching. This pattern of crying, facial expressions, and more general motor responses continued over the next fifteen months. But by nine months many mothers mentioned pushing mom away as indicating anger. These mildly aggressive behaviors heralded a major qualitative change at the beginning of the second year. At this time, although crying still occurred, behavior was now viewed as involving purposefulness, willfulness, aggressiveness, or tantrums. At fifteen months all mothers but one described their infants as showing anger either by aggression toward another person, such as kicking or hair-pulling, or by throwing themselves onto the floor. Further, there was an increase in the reported number of angry incidents beginning at twelve months.

Parental responses paralleled infant behaviors. At all ages mothers reported frustration of wants or needs as the primary cause of anger, but at three months, mothers experience some urgency about alleviating the cause or about comforting, whereas this was not true later. Instead, by the time infants had reached twelve months, mothers typically distracted, ignored, or disciplined their infants under these circumstances.

For interest, enjoyment, and distress, the signaling system emerged during the earliest months, as was expected, and manifested a fairly continual progression over the next fifteen months of the study. For interest, visual attentiveness indicated the emotion was present, whereas for enjoyment, vocalization, smiling, and motoric behaviors such as wriggling were most prominent. In general, causes of interest were objects or noninteracting people, whereas interacting with people was the most common cause of enjoyment. For both emotions, typical eliciting stimuli increased in complexity with age. Distress was present from early infancy and was perceived as an emotion when infant cries (usually whimpering or wailing) were unaccompanied by further cues such as red faces or startled reactions. Most mothers attributed these kinds of emotional reactions to physical illness or discomfort.

Thus, overall, mothers perceived consistent

patterns of affective behaviors in their own infants. These occurred in certain situations and not in others, were capable of being labeled discrete emotions, and led to particular sets of maternal responses. Although infant behaviors became increasingly complex and organized with age, there was a perceived clarity of infant signaling and a regularity of maternal response from three through eighteen months. From the mothers' point of view, continuity was impressive. But further inference seems warranted. Our data indicate there was continuity at the level of interpersonal affective interaction, and it seems likely that such a continuity would contribute substantially to infant experience. Early in infancy, mothers seem to provide more of the integration and extended meaning for early affective experience;[5] later, the organizing capacity of the infant is such that more is coherent and sustained outside of the caregiving interaction.

Transformations in Infancy

Another challenge that presents itself to the theory of an affective self concerns transformations in infancy. We now know there are nodal times of qualitative change when behavior is reorganized and when new modes of activity emerge. Since these involve widespread changes in state or arousal development, in cognition, in perception, and in motor and affective development, there is reason to believe that these times reflect normative central nervous system (CNS) regulatory shifts. In his *Genetic Field Theory of Ego Formation,* Spitz (1959) referred to these as new "psychic organizers"; in our earlier longitudinal study we referred to them as times of "biobehavioral shift" (Emde et al., 1976). Others have referred to them as times of developmental discontinuity or as representing stage boundaries in cognitive development (McCall, 1979; Uzgiris, 1976).

---

[5]Both in this and in mother's help in regulating extremes of emotions, one is reminded of Bion's (1962) concept of the "mother as a container" for early infantile experience.

A RESEARCH PERSPECTIVE: FOUR
BIOBEHAVIORAL SHIFTS

There is now a remarkable convergence of thinking among researchers about the times of such normative transformations. These are observed to occur at two months, at seven to nine months, at twelve to thirteen months, and at eighteen to twenty-one months.

In each of these developmental transformations affect is salient. Spitz referred to affect as the "indicator" of the new organizer. I look to the next decade of research to elucidate our understanding of these transformations, not merely because of a convergence of thinking, but because of a new generation of measures. These include measures of behavioral processes, such as those related to affective organization and social interaction, and measures of physiological processes, such as those related to the electrophysiology of CNS maturational events and those related to the endocrinology of physical growth spurts (Lampl and Emde, in press). That affect may have a crucial role in these regulatory shifts can be highlighted by a brief review of some of the phenomena.

FIRST-YEAR SHIFTS

The developmental transformation at two months occurs against a background of an increase in the amount of wakefulness that has been occurring over the first two postnatal months. The distribution of wakefulness also changes, with more of it occurring during the day and less at night. Further, there is a change in the quality of wakefulness; less of it is complicated by fussiness and, as some observers have put it, wakefulness becomes used "in a new way" with increased exploratory activity, whether with tous or people (Dittrichova and Lapackova, 1964). In fact, enhanced learning has been shown in the three experimental realms of operate conditioning, classical conditioning, and habituation. After two months the infant can learn in a variety of ways, can accommodate and change behavior in a social situation and adjust to what is familiar, thereby completing learned activities so that exploration of the new is possible. It is a time when Piaget, in his scheme of cognitive development, notes that the infant becomes increasingly involved in activities "designed to make interesting spectacles last" (see review in Emde and Robinson, 1979).

Beginning around two months new parents often state that their baby seems more human and less a doll-like creature. But while the cognitive and state changes noted earlier contribute to this new sense, these are minor compared with changes in the affective realm. I think of a triad of changes, which appear quite dramatically at this time and which are apt to give pleasure and incentive for continuing to be with the baby. These include (1) enhanced eye-to-eye contact, (2) social smiling, and (3) social vocalizing. Enhanced eye-to-eye contact around two months has not only been described in the naturalistic setting (Robson, 1967) but has been documented experimentally (Haith et al., 1977). The social smile also blossoms around two months. Although smiling has developmental antecedents, there is a shift from endogeneous (state-related) smiling to exogeneous smiling at this time, and this response becomes predictable and social (Emde and Harmon, 1972). Social vocalization, or cooing in response to the face of another, begins within one to two weeks after the flowering of the social smile. Altogether, parents now begin to think of their baby as playful. When they approach during wakefulness there is apt to be back-and-forth smiling, vocalizing, and looking, which give an affirming, fun-filled encounter—an exchange that is a welcome addition to the routines of caregiving.

At seven to nine months another major shift occurs. Leading up to this, the infant sits up and begins to crawl. With self-produced locomotion the infant's world changes again. In the realm of cognition the infant shows a beginning of understanding means-ends relationships and of intentionality in the sense of anticipating an event independent of action (the onset of Piaget's stage IV of sensorimotor development). Further, out of sight is not out of mind. The infant can purposefully remove a cloth covering a hidden object that was seen to disappear under it. Related to this accomplishment is an advance in emotional capacity. We can see that an infant can now demonstrate fearfulness expressions in advance of avoidance and pleasure in advance of approach. There is thus now play in addition to playfulness. Simple games begin with peek-a-boo, social games, and give and take with balls or favorite toys. Freud (1920) and Spitz (1957) have discussed how these games seem to have a theme of withdrawal and return and may bear a relationship to the comings and goings of caregivers as well as to the infant's beginning sense of mastery and coping with such experiences.

This change is also heralded by another shift in wakefulness and sleep-state organization between seven and nine months (Emde et al., 1976). But there is another change, now well studied (for a review see Horner, 1980), which has special emotional significance to parents. Up to this time, although their baby may have smiled or reacted more pleasantly to them as compared to strangers, substitute caregiving was relatively uncomplicated. Now things are apt to be different. The baby may cry when mother or father leaves and often manifests distress or even fearfulness when a stranger approaches. A recent experimental study (Fouts and Atlas, 1979) documents the change in still another way; while infants at six and nine months experienced mother's face as rewarding, they experienced a stranger's face as neutral at six months and negatively reinforcing at nine months. After this shift, substitute caregiving is more difficult, but parents feel needed and special. The developmental message is generally compelling: no one else will do.

We have sometimes referred to these nodal transformations in the first year in terms of their social properties, referring to the two-month shift as "the awakening of sociability" and the seven-to-nine-months shift as "the onset of focused attachment." Whatever else, these shifts inaugurate new levels of organization in the infant's social world—in terms of what is demanded, what is rewarding, what is expectable, and what is reciprocated.

SECOND-YEAR SHIFTS

The second-year transformations have not yet been studied in the same detail as the first-year transformations. Nonetheless, striking features have been documented.

At twelve to thirteen months walking usually has its onset and toddlerhood begins. In terms of cognition, the infant begins to appreciate the independence of entities in the world and understand that they carry with them their own independent properties. In terms of language, the infant can now comprehend that a word is agreed upon to designate a specific object. Symbolic functioning enters a new domain (see Kagan, 1981; McCall, 1979). The infant can imitate totally new behaviors not previously seen and not currently in the response repertoire. In the realm of affect there are also important changes. The year-old infant's frequent mood of "elation" in exploring the world has been commented upon by many (Mahler et al., 1975; Sroufe, 1979). Experimentally, it has been shown that an infant's control over activating a potentially fear-provoking toy can reduce distress at twelve months, but not earlier (Gunnar, 1980). As we have noted, social referencing is prominent in situations of affective uncertainty. Further, this is a time when the infant begins to use affect expressions instrumentally or purposefully. Parents note that smiling and pouting expressions can be used by babies in order to "get their way." As we have discussed, anger is now often directed at a person. Correspondingly, the infant is now held more accountable, and parents begin to take on the role of "disciplinarians" in addition to caregivers. Parents become concerned about socializing emotions (whether to encourage or inhibit anger or sadness, for example).

Eighteen to twenty-one months is another time of transformation. Mahler and her colleagues (1975) describe that the child, while energetically exercising growing autonomy also frequently both pushes mother away and clings to her. In terms of cognition, the child is capable of remembering and imitating sequences of actions, and of understanding symbolic relationships between entities. Two-word utterances with a subject and a predicate become possible. In terms of affect, this is the time of the upsurgence of "willfulness," of the exercising of the "semantic no," and of increased temper tantrums. There may be, as Mahler and her group have pointed out,

swings of mood and evidence of sadness—mood changes they relate to the beginnings of the rapprochement crisis (Mahler et al., 1975). In observed interaction with mother there are apt to be "shadowing and darting-away patterns"; the earlier "emotional refueling" type of interactions with mother tend to be replaced by a deliberate search for or avoidance of close bodily contact. It is as if toddlers are keenly aware of their separateness and the obstacles to mastering the world on their own. Obviously, this brings forth further changes in the child's social world. Caregivers react to these affective changes in a variety of ways, often reflecting their own developmental experiences with separation-individuation. Some may feel prideful and encourage autonomy, others may feel uneasy and protective.

THE ROLE OF EMOTIONS IN DEVELOPMENTAL TRANSFORMATIONS

As we have seen, it is typical that a change of affect accompanies each shift to a new developmental level of organization. At first we thought that affective change might herald or "lead" the shift, but longitudinal observations have indicated this is not so (Emde et al., 1976). In fact, we have found that changes in affective behavior seem clearest at the concluding phase of the shift, after motoric, perceptual, and cognitive changes have taken place. In thinking about the mysteries of developmental transformation, I have come to the view that affective changes may occur during the final phase of a developmental transformation in order to provide an incentive for the consolidation of other changes. If this is so, it would identify still another adaptive role for our emotions—namely that of guiding integration. Emotions would here sustain adaptive functioning at a higher level of organization through two modes. One would be through *social feedback* (what is attended to and rewarded) and the other would be through *internal feedback* (what is experienced as new, interesting, and pleasurably mastered). Both of these modes provide incentives for engagement with the world at a new level; they, thus, promote a wider world of being and interaction.

To recapitulate my view: because of maturational events, a group of transformational changes occurs in the organization of state, perception, cognition, and motor and language development. Affective changes, often dramatic, may also reflect these maturational events but are seen to have an adaptive role in providing integration and sustained functioning at a new level of organization. In the current presentation, I have emphasized the social mode of feedback and integration; more needs to be elaborated concerning the experiential mode. In addition, I have discussed affect in general terms only (what is pleasurable and unpleasurable); more needs to be elaborated concerning specific features of discrete emotions.

The Overall Transition from Infancy to Early Childhood

Because much research needs to be done, considerable uncertainty exists regarding the times of transformation in the second year. But beyond this, we have reason to be excited about the opportunities for research in a broader period—namely, the transition from infancy to early childhood during the second and third years. This is so for several reasons. First, it is a period when there are major developmental acquisitions whose emergent qualities differentiate man from other primates; the timing and mode of onset of these acquisitions are still not understood. Second, it is a period when behavioral continuities from infancy to childhood start to become convincing. Third, it is a period in which a second transformational role of affect emerges, one that brings a new dimension to the affective self.

A RESEARCH PERSPECTIVE: TRANSFORMATIONS
LEADING TO CONTINUITY

Let me enumerate some of the developmental acquisitions of this period which are now becoming the subject of intensive interdisciplinary research. We have already alluded to the emergence of self-awareness,

self-consciousness, and gender identity. Other acquisitions include language, symbolic play, and advanced cognitive capacities, such as the attribution of causality and the beginning awareness of social rules. Related to these intriguing acquisitions in social and affective development are becoming the subject of particular scrutiny.

In the social domain, the child begins to appreciate something about social relationships. Evidence suggests that in the presence of significant others the toddler becomes acutely sensitive to being included or "left out." Along with an increasing sense of autonomy, the child develops a sense of personal space and possession. These attributes have yet to be adequately described and understood.

There are also important affective acquisitions. Coincident with the child's greater representational capacities, this is a period when signs of anxiety can be seen in anticipation of task failure, and, correspondingly, pride can be seen following success obtained with effort. Now too, other, more complex emotions based on new cognitive capacities appear. These include shame and then what appear to be early forms of guilt. Also, emotional expressions begin to be used instrumentally; that is, particular expressions (such as smiling, sounding angry, or looking sad) are used to influence adults for a purpose. And corresponding to this, expressions of emotions become socialized so that some are at times inhibited or "masked" (especially with anger, sadness, and fear expressions).

But as laden with novel transformations as this period is, it is also a period when behavioral continuities begin to become manifest. As we have reviewed, recent research has suggested that individual variations in behavior observed during the first twelve months, however striking, are not directly predictive of later childhood behaviors except in extreme conditions. By contrast, the results of several longitudinal studies support the idea that some of the variation observed among three-year-olds is preserved, at least through school entrance. It seems probable that the self-organizing qualities that emerge during the one-to-three year period will allow us to see behavioral continuities, in contrast to the apparent lack of continuities between developmental events during the first year of life and later periods. Certainly, from what we know, it seems plausible to assume that during the second year children begin to relate their experiences to an inner executive and to evaluate themselves as competent or incompetent (see Bandura, 1981) and, in some ways, as "good" or "bad." The consolidation of self-awareness during the second and third years imposes a frame for experience that tends to promote preservation of particular behaviors and not others. There are indications that this is a time when reliable patterns of reaction to conflict, potential failure, violation of adult standards, social skills, and dominance by other children may emerge. Thus, there is promise that investigation of this period may reveal why some children are more resilient to conflict, anxiety, and privation than others.

Affect theory promises considerable usefulness in understanding self organization and in finding continuities during this age period, which bridges the experience of infancy to that of early childhood. As I have outlined, the child comes to this period with an affective core for self experience. Although this is a time when emotional signals assume less importance for social communication, as language takes over this function, organized feeling states continue to provide a context for social exchange and private experience. Thus, not only do affect expressions become "socialized" during this time (that is, they become an acceptable background for social discourse) but, more poignantly, *internal feeling states become increasingly organized.* This process occurs as emotional connections are made with internalized social "objects." It also occurs as patterned feeling states become connected in specific clusters which are also linked to memories of events, and which become used in anticipation or in internal affect signaling (cf. Emde, 1980; Engel, 1962; Freud, 1926). I believe there is promising evidence that such clusters begin during this time and include signal affects of anxiety, shame, depression, and forerunners of guilt. I hope it is apparent, however, that much research remains to be done. We need to know more about individual differences in family so-cialization practices and how different affective transactions influence what the child internalizes. Patterned feeling states and internal affective signaling systems need to be understood in relation to conflict, coping, and stress.

THE ROLE OF EMOTIONS IN EMPATHIC TRANSFORMATIONS

A second major transformational role of affect is acquired during this period through empathy. It is in empathy that the child "gets in touch" with the experience of another; experience is transformed by encountering something quite new and outside of one's own experience. Similar to the role of emotions in developmental transformations, emotions during empathy move one toward a new point of view, toward a new integration. Both kinds of transformation participate in a regulatory shift, but with empathy this is apt to be in the short time frames involved in human interaction, as contrasted with the longer time frames involved in development. Both transformational processes are analogous, however, in touching us to the core.

Much research remains to be done about empathy. Through the work of Zahn-Waxler and Radke-Yarrow (1982) and others we know that prosocial behaviors (and, by inference, empathic processes) begin during the second year. It may be that the capacity to empathize with the pain of another matures at this time, together with the emergence of other fundamental but complex capacities that link cognition and emotion (such as pride, shame, and anticipatory anxiety). It may also be that there is a required linkage with the ability to infer the causes of events and to recognize one's sense of agency in acts that harm or help another. These are only a few of the questions that need to be answered. It may even be, as Kagan (in press) and Hoffman (1983) have suggested, that young children have some tendency because of this empathic process to impose standards on aggressive behavior, regardless of their history of rewards and punishments. If this idea were found to be true, it would have profound implications for our understanding the origins of moral development. But we need more study of individual differences, especially of children who vary in aggressiveness, anger, and empathic abilities, and of individual differences in family socialization experiences.

Conclusion: Transformational Affect and Self Experience

We have inferred that affect is transformational, both for development and empathy. Spitz (1959) postulated that affective change served as the indicator of new psychic organization in infancy. We can now further postulate that affect is integrative. Affect allows the possibility of our experiencing a new level of understanding, a new "frame" for coping or behaving according to new principles. It is therefore a "resetting" but, to my mind, a resetting of a more sustaining kind than the temporary pause in action, as previously suggested by Pribram and Melges (1969).

Whether in developmental or empathic transformations, such affect is experienced as part of new and challenging information. At any given point the affect may be hedonically positive or negative, but it is dynamic by nature rather than fixed, and it propels us toward integrating diverse elements at a new level. Because it leads to the discovery of new relations, we might say that the transformational function of affect is epistemological. Thus, in its transformational role, an affect seems to guarantee that we will encounter the new and that we will change.

Now we are faced with a dilemma. How do we reconcile this transformational role of affect with the affective self, with a picture we have portrayed of an affective core providing continuity for human experience?

First, we must consider a "systems" principle: we function within multiple polarities in development. In addition to the *stage-related* developmental polarities described by Erikson (1950) and Sander (1975), there are *ongoing* developmental polarities which can be identified as differentiation/integration, perturbation/-

stabilization, and autonomy/interconnectedness (Werner, 1948).[6] Thus, at any given time, transformation and stability can be described in terms of the dynamic regulation of these polar tendencies. With a transformational affect there is movement toward novelty and change (an aspect of differentiation) but, at the same time, a stabilizing, self-consistent tendency (an aspect of integration). In terms of experience, we could state this as follows: as new relations are appreciated, there is a corresponding sense of what is human and familiar, of what is individually meaningful and coherent.

A second answer to our dilemma is related to the first. Affective functioning has self-stabilizing features, and, in fact, some of these become increasingly prominent during the second year as the transformational aspects of empathic processes increase. Our considerations have led us to the view that from earliest infancy, and based on a biological organization, affects have a stabilizing influence on experience. The affective core for experience influences the evaluation of perceptions, the guiding of information processing (see the recent work of Hoffman, 1978; Zajonc, 1980), and the selection of actions. These occur according to what is pleasant or unpleasant and according to specific aspects of the discrete emotions. Increasingly, affects also have a stabilizing influence because of their role in the storage and retrieval of the memories of past experience (see Bower, 1981; Rovee-Collier and Fagan, 1981). Certainly as self-awareness, representation, and symbolic functioning combine to generate the possibility of anticipatory signal-affect systems, one would expect the self-stabilizing role of affective memories to have increasing importance.

Much research remains before us, and we have become quite abstract. Let me close with something vivid. Recall the one-year-old infants in social referencing. They are engaged in some sort of activity and then encounter a situation of uncertainty. They pause, they puzzle,

---

[6]For a discussion of other developmental polarities, see Emde (1983).

and they look at another's facial expression of emotion. Then their feelings seem to change; behavior becomes altered, seemingly as a result of a transformation—as if through the feeling of another there has been a "vicarious" learning experience (Campos and Stenberg, 1981). As we view these infants, we feel a sense of familiarity and consistency, as though we are witnessing a fundamentally human process in which one affective core gets in touch with another. But we also have an impression of individuality, an impression made even clearer on observing this repeeatedly in large numbers of infants. As we see this phenomenon and experience it empathically, we are convinced that no two infants are alike. Although our research has not yet captured it, we know in our core that, even at this early age, there is both consistency and transformation in the affective self.

REFERENCES

Abelson, R. P. and Sermat, V. (1962). Multidimensional scaling of facial expressions. *Journal of Experimental Psychology*, 63:546–554.

Amsterdam, B. K. (1972). Mirror self-image reactions before age 2. *Developmental Psychology*, 5:297–305.

Arend, R., Gove, F. L., and Sroufe, L. A. (1979). Continuity of individual adaptation from infancy to kindergarten: A predictive study of ego-resiliency and curiosity in preschoolers. *Child Development*, 50:950–959.

Arnold, M. (1960). *Emotion and Personality*. New York: Columbia University Press.

Bandura, A. (1981). Self-referent thought: A developmental analysis of self-efficacy. In *Social Cognitive Development: Frontiers and Possible Futures*, ed. J. H. Flavell and L. Ross. Cambridge, Eng.: Cambridge University Press.

Bertalanffy, L. von (1968). *General System Theory, Foundations, Development, Applications*. New York: George Braziller.

Bion, W. R. (1962). *Learning from Experience*. New York: Basic Books.

Block, J. (1971). *Lives Through Time*. Berkeley: Bancroft Books.

Bower, G. (1981). Mood and memory. *American Psychologist*, 36:129–148.

Bowlby, J. (1969). *Attachment and Loss*, vol. I. *Attachment*. New York: Basic Books.

Bowlby, J. (1973). *Attachment and Loss*, vol. II: *Separation*. New York: Basic Books.

Brazelton, T. B. and Als, H. (1979). Four early stages in the development of mother-infant interaction. *The Psychoanalytic Study of the Child*, 34:349–369. New Haven: Yale University Press.

Bretherton, I. and Bates, E. (in press). The development of representation from 10 to 28 months: Differential stability of language and symbolic play. In *Continuities and Discontinuities in Development*, ed. R. N. Emde and R. J. Harmon. New York: Plenum.

Bridges, K. M. B. (1933). Emotional development in early infancy. *Child Development*, 3:324–341.

Butterworth, G. and Jarrett, N. (1980). The geometry of preverbal communication. Paper presented to the Annual Conference of the Developmental Psychology Section of the British Psychological Society, Edinburgh, Scotland, unpublished.

Campos, J., Emde, R. N., and Caplovitz, K. (in press). Emotional development. In *Encyclopedic Dictionary of Psychology*, ed. R. Harre and R. Lamb. Oxford: Blackwell.

Campos, J. and Stenberg, C. (1981). Perception, appraisal, and emotion. In *Infant Social Cognition*, ed. M. Lamb and L. R. Sherrod. Hillsdale, New Jersey: Lawrence Erlbaum Associates.

Clarke, A. M. and Clarke, A. D. B. (1976). *Early Experience: Myth and Evidence*. London: Open Books.

Darwin, C. (1877). A biological sketch of an infant. *Mind*, 2:285–294.

DeCarie, T. G. (1969). A study of the mental and emotional development of the thalidomide child. In *Determinants of Infant Behavior*, vol. 4. ed. B. M. Foss. London: Methuen.

Dittrichova, J. and Lapackova, V. (1964). Development of the waking state in young infants. *Child Development*, 35:365–370.

Ekman, P., ed. (1982). *Emotion in the Human Face*, 2nd ed. Cambridge, England: Cambridge University Press.

Ekman, P. and Friesen, W. (1975). *Unmasking the Face*. Englewood Cliffs, New Jersey: Prentice Hall.

Ekman, P., Friesen, W., and Ellsworth, P. (1972). *Emotion in the Human Face*. New York: Pergamon Press.

Emde, R. N. (1980). Toward a psychoanalytic theory of affect: I. The organizational model and its propositions. In *The Course of Life: Psychoanalytic Contributions Toward Understanding Personality Development*, vol. 1: *Infancy and Early Childhood*, ed. S. Greenspan and G. Pollock. Washington, D.C.: U. S. Government Printing Office.

Emde, R. N. (1981). Changing models of infancy and the nature of early development. *Journal of the American Psychoanalytic Association*, 29:179–219.

Emde, R. N. (1983). The prepresentational self and its affective core. *The Psychoanalytic Study of the Child*, 38:165–192. New Haven: Yale University Press.

Emde, R. N., Gaensbauer, T. J., and Harmon, R. J. (1976). *Emotional Expression in Infancy: A Biobehavioral Study*. *Psychological Issues*, Monograph 37. New York: International Universities Press.

Emde, R. N. and Harmon, R. J. (1972). Endogenous and exogenous smiling systems in early infancy. *Journal of the American Academy of Child Psychiatry*, 11:177–200.

Emde, R. N., Kligman, D. H., Reich, J. H., and Wade, T. D. (1978). Emotional expression in infancy: Initial studies of social signaling and an emergent model. In *The Development of Affect,* ed. M. Lewis and L. Rosenblum. New York: Plenum.

Emde, R. N. and Robinson, J. (1979). The first two months: Recent research in developmental psychobiology and the changing view of the newborn. In *Basic Handbook of Child Psychiatry,* vol. 1, ed. J. Call, J. Nosphitz, R. Cohen, and I. Berlin. New York: Basic Books.

Emde, R. N. et al., (in preparation). Adult judgments of infant emotions.

Engel, G. (1962). Anxiety and depression-withdrawal: The primary affects of unpleasure. *International Journal of Psycho-Analysis,* 43:89–97.

Erikson, E. H. (1950). *Childhood and Society.* New York: W. W. Norton.

Erikson, E. H. (1959). Growth and crises of the healthy personality. In *Identity and the Life Cycle. Psychological Issues,* Monograph 1. New York: International Universities Press.

Erikson, E. H. (1968). *Identity: Youth and Crisis.* New York: W. W. Norton.

Feinman, S. and Lewis, M. (1981). Social referencing and second order effects in ten-month-old infants. Presented at Society for Research in Child Development, Boston.

Fouts, G. and Atlas, P. (1979). Stranger distress: Mother and stranger as reinforcers. *Infant Behavior and Development,* 2:309–317.

Fraiberg, S. (1977). *Insights from the Blind.* New York: Basic Books.

Freedman, D. A., Cannady, C., and Robinson, J. S. (1971). Speech and psychic structure. *Journal of the American Psychoanalytic Association,* 19:765–779.

Freud, S. (1905). Three essays on the theory of sexuality. *Standard Edition,* vol. 7, ed. J. Strachey, pp. 125–243. London: Hogarth Press, 1953.

Freud, S. (1915). Instincts and their vicissitudes. *Standard Edition,* vol. 14, ed. J. Strachey, pp. 111–140. London: Hogarth Press, 1957.

Freud, S. (1920). Beyond the pleasure principle. *Standard Edition,* vol. 18, ed. J. Strachey, pp. 3–64. London: Hogarth Press, 1955.

Freud, S. (1926). Inhibitions, symptoms, and anxiety. *Standard Edition,* vol. 20, ed. J. Strachey, pp. 87–172. London: Hogarth Press, 1959.

Frijda, N. (1970). Emotion and recognition of emotion. In *Feelings and Emotions,* ed. M. B. Arnold. New York: Academic Press.

Frijda, N. and Phillipszoon, E. (1963). Dimensions of recognition of expression. *Journal of Abnormal Social Psychology,* 66:45–51.

Gaensbauer, T. and Hiatt, S. (1983). Facial communication of emotion in early infancy. In *The Psychobiology of Affective Development.* Hillsdale, New Jersey: Lawrence Erlbaum Associates.

Galenson, E. and Roiphe, H. (1971). The impact of early sexual discovery on mood, defensive organization, and symbolization. *The Psychoanalytic Study of the Child,* 26:195–216. New York/Chicago: Quadrangle Books.

Galenson, E. and Roiphe, H. (1979). The development of sexual identity: Discoveries and implications. In *On Sexuality,* ed. T. B. Karasu and C. W. Socarides. New York: International Universities Press.

Gallup, G. (1979). Self-recognition in chimpanzees and man. In *The Child and Its Family,* vol. 2, ed. Lewis and Rosenblum. New York: Plenum.

Gladstone, W. H. (1962). A multidimensional study of

facial expressions of emotion. *Australian Journal of Psychology,* 14: 95–100.

Gunnar, M. R. (1980). Control, warning signals and distress in infancy. *Developmental Psychology,* 16:281–289.

Haith, M. M., Bergman, T., and Moore, M. J. (1977). Eye contact and face scanning in early infancy. *Science,* 198: 853–855.

Hiatt, A. S., Campos, J., and Emde, R. N. (1979). Facial patterning and infant emotional expression: Happiness, surprise, and fear. *Child Development,* 50:1020–1035.

Hoffman, M. L. (1978). Toward a theory of empathic arousal and development. In *The Development of Affect,* ed. M. Lewis and L. Rosenblum. New York: Plenum.

Hoffman, M. L. (1983). *NIMH Task Force Paper.* Washington, D. C.

Horner, T. M. (1980). Two methods of studying stranger fearfulness in infants: A review. *Journal of Child Psychology,* 21:203–219.

Izard, C. (1971). *The Face of Emotion.* Meredith, New York: Appleton-Century-Crofts.

Izard, C. (1977). The emergence of emotions and the development of consciousness in infancy. In *Human Consciousness and Its Transformations,* ed. J. M. Davidson, R. J. Davidson, and G. E. Schwartz. New York: Plenum.

Izard, C. (1978). Emotion as motivation: An evolutionary-developmental perspective. *Nebraska Symposium on Motivation,* 26. Lincoln: University of Nebraska Press.

Izard, C. (1982). Measuring emotions in human development. In *Measuring Emotions in Infants and Children,* ed. C. Izard. Cambridge, England: Cambridge University Press.

Izard, C. et al. (1980). The young infant's ability to produce discrete emotional expressions. *Developmental Psychology,* 16:132–140.

Jacklin, C. N. and Maccoby, E. E. (1978). Social behavior at thirty-three months in same-sex and mixed-sex dyads. *Child Development,* 49:557–569.

Jung, C. (1939). *Integration of the Personality.* New York: Farrar and Rinehart.

Kagan, J. (1981). *The Second Year.* Cambridge: Harvard University Press.

Kagan, J. (in press). Continuity and change in the opening years of life. In *Continuities and Discontinuities in Development,* ed. R. Emde and R. Harmon. New York: Plenum.

Kagan, J., Kearsley, R., and Zelaso, P. (1978). *Infancy, Its Place in Human Development.* Cambridge: Harvard University Press.

Kagan, J. and Moss, H. A. (1962). *Birth to Maturity.* New York: John Wiley.

Klinnert, M. D. et al. (1982). Social referencing: Emotional expressions as behavior regulators. In *Emotions in Early Development,* ed. R. Plutchik and H. Kellerman. New York: Academic Press.

Kohut, H. (1977). *The Restoration of the Self.* New York: International Universities Press.

Lampl, M. and Emde, R. N. (in press). Episodic growth in infancy; A preliminary report of length, head circumference and behavior. In *New Directions for Child Development,* ed. K. Fischer. San Francisco: Jossey-Bass.

Lazarus, R. S. (1968). Emotions and adaptation. In *Nebraska Symposium on Motivation,* ed. W. Arnold. Lincoln: University of Nebraska Press.

Levinson, D. (1978). *The Seasons of a Man's Life.* New York: Ballantine Books.

Lewis, M. and Brooks-Gunn, J. (1979). *Social Cognition and the Acquisition of Self.* New York: Plenum.

McCall, R. B. (1979). The development of intellectual

functioning in infancy and the prediction of later I. Q. In *Handbook of Infant Development*, ed. J. Osofsky. New York: John Wiley.

Mahler, M., Pine, F., and Bergman, A. (1975). *The Psychological Birth of the Human Infant*. New York: Basic Books.

Matas, L., Arend, R., and Sroufe, L. A. (1978). A continuity of adaptation in the second year. *Child Development*, 49:547–556.

Money, J. and Ehrhardt, A. (1972). *Man and Woman, Boy and Girl*. Baltimore: Johns Hopkins University Press.

Moss, H. (1983). Review of longitudinal research. *NIMH Task Force Paper*. Washington, D.C.

Osgood, C. (1966). Dimensionality of the semantic space for communication via facial expression. *Scandinavian Journal of Psychology*, 7:1–30.

Oster, H. and Ekman, P. (1977). Facial behavior in child development. In *Minnesota Symposia on Child Psychology*, vol. 11, ed. A. Collins. New York: Crowell.

Papoušek, H. and Papoušek, M. (1982). Integration into the social world. In *Psychobiology of the Human Newborn*, ed. P. M. Stratton. New York: John Wiley.

Plomin, R. (1983). Childhood temperament. In *Advances in Clinical Child Psychology*, vol. 6, ed. B. Lahey and A. Kazdin. New York: Plenum.

Plutchik, R. (1980). *The Emotions*. New York: Harper and Row.

Pribram, K. H. and Melges, F. T. (1969). Psychophysiological basis of emotion. In *Handbook of Clinical Neurology* vol. 3, ed. P. J. Vinken and G. W. Bruyn. Amsterdam: North-Holland Publishing Company and New York: American Elsevier.

Robson, K. S. (1967). The role of eye-to-eye contact in maternal-infant attachment. *Journal of Child Psychology and Psychiatry*, 8:13–25.

Rovee-Collier, C. and Fagen, J. W. (1981). The retrieval of memory in early infancy. In *Advances in Infancy Research*, vol 1, ed. L. P. Lipsitt and C. K. Rovee-Collier. Norwood, New Jersey: Ablex.

Russell, J. A. and Ridgeway, D. (1983). Dimensions underlying children's emotional concepts. *Developmental Psychology*, 19:795–804.

Sackett, G., Sameroff, A. J., Cairns, R. B., and Suomi, S. J. (1981). Continuity in behavioral development. In *Behavioral Development*, ed. K. Immelmann, G. Barlow, L. Petrinovich, and M. Main. Cambridge, England: Cambridge University Press.

Sameroff, A. J. and Chandler, M. (1976). Reproductive risk and the continuum of caretaking casualty. In *Review of the Child Development Research*, vol. 4, ed. F. D. Horowitz et al. Chicago: University of Chicago Press.

Sander, L. W. (1962). Issues in early mother-child interaction. *Journal of the American Academy of Child Psychiatry*, 1: 141–166.

Sander, L. W. (1964). Adaptive relationships in early mother-child interaction. *Journal of the American Academy of Child Psychiatry*, 3:231–264.

Sander, L. W. (1975). Infant and caretaking environment: Investigation and conceptualization of adaptive behavior in a system of increasing complexity. In *Explorations in Child Psychiatry*, ed. E. J. Anthony. New York: Plenum.

Sander, L. W. (1983). Polarity, paradox, and the organizing process in development. In *Frontiers of Infant Psychiatry*, ed. E. Galenson, J. Call, and R. Tyson. New York: Basic Books.

Sandler, J. and Rosenblatt, B. (1962). The concept of the representational world. *The Psychoanalytic Study of the Child*, 17:128–146. New York: International Universities Press.

Scherer, K. R. (1979). Nonlinguistic indicators of emotion and psychopathology. In *Emotions in Personality and Psychophysiology*. New York: Plenum.

Schulman, A. H. and Kaplowitz, C. (1977). Mirror-image response during the first two years of life. *Developmental Psychobiology*, 10:133–142.

Sorce, J. F. and Emde, R. N. (1981). Mother's presence is not enough: The effect of emotional availability on infant exploration. *Developmental Psychology*, 17:737–745.

Sorce, J. F., Emde, R. N., Campos, J., and Klinnert, M. D. (in preparation). Maternal emotional signaling—its effect on the visual cliff behavior of 1-year-olds.

Spencer, H. (1890). *The Principles of Psychology*. New York: Appleton.

Spitz, R. (1957). *No and Yes*. New York: International Universities Press.

Spitz, R. (1959). *A Genetic Field Theory of Ego Formation*. New York: International Universities Press.

Sroufe, L. A. (1979). Socioemotional development. In *Handbook of Infant Development*, ed. J. Osofsky. New York: John Wiley.

Stenberg, C. (1982). The development of anger expressions in infancy. Unpublished.

Stenberg, C., Campos, J., and Emde, R. N. (1983). The facial expression of anger in infancy. *Child Development*, 54: 178–184.

Stern, D. (1977). *The First Relationship. Mother and Infant*. Cambridge: Harvard University Press.

Thomas, A. and Chess, S. (1977). *Temperament and Development*. New York: Brunner/Mazel.

Tomkins, S. S. (1962–1963). *Affect, Imagery, Consciousness*, 2 vols. New York: Springer.

Tronick, E. (1980). The primacy of social skills in infancy. In *Exceptional Infant*, vol. 4, ed. D. B. Sawin et al. New York: Brunner/Mazel.

Uzgiris, I. (1976). *Organization of Sensorimotor Intelligence*. New York: Plenum.

Waddington, C. H. (1962). *New Patterns in Genetics and Development*. New York: Columbia University Press.

Werner, H. (1948). *Comparative Psychology of Mental Development*, revised edition. New York: International Universities Press, 1957.

Woodworth, R. W. and Schlosberg, H. S. (1954). *Experimental Psychology*. New York: Holt.

Wundt, W. M. (1896). *Grundriss der Psychologie*, (quoted in Izard, 1971).

Zahn-Waxler, C. and Radke-Yarrow, M. (1982). The development of altruism: Alternative research strategies. In *The Development of Prosocial Behavior*, ed. N. Eisenberg. New York: Academic Press.

Zajonc, R. (1980). Feeling and thinking: Preferences need no inferences. *American Psychologist*, 35:151–175.

5

Early Infant Development from a Biological Point of View

Thomas F. Anders, M.D. and Charles H. Zeanah, M.D.

One might ask why clinicians or psychological theorists and researchers should be interested in biology. What is its relevance to practice? Although these questions may appear contrived, and the answers obvious, it is unfortunately true that most of us are too busy or too singularly focused to think in terms of the methods and objectives of other disciplines. Yet it is just in these intersections that new ideas, knowledge, and progress appear.

Three of the most comprehensive theories of human psychology were developed by men who began as biologists: Pavlov, Freud, and Piaget. They relied on biological principles in the construction of their theories, but used psychological explanations when limitations of investigative biotechnology precluded the empirical testing of their hypotheses. They never abandoned biology, however, as they attempted to link behavior and brain function. An understanding of biologic mechanisms helps in determining the limits and adaptive significance of behavioral responses.

The division of human behavior into biological and psychological components is of course artificial. The two are inseparably related. Yet the past twenty years have witnessed a plethora of research on the biological determinants of behavior. Infant studies have led the way. The approaches have been diverse: from basic neurochemical and neurophysiologic processes that underlie cellular function to the biologic substrates of specific psychological phenomena, such as attachment, dreaming, learning, and play. And the gains have been great: from advances in biological psychiatry to a greatly expanded understanding of the developmental process. The fields of ethology, neurobiology, neurophysiology, neurochemistry, and chronobiology have participated in this exciting effort. Two recent books, *The Roots of Human Behavior* (Hofer, 1981) and *Biological Psychology* (Groves and Schlesinger, 1982), comprehensively review the contributions of biology to an understanding of human behavior.

In this paper we provide an overview, derived in part from these two books, and attempt to integrate some of the work as it pertains to infancy. We focus on four areas: (1) the structural development of the brain; (2) the emergence of prenatal and early infant behav-

The preparation of this paper was supported, in part, by the W. T. Grant Foundation, C. Voorsanger, The Irving Harris Foundation; NIMH (MH14440); NIMH (MH16744); and The Ehrman Infant Psychiatry Fellowship program (CZ); its presentation was supported by the Thrasher Research Fund. The authors appreciate the critical reviews and helpful suggestions of Drs. Constance Bowe, Marcia Keener, and Judith Williams.

ior; (3) the ontogeny of attachment; and (4) the role of timing in infant behavior, all in the context of the biological substrates of behaviors that are often viewed as psychological.

There are at least three general properties of behavior that have biological concomitants at the cellular level: action, temporal organization, and coordination. Cells act spontaneously, although the action may be modified by sensory input. Nerve and muscle cells generate electrochemical impulses, called action potentials, without any environmental input. These action potentials result from the "behavior" of large molecules that change shape to open or close channels in the cell membrane for the transport of charged ions. Temporal organization implies, at the level of the cell, a process by which actions are turned off and on.

The coordination of action between cells is accomplished by communication. The capacity of molecules to bind to other molecules at specific sites, known as receptor sites, provides the basis for all forms of communication between cells. The discharge of one cell becomes a signal affecting the activity of the next. Two kinds of membrane changes are possible: excitatory discharges in a silent cell and inhibitory discharges in an active cell. The orchestration of receptivity and action is carried out by a complicated system of interconnections, which composes the "wiring diagram" of the nervous system, and by the many categories of chemical messengers, including neurotransmitters, which communicate across synapses, and hormones, which communicate via the circulatory system.

Critical periods during brain development are characterized by accelerated periods of differentiation and growth. They provide the opportunity for functional specialization and enhanced competence. Positive or negative stimuli are especially important during these periods. Once a system becomes organized, whether a cellular or behavioral system, the susceptibility to environmental influences declines. Critical periods vary among animal species; for example, rate curves of brain growth in relation to birth show that major growth occurs at midgestation in the guinea pig, in the first two weeks after birth in the rat, and during the first year in the human.

Brain Development

The biological properties of both cells and behavior: action, temporal organization, and coordination, need first to be reviewed in terms of the ontogeny of brain structure; that is, cell differentiation, cell migration, and the establishment of synapses between cells. Between seventeen and nineteen days of gestational age the neural plate is formed on the embryo's dorsal surface. Three principal cell types appear: neurons, neuroglia or support cells, and ependymal cells that line the ventricles and spinal canal.

The factors most important in determining the direction of neuronal migration are mechanical, chemical, and electrochemical (Ciaranello et al., 1982). Once the cell is in place, the elaboration of dendritic and axonal architecture begins. In both axon and dendrite growth, the membrane of one cell appears to be able to recognize the membrane of another. More neurons are made and axons sent out than there are terminal sites to innervate. Only neurons that make functional connections survive. The geometry of dendritic trees develops precisely. Several kinds of dendrite patterns appear as a result of carefully determined branch angles and segment lengths.

Synapse formation between axons and dendrites results in neurochemical specifity of pathways. Prior to contact by the presynaptic axon, the postsynaptic nerve cell membrane demonstrates global neurotransmitter sensitivity over its entire surface. With synaptic contact, however, a gradual development of specialized morphology and high regional density of receptors occurs. Thereafter, the cell is only sensitive to specific neurotransmitter stimulation, and only in regions where synaptic contact has been made.

Cell number increases to the end of the first year, after a rapid rise between ten and twenty weeks of gestational age. The spinal cord and brain stem cease cell division before the cerebrum and cerebellum begin. Large cells with long axons mature first, followed by the smaller interconnecting neurons, and, finally, the neuroglial cells. The brain more than doubles in volume in the first year, reaching 60 percent of its adult size. (Yakovlev, 1962).

Neurons, particularly in sensorimotor systems vital to life, are formed and function for months before birth. For neuronal cells and connections that arise early in ontogeny, autonomous gene expression serves a major role. For cells and pathways that arise later in development, extrinsic influences significantly affect the outcome.

Myelination is not influenced significantly by external factors other than nutrition. The vestibular system, responsible for the detection of postural orientation, is myelinated before birth. As Korner (1972) has noted, this may explain the effectiveness of rocking in quieting the newborn. The major tracts of the visual system begin to show evidence of myelin staining before birth and complete myelination rapidly in the first few months of life. This contrasts with myelination of auditory projections to the cortex which requires several years, a time during which the acquisition and comprehension of language and speech develop. Some cortical association areas continue to gain myelin up to the age of three.

The major tracts of the limbic system, which mediate emotions, do not begin to stain for myelin until weeks or months after birth. The cingulum, linking the frontal lobes and the limbic system, myelinates between two and ten months. The fornix, a tract emanating from the hippocampus, myelinates in the second half of the first year and later. Still other connecting tracts myelinate through the first, second, and third years (Konner, 1982).

Nutrition affects cellular growth of the brain, the formation of the fatty myelin axon sheaths, and the glycoproteins necessary for synaptic membranes. Since different regions of the central nervous system mature at different periods, nutritional insults affect growth and development differentially, depending on the stage of development in which the insult occurs.

Studies by Wurtman and his group (Wurtman and Fenstrom, 1974; Wurtman and Wurtman, 1977) have demonstrated that mere shifts in the carbohydrate-protein balance or in the amino acid composition of protein in the diet affect levels and balance of neurotransmitters in the brain. There is no evidence that structural changes are induced by such deficiencies, but the biochemical changes affect synaptic function. It is not known whether such alterations of diet in humans produce comparable neurotransmitter changes, whether such changes early in development affect neurotransmitter levels in adulthood, or whether the effects are reversible after return to a normal diet.

As described by Timiras (1982), hormones have been shown to play both organizational and regulatory roles in central nervous system development. Sex hormones appear to be indispensable during early maturation for the differentiation of such selected brain areas as the hypothalamus and limbic structures into a female or male type. Current observations support the concept that many but not necessarily all actions of androgens on the brain may be carried out by a conversation to estrogens at the cellular level. The metabolism of androgens by reduction and aromatization leads to the formation of testosterone metabolites and estrogen. The hypothalamic area of the brain appears to develop differently, depending on whether these substances are present at a critical period in late fetal life. Similarly, the presence of thyroid hormones pre- and postnatally is necessary for optimal brain maturation as manifested in myelinogenesis, dendritic and synaptic growth, development of membrane structural characteristics, and the synthesis, release, and uptake of neurotransmitters.

Some hormones (epinephrine, peptide hormones) act primarily at the surface of the cell where they bind to receptors and activate a second messenger (cyclic adenosine monophosphate (AMP), which in turn acts to change intracellular processes. Other hormones (steroid and thyroid hormones) enter the cell and bind directly to the nucleus, activating the synthesis of a different second messenger, ribonucleic acid (RNA), which directs intracellular processes. Still other hormones, such as growth hormone, do not cross the placenta but change placental function by inducing the release of a still different form of second messenger that travels from the placenta to the fetus.

Stresses in the intra- and extrauterine environment can produce changes in brain development. The evidence to date favors the idea that maternal hormones, changed in amount and pattern during stress, act directly on the fetal brain and/or the fetal endocrine glands to modify the characteristics of the developing neuronal networks. For example, if normal infant rats are separated prematurely from their mothers, they have, under stress, an increased susceptibility to stomach ulcers as young adults. When these early-weaned females are then mated, their offspring will also show susceptibility to ulcers, even though they have been reared normally. Cross-fostering studies demonstrate that these effects are transmitted to the next generation during the prenatal period rather than by changes in the mother's behavior toward her infants after birth. This does not imply genetic transmission of acquired characteristics but that the uterine environment instead of genetic material is responsible (Skolnick et al., 1980).

Prenatal Behavior

Before seven weeks of conceptional age, during the embryonic period, movement first appears in the beating of the heart. These movements are at first sporadic and random but gradually become regulated as temporal organization is established. The first discontinuity in development occurs between seventeen and twenty-two weeks of gestational age. The level of motor activity that has progressively risen over the preceding two months is reduced. The period of inhibition lasts until about the twenty-fourth week of gestation when the trend toward increasingly complex activity is resumed. It has become clear that the period of quiescence reflects the maturation of descending regulatory fibers, originating in the dorsal thalamus and striatum. As these higher regions become dominant, the midbrain systems previously regulating movement are brought under control (Hofer, 1981). The implication is that the brain is organized for behavior at several different levels. With maturation of progressively higher centers, new capacities and new forms of organization are

brought to bear upon behavior. Intrauterine events such as anoxia or drug ingestion have their effect on the most recently developed systems and capabilities.

Sensory receptors begin to function during the first trimester. The fetus first responds to tactile stimulation; strong direct stimulation produces local contraction of muscles. The sensory system develops in the following order: cutaneous, gustatory and olfactory, vestibular, auditory, and visual. The fetus can probably hear by midgestation, as evidenced by fetal movements following sudden loud noises. Recordings of sound level in the human uterus have shown that the fetus is exposed to a constant low-frequency rumble of at least sixty decibels, produced by the turbulance of blood flowing through the uterine arteries. Microrhythmic patterning is introduced with the ten-decible rise in sound level after each maternal heartbeat. Sounds from the outside need to be quite loud to elicit a behavioral response from the fetus (Walker et al., 1971).

The visual life of the fetus is more restricted, but the uterus is not as dark as had been supposed. Bright light flashed on the abdominal wall of the pregnant woman will result in changes in fetal heart rate and body position. Retinal structures appear to be adequate for function by five months of gestation, and the eyelids open at seven months.

Taste and olfactory receptors can be stimulated by substances present in the amniotic fluid. Infants will increase or decrease their rate of swallowing if saccharin or an iodinated dye are injected into the amniotic fluid.

The placental circulation is still another avenue of communication between the outside world and the fetus. The mother's behaviors and emotions affect the developing fetal nervous system through this channel. Substances diffuse and are actively transported across the placental membranes. The placenta also acts as a heat exchanger, distributing some of the fetus's metabolic heat to the maternal circulation. When the mother has a fever, the fetus's temperature is higher, an effect that alters biochemical rates of metabolism in the fetal brain. It is clear that the behavior and development of the fetus are influenced by excessive alcohol intake, smoking, drugs, or exposure to chemical pollutants during pregnancy (Streissguth et al., 1980).

One approach that has been used to assess the role of environmental stimulation on brain organization has been the removal of a particular sensory receptor or system, resulting in total deprivation of that particular perceptual experience. If such an insult occurs during early phases of cell differentiation, migration or synapse formation, atrophy or shrinkage of neurons, degeneration of fine structure, and even cell death result. Similar insults later in development lead only to mild signs of cortical cell degeneration, and only after months, presumably because of multiple redundant inputs to single cells and their axonal and dendritic processes. The effects of partial sensory deprivation are more equivocal. Neurons generally appear to remain intact, differentiate, migrate, and develop some branching and synaptic contacts, despite significant reduction of sensory stimulation. Hubel and Wiesel's (1971, 1977) classical studies of organization of visual behavior in newborn kittens, following selective visual deprivation, have clearly distinguished between synaptic integrity and functional organization.

Newborn Behavior

What about the neonate's biological endowment and capacity for behaving in an organized manner? At birth, some nervous system tracts are fully functional, most are rapidly developing, and only a few remain undifferentiated. It is not surprising to find, therefore, that research on infant behavior in the past two decades has substantiated a sophisticated set of capacities. Neither the Jamesian view of the infant as a mass of confusion, nor the Freudian view of the infant as predominantly narcissistic and reactive, nor the Watsonian view of the infant as a *tabula rasa* comprehensively explains the behavior of the human newborn. The sophisticated biological endowment of the infant enables it to seek stimulation actively, to regulate its environment, and to interact with adult caretakers (Moss and Robson, 1968; Stern, 1977).

At birth, physiological cardiopulmonary and nutritional changes set in motion a wide variety of biobehavioral adjustments. The infant loses 6 to 9 percent of its body weight. Its state is highly variable the first day or two, fluctuating between irritability and somnolence. Irregular breathing, regurgitation, and oscillations of body temperature and skin color suggest instability of autonomic physiologic regulation. But physiologic stability appears relatively quickly.

Rhythmic organization of behavior, through interaction with the environment, occurs early. Feeding is the first regularly recurring postnatal temporal event. A cycle of behavioral and physiologic regularity becomes organized around the interval between feedings. Although feeding is as frequent as every hour in some cultures, it usually occurs every three to four hours in ours. Thus the human infant seems able to adjust its rhythms to cycle lengths varying from one to six hours.

The neonate's day and night are spent shifting between six states of arousal: the Fussy/Cry state, Active Wakefulness, Alert Inactivity, the Drowsy state, the REM state, and the NREM sleep state (Wolff, 1966). At first, there is little stability in the durations of these states, although from birth there is some order in the directions of transition between them (Anders et al., 1983). Compared to the two sleep states, which occupy two thirds of the newborn's day, the awake states are particularly unstable. The newborn infant is quietly awake for only a fraction of the day, though this is the state in which it is most receptive to environmental stimulation. Quiet sleep and crying seem to buffer the infant from environmental input. Only sudden vestibular stimulation elicits a response in these states, producing startles in quiet sleep and calming the crying infant.

The wide variety of spontaneous behaviors in the neonate, including diffuse motility, crying, smiling, startles, mouthing movements, and penile erections in males, guarantees that the infant will have an impact on its environment. The recurrence of these behaviors during the different states of sleep and wakefulness provides a periodic opportunity to relate. Because these behaviors occur spontaneously, infants appear to initiate an interaction and not simply to respond. This capacity is a crucial ingredient for the discovery of cause and effect, the basis for the development of learning and thought (Trevarthen, 1977).

Social smiling emerges in the first few months after birth as central connections between perceptual mechanisms and the spontaneous smile mature. A key role for associative learning or operant conditioning seems unlikely. The average age of onset of social smiling is better predicted from postmenstrual than postnatal age; and monozygotic twins are significantly more concordant in the emergence of social smiling than are dizygotic twins. Some genetic contribution to individual variation therefore seems plausible (Brachfeld et al., 1980; Freedman, 1974).

What is the role of learning in shaping behavior? And what can be said of the biological foundations of learning? Much evidence demonstrates the human infant's remarkable ability to learn and to learn quickly. Many years ago it was demonstrated that the human fetus can be conditioned *in utero* (Spelt, 1938, 1948). Papoušek (1967) has demonstrated that newborns can be successfully and reliably conditioned, and MacFarlane (1975) has reported that six-day-old infants discriminate reliably the smell of their mother's milk. When the breast pad of an infant's mother and that of another lactating woman are placed on either side of its head, the infant turns toward the mother's pad.

Three-day-old infants not only discriminate their mother's voice, they also will work, by non-nutritive sucking, to produce their mother's voice in preference to the voice of another female (DeCasper and Fifer, 1980). Preliminary data indicate that this preference develops as a result of prenatal experience with the mother's voice. Spence and DeCasper (1982) have asserted that newborns are able to distinguish between a story their mothers read to them during pregnancy and a story they have not heard before. If these results are confirmed by replication, we must conclude that by the last trimester fetuses perceive maternal speech and learn to distinguish its sound.

The capacity for rapid learning depends upon the infant's biological endowment. Stern (1982) has termed this endowment "prewired knowledge of the world." The knowledge consists of various perceptual capacities which are enhanced and extended but not created by early experience. The inhibitory effect of visual stimulation on levels of spontaneous behavior may represent a precursor of later attention. Gaze fixation and visual following of the face, documented by Fantz (1961, 1963, 1964) and others, demonstrate that infants possess an unlearned preference for visual stimuli which conform to the characteristics of the human face (Fantz, 1965; Haaf and Bell, 1967; Haith et al., 1969; Stechler and Latz, 1966). At birth, infants will follow an ungarbled representation of a face for one hundred eighty degrees, but following is significantly less and briefer if the face is garbled (Goren et al., 1975). By one month of age infants demonstrate, by differential looking times, that they can distinguish the features of their mother's face from that of a strange woman (Carpenter et al., 1970). Similarly, from birth infants are able to distinguish the perceptual boundaries of colors in the same way as adults (Bornstein, 1975), that is, the infant learns the name of the color orange, but knows without learning that orange is qualitatively distinct from red.

A similar case holds for audition. Infants are born not only with a preference for the human voice (DeCasper and Fifer, 1980) but also with an ability to perceive speech categorically (Eimas et al., 1971). One-month-olds demonstrate that they recognize the phonemic change from a "ba" sound to a "pa" sound by an increase in non-nutritive sucking. Eimas (1975) concludes from this work that a neural speech-processing mechanism is activated by the human voice and analyzes speech into discrete units, namely, phonemes. Thus, infants recognize innately that speech is a special class of acoustic signals and that language is composed of discrete units.

Even more sophisticated forms of prewired knowledge demonstrate that the infant has remarkable competence as an interactional partner. Such capacities are referred to as intermodal matching (Meltzoff and Borton, 1979) or cross-modal fluency (Stern, 1982). Meltzoff and Moore (1977) first described the ability of two- to three-week-old infants to imitate human facial expressions. This visual-proprioceptive cross-modal translation has been replicated recently in infants thirty-six hours old (Field et al., 1982). In another study, one-month-old infants were given either a smooth or a rough pacifier to mouth. When shown both pacifiers, infants looked preferentially at the pacifier they had mouthed. This tactile-visual matching seems to be innate rather than learned (Meltzoff and Borton, 1979).

Finally, infants are able to match the intensity of events across modalities. For example, infants can indicate that a light of certain brightness is comparable to a sound of certain loudness (Lawson and Turkewitz, 1980; Lewkowicz and Turkewitz, 1980). Stern (1983) has emphasized the importance of matching intensity across modalities for interactional synchrony. Thus, there is no doubt that neonatal capacities are sophisticated at birth or shortly thereafter and develop rapidly. For what reason? Learning about the world through the vehicle of early socialization is critical for survival. And the roots of early socialization lie in the establishment of attachment bonds.

Attachment

The attachment process serves as an excellent model for examining how biologic and psychologic components of a dyadic behavioral system become integrated. Birth not only alters the neonate's physiologic adaptation but also its relationship to its mother from predominantly biologic to biopsychosocial. The importance of attachment stems from a combination of factors, including the immaturity of the nervous system, the associated helplessness of the infant over a prolonged period, and the evolutionary advantage of allowing environmental circumstances to influence postnatal development. Attachment is also important for the acquisition of social skills and, presumably, in *homo sapiens,* for the attainment of the highest human qualities, love and empathy. Disturbances in the establishment of, or in the later dissociation from, the attachment bond are thought to underlie many conditions

of clinical psychopathology or developmental delay (Emde and Harmon, 1982).

All parent-infant interaction does not necessarily constitute attachment. Attachment has been defined by three characteristics: (1) the ability of young to discriminate and respond differentially to the object of attachment; (2) a preference by the young for the attachment figure, manifested by differential proximity-seeking; and, (3) a response to removal of the attachment object that is distinct from responses to the reduction of social stimuli per se (Rajecki et al., 1978). Unfortunately, this definition considers only the infant partner and not the characteristics of attachment in the parent.

Studies of domestic cats, rats, and monkeys have shown that species-typical maternal responses to young can be elicited in both sexes, starting in the juvenile period of development. But such maternal behaviors do not necessarily constitute attachment. The rapid rise in estrogen levels during the end of pregnancy is thought to mediate the onset of intense maternal behavior after birth in some species. The continuation of the behaviors, however, requires the experience of interaction with the young. A few days of interaction with rat pups after birth fixes maternal behavior. If the pups are removed for three to four days maternal behavior immediately resumes on their return.

In rodents and ungulates, mother-infant interaction seems based primarily upon olfaction. Rat pups show behavioral and physiological responses to removal of the mother, which include temperature changes, cardiac and respiratory depression, and behavioral arousal. These responses can be prevented by providing a nonlactating female substitute (Hofer, 1975a, 1975b). Thus the response is alleviated by any female, not only by the mother. Similarly, when the maternal response to the pups is examined, there is evidence of differential treatment of her own and strange pups and of male and female pups. Yet there is no evidence that individual recognition and preference play a role in the mother's behavior.

Dogs of several breeds will exhibit separation distress upon removal from their mother, but again the response does not appear to be specific to the mother. The puppy's distress vocalizations will be quieted if a strange female of the same breed is substituted. In primates, on the other hand, infant monkeys of several species discriminate and prefer their own mother and vigorously protest her departure. Primate behavior, therefore, fulfills the criteria of attachment. The process by which these early experiences have their effect is probably associative learning. Individual variations in the mother's appearance, behavior, and odor repeatedly paired with broader prewired perceptual expectancies become highly specific and unique cues in alleviating distress.

During the initial stage of attachment, the infant is aroused by stimuli that are appropriately novel, yet not too discrepant. Arousal and attention become easier to elicit with repetition of the familiar stimulus, such as a parental behavior, as the infant comes to recognize slight shifts in stimulus quality. Stimuli vary in intensity, quality, dynamics (rise and fall time), and duration. The variations in stimulation provided by the parent need to be examined, as do the responses of the infant, particularly the change of state produced by the interaction. The infant's responses shape the parent's behavior and vice versa. In both humans and nonhuman primates, parental behavior is dependent on the parent's own experiences as an infant and on previous experiences of parenting.

Later in maturation, fearful and even aggressive responses may be elicited by novel stimuli, bringing the early period of attachment to a close. Such changes are not necessarily functions of the growth of fear, but they make specific individuals more attractive and others less so. The association of active imitation and attachment and of independent locomotion and the growth of social fear have been clearly demonstrated in several species. If attachment is the result of repeated stimulation at a stage of development before avoidance responses develop, then abusive interactions at this stage may actually increase attachment simply because of the intensity of repetitive stimulation, regardless of its quality.

In view of the relationship between emotions and the limbic system, this system would seem an appropriate place to look for developmental changes associated with the rise of at-

tachment behaviors, including social fears (Kling and Steklis, 1976). Interestingly, myelination of portions of the limbic system in man parallels the emergence of separation protest and stranger anxiety, two milestones of human attachment. At four months of age, there is little or no myelin in the striatum, fornix, or cingulum. By the end of the first year, these areas have achieved an almost adult level of staining (Yakovlev and Lecours, 1967).

In humans, the emergence of cognitive processes such as symbolization, identification, and abstract thought may be responsible for the special and uniquely human attributes of attachment, such as object permanence and the ability to love. But, even in humans, attachment is built upon a biological substrate of simpler processes.

As cognitive development proceeds, the gradual replacement of interaction with parents by interaction with the environment and the formation of new attachments to peers bring to an end the primary attachment process. Careful studies in rhesus monkey pairs on the roles of mother and infant in the gradually changing attachment relationship have shown the complexity of initiation, establishment, and dissolution of the process (Hinde and Spencer-Booth, 1971).

The absence of an opportunity for attachment has been best described in institutional children and infant monkeys reared in social isolation. Severely isolated children walk on all fours, are mute, and fail to learn a spoken language. They have a remarkably acute sense of smell, which is used to recognize familiar people, and a remarkable insensitivity to cold and pain. The most devastating effects are in emotional development. Laughing and smiling are absent.

These effects, for the most part, also have been demonstrated in socially isolated infant monkeys. The deficits in monkeys can be viewed as disordered regulation of arousal states. Excessive fearfulness, unexpected aggressive attacks, withdrawn self-clasping, and stereotyped repetitive behaviors represent pathological states of arousal and lead to fragmentation of sexual and maternal behavior and the inability to play. These deficits may be partially overcome, however. Rhesus monkeys raised in total isolation for six to twelve months develop competent social behaviors when forced to interact with much younger "therapist" monkeys (Suomi et al., 1976).

Isolated infant monkeys must be differentiated from infants who have been separated from their mother but who have been provided with other sources of stimulation such as a cloth surrogate, a foster mother, or peers. A depressive-like behavioral syndrome occurs in infant monkeys of some species following maternal deprivation. Sackett et al. (1981) and Kaufman and Rosenblum (1967) have shown that the different patterns of response to deprivation depend on the species of monkey. Such data seem incompatible with any single theory of deprivation effects. Sackett's group concludes that the deprivation effects in primates involve at least two independent mechanisms: genotypic differences in risk for developing deprivation syndromes during the rearing period and genotypic differences in the amount or quality of experience required to maintain exploratory behaviors and to develop species-typical social behavior after deprivation terminates.

Kaufman and Rosenblum (1967) have suggested that the depression-like syndrome in separated infant monkeys reflects an adaptive response akin to the conservation–withdrawal response described by Engel (1962). In humans, they postulate, the conservation-withdrawal response serves as the biologic substrate of depression, which, when present in full force, represents an example of adaptation gone awry.

The studies by Spitz (1945) and by Bowlby (1969, 1973) of infants in institutions have suggested that infancy experiences influence later social behavior. However, recently the primacy of early experience has come under attack. Follow-up studies of humans reared in impoverished institutional settings have shown that intellectual and behavioral deficits seen in infancy often disappear later in life. Whether social deficits remain is still controversial (Rutter, 1979; Tizard and Hodges, 1978). Another compelling case for a lack of continuity between early behavior and later performance is seen in the area of human newborn assessment, where consistency is found only when extremely abnormal behavior is present (Clarke and Clarke, 1976).

Biorhythmic Organization

CIRCADIAN RHYTHMS

Temporal structure is an integral part of the infant's life, from the organizing effects of the recurrent light–dark cycle and the three- to four-hour feeding pattern to the millisecond microrhythmic organization of dyadic interaction involved in establishing attachment. In this final section, certain aspects of timing are examined in more detail.

In 1729, the French astronomer DeMairan observed that the daytime leaf movements of a plant persisted when it was placed in constant darkness, suggesting an endogenous rhythm. Two hundred years later the persistence of periodicity in the activity of wild mice housed in constant light led Johnson (1939) to postulate the presence of a "self-winding and self-regulating, internal physiological clock." The existence of endogenous clocks did not become widely accepted, however, until the 1950s. Halberg (1969) has defined a biological rhythm as a statistically validated, physiologic change that recurs with a reproducible wave form; and chronobiology as the quantitative description of biological time structures.

The term *circadian* refers to self-sustained oscillations that recur once in twenty to twenty-eight hours; *ultradian* rhythms occur within a shorter period, and *infradian* cycles occur at monthly, seasonal, or yearly intervals. The peak of a rhythm is referred to as its acrophase. If two separate rhythms are in phase, their acrophases coincide. However, phase shifts may occur, so that acrophases may lead or lag each other by a certain number of degrees. Phase maps can be constructed to describe these relationships. The fact that the periods of free-running rhythms (that is, those observed under constant conditions) differ from those of known environmental cycles and differ among individuals precludes the possibility that environmental cues drive these rhythms.

Temporal organization allows organisms to

anticipate periodic events and to initiate metabolic processes before they are required. For example, feeding behavior in nocturnal rodents is preceded by the mobilization of digestive enzymes in anticipation of eating. In humans, sleep and wakefulness, cognitive and motor performance, body temperature, serum-hormone levels, urinary excretion of metabolites, synaptic excitability, sensitivity of sensory and regulatory mechanisms, and receptor-mediated events are examples of processes that vary with a circadian periodicity.

Relatively little is known about the ontogeny of circadian rhythms in humans (Anders, 1982). During the immediate neonatal period, sleep and wakefulness follow each other in three- to four-hour cycles. Gradually, during the first year of life, wakefulness shifts to the daytime and sleep to the night, though a true diurnal pattern of sleep-wake cycling is not evident before the age of three, when naps are finally relinquished. Diurnal influences on the temporal organization of REM sleep, however, can be detected as early as six weeks of age (Hellbrugge et al., 1964).

Diurnal cortisol excretion patterns are established by one year of age (Tennes and Vernadakis, 1977). Abe and colleagues (1978) reported on diurnal variations of body temperature in a large group of subjects ranging in age from five days to forty-four years. They found no circadian variation in temperature in neonates, day-night differences by one month of age, and temperature rhythms similar to those of adults with respect to phase after ten to eleven months of age. The amplitude of the circadian oscillation up to the age of seven was significantly larger than in adults.

The control mechanisms for circadian rhythms are poorly understood. Some circadian rhythms may be genetically regulated, for single gene mutations have been isolated that alter period length in insects. Pharmacological data suggest that the key elements involved in regulating circadian rhythms are membrane potential, turnover of cyclic nucleotides, and rates of protein synthesis. Under ordinary conditions, the circadian pacemaker acts as a single oscillator. However, there is compelling evidence for the presence of multi-

ple circadian oscillators (Takahashi and Zatz, 1982).

In man, the sleep-wake cycle and the body-temperature rhythm occasionally dissociate from each other and free-run with different period lengths. The conceptualization and investigation of multi-oscillator systems is complex. Two general types of organization could underlie such systems: (1) a hierarchy in which a dominant pacemaker drives the system and imposes its period and phase upon subordinate oscillators; and (2) a nonhierarchical, mutually coupled system in which no single oscillator is dominant but redundant oscillators share a pacemaking role. The latter system seems more likely in man.

Although circadian rhythms are generated endogenously, they are regulated by exogenous cycles, especially those of light and darkness. The imposition of period and phase control by environmental cues or *Zeitgebers* is called entrainment. Only a few environmental variables can entrain circadian rhythms. Light and temperature are the dominant ones, although in humans social cues also may be important. In mammals, the photoreceptors responsible for entrainment are located in the retina. Impulses are transmitted by means of the retinohypothalamic tract to the suprachiasmatic nuclei of the thalamus.

Entrainment occurs through a process known as *phase advance* or *phase delay*, whereby a specific stimulus or "trigger," such as a light pulse, is presented at a predetermined point in the circadian cycle. For example, individuals whose free-running sleep period is shorter than the period of the dark cycle achieve entrainment by repeated light stimuli presented late at night (phase delays); and individuals with free-running periods longer than that of the light cycle entrain by way of earlier occurring light triggers (phase advances).

ULTRADIAN RHYTHMS

In addition to diurnal cycles, temporal organization involves faster periodic functions, referred to as ultradian rhythms. Respiratory patterns, heart-rate patterns, and the alternation of REM and NREM sleep states are examples of such ultradian rhythms. The recent pro-liferation of studies on temporal dimensions of infant capacities and dyadic interactions has sensitized us to the salience of ultradian rhythms in all behavior. This area was pioneered by Sander's descriptions of the rhythmic structure of the human "infant-caregiver system." Sander (1969) proposed that the interactive events of caregiving function as *Zeitgebers* to entrain the semiautonomous physiologic rhythms of the infant.

From the moment of birth, microrhythms in many infant behaviors can be observed. The REM-NREM cycle recurs every fifty to sixty minutes, a period that remains constant through the first year of life, gradually lengthening through childhood until it achieves its adult period of ninety minutes by adolescence. The very definition of infant states, including the REM and NREM sleep states, depends on the congruence in time of multiple physiologic parameters. In other words, a state exists if several physiologic patterns are temporally in phase. Ashby (1956) has defined a state as the *recurrence* of recognizable patterns of variables together. Recently, the whole concept of behavioral and physiological states and specifically their periodic recurrence, organization, and temporal structure has come under critical review, especially in premature infants (Nijhuis et al., 1982). Our own group has begun to reexamine the definitions and properties of ultradian cycles derived from discontinuous state data (Kraemer et al. in press).

Despite this controversy, timing, contingency, and synchrony characterize stimulation. Rhythm and reciprocity add extraordinarily complicated dimensions to the study of early development. Repetition of combinations of behavioral elements constitutes infant-caregiver interaction. Regulated sensory stimulation supplied through dyadic interaction is necessary for the development of neural mechanisms that modulate and control central nervous system arousal and for the development of consistent neural responses necessary for the processing of sensory information. Experimental findings suggest that the normal mechanisms for gating and filtering new sensory input are inadequately developed after rearing in isolation. A parent literally regulates the be-

havioral, neurochemical, autonomic, and hormonal functions of the infant by different aspects of the relationship: nutrition, warmth, sensory stimulation, and *rhythmic responsiveness.*

Less is known about the oscillators that regulate ultradian rhythms than those that regulate circadian cycles. Ashton (1976) proposes that the human newborn is equipped with a "central pacemaker," which serves to both encode and organize the external world as well as to regulate its behavior. The pacemaker, he proposes, is located in the hippocampus and beats at approximately one to two cycles per second. As evidence, Ashton points to the infant's sucking pattern, which is characterized by rhythmic, predictable sequence of bursts and pauses (Wolff, 1968), and makes the observation that periodic stimulation is superior to aperiodic stimulation in soothing an infant. Both the suck bursts and the optimal soothing stimulus demonstrate a period around one to two cycles per second. But more than one pacemaker must be present. Recently, human fetal movement, recorded *in utero,* and gross motility patterns immediately after birth showed temporal organization with spontaneous oscillations near one cycle per minute (Robertson, 1982; Robertson et al., 1982).

How do exogenous stimuli entrain endogenous ultradian rhythms during development? What are analogous mechanisms to circadian entrainment? Feeding schedules superimposed upon sleep-wake cycles serve as organizers that regulate behavior. In social interaction, prewired temporal expectancies and the rules of interpersonal turn-taking serve as organizational forces. Kaye (1977) has observed temporal signaling between mothers and infants during feeding, associated with the burst-pause sequence of sucking. The mother's behavior alternates from quiet attention as the infant sucks, to jiggling, vocalizing, and looking when the infant pauses. The cessation of action is a signal to the infant that sucking may resume. Over the first few weeks of life, the stop-jiggling to suck latency becomes shorter, suggesting that the infant is adapting to the mother's signals (Kaye and Wells, 1978).

Data relevant to the infant's ability to "estimate" time come primarily from studies of temporal conditioning. Stern and Gibbon

(1979) suggest that the infant possesses an innate capacity to estimate time per se. As the infant develops, it applies this capacity to an increasingly larger set of environmental events; that is, the infant begins to appreciate that social interactions and other forms of environmental stimulation can all be described and understood in the dimension of time.

Contingent pupillary dilatation and constriction have been demonstrated using varying temporal intervals as the conditional stimulus. It has also been observed that following repeated presentations of a signal at precise temporal intervals, the omission of that signal elicits heart-rate deceleration, suggesting the infant's sensitivity to temporal stimuli elicits an orienting response. Studies employing somatic response measures such as eye blinks or sucks have not been as successful in conditioning to temporal cues, supporting the conclusion that the autonomic nervous system is particularly sensitive to the time dimension (Miller and Byrne, 1983, personal communication).

Temporal discrimination of auditory stimuli is present in infants by two months, and visual temporal discrimination by four months. Following habituation to a particular rhythm in one modality, infants demonstrate dishabituation to a different temporal sequence, regardless of modality, but appear to treat similar temporal sequences as equivalent when presented in different sensory channels. Infants also recognize that events sharing a common temporal structure belong together. When four-month-old infants are shown two motion pictures projected side by side on a screen and the sound track for only one of the films is played, the infants prefer to watch the film whose sound track is playing (Spelke, 1976). Therefore, at a young age, infants are able to coordinate the visual and auditory characteristics of an object that they see for the first time by detecting a temporal relationship between the object's movement and its sound (Spelke, 1979). Infants also prefer synchronous relationships between speech and lip movements to asynchronous relationships (Dodd, 1979). Finally, manipulation of infant affect and arousal can be accomplished by varying or violating temporal expectancies in infant "games" (Stern, 1977).

In conclusion, a final note about temporal organization of social groups (Harcourt, 1978). In a study by Haynes and his group (1982), the achievement of temporal coherence between infant monkeys and their social group was observed. The Haynes group examined the degree to which the state of the adult population regulates the behavioral states of infant members in a group of pigtail monkeys and demonstrated that the immature members of the group were temporally coordinated with the activities of the adult members. Infant behaviors did not necessarily mimic the adult behaviors, but there was a predictable relation between the state of the adult group at a given observation session and the kinds of behaviors in which infants engaged. Similarly, adult monkeys who were strangers to each other rapidly synchronized their behaviors and came to share the same cyclical patterns of activity when caged together.

Conclusions

The work of the ethologists, the neurobiologists, and, more recently, the chronobiologists have added enormously to our fund of knowledge about human behavior. The basic properties of behavior—action, temporal organization, and communication—have been reviewed. These properties are observed in the single cell during development and in a most complex social behavior, the attachment process. Similarly, trauma, either physical or psychological, have their effects at multiple levels, from the cellular to the systemic. The effects will depend on the intensity, timing, and the amount of reorganization that occurs subsequently. In this regard, the notions of critical periods, nutritional status, and the presence of stressful or noxious agents during early development are relevant. Because areas of the brain continue to develop until the age of three, we need to recognize the importance of these relationships.

But what has been most exciting has been the role of temporal organizers. Again, their influences are broad, seeming to affect many levels from single cell, to cell networks, to dyadic interactions and social group behaviors. Timing is critically important for learning and for affective regulation. Biology has brought us back to the brain and to the study of clocks and temporal organization. It is possible that from further studies of the ramifications of the time domain, we may come to a better understanding of the psychological dimensions of the behavior in which we are all so interested.

REFERENCES

Abe, K. et al. (1978). The development of circadian rhythm of human body temperature. *Journal of Interdisciplinary Cycle of Research*, 9:211–216.

Anders, T. (1982). Biological rhythms in development. *Psychosomatic Medicine*, 44:61–72.

Anders, T., Keener, M., Bowe, T., and Shoaff, B. (1983). A longitudinal study of nighttime sleep-wake patterns in infants from birth to one year. In *Frontiers of Infant Psychiatry*, ed. J. Call, E. Galensen, and R. Tyson. New York: Basic Books.

Ashby, W. R. (1956). *An Introduction to Cybernetics.* London: Chapman & Hall.

Ashton, R. (1976) Aspects of timing in child development. *Child Development*, 47:622–626.

Bornstein, M. (1975). Qualities of color vision in infancy. *Journal of Experimental Child Psychology*, 19:401–419.

Bowlby, J. (1969). *Attachment and Loss,* vol. 1, *Attachment.* New York: Basic Books.

Bowlby, J. (1973). *Attachment and Loss,* vol 2, *Separation.* New York: Basic Books.

Brachfeld, S., Goldberg, S., and Sloman, J. (1980). Parent-infant interaction in free play at eight and twelve months: Effects of prematurity and immaturity. *Infant Behavior and Development*, 3:289–305.

Carpenter, G., Meece, J., Stechler, O., and Friedman, S. (1970). Differential visual behavior to human and humanoid faces in early infancy. *Merrill Palmer Quarterly*, 16:91–107.

Ciaranello, R., VandenBerg, S., and Anders. T. (1982). Intrinsic and extrinsic determinants of neuronal development. *Journal of Autism and Developmental Disorders*, 12:115–145.

Clarke, A. and Clarke, A., eds. (1976). *Early Experience: Myth and Evidence.* New York: Free Press.

DeCasper, A. and Fifer, W. (1980). Of human bonding: Newborns prefer their mothers voices. *Science*, 208:1174–1176.

DeMairan, J. (1729). *Histoire de L'Academie Royales des Sciences.* Paris.

Dodd, B. (1979). Lip reading in infants: Attention to speech presented in- and out-of-synchrony. *Cognitive Psychology*, 11:478–484.

Eimas, P. (1975). Speech perception in early infancy. In *From Sensation to Cognition*, ed. L. B. Cohen and P. Salapatek. New York: Academic Press.

Eimas, P., Sigueland, C., Jusczyk, P., and Viganto, J. (1971). Speech perception in infants. *Science*, 171:303–306.

Emde, R. and Harmon, R., eds. (1982). *The Development of Attachment and Affiliative Systems.* New York: Plenum Press.

Engel, G. (1962). *Psychological Development in Health and Disease.* Philadelphia: Saunders.

Fantz, R. (1961). The origin of form perception. *Scientific American*, 204:66–72.

Fantz, R. (1963). Pattern vision in newborn infants. *Science*, 140:196–297.

Fantz, R. (1964). Visual experience in infants: Decreased attention to familiar patterns relative to novel ones. *Science*, 146:668–670.

Fantz, R. (1965). Visual perception from birth as shown by pattern selectivity. In *New Issues in Infant Development, Annals of the New York Academy of Science*, ed. H.C. Whipple, 118:793–814.

Field, T., Woodson, R., Greenberg, R., and Cohen, D. (1982). Discrimination and imitation of facial expressions by neonates. *Science*, 218:179–181.

Freedman, D. (1974). *Human Infancy: An Evolutionary Perspective.* New York: John Wiley.

Goren, C., Sarty, M., and Wu, P. (1975). Visual following and pattern discrimination of facelike stimuli by newborn infants. *Pediatrics*, 56:544–549.

Groves, P. and Schlesinger, K. (1982). *Biological Psychology*, 2nd ed. Dubuque, Iowa: Wm. C. Brown.

Haaf, R. A. and Bell, R. Q. (1967). A facial dimension in visual discrimination by human infants. *Child Development*, 38:893–899.

Haith, M. M., Kessen, W., and Collins, D. (1969). Response of the human infant to level of complexity of intermittent visual movement. *Journal of Experimental Child Psychology*, 7:52–69.

Halberg, F. (1969). Chronobiology. *Annual Review of Physiology*, 31:675–725.

Harcourt, A. (1978). Activity periods and patterns of social interaction: A neglected problem. *Behavior*, 66:121–135.

Haynes, C., Wade, T., and Cassell, T. (1982). Infant monkeys' achievement of temporal coherence with their social group. In *The Development of Attachment and Affiliative Systems*, ed. R. Emde and R. Harmon. New York: Plenum Press.

Hellbrugge, T., Lange, J., Ruttenfranz, F., and Stehr, K. (1964). Circadian periodicity of physiological functions in different stages of infancy and childhood. *Annals of the New York Academy of Science*, 117:361–373.

Hinde R. and Spencer-Booth, Y. (1971). Effects of brief separation from mother on Rhesus monkeys. *Science*, 173: 111–118.

Hofer, M. (1975a). Infant separation responses and the maternal role. *Biological Psychiatry*, 10:149–153.

Hofer, M. (1975b). Studies on how early maternal separation produces behavioral change in young rats. *Psychosomatic Medicine*, 37:245–264.

Hofer, M. (1981). *The Roots of Human Behavior.* San Francisco: W. H. Freeman.

Hubel, D. and Wiesel, T. (1971). Aberrant visual projections in the Siamese cat. *Journal of Psychology*, 218:33–62.

Hubel, D. and Wiesel, T. (1977). Grass Foundation Lecture. *BIS Conference Report #45*. Los Angeles: Brain Information Service, pp. 9–24.

Johnson, M. (1939). Effect of continuous light on periodic spontaneous activity of white-footed mice. *Journal of Experimental Zoology*, 82:315–328.

Kaufman, I. and Rosenblum, L. (1967). The reaction to separation in infant monkeys: Anaclitic depression and conservation-withdrawal. *Psychosomatic Medicine*, 29:648–675.

Kaye, K. (1977). Toward the origin of dialogue. In *Studies of Mother-Infant Interaction*, ed. H. R. Shaffer. London: Academic Press.

Kaye, K. and Wells, A. (1978). Mothers' jiggling and the burst-pause pattern in neonatal feeding. *Infant Behavioral Development*, 3:29–46.

Kling, A. and Steklis, H. (1976). A neural substrate for affiliative behavior in nonhuman primates. *Brain, Behavior and Evolution*, 13:216–238.

Konner, M. (1982). Biological aspects of the mother-infant bond. In *The Development of Attachment and Affiliative Systems*, ed. R. Emde and R. Harmon. New York: Plenum Press.

Korner, A. (1972). State as variable, as obstacle and as mediator of stimulation in infant research. *Merrill Palmer Quarterly*, 18:77–94.

Kraemer, H., Hole, W., and Anders, T. (in press). Detection of behavioral state cycles and classification of temporal structure in behavioral states. *Sleep*, 7, March, 1984.

Lawson, K. and Turkewitz, G. (1980). Intersensory function in newborns: Effect of sound on visual preferences. *Child Development*, 51:1295–1298.

Lewkowicz, D. and Turkewitz, G. (1980). Cross-modal equivalence in early infancy: Auditory-visual intensity matching. *Developmental Psychology*, 16:597–607.

MacFarlane, J. (1975). Olfaction in the development of social preference in the human neonate. Ciba Foundation Symposium 33. *Parent-Infant Interaction*. Amsterdam: Elsevier.

Meltzoff, A. and Borton, R. (1979). Intermodal matching by human neonates. *Nature*, 282:403–404.

Meltzoff, A. and Moore, M. (1977). Imitation of facial and manual gestures by human neonates. *Science*, 198:75–78.

Nijhuis, J., Prechtl, H., Martin, C., and Bots, R. (1982). Are there behavioural states in the human fetus?. *Early Human Development*, 6:177–195.

Papoušek, H. (1967). Experimental studies of appetitional behavior in human newborns and infants. In *Early Behavior: Comparative and Developmental Approaches*, ed. H. W. Stevenson, E. H. Hess, and H. L. Rheingold. New York: John Wiley.

Rajecki, D., Lamb, M., and Obmascher, P. (1978). Toward a general theory of infantile attachment: A comparative review of aspects of the social bond. *The Behavioral and Brain Sciences*, 3:417–464.

Robertson, S. (1982). Intrinsic temporal patterning in the spontaneous movement of awake neonates. *Child Development*, 53:1016–1021.

Robertson, S., Dierker, L., Sorokin, Y., and Rosen, M. (1982). Human fetal movement: Spontaneous oscillations near one cycle per minute. *Science*, 218:1327–1330.

Robson, K. and Moss, H. (1970). Patterns and determinants of maternal attachment. *Journal of Pediatrics*, 77:976–985.

Rutter, M. (1979). Separation experiences: A new look at an old topic. *Journal of Pediatrics*, 95:147–154.

Sackett, G. et al. (1981). Genotype determines social isolation rearing effects in monkeys. *Developmental Psychology*, 17:313–318.

Sander, L. (1969). Regulation and organization in the early infant-caretaker system. In *Brain and Early Behavior*, ed. R. Robinson. London: Academic Press.

Skolnick, N., Ackerman, S., Hofer, M., and Weiner, H. (1980). Vertical transmission of acquired ulcer susceptibility in the rat. *Science*, 208:1161–1163.

Spelke, E. (1976). Infants' intermodal perception of events. *Cognitive Psychology*, 8:553–560.

Spelke, E. (1979). Perceiving bimodally specified events in infancy. *Developmental Psychology*, 15:626–636.

Spelt, D. (1938). Conditioned responses in the human fetus in utero. *Psychological Bulletin*, 35:712–713.

Spelt, D. (1948). The conditioning of the human fetus in utero. *Journal of Experimental Psychology*, 38:338–346.

Spence, M. and De Casper, A. J. (1982). Human fetuses perceive maternal speech. Paper presented to International Conference on Infant Studies, Austin, Texas.

Spitz, R. (1945). Hospitalism: An inquiry into the genesis of psychiatric conditions in early childhood. *Psychoanalytic Study of the Child*, 1:53–74. New York: International Universities Press.

Stechler, G. and Latz, E. (1966). Some observations on attention and arousal in the human infant. *Journal of the American Academy of Child Psychiatry*, 5:517–525.

Stern, D. (1977). *The First Relationship*. Cambridge: Harvard University Press.

Stern, D. (1982). Implications of infancy research for clinical theory and practice. Paper presented to the Second Annual Symposium on Infancy Research, Stanford, California.

Stern, D. (1983). The early development of schemas of self, of other, and of various experiences of self-with-other. In *Reflections on Self Psychology*, ed. S. Kaplan and J. D. Lichtenberg. Hillsdale, New Jersey: Laurence Erlbaum Associates.

Stern, D. and Gibbon, J. (1979). Temporal expectancies of social behaviors in mother-infant play. In *Origin of the Infants Social Responsiveness*, ed. E. Thoman. Hillsdale, New Jersey: Lawrence Erlbaum Associates.

Streissguth, A., Laudesman-Diver, S., Martin, J., and Smith, D. (1980). Teratogenic effects of alcohol in humans and laboratory animals. *Science*, 209:353–361.

Suomi, S., Delizio, R., and Harlow, H. (1976). Social rehabilitation of separation-induced depressive disorders in monkeys. *American Journal of Psychiatry*, 133:1279–1285.

Takahashi, J. and Zatz, M. (1982). Regulation of circadian rhythmicity. *Science*, 217:1104–1111.

Tennes, K. and Vernadakis, A. (1977). Cortisol excretion levels and daytime sleep in one-year-old infants. *Journal of Clinical Endocrinology and Metabolism*, 44:175–179.

Timiras, P. (1982). The timing of hormone signals in the orchestration of brain development. In *The Development of Attachment and Affiliative Systems*, ed. R. Emde and K. Harmon. New York: Plenum Press.

Tizard, B. and Hodges, J. (1978). The effect of early institutional rearing on the development of eight-year-old children. *Journal of Child Psychology and Psychiatry*, 19:99–118.

Trevarthen, C. (1977). Descriptive analysis of infant communication behavior. In *Studies in Mother-Infant Interaction*, ed. H. R. Shaffter. London: Academic Press.

Walker, D., Grimwade, J. and Wood, C. (1971). Intrauterine noise: A component of the fetal environment. *American Journal of Obstetrics and Gynecology,* 109:91–95.

Wolff, P. (1966). *The Causes, Controls and Organization of Behavior in the Neonate: Psychological Issues,* Monograph 17. New York: International Universities Press.

Wolff, P. (1968). The serial organization of sucking in the young infant. *Pediatrics,* 42:943–956.

Wurtman, C. and Fenstrom, T. (1974). Effects of diet on neurotransmitters. *Nutrition Reviews,* 32:193–200.

Wurtman, R. and Wurtman, J. (1977). Determinants of the availability of nutrients to the brain. *Nutrition and the Brain,* vol. 1. New York: Raven Press.

Yakovlev, P. (1962). Morphological criteria of growth and maturation of the nervous system in man. *Mental Retardation,* 39:3–46.

Yakovlev, P. and Lecours, A. (1967). The myelogenetic cycles of regional maturation of the brain. In *Regional Development of the Brain in Early Life,* ed. A. Minkowski. Oxford: Blackwell Scientific.

6

Structure, Somatic and Psychic: The Biopsychological Base of Infancy

Leo Rangell, M.D.

The contributions to this Congress have thus far centered, either alternately or with one or the other emphasized, on the early biological or early psychological determinants of behavior visible or detectable during the stage of infancy. I will continue this exploration of biological and psychological origins mainly with respect to the interrelationships and fusion between the two.

Dr. Anders (chapter 5, this volume) has brought up to date the somatic substrate of infant behavior. I wish to add the counterweight of the psychic aspects to complete and balance the psychobiological unity which this age we are studying, the beginnings of life, provides us the opportunity to understand further. By serendipity, I will also refer to the chronobiology contributed by Dr. Anders, but will add to the unfolding of neural events the sequential relationships from the somatic to the acquisition of psychic functions.

While this Congress is deliberately multidisciplined, I speak from the discipline that is multidisciplined in its basic theoretical orientation. Psychoanalysis, in its essence and principles, reciprocally fertilizes and is fertilized by the findings of Piaget, Watson, primatology, ethology, and neurophysiology, all of which have been mentioned at various times by previous speakers. With structure as the bridge, I continue and extend this multilogue to the progression from somatic to psychic structure with the goal of examining the fused functioning of both.

The term *structure,* as in "psychic structure," which was already implicit in "psychic apparatus," came with the development of psychoanalytic theory. Structures, as Freud applied the term to psychological elements, were defined by Rapaport and Gill (1959, p. 803) as "configurations of a slow rate of change." In this respect, psychic structures are not qualitatively different from somatic structures. Although psychic and somatic structures do not overlap, as Freud concluded when he moved from the "Project" to a more purely psychologically centered science, both are resistant to change, and neither is irreversible. Somatic structures also undergo less volatile changes than organic processes. And somatic structures are also subject to slow rates of change, toward atrophy or hypertrophy, growth or deterioration.

Psychic structure in early development results in the acquisition and retention of psychic elements which achieve the status of a gradually increasing psychic reality. These come with experience to be on a par with, if different qualitatively from, external reality, or the reality of the internal visceral body cavity or sensorimotor body space. This is in keeping with Freud's (1923) description of the two surfaces of the ego, one directed toward the external world and the other toward the border of the internal environment. In changing from his original seduction theory to the role of fantasy, Freud (1887–1902) did not abandon the former but added the latter. He did not, as some think, eliminate reality but expanded it; internal psychic reality took its place alongside of the external. The early phase-related fantasy of castration develops a reality of its own, with as profound an etiologic effect as a threat from without.

By serendipity or design, this gathering represents a bridging of three pairs of polar opposites.

The first such pair are infant observers and analysts of adults. One looks progressively forward, the other retrospectively toward early life, each toward the other to establish continuity. I am speaking today as an analyst of adult life whose view is toward the life lived in the past as far back as we can see. Can we see back to infancy? Already this is a theoretical question to discuss. We do certainly think about and aim toward that time.

The second polarity is between body and mind. It is accepted as a truism that at the origin of life, more than at any other time, the two are closest—if not one. If I could have chosen my place on this program, which I did not, it would have been in this psychosomatic section, to discuss psychobiologic origins.

Thirdly, this period of the beginnings of life is also prior to the divergent paths brought about by language and culture. From the moment the infant is born, the language around him—language, incidentally, so intrinsic a subject to French psychoanalysis[1]—immediately sets large groups and clusters apart, not only the words but the affects, the culture, the communicative styles. Infants who were the same —not completely of course as there are evolutionary built-in differences as well—become French, Spanish, or American children.

How far back toward infancy do we reach in

the clinical situation? To age five? Usually. To age three? Commonly. To two? Occasionally. Below that? Atypically, and rarely with surety. I think of a patient's dream which was quite clearly dated at age two because of the house he lived in. The dream occurred around the time his grandfather died. The patient dreamed of having two mothers, one in a loose nightgown with her hair down, the other in curlers, stiff, with her hair up. He had just lost his grandfather, who had served as his warmest maternal figure, much as the patient is at present to his own grandson.

In addition to looking backward as far as we can clinically, I will extrapolate to the period of infancy on the basis of data derived from both directions, filtered in each case through the understanding derived from total psychoanalytic theory.

Before doing so, as a comment on methodology, I wish to counter a commonly held fallacy that the unscientific approach of clinical psychiatry or psychoanalysis is made more scientific by direct observational studies, whether in young children or, as in the subject of this Congress, in our studies with infants. The fact is that, while both methods complement each other and are cumulative in their effects, one is neither more nor less scientific than the other. The method of direct observation actually operates in both instances—of infants in action and adult patients in words—as well as in the intermediate form of play therapy in child analysis or psychotherapy. At neither end does the observer have the controlled situations or quantitative or other hard criteria of the physical sciences. Both poles of human observation are equally within the soft and humanistic modes of science, subjective and contemplative rather than measured in their methods of understanding and in the means of their conclusions.

The data in each case are interpreted after having been filtered through the same theory of understanding, which is itself subject to change in accordance with observed and available data. Direct observations of psychological phenomena in statu nascendi do not make retrospective analysis a harder or more proven science. At each point, horizontally and vertically, there are synapses of understanding between data and explanations over which both the observer and analyst need similarly to provide bridges, which one of my patients hopefully described as constituting "the creative leap."

Extrapolations from the Theory of Anxiety

To advance the theoretical problems involved at the point in life we are gathered here to study, I would like to turn to the phenomenon most centrally involved in clinical psychoanalysis: the role of anxiety. Just as Freud (1926) considered anxiety "the fundamental phenomenon and main problem of neurosis," so do I feel that a challenging and indispensable subject in which to achieve clarity is the tracing of its origins and course from birth. And just as it has been traditional in analysis that understanding the pathological sheds light on the normal, so can this tracing of the origins of anxiety cast light on adaptive as well as maladaptive behavior, both in earliest life and its future course.

To start with a dynamic condition that will have psychological relevance for the remainder of life, the initial psychoeconomic state at birth is the traumatic state. I do not yet say the traumatic experience, but the existence of the traumatic state. At first there can only be, as Greenacre (1945) says, automatic reactions, reflex actions, and involuntary responses without psychological awareness or experience. It requires a rudimentary and nascent beginning of what will later become an ego structure to register what can at this stage be called an "experience." I would note that this original condition is generically not unlike the state of actual neurosis postulated by Freud (1926) as consisting of physicochemical processes reactive to an influx of stimuli without accompanying psychological content.

Approaching the subject of anxiety from the point of view of adult neuroses, Freud (1895) first described this state as occurring in a discrete type of anxiety neurosis "detached from" the psychoneuroses in etiology. In a unitary theory of anxiety in which I combined Freud's first and second theories of anxiety, I said (1955a, 1968) that this psychoeconomic state of actual neurosis occurs routinely during the intrapsychic sequences of conflict formation in the formative stages of every neurosis, a formulation in agreement with the views of Fenichel (1945).

At some very early point in neonatal life, probably in advance of the six-month (or earlier) stranger anxiety identified by Spitz (1950) and Benjamin (1961), psychological "experience," still not anxiety, enters life, a momentous achievement prior to those named by Spitz (1959) as the early "organizers" of psychic development in infancy. An organism heretofore serving as the locus of a state becomes a young, very young, "person" who suffers it. Such an awareness, probably preconscious, at first dimly, then more surely, becomes at some point the first actual psychological "experience." With it, a mental structure has been added to a somatic neuronal one, initiating what Mahler (Mahler et al., 1975) has called "the psychological birth of the human infant."

Does trauma thus become the first human experience? Or is the state of satiation—bliss, as it is called from an adultomorphic position —"felt" first? Does trauma become "known" because it interrupts contentment? Or is relief sensed only after trauma has been experienced? Such questions will remain subjects of debate in the realm of philosophers, or prove a fertile area for those who project their fantasies or preferences onto childhood.

Empirically we can say that, at least chronologically, the state of trauma comes first. The conditions of the first neonatal minute—Greenacre (1941) states that intrauterine stress can already predispose to the onset of this state— produce the helplessness of the traumatic state without the accompanying affect of unpleasure, which is still to come. The condition of helplessness is followed immediately by events which result in the cessation of this state as the neonate is warmed, covered, and allowed to sleep. The state of helplessness continues, but is inoperative for some minutes or hours, until mounting need repeats the process of birth, with somatic stimuli pressing again, this time from within, and the conditions which will soon bring on unpleasure reappearing. The cycle repeats: traumatic helplessness interrupted by external manipulation that brings satiation and contentment.

At moments of development, which can only be subjectively identified, affects of unpleasure and pleasure make themselves "felt," and from then on accompany these alternating states. While ontogenetically trauma antedates the state of homeostasis, the accompanying affects, in whatever sequence they begin, will alternate from that time on. Some might believe that a difference can already be laid down here for future character formation toward optimism or pessimism, in accordance with which affect comes first or at least comes to predominate: unpleasure or pleasure.

Grossman (personal communication, 1983) speculates that for Freud, the deepest abstract nature of the repetition compulsion results from "the imprint on the child of prestructural traumata damaging the child in the preverbal stages." Pine (1982) speaks of the opposite effect, of the potential resulting from gratifying experience for a future good self-awareness in the second year of life. Both observations relate to Emde's (chapter 4) description of an affective core of the developing self. For completeness and clarity, I would add that the same applies to the future self-representation and sense of self.

The first affective experience of unpleasure might well be the cornerstone prestructure of mental life (perhaps I have here stumbled upon the theoretical justification for Kohut's [1977] description of "tragic man"). From the moment of onset of the mental in human life, psychic "structures" are superimposed upon somatic ones. Psychoanalysts, psychologists, and neurologists have described the subsequent interdependence between the now rapid growth of the central nervous system and the psychological aspects of life. Just as the central nervous system takes time to mature and develop, so does the growth and development of the psychic apparatus. It is precisely this slow development and relatively long period of dependence of the human species that were given special importance by Freud (1905) as leading to the most advanced neuropsychological evolutionary outcome among living forms. These observations about psychic maturation relate to Anders's (chapter 5) chronobiological timetable with its innate temporal rhythms and organization and add to it a chronobiopsychological sequence.

Both psychic and somatic structures develop simultaneously from lesser to higher forms of organization. Among early built-in constitutional prestructures in the ontogenesis of affect described by Rapaport (1953) are discharge channels—psychological pathways connoting direction—and stimulus thresholds—obstacles limiting rates of discharge, analogous to neurological reflex pathways with their facilitators or resistances to neural discharge. Both become parts of a later developed ego. The id-ego matrix present at birth (Hartmann, 1939, 1950) gradually differentiates into separate id and ego structures.

Psychic structures undergo a gradual unfolding, from *anlagen* to forerunners or precursors to prestructures to more formed and cohesive structures, and from these to systems of unified and functionally cooperating structures. Maturational expectations and timetables are built into the constitutional givens, with psychic expansion inherent within the growth potential and expectable forward thrust of originally somatic structures. Sensory apparatuses contain within them the functional capacity for perception, which will lead to the perceptual images of mental life. Motor organs possess the potential and expectation for providing a function that will mentally fulfill Hendrick's (1942) "instinct for mastery." Propioceptive and kinesthetic functions, mediated by the central nervous system, provide the *sense* of balance and orientation that is an intrinsic part of original and subsequent affect, of basic pleasure or unpleasure, and the rudimentary beginnings of an awareness of a self. Visceral and enteroceptive stimuli contribute, even disproportionately at first, to the mental and bodily states of well-being or disharmony. Early perceptions, the first experiences of pleasure and unpleasure, the mnemic images of these original affects, and dimly perceived or felt external objects or conditions constitute original mental impressions en route to becoming more formed mental representations.

From unpleasure and pleasure, the first diffuse "experiences" of affect and the first affective prestructures to be laid down, a next major psychological organizer of development is the differentiation and experience of anxiety. Traumatic helplessness is not unpleasure but leads to it. Unpleasure is not anxiety but leads to it. Anxiety awaits the ability to anticipate. Necessary are the functions of memory and recall and, with these, the capacity to imagine the recurrence of unpleasure. Anxiety is the anticipation of the unpleasure of traumatic helplessness. At the point at which it is achieved by the human infant, anxiety brings with it the human capability to survive and to suffer.

The deprived children Brazelton (chapter 28) treated, in whom he observed "a worried look," were already advanced to the degree that they could anticipate danger. They were thus at a higher developmental level than the marasmic children studied by Spitz (1945), in whom apathy, rather than anxiety, was in evidence. The hospitalized children described by Spitz were in a chronic undefended traumatic state, while the infants Brazelton treated in his office or in their homes with their mothers present could already anticipate that state, as well as the condition that would ward it off (the presence of the mother).

The gradually evolving maturational process combines both integration and differentiation. At every stage the achieved position maintains the original bond between soma and psyche, a continuous union often overlooked, as well as resulting in a differentiation between the two. An intellectual oscillation throughout man's history has led to an alternating overvaluation of one or the other, either to a Cartesian duality of body and mind, in a philosophic and psychiatric-psychoanalytic sense, or to an undue fusion, leading, for example, to the attempt to explain both by the material and somatic. The result has been either an emphasis of mind over matter or an exaggerated organic bias. In actuality both psyche and soma evolve together and separately, with unity and differentiation, with independence and a separate course for each, as well as with an interdependence between man's corporeal being and his thinking and feeling.

The relations between functions and structures evolve gradually. Pathological defensive behavior can exist in infants without being continuous with pre-ego modes of defense, as Fraiberg (1982) pointed out on the basis of careful direct observations of a deprived infant population. Precursors and prestructures are more malleable, changeable, and fluid than psychic elements that have become structured and fixed. Perceptions and affects, before they enter into formed memories, are more subject to addition, replacement, obliteration, and modification than after they have achieved the status of structured fixity. Perhaps this is the basis for the clinically obtained understanding that the earliest influences, by which are usually meant the pregenital, have profound but still changeable effects, whereas by the oedipal period, which is quite synchronous with the formation of tripartite structures, a good deal of character formation and predictability of behavior has been laid down. New inputs, however, can still be continuously absorbed to affect the quality of the still-developing structures.

A psychopathologic developmental variation is the phenomenon of premature structuralization, a defensive maladaptive event occurring in the presence of an abnormal degree of trauma. This can result from either overstimulation or deprivation. With the young child having automatically to sacrifice the long and beneficial dependency period and to develop defensively a premature independence for survival purposes, early pathology can result from prematurely developing structures encapsulating insufficiently developed ego or superego nuclei. Variations of such processes result in developmental arrests, ego deficits, or pathological fixations, which will exert a backward pull for future regression.

Freud's (1923) observations of the early ego as being originally a body ego can be properly expanded or altered to refer instead to a body self, as Mahler and McDevitt (1982) have recently called it. While the self is a composite of somatic and mental, the ego is a mental structure. The self representation contained within it, however, in the early stages of development of the psychic structure "ego," does consist of confluent images of the body, affective and cognitive, sensory and motor, surface-exteroceptive and enteroceptive-visceral.

Infancy is connected to adult life within the psychoanalytic theory of anxiety. The traumatic state of helplessness of birth and beyond, until the point at which a beginning ego embarks upon the process of stemming the tide from within, is the feared state behind all anxiety. Rank's (1952) birth trauma is not the model of anxiety but the model of the state that anxiety is dedicated to avoid. It is for this reason that Freud was ambivalent to his own first theory of anxiety, neither willing to retain it nor able to discard it. Freud's actual neurosis was the traumatic state, which I described (1969) as a stage in the intrapsychic process en route to symptom formation or, in favorable situations, to a more adaptive solution. It is also helpful and necessary to distinguish the traumatic state from a traumatic neurosis. A state of trauma appropriate to the stimulus is not a neurosis. The latter obtains only to a reaction inappropriate to the current stimulus, stemming from a latent, cumulative readiness to react.

Anxiety is never without psychological content, as Freud felt in his first theory, but is always the sign of such content, the cognitive-affective anticipation of danger. "The biological factor . . . establishes the earliest situations of danger," Freud (1926, p. 155) stated, but a psychological factor is required to recognize and react to it. Arising at the point of development when danger can be foreseen, the capacity for anxiety, one of the organizing milestones described by Spitz (1959), along with the smile, which is its opposite and bespeaks safety, is called forth in every repetition of the sensing of danger from then on. Anxiety undergoes a complex developmental line, with both phase-specific and individual experiences throughout life. Developmental stages passed through ontogenetically and sequential phases passed through in rapid succession during the unconscious intrapsychic process, from the original impulse or perception to the final psychic outcome, are typically visible in derivative forms as the material in analysis unfolds during the psychoanalytic process.

Derivatives in Analysis and in Life

Switching again rapidly from infancy to adult life, I would like next to point to certain clinically observable phenomena seen in adult psychoanalytic patients, which, to my way of understanding, derive directly from the tension state of the intrapsychic arc and genetically recapitulate ontogenetic development. In accordance with a formulation I previously (1981) suggested, that anxiety results from an unconscious recapitulation of the traumatic states of life, the dangers behind the unconscious anxiety in the clinical instances to be cited represent a series of defended against and increasingly distorted derivatives of the individual life history of traumatic states. Extrapolating back to our interest in the period of infancy, these traverse, in reverse order, states of trauma experienced in infancy and beyond, and either repetitions or derivatives of these remembered preconsciously in childhood, fantasied consciously and unconsciously later, and feared unconsciously throughout life.

Data in themselves do not typically prove or confirm theories employed to explain them. The same data can be explained by structural theory, object relations theory, self theory and, not as close to the center of psychoanalytic theory today, theories of environmental conflict or interpersonal relationships. Nevertheless, in the view I am presenting here, the most convincing, enduring, experience-related, and time-resisting explanations for not some but all clinical and life observations, rest upon total basic psychoanalytic theory, which includes psychic structure, anxiety, conflict, and the explanations that derive from these for symptom formation and all other human behavior. In specific clinical cases, there are universal substrates upon which individual experiences of traumatic threats have been superimposed. The closer the danger situations approach the original states of infantile trauma, the more does clinical phenomenology rest on common experiential ground.

I would like now to describe some clinical observations of certain adult behavioral patterns which I have been accumulating in the past few years and which, I believe, trace their origins to the earliest period of life. These include myriad postures, mannerisms, and automatic actions occurring in a variety of analytic phases and moods, which came to be understood as they were interwoven with the surrounding accompanying material and dynamics.

These actions can be divided into two groups: one serving tension reduction, almost somatic, neurophysiologic, and similar to Freud's original clinical observations along the same line; and another in which these same functions were admixed with superimposed or parallel symbolic and hermeneutic significance. These activities, which typically involve the neuromuscular system or the skin or its hair, nails, or other appendages, traverse a complementary series of phenomena from what I regard as reflex psychosomatic transmission at one pole to increasingly symbolic meaning at the other.

Whereas the significance of these traits and actions can become known to the analyst, it may or may not be useful to bring them to the attention of the patient in the interpretive process. When and if pointed out, they are usually thought of consciously as "little habits," typically fused with the character and rarely egodystonic. Not only has learning "abiding change wrought by experience," brought about structure formation (Rapaport, 1960, p. 99), but effects that can be "environmentally syntonic" as well. To the extent that these have accrued symbolic meanings during the course of development, they are rendered accessible to the interpretive process and to analysis. Just as preoedipal conflicts become embedded in the oedipal, and can be carried along analytically by analysis of the later more available experiences, so can these more primitive and direct mental processes be included in later symbolic acts and actions, and in the capacity of the analytic ego of the patient to understand and master them. Such automatic and seemingly reflex psychomotor acts may in this manner turn out in practice not to be outside the reach of analysis.

As evidence of the type of behavior I have in mind, in some patients a periodic or at times more continuous restlessness on the couch becomes prominent during the analytic hour. This is not so much at times of verbal communication or during the revelation of the concrete contents of psychic conflicts as in between these times. Although it is difficult to convey the clinical "feel" that is the background for my theoretical understanding of its meaning and dynamics, I have come to regard such motor activity as direct unconscious or preconscious expression of psychophysical tension, which is a discrete segment of mental activity upon which the bursts of verbal activity are superimposed. This type of behavior, freely available to analysts generally, in my view, represents an attempt to dispell tension occurring when psychic conflict mounts toward a relative traumatic state which would strain the capacity of the ego. There is, to be sure, psychic conflict operative at the same time and indeed at all times, but the motor innervations during these periods of visible activity are, in my opinion, attempts to discharge not the psychic content but its somatic accompaniments.

One patient would alternately flex his knees and then straighten his legs, move his head from one position to another, lie on one side and then the other, or rhythmically clench and unclench his fists. From the same dynamic background, another patient at certain times would energetically crack his knuckles and then rest. One could of course say that these movements expressed aggression, even if this was not in the psychic content at the time. But with or without this added, I came to understand these activities regularly and typically as attempts to produce physical, along with mental, homeostasis.

To be sure, such complex psychomotor actions are multidetermined, as is all final outward behavior, and consist of inputs from all levels of development. One patient stretched and yawned whenever a crucial interpretation was about to be conveyed, usually closer and closer to the castration anxiety. He also exhibited and noted a shiver, which he stated he did not understand. Here tension reduction was also operative as the specific anxiety was being approached, but the generalized movements were then joined by and utilized for an acute increment of defense, this psychological meaning being added to the baseline physiological process. The syndrome of "restless legs," known to physicians, and usually attributed to vascular insufficiency, is probably seen here in a more generalized form as a restless body, due not to vascular pathology but to a chronic psychosomatic malfunctioning in conflict resolution. This is probably related to Freud's "discharge of drive tension into the soma," cited by Rapaport (1950, p. 315) as a stage in the development of affective behavior.

Actions and behavior at the sensorimotor periphery of the body are complex, overdetermined, and serve multiple functions (Waelder, 1936). One patient rhythmically clasps his fingers and presses his hands tightly together, doing and undoing this repetitive action. In this case the patient is holding on to himself as a substitute for holding another, psychologically reassuring himself by seeking support, superimposed upon physical muscular tension reduction. Progressing in this series, another patient, in whom hand-seeking was more solely psychological, hermeneutic, and meaning-oriented, would put her arms and hands behind her head toward the analyst, looking to hold on, but no pressing or muscular movements were in evidence. Here the movements served a wish. There was no tension discharge. Still another patient clearly added masturbatory impulses from a later stage of psychosexual development. This patient kneads the muscles and pats the skin on the inside of his thighs, first gently, then increasingly forcefully. At times when he comes to his sessions in shorts after jogging, a not uncommon custom in Southern California, these actions can be seen more directly and undisguisedly.

Behavior in this category can be varied and changeable. In one patient, bursts of muscular activity accompanied irregular verbal outbursts, with silence as well as muscular inactivity simultaneously evident in between. One had the feeling of witnessing complex verbal and muscular tics, reminiscent of and not unlike sudden spikes on an electroencephalogram. Or the behavior is more stereotyped and ritualistic. A patient entered analysis with the main complaint of hair-pulling—trichotillomania—which he engaged in to such an extent that his wife was afraid he would cause himself to become bald. During the course of analysis, this patient came to display in the analytic position, along with constant and distracting gross twisting and turning of his body, a continued series of unconscious "habits," moving from one to another with rarely a quiescent period in between. He would habitually tear his fingernails or produce hangnails on the skin, pick these off, and then engage in a slow ritual of playing with the remnants. He would roll the nail fragments and dead skin into a ball with his fingers, hold and rub them for a while, and eventually drop them, after some hesitation about which side—whether to his left on the couch or to his right on the carpet.

The total action here was composed of complex psychological components and meanings, sexual and aggressive, from all levels of libidinal and ego development—oral, anal, and phallic. In this patient, there was a combination of chronic general tension-reduction, along with a complex masturbatory and self-stimulating ritual. With nails and skin, as also with his hair-pulling, he could be seen to produce excessive stimulation, even pain, which was erotized and used as a displaced focus for sexual and aggressive motivational drives. This patient could never be alone or without bodily stimulation or reassurance. In spite of a successful, story-book marriage, he carried on a promiscuous extramarital sexual life, which was compulsive, automatic, and shallow. He had more total satisfaction, physical as well as mental, with his wife, but needed the constant reassurance of an available reservoir of stimulus satisfaction as a back-up system should he be left and need some one or some place to go to. Mainly, he wanted to snuggle into and feel attached to these partners and would go further toward sexual intercourse only because he felt it was expected.

Deutsch (1952) has written about such analytic posturology, and Feldman (1959) described mannerisms and gestures of speech and action in everyday life. Both of these authors wove such observations well and convincingly into the total conflictual fabrics of their patients. What I am adding, however, is another component behind this aspect of behavior, a somatic substrate upon which the psychological motivations are superimposed and with which they are fused. This link, which ties psychic content together, a psychophysical ground upon which conflicts and their derivatives become the figures, is confluent with what Pontalis (1977) writes in his emphasis on the "in-between," the spaces and absences and nonverbal links between or behind concrete groups of psychic content. Pontalis, coming from another direction, interestingly notes a similar renewed interest in Freud's original concept of actual neurosis by modern French psychoanalytic theorists.

The recent emphasis on early deficit states converging from many modern psychoanalytic directions are not centered on the same phenomena I have been describing. Kohut's (1971, 1977) theory of ego deficits resulting from deficient early mothering, and also Kernberg's (1975) more widely based theories of preoedipal pathology, relate specifically to more regressed and disturbed psychopathology. What I am pointing to, in reviving Freud's original observations and theory about the genesis of anxiety, involves a more universal mechanism and set of intrapsychic dynamics.

This does not concern abnormalities of psychic structure resulting from phase-specific traumata at later psychosexual stages of development, pregenital or oedipal. Nor am I speaking of cases of earlier traumatic events involving localized musculature or any other somatic structures, resulting later in derivative syndromes. Such a case was reported by Anthi (1983): an operation on an infant at a few months of age for a right neck muscle injured during birth, with subsequent physiotherapy to the age of three, resulted in sequelae which were detected in analysis of the patient as an adult. I am describing a more generalized failure, at an early prestructural stage of development, from the same events described by Anna Freud (1969) as affecting the transition from the early chaotic undifferentiated state to the first cornerstone of psychic structure. The result is an influence on future structural development with a specific but generalized later effect, a hyperalertness to anxiety and sensitivity to trauma. The traumatic state feared and avoided is the state of helplessness common to mankind, rather than specific traumata that

come from individual experiences of later life. Frustration tolerance is low, and the stimulus barrier fragile, vulnerable, and carefully guarded.

Since such pathological effects have occurred before structure formation takes place, they are subject to compensation and amelioration until structure with greater stability and fixity ensues. Such early pathology is therefore not incompatible with subsequent more normal development, including future object relations, or with the formation of any more circumscribed pathological syndrome, borderline or neurotic. The effects I am describing may constitute a general background prior to the differentiation of later specific symptoms, including in infancy any of the attachment syndromes listed by Call (1981) or the general or psychosomatic afflictions of infancy categorized in the nosology of Kreisler (chapter 49).

The Psychobiologic Unity

The main theoretical consideration I wish to point to, in an overall view of the clinical material cited, is the regression in common to the psychobiological unity from which we started. Anxiety itself, a center of this presentation, is a psychobiological phenomenon, a unity of opposites not routinely kept in mind or appreciated when being understood or treated from one side only, that is, either by the psychoanalyst from the point of view of conflict or by the pharmacologist who puts aside the psychological aspects. The fact is that, while the treatment may be legitimately limited to one side or the other, with theoretical complications resulting from combining the two, the complete understanding of the phenomenon of anxiety, encompassing in theory the total self which harbors it, can only be achieved by a unified psychobiologic view.

It is consonant with this total theoretical approach that I have combined Freud's two theories of anxiety, the first, which purported to be physiological, without the effects of psychological conflicts, and the second, which centered on psychological content, eliminating its organic base. Traumatic helplessness, feared and already partially present in the experience of anxiety, is a psychophysical or equally somatopsychic state threatening a physical as well as mental dissolution of the self.

Jones's (1929) aphanisis, Glover's (1938) fear of bursting from within, Kohut's (1971, 1977) fragmentation of the self, Winnicott's (1952) fragmentation of the ego, Waelder's (1936) fear of the ego being destroyed or overrun, and Anna Freud's (1936) "dread of the strength of the instincts," as well as Freud's (1920, 1926, 1937) ultimate "resistances of the id," all refer to the same primitively feared states of physical and psychological disintegration. Fraiberg (1982) sensitively described a group of babies from three months of age, whose mothers were chronically not "good-enough," in whom hunger, solitude, or a sudden noise set off a state of helplessness and disintegration, with screaming and flailing about, which in effect was an already present traumatic state. But disintegrative states, as Fraiberg also pointed out, "are an extreme danger in themselves." Anxiety is a fear of the traumatic state; the traumatic state begets anxiety. Brazelton's frail and worried little patients demonstrated the ongoing mutuality and reciprocity of these contiguous clinical states.

In a paper on the psychological aspects mediated by the snout or perioral region, another area of personal research in which I approached the infantile state from the viewpoint of adult psychopathology (1954), I described the fear in stage fright, which can be applied to universal social anxiety, in which there is a fantasy, both a wish and a fear, of disappearing into the ground, with only the nose and mouth remaining above it. When the wish turns to pure fear, the remaining few inches of corpus will also submerge. All anxiety, in my clinical experience with pathological anxiety states, is ultimately a fear of a claustrum, a respiratory panic of the unavailability of air to breathe.

The clinical phenomenology to which I pointed in these studies, proceeding from adult manifestations to their infantile origins, of skin and neuromuscular facial mechanisms involving the lips, tongue, chin, and the snout or perioral region generally, correlate well with the direct and experimental observations of affect attunement reported by Stern (chapter 1). These same areas of affective facial expression were involved in his direct observations of the reciprocal communicative responses between infants and mothers.

Regression in the panic state, which Schur (1953) refers to as maximum anxiety, the feared state behind milder and more-defended-against anxiety states, is associatively and etiologically linked by a series of decreasingly distorted derivatives to the original preverbal traumatic state. One patient's ultimate anxiety, manifesting her fear of loss of ego control, was of losing bodily control of every orifice—that she would fall in a faint after sweating, vomiting, defecating, menstruating, and choking. In another patient, who, behind a very successful social and professional façade, had what he referred to as a "jelly center," his vulnerable state traced back to the birth of his sister when the patient was two. Historically his life changed abruptly at that time from being his parents' Leonardo Da Vinci, the only son, grandson, and grandchild of a large and doting family to what should have been realistically a normal state of sharing, but which to him became an intolerable state of deprivation. He remembered a period in his early childhood when he did not speak to his mother for two years. When, during his analysis, he inquired of his mother about this, she was incredulous, remembered nothing of it, and repeated her antagonism to his analysis and his analyst. In groping for the reasons for his chronic, depressed, and angry state at that time (after coming up with a number of trite and unconvincing explanations), the best he could lamely offer was, "I think she just wasn't nice to me."

Derivatives of anxiety throughout life fall on a continuum with respect to bodily or psychological effects. As with all continua or complementary series, most instances are in the midrange and combine polar attributes, with a lesser number of pure examples at either end. Thus most symptoms or other final common pathways of behavior combine psychic and somatic manifestations. Affects, so much stressed in these studies of infants, are themselves on the boundary between soma and psyche, as Freud (1915) said about instincts, and utilize aspects of each in their composition and expressions.

Outcomes generally regarded as psychosomatic and nonsymbolic, such as ulcer, asthma, or hypertension, can express ideational contents as well, aggressive or libidinal motivations and intentions from various phases of development. And presumably solely hermeneutic and conflict-expressing symptoms, such as conversion, can and do utilize bodily organs as well, with direct relief of tension or other nonsymbolic purposes admixed. Delusions or hallucinations are generally thought of as on the cognitive and ideational side of the continuum, and asthma, ulcer, or tics as more on the somatic. Yet there can be somatic delusions, and hallucinations involve auditory or visual perceptual pathways. Asthma or ulcer can express distorted oral longings. A tic can be a pregenital conversion (Fenichel, 1945; Rangell, 1959). Gilles de la Tourette's disease, a syndrome Mahler and I (1943) described from a combined psychoanalytic and neurological standpoint, is a complex combination of automatic, kinetic, muscular involvement with pathological, indirect symbolic expressions of aggressive drives and destructive intentions.

Anxiety expresses the psychological content of danger, yet its physical accompaniments are themselves direct bodily derivatives of the tension segment of the intrapsychic arc of conflict I have described. The shiver, so commonly regarded as intrinsic to anxiety and which I noted earlier as prominent in a patient whenever an interpretation close to castration either came or was expected, is not a fortuitous occurrence but might also have meaning. Its meaning, however, is not necessarily ideational but can be physiological. It can routinely signify an attempt to diminish the tension of anxiety, which comes about from an unsuccessful attempt of the defenses to stave off mounting instinctual or external pressure. The anxiety reaction is both a suffering of trauma, limited and experimental, and preparedness for restitution. While anxiety is properly regarded as a psychological reaction, in the last analysis it is a mental plan for total—that is, physical and mental—survival. The other side of the fear of disappearing is the wish to disappear for protective purposes, leaving, as I said earlier, the snout exposed for air.

The perioral region is the "window to the emotions" (Rangell, 1954). It is both protected and kept exposed. It is also the area of the body through which attachment is achieved, from the time of the infant's first perioral grasping and holding of the maternal breast. Every experimental thought that tests for anxiety is both to achieve separateness and to be assured of the possibility of return to the source of security. The combined search for independence and attachment, noted by Mahler and McDevitt (1982) as already present in the neonate, is continued in derivative form throughout life. Anxiety, from the time that it appears, is a practicing separation as much as the practicing subphase of a year or more later. And the "niche" sought by the reflex action of the infant is repeated throughout life in what I have called (1955b) "the quest for ground," manifested as a permanent need to belong, whether to a person, group, institution, or idea.

REFERENCES

Anthi, P. R. (1983). Reconstruction of preverbal experiences. *Journal of the American Psychoanalytic Association* 31:33–58.

Benjamin, J. D. (1961). Some developmental observations relating to the theory of anxiety. *Journal of the American Psychoanalytic Association* 9:652–668.

Call, J. (1980). Attachment disorders in infancy. In *Comprehensive Textbook of Psychiatry*, vol. III, 3rd ed., ed. H. I. Kaplan, A. M. Freedman, and B. J. Sadock. New York: Williams & Wilkins.

Deutsch, F. (1952). Analytic posturology. *Psychoanalytic Quarterly* 21:196–214.

Feldman, S. S. (1959). *Mannerisms of Speech and Gestures in Everyday Life*. New York: International Universities Press.

Fenichel, O. (1945). *The Psychoanalytic Theory of Neurosis*. New York: W. W. Norton.

Fraiberg, S. (1982). Pathological defenses in infancy. *Psychoanalytic Quarterly* 60:612–635.

Freud, A. (1936). *The Ego and the Mechanisms of Defence.* New York: International Universities Press.

Freud, A. (1969). Difficulties in the path of psychoanalysis. *Writings of Anna Freud,* 7:124–156. New York: International Universities Press.

Freud, S. (1887–1902). *The Origins of Psycho-Analysis,* ed. M. Bonaparte, A. Freud, and E. Kris. New York: Basic Books, 1954.

Freud, S. (1895). On the grounds for detaching a particular syndrome from neurasthenia under the description 'anxiety neurosis.' *Standard Edition,* vol. 3, ed. J. Strachey. London: Hogarth Press, 1962.

Freud, S. (1905). Three essays on the theory of sexuality. *Standard Edition,* vol. 7, ed. J. Strachey. London: Hogarth Press, 1953.

Freud, S. (1915). Instincts and their vicissitudes. *Standard Edition,* vol. 14, ed. J. Strachey. London: Hogarth Press, 1957.

Freud, S. (1920). Beyond the pleasure principle. *Standard Edition,* vol. 18, ed. J. Strachey. London: Hogarth Press, 1955.

Freud, S. (1923). The ego and the id. *Standard Edition,* vol. 19, ed. J. Strachey. London: Hogarth Press, 1961.

Freud, S. (1926). Inhibitions, symptoms and anxiety. *Standard Edition,* vol. 20, ed. J. Strachey. London: Hogarth Press, 1959.

Freud, S. (1937). Analysis terminable and interminable. *Standard Edition,* vol. 23, ed. J. Strachey. London: Hogarth Press, 1964.

Glover, E. (1938). The psycho-analysis of affects. In *On the Early Development of Mind: Selected Papers on Psychoanalysis.* New York: International Universities Press, 1956.

Greenacre, P. (1941). The predisposition to anxiety. In *Trauma, Growth, and Personality.* New York: International Universities Press, 1952.

Greenacre, P. (1945). The biological economy of birth. In *Trauma, Growth, and Personality.* New York: International Universities Press, 1952.

Hartmann, H. (1939). *Ego Psychology and the Problems of Adaptation.* New York: International Universities Press, 1958.

Hartmann, H. (1950). Comments on the psychoanalytic theory of the ego. In *Essays on Ego Psychology.* New York: International Universities Press.

Hendrick, I. (1942). Instinct and the ego during infancy. *Psychoanalytic Quarterly* 11:33–58.

Jones, E. (1929). The psychopathology of anxiety. In *Papers on Psycho-Analysis.* Baltimore: Williams & Wilkins, 1948.

Kernberg, O. F. (1975). *Borderline Conditions and Pathological Narcissism.* New York: Jason Aronson.

Kohut, H. (1971). *The Analysis of the Self.* New York: International Universities Press.

Kohut, H. (1977). *The Restoration of the Self.* New York: International Universities Press.

Mahler M. S. and McDevitt, J. B. (1982). Thoughts on the emergence of the sense of the self, with particular emphasis on the body self. *Journal of the American Psychoanalytic Association.* 30:827–848.

Mahler, M. S., Pine F., and Bergman, A. (1975). *The Psychological Birth of the Human Infant: Symbiosis and Individuation.* New York: Basic Books.

Mahler, M. S. and Rangell, L. (1943). A psychosomatic study of maladie des tics (Gilles de la Tourette's Disease). *Psychiatric Quarterly,* 17:579–603.

Pine, F. (1982). The experience of self: Aspects of its formation, expansion, and vulnerability. *The Psychoanalytic Study of the Child,* 37:143–167. New Haven: Yale University Press.

Pontalis, J.-B. (1977). *Frontiers in Psychoanalysis. Between the Dream and Psychic Pain.* New York: International Universities Press.

Rangell, L. (1954). The psychology of poise, with a special elaboration on the psychic significance of the snout or perioral region. *International Journal of Psycho-Analysis* 35:313–332.

Rangell, L. (1955a). On the psychoanalytic theory of anxiety: A statement of a unitary theory. *Journal of the American Psychoanalytic Association* 3:389–414.

Rangell, L. (1955b). The quest for ground in human motivation. Address to the first Western Divisional Meeting of the American Psychiatric Association and the West Coast Psychoanalytic Societies, October 29.

Rangell, L. (1959). The nature of conversion. *Journal of the American Psychoanalytic Association* 7:632–662.

Rangell, L. (1968). A further attempt to resolve the "problem of anxiety." *Journal of the American Psychoanalytic Association* 16:371–404.

Rangell, L. (1969). The intrapsychic process and its analysis: A recent line of thought and its current implications. *International Journal of Psycho-Analysis* 50:65–77.

Rangell, L. (1981). From insight to change. *Journal of the American Psychoanalytic Association* 29:119–141.

Rank, O. (1952). *The Trauma of Birth.* New York: Robert Brunner.

Rapaport, D. (1950). On the psychoanalytic theory of thinking. In *The Collected Papers of David Rapaport,* ed. M. M. Gill. New York: Basic Books, 1967.

Rapaport, D. (1953). On the psychoanalytic theory of affects. In *The Collected Papers of David Rapaport,* ed. M. M. Gill. New York: Basic Books, 1967.

Rapaport, D. (1960). *The structure of psychoanalytic theory: A systematizing attempt. Psychological Issues.* Monograph 6. New York: International Universities Press.

Rapaport, D. and Gill, M. M. (1959). The points of view and assumptions of metapsychology. In *The Collected Papers of David Rapaport,* ed. M. M. Gill. New York: Basic Books, 1967.

Schur, M. (1953). The ego in anxiety. In *Drives, Affects, Behavior,* ed. R. M. Loewenstein. New York: International Universities Press, pp. 67–103.

Spitz, R. A. (1945). Hospitalism. *The Psychoanalytic Study of the Child* 1:53–74. New York: International Universities Press.

Spitz, R. A. (1950). Anxiety in infancy: A study of its manifestations in the first year of life. *International Journal of Psycho-Analysis* 31:138–143.

Spitz, R. A. (1959). *A Genetic Field Theory of Ego Formation. Its Implications for Pathology.* New York: International Universities Press.

Waelder, R. (1936). The principle of multiple function. *Psychoanalytic Quarterly* 5:45–62.

Winnicott, D. W. (1952). Psychoses and child care. In *Collected Papers. Through Paediatrics to Psycho-Analysis.* New York: Basic Books, 1958.

7

The Pleasures and Annoyances of Babies: Causes and Consequences

Lewis P. Lipsitt, Ph.D.

In his presentation to the First World Congress on Infant Psychiatry, Erikson spoke eloquently of his return to the nursery to observe very young babies after a long period of minimal contact. In his report of the experience, he said that he was struck by the *"sensitivity* of the little creatures" (Call et al., 1983, p. 425). As Erikson well knew, the term *sensitivity* has at least a double meaning and possibly multiple meanings. At the very least, human infants (even newborns) are capable of *sensing* their environments in all perceptual modalities. Beyond this basic biological capacity, inherent in all essentially normal infants from birth, infants reflect their "appreciation" of stimulation. They do this, first, by responding to it in a basically reflexive fashion, as in startling to a bright light or turning the head to the locus of a gentle sound. Second, they manifest qualitatively distinguishable signs of their pleasure or displeasure with the stimulation. Third, infants *act* to perpetuate satisfying states of affairs and to terminate those conditions of the environment which are annoying.

The human infant is born with the capacity, to a greater or lesser extent and unquestionably compromised in babies born at risk, for experiencing the pleasures and annoyances of sensation. These hedonic processes are mediated by physiological mechanisms which by now are fairly well understood. Nonetheless, we need to know much more about the necessary and sufficient stimulation for their activation, and the processes by which pleasure and annoyance alter subsequent adaptive behaviors of infants and thus lay the foundations for the enduring effects of early experience. This presentation provides some indication of the progress we have made in that direction in recent years.

A Conceptual Overview

Much of human activity is directed toward the enhancement of pleasure and the reduction of annoyance. Pleasures and annoyances of sensation and of social interactions accompanying sensations are the principal catalysts for learning. Those responses that are followed by a satisfying state of affairs will tend to be repeated, while those that are not or are followed by annoyance will not be. This "law of effect" enunciated by E. L. Thorndike (1913) has to be regarded as the cornerstone of all learning-theory accounts of human behavior and personality development (Dollard and Miller, 1950).

For Freud, too, "the pleasure principle" was of paramount importance in early behavior and development, and the achievement of maturity was a matter largely of acquiring mechanisms delaying, suppressing, sublimating, or otherwise achieving self-control of pleasure-strivings. That control is largely, if not entirely, learned. Thus it can be supposed that the experiencing of pleasure and the consequences of such experiences are of truly central concern to child developmentalists and child psychoanalysts regardless of whether their principal theoretical affinity is for the learning-theory or the psychodynamic orientations. Dollard and Miller (1950) dedicated their classic volume, *Personality and Psychotherapy,* to both Pavlov and Freud.

Given that the human is capable of experiencing and being affected by pleasures and annoyances from early infancy, precious little attention seems to be invested today in the ontogeny of pleasure reception and pleasure seeking. Infant caregivers are in prime positions to administer pleasure to infants judiciously and thus to teach infants that their own behavior determines the style in which, and extent to which, they are in the future pleasured. Much of the reciprocating interaction that occurs between mother and infant involves, in fact, mutual delivery of pleasant contact in the form of touches, smiles, and vocalizations (Stern, chapter 1, this volume). These reciprocating gestures are the rewarding conditions (Thorndike's satisfying states of affairs) that *enable* learning to occur. Yet the pleasure principle, so central to Freud's thinking about infant development in his original theorizing, is referred to in only one presentation in the report of the First World Congress on Infant Psychiatry (Steele, 1983).

Failure to learn that one's own behavior is instrumental in arranging one's environment for pleasure and removing annoyances from one's midst may well be critical in the etiology of some types of mental and behavioral disturbances. For example, through the work of Richter (1957), Seligman (1975), and Beck and his colleagues (1967), we can now understand depression as a condition of helplessness or hopelessness occasioned, in part at least, by failures in self-regulation of reinforcing or pleasant events. On the other side of the hedonic coin, failure to defend oneself adequately in situations requiring defensive ma-

neuvers (as in imminent accidents, threatened assaults, and the like) are frequent in adults and may not be uncommon in infancy. The defensive and appetitive reflexes with which the human is born are exceedingly important for early biological well-being and self-regulation and for the eventual development of mature patterns of behavior. Such patterns are acquired largely through mechanisms of learning embedded in the socialization process.

An aspect of the conceptual view presented here is that certain developmental disorders of infancy and early childhood may result, first, from aberrations in the hedonic dispositions of infancy, compromising the ability of the child to experience fully the sensations of pleasure and annoyance ordinarily characteristic of the earliest stages of development, and second, from diminished learning capacity due to this dilution of rewarding contingencies in the lives of such infants.

I have elsewhere suggested (1979a) that the failure-to-thrive and sudden-infant-death syndromes and other critical conditions of infancy may be the culmination of a pattern of behavioral incompetencies. Incapacities to cope with adverse environmental events are well known as critical precursors of death and debility in older persons and could be involved in unfortunate developmental outcomes in infants and young children as well. Initial constitutional deficits may result in delayed development of normal response regulation. Compounding this initial adversity, a noncompensating environment then conspires to create an inability to cope when environmental challenges require recruitment of appropriate defensive reactions. As with adults, hedonic modulation of behavior is required, and patterns of adaptive behavior must be learned under auspices of the sensations of pleasure and annoyance.

The Nature of Infancy as Revealed in the Neonate Laboratory

Beginning with the earliest scientific observations on the development of children's learning processes, the first year of life has held the greatest fascination. Initially, the question of the earliest ages at which specific learned responses could occur was the major concern. Thus even studies of *learned* behavior had a heavily maturationist emphasis (Lipsitt, 1963). Whenever an attempt to condition infants with Pavlovian or other techniques failed to yield the anticipated effect, it was inferred that cortical innervation was of insufficient maturity at that age to permit learning to occur (El-konin, 1957). Indeed, many studies of early conditioning have been carried out in the Soviet Union and in the United States with the expressed intent of utilizing tests of learning capacity as indirect assessments of nervous system maturation.

The rapidity of human physiological and anatomical development in the first year of life is so great that it is small wonder that early child developmentalists were eager to discover behavioral indices that would provide quantitative information about the rapidly changing mental status of the child as well. Physical growth rate is faster in the first months of life than it will ever again be. The human infant doubles in weight in the first three months, and triples its birthweight by one year of age. From birth to six months, babies increase in weight an amazing two grams every twenty-four hours. Growth rate then diminishes, from about .35 grams per twenty-four hours between six months and three years, to .15 grams between three and six years. The behavioral changes occurring during this period are no less striking. By two months of age the baby smiles broadly and reciprocatingly. Imitative tongue thrusts, frowns, and lip pursing are easily elicited by this time. Babies show clear recognition of significant persons in their lives by six months of age, they are closely attached to some of these persons by eight months, and they generally take their first independent steps and make their first meaningful utterances of words by the end of the first year.

Because these achievements are very reassuring to the infant's parents or other caregivers, they are in turn rewarded, and in this way the behaviors become further shaped and intensified. Because of parental concerns with the emergence of such landmark behaviors, it is not surprising that some of the earliest research fascinations of child developmentalists were with milestone achievements. The obvious synchronies in physical and behavioral development, moreover, led easily to the adoption of techniques initially unique to anthropometry for the observation and quantification of mental progress as well. Behavior of the infant was soon recorded in response to specific test items, consisting of standardized stimulus situations, to document mental age in much the same way as physical age could be assessed in terms of norms and deviations from the mean for each chronological age. The study of individual differences, the continuity of individual differences seen early in life to later ages, and the causes of these individual differences (in the genetic or experiential histories of the individuals) could now be carried out.

A natural progression exists from the study of developmental *status*, cast as a developmental quotient based on the ratio of mental and chronological age, to developmental *progress*. The shift is from description to an understanding of process. The early emphasis of the field of child development was on constitutional determinants of behavior. While the force of experience in the unfolding of the developmental milestones and the achievement of mature behavior was not denied, the clear emphasis of many early researchers such as Gesell (1948) was on the constitutional determinants of behavior and development.

The constitutional bias of the field, which held that all behavior waits upon structural development and neural tissue, has only gradually been supplanted by the more reasonable view that brain growth and development, on the one hand, and behavioral advances, on the other, are mutually dependent. Recent research findings indicate clearly that nervous system tissue change is sometimes *due to* environmental stimulation. Rats reared in enriched environments, for example, have greater depth of cortex and more dendritic spines than deprived control rats (Rosenzweig and Bennett, 1976). Similarly, the dendritic spines and branches of the neurons in fish have been shown to be influenced appreciably in their development by visual and tactile contact with others of the same species (Coss and Globus, 1978). Although comparable experiments cannot be conducted with humans, evidence exists that some features of sensory and neural mechanisms do require experience for their full development and that brain growth can depend upon behavioral development (Gottlieb, 1971; Purpura, 1975). Further research in this area should illuminate how experiential factors permanently affect behavioral outputs, hedonic processes, learning competencies, and individual differences in maturation itself.

THE STUDY OF ORAL AVIDITY IN THE
NEWBORN

In recent years the study of sucking behavior of the young infant has been pursued in rather fine-grained detail. These studies have generated interesting data on the approach and avoidance style of the newborn, and individual differences in the reactions of babies to stimuli that adults would regard as pleasant or unpleasant (Lipsitt, 1979c). On the basis of these studies the conclusions must be drawn that human newborns are keenly sensitive to gustatory stimulation even in the first few hours of life and that pronounced preferences exist for sweeter fluids. Babies *act* on their sensitivity to taste differences and changes either to perpetuate the experience or to diminish or terminate it, depending upon the palatability of the fluid delivered contingent upon their own sucking behavior. The newborn is a hedonic creature, responding to the incentive-motivational properties of reinforcers with concomitant changes in behavior, often accompanied by autonomic nervous system changes as well. Autonomic accommodations to pleasant and unpleasant stimuli, such as systematic changes in heart rate (Lipsitt, 1979a; Porges et al., 1982), may be seen as early manifestations of affect.

A brief description of the procedures used in these studies of infant oral behavior will suffice, along with mention of some exemplary studies. In our laboratory at Women and Infants Hospital of Rhode Island, the babies are placed in a special crib in which breathing is monitored with a pneumobelt, along with heart rate and bodily motility, all of these measures being transmitted through appropriate transducers to a polygraph, which provides a continuous recording throughout the testing period. Sucking is also recorded on one of the polygraph channels. A special sucking apparatus is used, consisting of a stainless steel housing covered with a commercial nipple. Polyethylene tubes run into the tip of the nipple from pump sources, which deliver fluids on demand of the infant. That is, small drops of fluid enter the infant's mouth contingent upon the occurrence of a suck of sufficient strength to trigger the pump. Most of our studies involve very small amounts of fluid delivery— .02 ml per suck—so that infants may be studied for twenty to thirty minutes relatively free of satiation effects.

The infant may receive a variety of conditions in one testing session. For example, a session may start with two minutes of no-fluid sucking, merely recording the infant's sucking behavior on the blank nipple. This may be followed by two minutes of 5 percent sucrose, with .02 ml drops of this mild sweet solution being delivered for each criterion suck. Then a 15 percent sucrose period of two minutes may occur, all of this followed by a repeat no-fluid condition. An event marker indicates on the polygraph record each time the infant sucks, whether below or above the criterion amplitude, and an on-line computer registers the criterion sucks and simultaneously records both the sucking rate and heart rate of the infant in real time. At the end of the testing session, the computer prints out the sucking data and heart-rate results for each two-minute period separately, so that individual differences in five separate sucking parameters, all of these in coordination with heart-rate changes, may be statistically analyzed for the diverse conditions of fluid delivery. In this way the self-regulatory behavior of infants may be studied in the first hours of life—in relation to time since last feeding, conditions of birth, including the presence of risk conditions, gestational age, sex, and so on. Only a few of the most salient and most replicated results are summarized here.

Newborns characteristically suck in bursts of responses separated by rests. Burst-length and rest-length both constitute individual-difference variables even under no-fluid-delivery conditions. Some newborns simply engage in reliably longer bursts or pauses than others. Both of these parameters, however, as well as the sucking rate within bursts, are significantly influenced by the experimental conditions prearranged to occur contingent upon the behavior of the baby. With a change from no-fluid to a fluid-sucking condition, or from sucking for a less-sweet to a sweeter solution, several behavioral consequences characteristically occur. The sucking bursts tend to become longer, the interburst intervals become shorter, and the intersuck intervals get larger. Because sucking rate within bursts becomes slower with increasing sweetness of the fluid, simultaneously with the infant taking fewer and shorter rest periods, more responses are typically emitted per minute for sweeter, or hedonically more positive, fluids. Most of these effects are compromised in high-risk infants, and the greater the severity of neonatal problems requiring special care, the less will be the effect of an incentive shift from a mild to a stronger solution of sucrose (Cowett et al., 1978).

One wants to know, of course, whether there are carryover effects of pleasant taste sensations from one period of time to another. The question may be asked whether, in processing the information (from the tip of the tongue) that leads to self-regulatory alterations in sucking behavior, the infant "holds" bits of information relative to the pleasantness or unpleasantness of the experience which might guide subsequent behavior. Although it is very difficult to study the persevering effects of early experiences of this sort over a long period of time because of a variety of changing conditions, including the changing state of the baby and the removal of the baby from the hospital setting, we have been able to study short-term effects.

In one study (Kobre and Lipsitt, 1972) we tested infants for two minutes on the nipple without any fluid delivery prior to implementing the following conditions. A total of twenty minutes of responding was recorded for each infant in four successive five-minute periods. Between each period, the nipple was removed for one minute, the child was picked up, and the feeding tube was flushed of its previous fluid. Infants three days old received one of

five reinforcement regimens for the twenty-minute period. One group received only sucrose solution, and a second group received only water. A third group received sucrose solution and water alternately in five-minute shifts. Comparison of these three groups, all of which had sucked for the same amount of time and under identical conditions with respect to the manner in which they self-delivered fluid with their own sucking behavior, revealed that sucking rate per minute for the group receiving sucrose throughout was greater than for that receiving water throughout. Moreover, both groups showed very stable response rates throughout the twenty minute period, with no decline of responding over time. The group of greatest interest was that which was alternated every five minutes between sucrose and water. This group showed marked effects attributable to the alternating condition. When sucking for sucrose, the sucrose-and-water group behaved comparably to the group that had been sucking sucrose throughout. When switched to water, however, response rate during each of those five-minute periods was significantly lower than in the counterpart controls in the water-throughout group. Thus, when newborns have experience in sucking for sucrose, an immediately subsequent experience with water "turns them off." (They did not actually turn off or away from the water; rather they continued to suck but at a significantly lower level than that of their peers who had not been pleasured with sucrose.) When the fluid was changed, from water to sucrose now, response rate returned to the normal level for sucrose-sucking. Comparable findings were made in comparing the fourth and fifth groups, one of which received no fluid whatever throughout the twenty-minute period and the other, sucrose alternated with no fluid.

Infants thus optimize taste-incentive experiences by modulating oral behaviors pertinent to receiving these incentives. The effects highlight the importance of multiple determinants of even very early infant behavior. Infants are born with congenital or constitutional dispositions that impel their approach and avoidance behaviors, but these endogenous characteristics, so subject to individual variation depending even on gestational age and other perinatal variables, immediately are married with environmental conditions that can have equal or overriding influence. The *capacity* to experience sensations of pleasure may be inborn, but the *opportunity* to occasion them is a matter of environmental permissions and constraints.

CONNECTIONS BETWEEN THE MOUTH AND THE HEART

Certain features of behavior in the newborn vary depending upon the incentive conditions to which the infant is subjected. The rudiments of affect and temperament are already present in the newborn and take the form of behavioral and autonomic nervous system changes contingent upon the availability of "incentive-motivational" events.

Two major classes of immediate events can be regarded as proximal causes of infant behavior. The first is composed of stimulus events that have an eliciting quality, so that fairly regular responses will be called forth by their presentation. Such stimuli would include touches near the mouth that produce ipsilateral head-turning responses and other rooting activities. Other examples would be loud noises producing startle reactions or a sudden occurrence of wind near the baby's eyes, producing the blink reflex.

In contrast to this class of stimuli, which elicits such unconditioned or congenitally mediated responses, a second class of stimuli is composed of environmental events occurring *after* the execution of a response and which tend to sustain or perpetuate the response or cause it to occur again. Such stimulus events, when they occur quite consistently and contingent upon a given response or behavioral pattern, can produce learning (called operant conditioning), whereupon the stimulus events are classified as reinforcers. The behaviors sustained by the second class of events are sometimes called operants, whereas the behaviors elicited by the first type of event are called respondents. Sometimes the two kinds of response process may occur conjointly. For example, one may touch the side of an infant's mouth and elicit a head-turning and mouth-opening response, and follow this with insertion of a sugar nipple in the baby's mouth. In such an instance, the caregiver capitalizes on the prior presence of a respondent to provide an incentive or reinforcing condition, which may ultimately increase the probability that the baby, on the next occasion of being touched on the lips, will turn its head appropriately.

Pavlovian or classical conditioning is based upon the presence of a neurally mediated respondent in the infant's repertoire. Skinnerian or operant learning is based upon the availability in the organism's behavioral repertoire of some response or class of responses that is emitted with some frequency greater than zero and can be followed systematically with a reinforcing event. Both types of learning are dependent upon the capacity of the infant to process environmental information, perhaps that which especially relates to hedonic processes and to behave differently in the future on the basis of past experience. Thus classical and operant conditioning are rudimentary cognitive processes whose presence and strength are dependent upon qualifying characteristics of the nervous system.

There are also built-in associations between different response parameters in the newborn, and sometimes one response system may be driven by the other. Such is the case with respect to the newborn's heart rate in relation to sucking behavior.

Infant sucking behavior occurs in patterns of bursts and pauses. The bursts are longer for sweeter fluids, and the rest periods less frequent and shorter. Beyond this fundamental periodicity of sucking behavior, which is so strikingly controlled by environmental events in addition to constitutionally based individual differences, the heart rate rises each time the infant engages in a sucking burst and decelerates during the rest periods or interburst intervals. Thus as the infant engages in increased oral activity, heart rate goes up. The situation is not entirely that simple, however. With increasing sweetness of the fluid for which the infant sucks, heart rate also increases systematically, despite the fact that within sucking bursts, as indicated previously, sucking is *slower* for sweeter fluids than for less sweet fluids.

Data from systematic studies in which we have explored these regularities (Ashmead et al., 1980; Lipsitt et al., 1976) have substantiated the supposition earlier expressed that a hedonic or "savoring" mechanism is operative even in the first minutes of life. The seemingly paradoxical increase in heart rate during sweeter-fluid sucking, where the sucking rate within bursts is slower, is of considerable fascination to us. We are continuing to explore this phenomenon to determine the range of hedonically positive experiences that produce enhanced heart rate, and to discover whether such heart-rate enhancements have any discernible effect on the social interactions of infants' caregivers. Recent studies by Porges and his colleagues (1982) have indicated that vagal tone, as quantified through spectral analyses of heart rate and respiratory sinus arhythmia, is markedly affected by a wide range of neonatal conditions, including a variety of environmental challenges. The autonomic nervous system responsivity of the young child is unquestionably regulated to a large extent by the maturity of the central nervous system and by the character of stimulation provided by the environment. In turn, the pleasures and annoyances of stimulation as reflected in the baby's behavioral and autonomic responses can be, and usually are, acted upon by the infant's caregivers. Adults act to quiet a crying baby, and they tend to impose and perpetuate conditions that the infant appears to find pleasant.

CAN BABIES IMITATE?

For many years, and long before there were disciplines of psychology, pediatrics, or child development, infants in their first year of life have been known to "ape" the behavior of others with whom they interact. Casual observation suggests that there is almost invariably a hedonic "flavor" associated with the imitative act. Babies genuinely appear to enjoy the mimicking process. Adults interacting with infants often include games involving imitation. Disruption of a series of imitative acts to which the infant has become entrained often produces surprise in the baby. The games of peek-

a-boo and pattycake, to which infants usually respond with smiles, excited vocalizations, and other manifestations of pleasure, are examples of this kind of response, seemingly so dependent upon the pleasures of sensation and surprise.

Imitative behavior normally is expected toward the end of the first year and is generally thought unlikely to occur before that time. Nonetheless, a number of recent studies have shown that very young infants do indeed respond imitatively, especially to human visual stimuli (Maratos, 1973; Meltzoff and Moore, 1977). Infants even as young as two to three weeks of age have been documented responding with tongue movements when another person stuck his or her tongue out. To be sure, there is disagreement as to the stimulation required for the production of such responsive behavior. Jacobson (1979), for example, believes that this is not true imitation. There is little question, in any event, that the very young infant is capable of engaging in reciprocating interchanges and seems to derive pleasure from the experience.

One of the pioneer imitation experiments with infants was that of Maratos (1973), in which control conditions were used to assure that the "imitative behavior" did not result merely from enhanced arousal. Maratos herself served as the model, performing one at a time the following responses, while the babies, seven to eight weeks old, were oriented toward the model: thrusting of the tongue, movement of the fingers, or vocalization. Several different responses were recorded simultaneously, including the type of behavior modeled. When Maratos thrust her tongue toward the infant within easy visual range, she found the infant's tongue movement to increase. When she changed her behavior and engaged in finger-waving, the infant reciprocatingly increased its own finger movement, and tongue movements waned. In recent replications of the Maratos study, under different conditions and with even younger infants, it has been demonstrated that imitative behavior is present at least by three weeks of age (Meltzoff and Moore, 1977, 1983), or by ten days of age (Bower, 1977) or by three days of age (Field,

1982). Babies as young as twenty-one days of age apparently can hold in memory the imitated model for at least 2.5 minutes (Meltzoff and Moore, 1983). An adult thrust his tongue toward infants while they were sucking on a pacifier and unable to engage, at that moment, in imitative tongue movements. Following an interval of 150 seconds after the demonstration, the pacifier was removed from the infant's mouth. A significant amount of tongue thrusting by the infants thereupon occurred.

These studies demonstrate that infants do engage in reciprocating interactions with other persons, and with objects, very early. Apparently neonates capitalize in their behavior on the basic pleasures of sensation. They seek, moreover, to perpetuate tasks that yield satisfaction as revealed through their gleeful behavior and surprise reactions.

HABITUATION IN INFANTS

We have spoken principally of behavior mechanisms involving the potentiation of responses. Mechanisms whereby response processes are enhanced in frequency or intensity include classical and operant learning, imitative interactions, and other instances in which the apparent pleasures of sensation maintain the response. Classical and operant-conditioning procedures result in experientially induced behavior enhancements, which are persistent if not permanent. Whereas conditioning processes clearly involve the development of new associations, habituation is a mechanism of response diminution with repeated experience. Habituation entails a gradual reduction in response with repetitive stimulation.

Provided the stimulus is mild or only moderately intense, the elicited responses of human infants gradually diminish in intensity with repetitive stimulation. Response strength may reduce to zero, even though initial presentations of the stimulus may have produced marked startle behavior, great accelerations in heart rates, and so on. If, after the behavior has waned considerably or completely, a period of time is allowed to pass before the presentation of the next stimulus, recovery of the habi-tuated response often occurs. Thus habituation tends to be an evanescent phenomenon. The subject becomes uninterested in the stimulus, provided it is not highly arousing physiologically or noxious, and ceases to pay attention to it. Habituation seems to be a psychobiological guardian against the constant intrusion of nonthreatening but potentially disturbing stimuli. It is tempting to suppose that some developmental anomalies, such as hypersensitivity, hyperactivity, and autism, are at least in part due to failure to habituate—or failure to develop the appropriate neural structures for the normal mediation of habituation processes.

Reviewers of studies on infantile habituation (Kessen et al., 1970) note that the habituation phenomenon provides a ready tool for the study of memory. Habituation, like classical and operant conditioning, can reveal the extent to which cortical functioning is present in the very young human, and might reveal as well behavioral aberrations due to deficits of the central nervous system. Hydrocephalic and anencephalic infants usually show no habituation at all (Brackbill, 1971), although one study with a single baby was an exception (Graham et al., 1978). Lewis (1967) showed that impaired infantile habituation is related to low Apgar scores and other measures of perinatal distress and brain damage. Even obstetrical anesthesia has been documented to affect habituation in infants (Bowes et al., 1970). In this study infants were examined at two and five days of age. Infants whose mothers had been administered high dosages of anesthesia required as many as four times more trials to habituate than those whose mothers received little medication. Amazingly, this difference still was present when the infants were retested one full month later.

The habituation paradigm taps the organism's capacity for processing information and for discriminating among diverse stimulus inputs. Because habituation is such a universal behavior process and because the paradigm for its study provides a window through which the young human's ability to process information can be seen, future research attention in this area should help to illuminate further the nature of infancy.

The Significance of Early Learning

Although much of the behavior of young organisms is generated endogenously, early human behavior is also elicited and modified by environmental stimulation, some of it planned and deliberate (as in playing mouth-opening games) and some inadvertent (as with the noise accompanying the closing of a door). The baby and its caregivers control each other's behavior. Each responds reciprocatingly, and each thus serves as a stimulant of the other in a continuing flow of communications involving sights, sounds, and touches. Such stimulation is often accompanied by affect in others as well as the pleasures of stimulation inherent in the experiences themselves. Thus the infant has vast opportunities for learning about his or her own feelings of satisfaction in the presence of selected sensory stimulation and of other people.

The essence of babyhood sometimes has been characterized as a period of dependency, involving passive assimilation of environmental inputs. The contrary view is taken here that the infant is an active participant in a fairly constant flow of reciprocating gestures, evoking response from others as much as reacting to their stimulation. It is in the context of mutually satisfying, often pleasant, transactions that the infant acquires coping skills and gestures, the capacity for increasingly complex manipulations of the environment and other people, and the learned "social graces" that are shaped by environmental rewards and punishments.

The early months of life are also a proving ground for the adequacy of the infant's congenital response repertoire, the eventual embellishment of which results from early practice. Even some types of learning disability and psychopathological conditions may well have their earliest origins in the interplay between constitutional and experiential factors impinging on the baby from the first days. Our knowledge about these processes remains woefully inadequate today.

Studies reviewed elsewhere (Lipsitt, 1983) have suggested recently that some of the first manifestations of developmental disability may be found in the earliest days of life. Many of these have their roots, of course, in events surrounding birth, such as maternal anemia, oxygen deficit, jaundice and, in general, conditions that jeopardize respiration and adequate blood circulation to the brain. Infants who are born prematurely, who are small and require prolonged administration of oxygen at birth, who are floppy or limp (or overly tense and tight) do less well, physically and behaviorally, during the first year of life and in later years than infants whose histories are not marked by these indicators (Sameroff and Chandler, 1975). Many prenatal and neonatal birth-risk conditions have their most debilitating effects upon the sensory systems and on central nervous system functioning. Behavioral deficits, and learning problems in particular, are therefore increased in such populations.

RAGE AND LEARNED ANGER IN THE NEWBORN

Aversive or avoidance behavior is much in evidence in newborn children. Moreover, babies in the first few days of life may be seen to engage in quite effective defensive behaviors against bright lights, loud noises, and threats to their respiration. Some of these responses, particularly when intense, have a quality of anger about them, and the close observer of babies soon appreciates that these patterns of aversion and protest must have real adaptive significance.

Mavis Gunther, the noted British pediatrician, has described how the "feeding couple," as she called the mother-and-suckling pair, affect one another in subtle ways that may have enduring consequences (Gunther, 1961). She noted that the newborn, quite naturally, can occasionally become smothered for brief moments during the course of feeding. The infant's nostrils are very close to the mother's breast and sometimes occluded while the baby has a tight latch on the nipple. This causes difficulty in breathing, at least for a few moments. The infant objects to this, often strenuously, and this frequently causes quiet (often undisclosed) tension in the mother. When briefly deprived of its air supply, the baby turns its head back and forth and pulls back from the nipple. The arms flail, the face reddens, and, rather as a last resort if the respiratory blockage continues, there is a burst of crying. This throws the nipple from the baby's mouth with a force and decisiveness that often causes chagrin in the mother. The mother may become quite annoyed herself after a few such occasions, frequently not knowing what has started this cycle of discontent and feeling herself a failure in coping with her baby's needs and frustrations.

From her extensive observations of newborns with their mothers, Gunther has outlined some simple behavioral maneuvers which the mother can adopt to adjust herself posturally and to present the nipple in such a way as to minimize respiration blockage in the infant. Bottle-fed as well as breast-fed babies can be plagued by the awkward-stimulation problem, for it is possible for the shield of the artificial nipple to come against the baby's nostrils while feeding. The newborn's lips are fatty, and the nostrils are close to the upper lip, enhancing the likelihood that some respiratory blockage will occur during feeding. When respiratorily occluded, the newborn usually goes through the described pattern of behavior, culminating in releasing itself from the nipple by crying out, then taking in air, and regaining physical and behavioral stability. Paradoxically, perhaps, this is a high-incentive consequence, or a pleasurable experience, and thus some learned changes in the baby's behavior may occur (Lipsitt, 1979a, 1979b). Indeed, it is very likely some aspect of this process through which babies by ten days of age become remarkably adept at moving their heads about the breast in such a way as to prevent anything more than very brief respiratory occlusion. The learning process involved results from the fact that the baby's aversion to occlusion produces escape from the breast and is thereby rewarded. The next time that the baby is put to the breast, the position will be found less desirable than previously, and the baby may adaptively decline another opportunity to be smothered!

Gunther's simple instructions to the mother concerning the necessity of helping the infant keep its air passages clear usually produces rapid change, first in the behavior of the mother and then in the satisfaction of the baby. Too few studies provide helpful information about these critical early moments of mother-infant interaction and about the possible lasting consequences of critical experiences with powerful hedonic overtones.

A PSYCHOLOGICAL PERSPECTIVE ON CRIB DEATH

Approximately 8,000 babies in America die each year in their first year of life, usually between two and four months of age, and are termed victims of the sudden infant death syndrome (SIDS). The life-long consequences of grief and despondency in thousands of close survivors compounds the tragedy enormously. Especially because of the absence of definitive answers regarding the basic biological, and possibly psychological, mechanisms underlying SIDS, these deaths can never be accepted as truly "caused" in some reasonable manner. The phenomenon of SIDS and popular understanding of it have been surrounded by elements of confusion, suspicion, superstition, and despair. The historical neglect of research attention to the underlying causes and the frequent confusion of SIDS with child abuse have only recently abated.

Some progress has been made over the past ten years toward the better understanding of the actuarial verities underlying SIDS. Several studies have sought to document the psychobiological conditions present prior to the death in those infants who have succumbed. Although such investigations do not provide real explanations for individual cases, descriptions of precursor conditions in groups of SIDS cases, contrasted with controls, are useful at this point. Even the casual and anecdotal reports of psychophysiological conditions of infants who have had apneic or "near miss" episodes provide some leads into the biological processes possibly operating in infants who die (Steinschneider, 1972). Psychobiological factors might well be involved in the final pathway to the condition that causes the death of the infant; we must consider that experience and the effects that early experiences have on the young infant might be implicated (Lipsitt, 1978, 1979b).

In one study (Lipsitt et al., 1979), the perinatal and pediatric records of fifteen crib-death cases were examined closely and compared with two control groups, one consisting of the very next births of the same sex in the hospital of the target case and the other consisting of the next birth matched for both sex and race. The deceased group varied from the controls in several ways, each of them in a manner suggesting greater perinatal stress and initial biological jeopardy in the crib-death group. For example, reliable differences in Apgar scores in the first few minutes of life were shown, perhaps not surprisingly, given that apnea—the phenomenon of respiratory shutdown, and the final cause of death in crib death—and respiratory abnormalities were found significantly more frequently in the deceased group than in either of the controls. In addition, more of the mothers of deceased infants had had periods of anemia reported in their records, and more of the deceased infants than controls had required intensive care. The deceased infants were hospitalized longer at birth and received more resuscitative attention than the controls. In general and on average, then, the SIDS babies already showed that they began life with some constitutional fragility. Much more needs to be known about this and, of course, the psychological consequences for the parent-infant relationship that follows from such fragility. It is of interest to note that despite the greater incidence of the aforementioned conditions of jeopardy in infants who succumb, this is essentially a group-statistical finding, and one would be hard pressed to assert that for any of these infants there was any condition present that should seriously alert health care professionals or parents to the likelihood that any of these infants would die. Indeed, most infants with these conditions, such as mild respiratory distress, do survive and do not show any adverse developmental sequelae by the end of the first year. The research task, then, requires that we learn much more about the essential fragility of those that do not survive and about the developmental events that apparently transform seemingly minor insufficiencies into morbid crises two or three months later.

One proposal has suggested that an eventual understanding of crib death might well implicate a basic learning disability that has its origins, or at least its first manifestations, in the perinatal period (Lipsitt, 1976, 1979a, 1979b, 1983). This suggestion stems principally from the facts that, first, crib deaths have their peak occurrences between two and four months of age, and second, that this is a critical time during development when many of the basic reflexes with which the baby is born are in transition (McGraw, 1943). These reflexes, like the grasp of the newborn, are very strong initially but begin to weaken soon after birth, with some of them disappearing by five months. As McGraw has observed in her meticulous studies, many of these reflexes, such as the grasp and swimming maneuvers, go through marked changes so that with increasing maturity they are executed much more slowly and on a seemingly voluntary rather than an obligatory basis. McGraw's findings indicate that the transitional period between the reflexive and voluntary phases of different reflexes occurs around the ages of 100–150 days, which is the age range within which infants are in greatest crib-death jeopardy. Remarkably enough, considering that McGraw did not study and does not mention crib death, she mentions that the transitional phases are indexed by "disorganized behavior" and "struggling activity."

The suggestion can be made that if infants do not endure the first developmental transition period of their lives smoothly, moving from the essentially reflexive character of the neonate to a more intentional and reflective disposition, adequate defensive maneuvers will not be available to them when, for example, threats to or occlusion of normal respiratory processes occur. Rather little is known about the origins of adequate defensive behaviors in the very young infant, but it seems clear on the basis of information currently available that normal infants are born with the capacity, in greater or lesser degree, for engaging in defensive maneuvers or protective behaviors when situations arise to threaten normal biological processes such as respiration. These acts seem mediated by hedonic considerations, in this case annoyance. Annoyance is the "other side" of the hedonic coin, with appetitive and other approach behaviors being mediated by pleasant sensations. Defensive behavior, including many patterns of reaction classified later as ego defenses, are probably learned in the context of these early and very basic psychobiological structures.

Concluding Comments

When a baby is born, the principal concern of parents and relatives and of professional caregivers is with the infant's survival. The concern for survival of the infant and mother and protection of their biological comfort quite naturally tends to overshadow the behavioral, psychophysiological, and psychodynamic features of early life, even those involving interactions of the mother and infant. Attention sometimes does get drawn, however, to the relationship of the mother and infant to the baby's psychological functions. This has become increasingly so as perinatal technological expertise has increased, thus rendering the birth process less hazardous than in years past. For example, observers can see the mother, although fatigued and pained, holding her baby with its face close to hers, saying something "silly" while shaking him or her gently. Epitomizing the psychological importance of these first experiences, at least for the mother and quite probably the infant as well, one mother was heard saying: "Come on, baby. Open your eyes. I know you're in there." Acknowledgment and recognition of the baby's "person-

hood" is an immense achievement for the mother and presages the eventual necessity for the child to become autonomous, a task on which he or she will be working throughout the first year, if not the rest of life. From the moment of these first interactions, the capacity of the infant for experiencing pleasures and annoyances is operative and will become exceedingly important in impelling and sustaining learning. Many of these learned behaviors will be based upon fundamental biological reflexes, some of them involving approach to positive, desirable stimulation (like tastes) and others of which will be put into the service of enabling the infant to escape from noxious experiences.

Only relatively recently in the history of medicine and the biomedical sciences, have sensory and behavioral features of infants been noted carefully and credited with relevance to later life outcomes. It has been suggested here that the infant's sensory and learning capacities have important roles in assuring the infant's survival. Indeed, it has been proposed that crib death and other critical conditions of infancy might result from a concatenation of risk factors, all conspiring to create a major deficit at the critical period of about two to four months of age. The initial deficits are considered in their origins to be constitutional, but with increasing experience during development they become clearly psychobiological. In any event, they can be lethal in their effects, and much more needs to be discovered about the psychodynamics of infancy in relation to initial constitutional markers.

REFERENCES

Ashmead, D. H., Reilly, B. M., and Lipsitt, L. P. (1980) Neonates' heart rate, sucking rhythm, and sucking amplitude as a function of the sweet taste. *Journal of Experimental Child Psychology,* 29:264–281.

Beck, A. T., Rush, A. J., Shaw, B. F., and Emery, G. (1979). *Cognitive Therapy of Depression.* New York: Guildford Press.

Bower, T. G. R. (1977). *A Primer of Infant Development.* San Francisco: Freeman.

Bowes, W., Brackbill, Y., Conway, E., and Steinschneider, A. (1970). The effects of obstetrical medication

on fetus and infant. *Monographs of the Society for Research in Child Development,* 35:3–25.

Brackbill, Y. (1971). The role of the cortex in orienting: Orienting reflex in an anencephalic human infant. *Developmental Psychology,* 5:195–201.

Call, J. D., Galenson, E., and Tyson, R. L., eds. (1983). *Frontiers of Infant Psychiatry.* New York: Basic Books.

Coss, R. G. and Globus, A. (1978). Spine stems on tectal interneurons in jewel fish are shortened by social stimulation. *Science,* 200:787–790

Cowett, R. M., Lipsitt, L. P., Vohr, B., and Oh, W.

(1978). Aberrations in sucking behavior of low-birth-weight infants. *Developmental Medicine and Child Neurology,* 20:701–709.

Dollard, J. and Miller, N. (1950). *Personality and Psychotherapy. New York: McGraw Hill.*

Elkonin, D. B. (1957). The physiology of higher nervous activity and child psychology. In *Psychology in the Soviet Union,* ed. B. Simon. London: Routledge & Kegan Paul, 1957.

Erikson, E. H. (1983). Concluding remarks: Infancy and the rest of life. In *Frontiers of Infant Psychiatry,* ed. J. D. Call, E. Galenson, and R. L. Tyson. New York: Basic Books.

Field, T. M., Woodson, R., Greenberg, R., and Cohen, D. (1982). Discrimination and imitation of facial expressions by neonates. *Science,* 218:179–181.

Gesell, A. (1948). *Studies in Child Development.* New York: Harper.

Gottlieb, G. (1971) Ontogenesis of sensory function in birds and mammals. In *The Biopsychology of Development.* ed. E. Tobach, L. R. Aronson, and E. Shaw. New York: Academic Press.

Graham, F. K., Leavitt, L. A., and Strock, B. D. (1978). Precocious cardiac orienting in a human anencephalic infant. *Science,* 199:322–324.

Gunther, M. (1961). Infant behavior at the breast. In *Determinants of Infant Behavior,* ed. B. Foss. London: Methuen.

Jacobson, S. W. (1979). Matching behavior in the young infant. *Child Development:* 50:425–430.

Kessen, W., Haith, M. M., and Salapatek, P. H. (1970). Human infancy: A bibliography and guide. In *Carmichael's Manual of Child Psychology,* vol. 1, ed. P. H. Mussen. New York: John Wiley.

Kobre, K. R. and Lipsitt, L. P. (1972). A negative contrast effect in newborns. *Journal of Experimental Child Psychology,* 14:81–91.

Lewis, M. (1967). The meaning of a response, or why researchers in infant behavior should be oriental metaphysicians. *Merrill-Palmer Quarterly,* 13:7–18.

Lipsitt, L. P. (1963). Learning in the first year of life. In *Advances in Child Development and Behavior,* vol. 1, ed. L. P. Lipsitt and C. C. Spiker. New York: Academic Press.

Lipsitt, L. P. (1976). Developmental psychobiology comes of age: A discussion. In *Developmental psychobiology: The Significance of Infancy,* ed. L. P. Lipsitt. Hillsdale, New Jersey: Lawrence Erlbaum Associates.

Lipsitt, L. P. (1978). Perinatal indicators and psychophysiological precursors of crib death. In *Early Developmental Hazards: Predictors and Precautions,* ed. F. D. Horowitz. Boulder: Westview Press.

Lipsitt, L. P. (1979a). Critical conditions in infancy. *American Psychologist,* 34:973–980.

Lipsitt, L. P. (1979b). Infants at risk: Perinatal and neonatal factors. *International Journal of Behavioral Development,* 2:23–42.

Lipsitt, L. P. (1979c). The pleasures and annoyances of infants: Approach and avoidance behavior. In *Origins of the Infant's Social Responsiveness.* ed. E. Thoman. Hillsdale, New Jersey: Lawrence Erlbaum Associates.

Lipsitt, L. P. (1983). Stress in infancy: Toward understanding the origins of coping behavior. In *Stress, Coping, and Development in Children,* ed. N. Garmezy and M. Rutter. New York: McGraw Hill.

Lipsitt, L. P., Reilly, B. M., Butcher, M. J., and Greenwood, M. M. (1976). The stability and inter-relationships of newborn sucking and heart rate. *Developmental Psychobiology,* 9:305–310.

Lipsitt, L. P., Sturner, W. Q., and Burke, P. (1979). Perinatal indicators and subsequent crib death. *Infant Behavior and Development,* 2:325–328.

McGraw, M. B. (1943). *The Neuromuscular Maturation of the Human Infant.* New York: Columbia University Press.

Maratos, O. (1973). The origin and development of imitation in the first 6 months of life. Unpublished doctoral dissertation, University of Geneva.

Meltzoff, A. N. and Moore, M. K. (1977). Imitation of facial and manual gestures by 2-week-old infants. *Science,* 198:75–78.

Meltzoff, A. N. and Moore, M. K. (1983). The origins of imitation in infancy: Paradigm, phenomena, and theories. *Advances in Infancy Research,* vol. 2, ed. L. P. Lipsitt. Norwood, New Jersey: Ablex.

Porges, S. W., McCabe, P. M., and Yongue, B. G. (1982). Respiratory-heart rate interactions: Psychophysiological implications for pathophysiology and behavior. In *Perspectives in Cardiovascular Psychophysiology,* ed. J. T. Cacioppo and R. E. Petty. New York: Guildford Press.

Purpura, D. P. (1975). Dendritic differentiation in human cerebral cortex: Normal and aberrant developmental patterns. *Advances in Neurology,* 12:91–116.

Richter, C. (1957). On the phenomenon of sudden death in animals and man. *Psychosomatic Medicine,* 19:191–198.

Rosenzweig, M. R. and Bennett, E. L. (1976). Enriched environments: Facts, factors, and fantasies. In *Knowing, Thinking, and Believing,* ed. L. Petrinovitch and J. L. McGaugh. New York: Plenum.

Sameroff, A. J. and Chandler, M. J. (1975). Reproductive risk and the continuum of caretaking casualty. In *Review of Child Development Research,* vol. 4, ed. F. D. Horowitz, M. Hetherington, S. Scarr-Salapatek, and G. Siegel. Chicago: University of Chicago Press.

Seligman M. E. P. (1975). *Helplessness: On depression, Development, and Death.* San Francisco: Freeman.

Steele, B. F. (1983). The effects of abuse and neglect on psychological development. In *Frontiers of Infant Psychiatry.* ed. J. D. Call, E. Galenson, and R. L. Tyson. New York: Basic Books.

Steinschneider, A. (1972). Prolonged apnea and the sudden infant death syndrome. Clinical and laboratory observations. *Pediatrics,* 50:646–654.

Thorndike, E. L. (1913). *Educational Psychology,* vol. 2, *The Psychology of Learning.* New York: Columbia University Press.

8

Affect Retrieval: A Form of Recall Memory in Prelinguistic Infants

Patricia A. Nachman, Ph.D. and Daniel N. Stern, M.D.

A controversial issue in memory research has been whether or not prelinguistic infants are capable of evocative memory. Evocative memory refers to memory in the absence of the event to be remembered as compared to recognition memory in which the stimulus must be physically present in order for the infant to remember having perceived it. Psychoanalytic writers such as Fraiberg (1969) have argued that the infant is not capable of true recall or evocative memory until approximately one and a half years of age, which is roughly when use of language is under way. Piaget (1936) held a similar view, claiming that recall memory is not evident until after mental imagery, language, or some form of symbolic encoding of experience has evolved.

An observational study by McDevitt (1975) on the development of object constancy suggests that as early as nine months infants show some evidence of retrieval processes from which a rudimentary mental representation of the absent mother can be inferred. Otherwise, how would separation reactions occur? Al-

This article is based on a doctoral dissertation by the first author submitted in partial fulfillment of the requirements for the Ph.D. degree, Columbia University. The study was supported by a grant from the Fund for Psychoanalytic Research.

though anecdotal reports (Ashmead and Perlmutter, 1980) also support an earlier timetable for the advent of recall or evocative memory, progress in this area has been hampered because traditional techniques have relied almost exclusively on a conventional verbal symbolic system to demonstrate recall memory.

One acknowledged memory system operating during the prelinguistic period that does not require symbolic mediation is the motor memory system. Investigators using an operant conditioning paradigm, (Rovee-Collier and Fagan, 1970; Sullivan et al., 1979) trained three-month-old infants to move an overhead crib-mobile by means of foot kicks and then, after delays of one to fourteen days, reassessed the foot-kicking-response rate to the same but nonmoving mobile. Upon re-exposure, the infants kicked more than at base frequency at intervals as long as eight days, even though the mobile remained unmoving. The visual presence of the mobile and the crib served as context cues that retrieved the original response. Thus a nonverbal motor response, kicking, was evoked from past experience and served to demonstrate long-term cued-recall motor memory.

Although almost all theories of normal and pathological psychic development assume the importance of emotional experience during the first twelve months of life, the possibility that affect as a form of experience can be encoded, stored, or recalled during this early period has been largely overlooked. Only one experimental report has addressed this question directly in infants. Levy (1960) studied infants returning to a well-baby clinic for their inoculations and found that, until the second year, infants showed no anticipatory fear or distress at the sight of syringes, white coats, characteristic smells, or other events that might have acted as cues to recalling the painful experience of the previous inoculation. The delay between injections in this experiment, however, was very long—three months.

The purpose of the present study is to present evidence that affects, like motor patterns, are a major nonverbal form of recallable experience. In order to address the overall issue of recall of affect in infants, the following question was asked: Can an affective response that occurs in a specific context be reactivated after a period of time with minimal cues from the original context? A paired-comparison paradigm was used to explore cued recall of an affect in seven-month-old infants. We tested the infants' likelihood of smiling to a silent, stationary puppet one week after the infant had smiled at the same puppet in a rousing peek-a-boo game. (Prior to the rousing peek-a-boo game the same silent, stationary puppet by itself did not elicit smiling.) Recall was measured by differential smile responses to familiar and novel stimuli during paired-comparison test trials after delays of two minutes and one week.

Method

SUBJECTS

One hundred and two infants participated in the present study. The final sample consisted of seventy-five infants (thirty-nine males and thirty-six females) who were seven months old (mean age 29.9 weeks). The infants were from middle- and upper-middle-class families; all were healthy and apparently normal and had been recruited from local groups in a metropol-

itan area who were preparing for childbirth. Twenty-seven infants were eliminated from the study because they did not respond appropriately to the familiarization procedure, or they fussed, or they had a puppet at home similar to the experimental puppets, or they did not keep the second appointment for the retest a week later.

PROCEDURE

Infants were placed on their mother's lap in front of an infant theatre designed for the paired-comparison visual-preference paradigm (Fagan, 1970; Spieker, 1981). For the pretest, the infants saw two silent and *stationary* hand puppets, a rabbit and a frog, through the left and right windows of the infant theatre for two fifteen-second periods, counterbalancing for side of presentation within each infant. A video camera placed between the windows recorded smile responses and direction of gaze. The rabbit and frog were equally preferred during the pretest across infants (rabbit, $p = .49$; frog, $p = .51$; $p > .10$). Immediately following the pretest, the infants, still on the mother's lap, were turned to face a puppet stage on the other side of the room for the familiarization procedure. The stage was a one-meter-high screen, behind which the experimenter hid while manipulating one of the puppets for the peek-a-boo game. A second camera recorded the infants' facial expressions and gaze during the familiarization procedure.

One of two familiarization procedures was used for each infant. A rousing procedure, designed to elicit smiling, consisted of a five-second cycle of disappearance and reappearance of the puppet behind the screen, accompanied by a brightly intoned "peek-a-boo" at each reappearance. A neutral procedure, designed *not* to elicit smiling, consisted of a five-second cycle of a back-and-forth horizontal movement with the puppet always in sight, with each return to center position accompanied by a monotonously intoned "peek-a-boo." Puppets were randomly assigned to the two familiarization procedures. We determined that infants were habituated to the puppet during the familiarization period when they performed two consecutive body/head turns away from the puppet. Each infant thus determined his own rate of habituation. Cohen (1972; Cohen et al., 1973) has described this procedure in detail, and Friedman and his group (1970), Horowitz (1975), DeLoache (1976), and Olson (1976) all concur that the best approximation of memory acquisition is to permit familiarization until a criterion of termination has been reached for each individual infant. Peek-a-boo games were terminated more rapidly in the neutral procedure, but since there was no disappearance phase, the total looking time at the game puppet for both familiarization procedures was not different ($t = 1.78$; $df = 90$; .08).

Two minutes after the familiarization trial and again one week later the infants were shown the two puppets in the infant theatre exactly as described for the pretest (that is, sight alone without motion or sound). These short-delay and long-delay posttests were designated posttests I and II, respectively.

Results

SCORING

Duration of visual preferences was scored by a digital display timer that enabled scorers to hand-operate a left-right directional switch in synchrony with the infant's eye fixations. One display recorded left-looking times, the other right-looking times. In this manner, the duration of looking time in seconds was scored for the two puppets in the paired-comparison pretest and in both posttests. These data, while of interest, do not affect the major findings of this study.

Smile responses as dependent measures occurring during the paired-comparison posttests were scored by recording the first stimulus smiled to during each fifteen-second test period. Smiles occurring during the peek-a-boo game were scored by totaling the number of trials that were smiled at during the game. A trial is one appearance/disappearance cycle with "peek-a-boo" said one time. Smiles were defined as any upturning of the corners of the mouth. If an infant smiled at least one time during the peek-a-boo game, the infant was classified as a smiler. Those infants who did not smile at all during peek-a-boo were classified as nonsmilers.

RELIABILITY

Reliability was gathered on a random sampling of both conditions. All visual responses and smile responses were scored from videotape recording of the infant's facial expressions. Two observers independently scored the data tapes. Reliability smile responses, based on 120 comparisons for twelve babies was .96.

SMILE DATA

Of the seventy-five infants in the sample, half were exposed to the rousing condition, which was intended to promote smiling, and the other half were exposed to the neutral condition, which was intended to promote neutral affects (neither smiling nor frowning). However, five of the infants failed to smile during the rousing condition, while twelve of the infants exposed to the neutral condition smiled despite the attempt to render the condition affectively neutral. Because the purpose of the conditions was to endure a known affective response and infants who were exposed to a particular condition were assumed to experience that response, the twelve and five infants who failed to behave affectively as expected were excluded from the study. Because this was not a study in individual differences, in "sense of humor," or some related construct, we needed to be assured so far as possible that we knew the nature of the infants' affective experience. Therefore, all of the infants in the study demonstrated the affective response that was expected for the condition they were assigned to. Forty-one experimental or rousing-condition infants and thirty-four neutral-condition infants composed the final groups of this study.

The question of whether infants in the rousing group smile more at posttesting was addressed in view of the fact that infants could refrain from smiling at either puppet at posttesting, could smile at both puppets, smile to the familiar puppet alone, or smile to the novel puppet alone. Table 8-I shows this distribution of infant's smile responses for the rousing and neutral groups. If an infant was in the rousing group he was likely (20 percent) to smile at the familiarizing puppet during posttest I, and even more likely (78 percent) to do so one week later during posttest II. Infants in the neutral group were less likely (6 percent) to smile during posttest I or II (15 percent). Smiling in general (at either puppet) occurred in 93 percent of the infants in the rousing condition and in 27 percent of the infants in the neutral condition during the second posttest.

Table 8–2 shows chi-square comparisons for the rousing and neutral groups, contrasting those who smile exclusively at the familiar puppet, with those who smile at both puppets and those who never smile at posttesting. These contrasts were significant at the first posttest ($\chi = 17.51, p < .001$) and were highly

significant at the second posttest ($\chi = 29.0$, $p < .0001$). The strength of this finding stems from the observation that members of the neutral group rarely smiled during posttesting while most of rousing group smiled only at the familiar puppet.

Discussion

It can be concluded from these findings that the posttests themselves (without the memory of a familiarizing test experience with the puppet) did not elicit the smiles; rather, the high preponderance of smiling on posttesting by the infants who smiled during familiarization lends substantial support to the view that the earlier peek-a-boo game and the concommitant positive emotional reactions to the game influenced the smile responses to the puppets on posttesting. The preponderance of repeated

TABLE 8–1

Infants Who Smiled During Posttests

Smile Responses (2-minute delay)	Rousing Group		Neutral Group	
	Posttest I	Posttest II	Posttest I	Posttest II
N =	41		34	
Did not smile	22	4	27	25
Smiled at novel only	4	3	4	1
Smiled at familiar & novel	7	2	1	3
Smiled at familiar only	8	32	2	5

TABLE 8–2

Smiling Responses in Both Posttests
(chi square)

	Posttest I					Posttest II			
	Never smiled	Smiled at novel or both	Smiled at familiar only			Never smiled	Smiled at novel or both	Smiled at familiar only	
Rousing Group	22	11	8	41		4	5	32	51
Neutral Group	27	5	2	34		25	4	5	34
	49	37	9			29	9	37	

$\chi^2 = 17.51, p = .001$ $\chi^2 = 29.0, p < .0001$

smiling after a period of one week suggests that affects were a readily retrievable source of memory after a long temporal delay.

One curious aspect of the findings was that 82 percent of the infants in the rousing group who did not smile at posttest I, smiled at posttest II, as compared to 7 percent of the infants in the neutral group. The greater retrieval at posttest II for those who smiled during familiarization is probably due to the fact that posttest I occurred shortly after the habituation criteria had been performed and habituation might still have been in effect. It may also be due to memory consolidation during the week between the two posttests.

The ease with which the infants smiled on posttesting to the puppet they initially smiled at during the peek-a-boo game a week earlier was remarkable, considering that they simply viewed the puppet in a window during the posttest without replaying any aspect of the peek-a-boo game. Because the infants were given no retrieval cues, except the sight of the puppet (no motion or vocal cue or disappearance-reappearance), their smile reactions under these circumstances were defined as cued recall (Spear, 1976, 1978). Thus, smiling in the situation is viewed as a form of recall memory in that it entails the activation of a memory for an original event (peek-a-boo) and demonstrates knowledge of the attributes associated with the original event that were absent as cues during retention tests.

An alternative explanation exists that would account for the posttest smiles as a form of recognition memory rather than recall memory (Kagan, 1971; McCall, 1972; Zelazo, 1972). According to this view, the infant might smile simply upon recognizing the familiarizing puppet. This would constitute an affect display that is the accompaniment of a successful cognitive operation rather than a recalled or reevoked emotion. To rule out this possibility, we compared the amount of time the infants looked at the game (familiar) puppet with the other (novel) puppet during the paired-comparison posttests. We calculated the change in looking time to the game puppet from the pretest to the posttests in order to control for any individual initial preferences. We reasoned that if the familiarization procedure, regardless

of whether the infant smiled, significantly altered the visual preferences for the game puppet during the posttests, then we would have evidence that the infants had recognized the game puppet (Fagan, 1970). Therefore, if recognition rather than recall memory determined posttest smiling, it would be expected that both groups of infants would smile at posttesting if they demonstrated visual recognition memory for the puppet. Table 8-3 shows the changes in looking time at the game puppet between the pretest and the posttests I and II as a function of the rousing or neutral procedure. The infants who received the rousing procedure preferred to look at the game (familiar) puppet at posttest I and at posttest II while the infants who received the neutral procedure preferred to look at the other (novel) puppet at each posttest. This difference in direction of visual preference, while of interest, does not affect the findings. Despite this divergence in direction of visual preference, both familiarizing procedures altered the posttest looking preference, indicating that in both cases recognition memory had occurred. Therefore, it would be expected that both groups of infants would smile at posttesting if recognition memory alone accounted for posttest smiling. Accordingly, we attributed the posttest smiles to recall rather than recognition memory.

TABLE 8–3

Within-Group Contrasts of Looking Time at the Familiar Puppet (in percentages)

Test	Group	
	Rousing (N = 41)	Neutral (N = 34)
Pretest vs Posttest I	49.91	50.97
	55.35† (*t* = 2.76)	46.14* (*t* = 2.05)
Pretest vs Posttest II	49.91	50.97
	59.46‡ (*t* = 6.01)	46.48† (*t* = 2.77)

*$p < .05$
†$p < .01$
‡$p < .001$, two-tailed

It can be argued that re-evoked smiling is another form of motor memory rather than a form of affect memory. This assumes that an affect display (such as smiling) is not different from any other motor act (for example, foot kicking). Affect memory would then be a special case of motor memory. Either it is a special case, but a very special case with implications for peripheral theories of affect experience, or, as we propose, the psychobiologically unique aspects of emotional facial displays with their presumed accompanying special subjective states argue sufficiently that affect memory is distinct from general motor memory.

Recent findings in adults have focused on a central role for affect in memory. The independent existence of an affect memory system which appraises and registers the hedonic valence of experience has been suggested (Za-

jonc, 1980). This memory system is proposed to operate in parallel with the more generally recognized semantic or cognitive memory system which appraises the nonhedonic qualities of stimuli. The two systems are highly integrated. Other research in adults suggests that emotional state or mood can act as the cardinal mnemic key or organizing theme that mediates the encoding and recall of related nonaffective attributes of an experience (Bower, 1981). Our findings suggest that in early infancy, when affective functioning is thought to be relatively more essential for adaptation, affect can be re-evoked by cues even after long delays. This finding suggests the presence of a memory storage system, including affects, that are recallable by cue very early in infancy, long before the emergence of a language or symbol-based semantic recall memory system.

REFERENCES

Ashmead, C. H. and Perlmutter, M. (1980). Infant memory in everyday life. In *New Directions for Child Development: Children's Memory*, ed. M. Perlmutter. San Francisco: Jossey-Bass.

Bower, G. H. (1981). Mood and memory. *American Psychologist*, 36:129–148.

Cohen, L. B. (1972). Attention-getting and attention-holding processes of infant visual preferences. *Child Development*, 43:869–879.

Cohen, L. B., Gelber, E. R., and Lazer, M. A. (1971). Infant habituation and generalization to repeated visual stimulation. *Journal of Experimental Child Psychology*, 11:379–389.

DeLoache, J. S. (1976). Rate of habituation and visual memory in infants. *Child Development*, 47:145–154.

Fagan, J. F. (1970). Memory in the infant. *Journal of Experimental Child Psychology*, 9:217–226.

Fraiberg, S. (1969). Libidinal object constancy and mental representation. *The Psychoanalytic Study of the Child*, 24:9–47. New York: International Universities Press.

Friedman, S., Nagy, A. N., and Carpenter, G. C. (1970). Newborn attention: Differential response decrement to visual stimuli. *Journal of Experimental Child Psychology*, 10:44–51.

Horowitz, F. D. (1975). Visual attention, auditory stimulation, and language discrimination in young infants. *Monographs of the Society for Research in Child Development*, 39, (5-6, Serial No. 158). Chicago: University of Chicago Press.

Kagan, J. (1971). *Change and Continuity in Infancy*. New York: John Wiley.

Levy, D. (1960). The infant's earliest memory of inoculation: A contribution to public health procedures. *Journal of Genetic Psychology*, 96:3–46.

McCall, R. B. (1972). Smiling and vocalization in infants as indices of perceptual-cognitive processes. *Merrill-Palmer Quarterly*, 18:341–347.

McDevitt, J. B. (1975). Separation-individuation and object constancy. *Journal of the American Psychoanalytic Association*, 23:713–742.

Olson, G. M. (1976). An information-processing analysis of visual memory and habituation in infants. In *Habituation: Perspective from Child Development, Animal Behavior, and Neurophysiology*, ed. T. J. Tighe and N. Leaton. Hillsdale, New Jersey: Lawrence Erlbaum Associates.

Piaget, J. (1936). *The Origins of Intelligence in Children*. New York: International Universities Press, 1952.

Rovee-Collier, C. and Fagen, J. W. (1979). Extended conditioning and 24-hour retention in infants. *Journal of Experimental Analysis of Behavior*, 32:15–27.

Spear, N. E. (1976). Retrieval of memories: A biological approach. In *Handbook of Learning and Cognitive Processes*, vol. 4, ed. W. K. Estes. Hillsdale, New Jersey: Lawrence Erlbaum Associates.

Spear, N. E. (1978). *The Processing of Memories: Forgetting and Retention*. Hillsdale, New Jersey: Lawrence Erlbaum Associates.

Spieker, S. (1981). Infant recognition of invariant categories of faces. Unpublished doctoral dissertation, Cornell University.

Sullivan, M. W., Rovee-Collier, C. K., and Tynes, D. M. (1979). A conditioning analysis of infant long-term memory. *Child Development*, 50:152–162.

Zajonc, R. B. (1980). Feeling and thinking. Preferences need no inferences. *American Psychologist*, 35:151–175.

Zelazo, P. (1972) Smiling and vocalizing: A cognitive emphasis. *Merrill-Palmer Quarterly*, 18:349–365.

9

Reflections in the Mirror: Mother-Child Interactions, Self-Awareness, and Self-Recognition

Paulina F. Kernberg, M.D.

Considerations about the development of the self and its relation to mother-child interaction have more than theoretical interest for me. In fact, this paper stems from some of my intuitive clinical interventions, which I later re-examined in the context of various theoretical propositions about the sequential development of self-awareness, its connection with mother-child interaction, and the child's reaction to its reflection in the mirror.

I begin with a clinical vignette, offer some preliminary assumptions, review some pertinent theoretical and research literature on the development of self-awareness and on self-recognition in the mirror, and finally, consider the implications of this material for clinical practice and research.

The Case of Derek

Derek, a five-and-a-half-year-old autistic child, was the youngest of three children. When I first saw him, he would no sooner enter the office than he would lie down on the floor —sometimes with his back to me, sometimes accidentally facing me, but always with his gaze averted. He had very little verbal communication. After a few weeks it dawned on me that perhaps, I, too, should lie on the floor and do exactly what he was doing. If he twirled around in the chair, I did the same; if he stopped, I followed suit. When he fleetingly glanced in a vacuous way at my face, I promptly returned his gaze. After twelve sessions (he came three times a week) Derek started to acknowledge my presence and looked at me with more interest, interrupting his repetitive activity for a few seconds to do so. He even began to play while sitting or standing. When we had mutual eye contact, I introduced more complexity into our interactions, moving from strictly parallel, mirrorlike feedback to a more sequential, reciprocal exchange. With this came his beginning awareness of myself and himself.

Derek's behavior when confronted by his actual mirror image also underwent a transformation. Early in the therapy he would look blankly at the mirror, giving it a fleeting glance with no recognition behavior. After a few months, avoidance behavior—rubbing his eyes, a faint smile of embarrassment—became more characteristic of his reaction to the mirror image. As his ability to play symbolically grew, he transferred to the mirror my mirroring of him and increasingly obtained pleasure from the experience. Now, in our fourth year of work, when he comes for his weekly session, he looks at himself in the mirror, smiles, and fixes his hair, all with noticeable pleasure. At times he even comments on my reflection.

What Derek recapitulated between ages five and a half and nine years were the stages that are normally covered between six and thirty-six months. He became more assertive, acknowledging my presence, and inviting me to participate. Not only did he begin to engage in symbolic play, but his play also became more and more populated by interactions. He was able to participate in activity therapy groups for children of his age and was described as having "object hunger."

Preliminary Assumptions

Some of the first experiences of oneself, the first inklings of self-awareness, may be linked to the recognition of the way one is perceived by another human being. The beginning sense of self grows in part out of a certain experience of self and object, in which the subject relates to the other, who looks and behaves as much as possible like the subject—an animated parallel. A corollary of this assumption is that the first object image is a picture of oneself as the object, reflecting more the self than the object. (A baby's stranger anxiety might then indicate an experience of the object as containing nothing of oneself in it and thus threatening the baby with a sense of nonexistence.) In the same vein, Abelin's (1971) observations of early triangularization could be seen as illustrating this hypothesis: when the baby sees that father exists in relation to mother, it sees an externalized echo of itself in relation to the mother, which it can now observe. Given this assumption, one would also postulate that the infant's emerging self-awareness depends in part on two critical factors—on the intactness of cognitive functions and on the mother-infant relationship and attachment to the

mother (Ainsworth, 1968; Bowlby, 1969). Certain components of the relationship to the mother are especially relevant, namely, those that entail similar or parallel reactions between mother and infant, such as mutual gazing or mutual smiling (Stern, 1982).

One would assume that a normal infant reaction to its mirror image would depend not only on the intactness of the child but also on a normal mother-infant relationship (Rutter, 1972). By *reaction,* I refer to affective and behavioral components, especially exploratory behavior. Conversely, an abnormal reaction would imply the existence of a pathological interaction between mother and infant. Mahler and McDevitt (1982), for example, have described the case of Harriet, whose exaggerated adverse reaction to her mirror image paralleled her poor relationship with her narcissistic, immature, and unempathic mother. In other words, in the reaction to looking at herself in the mirror, the infant betrays her relation with the mother. Moreover, if the mother is looking at the mirror simultaneously with the infant, the intensity of the reaction will be increased in either a positive or negative way according to the nature of their relationship.

Contrasting the positive and negative, the normal and the pathological reflections, two quotations from literature centuries and cultures apart are particularly meaningful to me. The first is Sylvia Plath's poignant poem, "Mirror:"[1]

I am silver and exact. I have no preconceptions.
Whatever I see I swallow immediately.
Just as it is, unmisted by love or dislike.
I am not cruel, only truthful—
The eye of a little god, four-cornered.
Most of the time I meditate on the opposite wall.
It is pink, with speckles. I have looked at it so
    long
I think it is a part of my heart but it flickers.
Faces and darkness separate us over and over.

Now I am a lake. A woman bends over me,
Searching my reaches for what she really is.
Then she turns to those liars, the candles or the
    moon.

I see her back, and reflect it faithfully.
She rewards me with tears and an agitation of
    hands.
I am important to her. She comes and goes.
each morning it is her face that replaces the
    darkness.

In me she had drowned a young girl, and in me
    an old woman
Rises toward her day after day, like a terrible
    fish.

[1981, pp. 173–174].

My second quotation comes from eighteenth-
century China:[2]

My little boy is looking at the mirror.
He so resembles his mother
That he breaks into laughter.

Mother as Mirror

Winnicott (1967) lucidly described the important mirroring function of the mother's face
in the development of the child's self. He
asked, "What does the baby see when he or she
looks at the mother's face?" (p. 112). And he
suggested that what the baby usually sees is
him- or herself; that is, "the mother is looking
at the baby and *what she looks like is related to what
she sees there."* "The self essentially recognizes
itself in the eyes and face of the mother and in
the mirror which can come to represent the
mother's face" (Winnicott, 1972, p. 16). Winnicott also noted that many babies have the
experience of not getting back what they are
giving: they look but they do not see themselves. If mother's face does not function as a
mirror, the baby experiences a menacing chaos.
The baby then withdraws or just looks at the
world, not into it. What Winnicott pointed out
is that mirroring in the mother's face contributes to the child's beginning a significant exchange with the world. It is a two-way process
in which self-enrichment alternates with the
discovery of meaning in the world.

Support for Winnicott's description comes
from more recent child-development data.

---

[2]Anonymous; personal communication from José Bar-
chilon, M.D.

Brazelton's group's (1975) violation experiments, for instance, illustrated how the infant's
behavior may be disrupted to the point of disorganization if the mother does not synchronously mirror her baby. After a few attempts
to re-establish contact, the infant averts its
gaze, moves erratically, yawns, cries, or falls
asleep. A positive or negative state of self reflected the responsiveness or lack of responsiveness in the mother's facial expression. Just
how important this mirroring aspect of the
mother-infant interaction is in the development of a sense of self becomes even clearer
when we examine one of the types of mother-
infant exchange that Stern (1982) describes.

Stern (1982) has distinguished three major
modes of "being with another": (1) the interaction between the subject and the other may be
complementary; (2) the "other" may appear *similar*
(this would correspond to our assumption of
mirroring); or (3) the action of the other leads to
a change in neurophysiological state or consciousness, that is, *the infant's state shifts via another.*
In the complementary self-other experiences,
the subject and the object act asymmetrically,
as in the infant's cuddling or molding in relation
to the mother's holding activities, an action-
response pattern. The second type of experience is most relevant here and has to do with
self-other similarity, where the activities of the
two partners are symmetrical or isomorphic.
Some examples are simultaneous vocalizing,
mutual gazing, mimicking, affect contagion (as
in smiling), and pattycake games. Stern indicated that early experiences of self-other
similarity tend to occur at times of positively
toned high arousal. While such experiences can
seem invasive to the subject and under some
circumstances decrease the sense of an individual self, in certain circumstances where imitation reflects admiration and love (as with lovers
or mothers and infants), they may lead to both
self-definition and positive intimacy. One
might say that what is more easily recognized in
the other is in part what one is already.

An awareness of the sense of self is thus
contributed to by the parallel interactions with
the other. Initially, this parallel type of interaction, coaction, or synchrony, in contrast to alternation or turn-taking (Durfee and Lee,
1973), occurs with the mother. The infant looks

at the mother and sees in her face what the mother is looking at, in addition to her offering the infant's image back to the infant (Schact, 1981). The object is a mirror in which the outlines of the infant's primary identity are reflected (Lichtenstein, 1977). This type of interaction constitutes the most stimulating factor in the infant's environment, as shown by the intensification of pleasurable affect and increased arousal and alertness (Burlingham, 1963; Leonard, 1961; Lewis and Brooks, 1978). The state of mutual engagement is not only the first form of parent-infant relationship, developmentally antecedent to a sequential type of relationship, but there is evidence that a state of mutual engagement is important in early peer relations. Prior mutual looking is predictive of peer response (Bleier, 1976), and of verbal interaction among two-year-olds (Mueller and Brenner, 1977) and three- to five-year-olds (Mueller, 1972).

In a similar vein, Lewis and Brooks-Gunn (1979) have stated that although the infant interacts with both animate and inanimate objects, the exchanges with the human others are most important in learning about the self. One reason for this is that caregivers tend to make their actions contingent on those of the child. To interact with an other is to learn about both the other and the self. The more similar the self and the other are, the more what one learns is related to knowledge about the self. In the opinion of these investigators, knowledge of the other gained through interactions must of necessity give information about oneself. Even the infant's beginning understanding that objects exist separately, on their own, suggests a parallel recognition that the infant itself exists separately from others.

ATTACHMENT

Attachment plays a pivotal role in the development of positively charged symmetrical experiences (Stern, 1982), in positive self-knowledge (Lewis and Brooks-Gunn, 1979), and consequently in the development of healthy self-representations and awareness. Bowlby (1969) defined attachment as those behaviors of the mother and the infant which are aimed at increasing or maintaining proximity. What is crucial for future development is that the principal attachment figure, the mother or mother substitute, behave in a "mothering way," by which Bowlby meant that she needs to engage in lively social interaction with the baby and respond readily to its signals and approaches. The interaction around feeding of Stern's complementary experience does not represent the main impetus for attachment. It is the person who gazes at, talks with, and smiles at the baby who becomes the most important attachment figure. It is this person who guarantees the repetition of mirroring exchanges through which the baby comes to see itself in the other.

Ainsworth (1968) emphasized the baby's ability to explore the world and expand its horizons to include other attachments. If attachment is mixed with anxiety and insecurity, the child may show exaggerated clinging and following behavior. In contrast, the happy, secure child comes to take mother for granted and to spend more time, and with greater distance, away from her. Greeting, smiling, touching, embracing, scrambling over the mother, burying the face in her lap, calling, talking, watching —these are all responses to the mother's interactional initiatives that maintain and augment the interactions. Again, the mother's behavior echoes the child's, matching its need for mirroring. On the other hand, following, clinging, and crying are all behaviors that focus on avoiding separation.

Ainsworth (1968) also suggested that the more secure the tie to the mother, the greater the exploratory behavior, and that activity per se enhances the sense of self. Exploration of the mother's face involves a reflection of oneself, thus enhancing the child's sense of self. As Escalona (1968) put it, the animating integrative function of the mother brings meaning to the object world, but it also brings meaning to a sense of self as the infant perceives mother perceiving it. The first mirror, then, would be that of the mother.

Self-Recognition in the Mirror

A mirror possesses unique properties. It is relatively distortion free (aside from the reversal) and reproduces one's actions simultaneously, with one-to-one correspondence between gesture and reflection. This quality reveals that other people do not produce behavior sequences identical to one's own, that only the reflected image of oneself does so. In other words, what children can discover through the characteristics of the mirror is what they (not another) are doing. With this knowledge, the unique features of oneself may be learned.

An interesting observation noted by Lewis and Brooks-Gunn (1979) is that the only adults who have difficulty with visual recognition of their own faces are psychotic patients and those suffering from sudden central nervous system dysfunction. Admittedly, visual recognition (of the face) and a concept of self are not synonomous, for it is possible to have a self-concept and not visually recognize oneself. Nevertheless, it is hardly possible to recognize oneself without a concept of self. In this regard, self-recognition provides a simple, straightforward way of exploring the development of the self.

In Gallup's (1970) systematic animal studies, the main factor of the mirror situation was the subject's complete control over the behavior of the mirror image and its predictability, rather than the social-stimulation properties of the reflection. Gallup found that chimpanzees marked with red dye seemed to be able to recognize themselves in a mirror—that is, they used the image to explore the red mark on their skin. Gallup's (1977) monkeys, in contrast, did not appear to have this ability, even with prolonged exposure to a mirror. Although the monkeys could learn to use mirrors to manipulate objects, they seemed incapable of integrating features of their own reflection sufficiently to use mirrors to respond to themselves. Gallup postulated that this inability represented a cognitive deficit, and concluded: "Because the identity of the observer and the mirror images are *one and the same* the ability to infer correctly the identity of *the reflection would seem to be predicated on an already existing identity on the part of an organism making that inference. Without at least a rudimentary sense of identity self-recognition would be impossible*" (1977, p. 283, emphasis added). Self-directed behaviors in front of a mirror, then,

appear to be related to self-recognition (implying a self-concept). And, as the Papoušeks (1974) have pointed out, self-recognition, in contrast to self-concept, begins early and can thus only be detected in nonverbal behavior.

In young children, Amsterdam (1972) has observed a developmental sequence of behaviors associated with reactions to the mirror image. She traced a progression from early interest, enjoyment, and acceptance of the image to a period of exploration and curiosity, followed by withdrawal from the mirror and avoidance of the image. During this last phase children show self-consciousness when looking at the image. Finally, toward the end of their second year, children demonstrate the experience of a new awareness and relatedness to the image. More specifically, in the beginning, there is little or no interest. The infant does not look, glances briefly, stares blankly, or turns instead to mother and other objects. What Amsterdam terms social behavior in front of the mirror follows: the child smiles, laughs, vocalizes in a pleased tone, and kisses or playfully touches the image. At the stage of comparison behavior, the child focuses on self and its image, along with the object and its image. Then the child begins to manipulate the image, to observe what happens to its image if it moves its body. In such self-comparative behavior the child alternates between looking at the body part and its image. With search behavior, the child attempts to reach into the mirror, touches it in an experimental way, looks behind the mirror, and generally shows perplexity or inquisitiveness. As the avoidance reaction sets in, the child cries, hides, or withdraws from the mirror image. Finally, there is more self-conscious behavior. The child struts, glances coyly, blushes, preens, clowns, or seems embarrassed. There may be clear recognition with the child saying its name, and pointing to itself and the image.

In connection with the discussion of attachment, it is important to stress that most of these various behaviors occur in front of the mirror, echoing, as it were, the attachment behaviors between child and mother. It is noteworthy that Amsterdam's (1977) sociable behavioral reactions of the infant, which peak at six to eight months, overlap with the attachment behaviors described by Bowlby. Indeed Amsterdam refers to smiling, laughing, pleasant nondistress vocalizations, touching, and patting. On this basis, we could assume that the child's reaction to the mirror includes its reaction to the mother. We might compare the behavior at six to eight months with the child's initial "mistake" with the mirror image. At first the child reacts to the picture in the mirror as if it were another child with the same characteristics, hence, its excitement and arousal. (The same might be said for the infant's reaction to the reflection of the mother.) After a peak of curiosity about this image, sociable behavior diminishes and is finally supplanted by avoidance and self-consciousness. In Amsterdam's study, every subject who showed recognition behavior manifested either avoidance or self-consciousness or both. But why, we might ask, would children show an avoidance reaction after the earlier enjoyable experience? As I suggested before, my assumption is that they are increasingly aware that the reflecting mirror is *not* mother, and they therefore show a type of stranger reaction to their images, reflecting their unstable sense of self. Fifteen out of eighteen subjects cried after they had been engaged in searching or displaying self-consciousness or recognition (seventeen to twenty-four months) (Amsterdam, 1972). In contrast, with young infants who literally take the image as another child and display a positive affect in their response, the context might be compared with the affirming, parallel type of interaction that Stern has described in experiences with the mother.

Of particular interest is the child's behavior in front of the mirror when its face has been marked with a dot. Lewis and Brooks (1978) defined behavior directed toward the mark as self-recognition. The infant had to recognize that the image in the mirror was in fact itself and that the mark resided not on the image's face but on its own. In 75 percent of children between twenty-one to twenty-four months of age, these authors observed self-recognition or mark-directed behavior. Papoušek and Papoušek (1974) reported that five-month-old infants, after a certain learning period, become

more interested in their mirror images than in a televised movie of themselves. Thus, although eye-to-eye contact is a potent factor, the infant is eventually more interested in the observation of the relation between his or her own movements and the movements in the mirror image.

Zazzo (1975) has observed, "The baby identifies the image in the mirror as himself when he becomes conscious of the solidarity of his own movement with the movement of the mirror image. 'The child I see in the mirror moves when I move, smiles when I smile. He doesn't do anything. I cause it to move when I move. It's me!' " (p. 399). I would say that the infant at eight months perceives, "It's exactly like me, my twin"; at three years, "It is me!"

The mirror is a way of understanding how the child may acquire self-awareness. Initially, during the symbiotic stage, the mirror is outside in the mother. In the period of differentiation, the child deals with his or her image as if it were another child; around eight months, the other person is a double, a clone as it were. "Customs inspection" occurs as much with the mother as with the mirror image. There are two individuals, but who is mother and who is baby is not clear. The presence of the mother in the mirror reconfirms this we-ness. Between eighteen and twenty-four months is the period of perplexity, with occasional fleeting fascination or outright avoidance. The awareness of the separateness begins to emerge in fleeting but definitive moments. The toddler loses the oneness—then the we-ness—but is not as yet entrenched and secure in the "you" and "I"; it is the period of practicing with an interchange of object and self images. In the rapprochement stage or in fixations to this stage, we have a twofold reaction to the mirror, which would correspond to fascination (the good mother) and awe and fright (the bad mother of separation). At three years, the image corresponds to the stabilized awareness of oneself, enhanced by a positive reflection of an internalized mother.

Table 9–1 correlates Mahler's separation-individuation stages, Amsterdam's observations, and my own assumptions.

TABLE 9–1

Stages in the Infant's Development: the Relationship with Mother, and Reactions to the Mirror Image

Developmental Stage (Mahler)	Symbiosis 2–4 Months	Differentiation 5–8 Months	Early Practicing 8–12 Months / Practicing Proper 12–18 Months	Rapprochement 16–24 Months	On the Way to Object Constancy 26–36 Months
Mirror Behavior (Amsterdam)	Clear interest in mirror-image movement. Pleasurable reaction.	Mirror image reacted to as a sociable playmate. Expression of delight and enthusiasm with a playful approach to the "other child." Smiling, laughing, vocalizing, touching, patting.	Search for the image. Comparison behavior. Efforts to enter mirror (12 months). Look and reach behind mirror. Apprehension and refusal to look at mirror.	Avoidance of the mirror (17–24 months) associated with self-consciousness and/or recognition of the image.	Self-consciousness showing embarrassment or some form of self-admiration. From 24 months, new awareness and relatedness to the mirror.
Mother-Infant Relationship	Mother an external source of self-awareness, induced by her presence and lost by her absence.	Self is in the object, experienced as a twin.	Mother and child experienced as interchangeable with each other, but both must be there at the same time.	Awareness of mother as separate—a threat to self existence, (self inconstancy).	Mother is introjected and identified with by child. Child contains mirroring function, (self constancy).
Mirror Reaction	Blissful state in mirror in mother's presence and disorganized state in her rigid face or absence.	The mirror image is considered the other. It is so stimulating because it is so much like oneself as seen by mother.	Infant points to mirror as mother; fleetingly as oneself.	Fascination with the mirror image (good mother) and avoidance of mirror (bad mother of separation). Infant looks for mother in the mirror.	The child can look at himself or herself as mother has looked at him or her.

Implications

Mahler has said, "Mirror reactions are most relevant for following the process of building self representations and differentiating these from object representations" (Mahler et al., 1975, p. 223n). Some examples from the work of Mahler and from my own observations lay the groundwork for my concluding discussion of implications. They illustrate the potential diagnostic and therapeutic application of these findings and of the mirror itself.

Shannon, a twenty-one-month-old whom I observed offered a surprising response when she was asked in front of the one-way mirror, "Who is there?" She faintly said her own name after some insistence on mother's part. More characteristically, though, during ten minutes of observation, she pointed to the mirror with her hand and said, "Mommy, Mommy." On several occasions when she was asked by mother, "Where is Shannon?", she would point neither to the mirror nor to herself but, instead, look around and behind her. Possessing a positive mutuality with her devoted and sensitive mother, Shannon illustrated that during the rapprochement phase, the recognition of one's body as integrated in the self is not yet accomplished. Self and object representations are interchangeable, and the child's visual reaction to the mirror is that the image is predominantly mother. With self-constancy, an identification with mother allows the child to express fully her sense of herself in the mirror as shown by her calling herself by her name, and with her clear sense of "That's me!" expressed verbally and nonverbally.

Mahler and her colleagues (1975) described a mirror reaction reflecting problems with the mother-child interaction. Once the symbiotic period ended, Wendy's mother was characteristically less comfortable with her children. She was unable to enjoy the playfulness of the individuating child, and her relationship did not grow into playful mutuality. Wendy's mirror reaction at the age of eight to nine months, in contrast to the normal gleeful one, was to burst into tears if she did not see mother's image beside her own.

A comparison between another of the cases cited by Mahler and her group and a child I observed does suggest the usefulness of the mirror reaction in developmental assessment. Donna (Mahler et al., 1975), who had a positive attachment to mother at age six months, touched her own mirror image with interest. She looked in the face of observers and developed a kind of stranger reaction. When mother returned to the room, Donna would periodically look at mother's face, as if to reassure herself. After a family trip when she was nine to ten months old, where she was handled by many people, she became more demanding of mother's presence. This included her now becoming upset on seeing her own mirror reflection without her mother. In the beginning of the rapprochement phase between fourteen and fifteen months, whenever mother left the room, Donna would quickly run to the door and cry. She became generally intolerant of frustration. Her way of coping with mother's absences was to want to go out of the door also; being allowed to go out seemed to relieve her distress.

In contrast was Jennifer, a twenty-one-month-old active, verbal, and loving infant, whose mother was involved, warm, and relaxed with her. During a separation-reunion experience, Jennifer did not go to the door in search of her mother but instead shook the freestanding mirror, attempted to go into the mirror, and finally hid behind the mirror herself, all the while muttering, "Mommy, Mommy." The mirror seemed to her to be where her mother was, and going behind the mirror, out of its scope, seemed to console her as did Donna's going out the door. Jennifer's case illustrates that the mother is in the mirror at a certain point of transition in the internalization process. For Donna, a younger child, mother only existed in the external space and in the mirror when she was actually facing it. Jennifer, being older, showed a more advanced reaction to the mirror as mother, indicating a growing capacity for internalization and symbolization.

I have found the mirror useful diagnostically and therapeutically with older children as well. Particularly when the child needs (as did Derek) to work through aspects of an incomplete or pathological mother-child relationship, the mirror can be an adjunct to the therapist's (mirroring) treatment interventions. Jerry, a four-and-a-half-year-old only child, suffered an intense separation anxiety infiltrating all areas of his life. I saw him for five months in brief psychotherapy. By the seventh session, Jerry had improved somewhat. Asked who was in the mirror which he faced, he exclaimed, "Mommy!" When I repeated the question three times, he responded the same way, and this incident helped me to convince his mother that he was not ready to terminate. Two months later, by the tenth session, he had begun to show age-appropriate behavior in all areas. Now, when he saw his image in the mirror and I asked him who was there, he stomped and jumped about with the playful glee typical of his age and exclaimed, "Cowboy! Cowboy!" Behaviorally and verbally, he showed in his reaction to the mirror that he was no longer one with his mother.

Returning now to my initial case vignette: Through a similar type of interaction with his therapist, Derek was able to recognize himself in the mirror of the other. By seeing himself in me, he began to crystallize a concept of himself. Subsequently, he progressed through the stages Amsterdam has described for mirror behavior. Indeed, the mirror aided the psychotherapeutic process.

The first and most natural route toward insight for a patient often entails learning by attributing similar traits to others. It is as if the self comes to know itself by projecting itself onto others and then retrieving this image. Not only does one see an affective image of oneself in the other's face, but one also receives a reflection of more abstract character or personality attributes through this process of projection and introjection. The human mirror interprets and integrates the image received; the processed image then is introjected and contributes to the sense of self. Given intact cognitive equipment and a positive mother experience, the actual mirror experience can contribute to the sense of self. As I have tried to show, this may have some practical application in psychotherapeutic technique with borderline and psychotic patients, and more important, as a means to diagnose mother-infant relationships in normalcy and pathology. Papoušek and Papoušek (1974) have suggested that, if proved sufficiently, the identity between the mirror image and the concept of self could be a criterion of self-recognition. Alternatively, in my opinion, the proposition might be reversed. Self-recognition can occur only if a self-concept exists, as Gallup postulated with chimpanzees, and self-recognition via the mirror could became a criterion of self-concept. Regardless of the direction of this effect, however, the mirror clearly has a place in further clinical and experimental research. It can help us to assess mother-child interaction, its intermediate stages of internalization and self constancy, and allow for more accuracy and effectiveness in therapeutic interventions.

REFERENCES

Abelin, E. (1971). The role of the father in the separation-individuation process. In *Separation-Individuation: Essays in Honor of Margaret S. Mahler*, ed., J. B. McDevitt and C. F. Settlage. New York: International Universities Press.

Ainsworth, M. D. (1968). The development of infant-mother attachment. In *Review of Child Development Research*, vol. 3, ed., B. M. Caldwell and H. N. Ricciuti. Chicago: University of Chicago Press.

Amsterdam, B. K. (1972). Mirror self-image reactions before age two. *Developmental Psychobiology*, 5:297–305.

Bleier, M. R. (1976). Social behaviors among one-year-olds in a play group. Unpublished doctoral dissertation, Boston University.

Bowlby, J. (1969). *Attachment and Loss*, vol. 1, *Attachment*. New York: Basic Books.

Brazelton, B. T. et al. (1975). Early mother-infant reciprocity. In *Parent-Infant Interaction*, Ciba Foundation Symposium 33 (new series). New York: American Elsevier.

Burlingham, D. (1963). A study of identical twins. *The Psychoanalytic Study of the Child*, 18:367–423. New York: International Universities Press.

Durfee, J. T. and Lee, L. C. (1973). Infant-infant interaction in a daycare setting. *Proceedings of the 81st Annual Convention of the American Psychological Association, Montreal, Canada*, 8:63–64.

Escalona, S. K. (1968). *The Roots of Individuality: Normal Patterns of Development in Infancy.* Chicago: Aldine.

Gallup, G. G. (1970). Chimpanzees: Self recognition. *Science,* 167:86–87.

Gallup, G. G. (1977). Absence of self recognition in a monkey (macaca fascicularis) following prolonged exposure to a mirror. *Developmental Psychobiology,* 10:184–281.

Leonard, M. R. (1961). Identification in twins. *The Psychoanalytic Study of the Child,* 16:300–320. New York: International Universities Press.

Lewis, M. and Brooks-Gunn, J. (1978). Self-knowledge emotional development. In *The Development of Affect,* ed., M. Lewis and L. A. Rosenbaum. New York: Plenum Press.

Lewis, M. and Brooks-Gunn, J. (1979). Toward a theory of social cognition: The development of self. *New Directions for Child Development,* 4:1–19.

Lichtenstein, H., (1977). Narcissism and primary identity. In *The Dilemma of Human Identity.* New York: Jason Aronson.

Mahler, M. S. and McDevitt J. B. (1982). Thoughts on the emergence of the sense of self, with particular emphasis on the body self. *Journal of the American Psychoanalytic Association,* 30:827–848.

Mahler, M. S., Pine F., and Bergman, A. (1975). *The Psychological Birth of the Human Infant.* New York: Basic Books.

Mueller, E. A. (1972). The maintenance of verbal exchanges between young children. *Child Development,* 43:930–938.

Mueller E. A. and Brenner, J. (1977). The growth of social interaction in a toddler play group: The role of peer experience. *Child Development,* 48:854–861.

Papoušek, H. and Papoušek, M. (1974). Mirror image and self recognition in young human infants: I. A new method of experimental analysis. *Developmental Psychobiology,* 7:149–157.

Plath, S. (1981). *Collected Poems,* London: Faber & Faber.

Rutter, M. (1972). *The Qualities of Mothering.* New York: Jason Aronson.

Schact, L. (1981). The mirroring function of the child analyst. *Journal of Child Psychotherapy,* 7:79–88.

Stern, D. N. (1983). The early development of schemas of self, of other, and of various experiences of "self with other." In *The Development of the Self: Infant Research,* ed., J. D. Lichtenberg and S. Kaplan. Hillsdale, New Jersey: The Analytic Press.

Winnicott, D. W. (1972). Basis for self in body, *International Journal of Child Psychotherapy,* 1:7–16.

Winnicott, D. W. (1967). Mirror role of mother and family in child development. In *Playing and Reality,* Harmondsworth, England: Penguin Books, 1980.

Zazzo, R., (1975). Des jumeaux devant le miroir: Questions de methode. *Journal de Psychologie,* 4:399.

10

Infant Development: Fictive Personality and Creative Capacity

Jay Martin, Ph.D.

"Good" and "Bad" Fictions

We all make use of fictions. The first fictions are fantasies concerning parents, the body, the self, others in the immediate vicinity, and then strangers. Later, through fictions—offered to us in books, films, and the mass media arts—we acquire imprinting experiences, introjects, and, at a more mature stage, models for identification; through experiment with imitations of identifications, people learn to develop and change. Fictions, then, are essential in maturation, providing a necessary arena for "trying on" personal identities and "trying out" relations with others.

Yet, at every stage of development, experience with fictions is ambiguous. Not all fictions serve development. Quite naturally, everyone acknowledges that some fictions are "good," while others are "bad." "Good fictions" are variously named: "play," "experiment," "improvisation," "imagination," "hypothetical thinking," and "creativity." "Self-deception," "delusional thinking," "impairment of reality

Parts of this essay were written while I was a resident scholar at the Rockefeller Foundation Study and Conference Center, Bellagio, Italy; The work was completed under a Senior Research Grant from the National Endowment for Humanities. I am grateful to both institutions.

testing," and "illusions" are the terms by which we characterize fictions that hinder or balk growth and development. "Good fictions" are called "healthy" and "adaptive" because they tend to prepare for action, compensate for loss, or make flexibility and inventiveness possible. "Bad fictions" are labeled "neurotic" or even "psychotic" because they lead to isolation, denial, or grandiosity; they make loss inevitable and block free experimentation.

Yet, what eventually in adult life becomes divided into "good" and "bad" fictions starts out as a single process in infancy. The source of fictions in infancy is the infant's experience of internal illusions, which are soon subjected to a steady stream of disillusionment, from within and without. Put in the simplest terms, the infant is "illusioned" by his internal push for pleasure. His "illusions" seem confirmed by the experience of gratification and realized in the internal feeling of cohesion and growth. What "dis-illusions" the infant is the failure of the environment to respond to his illusions, which the infant interprets as loss. Loss attacks growth, blocks pleasure, brings pain. Loss is all that binds and confines. Loss is what the process of disillusionment brings and means.

Necessarily, infancy *must* include both illusioning and disillusioning experiences—confirmations that the self coheres in itself and can adhere to others; and also experiences that involve loss, bringing on doubt and (in Goethe's phrase) "disorder and early sorrow." Illusionment and disillusionment are so mixed and balanced in healthy development that they are really part of a single process. Through apparent confirmation of internal illusions or fantasies, the self begins the process of self-acceptance and then of attunement to and negotiation with the outer world. From small but steady experiences of disillusionment comes a grudging acceptance of the claims of the object world, along with the origin of adaptive mechanisms for facing change, active talents for making change, and capacities for coping with disappointment.

Infants "recover" quite naturally from their inevitable disillusionment when it occurs in a phase-appropriate manner. Indeed, later adult pleasure in suspending disbelief in images, illusions, and fictions of all sorts is probably a recollection of the pleasure once derived from recovering from disillusionment through learning to believe, and then not believe, in fictions. For some people, this pleasure in manipulating fictions was so great in infancy and childhood that they later devote their lives to experiment and become creators—writers, painters, scientists, inventors, filmmakers. Others are content to be able either to believe or to suspend disbelief without being disappointed or overwhelmingly disillusioned. All these sorts of persons learn to see fictions as predominantly "good."

That, of course, is the optimum path of development—when illusionment and disillusionment flow together in a mutually facilitating manner. But what happens when the infant's involvement with fictions is not facilitating in these ways? When the infant is too suddenly, too massively, or too continuously disillusioned, loss, anxiety, and depression seize hold of the growing self. In this state of disillusionment, the infant—and then the child and later the adult—can neither risk belief nor tolerate disbelief. Instead of belief, loss gets embedded or "inscribed" within the developing personality: ultimately this means the self cannot believe in itself, and instead sees itself as an illusion, a fiction.

By this means originates what I call the "fictive personality" process of development (Martin, 1984). Instead of creating fictions, the fictive personality seeks ready-made fictions wherein to find identities. Instead of the creative pleasure of manipulating fictions from inside, the fictive personality seeks to adopt others' illusions from outside the self. The fictive personality process starts in infancy and forever after forces the fictive personality back to infantile feelings in a hapless and hopeless effort to regain the primary paradise of infant illusion, before disillusion spoiled the infant's world.

The distinction I am drawing between the infant who can manage illusions and the infant who seeks illusions to maintain him is vividly evident, at a slightly later age, in the freely experimenting play of some children and the empty, tentative behavior of children who are playing others' games, as if they were the others whose games they play.

Peter

Peter's parents were both well-educated professional people.[1] He was their first child. Around the age of one Peter experienced a double loss: first, his family moved from an apartment to a house; and second, his mother went to work in his father's office while Peter was left with a sitter. Shortly after this, Peter experienced sleep disturbances. A year later, the house was sold, and the family moved again. Somewhat more than a year and a half later, the family moved a long distance, taking three weeks to go by car. Peter expressed a fear of playing outside his new home and began to watch television, especially cartoon shows, for more than four hours each day. He saw *Pinocchio* and *The Wizard of Oz*. When Peter was four his mother gave birth to another baby boy. Shortly afterward, the family moved again. During the auto trip Peter injured his penis. In the autumn, at age five, Peter was sent to kindergarten. At this time, Peter's father went on a business trip, and Peter's mother became ill

---

[1]Peter's case is reported in Call (1975). I appreciate Justin Call's assistance and encouragement.

with the flu. His uncle took Peter to a magic and marionette show where he met the principal actress and narrator, the "Magic Lady," who was a friend of his uncle's. Three days later, Peter's father arrived home at 2:00 AM. Two hours later Peter woke in terror with a psychotic hallucination.

His main terror was that he was going to be taken away into a magic land where he would become an unreal, "pretend" being. His mother recorded some of his speech at this time

> I am a boy, a real boy. I want you to go away. Witches are not allowed. The queen, I promised, I promised, I would do it. No, I don't want to be make-believe. I am a boy. Boys don't wear lipstick. Boys don't get flowers. I am my mommy's and daddy's boy. No, don't get rid of anyone . . . you can't make magic. Don't make my food magic. No, you can't do that. You can't get rid of anyone. Don't get rid of me.

Peter's hallucination records the precise moment in which the person experiences himself as a hallucination—when both the realm of the self and the world of objects become so tenuous in themselves and in their connections that both become painful make-believes, fictions. Peter sees himself, his food, and his very being becoming unreal—and himself transformed into a fiction; mommy and daddy recede into the distance, while the witch prepares to take him to the Land of Make-Believe where everything is changed: boys there wear lipstick, get flowers, and eat magic food.

Obviously, a series of losses and separations and a castration-like experience occurring just before the onset of these hallucinations revived an earlier fault line, a crack, in object- and self-relatedness at the level of what Lacan (Schneiderman, 1980) calls the "imaginary," most likely connected with the frequent moves made by the parents and by his mother's return to work during Peter's second year. Seeing *The Wizard of Oz, Pinocchio,* and a magic show shortly before the hallucinations provided fictional materials by which the personality, fragmented and detached from its image of itself as whole and of others as real, could see itself in terms of the available fictions.

Why *does* he adopt fictions? Because, when the self suddenly seems unreal and reality is unavailable, fictions alone seem to offer preformed substitutes for the illusions that the self has lost. When the self sees itself as a fiction, it restores itself by fusing with the fictions that are closest to the fears, embracing them. It is better, the self seems to say, to be a fiction than to be nothing. Peter's case allows us to see Peter's personality seeking reflections and turning toward fictions; his anxiety shows us how psychotic that moment, internally experienced, must be.

Fictive Personality Development

In imaginative literature about children or adults, many stories exist to testify that imaginative writers have long recognized how powerfully fictions appeal to people, perhaps especially to children; and many writers have described personages who take their personalities from characters in fiction. Simply to mention a few titles will exhibit how often writers have explored the process and condition of fictive personality. The most famous book on this theme written about children and with a child audience in mind is *The Adventures of Huckleberry Finn* (1885), in which Tom Sawyer performs all his actions in accordance with romantic literature. *Don Quixote de la Mancha* (1605) is, of course, the best known literary work dealing with an adult who adopts and then tries to conform to a fictive personality. The Don's fictions, Cervantes writes, were "more real to him than anything else in the world." Many other books come to mind in which the main subject is the way that an empty adult, or sometimes a child in whom identity formation has scarcely begun, "imports" into the self, as a preformed whole, a character from fiction or history. Emma Bovary identifies with a whole series of romantic heroines. Pirandello's *Henry IV* is about a character who believes he is the King. The same idea often appears in films, most recently in Martin Scorsese's *The King of Comedy* (1983) and Woody Allen's *Zelig* (1983).

Peter, Huckleberry Finn, Don Quixote, and the others all suffer, though in different degrees, from a developmental disturbance which predisposed them toward adopting others' fictions. I conceive of this disturbance as one in which the infant or child becomes disillusioned about both the self and the external world. In the relative absence of or weakness of attachment to both normal narcissism *and* object love, the self strives to identify totally with characters in literary, historical, or mass-media fictions. These fictions temporarily "fill in" the empty self by providing ready-made self-concepts, producing an illusion of real being, but all too often reflecting, beneath the surface, the reactive anger that arises from the early frustration that originally left the self helpless and empty.

Literary critics, philosophers, and psychoanalysts, as well as writers, have all recognized that the power of fictions resides in their ability to promote identifications. Ordinarily identification processes are involved in identity formation, values, the development of ideals, personal maturation, and the growth of creative capacity. But in the instance of the fictive personality, the identification has a completely different quality, seeming almost to amount to possession. The identification does not stop at resemblances; it becomes total, incorporating the violent and depressive aspects of the fictional character without self-examination in a completely unscrutinized, indiscriminate manner. For the fictive personality, fictions do not *simulate* life, they are a *source* of life. People with fictive personalities find it easy to discover selves to adopt.

Several of my patients have made me vividly aware of how the personality can acquire a fictional source. Let me refer very briefly to two instances.

Mrs. M and Mark R

Mrs. M, thirty-four, came into analysis because she felt empty, lacking an identity. To her the world was radically split between her "real," vividly experienced fantasies, and disappointing reality. She clung to the idea that her father, dead for eighteen years, would come back to her.

Whenever reality and fantasy came into conflict, fantasy won. She stuffed herself with fantasy. She ran up huge debts, resorted to shoplifting, overate, and lied compulsively. She developed, on demand, a whole battery of related illnesses, and she faked fainting spells and simulated at least one suicide attempt in order to get the attention which she craved from her father. While of course these symptoms and behaviors were multidetermined, they were fundamentally designed to make fantasy seem to triumph over reality and to allow her to fill herself up with illusions of the love she felt she had lost earlier.

In analysis she expressed her belief that to understand the world only three books were required. Her theory was that the world had three shapes, corresponding to her three favorite books: *Little Women, Gone With the Wind,* and *The Wizard of Oz.* All she had to do was to identify the proper book to be used to interpret the special aspect of the world that any problem brought to hand, then act like its heroine, and the way of dealing with "reality"—her fictive reality—would soon become evident. Never mind if her strategy didn't work: the illusion remained right, though the world might be wrong. It was no accident that all three of the books that served her had heroines (Jo, Dorothy, and Scarlett) who were lost girls, alone and frightened, abandoned by men but yearning for strong men (or powerful wizards) to save them. Analysis showed that Mrs. M had very early, probably even as an infant, been disillusioned by her father, who was never emotionally available to her. Her core wish was to remain an infant and to return to the illusion that a strong father-figure would care for her.

Others among my analysands have exhibited similar fictive orientations, and reconstruction in analysis has shown that their fictive identifications reach far back into childhood and must ultimately be traced to a predisposition toward ficticity laid down in infancy. Disillusioned early and despairing of getting either real nourishment or solid introjects, they remained hungry for primal illusions. Even as adults they continued to stuff themselves with fictions.

Mrs. M was eventually able to dispense with

her fictive identifications through analysis. Mark R was not. The last of a large family of six children, he was born four years after his next older sibling. All of his older brothers and sisters achieved considerable success educationally and in business enterprises. Only Mark seemed unable, from a very early age, to "make contact."

When Mark was about one year old, his father, a career officer in the air force, was sent into combat overseas. A year later Mark's mother was killed in an automobile accident. Several weeks passed before Mark's father was able to return home; in the meantime, Mark was taken care of by a variety of friends and relatives. To his father he seemed listless and withdrawn. In a short period Mark's father arranged to distribute the children among various relatives; then he returned to combat. Well before the end of the war, when Mark was four, his father was reported as missing in action, his plane having failed to return to base.

During his school years, Mark made few friends, except for a brief period when he belonged to a street gang. Eventually he quit school, joined the army, and became a paratrooper. A few days after he first parachuted into combat, he became delusional, saying that he had been wounded all over. His delusions passed rapidly, but he was now obsessed with classical mythology, especially with the gods who lived on the heights of Mt. Parnassus. This too passed, but what remained was the feeling of having been dropped and a fervent interest in the figure of Icarus, who had flown so high that his wings had melted. He saw innumerable complicated parallels between Icarus and himself, often confusing Icarus with his son Daedalus. He saw himself as having also been "dropped from the heights."

The French psychiatrist and psychoanalyst Marcel Czermak, referring to the phenomena of "mental automatism,"[2] which is one of the impressions given by the fictive personality, speaks of fictive persons as "living by copying gestures, to the point where they have become . . . marionettes of pure seeming fabricated by

various random parts, mimicked from people who have crossed their paths" (Czermak, 1977, p. 181). "Marionettes of pure seeming": it is a fine phrase, one that reminds us of children, like Peter, who see themselves as Pinocchio, or of grown-up girls still seeking infant illusions. Should they give up their fictions, they fear they will lose their selves.

Transitional Phenomena, the Necessity of Illusions, and the Origin of Fictions

The basic questions in the development of personality revolve around the issue of boundaries. The crucial questions are: What is the me? Later, where does the me stop? Still later, what is not-me? Then, how do I relate to others, and how are we different? Finally, how do we achieve intimacy and sharing while still maintaining a sense of self? Such questions involve a concept of self *and* others, of inside *and* outside, of separation *and* individuation. Developmentally, deficits are as easily organized as capacities. With regard to fictive personality development, the crucial points of organization or "transformation" (Emde, chapter 4, herein) occur at two months and at twelve to thirteen and eighteen to twenty-one months; at these times, in different ways, the infant hovers between the claims of narcissism and love of others, attachment and intimacy, the inner and the outer world. I am thinking centrally of the times that Winnicott (1953) has described as filled with "transitional phemomena," when the infant seeks identification with what Anna Freud (1969) calls "something which is neither the body nor the outer world," but which helps in making the transition between the two. This is a time of illusions—both "good-enough" and "not-good enough" fictions; a time, Smirnoff (1980) says, "when the object is no longer solely fantasy but has not yet become a symbol." At such a time, in the infant's mind both mother *and* the self are images; neither has substantial reality as a separate entity, because to believe in the true reality of either would overly stress its separateness, and separateness

---

[2] The phrase was first employed by the French psychiatrist Gäetan de Clérambault. (See Miller, 1977.)

is charged with disintegrative anxiety when the self is reorganizing. At this stage the self is highly subject to deflection, distortion, and fixation into ficticity, since neither the self nor others seem solid (cf. Furer, 1964; Galenson, 1980; Kestenberg, 1968; Mahler et al., 1975; Roiphe and Galenson, 1981; see also Emde, Kernberg, and Stern in this volume).

The Hampstead Nursery provided some moving examples of distruptions at this stage, most centering around the way young children, deprived of mother, cling to clothing brought from home, as fictions of mother (Freud and Burlingham, 1944). When one of the children was told that "his mother would not come next Sunday, he began to cry, rushed to the drawer where the caps are kept, and called out: 'My Mummy does not come, me must wear a hat' " (p. 441). Freud and Burlingham comment that as they develop children must dispense with transitional phenomena and form new relationships.

But what if no such relationship is available? What if it is not so easy to dispense with transitional objects or to leave transitional phenomena behind? No child is going to continue to wear a hat all his life. But other, less concrete, substitutes for the twinned image of mother and of self are soon at hand, other less tangible fictions—from books, theatre, mass-culture media—fictions that satisfy the child's craving to retrieve the lost illusions.

One stage builds upon another. A good experience of "adhesive identification" (Bick, 1968) is likely to lead to a capacity to receive the comforts, while minimizing the terrors, of symbiosis; a good beginning of individuation and separation while still in the symbiosis stage becomes a healthy foundation for the future evolution of individuality, autonomy, self-confidence, and the ability to tolerate separateness and aloneness (Parens, 1980; Winnicott, 1958). Contrariwise, infants who are unable to experience a firm sense of self through adhesive identification are likely to have problems benefiting from the supporting, mirroring nourishment of the symbiotic stage; lacking a sense of a self that can lean against itself or that can lean upon a mother, they are unlikely, in turn, to feel mirrored and to be able to negotiate successfully the difficult tasks

of separation and individuation and the establishment of a cohesive sense of self (Kohut, 1971; Tolpin, 1971). Instead, they are likely to define themselves as transitional persons, attached or adhering to neither self nor others, but somehow floating between them. Here, the fictive personality is born: the child—later, the adult—who can lean only on fictions concerning his or her own and others' existence (see Isaacs, 1948). Winnicott and his followers allow us to see the origins of a fictive personality orientation in transitional phases and transitional phenomena. But to understand the consequent unfolding dynamics of the fictive personality process, the work of four other analysts is, from different angles, highly important.

The Dynamics of Fictive Personality

Fictive personality disorders are multifaceted and overdetermined and to describe their nature and dynamics at all briefly I have to simplify. It is scarcely surprising that several previous investigators have noted and described various aspects of the fictive personality. Helene Deutsch's (1942) "as if" personality, Guntrip's (1968) "schizoid emptiness," Anna Freud's (1936) "altruistic surrender" considered as a defense, and Kohut's (1977) concept of the narcissitic disorders, provide, when taken together, a reasonably comprehensive, if still oversimplified, understanding of the complex dynamics of the fictive personality.

"As if" individuals, Deutsch says, experience an inner feeling of unreality and then project that feeling defensively onto the world so that existence "seems strange, objects shadowy, [and] human beings and events theatrical and unreal" (Deutsch, 1942, p. 263). They are like technically well-trained actors, but without any inner warmth. Like Pinocchio or marionettes they relate by transitory fictive identifications. Deutsch's formulation is justly famous and must be the starting point for analysis of fictive personality.

Guntrip (1968) describes the sense of inner emptiness concomitant to the loss of object cathexes. "The schizoid person has renounced objects even though he still needs them" (p. 18) is Guntrip's central theme. He assumes, correctly I believe, that the self drives toward good objects—relations, beliefs, commitments, institutions—by way of pleasure, achieved early in relation to others. Lacking the capacity for such varied relations, the self reaches toward pseudorelations, and thus a false self, in fictions—fictions that seem manipulable and manageable, that will not disappoint or disturb. But that route leaves the initial strivings unsatisfied; though objects are renounced, they are still desired, and this produces the central, hidden depressive conflict of the schizoid. Identification with fictions provides a means of maintaining the boundaries of the ego through the containers provided by the fictions.

The defensive aspect of the fictive personality is effectively designated by Anna Freud's phrase "altruistic surrender" (1936). She describes a young governess who as a child had wished fevently for beautiful clothes, marriage, and many children. Though as an adult she wore modest dress and remained unmarried and childless, she fulfilled her original desires by taking an active interest in the clothes of her friends, being an insatiable matchmaker, and caring professionally for many children. "It looked," Anna Freud writes, "as if her own life had been emptied of interests and wishes. . . . Instead of exerting herself to achieve any aims of her own, she expended all her energy in sympathizing with the experiences of people she cared for. She lived in the lives of other people, instead of having any experience of her own" (p. 125).

Kohut's (1977) analysis of narcissistic personality disorders helps to illuminate the fictive personality process from yet another angle. Borderline personality, as treated by Kohut (1971) and Kohut and Wolf (1978), is seen as arising from a deficiency in the normal development of the structure of the self. The fictive personality process is one defense against this deficiency, by which a rigid, fully formed fictive organization is imported from without, into the self, to supply what is lacking —identity itself. A cohesive self from books or mass media is placed inside the self to guard against the terrors of a noncohesive self (see Goldberg, 1978).

Reillusionment and Creativity

Each in separate ways, Deutsch, Guntrip, Anna Freud and Kohut, defined aspects of fictive personality processes; but each also pointed to the creative aspects of the use of good fictions. Disturbances at transitional, transformational stages often have the distintegrative-decreative effect I have been investigating, but they can also introduce fecundative-creative consequences. It seems that when an infant or child who has experienced her- or himself as fictive through disillusionment, is reillusioned and allowed to believe in good fictions again through good object relations and the appropriate satisfaction of fantasies, this constitutes an early creative experience in dealing with the double character of fictions, "good" and "bad." Creators seem to have had an early experience of ficticity, the pain of disillusionment, followed by the pleasure of reillusionment. It is no accident, then, that Deutsch, Anna Freud, Guntrip, and Kohut (1957) all turned naturally to literature to exemplify their points—Deutsch (1937, 1955) to *Don Quixote* and Thomas Mann's *The Confessions of Felix Krull;* Anna Freud to Rostand's *Cyrano de Bergerac;* Guntrip to the work of Henry James; and Kohut (1957) to *Death in Venice.* I think Cervantes, Mann, James, and Rostand had deeply and personally experienced ficticity at some stage in time and some level of awareness, but it is Don Quixote, Krull, Strether, Cyrano, and Aschenbach who are the fictive personalities. How did these authors manage to achieve a capacity to manipulate illusions instead of being driven by them? How did they manage to pass from the feelings of surrender to another's fiction and from bondage to illusions to the capacity to free the imagination by creating their own illusions?

I would assume that as infants, Cervantes, Rostand, and the others had some satisfying, rather than merely terrorizing, experience with illusions; for each spent a considerable time in reliving that past pleasure through creating illusions in the present. At the same time, in creating their characters for themselves and for others, these writers preserved a memory of a disturbance in infancy, memorializing a trauma that they suffered, then overcame—but never, in the unconscious, forgot.

The way in which fictions can be productively used to reillusion, to "try out" behavior, and in this case, to use language hypothetically, experimentally, and freely, is well illustrated by Lori, a six-year-old traumatized girl.

Lori

At the age of six, Lori, apparently a normal, healthy child, suffered the trauma of seeing her mother stab her father, a nightclub comedian, to death. Lori was unable to talk about this incident or in any way to acknowledge what had happened. Her behavior became constrained, she appeared listless and uninterested but subject to sudden angers, and her sleep was disturbed.

The night before the stabbing, Lori had watched a televised performance of the circus. In order to allow her to give herself relief from her internal feelings of guilt and the horrible pictures reality offered, it was suggested to Lori that she draw a picture of the circus. Without hesitation, she made a clown's face. Then she "put" the clown in an airplane. She was unusually excited by her drawings. Could she tell a story about them, she was asked. She complied animatedly. The clown flew his plane high above while millions of people watched. He "made the plane go funny," in spins and dives, and everyone laughed. The clown is a great success. Then black birds who are angry with him because no one laughs at them fly up and peck holes in his wings, and his plane deflates like a balloon. The clown jumps out and tries to parachute, but he comes down too fast and hits the ground with such a hard bump he is all smashed up. "You really wish your daddy had gotten through OK," she is told. At that, Lori cried and, while crying, hallucinated her deepest wish, that her father was still alive and somewhere in the room. Later, she was able to talk about seeing the stabbing itself in its actual detail. She also remembered good times with her father and recalled that they had gone on a vacation in a plane. She said that she was going to grow up to be an airline stewardess.

In this case, "practicing" an approach to the real incident through creating stories allowed Lori to bring her internal disillusions into contact with a created fiction. And through making use of her ability to use transitional phenomena—in this case, stories—an ability she had obviously acquired as an infant or in early childhood—she was able to help in her cure through her own creativity.

Loss and Creativity in the Case of S

In the instance of S, even more dramatically than in that of Lori, it is possible to see how early disillusionment followed by reillusionment is related to the origin and subsequent unfolding of creative capacity. Eventually, S, was to become a famous writer. In his infancy and childhood, however, S experienced loss and disillusion to about the same degree as did Peter, Mrs. M, Mark R, and Lori. By the time S was born, his mother had become sick with fatigue and stress in caring for her dying husband. After some initial success she was unable to nurse her child and sent S out to a wet nurse, where he was weaned early. Seriously ill with enteritis himself, S was about a year old when his father died. Mother, now a stranger to her baby, reclaimed him from the nurse and moved to her father's house. The baby recovered from his early illness, but he was troubled by hallucinations and lack of trust. He slept in the same room with his mother, and both were treated as children by S's grandfather. S had no memories of his father, except for the photograph which his mother placed on the wall above his bed and for some marginalia in his father's books. His grandfather doted on the boy, and S showed considerable excitement in the old man's company. Vain and narcissistic, S's grandfather played at looking like Victor Hugo, and he loved to be photographed. The house was filled with photographs of him.

At age four, S began to experience a desire to be like his grandfather. Though he vowed to remain perfectly still in church, internally he was troubled by obsessive thoughts of soiling, of shouting out obscenities or urinating in the holy water basin. He was beset by death-anxieties and performed numerous compulsive ceremonials of expiation designed to protect him magically. He had a very strong feeling of being an imposter, empty and unreal. He felt himself powerless, yet he behaved grandiosely and treated his mother like a servant. He was, he felt, "a fake child," lacking a soul, an "object" much like "a flower in a pot," "running from imposture to imposture." He saw himself as a fiction—a bad fiction. Clearly his early loss of his father, literally, and of mother, figuratively, disillusioned S. No wonder he found the fictions provided by books and films so appealing. He became fascinated by silent movies; at home, alone, he played out all the roles he had seen on the screen. That he lived in a world of fantasy drawn from what he saw in films and what he read was evident, but there was also something wrong with his identifications, something hollow. His grandmother noticed this and called him a "clown and a humbug." At the age of seven, in imitation of the films and books that were the source of his fantasies, he decided to lose the power of speech and remained mute for long periods.

At the age of seven, then, S seemed to be following the path of the fictive personality process, ready for any available fiction to offer him an identity—or a new role to play. But instead, around this same time he was reillusioned; he was turned toward the creative use of his imagination by his idealized and beloved grandfather, who was real after all. "He drove me," S later wrote, ". . . into a new imposture that changed my life." Grandfather reillusioned him by believing in him as valuable, by loving him. This was achieved through the making of fictions. S's grandfather was an amateur poet, and when the old man went on a trip when the boy was eight, he sent his grandson a letter in verse. The boy replied with a poem. "I received by return mail a poem to my glory; I replied with a poem. The habit was formed; the grandfather and his grandson were united by a new bond." S was given La Fontaine's *Fables.* He rewrote them in alexandrines, a difficult rhythmic scheme. Soon he began to write tales of adventure. He found he could enter easily into the lives of others—so long as he himself had created these others—and that he had a knack for composing tales. He was

writing stories, it turned out, not to escape reality, but as a way of understanding it. Instead of simply swallowing others' fictions he created his own, and through them he made his way to reality; lacking a firm sense of reality due to his early object losses, he created a world of objects that he could trust precisely because they were his creations, and through them he learned to trust the world enough to gain a relation to it. Eventually, writing gave him a role in life and a relation to others, an audience; it taught him that his own psychic reality was fundamental, but that he had to account, in his creations of characters and in the response of his audience, for the psychic reality of others. At the age of eight, he says, by means of fiction, "I was beginning to find myself. . . . I was escaping from playacting. I was not yet working, but I had already stopped playing. . . . By writing I was existing."

All the information about S comes from Sartre's autobiography *The Words* (1964); for S grew up to be Jean-Paul Sartre. In his autobiography Sartre shows dramatically how lost he had felt as a child, and he gives us enough genetic material to trace these feeling to his early infant losses. But he also shows clearly how his capacity for self- and object-relations was restored. Through reillusioning or new "affect attunements" (Stern, this volume) with his grandfather, Sartre learned a productive activity that turned his ficticity into creativity of the highest kind. In this essay it is not possible to give elaborate demonstration (though the demonstration would certainly be possible) that in the work produced by Sartre as an adult the original wounds in infancy are still evident, though they are reworked and richly transformed. Whether in the philosophy of existentialism, with its emphasis that the imaginary is the core of choices; or in a novel such as *La Nausée,* with its portrait of a character empty at the self's core, Jean-Paul's early experience of ficticity persists in the work of Sartre.

Feeling empty, Sartre produced imaginary beings. Lacking a bridge to others, he created stories that made connections between one episode and another, one character and another. He created what he lacked and thereby discovered that he possessed a great deal. Like Lori, he achieved a real self by telling imaginary stories.

REFERENCES

Bick, E. (1968). The experience of the skin in early object relations. *International Journal of Psychoanalysis,* 49:484–486.

Call, J. D. (1975). Hallucinosis and *The Wizard of Oz:* Psychosis in childhood. Unpublished.

Czermak, M. (1977). Sur le déclenchement des psychoses. In *Ornicar?* 9:26–28. Translated as The onset of psychosis. In *Returning to Freud,* ed. S. Schneiderman. New Haven: Yale Universities Press, 1980.

Deutsch, H. (1937). Don Quixote and Don Quixotisms. In *Neuroses and Character Types.* New York: International Universities Press.

Deutsch, H. (1942). Some forms of emotional disturbances and their relation to schizophrenia. In *Neurosis and Character Types: Clinical Psychoanalytic Studies.* New York: International Universities Press.

Deutsch, H. (1955). The impostor: Contribution to ego psychology of a type of psychopath. In *Neuroses and Character Types.* New York: International Universities Press.

Freud, A. (1936). *The Ego and the Mechanisms of Defense. Writings of Anna Freud,* vol. 2. New York: International Universities Press. 1966.

Freud, A. (1969). Answering pediatricians' questions. In *Writings of Anna Freud,* vol. 5. New York: International Universities Press.

Freud, A. and Burlingham, D. (1944). *Infants Without Families.* vol. 3, *Writings of Anna Freud.* New York: International Universities Press, 1973.

Furer, M. (1964). The development of a symbiotic psychotic boy. *The Psychoanalytic Study of the Child,* 19:448–469. New York: International Universities Press.

Galenson, E. (1980). Characteristics of psychological development during the second and third years of life. In *The Course of Life,* ed. S. I. Greenspan and G. H. Pollock. Washington, D.C.: National Institute of Mental Health.

Goldberg, A., ed. (1978). *The Psychology of the Self: A Casebook.* New York: International Universities Press.

Guntrip, H. (1968). *Schizoid Phenomena—Object Relations and the Self.* New York: International Universities Press.

Isaacs, S. (1948). The nature and function of fantasy. In *Developments in Psychoanalysis,* ed. M. Klein. London: Hogarth Press, 1952.

Kestenberg, J. (1968). Outside and inside, male and female. *Journal of the American Psychoanalytic Association,* 16:457–520.

Kohut, H. (1957). *Death in Venice* by Thomas Mann. A story about the disintegration of artistic sublimation. In *The Search for the Self,* vol. 1, ed. P. H. Ornstein. New York: International Universities Press, 1975.

Kohut, H. (1971). *The Analysis of the Self.* New York: International Universities Press.

Kohut, H. (1977). *The Restoration of the Self.* New York: International Universities Press.

Kohut, H. and Wolf, E. (1978). The disorders of the self and their treatment: An outline. *International Journal of Psycho-Analysis,* 59:413–426.

Mahler, M., Pine, F., and Bergman, A. (1975). *The Psychological Birth of the Human Infant.* New York: Basic Books.

Martin, J. (1984). Clinical contributions to the theory of the fictive personality. In: *The Annual of Psychoanalysis.* New York: International Universities Press.

Miller, J. A. (1977). Enseignements de la présentation des malades. *Ornicar?* 10:13–24. Translated as Teachings of the case presentation. In *Returning to Freud,* ed. S. Schneiderman. New Haven: Yale University Press, 1980.

Parens, H. (1980). Psychic development during the second and third years of life. In *The Course of Life,* ed. S. I. Greenspan and G. H. Pollock. Washington, D.C.: National Institute of Mental Health.

Roiphe, H. and Galenson, E. (1981). *Infantile Origins of Sexual Identity.* New York: International Universities Press.

Sartre, J. P. (1964). *The Words.* New York: Braziller.

Schneiderman, S., ed. (1980). *Returning to Freud.* New Haven: Yale University Press.

Smirnoff, V. N. (1980). The fetishistic transaction. In *Psychoanalysis in France,* ed., S. Lebovici and D. Widlöcher. New York: International Universities Press.

Tolpin, M. (1971). On the beginnings of a cohesive sense of self. *The Psychoanalytic Study of the Child,* 26:316–352. New York/Chicago: Quadrangle Press.

Winnicott, D. W. (1953). Transitional objects and transitional phenomena. In *Collected Papers.* New York: Basic Books, 1958.

Winnicott, D. W. (1958). The capacity to be alone. In *The Maturational Processes and the Facilitating Environment.* New York: International Universities Press, 1965.

Winnicott, D. W. (1960). Ego distortion in terms of true and false self. In *The Maturational Processes and the Facilitating Environment.* New York: International Universities Press, 1965.

11

Developmental Lines and Infant Assessment

Phyllis Tyson, Ph.D.

The enormous increase in attention to infancy during the last two decades coincides with an intensifying quest for developmental origins of later personality configurations. There is a growing conviction that a baby's early experience affects the development of attitudes, fears, anxieties, conflicts, wishes, expectations, and patterns of interacting with others. Wide differences between children may reflect not only their genetic and temperamental differences, but also differences in early experience with caregivers; the resultant influences on personality development in turn may affect neurobiological patterning, making it impossible later to separate the effects of earliest experiences and genetic factors (Greenacre, 1941; James, 1960). If individual differences do indeed result from divergent patterns of endowment and experience beginning from earliest infancy, questions arise as to how early divergent patterns can be identified as they emerge.

The measurement of unfolding maturational processes was begun over sixty years ago by Gesell, Cattell, and Bayley, who constructed infant tests on the presumption that the motive force of development was provided by genetic factors. A strong correlation between maturational precocity or delay and intelligence was assumed, together with a genetic conception of intelligence. The study of the development of

mental and motor competence thus dominated child psychology during the first several decades of this century. The infant was seen as a socially isolated organism impelled by inevitable maturational forces, and research was directed toward correlating developmental quotients on infant tests with later IQ scores, though with disappointing results. From a medical viewpoint, the newborn was believed to function only at a brainstem level of nervous organization (Brazelton, 1983; Peiper, 1963). Consequently, neurological examinations were stereotyped assessments of reflex behavior from which only the grossest of abnormalities were diagnosed.

In the 1940s and 50s, psychoanalytic theory, with its emphasis on the early roots of later neurosis, began to have increasing impact on the way in which the infant was viewed. Early psychoanalytic ideas gave a central role to the drives. The infant was thought to develop an attachment to his mother as a consequence of her satisfying his hunger or relieving his discomfort. Attention was therefore directed to duration of nursing, characteristics of weaning, age and method of toilet training, attitudes toward masturbation, and the like. However, with the work of Spitz, Winnicott, Bowlby, and Mahler, another shift took place. Spitz (1945), after observations of hospitalized or institutionalized children, felt that apathy, retarded development, and poor health resulted from the lack of an affectionate relationship with a specific caregiver. He concluded that an affectionate attachment to mother provided the motivation for the infant to perceive and to learn. Increasingly, psychoanalytic theory placed the child in a dyadic context in which the mother's actions were seen to be a central determinant of the child's development. Attention shifted from the child's maturational process to an emphasis on learning and on those environmental factors which influence development. Because the infant was vulnerable to trauma and distress which might later evolve to the level of a neurotic disorder, the behavior of the caregivers took on new interest. As a result assessment expanded to include emotional distress within the family, or more specifically, in the mother-child unit.

Mother's love, or the lack of it, then became the *sine qua non* for emotional health or pathology. Attention was directed to the specific problems of institutionalized children (Provence and Lipton, 1962) and to the ways in which maternal deprivation was reflected by delays in the child's ego development. Bridges between academic psychology and psychoanalysis became possible as, for example, perception, cognitive development, and language development were increasingly studied in the context of the mother-child interaction. Through the study of deviant children and their mothers it was possible to demonstrate how certain functions that were thought to have primary autonomy (Hartmann, 1939) could become secondarily disrupted (Provence and Ritvo, 1961). Other psychoanalysts (Bowlby, 1951, 1969; Mahler, 1967; Mahler et al. 1975; Winnicott, 1960, 1962, 1967) have studied the emergence of object relations. This work has extended our knowledge of the importance of the mother's attitudes and behavior to other than ego and cognitive aspects of the child—for example, to the child's emerging sense of identity, ultimate self-esteem, and sense of trust in others.

Unfortunately, the mother's role in emotional development has been occasionally overemphasized and has led to the common practice of looking to mother's failures as *the* source of psychopathology. The popularity of self psychology (Kohut, 1971, 1977) demonstrates the appeal of this position.

Researchers have now begun to redress the balance. Just as Winnicott (1960) reminded us that there was no such thing as only the baby, Bowlby (1969) reminded us that the reverse is also true. He drew attention to specific behaviors of the infant, or attachment behaviors, which engage the mother. The Brazelton Neonatal Behavior Assessment Scale (1973) evaluates the subtle ways in which the infant organizes his behavior to modify and direct the course and amount of interaction with his mother. Attachment theory is further reflected in various scales designed to assess mother/infant attachment (the Massie-Campbell Scale of Mother-Infant Attachment Indicators During Stress [Massie and Campbell, 1983], Ainsworth's [1973] graded stress as a measure of parent-infant attachment), and Call's (1980) classification of attachment disorders.

There is growing appreciation of the fact that attachment is neither a "trait" of the baby or the mother, nor is it a static product. Attachment is now more fruitfully viewed in terms of reciprocal participation rather than in terms of two individuals sending discrete messages. The human infant is born prepared for and responds as an active participant in human social interaction (Condon and Sander, 1974), and the reciprocity established has been found to be crucial for the evaluation of the infant's earliest sensorimotor adaptations.

Newer approaches to neurological assessment of the infant also reflect attention to social interaction. The infant is increasingly viewed as part of a psychobiological system, and it is understood that the integrating infant's biological/neurological equipment, or lack of it, will have a profound effect on the interaction he is able to elicit from his caregiver. The nervous system has recently been described as "an information-processing apparatus which generates activity, receives, transmits, conducts, transforms, stores and compares messages" (Prechtl, 1982, p. 29). It thereby initiates and maintains neural activity, regulates autonomic systems, adapts social behavior and interaction, seeks and regulates stimuli, and adapts behavioral states to the demands of the environment. The goal of neurological assessment, therefore, must be to identify transitory or permanent central nervous system dysfunction. Although such dysfunction may appear to be minimal, it may become more grossly manifest later, or it may influence other systems in subtle ways. For example, CNS dysfunction may undermine mother-infant reciprocity, and early identification may maximize potential through early intervention (see Parmelee and Michaelis, 1971; Prechtl, 1965; Prechtl and O'Brien, 1982; Saint-Anne Dargassies, 1979).

An ideal infant assessment, as these comments suggest, will integrate the evaluation of mental and motor competence and the intensity and level of drive organization, incorporate Hartmann's (1952) and Jacobson's (1964) concepts of ego development, include the quality of reflex behavior as modified by higher brain centers, and take account of theories of object relations and attachment. Included in this assessment will be an evaluation of the mother and the family system, as well as a recognition that the mother's and father's relationship to the examiner may influence the results. Such an integrated view obviously makes the task of assessment far more difficult. Our measuring instruments need to be broadened to include the infant's variable response to discontinuity, for normal development may frequently appear to be disrupted pathologically during periods of regression. Such episodes of discontinuity with temporary loss of equilibrium or transient symptoms resulting from developmental conflict (Nagera, 1966) may actually signify the widening of adaptive capacity (Call, 1983) and indicate an approach to a new developmental level with equilibration (Piaget, 1936).

Clearly, there is no specific, all-encompassing psychometric instrument to perform all these tasks. Instead, a broad framework is needed within which we can fit the results of our psychometric measurements, neurological examinations, behavioral observations, and personality assessments. A modification of Anna Freud's developmental lines (1965) can well provide such a framework. The idea of "developmental line" is based on an epigenetic view of psychic structure formation resulting from successive interactions between the infant's biologically and genetically determined maturational sequences, on the one hand, and experiential and environmental influences, on the other. The outcome of each developmental phase is understood to depend on the outcome of all previous phases as well as on the interactions among a variety of developmental lines.

Viewing personality development according to its simultaneous progress along several developmental lines affords a greater understanding of personality dynamics and highlights disharmony as well as harmony. Anna Freud stressed that the concept of developmental lines made it possible to make inferences about a child's inner world on the basis of observable behaviors. The broad scope of this framework makes it possible to consider the interaction of psychic structures (id, ego, superego), conscious and unconscious motivation, genetic or developmental factors, object relationships, the development of the sense of identity (including gender identity), self-esteem, physical maturation, and adaptation to the inner world and to the external environment. Mapping a person's progress along the assemblage of developmental lines conveys a convincing picture of his or her achievements or failures in personality development.

The path of development is not, of course, as straightforward and linear as the metaphor "line" might imply. Changes over time involve a number of dynamic interactions, continuities and discontinuities, transformations, progressions, and regressions. At each new stage the system, while maintaining a degree of integrity or "wholeness" (Piaget, 1968), differs qualitatively from the preceeding stage. Each new stage cannot be predicted from the sum of the parts of the preceeding stage. Emde (personal communication, 1983) has suggested that "developmental line" should be understood more in terms of spirals; analogous developmental issues are worked and reworked at successive developmental levels, but each reworking results in advances in consolidation and integration, a process implied by Piaget's notion of vertical *décalage* (Piaget, 1932, 1966). While later developmental processes repeat patterns analogous to earlier ones, accomplishments and adaptations attained on one level must be reworked and reintegrated at each successively higher level. Earlier mastery, though it may be sufficient for one stage, is not adequate to meet later internal and external demands.

Assessment of the infant and young child now becomes directed toward a consideration of the many interacting developmental lines or spirals within the young child in interaction with the developmental spirals of his parents and siblings. It goes without saying that certain developmental lines are more dependent on others for their progress, while others are genetically predetermined and less subject to influence. However, each child progresses in his own time, with his own "individual-specific response pattern" (Call, 1979), along even those "lines" which are genetically predetermined.

In conclusion, the concept of developmental lines or spirals provides a powerful framework within which a variety of measures of infant competence, maturation, and other attributes can be combined. By comparing and contrasting developmental lines over time, disharmonies, discrepancies, and incipient psychopathology within the infant or within the family system can be determined, and possibilities for more effective interaction enhanced.

REFERENCES

Ainsworth, M. D. S. (1973). The development of infant-mother attachment. In *Review of Child Development Research*, vol. 3, ed. B. M. Caldwell and H. N. Ricciuti. Chicago: University of Chicago Press.

Bowlby, J. (1951). *Maternal Care and Mental Health*. Geneva: World Health Organization.

Bowlby, J. (1969). *Attachment and Loss*, vol. 1, *Attachment*. New York: Basic Books.

Brazelton, T. B. (1973). *Neonatal Behavioral Assessment Scale*. Philadelphia: J. B. Lippincott.

Brazelton, T. B. (1983). Assessment techniques for enhancing infant development. In *Frontiers of Infant Psychiatry*, ed., J. D. Call, E. Galenson, and R. L. Tyson. New York: Basic Books.

Call, J. D. (1979). Introduction. In: *Basic Handbook of Child Psychiatry*, vol. I, ed., J. D. Noshpitz. New York: Basic Books.

Call, J. D. (1980). Attachment disorders of infancy. In *Comprehensive Textbook of Psychiatry*, vol. 3, ed., H. L. Kaplan, A. M. Freedman, and B. J. Sadock. Baltimore: William & Wilkins.

Call, J. D. (1983). Toward a nosology of psychiatric disorders in infancy. In *Frontiers of Infant Psychiatry*, ed., J. D. Call, E. Galenson, and R. L. Tyson. New York: Basic Books.

Condon, W. S. and Sander, L. (1974). Neonate movement is synchronized with adult speech: Interactional participation and language acquisition. *Science*, 183:99–101.

Freud, A. (1965), *Normality and Pathology in Childhood*. New York: International Universities Press.

Greenacre, P. (1941). The predisposition to anxiety. In *Trauma, Growth and Personality*. New York: International Universities Press. 1952.

Hartmann, H. (1939). *Ego Psychology and the Problem of Adaptation*. New York: International Universities Press, 1958.

Hartmann, H. (1952). The mutual influences in the development of ego and id. In *Essays on Ego Psychology*. New York: International Universities Press, 1964.

Jacobson, E. (1964). *The Self and the Object World*. New York: International Universities Press.

James, M. (1960). Premature ego development. *International Journal of Psycho-Analysis*, 41:288–294.

Kohut, H. (1971). *The Analysis of the Self*. New York: International Universities Press.

Kohut, H. (1977). *The Restoration of the Self*. New York: International Universities Press.

Mahler, M. (1967). On human symbiosis and the vicissitudes of individuation. *Journal of the American Psychoanalytic Association*, 23:740–763.

Mahler, M., Pine, F., and Bergman, A. (1975). *The Psychological Birth of the Human Infant*. New York: Basic Books.

Massie, H. N. and Campbell, B. K. (1983). The Massie-Campbell scale of mother-infant Attachment Indicators During Stress (AIDS Scale). In *Frontiers of Infant Psychiatry*, ed., J. D. Call, E. Galenson, and R. L. Tyson. New York: Basic Books.

Nagera, H. (1966). *Early Childhood Disturbances, the Infantile Neurosis and the Adulthood Disturbances*. New York: International Universities Press.

Parmelee, A. H. and Michaelis, R. (1971). *Neurological Examination of the Newborn Exceptional Infant*, vol. II. New York: Bruner/Mazel.

Peiper, A. (1963). *Cerebral Function in Infancy and Childhood*. New York: Consultants Bureau.

Piaget, J. (1932). Moral judgment: Children invent the social contract. In *The Essential Piaget, An Interpretive Reference and Guide*, ed. H. E. Gruber and J. J. Vonèche. New York: Basic Books.

Piaget, J. (1936). *The Origins of Intelligence in Children*. New York: W.W. Norton, 1963.

Piaget, J. (1966). Moral feelings and judgments. In *The Essential Piaget, An Interpretive Reference and Guide*, ed. H. E. Gruber and J. J. Vonèche. New York: Basic Books.

Piaget, J. (1968). *Structuralism*. New York: Basic Books, 1970.

Prechtl, H. F. R. (1965). Problems of behavioural studies in the newborn infant. In *Advances in the Study of Behavior*, ed., D. S. Lehrman, R. A. Hinde, and E. Shaw. New York: Academic Press.

Prechtl, H. F. R. (1982). Assessment methods for the newborn infant: A critical evaluation. In *Psychobiology of the Human Newborn,* ed., P. Stratton. New York: John Wiley.

Prechtl, H. F. R. and O'Brien, M. J. (1982). Behavioural states of the full-term newborn—The emergence of a concept. In *Psychobiology of the Human Newborn,* ed., P. Stratton. New York: John Wiley.

Provence, S. and Lipton, R. C. (1962). *Infants in Institutions.* New York: International Universities Press.

Provence, S. and Ritvo, S. (1961). Effects of deprivation on institutionalized infants: Disturbances in development of relationship to inanimate objects. *The Psychoanalytic Study of the Child,* 16:189–205. New York: International Universities Press.

Saint Anne-Dargassies, S. (1979). The normal and abnormal neurological examination of the neonate: Silent neurological abnormalities. In *Advances in Perinatal Neurology,* vol. 1, ed. R. Korobkin and C. Guilleminault. New York: Medical and Scientific Books.

Spitz, R. A. (1945). Hospitalism: An inquiry into the genesis of psychiatric conditions in early childhood. *The Psychoanalytic Study of the Child,* 1:53–72. New York: International Universities Press.

Winnicott, D. W. (1960). Ego distortion in terms of true and false self. In *The Maturational Processes and the Facilitating Environment.* New York: International Universities Press, 1965.

Winnicott, D. W. (1962). The theory of the parent-infant relationship. *International Journal of Psycho-Analysis,* 43: 238–239.

Winnicott, D. W. (1967). Mirror-role of mother and family in child development. In *Playing and Reality.* New York: Basic Books, 1971.

12

Survey of the Infant's "Sound Envelope" and Organization of Parent-Infant Communication

Jacqueline Rabain-Jamin

The early mother-infant relationship has most often been considered to be a dyad, and study of the involved interactions has taken into consideration neither the time and place of the relationship nor its implied social context.

This relationship is paradoxical for it appears to be culture-free. For this reason, all societies have codified and tried to ritualize the caregiving relationship (Héritier, 1977: Rabain, 1979). In fact, this relationship brings us face to face with our own origins. It reveals what is usually hidden: the naked body, the influence of corporality, primary excitability, and erogeneity.

Language, through rules and cultural reverberations, mediates the mother-infant relationship. Similarly, the characteristic sounds, rhythm, and materiality of the caregiver's words respond to the infant's body expressions —indeed, they act as a sort of *verbal mirror.*

The mother, vocally as well as with support and contact, echoes her infant's excitation, which is expressed through the infant's motility, tonicity, mouth activity, lip vibrations, sighs, breathing, and so forth. The mother responds with body contact as well as through sight, hearing, and speech. She solicits

the infant's attention and replies to his or her first vocalizations. These first vocalizations are still largely expressions of body excitement, but they already exhibit an incipient organization of linguistic communication: through the sounds the infant emits and attempts to master and to reproduce, the infant seeks to interact with surrounding people.

With regard to the acquisition of language by infants, interest in maternal vocalizations initially emphasized deformations in conventional syntax; the focus of interest shifted subsequently toward the study of onomatopeias, intensity of voice variation, modulation, and nonsense sounds.

Stern (1977) studied maternal vocalizations within the framework of what he called "infant-elicited social behaviors." He described the syncopated mother-infant training by characteristics of rhythm, timbre, and vocal accentuations, one of whose poles (the effect induced by the infant in the mother) has long been underestimated. He pointed out that the mother's expressions and vocalizations are part of a pattern of signs and postural expressions. The bodily impulses coming from the infant (for example, the agitation of legs and arms, acceleration of breathing, intensity of look, and so forth) trigger captivating images in the mother's mind, which in turn elicit words. These words shape or contain the baby's "emotion" and are an outlet for infant-triggered "excitation" in the mother.

I intend to describe certain types of infant-mother interactions: specifically, the mother's playful addresses. I consider these to be a response created by the interaction between mother and infant in which one or the other becomes carried away by the rhythm of these corporeal or linguistic exchanges. Thus an area is created for play and cultural expression. This area permits the relationship between mother and infant to go beyond a traditional subject/object duality. This playful space constitutes a separate field for both mother and infant, within which the so-called "fantasying interaction"[1] (Kreisler and Cramer, 1981; Lebovici, 1983) may be given shape through a codified formula. *More* precisely, maternal language borrows fragments from popular or family mythology and leads to fantasy creation through a series of transformations. The evolving of this area enables the infant to adapt to the rules underlying linguistic activity.

I shall deal with three aspects of playful address: *the associative or incantatory aspect,* which obeys the rules of combination, variation, and transformation of sounds and signifiers (as opposed to the signified, according to Saussure's (1915) classic distinction); *disparaging forms of address,* which obey the rules of metaphor and metonymy; and *the pronominal aspect,* which obeys the rules of substitution between the pronouns: I, you, she, he, *on* (in English "we," "let's," "that's").

My hypothesis is that these three aspects define stages or references for symbolization—they are at the origin of language acquisition. By moving on from mere response or simple sonorous accompaniment (nonsense sounds, onomatopoeias) to direct address and metaphoric and metonymic designation (gibes, abuse, insults usually derived from animals,

allegorical or emblematic reproaches) and from thence to pronominal substitutions, the mother's language goes from the verbal image of the words to their rules of agreement, that is, from the specific (factual) to the general (the structural). Of course, these aspects are isolated for the purpose of analysis and in reality may be present in the same statement or behavior.

The data used here comes from the analysis of recordings of the language employed by French mothers (or fathers) to address their infants. Ten infant-mother pairs were observed at home between birth and twenty months.

The Associative or Incantatory Aspect

Much mother-infant verbal communication does not seem to serve a direct purpose in the sense of being a message that the mother is attempting to convey. As Stern (1977) noted, the quality of the produced sounds is more important than the content of the statement. Scansion[2] or rhythmic patterning is introduced by a series of distinct onomatopoeias, by progressive and repeated sequences, that is, thematic variations. Thus, rhythmic patterning is induced in the infant by the adult's responses to the infant's nonverbal expressions.

Through phonic variations and prosodic features (Garnica, 1977)—interrogative modulations, musical voice-playing on sounds such as in poetry or play on words—the mother's language constitutes from the beginning a rhythmic and sonorous envelope in the same way that body contact defines the body boundary, supports it, smooths it. The mother's language sets the tonality and the tempo of this sonorous envelope.

In the case of the young infant, the cadence of the mother's vocalizations is obviously closely linked to the baby's body movements; indeed, it may be said to give form, sound, and

---

[1]This term is a literal translation of the French expression "interaction fantasmatique" (Kreisler and Cramer, 1981, p. 243) which refers to the projective identification of the mother on her infant.

[2]Scansion, often used, for example, in the study of Greek and Latin poetry, is finding rhythmical groups in phrases.

even verbal expression to them. The caregiver tends to reflect the infant's body states and actions by systemizing responses in an incantatory way. The content of what is said is less important than the *sound effect of complicity.* These sound effects may be self-contained (only accompanying or amplifying) or may shift toward symbolization and the emblematic. Thus, a father echoes the gurgling sounds of his six-week-old child. The father's noises soon sound like a wild boar's grunts. The wild boar has an emblematic value for this father who was born in the Ardennes[3]. Hence for the father, what was initially mere sonority or simple body noises still closely linked to libidinal experience comes to meet a chain of significance and takes on an allegorical meaning referring to paternal origins. This noise, in fact, suggests an entire tradition, an original culture in which the wild boar is the symbol of a region of France. A basis of identification, a coat of arms or seal in heraldic terms, is reflected to the child. It makes him a subject within a genealogy as well as within a territory. It states in few words where the child comes from.

I have emphasized the nonverbal aspect of the sounds the father used. The father's noises in reply to the baby's grunts and movements are closer to the body than to language as they combine cultural and biological heredity.

In general terms, the "reduction" of language to what seems to be its incipient appearance is by no means a secondary or negligible phenomenon. The materiality of language, what Barthes (1982) called *"le grain de la voix"* (the texture of the voice) conveys pleasure. The child is able to make the sounds, re-create an aspect of the parent's presence, and identify with the parent by playing with sounds.

Disparaging Forms of Address

Noises, incomplete or attempted sounds, word images, isolated, sometimes deformed words together form a shifting, permeable field, which nevertheless constitutes the foun-

dation for the ultimate elaboration of metaphor and metonymy. In emblematic or allegoric reprimands (for example: "You wave your arms like a wind mill") a physical characteristic, a gesture, a mimicry, or an attitude of the child comes to stand out and emerges from mere tactile participation as a sign, henceforth designated by a metaphoric expression. The infant's body, probably because of its powerful capacity to generate or trigger fantasy, may reactivate a genealogical memory. Contact, care, and meals have not only phantasmic but also social and cultural connotations.

Besides allegorical language, I have also studied the range of disparaging terms which have, until now, been neglected; yet extreme words exist in all cultures and envelop the child.

Everyday language contains a series of demeaning terms which the caregiver uses to upbraid the child. However, the tone of voice prevents any ambiguity: the "abused" child is in no way rejected. These "insults" often consist of slang expressions for filthiness, names of household or farm animals, or obsolete insults.

These terms of address are usually not employed with children under three months of age, and they may be used well beyond the first year. They are not only employed during washing and dressing but also to seal and celebrate the return of a parent after a separation as well as during body contact or playfully to penalize a transgression. The insult or demeaning word (for example: pig, toad, idiot, scoundrel) seems to be a maternal or paternal prerogative and is part of a common cultural heritage. It is noteworthy that these abuses are usually addressed in the presence of others—they are the opposite of the whispered intimate word.

Rather than investigate the aspect alluded to: oral (glutton, greedy), anal (pig, slime) or reflective (emphasizing deformity or clumsiness: camel, monster) it seems more pertinent to study the sequence containing the abuse. My hypothesis is that the employed term positively underlines the intensity and tempo of the relationship. Many of these abuses are used in order to gain control over the child. This is in part an intrusion, a physical influence (the child will later on be able to reply with a game of running away). The invective an-

---

[3]The wild boar is the eponym of the inhabitants of the Ardennes (in the northeastern section of France).

nounces or delays this moment of contact (the evoked verbal image remains heavily saturated with motor and visual elements) as though recovery of the child should be preceded by recovery of speech. Elsewhere, the insult appears as an interruption or follow-up during body contact or just before the caregiver leaves the child. Moreover, the insult and rather intimate remark alternate and eliminate all distance within the same animated crescendo. By way of example: after washing and changing eight-month-old Eric, his mother tickles his foot and whispers, "Eat the little foot." Then, while kissing Eric's foot, says: "Mother is going to eat Eric, all of Eric." Later, after having played with Eric on her lap, she gets up, throws him up in the air, and shouts: "The crab, the lobster, anything you like, that! Throw it away! Throw it away!" These statements reverberate in a symmetric and complementary relationship (swallow/reject—food/waste) as though the fantasy of reincorporation can only be resolved through its opposite: the playful rejection (Winnicott, 1949). This basic alternative also corresponds to the two poles of the feeding child's experience (absorbing food/excreting).

The extreme verbal form is a way of qualifying the relationship induced by the situation rather than by the protagonists, in particular the baby. It tends to ward off the anxiety of abandonment by provoking a state of animation and by allowing for the expression of playful aggression.

The insult or demeaning remark is a sign of intimacy, of an unshakeable link. Only a parent can take care of "filthiness," enjoy a "sloppy kiss," and permit herself or himself to describe them as such, that is, almost as insults or abuse which, when uttered, paradoxically underline the intensity of the parent's affective investment. The proffered insult comes, in fact, to signify the intimacy and strength of the bond. The insult testifies to complicity as did the accompanying sound effects.

It is also noteworthy that the insult is in tune with the impulses through the paradoxical expression of "rejection" and echoes the autoerotic joy the child takes in his own body. It is important that the mother's more or less active participation in this process appear culturally

coded as an insult, admitting thereby the "archaic" by converting the undifferentiated ("filthiness") into reality, and establishing a limit or barrier through publicizing of the well-known (insults spoken at large).

THE PRONOMINAL ASPECT

Abuse, gibes, and allegorical names refer to a particular lexicon, which is peculiar to a given subject born in a certain family and belonging to a certain culture. We go from the specific to the general when dealing with the game of pronominal substitution in maternal language. Here, we encounter the grammatical skeleton, the general rule. The child spoken to is a potential speaker.

The mother's use of "he," "she," "we," "let's," "that's," and the French *on* to address her baby instead of "you" has long puzzled researchers. Wills (1977) notes that this usage appears to obscure the distinction between speaker and listener, between the subject and the group to which the subject belongs, whereas pronouns are usually used to accentuate the identity of the actors and facilitate role differentiation. However, the context of the play within which the mother uses these pronouns must make us wary of premature conclusions.

By recording maternal vocalizations during the first year of the child's life and studying them in context, we have noted the following:

1. The pronominal aspect is subject to substitution. The mother rapidly goes from "you" to "we," "let's," "that's," "she," "he," and back. When analyzing these possible transformations, it is necessary also to include the pronominal form "I." The mother may pretend to yield her assertive attitude by using the "I" in the child's place, for example, "Oh aren't I stretching!" (in French: *"Oh, je m'étire, moi"*), or "Oh, aren't I strong!" (in French: *"Oh, je suis fort, moi"*).

2. Use of "he," "she," "we," "let's," "that's," *(on)* instead of "you," differs in frequency. Those mothers who use them rarely, do so most often during intimate moments (for example, during baby's bath).

3. When used, the indefinite form *on*

("that's," "we," "let's") instead of "you" appears most often during the first months. Use seems to decrease after nine to ten months. "He" or "she," when used instead of "you," is often conjugated with demonstrative markers, for example: "He's a bad baby, that one is!" or "Oh! that's a bad baby," (in French: *"Il est vilain ce bébé-là!"*) and is used longer than the form "I."

4. As far as semantic relations are concerned, there seems to be little difference between use of the third person (and first person plural English) and the second person in order to address the baby. Substitution or conversion of one into the other seems to depend on the intensity and tempo of the mother-baby interaction, that is, it seems to depend on extralinguistic criteria. The pronoun *on* is most often used in order to evoke a body state or an action. It appears when the situation is less tense after the emergency where the appropriate response would be "you," for example: "We're angry!" (in French: *"On est en colère!"*) "We're upset!" (in French: *"On s'énerve!"*) "We're rubbing our eyes!" (in French: *"On se frotte les yeux!"*) "We don't sleep!" (in French: *"On dort pas!"*) "What do we want?" (in French: *"Qu'est-ce qu'on veut?"*). "You" points to the baby's perceptive activity or his specific actions.

Phrases introduced by *on* or "you" are not formally distinct. The circumstances under which they appear differ. In this way, the alternate play of "you" and "we," "let's," or "that's" can vary as well as govern the same syntagma: "You're asleep" (in French: *"Tu fais dodo"*) "We're asleep" (in French: *"On fait dodo"*). as a function of perceptible temporality (baby-induced) and as a function of rhetoric (mother-induced). A concurrence of body time and story time is sought by using "we," "let's," "that's." Going from "you" to "we" corresponds to passing from a mood of direct address or interrogation to a mood of representation.

Thus, "you" is used to designate a precise act ("You sneeze," "You're slipping about,"). In this way, the many questions regarding the visual attention and direction of gazing in the three- to four-month-old appear in the "you" form ("What are you looking at?"). The

mother tries to join, to "catch up with" the infant's fleeting interest. When the mother uses "we," "let's," "that's," or "he," "she," "it" in order to tell or ask the infant what he or she is seeing (a rather rare form), she expresses complicity: "Ah! We saw the telly!" "What has she seen, my angel?"

5. "We," "let's," "that's," "he," "she," "it" refer to the potentially social. Because of their precise aspect, "I" and "you" do not escape arbitrariness, whereas the other pronouns refer to a third party, who symbolizes the social group and certifies and validates the baby's experience.

The mother's use of *on* to address her baby is similar to its employment in adult conversations in certain French public places (markets, *cafés,* and so forth), where it is permissible to express familiarity (Lindenfeld, 1978). The pronoun *on* also appears in the relationship between nurse and patient. The French indefinite pronoun *on* does not imply speaker-listener confusion. It is a sign of existing social consensus.

6. "I" emphasizes the child's (fictive) presence in his speech. The mother appears to yield her assertive attitude, while the "I" is actually the subject of the statement. It is a complementary form of *on* insofar as the same consensus of opinion is achieved. The child's granted characteristic, the emphatically evoked action, refers to a well-known picture, to a social make-believe, to a strong semiological fabric.

7. It is paradoxical that the third person (and in English the first person plural) is used by the mother during intimacy as well as when social background is underlined or emphasized. A third party is referred to when the body is invested. This address, more than any other, enables babies to adapt to their own body. This is partly due to the approbation given to their feelings and partly due to the produced entry into physical space/time.

From this point of view, "I" and "you" have more immediate, more temporary expressive values. "We," "let's," "that's," (*on*), "he," "she," "it" are closer to narrative forms and insert what is happening into a temporal continuity: they are already the voice of the story.

The active adaptation of the child's states and actions depends on the mother's caregiving. The child perceives reality as bearing a value coming from maternal investment. Children can only reappropriate the reflection they get from what they express to others. Mother-infant recognition takes place within a play of sounds and words and, initially, body contact. Through noises, nonsense ounds, the subtle passage from "he" or "she" to "you" and from *on* ("we," "let's," "that's,") to "I," the parent, in fact, rediscovers his or her own process of language acquisition.

REFERENCES

Barthes, R. (1982). *L'Obvie et l'Obtus.* Paris: Seuil.

Garnica, O. K. (1977). Some prosodic and paralinguistic features of speech to young children. In *Talking to Children: Language Input and Acquisition,* ed. C. E. Snow and C. A. Ferguson. Cambridge, England: Cambridge University Press.

Héritier, F. (1977). L'Identité samo. In *L'Identité. Séminaire dirigé par Claude Lévi-Strauss.* Paris: Grasset.

Kreisler, L. and Cramer, B. (1981). Sur les bases cliniques de la psychiatrie du nourrisson. *La Psychiatrie de l'Enfant,* 24:223–263.

Lebovici, S. (1983). *Le Nourrisson, la Mère et le Psychanalyste.* Paris: Le Centurion.

Lindenfeld, J. (1978). Communicative patterns at French market places. *Semiotica,* 23:279–290.

Rabain, J. (1979). *L'Enfant du lignage. Du Sevrage à la Classe d'Age chez les Wolof du Sénégal.* Paris: Payot.

Saussure, F. (1915). *Course in General Linguistics.* New York: McGraw-Hill, 1966.

Stern, D. N. (1977). *The First Relationship: Infant and Mother.* Cambridge: Harvard University Press.

Wills, D. D. (1977). Participant deixis in English and baby talk. In *Talking to Children: Language Input and Acquisition,* ed. C. E. Snow and C. A. Ferguson. Cambridge, England: Cambridge University Press.

Winnicott, D. W. (1949). Hate in the counter-transference. In *Collected Papers.* New York: Basic Books, 1958.

13

The Relationship Between Infant-Parent Attachment and the Ability to Tolerate Brief Separation at Six Years

Jude Cassidy, M.A. and Mary Main, Ph.D.

A crucial aspect of healthy functioning in children and adults is the ability to tolerate separation and aloneness. Clinicians working within a variety of theoretical frameworks have agreed that this ability is anchored in a history of confident knowledge that a sensitively responsive attachment figure will be available when needed (Bowlby, 1969, 1973; Freud and Burlingham, 1943; Mahler et al., 1975).

Bowlby has built his attachment theory around thinking of this sort. A relationship with an attachment figure who provides true physical and emotional security is seen as creating an inner sense of confidence in the child which he or she can call upon in situations in which that attachment figure is not actually present. Bowlby stated that "when an individual is confident that an attachment figure will be available to him whenever he desires it, that person will be much less prone to either intense or chronic fear than will an individual who for any reason has no such confidence" (1973, p. 202).

Mahler's extensive observations also support the view that the child's ability to tolerate separation is dependent on the history of the mother-child relationship. She states that a relationship in which the mother is "consistently emotionally available" promotes "independence and autonomous functioning [by building] basic trust, confidence in mother and others, and sound secondary narcissism" (Mahler et al., 1975, p. 115).

And, of course, Winnicott dealt directly with this issue in his classic paper, "The Capacity to be Alone."

Maturity and the capacity to be alone imply that the individual has had the chance through good-enough mothering to build up a belief in a benign environment. . . . Gradually the ego-supportive environment is introjected and built into the individual's personality, so that there comes about a capacity actually to be alone. Even so, theoreti-

Funding for different portions of our six-year longitudinal study came from the Grant Foundation, the Alvin Nye Main Foundation, the Society for Research in Child Development, the Institute of Human Development at Berkeley, and Bio-Medical Support Grants 1-444036-32024 and 1-444036-32025. We thank Donna Weston, Carol George, Nancy Kaplan, Bonnie Powers, Ellen Richardson, Judith Solomon, Jackolyn Stadtman, and Stewart Wakeling for their valuable assistance.

cally, there is always someone present, someone who is equated ultimately and unconsciously with the mother. (1958, pp. 32–36)

These theoreticians not only predict healthy separation for children with confidence in a secure attachment figure but also difficulty with separation for children who lack this confidence. For example, Bowlby suggests that a child with "no confidence that his attachment figures will be accessible and responsive to him when he wants them . . . [adopts] a strategy of remaining in close proximity to them in order so far as possible to ensure that they will be available" (1973, p. 213). Mahler's observations led her to similar conclusions:

Maternal unavailability made the practicing and exploratory period of such children rather brief and subdued. Never certain of their mother's availability and thus always preoccupied with it, they found it difficult to invest libido in their surroundings and in their own functioning. After a brief spurt of practicing, they would return to their mother, with ever greater intensity and attempt by all possible means to engage her. (1975, p. 81)

Similarly, Anna Freud reported that "the child is all the more clinging, the more he has an inner conviction that separation will repeat itself" (Freud and Burlingham, 1944, p. 591). The home observations of Ainsworth and her colleagues (1978) provide data for this connection. Mother-infant interaction was observed for a period of approximately seventy-two hours over the first year of life in a sample of twenty-six infants. Infants who experienced insensitive or unresponsive mothering were less able than other infants to tolerate brief separations in the home by twelve months. These babies protested when their mothers left the room even in the course of daily activities.

In the late 1970s, Main and Weston undertook the first stages of study of the social development of a large number of white middle-class families residing in the Bay Area of California (the Berkeley Social Development Project). The early stages of the project included assessments of the quality of the infants' relationships to mother at twelve

months of age and to father at eighteen months. The assessment procedure used was the Ainsworth Strange Situation (Ainsworth and Wittig, 1969). The 20-minute procedure contains episodes during which the mother and a female "stranger" alternately leave and return to the baby who remains in a laboratory room containing an attractive pile of toys. There are two pre-separation episodes, two separations from mother, and two episodes of mother-baby reunion.

Ainsworth originally used this procedure at the end of her longitudinal Baltimore study; individual differences in infant response to the Ainsworth Strange Situation could be described as reflecting secure vs. insecure attachment. Infants who avoided mother on reunion were called insecure/avoidant; infants angry with mother on reunion were called insecure/resistant; and infants who sought proximity or interaction and seemed neither highly angry nor highly resistant were called securely attached. Examination of narrative records of the behavior of the original twenty-three infant-mother pairs in the home situation showed a strong relationship between security of attachment as assessed in the separation-reunion assessment and maternal sensitivity and responsiveness as observed in the home (Ainsworth et al., 1978).

Two recent studies have corroborated the positive relationship between "security of attachment," as assessed on the basis of the infant's response to this procedure, and maternal sensitivity and responsiveness to the signals and communications of the infant, as observed in the home environment (Belsky et al., in press; Grossmann and Grossman, in preparation). Laboratory studies have also shown a connection between secure attachment and maternal sensitivity (Main et al., 1979; Matas et al., 1978; Smith and Pederson, 1983).

Method

In 1982, the children who had been in the first group of babies seen in the Strange Situation at the Berkeley Social Development Project were nearing six years of age. During the course of a multifaceted follow-up project, we had the opportunity to observe the relationship between early assessments of attachment and the ability to tolerate a brief separation at six years of age. The question addressed was: Are children who are secure with mother at twelve months of age as assessed through this laboratory technique more likely to tolerate a brief laboratory separation at six years of age than children judged insecure in the same setting?

The Ainsworth classification system is based primarily, but not entirely, on infant behavior during the two parent-baby reunion episodes. Securely attached babies show strong initial proximity-seeking, or at least interaction-seeking, on reunion. They tend actively to seek contact from the parent and to strive to maintain it. They cuddle in and find the parent to be a source of comfort. Once comforted, they are able to use the parent as a "secure base from which to explore" and return to play with the toys.

Insecurely attached babies show quite different patterns of reunion behavior. The largest number of insecurely attached babies are quite avoidant on reunion. They either turn away or actively move away from the parent. They play busily with the toys throughout much of the reunion, seemingly finding this of greater interest than the parent's return. If the parent calls them or invites them to approach, they tend to ignore her altogether. If picked up, they hold their bodies away and are quick to initiate release.

A second group of insecurely attached babies is classified as resistant and ambivalent. They might repeatedly alternate contact-seeking with struggles to be put down. Angry, resistant behaviors, such as throwing toys or hitting mother, characterize these babies. These babies are inconsolable, and contented play with the toys is delayed significantly if not altogether.

The secure, the insecure/avoidant, and the insecure/resistant categories make up the original Ainsworth classification system. In addition, Main and Weston (1981) reported that within the Berkeley sample some 14 percent of the babies did not fall into any of the categories

described by Ainsworth but seemed insecure in their attachment relationships. They called these babies insecure/unclassified. A large proportion of insecure/unclassified babies were deliberately included in the present follow-up study.

While several studies have shown significant stability of attachment classification to the *same* parent throughout the second year for white middle-class samples (Connell, 1976; Main and Weston, 1981; Waters, 1978), the quality of the infant's attachment relationship to one parent is independent of that to his or her other parent (Grossmann et al., 1981; Lamb, 1977; Main and Weston, 1981). Quality of attachment reflects the history of a specific relationship and thus characterizes not the child but the child's relation with a particular parent.

The present sample of thirty-seven children was selected from the larger sample assembled in the course of Main's previous research. All children came from intact families and white middle-class homes. Selection from the larger sample was deliberately used to provide a close to equal representation of children whose attachment relationships to mother at twelve months had been judged secure ($n = 14$), insecure/avoidant ($n = 10$), insecure/resistant ($n = 2$), and insecure/unclassified ($n = 11$). Each child was also assessed for security of attachment to father at eighteen months of age, but attachment to father (20 secure, 11 avoidant, 1 resistant, and 5 insecure/unclassified) was not a basis of sample selection. There were few insecure/resistant babies in the larger sample, and only three were available for this first follow-up—two with mother and one with father. There had been, of course, too many of the securely attached group to include them all in the first year of follow-up, and a random selection was made.

The children, now approaching six years, came to the laboratory with their parents for a series of videotaped assessments which lasted approximately two hours. The separation came after an extended familiarization period with the room and the adult playmate in the presence of the parents. Midway through the visit, following a period when the parents and child had been alone in the room eating a snack, there was a prearranged knock on the door.

This was a signal for the parents to give the child paper and colored pens, request that he draw a picture of anything he liked, and explain that they had to leave for a while but that the familiar adult playmate would join the child "in a minute."

We saw this separation as a nonthreatening situation for several reasons: (1) it lasted only one minute; (2) the children had been in the same room with their parents for almost an hour; and (3) these kindergarten-aged children had all faced longer daily separations.

The data consisted of approximately two minutes of videotape for each child—the minute during which the parents were in the room announcing and preparing for the separation and the minute during which the child was alone in the room. We combined these two minutes to form a measure of the child's reaction to the process of being left, and in particular to being briefly left *alone* by the parents. One coder, blind to earlier attachment classification, noted the presence or absence of disturbance related to the separation or to preparation for the separation for all children. In order to assess intercoder agreement, a second coder, also blind to earlier attachment classification, coded twenty-one randomly selected separations. The two coders agreed for twenty of the twenty-one children.

Results

As we expected, most children showed no disturbance. When their parents gave them the drawing materials, they moved easily to the new activity. Some responded with brief curiosity about the separation, that is, "Where are you going?" Most children said good-bye and eagerly turned to the attractive array of bright marking pens, then spent the minute alone focused on their new task, drawing with active involvement.

While most children showed no disturbance, children who had been securely attached to mother at twelve months were better able to tolerate this brief laboratory separation than were those who had been insecurely attached to mother. Only two of the fourteen securely attached children (14 percent) seemed disturbed by the separation. One boy muttered angrily, "I want to go home," as his parents were leaving. This was the only child in the sample who showed direct anger. Another securely attached child was considered distressed because he stared vacantly around the room during the separation; he seemed unable to focus his attention.

On the other hand, eleven of the twenty-three children who had been insecurely attached to mother at twelve months showed a kind of anxious response to separation. For the previously insecure children, distress during the parents' leave-taking took the form of crying, clinging, agitated pleading with the parents not to leave, or requests to accompany the parents. One child burst into tears. One child said worriedly, "I hope I'm safe." One child became quite agitated, jumped up, and said, "Stay with me." One child followed his parents to the door, and pulling strongly on his father's arm, repeatedly pleaded with him not to leave. When his parents left, he stood in the middle of the room and stared at the door while whispering to himself and twisting his arms together. This child's distress was so great that the separation was terminated and the adult playmate returned after a few seconds.

Thus, there was a striking difference between the two attachment groups in their abilities to tolerate this brief laboratory separation. Only 14 percent of the children who had been secure with mother at twelve months showed distress on separation, and in one case the distress was qualitatively distinct from others (the direct expression, "I want to go home"). On the other hand, nearly half the children (48 percent) who had been classified as insecurely attached to mother at twelve months showed some difficulty with separation at six years of age. This included four of the ten children who had been insecure/avoidant with mother at twelve months,—children who in infancy had shown little or no distress upon separation. A chi-square test showed a significant difference between children who had been securely attached to mother as babies and children who had been insecurely attached $(X^2 (1) = 4.30, p < .05)$. There was no relationship between early security of attachment to father and separation behavior. Seven of the twenty babies securely attached to father (35 percent) and six of the seventeen babies insecurely attached to father (35 percent) showed disturbance related to separation (X^2 (1) = .09, ns.). There were no sex differences.

We used the Ainsworth Strange Situation procedure to represent individual differences in experiences of ready accessibility and responsiveness of mother during the first year of life. To the extent that this procedure accurately represents such early experience, our

findings suggest that ready accessibility does not result in heightened sensitivity to separation and the need for the parent to stay with the child. Rather, it seems that this accessibility provides the child with a basic trust that enables tolerance of separation at five years, at least in our brief laboratory setting. Our findings lend support to the assertion that "an unthinking confidence in the unfailing accessibility and support of attachment figures is the bedrock on which stable and self-reliant personality is built" (Bowlby, 1973, p. 322).

REFERENCES

Ainsworth, M., Blehar, M., Waters, E., and Wall, S. (1978). *Patterns of Attachment.* Hillsdale, New Jersey: Lawrence Erlbaum Associates.

Ainsworth, M.D. and Wittig, B. (1969). Attachment and exploratory behavior of one-year olds in a strange situation. In *Determinants of Infant Behavior,* vol. IV. ed. B.M. Foss, London: Methuen.

Belsky, J., Rovine, M., and Taylor, D. (in press). The origins of individual differences in infant-mother attachment: maternal and infant contributions. *Child Development.*

Bowlby, J. (1969). *Attachment and Loss,* vol. 1, *Attachment.* New York: Basic Books.

Bowlby, J. (1973). *Attachment and Loss,* vol. 2, *Separation: Anxiety and Anger.* New York: Basic Books.

Connell, D.B. (1976). Individual differences in attachment: An investigation into stability, implications, and relationships to structure of early language development. Unpublished manuscript.

Freud, A. and Burlingham, D. (1944). *Infants without Families. Writings of Anna Freud.* vol. 3, New York: International Universities Press, 1973.

Grossmann, K. and Grossmann, K. E. (in preparation). Maternal sensitivity and newborn orienting response as related to quality of attachment in northern Germany.

Grossmann, K. E., Grossmann, K., Huber, F., and Wartner, U. (1981). German children's behavior toward their mothers at 12 months and their fathers at 18 months in

Ainsworth's Strange Situation. *International Journal of Behavioral Development,* 4:157–181.

Lamb, M. E. (1977). Father-infant and mother-infant interaction in the first year of life. *Child Development,* 48: 167–181.

Mahler, M., Pine, F., and Bergman, A. (1975). *The Psychological Birth of the Human Infant.* New York: Basic Books.

Main, M., Tomasini, L., and Tolan, B. (1979). Differences among mothers of infants judged to differ in security. *Developmental Psychology,* 15:472–473.

Main, M. and Weston, D. (1981). The quality of the toddler's relationship to mother and to father: Related to conflict behavior and the readiness to establish new relationships. *Child Development,* 52:932–940.

Matas, L., Arend, R., and Sroufe, L.A. (1978). Continuity of adaptation in the second year: The relationship between quality of attachment and later competence, *Child Development,* 49:547–556.

Smith, P. and Pederson, D. (1983). Maternal sensitivity and patterns of infant-mother attachment. Presented at the meetings of the Society for Research in Child Development. April.

Waters, E. (1978). The reliability and stability of individual differences in infant-mother attachment. *Child Development,* 49:483–494.

Winnicott, D.W. (1958). The capacity to be alone. In *The Maturational Processes and the Facilitating Environment.* New York: International Universities Press, 1965.

14

The Boston University Longitudinal Study: Prospect and Retrospect After Twenty-Five Years

Louis W. Sander, M.D.

The Boston University Longitudinal Study was begun in 1954 by Dr. Eleanor Pavenstedt for the purpose of illuminating the art of taking histories for child-psychiatry trainees. Illustration and demonstration of those aspects of the child's early relationships and developmental history that must be included in an intake anamnesis were felt to be sorely needed. What *are* the details of the mother-infant relationship at different ages in a sample of normal families, and how can they be elicited? What variations do they show over time, and how does the interviewer gain access to them? The study was designed around the systematic selection of mothers from the prenatal clinic of a general hospital, so that the effect of differences in maternal character might be traced to their expression in caregiving behavior. The mother-infant pairs were then followed to the point in the development of the personality of these firstborn children when they reached the first grade of school. Simple criteria in the selection of the sample eliminated families with severe psychopathology or serious disturbance in family organization. It turned out that the sample was a highly stable one. Now after twenty-five years, with a gap in contact of al-

most twenty years, twenty-nine of the original thirty families are all living within approximately fifty miles of the subjects' birthplace. Clearly, the sample has represented a specific cohort in time over a particular two-decade history of the city of Boston. Such a cohort can never be replicated, nor can this two-decade history ever be repeated—another feature of uniqueness in long-term longitudinal study that shapes and constrains the questions we can ask and the generalizability of findings.

As social and economic climates have dramatically changed, intervening and contextual variables have demanded greater attention. As the phenomenon of the "invulnerable child," or the "superphrenics" of which Anthony speaks, has become more widely appreciated, a wider perspective of the richness of possible developmental solutions offered by a given environment has become evident. There is a new challenge to define which elements show continuity, which show change, and which become transformed in the developmental course. Interest in development as a life-span process is stimulating a search for new understanding of developmental potential at the distal end of the life span. One can wonder if there are general principles that will allow us to appreciate common organizing processes at the two poles of the lifespan.

As we have amassed detailed information on the long-term picture for each of the subjects in our sample, each child and family and twenty-five-year history is strikingly different. It is clear we begin with a unique infant, having a unique mother and a unique father, in a unique family system, each system with its unique dynamics, and each proceeding via a sequence of unique vicissitudes and changes in organization over the years, obviously leading to the life and organization of a unique individual at outcome. Given the full detailed data on a sample of nearly thirty unique lives that have been lived over their first twenty-five years, what are our questions? It is not in jest that the central question in a study of this duration and this detail on a sample of this relatively small size is, What is the question? Will it concern itself with cause or with process, with what can be found that is common among the subjects or with what differentiates them?

Many escape addressing this kind of challenge to understanding by limiting research to early development, but one can never escape the uncertainty that always plays on the long-term outcome of children so studied. What makes some life courses seem so predictable and others so vulnerable to the unexpected? It is conceivable, then, that even in as small a sample as some thirty families, such a long-term follow-up can give us a feeling for variety, similarity, and idiosyncrasy of the longer-term developmental process. It may allow us to formulate a different set of principles for the long term that can give perspective to the early developmental course. We have felt, at least, that it should provide an opportunity to develop a systematic method of description that will be comparable across cases.

The initial data of the Boston University Longitudinal Study was gathered by a large multidisciplinary team using naturalistic observation in the home and clinic, developmental testing, interviewing, systematic play observation, and pediatric examination. The most intensive data extended from the prenatal period to approximately forty months of age and was based on contacts with the subject or fam-

ily every two weeks over this time. A similar intensity characterized the initial outcome study during the first grade at school. Some idea of the extensiveness of the data over only the first twenty-four months of life is indicated by the data sets for that span that range from 1,000 to 1,500 typewritten pages for each subject. Following the first-grade-at-school study, there was a twenty-year gap in contact until approximately 1979 to 1980 when this present follow-up was initiated.

Much work has been carried out with these data of the first three years of life, and an appreciable bibliography has accumulated. The initial task was to arrange the descriptive data of interaction between the mothers and their infants over the first three years of life in a framework of a sequence of adaptations negotiated between the two. By systematic use of such a framework, outstanding differences between family systems or mother-infant systems in adaptive behavior or course of change in interaction are defined, compared, and can be communicated to other researchers (Sander, 1962, 1964, 1969, 1975). It was hoped that these differences could then be related, on the one hand, to variables of infant endowment or of maternal character organization or of the family system. On the other hand, they could be related to variables describing the child's outcome during the first year at school, the originally planned end-point of the study.

Some may be familiar with the sequence of issues that were proposed as a systematic way to compare the adaptations and coordinations achieved by the different mother and infant pairs over the first three years of life. The formulation of this sequence of adaptive issues was drawn from biological models of living systems, especially as described by Weiss (1969), von Bertalanffy (1949), Ashby (1952), and Waddington (1976). These viewpoints contributed to a picture of the living system as an open energy system, always in exchange with a larger context, endogenously active, goal-oriented, self-regulating, self-righting, and self-organizing, hierarchically ordered in the relation of subsystems to each other and to the larger system providing context. We recognized the family system as a particular instance of the biological system. The family system exhibits clear dialectic tensions in the exchanges within it, deriving from idiosyncratic polarities between parents, the present and the past, home and society. These tensions then shape the child's active adaptive strategies as he or she organizes them in struggling to experience some enduring coordination with the caregiving context. The sequence of adaptive issues was formulated in an attempt to capture this struggle and the coordinations reached on each new level of activity a child was observed to begin to initiate as time passed. Each new level of activity brought with it the necessity for new coordination to be reached between child and caregiver. The child's experience of an increasingly differentiated sense of "agency" emerges as unique individual preferences can be recognized and successfully exercised in an ever wider range in the caregiving system, building on the constraints of an increasingly complex base constructed of these mutually arrived-at coordinations.

Thus we developed an essentially active "constructionist" view of development, the individual infant being seen as actively participating in the creation of a world of perception and meaning as the repertoire of specific coordinations and adaptive strategies are built that achieve enduring harmony and integration with the child's own particular caregiving context. We had enough observational and descriptive material to ask about mechanisms of this adaptive process. We wanted to know, How does 'fitting together' take place? We observed paradoxical incongruencies and dialectic polarities going along side by side, as simultaneous forces, confronting the child's creative resources for integration in his or her problem-solving effort. The behavioral solution demanded an organization somewhere between these poles, one that was also mutually harmonious with the shared regulatory constraints of the family system.

Paradox characterized many of our research questions. How could *coherence* of a system be maintained as it increased in *complexity?* Mechanisms of integration then became of central interest. How could a sense of separateness as a new individual and as a self-initiating agent be gained without the suffering of separation? Togetherness and differentiation must go along together. These focused our attention, then, on the qualities of attention and affect between the partners and on the patternings of their employment as particular idiosyncracies of communication. The quality of the emergent self as a superordinate system was identified as part of a particular mechanism of coherence that integrated a recurrent contextual configuration with an inner perceptual world related to the infant's "state." This brings together awareness of one's own state, one's motivational set with its intentions and initiations in relation to the pattern of feedback expected in "meeting" the familiar caregiving context. These represent key elements of a complex of integrative mechanisms within an ongoing adaptive process.

We can turn now to the new data of the twenty-five-year follow-up. Our task now is to relate our active constructionist view of early development to an understanding of the subject in the construction of his or her ecologic niche at outcome. In addition to three to eight hours of interviewing each subject by a skilled psychoanalyst, outcome data consist of separate interviews with each parent, reviewing the child's development, reviewing the parents' perspective of their own development as persons and as parents, and the vicissitudes of the family organization over the twenty-five years: dates of births, marriages, deaths, job changes, moves, split-ups, personal or interpersonal victories or defeats. Detailed psychological testing of the subjects and of the mothers is included in these current outcome data.

The design of the follow-up investigation has been based on the unexpected good fortune of being able to have two teams of senior investigators who could be blind to each other's data. The first team consists of the interviewer and testers of the subjects and parents. The second investigative team consists of investigators unaware of the outcome, who have undertaken to reanalyze the first twenty-four months of developmental data collected in the 1950s.

The design of the analysis is in two major parts. The first part is based on a matching task, attempting to match the first twenty-four-month subject with the outcome subject. This is based on a hypothesis that it is in "recognizability" rather than in correlational identity that an individual's continuity over time is carried (formulated by Dr. Gerald Stechler). This "recognizability" is really an integration of the individual's endowment and that specific configuration of adaptive strategies characteristic for that individual in relation to situations of stress, motivation, frustration, and the like. The hypothesis proposes: that by two years of age, in reaching the adaptive solutions described in our sequence of issues, a recognizable style or set of characteristic strategies will have been established for the individual. This set then can be recognized as belonging to that same individual at a later point in life when constructing an ecologic niche in which similar interpersonal issues are set up, to be coped with by familiar and previously successful adaptive strategies. It is the organization of the early data as well as the outcome data from this constructionist point of view that allow us to propose recognizability as the basis for continuity and thus open a valuable entree into the study of process in development. The "misses" as well as the "hits" in this matching task will contribute to our understanding of continuity, change, and transformation over the twenty-five-year span.

A second and more detailed analysis is based on the clinician's statements, specifically characterizing individual adaptive, coping, and character styles at the early and later points. These will be subject to ratings and Q-sort analyses, using independent judges and multiple regression analytic techniques.

In regard to the design of the analysis, it is evident there are major tasks unique to long-term personality studies. One of the major tasks is simply that of description—how can one describe anything of such complexity without biasing the material with the particular framework of the individual investigator's preferences and logic of construction? It is similar to the task of describing the transition from spring to summer or summer to autumn. Where does one begin in the description? With the solar system? With the sap in the trees? With the chemistry of the peepers? Or with a young man's fancies? The ordering of the descriptive data here will reflect the way the in-

vestigator conceives the developmental process proceeding over the twenty-five years or over the first two years. Does one still try to fit the data into psychoanalytic metapsychology? If not, then what format is being implied? What will fall under the category of "outcome" today that won't be in the category of "process" tomorrow?

From its inception, this long-term study of personality development was intended and designed as naturalistic, hypothesis-generating research rather than hypothesis-testing research. It still remains so. In committing ourselves to confront the complexity of the naturalistic situation, and now a twenty-five-year window on it, we are requiring of ourselves the exploration of both new conceptual propositions as well as innovations of method. Such exploration is based on attention both to uniqueness and to commonality; to complexity and to coherence or unity; to the changing individual over time and to that individual's changing context over time. The initial task is that of systematic description—a means of arranging the data so that comparisons can be made not only across the sample and over time but in such a way that useful perspectives on such comparisons can be communicated to others.

The courage to launch such an endeavor springs from the conviction that developmental research is ready now to confront within the multivariable data of early life the matter of "organization"—a matter inescapable for every living system. The organization of the living system is a dimension for contemplation, inspiration, and an endless resource for ideas, conceptual models, and creative research designs.

It is the matter of "organization" and change in organization—the matter of process—that challenges both our traditional conceptualizations and the content of our naturalistic observation. We see what we are looking for. Often we are not asking that what we see should integrate the unique and the common. In the conceptual model provided by biological (living) systems, "organization" is a given. We begin with it. We begin with active, self-regulating, self-organizing functions, as basic to the logic of description as they are to ordering the thinking and observing of the naturalistic situation from which such description stems. We need a better grasp of this logic of biologic organization. In the struggle to describe the twenty-five-year course of some thirty different families, we are struggling to appreciate the clues that will allow us better to define that logic. It is a logic that begins with a set of inescapable constraints (in addition to the nonlinear self-regulatory functions just mentioned). Among these are an obligatory embeddedness of life process within lawful dynamic exchange between individual and context; hierarchy in that context; ongoing exchange between all levels of that hierarchy; an array of mechanisms for regulation, adaptation, and integration by which that hierarchical organization of exchange is maintained yet retains its potential for change and transformation; a further embeddedness of process over time within a trajectory—something called "the life span," with its implications for a lawfulness of regulations about that trajectory, or "homeorrhesis." The exciting new findings in brain organization concerning crossmodal mapping and the theory of neuronal group selection alert us now to thinking in terms of a biological substrate becoming more comprehensible as a basis for understanding the complex patterning of adaptive behavior.

Early developmental research has increasingly directed our attention to the necessity to think of biological design in terms of the "given" of organization from the outset. We see this, for example, in the complexity of the newborn's ready-made sensorimotor coordinations or in the initial capacities for perceptual categorization and preferences. In our task of description of family systems we have the opportunity to identify clues to the transmission of features of organization across generations and to document the constructionist viewpoint of development in the subtle combinations of each of these features the developing individual amplifies or minimizes. In the idea of the acquisition or construction of an organization of adaptive strategies coordinating infant and caregiving environment should lie some of the clues to a different model for lawfulness in the organization of awareness, of that which is conscious, and those regulations which are unconscious. The clues to the establishment of such higher functions of personality as the coherence of an inner frame of reference—the sense of self—will be searched for in the material, especially in the interactions of recognition and self-recognition by which we have proposed such construction can be accomplished. For example, continuity of sense of self, in the constructionist view, may be a continuity experienced as contexts are reconstructed—ones in which one can recognize one's own recurrent states, as the individual's familiar adaptive patterns will now confront situations that are recurrent. Self-recognition of one's own states is facilitated, inasmuch as this recurrence is also part of a contribution to the recurrent situation that that individual has constructed.

These propositions point to some of the additional hypotheses and questions that will be guiding the investigation. At the conclusion of the initial descriptive exploration, judgments by new and independent teams of investigators will be sought in order to confirm or reject our exploratory integrative propositions in reevaluations (now more precisely focused) of the primary behavioral data.

REFERENCES

Ashby, W. R. (1952). *Design for a Brain*, London: Chapman & Hall. 2nd ed., Science Paperbook. New York: Barnes and Noble.

Bertalanffy, L. von (1949). *The Problem of Life*. New York: Harper Torchbooks, 1960.

Sander, L. W. (1962). Issues in early mother-child interaction. *Journal of the American Academy of Child Psychiatry*, 1:141–166.

Sander, L. W. (1964). Adaptive relationships in early mother-child interaction. *Journal of the American Academy of Child Psychiatry*, 3:231–264.

Sander, L. W. (1969). The longitudinal course of early

mother-child interaction: Cross-case comparison in a sample of mother-child pairs. In *Determinants of Infant Behavior,* vol. 4, ed. B. M. Foss. London: Methuen.

Sander, L. W. (1975). Infant and caretaking environment: Investigation and conceptualization of adaptive behavior in a system of increasing complexity. In *Explorations in Child Psychiatry,* ed. E. J. Anthony. New York: Plenum.

Waddington, C. H. (1976). Evolution of the subhuman world. In *Evolution and Consciousness,* ed. E. Jantsch and C. H. Waddington. Reading, Massachusetts: Addison Wesley.

Weiss, P. (1969). The living system: Determinism stratified. In *The Alpbach Symposium, 1968—Beyond Reductionism—New Perspectives in the Life Sciences,* ed. A. Koestler and J. R. Smythies. Boston: Beacon Press.

PART II

Perinatal Research and Clinical Applications

15

Experience Following Premature Birth: Stresses and Opportunities for Infants, Parents, and Professionals

Peter A. Gorski, M.D.

Many individuals live or work in a stressful environment. Few persons are born into such settings loaded with constant noise, activity and crowds. This paper will attempt to illustrate this social experience and consider the consequences endured by more than 200,000 infants (one in twelve live births) and their parents in the United States each year as a result of premature birth (Perelman and Farrell, 1982).

Even in 1983, the magnitude of physical, cognitive, and psychological disabilities following prematurity remains high. While the vast majority of premature neonates survive infancy (from 35 percent of infants born weighing under 750 grams to over 90 percent

This work was supported in part by Social and Behavioral Sciences Research Grant No. 12–93 from the March of Dimes Birth Defects Foundation and a Mount Zion Hospital and Medical Center General Research Support Grant.

The following members of our research team are gratefully acknowledged for their devoted contribution to our ongoing project: Carol H. Leonard, Ph. D., John A. Martin, Ph.D., Pamela C. High, M.D., Margaret D. Lang, P.N.P., Robert E. Piecuch, M.D., Mr. David M. Sweet, and Sally A. Sehring, M.D. Special gratitude is acknowledged for the sustaining support of Roberta A. Ballard, M.D.

born over 1,500 grams [Britton et al., 1981; Cohen et al., 1982; Driscoll et al., 1982; Horwood et al., 1982; Kiely et al., 1981]), the price of survival is too often expressed through a range of sensory, motor, or behavioral handicaps including blindness, hearing deficits, movement disorders, expressive and receptive language communication blocks, mental subnormality, school underachievement, and behavior problems. Up to one third of the large population of children who survive prematurity suffer minor dysfunction in the areas cited above. Another 15 percent to 30 percent remain moderately to severely disabled. (Britton et al., 1981; Driscoll et al., 1982; Horwood et al., 1982; Kiely et al., 1981; Knobloch et al., 1982; Ruiz et al., 1981). Morbidity has remained relatively unchanged when compared with the progress in lowering mortality rates over the last decade (Horwood et al., 1982; Kiely et al., 1981; Knobloch et al., 1982; Ruiz et al., 1981).

Subsumed within these categories of developmental risk are psychological morbidities that are often functionally crippling beyond any real physical impairment. The awful fears parents retain from the initial life threat can pervade and influence a host of subsequent relationships to the child and to other close people. As a superficial example, a pediatrician once told me about a phone call from a frantic mother of a 250-pound high-school junior who wanted to ignore his mother's protest about joining his school's football team. The physician hesitantly inquired about the mother's concerns for the strappingly healthy young man. "But don't you remember," she pleaded, "he was a premie!" Constantly perceived anxiety about oneself can limit a person's independent growth and risk-taking in school, career, and love, in addition to football (Green and Solnit, 1964).

The foregoing discussion of consequent vulnerability following premature birth merely hints at the central theme regarding the role of social interaction on subsequent outcome from at-risk birth. The documented contribution of interactional care during infancy drives to the core of mysteries about premature-infant developmental outcome that are still unsolved. Extensive research (Francis-Williams and Davies, 1974; Parmelee and Haber, 1973; Sameroff and Chandler, 1975) demonstrates no single or compound perinatal factors consistently predictive of neurological behavior after the first postnatal year. Remarkably, however, socioeconomic and parent-infant interactional assessments (Beckwith et al., 1976; Brown and Bakeman, 1979; Field, 1979; Sigman and Parmelee, 1979; Werner et al., 1971) appear to be strong indicators of later health or lingering vulnerability.

The association between social caregiving and physical, emotional, and intellectual development seems undeniable. The burning question now becomes how early does this supportive versus disturbing influence begin to have lasting effects. And how can we even observe and measure the course of perinatal attachment behaviors in cases of prolonged hospitalization during infancy? The current investigation naturalistically recorded enormously detailed observations of caregiver behavior and infant responses during this fragile period when infants with neurobehavioral immaturities first interact with the extrauterine world. We believe that our careful approach to behavioral observation contributes to tracing

developmental influences from one point in time to the next. Historically, longitudinal behavioral research has sampled relatively few data points, usually by examination outside of naturally occurring contexts. By examining only developmental endpoints, we risk missing continuities that may indeed exist over a lifetime. This paper identifies the early experiential effects of intensive-care-nursery (ICN) hospitalization on infants, parents, and professionals and proceeds to discuss the challenges and opportunities parents and infants first face as they prepare to engage each other in succeeding stages of mutual attachment and development.

"The First Home"

One first must recognize the environmental characteristics of ICNs in order to appreciate their peculiar challenges to parent-infant attachment and infant behavioral organization. This "first home" for families of infants born at risk is not very different from Hollywood portraits of intergalactic spaceships. A place of constant bright light, stark color, and relentless sounds, an ICN bears little relationship to outer realities. Many nurseries, in fact, offer no windows to look toward life on the street, in the trees, or even in the heavens. Inside the units, infants and machines blend inseparably to the naive eye. Only the machines and caregivers create sound. The infants, isolated or intubated, are unable to speak for themselves. No obvious place exists for parents to enjoy privacy from everyone in the nursery. Caregiving opportunities for parents are, at best, limited and ably performed by professional staff.

Professionals recognize that change is necessary and are slowly proceeding toward designing environments that are technologically superior yet emotionally more supportive (Kellman, 1980). Still, researchers currently have rudimentary understanding of the physiological and psychological effects of the architectural design of ICNs.

The ICN is not just a physical space, but one operated by as many as fifty to a hundred people at any given time. Humans therefore contribute much of the activity, noise, and care experienced by infants and parents (Long et al., 1980). Our unit recently reported analyses of professional staff caregiving patterns that may directly influence an infant's early social experience and behavioral development (Gorski et al., 1983). Several analyses from our observational research dramatize the caregiving ecology of an ICN. These include: percentage of time infants are handled or observed by caregivers; comparative time spent intervening rather than observing infants; numbers, identity, and consistency of attachment figures; and frequency of positional changes affecting the child's proprioceptive and vestibular sensory experiences. Results are summaries of data collected from eleven preterm infants observed continuously over several days in the hours between 8:00 AM and 4:00 PM. Detailed description of the computer-assisted recording methods has been reported elsewhere (Gorski et al., 1983; High and Gorski, in press). Six of the observations recorded the experience of chronically ill babies, while five were of healthy infants. The results are presented as a portrait of social interaction experienced by hospitalized infants:

Percentage of time nurse was present. A nurse was within reach space of the infant a median of 35 percent of the total time observed with the sick infants, 18 percent with the healthy ones, and 28 percent combined total.

Interval between nurse completing a caregiving task and leaving the infant's care area. Nurses remained 2.5 minutes, 0.65 minutes, and 1 minute with sick, healthy, and total combined infants, respectively, following completion of a caregiving intervention. In this analysis, differences are not considered among medical, social, and custodial interventions.

Percentage of time when no caregiver was present. No caregiver of any kind stood by the isolette for 54 percent of total observation time with the sick infants, 76 percent with the healthy group, and 62 percent total combined.

Percentage of time in various positions. The sick, healthy, and total combined infants studied remained in the prone position for 84 percent, 92 percent, and 90 percent of total observation time respectively. Sick babies remained supine 7 percent of the time, healthy infants, 8 percent, and combined overall, 8 percent of total observation time. Only the chronically ill babies spent any time, 6 percent, positioned on their right side, while healthy infants and the combined total medians scored 0 percent. Median values for time positioned on left side were 0 percent for all—sick, healthy, and combined populations.

Several characteristics and implications about modern intensive care are suggested by the current study. While investigators recognize the abundant sources of sensory stimuli in these environments (Cornell and Gottfried, 1976; Lawson et al., 1977; Long et al., 1980), our continuous observational data surprisingly reveal that nurses are present at the infant's bedside a minority of time. Conversely, no caregiver at all is present the majority of time observed. Indeed, besides the nurse, all other caregivers combined, including parents (who admittedly visit more consistently during evening hours), physicians, and support staff are present merely between 6 and 11 percent of total time observed.

Interestingly, nurses attended closely to sick infants for twice as much time as to healthy premature neonates. This phenomenon may reflect the common experience that a nurse is often assigned to care for just one infant when that patient is quite sick, while a nurse usually splits time between two infants if they seem to be in more stable physical condition.

Some of the analyses delineate how nurses tend to use their time when attending to infants. Because we are keenly interested in discovering any infant behavioral signals that might herald more serious physiological irregularities, we looked to find how available professional caregivers themselves might be for observing and making use of such infant cues. In fact, a disconcertingly limited time seems to be devoted by staff to observing an infant's responses to caregiving interventions. Healthy infants were watched about forty seconds following a caregiving procedure of any kind before the nurse left the area. Even chronically ill infants received less than three minutes of observation time from nurses following interventions. If, as we already found (Gorski et al., 1983), distress signs following and associated with interventions can occur as long as five minutes after an intervention with caregivers, then nursery staff may be missing opportunities to realize and to utilize causal relationships between the timing, content, or manner of interventions and infant behavioral and physiological responses.

Our findings of positions maintained by infants suggest a most asymmetrical proprioceptive experience. Given the occurrence of rapid central nervous system organization during this period of perinatal life, such skewed sensorimotor conditioning might conceivably affect emerging motor patterns and sensory integrative capabilities in this high-risk infant population. Surprisingly, there appears to be little difference in caregiving approach to sick versus relatively healthy preterm infants with respect to offering them a variety of positions from which to experience their extrauterine world.

Finally, our observations beg comparisons between the nature of interactions for these preterm infants with their caregivers and those of healthy term neonates with their parents at home. Quantitatively, we would predict that home-reared infants receive significantly more handling and vocalizing from caregivers during daytime hours than do hospitalized preterm infants. Although both hospitalized and home-reared newborns apparently receive most of their care from one person, that individual changes from shift to shift, day to day, for the preterm infant in the nursery. The primary care relationship term infants enjoy at home is usually provided by the same person.

Qualitatively, the term infant and parent quickly negotiate an interactive relationship characterized by smooth modulation between periods of close contact and brief rest. The preterm hospitalized infant is often exposed to an "all or nothing" approach to care, swinging from no human contact to frequently uncomfortable or perhaps painful physical manipulations. However, our work cautions us not to berate the obvious differences in caregiver-infant interaction of hospitalized and home-reared newborns. The immaturely formed nervous system controls of behavioral and physiological responses in preterm infants may actually benefit from long rest periods from caregiver interactions. Indeed, the "all or nothing" character of care observed may be ideally tailored to the "all or nothing" responses to stimuli that characterize preterm behavior (Aylward, 1982).

Impact on the Newborn

As already acknowledged, neonatal care can now successfully provide preterm infants with those essential life supports they are too weak to master for themselves. Included in this most positive service are means for ensuring body temperature regulation, respiratory and circulatory controls, and nutritional alternatives to stressing immature intestinal systems.

Unfortunately, while securing these essential life supports, clinicians for the most part neglected to consider the need to protect central nervous system vulnerabilities. As previously described (Aylward, 1982; Dreyfus-Brisac, 1970; Gorski et al., 1979; Karch et al., 1982; Prechtl et al., 1979), preterm infants exhibit significant immaturities in their behavior. For example, we have previously reviewed evidence for disordered sleep/wake state patterns in preterms infants compared with fullterms (High and Gorski, in press). Similarly, these infants often suffer physiological consequences when presented with abundant sensory stimuli from the caregiving environment (Gorski et al., 1983; Long et al., 1980). Neurological weaknesses force very premature infants to communicate conditions of stability or distress at a subbehavioral level, relying instead on such strange interactive signals as changing pulse, respiration, skin color, or activity (Gorski et al., 1983; Long et al., 1980). Although caregivers can learn to interpret such cues, facility with these communicative modes requires patient, often frustrating, effort.

Impact on Parental Attachment

Behaviorally immature, the preterm infant can spend months as a weak social interacter, particularly when compared with his fullterm peer. Unlike the healthy infant born at term, the premature neonate has limited abilities to elicit, pace, or follow a dyadic interaction at a social level of behavior. This alone causes enormous strain on parents who must nurture these often fussy, inconsolable infants who are easily aroused from brief sleep periods yet are underactive and poorly attentive when awake.

Parents experience stresses other than their babies' condition. Premature birth and subsequent hospitalization exact a unique toll on the emotional strength and security of parents. Consider some or all of the stressors likely to befall parents of prematures. Mother may be physically fragile after extended bedrest, excessive bleeding, undernutrition, or medication taken to postpone delivery as long as possible. Early termination of pregnancy aborts the psychological process as well as the somatic one. As a result, parents incompletely resolve the usual stages of separation-individuation in preparation for giving birth (Bibring, 1959). The various social and cultural supports accompanying normal term births are strikingly absent—no celebrations, homecomings, or gifts attend the unfortunate birth of an infant born too weak to survive without hospital care. Parents of prematures endure months with no baby at home, yet no baby in the womb either. This creates a unique pregnant/not pregnant state of suspended emotional direction. What about every parent's well-earned maternity leave from work? When should it begin? How long should it last? Parents of prematures usually must opt for waiting until baby's discharge from hospital. This creates a disorienting and conflict-full period, often lasting months, when parents return to prepregnancy life patterns.

In the nursery itself, parents easily feel like an insignificant pair among a hundred competent caregivers for their baby. Moreover, no specified caregiving role appears obvious for them. Painfully coping with the situation, parents try somehow to learn about their infant. Too often their only access is through monitoring instruments and technical jargon shared with the nursery staff. Parents observe that the professional caregivers rely heavily on mechanical data for determining an infant's likes and dislikes. Unfortunately, the staff's example discourages many parents from their efforts to study their child's animate responses.

Even the ultimate experience of taking the child home from the hospital can strain optimal parenting responses to these initially vulnerable infants. Eventual discharge leaves parents suddenly responsible for the total care of their infant. No matter how well prepared, parents greet this long-awaited autonomy from hospital with anxiety well in excess of that felt by fullterm parents.

Our experience has recommended a few practical aids for supporting parents in their effort to love and nurture their premature infants. Above all, supporting the wide fluctuations of parental feelings, including hopefulness, depression, isolation, and anger, demands a variety of methods to suit a variety of parents. One-to-one staff-parent relationships, parent self-support groups, home visits, and regular follow-up appointments after discharge can all help parents recover realistic faith and confidence. However, just as infants respond individually to care provided, so parents also benefit from support offered at the right time and in a manner befitting their own needs. For example, I have witnessed parents repelling other parents' attempts to offer the sympathy of common experiences. Some parents feel it cheapens their personal sense of profound hurt to suggest that others have felt comparable despair.

When parents can tolerate repeated visits to the ICN, staff can help them identify behavioral stages of infant recovery. By learning to recognize developing movement patterns and emerging organization of sleep/wake states, parents might appreciate progress well before the infant can satisfy their deeper hopes for the social interactive rewards far down the road.

As reported above, close caregiver contacts with infants are few and far between in ICNs. Attachment behaviors in parents might then be fostered if visits were timed to include active or alert periods such as feedings. These attention-demanding events might increase parent involvement in infant care. We encourage ICN staff whenever possible to consider parent visitation schedules when planning procedures that would predictably drain or gratify infant and parents.

The real physical frailties of premature infants may persist beyond the period of critical hospital care. In this case, clinicians can help avert a prolonged syndrome of imagined vulnerability (Green and Solnit, 1964) by clearly indicating when physical risks no longer exist and will not be likely to influence the child's future life course.

Impact on Staff

The most casual observer of an ICN would recognize the professional staff as primary caregivers to the infants. Less obviously, these same staff members lead parents toward increasing comfort, understanding and reward as caregivers themselves of their premature infants. Staff serve as models for handling, feeding, and even social interaction for parents afraid to distress their small babies. Nurses are sometimes even more available than family members for listening, chatting, empathizing, or encouraging parents stunned by the terrible violation of their expectations for parenthood. If parents are eventually to influence developmental recovery following a precarious infancy, then staff have a crucial opportunity to build parents' faith in that future.

How well then does the ICN environment foster such vital interactive skills and qualities among its staff? The longer I observe behavior in this bizarre setting, the more impressed I grow with anyone able to absorb constant stress and still serve the needs of others. These people work eight- to thirty-six-hour shifts in a place that never rests, is never quiet. Nearly all decisions have lifesaving implications. No wonder then that the ability to endure stress becomes a major measure of evaluating performance. To describe someone who works in the nursery is to describe someone who is suffering from chronic fatigue, who has very low energy reserves, who is always concerned about self-preservation while simultaneously practicing real self-abuse. How far, then, can the individual professional extend his or her own sense of the nursery's impact in order to care how it affects the infant and parent?

Ironically, many ICN organizations offer no structured system for sharing or communicating personal feelings among peers. Professionals need to realize the added help they could provide to parents of premature infants through improving the physical and psychological conditions for their own staff members. Professionals, just like parents, need private facilities where pressures can be temporarily shed. In addition, nurseries with lowest staff turnover rates have established networks of individual or group support for workers. Lacking such outlets, staff commonly, though unwittingly, express inner conflicts in the parents' presence. I often overhear staff drawing parents into their own personal dramas. Though engaging, this practice additionally burdens parents. Parents repeatedly tell me they make extra effort to befriend their child's caregivers so that staff will consequently enjoy attending to their infant.

Finally, I am surprised to learn that staff undervalue the effects of their behavior on infants. We can readily apply our research by teaching staff to recognize how responsive infants are to their care. In our nursery, physicians and nurses in turn express heightened interest and respect for individual response patterns in babies.

However, while putting behavioral observations to good use increases interest in the work, it also increases the effort required to make subtle discoveries. This circumstance produces a complementary chance for the researcher to support the clinical program by valuing the staff's specific questions and insights about the infants studied. The investigator who provides research reports to colleagues at international meetings can also enhance the people whose work he observes so closely at home. I have come to realize how strongly research findings appeal to caregivers eager to improve their service to infants and parents. The research process itself can help amend the impact of stressful environments if we take care when tempting subjects with the promise of our research to leave them feeling not so much studied as educated, supported, and respected.

REFERENCES

Aylward, G. P. (1982). Forty-week full-term and pre-term neurologic differences. In *Perinatal Risk and Newborn Behavior*, ed. L. P. Lipsitt and T. M. Field. Norwood, New Jersey: Ablex.

Beckwith, L. et al. (1979). Caregiver-infant interaction and early cognitive development in preterm infants. *Child Development*, 47:579–587.

Bibring, G.L. (1959). Some considerations of the psychological processes in pregnancy. *The Psychoanalytical Study of the Child*, 14:113–121. New York: International Universities Press.

Britton, S. B., Fitzhardinge, P. M., and Ashby, S. (1981). Is intensive care justified for infants weighing less than 801 gm. at birth? *Journal of Pediatrics*, 99:937–943.

Brown, J.V. and Bakeman, R. (1979). Relations of human mothers with their infants during the first year of life: Effects of prematurity. In *Maternal Influences and Early Behavior*, ed. R. W. Bell and W. P. Smotherman. New York: Spectrum.

Cohen, R. S. et al. (1982). Favorable results of neonatal intensive care for very low-birth-weight infants. *Pediatrics*, 69:621–625.

Cornell, E. H. and Gottfried, A. W. (1976). Intervention with premature human infants. *Child Development*, 47:32–39.

Dreyfus-Brisac, C. (1970). Ontogenesis of sleep in human prematures after 32 weeks of conceptional age. *Developmental Psychology*, 3:91–121.

Driscoll, J.M. et al. (1982). Mortality and morbidity in infants less than 1,001 grams birthweight. *Pediatrics*, 69: 21–26.

Field, T. M. (1979). Interaction patterns of preterm and term infants. In *Infants Born At Risk*, ed. T. M. Field, A. M. Sostek, S. Goldberg, and H. H. Shuman. New York: Spectrum.

Francis-Williams, J. and Davies, P. A. (1974). Very low birthweight and later intelligence. *Developmental Medicine and Child Neurology*, 16:709–728.

Gorski, P. A., Davison, M. F., and Brazelton, T. B. (1979). Stages of behavioral organization in the high-risk neonate. *Seminars in Perinatology*, 3:61–72.

Gorski, P. A., Hole, W. T., Leonard, C. H., and Martin, J. A. (1983). Direct computer recording of premature infants and nursery care. *Pediatrics*, 72:198–202.

Green, M. and Solnit, A. J. (1964). Reactions to the threatened loss of a child: A vulnerable child syndrome. *Pediatrics*, 34:58–66.

High, P. C. and Gorski, P. A. (1984, in press). Womb for improvement: Recording environmental influences on infant development in the intensive care nursery. In *Environmental Neonatology*. ed. A. W. Gottfried and J. F. Gaiter. Baltimore: University Park Press.

Horwood, S. P., Boyle, M. H., Torrance, G. W., and Sinclair, J. C. (1982). Mortality and morbidity of 500–1,499-gram birthweight infants live-born to residents of a defined geographical region before and after neonatal intensive care. *Pediatrics*, 69:613–620.

Karch, D. et al. (1982). Behavioral changes and bioelectric brain maturation of preterm and fullterm newborn infants: A polygraphic study. *Developmental Medicine and Child Neurology*, 24:30–47.

Kellman, N. (1980). Risks in the design of the modern neonatal intensive care unit. *Birth and the Family Journal*, 7: 243–248.

Kiely, J. L., Paneth, N., Stein, Z., and Susser, M. (1981). Cerebral palsy and newborn care II.: Mortality and neurological impairment in low-birthweight infants. *Developmental Medicine and Child Neurology*, 23:650–659.

Knobloch, H. et al. (1982). Considerations in evaluating changes in outcome for infants weighing less than 1,501 grams. *Pediatrics*, 69:285–295.

Lawson, K., Daum, C., and Turkewitz, G. (1977). Environmental characteristics of a neonatal intensive care unit. *Child Development*, 48:1633–1639.

Long, J. G., Lucey, J. F., and Philip, A. G. S. (1980). Noise and hypoxemia in the intensive-care nursery. *Pediatrics* 65: 143–145.

Parmelee, A.H. and Haber, A. (1973). Who is the risk infant? *Clinical Obstetrics/Gynecology*, 16:376–387.

Perelman, R. H. and Farrell, P. M. (1982). Analysis of causes of neonatal death in the United States with specific emphasis on fatal hyaline membrane disease. *Pediatrics*, 70: 570–575.

Prechtl, H. F. R., Fargel, J. W., Weinmann, H. M., and Bakker, H. H. (1979). Postures, motility and respiration of low-risk preterm infants. *Developmental Medicine and Child Neurology*, 21:23–27.

Ruiz, M. P. D. et al. (1981). Early development of infants of birthweight less than 1,000 grams with reference to mechanical ventilation in newborn period. *Pediatrics*, 68: 330–335.

Sameroff, A. J., and Chandler, M. J. (1975). Reproductive risk and the continuum of caretaking casualty. In *Review of Child Developmental Research*, ed. F. D. Horowitz. Chicago: University of Chicago Press.

Sigman, M. and Parmelee, A. H. (1979). Longitudinal follow-up of premature infants. In *Infants Born at Risk*, ed. T. M. Field, A. M. Sostek, S. Goldberg, and H. H. Shuman. New York: Spectrum.

Werner, E. E., Bierman, J. M., and French, F. E. (1971). *The Children of Kauai*. Honolulu: University Press of Hawaii.

16

Perinatal Risk Factors for Infant Depression

Tiffany Field, Ph.D.

Although clinical cases of sadness or depression in young children have appeared in the literature for several decades (Abraham, 1911; Anthony, 1977; Freud, 1917), there is continuing debate among researchers and clinicians in the United States as to the existence of the syndrome of childhood depression (Kashani et al., 1981; Schulterbrandt and Raskin, 1977). Members of the European psychiatric community, in contrast, refer to the existence of depression as early as the infancy stage. Melanie Klein, for example, theorized (1935) that a "depressive position" occurs in the infant as young as six months of age as a result of a diminution in the splitting process. Anna Freud and Burlingham (1944) have described the grief reaction of infants and young children removed from their homes and families to nurseries in outlying regions of England during the German bombing of London during World War II. Although the majority of the nurseries were generally pleasant and the caregivers well trained, large numbers of these infants developed marasmus, several of the children did not survive, and several of the survivors experienced severe emotional dysfunction even into early adulthood (Maas, 1963). Spitz's

(1946) syndrome of "anaclitic depression" appeared substantially similar to Freud and Burlingham's grief reaction. Spitz described the institutionalized French infants who were separated from their mothers as sad, weepy, and apathetic with immobile faces having a distant expression. Those infants who were separated after six months of age also refused to eat or to interact with other adults or children, and several demonstrated severe psychomotor retardation. Similarly, the studies by Robertson and Robertson as summarized by Bowlby (1973) of institutionalized and hospitalized infants and children separated from their mothers suggested a syndrome of depression similar to that described by Spitz. All these reports showed the depression as occurring in the context of stressful early separation from the parent. Direct observation of infants suggests that factors other than separation from the parent can predispose infants to depression. Among those I would like to consider are the perinatal risk factors of being born with medical complications or being born to a depressed mother.

Infants with the most common perinatal complication, that of prematurity and Respiratory Distress Syndrome (RDS), have been noted to show social/emotional problems and expressive language deficits as they reach school age (Field and Dempsey, 1983). Although psychiatric evaluations were not made

This research was supported by a grant from the Administration of Children, Youth, and Families and an NIMH Research Scientist Development Award.

on this sample of children, a recent study by Widmayer and associates (1983) on a similar population suggests that affective disorders such as depression are more prevalent in this population than would be expected by chance. In a large sample of children between four and eight years of age who had been treated for prematurity and RDS as neonates, several displayed signs of emotional problems. These included withdrawal, apathy, flatness of affect, sadness, behavior disorders, and inappropriate or bizarre responses, such as echolalia or preoccupation with death, during cognitive tests.

In an attempt to determine the incidence and severity of suspected emotional problems among these high-risk children, 114 children between the ages of four and seven, as well as their mothers and fathers, were interviewed. Of these 114 children, 56, or 49 percent, demonstrated signs of severe emotional disturbance. A subgroup of 20 of these children were chosen for more intensive evaluation. They had a play session with a child psychiatrist and were given the children's aperception test, a sentence-completion test, and the draw-a-person test and were then compared with a group of nondepressed children who were matched on perinatal complication and demographic variables. The children who had been diagnosed as depressed were found to have previously experienced a traumatic event—a death, divorce, or prolonged separation. In addition, there was a greater incidence of depression of a family member and less parental involvement for those children who were depressed than with the control group.

Several studies (Cytryn et al., 1982; McKnew et al., 1979; Welner et al., 1977) that have investigated either the incidence of depression in children of depressed parents or, from the other direction (McKnew and Cytryn, 1973; Poznanski and Zrall, 1970), the incidence of depressed parents in samples of depressed children suggest that depression "runs in families."

Although it is certainly possible that children of depressed adults may be at greater risk for depression, owing to some mode of genetic transmission, several anecdotal descriptions of the behavior of depressed mothers toward their infants and young children suggest that environmental factors may also play a major role in the developing depression of their offspring. Weissman and Paykel (1974), for example, in their study of depressed women have documented in detail the impact of depression on parenting. They found that depressed women were inordinately involved in their children's daily lives, had difficulty communicating with them, and were aware of their own loss of affection for the children. They also reported considerable friction with the children who were the most frequent objects of their mother's hostility. A description by Haka-Ikse (1975) suggests that infants and children of mothers with severe depression usually present a common developmental pattern with delays or arrests in language and in gross motor and personal-social skills. Not only are they slow in learning to speak, they tend to use very little of whatever speech skills they have. Apart from slowness in attaining motor milestones, these children also have diminished gross motor activity. They are inactive, sober, and irritable and tolerate minor stresses poorly. This description is similar to that provided by Field (1979) and Widmayer and colleagues (1983) on premature infants. Haka-Ikse further describes the infants and children of depressed mothers as clinging to their mothers and as having very little eye contact or playful interchange with them. She describes the mothers as being passive toward their children, rarely talking, playing, or interacting with them.

Whereas we have anecdotal descriptions of this kind on depressed mothers and their children, as of this time there have been no systematic studies of the early social interactions between depressed mothers and their infants. Because relationships have emerged between early mother-infant interactions and later social/emotional behaviors of the same children (Field, 1982), it is possible that early interactions have a considerable impact on the social/emotional outcomes of children. Whether early separation is a factor in the infant's depression, as for example in the premature RDS baby who remains separated from the parent during the first month or so of life, whether the infant's reduced responsivity to the parent is due to perinatal complications, or whether the depressed parent contributes to the depression noted in young infants, the early interaction situation may be one that mediates the development of depression in young infants. It might thereby serve as a vehicle for studying the early emergence of depressed affect.

In this paper we report the data from two studies on infants we considered at risk for developing depressed affect. The first is a descriptive study of the early interaction behaviors of infants born with the perinatal complications of prematurity and Respiratory Distress Syndrome. The second study was of early interactions between postpartum depressed mothers and their infants. The data from these studies suggest the possible value of closely monitoring the early interaction behaviors of at-risk infants for early signs of depressed affect and emerging depression.

Affective Displays of Preterm RDS Infants during Early Interactions

As has already been mentioned, Widmayer's data suggest that preterm RDS infants may be at risk for developing early depression. Preterm RDS infants are typically considered at risk for disturbed interactions with their mothers, in part because they present atypical interactive behaviors at birth. On the interaction items of the Brazelton scale (Brazelton, 1973), preterm RDS infants have been noted to be less alert, less attentive to stimulation, and less active than term-normal infants (Field et al., 1978). Their interactive behavior continues to be atypical as is indicated by a number of studies in which we have recorded their emotional expressions such as smiling, laughing, frowning, and crying, as well as vocalizations, activity level, and heart rate (Field, 1977, 1979, 1982).

METHOD

Twenty preterm RDS infants and twenty normal-term infants were observed when they were approximately four months old (corrected age). Three minutes of spontaneous face-to-face interactions with their mothers were videotaped, and heart-rate activity of both infants and mothers was recorded via telemetry. The videotapes were coded for infant gaze and gaze aversion (or looking at and looking away from the mother), vocalizing, laughing, crying, and the expressions happy, sad, and interested. In addition the overall expressivity of the infants and their mothers was rated on a 5-point Likert-type scale with 5 representing a positive expression and 1 a negative expression.

RESULTS

The data were analyzed by multivariate analysis of variance followed by univariate analysis of variance and post-hoc comparisons by Bonferroni t tests (Myers, 1972). As can be seen in figure 16–1, the preterm infants exhibited happy faces significantly less frequently than the term-normal infants, showed sad faces significantly more frequently than the term-normal infants, and fewer interested faces than were noted for the term infants. Analyses of the 5-point Likert-type ratings of expressivity revealed that the expressions of the preterm RDS infants and their mothers were less positive than those of the term infants and their mothers (see figure 16–2). The data on vocalizations revealed that cooing occurred less frequently among the preterm RDS infants, who were noted to cry more frequently than the normal infants (see figure 16–3). Figure 16–4 shows the proportion of interaction time the mothers talked to their infants and the proportion of interaction time the infants gazed at their mothers. The mothers of the preterm RDS infants were noted to talk more than the mothers of the term-normal infants, and the preterm RDS infants were noted to gaze away from their mothers more frequently than the term infants. Finally, for the analysis of interaction heart-rate activity, ten seconds of baseline heart rate were averaged and compared to the mean heart rate for the three-minute interactions. A two (baseline and interaction)-by-two (group) repeated-measures analysis of variance was conducted with baseline and interaction heart rate as a repeated measure. Figure 16–5 shows the change in

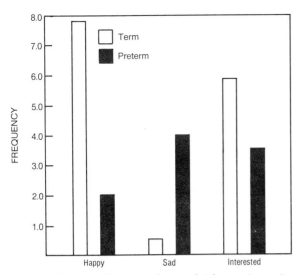

Figure 16–1 Frequency of various facial expressions emitted by normal and RDS infants during 3-minute spontaneous face-to-face interactions with their mothers.

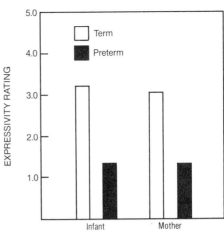

Figure 16–2 Expressivity rating (1 = negative expressivity, 5 = positive expressivity) of normal and RDS infants and their mothers during spontaneous face-to-face interactions

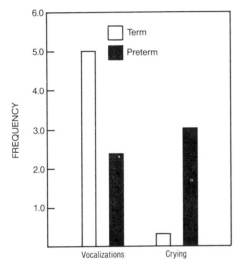

Figure 16–3 Frequency of contented vocalizations and crying by RDS infants during spontaneous face-to-face interactions with their mothers

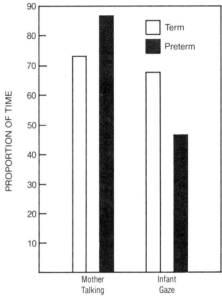

Figure 16–4 Proportion of interaction time during spontaneous face-to-face interactions

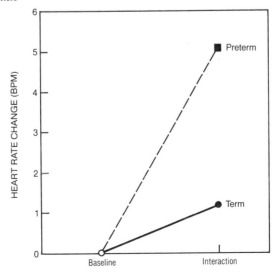

Figure 16–5 Mean tonic heart-rate change in beats per minute from baseline to spontaneous interaction.

beats per minute from baseline heart rate to interaction heart rate. The heart rate of the preterm RDS infants was significantly elevated during spontaneous interaction as compared to their baseline heart rate.

DISCUSSION

These data suggest that the preterm RDS infants spent less time looking at their mothers and appeared to "enjoy" their interactions less than the normal-term infants. Their smiles and contented vocalizations were notably less frequent and their frowns and cries more frequent than those of term infants. The more frequent negative affective behaviors together with elevated heart rate of the preterm RDS infants suggest that their interactions may have been more stressful. Their lesser attentiveness and their lesser affective responsivity to their mothers are consistent with the less alert, less responsive behavior noted in these infants at birth. Excessive stimulation on the part of the mother may have also contributed to the elevated heart rate, gazing away, and negative affect noted. The mothers' natural attempts to elicit positive affective behaviors appear to have been counterproductive.

The relationships reported between the early interaction behaviors of these preterm RDS infants and their mothers and the later behavior problems at school age (Field and Dempsey, 1983) together with the data on school-age depression in infants who experience prematurity and RDS by the Widmayer group (1983) raise the disturbing possibility that infants with perinatal complications of this kind may not only show depressed affect during their early interactions but may be at risk for later depression. Although the degree to which the infant's perinatal complications, the mother's responses to a less responsive baby, or the period of separation immediately following birth contributed to this picture of relatively depressed early interactions is not clear; these two groups of data nonetheless highlight the importance of monitoring the early affective displays of infants experiencing such perinatal complications as prematurity and Respiratory Distress Syndrome.

Early Interactions of Infants of Postpartum Depressed Mothers

In this study we investigated whether infants of mothers who are clinically depressed postpartum would behave in a depressed fashion during their early interactions. Tronick and his colleagues (1982) have observed early face-to-face play interactions in which nondepressed mothers have been instructed to "look depressed." These interactions result in disorganized, distressed behavior on the part of the infants. As compared to their behavior during spontaneous interactions, the infants more frequently looked wary, averted their gaze, protested, and attempted to elicit responses from the mother when she was asked to look depressed. The infants' distressed behavior continued even after the mothers resumed their normal behavior. Tronick and his group speculated that infants of naturally depressed mothers would behave in this fashion during their early interactions. However, it is possible that the normal infants' response to their mothers' looking depressed was merely their response to a violation of expectancy or their inability to elicit a response from their mother, just as infants also protest as they fail in their attempts to elicit responses from mother when she is asked to remain still-faced. Infants of naturally depressed mothers may become accustomed to their mother's depressed behavior and thus may not become distressed when she is invited to "look depressed."

METHOD

Twenty-four mothers (twelve depressed, twelve nondepressed) and their infants were videotaped during face-to-face interactions when the infants were three-to-four-months old. As in the previous studies the infants were placed in an infant seat on a table approximately eighteen inches from the mother's face. Two video cameras and a split-screen generator enabled simultaneous monitoring of the mothers' and the infants' facial behaviors. Three, three-minute face-to-face play interactions were recorded. For the first, spontaneous, interaction the mother was simply asked to play with her infant as she would if she were at home. This interaction was followed by one in which the mother was asked to look depressed, and finally, for the third interaction, the mother was asked to again behave spontaneously as if she were at home playing with the infant. The videotapes were then coded by research assistants naive regarding the hypotheses of the study. The same behaviors coded by the Tronick group were coded in this study. They included infant looking away (averting gaze), protesting (fussing, thrashing about in the seat, or crying), looking wary (gazing toward the mother with head partly averted and with a sad or sober face), monitoring (gazing toward the mother with a neutral facial expression), exhibiting brief positive displays, and being playful (showing positive facial displays of longer duration with or without vocalizations). Although Tronick did not code the behaviors of the mother, covariation in maternal behavior might be expected to alter the infant's behavior. Thus, we coded for the mother: positive facial expressions, vocalizations, looking at the infant, and tactile/kinesthetic stimulation. Interobserver reliability was assessed by the simultaneous coding of one half of the videotapes and ranged from .83 to .97.

RESULTS

A repeated-measures analysis of variance was conducted with group and sex as between-groups measures and interaction situation as a repeated measure. In brief, the data on the nondepressed mothers and their infants confirmed Tronick's results. A repeated measure by group-interaction effect revealed that the infants of nondepressed mothers behaved differently in the "looking depressed" interaction condition by showing significantly more distressed behavior (looking wary, looking away, and protesting) and more attempts to elicit maternal responses (showing brief positive facial displays). In turn, the nondepressed mothers were also different during the "looking depressed" condition, showing fewer positive facial expressions, less talking, and less

tactile stimulation. In contrast, the depressed mothers' behavior did not change across the three situations. Paralleling the unchanging behavior of the depressed mothers was the unchanging behavior of their infants. Group main effects suggested infants of depressed mothers showed significantly fewer positive facial expressions and vocalizations across all conditions (see figures 16–6, 16–7, and 16–8).

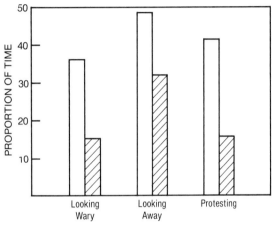

Figure 16–6 Proportion of time infants reacted negatively during the interaction in which mothers were asked to "look depressed"

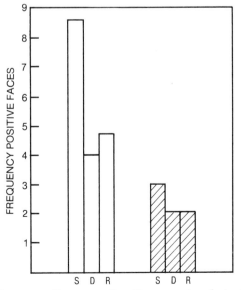

Figure 16–7 Frequency of positive expressions during the spontaneous (S), "looking depressed" (D), and return-to-baseline (R) interaction conditions

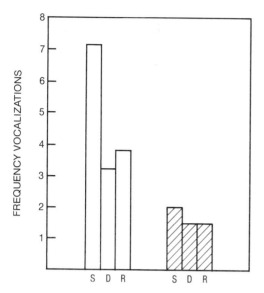

Figure 16–8 Frequency of contented vocalizations during the spontaneous (s), "looking depressed" (D), and return-to-baseline (R) interaction conditions

DISCUSSION

The data on the infants of nondepressed mothers suggest that they may be experiencing a "violation of expectancy" or an inability to elicit responses from their mothers. In contrast, the infants of postpartum depressed mothers appear to experience the "looking depressed" situation as no different from the spontaneous interaction they experience with their depressed mothers. The depressed mothers who are requested to look depressed appear to behave similarly across the spontaneous and the "looking depressed" interaction situations. The infants of depressed mothers may have learned to interact with their mothers in a similarly depressed-looking style of behavior. These data are reminiscent of infant primate studies in which infants do or do not have control in a stressful situation (Reite et al., 1981). During brief periods of stress, primate infants typically show agitated behavior. During more prolonged stressful situations, the infants become depressed. In the former situation, the primate infant has been said to be actively coping, and in the latter, passively coping. The behavior of the infants of depressed mothers as against that of those with nondepressed mothers in this study suggests a passive/active coping behavior contrast. The behavior of the infants of depressed mothers appears to "mirror" the behavior of their mothers and suggests that by experiencing frequent lack of control during early interactions, they have developed a passive coping, depressed style of interacting.

Although very little is known about the genetic transmission of depression in families, these data independently suggest that depression or depressed affect may emerge in very young infants as a function of their early interactions with postpartum depressed mothers. Whether the depressed affect of infants of depressed mothers derives from their "mirroring" of their mothers' behaviors or simply results from the minimal stimulation provided by their mothers is an empirical question. Nonetheless, these data suggest that depression in the mother may be transmitted to her offspring via their very early interactions. Although the diagnosis of childhood depression is still a matter of dispute, it would appear that depression may emerge as early as infancy even in the absence of separation or loss.

Although researchers in cognitive development have for the last few decades been looking at the early precursors of cognitive delays in children at high risk by virtue of perinatal complications and less than optimal environments, very few researchers have considered the origins of social/emotional deficits as occurring secondary to perinatal complications or nonoptimal environments. The data from these studies suggest that there should be a mandate for the International Congress of Infant Psychiatry to explore early precursors of infant and early childhood depression.

REFERENCES

Abraham, K. (1968). Notes on the psychoanalytical investigation and treatment of manic-depressive insanity and allied conditions. In *Selected Papers.* New York: Brunner/Mazel, 1979.

Anthony, E. J. (1977). Depression and children. In *Handbook of Studies on Depression,* ed. G. D. Burrows. New York: Excerpta Medica.

Bowlby, J. (1973). *Attachment,* vol. 2, *Separation: Attachment and Loss.* New York: Basic Books.

Brazelton, T. B. (1973). *Neonatal Behavioral Assessment Scale.* Philadelphia: J. B. Lippincott.

Cytryn, L. et al. (1982). Offspring of parents with affective disorders. *Journal of the American Academy of Child Psychiatry,* 21:389–391.

Field, T. (1977). Effects on early separation, interactive deficits, and experimental manipulations on infant-mother face-to-face interaction. *Child Development,* 48:763–771.

Field, T. (1979). Interaction patterns of high-risk and normal infants. In *Infants Born at Risk,* ed. T. Field et al. New York: Spectrum.

Field, T. (1982), Affective displays of high-risk infants during early interactions. In *Emotion and Early Interaction,* ed. T. Field and A. Fogel. Hillsdale, New Jersey: Lawrence Erlbaum Associates.

Field, T. and Dempsey, J. (1983). Five-year follow-up of preterm respiratory distress syndrome and postterm postmaturity syndrome infants. In *Infants Born at Risk: Physiological, Perceptual and Cognitive Processes,* ed. T. Field and A. Sostek. New York: Grune & Stratton.

Field, T. et al. (1978). A first-year follow-up of high-risk infants: Formulating a cumulative risk index. *Child Development,* 49:119–131.

Freud, A. and Burlingham, D. (1944). *Infants Without Families,* vol. 3, *Writings of Anna Freud.* New York: International Universities Press, 1973.

Freud, S. (1915). Mourning and melancholia. *Standard Edition,* vol. 14, ed. J. Strachey. London: Hogarth Press, 1957.

Haka-Ikse, K. (1975). Child Development as an index of maternal mental illness. *Pediatrics,* 55:310–312.

Kashani, D. H. et al.(1981). Current perspectives on childhood depression: An overview. *American Journal of Psychiatry,* 138:143–153.

Klein, M. (1935). A contribution to the psychogenesis of manic-depressive states. In *Contributions to Psycho-Analysis, 1921–1945.* London: Hogarth Press, 1948.

Maas, H. S. (1963). *The Young Adult Adjustment of Twenty Wartime Residential Nursery Children.* New York: Child Welfare League of America.

McKnew, D. H. and Cytryn, L. (1973). Historical background in children with affective disorders. *American Journal of Psychiatry,* 130:1278–1280.

McKnew, D. H. et al. (1979). Offspring of patients with affective disorders. *British Journal of Psychiatry,* 134:148–152.

Myers, J. L.(1972). *Fundamentals of Experimental Design.* Boston: Allyn & Bacon.

Poznanski, E. and Zrull, J. P. (1970). Childhood depression. *Archives of General Psychiatry,* 23:8–15.

Reite, M., Short, R., Seiler, C., and Pauley, J. D. (1981). Attachment, loss and depression. *Journal of Child Psychology and Psychiatry,* 22:141–169.

Schulterbrandt, J. G. and Raskin, A., eds. (1977). *Depression in Childhood: Diagnosis, Treatment and Conceptual Models.* New York: Raven Press.

Spitz, R. (1946). Anaclitic depression. *The Psychoanalytic Study of the Child,* 2:113–117. New York: International Universities Press.

Tronick, E. Z., Ricks, M., and Cohn, J. F. (1982). Maternal and infant affective exchange: Patterns of adaptation. In *Emotion and Early Interaction,* ed. T. Field and A. Fogel. Hillsdale, New Jersey: Lawrence Erlbaum Associates.

Weissman, M. and Paykel, E. (1974). *The Depressed Woman.* Chicago: University of Chicago Press.

Welner, Z., Welner, A., McCrary, M. D., and Leonard, M. A. (1977). Psychopathology in children of inpatients with depression: A controlled study. *Journal of Nervous and Mental Disease,* 164:408–413.

Widmayer, S. et al. (1983). Emotional dysfunction among children born prematurely. Paper presented at the annual meeting of the Southern Perinatal Association, New Orleans.

17

The Contribution of Twinship and Health to Early Interaction and Attachment Between Premature Infants and Their Mothers

Klaus Minde, M.D., F.R.C.P.(C)., Carl Corter, Ph.D.,
and Susan Goldberg, Ph.D.

The parent-infant attachment relationship has long been a focus for theories concerning the origins of mental health and disturbance; in the past two decades, it has also been the focus of a great deal of empirical research. In this paper, we briefly review certain theoretical approaches that have inspired much of the research; this review reveals several unresolved theoretical issues and some limitations of existing research. These questions are then related to our own study, which has examined the mother-infant attachment relationship developing under the biological risk factors of prematurity, illness, and twin birth.

Watching the developing relationship between a mother and her twin infants permitted a particularly revealing examination of the maternal side of the relationship. By observing how the mother interacted with two different infants at the same time, we were able to determine how infant characteristics affect the mother's behavior and how these effects are changed or maintained over time. In addition, by employing a larger number of measures of maternal functioning than most previous researchers have done, ranging from objective observations of maternal behavior to interview analysis of maternal attitudes and affect, we could capture a more lifelike picture of early development.

Although the parent-child relationship is generally recognized as a dynamic dyad, theorists have nevertheless simplified matters by analyzing it primarily from the point of view of one of the participants. Thus the term *attachment* has generally been applied to infants' behaviors, cognitions, and feelings toward the mother, while the term *bonding* has been used to describe mothers' earliest feelings and behaviors toward their infants. Because so much of the work on attachment and bonding is based on Bowlby's theory of development, we first consider his account of processes in the development of human attachment.

BOWLBY'S THEORY

Bowlby's belief in the importance of the attachment relationship has changed little since 1951 when he wrote that "what is believed to be essential for mental health is that the infant and young child should experience a warm, intimate, and continuous relationship with his mother" (p. 355). However, his theory of the mechanisms of that relationship has developed substantially, culminating in the sophisticated ideas presented in his three volumes of *Attachment and Loss* (1969, 1973, 1980). Although Bowlby states that he deals with the same phenomena as do the theories of "object relations" or "symbiosis-individuation," (1980, p. 389), his approach is fundamentally different and has inspired more empirical research.

According to Bowlby, attachment is a "system" composed of attachment behaviors, which operate to keep the infant and mother in proximity, as well as cognitions and affects, which operate to organize and select the behaviors. The term *system* is used in the sense of a control system, a concept Bowlby has borrowed from engineering. Smooth operation of the attachment system protects the infant in threatening circumstances, but allows other systems, such as exploration, to predominate in benign circumstances, thus permitting the child to acquire social and cognitive competence through interaction with the wider world. The organization of the attachment system runs a developmental course. For example, attachment behaviors become integrated and more "intelligent" as they are gradually brought under the control of cognitive expectations and plans. Affects play a role too. Insecurity or fear when the infant is out of contact with the mother serve as part of the appraisal process by which attachment behaviors are organized and activated. Although learning to discriminate mother and acquiring expectations by interacting with her are crucial to attachment formation, Bowlby described the attachment system as "instinctive" in the ethological, rather than psychoanalytic, sense. The particular innate features of the attachment system range from the initial reflexive behaviors such as sucking to a built-in aversion to being alone as a natural clue to danger. Thus the motivation for attachment is partly inherent in the system itself rather than stemming from some other source, such as need satisfaction.

Bowlby's radical departure from the traditional need-satisfaction explanation of attachment initially led to considerable controversy, especially in psychoanalytic circles. His theory has demonstrated its value, however, by directly stimulating research and by providing a useful model for integrating a wide variety of data on development. Thus even such critical research-oriented writers as Rutter (1977) have acknowledged that attachment as Bowlby conceptualized it may be an important determinant of later mental health.

Rutter reviewed two sets of data that demonstrate the importance of attachment. Tizard's (1977; Tizard and Hodges, 1978) long-term studies of children reared in modern residential nurseries without opportunity to develop attachment in infancy showed that the children were attention-seeking, restless, disobedient, and unpopular at school. This was true even for those children adopted after infancy, so that the absence of a continuous mother figure during infancy may have been the crucial variable. Rutter also showed the relevance of attachment for understanding the relative impact of parental death and divorce on children's adjustment. Rutter and others have shown greater deviance among children of divorce as against those experiencing a death, presumably because of the discordant family relations that precede divorce. Rutter suggested that attachment relationships may be damaged by marital discord, which in turn impedes the psychological availability of the parents to the child. Analogous findings are provided by Main and Weston (1981) and Crnic and associates (1983), who show that external stresses may impede maternal behavior, which in turn may offset the infant's later attachment behavior.

These findings are interesting for a number of reasons. They suggest, first, that, once a healthy attachment is formed and presumably internalized in some way, loss of a parent through death does not prevent healthy functioning. Second, even though almost all children reared in family circumstances develop attachments, the quality of the attachment varies depending on such factors as parental availability, which in turn may depend on social relationships and circumstances beyond the parent-child dyad. Finally, stress has many manifestations that offset the attachment relationship and adjustment differently; even the effects of a particular stress, such as parental loss, will depend on such factors as family functioning prior to the loss.

While Bowlby has taken the lead in theorizing about common processes in the development of attachment, Ainsworth and her colleagues (1978) have used his theory as a base from which to explore individual differences in the quality of attachment. A key contribution in this work has been the development of the Ainsworth Strange Situation as a reliable standardized procedure for assessing the quality of attachment in infants between one and one and a half years of age.

This objective assessment procedure has allowed Ainsworth and others to explore the correlates of attachment quality. These correlates suggest that quality of attachment has possible causes and consequences that help to refine our understanding of the development of attachment and have established the construct validity of the attachment assessment. Ainsworth's own longitudinal study of mother-infant interaction in the home during the infant's first year indicates that attachment quality at one year of age is foreshadowed by the degree of a mother's sensitivity to her infant's signals, but that early differences in *infant* behavior are not predictive of later attachment quality. For example, mothers of infants who were later classified as securely attached were, in the first three months, more responsive to crying than mothers of infants who were later classified as anxiously attached. The infant's crying behavior during the early months, however, was not correlated with later attachment status.

Although Ainsworth believes that influences within the mother-child relationship are reciprocal, she also thinks that her data indicate that "deep-seated patterns of maternal behavior do indeed have a strong influence on the way in which an infant's attachment to his mother becomes organized" (1978, p. 6). Thus, within her physically healthy, stable, middle-class sample, she finds evidence that the out-

come of an insecure attachment at one year of age is due primarily to maternal insensitivity, presumably based on relatively persistent patterns of maternal personality. It should be noted that in her middle-class sample there was little chance to see how stressful life events would affect the course of attachment. Furthermore, Ainsworth points out that her measures may have obscured the contribution of infant characteristics: "They cannot show the extent to which different mothers behaved differently because they were responding to infants with different characteristics" (p. 45).

In fact, several studies have indicated that infant characteristics assessed by the Neonatal Behavior Assessment Scale (Brazelton, 1973) may add to the prediction of later attachment classification (Crockenberg, 1981; Vaughn et al., 1980; Waters et al., 1980). Crockenberg found that highly irritable newborns were more often classified as anxiously attached at one year of age. Interestingly, Crockenberg found the connection between early irritability and later attachment only in families in which the mother had limited social support. Although these studies suggest that the infant's own characteristics may contribute to his or her later attachment status, they do not elucidate how the intervening transactions between mother and infant might "carry" the connection between early and later infant characteristics.

Potential consequences, as well as causes, of quality of attachment have also been examined. A number of studies have shown that attachment quality predicts behavior outside of the family setting (Lieberman, 1977; Waters et al., 1979). Waters and his colleagues also showed that attachment quality in the Strange Situation at fifteen months predicted blind ratings of interpersonal competence and ego strength/effectance in the children's playgroups almost two years later. Such cross-age, cross-situational, and cross-behavioral consistency in quality of social adaptation is a truly remarkable testimony to the power of the attachment-quality measure. Nevertheless, the mechanisms responsible for such consistency have not yet been demonstrated.

The explanation offered by Ainsworth, Waters, and others for such consequences builds on individual differences in the various processes outlined in Bowlby's systems approach to attachment. Briefly, a responsive mother builds feelings of security and expectations of ready availability should the child's attachment behaviors be activated. Such security and positive expectations permit the child more effective use of the mother as a base from which to explore the world and thus more opportunities to acquire competence.

There are alternative emphases to this one, which feature affective-cognitive internalization of a responsive mother. The stability of attachment quality could, for example, reflect stability in the *relationship* rather than in internalized qualities or cognition in the *child*. Secure attachment could thus be a measure of a sensitive relationship (or even a family network of sensitive relationships) in which the child acquires skills of reciprocal exchange which transfer to new situations, such as peer interaction in the preschool setting. A less likely but more parsimonious explanation would be that consistency is temperamentally based—the irritable newborn appears more insecure with her mother as a one-year-old, and these difficulties simply extend into other settings. Our study of mothers' responses to two different infants within the same family is a step toward disentangling these possibilities.

THE MOTHER'S ROLE

Although Bowlby and Ainsworth approach attachment as a system in the infant, they both assign the mother a major role in its development. But their analyses of the maternal side of the relationship are rather sketchy in comparison to the infant side. Bowlby describes the mother in terms of the mesh between her caregiving "system" and the child's attachment. Ainsworth's research rates and records a large number of maternal behaviors, but the mother's bond to her child seems to be influenced by a dimension of sensitivity that derives more from her personality than her current relationship with her infant.

Nevertheless, there would seem to be a place for affective and cognitive dimensions to the maternal side of the attachment relationship as well. Parke (1978) has argued strongly, for example, that a molecular consideration of parental behavior is not enough; we need to consider the expectations and interpretations of the adult since they are bound to modify the parent-child interaction. What is needed in the way of maternal measurement is multilevel measurement that goes beyond recording of caregiving. In our own research we have used additional measures, ranging from psychiatric interviews to records of mothers' spontaneous comments about their infants, to tap maternal interpretations and affect.

Klaus and Kennell's concept of bonding (1982) is essential to any consideration of the maternal side of the attachment relationship. Aside from its humanizing influence on hospital practices with parents and newborns, the concept has helped correct the overemphasis on the infant in the literature on infant-mother relationships, although there are problems in the concept, too. Here again the mother's role tends to be operationally defined only in terms of discrete caregiving behaviors; the analysis of affect and cognition is neglected. Most of the research concentrates on the first weeks of the infant-mother relationship and thus cannot elucidate the influence of early bonding on later interaction. The search for causes of individual differences in degree of bonding generally has been limited to studies of the role of contact, even though Klaus and Kennell acknowledge the potential importance of numerous other factors, such as the medical status of the infant.

Some of the potential limitations of Klaus and Kennell's concept of bonding stem from their adoption of a biological perspective on early mothering. They think that contact is important because it acts as a releaser of species-specific maternal behaviors and that *early* contact is important because there may be a sensitive period during which the releasing mechanism operates most efficiently. Whereas there are obvious biological elements in mothering, the evidence that contact acts as a releaser of human maternal behavior is not convincing.

One biologically inspired idea of Klaus and Kennell, that of monotrophy, is particularly relevant to our research. It states that there may be a propensity for bonding to be "developed and structured so that a close attachment can optimally be formed to only one person at a time" (p. 83). This idea stems partly from anecdotal observations of three sets of twins in which the smaller twin stayed in the hospital after the larger twin had gone home and parenting disorders with the smaller twin ensued. According to Klaus and Kennell, the principle of monotrophy "has obvious clinical implications that twins should be kept together and should be discharged at the same time so that simultaneous attachments may be possible" (p. 84).

The work on bonding raises a number of questions. Is monotrophy a factor in a mother's relationship with twins, and if so, what are its consequences? What is the relation between the mother's early investment in her children and later interaction or later attachment quality? Aside from contact, what factors feed differences in the degree of a mother's early investment in her infant(s)?

Our research strategy of employing multilevel measures of both mothers and infants and of comparing interaction between a mother and each of her twins has enabled us to provide new information on these questions and others stemming from the attachment literature.

Method

SUBJECTS

The overall design of our study includes a comparison group of singleton infants, but here we consider only twins. We drew our sample from small premature infant twins and singletons who were admitted to the Neonatal Intensive Care Unit at The Hospital for Sick Children within twelve hours after birth, between January 1980 and December 1981, and who had an average birthweight of less than 1,501 grams. This unit has sixty-four beds and in 1981 admitted about 1,600 infants, with approximately 120 babies weighing 1,000 grams or less and 200 infants weighing between 1,001 and 1,500 grams on

admission. About 10 percent of all admissions are twins. Parental visiting is permitted on a twenty-four-hour basis, and stimulation of the infant is actively encouraged. Infants were included in the study if both members of the twin pair survived for at least seventy-two hours after birth and neither had any physical malformation. Further requirements were that the parents spoke English, lived within twenty-five miles of the hospital, intended to keep their babies, and gave verbal consent to participate in the study.

Twenty-nine infant twin pairs satisfied all the foregoing criteria. Three twin pairs were excluded from the present analysis, however, because one twin in each pair died within the first weeks of life. All the parents we approached agreed to participate in the study.

There were no significant differences in birthweight, gestational age, total illness score, days of hospitalization, or sex distribution between first- or second-born twins, as shown in table 17–1. The zygocity of the twins was not studied hematologically because this would have involved costly and medically unnecessary procedures. However, fifteen of twenty-two same-sexed twin pairs were described in the medical records as sharing one placenta, and twelve of these were perceived as identical by their parents.

PROCEDURE

A summary of the measures employed in the present study is given in table 17–2. In what follows we focus on data for the hospital observations, the first two home visits, and attachment assessments.

Direct Observations of Parent-Infant Interactions. All infants were observed (a) in the hospital together with their mothers and fathers during two parental visits per week, provided the parents visited that often; and (b) at home with their mothers during feeding situations at six weeks and three, six, and nine months postterm. These observations lasted up to forty minutes. One observer continuously recorded infant behaviors, which included arm, head,

TABLE 17–1

Background Data

Parents	Infant Twin Pairs (N = 26)			Singletons (N = 27)		
	Mean	N	SD	Mean	N	SD
Age of mother	26.7		5.2	26.7		5.3
No. children	0.2		0.4	0.4		0.5
Marital status:						
Married		21			21	
Other		5			6	
Socioeconomic class:						
Upper		7			8	
Middle		10			9	
Lower		9			10	
Previous abortions:						
None		16			19	
1 or more		10			8	

Infants	Twin A			Twin B			Singleton		
	Mean	N	SD	Mean	N	SD	Mean	N	SD
Birthweight (grams)	1099		251	1108		212	1073		180
Gestational age (weeks)	29.3		2.0	29.3		2.0	28.4		1.7
Total illness score	71.8		77.0	85.2		70.2	81.2		59.2
Days of hospitalization	70.8		24.9	76.3		20.6	77.3		13.9
Sex:									
Male		16			17			17	
Female		10			9			10	

TABLE 17–2

Data Collection Schedule

Measure	Time of Data Collection					
	Hospital	6 weeks	3 months	6 months	9 months	1 year
Direct observations	X	X	X	X	X	
Interviews	X	X	X	X	X	X
Morbidity score	X					
Bayley Scales				X		
Temperament Assessment (Carey)			X	X		
Ainsworth Strange Situation (attachment)						X

leg, and hand-to-mouth movements, eyes opening, crying, vocalization, smiling, and yawning. A second observer recorded maternal behaviors—looking, looking *en face*, verbalizing to baby, verbalizing to others, instrumental and noninstrumental touching, feeding, smiling, and standing further than one meter away from the baby. A more detailed description of the observational technique can be found elsewhere (Minde et al., 1980).

Psychiatric Interview. Three to four weeks after each infant's admission, his parents were interviewed by a psychiatrist (K. M.). This semistructured interview focused on the personal and social backgrounds of both parents and their experiences during the pregnancy, delivery, and the postnatal period. In addition, the interviewer wrote a clinical case summary of each family, outlining the parental bonding experiences and expectations of their twins.

Parental Interviews. Parents were interviewed during the hospital stay to tap parental perceptions about each baby, the baby's illness, and how anxious they were about the baby's health and welfare. These interviews were carried out by one of the observers who recorded mother and infant behavior. At discharge, parents were interviewed about the hospital experience, their knowledge of resources available to them in their communities, and their feelings about bringing the baby home. At each home visit, parents were again interviewed about their experiences with each baby and their feelings about caring for their infants. All interviews were semistructured and coded systematically immediately following the interview.

Morbidity Scale. The Scale identifies and measures the nineteen most common diseases or pathophysiological states encountered in infants under 1,501 grams in our Intensive Care Unit (for example, Respiratory Distress Syndrome, pneumothorax, cardiac failure, necrotizing enterocolitis). It was developed by a neonatologist in our unit and is described in detail elsewhere (Minde et al., in press). In brief, to obtain the morbidity score, the medical chart of each infant is reviewed, and each of the nineteen medical conditions is rated for each day of the infant's hospitalization. Each medical condition is given a score from 0 (absent) to 3 (severe, if the condition is acutely life-threatening and requires immediate and intensive treatment). Each infant receives a "total daily score." The sum total of daily scores for the entire hospitalization reflects both the severity and duration of an infant's neonatal course in our hospital.

Ratings of Mother-Infant Interaction. After each home visit mother-infant interactions were rated on thirty-three scales (Egeland and Brunquell, 1977; Egeland et al., 1979). Infant ratings assess such characteristics as state of arousal, temperament, and social responsiveness; the maternal ratings assess such characteristics as the mothers' quality of physical contact, caregiving skills, and delight in their infants.

Attachment Assessment and Classification. At one year corrected age each child was seen in Ainsworth's Strange Situation paradigm (Ainsworth et al., 1978). This session was videotaped, and classifications were made from the videotapes. According to Ainsworth's classification scheme, the majority of children at one year are able to use the mother as a secure base for exploring a new environment or person, may or may not be visibly distressed at separation, but greet the mother positively on return and make clear efforts to reestablish and maintain contact with her. These children are considered securely attached (Group B). There are two patterns of behavior seen in insecurely attached children. One is avoidance of the mother as seen in delayed greeting or in ignoring her after separations (Group A). The other is an angry response, displayed as refusal to be comforted in spite of strong contact-seeking and prolonged contact, or outright tantrum behavior (Group C).

Results

DIFFERENTIAL TREATMENT OF TWINS

Our first question was whether mothers responded differently to their individual twin infants both in the nursery and at home. Furthermore, we wondered whether differences in behavior would be related to specific infant characteristics. Although we expected that particular characteristics in the infants might evoke particular kinds of maternal responses, we did not expect broad differences in maternal behaviors toward the twins.

However, hospital observers reported that as early as ten days after birth mothers began to show a clear preference for one infant over the other. As we became more aware of this phenomenon, we devised three indicators of preference. The first of these was based on the mother's perception of infant characteristics. Infants were considered preferred if the mother described them as having more positive traits (more perceptive, more cuddly, more of a fighter). These positive traits included physical resemblance to self, spouse, or an especially beloved family member. The second indicator was based on parental behavior. Infants were considered preferred if mother spent more time in caregiving, play, or visual attention to them. During hospital visits this would be manifest by differences in visiting time or by the mothers' visually keeping track of one twin while interacting with the other. At home, the preferred twin was the one who received more close physical contact or more spontaneous pleasurable interaction. Twins were also considered preferred when mother spent more time talking about them or comparing them favorably against their twin sibling. The third indicator was based on material signs. Twins were considered preferred if they had newer or better equipment (crib, high chair, infant seat), better clothing, more toys, or received other special treats from mother. To be considered as exhibiting a preference, a mother had to show differences in behavior in each of two categories as judged by two independent observers.

Of the twenty-five pairs who were discharged from the hospital twenty mothers developed clear preferences. In two of these families, one twin subsequently died, leaving eighteen families in which mother preferred one twin over the other. During the ensuing home observations at six weeks, three, six, nine, and twelve months, eight mothers were judged to continue to prefer their initially favored twin (stable preferences). Ten mothers shifted their preference from one twin to the other (unstable preferences). Some of the mothers who changed their preference had done so as early as six weeks after discharge, while others shifted as late as six months.

We were interested in the basis for initial preferences and therefore examined birthweight and birth order as possible precursors of preference. Birth order did not differentiate between initially preferred and nonpreferred infants. There were twelve first- and eight second-born infants in the initially preferred group. The average birthweights of initially preferred and nonpreferred twins also did not differ. However, the total illness scores of the initially preferred infants were significantly lower than those of their nonpreferred siblings, indicating the preferred infants had experienced significantly fewer medical complications (see table 17–3). This finding confirms preliminary data from the same population (Minde et al., 1982). The five twin pairs whose mothers showed no preference in the hospital were most like the preferred twin group. Thus the twins in the no-preference group were healthier on average.

FACTORS AFFECTING PREFERENCE SHIFTS

A second question concerned the factors influencing shifts in preference. Were there specific infant or maternal characteristics associated with stability or instability of preference?

INFANT INFLUENCES

Table 17–4 presents illness scores for initially preferred and nonpreferred infants whose mothers had stable or unstable preferences. It indicates that infants who were consistently preferred by their mothers (stable preference group) had significantly fewer medical complications than their consistently nonpreferred siblings. Differences between twin pairs whose mothers changed preference during the first year (unstable preference group) were not significant.

When we examined infant behavior during maternal visits to the nursery, in order to control for infants' varying length of stay and to rule out behavioral differences attributable to differences in medical condition, we used only visits that occurred between the second and fourth week of the infants' stay in the hospital when all infants were still in incubators. In addition, we used only data from visits in which there were observations of the mother with both of her twins on the same day. These restrictions allowed us to include an average of 2.8 observations per infant ($SD = .9$) lasting an average of forty-three minutes (SD 24) in this analysis.

Table 17–5 summarizes infant behaviors during these observations. Of the behaviors we recorded, initially preferred and nonpreferred infants differed only in their visual alertness. The initially preferred infant in the stable preference group and the initially nonpreferred infant in the unstable preference group had their eyes open longer. Insofar as

TABLE 17–3

Medical Conditions and Initial Preference

	Initially preferred		Initially nonpreferred		No-preference group	
	X	SD	X	SD	X	SD
Birthweight	1181	273	1037	213	1189	158
Illness score	68.7	66.1	119.3	71.7	67.1	61.6

$df = 38$
$t = 3.12$
$p < .01$

TABLE 17–4

Illness Scores and Maternal Preference in Twins During First Year

	Stable Preference (N = 16)		Unstable Preference (N = 20)	
Illness score	Preferred	Nonpreferred	Initially preferred	Initially nonpreferred
X̄	49.9	99.0	98.6	119.4
SD	39.6	44.7	80.6	95.5
	$df = 14$ $t = 2.17$ $p < .05$		$df = 18$ $t = 0.51$ NS	

TABLE 17–5

Infant Behaviors During Mothers' Visits in Hospital

	Stable Preference (N = 16)				Unstable Preference (N = 20)			
	Preferred		Nonpreferred		Initially Preferred		Initially Nonpreferred	
Behaviors	X̄	SD	X̄	SD	X̄	SD	X̄	SD
Eyes opening	14.3	10.1	5.4	3.5*	10.3	8.9	17.2	8.3†
Arm movement	20.9	13.2	21.7	12.7	16.0	7.0	14.8	7.3
Leg movement	26.3	12.2	26.2	12.8	15.8	7.3	14.2	9.7
Mouth movement	12.9	10.3	10.7	8.8	12.4	10.9	9.4	7.7
Vocalization	0.3	0.4	1.3	1.9	0.4	1.2	0.3	0.8

Mann Whitney U Test
$* = p < .1$
$† = p < .05$

infants were placed in these groups on the basis of maternal preference in the hospital, it indicates that infants who were initially not preferred but who subsequently became the favorite were more alert during nursery visits. Hence they were more likely to engage in one of the behaviors mothers may consider especially attractive or appealing.

To see whether these patterns continued after discharge, we next looked at the behaviors of these infants during feedings at six and twelve weeks after term. At these visits, the average feeding observed ranged from sixteen to twenty-three minutes. Table 17–6 shows the behaviors for infants in the stable preference group while Table 17–7 shows data for those in

TABLE 17–6

Infant Behaviors During Feedings, Stable Preference Group at 6 and 12 Weeks

	6 Weeks				12 Weeks			
	Preferred		Nonpreferred		Preferred		Nonpreferred	
Behaviors	$\overline{X}$	SD	$\overline{X}$	SD	$\overline{X}$	SD	$\overline{X}$	SD
Looking at mother's face	19.7	22.7	4.9	6.7†	10.6	12.6	15.4	12.4
Eyes opening	62.2	18.6	44.6	18.2*	89.6	4.0	75.9	14.0†
Arm movement	28.6	16.5	22.5	8.7	48.1	19.8	35.6	15.5
Leg movement	19.6	8.6	14.2	9.7	12.2	12.7	25.5	27.3
Mouth movement	56.3	30.9	48.8	34.8	68.9	18.4	59.7	26.6
Vocalization	5.1	4.4	8.4	6.5	4.3	4.5	2.4	2.2

Mann Whitney U Test
* = $p < .1$
† = $p < .05$

TABLE 17–7

Infant Behaviors During Feedings, Unstable Preference Group at 6 and 12 Weeks

	6 Weeks				12 Weeks			
	Initially Preferred		Initially Nonpreferred		Initially Preferred		Initially Nonpreferred	
Behaviors	$\overline{X}$	SD	$\overline{X}$	SD	$\overline{X}$	SD	$\overline{X}$	SD
Looking at mother's face	16.3	17.9	16.8	12.6	12.3	11.8	7.1	7.7
Eyes opening	74.2	22.5	74.3	14.2	91.8	7.0	91.4	6.7
Arm movement	43.2	18.5	40.4	16.7	62.7	28.8	49.0	25.4
Leg movement	21.3	15.7	10.1	4.5	25.4	26.0	18.1	12.9
Mouth movement	62.6	14.7	63.6	15.2	67.8	21.2	72.0	10.7
Vocalization	4.4	6.3	2.5	3.4	6.9	7.6	3.7	5.2

the unstable preference group. The tables indicate that initially preferred infants of mothers with stable preferences continued at six and twelve weeks to have their eyes open more and to focus significantly longer on the mother's face than did their nonpreferred siblings. In contrast, in the unstable preference group there were no behavioral differences. However, when we reconsidered our raw data, we noticed that four of ten mothers in this group had already shifted preference by six weeks and five by twelve weeks. In keeping with our hunch about the characteristics of the infants in the unstable preferences group, we expected those four or five infants had already "won the battle" for their mother's attention. Consequently we reanalyzed the feeding data by placing babies in groups according to preference at the time of observation. The results of this analysis are shown in table 17–8. They

indicate that the initially nonpreferred infant who will later be preferred focuses significantly more on the mother's face than the twin who will lose favored status.

While these observations provided us with some data, we were concerned that our conclusions were based on comparatively short observation periods. Therefore our confidence in these data would be strengthened if they could be confirmed by the more global ratings (Egeland and Brunquell, 1977; Egeland et al., 1979) used by the observers following each of the home visits. In the stable preference group (table 17–7), the consistently preferred infants spent more time looking at mother's face and were rated as more sociable. In the unstable preference group (table 17–8), the nonpreferred twin destined to become preferred was found to do more looking at mother and to be rated as more sociable. The findings from

TABLE 17–8

Infant Behaviors During Feedings, Unstable Preference Group at 6 and 12 Weeks, New Way[a]

	6 Weeks				12 Weeks			
	Preferred		Nonpreferred		Preferred		Nonpreferred	
Behaviors	X̄	SD	X̄	SD	X̄	SD	X̄	SD
Looking at mother's face	11.9	11.7	21.8	12.6*	4.4	5.2	15.0	11.3†
Eyes opening	71.1	21.5	76.6	15.3	90.7	7.2	92.6	6.3

Mann Whitney U Test
* = $p < .1$
† = $p < .05$
[a]Preference based upon status at the time of observation.

TABLE 17–9

Ratings Stable Preference Group of Twins at 6 and 12 Weeks

	6 Weeks				12 Weeks			
	Preferred		Nonpreferred		Preferred		Nonpreferred	
Behaviors	X̄	SD	X̄	SD	X̄	SD	X̄	SD
Amount of looking at mother's face	6.0	2.0	3.8	1.5*	5.4	1.3	4.0	1.5*
Social behavior	3.7	2.4	2.0	1.0	6.2	1.2	5.4	1.3
Muscle tone	4.6	1.9	5.0	1.3	4.4	0.7	5.0	1.2

Mann Whitney U Test
* = $p < .1$

the ratings are consistent with the coding of specific behaviors.

MATERNAL BEHAVIORS

We next examined maternal behaviors to determine whether mothers whose preferences were stable differed in any respect from those whose preferences were unstable. Table 17–11 summarizes observed maternal behavior during the hospital visits. While mothers in both groups spent significantly more time looking *en face* with their preferred infant, mothers whose preferences remained stable also touched their preferred infants more for both instrumental and affectionate purposes. Thus, mothers whose preferences remained stable showed different attention to the preferred twin in visual and tactile modalities whereas mothers whose preferences ultimately changed showed their preference only in the visual mode. In both groups, mothers looked more at

the nonpreferred infant although this difference was significant only in the stable preference group. (Since *en face* looking was excluded from the "looking" category, looking is a less accurate reflection of mother's attention to infant than *en face* alone or than looking plus *en face*).

Examination of the ratings of maternal behavior (table 17–12) shows that mothers with stable and unstable preferences were judged to vary in behavior toward their preferred and nonpreferred twins on only two of the eighteen scales: Mothers in both groups were judged more accepting of their preferred twin and as showing more negative regard toward the nonpreferred twin. This pattern occurred at both ages and in both groups of mothers, but the difference is statistically significant in only four of the eight comparisons. These data indicate that, for the most part, when mothers in both stable and unstable preference groups differentiate between the twins they are more positive toward the preferred twin. The main

TABLE 17–10

Ratings Unstable Preference Group of Twins at 6 and 12 Weeks, New Way[a]

| | 6 Weeks | | | | 12 Weeks | | | |
| | Preferred | | Nonpreferred | | Preferred | | Nonpreferred | |
Behaviors	X̄	SD	X̄	SD	X̄	SD	X̄	SD
Amount of looking at mother's face	5.0	1.6	6.6	1.5†	4.5	1.4	6.0	1.8*
Muscle tone	5.2	1.0	5.2	0.6	4.7	0.7	4.3	0.8
Social behavior	3.3	1.4	4.4	1.8	4.5	1.3	5.8	1.4*
Temperament	4.4	0.8	4.8	1.0	4.7	1.3	4.7	1.2

Mann Whitney U Test
* = $p < .1$
† = $p < .05$
[a]Preference based upon status at the time of observation.

TABLE 17–11

Maternal Behavior During Visits in Hospital

| | Stable Preference (N = 16) | | | | Unstable Preference (N = 20) | | | |
| | Preferred | | Nonpreferred | | Initially Preferred | | Initially Nonpreferred | |
Behaviors	X̄	SD	X̄	SD	X̄	SD	X̄	SD
Looking	53.1	18.7	68.6	9.1*	70.3	17.1	76.3	13.3
Looking *en face*	18.9	9.6	9.4	6.9†	10.7	12.5	1.3	2.4†
Touching	66.2	16.4	44.0	16.2†	49.6	18.8	54.4	21.9
Talking to infant	31.1	20.2	22.6	19.1	19.2	14.1	13.2	7.6
Talking to others	15.8	12.2	13.1	8.4	16.3	10.3	17.8	11.1
Smiling	10.3	8.1	6.7	6.3	5.1	4.3	3.1	3.4
Instrumental touching	10.5	8.7	4.6	3.3*	4.7	4.9	2.3	2.8

Mann Whitney U Test
* = $p < .1$
† = $p < .05$

feature which differentiated mothers with stable preferences from those whose preferences shifted was that in the hospital observation differentiation for the stable preference group occurred in several behaviors. In the unstable preference group it occurred only for looking.

We next compared mothers who had a preference with those who showed no preference. On the one hand, the principle of monotrophy suggests that the task of forming a relationship with two babies at once handicaps the mother, and one of the babies necessarily "suffers" from less adequate care. On the other hand, our concept of a "good" mother under these circumstances would include the ability to respond to both babies and to care for them equally. We therefore examined ratings of maternal behavior for the five mothers judged to have no initial preference.

The ratings confirmed our initial impression of lack of preference, showing that these mothers behaved very similarly toward each infant during our hospital and home-feeding observations and were rated similarly with both twins. However, when we compared ratings of mothers with no preference and those with one, the findings were somewhat different. During their hospital visits the no-preference mothers talked, touched, and smiled at their infants 50 percent less than did the mothers with a preference. However, at the six-week home visits, the no-preference mothers

TABLE 17–12

Ratings of Mothers with Stable and Unstable Preferences

Behaviors at:	Stable Preference (N = 14)				Unstable Preference (N = 20)			
	Preferred		Nonpreferred		Initially Preferred		Initially Nonpreferred	
	X̄	SD	X̄	SD	X̄	SD	X̄	SD
6 weeks								
Negative regard	1.2	0.2	2.3	0.5‡	1.4	0.5	2.2	0.6†
Acceptance rejection	7.8	0.8	6.7	0.6§	7.1	0.6	6.3	0.9
12 weeks								
Negative regard	1.5	0.7	1.9	0.8	1.3	0.4	2.3	1.1†
Acceptance rejection	6.6	1.2	6.0	1.1	7.2	0.6	6.1	1.3*

Mann Whitney U Test
* = $p < .1$
† = $p < .05$
‡ = $p < .02$
§ = $p < .01$

received more optimal ratings on twelve of thirteen scales ($p < .003$ by sign test). Yet by three months this pattern had reversed, and the mothers with a preference received more optimal ratings on twelve of the thirteen scales ($p < .003$). Furthermore, this last shift was accounted for by an overall increase (toward more optimal) in ratings for the preference group and a decrease for the no-preference group. The mothers, then, who had a preference maintained a consistent involvement over time, while mothers in the no-preference group started out poorly in the hospital, rallied at the six-week observations, but had lost interest again at three months.

PREFERENCE AND ATTACHMENT

Our third major question concerned the relationship between maternal preference and later security of attachment. On the one hand, our data show that while mothers differed in the treatment of their twins, the variation between mothers was far greater than that shown by the same mother within the twin pair. One could argue, however, that the nonpreferred baby may perceive the mother as being less responsive and may therefore be more likely to become insecurely attached. If it is absolute amount or quality of maternal care that deter-

mines attachment status, then preference should have little to do with attachment. If the relative amount or relative quality of care is important, then preferred infants should be more likely to be secure.

An examination of our total sample revealed the following. Of sixty infants who were seen in the Strange Situation paradigm (including twins, singletons, and single survivors) five (8 percent) could not be categorized because of severe developmental delays or handicaps. Of the remaining fifty-five, thirty-nine (7 percent) were securely attached (Group B) infants, while sixteen (29 percent) were insecurely attached (Groups A or C). Of the latter group there were five C and eleven A babies. This distribution is not strikingly different from that seen in full-term populations. Furthermore, there was no difference in the proportion of securely versus insecurely attached infants in the twin and singleton groups. For the twins, 77 percent were secure and 23 percent were insecure, while for the singletons the comparable figures were 75 percent and 25 percent.

We noted that there was a tendency for twins to be in the same attachment category. Of fourteen securely attached babies, ten were from five twin pairs. Among the insecurely attached group of nine infants, six came from three twin pairs. In addition it appeared that the existence of maternal preferences was related to security of attachment. All five pairs of securely attached twins came from families in which mothers had an initial preference, while the remaining four securely attached infants were preferred at one year, although they had not been consistently preferred. In the insecurely attached group eight of nine infants came from families in which mothers had not shown an initial preference. One insecurely attached infant was the nonpreferred twin whose preferred sibling was securely attached.

These data suggest that there are relationships between the pattern of attachment behavior in the Ainsworth Strange Situation and the absence or presence of a maternal preference. Mothers who did not have an initial preference were likely to have relationships with their infants that led to insecure attachments. The data in the previous section indicated that mothers who did not have an initial preference were rated at all except one of our early observation points as being less actively and enthusiastically involved with their infants. This suggests that mothers who do not develop a preference early on may possibly be less interested in both their children, a suggestion that seemed to be substantiated by two findings.

First, clinical descriptions of the five families who developed no preferences toward their twins revealed three of them to have many characteristics of psychosocial difficulties. The mothers had poor relations with their respective spouses; one mother had even placed the children in foster care for three months and appeared generally overwhelmed and uninterested in taking care of them. Second, as previously noted, ratings of maternal behavior also indicated that this group of mothers received less consistent and less optimal ratings than those who had an initial preference.

We felt the need to examine one remaining question. This pertained to the extent of the shift in maternal caregiving activity that took place when a previously nonpreferred infant became the preferred one. This shift could come about in different ways: theoretically, there were two possibilities. The infants could simply change positions, leaving the mother giving similar levels of care to the two infants.

It was also possible, however, that the initially preferred infant continued to receive consistent care, even as the care of the newly preferred baby surpassed this level after the shift in preference had occurred. In this case the overall quality of mother's investment vis-à-vis her infants would increase.

Therefore we compared the sum of the qualitative ratings of maternal behavior for the ten mothers who exhibited an unstable preference during the observation preceding and following the change of preference. Results indicated that the infants simply changed positions. The preferred infant received an average rating of 5.9 before and 6.0 after the switchover, while the mean maternal ratings for the nonpreferred infant were 5.5 and 5.6 respectively.

Discussion

The present data document that these very low birthweight babies, even with all the problems and risks that attend their birth and development are not more likely to be insecurely attached than normal full-term infants. Whereas this has been noted for other samples of preterm infants (Field et al., 1978; Rode et al., 1981), our infants were younger, smaller, and more seriously ill than those in the previous studies. Nevertheless, like their stronger counterparts, a substantial majority were securely attached to their mothers by one year corrected age, indicating that the propensity to form a secure attachment is an extremely robust developmental phenomenon that is not readily disrupted even under highly adverse conditions.

Second, our data document that the parental task of forming an emotional bond with two babies simultaneously is not an insurmountable one. Twins were no more likely than singletons to be insecurely attached. Furthermore, although the numbers were small, all of our single survivor twins were securely attached, indicating that the loss of one infant need not impair a mother's ability to form a positive relationship with the surviving twin.

Although these findings may be of general

interest, we feel that an especially challenging result of this study was the strong tendency of mothers to have a preference for one of the twins and for the existence of such preferences seemingly to enhance the likelihood of secure attachments. The final interpretation of this finding is not yet possible, but such preferences may, in fact, reflect a variant of the principle of monotrophy in that it is natural for a mother who is required to form more than one attachment simultaneously to be more invested in one child than the other. Insofar as in our study the majority of mothers developed definite preferences and, at least initially, these were related to the medical status of the infant, it would seem that the infant who is more robust and has a greater capacity to be awake and responsive to the mother is initially most likely to be preferred.

Why approximately half of the mothers maintained this initial preference and the remainder did not cannot be answered conclusively. Our study shows that when the infant who was initially not preferred was in fact more attentive and more sociable toward the mother, her preference was likely to shift. That the infants whose mothers shifted preference during the first year had a similar degree of initial medical complications suggests that in children with similar medical problems it is the behavioral concomitants of illness that interfere with the establishment of optimal early mother-infant interactions. We have previously shown that the amount of interaction a mother shows toward her infant in a nursery predicts her later relationship with this infant (Minde et al., 1980) and that medically more compromised infants show a different behavioral repertoire which is transmitted to their mothers (Minde et al., 1982). The present data substantiate the ideas of Brazelton and his colleagues about the early onset of powerful mother-infant transactions and the role the infant plays in these.

Furthermore, the present data suggest that the seemingly natural tendency to develop a preference may be associated with or even be a prerequisite for a later secure attachment in twins. In our sample all the twin pairs whose mothers showed no preference were later in one of the two insecurely attached groups.

While this may be an artifact of our comparatively small sample, a maternal preference may also suggest that a mother has truly identified the individualities of each infant and, in acknowledging this, demonstrates her commitment to their individual needs. Indeed, the fact that this preference often shifts suggests that these mothers do respond to differing needs at different times and invest in the infant who seems most likely to reciprocate at the time.

This sensitivity to the infant's needs and responsiveness is further illustrated by the fate of three twin pairs in which one twin developed a serious developmental delay. In all three of these pairs the mother had initially preferred the healthy infant. In two cases, however, mother shifted her preference to the retarded and handicapped infant by three or six months, in concordance with the baby's emerging abnormal symptoms. In both these cases the mother provided far more interaction for her retarded infant than she had for the initially preferred healthy infant. In the third case the mother shifted preferences at each observation point, and, as she herself had a multitude of medical and psychological problems, she never seemed to be very much engaged with either of her infants.

It should be noted that what we are calling preference is not an overt and conscious choice by the mother. Only one mother ever admitted her preference; this behavioral distinction seems quite unconscious and was, in fact, outwardly denied by all the other parents. We had the clinical impression from a number of cases, though not the majority, that the father would prefer the other infant and in that sense reestablish some balance.

We might have expected that a preference, though it might be advantageous for the preferred twin, would certainly have a detrimental impact on the nonpreferred twin. However, our findings indicate that rather than being disadvantageous, the existence of preferences is a generally positive feature and may serve to mobilize the developing mother-child relationship.

In contrast, a mother's apparent total egalitarian treatment of her infants was associated in our study with a generally lower rate of maternal caregiving and interactive activities and a preponderance of insecure infant attachment ratings at one year.

Because the majority of the no-preference mothers also faced a high number of psychosocial stresses, the lack of initial preference may simply reflect the mother's contingent general withdrawal from social interactions with both her infants. However, as two of the five mothers in the no-preference group developed a preference later on for one of their infants and yet at twelve months had insecurely attached infants, the answer to the impact of extreme egalitarianism early in life is probably more complex and needs further study. It does seem possible, though, that the association between an even slight preference for one infant over the other and later secure attachment may reflect a biological "need" to have some sort of hierarchy in one's interpersonal relationships. This idea would be consistent with Bowlby's concept of monotrophy but not with the narrower interpretation given to it by Klaus and Kennell, who asserted that one can only form one "successful" attachment at a time. Our data therefore provide only an initial step in the endless quest to learn more about ourselves and those around us.

REFERENCES

Ainsworth, M. D., Blehar, M. C., Waters, E., and Well, S. (1978). *Patterns of Attachment.* Hillsdale, New Jersey: Lawrence Erlbaum Associates.

Bowlby, J. (1951). Maternal care and mental health. *Bulletin of the World Health Organization,* 3:355–534.

Bowlby, J. (1969). *Attachment and Loss,* vol. I, *Attachment.* New York: Basic Books.

Bowlby, J. (1973). *Attachment and Loss,* vol. II, *Separation—Anxiety and Anger.* New York: Basic Books.

Bowlby, J. (1980). *Attachment and Loss,* vol. III, *Loss: Sadness and Depression.* New York: Basic Books.

Brazelton, T. B. (1973). *Neonatal Behavioral Assessment Scale.* Philadelphia: J. B. Lippincott.

Crnic, K. A. et al. (1983). Effects of stress and social support on mothers and premature and full-term infants. *Child Development,* 54:209–217.

Crockenberg, S. B. (1981). Infant irritability, mother responsiveness and social support influences on the security of infant-mother attachment. *Child Development,* 52: 857–865.

Egeland, B. and Brunquell, D. (1979). An at-risk approach to the study of child abuse: Some preliminary findings. *Journal of the American Academy of Child Psychiatry,* 18:219–235.

Egeland, B., Taraldson, B., and Brunquell, D. (1977). Observations of waiting room and feeding situations. (Mimeographed report.) Minneapolis: University of Minnesota.

Field, T. et al. (1978). A first-year follow-up of high-risk infants, formulating a cumulative risk index. *Child Development,* 49:119–131.

Lieberman, A. F. (1977). Preschoolers competence with a peer: Relations with attachment and peer experience. *Child Development,* 48:1277–1287.

Klaus, M. H. and Kennell, J. H. (1982). *Parent-Infant Bonding.* St. Louis: C. V. Mosby.

Main, M. and Weston, D. R. (1981). The quality of the toddler's relationship to mother and father: Related to conflict behavior and the readiness to establish new relationships. *Child Development,* 52:932–940.

Minde, K., Marton, P., Manning, D., and Hines, B. (1980). Some determinants of mother-infant interaction in the premature nursery. *Journal of the American Academy of Child Psychiatry,* 19:1–21.

Minde, K., Perrotta, M., and Corter, C. (1982). The effect of neonatal complications in premature twins on their mothers' preference. *Journal of the American Academy of Child Psychiatry,* 21:446–452.

Minde, K., Whitelaw, A., Brown, K., and Fitzhardinge, P. (in press). The effect of neonatal complications in premature infants on early parent-infant interactions. *Developmental Medicine and Child Neurology.*

Parke, R. D. (1978). Parent-infant interaction: Progress, paradigms and problems. In *Application of Observational-Ethological Methods to the Study of Mental Retardation,* ed. G. P. Sackett and H. C. Haywood. Baltimore: University Park Press.

Rode, S. S. et al. (1981). Attachment patterns of infants separated at birth. *Developmental Psychology,* 17:188–191.

Rutter, M. (1977). Sociocultural influences. In *Child Psychiatry: Modern Approaches,* ed. M. Rutter and L. Hersov. Oxford: Blackwell Scientific Publications.

Tizard, B. (1977). *Adoption: A Second Chance.* London: Open Books.

Tizard, B. and Hodges, J. (1978). The effect of early institutional rearing on the development of eight-year-old children. *Journal of Child Psychology and Psychiatry,* 19:99–118.

Vaughn, B., Taraldson, B., Crichton, L., and Egeland, B. (1980). Relationships between neonatal behavioral organization and infant behavior during the first year of life. *Infant Behavior and Development,* 3:47–66.

Waters, E., Vaughn, B., and Egeland, B. (1980). Individual differences in infant-mother attachment relationships at age one: Antecedents in neonatal behavior in an urban, economically disadvantaged sample. *Child Development,* 51: 208–216.

Waters, E., Wippmann, J., and Sroufe, L. A. (1979). Attachment, positive affect and competence in the peer group: Two studies of construct validation. *Child Development,* 50:821–829.

18

Ultrasound Scanning in Obstetrics: A Necessary View of the Child to Be Born

Maddy Brenot, M.D. and Jean-Louis Brenot, M.D.

In the last five years in France we have seen a considerable increase in the number of ultrasonic examinations performed during pregnancy. Previously this examination was limited to about 18 percent of all pregnant women, but now it has reached the point where it is performed on an average of four times during each pregnancy. Its huge popularity among professionals and expectant mothers is such that neither group can any longer imagine going without it.

Because of its simplicity and reliability, ultrasound is now administered to everyone, and it is this obligatory factor which is of interest to us here. Formerly, this examination was prescribed by the physician in charge of high-risk pregnancies and only after lengthy discussion between the doctor and the future mother. Today, on the contrary, it is no longer a question of choice. Ultrasound, now a routine part of the examination in prenatal consultations, exposes parents and doctors to a compulsory viewing of the child. Therefore we have wondered how those concerned have prepared themselves to cope with a technique that undermines the validity of the doctor's clinical examination and overturns all previous practice and experience by imposing on the viewers an animated image of the fetus, the clarity of which threatens the mother's capacity to dream and imagine. There have already been a few observations relevant to the emotional consequences of the widespread use of ultrasound (for example, Cornauau, 1982; Chadeyron, 1978; Soulé, 1982). Watching and listening to the participants, we have tried to pinpoint the compromises brought into play in order to preserve their pleasure in thought and imagination in spite of ultrasound, or even because of it.

Emotions Aroused by First Encounter with the Child's Image

The psychological reactions reported here are based on numerous interviews with many pregnant women in the Outpatient Department before, during, and after the ultrasound

This study was carried out in the Maternity Outpatient Department of the Children's Hospital, Dijon. The authors wish to thank all those there who made this work possible: mothers, and sometimes fathers, ultrasonographers, and obstetricians.

examination, at all stages of pregnancy, and with both newcomers to the examination and those who had previous experience with it.

The majority of pregnant women are not at all worried about the examination, for they are told how simple and harmless the technique is. It is interesting to observe how, in the first term of pregnancy, they react to the shock of suddenly seeing what was, until that moment, hidden from them, and how they fill in the gap between what they see of the child and what they feel in their bodies.

At this early stage of pregnancy, the mothers are not yet much encumbered by it. They make themselves comfortable, and, aware of having a flat stomach, they chat away with the ultrasonographer sitting beside them. This relaxed atmosphere contrasts with the silence that suddenly overtakes them when, in the semidarkness, the monitor screen lights up before their eyes. They become as if transfixed by the image and gaze in fascination as the ultrasonographer points out the fetal body. This initial encounter is always accompanied by deep emotion, which unfurls and unfolds as, little by little, they themselves discover the image of the body.

The build-up of feeling varies among women, and these variations in themselves seem to us to be a good indication that it is possible to escape the grip of the fascination with the technique itself, and for each one to react in her own way. Where we as observers see only the picture of a three-month-old fetus, closely resembling the preceding fetus, the mother's gaze and words, charged with an emotion that belongs to her alone, bring the image to life—that of a unique individual. The individuality of existence is in sharp contrast to the uniformity of images.

Some women sit entranced. They seem to touch the baby with their eyes, absorb its image, and fall into a deep contemplation without appearing to be interested in what is said to them. They give the impression of retaking possession of the child so momentarily projected out of them, and the mental bond they maintain with the image only ends with a deep sigh following its disappearance. Other women give themselves totally to the image and enter a sort of ecstasy. Their wondering gaze resembles nothing so much as that of the Virgin at the Annunciation. One of these patients came secretly once a month for the pleasure of seeing her baby and the joy of refinding it.

Many are astonished by the movements of the fetus, which they imagine curled up as though asleep in the hollow of their abdomen. Instead, they see a complete body which sometimes seems to swim, to jump, and bounce about with the agility and flexibility of an acrobat. The contrast between the activity of the fetus and the lack of awareness of movement by the mother can give her the feeling that the baby is totally outside her control, and in some way living its own life oblivious of her. So they exclaim, "I didn't realize I was so pregnant! It's already moving and you can't catch it. I'm worried by the movements because I can't see what's causing them. To see it move about so much and not to feel anything—it's so peculiar!" The gap between the two perceptions of sight and feeling, which creates a feeling of alienation in some women, leads to feelings of frustration in others, who will try to make up for it. For example, one such woman said, "At the ultrasound examination, I can see it but I can't touch it. It's just the idea of a child. At the delivery, I'll be able to see it and to touch it; then I'll be fulfilled. To see without being able to touch causes me such excitement that after the examination, I just have to tell everyone about it to make up for it."

However, some women cannot compensate successfully in this way, and in them a "minimizing" aspect of the image predominates, an image which they are unable to move and by which they are not moved. They may express their disappointment by saying such things as, "It was an image, no relief. He wasn't pink, but black and white—it was a few smudges where the doctor apparently saw something, but I didn't see anything. It was all wishy-washy, it wasn't like a month-old baby. It doesn't do anything to me." Nevertheless, in most cases the women's emotions turn to admiration when they see the child's vitality: "It's so reassuring to see him move about, he's so alive! I could spend hours watching him. It's a miracle!"

In the third month of pregnancy, the ultrasonic examination shows the mother the fetus moving with the heart at the center "like a pulsing smudge." This confirms to her the existence of her baby as being very much alive, and it gives her a feeling of security and confidence in the child's ability to live. In these circumstances, if the pregnancy is interrupted prematurely or if, later, an abnormality is discovered, the mother goes through a state of intense depression and retaliates by accusing the ultrasonographer, who is, in her eyes, guilty of having raised false hopes. One such mother could no longer go near the examination room, because for her the ultrasonographer who had confirmed the existence of the life was responsible for its loss.

During the first-term examination, the baby's image had a great impact on the mother, stressing vitality as it did. During the third-term examination, we see the mother taking the initiative, as she starts to discover the body of the child.

In Search of the Child's Identity

Near the end of pregnancy, the ultrasound image no longer shows the child's entire body; by moving the apparatus over the mother's abdomen, the ultrasonographer explores the different parts. Guided by him, the mother gives meaning to the patches drawn on the screen and familiarizes herself with the child. The mother is now no longer so absorbed by the picture, and her gaze shifts between the screen and the ultrasonographer's face, which she studies to discover his reactions. She is, of course, looking to assure herself that her baby is normal, with a complete and healthy body. She checks to make sure all four limbs are there, she asks to see the hands and feet, wants to locate the child's exact position by finding the vertebral column and ribs, and she asks for the head and abdominal measurements to reassure herself of the child's normal development. It is a very moving experience to discover the outline and profile of the face of a fetus sucking its thumb, swallowing, or stroking its forehead with its hand. As she looks at the child's face, the mother, by her remarks, shows she is trying to write the baby into the family history by establishing links between the baby and parents. "He's got a

pointed nose like me and big ears like his father." Moreover, she wants to reconstruct the body in its entirety from the more precise though partial pictures of the baby, and she wonders about the sex of the child. The mother knows that the ultrasonographer can actually reveal this to her, but here again there is a compromise between the temptation to know and the wish to retain the mystery. The parents thus preserve their freedom to play with technology without being governed by it.

However, we have noticed that when a father attends an examination it is nearly always in the hope of learning the child's sex. Indeed, the father often expresses his feeling of being a stranger to what the mother is experiencing in her body, even if psychologically he is very involved. Thus the lack of physical awareness provokes a wish to know the child's gender, but also to know how the machine works, how tall the child is, what the figures on the screen denote, and what the flashing lights mean—details that hardly ever interest the mother. For this reason, the father's presence changes the atmosphere in the examination room to a notable degree. Where the mother is passively attentive, the father is on edge, and he attempts to overcome his anxiety by trying to understand how everything works. When the father isn't present in person, he is often mentioned by the mother. It is her husband who wants to know the sex, and it is to please him that she is asking. If they are disappointed in their expectations, they will be able to make up for it together, to adopt the now definitely sexed image of the baby, to think about him or her in a more definite way, and prepare the other children.

Here again the parents tend to create a kind of freedom. They can do this by making a secret of it—a secret kept by the mother from her husband or a secret shared by the parents but of which the rest of the family, especially the grandparents, know nothing. There is a need to retain the element of surprise as a treat for everyone else. A certain need for autonomy can even be found by doubting the diagnosis, for the parents learn of mistaken forecasts and know that one can only be sure at the time of delivery. But apart from these cases, we have come across many women who resist the pressures on them to know the sex of the child, pressures which come not only from the father, but also from parents, friends, and society in general, as if one was obliged to use all the potential of a new technique. If they resist, it is always to protect their fantasy, to preserve the element of surprise, to keep the wonder of birth, something which one such family expressed this way: "Pregnancy is not knowing; it is doubt and the pleasure of giving birth. But it is also finding out the sex. To know that is to break the spell—it's like at Christmas when you know beforehand what's in the package."

The Imagined Child and the Image of the Child

We have noted the difficulties which some women have in evoking the imagined or fantasied child in the context of prenatal consultations centered on the ultrasonic examination of the real fetus. A certain number of women can only talk about the child after the examination, as if the image of the child on the screen acted as a foundation for the imagination and allowed the fantasies to develop. Once such woman said, "Since I've actually seen him, I can think about him, because you can't imagine something out of nothing. Around that crude ultrasonic image I saw I now invent the color of his eyes and hair, even his personality. Having seen his fingers move, I think he'll be a good guitarist." In other cases, some express the feeling of an unbridgeable gap between the ultrasonic image and the child they imagine, for the first is a developing fetus, and the second is a completed child.

For those women who found it easier to imagine the child and who could talk about it, we did not have the impression that the ultrasonic image interfered with their fantasying. However, we were probably not in the best circumstances to study this point in the context of the prenatal consultation. If, however, the two images seemed to merge for a moment during the examination, they appeared to move in two different directions immediately afterward, the imagined child surging beyond the image of the child, escaping the "minimizing" effect with a sudden leap.

The Ultrasonographer under the Mother's Eye

During the course of this study, we found it interesting to observe how the ultrasonographer uses the powerful tool at his disposal. He is not entirely dominated by its technical aspects. Indeed, he makes efforts to transform the examination into a real meeting with the mother, who then becomes a person carrying a child and not just an abdomen to explore. Even with the minimal time available of about fifteen minutes, he avoids rushing to complete the report and tries to make contact with the mother by asking simple questions relating to the pregnancy, the composition of the family, how tired she is, or by asking about her professional activities. He is able then to build up a picture of the mother for himself, one which he can later utilize when he talks with her about the ultrasonic image of the child.

During the course of the examination itself, the ultrasonographer is of course less available to the mother, his attention being concentrated on reading the images, and his overriding concern is not to miss a malformed fetus. While the mother goes over the outlines of the child with him, the ultrasonographer carefully explores the pictures and makes certain that the organs, the bladder, kidneys, heart, umbilical cord, etcetera are perfect, trying not to give away any possible concern he might have. During the exploration he remains fairly quiet, waiting for questions, pointing out certain landmarks, and letting the mother develop her own ability to fantasy while he concentrates on his own train of thought. He knows that one word too much, a hasty remark, a change in his facial expression would immediately alert the mother and could create real panic. Absorbed by the images before him, he tries to weigh up his fears and to find words to tell the mother without unduly alarming her. His position in the front line makes him particularly vulnerable because he is exposed to the mother's vision, whereas the obstetrician has the time to reflect. This watching will be hard to bear when the examination must be repeated in order to ascertain the development of abnormal images, since the mother will have her eyes fixed on him as she tires of looking at the screen. If he has taken the time to get to know her before the examination, it is easier for him to sense her ability to accept the information, and he can estimate the discrepancy between what he sees on the screen and what he can say to the mother. Thus each time he will have to find a compromise between unnecessary worrying and false reassurance.

Fortunately most of the time the picture is normal, and the ultrasonographer, himself reassured, can relax and be more available to answer the mother's questions. Moreover, he has kept a surprise for her. Suddenly he stops the video image to measure the child, and at the same time takes a photograph, which he gives her. It seems to us that it is essential at this point that the ultrasonographer not get carried away by the desire to show his power by revealing the child's sex to the mother when she has not asked for it.

The examination usually ends in a moving scene as, with a tender gesture, the ultrasonographer wipes away the jelly that covered the mother's abdomen, as if he wanted to tuck up the baby inside once more, the baby who was for a moment under the spotlight and illuminated. And the mother, too, who was made transparent by the ultrasonographer finds her opacity again in a flash.

Obstetricians and Ultrasonography

In ultrasonography, obstetricians have found a means to measure the fetus with precision, to control its development, and to verify its physical completeness, something that was almost impossible with the traditional clinical examination. A new world of research has evolved concerning the prenatal diagnosis of malformations. This research probably interests the radiologist, geneticist, and surgeon more than the obstetrician himself, and it already is causing ethical problems with regard to the eventual interruption of a pregnancy. We will not deal here with this very important issue, for our present concern is only with the way in which the obstetrician uses ultrasonography outside these special cases. Indeed, for the obstetrician there is a shift in focus from his traditional clinical examination, centered more on the mother, to ultrasound, which focuses on the actual presence of the fetus.

The obstetricians we have met retain their satisfaction as clinicians by always beginning with an examination of the mother, even if they have the ultrasound report in hand. The report is only consulted at a later date in order to verify their hypotheses or to support their opinions. Even if they recognize that ultrasound affords them valuable information, they use it primarily to stimulate their ability to think and not to avoid it.

When we began this study, we thought the use of ultrasound could have a mesmerizing effect and bring with it an exaggerated interest in technical data, while excluding the human element. Today we no longer have such a concern, for we have found that the obstetricians can put some distance between themselves and the ultrasonic scan. The essential part of medical work for obstetricians is still to build a firm relationship with their patients, a relationship now enriched by the use of the additional technical information. We hope we have been able to show in this work how the people who use obstetrical ultrasound manage to escape feelings of intrusion, thanks to the means they bring into play to protect themselves. Thus, patients and doctors use their creativity to turn a technical tool into a living experience.

REFERENCES

Chadeyron, P. A. (1978). Aspects psychologiques de l'echographie obstétricale. *Revue de Médecine Psychosomatique,* 20:187–193.

Cornuau, P. (1982). Echographie et enfant imaginaire. *Psychologie Médicale,* 14:1221–1224.

Soulé, M. (1982). L'enfant dans la tête: L'enfant imaginaire. In: *La Dynamique du Nourrisson,* eds., T. B. Brazelton et al. Paris: Les Éditions E.S.F.

19

The Influence of Electronic Fetal Monitoring on Perinatal Morbidity and Mortality

Kirk A. Keegan, Jr., M.D., Edward J. Quilligan, M.D., and Feizal Waffarn, M.D.

The past ten to twelve years have seen tremendous advances made in reducing perinatal morbidity and mortality, with mortality rates falling from 29.7 in 1,000 births in 1970 to 18.2 in 1,000 in 1979. Concomitant with this decline has been a literal explosion of technologic advancements—amniocentesis, L/S ratio, ultrasound imaging, respirator care, and neonatal and fetal-heart-rate (FHR) monitoring, to name only a few. Introduction of FHR monitoring in the late 1960s and its widespread clinical acceptance by the mid 1970s has led some authors to attribute much of the decline in neonatal morbidity and mortality to its use (Krebs et al., 1980; Parer, 1981; Paul and Hon, 1974). Others, however, have argued this point, claiming FHR monitoring to be meddlesome, of no benefit, to impact unfavorably on cost analysis, and to increase Caesarean section (C/S) rates (Haverkamp, et al., 1979; Neutra et al., 1978). Confounding the evaluation of the potential benefits of FHR monitoring have been changing philosophies in obstetrical and neonatal care, such as more frequent C/S for breech and the very low birthweight infant,

aggressive management of dysfunctional labor, newborn resuscitation, and neonatal intensive care, all of which have been shown to affect favorably neonatal morbidity and mortality statistics, perhaps independently of monitoring. While a direct cause-and-effect association between FHR monitoring and improved perinatal outcome may be difficult to demonstrate, clear relationships exist between the status of fetal and neonatal hypoxemia, acidemia, and both short- and long-term neonatal outcome. Normal oxygenation and metabolic status, in the absence of other predisposing conditions, rarely results in sequelae. However, the presence of hypoxemia and acidosis in the neonate has been correlated with low Apgar score, increased incidence of Respiratory Distress Syndrome (RDS), enterocolitis, encephalopathy, seizure activity, long-term neurologic handicap, and death (Garite, personal communication; Holden, 1982; Martin et al., 1974; Meyers, 1973).

Any technique that could provide information on fetal oxygenation and metabolic status could potentially alter, through some form of intervention, prolonged periods of hypoxemia and/or acidosis, thus avoiding their proven negative neonatal impact. Intrapartum electronic fetal monitoring provides this information more accurately and practically than any other known technique. Specific fetal-heart-rate patterns, late deceleration, severe variable deceleration, diminished beat-to-beat variability, and fetal tachycardia have been clearly associated with hypoxia and acidosis in both animal and human models (Hon and Quilligan, 1967; Martin et al., 1979; Myers, 1972; Paul et al., 1975).

The most significant FHR pattern suggestive of hypoxia is late deceleration. Alterations in uterine blood flow, whether acute (maternal hemorrhage) or chronic (maternal vascular disease), result in decreased placental blood flow and intervillous space perfusion and, thus, decreased fetal oxygenation. The resultant hypoxia leads to anaerobic glycolysis and acidosis. The addition of contractions during labor further reduces placental-fetal perfusion. The hypoxic fetus will then demonstrate, either through a chemoreceptor reflex vagal mechanism and/or direct myocardial depression, a slowing of the heart rate that begins after the zenith of the contraction and returns to baseline only after the contraction is completed. This deceleration pattern occurs most frequently in the normal fetal heart range, 120–150 BPM, and is usually undetectable by auscultation. Late decelerations occur rarely if O_2 saturation is greater than 31 percent and the PO_2 is greater than 20 mmHg. Mean fetal pH during labor, and in the presence of moderate to severe late deceleration, varies between 7.12 and 7.21, (normal > 7.25) (Kubli et al., 1969).

The most common abnormal FHR pattern occurring in 20 to 30 percent of laboring patients is variable deceleration (Krebs et al., 1979). It is a vagal reflex mediated deceleration associated with umbilical-cord compression during uterine contractions. The onset of the deceleration is variable, occurring during the ascent slope of the contraction and returning to baseline before the completion of the contraction. The transient nature of the cord occlusion results in varying but usually mild degrees of respiratory acidosis in the fetus, and intervention is usually not required. Prolonged periods of respiratory acidosis can lead to a combined respiratory-metabolic acidosis suggested by a mixed pattern of variable and late decelerations resulting in fetal acidosis with a fetal pH in the 7.13 to 7.22 range (Kubli et al., 1969).

Beat-to-beat fluctuations in FHR are controlled by the combined interaction of the sympathetic and parasympathetic nervous system (Krebs et al., 1979). This autonomic regulation provides both beat-to-beat short-term variability and cyclic long-term variability. These changes are undetectable, using auscultatory techniques. Alterations in baseline FHR variability can be decreased by factors such as fetal immaturity, maternal drugs, and normal fetal sleep cycles. Of greater concern, however, is the influence of hypoxia, which, too, reduces FHR variability. Variability acts as a modifier to FHR patterns. Both late deceleration and variable deceleration can be reflexly mediated and are indicative of minimal or no hypoxia or acidosis. These same patterns in the presence of decreased variability always indicate hypoxia and acidosis (Paul et al., 1975).

FHR tachycardia greater than 160 BPM is not infrequently seen in conjunction with other FHR changes compatible with hypoxia. Tachycardia can exist, however, without hypoxia, that is, in arrythmia, fever. Tachycardia fits the physiologic model for meeting the increased cardiac output demands of the fetus in the presence of hypoxia. Isolated tachycardia may indicate hypoxia, but this issue is controversial (Gimovsky and Caritis, 1982).

Electronic Fetal Monitoring (EFM) and Perinatal Mortality

Perinatal mortality in the United States is approximately 17 in 1,000 live births and is divided almost equally between fetal and neonatal deaths. Intrapartum fetal deaths account for about 20 percent of stillbirths and 10 percent of total perinatal mortality (Task Force, 1979). This relatively infrequent event, 2 to 4 per 1,000 births, dependent on patient population, makes evaluation of monitoring impact difficult because of the large numbers of patients required (40,000) to meet statistical significance. Reviews of retrospective studies comparing intrapartum stillbirths (IPSB) in monitored and unmonitored patients are of two types: parallel (same time-span) and sequential (two different periods). All but one of these retrospective studies have insufficient numbers to meet true statistical significance (Yeh and Paul, 1982). Furthermore, both study designs have inherent methodologic faults and biases which make conclusions drawn from them suspect. Despite these criticisms, most studies showed from a 1.8- to 2.4-fold drop in the IPSB rate when monitored patients were compared to unmonitored patients (Task Force, 1979). Combining the data from parallel studies during roughly the same period overcomes the deficit of sequential studies and provides sufficient numbers for evaluation (Amato, 1967; Chan et al., 1973; Kelly and Kulkarni, 1973; Paul et al., 1977; Tutera and Newman, 1975). A reduction in fetal death rate from 1.2 per 1000 to 0.7 per 1000 ($p > 0.01$) was noted. These combined data confirm the study by Yeh and Paul (1982), who demonstrated in over 115,000 patients during a ten-year period at the same institution, a difference in the intrapartum fetal death rate in infants over 1,500 grams corrected for anomalies of 0.2 in 1,000 in the monitored group, as compared to 0.7 in 1,000 in the unmonitored group.

Analysis of the beneficial effects of monitoring on neonatal death rates are hampered by study-design problems similar to those in IPSB research, although, since neonatal death occurs more frequently, study populations for analysis can be smaller. Unfortunately, events that may be unaltered by the presence or absence of EFM, such as mode of delivery, neonatal depression 2° to drugs, delivery trauma and nonasphyxial neonatal complications, have a significant impact on neonatal survival. Despite this fact, analysis of sequential studies shows an improvement and reduction in neonatal death rate from 4–13.3 per 1,000 to 1.7–7.2 in 1,000 after the introduction of monitoring (Eddington et al., 1975; Hughey et al., 1977; Shenker et al., 1975; Weinraub et al., 1978). This does not, however, prove a cause-and-effect relationship. Such an inference is strengthened, however, by the summation of

the parallel studies, which show a neonatal death rate (NDR) of 7.1 per 1,000 in the unmonitored group, as compared to 3.6 in 1,000 in the monitored group (Amato, 1967; Paul et al., 1977; Tutera and Newman, 1975). The ten-year monitoring experience at LAC/USC Women's Hospital showed similar results with the NDR in the over 1,500-gram monitored group to be 3.5 in 1,000, as compared to 4.6 in 1,000 ($p < .001$) in the unmonitored group.

The key to many of the problems in establishing a relationship between EFM and improved perinatal outcome clearly lies in the performance of well-controlled prospective studies. Unfortunately, these studies are difficult to perform for several reasons. The widespread acceptance of FHR monitoring, especially in high-risk patients, raises ethical questions of blinding a significantly at-risk group, even though concrete evidence for benefit by monitoring remains speculative. Furthermore, sample size remains a problem, large prospective studies are technically difficult, and long-term follow-up is extraordinarily expensive. Five controlled prospective studies have been performed to date. Four claim no benefit to monitoring, while one claims benefit in high-risk patients only (Haverkamp et al., 1979; Kelso et al., 1978; Renou et al., 1976; Wood et al., 1981). Despite their claims, individually or grouped, the number of patients reported is insufficient to warrant drawing meaningful conclusions.

Neonatal Morbidity

While intrapartum stillbirth or early neonatal death has a heavy impact on the family unit, neither imparts to the same degree the financial and emotional burden of significant short- and long-term neonatal morbidity. The cost of a stay in the neonatal ICU now approaches $1,000 a day. Survival in all too many cases may bring significant physical or mental handicap measured only by the tears and frustrations of the family and untold dollars to the health-care system. Excluding congenital anomalies, the incidence of which has been unchanged in the past ten years, the largest con-

tributor to neonatal morbidity is perinatal asy-
phyxia. Unquestionable relationships exist between the asphyxiated newborn, acidosis,
hypoxia, and abnormal FHR patterns. How,
then, do these sequelae of perinatal asphyxia
correlate with abnormal FHR patterns?

The earliest neonatal manifestation of
perinatal asphyxia is frequently a lowered
Apgar score. Normal FHR patterns correctly
predict vigorous, healthy Apgar over 7, nonas-
phyxiated newborns in 99 percent of cases.
Correlation with abnormal FHR patterns and
asphyxia is not as good, being 20 percent at five
minutes, with most infants doing better than
predicted (Schifrin and Dame, 1972). Despite a
high false positive rate for abnormal FHR patterns, lower Apgar scores are clearly more
prevalent when the FHR is abnormal.

Both parallel and sequential retrospective
studies show significantly better Apgar scores
in monitored versus unmonitored patients.
The inference is that abnormal FHR patterns
allow altering maternal position from side to
side or avoidance of the supine position, maternal oxygen, or delivery, resulting in an improved Apgar. No significant differences in
Apgar score were noted in the prospective
studies, although use of the NICU was more
prevalent in the ascultation group in one study
(Renou et al., 1976).

A significant contributor to perinatal asphyxia is prematurity. The preterm fetus may
be less tolerant of the stress of labor because of
decreased oxygen-carrying capacity, decreased
metabolic buffer ability, and decreased glyco-
gen reserves. It may therefore have a predisposition to acidosis and potential asphyxia. FHR
patterns in the preterm infant have been
shown to predict asphyxia, perhaps with
greater accuracy than in the term infant (Cibils,
1976; Martin et al., 1974; Schifrin and Dame,
1972).

A major contributor to the morbidity of the
premature infant is the influence of the Respiratory Distress Syndrome (RDS). Acidosis is
known to inhibit lecithin production via the
methylation pathway. The incidence of RDS
has been reported to be higher in fetuses
demonstrating abnormal FHR patterns during
labor when compared to infants of the same
gestational age with normal FHR patterns

(Martin et al., 1974). Whether the improved
survival of infants with RDS over the past decade is reflected solely in neonatal care or is
influenced by antenatal events, such as intervention for abnormal FHR patterns, remains
speculative. However, perinatal survival is improved in the monitored premature ≤ 1,500
grams, as compared with its unmonitored
counterpart (Amato, 1967; Yeh and Paul,
1982).

Asphyxia results in shunting of blood to
vital structures in the fetus, such as brain,
heart, and kidney. However, with increasing
hypoxia, vascular autoregulation of flow to
these areas may be hampered, resulting in decreased organ perfusion. Decreased blood flow
to the splanchnic bed has been incriminated in
the etiology of necrotizing enterocolitis. There
is evidence to suggest that fetuses developing
enterocolitis have a significantly increased incidence of abnormal FHR patterns (Garite, personal communication).

Perinatal asphyxia can alter function in all
organ systems. Unquestionably its greatest impact in terms of serious long-term morbidity is
its influence on the central nervous system.
The correlation between perinatal hypoxia and
neurologic deficit and cerebral palsy is well established (Adamsons and Myers, 1973; Volpe,
1974). In one study, evidence of hypoxia was
found in over half the cases of cerebral palsy
(Steer and Bonney, 1962). Despite a seeming
pathophysiologic correlation between perinatal hypoxic events, FHR patterns, and short-
and long-term neurologic outcome, information is scanty comparing the interrelationship
of the latter two observations. Myers (1972)
produced varying degrees of hypoxia in the
fetal monkey. FHR patterns characteristic of
late deceleration were produced. Evaluation of
monkeys who survived the asphyxial insult
and were later sacrificed revealed cortical brain
lesions similar to those present in patients with
cerebral palsy. Corroborative support in the
human fetus for an increased likelihood of
neurologic deficit following abnormal FHR
patterns has been provided (Painter et al.,
1979). Fifty high-risk infants were monitored
in labor and followed with frequent neurologic
testing through the first year of life. Abnormal
FHR patterns classified as moderate-severe

variable decelerations, severe variable decelerations, or late decelerations were noted in thirty-eight fetuses, with the remaining twelve fetuses acting as controls. A significantly higher incidence of abnormal neurologic examinations during the one-year follow-up was found in the abnormal FHR group (34.4 percent), as compared to the normal FHR group (7.4 percent). The most commonly found neurologic abnormality was hypotonia of the lower extremities. This fact agrees nicely with the functional anatomic lesions reported by Myers in the monkeys. All infants without FHR abnormalities were normal at one year, while seven in thirty-eight, (18 percent) with abnormal FHR patterns demonstrated neurologic abnormalities ranging from delay in gross and fine motor tone to severe spasticity and mental retardation. Of further interest is that FHR patterns appeared to be more predictive of one-year neurologic outcome than was Apgar score.

Recent data from our institution shed further light on the association of abnormal FHR patterns and neurologic sequelae. In our very mobile population, long-term follow-up of patients demonstrating abnormal FHR patterns is virtually impossible. Consequently a short-term indicator of potential long-term neurologic abnormality—neonatal seizure activity—was chosen for our at-risk population. Amiel-Tilson (1969) and Holden (1982) have shown that from 30 to 60 percent of neonates experiencing seizure activity in the newborn period will have long-term neurologic sequelae.

The etiology of neonatal seizure activity is varied and includes hemorrhage, infection, metabolic disturbances, CNS anomalies, and perinatal asphyxia. The latter has been incriminated in as many as 20 to 40 percent of cases but has heretofore been generally undocumented by FHR pattern analysis in any controlled fashion (Krauss and Marshall, 1972; Volpe, 1973).

The records of all infants with seizure activity, discharged alive from LAC/USC Women's Hospital and the University of California, Irvine Medical Center, 1977–1979, were reviewed, and each infant was matched in a case-control fashion by birthweight, gestational age, proximity of delivery, and availability of

FHR monitoring strips. The study group was composed of fifty patients and their controls, with twenty-five patients weighing more than 2,500 grams (Group I) and (coincidentally) twenty-five patients weighing less than 2,500 grams (Group II). The occurrence of perinatal asphyxia, as measured by neonatal events, and abnormal FHR patterns defined as moderate to severe variable deceleration, late deceleration, and prolonged deceleration were then compared in the study and control groups. Evidence for perinatal asphyxia as measured by Apgar score was present in the seizure infants in both term and preterm groups (table 19–1). Lower mean Apgar scores were present in seizure patients, as compared to controls, and, interestingly, term infants were more significantly depressed than their preterm counterparts. Comparison of fetal-heart-rate tracings revealed ominous patterns in 76 percent of term patients with seizures, as compared to 20 percent of their term controls. In a group of term patients with no postnatal etiology for seizure activity, this comparison was even more striking, with 94 percent of seizure patients revealing ominous patterns, as compared to 19 percent of controls. Similar differences were noted in the preterm group with 60 percent of seizure patients and 28 percent of the control patients revealing ominous patterns (table 19–2). Furthermore, episodes of absent variability were significantly more common, both alone and in conjunction with ominous patterns, in the term-seizure group, 48 percent versus 8 percent in the control group. The presence of absent variability in conjunction with late or severe variable deceleration has been clinically used as prima facie evidence of fetal hypoxia. This pattern occurred in 75 percent of term patients with no postnatal etiology for seizure activity. No correlation between decreased variability in preterm infants and their controls was noted (table 19–2). This may reflect fetal cardiovascular immaturity rather than fetal distress.

The labor patterns of each group were then analyzed by stage of labor (table 19–3). The percentage of all contractions associated with ominous patterns for each group was noted. While abnormal FHR patterns are occasionally present in patients with normal outcome, pa-

TABLE 19–1

Neonatal Seizures

Gestation Age	Group I $N = 25$	Group II $N = 25$
Seizure	39.2 ± 1.8	31.9 ± 3.6 *(NS)*
Control	39.4 ± 1.7	32.6 ± 3.5
Birth Weight		
Seizure	3417 ± 503	1577 ± 472 *(NS)*
Control	3363 ± 518	1666 ± 529
APGAR (One-Minute)		
Seizure	3.7 ± 2.8*	5.5 ± 2.5†
Control	7.9 ± 1.6	6.8 ± 1.9
APGAR (Five-Minute)		
Seizure	5.6 ± 2.7*	6.4 ± 2.5‡
Control	8.9 ± 0.5	7.8 ± 1.7

Mann Whitney-U Test
*$p < .0001$
†$p < 0.03$
‡$p < 0.05$

TABLE 19–2

Fetal-Heart-Rate Patterns

	Group I $N = 25$				Group IA $N = 16$				Group II $N = 25$			
	Seizure		Control		Seizure		Control		Seizure		Control	
	N	%	N	%	N	%	N	%	N	%	N	%
Ominous Patterns (OP)	19	76*	5	20	15	94*	3	19	15	60‡	7	28
Absent Variability (AV)	14	56†	3	14	12	75†	2	13	11	44	9	36
OP + AV	12	48†	2	8	12	75*	1	6	9	36	5	20

Chi square technique
*$p < 0.001$
†$p < 0.01$
‡$p < 0.05$

tients with neonatal seizures had consistently more ominous patterns during labor in both the term and preterm groups.

The onset of seizure activity was significantly different when Group I was compared to Group II. The majority of term patients (68 percent) had initial seizure activity within 48 hours of birth, whereas most preterm infants (92 percent) had initial seizure activity after 48 hours (p < 0.001), suggesting that causes other than hypoxia may have contributed to seizure activity in the preterm group. Onset of seizure activity was earlier in term infants with no postnatal etiology for seizure activity, earlier in infants with abnormal long-term neurologic follow-up, and earlier in neonates with abnor-

mal FHR patterns. These data, with, for the first time, confirmatory abnormal FHR patterns, support the idea that early onset seizure activity is associated with perinatal asphyxia (Dennis, 1978; Holden, 1982). The study was not originally designed to include long-term follow-up, but information was available on thirty-seven of fifty patients. A total of twenty-five of these thirty-seven patients (67 percent) had significant neurologic handicap. This confirms, albeit with incomplete follow-up, the significant potential for long-term neurologic damage following neonatal seizure activity. Critics of fetal monitoring claim no benefit to patients of low perinatal risk. Significantly, nine of twenty-five term patients in

TABLE 19–3

Percent Ominous Patterns

	Group I				Group 1A				Group II			
	Seizure		Control		Seizure		Control		Seizure		Control	
1st Stage	18.1	(17)*	10.2	(4)	21.1	(13)	15	(3)	12.6	(11)*	8.9	(5)
2nd Stage	69.9	(12)†	50	(3)	70.6	(10)†	48	(2)	44.6	(6)	34.1	(3)
TOTAL	26.5	(19)*	17.1	(5)	26.9	(15)	20.6	(3)	12.7	(15)†	9.3	(7)

Chi square technique
*$p < 0.01$
†$p < 0.05$
The numbers in parentheses are patients demonstrating abnormal patterns.

this study would have been classified as low risk, yet all had significant neonatal morbidity, and many had long-term neurologic sequelae.

The evaluation of fifty patients who subsequently developed seizures, and their controls, presents some interesting contrasts. Ominous FHR patterns were clearly more commonly found in the seizure groups. Yet, monitoring did not always provide a possible explanation if the seizure was attributable to perinatal asphyxia, and it certainly did not prevent a poor outcome. In regard to the latter, review of the FHR records suggested courses of action and more immediate interventions. In other cases, even with the aid of the "Retrospectiscope," management seemed appropriate. It is interesting that in the six term infants with normal FHR patterns, five had postnatal conditions associated with the potential for seizure activity. Another area of concern is that while the overall percentage of contractions associated with abnormal FHR patterns was 26 percent in the term group, some patients demonstrated intermittent, abnormal patterns in only 2–5 percent of all contractions. In other words, no persistent fetal distress was noted, yet perinatal morbidity was significant. A possible explanation is that these fetuses had experienced hypoxic episodes prior to the intrapartum period and were already neurologically damaged. They were, however, metabolically and cardiovascularly stable during labor. Hence, there was no evidence of fetal distress. Further credence to this theory is suggested by the fact that over 51 percent of patients with subsequent neurologic deficit reported in the Collaborative Perinatal Study had one-minute Apgars of ≥ 7, and 67 percent had Apgars ≥ 7 at five minutes. It is

not unlikely, however, that antenatal, intrapartum, and postnatal hypoxic events are additive, and anything that the obstetrician and neonatologist can do to minimize hypoxia will be beneficial.

The above data clearly demonstrate a correlation between hypoxic fetal-heart-rate patterns and short- and long-term neurologic abnormalities. To date, no large prospective study has been performed to show a reduction in neurologic sequelae specifically attributable to FHR monitoring. A sequential retrospective study by Ingemarssen (1981) does, however, shed some light in this area. Three consecutive time periods were chosen, during which the incidence of fetal monitoring in labor increased markedly. In the first period, only selected high-risk patients were monitored. In the second period, most high-risk and only a few low-risk patients were monitored. In period three, monitoring was employed routinely for most patients regardless of risk. Infants delivered with five-minute Apgars below 7 were then followed routinely for evidence of neurologic abnormalities. The incidence of neurologic handicap fell from 3.8 in 1,000 births to 0.3 in 1,000 births with the increase in FHR monitoring. Interestingly, the greatest reduction was found in preterm and low-risk patients.

The concept of routine FHR monitoring continues to be hotly debated, and evaluation of its impact on long-term neurologic sequelae remains speculative. Theoretic statistical data presented at the NIH Task Force on Intrapartum Fetal Distress (Task Force, 1979) suggest that universal monitoring would prevent one severe neurologically handicapped infant per 1,000 births in the United States, or approximately 3,000 severely affected infants per year. The cost of this prevention (universal monitoring), based on data by Quilligan and Paul (1975) corrected to 1983 dollars, would be approximately $133 million annually. The cost of institutionalization of a severely handicapped individual, depending on age of survival, is approximately $250 to $400,000—a long-term national cost of $1.2 billion. The financial impact of less severely handicapped patients would have to be added to this figure. The beneficial effects of monitoring in preventing intrapartum and neonatal deaths from cost analysis are, of course, immeasurable.

The ultimate proof of benefit from fetal monitoring remains unresolved until the per-

formance of large prospective, well-controlled, unbiased studies. Considering the widespread acceptance of electronic FHR monitoring and today's economic and medicolegal climate, it remains uncertain whether these studies will ever be performed. Yet, research such as ours strengthens the association of neonatal morbidity and hypoxic FHR patterns. Continuous measurement of fetal oxygen tensions from scalp blood, evaluation of fetal systolic time intervals, and measurements of fetal cerebral blood flow can be seen on the not-too-distant horizon. As additional research becomes available, the role of fetal monitoring in the fall in perinatal mortality will be more clearly elucidated.

REFERENCES

Adamsons, K. and Myers, R. E. (1973). Perinatal asphyxia: Causes, detection and neurologic sequelae. *Pediatric Clinics of North America,* 20:465–480.

Amato, J. C. (1967). Fetal monitoring in a community hospital—a statistical analysis. *Obstetrics and Gynecology,* 50(3):269–274.

Amiel-Tilson, C. (1969). Cerebral damage in full-term newborn infants: Etiology factors, neonatal status and continuous term follow-up. *Biologica Neonatorum,* 14:234–250.

Chan, W. H., Paul, R. H., and Toews, J. (1973). Intrapartum fetal monitoring. Maternal and fetal morbidity and perinatal mortality. *Obstetrics and Gynecology,* 41:7–13.

Cibils, L. A. (1976). Clinical significance of fetal-heart-rate patterns during labor: 1. Baseline patterns. *American Journal of Obstetrics and Gynecology,* 125:290–305.

Cibils, L. A. (1975). Clinical significance of fetal-heart-rate patterns during labor: 2. Late decelerations. *American Journal of Obstetrics and Gynecology,* 123:473–492.

Dennis, J. (1978). Neonatal convulsions, etiology, late neonatal status and long-term outcome. *Developmental Medicine and Child Neurology,* 20:143–148.

Edington, P. T., Sibanda, J., and Beard, R. W. (1975). Influence on clinical practice of routine intrapartum fetal monitoring. *British Medical Journal,* 3:341–343.

Gimovsky, M. L. and Caritis, S. N. (1982). Diagnosis and management of hypoxic fetal-heart-rate patterns. *Clinics in Perinatology,* 9:313–324.

Haverkamp, A. D. et al. (1979). A controlled trial of the differential effects of intrapartum fetal monitoring. *American Journal of Obstetrics and Gynecology,* 134:399–408.

Holden, K. R., Mellits, E. D., and Freeman, J. M. (1982). Neonatal seizures I., Correlation of prenatal and perinatal events with outcome. *Pediatrics,* 70:165–176.

Hon, E. H. and Quilligan, E. J. (1967). The classification of fetal-heart-rate II. The revised working classification. *Connecticut Medicine,* 31:779–783.

Hughey, M. J., LaPata, R. E., and McElin, T. W. (1977).

The effect of fetal monitoring on the incidence of cesarean section. *Obstetrics and Gynecology,* 49:513–518.

Ingemarsson, E., Ingemarsson, I., and Svenningsen, N. W. (1981). Impact of routine fetal monitors during labor on fetal outcome with long-term follow-up. *American Journal of Obstetrics and Gynecology,* 141:29–38.

Kelly, V. C. and Kulkarni, D. (1973). Experience with fetal monitoring in a community hospital. *Obstetrics and Gynecology,* 41:818–824.

Kelso, I. M. et al. (1978). An assessment of continuous fetal-heart-rate, fetal monitoring and labor. *American Journal of Obstetrics and Gynecology,* 131:526–532.

Krauss, T. A. and Marshall, R. E. (1977). Seizures in a neonatal intensive care unit. *Developmental Medicine and Child Neurology,* 19:719–728.

Krebs, H. B. et al. (1979). Intrapartum fetal-heart-rate monitoring, I. Classification and prognosis of fetal-heart-rate patterns. *American Journal of Obstetrics and Gynecology,* 133:762–772.

Krebs, H. B., Petres, R. E., Dunn, L. J., Segreti, A. (1980). Intrapartum fetal-heart-rate monitoring, IV. Observations on elective and non-elective fetal-heart-rate monitoring. *American Journal of Obstetrics and Gynecology,* 138:213–219.

Kubli, F. W., Hon, E. H., and Khazin, A. F. (1969). Observations on heart rate and pH in the human fetus during labor. *American Journal of Obstetrics and Gynecology,* 104:1190–1206.

Martin, C. B., Siassi, B., and Hon, E. H. (1974). Fetal-heart-rate patterns and neonatal death in low-birthweight infants. *Obstetrics and Gynecology,* 44:503–510.

Martin, C. B., Van der Wildt, B., and Jongsma, H. W. (1979). Mechanism of late deceleration in the fetal heart rate; a study with autonomic blocking agents in fetal lambs. *European Journal of Obstetrics and Gynecology Reproductive Biology,* 9:361–371.

Myers, R. E. (1972). Two patterns of perinatal brain damage and their conditions of occurrence. *American Journal of Obstetrics and Gynecology,* 112:246–276.

Myers, R. E., Mueller-Heubach, E., and Adamsons, K. (1973). Predictability of the state of fetal oxygenation from a quantitative analysis of the components of late deceleration. *American Journal of Obstetrics and Gynecology*, 115:1083–1094.

Neutra, R. R., Fienberg, S. E., Greenland, S., Friedman, E. A. (1978). The effect of fetal monitoring on neonatal death rates. *New England Journal of Medicine*, 299:324–326.

Painter, M. J., Depp, R., and O'Donoghue, P. (1979). Fetal-heart-rate patterns and development in the first year of life. *American Journal of Obstetrics and Gynecology*, 132:271–277.

Parer, J. T. (1981). FHR monitoring: Answering the critics. *Contemporary OB/Gyn*, 17:163–179.

Paul, R. and Hon, E. (1974). Clinical fetal monitoring, V. Effect on perinatal outcome. *American Journal of Obstetrics and Gynecology*, 118:529–533.

Paul, R. H., Huey, J. R., and Yaeger, C. F. (1977). Clinical fetal monitoring—its effect on cesarean-section rate and perinatal mortality: 5-year trends. *Post-Graduate Medicine*, 61:160–166.

Paul, R. H. et al. (1975). Clinical fetal monitoring, VII. Evaluation and significance of intrapartum baseline FHR variability. *American Journal of Obstetrics and Gynecology*, 123:206–210.

Quilligan, E. J. and Paul, R. H. (1975). Fetal monitoring: Is it worth it? *Obstetrics and Gynecology*, 45:96–100.

Renou, T., Chang, A., Anderson, I., and Wood, C. (1976). A controlled trial of fetal intensive care. *American Journal of Obstetrics and Gynecology*, 126:470–476.

Schifrin, B. S. and Dame, E. L. (1972). Fetal-heart-rate patterns, prediction of Apgar score. *Journal of the American Medical Association*, 219:1322–1325.

Shenker, L., Post, R. C., and Seller, J. S. (1975). Routine electronic monitoring of fetal rate and uterine activity during labor. *Obstetrics and Gynecology*, 46:185–189.

Steer, C. M. and Bonney, W. (1962). Obstetric factors and cerebral palsy. *American Journal of Obstetrics and Gynecology*, 83:526–531.

Task Force (1979). *Antenatal Diagnosis*. Bethesda, Maryland: Public Health Service, National Institutes of Health.

Tutera, G. and Newman, R. L. (1975). Fetal monitoring: Its effect on the perinatal mortality and cesarean-section rate and its complications. *American Journal of Obstetrics and Gynecology*, 122:750–754.

Volpe, J. (1973). Neonatal seizures. *New England Journal of Medicine*, 289:413–416.

Volpe, J. J. (1974). Perinatal hypoxic-eschemic brain injury. *Mead Johnson Symposium*, 6:48–59.

Weinraub, Z. et al. (1978). Perinatal outcome in monitored and unmonitored high-risk deliveries. *Israel Journal of Medical Sciences*, 14:249–255.

Wood, C. et al. (1981). A controlled trial of fetal-heart-rate monitoring in a low-risk obstetric population. *American Journal of Obstetrics and Gynecology*, 141:527–534.

Yeh, S., Diaz, F., and Paul, R. N. (1982). Ten-year experience of intrapartum fetal monitoring in Los Angeles County/University of Southern California Medical Center. *American Journal of Obstetrics and Gynecology*, 143:496–500.

20

Developmental and Temperamental Characteristics of Infants at Risk for Serious Psychopathology

Eugene J. D'Angelo, Ph.D., Lisa A. Krock, Ed.D.,
Linda D. O'Neill, M.A., M.P.H., and M. Patricia Boyle, Ph.D.

One of the current theoretical conceptualizations of schizophrenia is the "vulnerability model," which emphasizes the mutual involvement of genetic factors, organismic integrity, and environmental contingencies in the development of the psychosis (Zubin and Spring, 1977). According to this model, these interactions result in a global level of susceptibility which may eventuate in a schizophrenic episode when the experienced stress increases beyond a personal threshold (Zubin and Steinhauer, 1981). Hence, vulnerability is not considered a stable, unalterable trait, inasmuch as moderating variables may hypothetically serve to increase the threshold for a psychotic episode and/or potentiate the more noxious effects of an inborn factor.

While Erlenmeyer-Kimling (1978) and Zubin and Steinhauer (1981) have elaborated on the complexities of this model, a number of investigators (Fish, 1959, 1977; Mednick et al., 1971) have suggested that elements of vulnerability may be evident as early as infancy. As Anna Freud (1978) observed, what is vulnerable is less the child than the developmental process itself. For example, Fraiberg (1978) suggested that even with minimal genetic predisposition, severe disturbances in human attachment and the sense of self and object world render the infant susceptible to developing an unstable ego organization, a disturbance that could eventuate in psychosis. Fish (1963) identified the importance of an infant's ability to maintain a quiet and alert state, postural and motoric control, and focused attention as influencing the manner in which the perception of self and world are derived. Neuromaturational delays, for example, disturbances in arousal and motoric functioning, may render the infant susceptible to environmental influences that might lead to the development of the psychosis.

The present paper is an interim report from a longitudinal investigation of infants considered to be at risk for the subsequent development of schizophrenia because they are the offspring of psychotic mothers.

Neuromaturational Delay:
An Overview

Meehl (1962) speculated that a neurointegrative deficit underlies the development of the schizophrenic disorders. He posited that this inborn vulnerability, considered one of the central features of "schizophrenia," contributed to the development of the schizotypic personality organization characteristic of many prepsychotic individuals. Fish (1977) has suggested that "pandevelopmental retardation" represents this neurobiologic deficit, whereby the affected child is considered to be experiencing a disorganization of neurologic maturation manifested as periods of delay sometimes alternating with precocity in postural-motor, visual-motor, and physical development. These neuromaturational delays are evident as early as the first year of life and are often manifested despite the absence of significant neurological abnormalities. Instead, deviations in the timing and overall integration of both regulative and developmental functions, ranging from variable physical growth to irregular sleep patterns, are observed. Additionally, these infants exhibit abnormally quiet states associated with hypotonia, failure to adequately develop integrated bimanual skills, and decreased vestibular responses as part of the proposed neurointegrative deficit (Fish, 1977). Preliminary research suggested that the severity of these deficits during infancy corresponded with the type of psychopathology exhibited in later childhood (Fish, 1975, 1977; Fish and Hagin, 1973) (Ragins et al., 1975).

It is impressive that other prospective, at-risk studies have generally corroborated many of these findings. Ragins and colleagues (1975) reported that offspring of schizophrenic mothers had more problems related to sleep, neuromuscular development, perceptual competencies, and were more irritable during the assessment than were infants of unaffected women. Marcus and colleagues (1981) found that a subgroup of infants born to schizophrenic parents exhibited problematic motor and sensorimotor functioning. Within this subgroup, a cohort of infants had low to low-normal birthweights.

While the findings suggestive of neuromaturational irregularities among infants of schizophrenic parents are impressive, certain methodological issues appear to limit the generalizability and inferential nature of the existing data. Studies of infants at risk for schizophrenia have rarely investigated the environmental matrix—social and familial—in which these irregularities were manifested. Both Anna Freud (1967) and Eisenberg (1968) observed that disadvantage within the social environment may exacerbate or mute constitutional factors. They suggested caution in acceding to a purely genetic interpretation of these neuromaturational difficulties. For example, research has increasingly demonstrated that infants are significantly affected by the quality of their interactions with caregivers, which exerts influence over an infant's temperamental and behavioral organization (Brazelton and Als, 1979). Unfortunately, the existing studies of infants born to psychotic parents have provided limited information about infant-caregiver relationships and related environmental effects. Fish (1975) and Marcus and colleagues (1981) made brief reference to the out-of-home placements of several at-risk infants. Where environmental variables have been carefully studied, their relationships with developmental functioning have been noteworthy. For example, Sameroff and Zax (1978) reported that the poor developmental and emotional functioning of their group of genetically at-risk infants was more strongly associated with the chronicity/severity of parental illness and with the family's socioeconomic status than with maternal diagnosis.

Moreover, a number of studies have suggested that nonspecific pregnancy and birth complications (PBCs) were associated with an increased risk for subsequently developing schizophrenia (McNeil and Kaji, 1973; Mednick et al., 1971). Although Fish (1977) did not find a significant association between PBCs and neuromaturational delay, the Marcus group (1981) reported a relationship between low-normal birthweight and poor motor/sensorimotor functioning among infants with psychotic mothers. Investigators have tentatively implicated poor prenatal care (Garmezy, 1971), maternal emotional distress (Ferreira, 1965; McDonald, 1968), and the teratogenic effects of using psychotropic medication during pregnancy (Vorhees et al., 1979) as possible sources of these complications.

Investigators of infants at risk for schizophrenia need to document carefully both prenatal variables and concomitant environmental experience before asserting that pan-developmental retardation be considered a predominantly constitutional phenomenon. Focusing on the first year of life, and particularly the initial six months, in this paper we describe (1) the perinatal course, mental development, motor functioning, and temperamental characteristics; and (2) the familial relationships and recent life stresses impinging on infants born to schizophrenic mothers. Considered to be at genetic risk, this sample became naturally dichotomized when a subgroup of the infants was placed in foster care by four months of age. Comparisons on variables between the two subgroups and with infants of either depressed or unaffected mothers are described.

SUBJECTS

Mothers. Seventy-five first-time, expectant mothers, thirty-three with DSM-III diagnoses of schizophrenia, twenty-five with recurrent major depression, and seventeen in an unaffected control group, participated in the project. Eighteen of the schizophrenic mothers exhibited a nonparanoid psychosis, ten had a predominantly paranoid presentation, and five were undifferentiated in nature. Both clinical groups were recruited from private practice referrals, aftercare clinics, and community-based programs for previously hospitalized psychiatric patients. The unaffected women were selected from three obstetric and family medical practices. These control subjects were of comparable socioeconomic status, not exhibiting significant psychopathology as identified from completion of both

the Present Status Examination (Wing et al., 1973) and the Minnesota Multiphasic Personality Inventory. Neither they nor any of the expectant fathers had first or second degree relatives with a history of a schizophrenic spectrum disorder. Characteristics of the mothers can be found in table 20–1.

All of the mothers initiated their participation in the study during the first trimester of pregnancy, and each was provided with an assistant, who was responsible for data collection, for promoting ongoing prenatal medical care, and for monitoring familial interactions and life stresses. In this way, an attempt was made to minimize the variability within, or at least document in a prospective manner, the quality of the prenatal experience.

Each mother's psychiatric status and the nature of her manifest symptomatology were systematically documented during every period of data collection. The use of psychiatric medications during pregnancy was also monitored and recorded.

Infants. In all, there were forty-three male and thirty-two female infants in the study. No significant differences were found among the three clinical groups or between the two subgroups of infants born to schizophrenic mothers (foster versus home care) in prenatal nutrition and medical care, dosage of analgesic medication used during delivery, or pregnancy and birth complications. One infant of a schizophrenic mother was born in a psychiatric hospital. However, none of the babies was considered to be premature or required intensive medical attention during the neonatal period. Apgar ratings of all the infants were 8 and above at one and five minutes.

Significant differences were found in the birthweights among the three groups of babies ($F_{2,72} = 4.35$, $p < .025$). The Scheffé method revealed that the infants born to schizophrenic women ($\bar{x} = 2,823.54$ grams) were significantly lighter than those with either chronically depressed ($\bar{x} = 3,352.44$ grams) or unaffected mothers ($\bar{x} = 3,437.31$ grams). This finding is consistent with other studies reporting lighter birthweights in babies of schizophrenic parents (Mednick et al., 1971; Sameroff and Zax, 1978).

TABLE 20–1

Demographic Characteristics of the Mothers in the Study

	Age	Marital Status*	Education (years)	IQ	Length of Illness (yrs.)	Number of Hospitalizations	Dosage of Medication†	SES‡
Schizophrenic (n = 33)								
Foster Care (n = 16)	25.31	12M, 4S	12.13	98.36	6.11	3.41	.42	III
Home Care (n = 17)	24.26	13M, 4S	12.01	99.93	7.34	3.85	.51	III
Depressed (n = 25)	26.17	20M, 4S, 1D	12.82	98.25	6.69	2.87	.48	III
Control (n = 17)	25.57	9M, 4S, 4D	13.01	101.43	n.a.	n.a.	n.a.	III

*Marital status: M = married (including common law), S = single, D = divorced (including separated)
†Dosage of Medication I transformed into z scores
‡SES = Two-Factor Index Score for Socioeconomic Status

OUTCOME MEASURES AND PROCEDURE

All pregnancy, birth, and medical information was prospectively recorded on a medical questionnaire updated by the research assistants after every contact with the subjects. The infant measures included the Neonatal Behavioral Assessment Scale (NBAS) (Brazelton, 1973), the Bayley Scales of Infant Development (BSID) (Bayley, 1969), and the Infant Temperament Questionnaire (ITQ) (Carey and McDevitt, 1978). While the NBAS was scored only by health care professionals who had completed the prescribed reliability training, the rest of the data collection was completed by the research assistants.

The severity of maternal psychopathology was measured on the Short Clinical Rating Scale (SCRS) (French and Heninger, 1970). The global illness subscale of the SCRS was used as a measure of overall psychopathology.

The nature of the family's affective/interactive environment was measured on the relevant subscales of the Beavers-Timberlawn Family Evaluation Scale (FES) (Lewis et al., 1976). Each family's expressiveness, mood and tone, degree of conflict, and level of empathy was assessed. The parents and their children were observed during informal interaction (for example, at mealtime) for a minimum of half an hour before ratings were completed. Finally, the severity of life stresses was measured using the Schedule of Recent Experience (SRE) (Petrich and Holmes, 1977).

Infants and their parents were assessed beginning with two days after birth and at successive two-month intervals throughout the first year of life. Table 20–2 provides the temporal framework for the data collection. After the second-day evaluation, all of the data collection occurred in the subject's home. Although no normative data for the measure are available for this age, the Infant Temperament Questionnaire was administered at two months as well as during the usual four- to eight-month period.

As the longitudinal course of the project evolved, sixteen infants born to schizophrenic and five born to depressed mothers were placed in foster care. All of the sixteen infants were placed by 4 months of age, with the mean age of placement being 3.22 months. In contrast, the infants of depressed mothers were placed at a mean age of 8.31 months. When placement occurred, the foster care families were asked to participate in the study. Because all agreed, the family-affect and life-stress data were secured from the foster families during the remaining data-collection periods. Of note, MMPI profiles and clinical interviews revealed that none of the foster family members exhibited a schizophrenic spectrum disorder.

It is also important to note that none of the infants were considered physically abused or overtly neglected prior to placement. In fact, all

TABLE 20–2

Temporal Framework for Data Collection

	2 Days	Months					
		2	4	6	8	10	12
Infant							
NBAS	X						
BSID		X	X	X	X	X	X
ITQ		(X)*	X	X	X		
Mother							
SCRS	X	X	X	X	X	X	X
Family	X	X	X	X	X	X	X
SRE	X	X	X	X	X	X	X

*No normative data available at this age

of the babies were voluntarily placed after the mothers engaged in discussion with their therapists, physicians, and/or representatives of social service agencies. Of the schizophrenic mothers, 52.54 percent reported that they were placing their children because they were too difficult for them to parent; 20.54 percent felt that the babies were a disappointment to them "He is not what I expected, you know, he doesn't want me near him when I want to"); 16.07 percent expressed open dislike for the infant ("I think we just weren't made for each other . . . I hate her and she hates me"); and 11.19 percent reported that they perceived their babies as needing special care.

Results

ANALYSIS OF DEVELOPMENT AMONG THE THREE GROUPS

To facilitate the investigation of the foster versus home-care subgrouping of the babies born to schizophrenic mothers, an overview of the comparative functioning of the infants with schizophrenic, depressed, or unaffected mothers will be presented. Comparisons between the three groups were made using a one-way analysis of variance (ANOVA) and the Scheffé method. No sex differences were found among the groups on any variable.

Analysis of the reflex behaviors on the NBAS at two days of life revealed that the infants born to schizophrenic mothers had significantly poorer performances in sucking and crawling ($p < .05$). Behaviorally, these infants were more irritable; displayed significantly less alertness, consolability, cuddliness, and capacity to self-quiet; and exhibited inferior defensive movements, hand-to-mouth movements, general tonus, motor maturity, and pull-to-sit than did those of either depressed or unaffected mothers ($p < .05$).

Table 20–3 provides the Bayley mental (MDI) and motor (PDI) mean scores for the three groups of infants from two through twelve months of age. Significant MDI and PDI scale score differences between the infants of schizophrenic and unaffected mothers persisted from two through twelve months. While significance between PDI scores remained throughout the first year, no appreciable differences were found between infants of schizophrenic and depressed mothers on MDI scores at eight months and thereafter.

Utilizing the SCRS, a significant difference in global psychopathology between mothers in the two clinical groups was found to be significant only at ten months ($t = 2.61, p < .02$). No significant differences in life stress (SRE) were found at any data collection point among the three groups.

On the Infant Temperament Questionnaire (ITQ), infants of schizophrenic mothers were significantly less adaptive, active, and rhythmic than those of unaffected or depressed mothers ($p < .05$) at two, four, and six months. Infants of schizophrenic mothers continued to be less adaptive than those of unaffected mothers at eight months ($p < .05$).

Collectively taken, these results suggest that irrespective of the severity of postpartum maternal psychopathology and extant life stresses impinging on the family, the total group of infants born to schizophrenic mothers exhibited significantly poorer mental and motor development than did babies born of either depressed or unaffected mothers. These global results were generally supportive of those studies reporting the presence of neuromaturational delay in infants of schizophrenic mothers (Marcus et al., 1981; Ragins et al., 1975).

TABLE 20–3

MDI and PDI Mean Scores for the Sample (2–12 Months)

Months	2		4		6		8		10		12	
	MDI	PDI	MDI	PDI	MDI	PDI	MDI	PDI	MDI	PDI	MDI	PDI
Schizophrenic	96.5	88.9	94.1	88.3	96.15	89.1	98.1	89.4	98.0	91.2	97.5	90.4
Foster Care	95.4	88.4	91.6	85.3	93.7	84.6	95.3	86.6	94.1	87.8	94.6	87.4
Home Care	97.6	89.3	96.5	91.2	98.6	93.6	100.9	92.2	101.8	94.6	100.3	93.3
Depressed	101.3	103.6	103.6	104.2	108.6	104.4	103.2	102.5	104.7	103.6	103.5	103.9
Unaffected	103.4	105.2	107.8	105.7	107.3	106.1	108.2	109.4	107.7	110.9	109.5	109.8

COMPARISON OF HOME AND FOSTER CARE
INFANTS WITH SCHIZOPHRENIC MOTHERS

We then evaluated the data in light of the natural dichotomization of the groups of infants born to schizophrenic mothers. It was observed that no significant differences in global psychopathology, length of illness, marital status, or level of life stress significantly differentiated those schizophrenic mothers who placed their infants in foster care from those who continuously cared for their babies at home. Significant differences were observed in family affect, with foster placement being more strongly associated with elevations in family conflict and negative family mood ($p < .05$).

The infants of schizophrenic mothers placed in foster care ($\bar{x} = 2{,}404.08$ grams) were significantly lighter at birth than those who continued to live at home ($\bar{x} = 3{,}243.00$ grams) ($t = 6.23, p < .001$). Utilizing this dichotomy in the data analysis, the home care infants were not significantly lighter at birth than either the babies born to depressed or unaffected mothers. In contrast, the foster care infants continued to be significantly lighter than both groups of infants ($p < .01$).

Table 20–4 provides the mean scores and standard deviations for the NBAS reflex behaviors of the foster and home care infants. Table 20–5 provides similar data for NBAS behavioral items.

The home care infants exhibited significantly better sucking ($t = 3.59, p < .01$); more cuddliness ($t = 2.87, p < .02$); consolability ($t = 5.7, p < .001$); activity ($t = 7.55, p < .001$); and better general tonus ($t = 3.81, p < .01$) and defensive movements ($t = 3.16, p <$

$.01$) than did the foster care babies. The home care infants had significantly higher MDI and PDI scores than did foster care infants of schizophrenic mothers from four through twelve months ($p < .05$). However, home care infants continued to have significantly lower PDI scores (two to twelve months) than did babies of either depressed or unaffected mothers.

On the Infant Temperament Questionnaire, the infants in foster care exhibited significantly less adaptability ($t = 3.2, p < .01$), a lower threshold ($t = 7.3, p < .001$) at four months of age, and less rhythmicity at both two ($t = 9.6, p < .001$) and four months ($t = 6.06, p < .001$) than did their at-home counterparts. The foster care infants were perceived as significantly less active only at two months ($t = 5.89, p < .001$).

The natural mothers of the foster care infants were asked to complete the Infant Temperament Questionnaire on their babies during the day after making their decision for placement. Using the t-test for related samples, these mothers reported that their infants were less rhythmic, more negativistic, slowly adaptive, and exhibited a lower threshold to stimulation than was manifest at the two-month evaluation ($p < .05$). Similar t values, however, with scores occurring in a reversed direction, were found between the natural mothers' Questionnaire responses just after their decision to place the infants and those completed by the foster mothers during the four-month assessment ($p < .05$). It was interesting that no significant differences were found between natural mothers' Questionnaire responses at two months and the foster mothers' responses at four months. It is conceivable that a natural

TABLE 20–4

Means and Standard Deviations of NBAS Reflex Behaviors for Infants with Schizophrenic Mothers and Reared in Two Settings

Day 2 Reflex Behavior	Foster Care (n = 16)		Home Care (n = 17)	
	X	SD	X	SD
Plantar Grasp	2.00	0.00	2.00	0.00
Palmer Grasp	2.00	0.00	2.00	0.00
Ankle Clonus	2.00	0.00	2.00	0.00
Babinski	1.87	0.23	1.81	0.22
Standing	2.00	0.00	2.00	0.00
Automatic Walking	1.90	0.68	1.92	0.64
Placing	1.98	0.20	2.00	0.00
Incurvation	2.00	0.00	2.00	0.00
Crawling	1.13	0.88	1.43	0.79
Glabella	2.00	0.00	2.00	0.00
Tonic deviation of head and eyes	2.00	0.00	2.00	0.00
Nystagmus	1.86	0.68	1.98	0.89
Tonic Neck Reflex	2.00	0.00	1.87	0.76
Moro	2.00	0.00	1.93	0.46
Rooting	1.23	0.74	1.41	0.64
Sucking	1.49	0.92	1.77	0.79
Passive Movements				
Arms	1.89	0.57	1.34	0.34
Legs	1.81	0.21	1.79	0.85

mother's evaluation of her infant's temperament around the time of her decision to seek foster placement might reflect misattribution or selective perceptual distortion. However, as can be found in table 20–6, these perceived temperamental characteristics were also significantly associated with elevations in family conflict and negative family mood. No significant changes in life stress or increased severity of maternal psychopathology were observed in the mothers between the two-month-data-collection period and the time they decided to place their infants. A multiple regression analysis was performed on the MDI scores of infants placed in foster care and the significant temperamental and family affect variables at time of placement. This data can be found in table 20–7. Of the six variables entered into the multiple regression analysis, only family conflict, infant rhythmicity, and negative family mood achieved statistical significance. It was apparent that the environmental variable, family conflict, accounted for over half of the overall variance in MDI scores for the infants at the time of placement.

Ten of the sixteen foster care infants were placed after an outpatient visit to a pediatrician or family physician. During these medical evaluations, the infants were diagnosed as failure-to-thrive (FTT) because, among other concerns, their weight was under the third percentile for their age. Using the Mann-Whitney U-Test, the FTT infants ($\bar{x}$ = 2,316.78 grams) were found to be significantly lighter at birth, as well as exhibiting poorer sucking, hand-to-mouth activity, motor maturity, and greater irritability at day two than did the remaining infants ($\bar{x}$ = 2,491.37 grams) placed in foster care ($p < .05$). Although a trend was apparent, no significant differences were found between the two groups for Bayley scores, severity of maternal psychopathology (SCRS), level of life stress (SRE), and family affect during the two-through twelve-month data-collection periods.

Table 20–8 identifies those variables that discriminated between the total cohort, foster and home care infants born to schizophrenic mothers, and those babies whose mothers were either depressed or free from significant psychopathology.

TABLE 20–5

Means and Standard Deviations for NBAS Behavioral Items for Infants with Schizophrenic Mothers and Reared in Two Settings

Behavioral Items	Foster Care (*n* — 16)		Home Care (*n* = 17)	
	$\overline{X}$	SD	$\overline{X}$	SD
Dimension 1: Interactive Processes				
Orientation inanimate, visual	6.48	1.68	6.53	1.61
Orientation inanimate, auditory	5.37	1.49	5.40	1.33
Orientation animate, visual	5.82	1.35	6.05	1.21
Orientation animate, auditory	5.24	1.12	5.74	1.17
Orientation animate, visual and auditory	5.91	1.61	6.64	1.49
Alertness	5.14	1.27	5.43	1.35
Cuddliness	6.30	1.39	6.79	1.49
Consolability	6.11	1.38	6.73	1.32
Dimension 2: Motor Processes				
Defensive movements	6.49	1.11	6.92	1.24
Activity	4.81	1.38	5.98	1.51
Hand-to-mouth	4.78	2.22	4.88	1.97
General tonus	4.84	2.31	5.81	2.14
Motor maturity	4.15	1.40	4.41	1.53
Pull-to-sit	4.93	1.24	5.03	1.29
Dimension 3: Organizational Processes: Control of State				
Response decrement to light	6.89	1.61	6.66	1.55
Response decrement to rattle	6.83	1.33	6.71	1.29
Response decrement to bell	6.71	1.56	6.68	1.35
Response decrement to pinprick	4.84	1.48	4.71	1.42
Peak of excitement	4.93	1.69	4.82	1.53
Rapidity of build-up	3.56	.99	3.33	1.03
Irritability	3.94	1.63	3.82	1.79
Lability of states	3.15	1.31	2.95	1.29
Self-quieting activity	5.24	1.40	4.98	1.62
Dimension 4: Organizational Process: Physiological stability in response to stress				
Tremulousness	4.71	1.31	4.68	1.31
Startle	4.53	1.34	4.42	1.34
Lability of skin color	4.67	1.90	4.59	1.90

Conclusions

Our findings underscore the importance of comprehensively investigating the interactions among biological integrity, psychosocial status, and environmental matrix as they relate to the developmental functioning of infants born to schizophrenic mothers. Consistent with the observations of Marcus and his colleagues (1981), our results suggest that heterogeneous subgroups exist among these infants that, when not accounted for during global data analysis, might lead to inexact generalizations.

When the total group of infants born to schizophrenic women was compared with those of either depressed or unaffected mothers, the pattern of results was consistent with previous reports (Fish, 1977; Marcus et al., 1981; Ragins et al. 1975). However, when these infants were dichotomized into foster and home care subgroups, the comparative pattern of results diverged. In contrast to their foster care counterparts, the home care infants did not have significantly lower birthweights; exhibited fewer differences on the day-two NBAS assessment; and had significantly lower MDI and activity (ITQ) scores only during the two-month assessment, when compared with

TABLE 20-6

Significant Pearson Product-Moment and Multiple Correlations Between Temperament and Family Affect for Foster Care Infants at Placement

Temperament (n = 16)	Family Conflict* r†	Mood	Conflict & Mood R
Adaptability	.69	.73	.75
Negativism	−.63	−.57	.70
Threshold	.58	.54	.62
Rhythmicity	.74	.61	.75

*Scoring was reversed for purposes of this analysis.
†p < .05

TABLE 20-7

Multiple Regression of Identified Infant Temperament and Family Affect on MDI Scores for Infants in Foster Care (n = 16)

Item	R²	ΔR²	F
Total Identified Variable	.660	——	——
Family Conflict	.543	.543	16.84‡
Infant Rhythmicity	.422	.065	15.68†
Negative Family Mood	.414	.018	4.82*
Infant Adaptability	.282	.015	1.47
Infant Threshold	.193	.006	0.20

*p < .05
†p < .01
‡p < .001

infants of either depressed or unaffected mothers. As can be seen from table 20–8, the foster care infants began their lives in a developmentally more precarious state, which was apparently vulnerable to the type of family stresses that occurred around the time of their placement.

Despite these differences, certain similarities remained across the two subgroups. For example, both groups exhibited consistently inferior motor development when compared with the infants of either depressed or unaffected mothers. Further analysis of this data should provide us with a more accurate determination of the similarity between the types of motor difficulties exhibited in the present sample and those reported by Fish (1977). These motor problems might reflect the possible constitutional predisposition for schizo-phrenia. While the motor delays persisted for both groups throughout the first-year period, the behavioral/temperamental differences continued only for the foster care infants. These temperamental difficulties coexisted with their more pervasive developmental delays, greater family conflict, and increased negative family mood.

The Ragins group (1975) observed that the infants of schizophrenic parents who exhibited developmental difficulties and problematic temperaments also experienced less nurturance from their caregiver environment. In a video-taped investigation of a three-month old FTT infant, Alfasi (1982) reported that the infant's constitutional difficulties interacted adversely with the mother's overstimulating style and limited positive affect, promoting their asyn-chronous relationship. In our study, the foster care infants had mothers who expressed feelings of inadequacy, disappointment, and aggression similar to a subgroup of women with FTT infants (Evans et al., 1972). Of note, 62.5 percent of the infants in our study placed in foster care had a diagnosis of failure-to-thrive, with the condition no longer apparent by the six-month assessment.

While admittedly speculative, the findings from this study also suggest the need for investigators to examine the developmental course of those infants reared in adoptive homes who subsequently became schizophrenic (Heston, 1966; Rosenthal et al., 1968). If physical and/or temperamental difficulties were present prior to placement for this group and were not experienced by the home care babies, the samples would not be truly equivalent. This phenomenon might suggest that relatively discrete, etiological factors were operating in these groups that resulted in their both developing schizophrenia. Moreover, it would also be important to determine why a subgroup of these infants was ultimately placed with adoptive families. Sameroff and Zax (1973) have suggested that infants of schizophrenic parents who live in either foster or adoptive families bring more than elevated genetic risk to their new environments. Consistent with our study, the infants were reported to be lighter at birth, exhibited a

TABLE 20–8

Variables Discriminating Infants of Schizoprenic Mothers from Those with Depressed or Unaffected Mothers

Item	Global (n = 33)	Foster Care (n = 16)	Home Care (n = 17)
Birthweight	+*	+	−
NBAS:			
Sucking	+	+	−
Crawling	+	+	+
Alertness	+	+	+
Consolability	+	+	+
Cuddliness	+	+	−
Self-Quiet	+	+	+
Defensive Movements	+	+	−
Irritability	+	+	+
Hand-to-Mouth	+	+	+
General Tonus	+	+	−
Motor Maturity	+	+	+
Pull-to-Sit	+	+	+
Bayley:			
MDI2–12 mos.			
(unaffected)	+	+	2 mos. only
2–6 mos. (depressed)	+	+	2 mos. only
PDI 2–12 mos.	+	+	+
Temperament:			
Rhythmicity	+	+	−
Adaptability	+	+	−
Activity	+	+	2 mos. only
Threshold	−	+	−

*+ = variable significantly discriminates this group from either Depressed or Unaffected conditions

greater number of developmental difficulties, and had more problematic temperaments, which placed extra demands on and increased the possibility of having a negative relationship with their caregivers (Zax et al., 1977). In part, this might be one reason why the foster care infants were unable to live continuously with their psychotic mothers. Our findings indicated that at the time of placement, the foster care infants were perceived as more temperamentally difficult, their natural mothers were feeling increasingly negative about their relationship with them, and their family environments evidenced greater conflict and negative mood. Anthony (1983) observed that infants who exhibit constitutional/developmental difficulties and have both disruptive relationships with their caregivers and inconsistent family support systems are at particular risk for serious psychopathology. It is this encompassing chaos which may perniciously affect the developing child's sense of self and distort the integration of internal and external reality (Winnicott, 1959).

Despite its limitations, the present study attempted to realize the "meaningful interpenetration" (Anthony, 1983; Hartmann, 1959), of several investigative traditions as we simultaneously measured both developmental and environmental variables. Unfortunately, investigations that are primarily concerned with multiple interactions among variables rarely submit to easy description (Nisbett, 1965). However, Shakow (1973) has forcefully reiterated the importance of trying to appreciate the multifaceted aspects of schizophrenia rather than to settle for simple, but underinclusive, explanations. For the essence of the disorder may very well lie in its complexity.

REFERENCES

Alfasi, G. (1982). A failure-to-thrive infant at play: Applications of microanalysis, *Journal of Pediatric Psychology*, 7: 111–123.

Anthony, E. J. (1982). Infancy in a crazy environment. In: *Frontiers of Infant Psychiatry*, ed. J. D. Call, E. Galenson, and R. L. Tyson. New York: Basic Books.

Bayley, N. (1969). *Bayley Scales of Infant Development.* New York: Psychological Corporation.

Brazelton, T. B. (1973). *The Neonatal Behavioral Assessment Scale.* Philadelphia: J.B. Lippincott.

Brazelton, T. B. and Als, H. (1979). Four early stages in the development of mother-infant interaction. *The Psychoanalytic Study of the Child*, 34:349–367, New Haven: Yale University Press.

Carey, W. B. and McDevitt, S. C. (1978). Revision of the Infant Temperament Questionnaire. *Pediatrics*, 61:735–739.

Eisenberg, L. (1968). The interaction of biological and experiential factors in schizophrenia. In *The Transmission of Schizophrenia*, ed. D. Rosenthal and S. S. Kety. Oxford: Pergamon Press.

Erlenmeyer-Kimling, L. (1978). Vulnerability research: A behavior genetics point of view. In *The Child in His Family: Vulnerable Children*, ed. E. J. Anthony, C. Koupernik, and C. Chiland. New York: Wiley-Interscience.

Evans, S. L., Reinhart, J. B., and Succop, R. A. (1972). Failure to thrive: A study of 45 children and their families. *Journal of the American Academy of Child Psychiatry*, 11:440–467.

Ferreira, A. J. (1965). Emotional factors in prenatal environment: A review. *Journal of Nervous and Mental Disease*, 141: 108–118.

Fish, B. (1959). Longitudinal observations of biological deviations in a schizophrenic infant. *American Journal of Psychiatry*, 116:25–31.

Fish, B. (1963). The maturation of arousal and attention in the first months of life: A study of variations in ego development. *Journal of the American Academy of Child Psychiatry*, 2:253–270.

Fish, B. (1975). Biological antecedents of psychosis in children. In *Biology of the Major Psychoses*, ed. D. X. Freedman. New York: Raven Press.

Fish, B. (1977). Neurobiologic antecedents of schizophrenia in children: Evidence for an inherited, congenital neurointegrative defect. *Archives of General Psychiatry*, 34: 592–597.

Fish, B. and Hagin, R. (1973). Visual-motor disorders of infants at risk for schizophrenia. *Archives of General Psychiatry*, 28:900–904.

Fraiberg, S. (1978). The invisible children. In *The Child in His Family: Vulnerable Children*, eds. E. J. Anthony, C. Koupernik, and C. Chiland. New York: Wiley-Interscience.

French, N. and Heninger, G. (1970). A short clinical rating scale for use by nursing personnel. *Archives of General Psychiatry*, 23:241–246.

Freud, A. (1967). Comments on psychic trauma. In *Writings of Anna Freud*, vol. 5. New York: International Universities Press, 1969.

Freud, A. (1978). Foreword, In *The Child in His Family: Vulnerable Children*, ed. E. J. Anthony, C. Koupernik, and C. Chiland. New York: Wiley-Interscience.

Garmezy, N. (1971). Vulnerability research and the issue of primary prevention. *American Journal of Orthopsychiatry*, 41:101–116.

Hartmann, H. (1959). Psychoanalysis as a scientific theory. In *Essays on Ego Psychology*. New York: International Universities Press, 1964.

Heston, L. L. (1966). Psychiatric disorders in foster-home-reared children of schizophrenic mothers. *British Journal of Psychiatry*, 112:819–825.

Lewis, J. M., Beavers, W. R., Gossett, J. T., and Phillips, V. A. (1976). *No Single Thread: Psychological Health in Family Systems.* New York: Brunner/Mazel.

Marcus, J., Auerbach, J., Wilkinson, L., and Burack, C. M. (1981). Infants at risk for schizophrenia: The Jerusalem Infant Development Study. *Archives of General Psychiatry*, 38:703–713.

McDonald, R. L. (1968). The role of emotional factors in obstetric complications: A review. *Psychosomatic Medicine*, 30:222–237.

McNeil, T. and Kaji, L. (1973). Obstetric complications and physical size of offspring in schizophrenic, schizophrenic-like, and control mothers. *British Journal of Psychiatry*, 123:341–348.

Mednick, S. A., Mura, M., Schulsinger, F., and Mednick, B. (1971). Perinatal conditions and infant development in children with schizophrenic parents. *Social Biology*, 18:s103–s113.

Meehl, P. E. (1962). Schizotaxia, schizotypy, schizophrenia. *American Psychologist*, 17:827–838.

Nisbett, R. E. (1975). Interactions vs. main effects as goals of personality research. Presented at the Conference on Person-Situation Interactions, Stockholm, June 1975.

Petrich, J. and Holmes, T. (1977). Life change and onset of illness. *Medical Clinics of North America*, 61:825–838.

Ragins, N. et al. (1975). Infants and children at risk for schizophrenia: Environmental and developmental observations. *Journal of the American Academy of Child Psychiatry*, 14:150–177.

Rosenthal, D. et al. (1968). Schizophrenics' offspring reared in adoptive homes. In *The Transmission of Schizophrenia*, ed. D. Rosenthal and S. Kety. Oxford: Pergamon Press.

Sameroff, A. and Zax, M. (1973). Perinatal characteristics of the offspring of schizophrenic women. *Journal of Nervous and Mental Disease*, 157:191–199.

Sameroff, A. and Zax, M. (1978). In search of schizophrenia: Young offspring of schizophrenic women. In *The Nature of Schizophrenia*, ed. L. C. Wynne, R. L. Cromwell, and S. Matthysse. New York: Wiley-Interscience.

Shakow, D. (1973). Some thoughts about schizophrenia research in the context of high-risk studies. In *Schizophrenia: Selected Papers*. New York: International Universities Press, 1977.

Vorhees, C. V., Brunner, R. L., and Butcher, R. E. (1979). Psychotropic drugs as behavioral teratogens. *Science*, 205: 1220–1225.

Wing, J. K., Cooper, J. E., and Sartorius, N. (1973). *The Measurement and Classification of Psychiatric Symptoms.* London: Cambridge University Press.

Winnicott, D. W. (1959). The effect of psychotic parents on the emotional development of the child. In *The Family and Individual Development.* New York: Basic Books, 1965.

Zax, M., Sameroff, A., and Babigian, H. M. (1977). Birth outcomes in the offspring of mentally disordered women. *American Journal of Orthopsychiatry*, 47:218–230.

Zubin, J. and Spring, B. (1977). Vulnerability—a new view of schizophrenia. *Journal of Abnormal Psychology*, 86: 103–126.

Zubin, J. and Steinhauer, S. (1981). How to break the logjam in schizophrenia: A look beyond genetics. *Journal of Nervous and Mental Disease*, 169:477–492.

21

An Intervention Program for Mothers of Low-Birthweight Babies: Outcome at Six and Twelve Months

Barry Nurcombe, M.D., Virginia Rauh, Sc.D., A.C.S.W.,
David C. Howell, Ph.D., Douglas M. Teti, M.D. Paul Ruoff, M.D.,
Barbara Murphy, M.S., and John Brennan, M.B.B.S.

The preterm baby is prone to a number of developmental difficulties, particularly mental retardation and cerebral palsy. More subtle defects in attention and concentration, motor control, learning ability, and social competence may also appear in childhood (Caputo et al., 1981; Lubchenco et al., 1972).

In some instances, these developmental disabilities are clearly due to perinatal brain damage, particularly when the infant is very immature or sick at birth; however, the long-term follow-up of large samples of low-birthweight infants, such as that by Werner and colleagues (1971), indicates that, overall, the socioeconomic status of the family has the preponderant association with cognitive and psychosocial development, far outweighing that of perinatal biomedical factors. Such a finding could be accounted for on a genetic basis or explained on the ground that psychosocially disadvantaged families do not provide a favorable environment for the development of vulnerable infants, a situation Sameroff and Chandler (1975) call "the continuum of caretaking casualty."

The environmental theory has been expanded by Sameroff and Chandler in their transactional model. In this paradigm, mother and infant are described as affecting each other reciprocally, over time, as a result of innumerable interactions, which cumulatively enhance or impede both infant development and maternal adaptation. The theory is supported not only by the developmental difficulties of low-birthweight infants, but also by the disproportionately high incidence of child abuse in their parents (Thoman, 1980).

If the transactional theory is correct, and if disadvantaged parents are less likely to provide an environment that compensates for infant vulnerability, what is the nature of their failure to do so, and how could it be counteracted by intervention?

In general, there have been four approaches

The Vermont Infant Studies Project is funded by NIMH Grant #1-R01-MH-32924, and by March of Dimes 12–88.

to neonatal intervention, each related to a theory about the cause of poor outcome: the sensory-deprivation theory, the faulty-bonding theory, the emotional-crisis theory, and the theory that proposes that preterm infants are deficient in the capacity to elicit care.

The interactive, transactional model is not consonant with the first of these approaches, which describes neonates in intensive care as subject to early sensory deprivation, and in need of additional visual, kinesthetic, acoustic, or tactile stimulation (as, for example, in the intervention programs of Barnard, 1975; Kattwinkel et al., 1975; Korner at al., 1975). The intensive-care isolette is likely, in actuality, to provide an excess of, albeit unpatterned and uncontingent, stimulation.

On the other hand, the transactional model is consistent with the faulty-bonding theory, which suggests that, if there are obstacles to early mother-infant contact, a close relationship may not be established because the most favorable time for maternal bonding has passed. Although the irreversibility of faulty early bonding has yet to be demonstrated, a number of intervention programs have been planned according to this approach (for example, Barnett et al., 1970; Kennell et al., 1970; Leifer et al., 1972; Powell, 1974).

The transactional model is also consistent with the theory that premature birth represents an emotional crisis (Caplan, 1968, Kaplan and Mason, 1960), poor resolution of which can lead later to adverse mother-infant interaction. Minde and his group (1980) report one intervention program based on this approach.

Finally, the transactional model is consistent with the observation that premature infants are often deficient in the capacity to elicit and sustain social interaction (Brazelton, 1979). The immature infant often has feeble regulation of physiological homeostasis, motor activity, and state transition. Thus the baby is phlegmatic and hard to rouse, or irritable and easily distressed. The mother may respond by avoiding the unresponsive or aversive infant, or by overloading it with noncontingent stimulation. Such observations have been the basis of recent intervention programs that propose to teach mothers to respond more appropriately to their infants (for example, Widmayer

and Field, 1980). In this chapter we describe the implementation of an intervention program that was based conceptually on the work of the Boston Children's Hospital Medical Center group (Als et al., 1976, 1979, 1982).

The Mother-Infant Transaction Program

The intervention program implemented in the Vermont Infant Studies Project, the MITP, was designed to help mothers: (1) discern those changes in the infant's autonomically mediated physiological homeostasis, motor behavior, and state-regulation that indicate composure or distress; (2) recognize infant cues that indicate dawning attention and interaction; (3) respond promptly and appropriately to interactional cues, to signals of infant withdrawal, and to infant distress; (4) imbed the above responses in the course of everyday childrearing (waking, changing, bathing, playing, and feeding); and (5) enjoy the baby. The program thus aimed to promote contingent interaction and enjoyment in the context of daily care.

The MITP was implemented by a specially trained pediatric intensive-care nurse, according to the outline described in the appendix to this chapter. In general, the nurse followed the planned steps of the program; but she carefully varied its pace according to the parents' ability and readiness to follow the plan. Whenever possible, fathers were included; but daily scheduling problems often made it difficult for them to attend. The program was designed to be comparatively inexpensive, easily replicable, and suitable for implementation in other intensive-care nurseries.

Hypotheses

We hypothesized that as a result of the MITP the following *intermediate effects* would occur: (1) the mother would become more sensitive to the infant's signals of social interaction, withdrawal, and distress, and would respond more consistently and appropriately to these three signals by, respectively, social engagement, withdrawal, and consolation; (2) the mother would become affectively more involved with her infant in the course of daily care, leading to a higher level of dyadic involvement; and (3) the relatively greater degree of maternal sensitivity and responsiveness and the higher level of mutual affective involvement would lead to a greater synchrony between the dyadic partners.

It was hypothesized further that following the enhancement of mother-infant interaction, there would be an improvement in maternal adjustment and infant development during the first year of the infant's life.

Although detailed analyses of the intermediate dyadic interaction variables are in progress (Ruoff et al., 1983), they are not yet complete. In this contribution we will restrict ourselves to describing the effects of the MITP on maternal adjustment and infant development at six and twelve months.

Method

SAMPLE

The low-birthweight population consisted of all infants weighing less than 2,200 grams, of gestational age under thirty-seven weeks, and hospitalized for at least ten days in the Intensive Care Nursery of the Medical Center Hospital of Vermont between April, 1980, and December, 1981. Infants were excluded if they came from multiple births or single mothers and if they had severe congenital anomalies or neurological defects. Multiple births, congenital anomalies, and neurological defects prompted exclusion because of their confounding effect upon later development. Infants of single mothers were excluded because of the diversity of child-rearing arrangements in this group and the potential difficulty of follow-up.

This nursery, the only tertiary referral center for the Vermont Regional Perinatal Program, serves northern Vermont and northeastern New York State. The low-birthweight sample recruited is virtually a total sample of those born in the referral area who met the criteria for inclusion.

Eighty-six low-birthweight infants conformed to these criteria, and their mothers were approached one by one to participate in the Vermont Infant Studies Project. Eight of those approached refused to participate or were lost within several weeks of first contact. These cases did not differ from those who agreed to participate in terms of medical characteristics (birthweight, Apgar scores, perinatal complications, and neonatal behavioral assessment) or maternal age and parity; however, compared to participants, nonparticipants were of significantly lower socioeconomic class (Hollingshead and Redlich, 1958).

The study sample was compared with a local reference population to establish its representativeness. Table 21–1 compares the 1980–1982 population with low-birthweight statistics for the three-year period 1976 through 1978 at the Medical Center Hospital of Vermont. It shows that the populations did not differ significantly on a classification of low-birthweight deliveries by symptoms, although there were more caesarian deliveries in the study population.

A contrast group of fullterm, normal-birthweight infants (weighing more than 2,800 grams and over thirty-seven weeks in gestational age) was randomly selected from the regular nursery by recruiting the next fullterm baby born after the birth of each low-birthweight infant. Seven mothers refused to participate: three of them were unwilling to do so, and four were willing but unable. Mothers of fullterm infants were recruited up to a total of forty-one.

At recruitment, the seventy-eight low-birthweight mother-infant dyads were randomly assigned to experimental ($N = 38$) and control ($N = 40$) groups. Random assignment was used in order to control for birthweight, gestational age, size for gestational age, medical complications, and length of hospitalization. After they had been assigned to their groups, two experimental subjects moved out of the area. Two more experimental infants died of Sudden Infant Death Syndrome within the first two months of the program. During

Symptom[a]	1980–82 Vermont Infant Studies Sample (<2200 grams) (in percentages)	1976–78 Sample (<2,500 grams) (in percentages)
Premature rupture of membranes or premature labor	57.1	63
Small for gestational age	25.7	17
Medical termination	10.4	10
Caesarean section	35.7	25

[a]Categories overlap.

the course of the study, four low-birthweight infants (two in each low-birthweight group) developed severe neurological impairment and were dropped from the analyses. The characteristics of the sample are summarized in table 21–2. The expected differences between fullterm and low-birthweight groups are present. The groups are otherwise comparable in all respects except maternal education and socioeconomic status. In these respects there are significant differences among the three groups: the control group has a lower mean educational level ($F (2, 106) = 4.92, p = .009$) and social class ($F [2, 105] = 8.05, p = .001$) than the other groups.

MEASURES

Antecedent Variables. All mothers of low-birthweight infants were assessed, using the following three instruments at least one week before the infant's discharge, but prior to intervention: Rotter's (1966) scale of internality-externality, the Social Readjustment Rating Scale (Holmes and Rahe, 1967), and the Taylor Manifest Anxiety Scale (Taylor, 1953). Mothers of fullterm infants were assessed on the same three measures on the day before discharge. These tests allowed a comparison of experimental, control, and contrast groups in terms

of their locus of control, the life changes to which they had been exposed in the previous twelve months, and the anxiety they had experienced in the puerperium. These variables might be expected to affect or reflect the readiness for mothering of the women in this study. There were no significant differences between the three groups in these variables, except in anxiety, in which case control mothers were significantly more anxious than the fullterm contrast group: $F (1, 93) = 6.61, p = .012$.

Thus the two low-birthweight groups were comparable on all antecedent demographic, biomedical, and maternal variables other than maternal education and social class; and the fullterm group was comparable to the low-birthweight groups on all variables other than those referable to the preterm birth itself, and to anxiety, maternal education, and social class.

Following the neonatal period, all maternal and infant-outcome assessments were conducted or scored by staff who were unaware of the group to which the subjects belonged, except in those instances when the mother completed a self-administered questionnaire.

Maternal Adaptation. Toward the middle of the infant's first year of life, all mothers were assessed in regard to three variables: Satisfaction with the Mothering Role, Self-Confidence, and Attitudes to Child Rearing.

Satisfaction was assessed at the adjusted gestational age of six months in part of a longer semistructured interview (SSI) of 102 questions conducted with the mother in the home. The Satisfaction subscale of the SSI consisted of ten questions, the taped and transcribed responses to which were scored blind on Likert-type scales by two independent raters. The raters had high reliability (Pearson $r = .94$) on the composite scores of 72 percent of the sample, and the scale proved to be internally consistent (Cronbach's alpha = .80 on 86 percent of the sample).

Confidence was measured at four months by the Seashore Self-Confidence Rating Paired Comparison Questionnaire (Seashore et al., 1973). In this self-administered questionnaire, the subject is asked to compare her mothering ability with that of five other caregivers (spouse, own mother, experienced mother, nurse, and physician) on a number of specific tasks.

Attitudes to child rearing were measured by the Parent Attitude Survey (Herefore, 1963), which was completed in the home by the mothers when their babies were between four and twelve months adjusted gestational age. This instrument provides a total score by assessing attitudes in five areas: confidence in parenting, causation of the child's behavior, acceptance of the child's feelings, mutual understanding, and mutual trust.

All these measures—Satisfaction, Confidence and Attitudes—were significantly intercorrelated, absolute values of r varying from .33 to .52.

Maternal Psychopathology. This variable was assessed at the adjusted gestational age of six months by means of a twenty-item subscale of the semistructured interview already described in regard to the assessment of satisfaction. The psychopathology items of the SSI dealt with anxiety, phobias, somatic complaints, obsessionalism, depersonalization, depression, fatigue, irritability, and poor concentration. Cronbach's alpha was .81 on this scale on 86 percent of the sample, and the interrater Pearson reliability coefficient on composite scores was .95 on 79 percent of the sample.

Infant Temperament. Temperament was assessed at the adjusted gestational age of six months by means of the Carey Infant Development Questionnaire (Carey and McDevitt, 1978). An index of temperamental difficulty was provided by combining the Carey subscales of rhythmicity, approach, adaptability, intensity, and mood.

Infant Development. Infant cognitive development was assessed at the adjusted gestational ages of six and twelve months with the Bayley Scales of Infant Development (Bayley, 1969).

The Bayley Scales provide two developmental quotients, the Mental Development Index (MDI) and the Psychomotor Development Index (PDI). The Bayley Scales also allow the tester to rate the infant's behavior during testing on a number of subscales known as the Infant Behavior Record (IBR). Matheny (1980)

has found that these behaviors can be condensed by factor-analysis into three major dimensions: Task-Orientation, Test Affect-Extraversion, and Activity.

A principal components-factor analysis (VARIMAX rotation) was performed on the raw IBR scores in our sample. It yielded three factors which accounted for 87 percent of the variance, factors that proved to be similar to those described by Matheny. Factor scores were then derived from the complete factor-pattern matrix, using a regression-estimation procedure. We called the three factors: Task-Orientation, Cooperation, and Activity.

Hypothesized Outcomes

It was predicted that the intervention group would demonstrate a more favorable outcome than the control group in the following variables:

1. Maternal Adaptation (six months)
2. Maternal Psychopathology (six months)
3. Infant Temperament (six months)
4. Infant Development (six and twelve months)
5. Infant Behavior (six and twelve months)

It was also predicted that there would be systematic differences in outcome between the normal-birthweight and low-birthweight groups, the former being in advance of the latter in all measures. The low-birthweight intervention group was expected to demonstrate maternal adjustment and infant development intermediate between the other two groups.

Results

Maternal Adaptation. In view of the difference between the three groups in maternal education (see table 21–2), and because maternal education was significantly correlated with Satisfaction ($r = .28$, $p = .002$) and Attitudes ($r = .25$, $p = .005$), though not with Confidence ($r = .07$), the education variable was included as a covariate in the analyses of Satisfaction,

TABLE 21-2

The Sample: Demographic and Biomedical Variables

| | Low-Birthweight | | | | | | Normal-Birthweight Contrast | | |
| | Intervention | | | Control | | | | | |
	Mean	N	SD	Mean	N	SD	Mean	N	SD
Number		32			38			41	
Females		17			14			20	
First born		21			17			22	
Maternal age (years)	27.7		4.8	25.8		5.1	26.4		4.4
Birthweight (grams)	1610.1		393.7	1565.7		374.8	3472.6		430.0
Very low birthweight (1500 grams)		14			14		—		
Gestational age (weeks)[a]	32.5		2.1	32.1		2.6	39.9[e]		1.2
Apgar (1 minute)	6.7		1.6	5.8		2.3	8.4[e]		0.7
Apgar (5 minutes)	7.9		1.3	7.7		1.4	9.3[e]		0.6
Social class[b]	3.2		1.1	3.9		0.9	3.0		1.2
Maternal education (years)	13.7		2.4	12.4		1.6	14.0		2.8
Small for gestational age[c]		7			8		—		
Number of days hospitalized	36.7		25.6	34.1		24.6	3.4[e]		1.9
Caesarean delivery		11			14			8	
Brazelton scores (interactive processes)	4.5		1.0	4.8		.5	2.8[e]		1.3
Medical complications[d]	9.2		4.8	9.2		3.4	2.0[e]		1.8

[a]Determined by Dubowitz assessment (Dubowitz et al., 1970).
[b]Hollingshead and Redlich's (1958) Two-Factor Index of Social Position.
[c]10th percentile on Colorado Intreauterine Growth Charts (Lubchenco et al., 1966).
[d]Total number of ante-, peri-, and postnatal problems (Zax et al., 1977).
[e]$p < .01$ (Low-Birthweight versus Normal-Birthweight Group).

Confidence, and Attitudes in order to reduce its potentially confounding effect.

A multivariate analysis of covariance demonstrated significant intergroup differences in Satisfaction, Confidence, and Attitudes (F [6, 174] = 2.49, p = .025). Univariate tests revealed significant group differences on two dependent variables: Satisfaction (F [2, 88] = 3.24, p = .044) and Self-Confidence (F [2, 88] = 5.92, p = .004). However, the difference for Attitudes did not quite reach significance (F [2, 88] = 3.07, p = .051).

Table 21-3 shows the means for the three groups on the individual variables in this analysis. The multivariate contrast between the two low-birthweight groups on Satisfaction, Confidence, and Attitudes fell short of significance (F [3, 86] = 2.40, p = .073), although a univariate contrast between the low-birthweight experimental and control groups demonstrated a significant difference for Satisfaction (F [1, 88] = 4.74, p = .032) and Confidence (F [1, 88] = 6.14, p = .015), both in the direction predicted.

The multivariate contrast between the low-birthweight control group and the normal-birthweight contrast group was significant (F (3, 86) = 4.59, p = .005). Corresponding univariate tests between these two groups on the individual variables were also significant: Satisfaction (F [1, 88] = 5.47, p = .022); Confidence (F [1, 88] = 11.43, p = .001); and Attitudes (F [1, 88] = 5.93, p = .017).

Maternal Psychopathology. Because maternal education correlated with Psychopathology (r = −.29, p = .001), it was again used as a covariate in an analysis of covariance, in order to test group differences. There were no group differences in this measure (F [2, 100] = .325, p = .723).

Infant Temperament. Maternal education had no significant correlation with Infant Temperament. A one-way analysis of variance comparing group means on Temperament demonstrated significant overall differences (F [2, 94] = 5.57, p = .005). Subsequent contrasts on

TABLE 21–3

Maternal Outcome at Six Months

| | Low-Birthweight | | | | Normal-Birthweight Contrast | |
| | Intervention | | Control | | | |
	Mean	*SD*	Mean	*SD*	Mean	*SD*
Maternal Satisfaction[a]	14.97[c,e]	4.84	18.12	5.14	14.84[d,e]	3.71
Maternal Confidence[b]	8.86[c,e]	1.51	7.62	2.80	9.24[d,f]	1.06
Maternal Attitudes[b]	57.76	20.92	48.92	30.12	65.54[d,e]	21.56
Maternal Psychopathology[b]	26.83	4.34	28.75	6.18	27.46	6.02

[a]Lower scores are more favorable.
[b]Higher scores are more favorable.
[c]LBW Intervention versus LBW Control.
[d]NBW Contrast versus LBW Control
[e]$p < .05$.
[f]$p < .01$.

group means identified a significant difference between the two low-birthweight groups (F [1, 94] = 11.08, p = .001), but not between the low-birthweight control and the normal-birthweight groups (F [1, 94] = 2.29, p = .134) (see table 21–4).

Infant Development. Maternal education correlated with neither the Mental Development nor the Psychomotor Development Indices at six months. An analysis of variance demonstrated no overall difference on Mental Development (F [2, 105] = 2.60, p = .079); but there was an overall group difference on Psychomotor Development (F [2, 105] = 3.54, p = .033). No significant differences were found on contrasts between the Psychomotor Development Indices of the low-birthweight experimental and control groups (F [1, 105] = 1.74, p = .190), or between the Psychomotor Development Indices of the low-birthweight control and the normal contrast groups (F [1, 105] = 1.83, p = .180) (see table 21–4).

At twelve months, since maternal education correlated significantly with the Mental Development Index (r = .31, p = .001), it was used as a covariate in an analysis of covariance in order to test group differences. No significant difference was found (F [2, 101] = 2.40, p = .096).

Maternal education did not correlate significantly with the Psychomotor Development

Index. An analysis of variance demonstrated a nonsignificant group effect (F [2, 104] = 2.80, p = .066 (see table 21–5).

Infant Behavior. There were no significant correlations between maternal education and the three Infant Behavior dimensions at either six or twelve months. A one-way analysis of variance comparing group means demonstrated a significant group effect on Task Orientation at twelve months (F [2, 103] = 4.18, p = .018). A priori contrasts revealed that the normal-birthweight group demonstrated greater Task Orientation than the low-birthweight control group (F [1, 103] = 8.22, p = .005), whereas there was no significant difference between the low-birthweight experimental and control groups. No significant differences were found comparing the other group means on Infant Behavior, at either six or twelve months.

Discussion

In summary, by six months, the MITP had demonstrated a beneficial effect on maternal adaptation, as reflected by maternal satisfaction with and confidence in mothering. It had also produced a significant positive effect upon infant temperament; but there was no discernible effect upon maternal attitudes to child

TABLE 21–4

Infant Outcome at Six Months

| | Low-Birthweight | | | | Normal-Birthweight Contrast | |
| | Intervention | | Control | | | |
	Mean	*SD*	Mean	*SD*	Mean	*SD*
Mental Development[a]	113.48	11.53	110.61	13.36	117.07	12.32
Psychomotor Development[a]	101.81	11.75	105.86	12.36	109.73	13.29
Task-Orientation[b]	.07	.63	−.23	1.04	.15	.84
Cooperation[b]	−.01	.90	−.04	.99	.05	.90
Activity[b]	−.04	.83	.00	.90	.03	.94
Temperament[c,d]	1.93[e,f]	1.12	2.87	1.02	2.47	1.11

[a]Bayley Scales of Infant Development (Bayley, 1969).
[b]Factors derived from Infant Behavior Record (Bayley, 1969).
[c]Infant Temperament Questionnaire (Carey and McDevitt, 1978).
[d]Lower scores are more favorable.
[e]LBW Intervention versus LBW Control.
[f]$p < .01$.

TABLE 21–5

Infant Outcome at Twelve Months

| | Low-Birthweight | | | | Normal-Birthweight Contrast | |
| | Intervention | | Control | | | |
	Mean	*SD*	Mean	*SD*	Mean	*SD*
Mental Development[a]	113.53	11.42	108.78	12.80	117.02	10.41
Psychomotor Development[a]	99.40	11.39	103.00	12.38	106.42	12.93
Task-Orientation[b]	.05	.94	−.32	.96	.26	.79[c]
Cooperation[b]	.16	.56	−.22	1.06	.08	.83
Activity[b]	−.01	.91	−.01	.81	.02	.88

[a]Bayley Scales of Infant Development (Bayley, 1969).
[b]Factors derived from Infant Behavior Record (Bayley, 1969).
[c]$p < .01$, NBW versus LBW Control.

rearing or psychopathology. Neither at six nor twelve months was there support for an experimental effect upon infant mental and psychomotor development; nor was there evidence for such an effect upon infant behavior, as assessed by the Bayley Scales. The attrition of the sample, following the decision to drop infants with neurological impairment, appears to have caused a partial washing-out of the clearer experimental effect on maternal adaptation at six months (see Nurcombe et al., in press).

When contrasted with the low-birthweight control group mothers, it is apparent that mothers of normal babies were better adapted

at six months: they were more satisfied with and confident in and had more favorable attitudes to child rearing. Intervention mothers were intermediate between the other two groups. The mothers of the normal infants did not report their babies to have been temperamentally easier than low-birthweight control mothers reported theirs to have been; in fact, mothers who received intervention were at least equal to the mothers of normal babies in this regard; and there was no evidence, at six months, that the mothers of low-birthweight infants were subject to more psychopathology than the mothers of fullterm infants.

There was no support, at the adjusted gestational ages of six and twelve months, for differences between the low-birthweight control and normal-birthweight infants in regard to mental development, psychomotor development, task-orientation, cooperation, or activity, except that at twelve months the normal group significantly exceeded the controls in task orientation and the experimental group was intermediate between the two.

In those measures on which the experimental mothers or infants differed significantly from the controls (Maternal Satisfaction, Maternal Confidence, and Infant Temperament), the experimental group was either intermediate between the other two groups or, as in Temperament, at approximately the same level as the normal group.

There was no support for a programmatic effect on the cognitive or psychomotor development of the infant. Each measure in which there was significant experimental effect (Maternal Satisfaction, Maternal Confidence, and maternal perception of Infant Temperament) is psychosocial in nature; yet the MITP did not affect Maternal Psychopathology. In other words, although the effect of the MITP was primarily psychosocial in nature, its benefit was limited to those dispositions in mother and infant that are especially involved in the relationship between them. Maternal Psychopathology, though significantly associated with Maternal Satisfaction ($r = .72$), Confidence ($r = .44$), and Attitudes ($r = -.30$), does not appear to be a direct reflection of role strain. Probably all four dimensions of adjustment reflect a common, more fundamental fifth variable or set of variables.

The association, at six months, between Maternal Satisfaction, Attitudes, Psychopathology, and Education has an importance beyond the inconvenience it caused to the statistical analyses. Mothers of lower educational background were more liable to report poor adjustment during the first year of the baby's life, regardless of whether the infant had been of low or normal birthweight. This finding suggests that it may be possible to design an intervention program tailored for women who are most at risk of failure or breakdown in parenting, women who presumably could stand to benefit most from it. In further papers from this project we intend to explore the measurement of interaction, the follow-up of these infants into the third year of life, the identification of the vulnerable mother, and the interaction, if any, between maternal vulnerability and the infant's perinatal medical status.

Appendix

An Outline of the Mother-Infant Transaction Program[1]

Day 1. *Introduction* (getting acquainted with the baby): Demonstration of Brazelton Neonatal Behavioral Assessment Scale

Day 2. *Homeostatic Systems* (how the baby feels): Respiration, skin circulation, autonomically mediated movements, facial movement, and visceral activity

Day 3. *Motor Systems* (how the baby moves): Posture, tone, and movement

Day 4. *State Observation and Regulation* (how the mother can enhance organization): Predominant states, state changes, and consolability

Day 5. *Attention-Interaction System* (how the mother can engage her baby and sustain an interaction): Attention, alertness, and responsivity

Day 6. *Recognizing and Responding to Cues* (facilitating daily care): Waking, changing, feeding, and bathing

Day 7. *Initiating Activity* (getting ready for play at home): Alerting, timing, and methods

First Home Visit (three days after discharge): *Consolidation and Adjustment*

Second Home Visit (two weeks after discharge): *Mutual Enjoyment Through Play*

Third Home Visit (one month after discharge): *Temperament Patterns*

Fourth Home Visit (three months after discharge): *Review of Program and Termination*

[1]Details of the program are available from the authors.

REFERENCES

Als, H., Lester, B. M., and Brazelton, T. B. (1979). Dynamics of the behavioral organization of the premature infant. In *Infants Born at Risk*, ed. T. M. Sostek, S. Goldberg, and H. H. Shuman. New York: Spectrum.

Als, H., Lester, B. M., and Tronick, E. Z. (1982). Manual for the assessment of preterm infants' behavior (APIB). In *Theory and Research in Behavioral Pediatrics*, vol. I, ed. H. E. Fitzgerald, B. M. Lester, and M. W. Yogman. New York: Plenum.

Als, H., Tronick, E., and Brazelton, T. B. (1976). *Manual for the Behavioral Assessment of the Premature and At-Risk Newborn.* Boston: Child Development Unit, Children's Hospital Medical Center.

Barnard, K. (1975). *A Program of Stimulation for Infants Born Prematurely.* Seattle: University of Washington Press.

Barnett, C. R., Leiderman, P. H., and Grobstein, R. (1970). Neonatal separation, the maternal side of interactional deprivation. *Pediatrics*, 45:197–205.

Bayley, N. (1969). *Bayley Scales of Infant Development.* New York: The Psychological Corporation.

Brazelton, T. B. (1973). *Neonatal Behavioral Assessment Scale.* Philadelphia: J. B. Lippincott.

Brazelton, T. B. (1979). Behavioral competence of the newborn infant. *Seminars in Perinatology, 1:* 35–44.

Caplan, G. (1968). Patterns of parental response to the crisis of premature birth: A preliminary approach to modifying mental health outcome. *Psychiatry*, 23:365–375.

Caputo, D. V., Goldstein, K. M., and Taub, H. B. (1981). Neonatal compromise and later psychological development: A ten-year psychological study. In *Preterm Birth and Psychological Development*, ed. S. L. Friedman and M. Sigman. New York: Academic Press.

Carey, W. B. and McDevitt, S. C. (1978). Revision of the infant temperament and questionnaire. *Pediatrics*, 61:735–739.

Dubowitz, L. M., Dubowitz, V., and Goldberg, C. (1970). Clinical assessment of gestational age in a newborn infant. *Journal of Pediatrics*, 77:1–10.

Hereford, C. F. (1963). *Changing Parental Attitudes through Group Discussion.* Austin: University of Texas Press.

Hollingshead, A. B. and Redlich, F. (1958). *Social Class and Mental Illness.* New York: John Wiley.

Holmes, T. H. and Rahe, R. N. (1967). The social readjustment rating scale. *Journal of Psychosomatic Research,* 11: 213–225.

Kaplan, D. N. and Mason, E. A. (1960). Maternal reactions to premature birth viewed as an acute emotional disorder. *American Journal of Orthopsychiatry, 30:* 539–552.

Kattwinkel, J., Nearman, B. S., Fanaroff, A. A., and Klaus, M. H. (1975). Apnea of prematurity. *Journal of Pediatrics*, 86:588–592.

Kennell, J. H., Gordon, D., and Klaus, M. H. (1970). The effects of early mother-infant separation on later maternal performance. *Pediatric Research*, 4:473–474.

Korner, A. F., Kraemer, N. C., Faffner, M. E., and

Casper, L. M. (1975). Effects of waterbed flotation on premature infants: A pilot study. *Pediatrics*, 56:361–367.

Leifer, A. D., Leiderman, P. H., Barnett, C. R., and Williams, J. A. (1972). Effects of mother-infant separation on maternal attachment behavior. *Child Development*, 43:1203–1218.

Lubchenco, L. D., Delivoria-Papadapoulos, M., and Searls, D. (1972). Long-term follow-up studies of premature born infants II. Influence of birthweight and gestational age on sequelae. *Journal of Pediatrics*, 80:509–512.

Lubchenco, L. D., Hansman, C., and Boyd, E. (1966). Intrauterine growth in length and head circumference as estimated from live births at gestational ages from 26 to 42 weeks. *Pediatrics*, 37:403–408.

Matheny, A. P. (1980). Bayley's infant behavior record: Behavioral components and twin analysis. *Child Development*, 51:1157–1167.

Minde, K. et al. (1980). Self help groups in a premature nursery—a controlled evaluation. *Journal of Pediatrics*, 96: 933–940.

Nurcombe, B. et al. (in press). Intervention and transaction: Preliminary results of a program for the mothers of low-birthweight infants. *Journal of the American Academy of Child Psychiatry*, May, 1984.

Powell, L. F. (1974). The effect of extra stimulation and maternal involvement on the development of low-birthweight infants and on maternal behavior. *Child Development*, 45:106–113.

Rotter, J. B., (1966). General expectancies for internal vs. external control of reinforcement. *Psychological Monographs, 80:* 1–28.

Sameroff, A. J. and Chandler, M. J. (1975). Reproductive risks and the continuum of caretaking casualty. In *Review of Child Development Research*, vol. 4, ed. F. W. Horowitz. Chicago: University of Chicago Press.

Seashore, M. J., Leifer, A. D., Barnett, C. R., and Leiderman, P. N. (1973). Effects of denial of early mother-infant interaction on maternal self-confidence. *Journal of Personality and Social Psychology*, 26:369–375.

Taylor, J. A. (1953). A personality scale of manifest anxiety. *Journal of Abnormal and Social Psychology*, 48:285–290.

Thoman, E. B. (1980). Infant development viewed within the mother-infant relationship. In *Perinatal Medicine*, ed. E. Quilligan and N. Kretschmer. New York: John Wiley.

Werner, E. E., Bierman, J. M., and French, F. E. (1971). *The Children of Kauai.* Honolulu: University of Hawaii Press.

Widmayer, S. M. and Field, T. M. (1980). Effects of Brazelton demonstrations on early interactions of preterm infants and their teenage mothers. *Infant Behavior and Development*, 3:79–89.

Zax, M., Sameroff, A. J., and Babigian, H. M. (1977). Birth outcome in the offspring of mentally disordered women. *American Journal of Orthopsychiatry*, 47:218–230.

Discussion

Heidelise Als, Ph.D.

The developmental sequelae of prematurity are becoming increasingly apparent in the follow-up studies from various medical centers. The common theme that emerges points to significant decrease of mortality and the grosser morbidities of Cerebral palsy and mental retardation over the last ten years, presumably due to improved neonatal care (Brown, 1980; Davies and Tizard, 1975; Pape et al., 1978). The gestational age at birth and the weight at birth of babies that can be kept alive now have also significantly decreased over the last ten years. Twenty-five- and twenty-six-week-old preterms have a chance at survival now, when ten years ago survival at twenty-eight and twenty-nine weeks was an extraordinary feat. While these improvements are impressive, an increase in subtler dysfunctions such as learning disabilities and behavior problems is noted and is obviously cause for concern (Drillien et al, 1980; Herzig, 1981; Rubin and Balow, 1977; Saint-Anne D'Argassies, 1977). It appears that the prematurely born baby is not as easily able to take advantage of environmental opportunities, nor as readily able to express him- or herself gesturally, posturally, and vocal-verbally as flexibly and modulatedly as his or her full-term, full-weight peer. Although survival is increasingly assured, the quality of survival is still far from perfect. What is going awry in the unfolding of the organism's functioning?

Various factors may be at play, singly or, more likely, interactively, which make documentation of etiology very difficult. These fac-tors can be seen to be of three basic kinds: first, focal insults, often directly to the brain, or if to other organ systems, indirectly to the brain (for a review, see Chiswick, 1982; Cloherty and Stark, 1980); second, the effects of a hypothesized mismatch of CNS readiness of the immature brain in development and the demand of the nursery environment and care (Duffy and Als, in press); and third, the disruption of parental emotional competence and confidence due to having prematurely to let go completely of the up-to-then internalized child. Exacerbating factors presumably are the cumulative effect of already difficult social circumstances and/or the presence in the caregiver of physical, emotional, and mental stress of an ongoing nature.

Focal Insults to the Premature Brain

For many prematures, especially the younger age group (less than thirty-two weeks), there is the great danger of intraventricular hemorrhage frequently associated with subsequent ventricular dilatation, necessitating at times heroic efforts at spinal tapping or the insertion of a shunt. The formation of cysts is not uncommon after resolution of the acute bleed. The high incidence of intraventricular bleeds points to the great vulnerability of a brain in the process of massive cell proliferation when suddenly moved from an intrauterine environment, to which its development is evolutionarily adapted, to an extrauterine environment of quite different sensory demands. A similar threat to proper developmental progression is inherent in the immaturity of the lungs at the point of this transition from *in utero* to outside the womb, leading to asphyxia and its multiple direct and indirect CNS sequelae, and necessitating the use of mechanical ventilatory assistance with all its inherent complications, such as, for instance, the development of chronic lung disease. The effects on the brain of continuous, even if mild, hypoxemia, so often accompanying chronic lung disease, is difficult to estimate. Another frequent complication is inherent in the issue of nutrition in the presence of a hypersensitive, immature gut, heart, and—often compromised—lungs. How can appropriate nutritional input be assured to support the rapid brain development taking place, and how can fluid overload be prevented so as not to endanger the brain directly and indirectly? Among the myriad other threats is the high susceptibility to infection of the immature organism, complications due to immature cardiac function (e.g., patent ductus arteriosus) and many others. How preventable these events are is as yet unknown, and we are only beginning to appreciate their interrelatedness with the issue of mismatch of organism and caregiving environment. Control or prevention of focal insult would be a logical avenue for an intervention program.

Mismatch of Organism and Caregiving Environment

Our hypothesis concerning the etiology of the developmental compromise of the preterm organism, aside from the factors of focal insult, focuses on the continuous interaction of the developing central nervous system and the environment it finds itself in. There is increasing evidence that for normal development to occur, specific hormonal, neurochemical, and structural environmental conditions need to be met to ensure appropriate cell proliferation and migration (Kuffler and Nicholls, 1976). It appears that there are stages of heightened sensitivity

for proper formation of subcortical and cortical connections to occur. The shift from intrauterine to extrauterine environment certainly entails pervasive differences in all sensory modalities—auditory, visual, olfactory, gustatory, somasthetic, and kinesthetic—not to mention the irreversible triggering of autonomous respiratory function and the necessity for nutritional intake through another than the umbilical route. As we have pointed out elsewhere (Als and Duffy, 1982; Duffy et al., 1978, in press), there is evidence from experimental animal work showing that distorted or inappropriate sensory input during, for instance, the critical period of the visual system's development in the cat, will have the same effect as complete deprivation of input, namely, causing the visual cortical receptor cells to fail to fire, thus preventing the development of functional vision. This maldevelopment has been shown to be due to a neurotransmitter shift to increasingly active inhibition (Lewis et al., 1981). Furthermore, it has been shown that unavoidable, stressful stimulation produces an increase in endogenous opioid peptides leading to stress-induced analgesia (Madden et al., 1977). Furthermore, there is evidence from the primate that stereospecific opiate receptors increase in a gradient along hierarchically organized cortical systems, which sequentially process modality-specific sensory information of a progressively more complex nature. Aside from the posterior sensory processing areas, the highest densities were found in the frontal lobe and more specifically in the ventromedial frontal granular cortex, a frontal subdivision that has been implicated in autonomic and emotional functions and that is characterized by relatively rapid ontogenetic development and prominent interconnections with the amygdala and anterior temporal cortex (Lewis et al., 1981). It is of great interest that the inhibitory effects of sensory distortion and stress can be overcome by naloxone, an antagonist of opiates (Duffy et al., 1978). We have therefore speculated that the distortion and stress of prematurity may induce an endogenous overinhibition along hierarchically organized cortical systems by this mechanism. This would fit the picture of greatest risk for the subtle integrative capacities as they are evidenced in learning disabilities and behavior problems. Maladaptation of the frontal association cortex is strongly implicated in the learning disabilities by the recent work of Duffy and his associates (1980). Control, prevention, or reduction of the environment-organism mismatch would be a logical approach for an intervention program.

Disruption of Parental Emotional Competence and Confidence

The premature delivery of a baby requires the sudden and complete removal of the stimulus barrier that the parental organism provides for the *in utero* development of the newly unfolding organism at a time when this removal is unexpected and potentially harmful for the immature organism and when this removal and externalization of the fetus are possibly harmful to the adult organism. Normal parenting appears to be a process of continuous and gradual letting go, reduction of protection, and shielding of the fragile incorporated organism until complete autonomy of the externalized offspring has been reached. This process, in turn, demands of the parent organism complete confidence in that autonomy and self-reliance. In the premature birth, complete letting go is demanded of the parent at a time when neither the parent nor the infant is ready to accommodate smoothly to such externalization. As already pointed out, the fetal newborn is dependent for his survival on neonatal technology to substitute for the intrauterine environment. The parent is confronted with a sudden, complete premature separation and additionally is deprived of the normal transition phase afforded the fullterm parent, who naturally may mourn the loss of the pregnancy per se but moves to the next step of literally holding close and caring for the newborn baby by frequent body contact, albeit now outside the parental body but in immediate body space and contiguity. The normal transition from womb to arms to "Snugli" then typically progresses gradually to temporary infant chair, baby sitter, then to the floor and the world of objects, preschool, kindergarten, school, college or job, and then to the formation of an adult bond to another adult who is not the parent, thus arriving at the next spiral loop of the potential for new parenting and for grandparenting in turn, thus decreasing gradually the parental protective stimulus barrier to complete the letting go (Freud, 1920). In the premature birth, the parent, it appears, first needs to recapture the suddenly completely externalized infant and regain the base for a more normal progression of letting go. This recapturing is often hindered by the way we conduct the temporary substitute care and stimulus-barrier provision which the parent naturally provides in the fullterm situation. There is a competetive focus on the medical system's ability to provide survival assurance, a focus on the technical aspects of medical care's contribution, which probably comes out of the professional's difficulty in recognizing and accepting that his or her role is truly temporary and facilitative only and should be to reconnect developing parent and developing infant with each other onto a supported, normal trajectory of mutual development. The special care environment is nothing but an aid to making the adjustment of premature externalization of the fetus as productive as possible for fetus and parent in their negotiation of their mutual development, that is, gradually reducing the stimulus barrier provided by the parent for the fetus and infant in accordance with the infant's increasing autonomy. In this framework of parenting as a letting-go process, it becomes understandable that medical setbacks in the preterm's hospital stay are so devastating to parents, often quite out of proportion to the reality of the severity of the setback. The parent has begun to regain and reincorporate the infant by visiting, by attempts at caregiving, possibly even by physically holding the externalized fetus. The process is beginning to approach an equilibrium of accepting the initial total letting go and establishing confidence into a gradual regaining, and from there recapturing, the more gradual letting-go process. If this dynamic is not understood, each setback becomes a devastating replay of the original sudden disruption of the letting-go process. If these dynamics can be acknowledged and articulated to the parents by the health care professionals, it will free all those involved in the care of the baby to act on behalf of the optimal developmental progression of parent and infant.

It is obvious that the three points outlined above—endogenous distortion, environmental-organism mismatch, and parental emotional disruption—are not easily separable in identifying the relative risk a specific preterm infant finds him- or herself confronted with. It is likely that all three have a varying impact on the development of many preterm babies, and that, of course, there may be additional exacerbating factors in the parents (social, economic, mental stress, or emotional or physical illness) and/or the environment (poor care, and so forth) or the organism itself (genetic or congenital syndromes). If one then sets out to attempt to ameliorate or prevent the developmental sequelae so often associated with prematurity, one needs to structure one's approach as clearly as possible to affect the factors impinging upon that developmental process, and to control as well as possible for those factors one cannot address easily or directly. The prevention of endogenous organism interference (intraventricular hemorrhage, bronchopulmonary dysplasia, and the like) is still largely considered the domain of classical neonatology, although increasingly it is becoming clear that the continuous interaction of psyche and soma may well play a role in these entities also (see, for instance, studies on the decrease of hypoxemia by environmental modification, such as Hansen and Okken, 1979, 1980; Long et al., 1980; Long et al., 1980). The reduction of environment and organism mismatch and the decrease of distortion of the parental letting-go process have become increasingly the focus of studies by psychologists, psychiatrists, nurses, physical and occupational therapists, and infant educators involved in the care of the preterm infant in the special care nursery (see the work of Korner, Barnard, Burns, Minde, Pelletier, Vandenberg, and others).

THE BURLINGTON M.I.T.P. PROJECT

The project described by the interdisciplinary Burlington group addresses these latter two points. The approach taken, however, is global and at times internally contradictory. The main sequelae of prematurity named are mental retardation and cerebral palsy, yet babies beginning to show such severe distortions of development are excluded from the study. Babies are, however, selected to be neurologically intact, presumably to control for the factors outlined earlier under part one. The transactional model espoused by Sameroff and Chandler (1975) is invoked as rationale for working toward enhancement of the parents' understanding and appreciation of the premature infant in order to set in motion a positive interactive process with the expectation of ameliorating developmental sequelae. The exacerbating effect of low social-class status and low educational level is clearly spelled out. Two approaches toward influencing the parents' understanding of the infant are then intermixed and utilized conjointly, without clarifying implications of one versus the other. The first approach is based on the work of Brazelton with fullterms (1973) and the second is spelled out in our own theoretical formulation (1982) of synaction of development. Three groups of babies are selected, a fullterm control group, a relatively healthy preterm control group, and a relatively healthy preterm experimental group. The effects of the massive intervention effort are restricted to improvement in reported parental confidence, and there are no improvements in infant functioning at six and twelve months. Before discussing some of the possible reasons for the negative results, a few design problems need discussion. The laudatory approach of random assignment of preterms to a control and an intervention group yielded a skewed distribution of social class (SES) and education-level membership—the very variables that the study is so careful to spell out as highly significant in influencing development. Significantly higher SES and education levels were observed in the intervention group, thus making interpretation of even the few positive results very difficult. The effort to control statistically for this skewed distribution is illusory, since social class and educational status cannot be extracted from a person's attitudes, thinking, and behavior, but permeate all functioning continuously and thoroughly. This design flaw no doubt arose because of the relatively small number of subjects studied, which usually necessitates a modified approach of random assignment with matching for major variables.

A second problem with interpretation of the positive parenting confidence results consists of the fact that the interviewees in the experimental group knew that the interviewers were members of the project that had conducted the repeated intervention sessions. Parents are typically very good at picking up what an examiner or interviewer would like them to see, feel, or believe. It would have been better to have the parents interviewed by a completely separate interviewer who was not ostensibly connected to the project in the newborn period. Otherwise, one cannot be sure whether the parents' shift in attitude was genuine or reflected their acute reading and following of project expectations.

The negative infant findings may have various explanations. They might well be due to the outcome measures employed. The Bayley Scales of Infant Development (1969) are quite global and generalized assessments of relatively biologically based and maturation-dependent skills in the infant. Perhaps at later ages, due to improved parent confidence (which may be social-class and educational-level related), better results will be obtained.

The interventive approach per se instituted by the Burlington group requires further analysis. As the authors point out, it is based on Brazelton's work and it incorporates aspects of the synactive formulation of development, yet it also contradicts this formulation in a basic way. Brazelton's approach suggests the demonstration of a baby's behavior to the parent in the course of the Brazelton Neonatal Behavioral Assessment Scale (1973). It does not spell out how to interpret specifically the behavior and leaves it essentially up to the parents to derive their own conclusions from the demonstration. The Brazelton scale was developed to assess and quantify the behavior of the healthy fullterm newborn, and the component assessing alertness and social responsivity is usually given much attention. The Burlington group, in keeping with this thinking, places much emphasis on the hypothesized increase in social

interaction and increase in affective involvement, leading to a hypothesized higher level of dyadic involvement of parent and infant. This approach, adequate for a fullterm infant, presents developmental misunderstanding when applied to the other population without expansion of the conceptualizations, since in this approach alertness is largely judged in isolation of other behavioral subsystems and becomes the single representative criterion of developmental well-being. The Burlington group is nonspecific about its choice for application of the Brazelton scale to preterms and expands on this approach by pointing out that the intervention protocol is theoretically based on our own work, meaning the synactive formulation of development and the emphasis on behavioral subsystem interplay as it is documented in the Assessment of Preterm Infants' Behavior (APIB) (Als et al., 1982). The essence of this theoretical formulation lies in the focus at each stage of development, from the fetal stage on, on the current level of differentiation *and* modulation of functioning of various behaviorally observable subsystems in their interplay, namely, the autonomic system, the motor system, the state organizational system, and within it, the attentional interactive system, the self-regulatory capacity of the organism, and the organism's capacity to make use of environmental and caregiver facilitation (Als et al., 1979, 1982). Thresholds from smooth, well-differentiated, and well-modulated functioning of these systems in mutually supportive interplay to stressed, disorganized, subsystem-segmented functioning are continuously monitored. And, although stress in the opening up of previous balance and integration is necessary for a newly ascending developmental agendum, it must be containable without leading to costly maladaptations, and the subsequent return to a higher level of modulated differentiation need be assured. For instance, emphasis on eye opening and alert availability can be counterproductive in the preterm organism. In the fullterm, well-organized baby, alert eye-opening periods are usually accompanied and supported by a well-regulated, steady autonomic system and a well-organized, steady motor system, which assures ready intake of social stimulation from the caregiver without stress to the baby, in fact, often enhancing the baby's responsive state. In the immature organism, eye opening, even of a focused kind, may be accompanied by flaccid extremity, trunk, and facial tone (gape face), by pale color, and by uneven respiration. If the caregiver now pays differential attention only to alertness, disregarding the lack of simultaneous subsystem synaction from the autonomic and motor functioning, and proceeds to interact socially with the baby, that baby will be moved to more severe disruption of the autonomic and motor systems, leading, for instance, to vomiting and respiratory pause (for a dramatic example, see Gorski et al., 1983). The late Harvard professor of neurology, Derek Denny-Brown (1966, 1972), and in a different context, Schneirla (1959, 1965), have provided us with a basic biphasic principle of functioning that can be productively applied to learn about the thresholds from modulation to stress in the sensitive, immature preterm infant or, for that matter, in all developing organisms. When stimulation is currently appropriate to the organism in its intensity, complexity, and/or timing, the organism has strategies available to move toward that stimulation, take it in, and make it productive for its own developmental progression. When stimulation is currently inappropriate to the organism in its intensity, complexity, and/or timing, the organism has strategies available to move away from that stimulation, to defend against and avoid it. Thus, we must identify at each subsystem of functioning the current threshold of integration to defense and avoidance so that we do not inadvertently heighten the expense to one subsystem, while naively focusing on the seeming enhancement of another.

The Burlington group's intervention protocol consists of eleven sessions from the stay in the NICU to three months after discharge. In each session, a separate subsystem of functioning is focused on, first the autonomic system, a week later, the motor system, a week later, the state organizational system, and so forth. The infant is systematically examined in the first session only. The last several sessions then focus on daily activities such as bathing, diapering, and playing. It is not clear how the group arrived at the idea of sequential subsystem treatment when the essence of the theoretical model is the very integration of subsystems in the face of changing developmental demands and in the course of developmental progression. The first three or four months, after the initial critical period of ensuring survival, in the development of a preterm baby certainly are a considerable span of time during which much developmental progression typically is accomplished in the gradual emergence of subsystems and their increasing differentiation and beginning mutual modulation and support. A thirty-five-weeker now in an open isolette who had been born at twenty-eight weeks may still easily go into flaccidity, respiratory unsteadiness, bowel movement grunting, and a diffuse, drowsy, fussy state when handled, requiring prolonged times of resting and reorganization between manipulations; three months later, by seven weeks post due date, the same baby may now quite readily maintain modulated tone throughout a manipulation, may maintain steady color and respiration, and may, after a burst of focused animated attention, go into a brief episode of mild hiccoughs and recover him- or herself quickly by simply being held quietly for a few seconds. It is frustrating to realize that the Burlington intervention program pays no attention to the developmental progression of subsystem differentiation and integration and does not use the interpretation of this progression as a focus of their intervention. This, one surmises, could give the parent a handle on the developmental issues the baby and they are currently negotiating and would presumably free the parent to become confident in the observation of the infant's individuality, the degree of defense, and the emerging degree of approach and self regulation. In turn, one would expect that this would lead to increasingly creatively and autonomously formulated differentiation and modulation goals on the part of the parents, tailored specifically to their infant's thresholds of functioning. The satisfaction of the confidence of understanding the infant as an individual negotiating his or her own development would, one expects, enhance the provision of developmental modulation as necessary and of an ever decreasing stimulus barrier ensuring increasingly differentiated and smooth independent functioning. This would no doubt enhance the parent's sense of competence as a true parent in the process of developmentally appropriate letting go. It is, of course, an empirical question whether such an approach can work. Intervention truly based on this approach has not yet been tested, yet it is the logical approach derived from the theoretical underpinnings the Burlington project has chosen.

REFERENCES

Als, H. (1982). Towards a synactive theory of development: Promise for the assessment of infant individuality. *Infant Mental Health Journal,* 3:229–243.

Als, H. and Duffy, F. H. (1982). The behavior of the fetal newborn: Theoretical considerations and practical suggestions for the use of the A.P.I.B. In *Issues in Neonatal Care,* WESTAR. Obtainable from TADS, 500 NCNB Plaza, Chapel Hill, North Carolina, 27514.

Als, H., Lester, B. M., and Brazelton, T. B. (1979). Dynamics of the behavioral organization of the premature infant: A theoretical perspective. In *Infants Born at Risk,* ed. T. M. Field et al. New York: Spectrum.

Als, H., Lester, B. M., Tronick, E., and Brazelton, T. B. (1982). Towards a research instrument for the assessment of preterm infants' behavior (APIB), and Manual for the assessment of preterm infants' behavior (APIB). In *Theory and Research in Behavioral Pediatrics,* vol. I. New York: Plenum.

Bayley, N. (1969). *Bayley Scales of Infant Development.* New York: The Psychological Corporation.

Brazelton, T. B. (1973). *The Neonatal Behavioral Assessment Scale.* Philadelphia: J. P. Lippincott.

Brown, E. (1980). Procedures for follow-up. In *Manual of Neonatal Care,* ed. J. P. Cloherty and A. R. Stark. Boston: Little, Brown.

Chiswick, M. L. (1982). The newborn baby—adaptation and disease. In *Psychobiology of the Human Newborn,* ed. P. Stratton. New York: John Wiley.

Cloherty, J. P. and Stark, A. R. eds. (1980). *Manual of Neonatal Care.* Boston: Little, Brown.

Davies, P. A. and Tizard, J. P. M. (1975). Very low birthweight and subsequent neurological defect (with special reference to spastic diplegia), *Developmental Medicine and Child Neurology,* 17:3–17.

Denny-Brown, D. (1966). *The Cerebral Control of Movement.* Springfield, Illinois: Charles C Thomas.

Denny-Brown, D. (1972). *The Basal Ganglia and Their Relations to Disorders of Movement.* Oxford: Oxford University Press.

Drillien, C. M., Thompson, A. J. M., and Bargoyne, K. (1980). Low birthweight children at early school age: A longitudinal study. *Developmental Medicine and Child Neurology,* 22:26–47.

Duffy, F. H. and Als, H. (1983). Neurophysiological assessment of the neonate: An approach combining brain electrical activity mapping (BEAM) with behavioral assessment (APIB). In *Infant at risk: Toward Plasticity and Intervention,* ed. T. B. Brazelton and B. M. Lester. New York: Elsevier.

Duffy, F. H., Burchfiel, J. L., and Snodgrass, S. R. (1978). The pharmacology of amblyopia. *Journal of the American Academy of Ophthalmology and Otolaryngology,* 85:489–495.

Duffy, F. H., Denckla, M. B., Bartels, P. H., and Sandini, G. (1980). Regional differences in brain electrical activity by topographic mapping. *Annals of Neurology,* 7:412–420.

Duffy, F. H., Mower, G., Jensen, F., and Als, H. (in press). Neural plasticity: A new frontier for infant development. In *Theory and Research in Behavioral Pediatrics,* vol. II, New York: Plenum.

Freud, S. (1920). Beyond the pleasure principle. *Standard Edition,* vol. 18, pp 3–64, ed. J. Strachey. 1955.

Gorski, P. A., Hole, W. T., Leonard, C. H., and Martin, J. A. (1983). Direct computer recording of premature infants and nursery care: Distress following two interventions. *Pediatrics,* 72:198–202.

Hansen, N. and Okken, A. (1979). Continuous TcPO$_2$ monitoring in healthy and sick newborn infants during and after feeding. *Birth Defects: Original Articles Series,* vol. 15, pp. 503–508. Washington, D.C.: The National Foundation March of Dimes.

Hansen, N. and Okken, A. (1980). Transcutaneous oxygen tension of newborn infants in different behavioral states. *Pediatric Research,* 14:911–915.

Hertzig, M. E. (1981). Neurological "soft" signs in low birthweight children. *Developmental Medicine and Child Neurology,* 23:778–791.

Kuffler, S. W. and Nicholls, J. G. (1976). *From Neuron to Brain.* Sunderland, Massachusetts: Sinauer Associates.

Lewis, M. E. et al. (1981). Opiate receptor gradients in monkey cerebral cortex: Correspondence with sensory processing hierarchies. *Science,* 211:1166–1169.

Long, J. G., Lucey, J. F., and Philip, A. G. S. (1980). Noise and hypoxemia in the intensive care nursery. *Pediatrics,* 65:143–145.

Long, J. G., Philip, A. G. S., and Lucey, J. F. (1980). Excessive handling as a cause of hypoxemia. *Pediatrics,* 65:203–207.

Madden, J., Akil, H., Patrick, R. L., and Barchas, J. D. (1977). Stress-induced parallel changes in central opioid levels and pain responsiveness in the cat. *Nature,* 265:358–360.

Pape, K. E., Buncic, R. J., Ashby, S., and Fitzhardinge, P. M. (1978). The status at 2 years of low birthweight infants born in 1974 with birthweights of less than 1001 grams. *Journal of Pediatrics,* 92:253–260.

Rubin, R. A. and Balow, B. (1977). Perinatal influences on the behavior and learning problems in children. In *Advances in Child Clinical Psychology,* vol. 1, ed. B. B. Lahey and A. E. Kazdin. New York: Plenum.

Saint-Anne D'Argassies, S. (1977). Long-term neurological follow-up study of 286 truly premature infants. I: Neurological sequelae. *Developmental Medicine and Child Neurology,* 19:467–478.

Sameroff, A. J. and Chandler, M. J. (1976). Reproductive risk and the continuum of caretaking casualty. In *Review of Child Development Research,* ed. F. D. Horowitz and G. Siegels. Chicago: University of Chicago Press.

Schneirla, T. C. (1959). An evolutionary and developmental theory of biphasic processes underlying approach and withdrawal. In *Nebraska Symposium on Motivation,* ed. M. R. Jones. Lincoln: University of Nebraska Press.

Schneirla, T. C. (1965). Aspects of stimulation and organization in approach/withdrawal processes underlying vertebrate behavioral development. *Advances in the Study of Behavior,* 1:1–74.

A Reply to Dr. Als

Barry Nurcombe, M.D., Douglas Teti, M.D., Virginia Rauh, Sc.D.,
A.C.S.W., and Thomas Achenbach, Ph.D.

Dr. Als poses a number of searching questions, quite apart from her discussion of the causes of developmental morbidity. We welcome the opportunity to discuss the key issues, which we will address according to the following criticisms: (1) the allegedly inappropriate design of the Mother Infant Transaction Program; (2) the failure of randomization to control for maternal education; (3) the exclusion of certain groups from the cohort; (4) the failure to separate intervention from outcome evaluation; (5) the apparent failure of the intervention to affect outcome.

The Design of the Intervention

When the MITP was designed, we drew upon the following sources: Als and Brazelton (1975), Als, Tronick, and Brazelton (1976), Beckwith and colleagues (1976), Brazelton (1973), Bromwich (1976), Parmelee (1975), Prechtl (1974), Robson (1967), Sameroff and Chandler (1975), and Thoman (1975). The rather intricate concepts Dr. Als includes in her synactive theory were not available to us in 1976, when the program was conceived. Instead, the MITP was deceptively simple. The essence of the program was conveyed in daily sessions during the week before the discharge of the baby from hospital, when it was clear that the infant's medical condition had stabil-ized. The first five days were spent in helping the mother to appreciate the baby's potential, to detect the autonomic and motoric signs of stimulus overload, to help the baby organize her- or himself, and to recognize the state of quiet alertness that might indicate a readiness for interaction. The sixth and seventh days were used to prepare the mother to imbed her sensitivity, responsiveness, and interactional skill in the procedures of daily care. The purpose of the four home visits during the three months following discharge was to consolidate the knowledge and skills already learnt. Ultimately, the program aimed to promote maternal responsiveness, contingent interaction, and mutual enjoyment in the context of daily care.

We did not try to teach the process of subsystem differentiation, integration, and modulation or the concept of "threshold of integration to defense and avoidance." Given the wide SES range of our cohort, it would have been difficult to do so.

Dr. Als makes the point that the different subsystems function as a whole, so that to concentrate on one at a time is not only a distortion but potentially unbalancing. Quite so. But the same problem faces all educators who wish to foster the knowledge and skill that underlie a complex procedure: how to analyze the operation into sequential components and convey them in an integrated manner.

It should be stressed that the introduction,

the daily review of preceding days, and the consolidation of previous understanding and skill promoted after discharge were all specifically aimed at the practical synthesis of what had been learnt. At no time did we suggest, as Dr. Als says, that mothers should stimulate one subsystem at the expense of others (engaging in visual stimulation, for example, without concern for signs of autonomic or motoric distress).

Dr. Als describes our intervention as "massive." It is true that the MITP is more extensive than those programs which provide only a single demonstration of the Brazelton scale (for instance, Widmeyer and Field, 1980); but the eleven hours of intervention distributed over fourteen weeks and delivered by a pediatric nurse were designed to be practicable, replicable, and cost-effective.

Failure to Control for Maternal Education

We had originally planned to recruit forty subjects for each of the three groups: LBW intervention (Group 1), LBW control (Group 2), and NBW contrast (Group 3). This took twenty-two rather than the eighteen months we had anticipated, and a number of factors reduced the total sample to 111. Nevertheless, we expected that the number of subjects would be sufficient to allow a random assignment of LBW infants to control the most important variables. As it turned out, randomization was effective in all respects, except, unfortunately, maternal education; hence the necessity for the covariance analyses described in the text of our paper.

Dr. Als suggests that a statistical manipulation of this type is illusory, and that we have compared apples with oranges. A closer examination of the distribution of subjects throws light on this matter.

The difference between the LBW groups in mean maternal education is 1.3 years. When the three groups are stratified into levels according to years of education, the following distribution is revealed:

Maternal Education	LBW Intervention	LBW Control	NBW
More than 16 years	10	2	14
12–15 years	19	31	24
Less than 12 years	3	5	3

The difference in education, therefore, is caused by disproportionate numbers of highly educated women in groups 1 and 3. It is not due to a significant excess of lower-SES subjects in group 2; and it is women of lower SES who might be expected to have attitudes, feelings, and behavior that are qualitatively different from those of other subjects (Kohn, 1975).

Since the significantly lower mean educational level of the LBW control group was attributable mainly to an underrepresentation of mothers with a college degree or more, the original analyses were rerun on subjects with less than sixteen years of education. This procedure was used, with maternal education as a covariate, in order to rule out the possibility that group differences could be due to differences in SES and educational level. Elimination of highly educated mothers did indeed equalize groups by educational level (F [2, 80] = .8256, p = .192) and SES (F [2, 79] = 2.06, p = .13). Table 21–6 presents the mean educational levels and SES for this subset of the full sample.

Analyses on the subset of remaining subjects yielded findings that virtually replicated those on the full sample. Significant group differences were found in Satisfaction, Confidence, and Attitudes using a multivariate analysis of covariance, with maternal education as the covariate (F [6, 124] = 2.29, p = .040). Moreover, univariate tests demonstrated significant group differences on all three dependent variables: Satisfaction (F [2, 63] = 3.78, p = .028); Confidence (F (2, 63) = 4.91, p = .01); and Attitudes (F [2, 63] = 3.23, p = .046).

The multivariate contrast between the two LBW groups on Satisfaction, Confidence, and Attitudes was not significant (F [3, 61] = 2.14, p = .104). However, the univariate contrast between these two groups was significant for Confidence (F [1, 63] = 5.97, p = .017) and approached significance for Satisfaction (F [1,

TABLE 21–6

Maternal and Infant Outcome on a Subset of Mothers with Less than Sixteen Years of Education

	LBW Intervention		LBW Control		NBW	
	Mean	SD	Mean	SD	Mean	SD
Education (yrs.)	12.38	1.56	12.14	1.22	12.23	1.56
SES	3.76	0.62	3.91	0.89	3.46	0.98
Maternal Outcome						
Satisfaction[a]	15.52	4.49	18.25	5.33	14.83[c,e]	3.78
Confidence	9.21[b,e]	1.18	7.70	2.90	9.33[c,f]	1.01
Attitudes	53.68	19.50	47.38	30.82	65.42[c,e]	22.21
Psychopathology	27.10	4.35	28.88	6.34	28.40	6.70
Infant Outcome[d]						
Temperament[a]	1.88[b,f]	1.17	2.90	0.98	2.57	1.16
MDI (6 mos.)	115.09	10.47	110.18	13.57	119.00[c,f]	13.22
MDI (12 mos.)	113.95	12.38	108.51	13.11	113.64	8.96

[a]Lower scores are more favorable.
[b]LBW Intervention vs. LBW Control.
[c]NBW vs. LBW Control.
[d]Corrected for gestational age.
[e]$p < .05$.
[f]$p < .01$.

63] $= 3.43$, $p = .069$), both in the predicted direction (see table 21–6). The multivariate contrast between the LBW control group and the NBW group was significant (F [3, 61] $= 3.93$, $p = .012$). The univariate contrast between these two groups was also significant for all three dependent variables: Satisfaction (F [1, 63] $= 7.10$, $p = .01$); Confidence (F [1, 63] $= 8.30$, $p = .005$); and Attitudes (F [1, 63] $= 6.20$, $p = .015$).

Also consistent with previous findings on the full sample were results on maternal psychopathology, infant temperament, and infant cognitive development. Table 21–6 presents the group means for these variables. No group differences were found in maternal psychopathology (F [2, 75], $= .319$, $p = .727$). Significant group differences were found in Infant Temperament (F [2, 66] $= 4.67$, $p = .013$). A priori contrasts revealed a significant difference in the predicted direction between the two LBW groups (F [1, 66] $= 9.32$, $p = .003$); but not between the LBW control and fullterm groups (F [1, 66] $= 1.19$, $p = .279$). An overall group difference was found in Bayley Mental Development scores at six months (F [2, 78] $= 3.60$, $p = .032$). A priori contrasts demonstrated a significant difference between the LBW control and fullterm groups, (F [1, 78] $= 7.08$, $p = .168$). An analysis of covariance, with maternal education as the covariate, revealed no group differences in Bayley MDI at twelve months (F [2, 76] $= 1.64$, $p = .201$), nor were any a priori contrasts significant.

The Exclusion of Certain Groups from the Cohort

Dr. Als comments on the absence from our program of single mothers, multiple births, and clearly brain-damaged infants. We excluded them because we reasoned that these groups are qualitatively different from others and because they were not available in a large enough sample for meaningful analysis, given the time allotted for recruitment.

Failure to Separate Intervention from Outcome Evaluation

Dr. Als has correctly indicated a flaw in our design: subjects were aware that the evaluation staff were part of the research program. Intervention mothers, perhaps grateful for the help given, may have been induced to inflate their reports of personal satisfaction and confidence and to minimize their infants' temperamental difficulty.

The project director recruited all subjects. Subsequently, she had one more contact with them, at six months, when she conducted the semistructured interviews from which the Satisfaction and Psychopathology scores were derived. These interviews were recorded, typed, and scored by two raters unaware of the groups to which the subjects belonged. It should be pointed out that, whereas an intervention effect was found for Satisfaction, there was no such effect for Psychopathology (as might be expected in the case of an illusory "halo" effect). The Confidence, Attitudes, and Infant Temperament scores were derived from self-administered, mailed questionnaires. The Bayley scales were administered by a psychologist who had not had previous contact with the subjects, and who was blind as to group.

However, the possibility of a "halo" effect remains. We submit that it would be impossible to eliminate "halo" entirely from an action-research project of this nature. A more serious flaw, not mentioned by Dr. Als, is our failure to control for Hawthorne effect. To do so, a "dummy" intervention would have been required. We decided that, given the time constraints and relatively limited pool of subjects, it would not be practicable to recruit two control LBW groups.

The Apparent Failure of the MITP to Affect Outcome

By twelve months, our results were modest: an intervention effect on maternal role satisfaction and confidence, and on infant temperament, but none on maternal attitudes, psychopathology, or infant development.

We are now able to report two-year infant-development results on a nearly complete sample ($N = 85$). Table 21–7 displays the mean mental development indices of the three groups at twenty-four months.

An analysis of covariance with maternal education as covariate was significant between the MDI scores of the three groups (F [2, 79] = 13.78, $p < .001$). Univariate contrasts were significant between the two LBW groups (F [1, 79] = 18.45, $p < .001$) and between the LBW control and the NBW groups (F [1, 79] = 46.2, $p < .001$). Significant, but less impressive, experimental effects were found for twenty-four-month Bayley Psychomotor Development Indices (see table 21–8). An analysis of covariance with maternal education as a covariate was significant between the PDI scores of the three groups (F [2, 79] = 6.04, $p < .004$). Univariate contrasts were significant between the two LBW groups (F [1, 79] = 12.41, $p < .001$), and between the LBW control and the NBW groups (F [1, 79] = 12.41, $p < .001$).

The significant intervention effect on Bayley Mental Development remained when highly educated mothers were excluded. An analysis of covariance with maternal education as covariate was significant between the MDI scores of the three groups (F [2, 57] = 12.84, $p < .001$). Univariate contrasts were also significant between the two LBW groups, (F [1, 57] = 5.24, $p = .026$) and between the LBW control and the NBW groups (F [1, 51] = 25.60, $p < .001$).

Conclusions

In designing the MITP we drew upon a number of sources. Prominent among them was the work of the Harvard Child Development Unit, of which Dr. Als was a member. At that time (1976) the synactive theory had not been completely formulated; and, as Dr. Als points out, the conceptual sequence underlying the MITP is not consistent with the synactive formulation, although it clearly shares similar theoretical roots.

Randomization did not control for maternal education: there was an excess of highly educated women in the LBW intervention and NBW groups. However, when the groups are equated for maternal education by excluding these women from the outcome analyses, substantially the same results are obtained.

TABLE 21-7

Infant Outcome: Bayley MDI

Age	LBW Intervention		LBW Control		NBW	
	Mean	SD	Mean	SD	Mean	SD
Two Years[a]	117.33[b,d]	13.57	101.93	12.62	124.66[c,d]	15.41

[a]Adjusted for gestational age.
[b]LBW Intervention vs. LBW Control.
[c]NBW vs. LBW Control.
[d]$p < .001$.

TABLE 21-8

Infant Outcome: Bayley PDI

Age	LBW Intervention		LBW Control		NBW	
	Mean	SD	Mean	SD	Mean	SD
Two Years[a]	108.91[b,d]	8.21	100.07	11.70	108.34[c,d]	6.20

[a]Adjusted for gestational age.
[b]LBW Intervention vs. LBW Control.
[c]NBW vs. LBW Control.
[d]$p < .001$.

There are two flaws in the methodology. We failed to separate intervention from outcome assessment completely, and we did not control for the Hawthorne effect. However, the pattern of results is not consistent with a pure "halo" effect; and, in any case, it would not be possible to exclude "halo" fully in action-research of this kind. The control of a Hawthorne effect would require a more intricate methodological design.

The lack of an intervention effect upon infant outcome by twelve months is not surprising. It emphasizes the need for follow-up of cohorts like ours into early childhood, if environmental influences are to be detected.

In summary, an early intervention program of moderate intensity has produced significant changes in the mothers of LBW infants by six months and in the infants by two years. These results are not consistent with some reports of early effects on infant cognition following neonatal intervention. Perhaps the Bayley Scales are not sufficiently sensitive in the first year. Indeed, it is noteworthy that the relative cognitive deficits associated with low SES are not apparent in Bayley scores until the second year of life (Bayley, 1965).

The gradual deterioration of LBW control performance over two years contrasts with the upward "sleeper" trend of the LBW intervention group between one and two years. This differential trend, which is of great interest, awaits explanation.

Intervention programs, like the theoretical ideas on which they are based, are proper subjects for criticism or debate. Invariably, they could have been better designed, implemented more faithfullly, delivered to a more appropriate population, or tested with tighter control and more elegant evaluation techniques.

Searching for a rationale, interventionists tend to borrow from a number of sources. Theoretical ideas may thus be merged and modified in accordance with the scientific question at hand.

We hope that the success of the MITP will encourage others to implement early intervention for mothers and infants who are at risk of developmental problems. A logical next step would be to design and test an intevention based on the synactive formulation, and to do so in a replicable and economical manner. We would welcome the opportunity to compare our findings with those of an intervention derived directly from Dr. Als's theory.

REFERENCES

Als, H. and Brazelton, T. B. (1975). Comprehensive neonatal assessment (Brazelton Neonatal Behavior Assessment). *Birth and the Family Journal,* 2:3–9.

Als, H., Tronick, E., and Brazelton, T. B. (1976). *Manual for the Behavioral Assessment of the Premature and At-Risk Newborn.* Unpublished Manuscript. Child Development Unit, Children's Hospital Medical Center, Boston.

Bayley, N. (1965). Comparisons of mental and motor test scores for ages 1–15 months by sex, birth order, race, geographic location and education of parents. *Child Development,* 36:379–412.

Beckwith, L. et al. (1976). Caregiver-infant interaction and early cognitive development in preterm infants. *Child Development,* 45:579–587.

Brazelton, T. B. (1973). *Neonatal Behavioral Assessment Scale.* Philadelphia: J. B. Lippincott.

Bromwich, R. M. (1976). Focus on maternal behavior in infant interaction. *American Journal of Orthopsychiatry,* 46: 439–446.

Kohn, M. L. (1975). Social class and parent-child relationships: An interpretation. In *Influences on Human Development,* ed. U. Bronfenbrenner and M. A. Mahoney. New York: Dryden Press.

Parmelee, A. H. (1975). Neurophysiological and behavioral organization of the premature infant in the first months of life. *Biological Psychiatry,* 10:501–512.

Prechtl, H. F. R. (1974). The behavioral states of the newborn infant. *Brain Research,* 76:185–212.

Robson, D. S. (1967). The role of eye-to-eye contact in maternal infant attachment. *Journal of Child Psychiatry, Psychology and Allied Disciplines,* 8:13–25.

Sameroff, A. J. and Chandler, M. J. (1975). Reproductive risk and the continuum of caretaking casualty. In *Review of Child Development Research,* vol. 4, ed. F. H. Horowitz. Chicago: University of Chicago Press.

Thomas, E. G. (1975). Development of synchrony in mother-infant interaction in feeding and other situations. *Federation Proceedings,* 34:1587–1592.

Widmayer, S. M. and Field, T. M. (1980). Effects of Brazelton demonstrations on early interactions of preterm infants and their teenage mothers. *Infant Behavior and Development,* 3:79–89.

22

Improving Outcome of Children Born to Drug-Dependent Mothers

Loretta P. Finnegan, M.D., Karol A. Kaltenbach, Ph.D., Matthew Pasto, M.D.,
Leonard Graziani, M.D., Dianne O'Malley Regan, R.N., M.S.W.,
and Sandra L. Tunis, Ph.D.

Numerous investigators have reported an extremely high incidence of medical and obstetrical complications among pregnant drug-dependent women and high levels of morbidity and mortality among passively addicted infants. Opiate dependence in the pregnant woman is overwhelming to her own physical condition as well as to that of the fetus and eventually the newborn infant. In addition, drug-dependent mothers tend to neglect prenatal care as well as their general health care, and many abuse more than one drug (Connaughton et al., 1977; Finnegan, 1978; Finnegan and Fehr, 1980; Finnegan et al., 1977; Wapner and Finnegan, 1982). Perinatal management of drug-dependent women is further complicated by the frequency with which they experience psychiatric, psychological, and social difficulties.

In an effort to provide comprehensive services for this high-risk population of drug-dependent women and their infants, the Family Center Program was established to provide necessary medical, psychiatric, and social services as well as a variety of clinical assessments. Outpatient methadone maintenance is available for the drug-dependent women and, where appropriate, for their husbands or partners. Within the clinical setting of the Program, our studies have taught us much about the characteristics and needs of these women and about the medical and developmental outcome of their children. This report summarizes four aspects of our research: (1) the incidence of violence and depression among women enrolled in the Program and its possible relation to parenting effectiveness; (2) maternal perceptions of their newborns; (3) brain growth and cerebral ventricular development in the passively addicted infants; and (4) long-term outcome measures of mental development.

Incidence of Depression and Experiences with Violence in Drug-Dependent Women

DEPRESSION

In treating pregnant drug addicts, it is particularly important to assess the degree to which depression is present. Among addicts, women experience substantially more depression than do men (Reed et al., 1977). Furthermore, depression levels are usually higher on intake into a methadone program than in later stages of treatment (DeLeon et al., 1973; Dorus and Senay, 1980).

Assessing depression among drug-dependent women is also important in terms of the quality of the mother-child interaction. For example, in one study (Weisman et al., 1980), depressed women were found to experience higher levels of discord with their children than with members of their extended family, friends, neighbors, or work associates. These women showed an impaired ability to parent, which included diminished emotional involvement, impaired communication, disaffection, increased hostility, and resentment. Depressed mothers of infants expressed feelings of helplessness in caring for their children and became either overly concerned or directly hostile. Depressed mothers of school-age children were irritable, uninvolved, and intolerant of their children's noise and activities. Also, a relationship has been found between maternal depression and hostility, on the one hand, and child deviant behavior such as truancy, drug abuse, and theft, as well as childhood depression, on the other (Poznanski and Zrull, 1970; Weisman et al., 1972).

In order to assess the levels of depression in women enrolled in Family Center, the Beck Depression Inventory (Beck and Beck, 1972) is administered to all patients upon admission to the program, postpartum, and upon discharge. This thirteen-item, self-administered questionnaire measures levels of depression through endorsement or rejection of self-descriptive items such as, "I do not feel sad," "I get tired more easily than I used to," and "I hate myself." Depression levels are interpreted as none, mild, moderate, or severe with a possible range of scores from 0–39 (the higher the score, the more depression).

The study reported here was designed to compare the depression levels of a sample of pregnant drug-dependent women ($n = 149$) admitted from 1979 through 1982 with that of a sample of pregnant, drug-free control women ($n = 26$) who were comparable socioeconomically and attended the regular prenatal clinic of the hospital. Results revealed that the drug-dependent women showed significantly more depression ($p < .05$): 75 percent showed some level of depression, with 21 percent rated as mild, 39 percent as moderate, and 15 percent as severe. Mild depression was reported by 50 percent of the control women. Ethnic group, marital status, and number of children were not found to be significantly related to maternal depression.

In a previous study (Finnegan et al., 1981) we investigated the relation of depression in the drug-dependent group to a measure of ineffective parenting. The legal placement of children outside the home was the measure used for the comparison. Of the study women who had relatively high Beck scores, 41 percent had children currently in placement with relatives or foster parents. Furthermore, when compared with women whose children were in their own care, those with children who had either been placed in a foster home or referred to a child welfare agency were characterized by a significantly higher incidence of moderate or severe depression ($p < .01$). Thus legal actions associated with the placement of children appear to be highly related to maternal depression. Based upon these findings, it would appear that addressing depression as early as possible in the pregnancy is crucial in helping to ensure that the drug-dependent woman will be an effective parent.

VIOLENCE

Another variable associated with poor parenting is maternal experience of violence. Gayford (1975) reported that of those parents in his British nonaddicted sample, 54 percent of abusive husbands and 34 percent of abused wives had also abused their children. In a study of 200 Boston families (108 in which at least one parent was opiate-addicted and 92 with an alcoholic parent), Black and Mayer (1980) reported that physical or sexual abuse of a child occurred in 25.5 percent of the families. These investigators also found that serious neglect occurred in 30.5 percent of the 200 families and that violence between the parents was the strongest predictor of violence between parents and children.

Based on findings such as these, Family Center has addressed the issue of violence in the lives of its drug-addicted women. Violent experiences, both past and present, raise serious concern for the women's safety as well as for the safety and emotional development of their children. A questionnaire on the topic of violence was developed and is routinely given to women enrolled in the program. For this study, the questionnaire was administered to: a sample of seventy-eight Family Center women and a sample of forty-three drug-free control women recruited from the hospital's prenatal clinic.

Analysis of the questionnaire responses showed that compared to control women those enrolled in Family Center have experienced and continue to experience significantly more violence in their lives. A greater proportion of the drug-dependent women reported having been beaten as children (27 percent vs. 14 percent, p <.05). Mothers were most often identified as the perpetrator of the beatings. The experience of having been beaten as an adult (usually by the husband or partner) was reported by a significantly greater proportion of Family Center women than controls (73 percent vs. 20 percent, p <.001). Also, significantly more Family Center women have been raped as adults (23 percent vs. 3 percent, p < .001). Finally, there was a significant difference between the proportion of drug-dependent women (29 percent) and the proportion of those in the control group (6 percent) reporting the experience of childhood rape or sexual molestation (p <.001). The high incidence of violent experiences, both sexual and nonsexual, among the Family Center women appears particularly critical for the welfare of their children, considering that this group may already be at risk for child abuse according to other criteria such as chaotic lifestyle, extreme poverty, and drug abuse. Evidence that violence and abuse tend to be intergenerationally transmitted underscores the need for early and effective intervention.

Maternal Perceptions of Newborns

It has been demonstrated that a mother's perception of her child is an important factor in the psychological and social development of the child. Moreover, when maternal perception is not in concordance with the child's actual behavior, it is the perception that is the better predictor of risk (Broussard and Hartner, 1970). Therefore, in order to delineate the environmental risk factors for infants born to drug-dependent women, we have investigated these mothers' perceptions of their newborn infants. Sixty drug-dependent women and twenty-one non–drug-dependent women of comparable socioeconomic and medical backgrounds were administered the Broussard Neonatal Perception Inventory (Broussard and Hartner, 1970) twenty-four hours postpartum. The Broussard requires each woman to check such items as the amount she anticipates her baby will cry, how much trouble the infant has with sleeping and feeding, and the like in relation to the "average" baby. Results of this study revealed that drug-dependent mothers had significantly more negative perceptions of their newborns than did non–drug-dependent mothers ($X^2 = 4.7, p$ <.05). In addition, differences in maternal perceptions within the drug-dependent group were found to be a function of severity of abstinence. Mothers of infants who subsequently required pharmacotherapy for neonatal abstinence had significantly more negative perceptions than mothers of infants who did not require therapy ($X^2 = 7.38, p$ < .01).

The finding that drug-dependent women had more negative perceptions than did non–drug-dependent women is provocative. It is conceivable that drug-dependent women had more negative perceptions because they expected their infants to undergo neonatal abstinence. This would appear to be supported by the differences observed within the drug-dependent group. There are several reasons, however, why this explanation must be questioned. Because the mothers completed the inventory within twenty-four hours postpartum, most mothers had no indication of whether their infant would require therapy. Second, studies with normal infants and non–drug-related perinatal risk factors have found that maternal perceptions are often unrelated to the actual condition of the child (Broussard and Hartner, 1971). And third, Broussard and Hartner found a relationship between maternal perception and maternal depression. Mothers who had very positive perceptions of their infants tended to score lower on depression scales than mothers who had negative perceptions of their infants. This relationship is especially salient inasmuch as depression has been found to be prevalent among drug-dependent women.

We suggest, therefore, that these findings point to the importance of the early assessment of maternal depression, experience of violence, abuse, and molestation, and of mothers' perceptions of their infants in order to guide intervention and services for drug-dependent women and their infants.

Brain Growth and Cerebral Ventricular Development in Infants of Drug-Dependent Mothers

BRAIN GROWTH

Infants exposed prenatally to narcotic agents become passively addicted *in utero* and usually undergo the Neonatal Abstinence syndrome. This syndrome is characterized by signs and symptoms of central nervous system hyperirritability, gastrointestinal dysfunction, respiratory distress, and vague autonomic symptoms, which include yawning, sneezing, mottling, and fever. Sucking and swallowing reflexes are uncoordinated and ineffectual. Careful assessment of abstinence and appropriate treatment are essential in bringing the infant to a general state of good health (Finnegan, 1979; Finnegan et al., 1975; Finnegan and MacNew, 1974; Glass, 1974; Hill and Desmond, 1963; Kahn et al., 1969; Kandall and Gartner, 1972; Kron et al., 1975; Rajegowda et al., 1972; Rosen and Pippenger, 1974; Rothstein and Gould, 1974; Zelson et al., 1971). Incidence, clinical symptomatology, and treatment regimens have been evaluated by many investigators, but few studies have evaluated the effects of maternal perinatal drug intake on the brain of the developing fetus or that of the neonate. Ultrasound is now an established method of viewing and measuring the infant's brain.

In our study, in order to evaluate brain growth and cerebral ventricular development of infants born to drug-dependent women compared with those born to a group of medically and socioeconomically matched control women, samples of infants were studied, using ultrasound in the transaxial plane to measure the lateral and intracranial hemidiameter. Scanning through the temporal bone enabled the identification of the superolateral borders of the lateral ventricles, the brain stem, the basal ganglia, and the midline structures of the brain. In the latter part of the study, high resolution real-time sector scanning was added to the protocol. The 5 MHz transducer enabled coronal and parasagittal images to be scanned through the anterior fontanelle, which allowed visualization of the midline structures of the brain, the lateral ventricles and the caudate nucleus immediately below them, the choroid plexus, and the cerebral spinal fluid within the lateral ventricles. The thalami were well visualized below the caudate nuclei. The Sylvian fissures can be visualized on either side and, because the examination is in real time, arterial pulsations can be visualized within the Sylvian fissure and within the interhemispheric fissure as well as around the brain stem. To date, no documented abnormalities of the underlying structure of the brain or of the echogenicity of the white or gray matter have been documented.

The first parameter of interest was the brain growth of infants experiencing neonatal abstinence versus that of control infants. The widths of the left and right lateral ventricles (distances from the echo of the superolateral margin of each ventricle to the strong midline echo) were measured, as was the intracranial hemidiameter. The latter was measured from the center of the middle echo to the first strong echo of the inner table of the skull. Brain growth was defined as the ratio of the width of the left and the right lateral ventricle to the intracranial hemidiameter. This ratio was chosen because previous research had documented its usefulness in the detection of brain atrophy and of hydrocephalus and has also suggested that the cerebral lateral ventricles may be compressed in infants born to drug-dependent women (Tenner and Wodraska, 1975).

The lateral ventricles and the intracranial hemidiameter measurements were studied at twenty-four hours, seventy-two hours, one month, two months, and six months after birth. Sample sizes for the various studies ranged from fifty-two to nineteen. Preliminary analyses revealed no significant differences between the two groups (drug-exposed and controls) in the right or left lateral ventricle/intracranial hemidiameter ratios for any of the developmental categories. These results suggest that neonatal brain growth, as estimated by ultrasound measurements, is similar in both study and control infants, and that neither cerebral atrophy nor hydrocephalus were present as an explanation of abstinence symptomatology or as evidence of brain sequelae after prenatal exposure to narcotics.

SLITLIKE VENTRICLES

The high-resolution ultrasound examinations revealed a lack of separation of the walls of the lateral ventricles, creating a slitlike appearance in most of the prenatally drug-exposed infants but in few of the controls. Only the two- and six-month images failed to reveal significant differences comparing the infants undergoing abstinence to the control infants. The specific finding is a lack of a fluid space visualized between the walls of the ventricles in both the coronal and parasagittal views. The medial and lateral walls of the ventricles appear opposed on the coronal view, and the roof of the lateral ventricles appears opposed to the floor of the same ventricle in the parasagittal view. In the control infants, a fluid space is generally visualized throughout the length of the lateral ventricle in the parasagittal view.

The presence of slitlike ventricles may result from: (1) diffuse compression of the ventricles bilaterally, (2) a periventricular abnormality causing some compression of the ventricles, or (3) an abnormality in cerebrospinal fluid production or reabsorption. One might expect to see some dampening of the arterial pulsations within the cranium if increased intracranial pressure is indeed present. However, there has not yet been any consistent evidence of decreased pulsations. In addition, a series of transfontanelle measurements of intracranial pressure have been obtained. These have not revealed a statistical difference between drug-exposed and control infants. The possibility of edema localized to the periventricular regions has not been entirely excluded. Computerized axial tomography may offer more information in this regard. Developmental abnormalities of the ventricular system and ependymal adhesions are not plausible etiologies as the configuration of the lateral ventricle returns to normal generally by six months of age. Decreased cerebrospinal fluid production, or perhaps increased absorption, may result in decreased volume of fluid in the lateral ventricles resulting in the slitlike appearance. This is conjectural at present and requires further investigation. Interestingly, many studies have reported that symptoms of neonatal abstinence, including signs of central nervous system irritability, appear shortly after birth in infants born to drug-dependent women and that these symptoms are frequently manifested for as long as four to six months after birth. Thus the timing of the change in ventricular configuration suggests a relationship between abstinence symptomatology and the presence of slitlike ventricles in infants born to drug-dependent women.

In summary, ultrasound studies suggest no statistically significant difference in the brain growth of infants experiencing abstinence and that of control infants. However, high-resolution sector scanning has revealed the presence of slitlike ventricles in the majority of drug-exposed infants when scanned up to two months of age. Further study is needed to elucidate the pathogenesis of these slitlike ventricles and to determine its relationship to neonatal abstinence symptomatology.

Outcome Measures of Mental Development

The developmental outcome of children born to drug-dependent women has also been an area of special concern for health professionals. Although the abstinence syndrome is a temporally limited phenomenon, a major question is whether or not prenatal exposure to narcotics causes permanent sequelae. In a study of the long-term development of children born to opiate-dependent women, infants are evaluated at six, twelve and twenty-four months of age with the Bayley (1969) Scale of Mental Development and with a neurological examination. Sixty-five infants have been evaluated at six months of age. Of these, thirty-five have been evaluated at twelve months of age, and twelve have reached the twenty-four-month assessment. The neurological examinations for all infants were normal with the exception that a number of infants were found to have strabismus.

At six months of age, infants were found to function well within the normal range of development. The mean Mental Developmental Index (MDI) was 106. Infants also functioned within the normal range at twelve months ($\bar{x}$ MDI = 100) and twenty-four months of age ($\bar{x}$ MDI = 94) although the scores at each age were progressively lower. Of the thirty-five infants examined at six and twelve months of age, the decline in MDI scores was significant ($t = 2.06$, $p < .05$). However, when the data were analyzed according to sex, only the performance of the male infants was found to decline. Mean MDI's for males ($n = 17$) at six and twelve months of age were 107 and 97 respectively, and for females ($n = 18$), 104 and 102 respectively. The difference in performance for males was significant ($t = 2.22, p < .02$).

A progressive decline in the MDI's was also found for the twelve infants who had reached twenty-four months of age. Their mean MDI's at six, twelve and twenty-four months of age were 111, 100 and 93 respectively. The decline in the MDI was most pronounced between six and twenty-four months of age ($t = 4.53, p < .001$). Although not as dramatic, there was also a decline between each age level: six to twelve months of age ($t = 2.53, p < .01$) and twelve to twenty-four months of age ($t = 1.93, p < .05$). Due to the small sample and disproportionate distribution of sex (four males, eight females) these data cannot be analyzed for sex differences.

Overall, these data suggest that infants born to drug-dependent women do not exhibit any demonstrable developmental sequelae during the first two years of life. Several other studies (Rosen and Johnson, 1982; Strauss et al., 1976) report similar findings. The decline in developmental scores is also consistent with findings in the literature that a decrease in performance is characteristic for infants from low socioeconomic groups. However, the observed sex differences and the overall decline in performance warrant further investigation. Although development is within the normal range, methadone-exposed infants have been found to have lower MDI scores than comparison infants (Kaltenbach et al., 1979; Rosen and Johnson, 1982). It is feasible, therefore, that the decrease in performance reflects subtle cognitive dysfunction unrelated to socioeconomic level, or it may reflect the environmental milieu specific to this population.

In summary, Family Center provides a comprehensive clinical treatment setting that enables the pregnant addict to care for herself prenatally and her infant postpartally, within this setting, intervention is provided and research addresses: 1) medical complications in the mother and infant, 2) the short and long-term effects of maternal drug dependence on the infant and child through neurological, developmental, and psychological testing, and 3) the social and psychological issues associated with maternal poverty and addiction and their relationship to parenting. The results of the studies reported in this presentation indicate the following:

1) Drug dependent women at Family Center are significantly more depressed than are women in a drug-free control group and have significantly more violence in their lives.

2) Drug dependent women have more negative intrapartum perceptions of their newborns, with perception being related to the severity of subsequent withdrawal.

3) Although the brain growth of passively addicted and drug-free control infants is similar, the addicted infants have been shown to have slitlike lateral ventricles corresponding to the presence of abstinence symptomatology.

4) Developmental assessments of infants and children born to drug dependent women at six, twelve, and twenty-four months of age show normal functioning with declines in scores consistent with those expected for children from low socioeconomic groups.

Furthermore, data from Family Center have shown that if pregnant, drug-dependent women are maintained on methadone, provided with adequate prenatal care, and given needed intervention in the form of prenatal and parenting classes and social counseling, the possible complications associated with pregnancy, childbirth, and infant development can be markedly diminished in this high-risk population of mothers and children.

REFERENCES

Bayley, N. (1969). *Manual for the Bayley Scales of Infant Development.* New York: The Psychological Corporation.

Beck, A. and Beck, R. (1972). Screening depressed patients in family practice: A rapid technique. *Postgraduate Medicine,* 52:81–85.

Black, R. and Mayer, J. (1980). Parents with special problems: Alcoholism and opiate addiction. In *The Battered Child,* ed. C. H. Kempe and R. E. Helfer. Chicago: The University of Chicago Press.

Broussard, E. R. and Hartner, M. S. (1970). Maternal perception of the neonate as related to development. *Child Psychiatry and Human Development,* 1:16–25.

Broussard, E. R. and Hartner, M. S. (1971). Further considerations regarding maternal perception of the first born. In *The Exceptional Infant,* vol. 2, ed. J. Hellmuth. New York: Brunner/Mazel.

Connaughton, J. F., Reeser, D. S., and Finnegan, L. P. (1977). Pregnancy complicated by drug addiction. In *Perinatal Medicine,* ed. R. J. Bolognese and R. H. Schwartz. Baltimore: Williams & Wilkins.

DeLeon, G., Skodol, A., and Rosenthal, M. (1973). Changes in psychopathological signs for resident drug addicts. *Archives of General Psychiatry,* 28:131–135.

Dorus, W. and Senay, E. C. (1980). Depression, demographic dimensions, and drug abuse. *American Journal of Psychiatry,* 137:699–704.

Finnegan, L. P., ed. (1978). *Drug Dependence in Pregnancy: Clinical Management of Mother and Child.* A manual for medical professionals and paraprofessionals prepared for the National Institute on Drug Abuse, Services Research Branch. Washington, D. C.: U.S. Government Printing Office.

Finnegan, L. P. (1979). Pathophysiological and behavioral effects of the transplacental transfer of narcotic drugs to the fetuses and neonates of narcotic dependent mothers. *United Nations Bulletin on Narcotics,* Vol. XXXI, Nos. 3 & 4, July–December, 1–58.

Finnegan, L. P. and Fehr, K. (1980). The effects of psychoactive drugs on the fetus and newborn. In *Research Advances in Alcohol and Drug Problems,* vol. 5, ed. O. Kalant. New York: Plenum.

Finnegan, L. P., Kron, R. E., Connaughton, J. F., and Emich, J. (1975). Neonatal abstinence syndrome: Assessment and management, *Addictive Diseases* 2:141–158.

Finnegan, L. P., and MacNew, B. (1974). Care of the addicted infant. *American Journal of Nursing,* 74:685–693.

Finnegan, L. P., Oehlberg, S., Regan, D., and Rudrauff, M. (1981). Evaluation of parenting, depression and violence profiles in methadone-maintained women. *Child Abuse and Neglect,* 5:267–273.

Finnegan, L. P., Reeser, D. S., and Connaughton, J. F. (1977). The effects of maternal drug dependence on neonatal mortality. *Drug and Alcohol Dependence,* 2:131–140.

Gayford, J. (1975) Wife battering: A preliminary survey of 100 cases. *British Medical Journal,* 1:195–197.

Glass, L. (1974). Narcotic withdrawal in the newborn infant. *Journal of the National Medical Association,* 66:120–177.

Hill, R. M. and Desmond, M. M. (1963). Management of the narcotic withdrawal syndrome in the neonate. *Pediatric Clinics of North America,* 10:67–87.

Kahn, E. J., Newman, L. L., and Polk, G. A. (1969). The course of heroin withdrawal syndrome in newborn infants treated with phenobarbital or chlorpromazine. *Journal of Pediatrics,* 75:495–500.

Kaltenbach, K., Graziani, L. J., and Finnegan, L. P. (1979). Methadone exposure *in utero:* Developmental status at one and two years of age. *Pharmacology, Biochemistry and Behavior,* Suppl. 11:15–17.

Kandall, S. R. and Gartner, L. M. (1972). Late presentation of drug withdrawal symptoms in newborns. *American Journal of Diseases in Children,* 127:58–61.

Kron, R. E., Kaplan, S. L., and Finnegan, L. P. (1975). The assessment of behavioral changes in infants undergoing narcotic withdrawal: Comparative data from clinical and objective methods. *Addictive Diseases,* 2:257.

Poznanski, E. and Zrull, J. P. (1970). Childhood depression: Clinical characteristics of overtly depressed children. *Archives of General Psychiatry,* 23:8–15.

Rajegowda, B. K. et al. (1972). Methadone withdrawal in newborn infants. *Journal of Pediatrics,* 81:532–534.

Reed, B. et al. (1977). *Addicted women: Family Dynamics, Self-Perceptions and Support Systems.* Institute for Social Research at the University of Michigan.

Rosen, R. S. and Johnson, H. L. (1982). Children of methadone maintained mothers: Follow-up to 18 months of age. *Journal of Pediatrics,* 101:192–196.

Rosen, T. S. and Pippenger, C. E. (1974). Disposition of methadone and its relationship to severity of withdrawal in the newborn. Presented at the NIDA Perinatal Research Conference, Nashville, Tennessee.

Rothstein, P. and Gould, J. B. (1974). Born with a habit. Infants of drug-addicted mothers. *Pediatric Clinics of North America,* 21:307–321.

Strauss, M. E. et al. (1976). Behavioral concomitants of prenatal addiction to narcotics. *Journal of Pediatrics,* 89:842–846.

Tenner, M. S. and Wodraska, G. M. (1975). Diagnostic ultrasound in neurology: Methods and techniques. New York: John Wiley.

Wapner, R. J. and Finnegan, L. P. (1982). Perinatal aspects of psychotropic drug abuse. In *Perinatal Medicine,* ed. R. J. Bolognese et al. Baltimore: William & Wilkins.

Weissman, M., Paykel, E., and Klerman, G. (1972). The depressed woman as a mother. *Social Psychiatry,* 7:98–108.

Zelson, C., Rubio, E., and Wasserman, E. (1971). Neonatal narcotic addiction: 10-year observation. *Pediatrics,* 48:179–189.

23

Impediments to the Formation of the Working Alliance in Infant-Parent Psychotherapy

Stephen P. Seligman, D.M.H. and Jeree H. Pawl, Ph.D.

"Infant-parent psychotherapy," an original model of intervention into the problems in the relationship between infants and parents, was designed by Selma Fraiberg (1980) and her colleagues (Fraiberg et al., 1981) to accommodate the usual techniques of psychoanalytic intervention to the special situation of parents who face multiple difficulties. This model includes some of the more concrete, supportively oriented and educative techniques of nonpsychodynamic workers, such as developmental guidance and direct facilitation of social services, specifically applied in treating the social and psychological blocks that can be so destructive to the developmental potential of children in the first few years of life.

In this paper we describe some of the particular problems we have encountered in attempting this type of work with parents. We call special attention to the collaborative working alliance between parents and practitioners, and we hope to show how an understanding of the factors that impede the formation of such an alliance can make interventions more effective. In all intervention modes, successful work requires such rudimentary cooperative conditions as patients' confidence in our concern and ability to help, their willingness to consider our advice, information, or treatment plans, and a minimal adherence to appointment times. Moreover, when psychological exploration is attempted, patients must be willing to tolerate the effort and discomfort of painful self-examination (Sandler et al., 1980).

Unfortunately, the multiple and nearly overwhelming difficulties many families face as they try to raise their children—for example, economic vulnerability, sociocultural disadvantage, troubled family life, and tortured personal histories—thwart the use of proffered help. Effective and empathic responses to these difficulties can help establish the preconditions necessary for patients to accept the good will and specific skills professionals make available. Such understanding may relieve some of the frustration experienced by workers attempting to intervene with infants and their parents.

The Working Alliance in Infant-Parent Psychotherapy

The establishment of a trusting relationship and the work needed to maintain it can provide the basis for a variety of interventions, including the kind of psychological exploration that is often so difficult for parents whose parenting efforts are thwarted by their own personalities and conflicts. Only when an effective alliance has been established can such difficulties be understood in the context of the parents' personal histories. Parents are then able to see how they are repeating their own negative childhood experiences with their children. The recalling and reprocessing of these negative experiences help parents find their own more constructive parenting potential, in much the same way that analysis of transference brings relief in psychoanalysis.

Two dimensions of the therapeutic context in infant-parent psychotherapy—the home visit and the inclusion of the infant—create special opportunities for a more immediate response to intervention. Although home visiting engenders some unusual problems, parents appreciate the recognition of their strained situation (which home meetings signify) and more readily include the infant-parent psychotherapist into the flow of their troubled relationships. Taken together, the home visit and the presence of the infant provide patients and therapists with a richness of data that may be excluded in the clinic visit. The difficulties in the parent-child relationship can be observed and understood immediately in the home in a way that allows for faster and more precise exploration of critical issues than can be achieved in the consultation room or in the once-removed parental description. In addition, parents are sometimes able to use their relatively inarticulate infants as vehicles to express otherwise warded-off feelings about themselves, their histories, or their relationship to the therapist. One mother of a baby girl said, "I guess she's angry with you," when she herself felt critical of the therapist. Conversely, the therapist may use the infant as a mediator to soften the blow of a comment about the parents' negative feelings about themselves or about the infant; for example, one therapist commented that an observant four-month-old was "checking him over" during the early moments of a first session with a wary mother.

Despite the therapist's flexibility and best intentions, parents often do not experience interventions as simple attempts to promote their infants' development. Often they see professionals through the template of a variety of social conditions and personality constellations. Considering these complex determinants of a parent's responses to intervention is essential in developing a treatment approach. Communicating this understanding often leads to the development of a working alliance. Additionally, these determinants are so essential to the parenting context that understanding of this fact may generate realignment in the parent-infant relationship or in other relationships that support the central relationship, such as familial ties, parent-physician contacts, and interaction with social service agencies.

Impediments to the Working Alliance

Although parents present their difficulties when accepting offers of assistance in complex and multiply determined ways, it is useful to classify some of the various factors that may limit their ability and willingness to form a successful working relationship. These difficulties range from those which at first glance may seem extrinsic to the immediate therapist-patient relationship—economic, cultural, language, bureaucratic, and sociosexual constraints—to those which seem most intrinsic, such as the transferencelike ways in which the parent-patient experiences the therapist as he or she had once experienced his or her own parents. Four broad categories can be described: socioeconomic and sociocultural variables, prior experience with professionals and social agencies, the family situation, and personal history and psychology.

SOCIOECONOMIC AND SOCIOCULTURAL CONDITIONS

The socioeconomic determinants of parents' lives should not be underestimated. The strains of such conditions as demanding, unrewarding work, joblessness, poor housing, acute economic insecurity, racial and sexual discrimination, and loneliness all make it difficult for the best-intentioned parents to take good care of their infants. These conditions also militate against maintaining hope and accepting the emotional and practical demands that effective intervention requires. The single mother who works ten hours a day and then must overcome her exhaustion to provide a few hours of attention to her baby will find it difficult to make an appointment during working hours. She may well doubt whether she "has the energy" to attend weekly sessions. The therapist should recognize that the mother's fatigue, despair, and anxiety are indicators of a psychologically determined depression, and empathize with her about the stresses that produce them.

Similarly, the related social contexts of class, ethnicity, language, and sexuality are powerful determinants of how a parent experiences offers of help. These factors often evoke tensions that inhibit the formation of a trusting relationship. Resentment, suspicion, and envy are often experienced in tandem with the wish for help, especially when exacerbated by differences of race, sex, or class. Home visiting, despite its many advantages, presents particular difficulties with respect to these issues.

PREVIOUS EXPERIENCE WITH INTERVENTION

Another related type of difficulty arises when parents expect that offers of help will lead to the repetition of previous negative experiences with professionals or social agencies. Many patients expect professionals to solve all of their problems or are wary because other encounters with so-called helping professionals or agencies have left them feeling helpless, exploited, or abused. Often, the strained social conditions under which help is offered by such organizations as welfare departments and public clinics create a climate in which parents experience their requests for help as engendering further disappointment, frustration, and even increased feelings of helplessness and anger. Professionals may be viewed by some patients as intruders with hidden agendas, such as evaluating their parenting skills in order to take their children from them. Other patients expect only brief and often incomprehensible answers to their heartfelt and bewildered questions.

It has proven useful to anticipate these problems, to listen carefully for their derivatives, and to respond to them as quickly as possible and as frequently as necessary. Alertness to subtle expressions of negative feelings, and willingness to listen and empathize with frustrations and disillusionments, are essential. More than one alliance has been fostered by a therapist saying something like, "It must be hard when all these people on whom you count for answers just leave you in the lurch."

In addition to sympathizing with the often frustrating complexity of bureaucratic arrangements, professionals may concretely alleviate these difficulties through such steps as early and explicit explanation of the intervention program and the tactful consideration of patients' concerns with issues of confidentiality and lines of interagency communication. Where more than one agency or professional is involved, much confusion may be avoided by coordinating the multiple intervention efforts. Clarifying for parents the sometimes puzzling bureaucratic or medical procedures may also be helpful.

Sometimes the analysis of these socioemotional residues promotes further understanding about parents' blocks to professional help. The mother of a five-month-old boy with cerebral palsy, for example, complained that her son's neurologist never answered her questions about his developmental status. After consultation with the physician, the therapist was able to provide some information and to explain that, regrettably, many prognostic questions just could not be answered. Amid the tears that followed, the mother and therapist began to see that she did not ask questions directly because she dreaded to know the extent of her baby's brain damage. She subsequently showed an increased readiness to consult the pediatrician and to make use of the developmental assessment our clinic offered.

THE FAMILY SITUATION

Another general type of difficulty impeding effective work with parents involves the particular dynamics of their family lives. Although family dynamics cannot be completely separated from socioeconomic conditions and personal character and conflicts, the network of family relationships may be considered a semiautonomous system with a critical impact on the lives of infants, their parents, and on parents' abilities to accept interventions. The effect of these dynamics on work with families is extremely varied. For example, when a father and mother fight constantly, too preoccupied with their own opposition to cooperate with one another, it is difficult to establish the collaborative atmosphere necessary to consider the best interests of the child. Another such difficulty may occur when the parents see the infant as having come between them, particularly when they had hoped that the appearance of a baby would cement a shaky relationship.

In general, flexibility in response to these complicated configurations has seemed to be most useful in promoting the working alliance. Listening to a couple's nonparental concerns and offering help in sorting out their differences can improve the child-rearing climate as well as increase the couple's ability to use developmentally oriented intervention. It is sometimes necessary to meet with the parent who appears most interested or most involved in caregiving, or with the other family members when it seems appropriate. Then it is crucial to attempt to make the boundaries of inclusion explicit and to use this inquiry to understand as much as possible about the entire family situation.

The importance of extended family members who play significant roles in the life of the child or the family should not be underestimated; care should be taken to avoid the pitfall of seeing their presence as intrusion or distraction. The professional's respect, interest, and even deference to such essential people may ease the difficulties of entry into complex family systems. Sometimes a senior extended-family member, such as a grandmother, may see the therapist's inclusion in the family's attempt to cope with its difficulties as an infringement on her prerogatives as the counselor or ultimate authority on family problems. When this problem cannot be addressed directly, it may be useful to enlist the parents' help to figure out how to describe the intervention to that family member. This strategy may lead to therapeutic reflection of the parents'

relationship to their own families of origin as well as to their own relationship to treatment.

In one instance, a young mother was gradually abdicating responsibility for her infant son to her own mother. The therapist had increasingly long phone conversations with the grandmother when he called the family home to inquire about the mother's missed appointments. Those conversations eventually led to a series of meetings with the grandmother, who declared her appreciation that this therapist was the first of her daughter's many therapists who had ever listened to *her*. By the time formal custody of the infant was transferred to the grandmother, a firm working alliance had been established. The grandmother's relationship with her daughter has continued to be a primary focus of the weekly sessions, completing the exploration of her relationship to her own parents and to her infant son.

TRANSFERENCE AS AN IMPEDIMENT AND AN OPPORTUNITY

The critical importance of transference phenomena in the process of building and maintaining a working relationship has always been recognized as central to psychoanalytic technique but has often been underestimated in many other forms of intervention. Yet, the essential character of parents' experience of interventions is determined by their histories and conflicts, and attention to the persistent expression of these determinants is essential in speaking to parents' often pressing needs and fragile self-images. Attention to these factors may also present critical opportunities to understand and ameliorate the ways in which parents' personalities impede them from providing optimal care for their children.

The same difficult childhood experiences that mar parents' relationships with their children often provide the background for a readiness to see potential helpers as bad, or at least not-so-good parents. As ready objects for latent negative transference feelings, professionals may be treated with great defensiveness, wariness, covert aggression, avoidance, and the like, warded off by parents who simultaneously profess a great willingness to use assistance. As in any psychoanalytically oriented psychotherapy, the same difficulties for which parents need help are those which get in the way of their using this help.

These difficulties have emerged with particular vigor in work with parents with relatively severe character pathology, especially in the beginning phases of treatment. With such people, the hope engendered by the prospect of a supportive relationship is often inextricably bound up with the expectation of disappointment and rejection, paralleling their own parents' tendency to mix love with withdrawal, unreliability, and various forms of psychological and physical abuse. In response to these fears, patients keep themselves at a distance through such maneuvers as missing appointments, not hearing what is said, and not saying what they mean. The forms of these difficulties are as varied as the forms of defense and resistance which have been described so thoroughly elsewhere (Greenson, 1967).

This picture is further complicated by the fact that many of these parents are prone to an impulsive, acting-out style of coping with anxiety which may preclude or delay the establishment of the regularity, trust, and collaborative analytic stance which is the precondition for appropriately handling these counterproductive expressions of deprivation and inner rage. Such situations may be particularly difficult for professionals who are committed to making every effort to help the infant even when the parent seems unwilling or unable to form the basic attachment required to use this help.

Close attention to these issues may often lead to the beginnings of a working alliance with some very troubled parents. With a suspicious or paranoid mother, for example, caution, tactful information, and emphasizing her control of treatment procedures may be indicated. With a passive and dependent mother, quick establishment of a consistent, regular structure that emphasizes the therapist's reliability might be stressed. With a repressive, intellectualized parent, the therapist might spend hours listening to the details of her work or home life, employing the language of feeling only when confident that this will not excessively threaten much-needed defenses. Again, the variety of examples is as vast as the array of personalities that may be encountered.

Once the working alliance has been established, it is crucial to be alert to opportunities for clarifying and interpreting impeding feelings as they arise. With the emotionally hungry mother who feels that she is suddenly the object of attention because of her child rather than in her own right, the therapist may tactfully inquire about her feeling jealous or excluded. With a suspicious mother, it might be helpful to imagine with her how puzzling it must be to have all these offers of help when it is so hard to tell what people are really after. Sometimes the sense of being understood and accepted that is conveyed by these questions brings a bit of relief and trust, even when such questions are met with immediate denial.

It is also important to attend to the many ways in which the infant, who represents such a potent transference object, serves as a projective mediator through which parents express their feelings about themselves, their early objects, and their therapist. By speaking about the baby, or even through the baby, parents may express feelings and ideas they would otherwise find too threatening either to their self-esteem or to the therapeutic relationship. During an early stage of therapy, for example, one mother responded to the therapist's announcement of his upcoming vacation by telling her six-month-old daughter, "I guess he doesn't like us any more." When the therapist interpreted this as an expression of her current feelings of rejection, she remembered her own mother's abandonment of her when she was three. This, in turn, led to a greater understanding of her continued reluctance to become dependent on the therapist.

Thus, attention to the parents' transference feelings may weave a fabric of understanding, correlating the transference to the therapist and the transference to the child. This enables the therapist and patient to move from reflection on one context to reflection on the other, thereby gaining an unusual degree of progressive insight. For example, in the session just described, the mother was next able to consider whether her early and persistent experience of rejection was a determinant of her highly overprotective stance toward her daughter.

In another case, the movement went in the

opposite direction. When the mother of an eighteen-month-old boy who had great difficulty setting limits for her son seemed unable to stop him from grabbing at her coffee cup, the therapist's comment that she seemed to feel terribly helpless brought great relief, in contrast to the anger and frustration that had been overwhelming her. She then found it easier to experience her own need to protect herself by keeping her son in check. She was able to acknowledge the therapist's suggestion that she was resisting meeting with him because she feared that he would leave her feeling as helpless as had all the other "helping people." In addition, she became aware that she had felt blamed by them for the feelings of assault that had characterized her experience with this genuinely difficult infant during his first year. With this understanding she was able to use the important developmental guidance the therapist offered.

Our experience then has been that even where the focus is on supportive and guidance efforts, the transference elements of the parents' experience must be carefully attended to. Parents' reactions to offers of help by all kinds of professionals are determined by their characters and conflicts and will be expressed in transference reactions. By its very nature, the extended time format and psychological orientation of infant-parent psychotherapy encourages extensive exploration of these reactions. Nonetheless, it is critical for professionals working in other modes to be aware of how their interventions are experienced through the template of patients' past histories. Even in the relatively structured encounters of the pediatric clinic, social service agency, or parent education class, interventions may be more effective when workers can orient their approaches to the parents' specific psychological needs and worries. This approach allows parents to experience directly these anxieties, appreciate their sources, and better appreciate the understanding and acceptance offered them. In addition, this way of thinking helps to clarify some of the puzzling feelings of helplessness, anger, guilt, frustration, and anxiety which professionals often experience, and to relate them specifically to the transferential ways that assistance can be deflected, thwarted, or otherwise negated (Sandler, 1976).

REFERENCES

Fraiberg, S., ed. (1980). *Clinical Studies in Infant Mental Health: The First Year of Life.* New York: Basic Books.

Fraiberg, S., Lieberman, A. F., Pekarsky, J. H., and Pawl, J. H. (1981). Treatment and outcome in an infant psychiatry program *Journal of Preventive Psychiatry,* 1:89–111, 143–167.

Greenson, R. (1967). *The Technique and Practice of Psychoanal-* ysis. New York: International Universities Press.

Sandler, J. (1976). Counter-transference and role responsiveness. *International Review of Psycho-Analysis,* 3:34–47.

Sandler, J., Kennedy, H., and Tyson, R. L. (1980). Treatment alliance. In *The Techniques of Child Psychoanalysis: Discussions with Anna Freud.* Cambridge: Harvard University Press.

24

Factors Influencing the Psychological Adjustment of Mothers to the Birth of a Preterm Infant

Deborah B. Rosenblatt and Margaret E. Redshaw

The birth of a preterm baby is a shock for most parents and usually sets into motion a series of events which includes separation from the baby, anxiety about his survival and future health and development, and exposure to an area of medical care that is unfamiliar to them.

The literature contains many reports on the effects of admission to a Neonatal Unit (NNU) on maternal confidence (Barnett et al., 1970), mother-infant interaction (Brown and Bakeman, 1980; Marton et al., 1980), and family relations (Lynch and Roberts, 1977).

Although many professionals acknowledge the intrusiveness of the typically busy technological NNU, it has not been systematically studied in the way other aspects of neonatal care have been. A notable exception is a study wherein mothers were interviewed about their satisfaction with the care their baby received and their adjustment to the baby's stay (Jeffcoate et al., 1979). Over the past ten years neonatal care has become more sophisticated, resulting in greater success in saving small and sick infants, At the same time health professionals have become aware of the need for sensitive staff who can also deal with parents'

emotional needs in adjusting to the early birth of their baby and gradually assuming the more appropriate role of full-time parents to a healthy growing son or daughter. The current study attempts to document how well we are achieving some of these aims.

SUBJECTS

Over a one-year period, mothers of preterm infants (< thirty-seven weeks) were asked to complete a short questionnaire about their initial experience in the neonatal unit. The data presented here are drawn from the first fifty questionnaires filled out between day four and day seven, excluding outborn infants (very few in this unit), subsequent neonatal deaths, and those infants with congenital malformations. There were fifty-two infants because the sample included two sets of twins.

Details of maternal and infant characteristics are presented in tables 24–1 and 24–2. A few of these statistics are worthy of comment. We serve a very disadvantaged inner-city population in an area with a high proportion of West Indians, Africans, and Asians. There are a sub-

TABLE 24–1

Maternal Characteristics

	Number	Mean	SD
Maternal age		27.2	6.7
Marital status:			
Married	31		
Single	15		
Unknown	4		
Pregnancy 'Failures':			
1 or more miscarriages	9		
Neonatal death	3		
Previous infant in NNU	10		
Children at home:			
1 only	17		
2 or more	9		

(*N* = 50 mothers)

TABLE 24–2

Neonatal Characteristics

	Mean	SD
Birthweight	1826.8	521.8
No. < 1500 gms	14	
No. = SGA (< 10% tile)	19	
Gestation (completed weeks)	32.8	2.4
No. ≤ 30 weeks	6	
Apgar 1 minute	6.2	1.9
Apgar 5 minutes	8.2	1.4
Age (days) at discharge	33.7	21.1

(*N* = 52 infants)

stantial number of unbooked or poor antenatal-care attenders. Despite this, the sample under study is not particularly young—the mean maternal age here was twenty-seven; only six mothers were under twenty, nine were thirty-five or over. One third of the mothers were unmarried, although only two had no contact with a partner. Half of the mothers had at least one other living child. A quarter had "failed" in at least one previous pregnancy with the death of a fetus or neonate, or a requirement for "special care."

THE NEONATAL UNIT

Our unit is small (sixteen beds) but includes intensive-care facilities for up to six infants. Immediately after delivery the parents are given an instant photo of their baby and a de-

tailed booklet describing and illustrating aspects of the unit's policies and procedures, which includes suggestions for getting to know their baby, and indications of what to expect in terms of his or her behavior as the weeks go by. Visiting, as in most units in the U.K., is unrestricted for father or partner; we also encourage siblings to come. There is regular support from maternity social workers and a good liaison arrangement with health visitors in the community.

"MEETING" THE BABY

Because our sample was inborn we expected that parents would have contact with their infant as soon as possible. Almost half of the mothers had seen and touched the baby within two hours; three quarters of the fathers had seen their new offspring. Although only about 10 percent of parents had not seen or touched their infant by forty-eight hours, this is still too many!

Only half of the mothers and one third of the fathers had held their infant by the end of the first day. Most parents of sick infants were deprived of this intimate contact; one quarter of the mothers and half of the fathers had not held their infant by the fourth day.

PATTERNS OF VISITING AND CAREGIVING

As mentioned earlier, both parents are encouraged to visit the NNU at any time and to participate in their infant's care as much as possible. Certainly during this first week mothers were regular visitors, most likely because they remained inpatients (table 24–3). With the exception of two mothers who were still rather ill, the rest were spending one period a day, and 78 percent were visiting twice or more. All the fathers had seen their infants by this time, and most of them (94 percent) had visited the NNU. A quarter of the fathers were not able to come in every day although their visiting pattern was not significantly different. This highlights the difficulties of fulfilling obligations at work, perhaps arranging care for other children, and then setting out again (usually by public transport) to see the baby. Hav-

TABLE 24–3

Frequency of Parental Visiting
(in percentages)

	Mothers	Fathers[a]
Not every day	4	24
Once a day	18	49
Twice a day	12	27
Several times a day	66	—

[a]By maternal report

TABLE 24–4

Parents' Usual Activities with Their Infant
During Visiting
(in percentages)

	Mothers	Fathers[a]
Looking	100	98
Touching	96	79
Talking to	96	60
Holding	77	43
Feeding	65	36

[a]By maternal report

ing other children at home did not necessarily reduce their visiting frequency.

When asked about their activities during their visits with the baby, virtually all the mothers reported looking at, touching, and talking to their baby, and about three-quarters usually held or fed him or her. (table 24–4). Fathers did not seem to participate as fully, although these differences were not significant. Two mothers had no partner at the time of delivery. One explanation may be that because of work commitments, fathers were unable to come at an optimal time for interaction; another is that the mother holds and feeds the baby while dad is an onlooker. It does seem that fathers have greater opportunities to perform caregiving tasks (feed, change a nappy, and bathe the baby) in a neonatal unit than on a postnatal ward (Marton et al., 1981), but it is still most unusual for a father to come in on his own to do this. It mainly happens here when the mother is too ill to visit (or is still at a referring hospital), thus designating the father as substitute caregiver. Stereotyped attitudes about the paternal role are probably still too strong for a father to adopt a separate and competitive role by performing maternal duties when his wife is capable of doing so.

FEELINGS ABOUT DELIVERY

Mothers were asked several questions about the delivery and their feelings after the premature birth. The sample was evenly divided between those who had had a normal vaginal delivery (46 percent) and those who had a Caesarean section (C.S.) (50 percent). Very few (4 percent) had a breech extraction or forceps delivery, which probably reflects preference in this unit for delivering preterm breeches by C.S. More than half of the mothers (56 percent) replied that this was the type of delivery they had expected, which was true even when the C.S. group was examined separately. Their comments suggest that the obstetrician had often given a warning or explanation antenatally of a likely C.S., and there were no critical remarks about being misled. About 10 percent were pleasantly surprised to have a normal delivery when they had anticipated something worse, and one mother was also relieved not to have had her worst fears realized: "People tell you how they tied up your feet so you can push, but mine was no way like that."

Mothers were then asked whether they and their partners were "disappointed when your baby was born too soon." This phrase was chosen deliberately since the literature (Bibring, 1959; Kaplan and Mason, 1960; Klaus and Kennell, 1976) suggests that feelings of longing for a healthy, robust baby, and guilt at not carrying the baby to term can contribute to feelings of loss that are not simply a reflection of anxiety about the baby's survival.

From the distributions in Table 24–5, it is clear that half of the sample did not seem disappointed. Many of this group explained that previous pregnancies had ended in disaster and that *planned* intervention had been carried out this time—obviously with success, in their eyes, because the baby had survived. A quite different component of the "not"-disappointed group had delivered large, more mature babies between thirty-four and thirty-six weeks gestation, commenting, "Pleasant surprise, prefer to be early than late," or "Happy to get it over with." And one mother seemed delighted to be removed early from the temptations of pregnancy gluttony, and was "not at all disappointed because I was eating too much."

Most of the disappointed mothers were those who delivered babies of less than thirty-three weeks, and all cited their fears about the infants' survival, remarking how they "know that every day or week counted." Very occasionally, differing points of view from the medical staff made such fears all the more acute:

> My doctor [obstetrician] does not have the knack of telling me about the baby. . . . However cheerful I am when he comes in, he leaves me in tears. . . . He seems to want to put across the black side of Anne's condition.
>
> This is in direct contrast to the NNU staff who deal with the situation calmly and explain everything in rational terms. Maybe he wants to protect himself from a sense of failure. . . . Could he be trained in psychological techniques?

According to the mothers, their partners usually showed the same degree of disappointment as themselves. Only one father wrote in his own feelings and in justifying the response tended to cite the same reasons given above. A few mothers remarked that their partner was slightly less disappointed because "he was more worried about me" and felt that "getting the baby out was safer."

One mother, regarding her husband's extreme disappointment, voiced the sentiments alluded to in the literature: "I think he does not like the abnormal or imperfect. He did not want a baby that did not conform to his image of a bouncing eight-pounder."

MEDICAL PROCEDURES IN THE FIRST WEEK

Mothers were asked to mark the procedures carried out on their infant and then to rate the degree of upset that this had caused. Most of the infants under study had experienced a number of intrusive though necessary medical interventions (table 24–6). These included blood samples, nasogastric feeding, monitoring wires, and a drip in the arm or leg. One third

TABLE 24–5

Degree of Disappointment at Preterm Birth (in percentages)

Disappointment	Mothers	Fathers[a]
Very much	22	23
Quite a lot	8	5
A bit	29	29
Not at all	41	43

[a]By maternal report

TABLE 24–6

Percentage of Infants Experiencing Medical Procedures (as Noted by Mothers)

Nasogastric Feeds	94
Blood Samples	88
Monitoring Wires	83
"Drip" in the arm or leg	65
Nursed naked	58
Oxygen by mask	36
Oxygen in a headbox	35
Phototherapy for jaundice	25
Head shaved for medical procedures	6

had required oxygen via headbox or mask. Half had been nursed naked at some point, but only a few needed their hair shaved for a scalp drip (an event possibly more likely to occur after the first week). According to their mothers, only a quarter had received phototherapy for jaundice, but many mothers indicated "not sure" to this question.

We were particularly interested to know to what extent mothers were disturbed by these procedures, since extreme distress might serve to "distance" the mother from her infant and make it more difficult to accept an eventual healthy status. Again we were surprised that the majority of mothers reported only "slight" or "no" upset by any of the medical interventions. For simplicity of comparison, categories of "extremely," "very," and "quite" upsetting were combined, and the rank order of the most distressing is presented in table 24–7.

It is likely that such feelings differed concerning the various procedures, although we did not probe this further. For instance, frequent blood sampling or a drip might evoke sympathy for the infant's pain or discomfort but also anger at the medical staff for being cruel or unfeeling in intruding on his or her

TABLE 24–7

Percentage of Mothers Who Found Medical Procedures on Their Infant "Upsetting" During the First Week

Oxygen by mask	50
Drip in arm or leg	49
Headbox for breathing	37
Hair shaved for medical procedures	33
Monitoring wires	33
N.G. feeding tube	32
Blood samples	24
Phototherapy	15
Baby being nursed naked	9

TABLE 24–8

Percentage of Mothers "Bothered" by the Technological Environment of the Neonatal Unit

	Great Deal	A Bit	Not at All
Handwashing and aprons	0	0	100
Noise from monitors	8	32	30
High temperatures	4	40	56
Busy atmosphere	4	10	86

TABLE 24–9

"How Ill Does Your Baby Seem to You?"
(in percentages)

Very ill	12
Quite ill	16
Not very ill	33
Not ill at all	39

sleep. On the other hand, parents occasionally referred to oxygen therapy in a headbox as soothing and also "essential" for the baby's survival. There were a few mothers who ignored this question, adding such comments as "I try not to upset myself because I know it is for the baby's own good." Such *denial* of one's own feelings, however, may not be in the mother's best interests.

Some mothers found aspects of the NNU environment somewhat of a nuisance. High temperatures and noise from the monitors bothered them the most, whereas handwashing, wearing aprons, and the busy atmosphere were not seen as very intrusive (table 24–8).

PERCEPTION OF THE INFANT'S NEEDS AND FEELINGS

Pediatric staff take great care in explaining to parents the baby's condition and outlook in the first few days. Inevitably, however, parents may misinterpret what is being said, or may perceive the baby's status to be different from what they have been told. A series of questions probed the mother's perceptions of her baby's medical needs, her involvement in the baby's care and degree of comfort.

We expected that mothers would be overanxious and pessimistic in the first week; we were thus surprised that three quarters of the group marked that their baby was "Not very ill" or "Not ill at all."

In order to check the accuracy of these perceptions, a similar four-point rating scale was devised to reflect clinical criteria of the severity of illness. This was mainly based on respira-

tory status, not only because length of ventilatory support, high oxygen requirements, and apnea have been related to outcome, but because the level of intrusiveness of the therapy probably mirrors the mothers' concerns. The scale was applied to information in the notes between birth and day four. These criteria are set out in table 24–10 along with the percentage of infants in each group. Groups 1 and 2 could be viewed as needing intensive care; categories 3 and 4 would be easily managed in any NNU; and many babies in group 4 would now be nursed in our transitional-care ward with their mothers.

In fact, maternal judgments were better than we had intuitively expected (table 24–11). About half the ratings were in complete agreement. Of those who felt their infant was sicker than the doctors did, most replies fell into the much worse (2 or more point difference) category. Of the one quarter who had a more optimistic outlook, "slightly better" was a more frequent reply. However, it is not easy to interpret this discrepancy. If the questionnaire was filled out on day six or seven some babies may have made rapid progress from the period of the medical rating. Other mothers may have interpreted any slight improvement over the first few days as an indication that the baby was out of the woods and rated him more favorably.

TABLE 24–10

Medical Rating of the Infant's Condition in the First Four Days after Birth (in percentages)

Very Sick: Ventilated, $O_2 > 70\%$, and/or critically ill with other problems;	16
Moderately Sick: CPAP/ventilated > 24 hours and/or treatment for apnea;	18
Not Very Sick: O_2 in headbox and/or jaundice $>$ phototherapy level	39
Not Sick at all: Preterm infant but no other problems	27

TABLE 24–11

Agreement Between Mothers' Perceptions of the Severity of their Baby's Illness and Medical Ratings of his Condition (in percentages)

Mother perceived baby *as much worse* than doctors thought	13
Baby perceived as *slightly worse*	4
Absolute agreement	56
Baby perceived as *slightly better*	17
Baby perceived as *much better* than doctors thought	10

One of our concerns, however, is that sometimes a parent's optimistic interpretation of the baby's medical status is very out of line with how ill the baby really is—our questionnaires over the past year have revealed a number of mothers who marked "Not sick at all" for critically ill infants of less than twenty-eight weeks on a ventilator. Two mothers (not in the present sample) had been devastated when their infants—who they mistakenly believed were not very sick—died. We agree with Klaus and Fanaroff (1973) that doctors should be optimistic—most preterm infants survive unscathed by their unpropitious beginning. But it always behooves the doctor to ascertain (a) how each parent thinks the infant is doing and (b) how he or she has assimilated the most recent information, *before* discussing the baby's current status.

We have often wondered what mothers think about the baby's rather artificial experience in an incubator. As a crude attempt to tap this dimension, categories were suggested to mothers that reflected positive, neutral, and negative aspects (table 24–12). It was interesting that the majority considered their baby to be warm and cosy, while fewer noted negative

TABLE 24–12

"How Do You Think Your Baby Feels Now?" (in percentages, categories not mutually exclusive)

Warm and cosy	60
Lonely	25
Uncomfortable	17
Doesn't mind	10
Don't know	15

experiences such as being lonely or uncomfortable.

Babies perceived as very or quite ill were seldom considered to feel warm and cosy (X^2; $p < 0.01$). The degree of illness was not related to either perceived discomfort or loneliness in the baby. The attribute *warm and cosy* was significantly more often applied to infants in incubators, irrespective of their medical status (X^2; $p < 0.01$). However, the infant in an incubator was also the most likely to be described as lonely (X^2; $p < 0.02$), a word never applied to infants on an "open platform bed." This confirms our clinical impression that parents often see the incubator as a barrier to involvement with their infant. Even mothers who automatically caress and stroke their critically ill infant on an open bed think twice about disturbing him or her when behind the closed doors of an incubator, even though the transfer is a promotion in medical terms.

The parental role in a NNU can be almost nonexistent for an infant with high dependency on artificial ventilation, phototherapy, parenteral nutrition, and scrupulous attention to temperature and fluid balance. Although we rarely apply a minimal handling policy to parents, many hesitate to touch their baby lest they trigger an acute apneic spell or potentiate a more gradual deterioration in the baby's condition.

We probed how much mothers felt they were contributing to the baby's care. Sadly, one third felt that they were not as involved as they could be. However, this response was probably related to the baby's condition, since mothers who considered their baby to need a great deal of specialized care (60 percent of the sample) were the ones who were most satisfied with their own limited participation. Some violation of the caregiving role is to be expected initially when a baby is sick, but determined efforts must be made to overcome this. Mouth care, gentle physiotherapy, and tube feeding can often be given by skilled parents even in the early days.

PREVIOUS KNOWLEDGE ABOUT NEONATAL UNITS

Special care for neonates—the dramatic salvage of six-month fetuses and emergency surgery for newborns—has become an acceptable topic for the media. Two thirds of this sample knew something about special care before they had their baby (table 24–13).

Our own antenatal classes employ slides, discussion, and a visit to the neonatal unit but, ironically, the topic is usually covered too late in the series to be of use to mothers who deliver prematurely! One quarter of the mothers knew someone whose baby had been in such a unit, possibly because inpatient antenatal friendships had also culminated in a preterm or high-risk infant.

Surprisingly, knowledge and experience were not always viewed as helpful—just over half of the sample said it had made a difference to their reactions to the baby being in the neonatal unit. On the positive side, mothers often mentioned that the machinery and procedures (especially tube feeding) were familiar, or that they discovered that preterm infants were not as delicate or fragile as they had imagined.

Nevertheless, one mother who had read about special care for neonates, seen pictures and a television programme, *and* had a friend whose baby had been in a unit, commented: "It doesn't seem real when you read about babies that are born like dolls 'til you have to care for one; then you realize that it's harder to face when your own baby is one of them." Regrettably, the mothers who did not feel antenatal classes helpful usually did not elaborate, so we are none the wiser, although as in the remarks just quoted, real-life situations may be so sudden and traumatic that they relegate useful pieces of advice to the back of the mind. As one mother of a critically ill infant (not included in this sample) wrote, "No, it didn't help because I feared, and still fear, that it might die."

Ten mothers had an older child who required special care and survived; three others had experienced a neonatal death in the unit. This group was equally divided as to whether previous experience made the present situation easier.

Conclusion

These data have drawn our attention to some of the strengths and weaknesses inherent in a typical supportive neonatal unit of the 1980s. On the plus side, it is obvious that to some extent preparation and liaison pay off. Discussion with the obstetric team about an impending high-risk labor resulted in greater satisfaction with the delivery and less disappointment about the early birth for many mothers. Extreme disappointment about the birth of a preterm baby was most evident in the parents of the real "tinies"; this is probably resolved only as the infant's condition improves. An open door policy did seem to promote early contact with the baby or an increased level of visiting and parental caregiving in the first week.

Media exposure of the success of neonatal units and their functions reduced apprehension in many mothers when their own baby required admission. Regular discussion with medical staff led to fairly accurate parental perceptions of their baby's condition, inducing a bias toward an optimistic outcome. The majority of mothers could identify the procedures being carried out on their baby and were not unduly frightened or distressed by them. And though some babies required sophisticated care in a

TABLE 24–13

Previous Knowledge about Neonatal Units
(in percentages, categories not mutually exclusive)

Seen pictures or articles about NNU	30
Known someone whose baby had required such care	28
Watched a TV programme about it	22
Visited a NNU before the birth	16
Any one of the above	68

neonatal unit, the mothers' perceptions of the infants' state were primarily positive—half the babies were felt to be warm and cosy, with loneliness and discomfort cited less often.

On the negative side, a substantial number of mothers felt they could be taking a more active role in caring for their baby. Whether this is true is probably less important than their *feelings* of being superfluous, inept, or simply in the way. Even when an infant is entirely dependent on intensive nursing and life-support systems, staff must be able to convey by their manner and their words that parents are only *temporarily* taking a back seat and will soon be able to claim their rightful role.

A few mothers spontaneously remarked about the unwittingly insensitive comments from busy staff, feeling that their genuine questions were sometimes laughingly brushed aside as trivial. It was also made clear that the lack of privacy and general amenities in our cramped neonatal unit sometimes affected parent's expectations of the medical establishment's overall role as provider of their family's needs. As one mother said, "If you can give such sophisticated and expensive care to our baby, surely you could manage to have cold drinks or coffee for the parents and a play area for brothers and sisters!" Although as medical staff we are not able to do much about our layout or budget, it is surely our professional duty to see that administrators and hospital planners *are* aware of the full implications of family-centered pediatrics.

This study has not dealt with the major influences of personality, social circumstances, and family background on the mother's adjustment to her baby's need for specialized pediatric care immediately after birth (Leiderman and Seashore, 1975; Sherman, 1980). What we have tried to do instead is to highlight some of the practices and attitudes in the neonatal care setting which also contribute to parental well-being and feelings of competence and autonomy. Only by periodically reviewing our successes and failures can we be certain that we are serving the individual needs of our newborn patients and their families.

REFERENCES

Barnett, C., Leiderman, P., Grobstein, R., and Klaus, M. (1970). Neonatal separation: The maternal side of interactional deprivation. *Pediatrics*, 45:197–205.

Bibring, G. L. (1959). Some considerations of the psychological processes in pregnancy. *The Psychoanalytic Study of the Child*, 14:113–121. New York: International Universities Press.

Brown, J. and Bakeman, R. (1980). Relationships of human mothers with their infants during the first year of life: Effects of prematurity. In *Maternal Influences and Early Behavior*, ed. R. Bell and W. Smotherman. New York: Spectrum.

Jeffcoate, J. A., Humphrey, M.E., and Lloyd, J. K. (1979). Disturbance in parent-child relationships following preterm delivery. *Developmental Medicine and Child Neurology*, 21:344–352.

Kaplan, D. M. and Mason, E. A. (1960). Maternal reaction to premature birth viewed as an acute emotional disorder. *American Journal of Orthopsychiatry*, 30:539–552.

Klaus, M. H. and Fanaroff, A. A. (1973). *Care of the High-Risk Neonate*. Philadelphia: W. B. Saunders.

Klaus, M. H. and Kennel, J. H. (1960). *Maternal-Infant Bonding*. St. Louis: C. V. Mosby.

Leiderman, P. H. and Seashore, M. J. (1975). Mother-infant separation: Some delayed consequences. *Ciba Foundation, Parent-Infant Interaction*, No. 33. Amsterdam: Elsevier.

Lynch, M. and Roberts, J. (1977). Predicting child abuse: Signs of bonding failure in the maternity hospital. *British Medical Journal*, 1:624–626.

Marton, P., Minde, K., and Ogilvie, J. (1980). Mother-infant interactions in the premature nursery—a sequential analysis. In *Preterm Birth and Psychological Development*, ed. S. I. Friedman and M. Sigman. New York: Academic Press.

Marton, P., Minde, K., and Perrotta, M. (1981). The role of the father for the infant at risk. *American Journal of Orthopsychiatry*, 51:672–679.

Sherman, M. (1980). Psychiatry in the neonatal unit. In *Clinics in Perinatology: Symposium on Neonatal Intensive Care*, vol. 7, no. 1, ed. P. A. M. Auld. London: W. B. Saunders.

25

Medical and Nursing Staff at Risk: Very Early Prevention of Psychosomatic Illness in Infancy

Michel Soulé, M.D.,

The increased understanding of psychosomatic illness in infancy has made it clear that preventive measures need to be taken at increasingly earlier stages and should include the infant and both parents. Intervention should focus on the newborn, on the fetus, on the pregnancy, on the conditions of fertilization and generation by the parents, and finally on the adolescence of future parents. It is now better understood that there are crucial interactions on a real, interpersonal level and on the level of fantasy between the infant and its parents, as well as between the parents themselves. It is perhaps less well appreciated that these interactions involve a third "partner," for in addition to the infant and the parents, there is the medical and nursing staff who play an active role at all stages in this period of life, becoming progressively more involved with these real and fantasy interactions in many and complex ways. The staff participants include all personnel, including receptionists.

It is common knowledge now that there have been vast changes in family life and in the way couples live together. These changes, together with the fact that there is a comparatively small number of children in kinship groups, affect a young woman so that she cannot summon memories of childhood experiences to use in maternal identifications, or as a basis for intuitively sensing a reciprocal relationship with her child, or to plan maternal tasks in a confident and flexible way. In addition, at certain times during the pregnancy and after delivery, most mothers must confront anxiety, regression, and dependency in relation to whatever images of maternal functioning they possess. At these times the mother is much more sensitive to external interventions by anyone—man or woman—who provides actual treatment or assistance, and who at the same time embodies parental images and is therefore vested with all the concomitant emotional burdens. Consequently, this interaction also takes place on the level of fantasy between two individuals, one of whom, the mother, has recently undergone considerable change in psychological status. While the interaction between adults has aspects comparable to the interaction between mother and infant, it functions on a different plane.

The mother's fantasy life has been unconsciously affected by her pregnancy and by the birth and the proximity of the baby. Of course, this point has been preceded by the development of her fantasy of an imaginary child ever since her oedipal period. The medical or nursing staff person involved has also changed, but the professional role confers on him or her a more stable position under the circumstances. Nevertheless, the staff may have been influenced by a number of factors: earlier life experiences, particularly those connected with children; relationships with parents, particularly the mother; fulfillment from relationships with spouse and children; and whatever fantasied relationships the staff person has established with the imagined child.

This fantasy interaction between the mother and the staff person emerges when treatment is carried out during the mother's pregnancy, at the time of labor and delivery, and in the course of treatment given to the infant. It also takes place when advice is given to the mother. It follows that this fantasy interaction can have very important repercussions, which may either facilitate the mother-infant interaction, or inhibit and unsettle it. A common example of such interplay between fantasy interaction and the consequences for infant development is in making the decision to breast-feed and in implementing this decision. In addition to the part played by the mother, there are important roles that involve the father, the mother's parents, and the previous relationships and experiences of all of them, as well as the influences brought to bear by the medical and nursing personnel. Clinical experience demonstrates that both direct advice and, more subtly, covert attitudes affect young mothers and in some extreme cases actually interfere partially or altogether with breast-feeding.

The Doctor or Nurse at Risk

In order to carry out very early preventive interventions, doctors and nurses need to know a great deal, including the current personality of the infant in terms of its identity and potentials, the influence of the mother's role at various levels, and the history of early interactions between the infant and its mother and the infant and its father. In fact, doctors and nurses are now called on to carry out a very different task from the one they had trained for and which, to a certain extent, is supposed to protect them. In order to make effective early interventions, they need to identify themselves totally with the mother of the infant. Thus their vocational models, which include the act of giving reassurance, are being questioned. Most physicians and nurses see themselves quite differently; they see themselves as givers of medical treatment to prevent illness and death. Accordingly, they accept an idealized image of maternity as being exclusively good and protective, thus defending themselves against the anxiety and depression of the new mother, and avoiding confrontation with the ambivalence inherent in maternity, which plays a dominant role in the disturbances of maternal care. Many of these phenomena may easily be seen in neonatal and intensive-care units where machines without consciences or ambivalence keep people alive, but leave all other care up to the medical and nursing staff.

Some doctors and nurses, confronted by their new task, find themselves without freedom of choice over this "forced identification" and are unable to cope adequately with the interactions required of them. A number of problems may then arise, including: giving way to verbal criticism of the mother or infant, giving way to physical activity in therapeutic endeavors, automatically carrying out stereotyped technical gestures without enthusiasm, or allowing the standard of treatment to vary. Also the doctors and nurses frequently suffer from such psychological disturbances as bad dreams and nightmares, uncontrollable fatigue, lack of interest in their own personal life, and aggravation of certain illnesses, which are often associated with unpredictable behavior and with carelessness in regard to their commitments.

Preventive Policy for Those Responsible for Prevention

There is, of course, a large group of highly qualified physicians and nurses who have always acted intuitively, drawing upon their own resources and personal lives in establishing effective relationships with mothers and infants. Nevertheless, it is important to encourage *all* those involved in early preventive measures with infants and their families to work well with them. The following procedures are suggested: (1) personnel training with revised teaching programs that inform students of the tasks they will actually have to carry out; (2) training courses that confront the students with the real nature of their future work; (3) guidance at the end of studies directing some staff toward strictly biological and medical work, and others, who have shown themselves to be specifically suited, toward areas requiring a greater degree of psychological understanding.

After assuming their professional positions, senior members and departmental heads should pay particular attention to the activities of their personnel and to their state of health. They should consider not only the length of the working day and the predictable fatigue, but also the difficulties resulting from confrontation with serious psychological tensions; for example, those following the death of patients. While continued training and improvement in technical as well as theoretical matters is the rule in most departments, additional means are necessary in order to accomplish what is being proposed here. Private group meetings should be encouraged to involve people to a greater extent and to discuss in depth recent observations and events. Personal problems should not be mentioned or investigated in such meetings, but should be dealt with in a more personal way elsewhere.

26

A Projective Technique for Investigating Parental Attitudes: A Preliminary Report

Serge G. Stoleru, M.D., Marianne Reigner, Ph.D., and Martine M. Morales, Ph.D.

This is a preliminary report of our efforts to develop and validate an instrument with which to assess parental attitudes, during pregnancy and the early months, of interaction between an infant and his or her parents. Specifically we describe the results of comparing parental responses to various photographs of infants and toddlers with data from clinical interviews with the same subjects. The project has been undertaken with a view to providing a clinical tool to illuminate those parental attitudes which constitute a major aspect of the psychology and psychopathology of pregnancy and of the early months following the baby's birth. Such an instrument could also be useful in helping determine for which cases and on which grounds early intervention is required.

We have considered parental attitudes from two theoretical viewpoints, the first in relation to the mothers' general psychic functioning, to their own childhood, to their psychological conflicts, and especially to the Oedipus complex. The second is a developmental viewpoint in which parenthood, most particularly with the first child (Benedek, 1959, 1975), is seen as a step toward the maturation of the personality. These two views are complementary in delineating the way in which a person organizes the course of his or her life, given that person's individual and specific personality and psychological functioning (Erikson, 1980).

Material and Method

Data is reported here from the first of three planned clinical "contacts," the first being during pregnancy, the second within the first postpartum week, and the third during the infant's sixth month of life. Each contact is composed of a clinical interview focused on the experience of pregnancy and attitudes related to the baby, and the presentation of twenty photographs of parent-child dyads or of infants and toddlers in various situations (playing, feeding, and so forth). The examiner asks the subjects to describe their responses to the pictures and to tell a story that might account for the scene observed. A similar projective technique was used by Bibring and her colleagues (1961) with a set of pictures called the Pregnancy Evaluation Test. In the present investigation, both the clinical interviews and the picture presentations were videotaped.

This work has been supported by a grant from the Fondation pour la Récherche Médicale Française.

The technique of picture presentations was as follows: each spontaneous response to each picture (RP) was allowed to proceed until it was completed, that is, until a silent interval of twenty to thirty seconds or when the subject stated she was finished. This segment of data collection provided a measure of the subject's characteristic RP in regard to length, clarity, organization, and richness of detail. For the last ten RP's, interventions were made in order to obtain further clarity, and to increase the depth and breadth of understanding of the subject's perceptions. All interventions were in relation to the pictures, and no personal comments were made about them by the examiner. Typical interventions were the repetition of the subject's last sentence, asking for the clarification of a point, or asking what a character in the picture might be feeling or thinking.

A categorization of information obtained from the study of the videotaped clinical interviews was made according to the eleven categories listed in table 26–1. Of the three cases, the data for Case 2 were categorized by one researcher, the data for Cases 1 and 3 were categorized by comparing and combining the results of two researchers who studied the videotapes independently.

The videotaped RP's were analyzed by a researcher who had not participated in that particular subject's clinical contacts and who was

TABLE 26–1

Organization of Data Collected During the First Clinical Contact

1. Wish (or absence of wish) to have a baby
2. Relationship with the father of the baby
3. Relationship of the subject with her own parents (past and present relationships)
4. Relationship with other significant persons
5. Affective experience and mood
6. Images, feelings and fantasies related to the baby *in utero*
7. Anxieties related to the physical and mental condition of the baby
8. Narcissistic aspects of the pregnancy
9. Childbirth: Thoughts related to
10. Images, feelings and fantasies related to specific aspects and phases of child rearing
11. Integration of the pregnancy in the course of the subject's life

therefore blind as to that material. The same categories were used as for the clinical interviews.

Case Reports

For each case, the data of the clinical interview were compared with the RP's in each of the eleven categories. For the purposes of this presentation specific categories are given in order to demonstrate the importance of particular items and to show how the data thus collected from the two sources may overlap, complement one another, and, rarely, contradict each other.

Case 1

Miss D, age thirty-five, had been pregnant for eight months with her first child. She had been living with the baby's father since she learned she was pregnant.

CLINICAL INTERVIEW

Wish (or Absence of Wish) to Have a Baby. Miss D reported she became anorectic when she was ten months old. At age fifteen she again became severely anorectic and had psychiatric treatment on several occasions. She insisted that it was not until age thirty-four that she wanted a baby. In her mind, having a baby was linked to the idea of her own death: "To me it seemed that as the child grows, the mother disappears and is engulfed. I'm sure I concluded that anorexia meant the fear of dying." Other related comments she made: "I'm bored when I'm with a child . . . for instance, my best girlfriend's daughter, though a very good girl, gulps down our space, and she interferes when my friend and I have a lot to talk about."

On the basis of this and similar comments it may be inferred that Miss D experienced the baby inside her as devouring her from within and feeding on her so as to grow. Her linking pregnancy with anorexia as a fear of dying suggests that she was connecting her earlier wish not to have a baby to remnants of her past anorectic syndrome. The avidity she ascribed to the baby seemed to be a projection of the avidity she herself might have felt in her early relationship with her own mother. Her attitude toward children was striking in that her own needs were competing with needs related to her child. While a mother is able ordinarily to integrate her child's growth with her narcissistic interests and to use them as reasons for being proud, in Miss D's case there was now a conflict reflected in her tendency to a reciprocal exclusion of one type of interest by the other.

Conception occurred after Miss D stopped taking oral contraceptives and replaced them by an irregular use of a spermicidal agent (in fact, she said, "an antispermicidal agent"). She became aware during the interview that discontinuing the oral contraceptives might have a meaning she had previously not seen: "I think I have not wanted this child and wanted it at the same time."

Relationship of the Subject with Her Own Parents: The Pregnancy and the Relationship with the Mother. Miss D's idealized mother died three years before her pregnancy, and the conception was the fulfillment of a wish the mother had expressed to her daughter. Major aspects of their relationship were clinically characterized as being symbiotic. Miss D stated that her earlier wish not to have a baby expressed her desire to remain her mother's "eternal child," since she had been deprived of her father's love. The father was described as selfish and childish, aggressive with the mother, and jealous of the loving relationship between Miss D and her mother. Miss D reported a recent dream: "I was in sort of a paved yard, a vault, and there was a heap of ashes. Someone pushed me into the ashes, and they were the ashes of a girl, a schoolmate."

It seemed Miss D's wish to have a child was part of her mourning the loss of her mother. It appeared justified to agree with Miss D that the ashes in the dream represented her mother, who had been cremated, and that her fall expressed her fear of dying when, being pregnant and close to delivery, she was dangerously near to making an identification with her mother.

Images, Feelings, and Fantasies Related to the Baby in utero. Miss D's symbiotic relationship with her mother was duplicated in her relationship with the fetus. She seemed not to have images or expectations about the baby except those expressed as if the child were not autonomous in any respect. For instance, after she first heard the baby's heartbeat she said, "I have got two hearts, I have four feet, four hands. I am completely two-fold! I saw a TV film about a snake with two heads." Thus the child seemed a narcissistic double of herself and its conception like a parthenogenesis.

The Relationship with the Father of the Baby. Miss D's relationships with males were unusual. She spoke of a first passionate relationship with a partner she called "an eternal adolescent" who lived more in his dreams than in reality. Her present partner was a homosexual and "very young, psychologically speaking." When she told him she was pregnant he asked her to live with him, though she thought he was afraid she would love him less because she was now pregnant. She spoke about him as the agent of her reproductive function rather than as someone with whom she had a significant relationship.

Images, Feelings, and Fantasies Related to Specific Aspects and Phases of Child Rearing. Adolescence was referred to several times. Miss D said she kept this baby because "Maybe some day I will regret adolescence because I think it is a fascinating period." She reported that her first anorectic episode in adolescence began the day she learned, with a feeling of disgust, that her sister was pregnant. It appeared that she was tied to the conflicts of adolescence, though her own adolescent years were probably fraught with the revival of earlier conflicts, most likely those centering on oral and genital issues.

RESPONSES TO THE PICTURES

Wish (or Absence of Wish) To Have a Baby. Three RP's suggested to the examiner that Miss D might have been anorectic at some time. For example, the response to the photograph shown in figure 1: "This picture does not make me think of anything, once again; it is the third time! Just everyday life. It is the yoghurt, he has plenty of yoghurt all over his mouth. No, this again doesn't interest me at all. It is like dogs and cats that get their pictures taken, there is nothing to say, but some people will be ecstatic for hours." The examiner noted that the violent feelings of disgust and the difficulties experienced in producing a story led to the consideration that Miss D might have been anorectic.

Relationship of the Subject with Her Own Parents: The Pregnancy and the Relationship with the Mother. Miss D's responses indicated that she and the baby were united in her mind and that one of the baby's functions was to be a source of pleasure for Miss D's mother.

Images, Feelings, and Fantasies Related to the Baby in utero. Several RP's suggested the relationship with the baby was symbiotic in nature. One RP was interpreted as manifesting cannibalistic desires to devour the child she was bearing as a way to be pregnant again after an oral fertilization. In the clinical interview the subject perceived her baby as devouring her from within, appeared to express aggressive avidity against her own mother, and stressed fantasies about parental images, while the RP's showed her avidity toward and fantasies about the child to be born.

The Relationship with the Father of the Baby. The RP's raised questions in the examiner's mind about the quality of Miss D's relationships, including the one with the baby's father, who appeared as if only a friend or a reproductive agent.

Images, Feelings, and Fantasies Related to Specific Aspects and Phases of Child Rearing. In response to the only picture showing an adolescent male, Miss D expressed pleasure and interest. Other RP's contained comments that she felt much better with teenagers than with young children. The examiner inferred the presence of fixations to the adolescent phase, surmised that Miss D did not feel herself to be an adult woman able to become a mother, and considered that oral fixations in particular determined the crisis she experienced during adolescence. Miss D was greatly affected by viewing the picture of a child sitting on a chamberpot. She could not imagine herself as a mother in this scene. She criticized the attitude of mothers who want to train their child, and declared she preferred to show no interest in this aspect of child rearing lest she become as harmful as she thought her own mother had been. It was later noted that Miss D was critical of her mother at this point, whereas in the clinical interview she had referred to her mother only as an idealized figure.

Case 2

Mrs. K, age thirty-one, had been pregnant four and a half months. She was married and had a son, age two, and a daughter, age four.

CLINICAL INTERVIEW

Wish (or Absence of Wish) to Have a Baby. Mrs. K made it clear that children were a means to avoid feeling alone and helped in her struggle against depression. "One has children so as not to be alone when getting old; the more children we have, the more likely it is we can keep one nearby." In addition, Mrs. K's choice of names for her children indicated they served her ambitious expectations. The names were either

Figure 26–1

those of glorious or well-known figures, or very rare and connected to legendary characters notable for some defect amid their glory, or else for meeting a tragic end. Her daughter's name was that of an extraordinary woman who founded Malta. It was also the name of a fairy who could turn the lower part of her body into the tail of a snake; the fairy's husband, however, discovered the secret, and she had to leave her children. This material was interpreted in view of the fact that Mrs. K's father was mayor of the village in which she grew up. She felt her social position had now declined, and so she put her ambitions into her children, wishing they would repair her previous failures. It appeared that the magnitude of her ambition and its phallic aspects were associated with threats of failure and punishment.

Anxieties Related to the Physical and Mental Condition of the Baby. Mrs. K's fear that her children would not be normal was linked with her older brother's psychiatric problems, which she interpreted as hereditary. She was intolerant of his passivity and dependence on their parents and herself and seemed to view him as a threat to the baby to be born. She wished her brother would die "because he realizes what his condition is, he is very unhappy, and our parents are too." Her next words were: "I think that if when the baby is born it is abnormal I would rather . . . one should be able to sign a paper before birth so the baby is left to die by itself and nobody ressuscitates it."

The Relationship with the Father of the Baby. Mrs. K declared she would not allow herself to be "crushed" as her mother had been by her father and said that she and her husband made conjoint decisions about the household. However, she felt her husband devoted too much time to his work, and she insisted he be at home for her and for the children. They were happy to see him, and he admired them, but when they were infants he did not want to be much involved with them. Still, she felt neglected by him, complaining that he made no comments about her new dresses although he did about those of their daughter. These remarks seemed linked to her description earlier in the interview of the very close relationship she herself had had with her father.

RESPONSES TO THE PICTURES

Wish (or Absence of Wish) to Have a Baby. In several responses the child in the pictures was described as being alone, abandoned, left to himself, and unrooted. Mrs. K mentioned her father only once and said he did not show enough interest and affection to her children. Once she mentioned her mother and commented that she, Mrs. K, had never shown affection to her. The examiner interpreted the responses as the expression of attempts to overcome experiences of childhood deprivation and a lack of parental affection. The mother figure appeared an emotionally cold person who might leave her children. Having a baby suggested an effort on Mrs. K's part to "do better" than her mother had done with her, in an attempt to identify with the maternal aspect of her ego ideal. The wish for a baby, therefore, served an antidepressive function but was counteracted by feelings of inadequacy in the face of this ideal.

Anxieties Related to the Physical and Mental Condition of the Baby. Mrs. K was quite responsive and sensitive to situations in which it appeared the child in the pictures might be in danger. The quality of her responses caused the examiner to wonder whether they expressed Mrs. K's aggressive feelings toward the children.

The Relationship with the Father of the Baby. The husband's role in child rearing was mentioned with the first picture and also later. From the responses, the examiner noted the father was maintained at some distance from the children while they were very young, and the marital relationship was represented as stable.

Case 3

Mrs. A, age twenty-eight, was seven-months pregnant at the time of the interview. Her marriage of six years had been infertile until the husband underwent surgery for a varicocele. A pregnancy followed, terminated by a spontaneous abortion eight months before the present pregnancy. Mrs. A had clear doubts at this time about her capacity to conceive and keep a baby alive until term.

Relationship of the Subject with Her own Parents: The Pregnancy and the Relationship with the Mother. Mrs. A's parents divorced when she was two years old, and her father returned to his native India. Thereafter she was raised by her mother and maternal grandparents. The grandfather compensated for the loss of her father and appeared as an idealized and reassuring figure in contrast to a later prototype of men as selfish and not dependable. Mrs. A talked so little about her mother that it appeared at first that she did not live in the same house with her and her grandparents.

The Relationship with the Father of the Baby. Mrs. A had her first significant adult relationship with a man at age eighteen when she met her husband-to-be. Their relationship developed as stable and continuous, but she felt there had not been a deep intimacy between them. As Mr. A hesitated for some time whether to have the operation for varicocele, she suspected him of being "selfish." After he finally accepted the operation, their relationship was considerably strengthened and deepened, and she thereafter considered him a dependable person. The operation and conception apparently represented for her a test of her husband's dependability, a resolution of the mistrust originating in her parents' divorce and the loss of her father.

Images, Feelings, and Fantasies Related to the Baby in utero. Mrs. A perceived her infant as already distinct from her, and she took its movements as messages: "I am here, I am coming soon, everything is all right". She felt the baby as a reassuring figure and, like her husband, a dependable person, suggesting she was using the baby to overcome anxieties related to her infantile experience of loss. When she imagined her baby's future, she saw him as a toddler trying to walk and playing in a garden, just as she herself

had as a child. This was also the time when her father had left, and she said she used to "play Indians" perhaps in an effort to work through her feelings of loss. However, she did not speak at all about the early months of the baby's life, suggesting she might be anxious and uncertain about her competency as a mother.

RESPONSES TO THE PICTURES

Relationships of the Subject with Her Own Parents. Mrs. A made no reference to her father, but did refer in an idealized way to her grandfather. She repeatedly pointed to the existence of a past traumatic experience of abandonment. Contrasting perceptions of maternal figures were expressed, sometimes as a very severe or cruel figure, or less often as helpful and caring. The perception of an intrusive mother was in response to the picture showing a toddler sitting on a chamberpot. It elicited the memory of a Teddy bear that had an operation in the back and all the insides had been taken out.

Comparing this material with the clinical history led to the idea that the loss of the father at age two might have been experienced in the context of the anal phase and so as a loss of the contents of her body. The RP's suggested these unconscious fantasies might be currently active in her perception of real infants and thus possibly influence the way she herself would cope with her child's toilet-training.

The Relationship with the Father of the Baby. From the RP's, the examiner inferred that communication between Mrs. A and her husband had been uneasy before the pregnancy and that she was still concerned the baby might be an obstacle between them. She seemed to keep her husband at some distance from the baby, and it was difficult for her to imagine herself and her husband in their new roles.

A discrepancy between the RP results and the material of the clinical interview can be noted here. While the RP's indicated a number of areas of anxiety, the clinical interview suggested the baby was strengthening the marital relationship. It is possible that the clinician might have been more sensitive to Mrs. A's anxieties had he not been blind to the RP results.

Images, Feelings, and Fantasies Related to the Baby in utero. Responding to the picture of a happy toddler throwing cards up in the air (figure 26–2), Mrs. A said that in her dreams she heard her baby burst into laughter, and she saw it in a garden trying to take its first steps, happy to be able to do it all by itself. However, she seemed anxious about her ability to provide adequate care and to respond appropriately to her baby's cries.

Discussion

The principal aim of this study has been to investigate the relationships between the data

Figure 26–2

of the clinical interviews and the results of the analysis of the RP's for individual subjects. The individual differences in the results undoubtedly reflect the wide variation in the preconceptional experiences of the subjects, and these factors are not examined here.

For Case 1, the RP data suggested antecedent anorexia, a correct inference on the basis of the clinical interview. The RP's also traced connections between some aspects of the interview (oral strivings related to her mother) and some of her attitudes toward a baby (avidity directed toward the baby and perception of the baby's avidity). Thus RP's might be useful in understanding connections between a mother's various psychological traits and her perceptions of an infant.

For Case 2, comparing the data from both sources indicated that the RP's emphasized Mrs. K's depressive feelings and her past feelings of deprivation. This was confirmed in the interview, though not so clearly, and possible connections to a cold and unreliable mother figure appeared.[1] Also, the RP's reflected her wishes related to her maternal ego ideal, whereas the clinical interview emphasized Mrs. K's wishes to identify with the paternal aspects of her ego ideal. Thus it seemed the pictures elicited more painful material, probably linked to earlier experiences, than the material that appeared during the clinical interview.

For Case 3, the RP's provided important information regarding the mother figure, something she had not said much about during the clinical interview. The RP data also pointed to the way in which these perceptions of the mother might influence Mrs. A's future maternal behavior. A discrepancy appeared between the information from the RP's and the clinical interview with regard to the effect of the baby's arrival on the marital relationship. One explanation of this discrepancy might be a common feature of the RP's to uncover anxieties defended against by some patients during the first interview.

---

[1]The third clinical contact is now being studied, and it seems to support the RP analysis. In this last contact, Mrs. K spoke more about her mother, a pessimistic person who had never offered her grandchildren a present.

Conclusion

The preliminary study of a projective method to investigate parental attitudes during pregnancy demonstrates that the information provided by its use is complementary to the information obtained by clinical interview, though not identical. Generally speaking, items considered to be major issues by the clinical interviewer were also referred to as such by the examiner of the RPs. Only rarely were discrepancies found. It is suggested that this instrument can be used as an adjunct to the clinical interview in the assessment of a mother's perceptions and attitudes toward her future baby.

REFERENCES

Benedek, T. (1959). Parenthood as a developmental phase. *Journal of the American Psychoanalytic Association*, 7:389–417.

Benedek, T. (1975). Parenthood during the life cycle. In *Parenthood: Its Psychology and Psychopathology.* ed. E. J. Anthony and T. Benedek. Boston: Little, Brown.

Bibring, G. C., Dwyer, T. F., Huntington, D. S., and Valenstein, A. F. (1961). A study of the psychological processes in pregnancy and of the earliest mother-child relationship. *The Psychoanalytic Study of the Child,* 16:7–92. New York: International Universities Press.

Erikson, E. H. (1980). Elements of a psychoanalytic theory of psychosocial development. In *The Course of Life,* vol 1, ed. S. I. Greenspan and G. H. Pollock. Washington, D.C.: U.S. Government Printing Office.

PART III

Clinical and Research
Aspects of the
Infant-Caregiver Relationship

27

The Influence Babies Bring to Bear on Their Upbringing

E. James Anthony, M.D.

A baby exerts a huge influence on the household he enters, dominating the outer and inner lives of all the members. He is a developmental impetus. To quote Erikson (1968):

> Because [the family] members must reorient themselves to accommodate [the baby's] presence, they must also grow as individuals and as a group. It is as true to say that babies control and bring up their families as it is to say the converse. A family can bring up a baby only by being brought up by him. His growth consists of a series of challenges to them to serve his newly developing potentialities for social interaction. (p. 96)

What is being considered here is *not* the introduction of a helpless member into a group. In fact, quite a different view from the time-honored one that sees the infant as someone in need of total care is presented. The infant is now seen as a mediator of interpersonal contact and communication. The group's dynamics undergo a radical change because the new member automatically has top priority where needs are concerned. In fact, the baby restructures the family, disorganizes established modes of living, and provokes disturbing fantasies in the other children because of his primitive behavior. For nine months the baby has been an invisible but disquieting presence, and the pregnant mother's growing preoccupation with her fetus provides the family a foretaste of what is to come when the baby eventually enters the arena of real life. To everyone, the event is a mixed blessing, and feelings of love and hate surround the newcomer although, in the arms of his mother, he is relatively impervious to these reactions.

The idea of a baby bringing up a family is more than just an eccentric thought: it is a comment on the subtle nature of influence and the paradoxical way in which it often functions. The smallest and weakest can be as psychologically influential as the most powerful. Everyone in the family is a parent or surrogate parent as far as the baby is concerned, and this may lead to the members vying with one another as caregivers in their efforts to reap a rewarding smile—that elusive crowning of the coaxing effort.

The baby's cry, especially one of hunger, can be as potent as his smile; its strength and insistence can be heard everywhere in the house, and everyone responds. The mother's breasts drip with milk, the toddler becomes cranky, the six-year-old sister runs to comfort him, and even the father grows grouchier as he makes his way to the refrigerator (Brazelton, 1969). No one can remain immune to the raucous appeals that sound so imperative.

After the "King," as Freud humorously but

shrewdly referred to him, is satiated with milk, he holds court, and his subjects, young and old, drop their occupations to cater to his every whim. In doing so, they gradually learn the language of his needs. It is the infant's business to express and everyone else's to understand. Only the displaced toddler finds it hard to control envy and jealousy, and his feelings occasionally get the better of him, causing him to reach up to the "throne" to take a poke at the "King" amidst universal consternation and condemnation.

Breast-feeding, if done within the family circle, inevitably evokes fantasies in the other children who may not find it easy to concede, depending on their ages, that this cornucopian reservoir is the sole possession of one fortunate individual while they must make do with the cow. Even the mother vicariously enjoys the sensuousness of the occasion. Anni Bergman (in press) quotes an expatient who became a mother and was intensely involved in the pleasure of her baby sucking at her breast. For her, it was analogous to sexual gratification.

> It is impossible to describe what a lovely feeling goes through your whole body when your baby sucks; you are right away from this world. You are absolutely satisfied, and happy beyond desire. It is a wonderful feeling; you long for nothing but peace—uninterrupted peace. It is just unspeakably lovely: You feel no pain and no sorrow, and ah! You are carried into another world.

But this "alimentary orgasm" is not confined to the mother; it is also experienced by the infant. So each family member probably has a dim "organic" memory of this past excitement which, reactivated dramatically in his or her presence, stimulates greed, envy, and longing. At such moments, orality is the major psychosocial modality in the family.

All this implies that babies are not only represented in every psyche where they are invested with intense positive and negative feelings, but also that their various activities, polymorphous and incontinent, are a source of both wonder and disgust. Who is this being who can freely do all the things forbidden to everyone else and who is also such a potent stimulus for the internal system of unconscious fantasies? The baby, as Freud (1918) pointed out, is not only a baby but a symbol, and it is as a symbol that the baby can become disliked and repudiated; but it is also as a symbol that the baby gets accepted. Of course, the baby is not only a symbol to the family, but also a person in the process of personification; the baby's amorphousness is what renders him serviceable as a symbol.

A baby is a gift to the family who brings with him his own special gift of feces. In dispensing this gift, as with his smiles, he is not an indiscriminate giver. Freud did not find it difficult to believe that infants only soil people whom they know and love; apparently strangers are unworthy of this distinction. Furthermore, like feces, babies are believed by the younger children to be born through the anus; in a more roundabout way babies also connote money in the sense that both are gifts. A person's love of his penis is thus not without an element of anal erotism because the penis can also be given as a gift (Freud, 1918). These unconscious equations of baby, feces, penis, money, breast may form a unity that circulates within the unconscious life of the family and stirs up an assortment of resentment, envy, disgust, avarice, and castration anxiety. But there is also an overevaluation. As with many kings, the baby's reign is relatively brief: dethronement is predictable within a short period of time.

We therefore need to consider six interesting reversals regarding the role of infants in the family: (1) Far from being physically the weakest and most helpless member of the household, the baby is the most powerful and most influential—the "King" whose every need is rapidly attended to. (2) Far from being a psychological nonentity in the household, the infant's symbolic significance floods the unconscious minds of the family members, and the primitive behavior reactivates similar yearnings in all of them. (3) Succumbing to the infant's "ruthlessness" (Winnicott, 1954), all the family members to some extent undergo a regression in the service of the baby: they will act down, talk down, and think down for the baby's pleasure. (4) Far from being largely a "mid-brain specimen" with an incomplete cortical development, the infant manifests discriminatory responses that lead the rest of the family to credit him with extraordinary ingenuities. The "wise baby" lies there perceiving everything, understanding everything, but saying nothing—the quintessence of wisdom. The modern scientific attitude toward the first year of life is equally enthralled with any demonstrated competence. The baby may be the product of the family, but the family to some extent is what the baby makes of them. (5) The upbringing of babies has hitherto been regarded as the sacred duty and responsibility of parents and parent-surrogates, but today upbringing is regarded as complementary. The parents bring up their babies and babies also bring up their parents. Babies undergo sequential stages of development and so do parents. The effects on psychological growth are bidirectional, with both infants and parents exercising profound influences on one another. Infants grow up to care for their parents at a later stage of the life cycle, but when parents are mentally or physically ill or handicapped, the parenting of the parent by the child may begin very early. (6) Although babies eventually learn to speak the language prevalent in the family, they also train the family in the subtle art of nonverbal communication, making them conscious of "the second great language system." As Brazelton (1974) and Stern (1974) have shown, adults adapt themselves to an unusual degree in communicating with infants and toddlers, altering their intonation patterns, trimming their vocabularies, and stereotyping their facial expressions. Babies not only train parents in mothering and fathering but to a large extent dictate the patterns of feeding and caregiving.

The patterns of parenting are markedly affected by the characteristics of the infant. Sex differences evoke marked differences in child-rearing behavior which can only be in part accounted for by cultural attitudes toward male and female children. Although the statistical associations between parental practices and children's sex-typed characteristics are modest, some tentative conclusions do emerge: (1) Parental permissiveness appears to be related to aggressiveness, assertiveness, achievement orientation, independence in the offspring; such permissiveness could be looked upon as a reaction to childrens' goal-oriented, competent, and autonomous behavior. (2) Parental restrictiveness is associated with children who are dependent, compliant, conforming, fearful, and polite.

Although these findings have been interpreted traditionally as parental effects, more recent work has suggested that parental behavior is sensitive to and, even to some extent, controlled by the child's behavior; influence is not a one-way process.

This has even been claimed, with less supporting evidence, for sex roles: Sex roles were thought to be learned almost exclusively through identification with the like-sexed parent, but recently it has been suggested that children may serve as models for their parents as well as emulating them and their own peers and siblings.

Attachment Behavior

Much of the infant-mother interaction, even within the caregiving system, involves mutual and reciprocal exchanges within the context of play and imitation. These occur best when the infant is at a moderate level of arousal and the parent is fully engaged with the child. Hartmann has suggested (1956) that the infant was "preadapted" to the administrations of the mother. Chess (1973) has elaborated on this in her concept of matching and mismatching. For example, the clinging of a chimpanzee infant is so tight and close that it is experienced as oppressive by the human caregiver.

One of the factors that permits infant-mother interaction, pointed out by Emde and his group (1976), is the drop in fussiness that occurs before the third month, which is also associated with the amount of time that the infant is in an alert state. This releases the mother's energies from caregiving and allows her to interact socially with her baby. When this fussiness fails to decrease, maternal attachment also ebbs. Abusing parents sometimes complain that they felt stressed by the infant's fussing and crying to the point that exceeded their tolerance.

Crying and smiling are the two main tools used by the infant to communicate demands.

As Emde puts it, the crying relays the message: "Come, change what's happening." The smile communicates: "Keep up what you're doing. I like it." Although the majority of infants show a marked reduction in fussiness by the seventh month, a few develop a vicious cycle with the mother that leads to her detachment (Emde and Harmon, 1972).

The "correlation of organisms" has its own natural history. As the infantile system shifts from predictable interchanges to an unpredictable phase, which then slowly stabilizes as a predictable system again (Sander, 1970), the mother's behavior also undergoes restructuring in correlation with these changes. Korner (1974) and Sander (1970) each concluded that the caregiver's behavior is substantially determined by the infant's ontogenetic level of development. As infants become less endogenous and more reactive, they respond more to the caregiver while at the same time they influence her attitudes and behavior to a greater extent. By the end of the first year, they can be highly reactive organisms, and the mother, too, may feel more capable of influencing them. She reacts to the neonate with a maximum of care and preoccupation, but later the infant, according to Winnicott (1956), gradually releases her from this total concern, allowing her to bring her socializing, educating, and stimulating activities into play (Korner, 1974). So enthralling can this become that it sometimes seems as if mothers turn to their babies when bored or at a loss for something to do. At such times they appear to use them for their own needs. From time immemorial, mothers have found that these little creatures can be great fun especially when husbands are absent or neglectful. In turn, the babies have discovered mothers to be highly reactive organisms, much more amusing than their own fingers, toes, or rattles.

As with all nursery phenomena, attachment is a two-way process: the infant grows increasingly attached to the mother and suffers when she leaves. The mother becomes increasingly attached to her infant and may experience a sense of loss when the infant is taken from her. Similarly, when the process of attachment fails, the infant may turn away from the mother, and she may detach herself from him.

However, the separation disorders of the mother have been less assiduously studied, although there is some support for the observation that there are antecedents of separation traumata in the mother's early life. The infant's response to being left may reactivate the mother's own infantile responses, and these set up a morbid interaction infused on both sides with doubt, wariness, mistrust, and ambivalence.

These new studies of infancy appear to reverse all former notions of the baby as a passive recipient or an empty container waiting to be filled from the outside. Current research tends to ignore this helplessness and instead focuses a good deal of attention on competence and bidirectionality with its key concepts of mutuality and reciprocity. There are also those who would be prepared to push the infant's controlling and shaping capacities even further, contending that it is equally parsimonious to attribute correlations found between parent and child to the effect of the child on the parent as the other way around (Bell, 1968, 1974). As one of the main proponents of this movement to develop a theory of child-effects, Bell (1974) realizes that either interpretation may be extreme and that his own viewpoint undermines three decades of socialization research committed almost entirely to studying the effects of parents on their children. He acknowledges that his position is "frankly speculative" yet challenging. The opposition of extremes is apt to generate creative tensions as part of a dialectic, whose thesis is that babies lie on a continuum of effectiveness in the mother-infant relationship depending on traits inherent in the two partners plus the added activity of the father. Thus, a very passive, trouble-free, easygoing infant, who offers little or no resistance to the mother's procedures, may permit his mother to determine most aspects of their interactional life, while at the other end of the continuum babies who are vigorous, robust, and strong-willed, are highly resistant to any interference with their freedom. The latter can become highly controlling of the mother's behavior particularly if she is passive, anxious, and unsure of her mothering. Because of their outgoingness, activity, and curiosity, these infants learn rapidly from the environment and display new behaviors that excite the mother and keep her attentive and obedient to the infant's wishes. They can also intimidate the primiparous mother and reduce her to a nervous state of apprehension, in which she is always wondering what will be demanded of her next. As the baby enters the early toddler stage, this controlling behavior is aggravated, and these uncertain women may make ineffectual attempts to modulate it. By this time, however, the baby has diagnosed the mother correctly and treats her pathetic efforts with the assurance of someone in command of the situation. In the ordinary course of infancy, babies can be "extraordinarily good elicitors of maternal attention" (Korner, 1974), but with extremely outgoing infants, control by crying is soon replaced by the more powerful forces of negativism.

The Infant's Point of View

Clearly, infants are not at the developmental stage when they can apprehend the environment with the profundity that comes later, but they do seem able to turn their sensorimotor intelligence to the appraisal of the emerging world around them in terms of interest, avoidance, and attractiveness. For example, babies begin to differentiate the particular holding and handling techniques used by their mothers from those of other caretakers and regard these gestures as much a part of her as her person. They thus perceive and respond to her as different, a distinction that may be compounded of actual differences and those stemming from his infantile perspective. The mother herself behaves differently when her baby is quiet or excitable. The baby's excitement can reach a level of provocation that can compel her into extreme and often guilt-producing reactions. Hyperexcitable babies with exaggerated responses and low thresholds of frustration are difficult for any mother to pacify and control. Some mothers, under such circumstances, may begin to doubt their mothering capacities. They feel guilty and ashamed at not meeting

the infant's insatiable needs and demands and are left with the dismal conviction that they are failing the baby. Such hyperactive and hypersensitive infants can rapidly demoralize the best of mothers. Children with brain dysfunction can cause their mothers to feel rejected and overanxious regarding their apparent mismanagement, whereas it is the baby who is overtaxing the parent's capabilities.

Babies who get the upper hand on their caregivers can become "ruthless." Winnicott (1945) sees this ruthlessness as a normal stage in the infant's development; its persistence, however, not only leads to clinical states in the infant but may also make for clinical disturbances in the mother. As Winnicott puts it: "The normal baby enjoys the ruthless relationship with his mother, mostly in play, and one reason why his mother is so necessary for him is that he expects her to tolerate his ruthlessness *even when he hurts her and wears her out"* (my italics, p. 154). At the extreme end of the spectrum, this ruthlessness takes the manifest form of pleasure in dominating, controlling, and hurting the mother. As with all victims, there is something in the mother that "asks for it" and gets it. She is tormented by the child but masochistically offers herself to sadistic attacks. In such instances, a baby is able not only to control the upbringing milieu but to generate morbid conditions in the mother.

Brazelton (1961) describes the case of a difficult neonate with deviant state patterns who completely demoralized his mother to the point of depression and ineffectuality. The young professional mother had looked forward to the birth of this baby with eager delight. Her newborn infant, however, was capable of only two extreme states: deep sleep from which it was difficult to arouse him, and a hyperactive, hypersensitive state during which he screamed continuously. The mother felt totally "rejected" by the infant and overwhelmed by the task of mothering, but only understood the situation in terms of her own mismanagement. A period of psychotherapy enabled her to see the infant's problem as his own. Later she had a second "easy" baby and demonstrated that she was capable of having a normal mother-infant relationship.

The Infant's Impact on the Family's Unconscious Life: Two Vignettes

The first vignette emphasizes the regressive aspects I discussed earlier. A forty-year-old man had entered psychoanalytic treatment because of difficulties he was experiencing at work and at home. There were three children: a boy aged eight, another boy, aged three, and a nine-month-old girl. The patient's personality was not easy. He was strongly anal-sadistic, oppressive in dealing with his family, and authoritarian at work, especially with women. At the same time, he was unduly compliant with his superiors. He felt himself to be a chronically angry man with a constant need to control his rage, which usually dribbled out in biting criticisms. On the couch, he struggled for a long period with his predominantly cognitive stance; all his communications were rigidly delivered, usually in impeccable grammar. It was a difficult analytic task to get past his intellectual defenses.

On one particular day, he came somewhat shaken by "an incredible dream." It had wakened him and kept him up for the rest of the night. In the dream, he was walking along a corridor with another man whom he immediately associated with the analyst. All of a sudden, he found himself lying on the floor having a huge bowel movement. He seemed to be naked below the waist and attempted to control the defecation with his hand. He was aware of people passing by and staring at him while the feces gradually covered his buttocks and legs. He attempted to crawl toward a restroom, feeling very humiliated. He imagined that everyone was disgusted with him. The man in the corridor was doing nothing at all to help him control or clean himself. When he finally got to a toilet, he had shrunk down to about two feet in height so that his eyes only came up to the toilet bowl. There still seemed to be more feces on their way out as if his entire insides were coming out. There were feces everywhere. In his associations, he brought up a number of day residues. He thought that at the end of the last session, he had begun to associate more freely and that

his analyst was pleased at his effort. He felt that good insights had emerged, but later when he came to reconsider the session, he had wondered what would really happen if he let go and inundated the analyst with "crap." Would the analyst stand it or would he be disgusted?

When he went home that same evening from work, the family were sitting together with the baby lying naked on his mother's lap. Quite suddenly, without warning, the baby defecated. The eight-year-old had held his nose and closed his eyes, and the three-year-old (with whom he identified, since he too had been displaced by his sister's birth at about the same age) had screamed with excitement and jumped up and down. His wife was surprisingly tolerant, simply saying, "Oh dear, you are a messy little thing!" He had not got up to help her, for at first he felt fascinated by the scene and could feel his own guts rumbling. He was surprised at the amount of feces the baby produced and the fact that it simply gurgled with pleasure and was rubbing its hands in it. He wondered what it felt like to be so unconcerned about convention. When he did speak, he remarked critically to his wife that they should never sit in the best room without the baby being completely diapered.

He then recalled that earlier that morning he had griped to his wife about sleeping late and not getting up to serve him coffee and breakfast before he started to work. He had been half way through his meal when she emerged. He said coldly that he appreciated her appearance, but it was somewhat late. She interrupted him to say that nothing she ever did satisfied him. In precise, measured terms he continued to tell her that half a loaf was better than none, but that occasionally he would be glad to have a whole loaf. She exploded with anger and said that it was another indication of his tyrannical attitude and behavior. He ignored her anger and continued to talk pedantically in the manner of an adult to a child. But his hands were trembling with the tension he felt, and suddenly some coffee from his cup spilled onto his thigh. He fell completely to pieces, screaming with rage while rushing into the bathroom to wash off the coffee stain. He felt beside himself with fury and wanted to throw himself onto the floor and kick wildly. When he eventually pulled himself together, his wife softened completely and went solicitously to help him with cleaning. She had a small smile on her face, which afterwards he associated with the smile she showed when the baby soiled all over her. He understood her pleasure in both situations as being alike: he and the baby had both "let go": he had cast aside his armor-plated defenses to reveal the screaming and dirty little toddler inside him.

The second vignette is concerned with the impact of an infant's orality on her parents. A twenty-eight-year-old woman had given birth to a female infant whom she brought to see me during her treatment session when the baby was one month old (because she knew that I was a child analyst who would be crazy about babies!). She told me somewhat euphorically that the baby had transformed the lives of herself and her husband, and she went on to give me three examples of the radical changes that had been brought about in this young family by this third member.

The first shift in the family dynamics was ushered in by a dream that the mother had on the third day following the birth. She, her husband, and the new baby were in bed together, and the husband was feeding the baby semen from his penis while she looked on contentedly. Her reaction to the dream was one of shame because the content was "perverted," but it also signified something good for the little family. Her husband was pictured as participating fully in the care of the baby by doing his share of feeding. Since she herself was accustomed to sucking semen from her husband and was in the process of breast-feeding her baby, she felt that it was an intimate mutuality of sustenance. On the night before the dream the husband had sipped from her breast and had expressed pleasure doing so. There seemed to be two sides to the semen, just as there were two sides to milk. Semen was wonderful stuff that created babies, and yet the taste disgusted her and made her feel that it might sicken her if she swallowed it. Her milk was good for the baby but it also seemed to give the baby colic and make her throw up. She herself often threw up after meals, in order to control her

weight, by putting her finger down her throat. Everything was good and bad at the same time. She sometimes felt good about her baby and sometimes bad. She recalled the nightmarish dream she had toward the end of her pregnancy when she was swinging her baby around and dashing it against the wall. In the dream this did not hurt it at all, but she wondered whether deep down she was a child-abuser.

The dream also implied a real change in her husband. He had become much more nurturing in his attitude toward the baby as well as toward her. He seemed to be constantly "mothering" both of them, and she was very grateful to her baby for increasing the amount of tenderness that was coming her way. She wondered whether the dream was simply an expressed wish. Her nipples had been cracked and painful at the time of the dream, and she would have liked to have been relieved of the agonizing breast-feeding. The dream not only had her husband feeding the baby but the baby sucking from his penis, thus relieving her of the revolting task of doing so herself. But she was too timid to tell her husband her feelings because he seemed to enjoy oral sex so much. She recalled that at the hospital a nurse had commented on her baby's huge "orality" because the infant had sucked voraciously on her husband's hairy chest as he held it. She said that since the baby's arrival, both she and her husband had become much more oral themselves: not only did they eat too much, drink too much, kiss too much, and help themselves to candy, but they also seemed to be perpetually hungry. The baby, she thought, had "oralized" the family, as if by making them aware of their own oral needs they would be more likely to consider the baby's.

The baby also brought about another dramatic change by effecting a symptomatic cure of the mother's "oral syndrome" of bulimia. She was smoking much less pot and had given up cigarettes. This was partly because she felt that these "toxic" activities might endanger her care of the baby: she did not want to be "high" while carrying her baby around. She now seemed to be more addicted to her baby than to her old addictions and talked about wanting to eat her baby up because she was so adorable. She said slyly to the analyst: "She is my best therapist and is curing me of all my bad habits." She added that her baby seemed to know intuitively how to make her parents do what she wanted them to do in order to make her life more comfortable.

The third dramatic change ("almost a miracle") was in their sex life. She had never before experienced an orgasm in intercourse, only through masturbation. When they tried intercourse on the seventeenth day, she was very wary because her clitoris was still bruised and raw at the base and had in fact stopped her from masturbating. However, to her intense surprise, she reached a climax during intercourse, and this happened two more times. It was what she had always wanted, and it had been one of her major frustrations. Now her baby had brought it about. This wonderful infant had changed her husband's behavior toward her, improved her sexual life beyond expectation, and had rid her of a whole host of disturbing symptoms. She was now a much more contented and happy woman than she had ever been before. Why? Because, as she put it: "This baby knows that a happy mother makes for a happier baby!"

There is a passage in Plutarch's *Lives* stating that the ancient Greeks were very much aware of the baby's invisible power. Themistocles, the hero of the Persian Wars, had this to say of his infant son: "He was the most powerful of all the Hellenes; the Hellenes were commanded by the Athenians, the Athenians by myself, myself by the infant's mother, and the mother was commanded by her little baby."

REFERENCES

Bell, R. Q. (1968). A reinterpretation of the direction of effects in studies of socialization. *Psychological Review,* 75: 81–95.

Bell, R. Q. (1974). Contributions of human infants to caregiving and social interaction. In *The Effect of the Infant on its Caregiver,* ed. M. Lewis and L. Rosenblum. New York: John Wiley.

Bergman, A. (in press). The experience of the mother during the earliest phases of infant development. In *Parental Influences,* ed. E. J. Anthony and G. Pollock. Boston: Little, Brown.

Brazelton, T B. (1961). Psychophysiological reactions in the neonate. The value of observation of the neonate. *Journal of Pediatrics,* 58:508–512.

Brazelton, T. B. (1969). *Infants and Mothers: Differences in Development.* New York: Delacorte.

Brazelton, T. B. (1974). The origins of reciprocity. In *The Effect of the Infant on its Caregiver,* ed. M. Lewis and L. Rosenbaum. New York: John Wiley.

Chess, S. (1973). Temperament in the normal infant. In *Children with Learning Problems.* New York: Brunner-Mazel.

Emde, R. and Harmon, R. J. (1972). Endogenous and exogenous smiling systems in early infancy. *Journal of American Academy of Child Psychiatry,* 11:177–200.

Erikson, E. H. (1968). *Identity, Youth and Crisis.* New York: Norton.

Freud, S. (1908). On the sexual theories of children. *Standard Edition,* vol. 9, ed. J. Strachey. London: Hogarth Press, 1959.

Freud, S. (1918). From the history of an infantile neurosis. *Standard Edition,* vol. 17, ed. J. Strachey. London: Hogarth Press, 1955.

Hartmann, H. (1956). Notes on the reality principle. In *Essays on Ego Psychology.* New York: International Universities Press, 1964.

Korner, A. F. (1974). The effect of the infant's state, level of arousal, sex, and ontogenetic stage on the caregiver. In *The Effect of the Infant on its Caregiver,* ed. M. Lewis and L. Rosenblum. New York: John Wiley.

Sander, L. (1970). Regulation and organization in the early infant-caretaker system. In *Brains and Early Behavior,* ed. R. Robinson. New York/London: Academic Press.

Stern, D. (1974). Mother and infants at play. In *The Effect of the Infant on its Caretaker,* ed. M. Lewis and L. Rosenbaum. New York: John Wiley.

Winnicott, D. W. (1945). Primitive emotional development. In *Collected Papers.* New York: Basic Books, 1958.

Winnicott, D. W. (1949). Hate in the countertransference. In *Collected Papers.* New York: Basic Books, 1958.

Winnicott, D. W. (1954). The depressive position in normal emotional development. In *Collected Papers.* New York: Basic Books, 1958.

Winnicott, D. W. (1956). Primary maternal preoccupation. In *Collected Papers.* New York: Basic Books, 1958.

28

Why Early Intervention

T. Berry Brazelton, M.D.

We need more sophisticated methods for assessing neonates and for predicting their contribution to the likelihood of failure in the environment-infant interaction. The possibilities for synergism toward a failure in interaction between an infant who is not rewarding and an already stressed environment seem obvious. We also must be able to assess at-risk environments, for the impracticality of spreading resources too thinly points to the necessity of selecting target populations for our efforts at early intervention. With better techniques for assessing strengths and weakness in infants and the environment to which they will be exposed, we might come to understand better the mechanisms for failures in development. Even when desperate socioeconomic conditions produce comparable stresses, in many families children do not have to be salvaged from the clinical syndrome of child abuse, failure to thrive, and Kwashiorkor syndrome. Minimally brain-damaged babies do make remarkable compensatory recoveries in a fostering environment. Understanding the infant and the problems he will present to his parents may enhance our value as supportive figures for them as they adjust to a difficult child.

This paper was written while the author was partially funded by the Robert Wood Johnson Foundation, Carnegie Corporation, Saul C. and Amy S. Cohen Foundation, and National Institute of Mental Health.

The work reported here was done in close collaboration with Heideliese Als, Ph.D., Barry M. Lester, Ph.D, and Edward Tronick, Ph.D.

In other words, there appear to be at least two sources of vulnerability that contribute to the risk of failure in developmental outcome, the baby's own organizational system and capacity for growth—central nervous system and autonomic as well as physical—and the capacity of the environment (usually represented by the parents) to adjust to and nurture the at-risk infant in ways that are appropriate to individual needs. If the interaction between these two is positive, the opportunities are significantly increased for fueling feedback cycles necessary to the baby for developing energy for developmental progress.

Forces for Normal Development in the Infant

An understanding of the forces that work toward a child's development is critical to an understanding of the child's failure and toward any effort to prevent such failure. At least three forces are constantly at work (see figure 28–1.).

MATURATION OF THE CENTRAL AND AUTONOMIC NERVOUS SYSTEMS

Maturation of the central and the autonomic nervous systems, which regulate the baby's capacity to control reactions to incoming stimuli,

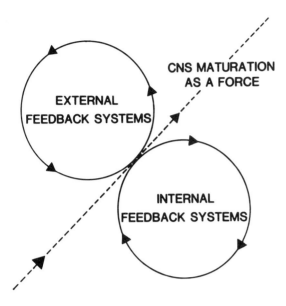

Figure 28-1   Three Sources of Energy for Development

is one of these forces. If infants are at the mercy of an overreaction of either a motor (Moro or startle) or autonomic reaction (as is seen in an overstressed pulmonary or cardiac system), they cannot learn to maintain attention or to react appropriately to a sensory stimulus or to other information necessary for development. The ability to pay attention is necessary to future learning. This force, when it is successful, will then press the baby forward to want to go on learning and adapting.

The developing nervous system constantly drives the infant on from one level of adjustment to another. This is an expensive and demanding system and needs to be fueled by the other two forces.

REALIZATION OF COMPETENCE IN THE BABY

A second force is that of the infant's competence, which is fostered by a feedback system relying upon the completion of a task that the infant has done. White (1959) called this a "sense of competence." The energy which has been mobilized to complete the task now fuels the realization of mastery and in turn reinforces the infant to press on to the next step in development. In hospitalized or institutionalized children who do not have the opportunity for completing new developmental tasks, one

sees the waning of this kind of inner excitement (Provence and Lipton, 1962).

REINFORCEMENT FROM THE ENVIRONMENT

The third force is the reinforcement from the environment that feeds the infant's affective and cognitive needs. The feedback cycles necessary for normal affective growth were pointed out by Spitz (1945), later by Harlow and Zimmerman in monkeys (1959), and conceptualized as "attachment" by Bowlby (1969). That this affective base is critical to cognitive and motor development was well documented in the institutionalized infants observed by Provence and Lipton (1962). We had not understood how critical this environmental nurturance was to all of the infant's development until the pathology was identified in environmentally deprived infants. The environmental forces can work powerfully to retard or to enhance the infant's progress. In our laboratory we are attempting to identify and conceptualize some of the ingredients of these interactive forces as they combine to fuel the child's recovery from severe deficits of prematurity, respiratory distress syndrome, and central nervous system dysfunction.

Developmental Model

As we began in the early 1950s to attempt to document and understand neonatal behavior, very powerful mechanisms appeared to dominate the neonate's behavior (Brazelton, 1961). In the tremendous physiological realignment demanded by the change-over from intrauterine to extrauterine existence, it has always amazed us that there is any room for individualized responses, for alerting and stimulus-seeking, or for behavior that indicates a kind of processing of information in the neonate, and yet there is. Despite the fact that the newborn's major job is that of achieving homeostasis in the face of enormous onslaughts from the environment, we can see evidence of affective and cognitive responses in the period after delivery.

This very capacity to reach out for, to respond to, and to organize toward a response to social or environmental cues seems so powerful at birth that one can see that even newborns are "programmed" to interact as they wade from sleep on their way to a disorganized crying state: to turn their head to one side to set off a tonic neck reflex, to adjust to this with a hand-to-mouth reflex and sucking on the fist. All of these can be called primitive reflex behaviors. But as soon as newborns have completed this series, they sigh, look around, and listen with real anticipation, as if to say, "This is what I'm really here for—to keep interfering motor activity under control so that I can look and listen and learn about my new world."

Our own model of infant behavior and of early infant learning goes like this: The infant is equipped with reflex behavioral responses which are established in rather primitive patterns at birth. These are soon arranged into more complex patterns of behavior that serve as goals for organization, at a time when the infant is still prone to a costly disorganization of neuromotor and physiological systems, and then for attention to and interaction with the world (Als et al, 1979). Thus, infants are set up to learn about themselves, for as they achieve each of these goals, their feedback systems say to them, "You've done it again! Now go on." In this way, each state of homeostatic control fuels the infant to go on to the next stage of disruption and reconstitution—a familiar model for energizing a developing system. We also believe that the infant's quest for social stimuli is in response to a need for fueling from the world outside. As infants achieve a homeostatic state, and reach out for a disruptive stimulus, the reward for each of these states of homeostasis and disruption is reinforced by social or external cues. Thus, they start out with the behaviorally identifiable mechanisms of a bimodal fueling system: (1) the attainment of a state of homeostasis and a sense of achievement from within; and (2) the energy or drive to reach out for and incorporate cues and reinforcing signals from the surrounding world which fuels from without. They are set up with behavioral pathways for providing both of these for themselves for adaption to their new world, even in the neonatal period. Since very

little fueling from within or without may be necessary to set these patterns and press the baby onward, they are quickly organized and reproduced over and over until they are efficient and incorporated and can be utilized as the base for building later patterns. Greenacre's (1959) concept of early pathways for handling the stress and trauma of birth and delivery as precursors for stress patterns later on fits such a model. It is as if patterns or pathways that work are "greased up" for more efficient use later on. Our own concept is that other patterns are available too, but that these are just readied by successful experience.

With this model of behavioral response systems, which provides an increased availability to the outside world, one can then incorporate Sanders's (1977) ideas of early entrainment of biobehavioral rhythms, Condon and Sander's (1974) propositions that the infant's movements match the rhythms of the adult's voice, Meltzoff and Moore's (1977) work on a kind of matching imitation of tongue protrusion in a three-week-old, and Bower's (1966) observations on early reach behavior to an attractive object in the first weeks of life. As each of these responsive behaviors to external stimuli fuels a feedback system within the baby toward a whole adult behavioral set—the baby becomes energized in such a powerful way that one can easily see the base for the entrainment. The matching of the infant's responses to those in the external world must feel so rewarding that whole sequential trains of behavioral displays in the environment quickly become available and the infant begins to entrain with them. Infants become energized to work toward inner controls and toward states of attention which maintain their availability to these external sequences. From the simpler form of attention to discrete stimuli, they are able to move toward prolonged periods of attention. In these periods, the prolonged attention is marked by sequential reactions to each stimulus. The sustained attention is modulated by brief but necessary periods of decreased attention. In this way, entrainment becomes a larger feedback system, which adds a regulating and encompassing dimension to the two feedback systems of internalized control and externalized stimulus-response. Hence entrainment

becomes an envelope within which one can
test and learn about both fueling systems.
Thus, infants can learn most about themselves
by making themselves available to entrainment by the surrounding world. This explains
the observable drive on the part of the neonate
to capture and interact with an adult interact-
ant—and the neonate's need for social interaction. Figures 28–2 and 28–3 show a schematic
presentation of this mutual fueling process
(Brazelton and Als, 1979).

Forces for Normal Development in the Parent

The parents' own genetic potential is influenced by past experiences, and these form
the most powerful base for their capacity to
nurture a new baby. When this base is intact,
as with healthy parents who themselves have
been well nurtured, one can expect them to
mobilize resources to adapt to the individual
baby. When, however, this base is stressed, for
example, in parents who are severely stressed,
the baby's individual needs may well be dominated by the parents' own needs and their own
past experience. In culturally deprived groups
or in those whose energy (physical and psychological) is limited by the demands of poverty and its concomitants—disorganization,
undernutrition, a sense of failure—it is no
wonder that we find limitations in ability to
adapt to the individual child, especially if that
child is not rewarding or has special needs. It
is not surprising, then, that one of the most
important marker variables of this process in
predicting the recovery of at-risk children—at
risk for all conditions physical and psychological—is socioeconomic status (Drillien, 1964;
Neligan et al., 1976).

What is surprising is the existence of energy
in most parents to adapt to a new baby, as well
as the ready availability of this energy. In order
to understand the forces for adaptation to a
new baby at delivery and in the immediate
perinatal period, we studied a group of
primiparous mothers and fathers in psychoanalytic interviews in the last months of

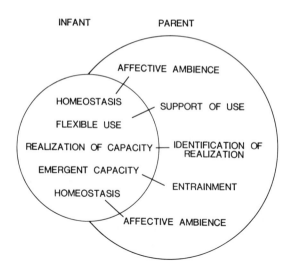

Figure 28–2 Infant-Parent Interaction
SOURCE: Brazelton, T. B. and Als, H. "Four
early stages in the development of mother-infant interaction," *The Psychoanalytic Study of the Child* 34 (1979): 349–69.

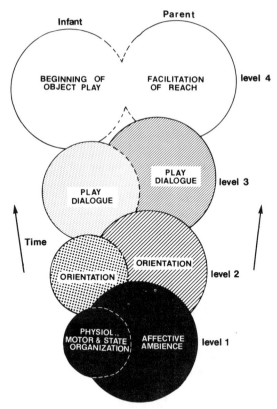

Figure 28–3 Stages of Organization in Parent-Infant Interaction
SOURCE: Brazelton, T. B. and Als, H. "Four
early stages in the development of mother-infant interaction," *The Psychoanalytic Study of the Child* 34 (1979): 349–69.

pregnancy at the Putnam Children's Center in the 1950s. We found that the prenatal interviews with normal primiparas uncovered anxiety that seemed to be of almost pathological proportions. The unconscious material was so confused, so anxious, and so near the surface that before delivery one felt an ominous foreboding about the woman's capacity to adjust to the role of mothering. Yet when we saw her in action in the postpartum month as a mother, this very anxiety and the distorted unconscious material seemed to become a force for reorganization, for readjustment to an important new role (Bibring et. al., 1961; Brazelton, 1963). I began to feel that much of the prenatal anxiety and distortion of fantasy was a healthy mechanism for bringing the mother out of the homeostasis she had achieved to a new level of adjustment. The "alarm reaction" we were tapping in on was serving as a kind of "shock" treatment for reorganization to her new role. I do certainly agree with Bowbly's concept of attachment and of the importance of providing opportunities for the mother to get to know her new infant early. I now see the shake-up in pregnancy as readying the circuits for new attachments; as preparation for the many choices she must be ready to make in a very short, highly sensitive critical period (Klaus and Kennell, 1970); as a method of freeing her circuits for a kind of sensitivity to the infant's individual requirements that might not have been easily or otherwise available from her earlier adjustment. Thus this very emotional turmoil of pregnancy and of the neonatal period can be seen as a positive force for the mother's healthy adjustment and for the possibility of providing a more individualizing, feasible environment for the infant (Bibring et al., 1961).

Prospective fathers must be going through a very similar kind of turmoil and readjustment. In an ideal situation we would be offering both parents much more support and fuel for their new roles than we do. So far, we in medicine have not done well in substituting for the extended family in this earliest period, but we are surely just on the brink of exercising our potential as supports for young parents. This energy is mobilized around the new infant. When the parents' needs are rewarded appropriately by responsiveness from the infants, the parents will develop in parallel with the infant. Because of the available energy disrupted from old pathways in pregnancy—anxiety, if you will—the new parents are as ready to learn about themselves as is the neonate. Just as they learn about each new stage in their development, find the appropriate control system, and experience the excitement of the baby's responsiveness, the father and the mother are forced to learn about themselves. As each new stage in the infant's development presses them to adjust, they learn about the excitement and the pain of disruption and, as they hit a plateau, about the gratification of homeostasis. In this way, we see mothers and fathers learning about themselves as developing people while they learn about their new baby. This is also the way in which the fueling for both nurturance and learning comes about at each new stage in the baby's development. Otherwise, nurturing a new infant would be too costly and too painful. In a reciprocal feedback system, the rewards are built in for the parents as well as for the infant. The pain can be seen as a preparation for detachment later on when that becomes necessary to the baby's developing autonomy.

Forces for Failure in the Interaction

The pressures on parents, both internal and external, to succeed with their infant can cause failure. We have been impressed with the power of violations of expectancy in the mother-father interaction when the feedback systems are not being completed in an expected way. The potential for withdrawal from each other and for ensuing failure in the interaction in caring people has been illustrated in our "still-face" experiment (Tronick et al, 1978) in which the mother violates the baby's expectation for interaction in a face-to-face play situation in our laboratory by remaining alert but unresponsive. She is instructed to follow a three-minute play period with a second three minutes in which she sits in front of the baby but remains unresponsive, staring at the baby with her face perfectly still. When the interactive system is violated by the parent's non-reciprocity, the infant responds in a predictable manner indicating the powerful effect of violating the baby's expectation for playful interactive responses in this situation.

Social interaction appears to be a rule-governed, goal-oriented system in which both partners actively share from the very beginning. The still face violates the rules of this system by conveying contradictory information simultaniously about one partner's goal or intent.

An infant's recognition of the mother's violation of reciprocity in the still-face condition begins very early. Along with Stechler and Latz (1966) and Carpenter (1974), we have seen evidence of it as early as two to three weeks. The pattern described is clearly established by four weeks and becomes increasingly complex. For instance, a three-month-old infant began reacting to the still face by showing the characteristic wary pattern of behavior. About a minute and a half into the interaction he looked at his mother and laughed briefly. After this brief tense laugh, he paused, looked at her soberly, and then laughed again, loud and long, throwing his head back as he did so. At this point, they would no longer have been able to engage in normal interactional behavior. The intentions and emotions of the older infant are similar to those of a younger infant, however, the richness and skill in reestablishing a reciprocal interaction are greater.

The strategies infants employ to bring the mother out of her immobility demonstrate a growing confidence in their effectiveness as social partners, and the seriousness of the infants' reaction when the mother remains unresponsive despite their efforts demonstrates how critical reciprocity is to them. The final withdrawing of the young infant who no longer seeks to pull the mother into the interaction reminds us of the withdrawn behavior and huddled postures of isolated monkeys (Harlow and Zimmerman, 1959) and of Bowlby's (1973) description of the withdrawn behavior of children separated from their caregivers.

The still-face mothers in our study remained unresponsive for only three minutes, yet their infants found even such a temporary violation greatly disturbing. Within fifteen seconds the babies had recognized the violation and had begun to try to master it. Their efforts included several programs aimed at eliciting her usual responses, suggesting that reciprocity and mutual achievement of the goals of social interaction form a necessary basis for the growth of affective well-being in early infancy.

The ability of the baby to precipitate and encourage the mother's attachment and caregiving behavior must be taken into account from the newborn period (Brazelton, 1961). With an unresponsive neonate, the feedback mechanisms necessary to fuel mothering behavior are severely impaired. In a series of medicated newborns of normal mother-infant pairs, the effect on neonatal sucking, coupled with the physiological effect of the medication on the mother's milk production, delayed recovery of weight gain by thirty-six to forty-eight hours in a normal group (Brazelton, 1961). Because this is an observation at a rather gross level, interferences in the interaction dyssynchrony and more subtle lack of fit in the earliest mother-infant attachment interaction should be carefully sought and observed over time.

The vulnerability of the parent to even mildly distorted cues from the infant can best be understood as "grief reaction" in the parent (adapted from Lindemann, 1944). Because of the heightened expectations at birth, the opportunity for grieving is enhanced by any minor violation of this expectancy. The very energy that has been mobilized to relate to a baby can turn inward into grieving in such cases.

The forces for grieving, as described by Lindemann (1944) in his studies of adults who experienced an unexpected loss of a beloved one at the time of the Cocoanut Grove fire, were those of overwhelming despair, self-incrimination, and guilt. Expected mechanisms were those of feeling guilty at not having "cared enough." The self-incrimination and depression were so intolerable that defenses were set up to preserve the adult survivor's emotional integrity. Expected defenses were denial, projection of guilt onto others, and detachment from the loved ones. The feelings and the defenses against them can be seen in all parents of a damaged or sick infant. Denial is used to handle the violations of expectation in behavior or in responsiveness. The mother denies that these matter, thereby covering up for herself and for others how deeply affected she really is by the inadequate responses she is receiving. Projection is also a common mechanism. The mother projects onto those around her the inadequacy she feels about having produced such a baby and about her inability to care for the baby properly. By projecting these feelings onto others, she can tolerate them better in herself. But this very projection makes her less available for interaction with a helping person. Detachment is understandable in that the caring mother, who feels she has already damaged the infant, feels also that if she were out of the way or detached the infant might be less at risk. This serves to make her less available to the infant.

If the parents' resources are turned inward in the grieving process, they become encapsulated and the defenses strengthened to turn the available energy away from the baby. In the period of acute grieving, this self-protective mechanism may be necessary. When the reorganization of the parents' ego has been accomplished, this energy can be made available to the baby and toward the baby's recovery (Greenberg, 1979). It has constantly surprised us that, even in the face of a devastating diagnosis of retardation in the baby, a parent can have the energy available to search for and work with the baby's more hopeful, positive behavior. With this as a base, parents of babies with Down's syndrome work to achieve an interactive alert state in the baby, and, within this state, they can teach the afflicted infant to achieve remarkable developmental steps. Unless they can be captured to turn their grieving around, to turn its energy outward in the service of the child's best recovery, it is probable that these parents can remain permanently withdrawn and unavailable to an at-risk child. The job of intervention is to accept the negative forces of grieving, but to work to free positive forces for interaction with the child as well. This work can best be done early and by utilizing the best behavior in the child as a demonstration to capture hope and reciprocity in the parents.

The danger of fixation in these defenses and of the parent's developing insensitive, inappropriate patterns in dealing with the infant at risk makes it critical that we be ready to intervene early in their development together. Time is of the essence. The emotional availability and flexibility of parents of normal infants can be seen as a sign for capturing this availability to the less-than-expectably normal infant as soon as possible. Before fixation can occur, we must be ready to capture and reinforce for the parents the positives in the infant's behavior, and we must be ready to set up a working relationship to help them to work around their predictable grief at the violations in expectation. This energy becomes a force for the baby's recovery—not only as it fuels the parent but as it serves as an external source of energy for the infant.

Anyone interested in intervention must understand the process of and defenses against grief in parents as well as those of attachment. He or she must also understand the processes of behavioral reactions, their violation, and the potential for recovery in the baby. This is a large order.

We have been struck with the power our own behavior has to energize and teach parents. Because the parents care so much and the energy of caring makes them available to the baby, they can watch us produce the baby's best performance and can use our efforts as a model to produce this performance themselves. As they produce an optimal performance, the internal feedback systems in the baby couple with and are reinforced by delighted responses in the parents. These two systems (internal and external) signal and reinforce the achievement again and again. The experience of completing such a curcular process might act as an organizer for the central nervous system, and real recovery from deficits becomes more likely.

Since the examination is a dynamic one and is clearly based on the baby's potential for organization with nurturing interaction, the skills and sensitivity of the examiner are critical for bringing the baby to an optimal performance. The amount of effort required from the adult to produce organization and reactivity may be an important gauge of the infant's developmental status. Of course, examiners must be trained to a reliable level of awareness of the neonate's potential for organization and performance, and the examiners' performance and scoring must be uniform or the data collected will not be of value, and the insight into the neonate's capacity for interaction with the environment will suffer as well.

Our experience in demonstrating the behavior of the high-risk premature infant as we perform the behavioral assessment in the presence of the parents shows that they watch carefully as we work with their infants. Our efforts to contain the infants, to adapt stimuli to them, to elicit responses that do not exhaust them are not overlooked. The parents observe in complete silence, ask us questions afterward, and often even make their own correct observations, such as, "I never knew he could see and would follow your face, but he can," "She gets exhausted if you do too much," "I see that you need to contain him so he won't get too excited," "You make your voice soft and insistent to get her to turn to you." All these observations have come from uninstructed parents, who then reproduce our techniques with their fragile babies to elicit attention and to teach them how to maintain their own inner controls. Over time, they not only identify with us as we work with the baby to produce optimal performance, but they begin to tell us how the baby functions best. In other words, in the face of an expectable reaction to their fragility and even in the case of identified damage to the central nervous system, parents have been able to lock onto the two aspects of these high-risk babies' behavior with which they can work: (1) helping the fragile baby maintain physiological control in order to produce alert behavioral responses; and (2) the attentional responses themselves, which are often difficult to elicit but so rewarding for the parents. The fragile infant's long latency to response, alternating high or low threshold for receiving stimuli, and tendency to overshoot with an unexpectedly total response or to overload from the cost of such a response—all of these make such infants difficult to work with. When they do respond, they often violate a parent's expectancy. In other words, behavioral responses are so extranormal that they set up the ingredients for a failure in their interaction, both because of the cost of responses and because of the grief reaction in the parent, which is likely to be engendered by the unexpectedly deviant response. But the parent can begin to understand these responses by observing us. And we have come to realize that the most powerful therapy for grieving parents is to set them to work in an appropriately sensitive way with such an infant. As they see their infants learn about their own inner organization, learn to control overreactions; as they see them coming to accept and respond to their social stimuli, geared especially to them, they can begin to find techniques for stimulation and for helping the children toward recovery that we have not thought of ourselves.

The energy for plasticity for recovery comes from two sources: (1) from within, as the baby learns to achieve control and maintain an alert state, providing an inner feedback cycle of completing an attentional or motor task which gives a "sense of competence"; and (2) from without, as the parents get to know their infant, to understand the infant's need for containment and homeostasis, as well as for social and motor stimuli which are appropriately and individually geared to the infant's capacity to utilize them (Als et. al., 1979). Of course, this kind of fueling is most appropriate to early infancy and to the early parent-infant interaction. Whether it serves a comparable purpose in older children remains to be tested.

REFERENCES

Als, H., Lester, B. M., and Brazelton, T. B. (1979). Dynamics of the behavioral organization of the premature infant. In *Infants Born at Risk,* ed. T. M. Field, A. M. Sos-

tek, S. Goldberg, and H. H. Shuman. New York: Spectrum.

Bibring, G. L., Dwyer, T. F., and Valenstein, A. F.

(1961). A study of the psychological process in pregnancy and of the earliest mother-child relationship. *The Psychoanalytic Study of the Child,* 16:9–72. New York: International Universities Press.

Bower, T. G. R. (1966). Visual world of infants. *Scientific American,* 215:80–92.

Bowlby, J. (1969). *Attachment and Loss,* vol I: *Attachment.* New York: Basic Books.

Bowlby, J. (1973). *Attachment and Loss,* vol II: *Separation.* New York: Basic Books.

Brazelton, T. B. (1961). Psychophysiological reactions in the neonate, 1: The value of observation of the newborn. *Journal of Pediatrics,* 58:508–516.

Brazelton, T. B. (1963). The early mother-infant adjustment. *Pediatrics,* 32:931–937.

Brazelton, T. B. and Als, H. (1979). Four early stages in the development of mother-infant interaction. *The Psychoanalytic Study of the Child,* 34:349–369. New Haven: Yale University Press.

Carpenter, G. C. (1974). Visual regard of moving and stationary faces in early infancy. *Merrill-Palmer Quarterly,* 20:181–195.

Condon, W. S. and Sander, L. W. (1974). Neonate movement is synchronized with adult speech. *Science,* 183: 99–101.

Drillien, C. M. (1964). *The Growth and Development of the Prematurely Born Infant.* Baltimore: Williams & Wilkins.

Greenacre, P. (1959). On focal symbiosis. In *Dynamic Psychopathology in Children,* ed. L. Jessner and E. Pavenstedt. New York: Grune & Stratton.

Greenberg, D. (1979). *Parental Reactions to an Infant with a Birth Defect.* Doctoral dissertation, Smith College, School of Social Work.

Harlow, H. F., and Zimmerman, R. R. (1959). Affectual responses in infant monkeys. *Science,* 130:421–432.

Klaus, M. H. and Kennell, J. H. (1970). Mothers separated from their newborn infants. *Pediatric Clinics of North America,* 17:1015–1030.

Lindeman, E. (1944). Grief. *American Journal of Psychiatry,* 101:141–149.

Meltzoff, A. N. and Moore, M. D. (1977). Imitation of facial and manual gestures by human neonates. *Science,* 198:75–78.

Neligan, G. A., Kolvin, I., Scott, D., and Garside, R. F. (1976). Born too soon or born too small. *Spastics International Medical Publications.* London: William Heinemann.

Provence, S. T. and Lipton, R. C. (1962). *Infants in Institutions.* New York: International Universities Press.

Sander, L. W. (1977). The regulation of exchange in the infant-caregiver system and some aspects of the context-content relationship. In *Interaction, Conversation, and the Development of Language,* ed. M. Lewis and L. A. Rosenblum. New York: John Wiley.

Spitz, R. (1945). Hospitalism. *The Psychoanalytic Study of the Child,* 1:53–74. New York: International Universities Press.

Stechler, G. and Latz, M. A. (1966). Some observations on attention and arousal in the human neonate. *American Academy of Child Psychiatry,* 5:517–525.

Tronick, E. et al. (1978). The infants' responses to entrapment between contradictory messages in face-to-face interaction. *Journal of the American Academy of Child Psychiatry,* 17:1–13.

White, R. W. (1959). Motivation reconsidered: The concept of competence. *Psychological Review,* 66:297–333.

29

The Evolution of Parent-Infant Attachment: New Psychobiological Perspectives

Hanuš Papoušek, M.D., Sc.D., and Mechthild Papoušek, M.D.

A recurring theme in infant psychiatry has been the elucidation of the role of mother-infant attachment in human development. Although extensively researched, our knowledge of the role of mother-infant attachment shows broad gaps and has generated increasing theoretical controversy, as is evident in contemporary discussions of this concept.

In an attempt to narrow these gaps with the help of a cross-disciplinary approach, we want to review some psychobiological aspects of mother-infant attachment. When looking at psychological phenomena a psychobiologist also tries to consider their evolutionary past, adaptive meaning, and biological roots, as these may be seen in paleontological or comparative analogies of the observed phenomena.

The psychobiological view is not new in the research on mother-infant attachment. Bowlby (1969) attempted to elucidate the evolution of mother-infant attachment in his pioneering book. However, the increase in available evidence since the late 1960s has brought about new conceptual impulses. What

The following foundations have kindly supported our research: Die Deutsche Forschungsgemeinschaft, and Die Stiftung Volkswagenwerk. We owe special thanks to April Benasich of New York University for her valuable comments and editorial help.

used to be a realm of speculative interpretations has become accessible to exact documentation. Hypotheses can now be experimentally verified. Superficial views and vaguely defined terms have gradually been replaced with detailed microanalytic approaches and a differentiated terminology. Thus, no matter how far we may be from the full truth, there are good reasons for a critical look at some fundamental aspects of mother-infant attachment.

The Specificity of Human Evolution

One way of approaching the fundamental phenomena of human evolution is to raise the question of similarities and dissimilarities between man and other animals—that is, the question of specificity—and to study the ways in which evolution might have favored the emergence of features specific to humans. *Consensus omnium* on the species-specific importance of thought, language, and culture in human evolution has not essentially changed in the last few decades. The human capacity to symbolize the real world in words enormously improved man's chance to profit from a cultural heritage, to communicate across distances and cultural, if not planetary, borders, to integrate the past experience of many generations, and to develop concepts and make predictions beyond the limits of concrete experience. However, the explanation of factors determining these complex capacities has changed in a way relevant to the question of mother-infant attachment.

Until the early 1970s, the most commonly cited interpretation of the divergence in hominids was the belief initiated by Darwin (1871) that tool use and material culture had played the pivotal role in the evolution of both bipedality and a large neocortex. The earliest recognized tools are about two million years old. The marked expansion of the hominid cerebral cortex took place during the last two or three million years. If tools were the primary determinant, then only two million years were required for bringing about the modern industrial revolution. According to recent findings accumulated in the 1970s, however, the phyletic origin of hominids can be placed in the middle to late Miocene, twelve to six million years ago, and a complete morphological adaptation to bipedality to the period of Australopithecus afarensis, four million years ago.

Lovejoy (1981) concludes a detailed analysis of recent paleontological findings with a suggestion of another interpretation of human evolution. Bipedality, an unusual and disadvantageous nonsaltatory form of walking, originally resulted from a mere variation in the genetic reproduction, according to Lovejoy, but was adopted due to advantages related to the demographic strategy, that is, to the reproductive rate, birth spacing, and longevity, on one hand, and to monogamic tendencies, strong social bonds, longer period of infant dependency, and intense parenting, on the other. Lovejoy's interpretation of human evolution has thus brought the evolutionary roots of parent-infant interactions into the focus of theoretical attention. An excursion to modern paleontology has suddenly become particularly exciting to all students of parenting and child development. Even if it may be too early to predict the outcome of the confrontation between the theories of tool use and of demographic propagation, Lovejoy's arguments cannot be disregarded.

One argument points out that birth spacing is shorter in man (two to four years) than in other primates (five to seven years in chimpanzees), if seen in relation to longevity, and that this difference increased the demographic propagation in hominids. Whereas the great apes have occupied only minor areas with minimal environmental change, hominids were capable of expanding into novel and varied habitats. The continuous sexual receptiveness of hominid females, the absence of an externally recognizable estrous cycle, and an equally stable male approach might have caused little or no synchronization of copulation with ovulation and the unparalleled (among primates) necessity to care for two or more dependent offspring simultaneously. Bipedality would prove advantageous from this point of view, while the disadvantage in slower locomotion would call for the selection of other forms of protection against predators, such as closer social bonding or advanced social organization and communication.

Lovejoy considers the interrelation between reproductive competence and social structures a contribution to further divergence in hominids from pongids. For example, the shift from external signs of estrous cycle to more variable epigamic features and to sexual uniqueness seems to be related to pair bonding and to the direct involvement of males in the survivorship of offspring. Put another way, during Miocene, the changing environmental conditions pushed the hominoid males toward intense participation in parenting and favored the selection of monogamous mating structures. Consequently, this led to the gradual replacement of the matrifocal group by a bifocal group, including paternity next to maternity.

Such an interpretation of human evolution provides a very different base for the concept of parent-infant bonding from the theoretical climate influencing the concept of mother-infant attachment in the 1960s. The current level of knowledge helps correct the one-sided overestimation of matrifocal bonding which is otherwise typical for some monkeys or, for instance, for chimpanzees. An orphaned chimpanzee must be around five years old in order to survive the loss of its mother. A bifocal distribution of parenting and the survival of a second parent may have been a crucial reproductive advantage in early hominids. As Lovejoy points out, monogamy can be found only among those primates in which the male is clearly and directly involved in the parenting process, for instance, in gibbons or siamangs.

These arguments remind us of the risk connected with using animals as models for interpretating human behavior. Bowlby's concept of human mother-infant attachment was doubtless very much influenced by Harlow's (1961) pioneering studies of social development and maternal deprivation in rhesus monkeys. However, although the specific consequences of maternal deprivation in rhesus monkeys is compelling, extrapolation of a general model of maternal deprivation to human affectional attachment is not necessarily justified. Comparative animal research offers a variety of models of deprivation among primates with other outcomes (Kaufman, 1982) and even a greater variety of models of the distribution of parenting between maternal and paternal partners (Ridley, 1978).

Considering the continuous sexual receptiveness and the missing synchronization between copulation and estrous cycle, one may ask what regulated birth spacing in the human past so that a new pregnancy did not interfere with nursing as long as the youngest infant depended on maternal milk. Here, modern cross-cultural anthropology helps us fill the gaps in paleontological evidence. Konner (1982) studied the factors of birth spacing in the !Kung San hunters-gatherers of the Kalahari Desert in Botswaana. His reports throw light on another important aspect that may have influenced the selection of mother-infant bonding, in addition to the protection against predators. The birth spacing in the !Kung San population is around forty-four months in spite of nonabstinent and noncontraceptive modes of sexual life. A mild seasonal caloric undernutrition alone cannot explain the delay of the next pregnancy.

Another factor considered by Konner was the unusual temporal pattern of nursing. Unlike the Western populations, the !Kung San mothers nurse children up to two or three years and, during the first two years, so many times a day that the average intervals are shorter than fifteen minutes. Because in human

females the hormone prolactin is promptly secreted in response to nipple stimulation and suppresses gonadal functions, the higher frequency of nursing may contribute to the control of fertility. The half-time of prolactin in plasma is around thirty minutes. Longer intervals in nursing therefore cannot help to suppress ovarian function. Only late in the second year of age do !Kung San children occasionally separate from mothers for a longer period of time during play. The level of prolactin can then fall so that its suppressive effects are decreased and ovarian cycling can be reinstated. Persisting irregularity in the ovarian cycle with additional suppressive effects, such as a seasonal undernutrition, may lengthen the birth interval to more than three years. Interestingly, the !Kung San women experience their suckling patterns as physically very pleasant.

Thus from a biological perspective, Bowlby's (1969) concept of maternal bonding as a mechanism for the protection of progeny against predators appears to be too narrow. Lovejoy's arguments suggest that shared participation by both parents in the care for progeny had already evolved in hominids. Konner's arguments clearly indicate that more selective pressures might have played important roles in the evolution of maternal bonding than merely the protection against predators. Consequently, birth spacing and demographic propagation should be regarded as additional factors closely interrelated with the evolution of maternal bonding.

To see the biological factors in human evolution as independent of the cultural ones would of course be as false as to believe that culture alone may have dictated the direction of human development in the past or in the present. We can hardly imagine that culture may have emerged independently of biological selection pressures or could neglect them without dangerous consequences. If man's capacity for symbolization and effective sharing of experience may have been interrelated with biological determinants during evolution, then this capacity has probably unfolded together with the development of cultural institutions which have extended the possibilities for integration of experience beyond the limits of individual territory and life span.

Parent-Infant Bonding and Intellectual Development

One of the main assumptions for the successful survival of the primate species is its capacity to reduce losses caused by environmental interaction—deaths caused by predation, accidents, hunger, infection, or parasitism. Strong social bonds, high intelligence, intense parenting, and long periods of learning may allow primates to fulfill this assumption. In this context, parent-infant bonding has been considered as interacting with the expansion of the neocortex in hominids (Lovejoy, 1981). Paleontology offers clear physical evidence for the enlarged cranium; however, fossil relics cannot tell us enough about the forms of parent-infant interactions that may have contributed to the intellectual growth of progeny.

A potential relationship between parent-infant bonding and the selection of intellectual capacities during evolution was not considered in former concepts on mother-infant attachment. In fact, in comparative animal research in general, parental care for the progeny's development of learning and cognitive capacities has not yet gained sufficient attention. It may therefore be helpful to devote a few paragraphs to this question.

For successful sharing of experience, the infant must be at least capable of processing parental information by means of some fundamental learning and cognitive operations. The parent can facilitate the infant's information processing by adjusting the mode, amount, and timing of information to the infant's actual state of integrative capacities. Both the parent and the infant must be able to use some means of communication, not necessarily verbal or subjected to conscious awareness.

These assumptions for experience-sharing can be favored in various ways during evolution. Integrative processes can be selected for as operators dominating behavioral regulation. The dominant role of integrative processes can be expressed in their earlier ontogenetic development, in a universal distribution within a given species, and in close ties to intrinsic rewarding mechanisms. Such a selection would then lead to the emergence of parents motivated not only culturally but also biologically for a didactic contribution to the infant's intellectual development. For the same reasons, the infant would be effectively motivated for successful learning from didactic interactions with the parent. Altogether, these arguments would provide a very meaningful interpretation of another aspect of parent-infant bonding, the importance of which need not be stressed to infancy psychiatrists.

Verification of these arguments in comparative studies is still insufficient in animals, perhaps due to a lack of evidence or, more probably, to a lack of attention paid to this aspect in theoretical concepts. The vast literature on various parental behaviors involved in nest-building, territory-defense, brooding, or prosocial care for progeny shows, among other things, that reproducing partners share parenting in manifold ways (Ridley, 1978) including complete role reversal. For instance, in Jacanidae, the female may defend a harem of males; among emus, the male may accumulate and incubate eggs from several females and exclusively care for the young; or among Osteoglossidae, the male fish alone may carry out mouth-brooding of eggs. In laboratory animals, systematic analyses of the regulations of maternal behavior were carried out by Rosenblatt (1975) in rats and elucidated the alternating roles of endocrine and psychological factors.

The richness of literature on these aspects of parenting contrasts with the paucity of studies concerning both the early ontogeny of integrative capacities and the parental didactic contribution. The present evidence merely confirms simple forms of conditioning in the young of some species and includes anecdotal material on parental teaching. Primates seem to show minimal inventiveness in teaching activities and no particular pleasure with the young's cognitive progress. Lawick-Goodall (1967), for instance, described situations in which young chimpanzees were obviously learning skills observed in parents, but parents merely tolerated the inquisitiveness of the young without any signs of didactic motivation.

With regard to parental didactic care for infants, the psychobiological progress has been nourished more by students of human behavior than by students of animal behavior. In our address to the International Ethological Conference (1977), we attempted to draw attention to this discrepancy.

According to our own evidence, human infants may well be receivers of didactic messages from the first postpartum days, if not prenatally. Having introduced the experimental method of head-turning in the studies of early integrative capacities (Papoušek, 1960) we found a tool for modeling learning situations and problem-solving situations as well as for analyses of spontaneous intentional acts (for a review see Papoušek, 1977). In those experimental models, instrumental learning was demonstrated during the first week of life and more complex capacities of discriminatory learning, detection, acquisition of rules, and concept formation, including numeric concepts, during the first three or four months. It also became obvious that successful learning and problem-solving was accompanied with affectionate signs of pleasure and that some form of intrinsic motivation resulting from successful integrative operations outweighed the effects of extrinsic rewards. Thus, capacities necessary for perceiving and processing information clearly play a fundamental role in the infant's behavioral regulation (Papoušek and Papoušek, 1979) and function in the newborn. Moreover, Solkoff and Cotton (1975) demonstrated operant head-turning in prematurely born infants at the postconceptual age of thirty-one weeks.

Only since operant learning in head movements was reported in one-day-old rat pups by Johanson and Hall (1979) could it be concluded that the very beginning of learning is not a species-specific feature in human infants. In the last decade of research on human infancy, a proliferating number of studies using sophisticated techniques has confirmed early functioning of cognitive operations, including categoric perception, equivalence classification, and prototypicality, as exemplified in Bornstein's studies (1981). However, this research has not been paralleled in animal infancy; consequently, the question of human specificity remains unanswered in this area.

In our later studies, we spent much time observing human infants in their naturalistic settings and looking for learning situations in which the further development of integrative capacities could be supported in everyday life. The physical environment does not offer a meaningful number of learning situations unless mediated or modified by the caregiver in response to the infant's sign of attention. However, the caregiver's interaction with the infant appears to consist of numerous episodes convincingly interpretable as learning situations.

The adaptive significance of infant learning may be questioned with respect to the existence of infantile amnesia. It is not yet sufficiently known to what degree human infants retain and benefit from early processing of environmental information. However, even if they may lose most of the data-based (declarative) information, they still may profit from the rule-based (procedural) information. Put another way, infants not only learn "that," they also learn "how." In one of our studies (Papoušek, 1977), the infant's ability to "learn how to learn" was significantly differentiated from age-dependent improvement in learning. Clinical studies of amnesia in adults showed, for instance, that in Korsakoff's syndrome, amnesia concerns only declarative data but leaves procedural information intact (Cohen and Squire, 1980).

Those who have deliberately tried to teach human infants something, perhaps for experimental purposes, will certainly agree that it is a very intricate task. In addition to communicative difficulties, we must be lucky enough to find the infant in an adequate general behavioral state, we must select an appropriate form of stimulation and repeat it usually many times while keeping the infant's attention on the necessary level. Instructions in this area are a rare find, not only in historical documents of human civilization but even in the contemporary scientific literature.

In our current studies, we have invested much effort in microanalyses of behaviors included in parent-infant interactions, and we have seen that parents cope with the intricate didactic tasks without difficulties but also without much conscious awareness (Papoušek and Papoušek, 1982, in press). The fact that meaningful didactic care for early intellectual development can be carried out unknowingly seems to us to suggest that this care has psychobiological rather than cultural roots and to serve as evidence regarding the probable course of its evolution, otherwise so difficult to detect in paleontology.

We can here only amplify the growing list of behavioral components involved in didactic interchanges with a few examples of microanalytic approaches, on one hand, and evolutionary relevance, on the other. Our instances will concern, first, the behaviors utilized to evaluate and to optimize the infant's behavioral states, and second, some particular modifications in the parent's vocal communication with the infant.

The classification of the general behavioral states in young infants is neither an easy methodological task nor a part of investigation regularly included in infancy studies (for a review see Prechtl and O'Brien, 1982). To students of infant development, behavioral state is one of the determinants of the infant's success in learning (Papoušek, 1977); to parents, it seems to be a determinant for many everyday practical decisions whether to entertain, feed, soothe, or lullaby the infant. We were struck by the frequency of behaviors interpretable as tests of muscle tone in situations where parents had to make such decisions, evidenced in the content of their babytalk. Comparing audiotaped parental babytalk with its situational context recorded on videotapes or films, we most often found parental attempts to open the infant's mouth or fists. We also found that these attempts could elicit distinguishable types of responses related to the infant's behavioral state. Moreover, we realized that the position and movements of hands alone could serve the parent as observable visual cues for interpreting the infant's general state.

In order to verify the hypothesis that parents process and adequately answer the cue signals observable in the infant's hands, we drew pictures of babies in which only two variables were modified in congruent or incongruent manners: the state of eyes (open or closed) and the state of hands (at mouth; firmly closed fists; half-stretched hands and fingers; dropping hands and fingers; position as in quiet sleep).

G. Kestermann (1982) tested schoolgirls and adults—both females and males—with different degrees of experience in parenting. She asked her subjects to respond nonverbally with one of four prearranged practical interventions (offering a milk bottle; offering a toy; turning off the light; signaling inability to decide) and measured latencies and qualities of such interventions. Kestermann concluded that parental responses were clearly differentiated according to selected cue signals and effected more by hand-cues than by eye-cues in incongruent pictures. The latency time of parental responses, as measured by Kestermann, significantly correlated with the degree of parental experience. No substantial differences were found between mothers and fathers so long as both were experienced in caring for infants.

In similar studies, we usually interview parents at the end of observations and frequently find interesting discrepancies in their rationales. For instance, parents may try hard to facilitate a visual contact and yet believe that newborns cannot see anything. Or else, they clearly respond to isolated hand-cues but believe that they saw a change of mood in the facial expression. Conversely, it may be very difficult for them to control their behaviors and not to answer a given cue with a specific response, if asked by the experimenter not to do so.

The same also holds true for the use of so-called babytalk or motherese in persons addressing infants. This specific modification of speech can often be used even by persons believing that babies should always hear only a correct form of adult speech in order to learn it from the very beginning. As another example of intuitive parenting, babytalk certainly deserves full attention. Its characteristic features are: (1) a higher average fundamental frequency (F_0) than that of narrative speech;[1] (2) a simple structure and syntax with frequent repetitions of utterances; (3) a slower rhythm with prolongated intersegmental pauses; and (4) strikingly pronounced melodic contours of

---

[1]Notice that "fundamental frequency" is a physics term. F_0 identifies pitch whereas additional frequencies F_1, $_2$, $_3$, and so forth give a tone "color" identifying an instrument, a voice, and the like. All are measured in Hz.

the so-called prosodic envelopes distinguishing fundamental categories of messages, such as questions, simple statements, alarm signals, or soothing.

These features of babytalk appear to be very meaningful if we realize that, to the infant, to acquire the language of the social environment is something very different from learning another language, since the infant is still naïve in any form of communication. Prior to teaching infants how to produce individual phonemes, syllables, or words, it may be very useful to help them to learn when a person is addressing them, to distinguish an invitation to a dialogue from a warning, to understand the basic rules of a dialogue, and to be motivated for vocal communication in general. Perhaps for the particular sake of this script, the caregiver unknowingly chooses a different pitch for an infant from the pitch used for adults, modifies the temporal and syntactic structures in the mentioned ways, and affectionately rewards the infant for every attempt to enter a dialogue and for every bit of progress in the emerging vocal communication.

A microanalysis of vocal interchanges between parents and young infants reveals an unpredicted differentiation of vocal sounds as early as two to three months, mutual imitations on both sides, and the first communicative functions in early prosodic contours (Papoušek and Papoušek, 1981). Further development leads not only to new phonetic skills but also to play with musical elements. Thus, numerous situations become manifest in which the parent makes herself or himself familiar, understandable, predictable, and contingent on the infant's behavior, whereas the little partner joyfully exercises predictions, concept formation, imitation, or playful modification. These sorts of interchanges may be very important for integrative growth and therefore should not be overlooked.

How much evidence do we have that similar forms of parent-infant interactions contribute to the infant's psychological development? There are no easy ways to study this question, which makes us appreciate the careful comparisons of singletons and twins in Bornstein and Ruddy's study (1983) which included naturalistic observations in homes. Both populations were first investigated at the age of four months. No difference was found in measures of information processing in infants, such as rate and amount of habituation, or in recognition memory. However, mothers of singletons encouraged attention to environmental objects, properties, and events more than twice as often as mothers of twins. Obviously, twins get much less didactic contribution in a dyadic form than singletons. Another investigation of these subjects at the age of twelve months revealed a much poorer verbal vocabulary in twins and a poorer performance on many items of the Bayley Scales of Infant Development. This finding supports the assumption that parental didactic tendencies play an important role in the infant's integrative development.

In the same vein, of course, the interpretative relevance of these interactional aspects to the evolution of parent-infant bonding should be considered. That babytalk in particular is universally distributed across cultures and that it is already developed around three years of age indicate that the interrelation between parent-infant bonding and the evolution of high symbolic and communicative capacities might have played a leading part in the selection of human behaviors. Hypothetically, we can construct exciting concepts on this premise; however, the inherent limits of the new approach cannot promise early verification of such concepts.

For instance, cross-cultural studies on the distribution of individual components included in intuitive parenting would contribute enormously to a better understanding of the evolution of specific human capacities. But only the close cooperation of new teams would make such studies possible in the future. We ourselves have not been able to schedule expeditions to other cultures. Only good luck helped us gain access to materials otherwise difficult to find. The Bavarian television wanted to prepare a series of films on the psychological development of infants and accepted our recommendation to do so in a cross-cultural comparative mode. They sent a team, naïve as to the problems of intuitive parenting but very skilled in collecting samples of interactions between infants and caregivers. The infants ranged in age from newborns to twelve-month-olds, and the caregivers included both parents, siblings, other peers, and strangers. This team brought back films on Mexican Indians (weavers, potters, and Lacandones), black families in New York and Senegal, nomadic Bedouins in the Sinai, white families in Sweden, Germany, Italy, Poland, and Israel, Hindu and Chinese families in Malaysia, and inhabitants of Bali. Access to this material, which is going to be distributed internationally, made it evident to us that both the universality of some interactional phenomena and cultural differences in others may enrich our knowledge and decisively influence future interpretations of parent-infant bonding.

In conclusion, we want to emphasize that there is proliferation of new approaches to what used to be studied as mother-infant attachment.

REFERENCES

Bornstein, M. H. (1981). Two kinds of perceptual organization near the beginning of life. In *Aspects of the Development of Competence,* ed. W. A. Collins. Hillsdale, New Jersey: Lawrence Erlbaum Associates, pp. 39–91.

Bornstein, M. H. and Ruddy, M. G. (1983). Infant attention and maternal stimulation: Prediction of cognitive and linguistic development in singletons and twins. In *Attention and Performance,* vol. X, ed. H. Bouma and D.G. Bouwhuis. London: Lawrence Erlbaum Associates.

Bowlby, J. (1969). *Attachment and Loss,* vol. 1, *Attachment.* New York: Basic Books.

Cohen, N. J. and Squire, L. R. (1980). Preserved learning and retention of pattern-analyzing skills in amnesia: Dissociation of knowing how and knowing that. *Science,* 210: 207–210.

Darwin, C. (1871). *The Descent of Man.* London: John Murray, 1898.

Harlow, H. F. (1961). The development of affectional patterns in infant monkeys. In *Determinants of Infant Behaviour,* ed. B. M. Foss. London: Methuen.

Johanson, I. B. and Hall, W. G. (1979). Appetitive learning in one-day-old rat pups. *Science,* 205:419–421.

Kaufman, I. C. (1982). Animal models in developmental psychobiology. In *The Development of Attachment and Affiliative Systems,* ed. R. N. Emde and R. J. Harmon. New York: Plenum.

Kestermann, G. (1982). Gestik von Säuglingen: Ihre kommunikative Dedeutung für erfahrene und unerfahrene Bezugspersonen (Doctoral dissertation, the University of Bielefeld, Department of Biology, unpublished).

Konner, M. (1982). Biological aspects of the mother-infant bond. In *The Development of Attachment and Affiliative Systems,* ed. R. N. Emde and R. J. Harmon. New York: Plenum.

Lawick-Goodall, J. van (1967). *My Friends the Wild Chimpanzees.* Washington, D. C.: National Geographic Society.

Lovejoy, C. O. (1981). The origin of man. *Science,* 211: 341–350.

Papoušek, H. (1960). Conditioned motor alimentary reflexes in infants, II. A new experimental method of investigation, *Československá Pediatrie,* 15:981–988 (in Czech).

Papoušek, H. (1977). Entwicklung der Lernfähigkeit im Säuglingsalter, In *Intelligenz, Lernen und Lernstörungen,* ed. G. Nissen. Berlin/ New York: Springer Verlag.

Papoušek, H. and Papoušek, M. (1977). Biological Aspects of Early Social and Cognitive Development in Man. The 15th International Ethological Conference in Bielefeld, August 23–31.

Papoušek, H. and Papoušek, M. (1979). The infant's fundamental adaptive responsive system in social interaction, In *Origins of the Infant's Social Responsiveness,* ed. E. Thoman. Hillsdale, New Jersey: Lawrence Erlbaum Associates.

Papoušek, M. and Papoušek, H. (1981). Musical elements in the infant's vocalization: Their significance for communication, cognition, and creativity. In *Advances in Infancy Research,* ed. L. P. Lipsitt and C. K. Rovee-Collier. Norwood, New Jersey: Ablex.

Papoušek, H. and Papoušek, M. (1982). Integration into the social world: Survey of research, In *Psychobiology of the Human Newborn,* ed. P. Stratton. Chichester: John Wiley.

Papoušek, H. and Papoušek, M. (1983). The psychobiology of the first didactic programs and toys in human infants. In *The Behavior of Human Infants,* ed. A. Oliverio and M. Zappella. New York: Plenum.

Prechtl, H. F. R. and O'Brien, M. J. (1982). Behavioural states of the full-term newborn. The emergence of a concept, In *Psychobiology of the Human Newborn,* ed. P. Stratton. Chichester: John Wiley.

Ridley, M. (1978). Paternal care. *Animal Behavior,* 26: 904–932.

Rosenblatt, J. S. (1975). Prepartum and postpartum regulation of maternal behavior in the rat. In *Parent-Infant Interaction,* ed. M. O'Connor. Amsterdam: Elsevier.

Solkoff, N. and Cotton, C. (1975). Contingency awareness in premature infants. *Perceptual and Motor Skills,* 41: 709–710.

30

Biological Bases of the Mother-Child Relationship

Robert A. Hinde, Sc.D.

That either data from animals or evolutionary theory could be of any value to child psychiatry might well be doubted. Our cognitive abilities and capacity to communicate by a spoken language set us apart from other species. The influence of biology on the behavior of mothers is often shrouded by that of culture, and the diversity of human cultures has no parallel among animals. Simple comparisons between the behavior of people and that of animals are misleading if only because, given the diversity of animals and the diversity of cultures, it is nearly always possible to find a parallel to prove whatever you wish. Nevertheless, I argue here that principles abstracted from comparative data on lower species can provide a perspective not without value for child psychiatry.

Two general points must be emphasized. First, the discussion will move repeatedly between nonhuman and human primates. The issue is not whether there are resemblances between the two but whether, at a more abstract level, data on or theories about nonhuman primates can facilitate our understanding of our own species. Second, it is possible to produce

reasonably strong evidence about the selective forces that have shaped the behavior of monkeys and apes. The view that comparable selective forces have shaped a particular aspect of our own behavior invariably rests on much less secure evidence, though there is often a strong *prima facie* case. Clearly there is an enormous danger of armchair theorizing. Yet I hope to show that the approach gives us useful additional insights about human behavior and helps to integrate numerous apparently independent human characteristics.

For brevity I shall focus mainly on the parent-offspring relationship, though of course that relationship can be considered only in the social context in which it is embedded. Furthermore, this will usually mean the mother-offspring relationship, since in the nonhuman primates that have been most studied paternal care is not well developed. There are in fact few extant nonhuman primates in which the father plays a substantial role in the care of the offspring—principally the gibbons and some South American species. Nevertheless, evidence from comparative anatomy and physiology strongly suggests that our species has been adapted to sustain a pair-bond between male and female (Alexander and Noonan, 1979; Short, 1979). This bond may have been adaptive because the father's presence was impor-

This work was supported by the Medical Research Council and the Royal Society.

tant for the development of the offspring. Alternatively, if bonds led to polygynous units in which mothers cooperated in caring for each other's offspring, each would have been able to breed more often (Mellen, 1981).

The examples I select move from relatively simple characteristics of individuals to more complex issues concerned with the social network, and from relatively simple to more complex biological arguments.

Mammals vary greatly in the frequency with which they suckle their young: in some species the young spend the greater part of the day attached to the nipple, while in other species they are suckled once a day, or even less often. Comparative study shows that suckling frequency is inversely related to the protein content of the milk. Human milk has a relatively low protein content, suggesting that neonates should be fed more frequently than the four-hourly feeds common in many maternity hospitals. In harmony with this view, mammalian babies that are suckled infrequently suck faster and for a shorter period than those that are suckled frequently: human babies suck very slowly (Blurton Jones, 1972). Thus by comparing man with a range of other species, we get a new perspective on the appropriateness of schedule feeding. The view is confirmed by a comparison of breast- and bottle-fed babies: bottle milk tends to be more concentrated than breast milk, and bottle-fed babies demand food less often (Bernal, 1972).

Thus comparative data from other species can throw light on the adaptive nature of particular human characteristics. But such characteristics do not exist in isolation from each other. In every species structure, physiology, and behavior form a harmonious whole suited to the species' way of life and to the environment in which it lives. Newborn primates are relatively helpless, but their mothers must move about in search of food. Unlike some ungulates, most of them carry their babies with them. It seems likely that this was the case also with early man. Such a view would be compatible with the evidence for frequent suckling cited above. Furthermore, while some mammalian mothers with relatively helpless young cache them in a nest or hiding place for long

periods, this is unlikely to have been the case in early humans: infants of caching species usually do not urinate or defecate unless stimulated by the mother, and this is not the case with human babies. Furthermore, the poor thermoregulatory ability of human infants is more compatible with their being carried than with their either being cached or following their mothers (Blurton Jones, 1972). The continuing presence of the Moro reflex (Prechtl and Lenard, 1968) and the vestigial grasping reflex of human infants indicate that they originally held on to their mothers like other primates. With reduction of maternal body hair this must have become difficult, and carrying must have posed problems to the mother especially as, by analogy with modern hunter-gatherers, she was probably responsible for a high proportion of food-gathering (Blurton Jones and Sibley, 1978). Presumably the establishment of home bases (Isaac, 1979) somewhat ameliorated this issue.

Thus the dilute milk and frequent nursing would have been associated with more or less constant maternal availability—though there is no implication that either of these issues was primary. Maternal availability would have been associated also with maternal protection and with infant dependence on that protection. As Bowlby (1969) pointed out, the so-called "irrational fears of childhood" made good sense in our "environment of evolutionary adaptedness," where dangers from predators, from infanticidal fellow-members of the species (Hrdy, 1977), and from just getting lost were constantly present. Mortality before the age of fourteen was probably between 55 and 68 percent (Acsádi and Nemeskeri, 1970). For an infant attached to an at least partially arboreal mobile mother, falling, darkness, and solitude signify real dangers and contact comfort is properly reassuring.

Nurturance and protection are but two of the resources a primate infant needs from the mother: she also cleans, guides, "teaches," and so on. Natural selection ensures that each female directs her maternal care primarily to her own infant (or, as we shall see shortly, to those of her close relatives). It would not be in a female's interests to devote her primary care to another's offspring. On the contrary, in some circumstances another's infant may be a potential competitor to her own, so that a female would do better not to aid and even to harm unrelated infants. Two things follow. First, it is in an infant's interests to avoid unfamiliar individuals: fear of strangers will be conducive to survival. Fear of strangers is in fact found in a wide range of species (Freedman, 1961), and it is no coincidence that in our own it appears at about the same time as the capacity for independent locomotion.

Second, if strangers may be hostile, it will be in the infant's interests to seek nurturance and succor primarily from its own mother: the formation of a close mother-infant relationship is thus in the evolutionary interests of both. This is the key to the significance of much behavior that seems at first sight to contribute little to the long-term well-being of either party. In the human case the smile and the games that mother and infant play (for example, Stern, 1977) function to cement and deepen the bond between them. The smile is elicited preferentially by stimuli with the configuration of the human face (Ahrens, 1954), and an interest in such a configuration is present from birth (Jirari, cited in Freedman, 1974). Many mothers say that they feel their babies become "real persons" when they start to smile. The games show considerable cultural diversity, but the propensity to play such games is certainly pancultural.

Although it is the relationship with the mother that is of primary importance to the very young primate, other relationships soon come to be important. One reason for this requires a slight digression. In caring for their own young, parents promote the survival and chances of reproduction of an individual who is genetically very similar to themselves. In evolutionary terms, parental care is but an example of a much wider principle, generally referred to as kin selection. Darwin focused on individual selection operating through the survival and reproduction of individuals. Those that reproduced most effectively were responsible for a higher proportion of the next generation. Yet natural selection can be seen not just as perpetuating viable or fertile individuals, but as operating to ensure the survival of genes. Suppose a mutation gave rise to a gene

that caused an individual to give up his life for others. If that individual died, one copy of that gene would disappear, but if in dying he saved the life of more than one individual who also carried the gene, then the new gene could still increase in the population. Death is, of course, an extreme case, but the same principle applies to acts that decrease the actor's chances of reproduction but augment those of others carrying the same gene (Hamilton, 1964). Thus natural selection acts to ensure that individuals not only maximize their own reproductive success, measured in terms of their descendants in subsequent generations, but also that of their relatives, who share a very high proportion of their (rare) genes, to an extent devalued according to their degree of relatedness. This is referred to as maximizing "inclusive fitness." Selection can thus favor acts that benefit related individuals and is more likely to do so the closer the degree of relatedness and the smaller the cost to the actor. An individual's offspring are among his or her closest kin, so acts that favor them promote the perpetuation of genes, half of which are identical with the individual's own. Hence selection for parental care. But individuals are equally closely genetically related to their parents and (full) siblings, so altruistic acts directed toward them may also be in an individual's evolutionary interests. This is more the case with siblings than parents since, given two individuals equally closely related, natural selection will favor more strongly altruistic acts directed toward the one with the greater reproductive potential, and this usually means the younger. (This also implies that parents have more interest in the well-being of their young than vice-versa).

There are in fact many primate species in which siblings take part in infant care (Ingram, 1977), and in many others aid in agonistic encounters comes primarily from close genetic relatives (Datta, 1983). Acts that favor less closely related individuals (aunts, cousins) may also be favored if the cost to the individual is not too great. The cohesion of interrelated individuals in a family-like structure is thus firmly rooted in the forces of natural selection. It may well be doubted whether nonhuman primates "know" who is related to them. But in many species female relatives tend to stay together, so familiarity is an index of related-ness. This lends further force to the "fear of strangers." Archaeological evidence is in har-mony with the view that early human social groups contained twelve to fifty individuals (Mellen, 1981), most of whom would probably have been relatives. Strangers would be likely to be unrelated. However, in many human so-cieties primary allegiance goes to a group of individuals *perceived* to be related, even though genetic relatedness is not always all that close.

We have seen that it is in the interests of both parent and infant to promote the bond between them. Infants thrive better with mothers who are sensitively responsive, (Ains-worth et al., 1978; Bowlby, 1969); not only because such mothers provide for their needs in the short term, but because sensitive respon-siveness promotes a better long-term relation-ship. However that is not the whole story, for the positions of parent and child are not pre-cisely similar. Natural selection promotes par-ental care because the offspring carries the par-ents' genes, and gene survival is contingent upon the offspring's well-being. At the same time the parent expends resources in caring for the infant, and this may reduce its chances of rearing further young subsequently.

The relative importance of these two issues changes with time. When the infant is initially born, parental care is essential for its survival. As it grows, it demands more milk, and thus the cost of parental care to the parent (mea-sured in terms of the parent's inclusive fitness) increases. At the same time parental care becomes less essential to the offspring, so the benefits conferred by a given parental act on the offspring (measured in terms of the off-spring's inclusive fitness) decrease. There thus comes a time when the costs to the mother exceed the benefit to her in terms of their effects on the young. Yet the infant will con-tinue to benefit from maternal care in its own right, and the cost to the mother will affect the infant's inclusive fitness less than the mother's, since only some of their genes are shared. Thus the continuation of maternal care favors the infant's evolutionary fitness and diminishes the mother's. Natural selection will favor the mother's halting maternal care and the infant's eliciting it. (In addition, continued suckling

may delay the mother's next pregnancy and hence the arrival of a competitor for the in-fant.) And so the infant is selected to elicit more parental investment than the parent is selected to give (Trivers, 1974). Weaning con-flict is thus based firmly in the processes of evolution.

Data on the mother-infant relationship in a wide range of species support this view. The rate at which an infant monkey becomes inde-pendent of its mother seems at first sight to be determined by the infant's increasing physical capacities and exploratory tendencies, but this is a misleading impression. As an infant rhesus gets older, it spends more and more time off its mother. If this were due solely to a change in the infant, we should expect the frequency with which the mother rejects the infant's at-tempts to gain contact to decrease. In fact the rejections increase, so the opposite must be the case—the increase in the time the infant spends off the mother is controlled more im-mediately by changes in the mother than by changes in the infant. This of course does not imply that the infant could not achieve inde-pendence on its own: infants reared on inani-mate mother surrogates do in fact leave them more and more as they grow older, though in-dependence is achieved more slowly than by mother-reared infants (Hansen, 1966). Nor does it imply that the changes in the mother arise endogenously: they may be initiated by the infant's increasing demand for milk or its more vigorous locomotor play. However, these in turn depend on maternal care, which in turn depends on signals from the infant, and so on. Development depends on a complex interac-tion between parent and offspring, and the present analysis shows only that changes in the time the infant spends off the mother are im-mediately due primarily to changes in the mother. Reflection does suggest that a similar principle operates in our own case: many human mothers push the baby on from breast to solid food, from crib to bed, or from home to school faster than the child, if allowed to make these decisions, would proceed (Hinde, 1974, 1979).

This emphasis on the biological advantages to the mother in promoting the offspring's in-dependence, and on the role of changes in the mother in bringing it about, is in no way contrary to the emphasis placed on sensitive mothering by many writers. But it does imply that infants are unlikely to be adapted to mothers who are infinitely compliant. If it is in the biological interests of the mother to reject the infant before it is in the interests of the infant to be independent, we can be sure that infants must be adapted to cope with mothers who wean them before they would otherwise prefer it, and to emerge from the relationship as individuals able to cope with the society into which they have been born. Similar considerations may well apply to our own species, where children whose parents have used a degree of measured control seem better adjusted (Baumrind, 1967, 1971).

This brings us to the nub of the issue so far as child psychiatry is concerned—the question of individual differences. Early attachment theory (Bowlby, 1969), taking some cues from ethology, was concerned with the adaptedness of particular responses or response systems, given an ideal partner: the implication was that mothers who behaved in an ideally sensitive way would raise an ideally well-adjusted infant. We have seen that the evolutionary viewpoint of Trivers and the data on weaning in monkeys complicate the issue by indicating that the partner in the mother-infant (or any other) relationship is unlikely to be ideal because he or she is likely to have slightly different interests. Now we reach a third stage in the argument—partners are likely to depart from the ideal (if it makes sense to talk in such terms) in varying ways. Are these individual differences to be seen as mere noise in the system that come to the psychiatrist's notice when they pass acceptable limits? Or is there more to it than that? Even if they are in part the products of chance events, perhaps the *effects* of those events are not chance, but are guided by the forces of selection.

Variation between individuals and between relationships is pronounced in animals just as it is in man. For example, at fifteen weeks infant rhesus monkeys in our colony may spend anywhere from 40 to 80 percent of the morning hours off their mothers. By an argument similar to that used earlier for age changes, we can

ascribe responsibility for these differences in the mother-infant relationship primarily to the mother or primarily to the infant. If the infants who were off the most are those who were rejected the most, interdyad differences could be primarily due to differences between mothers, but if such infants were rejected the least, interdyad differences would be primarily due to differences between infants. In fact the data show that interdyad differences are due more to differences among mothers in the early weeks and to differences among infants later. This suggests that variance in the inclusive fitness of both partners depends more on the mother's characteristics and circumstances early on, and more on the infant's later.

Before proceeding further, it is necessary to emphasize the general importance of thinking of behavior as involving "alternative strategies." Recent studies of monkeys and other species have shown that, rather than describing the behavior of members of a species as involving a "normal," mean, or modal behavioral style, with variance about it regarded as mere "natural" variability, it is more profitable to relate the behavior of individuals to their circumstances, assessing how far the variation represents alternative strategies for use in different circumstances—the word *strategy* carrying no implication of conscious planning. Consider the familiar dominance hierarchy. It may be better to be at the top because that brings better access to mates and food. But animals that find themselves to be subordinate do not spend all their time striving to be at the top. It may be better for them to bide their time, hoping for better circumstances later (Lack, 1954). Individuals thus develop in such a way that they strive for dominance if they are likely to be successful but bide their time if they are not. Natural selection has operated not to produce a stereotyped mode of behavior but flexibility appropriate to the circumstances.

Similar issues arise with maternal styles. Altmann (1980), studying baboons in Africa, found she could divide the mothers into those who were "restrictive" and those who were "laissez-faire." The former had infants who might be more likely to survive in the early months because they were less exposed to kidnapping, predation, and so on. However, such mishaps were less likely to happen to infants of high status females than to those of low status. Furthermore, "restrictive" mothering tends to lead to independence being achieved more slowly, and a laissez-faire style could lead to infants better able to survive if orphaned. It may therefore be better for high-status mothers to be laissez-faire and low-status ones to be restrictive. On this view there would be no best mothering style, and natural selection would act to favor individuals who showed a mothering style appropriate to the situation in which they found themselves.

Recently a comparable argument has been applied to the behavioral styles of human infants with their mothers. In the Ainsworth Strange Situation procedure (Ainsworth et al., 1978) infants are separated from the accompanying parent for about three minutes. On reunion, most infants go straight to the mother and make physical contact with her before continuing to play with the toys provided. However, some infants actively avoid and ignore the parent even when he/she seeks their attention, and focus on toys and the inanimate environment instead. In view of the importance of the mother-child relationship to the infant, such behavior seems maladaptive. The mothers of such children often have an apparent aversion to physical contact with their child and are restricted in emotional expression (Main and Stadtman, 1981). In addition, the child's avoidance is often associated with traces of maternal "anger" (George and Main, 1979). Recently Main and Weston (1982) have suggested that avoidance is a strategy that permits the offspring of such mothers to maintain organization, control, and flexibility in behavior. If the infant were to attempt to cling to the somewhat rejecting mother, distress and behavioral disorganization would be likely. The child thus employs alternative strategies according to the nature of the mother.

Cases such as these show that there is sense to be made of individual variation in behavior, for at least some variants may result from the pursuit of strategies evolved as adaptive in particular contexts. This argument must not, of course, be taken too far; it does not imply that all aberrations should be regarded as socially acceptable. But it does indicate that there can be a danger in idealizing particular behavioral styles—a mother ideal in some circumstances may not be so in others.

We may now consider four ways in which differences in the effects of maternal care for sons and for daughters affect the inclusive fitness of the mother. In general, in most organisms, variance in the reproductive success of males is higher than that of females. A male may fertilize many females or none, but most females reproduce. A female who is likely to have high reproductive success would have more descendents in the second generation if she had mostly male offspring, but a female whose offspring were likely to be of poor quality might do better to make sure of leaving at least a few descendants by having mostly daughters (Alexander, 1974; Trivers and Willard, 1973). There is evidence in some species that the sex of the offspring is actually controlled according to these principles. The female coypu with larger-than-average fat reserves show a significant tendency to abort small female-dominated litters, presumably because they would enhance their inclusive fitness by producing a higher proportion of males (Gosling and Petrie, in press). (This issue is discussed further in an important review by Clutton-Brock and Albon, 1982.)

In man, so far as we know, there is no mechanism for controlling the sex of the offspring, but there is evidence that differential infanticide can play a similar role. Surveying data from a wide range of societies in India and China, Dickemann (1979) has shown that female infanticide occurred predominantly in the higher social strata. Male reproductive success tended to be greatest at the top of the social hierarchy, where there was a greater incidence of female infanticide, suicide, and celibacy. Middle- and upper-class females competed for the high-status grooms and were transferred up the hierarchy by means of dowries. At the bottom of the scale women had greater reproductive expectations than men, and men even competed for the purchase of brides. Polygomy and female infanticide in the upper classes, and the upward movement of women could produce a marked shortage of women lower down. Male infanticide was not practiced, perhaps because the extra males assisted economically (Irons, 1979). Polyandry sometimes occurred (Crook, 1980).

A second possibility is that the social structure could be such that an increment in maternal care would have a greater effect on the reproductive potential of the mother and her close relatives if expended on an infant of one sex than on an infant of the other. This appears to be the case in rhesus monkeys and baboons where, as we shall see, daughters remain in the troop but males leave. The daughters acquire and augment their mother's status, thus enhancing their mutual reproductive success. Thus a middle- or high-status female might do well to keep her daughter with her, whereas a low-status female, whose reproductive success tends to be low, might do better to have males who might acquire high status and achieve high reproductive success in another troop (Simpson, 1983). There is evidence that this principle does operate. In at least some circumstances the birth ratio is weighted toward females in high-status mothers and toward males in low status ones (Altmann, 1980; Simpson, 1983). (The means by which sex of offspring is controlled is not yet known in these species: in others the incidence of copulation with respect to ovulation may be important [Verme and Ozogo, 1981].)

A related finding is that, again in at least some situations, mother rhesus monkeys tend to be slower to breed again after giving birth to daughters than after giving birth to sons (Simpson et al., 1981). This also could be interpreted in terms of a greater payoff (in terms of the reproductive success of herself and her offspring) a mother gets from successfully rearing daughters rather than sons. This is compatible with the view that it is in the interests of the mother's inclusive fitness to invest more in daughters.

A third issue arises when property can be passed on. A female monkey can pass on her status equally to all her offspring. In humans, where property as well as, or instead of, status becomes important, this is no longer so. In most societies property passes primarily to one sex or the other, and either it must be divided between individuals, or given to some at the expense of others. Reproductive strategies in

the higher classes may seem to be directed toward ensuring that the young do not drop in status (for example, by limiting the number of offspring so that the property is not too much divided or by passing property only to the eldest offspring, while the younger one(s) become celibate but "respected" priests). Whether such strategies do in fact lead to greater ultimate inclusive fitness for the property owner and his relatives is an open issue. In any case, it does not apply to the relatively propertyless classes, who thus tend to have a greater reproductive output.

It is perhaps unnecessary to emphasize again here that I am not suggesting that monkeys are like man—indeed, rather the reverse, because higher-status rhesus monkeys seem to put greater reproductive effort into daughters than sons, while for higher-status humans in many societies the reverse is the case. The common principle is that parental investment may differ according to the sex of the offspring, and the direction of the effect may depend on the social structure and/or norms. Thus we must expect not only sex differences in the behavioral propensities of individuals but differences in the ways in which parents behave toward sons and daughters.

A further issue is that the behavioral styles conducive to reproductive success in males may be different from those in females. We should thus expect natural selection to favor mothers who act so as to enhance the sex-appropriate behavior in their offspring. I know of no clear examples of this in monkeys, though the tendency of rhesus monkey mothers to promote the independence of their daughters (who will stay in the troop) less than that of their sons (who will leave the troop), referred to later in another context, may be partially explicable in these terms.

An example of the way in which human mothers encourage culturally sex-appropriate tendencies in their offspring has recently come up in a study of mother-child relationships. Children's temperamental characteristics were assessed by a modification of Thomas and Chess's (1977) technique at forty-two months and fifty months. Interview and observational data were also obtained at each age. At the latter age both interview (Stevenson-Hinde and Simpson, 1981) and observational data (Hinde et al., 1982) indicated that Shy girls had a more positive relationship with their mothers than non-Shy girls, but Shy boys had a more negative one than non-Shy boys. The differences in this respect at forty-two months had been minor. It seems that over this age range the mothers in the sample came to encourage shyness in girls and discourage it in boys. A rather different picture emerged for the characteristics Moody, Intense, Unmalleable, Irregular, and Assertive: high scores on these were associated with tensionful mother-child relationships more in girls than in boys. It seemed as though mothers found these characteristics less tolerable in girls than in boys (Hinde and Stevenson-Hinde, in press). Of course we are concerned here with the differential desirability of characteristics in the two sexes in a particular culture. How far these are linked to reproductive success is an open issue.

We may now move beyond the mother-infant relationship to consider some of the relationships of mothers and infants with others, and their impact on the mother-infant relationship. We shall find that these issues are powerfully influenced by the sex of the infant.

It is first necessary to say a word about social structure in nonhuman primates. In fact this shows great diversity: some species are monogamous, some almost solitary, some live in groups containing females and a single male, some in groups containing a number of males. We will focus on one pattern, that is found in a number of species of baboons and macaques. In these species the core of the troop consists of adult females and their young. The females belong to one or more matrilines, all individuals in one matriline being dominant to those in the next. There is also a dominance hierarchy within each matriline, each female's daughters being arranged in inverse order of age. The males leave their natal troop when a few years old and usually join another. Each troop thus contains a number of adult males which stay for a number of years before moving on.

Potent sources of differences in maternal style, which also interact with the infant's sex,

lie in the social situation. Mother rhesus monkeys living with their infants but segregated from other individuals are much less restrictive than group-living mothers (Hinde and Spencer-Booth, 1967); in this species, other individuals can covet or be aggressive to young infants, and mothers tend to keep their infants close to them. This tendency is more marked among the more subordinate mothers, who are less able to threaten other females away from their infants. But group companions also respond differently according to the sex of the infant. In bonnet (Silk et al., 1981) and rhesus macaques (Simpson, 1983) other adults tend to be more aggressive to mothers with infant daughters than to those with infant sons, and even to females pregnant with a female foetus than to mothers pregnant with a male (Sackett et al., 1974). (This may be related to the fact that daughters of unrelated mothers in the troop will remain in the troop and become competitors, whereas sons will move away.) Not surprisingly, mothers tend to restrain their young daughters more than their young sons.

Here again is an interaction with maternal rank. High-status mothers reject sons more than daughters, but this is not true of low-ranking mothers. Since high-ranking mothers tend to receive less aggression than low-ranking ones, they may be better able to afford to promote their son's early independence (Simpson, 1983).

One of the most potent sources of difference in maternal style comes from the presence (or absence) of other offspring. It is easy to presume that primiparous mothers adopt a maternal style different from multiparous ones (Hooley and Simpson, 1981) because they are more inept, but we must remember that this in itself may involve an adaptation: their ineptness requires them to take more care. We should also expect that parents would promote the independence of early-born offspring in order to rear more and to invest most in a last-born infant. An elder sibling may be jealous, requiring the mother to take more care of a new infant (Hooley and Simpson, 1983), or it may assist the mother and thereby reduce her load (Ingram, 1977). This effect may vary with the elder sibling's sex. Young females are often intensely interested in young infants; presumably this is in their own interests, for exposure to mother-infant dyads can affect their own capacity to behave maternally (Dienske et al. 1980): it may or may not be in the mothers' interests. The presence of daughters especially may affect the amount of aggression directed toward the family triad by other females (Simpson, 1983).

Hooley and Simpson (1981) found that primiparous mothers protected their daughters more than their sons—presumably because daughters attract more aggression from adult females than do sons. Multiparous mothers, however, protected sons more than daughters, especially when the siblings were two, three, or four years older than the infants. This may be because siblings tend to be especially attracted to young males, and the mother may need to limit their interactions, especially those of the larger siblings, with the infants.

In rhesus monkeys it is in a female's interests to support a daughter in encounters with unrelated or distantly related females, for rank is related to reproductive success, and she is thereby enhancing the reproductive expectations of individuals who carry many of her genes over those of individuals who carry fewer. It is for this ultimate reason that daughters tend to acquire their mothers' ranks. It is also in a mother's interests to support her younger daughters (within limits) over older ones, because the former have a longer potential reproductive life ahead of them (Chapais and Schulman, 1980; Schulman and Chapais, 1980).

We have seen that relationships are especially likely to form between individuals who are closely related to each other genetically. It may also be in an individual's long-term interests to form relationships with others who will be useful subsequently, even if they are unrelated. An example is provided by the behavior of adolescent baboons. Young female baboons tend to direct their grooming behavior toward the more dominant adult females in the troop, and young males to the more subordinate ones. While grooming may have some function in cleaning the fur there is considerable evidence that it is also important in furthering interindividual relationships,

analogous to the bestowal of social approval in man (Hinde and Stevenson-Hinde, 1976). The manner in which each sex distributes its grooming may be appropriate to its long-term needs. The young females will stay in the troop and may later profit from aid given by more dominant individuals; the young males will later leave the troop, but in the meantime can profit from practicing copulation, and they are more likely to be able to mount the subordinate females without interference from adult males (Cheney, 1978). In a similar way much of the social life of nonhuman primates is best understood as involving individuals furthering their own interests by fostering relationships with particular other individuals (Datta, 1983). If we are unwilling to ascribe to nonhuman primates foreknowledge of who will later be useful, we must presume that natural selection has predisposed individuals to form relationships with those others who are likely to be of use to them in the future. This of course in no way denigrates the concept of friendship; humans can behave altruistically, but most friendships involve expectations of dividends.

Clearly one could follow these complexities further. But in conclusion it is necessary to sound again the warning that it is nearly always possible to find an animal parallel to almost any human practice. And we must remember that the biologist, concerned with the breeding success or inclusive fitness of individuals, is operating on a different set of premises from the anthropologist, who is often concerned with the transmission of property. And the man in the street, concerned with the desiderata of power, happiness, or "adjustment" to a particular culture, may see individual strategies from yet a different viewpoint. How far property, power, or happiness are in fact related to reproductive potential is an open issue. The biologist's approach will thus certainly not solve all the psychologist's problems. What can be claimed is that it does help to integrate our knowledge of many, if not all, of man's behaviors and propensities in general and of the mother-child relationship in particular.

REFERENCES

Acsádi, Gy. and Nemeskeri, J. (1970). *History of Human Life Span and Mortality.* Budapest: Akademiai Kiado (translated from Hungarian).

Ahrens, R. (1954). Beitrag zur Entwicklung des Physiognomie und Mimikerkennens, tiel 1, 11. *Zeitschrift für Experimentelle und Angewandte Psychologie,* 2:412–454, 599–633.

Ainsworth, M. D. S., Blehar, M. C., Waters, E., and Wall, S. (1978). *Patterns of Attachment.* Hillsdale, New Jersey: Lawrence Erlbaum Associates.

Alexander, R. D. (1974). The evolution of social behavior. *Annual Review of Ecology and Systematics,* 5:325–383.

Alexander, R. D. and Noonan, K. M. (1979). Concealment of ovulation, parental care and human social evolution. In *Evolutionary Biology and Human Social Behaviour: An Anthropological Perspective,* ed. N. A. Chagnon and W. Irons. North Scituate, Massachusetts: Duxbury Press.

Altmann, J. (1980). *Baboon Mothers and Infants.* Cambridge: Harvard University Press.

Baumrind, D. M. (1967). Childcare practices anteceding three patterns of preschool behavior. *Genetic Psychology Monographs,* 75:43–88.

Baumrind, D. M. (1971). Current patterns of parental authority. *Developmental Psychology Monographs,* 41:1–103.

Bernal, J. (1972). Crying during the first 10 days of life, and maternal responses. *Developmental Medicine and Child Neurology,* 14:362–372.

Blurton Jones, N. (1972). Comparative aspects of mother-child contact. In *Ethological Studies of Child Behaviour,* ed. N. Blurton Jones. Cambridge, England: Cambridge University Press.

Blurton Jones, N. and Sibley, R. M. (1978). Testing adaptiveness of culturally determined behaviour. *Symposia for the Society of Human Biology,* 18:135–157.

Bowlby, J. (1969). *Attachment and Loss,* vol. 1. *Attachment.* New York: Basic Books.

Chapais, B. and Schulman, S. R. (1980). An evolutionary model of female dominance relations in primates. *Journal of Theoretical Biology,* 82:47–89.

Cheney, D. (1978). Interactions of immature male and female baboons with adult females. *Animal Behaviour,* 26: 389–408.

Clutton-Brock, T. H. and Albon, S. D. (1982). Parental investment in male and female offspring in mammals. In *Current Problems in Sociobiology,* ed. King's College Sociobiology Group. Cambridge, England: Cambridge University Press.

Crook, J. H. (1980). *The Evolution of Human Consciousness.* Oxford, England: Clarendon.

Datta, S. B. (1983). Patterns of interference. In *Primate Social Relationships: An Integrated Approach,* ed. R. A. Hinde. Oxford, England: Blackwell.

Dickemann, M. (1979). Female infanticide, reproductive strategies and social stratification: a preliminary model. In *Evolutionary Biology and Human Social Behaviour: An Anthropological Perspective,* ed. N. A. Chagnon and W. Irons. North Scituate, Massachusetts: Duxbury Press.

Dienske, H., Vreeswijk, W. van, and Koning, H. (1980). Adequate mothering by partially isolated rhesus monkeys after observation of maternal care. *Journal of Abnormal Psychology,* 89:489–492.

Freedman, D. G. (1961). The infant's fear of strangers and the flight response. *Journal of Child Psychology and Psychiatry,* 4:242–248.

Freedman, D. G. (1974). *Human Infancy: An Evolutionary Perspective.* Hillsdale, New Jersey: Lawrence Erlbaum Associates.

George, C. and Main, M. (1979). Social interactions of young abused children: Approach, avoidance, and aggression. *Child Development,* 50:306–318.

Gosling, L. M. and Petrie, M. (in press). The economics of social organisation. In *Functional Ecology: An Evolutionary Approach,* ed. P. Calow and C. R. Townsend. Oxford, England: Blackwell.

Hamilton, W. D. (1964). The genetical theory of social behaviour. *Journal of Theoretical Biology,* 7:1–52.

Hansen, E. W. (1966). The development of maternal and infant behavior in the rhesus monkey. *Behaviour,* 27:107–149.

Hinde, R. A. (1974). *Biological Bases of Human Social Behaviour.* New York: McGraw Hill.

Hinde, R. A. (1979). *Towards Understanding Relationships.* London: Academic Press.

Hinde, R. A., Easton, D., Meller, R. E., and Tamplin A. (1982). Temperamental characteristics of 3–4-year-olds and mother-child interaction. In *Ciba Foundation Symposium 89—Temperamental Differences in Infants and Young Children.* London: Pitman.

Hinde, R. A. and Spencer-Booth, Y. (1967). The effect of social companions on mother-infant relations in rhesus monkey. In *Primate Ethology,* ed. D. Morris. London: Weidenfeld & Nicolson.

Hinde, R. A. and Stevenson-Hinde, J. (1976). Towards understanding relationships: Dynamic stability. In *Growing Points in Ethology,* ed. P. Bateson and R. A. Hinde. Cambridge, England: Cambridge University Press.

Hinde, R. A. and Stevenson-Hinde, J. (in press). Relationships, personality and the social situation. In *Key Issues in Interpersonal Relationships,* ed. R. Gilmour and S. Duck. Hillsdale, New Jersey: Lawrence Erlbaum Associates.

Hooley, J. M. and Simpson, M. J. A. (1981). A comparison of primiparous and multiparous mother-infant dyads in Macaca mulatta. *Primates,* 22:379–392.

Hooley, J. M. and Simpson, M. J. A. (1983). The influence of siblings on the infant's relationship with mother and others. In *Primate Social Relationships: An Integrated Approach,* ed. R. A. Hinde. Oxford, England: Blackwell.

Hrdy, S. B. (1977). *The Langurs of Abu.* Cambridge, Massachusetts: Harvard University Press.

Ingram, J. C. (1977). Interactions between parents and infants, and the development of independence in the common marmoset (Callithrax jacchus). *Animal Behaviour,* 25: 811–827.

Irons, W. (1979). Culture and biological success. In *Evolutionary Biology and Human Social Behaviour: An Anthropological Perspective,* ed. N. A. Chagnon and W. Irons. North Scituate, Massachusetts: Duxbury Press.

Isaac, G. L. (1979). Casting the net wide: A review of archaeological evidence for early hominid land-use and ecological relations. In Nobel Symposium. *Current Argument on Early Man.* Oxford, England: Pergamon.

Lack, D. (1954). *The Natural Regulation of Animal Numbers.* Oxford, England: Clarendon.

Main, M. and Stadtman, J. (1981). Infant response to rejection of physical contact by the mother: Aggression, avoidance, and conflict. *Journal of the American Academy of Child Psychiatry,* 20:292–307.

Main, M. and Weston, D. R. (1982). Avoidance of the attachment figure in infancy: Descriptions and interpretations. In *The Place of Attachment in Human Behavior,* ed. C. M. Parkes and J. Stevenson-Hinde. New York: Basic Books.

Mellen, S. L. W. (1981). *The Evolution of Love.* Oxford, England: W. H. Freeman.

Prechtl, H. F. R. and Lenard, H. G. (1968). Verhaltensphysiologie des Neugeborenen. In *Fortschritte der Paedologie.* Berlin: Springer Verlag.

Sackett, G. P., Holm, R. A., Davis, A. E., and Fahrenbruch, C. E. (1974). Prematurity and low birth weight in pigtail macaques: Incidence, prediction, and effects on infant development. *Symposium of the 5th Congress of the International Primatological Society,* pp. 189–206.

Schulman, S. R. and Chapais, B. (1980). Reproductive value and rank relations among macaque sisters. *American Naturalist,* 115:580–593.

Short, R. (1979). Sexual selection and its component parts, somatic and genital selection, as illustrated by man and the great apes. *Advances in the Study of Behavior,* 9:131–158.

Silk, J. B., Clarke-Wheatley, R. P. S., and Samuels, A. (1981). Differential reproductive success and faculative adjustment of sex ratios among captive female bonnet macaques (Macaca radiata). *Animal Behaviour,* 29:1106–1120.

Simpson, M. J. A. (1983). The effect of the sex of an infant on the mother-infant relationship and the mother's subsequent reproduction. In *Primate Social Relationships: An Integrated Approach,* ed. R. A. Hinde. Oxford, England: Blackwell.

Simpson, M. J. A., Simpson, A. E., Hooley, J., and Zunz, M. (1981). Infant-related influences on birth intervals in rhesus monkeys. *Nature,* 290:49–51.

Stern, D. (1977). *The First Relationship: Infant and Mother.* Cambridge, Massachusetts: Harvard University Press.

Stevenson-Hinde, J. and Simpson, M. J. A. (1981). Mother's characteristics, interactions, and infant's characteristics. *Child Development,* 52:1246–1254.

Thomas, A. and Chess, S. (1977). *Temperament and Development.* New York: Brunner/Mazel.

Trivers, R. L. (1974). Parent-offspring conflict. *American Zoologist,* 14:249–264.

Trivers, R. L. and Willard, D. E. (1973). Natural selection of parental ability to vary the sex ratio of offspring. *Science,* 179:90–92.

Verme, L. J. and Ozoga, J. J. (1981). Influence of temporal relationships during oestrus on deer sex ratio. *Journal of Wildlife Management,* 45:710–715.

31

Observations on the Nature of the Infant-Grandparent Relationship: A Preliminary Report

Arthur Kornhaber, M. D.

Introduction

James M. Herzog, M. D.

The more things change, the more they remain the same. Dr. Kornhaber's paper introduces us to the important nurturing and developmentally facilitating role that the extended family plays in the life of a small child. He focuses on the positive aspects of these interactions and on the joy that such interchange can bring to all involved. His findings are consonant with those that suggest that support networks for new parents aid good parenting (Brown, 1975) and with clinical impressions suggesting that the birth of a grandchild may be a critical consolidating experience in adult development (Cath, 1982).

Kornhaber focuses on facilitation and complementarity. He does not address the frequently reciprocal issues of competition, conflict, restitution, and revenge. In this regard a study of the parent-grandparent relationship becomes an imperative correlative for the study of the grandparent-infant one. It has been generally accepted that motherhood brings an opportunity to rework in a somewhat expanded way daughter-mother issues (Bibring et al., 1961), work that is often not completed until the second or subsequent pregnancies. Similar observations have been made with regard to expectant fatherhood (Herzog, 1982). In a longitudinal observational study of eight families (Herzog, chapter 36, this volume) it became abundantly clear that complicated dynamic interplays between parents, parental representations, and grandparents occur frequently in many families. The converse is also true. Grandparents must deal with the reawakening of many vestigial conflicts their children's fecundity and the very presence of a new infant may stimulate.

For these reasons it seems very critical to me that Dr. Kornhaber's excellent work be continued and enlarged to examine the grandparent-infant relationship in light of the grandparent-parent relationship—past, present, actual, and desired. It seems to me that this is particularly critical if one wishes to prescribe grandparent involvement in the family life. This ancient and seemingly universal good needs to be understood as an opportunity that is predicated on more than the appearance of a new child. As with all such psychobiological happenings, it is an occasion when new and beneficial reorganizations can be accomplished by all concerned. As clinicians, however, we know that such occurrences present a fertile ground for the perpetuation or elicitation of less favorable development as well.

REFERENCES

Bibring, G. L., Dwyer, T. F., Huntington, D. S., and Valenstein, A. F. (1961). A study of the psychological processes in pregnancy and of the earliest mother-child relationship. *The Psychoanalytic Study of the Child,* 16:9–73. New York: International Universities Press.

Brown, G. W., Bhrolchain, M. N., and Harris, T. (1975). Social class and psychiatric disturbance among women in an urban population. *Sociology,* 9:225–254.

Cath, S. (1982). Vicissitudes of grandfatherhood: A miracle of revitalization. In *Father and Child—Developmental and Clinical Perspectives,* ed. S. H. Cath, A. R. Gurwitt, and J. M. Ross. Boston: Little, Brown.

Herzog, J. M. (1982). Patterns of expectant fatherhood: A study of the fathers of a group of premature infants. In *Father and Child—Developmental and Clinical Perspectives,* ed. S. H. Cath, A. R. Gurwitt, and J. M. Ross. Boston: Little, Brown.

Interest in the grandparent-grandchild relationship has recently increased. Previous neglect is probably the result of greater attention to the parent-child bond and because we live in an "ageist" era in which the elderly and their skills and gifts are not valued as they once were. Recent studies have shown that the grandparent-grandchild relation has significant value for both the old and young.

Wood and Robertson (1976) studied the importance of grandparenthood to middle-aged and older adults and found that involved grandparents tended to have slightly higher levels of life satisfaction. Findings from an ongoing research project (Kornhaber and Woodward, 1981) have shown that

> the grandparent-grandchild bond is second only in emotional importance to the bond between parents and children. Problems that are passed on from grandparent to parent are not directly passed on from grandparent to grandchild (although children are profoundly affected by their parents' attitudes toward their grandparents). Grandparents and grandchildren affect one another simply because they exist. (p. 279)

That study also showed that children with close relationships to at least one grandparent were different from children with intermittent or infrequent grandparent contact. The youngsters with close relationships to grandparents had a deep sense of belonging to a family and community. They were not ageist, because of the older people who loved them, and they were not sexist, because grandfathers and grandmothers had similar activities. They did not fear old age, because their grandparents served as positive role models. Grandparents offered these children an emotional sanctuary from the everyday world, an atmosphere where they were accepted for just being alive, and a place to go, apart from the world of their peer group and their parents, to learn about other times and other ways of living. Thus, these youngsters felt deeply connected to their families and were highly socialized. They knew that their behavior reflected upon their families, and they lived in a loving and emotionally secure world.

Among early investigators, Neugarten and Weinstein (1964) examined grandparenting styles and identified five types of grandparents: formal, funseeker, surrogate caregiver, reservoir of wisdom, and distant figure. Kahana and Kahana (1970) explored the changing meaning of grandparents for children of different ages, reporting that indulgence was of value to younger children, fun-sharing qualities to latency children, while adolescents reflected distance from their grandparents. These authors found that grandparenting was a natural instinct or response demonstrated by thoughts, feelings, and action, and affected by the culture. Before the child is born, the anticipating grandparent mentally rehearses future grandparenting. The way in which a given individual experiences grandparenthood is based on his experience as a grandchild, the attitudes of his society toward grandparenthood, and his own altruistic orientation. When a grandchild is born, new grandparents experience strong feelings and unique thoughts. There is an urgency to make contact with the new child, a need for intimacy.

Kahana and Kahana also called attention to the unique roles that grandparents play. They are similar to parents' roles because a grandparent has already been a parent and can fulfill that role. They are different because a parent cannot be a grandparent. At first, a grandparent's role is "titular," conferred by the birth of a grandchild. Immediately, a grandparent becomes a living ancestor and a role model for the child. When an intimate relationship is established, a grandparent becomes a living historian and family archivist. As mentors, grandparents teach children things they learn nowhere else in an atmosphere of acceptance. As nurturers, grandparents are the second line of defense, a safety net for the child when parents fail. The nurturing role is twofold—indirect, by supporting the child's parents, and direct, by caring for the child. When grandparents and grandchildren spend a great deal of time together, grandparents become wizards in the eyes of the young child and cronies to the older child. These roles give meaning to the grandparents' lives and exemplify "generativity" in its most powerful form—the application of a lifetime of wisdom and experience to a relationship with their progeny.

The object of the present study was to observe the grandparent-infant relationship in order to examine the nature of the interaction and to plan future and more specific research designs. The inherent difficulties in examining an emotional attachment are obvious. To illustrate: an eighteen-month-old child had grandparents from different cultures, one set Latin, the other Nordic. Her Latin grandparents tickled, frolicked with, and cajoled her. Her Nordic grandparents, who loved her no less, let her "be." Her Latin mother thought her in-laws were "cold and hard;" her Nordic father thought her Latin grandparents were "driving her crazy." The youngster was perfectly content, although different, with both sets of grandparents.

Many complex variables affect the relationship. There are "special" grandchildren, from the firstborn to grandchildren who resemble the "other side" of the family. Fortunately, the infant's charm usually overcomes any ephemeral prejudices. The parent-grandparent relationship also profoundly affects the grandparent-infant relationship. A healthy grandparent-parent relationship facilitates a close attachment between elders and infants. Adversary relationships between the older and middle generations can destroy a grandparent-infant relationship. On the other hand, the grandparent-infant relationship inextricably involves all three generations. The family is thus bonded together by the birth of a new child.

Subjects and Methods

For the purposes of this study, we decided to observe the grandparent-infant relationship as it is lived in emotionally close families. We studied thirty grandparent-infant dyads (eighteen grandmothers and twelve grandfathers), 35 percent of whom came from a low socioeconomic background, 45 percent from the middle class, and 29 percent from a high socioeconomic background. The ethnic distribution was 65 percent white, 15 percent black, 10 percent Hispanic, 5 percent Indian, and 5 percent Asian. All the grandparents lived within one hour's driving time of the child and spent at least ten hours per week with the child. All infants lived with their parents. Eighteen mothers worked full- or part-time; all fathers worked. Ten grandmothers and two grandfathers worked full-time, eight grandmothers and five grandfathers, part-time. We directly observed grandparents and infants at the clinic, the parents' home, the grandparents' home, and "outside" (parks, and the like). The dyad was observed from the infant's birth for a minimum of four hours a week for three years. Only one brief example from the study will be given for purposes of illustration.

The Case of Dawn

Mr. and Mrs. W. not only accompanied their daughter and her husband to the hospital in order to await the birth of their new grandchild, they outfitted a nursery in their own home for "when the baby would come and visit." They became involved with the new baby in a supportive and nonintrusive way. Mrs. W. spent several hours a day at her daughter's home during the first six months of Dawn's life. (We found that grandmothers and mothers consistently became emotionally closer and shifted their relationship for the better when a new child was born and the grandmother was present, a view confirmed by Harmon [1978].)

Dawn was moved freely between her parents and her grandmother during her first six months. She was more withdrawn in feeding and play with her grandfather and averted her eyes from his gaze more frequently than from her parents' or her grandmother's. At eight months she showed no stranger anxiety with her grandparents. She became closer to her grandfather as soon as she became mobile. The more active she became, the more her grandfather became involved with her. "The less fragile she is, the more that I can do with her," he said. Grandmother spent a great deal of time in calm and soothing activities—rubbing, petting, stroking, grooming, rocking, feeding, and toilet-training. Grandfather spent time in more physical activities, such as wrestling on the floor, prancing, and "showing off" by taking her to his church. Dawn was at ease with her grandmother and mimicked her gestures and activities. They engaged in quiet and peaceful doll play together. Dawn became "hyper" with her grandfather, and the family commented on the way she was overcome with joy when he walked into the room. They also noted that she "had Grandpa in the palm of her hand" and that "he never treated his own kids that way" (infant power). Although Dawn preferred her mother at bedtime and when injured, she could interchange her parents for her grandparents with no distress. She went freely to her grandparents' home and stayed overnight with no difficulty.

Discussion

Like other infants in this study, Dawn exhibited no signs of regression or other disturbance when separated from her parents and cared for by her grandparents. Play patterns, eye contact, feeding, and bowel functions were stable. Most of the children were observed to be at ease with their grandparents, especially when alone with their grandmothers. Of all the adults in the study, nonworking grandmothers were most patient and tolerant and gave their grandchildren the greatest amount of undivided attention.

Many of the infants were more relaxed with their grandmothers than they were with their parents, and they seemed to explore less when with the grandmothers. When parents were present, the infants sought intimate contact but interacted less intensely with grandmother. Infant-grandfather interactions were as intense as the parent-child interaction.

Grandparents did not appear to encourage the infant's individual strivings. Grandparents appeared to teach by "showing" rather than by "telling." Also, infants sought out bodily contact with grandmothers, although not with the same urgency as with the parents.

Preliminary Clinical Impressions

The emotional tone of the grandparent-infant relationship is different from that of the parent-child relationship, and intellectual and social learning are accomplished differently in the two relationships. Grandmothers and grandfathers appear to relate differently to their grandchildren than they did to their own children. Infants and grandparents are greatly attracted to one another, and those children with absent fathers are especially attracted to grandfathers. While infants can easily interchange parents for close grandparents, the grandparent-infant relationship is unique unto itself. The birth of a child establishes a three-generational family in which grandparents are the second level of the physical and emotional support system of the newborn infant—a natural welfare system. Because of their enormous helping potential, grandparents should be routinely interviewed and included in the child psychiatric assessment process.

REFERENCES

Harmon, R. J. (1978). Perinatal influences on the family: Some preventive implications. Paper presented at the Meetings of the American Academy of Child Psychiatry, unpublished.

Kahana, B. and Kahana, E. (1970). Grandparenthood from the perspective of the developing grandchild. *Developmental Psychology*, 3:98–105.

Kornhaber, A. and Woodward, K. L. (1981). *Grandparents/Grandchildren—The Vital Connection*. New York: Doubleday.

Neugarten, B. and Weinstein, K. (1964). The changing American grandparent. *Journal of Marriage and the Family*, 26: 49–61.

Wood, V. and Robertson, J. F. (1976). The significance of grandparenthood. In *Times, Roles and Self in Old Age*, ed. J. Gubrium. New York: Human Sciences Press.

32

Improving the Psychological Prognosis for Offspring of Adolescent Mothers

Peter Barglow, M.D., Roger Hatcher, Ph.D., and Lyle Joffe, Ph.D.

In 1979 there were over a quarter of a million births to unwed teenage mothers in the United States, an increase of 44 percent from a decade earlier. The child resulting from an adolescent pregnancy is subjected to a high degree of medical and psychological risk, as is the mother herself (Fried, 1980, Peterson et al., 1982). Measurements used to evaluate these infants include birthweight, the Brazelton (1973) neonatal examination, the Bayley (1969) Mental and Motor Scales, and the Graham Behavior Test (1956). Later sequelae of adolescent parenting are measured through rating how the mother talks to and holds the infant. Subsequently, the incidence of child abuse and neglect has been measured, and the child's IQ, reading ability, and educational attachment have been checked. Research conclusions that offspring deficits result from adolescent pregnancy are not unanimous (Sandler, 1977), but there is sufficient recent evidence to warrant caregiver intervention to minimize long-term damage, particularly among poverty populations.

Sameroff's studies (1975) have indicated that, regardless of maternal age, socioeconomic milieu is the single most important variable determining the long-range sequelae of early mother-infant pathology. But poverty is not the only influential factor. Werner's group (1969) has shown that resilience in children of the poor depends on a wide variety of factors —family size, the presence of alternative caregivers, family cohesiveness, and the infant's capacity to stimulate positive parental response. Over the past decade we have had the opportunity to scrutinize and evaluate the positive effects of the interventions described below.

Precision in Diagnosis

Effective intervention always requires skilled and detailed psychological interviewing. The regressive tendencies and fear of the unknown that usually characterize adolescent pregnancy, and age or sociocultural and ethnic gaps between client and interviewer make obtaining emotional data both difficult and time-consuming. When the adolescent girl first discovers that she is pregnant, denial and disbelief ("How could this could happen to me?") are common defense mechanisms contributing to a typical withholding of vital psychological information. The pregnant girl often has fantasies that she will be a better mother than her own mother, incorporating intense feelings of bitterness, disappointment, and anger toward her mother (Schaffer and Pine, 1972). These feelings are usually displaced onto mental health professionals, thereby complicating the interview process. Verbal as well as nonverbal clues may be helpful in eliciting the history. Further, the interviewer should keep in mind that the adolescent may have overt psychiatric symptoms and that her psychological and psychosocial history should be carefully explored. Extra time is required with the pregnant adolescent in order to become fully acquainted with her in an unhurried manner. It is crucial to inquire about her sexual activity and her attitude and concerns about the pregnancy. Often the teenager is so anxious, shy, or intimidated by the examination that she forgets or suppresses her own questions. We have found that invariably the teenager has special feelings toward caregivers that can be used to enhance the alliance.

Asking a mother how she has picked the baby's name is essential. Often it has a specific meaning that may be important to explore. For example, we encountered a teenager who wanted to name her baby "My Own." Some mothers may not have thought of a name even by the third trimester. The expected or desired sex of the baby, anxieties concerning the health of the baby, and hopes and aspirations of the parents always need to be explored. Occasionally, a patient will reveal a dream that will aid the helping professional learn more about the patient. For example, an eighteen-year-old girl pregnant for the third time dreamed that her boyfriend's mother was scratching her swollen abdomen. Only with further exploration did the interviewer discover that she had a conflictual relationship with her boyfriend, whose mother was trying to force her son to end the relationship. As a consequence she was contemplating an abortion.

Early Identification of Risk Factors

Although the youthfulness of these girls alone justifies the provision of special social, psychologic, and medical services, the presence of several other factors implies the need for intense psychological scrutiny and intervention. Concurrent existence of chronic medical illness such as orthopedic disability, asthma, or sickle cell disease always increases the likelihood of severe psychic vulnerabilities. Conclusions drawn from our own experience with pregnant diabetic adolescents (Barglow et al., 1981) may be generally applied to other chronic conditions. Our youthful patient population clearly was lower in medical adherence than adult patients. The pregnancy had revived overwhelming feelings of psychic helplessness. These frightening perceptions were then warded off by attitudes of negativeness, bravado, and defiance toward family, friends, and medical caregiver alike. We also noted much conscious and unconscious competition with the fetus for special attention, care, and demonstrations of love and devotion.

A high proportion of our adolescent pregnant population could be characterized by what the obstetricians refer to as "socioeconomic-family-chaos-stress syndrome." This condition produces scheduling conflicts in obstetrical clinic routines, loss of educational materials, boyfriends that disappear, mishandled finances, and multiple patient errors in following obstetrical and medical instructions. This population also had an increased incidence of perinatal and postnatal morbidity. To offset these factors, Michael Reese Hospital established a four-hour sequence of educational and clinical experience scheduled at convenient times exclusively for adolescent pregnant girls. Using a team approach, including specially trained social workers, this program produced some amelioration of the aforementioned problems. We have found the *Coddington Stress Scale* to be a valuable instrument to predict poor diabetic adherence and control in adolescent subjects (Barglow et al., 1983) a finding probably also applicable to pregnant adolescents.

Dr. R. Klue (personal communication, 1981) has noted that many pregnant adolescents failed to form mental representations of their unborn children and could not distinguish fetal movement from other sensations. She suggested that this phenomenon might account for the "sparse and disaffected" comments some adolescents, who later seemed not to bond to the baby, made about pregnancy and the fetus. We have noted that third-trimester absence of fantasizing about the gender of the future baby and a lack of planning for the physical environment of the infant—for example, not attempting to obtain clothing, furniture, or living space—were clues predicting future rejection of the child (Barglow et al., 1968). More recently we found the Loevinger Scale could predict poor compliance secondary to immaturity in diabetic adolescents (Barglow et al., 1983). We believe it to be an excellent screening device to identify teenagers likely to ignore, neglect, or abuse infants. In these situations remedial measures could be taken, with identification of ancillary or alternative caregivers for the child.

The presence of overt psychopathology in the pregnant teenager is a clear-cut signal for active intervention. This fact is illustrated by the case history of a nineteen-year-old unmarried pregnant adolescent living with her boyfriend. She had been referred to a drug-abuse pregnancy program. She regularly used phencyclidine ("Angel Dust") and was described as having multiple physical fights with her male partner. She had mood swings and a documented record of antisocial and irresponsible sexual behavior. There was a history of suicide attempts, multiple changes of residence during pregnancy, and failure to follow medical recommendations. She gave birth to a normal female infant, but was described as easily frustrated and enraged by the demands of the infant who progressively lost weight. She dropped out of a couples-psychotherapy program in the weeks following delivery, and continued to use drugs. At eleven months of age her infant suffered irreversible brain damage upon swallowing an overdose of lithium. Someone had opened a capsule, put powder on the infant's tongue, and given the child a bottle of milk. A legal investigation failed to prove maternal child abuse or negligence, but accidental use of lithium was ruled out as a possibility, and the patient was the most likely suspect. This case dramatically illustrates the need to provide this population with extensive and intensive psychiatric service.

While there are no hard and fast rules for deciding which symptom constellation is normal and which reflects psychopathology, it should be remembered that the pregnant adolescent does have many emotional problems. In a study comparing symptoms of distress in teenage and adult mothers, 23 percent of adolescent mothers (childbearing before age eighteen) reported frequent feelings of sadness, compared with 13 percent of mothers who began childbearing between twenty and twenty-four years of age. Feelings of tension were reported in 44.7 percent of the adolescent mothers compared with 30 percent of the older group (Brown et al., 1980). In addition, the suicide risk rises among teenagers who become pregnant. Those who are Catholic show a greater tendency toward suicide than do Protestant adolescents, a risk that persists for as long as five years after pregnancy (Gabrielson et al., 1970).

General Antenatal Interventions

The following procedures help the teenager complete pregnancy while facilitating a favorable emotional environment for the future child (Barglow, 1980): (1) evaluation of the emotional and economic strengths and weaknesses of the home environment; (2) identification of one responsible adult parent or friend who is stable and supportive of the continuation of the pregnancy (particularly important for the very young pregnant child; a working alliance with such an adult can be a life-saving crisis intervention); (3) maximal involvement of the man or boy who is to become father of the baby; (4) linkage to a suitable medical facility near the patient's home capable of providing nutritional, dental, and social services, psychological counseling, and comprehensive obstetrical care and postnatal follow-up; (5) delineation of prior educational accomplishment and establishment of a provisional time schedule for school continuation (in our first study of pregnant adolescents [1968], we found that pregnancy enhanced learning capacities as often as physical discomfort and psychological distress interfered with study procedures); (6) facilitation of contact with appropriate community resources offering specialized assistance to the pregnant adolescent; and (7) family planning, education, and advice beginning during pregnancy, with routinized, careful, concentrated planning of postdelivery contraceptive activities (Michael Reese Hospital has pioneered interventions that rely on peer-group leaders to help sexually active adolescents to clarify personal values, learn decision-making skills, and obtain practice in trying out behavior that leads to effective contraception). (Rogel et at., 1981).

Specific Types of Intervention

PARENTING THE INFANT EFFECTIVELY

Preparation for parenting, as with adults, must begin during pregnancy. The Adolescent Parenting Program of Michael Reese Hospital Dysfunctioning Child Center utilizes the following principles during pregnancy to facilitate later adolescent parenting.

Nurturance. Adolescent mothers-to-be require positive, optimistic (even enthusiastic) emotional support to facilitate their full involvement in childbirth preparation. Only this kind of milieu ensures patient follow-through with the multiple pregnancy-related recommendations of the medical facility. Such an atmosphere is created by high staff-patient ratios, personal and individualized physical contact during pregnancy exercise, twenty-four-hour availability of staff in person or by phone, and joint participation in snacks and some social activities.

Concentrated Childbirth Preparation. Accurate information is given to individuals and groups, using sound, visual, and reading materials which describe in depth the course and potential complications of pregnancy, labor, and delivery. Questions are encouraged and patient learning evaluated. Visits to labor and delivery rooms, full explanation of laboratory tests and special diagnostic procedures, such as stress-testing, produce familiarity and reinforce cooperation between patients and staff. Relaxation and breathing techniques taken from the Lamaze method are prescribed for suitable participants, and obstetrical anesthesia methods are discussed. These considerations and steps reduce the fear of pain and enhance a perception of active participation in future labor and delivery.

Pregnancy as a Growth Experience. Through specific physical exercises, sometimes including dance, adolescents can explore (in fantasy) aspects of their changing identity. Perceptual-motor exercises facilitate the process of learning from others—older teenagers, staff, and sometimes parents. Maintenance of body tone, development of stamina, and a sense of competence are vital for both childbirth and effective parenting. Optimal adolescent self-care prepares the future mother to care better for her baby's needs.

FACILITATION OF BONDING FOLLOWING DELIVERY

In 1978 Lester compared infants of adolescent mothers with those of older mothers two days after birth, using the complex neurobehavioral Brazelton examination. He found babies of adolescent mothers to be either significantly underaroused or overaroused when compared with babies of older mothers. He also suggested that in cultures where early marriage and childbearing are accepted as part of normal adolescent development (for example, in Puerto Rico), teenage mothers are likely to experience less stress. Field (1980) noted that teenage mothers were less vocal, less contingently responsive, and engaged in less game-playing during face-to-face interactions with their infants, as opposed to older mothers' behavior. During feeding, adolescents held their infants in a less beneficial position and gazed at their babies less often. Sandler (1977) found that older mothers spent more time talking to and looking at their babies than did young mothers. The more attentive interactions were associated with infants' higher scores on motor and mental development tests at nine months of age. Self-preoccupation seems to contribute to the teenage mother's inadequate stimulation of her child during the first six months of the infant's life. Adult mothers tend to be more nurturing and concerned with the well-being of their children. These observations emphasize the importance of diagnosing and treating bonding deficiencies in the evolving adolescent mother-infant relationship.

If difficulties in bonding exist, intervention is indicated. Enhancement of attachment can be facilitated by early and also prolonged periods of contact between the infant, mother, and father in a relaxed atmosphere, with a nurse or midwife available as consultant. The mother should be encouraged to touch, stroke, hold (particularly in a face-to-face position), fondle, and feed the baby, and to visit regularly and take an active part in the baby's care. There are many reasons for failure of attachment, some easily correctable and some extremely difficult to treat. No simple methods exist for treatment of attachment failure; only careful psychological identification of the impediment leads to the correct course of action. Methods of intervention may include any combination of the following: encouragement of contact, modeling of methods of handling infants, use of surrogate mothers, adoption, and in rare instances, placement of the infant with or without legal involvement. Caplan (1981) has stressed that disorders of bonding can be prevented if special efforts are made to ensure proper contact between infant and mother, and he has commented on the role of modeling to facilitate bonding.

Zimrin, (1978), evaluating methods of changing infant-battering behavior of mothers, has demonstrated the beneficial effect of modeling over placebo intervention and nonintervention. If possible, the infant should be discharged only after attachment has been demonstrated according to the criteria already mentioned. Even after discharge, caregivers need to be alert for signs of inadequate home nurturance, evidence of the infant's failure to thrive, recurrent unexplained infections in the infant, or of minor child abuse indicating serious problems in attachment. A visiting nurse or professional home help in selected cases may be indicated. If, however, serious problems in attachment continue, the obstetrician may have to call upon a mental health worker expert in effecting maternal emotional care for the infant or may have to involve the extended family or a community support system.

PROMOTION OF BREAST-FEEDING

To establish the superiority of breast-feeding over modern formulas for infants of adult mothers is not as simple as many breast-feeding advocates indicate. The matter is even less clear-cut for adolescent mothers. Random assignment of infants to breast-feeding or bottle-feeding research cohorts is impossible, and changes in feeding method are almost always in the direction away from breast-feeding, adding "nonhealthy infants" to the bottle-fed study population. Although considerable evidence suggests that breast-feeding reduces infant morbidity and mortality and enhances mother-infant attachment, adolescents are the one population least likely to breast-feed.

The scarcity of psychological data about the aversion to breast-feeding of adolescent mothers is remarkable. The Reese Department of Psychiatry has therefore initiated a long-range study of the phenomenon (Stetland, personal communication, 1983). Preliminary findings document the complexity of the decision-making process and the need to understand the unique circumstances of each young mother with regard to the following questions. If the adolescent's mother is primary caregiver for the infant, does breast-feeding complicate bonding to the grandmother? Are medical or nursing staff sabotaging breast-feeding because of their reactions to the mother's youth? Has the adolescent had exposure to at least one peer-group member who was successful in breast-feeding? Are the family and school systems flexible enough to allot the time required for mother-infant intimacy? What are the attitudes of the baby's father toward breast-feeding? In answering these questions, all information relevant to other interventions should have been obtained. Unfortunately, data mobilized at our institution, do not yet offer final conclusions about the feasibility of breast-feeding success for this population (Goodman, 1975).

PSYCHOLOGICAL MANAGEMENT OF PREMATURITY

Prematurity is the one neonatal risk factor most clearly linked statistically with adolescent pregnancy. Infants weighing less than 2,500 grams are born from 15 to 20 percent of adolescent mothers compared to 10 to 15 percent from older women (Peterson et al., 1982). The premature infant signifies to the infant's mother the possibility of permanent disability or death. Goodman (1975) has described the following early signs of anticipatory grief and mourning that indicate the mother has given up hope: fatigue, loss of appetite, sighing, and feelings of remorse and guilt. It has often been noted that even if it appears that the baby will live the mother mourns for the normal fullterm infant she never had.

Solnit and Stark (1961) have described a frequent depressive reaction precipitated by the birth of a defective child. Mothers displayed a mourning reaction to the loss of a fantasied child and an adaptation to the reality of the existing child. Responses to a premature infant also differ from reactions to a clearly disabled infant. Cummings and colleagues (1966) have emphasized the marked diversity of parental adjustments to a child's deficiency state. In their study, mental retardation seemed to produce greater psychic stress than chronic physical illness. The visibility of the organic defect and its implications for longevity were considered important factors in maternal adaptation.

The deleterious effects of prematurity can be counteracted by appropriate interventions. Klaus and Kennel (1974), for example, have suggested that harmful effects of the early mother-infant separation, which often accompany prematurity or infant morbidity, can be almost completely neutralized by special efforts of hospital helping personnel. However, their claim of long-range beneficial consequences of early skin-to-skin contact between mother and newborn has been corroborated by only a few studies (de Château and Wiberg, 1977). Rheingold (1956) showed that home care for infants was associated with much more human intervention—handling, talking, body contact—than was true of institutionalized infants, but he could not demonstrate behavioral differences in two small infant groups. Some investigators, impressed by the need for early intervention, have pioneered the development of nursery and home stimulation-programs for low-birthweight infants. Nurses provide extra talking, rocking, and tactile contact. Social workers later make regular home visits to encourage the mother's continuous optimal child care and stimulation. The experimental group was later found to have a higher developmental status than a control group (Scarr-Salapetek and Williams, 1973). Powell, (1974) who duplicated this intervention effort with prematures, also found higher mental scores on the Bayley scales at six months, but found no differences in weight, height, or other developmental indices at two, four, or six months of age. Rice (1975) provided tactile-kinesthetic stimulation to thirty premature infants with a gestational age of thirty-seven weeks or less and a birthweight of 2,500 grams or less. Severely compromised infants (physically or neurologically) were excluded. These stimulated infants gained more weight and showed more advanced developmental scores on the Bayley mental and motor scales than a control group.

A scrutiny of stimulation studies of premature infants has led us to conclude that recent evidence clearly justifies the use of intensive infant stimulation (Schaefer et al., 1980). Our approach to helping the premature infant utilizes intervention that consists of weekly structured and sequential individual tutoring sessions, including a step-by-step program of maternal activities designed to promote specific behavioral sequences (social skills, language attainment, motoric capacity, group-play learning). Infant groups are assessed periodically (four times) until two years of age using instruments such as the Bayley (1969), Uzgiris and Hunt (1975), and Bell (1971) developmental profiles. Considerable effectiveness of intervention can be demonstrated. If all the preceding approaches are consistently utilized, beginning early in adolescent pregnancy, the infant's prognosis may well be as favorable as that of the older mother's offspring.

REFERENCES

Barglow, P. (1980). When to help—when to refer. *Transitions* 3:2–4, (Syntex Labs).

Barglow, P. et al. (1968). Some psychiatric aspects of illegitimate pregnancy in early adolescence. *American Journal of Orthopsychiatry,* 38:672–687.

Barglow, P., Edidin, D., Budlong-Springer, A., and Berndt, D. (1983). Diabetic control in children and adolescents: Psychological factors and therapeutic efficacy. *Journal of Youth and Adolescence,* 12:77–94.

Barglow, P. et al. (1981). Psychiatric risk factors in the pregnant diabetic patient. *American Journal of Obstetrics and Gynecology,* 140:46–52.

Bayley, N. (1969). *Bayley Scales of Infant Development,* New York: The Psychological Corporation.

Bell, R. Q., Weller, G. M., and Waldrop, M. D. (1971). Newborn and preschooler: Organization of behavior and relations between periods. *Monographs of the Society for Research in Child Development.*

Brazelton, T. B. (1973). The Neonatal Behavior Assessment Scale. Philadelphia: J. B. Lippincott.

Brown, H., Adams, R., and Kellam, S. (1980). A longitudinal study of teenage motherhood and symptoms of distress: The Woodlawn Community Epidemiological Project. In *Research in Community and Mental Health,* vol. 2, ed., R. Simmons. Greenwich, Connecticut: JAI Press.

Caplan, G. (1981). The first year of life: Mother-infant bonding. Paper read at a conference at Michael Reese Hospital, Chicago, Illinois, May 29.

Cummings, S. T., Bayley, H. C., and Rie, H. E. (1966). Effects of the child's deficiency on the mother: a study of mothers of mentally retarded, chronically ill and neurotic children. *American Journal of Orthopsychiatry,* 36:595–608.

de Château, P. and Wiberg, B. (1977). Long-term effect on mother-infant behavior of extra contact during the first hour postpartum. *Acta Paediatrics in Scandinavia,* 66:137–143, 145–151.

Field, T. M. (1980). Interactions of preterm and term infants with lower- and middle-class teenage and adult mothers. In *High-Risk Infants and Children,* ed. T. Field. New York: Academic Press.

Gabrielson, W., Klerman, L. V., and Curne, J. B. (1970). Suicide attempts in a population pregnant as teenagers. *American Journal of Public Health,* 60:22–29.

Goodman, M. D. (1975). Two mothers' reactions to the deaths of their premature infants. *Journal of Obstetrics and Gynecology Neonatal Nursing,* 4:25–27.

Graham, F. K., Matarazzo, R. G., and Caldwell, B. M. (1956). Behavioral differences between normal and traumatized newborns: II. Standardization, reliability and validity. *Psychological Monographs,* 70, (No. 428).

Klaus, M. H. and Kennell, J. H. (1974). Evidence for a sensitive period in the human mother. In *Maternal Attach-*ment and Mothering Disorders: A Round Table, ed. M. H. Klaus, T. Leger, and M. H. Trause. Sausalito, California: Johnson & Johnson.

Lester, B. M. (1978). Relations between teenage pregnancy and neonatal behavior. Washington, D. C.: *National Institute for Child Health and Development.*

Loevinger, J. (1976). *Ego Development: Conceptions and Theories,* London: Jossey-Bass.

Peterson, C., Sripada, B., and Barglow, P. (1982). Psychiatric aspects of adolescent pregnancy. *Psychosomatics,* 23: 723–733.

Powell, L. F. (1974). The effect of extra stimulation and maternal involvement on low-birthweight infants and on maternal behavior. *Child Development,* 45:106–113.

Rheingold, H. L. (1956). The modification of social responsiveness in institutional babies. *Child Development,* Monographs 21:2:Serial 63.

Rice, R. (1975). The effects of tactile-kinesthetic stimulation on the subsequent development of premature infants. Dissertation, University of Texas, Austin.

Rogel, M. et al. (1981). Contraceptive behavior in adolescence—a decision-making perspective. *Journal of Youth and Adolescence,* 10:491–506.

Sameroff, A. (1975). Early influences on development: Fact or fancy? *Merrill-Palmer Quarterly,* 21:267–294.

Sandler, H. M. (1977). Effects of adolescent pregnancy on mother-infant relationships: A transactional model. Washington, D. C.: *National Institute of Child Health and Development.*

Scarr-Salapetek, S. and Williams, M. (1973). The effects of early stimulation on low birthweight. *Child Development,* 44:94–104.

Schaefer, M., Hatcher, R., and Barglow, P. (1980). Prematurity and infant stimulation: A review of research. *Child Psychiatry and Human Development,* 10:199–212.

Schaffer, C. and Pine, F. (1972). Pregnancy, abortion and the developmental tasks of adolescence. *Journal of American Academy of Child Psychiatry,* 11:511–536.

Solnit, A. J. and Stark, M. H. (1961). Mourning and the birth of a defective child. *The Psychoanalytic Study of the Child,* 16:523–537. New York: International Universities Press.

Werner, E., Simonian, K., Bierman, J. M., and French, F. E. (1967). Cumulative effect of perinatal complications and deprived environment on physical, intellectual and social development of pre-school children. *Pediatrics,* 39:480–505.

Zimrin, H. (1978). Intervention aimed to change battering behavior of mothers towards their children. Doctoral dissertation, Hebrew University of Jerusalem.

Uzgiris, I. C. and Hunt, J. Mc V. (1975). *Toward Ordinal Scales of Psychological Development in Infancy.* Champaign, Illinois: University of Illinois.

33

Teasing as an Inducer of Violence

Richard Galdston, M.D.

This paper is based upon the observation that teasing is prominent as a mode of relating favored among the 85 families and their 125 children between the ages of one to four years who have been the subjects of a fourteen-year investigation into domestic violence. These families were included in the study on the basis of their demonstrated tendency toward recurrent physical assaults. The *Concise Oxford Dictionary* of 1923 defines teasing as "to assail playfully or maliciously, to vex with jests, questions or petty annoyances . . . to pick into separate fibres."

Detailed study, including a videotaped record, reveals four steps of interpersonal exchange in an episode of teasing: (1) excitement of desire is stimulated by word or sight; (2) incitement to action is elicited by one party, who offers a part of his or her body as bait to be acted upon, to get a "rise" out of the other; (3) provocation is put forth by the one who has been excited and incited to respond: "You asked for it!"; and (4) retaliation is the response: "I'll fix you!" Aggression is discharged as violence or as flight to avoid violence. The cycle of engagement in teasing is concluded

The Parent's Center Project for the Study in Prevention of Child Abuse was begun in 1968 with members of the staff of the Parents and Children's Services, Boston, Mass. The author is Principal Investigator (Galdston, 1981). Donald S. Zall, ACSW, and Patricia O'Connell, MSW, LICSW, made significant clinical observations upon which parts of this paper are based.

with the disappointment of desire followed by attack or retreat.

Teasing lies midway between threat and bribe on the spectrum of interpersonal manipulation. Because it can be defined only by intent, it is difficult to measure for purposes of comparison. The prominence of teasing among our study group derives from a lack of other modes of relating between these parents and their children. Tenderness is scant. Mutuality of respect conveyed by permission asked and gratitude granted is lacking. Neither requests nor thanks are verbalized. Needs are negotiated as demands ordered or as nonverbal communications acted out with others. Adults teasing each other use children in a special role as go-betweens, as agents carrying behavior back and forth between the mates. In some instances the child gets caught up in the ensuing violence and is used literally as a shield to protect one parent from the blows of the other. Within this context, teasing as relating looms the larger by default.

A mother invited her four-year-old daughter to awaken her sleeping father. When the child did so, the father flew into a rage at the child, who burst into tears. The mother then confronted her husband with their sobbing daughter, saying, "See? Lookit her! That's how you make me feel all the time!"

Between adults, teasing can serve as a proximal stimulus to kindle and ignite violent behavior. Between adults and their children, the teasing experience can have significant consequences upon the young child's development.

Disappointment and Comforting

The typical apology offered the child by the teasing adult is, "I was only kidding!" "Can't you take a joke?" "I didn't mean it . . . don't be so silly!" Such explanations consign the experience to the realm of play—a transitional area where things may or may not be what they seem (Winnicott, 1971). A mother told her four-year-old son to "go out and play on the turnpike!" When asked why she invited such danger upon her son, she responded that she was "only kidding," and "didn't mean it!" This mother had previously complained that her son never listened to her and was chronically disobedient.

For the young child, excited to desire and incited to act as if by reality, the revelation of an illusion has the effect of a disappointment of desire: "Now you see it—now you don't!" (Jacobson, 1946). In the immediate aftermath the child turns away from the disappointing object. The disappointment often precipitates temper tantrums, the release of a tumult of energies that can erupt when a child's behavior "falls to pieces." Study of the "pieces," the tears of rage and grief, the gnashing of teeth, the pulling of hair, and attacks upon those near and dear reveal these to be the expressions of libidinal and destructive instincts that have been deprived of their expected object by the teasing experience. The child's attainment of a composition of libidinal and destructive instincts into a stage-appropriate endeavor has been disrupted. The child's ego structure decomposes temporarily, allowing less organized instinctual discharge.

Under optimal conditions, the tantrums evoke a response from the mother. Her attentions provide the child with a comforting presence, which she lends through her body and voice. By being with the child through the disintegration of the tantrum into the restoration of composure she puts "the pieces" back together again. She affords the child a prototype of comforting as the remedy for disappointment. The strengthening potential of experience at receiving comfort goes far to promote the development of courage, the child's faith that something can be done to contend with the dangers of disappointment.

Armed with the idea of comforting as a precursor for courage, the young child is better prepared to overcome the affective and instinctual consequences of disappointment. This preparation is needed to support the vigorous exercise of aggression sufficient to gain a sense of reality and to relinquish the primacy of the fantasies of omnipotence that prevail during early toddlerhood. In such fashion, the toddler can come to know the limitations of his or her competence to contend with what lies about.

Normally, the child's drive to master aggression through work toward personal accomplishment is a force for ego growth sufficient to contend with the ravages of disappointed desire. The toddler's exercise of aggression in pursuit of adventures into reality is greatly supported by access to a reliable comforting presence to draw upon as need be. Occasionally, one may overhear children of three to four years of age speaking softly to themselves, "Now don't you worry . . . Everything is gonna be all right." These children have developed the means to comfort themselves when the objects of their instinctual energies fail to live up to their expectations.

When the capacity to comfort is deficient, as it is among most of the parents in our study, the child is left to his or her own devices to contend with disappointment. We have studied the ways by which children in the Project manage disappointment through the fabrication of comforting devices, mental imagery, bodily practices, and fictitious figures from which they can draw comfort. These practices can go far to support the child in distress. However, the addition of parental teasing to a limited capacity to offer comfort places a burden upon the child that is beyond his or her tolerance.

Teasing as Premeditated Disappointment

The stress of chronic teasing without comforting results in a restriction in ego development that can have far-reaching effects upon the subsequent formation of character structure. As a mode of interaction, teasing serves to detach the child's instinctual drive derivatives from the objects with whom he or she seeks to engage the world. Insofar as early ego growth depends upon the child's capacity to act upon the object world (Modell, 1968), teasing exerts a disintegrative effect upon ego functioning. When reintegration is promoted by parental comforting, the child can use the teasing-comforting sequence as a means of separating his or her self out of the matrix of the object world by recognizing and acknowledging the boundaries of each—the "me" and the "not me" of experience. But teasing without comforting turns the aggression back upon its source instead of directing it to the objects that lie beyond the child. It exerts a diabolic rather than a symbolic influence upon the development of the child's ego (May, 1975).

In order to adapt to chronic teasing, the child must learn to operate at a more primitive level in which both object and instinct remain largely within the child's psychic domain. Curiosity is constricted and aggression limited largely to the exercise of control through compulsive repetition. With a reduced capacity to sublimate aggression toward the mastery of ego functions through work (Hendrick, 1943), the child becomes vulnerable to violence as the result of aggression that exceeds ego competence to administer.

OBJECT INCONSTANCY AND THE SPREAD OF NARCISSISM

Teasing by parents confronts the child with primary objects who are willfully fickle. The parents' conversion of pleasurable stimuli into painful experience confounds the child's association of affects with objects. Reliance upon protection from a personal pain barrier (Hoffer, 1950) is rendered untrustworthy, and the child must develop other attitudes and practices to attain a sense of safety.

The teased child presents a picture of constricted apathetic behavior marked by outbursts of tears or assaults against whoever gets too close. The child tends to substitute auto-

erotic practices for social activity, often with the admonition to others to "Get outta here . . . !" Curiosity suffers as withdrawal from the object world limits experience to what lies largely within the established domain of the child's control. The boundaries of the child's narcissistic space become almost perceptible to the adult observer and to other children, who may comment, "Best leave him alone . . . something is bothering him." The child may maintain a sort of "free-fire zone." Anyone who enters it will occasion outcries of alarm or physical attack.

The male children tend to pursue repetitious activities, such as taking off and putting on shoes or the aimless waving of a vacuum cleaner hose. The child is absorbed in an activity with no apparent purpose other than the stereotyped exercise of an idiosyncratic effort that appears to afford relief through compulsion.

The girls tend to become absorbed in the private enactment of fantasy, pursued as if determined by a need to repair some wrong. The activity may be elaborate, involving imagined others, writing pretend notes of instructions, whispering commands to perform deeds—all pressed with a fervor that precludes distraction or participation by others. As play, it is joyless, solitary, and very important to the child. The children, male or female, engaged in such behavior are avoided by the others as if it were tacitly understood that the child was engaged in some solo mission that should not be disturbed.

The teased child develops a sense of object inconstancy—important objects are not what they appear to be. The issue of "turning into," of magical transformation, remains a source of wonderment and a lasting preoccupation for many of these children. The themes most favored by the children as stories or films are those that deal with the question of how good and bad can be made into the other, by whom, and under what circumstances. This concern has an obsessional quality—recounted, reviewed, and acted-out in make-believe forms, incarnations of animals, Superman, the Hulk, and the like. All manner of being, with benign and evil affects changing back and forth before one's very eyes, become matters of imagery for enactment by the children as they attempt to order their experience of the ways things change in their lives.

When a child's most predictable experience is of the unpredictability of pleasure turning into pain or of pain into pleasure, emotional ambivalence is the affective state most likely to prevail. Acceptance of object inconstancy becomes congruent with experience of the external world. As a construct of expectation it is consonant with the burgeoning of emotional ambivalence.

SPLITTING, AMBIVALENCE, AND MANIPULATION

The persistence of intensely ambivalent emotions requires the child to split his or her perceptions of objects and to segregate them according to the qualities of "good" or "bad" to attain some sense of harmony among the introjects of experience (Horowitz, 1977; Klein, 1932). The consequence of splitting upon the child's object relations is demonstrated by the recurring need among many of the children to develop relationships with different child-care workers according to the various ego functions and affect states these workers serve. Most common is the selection of one child-care worker with whom to have fights and another to make up with. Others are selected to be fed by and to cuddle with, to be taken to the toilet by, and to be put down for naps by. Splitting becomes more than a cognitive or perceptual adaptation. What begins as an intrapsychic accommodation to the demands of ambivalent emotions becomes, in time, a way of life.

The splitting of perception and the segregation of affects becomes a prototype for ego functioning that shapes character structure and determines lifestyle. Splitting makes it possible for the child to avoid the hazards of contending with emotional ambivalence and solving internal conflict through the substitution of interactions with others instead of developing ego functions to master self-care.

The adults studied in the Project manifest certain habits of behavior that can be understood to be the result of chronic splitting and the compartmentalization of experience. A number of women have had two men to whom they related at the same time for different purposes. Others repeated a series of relationships with similar men and similar outcomes. Many of the men have fathered other families previously. Each relationship is replaced by the next as if nothing had gone before from which the participant might learn something of personal value. They have the experience but miss the meaning.

Objects are chosen to fit affects—someone to love, someone to hate, and other "someones" chosen to manipulate in accordance with the rise and fall of anxiety. Objects who agree to correspond to the affects for which they were selected lend themselves to manipulation into a network of relationships fabricated as the external representation of intrapsychic conflict. One mother described her skill at this process by likening her manipulations to those of Archie Bunker in the TV series, "All in the Family." A father observed about himself that "when things get too hot for me, why then I crank up the old chaos machine . . . and the beat goes on!"

THE SEARCH FOR INTEGRITY: CRISIS AND VIOLENCE

The creation of a crisis among these violence-prone adults follows a course that points to an underlying pattern. In many respects, it resembles the teasing behavior between parent and child, except that it is more elaborate and involves a number of participants. The sequence of exciting, inciting, provocation, and retaliation can be recognized as the motif played out within the context of relationships arranged to camouflage flaws in ego structure. Deficits in ego functioning are supplemented and concealed through the manipulation of others.

The observer can trace the spread of anxiety as it is propagated from intrapsychic conflict to interpersonal crisis, which can erupt into domestic violence that rapidly spreads to acquire social dimensions through the intervention of the police or the other agencies with which society attempts to control the unacceptable behavior of its members.

The stability of the system of interpersonal manipulation depends upon the willingness and ability of the various "someones" selected to fit specific affects to fulfill their assignments. Because the selection process is based upon the specifications of unmastered shifting ambivalence, the requirements are bound to change. The man chosen to be strong is shortly hated for it. The child assigned to be docile is faulted for being a wimp. The tides of ambivalence rise and fall. The objects chosen to correspond to feelings are swept in and out of favor with an ebb and flow of affects that is bewildering and confusing. One of the adults likened the experience to being on a "merry-go-round with a drunken driver." Another described her situation as resembling that of the tigers in *Little Black Sambo* who chased each other's tails around a tree at such a dizzying pace that they were turned into butter.

As long as the participants perform according to their requirements of each other, the system of interpersonal manipulation serves to stabilize a balance of affects. Sooner or later, someone doesn't do what he or she is supposed to. There is a breakdown in the provision of mutual ego support through manipulation. An eruption of emotion and an outburst of activity ensues in the form of a crisis. The crisis threatens to confront the participants with the ambivalent emotions that they bear toward their objects, a demand upon their egos that they are not prepared to meet.

At this point, the emerging ambivalence of emotion and the mounting activity are apt to collide in an attack of violence. An alternative course can be observed in the diffusion of the crisis to involve others. The original partners become crisis-mongers, recruiting other parties to take sides and join what will shortly become a reconstitution of an external representation of ambivalence. A polarization occurs among those who have intervened in the crisis only to find themselves parties to a new version of an old conflict in which they have become the new "someones" chosen to correspond to the affective needs of the original manipulators.

It is of note that the phrase favored to announce imminent violence is "I'm gonna fix him (or her)!" The verb *to fix* has at least three meanings: to *repair* a break, to make whole; to *locate* in a position; and to *castrate*. The act of violence functions as a fixative in the three senses of the word. The ambivalent emotions and the underlying drives are joined to the same object through the process of assault and making up. The cycle of love and hate chasing each other is aborted. The discharge of aggression in violence stops the movement and releases the tension of ambivalent emotions bestirred through teasing behavior.

The role of violence in the sexual relations of the adults in our study is complex. For many of the couples, the idea or act of violence is an aphrodisiac. Typically, the sequence begins with teasing that escalates to a threat or act of violence, followed by sexual intercourse. Partners unwilling or unable to engage in violence are soon discarded as "boring" or "too nice." The postures of assailant and victim, usually alternating between the partners, appear to function as a means of temporarily reconciling sexual ambivalence. Violence appears to "clear the air" of personal doubts and hostilities, to allow for a "fix" on gender as male or female sufficient to enable the couple to consummate intercourse, an act otherwise difficult for them to achieve.

The pattern of chronic teasing of children and adults, cyclical crisis-making, and periodic violence remains singularly constant over years. The devotion of the partners is structured upon the process of interpersonal manipulation in the service of propagating unacknowledged and unmastered ambivalence. When one drops out of the relationship, another quickly appears to take his or her place. The ego-sparing effects of this arrangement can be detected in the absence of signs of personal distress among the participants, whose blithe indifference to recurring crises as a way of life bespeaks their relief from the burden of having to contend personally with their own ambivalence.

The status of chronic victimhood is not only accepted but defended against attempts by outside parties to bring change. The intervention of others in the cycle of crisis and violence is both sought out and rejected. The position of victim affords an order of psychic security from the responsibility for the resolution of personal ambivalence.

REFERENCES

Galdston, R. The domestic dimensions of violence, *The Psychoanalytic Study of the Child*, vol. 36, pp. 391–413. New Haven: Yale University Press.

Hendrick, I. (1943). Work and the pleasure principle, *Psychoanalytic Quarterly*, 12:311–329.

Hoffer, W., (1950). Oral aggressiveness and ego development, *International Journal of Psychoanalysis*, 31:156–160.

Horowitz, M. (1977). Cognitive and interactive aspects of splitting, *American Journal of Psychiatry*, 134:549–553.

Jacobson, E. (1946). The effect of disappointment on ego and super-ego development in normal and depressive development. *The Psychoanalytic Review*, 33:129–147.

Klein, M. (1932). *The Psychoanalysis of Children*. London: Hogarth Press.

Mahler, M. (1972). On the first three subphases of the separation-individuation process. *International Journal of Psycho-Analysis*, 53:333–338.

May, R. (1975). Values, myths and symbols. *American Journal of Psychiatry*, 132:703–706.

Modell, A. (1968). *Object Love and Reality*. New York: International Universities Press.

Winnicott, D. (1971) *Playing and Reality*. New York: Basic Books.

34

Three-Year Follow-Up of Early Postpartum Contact

Peter de Château, M.D. and Britt Wiberg

Introduction

John Kennell, M.D.

When the results of the de Château and Wiberg study were first published, Marshall Klaus and I were greatly interested because the study had some of the features of research design, and also vivid contrasts, of our original study on full-term infants reported in 1972. Our study showed that mothers who had one hour of contact with their baby in the first three hours and five additional hours of contact on the first three hospital days showed differences in behavior as a group at one month and at one year.

Our study in Cleveland had been carried out with poor mothers, primarily black and single, who were bottle-feeding their babies. The Swedish mothers de Château and Wiberg studied came from middle-class backgrounds, were married, and planned to breast-feed in the hospital. Prior to the de Château and Wiberg report, two studies of Guatemalan mothers with their infants in the first two days of life (Hales et al., 1976, 1977) had revealed significant differences in behavior with and without early contact. However, we were not surprised at the small number of differences detected in the Swedish mothers thirty-six hours after delivery during breast-feeding because of the technical difficulties of detecting differences in holding and feeding behavior when the mother is breast-feeding.

De Château and Wiberg's observation that there were significant differences in the behavior of the mothers in the two groups at three months confirmed that other investigators could find differences in a totally different population in a home visit. At that time we did not have the technology to make precise observations of the infant's behavior, so the significant differences in infant behavior that they found in the two groups added a new dimension. In their introduction to the paper that follows here, de Château and Wiberg suggest that the exposure of the newborn infant "at an early stage to certain modalities like skin and suckling contact . . . may perhaps be an important precursor for integration of one's personality and subsequent capacity to relate to other individuals." This is different from our original concept. It was our hypothesis that the events in the first minutes and hours after delivery might affect the later attachment and parenting behavior of the mother and father, and in turn their greater interest, affection, and attention to their infant repeated over and over again would result in differences such as were found at three months. This constitutes an important area for further study and discussion.

The new details provided in this paper are helpful for those interested in parent-to-infant attachment. As time has passed and other studies of early parent-infant contact have been conducted, it has become clear that it is extremely important for investigators to record in their publications precise details about the "routine care," the characteristics of the patient population, and exactly what happened to each mother. All of us tend to think of our hospital routine as being the same as that of other hospitals. Even when we consider two hospitals under the direction of the same Department of Obstetrics or Pediatrics in any one city, a careful observer who moves from one hospital to the other will see myriad differences. We gained a new understanding of our own data when we looked at pictures taken during the period of early contact in our original fullterm study. Surprisingly, the differences in the behavior of the mothers in the experimental group were accounted for entirely by the women who were awake and interacting with their babies throughout the one-hour period of early contact. Further analysis showed that the mothers in the experimental group who slept through much of that experience had received larger doses of medication closer to the time of delivery. Our subsequent studies of human support during labor (Sosa et al., 1980) have made it clear that human support provided to a mother during her labor may affect her interaction with her baby during the period of early contact. It would be helpful to know which mothers in the Swedish study had the father present in the delivery room and during the time after delivery when the baby was placed in the mothers' bed.

In examining studies of early mother-infant contact, it is essential to appreciate the words of a student of the sensitive period, P. Bateson (1979), who notes, "The extent to which a sensitive period is replicated may frequently depend on the degree to which conditions in which it was first described are copied. Even small changes can cause the evidence to evaporate. These alterations in conditions are worth

investigating because they probe the system" (p. 482).

Thus the slight but possibly important alterations in conditions in different hospitals may account for some of the apparent inconsistencies in outcome across studies. These variables include whether both the control and experimental infants are either dressed or undressed, whether the father is present or absent, and the conditions of privacy or no privacy. What is surprising is how similar the changes in maternal behavior are, even from widely varying cultures.

A listing of the medical criteria is also necessary in making comparisons across studies. The restriction on patients not receiving "more than 200 mg. of pethidin" suggests a use of this medication that far exceeds the dosage used at the time of our 1972 study. And the use of this drug has been significantly decreased since then.

It is also interesting to compare the timing of contact across studies. Our own experience may help with "probing the system," to use Bateson's term, and relieving the concerns of parents who do not have contact with their infant in the first sixty minutes. In the study we reported in 1972, the earliest any experimental mother received her undressed baby (for the one-hour period of contact in privacy under a heat panel) was sixty-one minutes. For the majority the delay in contact was between one and two hours. In that study the mothers said they planned to bottle-feed, so all the mothers were gowned during the early and extended contact and there was no skin-to-skin contact.

De Château and Wiberg emphasize the important point that it is necessary to present the number of observations made and the details of the statistical analysis because "when we look at the results of the study, it is obvious that only a few of the many observed behaviors differed among the groups."

The major area of disagreement concerning studies of parent-infant bonding have revolved around whether for a small number of mothers there are any lasting effects of early maternal-infant contact on the mother's behavior toward her baby and on their subsequent relationship. A parent's behavior is affected by cultural and socioeconomic background, genetic endowment, parenting received by his or her own parents, hospital care practices, the nature and health of the baby, family relations, experiences with past pregnancies, as well as the presence or absence of mother-newborn contact in the early days after birth. The paper by de Château and Wiberg suggests the possibility of effects that last as long as three years. With all the complex factors influencing a parent's behavior, it should not be surprising that our present techniques do not show significant differences after thirty-six months. However, future studies may focus on features of the child that more sensitively detect the effects of the parents' early postpartum experience. If early and extended contact makes a difference in the incidence of abuse, failure to thrive, abandonment, and neglect, as is suggested by the study of O'Connor and colleagues (1980), but not confirmed by the study of Siegel and colleagues (1980), more striking differences in parent-infant interaction and in the behavior and development of some children can be anticipated.

REFERENCES

Bateson, P. (1979). How do sensitive periods arise and what are they for? *Animal Behavior*, 27:470–486.

Hales, D. J., Lozoff, B., Sosa, R., and Kennell, J. H. (1977). Defining the limits of the maternal sensitive period. *Developmental Medicine and Child Neurology*, 19:454–461.

Hales, D. J., Trause, M. A., and Kennell, J. H. (1976). How early is early contact? Defining the limits of the sensitive period. *Pediatric Research*, 10:448.

Klaus, M. H. et al. (1972). Maternal attachment: Importance of the first postpartum days. *New England Journal of Medicine*, 286:460–463.

O'Connor, S. M. et al. (1980). Reduced incidence of parenting inadequacy following rooming-in. *Pediatrics*, 66:-176–182.

Siegel, E. et al. (1980). Hospital and home support during infancy: Impact on maternal attachment, child abuse and neglect, and health care utilization. *Pediatrics*, 66:183–190.

Sosa, R. et al. (1980). The effect of a supportive companion on perinatal problems, length of labor, and mother-infant interaction. *New England Journal of Medicine*, 303:597–600.

Discussion

In recent years the number of research programs dealing with the perinatal period and its impact on future psychosocial development of children and their families has been increasing. One reason for this interest may be a general trend in our western societies toward a more natural way of living. Several studies examining specific caregiving procedures around the time of delivery reflect this more natural attitude to the process of childbirth, (de Château and Wiberg, 1977a, 1977b; Kennell et al., 1974; Klaus et al., 1972; Larsson et al., 1979; Leifer et al., 1972; O'Conner et al., 1980; Taylor et al., 1979). They have documented that the early hours, days, weeks, and months after birth are of special importance for the development of the infant's state of stability, adaptation, and functional affection in relation to the parents. To be exposed at an early stage to certain modalities like skin and suckling contact, and also to experience hunger, pain, and distress, may perhaps be an important precursor for integration of one's personality and subsequent capacity to relate to other individuals. Other adult behavior such as holding, carrying, touching, talking, and showing different objects may be equally important to meet the needs of the neonate. The alertness of the newborn is highly significant and complements parental receptivity, thus preparing for a sensitive synchrony of responsiveness of infant and caretaker. In fact, the early parent-infant interaction is felt to determine the amount and quality of sensory stimulation received by the newborn later on.

This study was supported by the Swedish Medical Research Council (grant no. 5443), the University of Umeå, the Karolinska Institute, the Swedish Save the Children Fund, and the March of Dimes Foundation, New York.

The present communication is part of an ongoing longitudinal study on possible effects of early mother-infant contact. An extra naked, skin-to-skin, and suckling contact was given during the first hour postpartum to one group of mothers and infants while a control group received routine care. A summary of the results of follow-ups at thirty-six hours, three months, and twelve months are presented. More detailed information is given on follow-up three years after delivery.

Procedure

The study was performed in a university hospital and included forty-two mother-infant pairs divided into two groups: *P group (n = 20):* primiparous women, given routine care with their newborn infants; and *P+ group (n = 22):* primiparous women, given an extra twenty minutes of skin-to-skin and suckling contact with their newborn infants, followed by routine care.

A schedule of the postpartum care in the two groups is given in table 34–1. The basic conditions for participation in the study were that mothers and infants should be healthy and live in our hospital area and that pregnancy and delivery should have been normal and the neonatal period uncomplicated. Medical criteria that all mother-infant pairs had to meet were: maternal age twenty to twenty-nine years; length of pregnancy thirty-eight to forty-two weeks; no history of previous abortions or miscarriages; no use of drugs except iron medication and vitamins during pregnancy; normal weight gain; normal blood pressure and HB percentage; and no proteinuria. The mother had to have come into labor spontaneously at full term, to have had a labor of less than twenty-four hours, and not have received more than 200 mg. pethidin (or equivalent) one to six hours before parturition. All infants had to have been born by vertex presentation and to have no signs of intra- or extrauterine asphyxia. The apgar score was to be more than 7 at one minute pp, infant weight between 3,000 and 4,000 grams. None of the infants had any congenital mal-

formation and all were healthy one and six days postpartum.

Because the selection procedure is essential for the evaluation of this study, it will be described in some detail. When the mother arrived at the hospital for delivery the midwife made a preliminary selection based on previous obstetric history, present pregnancy, and residence. The records of these mothers were marked and numbered in order of arrival. By this preliminary procedure, fifty mothers were selected for the study. General care, observation, and preparation for delivery were carried out according to standard routine procedures. All women were delivered by the midwife on duty. Immediately after delivery, the midwife or nurse's aid matched the number on the mother's record with a table of random numbers. According to this table, the primiparous mothers were randomly assigned to either the "routine care" group (P) or the "extra contact" group (P+). Eight mother-infant pairs who did not fulfill the established criteria concerning residence, delivery, infant, and neonatal period were excluded from the study. The final study groups thus were composed of forty-two mother-infant pairs. The groups were comparable as to mean maternal age, civil and socioeconomic status, education, mean number of visits to antenatal clinics, maternal weight-gain during pregnancy, and mean gestational age. An equal proportion of the fathers were present at delivery, and the mean duration of labor and amount of analgesia used were comparable in the two groups.

ROUTINE CARE IMMEDIATELY FOLLOWING
DELIVERY (P)

After delivery the baby lies on the delivery table, between the legs of the mother. Mouth and upper airways are rinsed and the stomach emptied. Face, trunk, and legs are wiped dry with a towel. The infant is then shown to the mother for a brief glance, but usually she does not touch him. A numbered bracelet is put around the wrist of both mother and infant. After cord clamping, two–six minutes postpartum, the baby is taken to another part of the delivery room for weighing, bathing, physical

TABLE 34-1

Schedule of Postpartum Care of Infant

Time	Group	
	P (N = 20)	P+ (N = 22)
0–30 min. pp	Weighing, measuring, bathing, Credé-prophylaxis, dressing, etc.	Naked skin-to-skin and suckling contact with mother
next 15–30 min. pp	Resting dressed in crib or mother's bed	
45–120 min. pp		

P = primiparous mothers and infants with routine care after delivery
P+ = primiparous mothers and infants with extra contact following delivery

examination, Credé prophylaxis, and dressing. This takes approximately thirty minutes. In the meantime the mother is helped to deliver the placenta, washed, and cleaned. The baby—with clothes on—is put in a crib and covered with a blanket. The crib is placed beside the mother's bed so that she can watch her baby and touch the face. In some instances the baby, dressed and wrapped in a blanket, is placed in the mother's bed. The mother, the infant, and the father, who has often attended the delivery, remain together in the delivery room until approximately two hours after the actual time of birth, when they are transferred to the maternity ward.

"EXTRA CONTACT" IMMEDIATELY FOLLOWING DELIVERY (+)

Mouth and upper airways are rinsed, the stomach emptied, the body dried with a towel, and a numbered bracelet fastened around the wrists of infant and mother as in routine care. After clamping of the cord two to six minutes following delivery, the midwife puts the naked baby onto the mother's abdomen and the infant's back is covered with a blanket. This skin-to-skin contact begins approximately ten minutes postpartum. Some five minutes later the midwife moves the baby upwards on to the mother's chest and helps it to suckle from the mother's breast. It is now approximately fifteen minutes postpartum. This "extra contact" lasts for about ten to fifteen minutes. After this period, when the baby was about twenty-five to thirty minutes old, the normal

routine procedure just described was continued.

ROUTINE CARE AT THE MATERNITY WARD FROM ABOUT TWO HOURS AFTER DELIVERY UNTIL DISCHARGE FROM HOSPITAL SIX TO EIGHT DAYS LATER (P AND P+)

During the first three days the mother sees and nurses her infant every four hours during the day. During the night and most of the day the infant stays in a separate baby room. During the second half of the postpartum week the infant is placed in the mother's room during the day. The mother takes a more active part in the care of her infant, bathing, changing nappies and clothes, and so on. Most rooms have accommodation for four mothers and their infants.

FOLLOW-UPS

Table 34-2 shows the design of the follow-up studies at thirty-six hours, three, twelve, and thirty-six months. Observation of behavior of all subjects was made thirty-six hours after delivery in the mother's own room during breast-feeding (de Chateau and Wiberg, 1977a). At three months during a home visit, observations were made of mother-infant free-play and an unstructured personal interview with the mothers was carried out. The interview covered mother's preparation for and perception of pregnancy, delivery, the neonatal week, and the first three months at home (de Château and Wiberg, 1977b). When

TABLE 34–2

Design of Follow-up Studies of Extra Contact Postpartum

1. At 36 hours on the maternity ward	Mother-infant behavior during breast-feeding
2. At 3 months during a home visit	a. Mother-infant behavior during a free-play observation b. Interview with mother c. Assessment of the duration of breast-feeding
3. At 12 months at the outpatient clinic	a. Mother-infant behavior during a physicial examination of infant b. Gesell Development Schedules c. Vineland Test d. Interview with mother e. Mother's diary on infant sleeping and feeding habits f. Assessment of the duration of breast-feeding g. C.M.P.S. Test
4. At 36 months at the hospital	a. Videotape of mother-child free play b. Interview with mother c. Interview with father d. Denver Developmental Screening Test e. Observation of child play f. Language analyses

the babies had reached the age of one year, they were seen again, this time in the outpatient clinic. Again, observation of maternal and infant behavior followed a standard pattern. All the observations took place in the same examination room during a routine physical examination of the infant by a pediatrician. The children's social development and maturity were measured with the Vineland Social Maturity Scale (Doll, 1936) and their psychomotor development with the Gesell Development Schedules (Gesell and Amatruda, 1947). The psychological needs of the mothers were further explored with the help of the Cesarec-Marke Personality Scale (Cesarec and Marke, 1968). The duration of breast-feeding was calculated with the help of data collected during the interview with the mothers at three and twelve months and checked through scrutiny of the Child Health Center Records. At three years the families were contacted again. Altogether, thirty-eight families participated, including the child, parents, and any new siblings. The family arrived at the hospital at approximately 9:30 A.M. A short introduction of what would happen during the day's visit was given. After this introduction the parents were, each separately, interviewed. Meanwhile the child was taken to another room for a standardized, structured play using the Erica Method, a

kind of projective play technique for children (Danielsson, 1968). While the parents were still being interviewed the child was given the Denver Developmental Screening Test (Frankenberg and Dodds, 1967). At noon the family met again to have lunch in a private room and remain together for a scheduled rest. After lunch mother and child were invited to play with dolls, representing their own family, in a doll's house. A videotape recording of this session of thirty minutes was made. The father was asked to wait outside the room. As soon as the recording was completed, the family was asked to watch a playback. At the end of the day, child play was again observed using the Erica Method (Danielsson, 1968), while the parents had a final discussion about what had been studied during the day.

Results

A summary of the results of the behavioral studies at thirty-six hours, three months, one year, and three years is given in table 34–3. The mother's position differed greatly between the two groups at thirty-six hours: mothers with extra contact (P+) were sitting up, leaning on one elbow and holding their infants more frequently, and this was correlated with holding being slightly more encompassing and including more *en face* gaze.

A comparison of the two groups three months after delivery during a home visit revealed a number of significant differences in maternal behavior: Mothers in the contact group spent more time looking *en face* and kissing their infants at this time. Infant crying was more frequently observed among control infants and occurred with mother rocking more frequently. Infant smiling and/or laughing appeared significantly more often in the extra-contact group.

At one year, during a physical examination of the infant by a pediatrician, maternal behavior was again observed. Mothers with extra contact significantly more often held their infants with an expression of positive feelings as shown by body posture; they also exhibited more affectionate touching (defined as any extra touching of infant or infant's clothes by mother's fingers, not in connection with feeding or caregiving). In contrast, mothers with routine care more often held their infants with an expression of negative feelings as demonstrated by body posture (table 34–3).

A quantitative analysis of videofilms of mother and child interaction during play at follow-up three years after delivery showed that mothers with extra contact smiled more often at and had more body contact with their children than did the mothers with routine care.

A summary of the main results of personal interviews with the mothers at three months, one year, and three years after delivery is given in Table 34–4. No differences between the two groups were found in the obstetrical history and the first postpartum week. The mothers of the two groups had equally many difficulties during the first week at home. However, mothers in the control group (P) had household help for a longer period after discharge from the maternity ward than mothers in the study group (P+). The infants in both groups slept equally long at three months, and woke up

TABLE 34–3

Results of Behavioral Studies at 36 Hours, 3 Months, 1 Year, and 3 Years *

Behavior	Mean Frequencies		*p*-values T-test
	P	P+	
At 36 hours:	(*n* = 20)	(*n* = 22)	
Mother holding infant	2.9	10.9	0.001
encompassing	5.3	9.3	0.1
sitting up	3.3	10.1	0.009
leaning on elbow	7.9	2.4	0.02
looking *en face*	1.6	2.6	0.2
At 3 months:	(*n* = 19)	(*n* = 21)	
Mother looking *en face*	0.8	3.1	0.008
kissing	0.3	1.1	0.009
Infant smiling	1.4	2.7	0.02
crying	1.2	0.2	0.02
At 1 year:	(*n* = 15)	(*n* = 16)	
Mother holding infant positively	2.93	4.43	0.01
holding infant negatively	0.33	0	0.03
touching affectionately	0.46	1.31	0.04
At 3 years:	(*n* = 18)	(*n* = 20)	
Mother smiling	4.2	6.6	0.05
touching child	2.4	3.9	0.05

P = primiparous mothers with routine care
P+ = primiparous mothers with extra contact
*For each behavior category, approximately 20 observational periods of 10–15 seconds each were recorded for each mother-infant couple. The number of times each behavior was observed in each period was recorded, and the mean frequencies calculated.

equally often during the night and during the day. In both groups an equal number of infants had suffered from colic and received medication for it. At three months, mothers in the P + group found adaptation to the infants somewhat easier than mothers in the P group. More P+ mothers also still breast-fed their infants, whereas mothers in the control group (P) reported more problems with night-feeding than mothers in the extra-contact group (P+).

At one year the groups were interviewed again and were still comparable with regard to civil and socioeconomic status. Fewer mothers with extra contact (P+) immediately following delivery had returned to their employment outside the home than had routine-care mothers (P). A greater proportion of extra-contact children (P+) were reported to sleep in a room of their own. Both groups lived in comparable housing. Ten control mothers (P) as opposed to five extra-contact mothers had started bladder-training of the infant at one year (P+). According to the mothers, fathers in the P+ group participated to a lesser extent in the daily care—feeding, changing nappies, playing, putting to bed—of their children than did fathers in the control group.

The mean duration of breast-feeding for the mothers in the P+ group was 175 days, compared with 108 days for mothers in the P

group. The mean duration of breast-feeding is in full concordance with data collected from a larger sample during the same period and in the same area (de Château et al., 1977). However, the range (P+: 14–365 days; P: 10–240 days) was very wide.

At three years some differences were still found during an interview with the mothers. For example, 60 percent of the mothers in the control group (P) found the time they had with their infants immediately after delivery to have been insufficient. In contrast only one in five mothers in the study group (P+) shared this opinion. The general health and development of the children and the number of visits to hospitals and well-baby clinics was comparable in both groups. However, mothers in the extra-contact group (P+) judged their infants to have a faster language development. The number of siblings born during the three-year follow-up period was twice as many in the extra-contact group (P+) as in the control group (P).

At one year psychomotor development was measured by the Gesell Developmental Schedules. A comparison of all subjects in the routine-care group (P) with all subjects in the extra-contact group (P+) revealed no significant differences in any of the five parts of the test. However, in four of the five parts of the

TABLE 34–4

Summary of Results of Personal Interviews with Mothers, 3 Months, 1 Year, and 3 Years After Delivery

	P	P+
At 3 months:		
Help at home (in days) pp	19.5	7.6
Night feeding (in days)	24	42
Problems with night feeding	6/20	1/22
At 1 year:		
Returned to gainful employment	14/17	10/18
Infant sleeps in own room	4/17	9/18
Started bladder-training of infant	10/17	5/18
Father participates in daily care of infant	14/17	10/18
Breast-feeding (in days)	108	175
At 3 years:		
Time spent together with infant after delivery insufficient	12/19	5/20
Number of siblings born during follow-up period	4/19	9/20
Language development "two-word sentences" before 18 months	9/19	15/20

P = primiparous mothers with routine care
P+ = primiparous mothers with extra contact

test (exception: adaptive factor), children with extra contact immediately after delivery (P+) were ahead of children in the routine-care group (P). The social maturity of the children in both groups was measured on the Vineland Social Maturity Scale. Both control mothers (P) and study-group mothers (P+) rated their children somewhat more highly than was to be expected from their actual biological age. No significant differences between the two groups as a whole were found.

There were also no differences in the results of the Denver Developmental Screening Test at three years.

Discussion

The interpretation of studies of early stimulation is still difficult and should be approached with great caution (de Château et al., 1979). For example, because some mothers and infants may have special needs, they may not benefit from an early intensive interaction. Thus our attitude that hospital staff should apply firm rules and routines may in fact limit adaptability. For this reason we should offer early interaction to parents with an open mind and be sensitive to their individual needs and capacities. Thus parents should be permitted to make their own decision about neonatal extra contact and be prepared for it during pregnancy. This would allow a flexible approach and optimal use of our knowledge. Together with the parents we would then be able to create the best possible atmosphere for acceptance of the newborn.

When we look at the results of this study, it is obvious that only few of the many observed behaviors differed between the groups. Yet even so, the relatively short period of extra contact during the first hour following delivery can hardly in itself explain the differences in maternal behavior and the differences found in parental attitudes later on. In this study mothers and infants during this early contact might, however, have had an opportunity to exchange signals, which may be of importance for the establishment of mother-infant synchrony later on. Conse-

quently the early development of the mother-infant relationship may proceed more smoothly. For instance, at one year more mothers with routine postnatal care had returned to their gainful employment outside the home than mothers with extra contact. Because there were no actual differences between the two groups on any social parameters, an equal proportion of mothers in both groups were in a position to resume work if they wanted to do so. Yet mothers in the extra-contact group preferred and consciously chose to stay at home with their children for a longer time than mothers in the routine-care group. This could also be seen as a sign of maternal overinvolvement. Yet the fact the mothers in the experimental group put their children to sleep less frequently in the parental bedroom would weigh against this interpretation. A relatively large number of mothers had started bladder-training of their children before the age of one year, twice as many in the control group as in the extra-contact group. This might possibly indicate greater need for firm rules and training in the control mothers. However, the clearest effect of the extra-contact was seen in the duration of breast-feeding. Thus, while breast-feeding was more common in extra-contact mothers, these mothers also gave night-feeds for a considerably longer time and experienced fewer problems with night-feeds than routine-care mothers. This might indicate that the early contact had influenced mother-infant cooperation in feeding.

Factors unrelated to early interaction after delivery may possibly also have great impact upon later development of parent-infant relations. Examples of such factors have been given elsewhere (de Château and Wiberg, 1977a, 1977b; de Château et al., 1979). Here we will only comment upon the fact that some mothers were specially selected for an unusual treatment. All mothers were selected for the study at the same time in relation to their delivery and in the same way. At the time of selection it was not discussed whether mothers were going to belong to one group or the other. All mothers were informed that they would participate in a longitudinal study concerning infant development, general health, and family relations and that existing routines in the maternity ward were part of this study. *Insofar* as no mother refused to participate, a selection bias is unlikely. Because blind observers were used during follow-up visits and the staff in the maternity ward were not informed about the fact that two groups of mother-infant pairs with different postnatal experiences were studied, bias here is also quite unlikely.

At three years we discussed at greater length the early postnatal experiences with both mothers and fathers. It was then obvious that parents with early interaction were more satisfied than parents with routine care. Parents in both groups, however, felt special because they were part of a study concerning infant development, health, and family relations.

In a review article Rutter (1980) discussed the theoretical and empirical aspects of long-term effects of early experience. He concluded that in some circumstances early experience can and does have important effects on intellectual and psychosocial development. However, permanent damage after severe maternal deprivation during the first years of life is not inevitably present. In our opinion, these conclusions are in full accordance with the results of this study. One has therefore to bear in mind that a great number of other factors, prenatally, postnatally, and during childhood, adolescence, and adult life may affect and change later psychological functioning. Thus, early parent-infant interaction is but one of many factors in normal socialization and cannot be considered to be more than that.

REFERENCES

Cesarec, Z. and Marke, S. (1968). *Cesarec Marke Personality Scale Manual.* Stockholm: Skandinaviska Testförlaget.

Danielsson, A. (1968). Sandlådeobservationer enligt Erica Moteden. *Nordisk Medicin*, 68:1197–1202.

de Château, P. (1979), Effects of hospital practices on synchrony in the development of the infant-parent relationship. *Seminars in Perinatology*, III:45–61.

de Château, P., Holmberg, H., Jakobsson, K., and Winberg, J. (1977). A study of factors promoting and inhibiting lactation. *Developmental Medicine and Child Neurology*, 19:575–584.

de Château, P. and Wiberg, B. (1977a). Long-term effect on mother-infant behavior of extra contact during the first hour postpartum, Part I, First observations at 36 hours. *Acta Paediatrica Scandinavica*, 66:137–144.

de Château, P. and Wiberg, B. (1977b), Long-term effect on mother-infant behavior of extra contact during the first hour postpartum, Part II, A follow-up at three months. *Acta Paediatrica Scandinavica*, 66:145–151.

Doll, E. A. (1936). *The Vineland Social Maturity Scale.* Circle Pines, Minnesota: American Guidance Service.

Frankenberg, W. K. and Dodds, J. B. (1967). The Denver Developmental Screening Test. *Journal of Pediatrics*, 71:181–189.

Gesell, A. and Amatruda, C. S. (1947). *Developmental Diag-*

nosis: Normal and Abnormal Child Development, 2nd Ed. New York: Harper & Row.

Kennell, J. H. et al. (1974). Maternal behavior one year after early and extended postpartum contact. *Developmental Medicine and Child Neurology*, 16:172–179.

Klaus, M. H. et al. (1972). Maternal attachment—Importance of the first postpartum days. *New England Journal of Medicine*, 286:460–463.

Larsson, K. et al. (1979). Effects of various amounts of contact between mother and child on the mother's nursing behavior: A follow-up study. *Infant Behavior and Development*, 2:209–214.

Leifer, A., Leiderman, P. H., Barnett, C., and Williams, J. (1972). Effects of mother-infant separation on maternal attachment behavior. *Child Development*, 43:1203–1218.

O'Connor, S. M. et al. (1980). Reduced incidence of parenting inadequacy following rooming-in. *Pediatrics*, 66:176–182.

Rutter, M. (1980). The long-term effects of early experience. *Developmental Medicine and Child Neurology*, 22:800–815.

Taylor, P. M. et al. (1979). Effects of extra contact on early maternal attitudes, perceptions, and behaviors. Paper presented to the Biennial Meeting of the Society for Research in Child Development, San Francisco.

35

Comments Concerning the Concept of Fantasmic Interaction

Serge Lebovici, M.D.

A discussion of the concept of interaction of the fantasies of two individuals (fantasmic interaction) may be puzzling. Behavioral scientists use the term *interaction* to designate transactions between two separate people, whereas fantasies are wishes representing drive at a psychological level. The aim of the drive is to establish a connection between the mental representation of the self and the mental representation of the internal object, the internal object being essential for a major portion of the organization of drives by means of satisfying needs and wishes.

Psychoanalytic theory offers a clear and coherent explanation of the genesis of fantasies. Satisfaction of the needs of the very young infant cannot be maintained permanently. The baby can, however, reactivate the mnemonic traces of pleasure by stimulating (or utilizing) the autoerotic zones which have given rise to pleasure previously. This takes place during the anaclitic phase. In other words, children can hallucinate pleasure and can create the outlines of the object that has provided satisfaction of their needs by means of a wish. This hallucination partly soothes the internal drive excitation and *creates, from a psychological point of view,* the object that has provided satisfaction. More likely than not,

there is no relation between the actual pleasure experienced and the fantasy satisfied by the fantasied object that was produced by the hallucination of pleasure experienced at an earlier time. At the beginning of life, children who are learning to live psychologically after being separated physically from their mothers have at their disposal the narcissistic power that derives from the unity between them and the maternal care received. Children have to differentiate, in their internal reality and the objects of their external reality, the notion of what they reject and experience as harmful. Fantasies are also influenced at this time by early perceptual capacities and by the double processes of projection and negation.

This brief summary of the fundamental concepts of Freudian metapsychology illustrates the indissoluble relationship between the fantasmic representation of the object, perception, and the early object representations.

It should be noted that for Anna Freud, Spitz, and Winnicott, the initial unit is composed of the newborn and the maternal care received by the newborn. This introduces both the concept of total dependence and of narcissism and development: that is, (1) the ontogenesis of object relations and of fantasy; (2) a dialectical contradiction between the experience of pleasure and the experience of reality; and (3) the development of thought and of the mental representations that characterize the emergence of secondary-process mentation as compared to primary-process thought which is both prerepresentational and affective in nature.

Two schools of psychoanalysis, however, do not recognize this Freudian view of development. Melanie Klein considers drives and fantasies to be the same and their appearance the starting point of a genetic continuity, independent of the nature of the external object in reality. And the Hungarian school of psychoanalysis believes that the initial bond will be the prototype of all subsequent relations between the baby and its mother and that this fantasy underlies all search for pleasure. This is the desire to return to this "oceanic" fusion, which other authors have called an intrauterine fantasy.

Imre Hermann (1972), trained by the Hungarian school, described what he called *agrippement* behavior. He was the first psychoanalyst to introduce confusion between observations based on behavioral studies in animals and descriptions of the mental operation concerning what he calls the "filial" instinct. The interpersonal and interactive levels of behavior can be confused with the study of psychic conflict; this failure to distinguish between the two levels must be guarded against when describing fantasy interactions.

Bowlby's (1981) study of the nature of the bond between mother and child cannot be criticized from a methodological point of view. Bowlby describes the affective bonds and their vicissitudes as the substrate of human relations. Some distortions in development act as points of fixation and play a hidden role in psychic life and in human behavior, leading to unconscious conflicts. The description of affective bonds is based on the study of interactive behavior in animals and of Piaget's concept of development, gradually focusing on (perceptive) units which have become clearer. Many studies have examined in depth the study of early social interaction and of the important capacities which contribute to its organization and evolution.

Contributions of Psychoanalysis to the Study of these Interactions

Many psychoanalysts who have been interested in the description of early interactions between mother and infant have had to bridge their knowledge of the psychoanalytic reconstruction of development with the results of their infant observations. Anna Freud (1965) devoted most of her later scientific work to the study of normal and abnormal development, and the longitudinal studies by Ernst and Marianne Kris and Sally Provence at Yale all led to the theoretical concepts of Hartmann and Spitz, who systematized our knowledge of the genesis of object relations.

Although the 1960s and 1970s saw an increase in these contributions, it has been surprising how little has been done to link all of these data of infancy research with psychoanalytic practice and an underlying theoretical framework. Solnit (1982) believes that the data from direct observation of young children in regard to their object relations and the reconstruction of the earliest periods of their lives can contribute only to some evaluation of the influence of the past on the future, even in cases followed over several decades. Nevertheless, the early organization of drives and of the nature of early relations with primary objects influences personality structure in a definitive way and influences, too, the results of psychoanalytic treatment. This is demonstrated by the case studied by E. Kris, first alone, and later in collaboration with Ritvo and Provence. The primary qualities of the affective bond of this patient as an adult toward her mother had been previously investigated. However, the threat of regression and the presence of a large range of defenses to ward off these regressions were described by the authors as evidence of the importance of the early qualities of the affective bond. The type of interaction described in the Yale longitudinal study persisted into adulthood, limiting the subject's ability to find happiness in affective relationships. Thus, according to Solnit, these early ego characteristics represent the "nonanalyzable" aspect of the personality during the course of treatment of the adult patient.

This prospective and retrospective study therefore shows the importance of observing early interactions. In this case, there was the contradiction between the particular type of affective bond already established and the analysis of unconscious conflicts which leads to clinical, technical, and theoretical reflections.

The psychoanalysts who have contributed so much to the study of early interactions have not been concerned with a revision of the metapsychological framework which should derive from the new description of social attachment bonds and from the abandonment of developmental theory in favor of the concept of dependency.

The psychoanalytic theory of drives has been criticized, but not by psychoanalysts who work with children and babies. Kaufman (1981) emphasized the importance of studying animal behavior for a better understanding of the theory of instinct, energy, and drives. The "hydraulic theory" of the Freudian concept of drives has also been criticized (Klein, 1976).

Another critic of the psychoanalytic theory of drives, Schafer (1976), refers to action language and writes:

> The terms of Freudian metapsychology are those of natural science. Freud, Hartmann, and others deliberately used the language of forces, energies, functions, structures, apparatus, and principles to establish and develop psychoanalysis along the lines of a physicalistic psychobiology.
>
> It is inconsistent with this type of scientific language to speak of intentions, meanings, reasons, or subjective experience. Even though in the first instance, which is the psychoanalytic situation, psychoanalysts deal essentially with reasons, emphases, choices, and the like, as metapsychologists they have traditionally made it their objective to translate these subjective contents and these actions into the language of functions, energies, and so forth. . . . They have suppressed the intentionalistic, active mode. In line with this stragegy, reasons become forces, emphases become energies, activity becomes function, thoughts become representations, affects become discharges or signals, deeds become resultants, and particular ways of struggling with the inevitable diversity of intentions, feelings, and situa-

tions become structures, mechanisms, and adaptations. And, in keeping with the assumption of thoroughgoing determinism, the word *choice* has been effectively excluded from the metapsychological vocabulary. (p. 103)

Schafer tends to refer to interaction, but he defines psychoanalytic interaction as occurring between one person who is the agent and one who will not be concerned with mechanisms but with another person.

Bettelheim (1983) offers a similar type of criticism against the influence of physics in the *Standard Edition* of Freud's works. In France, Widlöcher (1981, 1983) describes the psychoanalytic process as a communication which is informative and interactive. It is informative in the sense that the reality of the lived self as a continuity of experiences (which from a neurobiological point of view implies a reconstitution and even a reconstruction) is opposed to the mental representations stored in the preconscious. It is interactive in the sense that the psychoanalyst's interpretation induces an interactive process of thought: the psychoanalyst "coparticipates" in establishing this process by proposing mental representations (rather than actual) of interactions and appealing to the "observing ego" through the therapeutic alliance.

However, these interesting proposals to revise metapsychology neglect the economic aspects, the investments, the affects and their roles in mental processes. In support of this aspect are the important contributions of Daniel Stern, particularly those concerning the transmodal attunement of affects (see Chapter 2). These ideas coincide with my own idea of interactions which are also fantasies and therefore affective in nature.

Types of Early Interactions

Descriptions of the early competencies of babies enable us to describe in detail the complex interactions, the evolution of which is dependent on the state of both partners. The ethological theories of imprinting and of the sensitive periods during which imprinting is specifically active help us understand the mechanisms of the interaction. The state of each partner operates to optimize these reactions. On the baby's side, there is the advantage to be gained from interactions during the baby's awake period (Brazelton, 1982), and the baby's need for feedback in the internal feedback circuits. Brazelton has also shown the staggering effects on the baby of changes in the mother's facial expressions (Brazelton et al., 1975). The unit of observation must therefore be the "dyad" (Flament, 1982).

In France, the theory of interactive epigenesis is applied to the study of the dyad (Cosnier, personal communication), a theory that corresponds more or less to the synchronous units between infants and their others described by Condon and Sander (1974). This latter work illustrates how affective exchanges between both interactional protagonists are influenced by the infant. The infant's sounds, expressions, postures, and movements coalesce onto contagious affects which are shared with the maternal environment. The relationship between emotional sequences of the dyad and the variations in tonus have been studied by de Ajuriaguerra, who has termed this interaction "the tonic dialogue" (de Ajuriaguerra et al., 1979).

French psychoanalysts have been emphasizing what we have called the "creative anticipations" of the mother (Lebovici, 1983; Diatkine, in press). Our hypothesis is that the imaginary life and fantasies of the mother enable her to attribute a psychological and meaningful significance to the first modes of expression of the baby; programmed, transitory, and nonsignificant behavior takes on a significant value for the mother. On the baby's side, there is an affective reaction to the mother's affect, laying the groundwork as a protorepresentational system which may then develop into anticipation, starting in the second half of the first year of life.

This system is set up by the baby and mother together and involves a transaction, the genesis of which is highlighted by the following points. We have already discussed the role that the hallucination of pleasure still plays for psychoanalysts. The anaclitic desire for the satisfaction of the need can be represented, as suggested by Mahler, by the "negative hallucination" of the mother (Mahler et al., 1975). Winnicott has said that the mother, originally nearly perfect in her concern (the maternal concern), becomes a "good enough" mother, leading to an organization of the self. In this transaction, the baby acquires a sense of continuity of what it has experienced because of disappointment and depression. It should also be noted that the difficulty in maintaining a bond with a differentiated object during the second half of the first year of life leads to the concept of a third component in the early interaction and in the object relationship being established. Spitz (1965) has called this phenomenon "stranger anxiety," and it results from the fact that the mother's absence becomes a source of danger which is then projected onto the unusual. Fain (1971) has described it as "a process of fantasy."

The narcissistic gratifications provided by the baby to mother strengthen her sense of creative anticipation and make her a mother. Winnicott was right when he stated that when babies watch their mothers, they see her looking back in an infinite exchange of mirror effects.

Gratification of the mother's needs may have another role through her reinforcement of "the contact' barrier" essential for the baby's feedback. She can act as a "protective shield mother." It is by means of these conditions that the early interactions create a state of temporospatial awareness for the baby. Everything that is unorganized, that impedes the baby's ability to distinguish the representation of the self from the object, that allows the baby to experience masochistic pleasure, will lead the baby to project these negative aspects of the mother-infant interaction onto the external reality.

Affects

The earliest relations between the baby and its mother are formed in an affective environment, which becomes increasingly represented in a mental form for the child. When the mother talks to the baby, it is usually in a paradoxical way in that the tones and the rhythms of her speech are more important than the words themselves. She lives in a state of tonic excitement and satisfaction, induced by her state of motherhood. The baby begins to communicate with the mother very early, by way of changes in tonus, expressions, and sounds.

A number of studies have shown that affects are understood through changes in the mother's expression, tonus, sound, and so forth (Emde, 1980). The baby can learn to recognize the maternal communication only by integrating affectively what she says or does: in other words, Emde has developed a theory concerning discrete emotions which form a mode of affective communication. The affect is for the mother or child a question or an answer before it attains psychological value. On the basis of Emde's studies, I propose the following concept: These affects of communication are extremely important for survival after birth. They foster the development of a significant relation between the mother and baby by means of an apparatus already present in the baby but still in the process of development. The affects are not due to the social interaction, but are concomitant with it, organizing it and aiding in the formation of mental representations of the sense of organization of time and space.

I have recently discussed (1983) some cases of babies several months old who have reacted significantly and appropriately to their mothers' complex statements, particularly those with an aggressive or hostile component. The maternal expression and the changes in her tonus as she "holds" the baby probably play a decisive role in the baby's comprehension of the mother's real intent.

The development of language (Bruner, 1982) can be traced as it evolves in forms of affective action where the mother and baby interact following the line of the mother's creative anticipation and the child's protomental representations. This has to be taken into account in order to understand the evolution of pointing. Newborns held by their heads can direct their hands toward an object; later on, they point at the object and want it, at least according to the mother's attribution of meaning, and still later on, pass it from hand to hand. At the end of the

first year, they voluntarily let it drop. Winnicott (1953) says that the babies are demonstrating that weaning has taken place, that is, the ability to dispense with an object linking them to their mothers. However, this toy takes on a symbolic value for the baby and, as in the reel game, the toy may symbolize someone whom the infant can bring back, thus overcoming separation anxiety.

Fantasmic Interactions

Social interactions are associated with affective exchanges, which play, as we have seen, a decisive role for mother and child. Affects convey emotion and words give them meaning. The representation of the things and words creates the fantasies associated with these affects in the various mental representations of external and internal reality. This explains the origin of the term *fantasmic interactions* proposed nearly simultaneously by Kreisler and Cramer (1981) and myself.

The mother's conflicts over motherhood have evolved and are resolved by her version of the "family romance" which derived from her primal-scene fantasies. Her conflicts over motherhood are also resolved through secondary identification with her mother and her wish to be a mother. This resolution of conflict nearly always parallels the desire to become pregnant. This universal desire—present in both young girls and young boys—is obviously present in the infantile fantasies. On the other hand, it is reinforced or inhibited by the special features of the mother's history, the vicissitudes of her relationships with men and the child's father, and the transmission over generations of the concept in which the child has a specific place in the equilibrium of the familial system.

Two kinds of "children" exist in the mother's mind: the "fantasmic" child—the one resulting from and formed by infantile and unconscious conflicts—and the imaginary child who has a specific place in the familial system.

On the baby's side, without going into the psychoanalytic theory of development, we merely emphasize that the study of interactions shows the need to go beyond psychoanalytic reconstruction concerning the genesis of the id and ego. It is useful to understand the fantasmic life and thoughts of the child and to consider the effects of the baby's action on the mother. Babies' narcissistic rage of helplessness contrasts with pleasurable excitement when they know they have produced affective changes in the mother. Then communication becomes symbolic. For example, pointing becomes a ritual, and the functional games become systematic. From this evolves a relatively early form of meaning, and socially conventional codes are accepted.

This whole development becomes more definite by the fourth trimester of the first year, before the development of social language, as the baby becomes "a subject," the *self* becomes an *I.* Winnicott (1953) locates fantasmic interactions in the "transitional" area. I prefer to describe them as means of maternal investment, in the course of which various processes lead to the differentiation between the internal object (the mental representation of which implies the presence of memories and of fantasy construction) and the external object, which is recognized by its permanency, its protective and soothing value, and also by the anger it induces.

Of course, affective exchanges with the mother continue to maintain primary-process thinking, implying a continuing lack of distinction between affects and perception. Children feel that their remarkable capacities are dependent on their mother's own wishes, wishes that the child cannot control. On the other hand, babies can be their mothers' "therapists" in regard to the mothers' lack of positive affects and "white" depression.

The concept of fantasmic interaction aims at describing primary transactions between both partners. Although Brazelton (1983) has developed his concept of homeostasis between mother and baby from a theoretical basis very dissimilar to mine, he illustrates what I am discussing. I conceive of these observations as the proof of the first steps of an emotional and cognitive consciousness in the baby and in the mothering "other." A baby learns in part on its own, developing a basis

for its "id." The mother and father who are attached and intimately linked to the baby go, consciously and unconsciously, through the parallel steps of their own development as parental units. Freud (1925) described babies' holds on their mothers; he believed it is the cause of the child's cruelty. I prefer to ascribe this hold on the parent by two aspects of the baby: one is directed toward the mother as an external reality and is demonstrated by the infant's clinging to the mother in their social interaction; the other pertains to the drives and is directed toward the internal object which the baby will control.

The mother has a definite maternal power and hold over her baby; she is capable of anticipating the baby's wishes and needs; she can lull her baby to sleep, understand her baby's behavior, and so forth. The mother's capacity to anticipate therefore confirms the baby's triumphant narcissism. However, at the same time, the baby, who by now represents the mother's fantasied baby, creates internal objects that are not solely the product of the baby's own hallucination of pleasure; the internal object also depends on the mother's fantasies and abuses.

Fantasmic Interactions and their Observer-Interpreter

If an observer becomes identified with either partner of the interaction, the observer can make certain predictions. If he or she becomes identified with the baby, he or she can imagine and predict the ways object relations will develop in the baby; if he or she becomes identified with the mother, he or she can predict what has controlled the genesis of object relations in the mother. In fact, it might not even be necessary to separate the description of the genesis of object relations from that of the early interactions. The psychoanalyst can later reconstruct the interactions (Lebovici, 1982), while the psychiatrist can intervene at the level of the repertoires of reciprocal behavior which are also identificatory in origin. It is therefore necessary to have therapeutic consultations concerning these fantasmic interactions.

The knowledge of these fantasmic interactions facilitates the use of a double repertoire, one pertaining to the observation of the child and the mother together, and the other the kind of interaction that exists between them by the way they express themselves in words and various types of nonverbal behavior. This is a very specific situation, for the mother does not talk about herself in the same way when she is alone as when she is with her baby. It is particularly different when she holds the baby in her arms and tries to pay attention to both her questioner and her baby.

This is probably the only situation in which a psychoanalyst can directly examine behavior in interactions. In the usual clinical situation, the fantasies are known: in the adult, because of what the adult says, does, and dreams; in the child, because of the way the child plays and expresses itself in words. In contrast, a short circuit is established in this specific situation between behavior and fantasmic life. I shall illustrate this briefly with a few examples.

A seven-month-old male baby is very agitated and cannot fall asleep. He quiets down when I put him in his mother's arms. She used to hold him with his head hanging over her shoulder, but changed this position when I told her: "Up to now, you have not enabled your baby to take you in as his mother when watching you, because he couldn't allow you to allow him to watch you while watching him." Obviously, the new outlook of the mother stimulates affective, tonic, and fantasmic changes which are decisive in calming the baby's motor and psychological excitation.

A thirteen-month-old baby, also a boy, was brought because of severe and constant difficulty in falling asleep. I set up with him a game of peek-a-boo, first with a toy dog and then directly with him. I then bring his mother into the room. He climbs onto her knees. At my signal, the mother sings a lovely lullaby and, while sitting by her side, I mention that I would really appreciate having someone sing me such a nice song. The baby gets down, leaves us, a bit tipsy, but watching us from behind all the time, and falls asleep on a pile of clothes. I believe he had established a new mode of functioning of his "self" and had acquired a certain notion of continuity of life even when he no longer had us in view. My reciprocal identification with his mother established in him a fantasy of a primal scene which his mother and I shared.

A five-month-old infant is constipated, although he is breast-fed. The mother lulls him to sleep in her arms while speaking peacefully about her happiness in living with the baby even though the child's father has left her. When, in the course of this conversation, I ask her how she imagines this baby as a grown-up man, she first says that she cannot imagine, moves him away with a pushing gesture, and then declares that he will be a quiet and good man like her father. Suddenly the child wakes up, anxious and agitated: this is when she is discussing his future adolescence, and she gestures to show that he will have to be closely watched to avoid becoming a delinquent. There are really two mothers here, each with different fantasies: one assumes the right to realize in a fantasmic way an incestuous oedipal fulfillment with her baby sleeping on her bosom as a symbol of her own father; the other utilizes the defenses which have been established against her own drives from the anal level of development when she clutches her baby, wakes him up (and constipates him?).

Conclusion

We have described two conclusions drawn from the study of mother-child interactions, specifically from the interactions of their fantasies: (1) fantasies are an integral part of the mother's caregiving activities; (2) the baby invests the mother with affect even before knowing her cognitively. This in turn helps the mother to establish her concept of herself as a mother.

The mother actually has three different babies. First is the fantasmic baby, formed out of the mother's wish to have a baby. This has to do with the relationship of the mother with her image of the baby and reflects the oedipal aspect of her fantasies and her mourning for her oedipal object. The child, which replaces an incestuous object, enables the mother to identify with her own mother and assuages her superego.

Second, the imaginary baby arises from the mother's wish for pregnancy and for children. It represents what the mother and child's father plan for their future and also their concern about the here and now. This is the child of the familial system. It occupies a position in the transmission of continuity between generations. Its presence means that postoedipal inhibitions have played their expected part.

Finally, one could define a third child, the child of reality, as the one who, because of its early competence, interacts with the mother. This child is hard to delineate because its behavioral repertoire is determined by social bonds and expectations. This is the child who perceives the mother in her different aspects and has to construct early mental representa-

tions from her negative aspects while appearing to the mother quite different from what the mother dreamt of.

We have tried to unify the complex aspects of the developing infant through psychoanalytic observation and understanding. This approach can identify the basis of the problems to come and possibly make them more amenable to change during the process of formation of the various aspects of the baby.

It is therefore possible to talk of therapeutic consultations concerning the study of early interactions because of our ability to identify with and empathize with the babies, mothers, and families.

The clinical study of interactions has certain special features which make it unique; while a mother holding her baby can explain its behavior and link it to her own emotional and fantasmic life, in the course of the study of the reciprocal actions, one can observe the helpful aspect of what the baby does for its mother.

REFERENCES

Ajuriaguerra, J. de, Cukies-Memeury, F., and Lezine, I. (1979). Les postures de l'allaitement au sein chez les femmes primipares. *Psychiatrie de l'Enfant*, 22:503–518.

Bettelheim, B. (1983). *Freud and Man's Soul*. New York: Knopf.

Bowlby, J. (1981). Psychoanalysis as a natural science. *International Review of Psycho-Analysis*, 8:243–256.

Brazelton, T. B. (1982). Le bébé: Partenaire de l'interaction. In *La Dynamique du Nourrisson*, ed. M. Soulé. Paris: Les Editions ESF.

Brazelton, T. B., Tronick, E., Adamson, L., and Als, H. (1975). Early mother-infant reciprocity. *Parent-Infant Interaction*. Ciba Foundation Symposium 33. Amsterdam: Elsevier.

Bruner, J. (1982). Development of language. In *Frontiers of Infant Psychiatry*, ed. J. D. Call, E. Galenson, and R. L. Tyson. New York: Basic Books.

Condon, W. S. and Sander, L. W. (1974). Neonate movement as synchronized with speech: Internal participation and language acquisition. *Science*, 183:99–101.

Diatkine, R. (in press). La genèse de la psychopathologie de l'enfant. In *Traité de Psychiatrie de l'Enfant et de l'Adolescent*. ed. S. Lebovici et al. Paris: Presses Universitaires de France.

Emde, R. N. (1980). Toward a psychoanalytic theory of affect. In *The Course of Life: Psychoanalytic Contributions Toward Understanding Personality Development*, vol. I: *Infancy and Early Childhood*, ed. S. I. Greenspan and G. Pollock. Washington, D. C.: U.S. Goverment Printing Office.

Fain, M. (1971). Prélude à la vie fantasmatique. In *Eros*

et Anteros, ed. D. Braunschweig and M. Fain. Paris: Payot.

Flament, F. (1982). *Colloques de l'Association des Psychologues de Langue Française*.

Freud, A. (1965). *Writings of Anna Freud*, vol. 6, *Normality and Pathology in Childhood*. New York: International Universities Press.

Freud, S. (1905). Three essays on the theory of sexuality. *Standard Edition*, vol. 7, ed. J. Strachey. London: Hogarth Press, 1953.

Hermann, I. (1972). *L'Instinct Filial*. (French translation by N. Abraham). Paris: Denoël.

Kaufman, I. C. (1961). Quelques implications théoriques tirées de l'étude du comportement des animaux et pouvant faciliter ma conception de l'instinct, de l'énergie et de la pulsion. *Revue Française de Psychanalyse*, 25:633–649.

Klein, G. S. (1976). *Psychoanalytic Theory: An Exploration of Essentials*. New York: International Universities Press.

Kreisler, L. and Cramer, B. (1981). Sur les bases cliniques de la psychiatrie du nourrisson. *Psychiatrie de l'Enfant*, 24:233–263.

Lebovici, S. (1982). L'après coup et l'organisation de la nevrose infantile. In *Traumatismes et Après-Coup*, ed. J. Guillaumin. Toulouse: Privat.

Lebovici, S. (1983). *Le Nourrisson, la Mère et le Psychanalyste*. Paris: Le Centurion.

Mahler, M., Pine, F., and Bergman, A. (1975). *The Psychological Birth of the Human Infant*. New York: Basic Books.

Schafer, R. (1976). *A New Language for Psychoanalysis*. New Haven: Yale University Press.

Solnit, A. J. (1982). Early psychic development as reflected in the psychoanalytic process. *International Journal of Psycho-Analysis,* 3:23–38.

Spitz, R. (1965). *The First Year of Life.* New York: International Universities Press.

Widlöcher, D. (1981). Genèse et changement. *Revue Française de Psychanalyse,* 45:889–976.

Widlöcher, D. (1983). L'étude des déterminations du comportement humain. *Psychiatrie de l'Enfant,* 26:141–158.

Winnicott, D. W. (1953). Transitional objects and transitional phenomena. In *Collected Papers.* New York: Basic Books, 1958.

Winnicott, D. W. (1956). Primary maternal preoccupation. In *Collected Papers.* New York: Basic Books, 1958.

PART IV

The Infant-Caregiver

Relationship:

Fathers and Infancy

36

Fathers and Young Children: Fathering Daughters and Fathering Sons

James M. Herzog, M.D.

For several years now, I have been conducting a home-based naturalistic study of eight families. When I began, each family consisted of a mother, father, and child in the second year of life. Four of the children were boys; four were girls. All were first children. The parents, all volunteers, were middle-class professionals. In six of the eight families, there is now a second child. It has thus become possible to compare the behavior of some fathers and mothers with children of each sex, although not to control for birth-order effects or for the possibility, as some epidemiological data suggest, that parenting improves with practice (Rutter, 1979). There are thus fourteen father-toddler dyads. In earlier communications (Herzog, 1980, 1982) I detailed my initial conclusions obtained from observing each family for about fifty hours in situations in which mother, father, and child were present. Previously I focused primarily on father-son interaction in this setting and described the way the father disrupts the more homeostatic activities between mother and child and introduces a new and different interactive style. This mode has been noted by other observers and experimentalists using more diverse populations in other settings (Lamb, 1981).

Here I present some material pertinent to father-daughter interaction, augmenting the observational material with analytic and clinical material designed to illustrate some of the enormous complexity involved in understanding paternal function and in particular the different ways it manifests itself with sons and daughters. It is my contention that it is not enough to state that fathers play an important role in sex-role stereotyping or in the consolidation of core gender identity. One must rather begin to explore the principles underlying this and other parenting or transacting functions attributed to men. I consider this inquiry to be somewhat in the spirit of Radin's (1981) attempts to explore some of the antecedents of "androgeny" in child-rearing fathers, although what I choose to examine and what I learn is very different from what she reports. I present observations from two families, which I have selected because, in a particular way, they balance some of the demographic variables one must consider. In the first family my initial observations involved a triad consisting of mother, father, and firstborn son; thirty-seven months later a daughter was born. In the second family the original constellation was father, mother, and firstborn daughter; thirty-eight months later a son was born. As you will see, these families, although matched for age, socioeconomic status, religion, occupation, cultural interests, and even training institutions, encompass great variability in parental behaviors, particularly on the interrogative and meaning levels of reality. On the level of what I call videotaped reality (what a camera would record) there is, however, considerable overlap.

FIRST FAMILY

Daniel was the firstborn son of thirty-year-old parents. David, a lawyer, and Miriam a pediatrician, had been married three years prior to his birth. They described their relationship as close and growing. The pregnancy had been planned and had proceeded smoothly. The delivery had been uncomplicated, and 7 lb., 12 oz. Daniel was welcomed, seemingly unambivalently. Miriam went back to work when Daniel was three months old. She worked part time until he was nine months old and then decided to stay home full time. "He will only be a baby once, and I want to be here," she said, arranging a leave of absence. Miriam seemed warm and friendly toward her husband and toward her son, although she was occasionally critical of her husband's indecisiveness. She was a careful, mildly obsessional woman, clearly very invested in her mothering. David, Daniel's father, seemed even more obsessional than his wife. When I began my Sunday afternoon visits, he seemed quite nervous. He would advance very strong opinions and then, under his own scrutiny or his wife's, he would reconsider. He felt that someone interested in fathers might find fault with his fathering. By my third visit, however, he had noticeably relaxed. A typical observation follows.

Danny is seventeen months old. He and Miriam are sitting on the floor playing with some blocks. Miriam is following Danny's lead. He is sort of arranging the blocks. Some are placed on top of each other, some next to each other. Miriam tries to be the assistant contractor-engineer. David is on the phone. He hangs up and comes barreling over. Danny looks up. David gets down on his hands and knees. He tousles Danny's hair and says, "No,

no, come on, let's go." He pushes over the assembled blocks. Danny squeals with laughter. Miriam's face breaks into a smile. Now Danny starts to hit the blocks. Both father and son are pushing them around. About a minute later Danny picks up a block and throws it. It doesn't travel very far. Miriam says, "Oh no!" David says, "Stop it, Dan." A second block is picked up. "I said stop it now. That's dangerous." His father speaks more quietly than he did when playing raucously. He sounds very serious. Danny puts down the block. He smiles, as do his parents. Less than thirty seconds later David gives the blocks another jab. Round two has begun, and almost immediately Danny is once again convulsed by giggles and squeals of delight.

Subsequent observations revealed many different kinds of interactions, but the pattern just described was often repeated. David would disrupt what Danny was doing. Danny would welcome this assault, and his spirits would rise dramatically as the active and exciting play commenced. Often the intensity of his affect would escalate until he lost control. At this point his father, who had initiated the sequence, would bring it to a close. Whereas at seventeen months these second and third rounds of play were initiated by David, by twenty-four months successive rounds were initiated by Danny himself.

Danny is twenty-one months of age. He is playing with the vacuum cleaner. He is in high spirits, making whooshing sounds as he goes about his work-play. He bangs into some plants. David says, "Easy does it, Cowboy." Danny regards him with an intense look and resumes his play. David intervenes again. "If you want to be a Boston Bruin, you'll have to go into the living room," he says. Danny puts down the vacuum cleaner, begins to suck on his thumb, and then quite clearly puts his hand in his diaper and begins to masturbate. Miriam, who has been reading during the preceding dialogue now looks up as her husband says: "That's the spirit, you big stud, take matters into your own hands." He smiles at Danny, who smiles back. Miriam remarks, "You're a good boy Danny."

SECOND FAMILY

Rachael is the firstborn of her parents, Arthur, a thirty-four-year-old psychiatrist, and Nora, a thirty-year-old researcher. Rachael was a planned child, and the pregnancy was uneventful, but a Caesarean section was performed after sixteen hours of labor. Although Rachael was observed in the neonatal intensive care nursery for forty-eight hours, she went home with her mother at six days of age. Unlike some of the other families, the transference reaction evoked by my presence was not obvious with Arthur and Nora. Arthur did not appear to be either competitive or compliant. As a dynamically oriented psychiatrist of adults, he remarked that the relevance of normative data to reconstruction was quite critical. Nora was often quiet during my visits. She seemed less uneasy than retiring. Both parents told me at the beginning of the study that Rachael was enormously committed to her mother and would go to no one else—sometimes not even to her father. Both grandmothers had expressed concern about the tightness of this bond. Arthur said, in Nora's presence, that she had found her niche as a mother, that she loved being at home, that he loved her being there, and that Rachael was the luckiest little girl in the world.

At the beginning of my observation, Rachael, at fourteen months, would often look warily at me as she held tightly to her mother. They played together or Nora read to her. Arthur sometimes waved at his daughter or drew close to mother and daughter to complete the family tableaux. Rachael would smile attentively at him and sometimes draw closer to her mother. Occasionally Arthur did something that created noise. During my first observation of this sort, he put on some music and invited Rachael, who was being quietly read to, to dance. Rachael looked perplexed. Her father, on his knees and smiling, waltzed her gently around the floor and then lifted her up into the air. "Be careful," Nora cautioned, noting that the little girl's smile diminished as she became airborne, "she's not such a great flier." Arthur responded to his wife's suggestion and stopped. Rachael did not immediately toddle

back to mother, and as the music played on, Arthur resumed the waltz. "You lovely dancer —what a joy to squire you," he said and then looked over at me with obvious embarrassment.

At eighteen months Rachael is lying somewhat dreamily with her mother while Nora reads her a story. Arthur gets up from his reading (it's about thirty minutes into the observation) and heads over toward them. He hums— the tune is "Who's Afraid of the Big Bad Wolf?" "What's my beautiful girl up to?" he asks. Rachael looks up; she smiles. "Beautiful dreamer," the musical Arthur begins to sing. Rachael rises and walks toward her father. Mother smiles. As Rachael approaches, her diaper falls off. "Pretty girl," says Arthur. "Put the diaper back on," says Nora. "Da Da," says Rachael, "Da Da." She is beaming now as she reaches her father. He sweeps her up in his arms and again waltzes with her around the room. Nora follows with the diaper. "She'll get you all wet," she says to her husband. Rachael is very excited and tries to sing along with her waltzing, crooning papa. This continues for about a minute, and then Nora puts on the diaper and says, "Let her calm down, Art." The oomph in father's singing is decelerated. His volume decreases, and the speed at which he is going around the room diminishes. Rachael also quiets down. Arthur puts her down. She stares expectantly in his direction. He smiles, first at Nora and then at Rachael. "May I have the pleasure of the next dance?" he asks, bowing archly and speaking with a mock English accent. Rachael squeals with delight, resumes singing, and rushes toward her father. Once again she is transformed by the excitement of the situation.

Rachael at twenty-one months is approaching her father who sits at his desk. Her hand is at her crotch. Arthur looks up. "Do you have to go to the bathroom?" he inquires smiling. "Uh, uh," smiles Rachael. Arthur gets up and goes to her. She puts her arms around his legs. "Hey, little one, want to play?" asks Arthur. Rachael smiles in assent. Arthur leans down and picks her up. "Ay, ay," she says. "That's right, fly," responds her father and whooshes her around over his head. "Ay, ay," laughs Rachael, "Ay, ay." Notice that daughter approaches father.

Two weeks later, Rachael is sitting quietly between her parents on a couch. One parent after the other is reading *Goodbye Moon* to her. Rachael's hand is in her diaper. She appears to be masturbating. She pulls out her hand and smells her finger. She then puts her finger in front of her mother's nose. Her mother frowns and says, "Don't do that, Rachael, it's not nice." Rachael looks troubled, then moves her hand over to her father. "My pretty girl," he smiles, "My fetching fragrant filly." Rachael smiles, then looks back toward her mother somewhat questioningly. Nora seems not to notice and continues reading. Rachel snuggles up close to Arthur.

Now let us observe each of these families with the second child. An important aspect of these observations is that they often involved four people, both children usually being at home during my Saturday or Sunday afternoon visits. First, father David and family.

Rebekah is fifteen months old. Danny is four years, four months. He is very much an oedipal child, attached to his mother, often quite rivalrous and angry with his Dad. Miriam, who has still not gone back to work, is reading to Rebekah. They are sitting on a couch. David and Danny are tossing a football. "Throw it right, Daddy," Danny shouts when he misses the ball. The football game continues until Danny gives up in at least mock disgust and switches on the TV. David then approaches the couch with the football. He tosses it gently toward Rebekah. "What are you doing?" asks Miriam. "Just playing." Rebekah reaches for the ball. She smiles broadly and leans over to her father. She applies her body to his. The reading is over. Miriam puts down the book and goes to the kitchen. David, who has appeared somewhat rattled, seems to relax as he and Rebekah snuggle. Shortly thereafter, he asks her if she wants to play horsey. She nods excitedly, and he picks her up, neighing noisily as both go

galloping across the floor. "Be quiet, I can't hear," shouts Danny from in front of the TV. Rebekah is giggling and excited; she seems to be enjoying herself immensely. Two minutes later Miriam returns from the kitchen. "Whoa, Horsey," she says with a smile. "That little girl needs to take her nap shortly."

Rebekah is 21 months; Danny is 58 months. Danny has just been naughty, throwing something at his sister. He has been sent to his room, from which loud bangs occasionally issue. Rebekah is sitting between her parents. She and Miriam are playing with some loops of material with which one can weave potholders. "Pretty one, come here," her father says. "I can't believe it, you're not only beautiful, but you can sew." He scoops his daughter up. All the potholder material falls to the floor. Rebekah laughs and grows excited. Shortly thereafter, David puts her down. "She is so beautiful," he says to his wife, "and so easy to be with." Miriam nods assent and then notices that Rebekah is wet. David goes to get a diaper. He returns and watches as Rebekah touches herself while her mother is changing her. "She is so beautiful," he murmurs. "She'll make some man a lovely wife." "Move your hand dear," says Miriam to her daughter. "I need to fix your diaper." She gives Rebekah a kiss. Then she turns to her husband and says, "And she makes a certain father a wonderful daughter, particularly in comparison to what you're going through with Danny." The last words are practically drowned out by a loud crash from Danny's room. Everyone rushes in that direction.

We return to Father Arthur and his family. Gideon is seventeen months, Rachael is four years, seven months. Nora is at home full time. She is editing a book in the evenings. Arthur is now an academic psychiatrist and has become an analytic candidate. Rachael and her father are sitting, talking. Gideon and Nora are on the floor playing with blocks. Rachael is talking to her Dad about how cute Gideon is. "Babies are wonderful," she says, smiling. This grouping, father with daughter, mother with son, continues for about fifteen minutes. All eyes are on Gideon. Then Rachael (who is a very good reader and often wants to read to me) gets up and says she will read. Arthur joins Nora and Gideon. "So you want to be an architect," he says to his son, "Gideon, the builder." Gideon stares at him intently. "Let's see," Arthur continues, "shall we build a skyscraper?" He piles block on block. Gideon is still staring. "Nah, this is no good, let's start again," says Arthur, and he knocks over the tower. Gideon laughs and knocks some of the blocks too. "That's fun, old man, isn't it," says Arthur. "Can you push it further?" Father and son are now both pushing blocks quite vigorously. "Art, he was playing so nicely, so quietly," says Nora. "Rachael won't be able to read." Gideon, we've got to cool it," says Arthur. "You heard mother. Let's build our Empire State Building." The construction recommences, and one can almost feel Arthur's urge to knock over the building. There is a look of excited anticipation on Gideon's face. "One two, three— now!" shouts Arthur and the building goes over. "Boo, boo, boo!" shouts Gideon and begins pushing the blocks. "Sh," says Rachael loudly. "You see," says Nora to her husband, "She can't read," and then to Rachael, "Boys will be boys, my dear. Why don't you go into the library and close the door?"

Six months later, Gideon is walking around the room holding his penis. "My wee wee," he says. Rachael looks up, "Mom, tell him to stop," "Gideon, no." Gideon says, "Da Da wee my wee. Da Da wee wee, my wee." He beams. Nora looks uncomfortable. "Let's do something Gideon," she says, "Would you like to read?" "My wee Da Da wee," sings Gideon. Arthur is smiling broadly. "If you've got it, flaunt it," he says. "Yes, Gideon, we wee wee the same." He then turns to Rachael, who is quite upset, and explains, "Little boys like Gideon are just figuring out important things like whether they're boys or girls." "He's so stupid, Daddy," Rachael answers, "Everyone knows he's a boy and I'm a girl." "And I am delighted that you are, a wonderful girl who brings your mother and me much joy. Carry on, you wee wee soldier," he says to his son and simultaneously hugs his daughter. Nora smiles.

Discussion

Despite the fact that many children today grow up without one, there is much clinical evidence to support the idea that children need a father. In previous work (1980), I introduced the idea of father hunger—an affective state experienced when the father is felt to be absent. I postulated, on the basis of the symptoms, play, and dreams of fatherless children, that the father's principal intrapsychic role was as the modulator and organizer of aggressive drive and fantasy. Much earlier, Hans Loewald (1951) had posited another critical but related function as a protection against the threat of maternal engulfment. Mahler's (1955) seminal contribution on psychological separation-individuation also favored this paternal function. Ernst Abelin (1975) has followed this fecund lead in his research and theorizing on the father's role during this important period of late practicing and rapprochment.

The father is the organizer and modulator of intense affect paradigms. He beckons to the child like a knight in shining armor, not only pulling him or her out of, or assisting in the dissolution of, the intense mother-child relationship that Mahler has called symbiosis, but actively intruding upon it; he breaks up the intimate, homeostatically attuned, resonating empathy (Herzog 1979). The disruptive caregiver, when asked what he is doing (the interrogative level), often portrays himself at such times as a sibling. He can play with his child under the benevolent auspices of the mother. She remains the adult. "It's fun," David said, "just knocking around like a kid." "Boys will be boys," the astute Nora observed. This is more true for isogender interactions, fathers with sons. On a deeper level, there is often a simultaneous raging against the mother-child union and a desire to be included in it. "If I am an eighteen-month-old too, maybe Maria will take me to her bosom," a forty-year-old physicist in analysis told me. He had dreamed that two peas in a pod were warm and snug in the palm of the jolly green giant. This dream followed closely upon his telling me that he felt young and free when he romped with his

seventeen-month-old son, as he had been before all of the trouble in his family of origin
began. The green giant also signified his envy
of his wife's power and fecundity and his fear
of her disapproval that he was endlessly a little boy and not an adult.

Fathers of sons disrupt by the use of gross
motor activity, which introduces escalating
affect. Fathers of daughters tend to use less
disruptive large motor modes of entrée and to
key their pitch to the protoheterosexual aspects of the exchange. There are thus numerous uses of terms referring to physical beauty,
invitations to dance, and other descriptions of
courtship. Some of these ways, as well as some
of the ways in which fathers interact with boys
—"So you want to be an architect, do you,
Gideon"—have an almost peculiar out-of-
synch temporal quality. It is as if the father
were disrupting with content that reveals his
future plans or aspirations for the child. That
there should be sex-typing in these aspirations
is highly interesting. All the fathers of girls in
my study roundly insisted that they favored
total freedom of choice for their daughters professionally but tended to interact with them
predominantly in a mode I would call proto-
erotic endorsement. Notice, however, that
David tossed a football to Rebekah as he had
with his son as his initial invitation for her to
leave Miriam and join him.

As I talked in considerable depth with the
fathers, I found that on the interrogative level
this future-oriented empathy was fairly prevalent. Fathers see their children not only as they
are (and perhaps not so clearly as they were; cf.
Earl's (1980) work on fathers as observers of
their children), but as they would like them to
be. Their empathy seemed in part to be focused
on a developmental goal. Sometimes this was
explicit. Arthur said, "My dad is an architect.
If I hadn't decided to study psychoarchitecture
I would build buildings. It would be nice if
Gideon wanted to do that too." In 1973, Dorothy Burlingham reported something about this
aspect of fatherhood. "According to my own
experience in direct observation and analytic
treatments of a number of fathers, their fantasies concerning the expected child were built
around the wish that the boy should be a
strong powerful male like the ideal of himself:

if a girl, that she would respond to his own
loving feelings" (p. 30). So the disruption of
the father is Janus-like. It appears to have regressive determinants—identification as a
rival, as a sibling longing to dislodge and longing to unite, fearing re-engulfment and simultaneously courting it—and progressive ones—
pushing or enabling development by introducing future-oriented content and attuning oneself with that part of the child which is gazing
in the direction of further differentiation, individuation, and growth.

The situation is even more complex with a
second child. The first child is still very much
present, and his or her developmental issues
exert a powerful effect on the father. Daniel's
struggle with David affected his relationship
with Rebekah. The same is true of the Rachael-
Arthur dyad and the Arthur-Gideon interaction. In some ways there is a generalizable conclusion. First-time fathers of boys tend to be
more large-motorish with subsequent children
—either male or female. First-time fathers of
girls tend to be less so with subsequent offspring, either male or female. As I have previously wondered if there is a connection between the degree of gear-shifting between
fathers and sons and the tendency of boys to
favor the accommodative cognitive mode—for
example, changing to something new rather
than fitting new data to old schemes—I must
now ask whether the first child sets an interactive disruptive style and if one should look for
familial cognitive modes with greater or lesser
expressivity according to gender.

With the second child, there is also another
phenomenon of note. Father tends to have a
special relationship with the first-born.
Shapiro (1980) has reported that this is related
in middle-class families to the need for him to
care for the first child while mother is occupied
with the newborn second child. On the interrogative level and the level of meaning, there
is a clear connection to the sibling motif and to
the conflict over viewing and sensing the
mother-infant unity—the wish to be one with
it, and the fear of being engulfed by it. Mothers
do not report this fear when watching father
and child together, in my experience, not even
in analysis. Fathers report it frequently.

I wish also to comment ever so briefly on the

interesting reaction to genital discovery and manipulation. There was much variation, but, in my admittedly unrepresentative sample, both mother and father applauded genital play on the part of boys. Fathers were more enthusiastic than mothers about this phenomenon in girls. Mother most often mentioned dirtiness and the proximity of the anus when discussing this matter—a cloacal reference, perhaps. Obviously, this enthusiasm of the fathers for their daughters' self-exploration may be determined by culture, class, and time. It would be hard to imagine a Victorian parent approving of any such thing in either a son or a daughter. The implications of this data for the development of painful self-consciousness (Amsterdam and Leavitt, 1980) in the second year of life and on the affect of shame in so many women are particularly provocative. Galenson's paper (1982) on this topic, as well as Anthony's (1981), is particularly germane. Notice in Arthur's case that this aspect of father-child interaction is also influenced by the presence of a sibling. Loyalty to the first child may affect libidinal and aggressive availability to the second.

I illustrate with a brief vignette from an analytic patient. "My father and I get doughnuts every Sunday morning," seven-year-old Tanya tells me. "He knows that I love them. He doesn't mind if my fingers get sticky. He likes my doughnut hands. Mommy doesn't. 'Wash your hands, wash your hands, don't be dirty," she always says." Tanya is in her third month of analysis. She has an older and a younger brother. She fights with her mother constantly and longs for her father, who is frequently traveling, to be at home. Tanya is often ashamed of herself. She is always messy or messing up. When she draws pictures of faces, they always lack noses. "I don't like to draw noses," she says sadly. "Mommy says I stink," Analytic data is always multidetermined and draws its meaning from many levels, but I wonder about the connection between these constellations of feelings and my observation of father-daughter and mother-daughter interaction in the second year of life.

I close with a poem written by a nine-year-old boy in his second year of analysis with me. In it he describes the son of a knight at the time of King Arthur. I take this to be a commentary on the antiquity of the issue and on the complexity of paternal representations and their relationship to father-child interactions and transactions.

The night swoops down
It helps me to get my guts up
I want to stay at home
But I have to learn to fight to grow up right
My father loves to wrestle
He can run fast too
He shows me how to get my guts up
Then I don't have to stay still
If it gets very noisy I won't be ill.

REFERENCES

Abelin, E. (1975). Some further observations and comments on the earliest role of the father. *International Journal of Psycho-Analysis,* 56:293–302.

Amsterdam, B. K. and Leavitt, M., (1980). Consciousness of self and painful self-consciousness. *The Psychoanalytic Study of the Child,* 35:41–46, New Haven: Yale University Press.

Anthony, E. J., (1981). Shame, guilt, and the feminine self in psychoanalysis. In *Object and Self: A Developmental Approach. Essays in Honor of Edith Jacobson,* ed. S. Tuttman, C. Kayes, and M. Zimmerman. New York: International Universities Press.

Burlingham, D. (1973). The preoedipal infant-father relationship. *The Psychoanalytic Study of the Child,* 28:23–48, New Haven: Yale University Press.

Earls, F. (1980). The prevalence of behavior problems in three year old children: Comparison of the reports of fathers and mother. *Journal of the American Academy of Child Psychiatry,* 19:439–452.

Galenson, E. (1982). The preoedipal relationship of a father, mother, and daughter. In *Father and Child, Developmental and Clinical Perspectives,* ed. S. Cath, A. Gurwitt, and J. M. Ross. Boston: Little, Brown.

Herzog, J. M. (1980). Sleep disturbance and father hunger in 18–28 month old boys: The Erl Konig Syndrome. *The Psychoanalytic Study of the Child,* 35:219–236. New Haven: Yale University Press.

Herzog, J. M. (1982). *Fathers and young children.* Plenary Address, Tenth International Congress on Child and Adolescent Psychiatry and Allied Professions, Dublin, Ireland.

Lamb, M. (1981). *The Role of the Father in Child Development.* New York: Wiley Interscience.

Loewald, H. W. (1951). Ego and reality. *International Journal of Psycho-Analysis,* 32:10–18.

Mahler, M. (1955). On symbiotic child psychosis. *The Psychoanalytic Study of the Child,* 10:195–212. New York: International Universities Press.

Radin, N. (1981). Childrearing fathers in intact families: Some antecedents and consequences. *Merrill-Palmer Quarterly,* 27:489–514.

Rutter, M. (1979). Maternal deprivation, 1972–1978. New findings, new concepts, new approaches. *Child Development,* 50:283–305.

Shapiro, E. (1980). Unpublished doctoral dissertation.

37

Mothers, Fathers, and Child Care in a Changing World

Michael E. Lamb, Ph.D.

In the 1970s, there occurred an explosion of interest in the topic of socialization and socio-emotional development in infancy, returning to prominence an issue that had fallen from favor in the preceding decades. Like the research and theorizing that dominated the earlier era of concern with this topic, most of the attention during the 1970s was on the family, inasmuch as many of the more important aspects of socialization were believed to take place early in life when extrafamilial experiences were few. Thus it was with parental—especially maternal—influences that psychologists were concerned.

In order to make their hypotheses testable and their models concise, however, students of socialization made a number of simplifying assumptions about the sorts of families in which children were being raised. Prominent among these was the assumption that "normal" socialization took place in the context of two-parent families in which fathers assumed responsibility for financial support while mothers eschewed employment in order to assume responsibility for the care of children, homes, and families. This simplifying assumption was never wholly satisfactory because it failed to take into account the many families that violated the supposed norm. Moreover, this "model" of the family has become increas-

ingly unsatisfactory as the number of deviant families has continued to mount. Mothers are employed outside the home in the majority of American families today, for example, and the continuing rise in divorce rates means that many children spend at least part of their childhood in single-parent homes. Unfortunately, psychologists have only recently recognized that the "average" or "traditional" American family is no longer normative and that we must therefore consider the effects of various family forms more systematically and carefully than in the past. This realization has been achieved slowly, and there have thus been few studies designed to explore the effects of changing family forms. Scholars have been satisfied to assume that any deviations from traditional patterns of child care must have adverse consequences.

My goal here is to review the available evidence concerning the effects of new forms of family and child-care arrangements on the development of young children. To do this, I first review our current understanding of the ways in which socialization proceeds in traditional (mother as caretaker, father as breadwinner) two-parent families, summarizing the information without detailed analysis of specific studies and without discussion of topics regarding which much uncertainty remains.

Then I focus attention on three major deviations from the traditional pattern: maternal employment and the increased use of out-of-home care, increased paternal participation in child care, and divorce and single parenthood. Because we still have only a sketchy understanding of the way in which these deviations affect child development, it is often necessary for me to speculate about the effects of these deviations on the basis of our knowledge concerning socialization in traditional families.

Socialization in Traditional Families

In this section, I briefly summarize what we know about maternal and paternal influences on development in infancy, starting with a discussion of the formation of infant-parent attachments: To whom do infants form attachments? Why? Are there sex differences in the patterns of infant-parent interaction? I then turn to individual differences in the security of infant-parent attachment: What factors affect these? How can we assess the quality of relationships? What long term effects, if any, do they have on child development?

TO WHOM DO ATTACHMENTS FORM?

Mere exposure seems to be the most important factor determining to whom infants form attachments: Infants apparently become attached to those people who have been available to them extensively and consistently during the first six to eight months of life (Ainsworth, 1973; Rajecki, et al., 1978). Presumably, it is also important that adults and infants interact, with the adults responding to the infants' signals appropriately and providing for some of their needs (for example, for contact comfort). Unfortunately, this has not yet been established empirically.

In most societies, mothers assume primary, if not sole, responsibility for infant care. It is their faces that infants are most likely to see when they are alert; mothers are likely to pick up and comfort infants when they are distressed and feed them when they are hungry. By virtue of their mothers' consistent availa

bility and responsiveness, one would expect infants to form primary attachments to them, as indeed most infants seem to do (Lamb, 1980). From around six to eight months, infants begin to respond differentially to separations from their mothers (Stayton, et al., 1973), and they begin to retreat to their mothers when alarmed by the appearance of strangers or by other stressful circumstances. Mothers are better able to soothe their infants than other women are (Ainsworth, 1973). Less self-evident, perhaps, is the fact that most infants form attachments to other figures—fathers in traditional western cultures (Lamb, 1977c; Schaffer and Emerson, 1964) or consistent substitute caretakers in others (Fox, 1977)—at about the same time that they form attachments to their mothers, even though the amount of time infants spend interacting with their fathers is substantially less than the amount of time they spend with their mothers (Lamb and Stevenson, 1978). At least within those families willing to participate in research projects (a somewhat selected sample, one suspects), infants discriminate both mothers and fathers from strangers (Lamb, 1977a, 1977c, 1980). They seek proximity, contact, and comfort from their fathers with the same intensity and frequency as from their mothers, without apparent preference (Lamb, 1976b, 1977a). By the end of the first year, however, the situation changes somewhat. Although infants continue to show no preference for either parent in familiar or stress-free situations, they turn to their mothers preferentially when distressed (Lamb, 1976f). This tendency is still evident at eighteen months of age (Lamb, 1976a) but appears to have disappeared by twenty-four months (Lamb, 1976c).

SEX-OF-CHILD DIFFERENCES

A rather different shift in preference occurs in the stress-free home environment during the second year of life. Although parents respond preferentially to neonates of their own sex (Parke and Sawin, 1980), these preferences diminish during the early part of the first year. There are no major sex differences in the behavior of either parents or infants throughout most of the first year (Lamb, 1977c; Pedersen et al., 1980), but the situation changes by the second year. Starting around the first birthday if not before, fathers begin to pay greater attention to sons than to daughters, and, apparently as a result, boys start to focus their attention and proximity/contact-seeking behaviors on their fathers (Lamb, 1977a, 1977b). By the end of the second year, all but one of the boys in one small longitudinal study were showing marked and consistent preferences for their fathers on a number of attachment-behavior measures (Lamb, 1977b). Girls were much less consistent: by age two, some preferred their mothers, some their fathers, and some neither parent. This is consistent with other evidence suggesting that parents are initially less concerned about establishing sex-appropriate behavior in daughters than in sons (cf. Lamb, 1976e, 1981c). A similar pattern of sex differences was not observed in a sample of Swedish mothers, fathers, and firstborns (Lamb et al., 1982b, 1983), however, while in a group of kibbutz-dwelling Israeli families, both mothers and fathers showed preferences for firstborn children of their own sex (Sagi et al., 1983). It is not clear whether these findings reflect sampling or cultural variations, but the preferential treatment of same-sex infants seems to be fairly widespread.

SEX-OF-PARENT DIFFERENCES

Because attachment figures are by definition sources of protection and comfort (Bowlby, 1969), the infants' preferences for mothers when distressed, alarmed, or frightened are especially pertinent in defining mothers as the primary attachment figures. However, this does not mean that mothers are preferred in all circumstances and for all types of interaction. Rather, mothers and fathers engage in different types of interaction with their infants and thus come to represent different types of experiences. Mothers, as primary caretakers, are much more likely to engage in caretaking routines than fathers are; for their part, fathers are relatively more likely than mothers to play with their infants, and the play itself is likely to be more unpredictable and physically

stimulating than mothers' play is (Belsky, 1979; Lamb, 1976b, 1977c; Power and Parke, 1982). Infants respond more positively to play bids from their fathers (Lamb, 1977c) and, through thirty months, prefer to play with their fathers when they have a choice (Clarke-Stewart, 1978). Boys continue to show this preference through four years of age, whereas girls switch to a preference for their mothers between two and four years of age (Lynn and Cross, 1974).

The formative significance (if any) of the distinctive behavioral differences between mothers and fathers remains to be established. I have suggested elsewhere that they may permit infants, especially boys, to learn socially sanctioned sex differences and begin establishing a sense of gender identity (Lamb, 1977b; Lamb and Lamb, 1976). However, this speculation is based solely on the rather weak evidence that gender identity is established in the first two to three years of life (Money and Ehrhardt, 1972) and that boys may have difficulty establishing masculine sex roles when their fathers are absent early in their lives (Biller, 1981; Lamb, 1981c). Unfortunately, there have yet to be longitudinal studies in which outcome measures are used to determine whether variations in maternal and paternal roles have long-term developmental implications.

INDIVIDUAL DIFFERENCES IN PARENT-INFANT ATTACHMENTS

At this point, let us turn from normative characteristics of parent-infant interaction to the origins and implications of individual differences. It is widely believed that the responsiveness, or unresponsiveness, of adults influences the quality or "security" of attachment relationships (Ainsworth et al., 1978). Ainsworth and her colleagues reported that when mothers were sensitively responsive to their infants during the first year of life, their infants formed secure attachments to them. When the mothers were insensitive, insecure relationships resulted. As yet, no one has asked whether the same factors account for individual differences in the security of infant-father and infant-mother attachments.

In order to assess individual differences in the quality of infant-adult attachments, Ainsworth and Wittig (1969) devised a laboratory procedure, the Strange Situation, which permitted researchers to observe how infants organize their attachment behaviors around attachment figures when they are distressed. The primary focus in the Strange Situation is on the infant's responses to reunion with the attachment figure following two brief separations. Securely-attached infants behave in the manner predicted by ethological attachment theory: they use their parents as secure bases from which to explore, especially in the preseparation episodes, and they attempt to reestablish interaction (often by seeking proximity or contact) when reunited with their parents following the brief separations. Some insecurely-attached infants are labeled "avoidant" because they actively avoid their parents when reunited; others are called "resistant" because they respond to reunion with angry ambivalence, both seeking contact/interaction and rejecting it when it is offered.

Ainsworth's reports concerning the consistent relationship between early parental behavior and infant behavior in the Strange Situation have elicited a great deal of attention, particularly in light of evidence that the patterns of behavior observed in the Strange Situation are characteristic of the relationship rather than the infant, that is, the same infants may behave differently with their mothers and fathers (Lamb, 1978; Lamb, Hwang, et al., 1982; Grossmann et al., 1981; Main and Weston, 1981) and that the patterns of behavior can be remarkably stable over time (Connell, 1976; Waters, 1978). Some caveats are in order, however. First, the relationship between parental behavior and behavior in the Strange Situation was established in only one small longitudinal study—the very study from which the hypotheses grew. There is thus a clear need for replication in larger, hypothesis-testing studies and for more serious consideration of the role played by initial differences among infants in determining security of infant-parent attachment (see Lamb et al., 1984). Second, the stability of Strange Situation behavior over time is not always as high as Waters and Connell reported: two research groups (Vaughn et al.,

1979; Thompson et al., 1982) reported substantially lower stability (62 percent and 53 percent respectively) over a comparable period of time. In both cases, temporal instability was systematically related to stress and major changes in daily circumstances and caregiving arrangements. This suggests that the security of attachment, as assessed in the Strange Situation, reflects the *current* status of the infant-adult relationship. When patterns of interaction change for any reason, the quality of the relationship may also change, and thus we observe changes in the organization of the infant's attachment behavior. Only in especially stable circumstances are we likely to find long-term stability or consistency (Lamb et al., 1984). There does *not* appear to be a sensitive period during which infants establish relationships that will remain secure or insecure from that point on, but the degree of flexibility and the consequences (if any) of repeated changes in the security of attachment remain to be established.

INTERPRETING INDIVIDUAL DIFFERENCES IN STRANGE-SITUATION BEHAVIOR

Another critical issue for researchers is to determine *why* and *how* differences among parents produce differences in attachment security, assuming that Ainsworth's findings are replicated. Adults, of course, do differ in their responsiveness to infant signals (for instance, signals of distress), and I have speculated that these individual differences among parents probably produce distinctive expectations on the part of infants' regarding their parents' behavior, which may in turn account for individual differences in the way infants behave in the Strange Situation (Lamb, 1981a, 1981b). Specifically, adults may differ along two dimensions—predictability and appropriateness—with deviation along either dimension constituting insensitivity (Ainsworth et al., 1974; Lamb and Easterbrooks, 1981). Adults who respond predictably and appropriately should have infants who turn to them unhesitatingly when alarmed or in need of comfort and who are able to use the adults as secure bases from which to explore. This is the secure pattern of behavior described earlier. By contrast, adults who are fairly consistent but often behave inappropriately or aversively should have infants who expect inappropriate responses from their parents and who thus turn away from rather than toward them when distressed. Such avoidant patterns of behavior are also observed in the Strange Situation. Meanwhile, adults who are unpredictable and who sometimes respond aversively should produce uncertainty and ambivalence in their infants, and this is in fact the third major pattern of behavior ("resistant") observed in the Strange Situation. From the limited data currently available (Ainsworth et al., 1972, 1974), it appears that the major patterns of behavior observed in the Strange Situation are associated with the styles of parental behavior described here, but, as emphasized earlier, we still need to see these associations replicated in independent samples.

Although it is assumed by most researchers that the infant's behavior in the Strange Situation is determined by the adult's prior behavior, there is some evidence that the adult's behavior in the *immediate* situation may provide cues for the infant. For example, Estes and his colleagues (1981) found that the mothers of securely attached infants were more expressive and affectively involved than the mothers of insecurely attached infants. Cross-lagged correlations suggested that the direction of influence ran from mothers to infants, with infants becoming more attentive to their mothers' cues as they grew older. It remains to be determined, however, whether the mothers' immediate behavior in the Strange Situation directly causes the infants' behavior, simply reminds infants of their mothers' typical mode of behavior, or is causally unrelated to the infants' Strange Situation behavior but is correlated with the aspects of maternal behavior that are causally important.

While developing specific expectations about the behavioral propensities of attachment figures during the first year of life, infants are also learning about themselves—specifically, about their ability to elicit responses from others and thus to help shape their own experiences. Recognition of one's own efficacy, which I call perceived effectance, is as important developmentally as a sense of trust in others. Once

again, I expect individual differences in the perceived effectance of infants to be correlated with variations in their parents' behavioral propensities. When adults respond promptly and consistently to their infants' signals, the infants should develop high perceived effectance. When the adults' responses are less predictable, lower perceived effectance should result.

PREDICTIVE VALIDITY OF SECURITY OF ATTACHMENT

Because expectations about oneself and about important others are developmentally important, one would expect them to anticipate later differences in child development. In fact, there is surprisingly good evidence that individual differences in Strange Situation behavior are related to aspects of the children's behavior in a variety of contexts months and even years later, at least when there is stability in family circumstances and child-care arrangements (Lamb et al., 1984).

In an early study, Main (1973) reported that infants who were securely attached to their mothers at one year of age were more cooperative with and friendly toward an unfamiliar woman eight months later than were insecurely attached infants. Similarly, Thompson and Lamb (1983) found that securely attached infants were more sociable with unfamiliar females at both twelve and nineteen months of age. Furthermore, sociability was stable over time when the security of attachment was temporally stable, but not when attachment security changed between twelve and nineteen months. Both Waters and his colleagues (1979) and Pastor (1981) showed that securely attached infants were later more socially competent in interaction with peers than insecurely attached infants were. Securely-attached eighteen-month-olds later displayed more persistence and enthusiasm in problem-solving situations than insecurely attached infants did (Matas et al., 1978; Sroufe and Rosenberg, 1982). Finally, Arend and his colleagues (1979) and Sroufe (in press) reported that securely attached infants demonstrated more ego control and ego resiliency than insecurely attached infants did several years later.

Main and Weston (1981) sought to determine what would happen when infants were securely attached to one parent and were insecurely attached to the other. They found that the nature of the attachment to the mother (primary caregiver) has the greatest impact on the infants' responses to a strange adult, although the quality of the infant-father attachment also had an independent influence. Unfortunately, the assessments of sociability all took place in the mothers' presence, six months before the father-infant attachment was assessed. This may explain why these results were not replicated by Lamb, Hwang, and their colleagues (1982) in a study I will describe more fully.

Nevertheless, the long-term effects of individual differences in the security of attachment appear to be well established. It is important to recognize, however, that these "effects" are found *if and only if* there is temporal stability in family circumstances and/or the security of attachment (Lamb et al., 1984). This suggests that it is the current status of parent-child relationships, rather than the quality of these relationships during some early critical period, which affects the child's later behavior. These findings stand as testimony to the resiliency of young children and to their ability to adapt to changing circumstances.

Clearly, we still need much more research if we are to understand the long-term formative significance of individual differences in attachment. I am optimistic that the behavior observed in the Strange Situation will prove to be important, but I doubt whether the significance will be as great as some now seem to believe (Sroufe, 1978, 1979, in press). Infant experiences are formatively significant, but so too are the other experiences that children encounter as they mature. An infant who has established insecure relationships with both of its parents is more likely to develop in a suboptimal way than is one who is securely-attached to both parents, particularly if the parents' behavior and circumstances remain reasonably consistent over the years. Parents *do* change, however, either because their circumstances change, because they find it easier or harder to relate to infants than to preschoolers, or because they have adjusted to their child's temperament. As their behavior changes, so too may the security of the infant-parent attachments. Furthermore, a variety of people other than parents affect the socialization process, and this makes it highly unlikely that one will find strong linear continuity from infancy.

Nontraditional Family Forms

In the preceding section, I focused on the processes and outcomes of socialization in traditional two-parent families. As noted earlier, however, such families are becoming increasingly uncommon. The most recent estimates suggest that only 23 percent of the households in the United States now fit the traditional pattern, with father as sole breadwinner and mother at home caring for one or more children (Pleck, 1983; Pleck and Rustad, 1980). Contemporary families tend to deviate from the traditional norm in three major ways: maternal employment, increased paternal participation, and divorce and single-parenthood. My goal in this section is to describe both the ways in which socialization processes may be changed by these nontraditional family conditions and their likely or demonstrated effects on child development.

MATERNAL EMPLOYMENT AND OUT-OF-HOME CARE

Recent statistics demonstrate that an increasing number of women now either choose to or feel they have to remain in paid employment after their children are born. By 1978, 50 percent of the women in the United States and 44 percent of the married women with husbands present were in the paid labor force, with the proportion of married women who are employed expected to rise to 57 percent by 1995 (Glick, 1979). Employment rates are not substantially lower for married mothers in intact families than for women in general: in 1979, 52 percent of the mothers of school-aged children (six to seventeen years old) and 36 percent of the mothers of infants and preschool-aged children were employed (Glick and Norton, 1979). For obvious economic reasons, employment rates are even higher among single mothers and black mothers—both single and married (Glick and Norton, 1979). Clearly, therefore, *most* American children now grow up in families in which both parents, or the single resident parent, are employed outside the home.

I have elsewhere critically reviewed the literature concerned with the effects of maternal employment on child development (Lamb, 1982), so I will not review the many relevant studies in detail here. Nor will I discuss the evidence concerning the effects of maternal employment on school-aged children, even though this topic has been most thoroughly explored. Instead, I prefer to focus on evidence concerning the effects of maternal employment on the security of *infant*-mother attachment. Research on this topic is of special importance because of the long-term implications of security of attachment and because of the widespread assumption that maternal employment is certain to have more deleterious effects on infants than on children of any other age. Unfortunately, developmentalists have felt so confident about this assumption that there have been relatively few empirical studies. Further, most of them have considered the effects of maternal employment and of alternative care separately even though these conditions often occur together.

Maternal Employment. Concerns about the effects of alternative (extrafamilial) care on socioemotional development were initially stimulated by evidence concerning the harmful effects of major maternal separations on child development, for example, maternal separations resulting either from hospitalization or institutionalization (Bowlby, 1951; Robertson and Bowlby, 1952; Schaffer, 1958; Schaffer and Callender, 1959; Spitz and Wolf, 1946). Initial reports suggested that the reactions of young children to major separations are extremely alarming: children show a phase of active protest immediately following separation, then a phase of withdrawal and apathy, and finally a phase characterized by either detachment or anxious attachment (Bowlby, 1969, 1973; Yarrow, 1964). However, children's reactions to

hospitalization or institutionalization are influenced by a number of other factors apart from the separation experience per se (Yarrow, 1964). These factors include the quality of the institution, the number of substitute caretakers, the duration of the separation, and the age of the child. Consequently, although major separations clearly place children at risk, it cannot be assumed that adverse effects are inevitable, although this assumption is commonly made.

Despite these limitations, several developmentalists have concluded that any separation in the early years, including regular minor separations, as when the child is left with another caretaker, may weaken the attachment relation to the mother and/or make the child less secure and trusting (for example, Blehar, 1975). During the past ten years, however, theorists have come to questions the analogy between institutionalized and daily supplementary care. Most of the published research in fact shows that day care and/or maternal employment *need not* have harmful effects on children.

Although Hock (1980) reported no significant effects of maternal employment on the security of infant-mother attachment in the Strange Situation, three recent studies suggest that the likelihood of insecure (especially avoidant) attachment relationships may increase when the mothers of young infants are employed (Owen et al., 1982; Thompson et al., 1982; Vaughn et al., 1980). Although none of these studies considered maternal employment in the context of alternative-care characteristics, their findings nonetheless highlight a number of factors that need to be taken into account when assessing the effects of maternal employment.

Most important, maternal employment does not necessarily have adverse effects on the infant-mother attachment. Taken together, these studies show that perhaps half of the children whose mothers were employed have secure attachments, compared to the usual rate of 65 percent. In fact, one has to combine the data across studies to reveal any real effect on the security of attachment. In Owen's study, maternal return to employment before the babies were six months old did not affect the likelihood of insecure infant-mother attachment. Thompson and his colleagues reported that 40 percent of the fifteen infants with employed mothers were insecurely attached at nineteen months, compared with 29 percent of the twenty-eight infants with unemployed mothers. Vaughn's group found that the proportion of insecure attachments at twelve months was 47 percent and at eighteen months 50 percent when mothers returned to work during the first year; most of the insecurely-attached infants were avoidantly attached. Return to work when the infants were between twelve and eighteen months had no significant effect.

Presumably the mothers' attitudes and circumstances, along with the quality of alternative care, determine whether secure or insecure relationships will result. This was demonstrated quite clearly by Owen and her colleagues (1982) who explored both mothers' and fathers' attitudes thoroughly in a longitudinal study of eighty-one families, followed from the third trimester of pregnancy until the infants were over a year old. They found that infants who were securely attached had mothers who valued parenthood highly, whereas the mothers of those who were insecurely attached tended to value work highly and parenthood less. When mothers values parenthood highly, they tended to have securely attached infants—*regardless of whether or not they were employed.* This suggested that maternal employment per se was a less important determinant of the security of attachment than were the mothers' attitudes and values. This is important because it underscores the inappropriateness of the assumption that employed mothers constitute a homogeneous group. Clearly, we will only understand the effects of maternal employment when we take into account the attitudes, values, motivations, and circumstances of both employed and unemployed mothers and stop viewing them as homogeneous groups.

Further, Thompson and his colleagues (1982) showed that, although maternal employment was associated with attachment insecurity, there was an even clearer relationship between maternal employment and *changes* in the security of attachment. In other words, the mothers' return to work appeared to affect the interaction between mothers and infants, but these effects could be both positive and negative. In some cases, maternal employment seemed to make insecure relationships into secure ones; in other families, the reverse occurred. Again, therefore, we need to consider not only *whether* mothers work, but *why* they work. Presumably, if mothers dislike being home and feel more fulfilled when employed, then the return to employment may have positive rather than negative effects.

The evidence thus suggests that, whereas maternal employment has a fairly clear-cut effect on the sex-role attitudes of boys and girls (Lamb, 1982), effects on the quality of parent-child relationships, and hence on the children's psychosocial adjustment, are less consistent. Their presence and nature depends on a number of factors—including the values and attitudes of the mothers, their spouses, and the members of their social networks. Presumably, effects also differ depending on the types of nonmaternal care to which children are exposed, but unfortunately this issue has not been explored empirically. The evidence available thus far demonstrates that—contrary to popular belief—maternal employment does not necessarily have harmful effects on child development. In fact, the effects may in many circumstances be beneficial.

Effects of Out-of-Home Care on Parent-Child Relationships. In addition to parental attitudes and motivations, the quality of the care obtained when the child is not with the mother must surely affect the reaction to maternal employment. Unfortunately, although there have been several studies concerned with the effects of extrafamilial care, quality of care has never been considered. Instead, focus has been on whether or not day care affects child development. The first attempt to compare the effects of nonparental and home care was performed by Caldwell and her colleagues (1970), who studied two groups of two and one-half-year-old children, half attending a high-quality day-care facility and the others home reared. Ratings of child-mother, child-other, and mother-child interactions revealed no differences between the day-care children and home-care children on any of the measures.

In a widely-cited study, Blehar (1974) then compared twenty two- and three-year-old children receiving full-time group day care with twenty home-reared children of similar ages. The children were observed with their mothers in Ainsworth's Strange Situation, and Blehar reported disturbances in the day-care children's attachments. More specifically, the two-year-olds exhibited "detachment-like behavior" (that is, avoidance) and the three-year-old children exhibited "anxious, ambivalent attachment behaviors." They explored less, were more distressed by separation, and sought more proximity to and contact with their mothers upon reunion than did the home-care controls.

Because these findings seemed to confirm that day care had effects similar to long-term separation, several investigators have attempted to replicate Blehar's study. Portnoy and Simmons (1978), for instance, compared three groups of three and one-half- to four-year-old children. These groups were composed of children who were cared for at home by their mothers until three years of age and were then enrolled in a group day-care center; home-reared children; and children who stayed in family day care between the ages of one and two and were then enrolled in a group day-care center. Despite the fact that Portnoy and Simmons used the same observational procedure as Blehar, they found no significant group differences in attachment patterns. In another attempt to replicate Blehar's results, Moskowitz and her colleagues (1977) compared a group of three and one-half-year-old children who had approximately six months of day-care experience with a matched group of home-reared controls. This study was (in contrast to Blehar's) designed to minimize experimenter bias: the experimenter, interviewers, strangers, and coders were all unaware of the hypotheses and of the children's backgrounds. The Moskowitz group found that day-care children showed less distress than the home-reared children in the latter parts of the Strange Situation. Apart from this, the two groups were not different on any other measures, including measures of attachment behavior to their mothers.

Several other attempts to replicate Blehar's findings with both two-and three-year-olds have been unsuccessful (Barahal, 1977; Brookhart and Hock, 1976; Cornelius and Denney, 1975; Doyle, 1975; Ragozin, 1977, 1980; Roopnarine and Lamb, 1978). Most recently, Blanchard and Main (1979) reported that the effects Blehar (1974) observed may represent temporary adjustment problems rather than long-term maladjustment in parent-child relationships.

In Cochran's (1977) Swedish study, mother-child separations were observed in the home rather than in the laboratory. Cochran reported that the center- and home-reared children responded very similarly to these brief separations. Fewer than 60 percent of the children in both groups followed their mothers to the door and fewer than 35 percent cried when their mothers left. Kagan's group (1978) compared thirty-two pairs of children matched for sex, ethnicity, and social class; half were enrolled in full-time day care between the ages of one and one-half and three and one-half. They found that the children reared at home did not cry more or less when separated from their mother in a laboratory situation than did those who had been in day care.

Roopnarine and Lamb (1978) adopted a somewhat different strategy when comparing day-care with home-reared children. Three-year-old children were observed in the Strange Situation immediately prior to enrollment in day care and again three months later. When comparing this group to another group of children, matched in all respects except for the fact that their parents had no plans to enroll them in day care, they found that the day-care children were more concerned about the brief separations than the home-care children were. After three months of day care, however, these group differences had disappeared. This study thus underscored the need for preenrollment assessments: group differences observed in a single posttest assessment cannot be interpreted as effects of substitute care, and the absence of group differences in a posttest does not mean that substitute care has had no effects. Roopnarine and Lamb (1980) later replicated these findings, showing that group differences in responses to separation were greater in preenrollment than in postenrollment assessments. They thus urged that researchers turn attention from group comparisons to studies in which initial differences are related to effects of substitute care.

Relationships with Caretakers. Instead of studying reactions to brief separations, several researchers have asked whether children in substitute care develop attachment-like relationships with caretakers, and, if so, how these relationships compare with mother-child relationships. In one such study, Ricciutti (1974) found that children responded more positively to the approach of their regular caretakers than to the approach of strangers. They also became less upset when left alone with their mothers, indicating that the relationships to mothers were more important than those to either strangers or familiar caretakers. Later, Farran and Ramey (1977) observed twenty-three children interacting with their mothers and teachers and reported that the children showed an overwhelming preference for proximity to and interaction with their mothers. Similarly, in a Norwegian study (Martinson et al., 1978), seventeen infants aged between ten and twenty-three months were observed twice in a laboratory situation, once with their mothers and once with a familiar preschool teacher. To the investigators' surprise, the children behaved similarly with the two adults. Cummings (1980) compared reactions to: irregular caretakers, regular caretakers, and mothers. In the day-care setting, the children revealed a preference for regular over irregular caretakers. In the laboratory, however, the children rarely approached caretakers, preferring instead to spend time in the proximity of their mothers; they were often upset when left alone with one of the caretakers. Anderson and her colleagues (1981) reported more contact-seeking distance interaction and exploration in the presence of highly involved caretakers than of strangers, whereas all these behaviors were more common in the presence of strangers than of less-involved caretakers. Finally, home observations of parents and two- to three-year-old children in Clarke-Stewart's (1980) detailed study revealed no differences in the behavior of either parents or children. In all, even though no one has attempted to describe the

nature of the relationship between the child and the caretaker, it seems that the enrollment of children in day care does not lead to the replacement of the mother by the caretaker as the child's primary object of attachment.

Effects of Supplementary Care on Relationships with Others. In another line of research, interactions with unfamiliar adults have been studied, but here consistent group differences between home-reared and center-reared children have not been found. One study, (Schwarz et al., 1974), for instance, reported that day-care children were more aggressive (both physically and verbally) toward, more motorically active, and less cooperative with adults than home-reared children. This finding, however, was not replicated in two other studies (Lay and Meyer, 1972; Macrae and Herbert-Jackson, 1976). McCutcheon and Calhoun (1976) showed that increased interaction with peers led day-care children to interact less with adults. An earlier study (Raph et al., 1964) reported that negative behavior toward teachers varied depending on the amount of prior group experience. In two other studies, home-reared and family-day-care-reared children were found to interact (Finkelstein and Wilson, 1977) and to verbalize (Cochran, 1977) with their caretakers more than day-care children did. Day-care children, on the other hand, were found to interact more with unfamiliar adults than did children in the other groups. Insofar as none of these studies used standardized measures, however, it is difficult to appraise or compare their findings. Clarke-Stewart (1980) found that two- to three-year-old children in alternative-care settings were more compliant, prosocial, and socially competent than children being raised at home, who appeared "more attached" to their mothers. Those in family day care fell between those in centers and those cared for exclusively at home. However, none of these studies involved pretest assessments, making interpretation of the findings difficult at best.

Surprisingly little attention has been paid to the effects of day care on peer relationships, even though children in group-care settings typically have more experience with peers than do home-reared children. Becker (1977) reported that regular contact with peers increased peer competence, but none of her subjects were in alternative care. Schwarz and his colleagues (1974) reported that center-reared children were more aggressive than home-reared age-mates. However, these effects appear to be culture-specific—at least according to informal accounts—for similar effects are not observed in China (Kessen, 1975) or in the USSR (Bronfenbrenner, 1970). They were also not reported by Clarke-Stewart (1980), who found that children in alternative-care settings were more cooperative with unfamiliar peers than those raised exclusively at home. However, no researchers have systematically examined the effects of alternative care on peer competence using standardized measures of known reliability and validity in a pretest/posttest design.

Limitations of the Research. Research on the effects of substitute care is severely limited in several respects. First, many of the studies have focused upon optimal, university-affiliated programs, in which there is a high staff-child ratio (3:1 or better) and a well-designed curriculum for tutoring cognitive, emotional, and social development. The care provided in these settings is probably not representative of the care most children receive, making generalization of the findings impossible. It is imperative that quality of care be treated systematically if we are to understand the effects of substitute care on children (Anderson, 1980).

Second, most studies have involved only one postenrollment assessment, without any assessment of long-term effects. Moore (1975) and Cochran (1977) examined longer term outcomes, but in Moore's study, family instability was confounded with type of early care, and many of Cochran's subjects changed group status, making it hard to interpret evidence regarding long-term effects. Thus we really have no information on this score.

Third, many of the published studies have not matched the family backgrounds of children in the different groups, even though (at least in the United States) families using nonfamily care may differ in important respects from families rearing their children at home (Hock, 1976).

Fourth, the overwhelming majority of stud-

ies have been carried out in the United States. This fact also limits the generalizability of the reported findings. Further research in other countries is important not only for what it tells us about children in these countries, but also because the study of diverse cultures helps us to identify general processes of development as distinct from those that are unique to a specific culture.

Fifth, most studies investigating socioemotional effects of nonparental care have focused on group day-care centers. Scant attention has been focused on family day-care homes (cf. Cochran, 1977; Portnoy and Simmons, 1978). This is important because family day care is a much more common type of substitute care than is enrollment in a day-care center. Even though family day care also involves separation from the parents, care is provided by a single adult in a home setting and the number of peers is smaller than in day-care centers. Thus, the effects of family day care and center day care are likely to be different, yet the differences have yet to be explored.

Sixth, despite clear-cut evidence that children form attachment bonds to their fathers, no researchers have investigated the effects of extrafamilial care on father-child relationships. Progress toward understanding early socioemotional development requires at the least an acknowledgment that infants are socialized in the context of a complex, multidimensional social system. This means that broader assessments of the effects of substitute care are needed.

Seventh, most previous studies have assessed only selected aspects of the child's socioemotional development, using laboratory assessments whose ecological and predictive validity is questionable. No researchers have attempted to assess multiple aspects of socioemotional development using ecologically and predictively valid measures.

Finally, researchers have sought only to compare groups of children (for example, those who are versus those who are not in day care), usually with the goal of determining whether substitute care is good or bad for children. Researchers have yet to recognize, apparently, that what is good for one child or one family may be bad for another. What is now needed are studies that explore the effects of different types of early rearing experiences on children whose socioemotional characteristics differ initially. Only in this way will we get a more differentiated understanding of the ways in which different experiences can affect early socioemotional development. Similarly, we need studies in which the quality of extrafamilial care is related to measures of the children's adjustment. It seems reasonably safe to predict that poor quality care will have adverse consequences, but the relevant research has yet to be conducted.

INCREASED PATERNAL PARTICIPATION

As in the case of maternal employment, day care, and single parenthood, developmentalists have expressed concern about the implications of increased paternal involvement, particularly when this leads fathers to be as involved as, or more involved than, their wives. Psychoanalysts have been especially clear about the need for fathers to avoid extensive involvement in feminine activities such as caretaking, lest they confuse the child and deny it a more psychologically distant figure to help it separate and individuate, to use Mahler's terms (Abelin, 1980; Cath et al., 1982). Others have expressed concern that if fathers become associated with feminine activities their effectiveness as sex-role models will be compromised and their children's psychological adjustment will be threatened.

Although the empirical evidence is lacking, these concerns are probably not warranted. First of all, there is no reason to believe that father (rather than mother or a regular babysitter) needs to be the person who helps the child through the process of separation-individuation in the second year of life. Nor are women any better qualified than men to serve as primary caretakers. Second, there is no reason to believe that men are less masculine in their children's eyes because they are extensively involved in child care. Indeed, my research in Sweden showed that there were distinctive differences between maternal and paternal behavioral styles *regardless* of the parents' relative involvement in child care (Lamb,

Frodi, et al., 1982a, 1982b). Third, even if the parents' gender roles are blurred in role-reversed or role-sharing families, there is no reason to believe that the child's sense of gender identity and personal adjustment will be affected. There is in fact no relationship between traditionality of gender role and security of gender identity. Fourth, one could argue that in our more egalitarian contemporary world, it is advantageous rather than harmful for children to develop androgynous gender roles rather than traditionally masculine and feminine roles.

The few empirical studies concerned with increased paternal involvement in child care have had to do with job sharing or temporary role-reversal. As noted earlier, the mother-child relationship in traditional families appears to have a greater impact on most aspects of socioemotional development, presumably because mothers typically serve as primary caretakers and socialization agents. If this were true, then we would expect the relative importance of the father-child relationship to increase as the extent of paternal involvement increased. To my surprise, our recent research in Sweden failed to show this: there was no relationship between degree of paternal involvement and the predictive validity of the infant-mother and infant-father attachment relationships (Lamb, Hwang et al., 1982). Correspondingly, degree of paternal involvement was unrelated to the children's patterns of preferences (Lamb, Frodi, et al., 1983).

Studies of older children have yielded different results, however. Russell's (1982a, 1982b) highly involved fathers reported that they felt much closer to their children as a result of their role-sharing or role-reversal, but unfortunately no effects on the children were assessed. Radin (1982); Radin and Sagi, 1982) reported that increased paternal involvement had positive effects on the locus of control and academic achievement of preschoolers. Children with highly involved fathers, like those with employed mothers, had less stereotyped attitudes regarding male and female roles. In a later study of Israeli fathers in which Sagi employed Radin's measures, results similar to but stronger than those obtained in the United States were reported (Radin and Sagi, 1982;

Sagi, 1982). Presumably, the effects on sex-role attitudes occurred because the role-sharing parents provided less stereotyped models with which their children could identify and also encouraged their children to have egalitarian attitudes. The effects on intellectual performance may reflect fathers' traditional association with achievement and occupational advancement, or it could reflect the benefits of having extensive stimulation from two highly involved and relatively competent parents.

Attempts to explain increased paternal participation usually identify two factors associated with extensive paternal involvement —maternal employment and unusually high or low involvement by the fathers' own fathers. Much more attention has been devoted to the relationship between maternal employment and paternal involvement. It is widely suggested in both the popular and professional literature that maternal employment affects family life by leading to a redistribution of the family work-load (L. Hoffman, 1977). When mothers and wives are employed, the argument goes, their husbands start to play a greater role in child care and housework. The empirical evidence, suggests, however, that men do not do much more housework and childcare when their wives are employed than when their wives are full-time homemakers and mothers. In fact, the results of a recent national time-use survey revealed that the increased male involvement in child care associated with maternal employment amounted to only a few extra minutes per day; prior to this survey in the mid-1970s there was no evidence that maternal employment had *any* effect on the amount of time that men devoted to child care (Pleck, 1983). However, fathers' relative involvement certainly increases simply because their wives spend much less time with child care.

The fact that absolute levels of paternal involvement increase so little when mothers are employed is rather surprising, given the widespread claims that men today *want* to be more involved in child care than their own fathers were (Sheehy, 1979). Perhaps these men are only espousing these values because they are now socially approved, or perhaps our social and economic system is still too rigid to permit

men to assume a greater role in child care without risking great personal and professional costs. At first glance, this seems unlikely, since (at least in Sweden) the provision of paid paternal leave with a guarantee of reemployment at or above the preleave level has induced remarkably few eligible fathers to request even small amounts of paternal leave (Lamb and Levine, 1983). On the other hand, the attitudes of peers and employers may still inhibit fathers from seeking parental leave, as may the attitudes they have internalized during years of living in a sex-stereotyped society. In addition, it is possible that men are biologically designed to be less interested and competent in child care than women are. My colleagues and I are currently engaged in a multinational effort to identify the circumstances that limit or facilitate paternal involvement (Levine et al., 1983). We expect our efforts to advance our understanding of paternal involvement while also identifying ways in which we could facilitate involvement by those fathers who wish to be more involved.

Other than maternal employment and institutional practices, discussions of paternal participation often identify the earlier involvement of the father's father as a key determinant of the level of involvement. Some have hypothesized that fathers became highly involved in an attempt to compensate for the limited involvement of their own fathers (Gersick, 1975; Mendes, 1976) whereas others have argued that highly involved fathers themselves had unusually involved fathers, whom the younger fathers attempt to emulate (Manion, 1977). One recent study of Israeli fathers by Sagi (1982; Radin and Sagi, 1982) provided clear support for the identification hypothesis: highly involved fathers reported that their own fathers had been unusually involved in child care. There is little empirical support for the compensation hypothesis.

Obviously, considerably more research is needed before we will fully understand the effects of increased paternal involvement. Based on the available evidence, however, we can discount popular fears that the personal adjustment and gender identity of children will be seriously disturbed if their fathers assume an extensive role in child care. True, many of Russell's (1982a, 1982b) subjects returned to more traditional lifestyles when they had the opportunity to do so, but none of the children in this or any of the other studies reported here appeared to suffer adverse consequences. Several researchers are currently engaged in studies designed to explore the effects of these nontraditional child-rearing styles on children, so we should be much better informed a few years from now than we are today.

DIVORCE AND SINGLE PARENTHOOD

Of the deviant family forms being considered here, single parenthood is the one about which there is most reason for concern, particularly since, over the last few decades, the number of single-parent families has risen dramatically. National statistics now suggest that about a third of the children in the United States will spend some portion of their childhood in a single-parent family (Glick and Norton, 1979). For 90 percent of them, the single parents will be their mothers. Unfortunately, none of the studies on this topic have involved infants and very young children, so we are able only to speculate about the effects on very young children.

To the extent that they do not have a spouse to supplement their parenting efforts, single mothers and fathers are in a similar predicament, with lack of supervision and control over children being possible consequences. Further, in all single-parent families one major sex-role model is absent. On the other hand, many single mothers lack the training and experience to obtain satisfying and financially rewarding jobs, so they are likely to be in worse economic circumstances than single fathers. Especially when the children involved are young, community attitudes are often less supportive of single mothers working than of single fathers. Social isolation is commonly experienced by both divorced parties, but may be especially serious for mothers whose social network was largely defined by their exhusbands' work associates. For these reasons, single mothers may often be in worse straits than single fathers.

As long as these social and economic stresses remain, single parents are apt to be less effective, consistent, and sensitive as parents, and this is likely to distort relationships with their children and have adverse effects on their psychological adjustment regardless of the children's ages. Unfortunately, we cannot say what proportion of the adverse effects of father absence would be eliminated if single mothers could count on less financially stressful circumstances and were less isolated from social networks. We do know, however, that increasing numbers of women combine working and mothering, and these women thus retain independent sources of income and access to social networks. Divorce is substantially less stressful and disruptive for these women (Hetherington, 1979) than for previously unemployed mothers. Marital dissolution is inherently stressful for almost all people, however, making at least temporary disturbances of psychological functioning almost inevitable (Hetherington, et al., 1978).

There have been numerous studies of children raised by single mothers and substantially fewer studies of single fathers (see Lamb, 1976e, 1981c, and Biller, 1976, 1981, for reviews). Although researchers now question whether the absence of a male model satisfactorily accounts for the effects observed, it is fairly clear that children (especially boys) raised by single mothers are "at risk." Boys raised by single mothers are more likely than those from two-parent families to be less "masculine," more psychologically maladjusted, delinquent, hypo- or hyperaggressive, and to perform more poorly at school (see reviews by Biller, 1981; Lamb, 1981c; Radin, 1981; Shinn, 1978). Although the evidence is not clear cut, it seems that these effects are exaggerated when the father's absence begins early in the children's lives. Girls, too, may reveal deficits in their ability to interact with males, although these effects may not be evident prior to adolescence even when the fathers' absence occurred much earlier (Hetherington, 1972). The availability of alternative male models (stepfathers, older brothers, uncles, grandfathers) can reduce the adverse effects on sex-role development (Biller, 1974) although few substitute relationships match the intensity of close father-child relationships.

Interestingly, the only comparative study of single fathers of which I am aware (Santrock and Warshak, 1979; Santrock et al., 1982) indicated that girls adapted more poorly than boys in the care of single fathers. This finding is consistent with evidence suggesting that fathers are embarrassed when called upon to purchase clothing for and to discuss menstruation and sexuality with their pubescent daughters, and this is likely to be especially problematic for single fathers (Fox, 1978; Hipgrave, 1982). Together with the results of studies concerned with the children of single mothers, these findings suggested that single parents are more successful raising children of the same than of the opposite sex, but we obviously need further documentation of this assumption.

Nevertheless, although most social scientists seem to consider single fathers to be in an especially invidious position because they typically have to assume sole parental responsibility without adequate warning or preparation, I suspect that *on average,* today's single fathers are more likely than single mothers to succeed in meeting the extensive demands placed on them. Excepting widowers, they are a highly selected and self-motivated group, simply because popular and judicial skepticism regarding their motivation and ability ensures that they have to fight to obtain custody, whereas mothers often gain custody by default. In addition, society either tolerates or expects single fathers to work full time and to employ others to assist in child and home care, whereas both of these practices would be viewed as indices of incompetence on the part of single mothers.

Nonetheless, the potential for deviant outcomes among the children of single mothers and fathers is considerably greater than with any of the other nontraditional family forms discussed here. As Maccoby (1977) has said: "Child rearing is something that many people cannot do adequately as single adults functioning in isolation. Single parents need time off from parenting, they need the company of other adults, they need to have other voices joined with theirs in transmitting values and maturity demands to their children." The so-

cialization process *need* not fail, of course. Its success depends on the availability of emotional, practical, and social supports for single parents and their children.

Three other issues must also be mentioned. First, marital disharmony appears to have more deleterious effects, especially on boys, than does divorce and father absence (Block, et al., 1981; Lamb, 1977d; Rutter, 1972, 1979). It is conceivable, therefore, that some of the "effects of single parenthood" may be consequences of the marital hostility that preceded divorce, rather than of the divorce and subsequent period of single parenthood. Thus, if our goal is to minimize the psychological damage to developing children, single parenthood may be the most desirable of the realistic alternatives. Second, psychological father absence (which occurs when fathers are seldom available to their children) and physical father absence have qualitatively similar effects on sex-role development (Blanchard and Biller, 1971). Likewise, distant or hostile fathers and absent fathers have qualitatively similar (though quantitatively different) effects on moral development (M. Hoffman, 1970). These findings again imply that single parenthood may not have less desirable consequences than the alternative arrangement. Finally, it is important not to exaggerate the ill-effects of divorce or single parenthood. Even though many studies have demonstrated statistically significant group differences between children in single- and two-parent families, many of the individuals in the groups do not deviate from the norm. In other words, we must not let the evidence of development problems in *some* children of divorce lead us to unfounded statements about the *inevitable* effects of divorce.

Conclusion

We have substantial evidence that experiences within the family have a major impact on social, personality, and intellectual development. Of course socializing agents outside the family—television, peers, teachers, for example—also affect development, and later experiences can either reverse or accentuate the effects of earlier experiences: there are no magic periods during which specific experiences have irreversible effects on subsequent development. Nevertheless, it is reasonable to conclude that children who have good and rewarding early relationships within the family are probably at an advantage relative to those whose initial experiences are less satisfactory.

It is also clear that the socializing experience differs when children are raised in families that deviate from the two-parent, traditional norm, and that the differences indeed affect children's development. At this point, we still need much more work designed both to identify the effects more precisely and to define the processes by which these effects are mediated. However, we know enough to underscore some of the points made earlier. First, there is no justification for assuming that any family forms that deviate from the traditional form necessarily have harmful consequences. In fact, as I have suggested, some of these deviant styles—for example, those involving maternal employment—have what may be seen as positive effects on children. Second, we must be careful to distinguish between the objective description of findings or effects and the subjective evaluation of those findings. It is one thing to say that girls whose mothers are employed are less stereotypically feminine; a value judgment is involved if we then describe this effect as either desirable or undesirable. Finally, we need to remember that families do not exist in isolation: they are embedded in and influenced by a wider social context. Consequently, the attitudes and values of others affect both the behavior of parents, and thus indirectly their children, and may also have direct effects on the latter. Because societal attitudes change over time, the same "deviant" family form may have different effects in different historical epochs or in different social contexts. Maternal employment was formerly viewed very negatively; three decades later, maternal employment is the normative practice, and it is the unemployed mother who must often cope with questions about how she can be fulfilled if she is "only a mother." Maternal employment is thus likely to have had different effects in the 1950s than in the 1980s.

REFERENCES

Abelin, E. L. (1980). Self-image, gender identity, and the early triangulations. Manuscript in preparation.

Ainsworth, M. D. S. (1973). The development of infant-mother attachment. In *Review of Child Development Research*, vol. 3, ed. B. M. Caldwell and H. N. Ricciuti. Chicago: University of Chicago Press.

Ainsworth, M. D. S., Bell, S. M., and Stayton, D. J. (1972). Individual differences in the development of some attachment behaviors. *Merrill-Palmer Quarterly*, 18:123–143.

Ainsworth, M. D. S., Bell, S. M., and Stayton, D. J. (1974) Infant mother attachment and social development: "Socialization" as a product of reciprocal responsiveness to signals. In *The Integration of a Child Into a Social World*, ed., M. P. M. Richards. Cambridge, England: Cambridge University Press.

Ainsworth, M. D. S., Blehar, M. C., Waters, E., and Wall, S. (1978). *Patterns of Attachment*. Hillsdale, New Jersey: Lawrence Erlbaum Associates.

Ainsworth, M. D. S. and Wittig, B. A. (1969). Attachment and exploratory behavior of one-year-olds in a strange situation. In *Determinants of Infant Behaviour*, vol. 4, ed., B. M. Foss. London: Methuen.

Anderson, C. W. (1980). Attachment in daily separations: Reconceptualizing day care and maternal employment issues. *Child Development*, 51: 242–245.

Anderson, C. W., Nagle, R. J., Roberts, W. A., and Smith, J. W. (1981). Attachment to substitute caregivers as a function of center quality and caregiver involvement. *Child Development*, 51:53–61.

Arend, R., Gove, F. L., and Sroufe, L. A. (1979). Continuity of individual adaptation from infancy to kindergarten: A predictive study of ego-resiliency and curiosity in preschoolers. *Child Development*, 50:950–959.

Barahal, R. M. (1977). A comparison of parent-infant attachment and interaction patterns in day care and non-day care family groups. Unpublished doctoral dissertation, Cornell University.

Becker, J. N. T. (1977). A learning analysis of the development of peer-oriented behavior in nine-month-old infants. *Developmental Psychology*, 13:481–491.

Belsky, J. (1979). Mother-father-infant interaction: A naturalistic observational study. *Developmental Psychology*, 15:601–607.

Biller, H. B. (1974). *Paternal deprivation: Family, School, Sexuality and Society*. Lexington, Mass.: D. C. Heath.

Biller, H. B. (1976). The father and personality development: Paternal deprivation and sex-role development. In *The Role of the Father in Child Development*, ed., M. E. Lamb, New York: John Wiley.

Biller, H. B. (1981). Father absence, divorce, and personality development. In *The Role of the Father in Child Development*, rev. ed., ed. M. E. Lamb. New York: John Wiley.

Blanchard, M. and Main, M. (1979). Avoidance of the attachment figure and social-emotional adjustment in day-care infants. *Developmental Psychology*, 15:445–446.

Blanchard, R. W. and Biller, H. B. (1971). Father availability and academic performance among third grade boys. *Developmental Psychology*, 4:301–305.

Blehar, M. C. (1974). Anxious attachment and defensive reactions associated with day care. *Child Development*, 45: 683–692.

Blehar, M. (1975). Anxious attachment and defensive reactions associated with day care. In *Influences on Human Development*, ed. U. Bronfenbrenner and M. A. Mahoney. New York: Holt, Rinehart & Winston.

Block, J. H., Block, J., and Morrison, A. (1981). Parental agreement-disagreement on child-rearing orientations and gender-related personality correlates in children. *Child Development*, 52:965–974.

Bowlby, J. (1951). *Maternal Care and Mental Health*. Geneva: World Health Organization.

Bowlby, J. (1969). *Attachment and Loss*, vol. 1, *Attachment*. New York: Basic Books.

Bowlby, J. (1973). *Attachment and Loss*, vol. 2., *Separation: Anxiety and Anger*. New York: Basic Books.

Bronfenbrenner, U. (1970). *Two Worlds of Childhood*. New York: Simon & Schuster.

Brookhart, J. and Hock, E. (1976). The effects of experimental context and experiential background on infants' behavior toward their mothers and a stranger. *Child Development*, 47:333–40.

Caldwell, B. M., Wright, C. M., Honig, A. S., and Tannenbaum, J. (1970). Infant day care and attachment. *American Journal of Orthopsychiatry*, 40:397–412.

Cath, S., Gurwitt, A., and Ross, J. (1982). *Fatherhood: Developmental and Clinical Perspectives*. Boston: Little, Brown.

Clarke-Stewart, K. A. (1978). And daddy makes three: The father's impact on mother and young child. *Child Development*, 49:466–478.

Clarke-Stewart, K. A. (1980). Observation and experiment: Complementary strategies for studying day care and social development. In *Advances in Early Education and Day Care*, ed. S. Kilmer. Greenwich, Connecticut: JAI Press.

Cochran, M. M. (1977). A comparison of group day and family child-rearing patterns in Sweden. *Child Development*, 48:702–707.

Connell, D. B. (1976). Individual differences in attachment behavior. Unpublished doctoral dissertation, Syracuse University.

Cornelius, S. W. and Denney, N. W. (1975). Dependency in day-care and home-care children. *Developmental Psychology*, 11:575–582.

Cummings, M. E. (1980). Caregiver stability and day care. *Developmental Psychology*, 16:31–37.

Doyle, A. B. (1975). Infant development in day care. *Developmental Psychology*, 11: 655–656.

Estes, D., Lamb, M. E., Thompson, R. A., and Dickstein, S. (1981). Maternal affective quality and security of attachment at 12 and 19 months. Paper presented to the Society for Research in Child Development, Boston.

Farran, D. C. and Ramey, C. T. (1977). Infant day care and attachment behavior toward mothers and teachers. *Child Development*, 48:1112–1116.

Finkelstein, M. and Wilson, K. (1977). The influence of day care on social behavior toward peers and adults. Paper presented to the Society for Research in Child Development, New Orleans.

Fox, G. L. (1978). The family's role in adolescent sexual behavior. Paper presented to the Family Impact Seminar, Washington, D.C.

Fox, N. (1977). Attachment of kibbutz infants to mother and metapelet. *Child Development*, 48:1228–1239.

Gersick, K. (1975). Fathers by choice: Characteristics of men who do and do not seek custody of their children following divorce. Unpublished doctoral dissertation, Harvard University.

Glick, P. C. (1979). Future American families. COFU Memo, 2(3):2–5.

Glick, P. C. and Norton, A. J. (1979). Marrying, divorcing, and living together in the U.S. today. *Population Bulletin*, 32:whole number 5.

Grossmann, K. E., Grossmann, K., Huber, F., and Wartner, U. (1981). German children's behavior towards their mothers at 12 months and their fathers at 18 months in Ainsworth's Strange Situation. *International Journal of Behavioral Development*, 4:157–181.

Hetherington, E. M. (1972). Effects of father-absence on personality development in adolescent daughters. *Developmental Psychology*, 7:313–326.

Hetherington, E. M. (1979). Divorce: A child's perspective. *American Psychologist*, 34:851–858.

Hetherington, E. M., Cox, M., and Cox, R. (1978). The aftermath of divorce. In *Mother/Child, Father/Child Relationships*, ed. J. P. Stevens and M. Matthews. Washington, D. C.: National Association for the Education of Young Children.

Hipgrave, T. (1982). Child rearing by lone fathers. In *Changing Patterns of Child Bearing and Child Rearing*, ed. R. Chester, P. Diggory, and M. Sutherland. London: Academic Press.

Hock, E. (1976). *Alternative Approaches to Child Rearing and Their Effects on the Mother-Infant Relationship* (Final report, Grant No. OCD-409). Washington, D.C.: Office of Child Development, Department of Health, Education and Welfare.

Hock, E. (1980). Working and nonworking mothers and their infants: A comparative study of maternal caregiving characteristics and infant social behavior. *Merrill-Palmer Quarterly*, 26:79–101.

Hoffman, L. W. (1977). Changes in family roles, socialization and sex differences. *American Psychologist*, 32:644–657.

Hoffman, M. L. (1970). Moral development. In Carmichael's *Manual of Child Psychology*, 3rd ed., vol. 2, ed. P. H. Mussen. New York: John Wiley.

Kagan, J., Kearsley, P., and Zelazo, P. (1978). *Infancy: Its Place in Human Development*. Cambridge, Massachusetts: Harvard University Press.

Kessen, W. (1975). *Child Care in China*. New Haven: Yale University Press.

Lamb, M. E. (1976a). Effects of stress and cohort on mother- and father-infant interaction. *Developmental Psychology*, 12:435–443.

Lamb, M. E. (1976b). Interactions between eight-month-old children and their fathers and mothers. In *The Role of the Father in Child Development*, ed. M. E. Lamb. New York: John Wiley.

Lamb, M. E. (1976a). Interactions between two-year-olds and their mothers and fathers. *Psychological Reports*, 36: 447–450.

Lamb, M. E. (1976d). Parent-infant interaction in eight-month-olds. *Child Psychiatry and Human Development*, 7:56–63.

Lamb, M. E. (1976e). The role of the father: An overview. In *The Role of the Father in Child Development*, ed. M. E. Lamb. New York: John Wiley.

Lamb, M. E. (1976f). Twelve-month-olds and their parents: Interaction in a laboratory playroom. *Developmental Psychology*, 12:237–244.

Lamb, M. E. (1977a). The development of mother-infant and father-infant attachments in the second year of life. *Developmental Psychology*, 13:637–648.

Lamb, M. E. (1977b). The development of parental preferences in the first two years of life. *Sex Roles*, 3:495–497.

Lamb, M. E. (1977c). Father-infant and mother-infant interaction in the first year of life. *Child Development*, 48:167–181.

Lamb, M. E. (1977d). The effects of divorce on children's personality development. *Journal of Divorce*, 1:163–174.

Lamb, M. E. (1978). Qualitative aspects of mother- and father-infant attachments. *Infant Behavior and Development*, 1:265–175.

Lamb, M. E. (1980). The development of parent-infant attachments in the first two years of life. In *The Father-Infant Relationship: Observational Studies in a Family Setting*, ed. F. A. Pedersen. New York: Praeger Special Studies.

Lamb, M. E. (1981a). Developing trust and perceived effectance in infancy. In *Advances in Infancy Research*, vol. 1, ed. L. P. Lipsitt. Norwood, New Jersey: Ablex.

Lamb, M. E. (1981b). The development of social expectations in the first year of life. In *Infant Social Cognition: Empirical and Theoretical Considerations*, ed., M. E. Lamb and L. R. Sherrod. Hillsdale, New Jersey: Lawrence Erlbaum Associates.

Lamb, M. E. (1981c). Paternal influences on child development: An overview. In *The Role of the Father in Child Development*, rev. ed., ed. M. E. Lamb. New York: John Wiley.

Lamb, M. E. (1982). Maternal employment and child development: A review. In *Nontraditional Families: Parenting and Child Development*, ed. M. E. Lamb. Hillsdale, New Jersey: Lawrence Erlbaum Associates.

Lamb, M. E. and Easterbrooks, M. A. (1981). Individual differences in parental sensitivity: Origins, components, and consequences. In *Infant Social Cognition: Empirical and Theoretical Considerations*, ed. M. E. Lamb and L. R. Sherrod. Hillsdale, New Jersey: Lawrence Erlbaum Associates.

Lamb, M. E., Frodi, A. M., Frodi, M., and Hwang, C.-P. (1982a). Characteristics of maternal and paternal behavior in traditional and nontraditional Swedish families. *International Journal of Behavioral Development*, 5:131–141.

Lamb, M. E., Frodi, A. M., Hwang, C.-P., Frodi, M., and Steinberg, J. (1982b). Mother-and father-infant interaction involving play and holding in traditional and nontraditional Swedish families. *Developmental Psychology*, 18:215–221.

Lamb, M. E., Frodi, M., Hwang, C-P, and Frodi, A. M. (1983). Effects of paternal involvement on infant preferences for mothers and fathers. *Child Development*, in press.

Lamb, M. E., Hwang, C. P., Frodi, A., and Frodi, M. (1982). Security of mother- and father-infant attachment and its relation to sociability with strangers in traditional and non-traditional Swedish families. *Infant Behavior and Development*, 5:355–367.

Lamb, M. E. and Lamb, J. E. (1976). The nature and importance of the father-infant relationship. *The Family Coordinator*, 25:379–385.

Lamb, M. E., and Levine, J. A. (1983). The Swedish parental insurance policy: An experiment in social engineering. In *Fatherhood and Family Policy*, ed. M. E. Lamb and A. Sagi. Hillsdale, New Jersey: Lawrence Erlbaum Associates.

Lamb, M. E., and Stevenson, M. B. (1978). Father-infant relationships: Their nature and importance. *Youth and Society*, 9:277–298.

Lamb, M. E. et al. (1984). Security of infantile attachment as assessed in the Strange Situation: Its study and biological interpretation. *Behavioral and Brain Sciences*, 7:127–147.

Lay, M. Z. and Meyer, W. J. (1972). Effects of early day-care experiences on subsequent observed program behaviors. Unpublished progress report, Syracuse University.

Levine, J. A., Pleck, J. H., and Lamb, M. E. (1983). The Fatherhood Project. In *Fatherhood and Family Policy*, ed. M. E. Lamb and A. Sagi. Hillsdale, New Jersey: Lawrence Erlbaum Associates.

Lynn, D. B., and Cross, A. R. (1974). Parent preferences of preschool children. *Journal of Marriage and the Family*, 36:555–559.

Maccoby, E. E. (1977). Current changes in the family and their impact upon the socialization of children. Paper presented to the American Sociological Association, Chicago, September.

Macrae, J. W. and Herbert-Jackson, E. (1976). Are behavioral effects of infant day care program specific? *Developmental Psychology*, 12:269–270.

Main, M. (1973). Exploration, play and cognitive functioning as related to child-mother attachment. Unpublished doctoral dissertation. Johns Hopkins University.

Main, M. B. and Weston, D. R. (1981). Security of attachment to mother and father: Related to conflict behavior and the readiness to establish new relationships. *Child Development*, 52:932–940.

Manion, J. (1977). A study of fathers and infant caretaking. *Birth and the Family Journal*, 4:174–179.

Martinson, H., Smorvik, D., and Smith, L. (1978). Effects of presence of mother versus preschool teacher on the behavior of infants in a strange situation. *Scandinavian Journal of Psychology*, 19:159–162.

Matas, L., Arend, R. A., and Sroufe, L. A. (1978). Continuity of adaptation in the second year: The relationship between quality of attachment and later competence. *Child Development*, 49:547–556.

McCutcheon, B. and Calhoun, K. (1976). Social and emotional adjustment of infants and toddlers to a day care setting. *American Journal of Orthopsychiatry*, 46:104–108.

Mendes, H. (1976). Single fatherhood. *Social Work*, 21:308–312.

Money, J. and Ehrhardt, A. A. (1972). *Man and Woman, Boy and Girl*. Baltimore: Johns Hopkins University Press.

Moore, T. W. (1975). Exclusive early mothering and its alternatives: The outcomes to adolescence. *Scandinavian Journal of Psychology*, 16:255–272.

Moskowitz, D., Schwartz, J., and Corsini, D. (1977). Initiating day care at three years of age: Effects on attachment. *Child Development*, 48:1271–1276.

Owen, M. T., Chase-Lansdale, P. L., and Lamb, M. E. (1982). Mothers' and fathers' attitudes, maternal employment, and the security of infant-parent attachment. Unpublished manuscript.

Parke, R. D. and Sawin, D. B. (1980). The family in early infancy: Social interactional and attitudinal analyses. In *The Father-Infant Relationship: Observational Studies in the Family Setting*, ed. F. A. Pedersen. New York: Praeger Special Studies.

Pastor, D. L. (1981). The quality of mother-infant attachment and its relationship to toddlers' initial sociability with peers. *Developmental Psychology*, 17:326–335.

Pedersen, F. A., Anderson, B., and Cain, R. (1980). Parent-infant and husband-wife interactions observed at age 5 months. In *The Father-Infant Relationship: Observational Studies in the Family Setting,* ed. F. A. Pedersen. New York: Praeger Special Publications.

Pleck, J. H. (1983). Husbands' paid work and family roles: Current research issues. In *Research in the Interweave of Social Roles,* vol. 3, *Families and Jobs,* ed. H. Lopata and J. H. Pleck. Greenwich, Connecticut: JAI Press.

Pleck, J. H. and Rustad, M. (1980). Husbands' and wives' time in family work and paid work in the 1975–76 study of time use. Unpublished manuscript, Wellesley College.

Portnoy, F. and Simmons, C. (1978). Day care and attachment. *Child Development,* 49:239–242.

Power, T. G. and Parke, R. D. (1982). Play as a context for early learning: Lab and home analyses. In *Families as Learning Environments for Children,* ed. L. M. Laosa and I. E. Sigel. New York: Plenum.

Radin, N. (1981). The role of the father in cognitive, academic, and intellectual development. In *The Role of the Father in Child Development,* rev. ed., ed. M. E. Lamb. New York: John Wiley.

Radin, N. (1982). Primary caregiving and role-sharing fathers. In *Nontraditional families: Parenting and Child Development,* ed. M. E. Lamb. Hillsdale, New Jersey: Lawrence Erlbaum Associates.

Radin, N. and Sagi, A. (1982). Childrearing fathers in intact families in Israel and the U.S.A. *Merrill-Palmer Quarterly,* 28:111–136.

Ragozin, A. S. (1977). Attachment behavior of day care and home reared children in a laboratory setting. Paper presented to the Society for Research in Child Development, New Orleans.

Ragozin, A. S. (1980). Attachment behavior of day care children: Naturalistic and laboratory observations. *Child Development,* 51:409–415.

Rajecki, D. W., Lamb, M. E., and Obmascher, P. (1978). Toward a general theory of infantile attachment: A comparative review of aspects of the social bond. *Behavioral and Brain Sciences,* 1:417–463.

Raph, J. B., Thomas, A., Chess, S., and Korn, S. J. (1964). The influence of nursery school on social interactions. *American Journal of Orthopsychiatry,* 38:144–152.

Ricciuti, H. (1974). Fear and development of social attachments in the first year of life. In *The Origins of Fear,* ed. M. Lewis and L. A. Rosenblum. New York: John Wiley.

Robertson, J. and Bowlby, J. (1952). Responses of young children to separation from their mothers. *Courrier de Centre International de L'Enfance,* 2:131–142.

Roopnarine, J. L. and Lamb, M. E. (1978). The effects of day care on attachment and exploratory behavior in a strange situation. *Merrill-Palmer Quarterly,* 24:85–95.

Roopnarine, J. and Lamb, M. E. (1980). Peer and parent child interaction before and after enrollment in nursery school. *Journal of Applied Developmental Psychology,* 1:77–81.

Russell, G. (1982a). Shared-caregiving families: An Australian study. In *Nontraditional Families: Parenting and Child Development,* ed. M. E. Lamb. Hillsdale, New Jersey: Lawrence Erlbaum Associates.

Russell, G. (1982b). *The Changing Role of Fathers.* St. Lucia, Queensland: University of Queensland Press.

Rutter, M. (1972). *Maternal Deprivation Reassessed.* Harmondsworth, England: Penguin.

Rutter, M. (1979). Maternal deprivation, 1972–1978:

New findings, new concepts, new approaches. *Child Development,* 50:283–305.

Sagi, A. (1982). Antecedents and consequences of various degrees of paternal involvement in child rearing: The Israeli project. In *Nontraditional Families: Parenting and Child Development,* ed. M. E. Lamb. Hillsdale, New Jersey: Lawrence-Erlbaum Associates.

Sagi, A. et al. (1983). Security of infant-mother, -father, and -metapelet attachments among kibbutz-reared Israeli children. In *The Strange Situation,* ed. I. Bretherton. Monographs of the Society for Research in Child Development, in preparation.

Santrock, J. W. and Warshak, R. A. (1979). Father custody and social development in boys and girls. *Journal of Social Issues,* 35:112–125.

Santrock, J. W., Warshak, R. A., and Elliott, G. L. (1982). Social development and parent-child interaction in father-custody and stepmother families. In *Nontraditional Families: Parenting and Child Development,* ed. M. E. Lamb. Hillsdale, New Jersey: Lawrence Erlbaum Associates.

Schaffer, H. R. (1958). Objective observations of personality development in early infancy. *British Journal of Medical Psychology,* 31:174–183.

Schaffer, H. R. and Callender, W. (1959). Psychological effects of hospitalization in infancy. *Pediatrics,* 24:528–539.

Schaffer, H. R. and Emerson, P. E. (1964). The development of social attachments in infancy. *Monographs of the Society for Research in Child Development,* 29: serial number 94.

Schwarz, J. D., Strickland, R. G., and Krolick, G. (1974). Infant day care: Behavioral effects at preschool age. *Developmental Psychology,* 10:502–506.

Sheehy, G. (1979). Introducing the postponing generation. *Esquire,* 92:25–33.

Shinn, M. (1978). Father absence and children's cognitive development. *Psychological Bulletin,* 85:295–324.

Spitz, R. A., and Wolf, K. M. (1946). Anaclitic depression. *The Psychoanalytic Study of Child,* 2:313–342. New York: International Universities Press.

Sroufe, L. A. (1978). Attachment and the roots of competence. *Human Nature,* 1:50–57.

Sroufe, L. A. (1979). The coherence of individual development. *American Psychologist,* 34:834–841.

Sroufe, L. A. (in press). Individual patterns of adaptation from infancy to preschool. In *Minnesota Symposium in Child Psychology,* vol. 16, ed. M. Perlmutter. Hillsdale, New Jersey: Lawrence Erlbaum Associates.

Sroufe, L. A. and Rosenberg, D. (1982). Coherence of individual adaptation in lower class infants and toddlers. Paper presented to the International Conference on Infant Studies, Austin, Texas.

Stayton, D. J., Ainsworth, M. D. S., and Main, M. B. (1973). The development of separation behavior in the first year of life: Protest, following and greeting. *Developmental Psychology,* 9:213–225.

Thompson, R. A. and Lamb, M. E. (1983). Quality of attachment and stranger sociability in infancy. *Developmental Psychology,* 19:in press.

Thompson, R. A., Lamb, M. E., and Estes, D. (1982). Stability of infant-mother attachment and its relationship to changing life circumstances in an unselected middle class sample. *Child Development,* 53:144–148.

Vaughn, B., Egeland, B., Sroufe, L. A., and Waters, E. (1979). Individual differences in infant-mother attachment at twelve and eighteen months: Stability and change in families under stress. *Child Development,* 50:971–975.

Vaughn, B., Gove, F., and Egeland, B. (1980). The relationship between out-of-home care and the quality of infant-mother attachment in an economically disadvantaged sample. *Child Development,* 51:1203–1214.

Waters, E. (1978). The reliability and stability of individual differences in infant-mother attachment. *Child Development,* 49:483–494.

Waters, E., Wippman, J., and Sroufe, L. A. (1979). At-

tachment, positive affect, and competence in the peer group: Two studies in construct validation. *Child Development,* 50:821–829.

Yarrow, L. J. (1964). Separation from parents during early childhood. In *Review of Child Development Research,* vol. 1, ed. M. L. Hoffman and L. W. Hoffman. New York: Russell Sage Foundation.

38

The Father's Role with Preterm and Fullterm Infants

Michael W. Yogman, M.D., M.Sc.

Ten years of research on the father's relationship with healthy fullterm infants has changed our thinking about the father's importance in early development and has offered a new starting point from which to study the father's relationship with premature infants. Therefore, I first briefly review the evidence for the competence of healthy fathers and infants to interact with each other, Highlighting the similarities in behavior and psychological experience between competent fathers and mothers. I then briefly describe what is known about what fathers and infants actually do together and discuss influences on actual paternal involvement. My major focus is on the influence of stress, particularly the stress of the birth of a premature infant on the father-infant relationship.

Competence of Fathers and Infants

Within contemporary Western society, the evidence that fathers and infants can and do

This research was supported by the National Foundation March of Dimes, with additional assistance from NICHD grant No. 10889 and MCH grant No. MGR—250400. I also thank my colleagues, Diana Dill, Joel Hoffman, Carey Halsey, Nancy Jordan, Barry Lester, and especially Dr. T. B. Brazelton for their support in this research.

develop a meaningful relationship right from birth is impressive. Fathers start out as similar to mothers in their competence and capability to interact with young infants. Their sensitivity to the baby's behavior and rhythms is almost identical to that of mothers. Even evidence from studies of primate behavior have demonstrated that caregiving is not exclusively maternal. In some species, such as the marmoset, a New World monkey, the male is the primary caregiver (Chivers, 1972; Hampton et al., 1966; Ingram, 1978).

Similarity between the psychological experience of infant care for mothers and fathers is striking and begins even prior to birth (Bibring, 1959; Gurwitt, 1976; Ross, 1975), and includes similarities in prenatal physical symptoms and complaints (Lipkin and Lamb, 1982).

Furthermore, fathers and mothers display similar behaviors when interacting with their newborns after birth. Studies by Parke and Sawin (1975, 1977) of father-newborn interaction in the postpartum period suggest that fathers and mothers are equally active and sensitive to newborn cues during the postpartum period. Not only do fathers and mothers share the exhilaration of the prenatal period, but they also share the lows or the normative postpartum blues of this period. In an interview study of men in the first few weeks postpartum, 62 percent reported feelings of sadness and disappointment (Zaslow, et al., 1981).

As infants begin to smile and vocalize, they are good elicitors of social interaction with fathers as well as mothers. In our studies of face-to-face social interaction of fathers with their infants of two weeks to six months of age, we have demonstrated similar rhythmic cycles of arousal and withdrawal for father-infant and mother-infant dyads (Yogman, 1977; Yogman et al., 1983).

Parents with healthy infants came to our laboratory for videotaping every week for six months. Infants were seated comfortably in an infant seat, and parents were instructed to play without using toys. Two cameras recorded adult and baby as described previously (Brazelton et al., 1975; Yogman, 1982). Our tapes of a three-month-old male infant interacting with his mother and father demonstrate the similarities in joyful affect, in timing, and in mutual regulation during interactions with both parents. Initial analyses demonstrated that infants as young as six weeks of age (mean age = 80 days) interact differently with their familiar parents than with unfamiliar strangers, as evidenced by differences in facial expression and limb movements (Dixon et al., 1981; Yogman, 1982).

The major analyses focused on the similarities in meshing and reciprocity achieved by the father with the infant as compared with the mother. By three months of age infants successfully interacted with both mothers and fathers with a similar mutually regulated reciprocal pattern characterized by transitions between affective levels that occurred simultaneously for infant and parent (Yogman, 1977, 1982). Parents were equally able to engage the infant in games (Yogman, 1981). Finally, using the technique of spectral analysis to study the rhythmicity in infant behavior and heart rate during social interaction with mother and father, we found that infant and adult behavioral rhythms are synchronous and similar only with father and mother, not with an unfamiliar stranger (Yogman et al., 1983). In sum, the studies of fathers and infants in the first six months of life support the hypothesis that fathers are competent and capable of skilled and sensitive social interaction with young infants.

The study of the father-infant relationship with infants aged six to twenty-four months has focused primarily on the development of attachment as Bowlby (1969) and Ainsworth (1973) have defined it. These studies have asked such questions as: Do infants greet, seek proximity with, and protest on separation from fathers as well as mothers? Such studies provide conclusive evidence that infants develop a focused selective attachment relationship with fathers as well as with mothers (Kotelchuck, 1976; Lamb, 1975, 1981).

Performance of Fathers and Infants

Regardless of their competencies, what fathers and infants actually do together seems increasingly variable and diverse as stereotypes for male roles shift. It is highly dependent on the surrounding context. In natural observations at home, the mother is clearly the predominant partner with the infant in terms of time spent together (Clarke-Stewart, 1980).

FATHER-INFANT PLAY

Regardless of the amount of time fathers spend with their infants, they are more likely to be the infant's play partner than the mother, and fathers have a qualitatively distinct style of play that tends to be more stimulating, vigorous, arousing, and state disruptive for the infant than play between mothers and infants. In our studies of infant games during the first six months of life, episodes of play in which parents used a repeating set of behaviors to either engage or maintain the infant's attention were identified from review of the videotapes, coded in narrative form and then categorized according to a predefined set of descriptions of adult behavior as tactile, limb movement, visual, or verbal (Yogman, 1981). Fathers engaged their infants in tactile and limb-movement games in which their behavior attempted to arouse the infant. Examples of such games included a father repeatedly pulling his six-week-old son to sit, tapping his three-week-old daughter at the corner of her mouth and on her chin, and playing a button-your-lip game with his two-month-old daughter. Mothers more commonly played visual games in which they displayed distal motor movements that were observed by the infant and appeared to be attempts to maintain visual attention (Yogman, 1981).

The visual games more often played by mothers may represent a more distal attention-maintaining form of interactive play than the proximal, idiosyncratic limb-movement games favored by fathers. Studies of the games parents play with eight-month-old infants show similar findings: mothers played more distal games, while fathers engaged more in physical games (Power and Parke, 1979). Stern (1974) has suggested that the goal of such games is to facilitate an optimal level of arousal in the infant in order to foster attention to social signals. The proximal games of infants and fathers may serve to modulate the infant's attention and arousal in a more accentuated fashion than occurs during the distal games of infants and mothers. These findings are surprisingly robust in that similar findings have been replicated with infants of different ages in different situations.

These differences in quality and stimulation level of play persist even in studies of primary caregiver fathers in the United States (Field, 1978; Yogman, 1982) and in studies of nontraditional fathers taking advantage of paternity leave in Sweden (Frodi et al., 1982; Lamb, et al., 1982). It is interesting to speculate that these play differences may become less tied to gender as socialization of young children changes. It is important to note that the performance of caregiving tasks seems more modifiable and more closely related to role than to gender.

Influences on Paternal Involvement

While our limited research allows some generalizations and speculations about the role of the father in infancy, the diversity of fathering styles suggests the importance of acknowledging that the father-infant dyad is embedded in multiple other systems, such as the triad with mother (the most frequent condition for the infant and father), the family, the culture, and even a particular economic, political, and historic era. Each of these contextual variables must be considered when attempting to unravel clinical issues involving an individual father and infant.

Forces within the family have a major influence on paternal involvement. Some of the major influences on father's involvement are mother's wishes and the marital relationship. High marital satisfaction has been associated with both parents' relationship with the baby. Conversely, heightened paternal feelings of competition with his spouse have been shown to occur with term infants, particularly if the father has a close relationship with the baby and the mother is nursing. Husbands of nursing mothers described feelings of inadequacy, envy, and exclusion, and the competition may actually undermine the mother's attempts at breast-feeding, unless these feelings are addressed (Lerner, 1979; Waletzky, 1979). Mother may play a critical role as a gatekeeper, either supporting or discouraging the father's involvement.

Fathers and Premature Infants

Forces outside the family, such as stress of any kind, may have a major impact on the father, either positively as a catalyst for growth, or negatively. The stress may result from loss (loss of a parent or a previous infant), from economic difficulties, from marital conflict, or from a problem with the baby, such as prematurity.

The birth of a high-risk premature infant confronts fathers as well as mothers with major stress. This may have a direct effect on the father-infant relationship, either facilitating or interfering with the relationship. It may also have an indirect effect on the infant mediated through its effect on the father's support of the mother. The utilization of supports is a major coping mechanism for dealing with stress, and the father is the most readily available source of support for the mother within the family. The father's support may involve four different areas: emotional support, help with caregiving tasks, financial support, and the mobilization and recruitment of additional resources from the community at large.

Evidence for the stressful effect of a premature birth is suggested by data from a study in England (Jeffcoate et al., 1979) in which mothers and fathers were interviewed in the first weeks after a premature birth. Both parents reported more depression, anxiety, emotional turmoil, and difficulty caring for the baby than a matched group of parents of fullterm infants.

Fathers especially need permission to express their feelings of fear and grief during this perinatal period, even if it violates the stereotype of masculinity. Zilboorg (1931) has examined the interaction of psychodynamic and sociocultural influences on postpartum reactions in men and women and suggested that men are more likely than women to develop symptoms of extreme regression, psychosis, or paranoia because depression is a socially unacceptable symptom in males. According to Zilboorg, society instructs men to view passivity, impotence, and crying as a threat to their self-image. While this attitude may be less prevalent today, professionals working with fathers in a premature nursery may still need to view bizarre and regressive behavior as less pathological than in other situations and as analagous to maternal depression.

Initially after a premature birth, fathers are often required to play a primary role in decision-making, either because the infant has been transferred to a different hospital or because of the physical incapacity of the mother. When they visit, parents are often terrified about basic questions of survival, and fathers will often focus on physiological data and laboratory values, perhaps as a way of fending off an emotional attachment to the baby before knowing anything certain about survival. Father may suffer a double burden in that extended family members may expect him to remain strong and even to recruit the help that will "fix" things and ensure the baby's survival. Once fathers begin to interact with their newborns in an intensive-care nursery, they do so with behaviors similar to those described for fullterm fathers: responding more to newborn limb movements and talking less to the baby than mothers (Marton et al., 1981; Parke and Tinsley, 1982).

Clearly, fathers who visit the nursery more often are a self-selected group, likely to be more committed to learning about the baby and to participating in caregiving. In the context of a longitudinal study of twenty preterm infants, we offered the fathers as well as the mothers the opportunity to observe an assessment of their neonate's behavior (Brazelton, 1973). Half of the fathers chose to participate. These self-selected fathers were younger and more likely to be having their first baby than those who did not choose to observe. Surprisingly, there was no association between neonatal medical complications and father participation. Compared with the fathers who did not observe this demonstration of neonatal behavior, the participating fathers had made more nursery visits in the subsequent month, and both they and their wives reported that they were performing more caregiving tasks after the infants were home for one month than fathers who did not observe a demonstration of their newborn's behavior.

In this current study, the indirect effects of stress on fathers' support of mothers were also assessed. Many of the fathers responded to this stress by providing much more support to their spouses, both emotional and physical, by helping with caregiving tasks.

Table 38-1 shows the percentage of fathers in the preterm and in a fullterm comparison group who said they participated at all in each type of caregiving task at one, five, and eighteen months postterm. While fathers still did far less caregiving than mothers, fathers of the preterm infants reported doing more of the caregiving tasks at each age than the comparison group of fathers of fullterm infants. These differences were significant at eighteen months and showed a trend to significance at five months. While all fathers helped with diapering, the preterm fathers were more likely to take the infant to a physician, to bathe the baby, and to get up at night to console their infant at eighteen months. The stress of premature birth appears to have encouraged fathers to provide more physical support to mothers (help with caregiving tasks).

Direct effects of the stress of premature birth on the interactions of fathers and their infants were also assessed. Interestingly, there was no

TABLE 38–1

Paternal Caregiving

	Preterm (in percentages)	Fullterm (in percentages)
One month:		
Gets baby up	44	20
Dresses baby	67	40
Bathes baby	33	20
Changes diapers	89	80
Puts baby to bed	78	60
Takes baby to doctor	67	20
Comforts baby when frets	89	100
Comforts baby when cries at night	67	60
Five months:		
Gets baby up	100	80
Dresses baby	71	60
Bathes baby	71	30
Changes diapers	100	80
Puts baby to bed	86	70
Takes baby to doctor	86	60
Comforts baby when frets	100	90
Comforts baby when cries at night	71	70
Eighteen months:		
Gets baby up	100	85
Dresses baby	89	85
Bathes baby	89	69
Changes diapers	100	85
Puts baby to bed	89	85
Takes baby to doctor	89	69
Comforts baby when frets	100	85
Comforts baby when cries at night	89	54

correlation between the indirect effect on paternal involvement in caregiving and the direct effect on father-infant games seen during a face-to-face play session at five months postterm.

For this comparison of father-infant games, we studied fathers of ten preterm and ten fullterm infants during a three-minute episode of face-to-face play in the laboratory, as described in earlier studies (Yogman, 1977, 1982). The two groups differed on the obvious perinatal measures but not on social class or demographic characteristics. Episodes of play defined as games were coded as in the earlier study (Yogman, 1981). The games were then categorized as arousing if they involved such proximal activities as tactile and limb-movement games or as nonarousing if they were assumed to maintain rather than arouse the infant's attention (verbal and visual games). The results (table 38–2) show that fathers of preterm infants played both fewer and shorter games and fewer arousing games, in particular, than did fathers of fullterm infants. Fathers were less able to directly engage their preterm infants in play compared to the fullterm infants. When they did, the play lasted for a shorter time, particularly if the game was an arousing one.

Other studies of direct paternal interaction with preterm infants have produced conflicting findings, in part because of different measures, because the infants are often quite heterogeneous in medical complications and behavioral difficulty, and because parental reactions are also variable. In two studies of preterm infants at three months postterm, their face-to-face play with fathers and mothers was fairly similar (Marton et al., 1981; Parke and Tinsley, 1982) except for more maternal instrumental touching, while a study at four months postterm found that fathers played more games than mothers with their preterm infants, although less than with fullterm infants (Field, 1979b).

One suggested explanation of these findings is that the infant's behavior exerts a strong influence on the parent. For example, a stressed infant having difficulty with motor activity and tone and with state regulation and hypersensitivity provides a parent with a much more difficult infant to interact with. The difficulties mothers have in interacting with a labile premature infant have been described by Field, (1979a), and Goldberg (1978). In such an instance, the tendency of many fathers to excite, play with, and vigorously stimulate their infant may stress an already vulnerable infant, interfere with social interaction, and lead a fa-

TABLE 38–2

Father—Infant Games

	Preterm		Fullterm	
	Number ($\overline{X}$)	Total Duration ($\overline{X}$) (seconds)	Number ($\overline{X}$)	Total Duration ($\overline{X}$) (seconds)
All games with father	0.8	11.3	1.9	27.7
Arousing games with father	0.6	6.0	1.5	20.9
Nonarousing games with father	0.2	5.3	0.3	5.1

ther to feel failure and to withdraw. Alternatively, a father may adapt to the baby's needs by limiting his arousing stimulation to specific periods when the baby can tolerate it. Describing the baby's cues (particularly when they are hard to read) may be of great help to a father in this situation and may offer him a more adaptive alternative to complete withdrawal. Unfortunately, most intervention programs for high-risk infants do not specifically address the father's role (Bricker and Bricker, 1976). The expectation that most fathers will withdraw may quickly become a self-fulfilling prophecy unless the father's participation is actively encouraged.

The diversity of the interaction of these fathers with premature infants is best illustrated by case studies of three families from the longitudinal study. Perinatal data from these families are summarized in table 38–3.

CASE 1

Allan was the third infant born to a family with two older boys, one of whom was born prematurely. He was delivered after a thirty-two-week uncomplicated pregnancy, weighed 1,820 grams, and had good Apgars of 7 and 7. He developed moderately severe hyaline membrane disease requiring intubation and ventilation for five days. He recovered rapidly, gained weight by day ten, and was discharged home after twenty-three days at thirty-six weeks postconceptional age. The father in this family was very involved, providing both emotional support for his wife and helping with caregiving. He was able to engage his baby in several games at the five-month session by waiting over a minute until the baby was ready, read-

justing his infant's position in the seat, and engaging the infant in a mildly arousing armwaving game eliciting responsive smiles and vocalizations. The father seemed sensitive to his infant's fatigue and need for periods of time out. The infant's outcome at nine and eighteen months postterm was good, as reflected in his Bayley scores.

CASE 2

The second case is a more severely ill infant and illustrates the difficulties faced by some fathers in making this adjustment. Jeffrey was born prematurely after a twenty-nine-week pregnancy, the first child of parents in their early thirties. He weighed 1,080 grams at birth. His Apgars were 1 and 7, and he was felt to be small-for-gestational-age. After a prolonged neonatal hospitalization complicated by mild hyaline membrane disease and more severe apnea, this infant was discharged home at thirty-six weeks of age postterm, weighing 1,500 grams after a fifty-two-day hospitalization. As a newborn, the baby was irritable and difficult to console. He had problems with sleep, feeding, and crying in the first few weeks at home. Both parents worked at a local TV/radio station, had variable and unpredictable schedules, returned to work rapidly, and were isolated from their extended families. In early interviews, father described feeling "left out and unnecessary" and noted the presence of marital conflict. Even when the baby was a month postterm, the father still felt the baby was "a guest rather than his." In spite of these feelings, father reported that he helped with a substantial portion of the caregiving. When the family was seen for

TABLE 38–3

Perinatal Case Summaries

	Case I 34 y.o. G$_3$P$_2$ Housewife 34 y.o. Statistician	Case II 30 y.o. G$_1$ Graphic Designer 32 y.o. Account Executive	Case III 27 y.o. G$_2$P$_0$ Editor 27 y.o. Engineer
Mother: Father:			
Birthweight (gms)	1820	1080	950
Gestational age	32	29	27
Apgar (1, 5 min)	7,7	1,7	5,7
OCS (Parmelee)	71	60	63
PNF (Parmelee)	67	77	55
Neurological (Parmelee)	12	12	5
Duration of hospitalization (days)	23	52	80
Bayley: MDI 9	111	99	111
PDI 9	96	100	100
MDI 18	117	—	107
PDI 18	113	—	113

a five-month face-to-face session, the father interacted with the baby, continually tapping and shaking the infant's limbs although the infant spent much of the interaction looking away from his father, squirming, and finally fussing and crying. At this time, the father could not respect the infant's need for time out. He continually shifted his behavior, never allowing this labile infant to organize around a specific pattern of play, and often interacted with intrusive and overwhelming stimulation. By the time the infant was nine months postterm, both parents were much calmer, more organized, and less in conflict. They were able for the first time to discuss their previous fears about brain damage. Mother was now pregnant again, and the infant was doing better than expected on the Bayley. The family then moved to California, and no further follow-up was possible.

CASE 3

The third case was one of the most severely ill infants in the study. Alva was the first baby born to twenty-seven-year-old dual-career parents who had had one previous miscarriage. She was delivered at twenty-seven weeks weighing 950 grams, with Apgars of 5 and 7. She developed severe hyaline membrane disease, required ventilatory support for a week, was intubated and in high oxygen concentrations for over six weeks, and devel-

oped apnea as well as bronchopulmonary dysplasia. She was thought to have a periventricular hemorrhage and had focal hypertonicity and hyperreflexia in her right leg. She was hospitalized over eighty days and was finally discharged home at thirty-nine weeks postterm. She also had a congenital esotropia of her left eye with strabismus that eventually required thick glasses and several operations. Needless to say, both parents were initially terrified. Once home, Alva had frequent periods of inconsolable crying, requiring swaddling and frequent feeding. The parents were unable to take her out, and mother decided not to go back to work. Father adjusted his schedule by leaving work a bit early each day and was very involved both in providing emotional and physical support and in direct interaction with Alva. Slowly she began to gain weight. When she was seen at five months postterm, she had difficulties with vision and maintenance of truncal motor tone. Yet father, by providing postural support, was able to engage his eight-month-old daughter by wiggling his fingers in front of her face saying, "Fingers; remember, *fingers,*" at which she would become quiet and still and eventually brighten. When she began to avert her gaze, he would sensitively back off, as he had learned to respect her need for time out.

Project staff were so concerned about her motor tone after this visit that they advised the parents to work with an early intervention program. After considering this, the parents followed through and began weekly visits.

Four months later, when seen in the laboratory, Alva had improved dramatically, and on a measure of social play she demonstrated a sense of persistence and mastery after pulling up to stand. When she turned her attention to a prohibited toy, a tape recorder, father anticipated her behavior and was able to distract her with an alternative wind-up toy. Her Bayley scores by eighteen months reflect the continued sensitive environmental structuring provided by her father as well as her mother. Although her motor tone was still slightly increased, her vision was now more adequate, she talked in phrases, her play was more creative, her sleep behavior was more organized, and she had even begun to have occasional tantrums.

In spite of the diversity of interactive play adaptations between fathers and premature infants and despite the low frequency of games fathers play with preterm infants, the father's ability to engage his preterm infant in play in the five-month sessions and the infant's developmental outcome at nine and eighteen months post-term on a Bayley test were significantly associated. Table 38–4 shows the correlations.

The total number of games played by father ($r = .79$), as well as by both parents combined ($r = .77$), were significantly correlated ($p <$ 0.05) with the Bayley (1969) Mental Development Index (MDI) at eighteen months. These correlations were higher than those for games with mother alone and were higher than correlations for measures of perinatal complications, which were not significant. The total duration of all games played with both parents was also significantly correlated with MDI scores at nine and eighteen months and with the Psychomotor Index (PDI) at eighteen months, while the duration of nonarousing games with both parents was correlated with the MDI at nine months and the PDI at eighteen months. Because correlation coefficients can be deceptive with small sample sizes, scatter plots were checked for spurious correlations due to outliers, and only correlations from valid scatter plots are reported.

The infants' sense of mastery during our assessment of social interaction at nine months was also correlated with the total duration of games played with both parents at five months. Perhaps these associations reflect the infants' behavioral robustness and capacity to engage in play with their fathers. Because of the small sample size, we could only look qualitatively at the relationship between neonatal behavior, five-month *en-face* play, and infant outcome. Figure 38–1 shows two scatter plots of neonatal behavior (the motor and regulation of state cluster, mean scores across three Brazelton exams) plotted against number of games with father. The infants with the best Bayley outcomes had high scores on both of

TABLE 38–4

Father-Infant Games and Premature Infant Outcome

	Bayley 9		Bayley 18	
	MDI	PDI	MDI	PDI
Number of all games	.61	.43	.77*	.59
With father	.45	.16	.79*	.15
With mother	.59	.45	.68	.63
Number of arousing games	.50	.15	.80*	.28
Number of nonarousing games	.55	.43	.44	.62
Duration of all games	.70*	.61	.85*	.72*
Duration of arousing games	.45	.03	.77*	.15
Duration of nonarousing games	.67*	.62	.40	.80*

*$p \leq 0.05$

these clusters and high game scores, supporting this hypothesis.

The measures of social interaction, games during *en-face* play, were significantly correlated with outcome, even though measures of obstetric and pediatric complications and a neonatal neurological examination showed no significant correlations with outcome. Beckwith and Cohen (1980) have reported similar findings for social interaction with mothers of preterm infants: infants with higher scores on reciprocal social interactions and severe medical complications performed better at two years of age than infants with lower scores on reciprocal social interaction and milder perinatal complications.

In contrast to this evidence suggesting that under the stress of prematurity the father's direct interactions with his infant are associated with outcome, the only correlation with paternal caregiving (at one month) was the infant's range of affect during an assessment of social interaction at nine months. There was no correlation between the measures of caregiving and support and Bayley measures of infant outcome. Perhaps the measures are inadequate,

perhaps the paths of influence are more complex, or perhaps the indirect effects were too variable in this small sample.

Conclusion

In conclusion, these studies of fathers with fullterm and preterm infants are beginning to form a basis for theorizing about the transition to parenthood in adult male development and about the nature of the father-infant relationship.

First of all, these studies suggest that fathers can have a meaningful and direct relationship with their infants right from birth and that the pregnancy experience is a time of developmental transition for fathers as well as mothers.

In spite of different research strategies and samples, the studies have shown considerable consistency in describing the nature of father-infant interaction. In the newborn period, fathers held and rocked their babies more than mothers and were more stimulating (Parke and Sawin, 1975). By three months of age, fathers and infants in our studies engaged in more proximal, arousing, idiosyncratic games, whereas mothers and infants were more likely to engage in smoothly modulated, soothing distal games, especially verbal ones. Others have found that fathers are more likely to play physical, arousing, idiosyncratic games with their infants at one and two years of age, while mothers are more likely to play conventional games (Clarke-Stewart, 1980; Lamb, 1977). Furthermore, infants respond to their fathers with more excitement. In sum, while fathers have been shown to be sensitive to infant cues (Parke and Sawin, 1975, 1977) and skilled interactants with young infants (Yogman, 1977), consistent differences in the quality of behavioral regulation have been demonstrated between father-infant and mother-infant interaction. Fathers are more likely to develop a heightened, arousing, and playful relationship with their infants (Clarke-Stewart, 1980; Parke, 1979; Yogman, 1982) and to provide a more novel and complex environment (Pedersen et al., 1979); while mothers are more

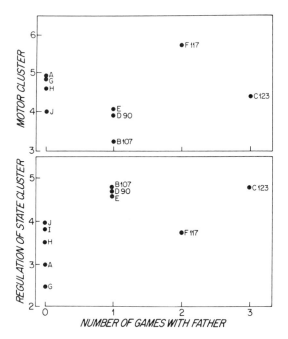

Figure 38–1 Scatter plot of neonatal behavior (mean cluster scores for 3 exams) U.S. paternal play, with infant Bayley MDI 18-month scores superimposed

likely to provide a more containing, protective, and nurturing experience. Not only do the two parents offer the infant two different kinds of stimulation, but the infant responds differently, as if expecting and reinforcing this dichotomy. One can speculate that the complementary experiences the two parents offer the infant parallel two fundamental processes in most developmental theories (Werner, 1948). One process usually emphasizes differentiation in which the infant actively seeks arousing and playful stimulation (differentiating new skills, including the capacity to experience intense affect), while the other process emphasizes integration in which the infant aims to reduce tension from drives and seeks soothing, integrative, nonarousing stimuli.

In understanding the effects of stress on fathers and premature infants, it is first important to emphasize the medical, behavioral, and interactional variability of these infants. The small sample size makes it impossible to draw firm conclusions but rather to generate more informed hypotheses. In summary, the father's direct role as a play partner for his premature infant seems to need to be timed to the recovery and physiological stability of the baby. His ability to engage the baby affectively requires a much greater sensitivity to the individuality of the baby than is usually required with a fullterm infant. When this occurs, it may illustrate the process of stress catalyzing growth whereby the father's vigorous interactive play with his infant may encourage the baby to maintain a moderately high level of arousal, which may, in turn, facilitate both the differentiation of sensorimotor skills, the capacity for experiencing intense affect, and the development of mastery motivation, persistence, and modulated assertiveness.

Because the lag in parental perceptions of fragility and the overprotectiveness that others have reported (Minde et al., 1978) did not occur, it is tempting to speculate that fathers' ability to engage their babies in games allowed them to counter a perception of the baby as fragile and vulnerable when that perception no longer fit.

The indirect influences of the father on the mother and on the infant's development are less clear from these data, since to be effective, the father's indirect role of providing emotional and physical support for the mother must truly fit her emotional needs. Clearly these infants are harder to feed, console, and care for, and they require more trips to the doctor for medical care. Fathers did provide more help with these tasks regardless of their capacities as play partners. However, these indices showed no association with the mother-infant relationship as assessed by measures of mother-infant games and maternal responsivity from the Caldwell HOME scale (Bradley and Caldwell, 1976), nor any association with infant outcome on the Bayley. Without more in-depth interviews with parents, it is not clear which mothers truly felt emotionally supported. Conversely, if the father's involvement was seen as competitive, it could have adversely influenced both the marital relationship and the infant.

As in previous studies, the data suggest that a coherent paternal role that fits the needs of both mother and father is more adaptive than simply high or low involvement. The outcome data, however, are all short term and inadequate in terms of understanding paternal influences on personality development.

Finally, as with fullterm infants, one must acknowledge not only the influence of the father on his preterm infant's development but also the effects of paternal participation on adult male development as well. At the end of the longitudinal study, when the father of one of the premature infants was interviewed and asked about his experience as a father, he replied, "It has fulfilled my life in every way. It has made me see myself better and deeper than I expected, and it has been far better than I ever could have dreamt." He then described what he liked best about his baby, quoting Wordsworth's "Lines Composed a Few Miles Above Tintern Abbey."

In hours of weariness, sensations sweet,
Felt in the blood and felt along the heart,
And passing even into my purer mind
With tranquil restoration:—feelings too,
Of unremembered pleasures: such, perhaps,
As have no slight or trivial influence
On that best portion of a good man's life,
His little, nameless, unremembered acts
Of kindness and of love.

REFERENCES

Ainsworth, M. D. S. (1973). The development of infant-mother attachment. In *Review of Child Development Research*, vol. 3, ed. B. Caldwell and H. Ricciuti. Chicago: University of Chicago Press.

Beckwith, L., and Cohen, S. E. (1980). Interactions of preterm infants with their caregivers and test performance at age 2. *In High Risk Infants and Children*, ed. T. Field, New York: Academic Press.

Bibring, G. (1959). Some considerations of the psychological processes in pregnancy. *The Psychoanalytic Study of the Child*, vol. 14, pp. 113–121, New York: International Universities Press.

Bowlby, J. (1969). *Attachment and Loss*, vol. I. New York: Basic Books.

Bradley, R. and Caldwell, B. (1976). Early home environment and changes in mental test performance in children from 6 to 36 months. *Developmental Psychology*, 12:93–97

Brazelton, T. B. (1973). *Neonatal Behavioral Assessment Scale*. Philadelphia: J. B. Lippincott.

Brazelton, T. B. et al, (1975). Early mother infancy reciprocity. In *Parent-Infant Interaction*, ed. R. Hinde. Ciba Foundation Symposium No. 33. Amsterdam: Elsevier.

Bricker, W. A. and Bricker, D. A. (1976). The infant, toddler, and preschool research and intervention research project. In *Intervention Strategies for High Risk Infants and Young Children*, ed. T. D. Tjossem. Baltimore: University Park Press.

Chivers, D. J. (1972). The siamang and the gibbon in the Malay Peninsula. *Gibbon and Siamang*, 1:103–135.

Clarke-Stewart, K. A. (1980). The father's contribution to children's cognitive and social development in early childhood. In *The Father-Infant Relationship: Observational Studies in a Family Setting*, ed. F. A. Pedersen. New York: Holt, Rinehart & Winston.

Dixon, S. et al., (1981). Early social interaction of infants with parents and strangers. *Journal of the American Academy of Child Psychiatry*, 20:32–52.

Field, T. M. (1978). Interaction behaviors of primary versus secondary caretaker fathers. *Developmental Psychology*, 14:183–184.

Field, T. M. (1979a). Interaction patterns of preterm and full-term infants. In *Infants Born at Risk: Behavior and Development*. ed, T. M. Field. New York: SP Medical and Scientific Books.

Field, T. M. (1979b). Games parents play with normal and high-risk infants. *Child Psychiatry and Human Development*, 10:41–48.

Frodi, A., Lamb, M., Hwang, C., and Frodi, M. (1982). Increased paternal involvement and family relationships. Paper presented to International Conference on Infant Studies, Austin, Texas.

Goldberg, S. (1978). Prematurity. Effects on parent-infant interaction. *Journal of Pediatric Psychology*, 3:137–144.

Gurwitt, A. R. (1976). Aspects of prospective fatherhood. *The Psychoanalytic Study of the Child*, vol. 31, pp. 237–271. New Haven: Yale University Press.

Hampton, J. K., Hampton, S. H., and Landsehr, B. T. (1966). Observations on a successful breeding colony of the marmoset. Oedipamidas Oedipus. *Folia Primatologica*, 4: 265–287.

Ingram, J. C. (1978). Social interactions within marmoset family groups. In *Recent Advances in Primatology*, vol. 1,

ed. D. Chivers and J. Herbert. New York: Academic Press.

Jeffcoate, J. A., Humphrey, M. E., and Lloyd, J. K. (1979). Role perception and response to stress in fathers and mothers following pre-term delivery. *Social Science and Medicine*, 1304:139–145.

Kotelchuck, M. (1976). The infant's relationship to the father: Experimental evidence. In *The Role of the Father in Child Development*, ed. M. Lamb. New York: John Wiley.

Lamb, M. E. (1975). Fathers: Forgotten contributors to child development. *Human Development*, 18:245–266.

Lamb, M. E. (1977). Father-infant and mother-infant interaction in the first year of life. *Child Development*, 48: 167–181.

Lamb, M. E. (ed.), (1981). *The Role of the Father in Child Development*. New York: John Wiley.

Lamb, M. et al., (1982). Mother and father-infant interaction involving play and holding in traditional and nontraditional Swedish families. *Developmental Psychology*, 18:215–221.

Lerner, H. (1979). Effects of the nursing mother-infant dyad on the family. *American Journal of Orthopsychiatry*, 49: 339–348.

Lipkin, M. and Lamb, G. S. (1982). The couvade syndrome: An epidemiologic study. *Annals of Internal Medicine*, 96:509–511.

Marton, P., Minde, K., and Perrotta, M. (1981). The role of the father for the infant at risk. *American Journal of Orthopsychiatry*, 51:672–679.

Minde, K. et al, (1978). Mother-child relationships in the premature nursery—an observational study. *Pediatrics*, 61:373–379.

Parke, R. (1979). Perspectives on father-infant interaction. *Handbook of Infancy*, ed. J. D. Osofsky. New York: John Wiley.

Parke, R. and Sawin, D. (1975). Infant characteristics and behavior as elicitors of maternal and paternal responsibility in the newborn period. Paper presented to Society for Research in Child Development, Denver.

Parke, R. and Sawin, D. (1977). The family in early infancy: Social interactional and attitudinal analyses. Paper presented to Society for Research in Child Development, New Orleans.

Parke, R., and Tinsley, B. (1982). The early environment of the at-risk infant. In *Intervention with At-Risk and Handicapped Infants*, ed. D. D. Bricker. Baltimore: University Park Press.

Pederson, F., Yarrow, C. J., Anderson, B. J., and Cain, R. L. (1979). Conceptualization of father influences in the infancy period. In *The Child and its Family*, ed. M. Lewis and L. Rosenblum. New York: Plenum.

Power, T. G. and Parke, R. D. (1979). Toward a taxonomy of father-infant and mother-infant play patterns. Paper presented to the Society for Research in Child Development, San Francisco.

Ross, J. M. (1975). The development of paternal identity: A critical review of the literature on nurturance and generativity in boys and men. *Journal of the American Psychoanalytic Association*, 23:783–817.

Stern, D. (1974). The goal and structure of mother-infant play. *Journal of the American Academy of Child Psychiatry*, 13:402–421.

Waletzky, L. (1979). Husband's problems with breast-feeding. *American Journal of Orthopsychiatry*, 49:349–352.

Werner, H. (1957). *Comparative Psychology of Mental Development,* rev. ed. New York: International Universities Press.

Yogman, M. W. (1977). The goals and structure of face-to-face interaction between infants and fathers. Paper presented to the Society for Research in Child Development, New Orleans.

Yogman, M. W. (1981). Games fathers and mothers play with their infants. *Infant Mental Health Journal,* 2:241–248.

Yogman, M. W. (1982). Development of the father-infant relationship. In *Theory and Research in Behavioral Pedia-trics,* vol. I, ed. H. Fitzgerald, B. Lester, and M. Yogman. New York: Plenum.

Yogman, M., Lester, B., and Hoffman, J. (1983). Behavioral and cardiac rhythmicity during mother-father-stranger-infant social interaction. *Pediatric Research,* 17:872–876.

Zaslow, M. et al. (1981). Depressed mood in new fathers. Paper presented to Biennial Meeting of Society for Research in Child Development, Boston.

Zilboorg, G., (1931). Depressive reactions related to parenthood. *American Journal of Psychiatry,* 10:927–962.

39

Children of the Fathermothers: Infants of Primary Nurturing Fathers

Kyle D. Pruett, M.D.

[Winnicott said] "There is no such thing as an infant because one never sees an infant without a crib, without arms holding it, without maternal care," [but] we in turn may say that an infant with its mother does not exist. A mother-child couple does not exist without a father somewhere. . . . Thus, we may state in the extreme that *there is no such thing as a dyadic relationship.*

—ANDRÉ GREEN

In André Green's (1975) cogent addendum to Winnicott's famous aphorism, we are gently reminded never to underestimate the ties that bind. Yet our research strategies have been less wise. In the quest for the seminal truth of our own personal development, we often fall prey to the seduction of investigating the minutiae of human development and behavior in ever increasing detail. One casualty of this naive myopia, now undergoing rehabilitation, has been the relationship between fathers and their children, their infants in particular. Important contributions have been made to this somewhat neglected data base by a number of researchers (Frodi and Lamb, 1978; Kotelchuk, 1976; Lamb, chapter 37, this volume; Lamb and Bronson, 1980; Lamb et al., 1982; Parke, 1979; Pedersen et al., 1980, 1979; Yogman, 1982, and chapter 38, this volume; Yogman et al., 1977). A subgroup I find of special interest is the primary nurturing father, functioning as, what one ambivalent man dubbed himself, a "fa-

thermother." In this paper I summarize some early observations made in the course of an ongoing investigation into the development of seventeen infants being raised primarily by their fathers in intact families. Two years after the work began, sixteen of the original families were available for a follow-up study. The first report of this work (Pruett, 1983) should be consulted for details and for a review of the literature.

Briefly stated, the study is concerned with the development of infants from two to twenty-four months, the psychodynamic characteristics of their fathers, their patterns of nurturing, and the relationships between the infants' mothers and fathers. The original group of seventeen families was recruited primarily with the aid of pediatricians practicing in the New Haven area. A family's admission to the study was based on the referring clinician's judgment that the father bore the major responsibility for and the commitment to parenting, although the parenting might be shared with the mother. Whatever the arrangement for infant care, it provided the opportunity for the formation of a primary affectional tie between father and infant. All the study infants were firstborn; sex distribution was eight males and nine females. The parents ranged in age from nineteen to thirty-six, with a mean age of twenty-four for fathers, and twenty-five for mothers. The family socioeconomic spectrum ranged from welfare recipients to professionals.

Review of Methodology and Initial Findings

An extensive discussion of methodology and of the initial findings is given in the previous report (Pruett, 1983). In summary, the fathers were first interviewed at home while caring for their infants. Retrospective analytically oriented interviewing techniques were employed. Extensive histories were taken, and naturalistic observations of the father-infant dyad in the process of typical "male-care" were recorded. After the initial interview, the babies were examined in a laboratory setting at the Child Development Unit of the Yale Child Study Center, using the Yale Developmental Schedules to assess in detail their developmental competence in gross and fine motor performance, adaptive problem-solving, language skills, and personal-social functioning. A final and extensive interview was conducted at home with both mother and father present. A marital history was obtained and further naturalistic observations about the family triad were recorded.

The findings were as follows. These infants raised primarily by men appeared to be vigorous, competent, and thriving, and they seemed especially comfortable with and interested in stimulation from the external environment. Many of these infants functioned well above the expected norms on the standardized test of development. The youngest group (age two to twelve months) performed problem-solving tasks on a level of four to twelve months older, while social skills were two to ten months in advance of the norm. The older infants (age twelve to twenty-two months) were similarly precocious.

The fathers easily formed and participated in the intense reciprocal nurturing attachment so critical in the early life of the human infant. The choice and style of caregiving appeared to be drawn from deep within the father's own adaptive and narcissistic wish to nurture and to be nurtured. The derived style was not merely

that of a mother's substitute, "wife-mirror," or *"in loco matris."* The father's nurturing style was seen to be a distillate of selected identifications and disidentifications with the important objects in his own life. His nurturing capacities did not seem to be determined wholly by genetic endowment or gender identity.

About one third of the study families decided on the caregiving system prior to the pregnancy, one third decided during the pregnancy, and a third in the neonatal period. The last group was usually pressed into the choice for economic reasons—the father lost his job and the mother did not. The timing of the decision could not be correlated with how well the infants did on the developmental examination.

Current Observations

Two years after entering the study, each family was studied again, using the original method of investigation. One family left the area and could not be contacted, leaving sixteen families. In this group, second children had been born in seven families. Fathers continued as the primary caregiver in eight, including four families in which there were now siblings. Mothers became the primary nurturing parent in three families, all of which had second children. In six families (three with second children), the fathers had returned to work or school and had ceased to function as the primary caregiving parent. There was one parental separation in which the father retained custody.

Impressive changes occurred within the family system as a whole, with special reverberations within each family member. To provide a preliminary indication of these families' solutions and adaptations to growth and change in infant and parents and in their relationships, a representative family will be described.

The Case of Sam

Mrs. S age twenty-four, reported that Mr. S age twenty-five, and Sam, now twenty-seven months old, composed "all the family we need," as she explained the couple's decision to not have a second child. Mrs. S had had a miscarriage one year before Sam's birth, and she had taken a full-time job "to get rid of my blues. Three months later I was pregnant again and scared, but this one felt right from the beginning." The parents decided during the pregnancy that Mrs. S would return to work after six weeks, and her husband would stay at home with the baby and leave his sales job, "which I didn't much care about anyway. Besides, I'd always been the one pushing to have kids."

Mrs. S was the second of seven children born to a working-class family. Her father held two jobs most of his life. Her mother suffered from chronic illness and "had never been able to do much of anything for us, so I was sure I was going to take care of myself."

At the initial interview twenty-two months earlier, Mr. S had said, "I was shocked by how close I felt to him right from the beginning. I had to hold myself back from picking him up and carrying him around all the time when my wife went back to work. It was like Sam took charge of *me,* not the other way around." When first seen at the age of six months, Sam was especially competent motorically and seemed to enjoy vigorous physical jostling about by his father (who prided himself on being an accomplished amateur athlete) without becoming distressed, disorganized, or overstimulated. Now, twenty-two months later, much the same could be said. Mrs. S continues to work and has enjoyed several promotions and raises. The father remains at home caring for Sam, though he has returned to some part-time weekend work as a salesman. As a couple, Mr. and Mrs. S were feeling generally more comfortable about their parenting choice, now that Sam was doing so well. Both extended families had expressed dismay and criticism initially, the mother's sister asking, "How can you leave your baby?" Now, however, both families were more accepting of them as Sam had turned into "such a charmer."

This toddler's use of his mother and father during his struggle for autonomy and independence over the preceding months was intriguing. For example, when Sam was about eigh-

teen months old, Mrs. S had assumed the job of putting him to bed, and the father had taken to sneaking out of the bedroom because Sam became so distressed at separations from him day or night. The couple theorized at the time that Sam was more accustomed to his mother's comings and goings. Shortly afterward, Sam had his first bona fide temper tantrum when he saw his father holding another infant at the family holiday gathering. This appears to be the father-infant counterpart of Abelin's (1979) "Madonna constellation" conflict, a term he used to describe the toddler's distress at seeing his mother holding another child.

At the time of the home visit, Sam was observed to make quite differential use of his parents. He brought dolls, stuffed animals, and doll clothes to his mother, who then became actively engaged in helping him clothe his "babies." He carried the baby bottle to his father after the babies were clothed. He *walked* to his mother, but *ran* excitedly to his father, initiating a tickling game while crawling up into his lap. Mrs. S made several attempts to pick Sam up to cuddle him, but he squirmed out of her grasp. At one such time his father commented, "I think he really prefers to get around by himself these days." The mother responded, "I really do feel he knows Sam better than I do. That took some getting used to at first, but now it just seems right. He was the one who heard Sam cry at night, not me. In fact, Sam and I really began doing better when, after he started walking [at ten months], I felt like he *required* less of me, and so I could *give* him more. We've been doing better ever since." The couple spontaneously reported that Sam seemed to be coming out of a period of being more compliant with mother than with father, making her authority seem more effective than his. Mr. S said, "It was like I meant *entertainment,* and she meant *business,* but we're over that now."

At twenty-seven months of age, Sam took great pleasure in the developmental assessment. His language and problem-solving skills were at the thirty-month level, with some successes in each part of the profile at thirty-six months. His personal-social skills were particularly prominent, and his capacity to play in a reciprocal, turn-taking complex fashion was more typical of a three- to three and one-half-year-old child. Motorically, he was already riding a tricycle, and he could ascend and descend stairs with the skill of a three-year-old.

The S's were fairly typical of those families who had achieved an increasing stability and adaptation to this nontraditional parenting arrangement. All three family members were progressing according to their own stages within the life cycle and coping well with the phase-appropriate developmental tasks. Sam was continuing to develop in the vigorous fashion seen in most of the children at the time of the first study. In reply to a friend's rather challenging inquiry and doubts about "his son growing up to be a man," Mr. S, his own philosphical preference for an androgynous sexual identification clearly evident, responded: "Any kid who bombs around the neighborhood in his Big Wheel with his baby doll in the jump seat is probably going to make out just fine."

Discussion

The mothers in this initially "father-prime" population who bore second children tended to find themselves more deeply involved with them than with their first. This seemed to be true both in terms of actual hours of care, and in a greater "attunement" to their infants. When asked to explain this phenomenon, these mothers often credited their husbands as providing nurturing role models, or some similar formulation. The parents offered interesting descriptions of behavior that, in their view, characterized primary parenting, for example, "the person who wakes up at night when the baby cries"; "the person who decides when the baby is really sick and calls the doctor"; "who decides to go home to take care of the baby when the day-care arrangements fall through." Usually these designations correlated with the overall time commitments to parenting as well.

Regardless of the socioeconomic status of the family, the mothers continued to report high satisfaction in the work place as they had at the time of entry into the study. Most of them attributed much of their positive feelings about work to feeling free from worry about the quality of care their babies were receiving.

One typical comment was, "It was nice to have someone who loved *you* looking after your baby too."

In the initial report (Pruett, 1983) it was suggested that these babies may have performed well on certain developmental tasks as a result of a particularly heightened, arousing and playful interactional quality between them and their fathers. This style has been reported by others (Clarke-Stewart, 1980; Parke, 1979; Yogman, 1982). In addition, Pedersen's group (1979) have remarked that this style may be "more novel and complex" than the more intimate style of maternal infant care. This quality of interaction was observed throughout the study, adding credence to its being primary to the father-infant dyad rather than a function of infrequent interaction or lack of familiarity with the infant. However, in a study of Swedish fathers who cared for their babies for portions of the first year of life under the provisions of a government insurance plan, Lamb's group (1982) found that these fathers played with or stimulated their infants less than did American fathers, and even as primary caregivers they were less preferred by their infants than were the mothers. Cross-cultural factors as well as the extent to which the father makes the choice to be the primary caregiver may make significant contributions to the quality of interaction between father and infant.

While almost all couples in the study group referred to their parents as "traditional" in the way they themselves had been reared, there were several who gave impressions of a possible predisposition. A number of those men who made an early choice to serve as primary parent reported their own fathers as "absent, gone a lot, distant." Their nurturant role identifications were more with their mothers, and they seemed to marry women with strong autonomous strivings who did not seek their primary or sole fulfillment in life through mothering. Those women who assumed the primary nurturing role after the second pregnancy often described their own mothers as being "unhappy, cold, unavailable"; they felt more strongly identified with their fathers, who were generally experienced as nurturing and supportive. Such women also reported feeling less competitive with their husbands and tended to identify positively with their spouse's nurturing of the first baby. While the majority of parents in the study group had described their own childhood in positive terms, thirteen of the original seventeen mothers had had mothers who worked outside the home during some period in their childhoods. In a recently reported study of role-sharing fathers, Radin (1982) found that "the notion that fathers of child-rearing men are unloving, unavailable and powerless was unsupported . . . [men described thus] may influence their sons in many ways, but apparently *not* toward becoming primary childrearers in intact families" (p. 197).

The typical father in the study group reacted to his wife's pregnancy in the profound ways described by Gurwitt (1976); strong affective responses to changes in his wife's physiologic and psychologic status, and preoccupation with earlier nurturing experiences of his own. Interestingly, fathers tended to gain weight with the first, but not with the second, pregnancy. It may be, as Catherine Cox (in a personal communication) suggests, that the father's more active availability to his neonate reflects a less conflicted commitment to fostering his child's autonomy because his body has never been truly filled and then emptied of his own baby, or made ill, or experienced a distorted body shape or image.

It was common to hear from both parents of how powerfully their infants affected or even "controlled" the fathers: "All of a sudden . . . she caught me by surprise . . . didn't expect what I felt . . . no one told me I'd ever feel that way about a baby." Some years ago Erikson (1964) commented on the infant's power to evoke caregiving wishes, tenderness, and "concern in those who are concerned with his well-being . . . and stimulate their active caretaking" (p. 113). Although some were initially ambivalent and uncertain, none of the fathers were at all reluctant in the fulfillment of their tasks. The power of the infant through the daily, even tedious, tasks of caregiving to somehow release in the father a profound commitment to its well-being dwarfs the issues of role, gender, or specific antecedent requirements for the job. Yogman (1982) has even suggested that the prolonged involvement

with an infant may have a biological concomitant in diminished androgen levels in such fathers.

No difficulties with sex role or gender identity have appeared in the study group. Lamb and Bronson (1980) have pointed out that "misguided predictions of negative consequences arise because of the continuing confusion of two concepts—gender role and gender identity . . . [the former] refers to behavior . . . [the latter] to an individual's satisfaction with his or her gender" (p. 349). In the group studied, the fathers' and mothers' gender identities were secure and stable, thereby allowing them to assume a broad repertoire of gender roles, often interchangeably. Consequently, strong identifications with same-sex parents appear to be proceeding typically. The oldest child in the study at this report is a forty-nine-month-old girl. Her oedipal rivalry has age-appropriate characteristics of this developmental phase typical in a family with a loving and intimate relationship between the parents.

While it is still early in the study, an interesting quality can be observed in a number of the children regarding sex role expressions. The "baby-doll toting, Big Wheel stunt driver" was not an unusual phenomenon among this population. One boy confidently labeled the sport-jacket card on the Stanford Binet Vocabulary Test as a "dress," in homage to his businesswoman mother's wardrobe. Because most of these parents appear to have relatively unconflicted cross-gender identifications with their own parents, it may be that they tend to differentiate less radically between sexual stereotypes.

In conclusion, the data reported from this study are inherently limited by virtue of the fact that they are confined to conscious, verbalized descriptions, observations, and recollections. There is little access to material beyond conscious awareness. Nonetheless, the data force us to reassess what now seem to be simplistic ideas of an exclusive primary love object, and to begin to consider the effects on ego growth and competence of a more complex mosaic of primary and secondary love objects. In addition, we must look beyond the conventional explanations for the intimate involvement of fathers with their infants, most of which are based on experience with psychopathology and which refer to womb envy, the wish for immortality, or the urge to create.

There is much yet to learn of such parenting styles and motives, and the children seem to be doing their best to help us along.

REFERENCES

Abelin, E. (1979). The role of the father in the preoedipal years. Panel reported by R. Prall. *Journal of the American Psychoanalytic Association,* 26:141–161.

Chiland, C. (1982). A new look at fathers. *The Psychoanalytic Study of the Child,* 37:367–379. New Haven: Yale University Press.

Clarke-Stewart, K. A. (1980). The father's contribution to children's cognitive social development in early childhood. In *The Father-Infant Relationship,* ed. F. A. Pederson. New York: Holt, Rinehart & Winston.

Erikson, E. (1964). Human strength in the cycle of generations. In *Insight and Responsibility.* New York: Norton.

Frodi, A. M. and Lamb, M. E. (1978). Sex differences and responsiveness to infants: A developmental study of psychophysiological and behavioral responses. *Child Development,* 49:1182–1188.

Green, A. (1975). La psychanalyse, son objet, son avenir. *Revue Française de Psychanalyse,* 39:103–134. Quoted by Chiland, C. (1982).

Gurwitt, A. (1976). Aspects of prospective fatherhood. *The Psychoanalytic Study of the Child,* 31:237–271. New Haven: Yale University Press.

Kotelchuk, M. (1976). The infant's relationship to the father: Experimental evidence. In *The Role of the Father in Child Development,* ed. M. E. Lamb. New York: John Wiley.

Lamb, M. E. and Bronson, S. (1980). Fathers and the context of family influences: Past, present and future. *School Psychology Digest,* 9:336–353.

Lamb, M. E., Frodi, A. M., Hwang, C. P., and Frodi, M. (1982). Varying degree of paternal involvement in infant care: Attitudinal and behavioral correlates. In *Nontraditional Families: Parenting and Child Development,* ed. M. E. Lamb. Hillsdale, New Jersey: Lawrence Erlbaum Associates.

Parke, R. D. (1979). Perspectives on father-infant interaction. In *Handbook of Infant Development,* ed. J. Osofsky. New York: John Wiley.

Pedersen, F. A., Anderson, B. J., and Cain, R. L. (1980). Parent-infant and husband-wife interactions observed at five months. In *The Father-Infant Relationship: Observational Studies in Family Context,* ed. F. A. Pedersen. New York: Praeger.

Pedersen, F. A., Yarrow, L. J., Anderson, B. J., and Cain, R. L. (1979). Conceptualization of father influences in the infancy period. In *The Child and Its Family,* ed. M. Lewis and L. Rosenblum. New York: Plenum.

Pruett, K. D. (1983). Infants of primary nurturing fathers. *The Psychoanalytic Study of the Child,* 38:257–277. New Haven: Yale University Press.

Radin, N. (1982). Role-sharing fathers and preschoolers. In *Nontraditional Families: Parenting and Child Development,* ed. M. E. Lamb. Hillsdale, New Jersey: Lawrence Erlbaum Associates.

Yogman, M. W. (1982). Development of the father-infant relationship. In *Theory and Research in Behavioral Pediatrics,* vol. I, ed. H. E. Fitzgerald et al. New York: Plenum.

Yogman, M. W., Dixon, S., Tronick, E., and Als, H. (1977). The goals and structure of face-to-face interaction between infants and their fathers. Paper presented to the Society for Research in Child Development, New Orleans, March (unpublished).

40

"Paternity Blues" and the Father-Child Relationship

Lisbeth F. Brudal, dr. philos.

To see the World in a Grain of Sand
And a Heaven in a Wild Flower,
Hold Infinity in the Palm of your Hand
And Eternity in an Hour.
—William Blake: *Songs of Innocence*

Margaret Mead once said that in those cultures in which men must leave home to contribute to the maintenance of society they are forbidden direct contact with their newborn children. The reason for this taboo, according to Mead, is perhaps the belief that, if new fathers came in contact with their newborns, the fathers would become so involved with the children they would never again go out into the world to work.

We are lacking in modern studies of this aspect of parent-infant relationship, in spite of the quantity of work already done on this early stage in life. Studies of infants' emotional needs by Anna Freud (1949, 1965), Bowlby (1969), and Mahler (Mahler et al., 1975) have been supplemented by investigations of the infant's states of consciousness (for example, Brazelton, 1973; Korner, 1972; Prechtl, 1964). Work on the *mother*-child relationship has achieved prominence (for example, Brazelton, 1963; Klaus and Kennell, 1976). The *parents' significance for the child,* especially that of the mother, has been examined too, for example,

by Biller (1974), and Klaus and Kennell (1976). The parents' own reactions as related to becoming growing and maturing adults have received less attention. Few investigators seem to have built on what Erikson (1950) termed the eighth stage of human development—generativity. Only in the last few years have the father's role and importance been systematically studied (see Cath et al., 1982; Lamb, 1976). Shereshefsky (1973) and Parke (1979) have examined the father's reaction in connection with the perinatal period. Benedek (1970) defined fatherliness as "an instinctually rooted character trend which enables the father to act toward his child or all children with immediate empathic responsiveness" (p. 175).

The parents' *abnormal psychological reactions* during the perinatal period have focused chiefly on the mother's reactions in the days after childbirth, for example, puerperal psychoses and the so-called "maternity blues" or "postpartum blues." Yalom and his group (1968) consider postpartum blues to be so ubiquitous and ostensibly benign as to have seldom been deemed worthy of serious study. Winnicott (1956), however, had a different view of the mother's special psychological state beginning near the end of pregnancy and continuing for some time after. He compares it with a fugue state, refers to it as "almost an illness," and terms it Primary Maternal Preoccupation, characterized by heightened sensitivity. Interestingly, Winnicott also mentions that fathers too can experience such heightened sensitivity, leading to the capacity for identification with the baby.

Recent studies by Shereshefsky (1973) and Brudal (1983) indicate that the way in which a man experiences the perinatal period is affected by, among other factors, the relationship he has with his father, in much the same way the woman's primary maternal model is important for her experiences during this time. It is also suggested that a man's dependency needs are activated as well. Retterstøl (1968) has shown that paranoid psychoses in some men are related to prospective or recent fatherhood.

In 1974, Greenberg and Morris interviewed eight first-time fathers during the first days after childbirth. They termed the fathers' emotional reactions to becoming fathers "engrossment," referring to "a sense of absorption, preoccupation and interest in the infant" (p. 521). The current study can be considered a replication and extension of the work of Greenberg and Morris.

SAMPLE

Sixty first-time Norwegian fathers were randomly selected from a normal population. Forty subjects had been present at a vaginal delivery without instrumentation, twenty others were present during scheduled Caesarean sections with epidural. These latter fathers had responded affirmatively when previously asked if they wished to be present during the Caesarean, for which the most usual indications were breech presentation, twins, older primipara, or herpes genitalis. Fathers came from different parts of Norway; their backgrounds were widely diverse.

METHOD

A semistructured interview and a twenty-four-item questionnaire (Norwegian translation of Pitt's [1968] work devised to register "atypical" depression in postpartum women) were administered within four days after delivery and the interviews recorded on cassette tapes. Most subjects (42 percent) were interviewed on the second day after delivery.

PROCEDURE

All interviews were conducted in the maternity ward. Requests to participate came from the midwife in charge. Four fathers declined to participate in the study. The subject was asked to tell in his own words about the situation immediately preceding the birth, the delivery itself, and the time between delivery and the interview. Then the semistructured interview was administered and finally the questionnaire. The procedure took one and a half to two hours. Interview data were control coded, and correlation between two raters ranged between .94 and .52, (median .74).

RESULTS

No significant differences appeared between those present at vaginal deliveries and those at Caesarean sections. The two groups are therefore combined (see table 40–1).

The subjects described cognitive changes, especially problems with concentration and forgetfulness, often to their uncomfortable surprise. Some insisted that the language did not have words for the experiences of depersonalization. The asthenia category includes those who described that everything now took

TABLE 40–1

Father's Reactions in Postpartum Period
(in percentages)

(i)	Birth has given new, unfamiliar feelings	72
(i)	Cognitive changes (forgetfulness, poor concentration)	57
(q)	Reduced sexual needs	51
(q)	Depersonalization	48
(i)	Delivery and time after are indescribable experiences	48
(q)	Tension	35
(q)	Reduced interest in food	31
(q)	Asthenia	31
(q)	Worried about the baby	30
(i)	Changed view of life	30
(q)	Insomnia	25

(i) = interview results, (q) = questionnaire, $N = 60$

TABLE 40–2

Fathers' Reactions During Delivery
(in percentages)

Emotional reactions:	
feelings more intense	65
feelings more distant	27
Cognition:	
could concentrate only on delivery	27
Depersonalization	32
Time perception:	
time disappeared	30
time stood still	28
Psychosomatic reactions:	
felt birth somatically	40
tension	38
sweating	35

$N = 60$

more effort, some even staying home and not accomplishing their usual tasks. It should be emphasized that the subjects' orientation and questionnaire focused on reactions directly related to the birth and thus on *changes*, not on preexisting experiences.

The results in table 40–2 are from the interview. Very few fathers escaped the experience of a new intensity of feeling during delivery, whether more intense or more distant. It was not unusual for them to say they felt like crying. Some even said that they cried for the first time in their lives. In some cases, changes in time perception were accompanied by experiences of "panoramic memory," that is, seeing one's life pass in review in a few seconds. Dep-

ersonalization experiences appeared more commonly postpartum (from 32 percent during delivery to 48 percent postpartum). In a study made by Stein and reported by Brockington and Kumar (1982), it is not clear whether primiparae only, or also multiparae, are included. Whereas there are clearly many similarities between some of the psychological reactions of new mothers and those of first-time fathers, more women have sleeping problems (see table 40–3).

Discussion and Conclusions

Because of the unusual circumstance of the twenty fathers who chose to be present at the Caesarean sections, there may be some selection factors not yet identified that distinguish this group. The others are not exceptional in Norway since almost all Norwegian fathers are present during childbirth. Another exploratory aspect of this study lies in the fact that verbatim reports were gathered in the subjects' spontaneous accounts, but have not been included in the data in any way. We hope to study the relationships between data gathered from the questionnaire, the semistructured interviews, and the spontaneous accounts.

The data strongly suggest that new mothers and new fathers have a number of reactions in common, such as forgetfulness and poor concentration, depersonalization, depression, and

TABLE 40–3

Comparison of "Maternity Blues" and Fathers' Postpartum Reactions
(in percentages)

"Maternity Blues"* N = 24				Fathers' Postpartum Reactions† N = 60	
Insomnia		79	(q)	Insomnia	25
Forgetfulness	29		(i)	Forgetfulness, poor	
		58		concentration	57
Poor concentration	29		(q)	Depersonalization	48
Feelings of unreality		50	(q)	Asthenia	31
Depression		38	(q)	Tension	35
Tension		37	(q)	Reduced interest in food	31
Anorexia		29			
			(q) = questionnaire, (i) = interview		

*Stein, reported in Brockinton, I. F. and Kumar, R. (1982). *Motherhood and Mental Illness.* London, Academic Press.
†Brudal, L. (1983). *Fødselens Psykologi Laerebok i Forbyggdende Arbeid.* Oslo: Aschehoug.

tension, lending further support to the idea that these reactions in mothers are based on emotional rather than hormonal factors. Although the evidence does not indicate that these reactions in men and women are identical, nevertheless the presence in new fathers of a clear-cut postpartum syndrome seems to justify the use of the term *paternity blues* comparable to *maternity blues*. Since the study of the psychological reactions in connection with the birth of a child may be fruitfully considered a separate field, it is here proposed that it be called *tocology,* derived from the Greek *tokos,* meaning to give birth or to be born.

REFERENCES

Benedek, T. (1970). Fatherhood and providing. In *Parenthood: Its Psychology and Psychopathology,* ed. E. J. Anthony and T. Benedek. Boston: Little, Brown.

Biller, H. (1974). *Paternal Deprivation.* Lexington, Massachusetts: D. C. Heath.

Bowlby, J. (1969). *Attachment and Loss,* vol. I. New York: Basic Books.

Brazelton, T. B. (1963). The early mother-infant adjustment. *Pediatrics,* 32:931–938.

Brazelton, T. B. (1973). *Neonatal Behavioral Assessment Scale.* Philadelphia: J. B. Lippincott.

Brockington, I. F. and Kumar, R. (1982). *Motherhood and Mental Illness.* London: Academic Press.

Brudal, L. (1983). *Fødselens Psykologi Lærebok i Forbygdende Arbeid.* Oslo: Aschehoug.

Cath, S., Gurwitt, A., and Ross, J. M., eds. (1982). *Fatherhood: Developmental and Clinical Perspectives.* Boston: Little, Brown.

Erikson, E. H. (1950). *Childhood and Society.* New York: W. W. Norton.

Freud, A. (1949). Certain types and stages of social maladjustment. In *Searchlights on Delinquency,* ed. K. R. Eissler. New York: International Universities Press.

Freud, A. (1965). *Normality and Pathology in Childhood.* New York: International Universities Press.

Greenberg, M. and Morris, N. (1974). Engrossment: The newborn's impact upon the father. *American Journal of Orthopsychiatry,* 44:520–531.

Klaus, M. H. and Kennell, J. H. (1976). *Maternal-Infant Bonding.* St. Louis: C. V. Mosby.

Korner, A. (1972). State as variable, as obstacle and as mediator of stimulation in infant research. *Merrill-Palmer Quarterly,* 18:77–94.

Lamb, M. E. (1976). *The Role of the Father in Child Development.* New York: John Wiley.

Mahler, M., Pine, F., and Bergman, A. (1975). *The Psychological Birth of the Human Infant.* New York: Basic Books.

Parke, R. D. (1979). Perspective on father-infant interactions. In *Handbook on Infant Development,* ed. J. D. Osofsky. New York: John Wiley.

Pitt, B. (1968). "Atypical" depression following childbirth. *British Journal of Psychiatry,* 114:1325–1335.

Prechtl, H. F. R. (1974). The behavioral states of the newborn infant (a review). *Brain Research,* 76:185–212.

Retterstol, N. (1968). Paranoid psychoses associated with impending or newly established fatherhood. *Acta Psychiatrica Scandinavica,* 44:51–61.

Shereshefsky, P. M. (1973). *Psychological Aspects of a First Pregnancy and Early Postnatal Adaptation.* New York: Raven Press.

Yalom, I., Lunde, D. T., Moos, R. H., and Hamburg, D. A. (1968). "Postpartum blues" syndrome. *Archives of General Psychiatry,* 18:16–27.

Winnicott, D. W. (1956). Primary maternal preoccupation. In *Collected Papers.* New York: Basic Books, 1958.

41

Contact with Intensive-Care Infants: Father's Sex Type, Infant Preference, and Frequency of Visits

Juarlyn L. Gaiter, Ph.D. and Alix A. S. Johnson, Ph.D.

In a review of literature on father influences on infants, Parke (1979) proposed a reconceptualization of the primacy of mother as "nurturer" of the infant and suggested a behavioral model that differentiated adult-infant interaction style. He concluded that historical, social, and economic conditions have dictated that men assume traditional roles but that men do not lack the ability to function as competent caregivers of infants.

Very little is known about the father's contact with preterm, sick babies. The early arrival of an unexpected sick newborn is a critical stressful event for both parents. For preterm infants who are transported to medical centers for specialized care, the father may immediately become the "primary" parent. If the mother remains hospitalized following a high-risk birth, the father is often the only parent able to visit the sick newborn and begin the early acquaintance process. In fact, the father may not merely substitute for the mother, he may assume full responsibility of parenting without her support.

The data reported in this paper are preliminary findings which describe the visiting patterns of fathers and their behavior toward their hospitalized preterm infants.

Review of the Literature

FATHERS AND PRETERM NEWBORNS

Some recent studies have described fathers' reactions to a preterm birth, although most of the investigators have used questionnaires rather than behavioral data. Benfield and colleagues (1976) reported that often fathers react with anticipatory grief toward the birth of a preterm baby. The level of grief may be unrelated to the severity of the infant's illness. Both Jeffcoate's (1979) and Marton's (1981) groups cited evidence that fathers are generally concerned not only with caring for their infant but also about coping with unexpected household responsibilities. In one behavioral study, Lind (1974) reported that fathers who visit and handle their hospitalized newborns remain involved by assuming an active caregiver role in the home. A particular personal benefit of this caregiver role for the father may be a deeper emotional involvement with the baby.

Empirical evidence suggests that early father-newborn interaction may influence the mother's attitude and behavior toward her child. Using a family systems model for investigating parent-infant relationships, Pedersen (1980) found that when the father has positive feelings about the infant, the mother is likely to have similar feelings. When the father's attitude and behavior are negative, however, the mother may either compensate for his behavior or also behave negatively toward the child. Pedersen showed that when fathers of four-week-old infants were supportive of the mother, she was more able to pace the infant's feedings, sense the baby's need for rest, and provide more stimulation or relief from ingested air. In contrast, when tension and conflict characterized the husband-wife relationship, the mother was less competent in feeding the infant. Pedersen concluded that one way in which the father may make his peculiar contribution to the infant's early development is by supporting the mother. Expressing this father-infant support system as a "triadic relationship," Belsky (1981) proposed a "family system model," contrasting with past studies which viewed fathers as peripheral to the mother-infant dyad. Earlier studies that viewed fathers within a family system model sought to explain the effect of their absence from the family on the behavior and socioemotional development of children (Biller, 1971, 1974; Hetherington, 1966).

MOTHER–PRETERM INFANT CONTACT STUDIES

In 1976, Klaus and Kennel hypothesized that early close physical contact between the newborn and mother produces positive and enduring effects for both. Lamb (1976) criticized the early mother-infant interaction studies on which Klaus and Kennell based their conclusions and provided evidence that immediate physical contact between the newborn and mother is neither a necessary nor a sufficient requirement for a long-term close relationship between parent and child.

In an earlier investigation, Prugh (1953) reported that mothers of preterm infants may have frightening fantasies, which stem from anxiety and guilt concerning causes of their preterm delivery and the condition of the newborn. Other investigators have suggested that the lack of early maternal contact with the preterm infant is associated with poor parenting experiences for these children (Barnett et al., 1970; Leifer et al., 1972). Typically, preterm infants who have been hospitalized for severe birth complications have behavioral deficiencies making them difficult to console, infrequently alert, and unreliably responsive to parental stimulation. Goldberg (1979) reported that preterm infants who have experienced respiratory illness rarely cry and are not likely to give parents clear distress signals. Consequently, such infants and their parents may have few mutually satisfying interactions. When parents begin to perceive their infants as "unreadable," unpredictable, and unsatisfying, their confidence as competent caregivers is threatened.

Sameroff and Chandler (1975) reported that the variability in subsequent developmental outcome of vulnerable infants is influenced more by the nature of their early socioemotional and cognitive environment than by adverse conditions at birth. However, if both parents are given the opportunity to learn about their infant's behavioral characteristics before hospital discharge (that is, to understand and accept the infant's level of behavioral organization) subsequent parenting difficulties may be minimized or eliminated.

Rubin (1963) described the initial nature of physical contact mothers have with their newborns as exploratory "fingertip touching." More recently, Klaus and his group (1970) outlined an orderly progression of maternal involvement on first meeting the newborn. This progression begins with visual inspection of the infant and quickly proceeds to fingertip contact; then mothers stroke the infant's abdomen with the palm of the hand. For term mothers there is a gradual decrease in fingertip contact coincident with an increase in palm contact with the infant during the first few meetings. Klaus and his colleagues (1970) report that, in contrast to the behavior of term mothers, mothers of preterm newborns tend to have more fingertip than palm contact with their babies. Minde and his co-workers (1978) note that mothers of preterm newborns spend more time passively looking at their babies than actively touching them during their first two visits to the preterm nursery. From behavioral observations, these investigators concluded that the mother's hesitancy to touch and handle the baby indicates a need to adjust to the unexpected physical appearance of their sick, small infant. The initial step in this acquaintance process seems to be visual.

The Minde group (1978) found that mothers who provide their infants with stimulation such as looking, talking, holding, kissing, or stroking are more likely to visit and telephone the nursery than mothers who do not stimulate their babies. These researchers reported that characteristics of the preterm newborn are important in determining how stimulating mothers are during their visits. Both the Minde group (1978), and the Prechtl group (1979) have observed that preterm infants of less than twenty-nine weeks gestation were less active and less likely to respond to maternal stimulation than infants born closer to term. These findings suggest that characteristics of both the mother and infant determine the nature of the mother's contact with the hospitalized newborn during visits. The nature of the father's contact with his preterm newborn may be similarly determined. However, no one has yet described the kind of contact fathers have on first meeting their preterm baby in the nursery.

FATHER'S SEX TYPE AND INFANT CONTACT

One of the most prominent influences on the behavior and attitudes of fathers has been an inhibition in Western culture for men to express tenderness and nurturance toward infants (Hartley, 1974; Lynn, 1974). In writing about the psychological aspects of motherliness and fatherliness, Josselyn (1956) stated that men might consider any nurturing feelings engendered in them by infants and chil-

dren as "evidence of suppressed femininity." This perception would then create anxiety in men who had been taught through their early socialization to scorn anything associated with femininity as indicative of weakness. The stereotyped male sex role is antithetical to the affective behavior generally regarded as "maternal"—kissing, fondling, holding, rocking, and feeding babies. Men tend to engage in more vigorous patterns of stimulation of normal infants than women (Lamb, 1976). Gentle, nurturant behaviors may be more suitable for handling physically fragile, preterm babies.

For many years, the psychometric conceptualization of masculinity and femininity reflected the assumption that these constellations were mutually exclusive but complimentary. Recently, however, several researchers have suggested that psychological adaptive functioning might in fact be related to the individual's possession of traits customarily associated with both sexes (Constantinople, 1973). The concept of psychological androgyny implies that an individual may successfully blend the complimentary modalities of masculinity and femininity, depending upon situational appropriateness (Bem et al., 1976).

In 1974 Bem published a sixty-item checklist of adjectives—the Bem Sex Role Inventory—composed of positively toned words selected as desirable traits for men and women in this society. The inventory was designed so that one could rate oneself as having masculine *and* feminine traits to varying degrees (along a seven-point scale). Respondents could be classified as masculine sex-typed, feminine sex-typed, and androgynous or undifferentiated (possessing traits characteristic of both men and women). Bem assumed that people who possessed both masculine and feminine traits were more flexible psychologically and thus better adjusted than those who endorsed items characteristic of only one sex. Androgynous individuals were not only likely to perform cross-sex behavior with little reluctance or anxiety (Bem and Lenney, 1976), but displayed both "masculine" independence when under pressure to conform and "feminine" nurturance in interactions with a baby kitten (Bem,

1975). Bem and her group (1976) also found that men classified as either androgynous or feminine interacted more with an infant than did "masculine" men.

In an initial report of the development of the Bem Sex Role Inventory, Bem (1974) presented data from a normative sample of over 800 college men and women on the internal consistency and correlations between the masculinity and femininity scales. Bem reported reliabilities of .80 or better for each scale, and correlations of .11 and −.14 between the scales. The two scales thus seem to be independent and reliable indicators of the subject's self-described sex-linked personality characteristics. Currently, no information is available on the stability of the Bem Sex Role Inventory, and it is not clear whether the scores reflect transitory psychological states or enduring personality characteristics.

In our observational study of early father-newborn contact in the hospital environment, an important question was whether fathers who regarded themselves as androgynous would engage in more physical contact with their infant than masculine sex-typed fathers. Also, since in Western culture, parents generally prefer first-born male children (Biller, 1971; Williamson, 1976), it was assumed that fathers would handle and visit first-born males more frequently than children born later.

The Observational Study

The objectives of this observational study of fathers and their preterm newborns were to describe the type of contact fathers had with infants in a hospital setting and the influence this contact had on father's subsequent visits. We hypothesized that: (1) fathers who touched their infants during the first nursery visit would visit more frequently than those who remained physically distant; (2) firstborn male newborns would be visited more frequently than later-born males and females; and (3) androgynous fathers (those who rate themselves high on both masculine and feminine traits) would be more psychologically flexible and therefore more able to relate to their newborn

than fathers whose sex-type ratings were rigidly masculine.

PROCEDURES

Three hundred and thirty preterm infants admitted to the intensive-care nursery of the Children's Hospital National Medical Center (CHNMC) in Washington, D.C., with the diagnosis of respiratory distress, from January 1979 through October 1980, and their fathers were potential subjects for study. Infants with the diagnosis of respiratory disease were chosen for study because this group represents a relatively homogeneous sample of sick infants requiring special medical management. Selection of father-infant pairs for observation depended upon the fulfillment of the following criteria: (1) the diagnosis by x ray and clinical impressions of severe respiratory disease requiring assisted ventilation and intensive-care therapy; (2) the absence of any other life-threatening disease or physical anomalies; (3) the determination by clinical examination that the infant was born at twenty-eight to thirty-seven weeks' gestation; (4) the infant was a singleton; (5) the birthweight was appropriate for gestational age; (6) this was the first preterm birth for the couple; and (7) parents resided together at the time of the baby's birth at a distance no greater than fifty miles from CHNMC.

The study sample was composed of thirty-five father-infant pairs. The age range for the fathers was twenty-one to forty, with a mean of twenty-nine years. All of the fathers had completed high school. Fourteen fathers were unskilled and skilled laborers; eighteen were clerical or professional workers, and three fathers were unemployed.

In the sample of thirty-five newborns there were twenty-two males and thirteen females. Of these, nineteen (twelve males, seven females) were firstborns. The mean birthweight of the sample was 1,485 grams, and the mean gestational age was 31 weeks. Nine of the thirty-five study infants weighed less than 1,000 grams at birth.

Each father was observed for the duration of his first visit to the nursery. One of five trained nurses who had attained interobserver reliability of at least .89 used an adaptation of the Maternal Assessment Tool (Cropley et al., 1976) to observe and record each father's behavior. Originally designed to evaluate the behavior of mothers during their first contact with fullterm healthy babies, the Maternal Assessment Tool is based on the experimental findings of Klaus and Kennell (1976), Rubin (1972), and parental observations made by experienced obstetrical and gynecological nurses (Cropley et al., 1976). The tool consists of thirty-seven items arranged in four categories of behavior indicative of the degree of parental involvement with the infant.

1. *Identifying Behaviors*—which denote parental statements about the infant's appearance, wholeness, and behavioral state, indicated by a comment such as "She looks very drowsy and weak."

2. *Locating Behaviors*—a category that notes whether the parent has placed the infant within a significant social system. For example, the parent might verbally associate characteristics of the infant with a family member.

3. *Modalities of Interaction*—which indicate how the parent, using visual, verbal, or tactile contact, begins to relate to the baby.

4. *Caretaking Behaviors*—activities that demonstrate that the parent supports or protects the infant by providing for the baby's physical needs, such as diapering and feeding.

All the behavioral items in the four categories were divided into distal (verbal) or proximal (physical) contact variables. Distal-contact variables ($N = 20$) were characterized by parental comments made concerning the infant's physical condition, characteristics, or behavior. Proximal-contact variables ($N = 17$) were parental behaviors such as fingertip touching, palm contact with the infant, and feeding the infant. Numerical scores for distal-contact variables ranged from 4 to 8. A total involvement score was obtained for each father by summing the frequency of proximal and distal contact. The higher the contact scores for both the distal and the proximal variables, the greater the parental involvement with the infant.

When the infants had been in the nursery for two weeks, the Bem Sex Role Inventory (Bem, 1974) was administered to each father.

The individual masculine and feminine mean scores can be used to examine the influence of masculine and feminine sex-type characteristics on father's behavior with infants. Twenty of the Bem items have been empirically classified as masculine, 20 as feminine, and 20 as social desirability indicators. A median split classification of fathers as sex-typed masculine, feminine, or androgynous was derived.

In addition to the Bem Sex Role Inventory scores for each father, the frequency of telephone calls and the number of visits fathers made to the nursery during the first four weeks of the infant's hospitalization was recorded. The frequency of calls and visits, sex type, and the father involvement scores were analyzed using t-test and chi square analyses (Winer, 1971).

RESULTS

As predicted, the fathers' scores for involvement with the baby during the first nursery visit and the number of daily visits over a four-week period were significantly related ($r = .40$, $df = 33$, $p < .01$). That is, fathers who had more contact (proximal and distal) with the infant during the first nursery visit returned to the nursery more often than fathers who made little contact with their infant at their initial visit. The mean score for father involvement during the first visit was 13 (range: 1 to 30 points). A majority of the fathers touched their infants during the first visit. More fathers used fingertip touching to explore their infants (proximal contact). Twenty-eight percent of the fathers did not touch their babies. Forty-eight percent of the fathers spoke directly to their infants (distal contact). This is shown in figures 41–1 and 41–2.

A significant question was whether the ten fathers who did not touch their babies were distinguishable from the twenty-five fathers who did. The two groups did not differ in terms of sex of the infant, socioeconomic status, race, number of first- and later-born infants, or calls to the nursery. However, a trend indicated that fathers who touched their babies stayed longer during their first visit than their nontouching counterparts. Six of the non-

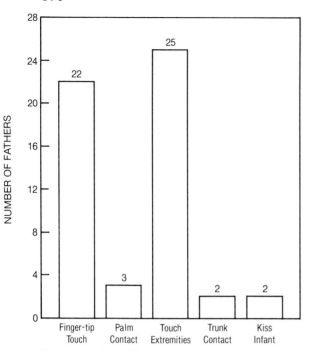

Figure 41–1 Type of Father Contact with Infant (Proximal)

SOURCE: Irvin, Nancy A., Kennell, John H., and Klaus, Marshall H. "Caring for the parents of an infant with a congenital malformation." In Klaus, Marshall H. and Kennell, John H., *Parent-Infant Bonding*, 2nd ed. St. Louis: C. V. Mosby, 1982.

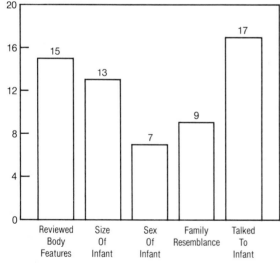

Figure 41–2 Comments by Fathers about Infants During Visit (Pistal)

touching fathers had babies whose birthweights were less than 1,000 grams. A majority of these fathers (six of ten) commented about their baby's size, but only three talked directly to their babies. The most significant difference by far between fathers who touched their new-

borns and those who did not was that the "touching" fathers made significantly more visits during the first weeks of the infant's hospital confinement ($t = 3.96$, $df = 33$, $p < .001$) than those fathers who did not touch their infants. The mean number of visits fathers made to the nursery was 11.8, $SD = 6.68$ with a range of 2 to 26 visits. The mean number of phone calls was 5.00 (median = 3 calls), $SD = 5.82$ with a range of 0 to 26 calls (see figure 41–3). Ten fathers did not call the nursery during the first four-week period that their infants were hospitalized (see figure 41–3).

Psychological androgyny in fathers was believed to underlie a high level of behavioral involvement of fathers with the newborn preterm infants. The impulse to caress and talk to his baby may be present in every father, but the actual expression of these impulses could be suppressed by men concerned with presenting a "masculine" image. In contrast, psychologically androgynous men with self-described masculine and feminine traits were hypothesized to be most likely to handle and talk to their babies. These behaviors were expected, in turn, to stimulate the development of other affectively expressive behaviors and an increased emotional investment in the infant. Consequently, this investment would be reflected in more frequent contacts with the infant during hospitalization.

In order to test the hypothesis that father's sex role would be related to behaviors with the

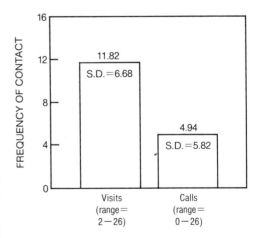

Figure 41–3 Father's Contact

infants and frequency of contacts, mean masculine and feminine scores were calculated for each father. These means were used in correlations with the variables of infant sex and birth order, the parental behavioral assessment of the first nursery visit, and the number of daily contacts. Because none of these correlations were significant, the median split classification of fathers was used. The fathers were then pooled into two sex-role-type groups: (1) differentiated, either high masculine-low feminine or high feminine-low masculine, and (2) undifferentiated (low masculine-low feminine) and androgynous (high masculine-high feminine). When the dichotomous sex-role rating (differentiated or androgynous) was assigned to each father, a significant relationship was obtained between sex type and number of daily contacts. Fathers who described themselves as predominantly masculine *or* feminine maintained more frequent contacts with their infants (mean = 18 contacts for differentiated sex-role-typed fathers, mean = 12.5 contacts for undifferentiated fathers, and a mean of 13.17 for androgynous fathers). Figure 41–4 shows the mean number of daily contacts and father sex type. These results therefore failed to support the hypothesis that androgynous fathers would show more involvement with their babies than masculine-sex-typed fathers. The relationship between sex-role type and fathers' behavior during the first nursery visit was not significant.

The infant's birth order and the number of father contacts were significantly related ($r = .42, df = 33, p < .01$). Although the correlation coefficient between the sex of the infant and daily contacts failed to reach significance, a t-test of the difference between the mean number of daily contacts for fathers of firstborn males and all other infants was significant ($t = 2.48, p < .01$). This result supported the second hypothesis that firstborn males would receive the greatest number of daily contacts from their fathers.

Discussion

The most illuminating finding of this study was that the fathers who touched their babies were those who talked to them, visited longer

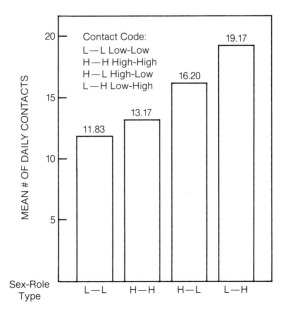

Figure 41–4 Undifferentiated and Differentiated Sex-Role Types and the Frequency of Daily Contacts

during their first visit, and were more frequent visitors than fathers who did not touch their babies. Frequent visitors saw their babies twice as often as the infrequent visitors during the first three weeks and three times as often during the fourth week. A noteworthy aspect of this finding is that the fathers who touched their babies visited on the average more frequently than mothers of similarly sick newborns (Leifer et al., 1972; Rosenfield, 1980).

A significant relationship was found between the fathers' sex type and the number of visits to the nursery ($r = .35, df = 33, p < .05$). That is, fathers who described themselves as predominantly high feminine-low masculine or low feminine-high masculine had more frequent contacts with their infants than undifferentiated and androgynous fathers. The androgynous low masculine-low feminine fathers were significantly less likely to maintain contacts with their babies. These two groups of fathers also touched and talked less frequently to their babies. Consequently, these results failed to support the hypothesis that androgynous fathers would show more involvement with their infants. Fathers who identified strongly with predominantly masculine or feminine traits had the greatest number of daily contacts with their infants.

A possible explanation for this finding is that the Bem inventory ratings may be indicators of a generalized response style. For example, in order to reduce anxiety generated by ambiguity some fathers may have rejected the feminine or masculine traits more definitively (choosing "never or almost never true" rather than "sometimes true" under less stressful conditions). Choosing one consistent set of traits, whether masculine or feminine, may have been the significant cognitive function relating Bem inventory ratings to frequency of daily contacts with the preterm babies. Another possible explanation is that fathers who discriminated consistently between masculine and feminine traits may also have been less anxious, more cooperative, and more inclined to reveal themselves on the questionnaire. No corroborative data, however, are available from this study to support this speculation.

Firstborn males are reportedly the preference for most American families (Biller, 1971; Williamson, 1976). Parke and Sawin (1976) have shown that parents of normal newborns tend to touch male babies more frequently than female babies and that fathers touched firstborn males more than any other infants. The results of our study support the general findings of the attraction of the firstborn son, whether preterm or fullterm.

Our observations of fathers took place during the most critical period of intensive care—within the first twenty-four to forty-eight hours of the infant's hospitalization. At this time, the newborn is incapable of engaging in reciprocal interaction (for example, looking and touching) believed to be so important in eliciting and rewarding parental behavior. Yet the majority of fathers touched their infants and employed fingertip contact, the typical mode of behavior mothers display toward preterm infants. Like mothers, very few fathers made palm contact or touched larger surfaces of the infant's body. Although the preterm infant's physical and behavioral characteristics probably had a significant influence on the father's interactive behaviors, most of the fathers visited the nursery and showed their support for the infant.

The ten fathers who did not touch their newborns had the smallest infants in the sample. During the initial visit these fathers commented about their baby's size. Only three of these fathers were motivated to speak to their newborns. This finding is congruent with reports (Klaus, Kennell et al., 1970; Minde et al., 1978) that a small, sick baby may be an anxiety-arousing stimulus for both parents.

These are several ways to interpret the effect that touching the infant has on the behavior of parents. The father's physical contact may initiate a feeling of greater familiarity and closeness to the infant; consequently, his interest in the infant may be heightened and reflected in the frequency of visits. Alternatively, it may be argued that fathers who touched their infants were predisposed to this form of interaction because of personality, situational, experiential, or cultural factors. Whatever the explanation for the differential behavior of fathers at first meeting their sick babies in the nursery, this study shows that fathers, when given the opportunity, display nurturant behaviors toward their preterm infants.

During their first visit, about half of the fathers spoke directly to their infants, despite their infant's behavioral deficiencies and the fact that various kinds of medical apparatus and monitoring equipment covered the infant's eyes, mouth, and limbs. A few fathers called their newborns by name, and one fourth commented that their infant resembled a family member. Such remarks conveyed an implicit acceptance and placement of the infant within the family system. Rheingold and Adams (1980) and Gaiter and colleagues (1981), have reported that it is not unusual for hospitalized infants to be spoken to in a personal manner by nursery staff. Modeling staff behavior may be a useful method in encouraging fathers to relate personally to their babies.

What emerges from the foregoing discussion is a tentative model of the development of paternal involvement with the preterm infant during its earliest weeks of life. For fathers, hormones do not play a priming function for "paternal" behaviors. Yet, looking at and touching the infant seem to act as powerful stimuli or releasers of responses directed toward the infant. The experience of physical contact with the newborn apparently leads to increased interest and contact with the infant.

Also to be considered is the possibility that the capacity to use tactile contact may be an important aspect of an overall capacity to "parent" an infant. Thus, those fathers who relate well to their preterm babies would be those who tend to touch them, in contrast to those fathers who visit their babies infrequently and who do not use tactile contact.

Pedersen (1980) offers evidence suggesting that opportunity for the father to become acquainted with his infant can be important for the whole family unit. Currently, the bulk of parent-infant studies still focus on the mother-infant dyad. Situational factors surrounding the early unexpected birth of a preterm infant can thrust the male parent into a critical role requiring nurturant and supportive behavior during the newborn's early hospitalization. In this way, the father has the opportunity to become the initiator of a triadic relationship involving mother, father, and infant. The role of the father in the gradual development of this triadic relationship in the context of a stressful preterm birth has not been studied.

Taken together, the findings of this study suggest a "family systems theory" defined by a network of interdependent relationships. If the father takes the opportunity to relate to his baby, he may play a more active role in uniting the mother and infant. He can prepare her to accept the fragile infant's appearance and temporary inability to perform expected reciprocal parent-infant behaviors. The father can actively support the mother and acknowledge her parenting role by giving her personalized information about their baby's behavior and characteristics. Probably most important for the father is the development of his own relationship with the baby without the competing presence of the mother. The change in father's behavior as a result of contacts with the baby is supported by Benfield and colleagues (1976), who report that fathers who visited their hospitalized infants made drastic changes in their daily activities in order to maintain family stability. Data from the present investigation show that when the mother is unable to serve immediately as the infant's caregiver, the father assumes this role and behaves very much like a mother toward his baby. Of equal importance is the potential that lies in the father's very early contact with the hospitalized newborn: it may contribute significantly to the bonding of the male parent to his offspring and stimulate his active participation in child rearing.

REFERENCES

Barnett, C. R., Leiderman, P. D., Grobstein, R., and Klaus, M. (1970). Neonatal separation: The maternal side of interactional deprivation. *Pediatrics*, 45:197–205.

Belsky, J. (1981). Early human experience: A family perspective. *Developmental Psychology*, 17:3–23.

Bem, S. L. (1974). The measurement of psychological androgyny. *Journal of Consulting and Clinical Psychology*, 42:155–162.

Bem, S. (1975). Sex-role adaptability: One consequence of psychological androgyny. *Journal of Personality and Social Psychology*, 31:634–643.

Bem, S. and Lenney, E. (1976). Sex typing and the avoidance of cross-sex behavior. *Journal of Personality and Social Psychology*, 33:48–54.

Bem, S. L., Martyna, W., and Watron, C. (1976). Sex typing and androgyny: Further explorations of the expressive domain. *Journal of Personality and Social Psychology*, 37:1016–1023.

Benfield, D. G., Lieb, S. A., and Reuter, J. (1976). Grief response of parents after referral of the critically ill newborn to a regional center. *New England Journal of Medicine*, 294:975–978.

Biller, H. B. (1971). *Father, Child and Sex-Role*. Lexington, Massachusetts: D. C. Heath.

Biller, H. B. (1974). *Paternal Deprivation*. Lexington, Massachusetts: D. C. Heath.

Constantinople, A. (1973). Masculinity-femininity: An exception to the famous dictum. *Psychological Bulletin*, 80:389–407.

Cropley, C., Lester, R., and Pennington, S. (1976). Assessment tool for measuring maternal attachment behaviors. In *Obstetrical and Gynecological Nursing*, ed. L. K. McHall and J. T. Galeemer. New York: C. V. Mosby.

Gaiter, J. L. et al. (1981). Stimulation characteristics of nursery environments for critically ill preterm infants and infant behavior. In *Intensive Care in the Newborn*, ed. L. Stern et al. New York: Masson.

Goldberg, S. (1979). Premature birth: Consequences for the parent-infant relationship. *American Scientist*, 67:214–220.

Hartley, R. (1974). Sex-role pressures and the socialization of the male child. In *Men and Masculinity*, ed. J. H. Pleck and J. Sawyer. Englewood Cliffs, New Jersey: Prentice-Hall.

Hetherington, E. M. (1966). Effects of paternal absence on sex-typed behaviors in negro and white preadolescent males. *Journal of Personality and Social Psychology,* 4:87–91.

Jeffcoate, J. A., Humphrey, M. E., and Lloyd, J. K. (1979). Disturbance in parent-child relationships following preterm delivery. *Developmental Medicine and Child Neurology,* 21:344–352.

Josselyn, I. M. (1956). Cultural forces, motherliness and fatherliness. *American Journal of Orthopsychiatry,* 26:264–271.

Klaus, M. H. and Kennell, J. H. (1976). *Maternal-Infant Bonding.* St. Louis: C. V. Mosby.

Klaus, M. H., Kennell, J. H., Plumb, N., and Zuehlke, S. (1970). Human maternal behavior at the first contact with her young. *Pediatrics,* 46:187–192.

Lamb, M. E. (1976). The role of the father: An overview. In *The Role of the Father in Child Development,* ed. M. E. Lamb. New York: John Wiley.

Leifer, A., Leiderman, P.D., Barnett, C. R., and Grobstein, R. (1972). The effects of mother-infant separation on maternal attachment behavior. *Child Development,* 43:1203–1218.

Lind, R. (1974). Observations after delivery of communication between mother-infant-father. Presentation to International Congress of Pediatrics, Buenos Aires, Argentina (unpublished).

Lynn, D. B. (1974). *The Father: His Role in Child Development.* Monterey, California: Brooks/Cole.

Marton, P., Minde, K., and Perrotta, M. (1981). The role of the father for the infant at risk. *American Journal of Orthopsychiatry,* 51:652–679.

Minde, K. et al. (1978). Mother-child relationships in the premature nursery: An observational study. *Pediatrics,* 61:373–379.

Parke, R. (1979). Perspectives on father-infant interaction. In *Handbook of Infant Development,* ed. J. D. Osofsky. New York: John Wiley.

Parke, R. and Sawin, D. B. (1976). The father's role in infancy: A re-evaluation. *Family Coordinator,* 25:365–371.

Pedersen, F. A. (1980). *The Father-Infant Relationship: Observational Studies in Family Setting.* New York: Praeger.

Prechtl, H. F., Fargel, J. W., Weinmann, A. M., and Bakker, H. H. (1979). Postures, motility and respiration of low-risk preterm infants. *Developmental Medicine and Child Neurology,* 21:3–27.

Prugh, D. (1953). Emotional problems of the premature infant's parents. *Nursing Outlook,* 1:461–473.

Rheingold, H. L. and Adams, J. L. (1980). The significance of speech to newborns. *Developmental Psychology,* 16:397–401.

Rosenfield, A. G. (1980). Visiting in the intensive care nursery. *Child Development,* 51:939–941.

Rubin, R. (1963). Maternal touch. *Nursing Outlook,* 11:828–831.

Rubin, R. (1972). Fantasy and object constancy in maternal relationships. *Maternal-Child Nursing Journal,* 1:101–111.

Sameroff, A. J. and Chandler, M. J. (1975). Reproductive risk and the continuum of caretaking casualty. In *Review of Child Development Research,* vol. 4, ed. F. G. Horowitz et al. Chicago: University of Chicago Press.

Williamson, N. E. (1976). *Sons or Daughters: A Cross-Cultural Survey of Parental Preferences.* Beverly Hills, California: Sage Publications.

Winer, B. J. (1971). *Statistical Principles in Experimental Design,* 2nd ed. New York: McGraw-Hill.

PART V

Psychopathological Issues

42

Helping Parents after the Birth of a Baby with a Malformation

John H. Kennell, M.D. and Marshall H. Klaus, M.D.

In 1957 Donald Winnicott commented,

... it is well you should know that it is entirely natural that a mother should want to get to know her baby right away after birth. This is not only because she longs to know him (or her), it is also —and it is this which makes it an urgent matter —because she has had all sorts of ideas of giving birth to something awful, something certainly not so perfect as a baby. It is as if human beings find it very difficult to believe that they are good enough to create within themselves something that is quite good. I doubt whether any mother really and fully believes in her child at the beginning. Father comes into this too, for he suffers just as much as mother does from the doubt that he may not be able to create a healthy normal child. Getting to know your baby is therefore in the first place an urgent matter, because of the relief the good news brings to both parents. (p. 24)

But what if the news is not good? The birth of a newborn blighted with a malformation is a crushing blow to the parents and to everyone else who has shared in the event. The baby is the culmination of the parents' best efforts and embodies their hopes for the future. To help parents develop ties to their malformed infant is difficult: parental reactions are turbulent, the child's birth often precipitates a major family crisis, and the usual pathways for the development of close parent-infant bonds are disrupted.

Bettelheim (1972) probably best describes the goal of efforts to help the parents of a malformed infant. "Children can learn to live with a disability. But they cannot live well without the conviction that their parents find them utterably loveable. . . . If the parents, knowing about the child's] defect, love him now, he can believe that others will love him in the future. With this conviction, he can live well today and have faith about the years to come" (pp. 34–35).

During the course of a normal pregnancy, the mother and father develop a mental picture of their baby. Although the degree of concreteness varies, each has an idea about the sex, complexion, coloring, and so forth. One of the early tasks of parenting is to resolve the discrepancy between this idealized image of the infant and the appearance of the real infant (Solnit and Stark, 1961). The dreamed-about baby is a composite of im-

This work was supported in part by The William T. Grant Foundation and Maternal and Child Health, Grant No. MC-R-390337.

The work for this report was done in close collaboration with Dennis Drotar, Ann Baskiewicz Mostow, Pauline Benjamin, Robin Geller, Nancy Irvin, Steven Robertson, Mary Anne Trause, Carolyn Rudd, and Michele Walsh. Their assistance made our study possible. Particular thanks go to Robin Geller and Michele Walsh for their patient and meticulous organization and analysis of the data, a small portion of which is included in this manuscript.

pressions and desires derived from the parents' own experience. If the parents have different cultural backgrounds, the tasks of reconciling the image to the reality is more complicated. And the reconciliation is even more difficult if the baby is born with a malformation (see figure 42–1).

The reactions of the parents and the degree of their future attachment difficulties depend in part on the properties of the malformation; for example: is it correctable or noncorrectable? visible or nonvisible? does it affect the central nervous system? is it familial?

A number of investigators have noted that the more visible the defects are the more immediate will be the resulting concern and embarrassment. Even a minor abnormality of the head and neck results in a greater anxiety about future development than an impairment of another part of the body (Johns, 1971).

In several studies parents have reported that when they saw their infants for the first time, the malformations seemed less alarming than they had imagined. Seeing the children reduced some of their anxiety. In our own studies (Drotar et al., 1975) one parent reported, "We had been conjuring up all kinds of things —that there could be something wrong with every organ. But then what I saw was a relatively normal baby."

Some parents were reluctant to see their babies at first, expressing a need to temper the intensity of the experience. When these parents did see their babies, it seemed to mark a turning point, and *caregiving feelings were elicited where previously there had been none.* The shock of producing a baby with a visible defect is stunning and overwhelming, but attachment can be facilitated by showing parents their newborn baby as soon as possible and as soon as the parents feel ready. The parents of a malformed newborn infant need everything we have found beneficial for bonding to a normal baby, and much more. For example, continuous human support during labor and delivery for every mother will make things go better for even the very young, very deprived woman.

We should keep parents and babies together whenever reasonable, and, if a separation is necessary, return the baby to the parents promptly. Most babies with anomalies have a wide array of attractive features. Would it be reasonable for the parents to have time to interact and hold such a baby, to begin an attachment? When first showing the infant with a visible problem it is important to show all the normal parts as well and to emphasize positive features such as strength, activity, and alertness. The physicians and nurses can determine the parents' view of such a baby by pointing

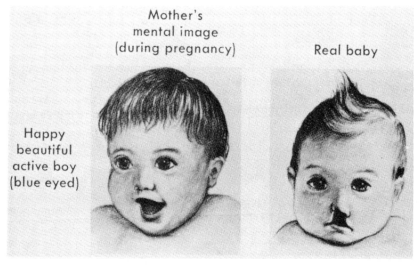

Mother's
mental image
(during pregnancy)

Real baby

Happy
beautiful
active boy
(blue eyed)

Figure 42–1   The change in mental image a mother of an infant with a malformation must make following childbirth.
Source: Drotar, D. et al. "The adaptation of parents to the birth of an infant with a congenital malformation: A hypothetical model," *Pediatrics* 56 (1975), p. 715. Copyright American Academy of Pediatrics, 1975.

out diagnostic features. For example, in a case where the positions of the thumbs and hands and the facial appearance suggest trisomy eighteen—a chromosomal problem associated with retardation and death within the first year —whether it would be best in the long run if the parents had a few minutes or hours with such an infant before they were told about the medical concerns is a controversial point that needs careful study.

Attachment is an interactive process. The contributions made by the infant are major. There is a spectrum of individual differences in the behavior and temperament of newborn infants and with malformed infants there may be deviations in the achievement of milestones in social and emotional development. Malformed infants present a spectrum of responsiveness, of disability, and of desirability.

We believe it is best to leave an infant with his mother for the first few days so that she can become accustomed to him, rather than rushing him to another division or hospital where the special surgery will eventually be done. Obviously, if surgery is required immediately, it must be performed without delay, but even in these cases it is desirable and usually safe to bring the baby to the mother and show her how normal the baby is in all other respects and to let her touch and handle her infant. The father should be included in this and in all other discussions with the mother. We try to arrange for the mother and father to have extended periods to become acquainted with all their infant's features, both positive and negative. The mother of a normal infant goes through a period of several days in which she gradually realigns the image in her mind of the baby she expected with the image of the actual baby she delivered. When the baby has a malformation, the task of realigning the images is more difficult, and the result is a greater need for prolonged mother-infant contact. Lampe and associates (1977) noted significantly greater visiting if an infant with an abnormality had been home for two weeks before surgery was required.

In our studies, despite the wide variations among the children's malformations and parental backgrounds, a number of surprisingly similar themes emerged from the parents' discussion of their reactions. Generally they could recall the events surrounding the birth and their reactions in great detail (Drotar et al., 1975). They went through identifiable stages of emotional reactions, as shown in figure 42–2 which is a generalization of the complex reactions of individual parents. Although the amount of time that a parent needed to deal with the issues of a specific stage varied, the sequence of stages reflected the natural course of most parents' reactions to their malformed infant.

FIRST STAGE: SHOCK

Most parents' initial response to the news of their child's anomaly was overwhelming shock. All but two of the twenty parents reported reactions and sensations indicating an abrupt disruption of their usual states of feeling. One of the fathers explained, "It was as if the world had come to an end." Many parents confided that this early period was a time of irrational behavior, characterized by much crying, feelings of helplessness, and occasionally an urge to flee.

SECOND STAGE: DISBELIEF (DENIAL)

Many parents tried either to avoid admitting that their child had an anomaly or to cushion the tremendous blow. Each reported that he or she wished either to be free from the situation or deny its impact. One father graphically described his disbelief: "I found myself repeating 'It's not real' over and over again." Other parents said that the news of the baby's birth did not make sense. One man said, "I just couldn't believe it was happening to me." Although every parent reported disbelief, the intensity of the denial varied considerably.

THIRD STAGE: ANGER, SADNESS, AND ANXIETY

Intense feelings of anger and sadness accompanied and followed the stage of disbelief. A significant number of parents reported

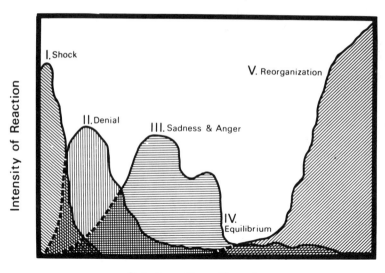

Relative Time Duration

Figure 42–2 Hypothetical model of sequence of normal parental reactions to birth of a child with congenital malformations
SOURCE: Drotar, D. et al. "The adaptation of parents to the birth of an infant with a congenital malformation: A hypothetical model," *Pediatrics* 56 (1975), p. 715. Copyright American Academy of Pediatrics, 1975.

angry feelings. One father said, "I just wanted to kick someone." A mother reported that she was angry and "hated him (the baby) or hated myself. I was responsible." The most common emotional reaction was sadness. One mother reported, "I felt terrible. I couldn't stop crying. Even after a long while I cried about it." In most instances mothers feared for their babies' lives, despite strong reassurance. One mother said that she at first perceived her child as "nonhuman." "Holding him with that tube distressed me. In the beginning I held him only because it was the maternal thing to do." Almost all the mothers were hesitant about becoming attached to their babies.

FOURTH STAGE: EQUILIBRIUM

Parents reported a gradual lessening of both their anxiety and intense emotional reactions. As their feelings of emotional upset lessened, they noted increased confidence in their ability to care for the baby. Some parents reached equilibrium within a few weeks after the birth, whereas others took many months. Even at best, this adaptation continued to be incom-

plete. One parent reported, "Tears come even yet, years after the baby's birth."

FIFTH STAGE: REORGANIZATION

During this period parents deal with responsibility for their children's problems. Some mothers reported that they had to reassure themselves that "the baby's problems were nothing I had done." Positive long-term acceptance of the child involved the parents' mutual support throughout the time after birth. Many couples have reported that they relied heavily on one another during the early period. However, in some instances the crisis of the birth separated parents. In one case the parents blamed each other for the baby's birth. Another mother wanted to be isolated from her husband. "I don't want to see anybody. I just want to be by myself."

Despite the similarities in parental reactions to various malformations, parents progressed through the various stages of reaction differently. Some parents did not report initial reactions of shock and emotional upset; they tended instead to intellectualize the baby's problem and focus on the facts related to the baby's condition. Other parents were unable to cope successfully with their strong emotional reactions to the birth and, as a result, did not achieve an adequate adaptation; they were in a state of sorrow that lasted long after the birth.

A lack of opportunity to discuss the infant's diagnosis can create a situation in which the parents feel overwhelmed and unable to gauge the reality of their child's abnormality. If the mourning process becomes fixed as a sustained atmosphere of the family, the ghost of the desired, expected, healthy child sometimes continues to interfere with the family's adaptation to the defective child. These findings confirm the original creative work of Solnit and Stark (1961), which has become the foundation of most therapeutic approaches to the parents of the malformed infant. Their brilliant analysis can be summarized as follows: (1) the infant is a complete distortion of the dreamed-of or planned-for infant; (2) the parents must mourn the loss of this infant—a process that may take several months—before they can become fully attached to the living defective infant; (3) the physician, nurse, and social worker should not interpret to the parents that the grief they are feeling is due to the loss of the expected perfect child, nor should they attempt to compare this mourning response with any others the parents might have experienced, for it may rob the mother of the full strength and depth of her own grief by intellectualizing it; (4) the mother's attempts to withdraw her strong feelings from the lost expected baby are disrupted by the demands of the living blighted child, and the task of becoming attached to the malformed child and providing for ongoing physical care can be overwhelming to parents at the time around birth, when they are physiologically and psychologically depleted; (5) along with this process of mourning is a large component of guilt that takes many forms and requires great patience from those helping the family, for the parents may repeat the same questions and problems many times; (6) those helping the parents should understand the resentment and anger, since it is sometimes directed toward them;

and (7) the mourning cannot be as effective when the damaged child survives, as the daily impact of this child on the mother is unrelenting and makes heavy demands on her time and energy.

It is remarkalbe that families who must cope with the intense emotional experience stirred up by the birth of a malformed infant can assimilate the child into the family and begin to respond to the child's needs as readily as they do.

The availability of the pediatrician, family physician, or health visitor throughout the child's early weeks and years puts them in a position to help with the family's adaptation. Parents have told of the importance of identifying the normal features of their child, which become increasingly evident as he grows. Pediatrician and family physicians have an excellent opportunity to nurture this. They can be sensitive to the relationship between the parents, can determine which stage of adaptation each parent has reached, can check how aware each partner is of the other's progress, and may be alert to evidence of asynchrony of the parents' mourning reactions.

In a carefully controlled prospective study in England, Gath (1977) compared thirty families with a newborn baby with Down's syndrome with thirty families with a normal baby. Marital breakdown or severe marital disharmony was found in nine of the Down's syndrome families and in none of the controls. To prevent this type of outcome with all its ramifications is the challenge we face in working with families with a malformed neonate. We have encouraged the parents to share their feelings and to move together as synchronously as possible.

The problems of fathers have been striking. Most of them are *in no way* ready for such a catastrophe—they don't express their sadness and they react to guilt differently from their wives. One of our colleagues has suggested that what we need in the United States is *men's liberation* to make it acceptable for men to feel and express their emotions when they are suffering from a tragedy.

From the time the defect is identified, the goal of the physician, nurse, social worker, or health visitor will be to enhance the parents' mourning by empathic available listening. The natural tendency is to support the parents' denial, but the parents need to appreciate their inner reactions of disappointment, resentment, humiliation, and loneliness. Roskies (1972) has suggested that the identity of the baby and his or her acceptance by the parents may be influenced by the way the baby is identified and accepted by society. When a newborn has a malformation, the parents find everything in life changed from what it was, including themselves. Those of us in hospitals make up the society for the parents and neonate in the first few days. We, too, have reactions to a malformed infant, and they are often powerful ones. Particularly young or inexperienced nurses and physicians may be overwhelmed by the sight of the malformed baby. Then after the initial excitement, there is a part in all of us that dreads seeing the parents and helping them. We would much prefer being with the happy and enthusiastic parents of a normal, healthy infant. We may go through the same stages as the parents, and we may need similar support—an opportunity to talk about our feelings with an experienced colleague or with a group of our associates.

Some guidelines for those who help parents of malformed infants come from a study by our research group. The study was of forty families; seventeen had infants with a cleft palate and twenty-three had infants with Down's syndrome. The study was done when the children were fifteen months of age.

When asked *what aspects of care were helpful,* two thirds said the emotional support provided by the doctors and nurses. Almost half replied that the doctors and nurses answered their questions about the child's condition. When questioned about *what was not helpful,* 40 percent said they were not told about the child's condition in an appropriate way. For most of them, that meant that the father and mother were not told about the news together. This response occurred most frequently with the Down's syndrome families.

When asked *what they would advise for doctors and nurses* working with families of a malformed infant, almost one half said that doctors and nurses should be humane, open, and honest with them and one third suggested that they be

supplied with information about the child's condition.

Responding to the circumstances surrounding the birth of an abnormal child in the best way is exceedingly difficult for parents because of the ambiguities involved. For example, what is the difference between overprotectiveness and responding to special needs? Daniels and Berg (1968) quote one mother as saying, "It is hard, sometimes, to figure out what is being motherly and what is taking over. I want to help him as much as he wants and needs, but I don't want to hold onto him." Realistically, the physical care required by such children is much greater than that required by normal children. Recurring hospitalizations for some, and uncertain developmental predictions for others, intensify parental concern and often frustrate consistent planning so that it is difficult to determine when parents cross the boundary into overprotective behavior.

Another feature to consider is the notion of just what characteristics constitute optimal adaptation. If sorrow, depression, and anger are natural responses to the birth, and if the infant evoking these feelings continues to live, what is the right balance between mourning and acceptance? Olshansky (1962) coined the term "chronic sorrow" to describe some of the enduring aspects of parental reactions in adapting to a retarded child. Chronic sorrow at some level may be constantly present in parents, especially if the child will always be dependent on them, as in some cases of retardation. To expect the disappearance of the painful impact of this child on a family, under the guise that these feelings must be "resolved," may force parents to deny their real feelings to professionals who want to help.

In summary, the parents of a baby born with a malformation go through turbulent and painful reactions, and the doctors and nurses may also do the same. For every parent and baby, we should do our best to provide what we have learned is helpful for all parents and their newborn infants: the presence of a supportive companion during labor and delivery plus early and extended parent-infant contact in the first few days if the baby's condition makes this feasible. The parents should be told about the problem together and kept together as much as possible. With support from their colleagues, caregivers can provide support, be patient, and listen empathically to the parents.

REFERENCES

Bettelheim, B. (1972). How do you help a child who has a physical handicap? *Ladies Home Journal,* 89:34–45.

Daniels, L. L. and Berg, G. M. (1968). The crisis of birth and adaptive patterns of amputee children. *Clinical Proceedings Children's Hospital of the District of Columbia,* 24:108–117.

Drotar, D. et al. (1975). The adaptation of parents to the birth of an infant with a congenital malformation: A hypothetical model. *Pediatrics,* 56:710–717.

Gath, A. (1977). The impact of an abnormal child upon the parents. *British Journal of Psychiatry,* 130:405–410.

Johns, N. (1971). Family reactions to the birth of a child with a congenital abnormality. *Medical Journal of Australia,* 1:277–282.

Lampe, J., Trause, M. A., and Kennell, J. H. (1977). Parental visiting of sick infants: The effect of living at home prior to hospitalization. *Pediatrics,* 59:294–296.

Olshansky, S. (1962). Chronic sorrow: A response to having a mentally defective child. *Social Casework,* 73:190–193.

Roskies, E. (1972). *Abnormalities and Normalities: The Mothering of Thalidomide Children.* New York: Cornell University Press.

Solnit, A. J. and Stark, M. H. (1961). Mourning and the birth of a defective child. *The Psychoanalytic Study of the Child,* 16:523–537. New York: International Universities Press.

Winnicott, D. W. (1957). *The Child, the Family and the Outside World.* London: Tavistock Publications, Penguin, 1964.

43

DSM-III and the Infantile Psychoses

William Goldfarb, M.D., Ph.D., Donald I. Meyers, M.D.,
Judy Florsheim, M.S., and Nathan Goldfarb, Ph.D.

Professional interest in the classification of the psychoses of childhood extends back four to five decades. Despite this fact, diagnostic confusion has prevailed. The diagnostic labels that emerged in this period included, among others, well-known and frequently employed designations, such as childhood schizophrenia (Bender, 1947; Fish, 1977; Potter, 1933) and infantile autism (Kanner, 1943). Each of these labels referred to subclasses of children whose symptoms were diversified; and all these subclasses obviously overlapped in the kinds of children they subsumed and the varieties of psychopathy manifested. Perhaps for this reason there was a tendency to include all the varieties of psychotic children in one large, frankly heterogeneous population; and the most usual global diagnostic classification assigned to the wide variety of psychotic children was childhood schizophrenia. Indeed, Kanner's relatively precise criteria for the clinical diagnosis of infantile autism, a condition he pointedly distinguished from schizophrenia, were incorporated along with others into the nine criteria proposed by the British Working Party for the diagnosis of a category termed "schizophrenic syndrome of childhood" (Creak, 1961). These criteria were the basis for selecting a diversified group of children, including some who exhibited all the characteristic features of infantile autism as originally defined by Kanner and others who shared fewer and less severe autistic manifestations.

The absence of precise, objective, and reliable criteria for the designation of nonoverlapping subclasses have been major hindrances to investigating the childhood psychoses.

Over the past decade, however, there has been a significant growth in information about psychotic children and consequent improvement in their objective classification into homogeneous subclasses of children. These classifications have been incorporated into the latest version of the American Psychiatric Association's (1980) Diagnostic and Statistical Manual—DSM-III.

The segment of DSM-III dealing with what are termed Pervasive Developmental Disorders of Childhood is a most significant effort to classify the childhood psychoses in a fashion that is objective, reliable, and universally acceptable. Already there is evidence that the DSM-III diagnoses of the Pervasive Developmental Disorders of Childhood are indeed reliable and usable, (Cantwell et al., 1979; Mattison et al., 1979; Russell et al., 1979). However, questions may reasonably be raised regarding the exhaustiveness of this diagnostic scheme and the degree of homogeneity of each of the subclasses of the Pervasive Developmental Disorders. We address ourselves here particularly to the capacity of this scheme to encompass the full range and diversity of infantile psychoses with onset below thirty months.

DSM-III provides operational criteria for the diagnosis of three subclasses of preadolescent psychoses, now termed the Pervasive Developmental Disorders of Childhood. These include Infantile Autism, Childhood Onset Pervasive Developmental Disorder, and Atypical Pervasive Developmental Disorder. In accord with Rutter's (1972) suggestions, disintegrative psychosis and schizophrenia of childhood are excluded from the Pervasive Developmental Disorders. Disintegrative psychosis with rapid dementia is classified as Organic Brain Syndrome. Schizophrenia of childhood with hallucinations, delusions, and loosening of associations is classified among the Schizophrenic Disorders.

Presumably, in DSM-III the category of Infantile Autism is designated the sole or certainly the major disorder of early onset (before thirty months of age) and is distinguished from the Childhood Onset Pervasive Developmental Disorders, with onset after thirty months of age. However, clinical experience would suggest that there is also a subcategory of pervasive disorders of early onset, other than Infantile Autism, that needs to be recognized. Rutter (1972) referred to a substantial group of psychotic children who did not fit any of his three proposed types (infantile autism, disintegrative psychosis, childhood schizophrenia) although he considered them a minority and described them as "a mixed bag." The informal, quasiclassificatory phrase *a mixed bag* is an unfortunate one because the fallacious conclusions may be drawn that the psychotic children so described are rare in the total universe of psychotic children, and also that their classification is imprecise and unreliable. Of course such children might be placed in the category of Atypical Pervasive Developmental Disorders of DSM-III. However, these children are a well-defined and sufficiently numerous group who, for practical reasons of research and treatment, should be retained as a subdivision of Pervasive Developmental Disorders of early onset. As will be seen, keeping them as a separate category has provided greater understanding.

In accord with these general considerations, we have adapted the DSM-III classification of Pervasive Developmental Disorders in order to reflect the hypothesized heterogeneity of the infantile disorders. In this system, Infantile Autism is seen as including only a portion of the early-onset disorders. Our adapted classification follows.

A. Infantile Onset Pervasive Developmental Disorders—Symptoms recognizable before thirty months
  1. Infantile Autism (All DSM-III criteria for Infantile Autism met.)
  2. Remainder (Not all DSM-III criteria for Infantile Autism met.)
B. Childhood Onset Pervasive Developmental Disorders—Symptoms recognizable after thirty months

The study to be reported here evaluated the capacity of DSM-III to encompass the full range of disorders heretofore termed infantile psychosis.

The following propositions were formulated:

1. Children with the pervasive developmental disorder of Infantile Autism are identifiable. (In our revised classification, they are labeled A1 children.)
2. Also identifiable is a more inclusive population of children with infantile psychoses, and by selecting from among them those with Infantile Autism (A1 children), one thereby also identifies the remaining children (A2 children), who show less social withdrawal.
3. The two subclasses of children with infantile onset Pervasive Developmental Disorders (A1 and A2) probably differ in other dimensions, such as sex distribution, adaptive capacity, IQ, neurological status, social class, family functioning, psychiatric status of the parents, and longitudinal course of the disorder.

The Subjects

The subjects of our study were twenty-four early-school-age children who were admitted to the Henry Ittleson Center for Child Research for residential treatment. The group included sixteen boys and eight girls. All had been originally diagnosed by two psychiatric observers as suffering from the "schizophrenic syndrome of childhood" on the basis of the nine criteria proposed by the British Working Party (Creak, 1961).

These criteria resulted in a selection of

twenty-four children in whom some or all characteristic autistic manifestations were evident. Thus the children have shown gross incapacities in human relationship, major disorders in personal identity, gross delays or impairments in language and speech, excessive anxiety provoked by change, and bizarre, stereotyped behaviors. Symptomatic manifestations were recognizable in the children before thirty months of age. Nevertheless, it has been our clinical impression that the sample of psychotic children under care at the Ittleson Center has also been more heterogeneous than implicit in an unequivocal diagnosis of early infantile autism. In contrast to those among the psychotic children with undoubted infantile autism, the remaining children seemed qualitatively less aloof, had greater capacity for communication, were less bizarre, and were less fixed in their obsessive, ritualistic, and stereotyped behaviors.

Although onset was noted to be below thirty months in all twenty-four cases[1] in the present study, the mean age at the time of initial psychiatric diagnosis of the children of the study was 5.4 years (*SD*, 1.1 years) and the mean age of admission to residential care was 6.9 years (*SD*, 0.9 years). Teachers who were impressed by the children's learning failures and social impairments were the primary agents for initiating psychiatric consultation in 75 percent of the cases.

Procedure

The twenty-four psychotic children were first evaluated to see if they met the six DSM-III criteria for the diagnosis of Infantile Autism.[2] In reviewing the symptoms of the chil-

---

[1]Employing our case records, two psychiatrists agreed in twenty-three of the twenty-four cases that recognizable symptoms occurred below thirty months. In the twenty-fourth case, one of the psychiatrists found the data insufficient to establish age at recognition.

[2]"(A) Onset before 30 months. (B) Pervasive lack of responsiveness to other people (autism). (C) Gross deficits in language development. (D) If speech is present, peculiar speech patterns such as immediate and delayed echolalia, metaphorical language, pronominal reversal. (E) Bizarre responses to various aspects of the environment, e.g., resis-

dren for this purpose, emphasis was placed on the children's developmental histories below thirty months of age. To meet the DSM-III diagnostic criterion of autism, or lack of responsiveness to other human beings, only the most extreme, pervasive, and impervious instances of aloofness and social distance were accepted. Weight was also given to a history of characteristic early manifestations of social aloofness such as conspicuous failure to cuddle, extreme avoidance of eye contact, indifference to affection and physical contact, absence of facial responsiveness, rare expression of feelings, and especially an absence of pleasurable feelings, caring and sympathy, and empathic response. Finally, the syndrome of Infantile Autism (A1) was diagnosed only if the child met all the six DSM-III criteria. On this basis the children were subcategorized as those with Infantile Autism (A1 children) and the remaining children (A2 children). A1 and A2 subgroups were then compared with respect to a variety of attributes of the child and family, described in the presentation of results.

Results

Twelve of the children (50 percent) met all six DSM-III criteria for Infantile Autism. They were designated A1 children. The remaining 12 children were designated A2 children.

A comparison of A1 and A2 subgroups on each of the six DSM-III criteria for Infantile Autism demonstrated a significant difference only in the one criterion of autism, that is, a pervasive lack of responsiveness ($p < .01$). By definition, of course, all twelve A1 children showed the extreme and characteristically pervasive "autistic" aloofness. Significantly fewer instances, two, of such extreme and very early aloofness were found among the A2 children. Nevertheless, the other DSM-III criteria for Infantile Autism were found fre-

---

tance to change, peculiar interest in or attachments to animate or inanimate objects. (F) Absence of delusions, hallucinations, loosening of associations and incoherence as in Schizophrenia" (pp. 89–90).

quently in both subgroups and did not distinguish them. It must also be understood that all twenty-four children in both subclasses showed serious impairments in social relationships prior to admission. For example, none had enduring friendships and none could participate spontaneously in cooperative group play. However, we did distinguish between the more extreme and impervious instances of early aloofness and the less extreme forms of social isolation in which the child's passivity was a major but not insurmountable hurdle hindering social contact or did not become extreme until after the age of thirty months. It might be reasonable to define the A1 subclass as autistic and the A2 subclass as less autistic.

The A2 subgroup had a distinct clinical and symptomatic resemblance to the DSM-III B subgroup of children with Childhood Onset Pervasive Developmental Disorder. Excluding age of onset as a criterion, the criteria for Childhood Onset Pervasive Developmental Disorder could be applied to all the A2 children.

AGE AT PROFESSIONAL DIAGNOSIS OF PSYCHOSIS; AGE AT ADMISSION TO TREATMENT

There are no significant differences in age at which the A1 and A2 children were admitted to residential treatment (table 43–1). By intake procedure, all children were admitted to residential treatment at approximately seven years of age. However, professional diagnosis of infantile psychosis was made at a younger age in the A1 group than in the A2 group ($p. = .05$). The age at diagnosis of the psychotic state in both groups was older than has been recorded in the Kolvin studies of childhood psychosis (Kolvin et al., 1971) and in the Ornitz and Ritvo studies of infantile psychosis and infantile autism (Ornitz and Ritvo, 1976; Ornitz et al., 1977). One may presume that the children in the latter group of studies had been observed in programs that provided service to preschool children, unlike the children at the Ittleson Center. The impact of this kind of selective influence on investigative data regarding the children and their families is difficult to evaluate but certainly needs to be explored.

SEX

Although there were relatively more boys in the A1 subgroup, these differences are not statistically significant at the .05 level (table 43–2).

EGO STATUS

For evaluating the adaptive competence of the children at admission to and during residential treatment, the treating psychiatrists rated the children on the Ego Status Scales for children of early school age (see Goldfarb et al., 1978, for scale definitions). The five ordinally arranged levels represent global judgments based on the child's recognition and differentiation of persons who are important in his life, his mode of contacting other humans, his communication and speech, his receptor behavior, his self-care, and his response to schooling. These levels are defined as: (1) very severely impaired; (2) severely impaired; (3) moderately impaired; (4) mildly impaired; and (5) normal. Ego ratings 1, 2, and 3 represent gross levels of

TABLE 43–1

Age of Autistic and Less Autistic Children at Diagnosis and at Admission to Residential Treatment (in Months)

Diagnosis	At diagnosis		At admission to treatment	
	Mean	Standard Deviation	Mean	Standard Deviation
Autistic group (A1)	59.8	11.7	83.2	9.8
Less autistic group (A2)	70.1	12.7	85.6	11.9

impairment, which in previous studies covered the range of disabilities noted in psychotic children on admission to the Ittleson Center. Ego ratings 4 and 5 characterize the functional level of children who are capable of accommodating to the expectations of family and community living, even if there are still eccentricities and a continuing need for environmental support. In adolescence and later, global judgments of ego status are made on the basis of the child's capacity for self-care, communication, relationship, and orientation. Two psychiatrists who knew the children and used all the available case information independently rated twenty-three of the twenty-four children in Ego Status at admission to treatment, discharge, and last follow-up in adolescence. (The three ratings, over time, by each psychiatrist are not independent because all three ratings were made by the same psychiatrist.) Using a binary system of coding the children as being either grossly impaired in Ego Status (ratings 1, 2, and 3) or mildly impaired to normal (ratings 4 or 5), the two raters agreed completely.

At admission, all children fell between levels 1 and 3. The children were divided into two categories for comparison of A1 and A2 children at admission to treatment: children rated level 1 and children rated ego-level 2 or 3 (see table 43–3). On this basis, the A1 children were inferior in ego status at admission ($p < .04$). Indeed, all children rated level 1, signifying lowest level of social relatedness, intelligence, and language, were found in the A1 subclass of children.

IQ

Table 43–4 presents mean Verbal, Performance, and Full IQ's on the Wechsler Intelligence Scale for Children at admission. The A2 children were superior to A1 children in mean Verbal IQ ($p < .01$), Performance IQ ($p < .05$), and Full IQ ($p < .02$). In each instance, the average IQ of the A1 subgroup was at retarded levels, whereas the A2 subgroup showed dull to average mean IQ's.

Bartak, and colleagnes (1975) have inferred from their data that the autistic child is typically characterized by failure in language capacity and by higher performance in visuospatial response. In support of our own emphasis on the specificity of samples of psychotic children under investigation as a function of selective intake processes, the A1 children with diagnosed Infantile Autism showed no significant difference between Verbal IQ and Performance IQ. In contrast, the A2 group showed a higher Verbal IQ than Performance IQ ($p < .02$).

TABLE 43–2

Sex Distribution of Autistic and Less Autistic Children

Diagnosis	Number of Children	
	Male	Female
Autistic group (A1)	10	2
Less autistic group (A2)	6	6
	16	8

TABLE 43–3

Ego Status at Admission of Autistic and Less Autistic Children

Diagnosis	Number of Children	
	Very Severely Impaired (Ego status 1)	Severely & Moderately Impaired (Ego status 2, 3)
Autistic group (A1)	5	7
Less autistic group (A2)	0	12
	5	19

NEUROLOGICAL STATUS

Each child was evaluated at admission by a child neurologist on the basis of neurological examination and history. The neurologist sought unequivocal and accepted signs of neurological impairment such as changes in normal reflexes, appearance of abnormal reflexes, asymmetrical failures in sensory and motor response, and EEG abnormalities. However, he also looked for "soft" disturbances in gait, posture, balance, coordination, muscle tone, perception, and speech. Congenital stigmata were also appraised. Examination and history were rated separately, with scores ranging between one and five, as follows: (1) unequivo-

TABLE 43–4

WISC IQ at Admission of Autistic and Less Autistic Children

Diagnosis	Verbal IQ		Performance IQ		Full IQ	
	Mean	Standard Deviation	Mean	Standard Deviation	Mean	Standard Deviation
Autistic group (A1)	66.3	19.8	62.5	19.8	62.8	18.6
Less autistic group (A2)	92.6	25.6	82.1	19.5	86.3	23.1

cally positive (3) equivocally positive, and (5) unequivocally negative. A child who received a rating between (1) and (3) in either physical examination or history was regarded as giving evidence of neurological impairment. As evident in table 43–5, at admission, more A1 children presented evidence of neurological impairment than did A2 children ($p. < .02$). All A1 children and 25 percent of A2 children presented such evidence of a neurological deficit.

SOCIOECONOMIC POSITION
(HOLLINGSHEAD–REDLICH SCALE)

Five classes are defined by this scale for statistical analysis. Because of small sample size, classes I and II, and IV and V have been combined to yield three classes—upper (I, II), middle (III), and lower (IV, V).

Although upper-class families ($n = 3$) were found only in the A1 subgroup, there were no significant differences between A1 and A2 children (table 43–6).

FAMILY ADEQUACY: THE ITTLESON CENTER
FAMILY INTERACTION SCALES (BEHRENS ET
AL., 1969)

These scales measure the functioning of family groups by evaluating interpersonal responses of the family as a whole, of the parents as marital and parental pairs, and among the children. The observer visits the family for three hours, including mealtime, and then rates the family on forty-four seven-point scales of family interaction. The forty-four scores are summed to yield a single score to represent family adequacy. The Spearman rank correlation coefficient between scores of two observers of thirteen families was .86.

Independent observation of the families was completed in twenty-two of the twenty-four families, including eleven families of A1 children and eleven families of A2 children (see table 43–7). The families of A1 children showed a significantly higher mean family adsequacy score than did the families of A2 children. ($p < .01$) A majority (64 percent) of the family adequacy scores in the A1 subgroup were higher than the highest score in the A2 subcluster.

PSYCHOPATHOLOGY OF PARENTS

Appraisals of the psychiatric status of the forty-eight parents of the twenty-four children in the present study were made by one psychiatrist who was unaware of the diagnostic subclassification of the children. For judging and classifying the parental psychopathology, the psychiatrist made use of detailed clinical reports of the mental status examination and psychiatric history of each of the parents. The diagnostic criteria and the system of classification were those defined in DSM-III.

Table 43–8 presents the primary diagnoses of the twenty-four parents of the twelve children with the unequivocal diagnosis of Infantile Autism (A1 subgroup) and the twenty-four parents of the remaining children (A2 subgroup).

In the A2 group, there were more mothers with psychosis, either Schizophrenic Disorder or Atypical Psychosis,[3] than among the mothers of A1 children ($p = .04$). None of the fathers in either subgroup had the diagnosis of

---

[3]Atypical psychosis was diagnosed because there were clear symptoms of psychosis, but there was no documented deterioration from previous level of functioning and key symptoms had been manifested as far back as early childhood.

TABLE 43–5

Neurological Status at Admission of Autistic and Less Autistic Children

Diagnosis	Number of children	
	Evidence of neurological impairment	No evidence of neurological impairment
Autistic group (A1)	12	0
Less autistic group (A2)	3	9
	15	9

TABLE 43–6

Socioeconomic Position of Families of Autistic and Less Autistic Children (Hollingshead-Redlich Scale)

Diagnosis	Number of children		
	Upper Class 1, 2	Middle Class 3	Lower Class 4, 5
Autistic group (A1)	3	6	3
Less autistic group (A2)	0	7	5
	3	13	8

TABLE 43–7

Family Scores (Family Interaction Scales) of Autistic and Less Autistic Children

Diagnosis	n	Mean	Standard Deviation
Autistic group (A1)	11	193.4	37.5
Less autistic group (A2)	11	151.0	28.7

psychosis. Sychizotypal disorders occurred with about the same frequency in both subgroups of mothers and fathers. Such schizotypal personality disorders were noted in one third of the A1 subgroup of parents and in a quarter of the A2 subgroup. More generally, the A1 subgroup contained more parents who were free of mental disorders.

LONGITUDINAL DATA

Patterns of longitudinal change are derived on the basis of findings at time of admission to residential treatment, discharge from residential treatment, and last follow-up after discharge from the residence. The children as a whole were 6.9 years of age at admission to treatment, 11.4 years at discharge, and 20.7 years at last follow-up.

Two criteria of normalcy were defined, the first being ego-status ratings 4 and 5 and the second being placement at home in the community rather than in institutions. There were no significant differences between A1 and A2 children in number who attained normalcy either in ego status or in placement at discharge and follow-up (tables 43–10).

It will be recalled that all five children who were rated on admission at level 1, the lowest level of adaptive competence, were found in the A1 group. These children remained at level 1 at discharge and follow-up.

DIAGNOSIS AT LAST FOLLOW-UP EXAMINATION

Diagnostic appraisals of these twenty-four subjects as adults or late adolescents were by psychiatric examination of the subjects aided by interviews of parents and caretakers and psychological tests. Because the DSM-III criteria for schizophrenia include deterioration from a previous level of function and because the DSM-III diagnosis of Infantile Autism, Residual State is not sufficiently descriptive, the simple diagnostic label of Psychosis is used to indicate the presence of delusions, hallucinations, loosening of associations, and illogical thinking as specified in DSM-III (p. 188), an alternative DSM-III label might be Atypical Psychosis (see Table 43–11). Evidence of an organic mental disorder and mental retardation may or may not be present. The DSM-III criteria for nonpsychotic disorders were followed without modification. Using this diagnostic scheme, the A1 subgroup had more subjects who as adults or late adolescents were mentally retarded (A1 = 9, A2 = 2, $p = .02$).

Discussion

In DSM-III, the Pervasive Developmental Disorders include only one subcategory with onset in infancy, namely, Infantile Autism,

TABLE 43–8

Mental Disorders of Parents of Autistic and Less Autistic Children

	Number of Parents			
	Autistic (A1) Children		Less Autistic (A2) Children	
DSM-III CLASSIFICATION	Mother	Father	Mother	Father
Axis I				
Psychoses				
Schizophrenic disorders	—	—	2	—
Atypical psychosis	—	—	3	—
Dysthymic disorder	—	—	1	1
Simple phobia	—	—	1	—
Axis II				
Personality disorders				
Schizoid	—	—	—	1
Schizotypal	3	1	3	1
Mixed				
-including schizotypal	1	3	1	1
-excluding schizotypal	2	1	1	3
Narcissistic	—	—	—	3
Compulsive	1	2	—	—
Passive-aggressive	—	—	—	2
Unspecified	2	1	—	—
Atypical	—	1	—	—
No diagnosis on Axis I or II	3	3	—	—
Total	12	12	12	12

TABLE 43–9

Attainment of Mildly Impaired to Normal Ego Status of Autistic and Less Autistic Children

	Time at which ego status 4,5 was attained			Number of children	
Pattern	Admission	Discharge	Follow-up	Autistic (A1)	Less autistic (A2)
A	no	no	no	8	5
B	no	no	yes	2	4
C	no	yes	no	0	0
D	no	yes	yes	2	3
				12	12

defined by criteria that are in accord with Kanner's (1943) original description. We have questioned whether this diagnostic category encompasses the full range of disorders which heretofore have been included among the infantile psychoses. To answer this question, we applied the DSM-III criteria to twenty-four children who had been classified earlier as instances of infantile psychosis on the basis of the British Working Party criteria (Creak, 1961). These children were representative of the Ittleson Center population of children who had histories of infantile onset of psychosis, but were first admitted to residential care at early school age. They were thus selectively different from children with infantile autism who are more typically brought to psychiatric attention and care within the first thirty months of life.

The diagnosis of Infantile Autism was made only if all six DSM-III criteria were met and only if the criterion of lack of responsiveness (autism) referred to the most extreme and pervasive kind of aloneness, manifested charac-

TABLE 43–10

Home Placement of Austistic and Less Autistic Children

	Time at which placement at home occurred			Number of children	
Pattern	Admission	Discharge	Follow-up	Autistic (A1)	Less autistic (A2)
A	no	no	no	2	4
B	no	no	yes	0	1
C	no	yes	no	4	0
D	no	yes	yes	6	7
				12	12

teristically before thirty months of age. On this conservative basis, half the children in the study were diagnosed as cases of Infantile Autism and designated A1 children. The remaining half of the children, designated A2 children, did not meet all the DSM-III criteria. It was noted that the A2 children were not totally devoid of autistic attributes and, indeed, differed significantly from the A1 children in only the one criterion referring to the most extreme form of social aloofness.

It is concluded that DSM-III does not provide for the full range of pervasive developmental disorders of infantile onset before thirty months of age. The group of children (A2) who show serious and pervasive developmental disorders of infantile onset but who are less severely disordered in social behavior than the group with Infantile Autism (A1) should also be delineated. In addition, this binary classification has practical diagnostic advantages, because a comparison of the A1 and A2 subgroups has resulted in new findings. The A1 and A2 subgroups did not differ in sex, socioeconomic position, and age at which treatment was initiated. Nor, at the time of discharge and at the time of last follow-up, did the two subgroups differ in number attaining normalcy in ego status and in their placement course. However, in comparison to A2 children, A1 children had been diagnosed at an earlier age, were lower in global adaptive capacity (Ego Status at admission), and in verbal and nonverbal aspects of intelligence. More A1 children gave evidence of neurological impairment. The families of A1 children showed more adequate levels of interactional behavior. More mothers of A2 children showed psychoses. A2 parents

also included more mothers and fathers with mental disorders more generally. Finally, as adults the A1 group showed mental retardation. All these differences would support the use of a binary system of classification of the Infantile Onset Pervasive Developmental Disorders.

These findings have theoretical as well as practical clinical import, inasmuch as inferences based on studies of subclasses of children with the diagnosed condition of Infantile Autism should not be generalized to the remainder of children in the larger, generic group with major disorders, hitherto included among the infantile psychoses. This error in generalization may becloud perspective when evaluating

TABLE 43–11

Follow-Up Diagnosis of Autistic and Less Autistic Children

Diagnosis	Autistic (A1)	Less Autistic (A2)
Psychoses	6	3
With Mental Retardation	5	1
Without Mental Retardation	1	2
Personality Disorders	6	9
Schizotypal	2	3
Borderline	0	1
Narcissistic	0	1
Dependent	3	1
Mixed		
Schizotypal & Narcissistic	0	1
Borderline, Schizoid, Paranoid	0	1
Borderline, Antisocial	0	1
Narcissistic, Schizoid	1	0
With Mental Retardation	4	1
Without Mental Retardation	2	8

some apparently discordant findings in the literature of infantile psychosis. One needs to keep in mind that specific samples of children with infantile or early onset psychosis contain varying proportions of at least two subgroups on an apparent continuum: one containing children with strong autistic manifestations and another containing children with less consistent or less severe autistic patterns. Since these two subclasses are found to differ in behavioral, biological, and interactional variables, discrepant experimental findings may represent differences among the study samples in degree of heterogeneity and in proportion of the two subclasses. The part played by such differences in sampling needs, for example, to be weighed in explaining divergences among investigators, in their observations of the psychiatric status of the parents, communication patterns of the parents, and adequacy of families of psychotic children.

To offer one example, Cantwell's studies (Cantwell et al., 1978) of the families of autistic children would seem to contradict the findings

and conclusions of Goldfarb and his colleagues (Behrens and Goldfarb, 1958; Goldfarb, 1961, 1962), based on studies of families of more heterogeneous groups of psychotic children. Quite apart from questions of procedures and controls, it is clear that Cantwell's findings, based on investigations of families of children with Infantile Autism, are not generalizable to the broader and more diverse group of psychotic children observed in the Ittleson sampling.

Finally, it is of interest that the A2 subgroup met the criteria for diagnosis of Childhood Onset Pervasive Developmental Disorders (Subgroup B), except for the age-of-onset requirement. Should further investigation comparing A2 and B subgroups support the finding of no difference between them in basic child and family attributes, then the ambiguous construct of age of onset would not be essential as a criterion for subclassification. In this circumstance, subclassification would merely refer to subclasses of children varying in level of autism.

REFERENCES

American Psychiatric Association (1980). *Diagnostic and Statistical Manual of Mental Disorders*, 3rd. ed. (DSM-III). Washington, D.C.: American Psychiatric Association.

Bartak, L., Rutter, M., and Cox, A. (1975). A comparative study of infantile autism and specific developmental receptive language disorder: I. The children. *British Journal of Psychiatry*, 126:127–145.

Behrens, M. L. and Goldfarb, W. (1958). A study of patterns of interaction of families of schizophrenic children in residential treatment. *American Journal of Orthopsychiatry*, 28:300–312.

Behrens, M.L. et al. (1969). The Henry Ittleson Center Family Interaction Scales. *Genetic Psychology Monographs*, 80:205–295.

Bender, L. (1947). Childhood schizophrenia: Clinical study of one hundred schizophrenic children. *American Journal of Orthopsychiatry*, 17:40–56.

Cantwell, D., Russell, A., Mattison, R., and Will, L. (1979). A comparison of DSM-II and DSM-III in the diagnosis of childhood psychiatric disorders: I. Agreement with expected diagnosis. *Archives of General Psychiatry*, 36:1208–1213.

Cantwell, D. P., Baker, L., and Rutter, M. (1978). Family factors. In *Autism: A Reappraisal of Concepts and Treatment*, ed. M. Rutter and E. Schopler, New York: Plenum.

Creak, M. (1961). Schizophrenic syndrome in child-

hood: Progress report of a working party. *Cerebral Palsy Bulletin*, 3:501–504.

Fish, B. (1977). Neurobiologic antecedents of schizophrenia in children. *Archives of General Psychiatry*, 34:1297–1313.

Goldfarb, W. (1961). *Childhood Schizophrenia*. Cambridge: Harvard University Press.

Goldfarb, W. (1962). Families of schizophrenic children. In *Mental Retardation*, ed. L. C. Kolb et al., *Association for Research in Nervous & Mental Diseases Research Publications*, no. 39. Baltimore: Williams & Wilkins.

Goldfarb, W., Meyers, D. I., Florsheim, J., and Goldfarb, N. (1978). Psychotic children grown up: A prospective follow-up study in adolescence and adulthood. *Issues in Child Mental Health*, 5:105–183.

Kanner, L. (1943). Autistic disturbances of affective contact. *Nervous Child*, 2:217–250.

Kolvin, I., Ounsted, C., Humphrey, M., and McNay, A. (1971). The phenomenology of childhood psychoses. *British Journal of Psychiatry*, 118:385–395.

Mattison, R., Cantwell, D., Russell, A., and Will, L. (1979). A comparison of DSM-II and DSM-III in the diagnosis of childhood psychiatric disorders: II. Interrater agreement. *Archives of General Psychiatry*, 36:1217–1222.

Ornitz, E. M. and Ritvo, E. R. (1976). The syndrome of

autism: A critical review. *American Journal of Psychiatry,* 133: 609–621.

Ornitz, E. M., Guthrie, D., and Farley, A. H. (1977). The early development of autistic children. *Journal of Autism and Childhood Schizophrenia,* 7:207–229.

Potter, H. W. (1933). Schizophrenia in children, *American Journal of Psychiatry,* 12:1253–1270.

Russell, A., Cantwell, D., Mattison, R., and Will, L (1979). A comparison of DSM-II and DSM-III in the diagnosis of childhood psychiatric disorders: III. Multiaxial features. *Archives of General Psychiatry,* 36:1223–226.

Rutter, M. (1972). Childhood schizophrenia reconsidered. *Journal of Autism and Childhood Schizophrenia,* 2:315–337.

44

On the Precursors to Psychic Structure: Notes on the Treatment of a Two-Year-Old Autistic Toddler

Ruth Codier Resch, Ph.D. and Stanley Grand, Ph.D.

The ego is first and foremost a bodily ego.
SIGMUND FREUD

The body, the body ego, and the ego represent a continuum in the transformation from the biology to the psychology of mental growth. The gradual emergence of thought, fantasy, and symbolization—the evolution of personal meaning and its content—from a biological matrix is a uniquely psychoanalytic concept of human development. The "psychological birth of the human infant" proceeds, in our view, through a complex set of changes in which primarily *biological* regulations are gradually transformed into structures and functions that are primarily *psychological.*

Sensory experience—the more or less perceptual aspect of mental representation—persists throughout life and is the moment-by-moment contribution of biology to the continuous stream of mental development. Indeed, infant research is increasingly showing the sophistication of the perceptual and social capacities of the neonate (Bower, 1977; Brazelton, 1973a; Carpenter, 1975) and the enormous importance for later development of these capacities in the micromomentary synchronies of very early dyadic relationships (Beebe and Stern, 1977; Condon and Sander, 1974; Stern, 1983; Wolff, 1963).

Mahler (1958), in a paper highlighting the importance of the early relationship between mother and infant, discussed the biological necessity of the "species-characteristic social symbiosis" between infant and mother. Although the importance of this conception of biosocial symbiosis in her early work was overshadowed by the more recent emphasis on the psychological development of the self representation, we think that this earlier concept of biosocial symbiosis is useful for clinical work with patients exhibiting more primitively organized pathology.

In this paper we distinguish two distinct aspects of the symbiosis by presenting the observation and treatment of a two-year-old toddler having a diagnosis of infantile autism. We describe a biosocial and a psychological aspect of the symbiotic bond. In normal babies the two aspects merge with great rapidity very early in development. However, the distinction between the two has particular importance for both the diagnosis and treatment of certain infant and child pathologies, as well as in later biosocial life crises.

Differentiating the two aspects of the symbiosis has enabled us to conceptualize the extraordinary changes that occurred in this toddler in a very brief time. We trace in those changes the gradual transformation of biological regulations to psychological regulations. We believe that in infantile autism this transformation process has been arrested at a primitive level of biological organization—that is, at an early stage in the symbiosis. Our treatment of this toddler was aimed at establishing or constituting biological regulation so that psychological development could proceed.

The distinction has further significance in allowing us to observe the beginning organization of the body ego, specifically as it is integral to the biosocial phase of the symbiosis. In presenting this unusual treatment we wish to highlight the *con*stitutive nature of work that occurs at the delicate interface between the biosocial and psychological aspects of the symbiosis and to emphasize the relevance to the concept of symbiosis of the bio-organic imperatives of infant immaturity.

Luisa

At our first evaluation of Luisa at twenty-four months of age, she shows almost classically clear symptoms of primary autism in the context of an extensive degree of retardation in functioning and a history of seizure activity. She is already beginning to collect a history of multiple referrals and multiple diagnoses, emphasizing yet again the issue of early psychiatric identification and diagnosis of such children (Call, 1963a, 1963b, 1975, 1977a, 1977b).

In the first four minutes of formal developmental testing, almost all of her major symptoms can be seen. She stares at length and blankly at the bright lights of the video-observation nursery. She does not spontaneously reach for the test toys or brighten with interest in them. She does not look at or show interest in any of the people in the room, including her mother. She assiduously avoids all eye contact. She rubs the backs of her nails (palms up) on any available surface as she wanders aimlessly around the room. Her face contorts into a strange grimace when she oscillates her splayed fingers across the end of a plastic string. Both the face and hand gestures are peculiar, mannered, and repetitive. Apart from these grimaces, her face is steadily and totally deadpan. There are very few flickers of interest and no brightening with emotion at all, either positive or negative.

Her age-equivalent performance on the Bayley Mental Scale of Infant Development (1969) is that of a six and one-half-month-old baby (the age at which her score equals 100). The range of her scores was 4.8 to 12 months.

Neurological examination at the time observed that:

> apart from the lack of speech, milestones all appear to have developed normally. She is hardly able to care for herself at all. There is no undressing, feeding is only done with a bottle, no toilet training. She is said to be hyperactive and destructive. The mother thinks she sees but has doubts about her hearing. She does not gesture when needed, just cries, and the mother somehow understands what she is after. Sleep is normal. Fits . . . started at six months of age . . . occurring three to five times a day, lasting only one to two seconds.

Luisa was hospitalized for three days at the age of 6 months for seizures, the nature of which were undetermined. She was subsequently maintained on medication (currently phenobarbitol, 30 mg., clonazepam, 4.5 mg. daily) and followed neurologically. Her birth and neonatal development are said to have been normal until the first seizure. Gross motor milestones continued to be normal afterward. Cognitive, social, and affective development and self-care were severely delayed. At our initial evaluation, the mother says that Luisa's complete lack of responsiveness and almost total lack of play has been the same for many months.

Luisa's mother is strikingly free of pathology related to this toddler, despite the baby's extreme symptomatology (cf. Mahler, 1952; Rutter, 1965). She is an attractive, vital young woman in her early twenties. She has an older child, a very bright and charming boy who bore testimony to her ability both to produce a normal baby and to mother successfully. The family, however, is not without other major psychological and social stresses; the mother is on a form of welfare, and the father is away "in the Islands."

It was the mother's perseverance in asking questions and requesting more help that resulted in her being evaluated by the senior author. She was remarkably willing to join into the treatment offered her and lent herself unflaggingly and enthusiastically to it. All of which speaks indirectly for her considerable care, patience, and concern for this child.

The pervasiveness of the pathology and the early gross impairment and retardation of function in this two-year-old toddler argue for the diagnosis of Pervasive Developmental Disorder: Infantile Autism (DSM-III 299.0x) associated with infantile seizures and mental retardation (319.0).

The following narratives are based on videotapes of evaluations made at twenty-four months and twice during the early treatment process, at twenty-six and twenty-seven months. The video observations were: play alone, play with mother, and the Bayley Scales of Infant Development.

Observation of Play Alone. Narrative Excerpts[1] Typical of the Fifteen-Minute Video Observation

Luisa sits in a small playpen containing a toy drum, a stuffed animal, and one or two other small toys. Moaning slightly, she alternately gazes at the drum held between her legs and the lights above her. While staring rather vacuously at the lights, she taps on the drum several times with one hand and then pushes it aside. With one hand, Luisa grasps the playpen railing, moans, and pulls herself up. She runs her hand along the top railing, moaning every few seconds; then her hand and gaze drop a few inches to her stomach which she pats several times. She looks up briefly, then shifts her gaze and hand to the buttons on her overalls, which she pulls at a couple of times, and then pats her stomach again.

Luisa takes a few steps, patting herself absentmindedly as she moves and looks down at the

[1]We express our appreciation to Betty Lefer for her care in writing the narrative sections of this paper.

floor. She moves slowly to the side of the playpen, leans over and bangs on the bare wall. She turns suddenly, runs her fingers along the railing and takes a few steps to the other side of the playpen. After a brief visual and tactual examination of the molding on the wall, Luisa runs her hand up and down a railing, her gaze diffuse and directed downward. She turns away and lowers her head to the railing, rubbing her teeth along it for several seconds. Then Luisa straightens up, moves slightly to the side, and turns around. She walks across to the opposite side of the playpen and promptly rubs her teeth along that railing for a bit over ten seconds. She straightens up, takes another step, and lowers her mouth to the railing again, rubbing her teeth back and forth a dozen times (120 seconds).

This segment is representative of the Fifteen-Minute tape; the play is arid for a two-year-old. It is mainly primary circular reactions, that is, actions *on* the body (Piaget, 1936). It has little content and no emotion; it is primarily self-stimulating, but even that aspect is fleeting.

Observations of Play with Mother. Narrative Excerpts Typical of the Fifteen-Minute Video Observation

Mother kneels in front of Luisa, who is seated in the playpen. She speaks softly to Luisa, who begins to cry. Mother leans over into the playpen, singing as she grasps Luisa by the hands and pulls her to a standing position. Luisa's cry becomes a wail, and mother gently pulls Luisa toward her, putting her arms around her daughter. She rubs the back of Luisa's head and Luisa strains to pull away, turning herself around in her mother's arms while continuing to cry. Still holding Luisa, mother talks to her in a soft, singsong voice and pats her on the bottom.

Luisa now stands with her back to her mother, whose hand is around Luisa's waist. Mother picks up a toy and brings it around in front of Luisa, who knocks it to the floor. Mother briefly lets go in order to retrieve the toy, and Luisa's cries escalate again. As mother reapproaches with the toy, Luisa turns to her but does not touch the toy, her cries continuing. Mother picks her up, sits her down, and begins banging on the drum that lies between them. Luisa looks but does not stop crying and does not respond to mother's invitation to play. Mother stops playing with the drum and, instead, sings and claps her hands in front of her daughter's face, about a foot away. Luisa cries louder and looks down and away, but then turns toward mother's smiling face. Crying stops for about five seconds as Luisa focuses on her mother, who continues to sing and clap. Luisa looks downward briefly and mother stops singing and clapping, lowers her head, and says, "Peek-a-boo." Luisa begins to cry again and rubs her fingernails along the edge of the drum. Mother immediately begins to clap again. Luisa looks away, still rubbing and crying, and mother crawls around to the other side of the playpen behind Luisa, calling Luisa's name as she goes. Luisa's cries become more intense as mother sits behind her, calling her name and talking, attempting to get Luisa to turn and look at her. Luisa does not turn around; instead, she cries louder and stares in front of her as mother moves from side to side, still trying to attract her daughter's attention (75 seconds).

Thus, the baby is fretful at the outset, seemingly inconsolable. There is little synchrony between mother and baby. Nothing the mother does attracts, satisfies, or comforts the baby. Nothing in what the baby does cues the mother or communicates to her what can be done. She avoids the mother, screening out stimuli, sometimes frenetically; she refuses everything. The mother, supported by the examiner's request, keeps trying valiantly and fairly flexibly, despite continuous failure and continued distress and avoidance in the baby.

Seven very long minutes later the two of them succeed in engaging in their first game. The mother works very hard for a few seconds of reciprocal play. Encouraged, she tries for more direct face-to-face intimacy. The problem of gaze avoidance is enacted vividly. The baby goes to great lengths to avoid face-to-face gaze. It is the chase-and-dodge sequence of an overstimulated baby that Beebe and Stern (1977) have so beautifully described. For the mother, eye-to-eye gaze is normal, and she seeks it with her baby, finally almost forcibly. Mother pulls Luisa's body around to face her, asking for a kiss and puckering her mouth. Luisa taps her mother's cheek softly at first, increasing pressure until she roughly slaps the mother's face away to the side. We see Luisa's efforts less as dynamic and meaning-laden and more as an organismic sensory protective device, a primitive effort to screen out a sensory field that has too many stimuli.

Luisa's object relations and play lack the essential qualities of the oral phase or of sym-biosis. Using either the psychoanalytic or Piagetian conceptions, Luisa's play is not object-differentiated.

What is also diagnostically striking is the sensoriattentional status of this infant. She mediated sensory input through defocusing and diffusion of her attention. She ignored many stimuli completely (self, things, or mother), as when she stared into space and aimlessly wandered. She modified some stimuli by reducing the amount of direct sensation, as in oblique gaze or rubbing with teeth or fingernails, or by reducing complexity by maintaining part-object perception. Thus, Luisa is predominantly and strikingly hypo-reactive to her environment. Either hypo- or hyperreactivity are, of course, seen in infantile autism and show striking parallels to the sensory-processing deficits seen in the later schizophrenias (Ornitz, 1969).

Shevrin and Toussieng (1965) have argued that sensory dysfunctions, such as we saw in Luisa, may serve as protective mechanisms and are quite different from psychic defense formations. Defense structures are directed against psychic *representations* of instinctual stimulation. Sensory structures, on the other hand, are directed against *real* stimuli, whether inner or outer, and are similar to what Mahler (1952) called "somatic defense mechanisms." We have presented in greater detail elsewhere our view of the aberrant arousal- and attention-regulating processes in this child (Resch et al., 1981).

Thus our treatment strategies, discussed later, are on specific neurosensory dysfunctions and are addressed specifically to the autistic aspect of her diagnosis.

The Biosocial Symbiosis

The biosocial aspect of the symbiosis has to do with survival via bio-organic regulation and the organization of sensation and attention. The bio-organic processes involve the regulation and cycling of the primary bodily functions—breathing, feeding, eliminating, waking, and sleeping. The sensory processes involve the organization of primary sensations

—internal deep sensations, surface sensations in skin, mucous membrane, and surface muscle, relatively distal sensations—sound and sight. The arousal-attentional processes involve the organization of the organism's awareness and mediation of these bio-organic and sensory processes in the promotion of bodily viability and optimum functioning.

These three processes are at birth neither differentiated nor undifferentiated. They are at some level of immaturity of function—or in such cases as this one, of dysfunction. These three classes of process are the biological regulations that are the necessary substrate for psychological regulation being discussed throughout this paper. The critical diagnostic procedures for these processes in this toddler were developmental performance, neuropsychological function, and medical history. These lead to the specification of the biological dysfunctions underlying the autism. In this child they were in the sensory and arousal/attentional processes.

A normal baby is to a very great extent able to participate both in producing stimulation for itself and in regulating much of its own arousal (Brazelton and Als, 1979); Milewski and Siqueland, 1975; Wetherford and Cohen, 1973). What the infant cannot manage for itself, the symbiotic partners must assume *and,* very important, gradually relinquish as the infant gains in competence—or they resume as competency diminishes (in relation to a particular transitory state or to developmental discontinuities). Thus in the immediate neonatal period both the infant and its symbiotic partners function differentially in the mediation of stimulation and arousal.

The goal of the biosocial symbiosis is the achievement of the primary structuring and organization of sensation and attention regulation. The dynamic achievement of this stage is the rudimentary organization of the experience of the body self (that is, the body ego). This rudimentary organization is not, of course, intrapsychic in the representational sense. However, we postulate that it is intrapsychic in the sense of a neurosensory *organization.* That is, the organizing character of ordinarily recurring cycles of sensation and routines in the infant's own body and in the sensory experiences of

the symbiotic partnership promote specificity of sensation (Resc et al., 1983). The accumulation of sensory experiences, of their regulation and increasing organization, together with the infant's attention to them: these constitute the basis for the sensoribiological experience of the body, the rudimentary body image or body self (Grand, 1982).

The normal mothering symbiosis functions to safeguard the infant's efforts at regulation and reciprocal regulation in the symbiotic dyad. This is a critical characteristic of the "optimum facilitating environment" (Winnicott, 1960) in the biosocial phase. Our patient's mother, in the position of attuned regulator, was simply "something there," an aspect of the singular event. She might be thought of as part of the action schema of the toys, or of herself having neither clearly animate nor inanimate status.

The infant's maturational capacity to participate effectively in the resonating characteristics of the symbiosis—and the accumulation of such experiences—then allows for the emergence of the *animate bio-organic other.* Again, the "other" at this stage is not intrapsychic in terms of a mental representation; it is a dynamic sensory representation. We believe that these structuralizing experiences of sensory self and sensory other are the biosocial precursors (substrate) for psychic structure.

THE FUNCTIONING BIOSOCIAL SYMBIOSIS

Observation of Play Alone. Narrative Excerpts Typical of the Fifteen-Minute Video Observations, Two Months into Treatment (Twenty-Six Months).

Luisa is now playing in the open nursery living room, no longer in the playpen. Mother is nearby on the couch; Luisa is deeply concentrated on coherent spontaneous play with toys.

> Luisa bends over to pick up a ball, which she fingers briefly and then drops, lowering herself to the floor to look at another toy—a flower mirror —lying there. She lowers her face to the mirror, then sits up with the toy in one hand, patting it with the other. She jiggles her leg as she looks around the room. She looks down at the flower mirror and runs her fingernails over it briefly. Luisa throws the toy to the floor, leans over, and

bangs on it; she picks it up and tosses it down again, moves toward it to retrieve it. As she touches it, her eyes catch sight of the Busy Box, and she crawls over to it, spins a wheel, and then moves back to the flower mirror. Luisa picks it up and taps on it repeatedly, gazing at it and the objects around her. She throws the flower mirror several feet away from her, sits and looks at it for a few seconds and then crawls over and picks it back up. Luisa stands with it and starts to walk around the room, tapping the toy as she goes. She stops briefly and looks up at the lights, then continues walking and tapping.

As Luisa moves to the edge of the play area, mother leans over and stretches out her arm to stop her. In response, Luisa turns and walks back to the center of the room. She sits down and bangs the toy against the floor, turns to look briefly at mother, and then looks back at the toy (eighty-five seconds).

To be sure, most of the autistic symptomatology is represented even in this brief segment: the wandering, the stare, and the finger rubbing. What is striking is that they are all represented only very briefly and fleetingly, in no way as dominant as they were when we first evaluated her.

The play is now organized; she is able to focus on toys, handle them, explore their sensory qualities. She can move among a number of toys and return to refocus on earlier activities.

Observation of Play with Mother. Narrative Excerpt Typical of the Fifteen-Minute Observation

> Luisa, with toy in hand, sits on the floor as mother kneels beside her and pulls the Busy Box toward them. Mother spins some of the objects and pushes the box in front of Luisa, taking the toy out of her hands. Luisa kicks the Busy Box and leans away; mother sits her back up in front of the box. Luisa leans forward and spins some of the objects in it. Mother leans forward and squeezes the horn, then moves the box closer as Luisa squeezes the horn too. Mother jiggles the arrow, and Luisa reaches out and places her hand on top of it, then makes sweeping moves with her hand, jiggling another object. She leans forward intently and spins a wheel several times. Mother then makes a noise with another object and stands the Busy Box up in front of her daughter. Luis leans forward, spins a wheel, and mother imitates. Luisa then touches another object and, with a rather diffuse gaze, looks toward mother

then back at the box with a more concentrated focus. She does lateral sweeps and spins for about ten seconds before mother leans over, takes Luisa's hand, and rings the bell with it. When mother lets go, Luisa pushes herself away from both mother and the Busy Box. Mother gently moves the toy closer to Luisa, who pounds on a nearby slide but then leans forward and plays again with the box (seventy-five seconds).

Mother is still sometimes abrupt in the things she does and sometimes rather intrusive, but clearly her sensitivity to the baby's pace is mostly synchronous. The baby responds to her cues and gestural "suggestions" for play. When the mother increases the stimulation perhaps too much, the baby is not disrupted, she copes. She maintains or lowers stimulation herself. She sometimes follows the mother's lead. At other times she clearly notices what mother is doing. Luisa is regulating herself and is now able to participate in dyadic regulation.

THE FUNCTIONING PSYCHOLOGICAL SYMBIOSIS

Observation of Play Alone. Narrative Excerpts Typical of the Fifteen-Minute Observation After Another Month of Treatment (Twenty-Seven Months)

In addition to the play alone and play with mother observations, Bayley testing was again done at twenty-seven months. The Mental Developmental Index was still well below 50, but Luisa's age equivalent rose from six and one-half months to nine and one-half months. In this three-month period, she advanced three months. This usually is a normal rate but for Luisa it represented a dramatic acceleration in development. The range of her scores at that time was seven to twelve months. Although her ceiling score did not change, the basal score moved up from 4.8 to 7 months, thus consolidating her range of scores at a higher level.

She was reevaluated at thirty-three months after four treatment sessions and the summer vacation break. (Details of this period can be found in Resch et al., 1981). Her age equivalent at this time was eleven and three quarters months, with a range of scores from 9.1 to 13, reflecting a slight change in ceiling, with a basal shift of four and three quarters months.

At thirty-seven months, she was again reevaluated with no further professional treatment. Mother was in a full-time training program, and Luisa, being cared for by her grandmother, was awaiting placement in a special nursery school. At this time, her age equivalent was thirteen months, range 10.5 to 14.6. Thus the gains made from the relatively brief treatment of the biosocial symbiosis and its dysfunctions were clearly maintained, advanced, and consolidated over time.

Unfortunately, further follow-up in this case was made impossible because of a major illness requiring the senior author to leave institutional practice for a long period of time. Ideally, the treatment of the biosocial symbiosis would have been resumed, tailored at a higher level, and very gradually expanded into a more psychological treatment of the symbiosis.

In the first two minutes, very shortly after she entered the room, Luisa is seen in quite concentrated self-directed play. Secondary circular reactions now dominate, and there is coordination of secondary circular reactions (Piaget, 1924). For the first time, Luisa smiled. Throughout the whole time, her facial expression was lightened, a continuous sweet expression of pleasure.

> Luisa is sitting on the floor surrounded by toys. She leans over to the drum and pulls it toward her, turning it upside down. Looking up at the lights, she briefly drums her fingernails on the drum, then looks back down at it. Luisa turns it over, and two balls roll out the hole on the side. She gets up, picks up one ball and drops it down into the top hole in the drum. She watches as it disappears, and she attempts to put her hand in the hole after it. Although there are people talking around her, Luisa seems not to notice, concentrating intently on the drum and balls.
>
> Luisa picks up the second ball and watches as it spirals down into the drum. She sits up, tips the drum over, and pulls it out of the side hole. She drops it onto the solid side of the drum and watches it roll around. Luisa picks it up, turns the drum over, and drops the ball into the hole. She looks away briefly and then tips the drum over, looks at the side, seeming to search for the ball. It doesn't appear, and Luisa rights the drum, then reaches her hand inside it, tips it over again, looks in the side, rights it again, and searches visually and tactually inside the top hole. After several attempts at sticking her hand into the hole, Luisa

leans back and crawls away. She walks to the edge of the play area, and mother reaches out her arm to stop her; Luisa turns immediately to a new toy (100 seconds).

> Luisa is examining a toy and looks up as someone says something to her mother, who is seated behind Luisa. Luisa turns and crawls over to mother, straining toward her. Mother leans over smiling, touches Luisa's face, blows a kiss, and leans back. Luisa leans forward again and seems to kiss mother's hand (ten seconds).

Observation of Play with Mother. Narrative Excerpts Typical of the Fifteen-Minute Observation

> Mother sits beside Luisa on the floor. The drum is in front of Luisa, and she drops a ball into the hole, then looks down after it. Mother hands Luisa a large bead, and she takes it, looking at it briefly before dropping it into the drum. She again looks into the hole. Mother hands Luisa another bead, and this whole process is repeated twice. Each time, Luisa looks at the bead as she takes it and then looks for it once it has disappeared. The third bead rolls away from Luisa; she looks for it in the drum hole. Mother immediately hands her daughter a fourth bead, which Luisa takes and drops in the hole. Given a fifth bead, she momentarily rubs her fingernails against it, and mother tries to distract her by tapping on the drum. Mother takes the bead from her daughter and brings it close to the drum, showing Luisa what to do with it. When she gives the bead back to her daughter, Luisa runs her fingernails rapidly back and forth against it. Someone says something to mother, who moves over next to Luisa. Luisa looks up with interest and then back down at the bead, which she continues to rub. As mother resettles herself, Luisa drops the bead in the drum (forty-five seconds).
>
> Luisa walks over and squats in front of a toy chime, rubbing her fingernails against the wheels. Mother leans over, spins, and counts again. Luisa looks aside at another toy as mother does this, but mother then takes her hand and moves it to spin the wheel, counting again. Luisa watches the toy as this goes on, but after six spins withdraws her hand and sits back with a tired and glum expression on her face. As mother pulls back, Luisa sits forward with interest, her body at attention, and runs her fingers across the toy. Mother says, "No," and quickly reaches over to guide Luisa's hand again. Luisa pulls back but then leans forward to spin a wheel on the Busy Box in front of her. Mother and Luisa then alternate manipulating various objects on the box, Luisa moving slowly and deliberately (sixty seconds).

Finally, toward the end of the fifteen-minute observation period, Luisa, looking tired, rubs her eyes and slowly crawls a few steps as mother bounces a rubber ball against her. Luisa looks up several times as she is hit, but continues over to the Busy Box and begins to play with it. Mother says something to her, and Luisa looks up, still spinning the ball on the Busy Box. Mother calls her name, and Luisa sits up, looks at her, and briefly rubs her eye as mother rolls the ball to her. From the opposite direction, another ball rolls in front of Luisa, thrown by her brother. Luisa tenses briefly, but then relaxes and looks at the ball her mother holds. The ball is rolled toward her. Luisa lowers her hand from her eye and places both hands on the ball, taps it twice, and rolls it aside, following it with her gaze. Mother pushes it back toward her. Luisa turns her head, begins rubbing her eye again, and rolls the second ball back and forth in front of her until it rolls away (forty seconds).

In their play together, it is still striking that the synchrony of the mother is not entirely smooth. But the synchrony is sufficient to advance their common intentions in play.

At the end of their fifteen-minute play together (actually now a full half hour of intensive play) Luisa is visibly tiring, but she continues scanning the space for what to do next. Modulating herself, she continues to play at a slower pace.

Modulation and screening of stimulation have shifted completely away from their former use of getting rid of stimulation. They are now used partially and selectively in the service of continuation of *her own intentions.* She has now achieved intentionality and self-direction throughout play alone and play with mother—a major hallmark of the stage of secondary circular reactions and of the practicing period of separation-individuation (Mahler et al., 1975). In the normal development of symbiosis in the early months, secondary circular reactions do not yet occur. They occur at "hatching," the transition to the subphase of practicing (Resch, 1979).

The Psychological Symbiosis

The psychological aspect of symbiosis is also concerned with survival, but via the organization of perception and the structuralization of psychological significance—that is, meaning—in the symbiotic partnership. The fundamental task in the psychological symbiosis is to establish and preserve the symbiotic partner intrapsychically—attachment if you will (Ainsworth, 1981; Ainsworth et al., 1981; Bowlby, 1969).

Just as the emergence of focal attention facilitates the awareness of a reciprocating partner, familiarity and gratifying reciprocal play facilitate the recognition of significant objects. The normal infant in reciprocal play with its mother, as well as with inanimate toys, repeatedly engages in primary circular reactions on its own body, and mother's body—feeling, touching, smelling, sucking, hearing, and seeing. Initially organized around the issues of bio-organic regulation (in the biosocial symbiosis), these experiences now gradually become transformed, through practice and emerging competence, into mutually gratifying play—a hallmark of this stage—for example, the playful dyadic gaze (Beebe and Stern, 1977) and familiarity (Haith and Campos, 1977; Piaget 1924).

In the biosocial phase the first representation of the partner was dynamic sensory. Now in the presence of the symbiotic partner the infant shows clear signs of *perceptual recognition* of the object (animate *and* inanimate). With this comes the affect, the sweet smile of pleasure (Spitz, 1959). In this relatively more psychological phase, the sensory representation evolves into a meaning representation. Its significance derives from the linking of recognition and affect.

Through the mother's supportive and validating efforts Luisa was enabled to progress to the stage where she could—herself—construct the inanimate object. *This* baby found the inanimate first, then the animate. We have elsewhere discussed in considerable detail Luisa's unique progress through the earliest construction of inanimate and animate objects [Resch et al., 1981].) It is of some importance to note here that, contrary to normal infant development, Luisa first constructed the inanimate object and then the person. This happened via the sense of instrumentality that was generated by the mother's sensitive and strenuous efforts in taking over the larger share of the symbiosis. So the biosocial symbiosis created a matrix of structuralizing experience that allowed Luisa to differentiate herself from the action of the toys and from the matrix of the biosocial symbiosis itself.

Such differentiating experience then enabled Luisa to make a truly creative discovery. It was *she herself* who made things happen. This sense of instrumentality is the essence of secondary circular reactions. It is also the sensoricognitive aspect of psychological differentiation (Mahler et al., 1975; Resch, 1979).

Treatment of the Biosocial Symbiosis

The hallmarks of traditional psychoanalytic therapy are metaphor, symbol, and meaning. However, in order to function with our very young patient in terms of her developmental status, techniques had to be aimed at the phase of development prior to the emergence of such representational hallmarks— at the "pre-object" phase. But, while our treatment medium was not specifically metaphor, symbol, and meaning, it was developmentally continuous with these representational structures. We conceptualize the treatment within the biosocial dyad as the process by which the representation of the object is transformed from a sensory object to an object of recognition. The mother, by undertaking bio-organic functions for the rudimentary ego in empathic sensitive and concrete forms, engages the baby in a constitutive process. To the extent that the mother is "good enough" (Winnicott, 1960, 1962) at giving herself to the process, she is capable of mediating a functioning biosocial symbiosis. To the extent that a mother in this form of treatment is ambivalent and harbors pathology of her own with regard to the child, even with perseverance and help, a functioning biosocial symbiosis may be hindered from developing and may require maternal psychological treatment quite apart from the baby-mother treatment described here.

In formulating the treatment of this autistic child, two objectives guided our techniques. The first was to organize a reciprocally regulating dyad. The second was to organize sensory perceptual processing structures in the infant capable of resonating with stimuli. To do this we worked in five concrete content areas: (1) momentary and periodic regulation; (2) sensory tactile experience; (3) primary manipulation of objects; (4) restriction of autisms; and (5) generalization to daily functioning. The treatment materials were the baby's range and use of perception, attention, stimulus thresholds, stimulus-modulating mechanisms (Anthony, 1958; Bender, 1947; Bergman and Escalona, 1949; Hutt et al., 1965; Ornitz, 1968a, 1968b, 1969; Ornitz and Ritvo, 1968). The crux of these is their functioning in the dyadic relationship: what each partner effectively brings to the process of pacing, synchrony, and integration on a moment-by-moment basis.

First, we worked with momentary and periodic regulation. Essentially, along with the mother, we played with the child, or tried to. It was as hard for us as it had been for the mother all these months. That difficulty, by the way, is enormously instructive and a touchstone for our own empathy for both mother and child. We intended, by means of play, to enter *with* the mother into this baby's very difficult arena of organism-environment exchange.

We studied intensively the moment-by-moment interplay of the child's attention to objects, her pace, her stimulus thresholds, her fleeting moments of receptivity, and her diffusion of attention. We sought to sharpen and attune the mother's awareness—to make objective for her this baby's attentional behavior, her specific sensory responses and intake patterns. To do this for the mother, we had to pay very close attention to attuning ourselves to Luisa's attention and pace.

Together with the mother, we searched for the baby's momentary rhythms to sense her movements of tentative reciprocation in play. We tried to put our own senses at the service of hers. This meant, on the one hand, being attentive to our own intelligence and, on the other hand, giving our own sensory responsive mechanisms entirely over to her. This is a seesawing process that is extraordinarily taxing with an autistic infant, a process of merging and unmerging with the child, and of being hypervigilant not to override her responses with our own ideas about her.

When Luisa was receptive to the various forms of play but her tolerance seemed to be failing, we introduced periodic "rest" times. We wanted to keep her as "with us" as possible, that is, not to allow her to fully dissociate. We sought to respect her disengagement but not to allow so much disengagement that she would begin staring or wandering. For example, she might lie on the floor while we deeply stroked her body or rubbed her back. We rocked her or swung her gently.

Second, we sought to engage Luisa in full sensoritactile experience, for instance, textures, rubbing, touching, skin-caressing, and pressing body to body. We used a soft fuzzy Teddy bear and had Luisa make long caresses of it with her hand. Her symptom of rubbing the backs of her nails across surfaces indicated some attentiveness to textures and patterns, but she was tactile defensive. We turned Luisa's hand over to the fleshy part of her fingers, being careful to do this initially more stimulating activity briefly and in small amounts. (She resisted having her hands touched, so we had to proceed slowly.)

She liked to press her face against our faces, with soft movements of one face against the other. But this had to be done in a side-to-side position, facing in the same direction (not toward one another) so as not to make eye contact. As in Burlingham's treatment of blind children (1972), we provided long, deep strokes on her body, arms, and legs.

Third, we tried to establish primary manipulations of toys as a prelude to increasing her interest in responding to sights and sounds, and then to an increase in actively producing manipulative play herself. Initially, she was resistant, particularly to having her hands handled; so we touched and moved her hands briefly and as smoothly as possible (continuous with the tactile work). We used ordinary toys: the bear, a chime (Playskool No. 42), a drum with a hole in it for balls (Playskool No. 47), a mirror with a rattle in it (Playskool No. 45), a Busy Box (Fisher Price), and our bodies. We did the actions ourselves, carefully watched the response, and then gently put her hands through the actions and carefully watched the response again. This doing-and-having-baby-do sequence is precisely what a mother of a normal two-to-three month-old baby *automatically* does in introducing and extending tactile and manipulative play. Our work with this child was anything but automatic. We took very much smaller pieces of play, holding, touching, shaking, dropping (instrumentally, as a ball into the drum), and built them slowly into sequences.

When we moved to secondary circular reactions (alloplastic actions on objects), we took up the drumming play that Luisa and her mother had done with so much effort in the first diagnostic session. Then we added dropping balls into the drum. We sought to make these repeated and familiar activities between them—in fact, they are examples of synchronous choreography. Then the mother and child alternated doing—that is, changing leadership in the mutual cueing process.

Fourth, there was a series of restraints that we discussed with the mother. We sought, gently, to discourage Luisa's specific autistic symptoms: the aimless wandering, fingernail- and tooth-rubbing on objects, and staring into space. (For the rationale for these in terms of their function as sensory isolating mechanisms, see Resch et al. [1981]). We asked the mother to refrain from pressing for mutual gaze and certainly to avoid "battles" over it.

Fifth and finally, we worked with the mother to generalize, that is, to do at home what we had learned together. The therapy sessions were intense and intensive; nobody could live that way for any length of time. We gave specific attention to organizing and recasting our work in terms that would fit with the mother's *ordinary routines* with the baby and the rest of her family responsibilities. Consequently, we gave her two or, at best, three specific things to concentrate on during her regular routines, daily or several times a day, for that week. We thereby actively and deliberately made the transfer of insight from the treatment setting to its application in the ordinary, mundane activities of family life.

Discussion

Psychoanalysis is the major developmental theory to address the importance of the organism's biology within its psychology, as well as its reverberations and implications throughout the life cycle. The biological substrate of the neonatal phase has only recently come into prominence through the pioneering work of infant researchers such as Als (1979), Brazelton (1973b, 1981), Sander (1977), Weil (1983), and many others. This, despite the early recognition by Freud (1923) that the core of the ego is the body ego. We now appreciate the enormous effort and sophistication that the normal infant brings to the process of interpersonal regulation and exchange (Brazelton and Als, 1979; Pine, 1981; Sander, 1977; Stern, 1976; Winnicott, 1960). It is this centrality of the intimate mutual exchange between infant and mother, that is, the multilevel biosocial, and psychological exchange, that organizes the core body-ego experiences of the infant and makes possible the emergence of representational structuring.

What biological and behavioral—and even psychoanalytic—rehabilitative treatments have fundamentally lacked in their own efforts in the treatment of childhood autism is a guiding theory regarding the transformation of biopsychological regulation in the intimate mutual exchange between infant and mother—that is, a theory specifically addressing the issues of psychological structure-building within the dyad (Nagera, 1981).

What we wish to highlight here is the extension of psychoanalytic treatment theory down into the neuropsychological and "transformational" aspects of the dyadic symbiosis. In a significant sense, the psychological birth of the human infant coincides with its biological birth; the two-person reciprocating, resonating symbiosis. Biological regulation assumes central salience in earliest neonatal development in the biosocial symbiosis (Brazelton, 1981; Emde, 1983; Greenspan, 1983; Greenspan and Lieberman, 1980; Weil, 1983). They are organized and structured by the biosocial symbiosis. They then become the basis for the dynamic organization of the body self and of the sensory representation of the object. Their special import is *never* fully replaced, however, by psychological regulations. They are rapidly transformed by *psychological significance*—perceptual recognition and affect—in the presence of the

symbiotic partner. The biosocial symbiosis organizes the primitive body-self and the sensory object. The psychological symbiosis organizes the primitive affective social self and the recognized object.

The human capacity to rebalance and to reorganize the biopsychological aspects of the symbiosis continues to reemerge and have adaptive functions throughout the normal life cycle. In a purely practical sense, biology asserts itself regularly in intrusive forms in illness, developmental lags, disabilities, dysfunctions, and finally, aging. The symbiosis is gradually in part replaced by internalized biopsychological regulations. Throughout childhood, the parenting system and, later, social systems function to reinstitute bioregulatory processes during periods of stress—they are specifically tailored to the biopsychological imperatives of the occasion and the developmental level of the person. These more normal rebalancings of the intimate dyadic relationship do not, of course, require the extreme expertise of a Luisa treatment. Yet the dyadic empathy, synchrony, and success of such episodes lay the groundwork for the cumulative experience of body self and body integrity.

Finally, we would like briefly to highlight the relevance of the biosocial symbiosis for the theory of psychoanalytic technique generally. Our conception of the biosocial symbiosis between infant and caregiver(s) is similar to a number of other conceptions of this very early and significant stage in the development of psychic structure. Spitz's *dialogue* (1965), Winnicott's *facilitating environment* (1960, 1962), Masud Khan's *protective shield* (1974) are a few conceptions that cover similar ground. While these analysts do not emphasize nearly so much as we do the reciprocity of the resonating symbiotic dyad, they do emphasize the relevance of the interaction between mother and infant in establishing the earliest roots of psychic structure and the prototypic regulations and controls of drive discharge. From our perspective, such early prototypes have enormous significance for the deeply affective core of human experience and subsequent psychic conflict.

The original failure in the establishment of the reciprocating biosocial interaction between Luisa and her mother represented a developmental failure heavily weighted toward the biological end of a continuum of biopsychological organization. In contrast, when reciprocating interaction is relatively successful, and a smooth transformation into psychic structure occurs, the outcome is heavily weighted toward the psychological end of the biopsychological continuum. We would suggest that between the two there occurs a variety of outcomes in which the relatively incomplete transformation of biological regulations into psychological regulations results in varying degrees of regulatory deficiency, most often characterized by the direct discharge of drive through the body or overt motor action. Thus we suggest that borderline, somatizing, psychosomatic, and acting-out patients all reflect this middle area of the biopsychological continuum where mental struggle and conflict are expressed by a relatively greater emphasis upon and participation in bodily channels of discharge.

It is therefore in this middle area of the continuum of dysfunctional biopsychological organization that therapeutic intervention often requires more emphasis upon *regulation* than upon *explanation*, a therapeutic aspect which was, in an extreme form, the focus of the work with Luisa. Loewald (1960) has described how this aspect of therapeutic intervention, that is, the organizing and regulating aspect, is related to the mother's earliest organization and regulation of the infant's instinctual discharge. We believe that the relevance of the biosocial symbiosis for psychoanalytic technique is in just this regulatory aspect of therapeutic work at the higher levels of psychopathology. Its relevance increases as a function of the extent to which the earliest transformation from biological to psychological regulation failed. From this perspective, then, psychoanalysis as a truly general biopsychological theory may reaffirm in modern terms Freud's significant insight that the ego is first and foremost a body ego.

REFERENCES

Als, H. (1979). Social interaction: Dynamic matrix for dynamic behavioral organization. In *New Directions for Child Development*, ed. I. C Uzgiris. San Francisco: Jossey-Bass.

Anthony, E. J. (1958). An experimental approach to the psychotherapy of childhood: Autism. *British Journal of Medical Psychology*, 31:211–225.

Ainsworth, M. D. (1981). The development of infant-mother attachment. In *Review of Child Development Research*, vol. 3, Chicago: University of Chicago Press.

Ainsworth, M. D., Blehar, M. C., Waters, E., and Wall, S. M. (1981). *The Strange Situation: Observing Patterns of Attachment*. Hillsdale, New Jersey: Lawrence Erlbaum Associates.

Bayley, N. (1969). *Bayley Scales of Infant Development*. New York: The Psychological Corporation.

Beebe, B. and Stern, D. (1977). Engagement-disengagement and early object experiences. In *Communicative Structures and Psychic Structures*, ed. N. Freedman and S. Grand. New York: Plenum.

Bender, L (1947). Childhood schizophrenia: Clinical study of one hundred schizophrenic children. *American Journal of Orthopsychiatry*, 17:40–56.

Bergman, A. and Escalona, S. (1949). Unusual sensitivities in very young children. *The Psychoanalytic Study of the Child*, 3/4:333–352. New York: International Universities Press.

Bower, T. G. R. (1977). *A Primer of Infant Development*. San Francisco: W. H. Freeman.

Bowlby, J. (1969). *Attachment and Loss*, vol. 1, *Attachment*. New York: Basic Books.

Brazelton, T. B. (1973a). *Neonatal Behavioral Assessment Scale*. Philadelphia: J. B. Lippincott.

Brazelton, T. B. (1973b). Introduction. In *Organization and Stability of Newborn Behavior. Monographs of the Society for Research in Child Development*, vol. 43, nos. 5–6, ed. A. J. Sameroff. Chicago: Society for Research in Child Development.

Brazelton, T. B. (1981). Precursors for the development of emotions in early infancy. In *Theory, Research and Experience*, vol. 2, ed. R. Plucik and H. Kellerman. New York: Academic Press.

Brazelton, T. B. and Als, H. (1979). Four early stages in the development of mother-infant interaction. *The Psychoanalytic Study of the Child*, 34:349–369. New Haven: Yale University Press.

Burlingham, D. T. (1972). *Psychoanalytic Studies of the Sighted and the Blind*. New York: International Universities Press.

Call, J. (1963a). Interlocking affective freeze between an autistic child and his "as-if" mother. *Journal of the American Academy of Child Psychiatry*, 2:319–344.

Call, J. (1963b). Prevention of autism in a young infant in a well-child conference. *Journal of the American Academy of Child Psychiatry*, 2:451–459.

Call, J. (1975). A quiet crisis. In *Emergencies in Child Psychiatry*, ed. G. Morrison. Springfield, Illinois: Charles C Thomas.

Call, J. (1977a). Autistic behavior in infants and young children. In *Practice of Pediatrics,* vol. 1. Hagerstown Maryland: Harper & Row.

Call, J. (1977b). Psychologic and behavioral development of infants and children. In *Practice of Pediatrics,* vol. 1. Hagerstown, Maryland: Harper & Row.

Carpenter, G. (1975). Mother, face and the newborn. In *Child Alive,* ed. R. Lewin. London: Temple Smith.

Condon, W. S. and Sander, L. W. (1974). Neonate movement is synchronized with adult speech: Interactional participation and language acquisition. *Science,* 183:99–101.

Emde, R. N. (1983). The prerepresentational self and its affective core. *The Psychoanalytic Study of the Child,* 38:165–192. New Haven: Yale University Press.

Freud, S. (1923). The ego and the id. *Standard Edition,* vol. 19, ed. J. Strachey. London: Hogarth Press, 1961.

Grand, S. (1982). The body and its boundaries: A psychoanalytic view of cognitive process disturbances in schizophrenia. *International Review of Psycho-Analysis,* 9:327–342.

Greenspan, S. I. (1983). Disorders and preventive intervention of affective development in infants. Presented at the Conference on Affective Development, Harvard University, Boston, Massachusetts.

Greenspan, S. I. and Lieberman, A. F. (1980). Infants, mothers and their interaction: A quantitative clinical approach to developmental assessment. In *The Course of Life: Psychoanalytic Contributions Toward Understanding Personality Development,* vol. 1: *Infancy and Early Childhood,* ed., S. I. Greenspan and G. H. Pollock. Washington, D.C.: Government Printing Office.

Haith, M. and Campos, J. (1977). Human Infancy. *Annual Review of Psychology.* 28:251–293.

Hutt, S. J., Hutt, C., Lee, D., and Ounsted, C. (1965). A behavioral and electroencephalographic study of autistic children. *Journal of Psychiatric Research,* 3:181–197.

Khan, M. (1974). The concept of cumulative trauma. In *The Privacy of the Self,* New York: International Universities Press.

Loewald, H. W. (1960). On the therapeutic action of psychoanalysis. *International Journal of Psycho-Analysis,* 41:16–33.

Mahler, M. (1952). On child psychosis and schizophrenia: Autistic and symbiotic psychosis. *The Psychoanalytic Study of the Child,* 7:206–305. New York: International Universities Press.

Mahler, M. (1958). Autism and symbiosis, two extreme disturbances of identity. *International Journal of Psycho-Analysis,* 39:77–83.

Mahler, M., Pine, F., and Bergman, A. (1975). *The Psychological Birth of the Human Infant.* New York: Basic Books.

Milewski, A. and Siqueland, E. R. (1975). Discrimination of color and pattern novelty in one-month human infants. *Journal of Experimental Child Psychology,* 19:122–136.

Nagera, H. (1981). *The Developmental Approach to Childhood Psychopathology.* New York: Jason Aronson.

Ornitz, E. M. (1968a). Perceptual inconstancy in early infantile autism. *Archives of General Psychiatry,* 18:76–98.

Ornitz, E. M. (1968b). The auditory evoked response in normal and autistic children during sleep. *Electroencephlography and Clinical Neurophysiology,* 25:221–230.

Ornitz, E. M. (1969). Disorders of perception common to early infantile autism and schizophrenia. *Comprehensive Psychiatry,* 10:259–274.

Ornitz, E. M. and Ritvo, E. R. (1968). Neurophysiologic mechanisms underlying perceptual inconstancy in autistic and schizophrenic children. *Archives of General Psychiatry,* 19:22–27.

Piaget, J. (1924). *The Construction of Reality in the Child.* New York: Basic Books, 1954.

Piaget, J. (1936). *The Origins of Intelligence in Children.* New York: International Universities Press, 1952.

Pine, F. (1981). In the beginning: Contributions to a psychoanalytic developmental psychology. *International Journal of Psycho-Analysis,* 8:15–33.

Resch, R. C. (1979). Hatching in the human infant as the beginning of separation-individuation. *The Psychoanalytic Study of the Child,* 34:421–441. New Haven: Yale University Press.

Resch, R. C., Grand, S., and May, M. (1983). Eye, hand, and mother. Presented at the Seventh Biennial Meeting of the International Society for the Study of Behavioral Development, Munich, West Germany, August 1983.

Resch, R. C., Grand, S., and Meyerson, K. (1981). From the object to the person: A case of infantile autism treated at two years of age. *Bulletin of the Menninger Clinic,* 45:281–306.

Rutter, M. (1965). The influence of organic and emotional factors on the origins, nature and outcome of childhood psychosis. *Developmental Medicine and Child Neurology,* 7:518–528.

Sander, L. W. (1977). Regulation of exchange in the infant caretaker system: A viewpoint on the ontogeny of "structures." In *Communicative Structures and Psychic Structures,* ed. N. Freedman and S. Grand. New York: Plenum.

Shevrin, H. and Toussieng, P. (1965). Vicissitudes of the need for tactile stimulation in instinctual development. *The Psychoanalytic Study of the Child,* 20:310–339. New York: International Universities Press.

Spitz, R. (1959). *A Genetic Field Theory of Ego Formation.* New York: International Universities Press.

Spitz, R. (1965). *The First Year of Life.* New York: International Universities Press.

Stern, D. N. (1976). Issues in early mother-child interaction. In *Infant Psychiatry: A New Synthesis,* ed., E. N. Rexford, L. Sander, and T. Shapiro. New Haven: Yale University Press.

Weil, A. (1983). Variations of affective development in infants. Presented at the Conference on Affective Development, Harvard University, Boston, Massachusetts, May 1983.

Wetherford, M. and Cohen, L. (1973). Developmental changes in infant visual performance for novelty and familiarity. *Child Development,* 44:415–424.

Winnicott, D. W. (1960). Ego distortion in terms of true and false self. In *The Maturational Processes and the Facilitating Environment.* New York: International Universities Press.

Winnicott, D. W. (1962). Ego integration in child development. In *The Maturational Processes and the Facilitating Environment.* New York: International Universities Press.

Wolff, P. (1963). Observations on the early development of smiling. In *Determinants of Infant Behaviour,* vol. 2, ed. B. M. Foss. London: Methuen.

45

An International Survey of Mental Health Professionals on the Etiology of Infantile Autism

Victor D. Sanua, Ph.D.

My purpose in this paper is to examine the causes attributed to infantile autism by psychiatrists, psychologists, and other professionals in the United States and Europe.

There is an extensive literature of studies conducted in the Western world, as well as in developing countries (Erinosko and Ayonrinde, 1978); Gallagher, 1977; Graves, 1971; Jaeckel and Weiser, 1970; Leighton et al., 1963; Lemkau and Crocetti, 1962; Nunnally, 1961; Rogan et al., 1973; Townsend, 1975, 1978) on the opinions held by laymen as well as the mental health workers on the etiology of mental illness, and specifically schizophrenia, but no surveys on infantile autism have ever been conducted.

A distinction must be made here between infantile autism, as described by Kanner (1943, 1973), and childhood schizophrenia. The general view is that the illness starts so early in life that environmental factors can play only a minor role. However, during the past decade William James's notion that the baby is a "blooming, buzzing bundle of confusion" has been weakened by the studies of developmental psychologists and psychiatrists. Their research has discovered a high sensitivity in ne-

onates soon after birth (Klaus and Kennell, 1982; Sanua, 1981b).

An intensive review of the literature revealed that there are eleven major etiological factors that could be implicated in infantile autism. To these eleven, I have added a twelfth one, the cultural factor (see Sanua, 1981a, b), which is scarcely mentioned in the literature.

Procedure

Approximately 500 questionnaires were mailed to psychiatrists, psychologists, and other professionals (speech therapists, teachers, social workers) who were attached to institutions and treated autistic children or to professionals who had published within the last five years. The basic aim was to discover the relative importance that these professionals attached to the etiology of infantile autism. The questionnaire also included other items about infantile autism which have remained polemical until today, such as the socioeconomic status and the intelligence of the parents of these autistic children, whether the illness is a variant of childhood schizophrenia, the autistic child's ranking among his siblings, the intactness of his perceptual abilities, and so forth.

The present analysis is based upon 280 questionnaires which were returned from the three groups of professionals in two major geographical areas, the United States and Europe. Respondents from other areas were too few in number to make any kind of analysis meaningful at the present time.

The twelve possible causes could be reduced to being placed in three major categories, as follows: biological or genetic (organic, genetic, constitutional, or metabolic factors); environmental in a physical sense (birth complications, viral infection, pollution, dietary hazard, receptive disorder); and environmental in a social sense (parental psychopathology, disturbed family interaction, deficient mother-child relations, cultural factors). Geographical differences on one etiology from each of the three major categories will be analyzed.

ORGANIC FACTORS

An analysis of the responses on the organic factors in the etiology of infantile autism elicited one dominant opinion among the professionals in the United States, as can be seen from table 45–1.

If we combine "somewhat important" and "very important" responses in the United States, we find that 97 percent of psychiatrists, 86 percent of psychologists, and 83 percent of other professionals believe that infantile au-

tism is organically determined. There is, however, a higher percentage of psychologists and other professionals who feel that organic factors are "very important" compared to psychiatrists, and the differences are significant. Europeans seem to attach less importance to the organic etiology of infantile autism.

One general conclusion that can be drawn from these findings and that was found to be consistent in the rest of the study is that there is a greater similarity of opinions among different professionals in the United States than with their respective counterparts in Europe. Thus discipline does not seem to play any major role in influencing one's thinking on the subject of infantile autism. It should be added that psychologists and other professionals, particularly in the United States, tend to be more organically minded than psychiatrists.

The insistence on the organic etiology of infantile autism also applies to adult schizophrenia. Bleuler (1978) found that "many clinicians and researchers are fully convinced that primary physical disorders (functional and structural) constitute the most essential onset conditions for schizophrenia, although they are unable to identify any clear symptoms indicating such supposed disorders" (p. 447).

BIRTH COMPLICATIONS

Table 45–2 provides in percentages the responses obtained on this specific question. More psychiatrists and psychologists in the United States subscribed to this factor than

TABLE 45–1

Opinions on Organic Etiology of Infantile Autism

	Psychiatrists		Psychologists		Other Professionals	
	U.S.A.	Europe	U.S.A.	Europe	U.S.A.	Europe
Organic Factor:	(in percentages)		(in percentages)		(in percentages)	
Did not answer	3	16	7	6	13	26
Not Important	0	21	7	11	4	3
Somewhat Important	35	41	8	47	13	42
Highly Important	62	22	78	36	70	29
$N =$	31	63	45	36	45	31
$\chi^2 =$	16.18		17.69		15.42	

the "other professional" group. The largest difference between the professions is to be found between psychiatrists in the United States and psychiatrists in Europe. By combining "very important" and "slightly important," we find 81 percent of the former group and 47 percent of the latter, ($X^2 = 11.6$) who believe infantile autism may be caused by birth complications. There was no statistical significance between psychologists and other professionals in the United States and their European counterparts.

PARENTAL PSYCHOPATHOLOGY

In view of the strong biological bias found in the earlier questions, it is not surprising to find a de-emphasis on the importance of parental pathology among all of the professionals in the United States.

As can be seen from table 45–3, psychologists were most numerous in indicating that

parental psychopathology had little to do with infantile autism. Following a similar pattern, European professionals of the three groups tended to attribute to parental pathology a greater degree of importance than their counterparts in the United States.

Discussion

The general finding of this international survey is that more professionals in the United States, irrespective of discipline, are convinced that infantile autism is caused primarily by *genetic/organic* factors than their European counterparts, who should historically, have a stronger organic tradition.

Professionals in the United States give priority to organic factors, followed by constitutional factors, genetic factors, and metabolic disorders. An analysis of the differences in responses on *environmental factors,* such as birth

TABLE 45–2

Opinions on Birth-Complication Etiology

	Psychiatrists		Psychologists		Other Professionals	
	U.S.A.	Europe	U.S.A.	Europe	U.S.A.	Europe
Birth Complications:	(in percentages)		(in percentages)		(in percentages)	
Did not answer	6	33	10	17	15	40
Not important	13	20	11	22	35	15
Somewhat important	65	37	52	50	40	30
Highly important	16	10	27	11	10	15
$N =$	31	63	45	36	45	31
$X^2 =$	11.6		N.S.		N.S.	

TABLE 45–3

Opinions on the Parental Psychopathology Etiology

	Psychiatrists		Psychologists		Other Professionals	
	U.S.A.	Europe	U.S.A.	Europe	U.S.A.	Europe
Parental Psychopathology:	(in percentages)		(in percentages)		(in percentages)	
Did not answer	6	22	4	16	16	36
Not important	58	24	70	34	47	29
Somewhat important	20	37	22	34	33	19
Highly important	16	17	4	16	4	16
$N =$	31	63	45	36	45	31
$X^2 =$	17.33		11.72		N.S.	

complications, viral infection, pollution, and receptive language problems, shows again that professionals in the United States tend to give more importance to these factors than their European counterparts.

It is only when we deal with *parental psychopathology* that we find a reversal in trends. If we combine the "somewhat important" and "highly important," 35 percent of psychiatrists in the United States and 54 percent of psychiatrists in Europe think that parental psychopathology may be a factor in infantile autism. For psychologists, the percentages were 26 percent and 50 percent respectively. No difference was found when "other professionals" in the United States and Europe were compared.

There are some contradictions in the findings. Although 97 percent of the psychiatrists in the United States think that organic factors are "somewhat" and "highly important" in causing infantile autism, 36 percent indicated that parental psychopathology might have some influence on the illness. Thus, while almost all the psychiatrists subscribe to an organic origin of the illness, about one third are not willing to discount the parental contribution completely.

This widespread belief in the organic etiology of infantile autism among professionals in the United States, in spite of the limited evidence (see Sanua, in press) could be attributed to the fact that the few researchers in the United States who have devoted their investigations to this field are exclusively organic in orientation. For example, Edward Ritvo, professor of psychiatry at the University of California in Los Angeles and at one time Chairman of the Professional Board of the National Society for Autistic Children, does not seem to differentiate in his research between children with Kanner's syndrome and other childhood psychoses. Ritvo has been criticized

(Cox et al., 1975, p. 155) for including in a sample of autistic children a "proportion of children with severe mental retardation and overt neurological disorders." In an earlier study Ritvo (Ornitz and Ritvo, 1968) indicated that they considered early infantile autism, symbiotic psychosis, and some cases of childhood schizophrenia, as well as cases of atypical development, all variants of the same disease.

Another investigator who has had a great deal of influence in the field is Eric Schopler, the current editor of the *Journal of Infantile Autism and Developmental Disorders,* who includes within the rubric of infantile autism other types of children's disturbances. The following quotation (Schopler et al., 1980) illustrates our point:

> The resulting instrument was initially called the *Childhood Psychosis Rating Scale* (CPRS). Because our scale reflected a broader conceptualization than Kanner's classic definition of autism, we had consciously chosen the term psychosis rather than autism, so as to minimize confusion. However, in light of increasing evidence that the definition of autism has expanded and is no longer restricted to Kanner's use of the term, we now call our instrument the *Childhood Autism Rating Scale.* (p. 92; author's italics)

Using Rimland's Check List (1968), which is very close to Kanner's criteria, Schopler's group (1980) found that out of the 450 cases of children in their sample only eight were considered autistic.

Thus, professionals on each side of the Atlantic, irrespective of discipline, seem to be influenced by different ideologies when they think of the causes of infantile autism. While journal articles and extended reviews (DeMyer et al., 1981) seem to support the organic point of view in the United States, European professionals tend to be either noncommittal (large number of no responses) or more flexible about the causes of infantile autism.

REFERENCES

Bleuler, M. (1978). *The Schizophrenic Disorder: Long-Term Patient and Family Studies.* New Haven: Yale University Press.

Cox, A., Rutter, M. Newman, S., and Bartak, L. (1975).

A comparative study of infantile autism and specific developmental receptive language disorders. II. Parental characteristics. *British Journal of Psychiatry,* 126:146–159.

De Myer, M. K., Hingtgen, J. N., and Jackson, R. K. (1981). Infantile autism reviewed: A decade of research. *Schizophrenia Bulletin,* 7:388–451.

Erinosko, O. A. and Ayonrinde, A. (1978). A comparative study of opinion and knowledge about mental illness in different societies. *Psychiatry,* 41:403–410.

Gallagher, B. J. (1977). The attitudes of psychiatrists toward etiological theories of schizophrenia. *Journal of Clinical Psychology* 33:100–103.

Graves, G. D., Krupinski, J., and Stoller, A. (1971). A survey of community attitudes towards mental illness. *Australian and New Zealand Journal of Psychiatry,* 5:18–28.

Kanner, L. (1943). Autistic disturbances of affective contact. *Nervous Child,* 2:217–250.

Kanner, L. (1973). *Childhood Psychosis.* New York: John Wiley.

Klaus, M. and Kennel, J. (1982). *Maternal-infant bonding.* St. Louis: C.V. Mosby.

Jaeckel, M. and Wieser, S. (1970). *Das bild des geisteskranken in der offentlichkeit.* Stuttgart: George Thieme Verlag.

Leighton, A. H. et al. (1963). *Psychiatric Disorder among the Yoruba.* New York: Cornell University Press.

Lemkau, P. V. and Crocetti, G. M. (1962). An urban population opinion and knowledge about mental illness. *American Journal of Psychiatry,* 118:692–700.

Nunnally, J. (1961). *Popular Conceptions of Mental Health.* New York: Holt, Rinehart & Winston.

Ornitz, E.M. and Ritvo, E. R. (1968). Neurophysiologic mechanisms underlying perceptual inconstancy in autistic and schizophrenic children. *Archives of General Psychiatry,* 19:22–28.

Rimland, B. (1968). Importance of accurage diagnosis stressed: Development of Form E-2. *Acta Paedopsychiatrica,* 35:146–160.

Ritvo, E. R. et al. (1971). Social class factors in autism. *Journal of Autism and Childhood Schizophrenia,* 1:297–310.

Rogan, E. N., Dunham, H. W., and Sullivan, T. M. (1973). A world-wide transcultural survey of diagnostic, treatment and etiological approaches in schizophrenia. *Transcultural Psychiatric Research Review,* 10:107–110.

Rutter, M. and Garmezy, N. (1983) Developmental Psychopathology. In *Handbook of Child Psychology,* ed. P. Mussen. New York: John Wiley.

Sanua, V. (1981a). Autism, childhood schizophrenia and culture: A critical review of the literature. *Transcultural Psychiatric Research Review.* 18:165–181.

Sanua, v. (1981b) Cultural changes and psychopathology in children: With special reference to infantile autism. *Acta Paedopsychiatrica,* 47:133–142.

Sanua, V. (1983a) The sociocultural aspects of infantile autism: A neglected area. In *Problems and Theory in Developmental Psychology,* ed. Marguerite F. Levy. New York: Irvington Publishers.

Sanua, V. (1983b) Infantile autism and childhood schizophrenia: Review of the issues from the sociocultural point of view. *Social Science and Medicine,* 17:1633–1651.

Sanua, V. (In press). L'étiologie organique de l'autisme (Syndrome de Kanner): Faits scientifiques ou opinions? *Revue Française de Neuropsychiatrie de l'Enfance et de l'Adolescence.*

Schopler, E. Reichler, R. J., Devellis, R. F. and Daly, K. (1980). Toward objective classification of childhood autism: Childhood Autism Rating Scale (CARS) *Journal of Autism and Developmental Disorders,* 10:91–103.

Townsend, J. M. (1975). Cultural conceptions of mental illness. *Journal of Nervous and Mental Disease,* 160:409–421.

Townsend, J. M. (1978). *Cultural conceptions and mental illness: A comparison of Germany and America.* Chicago: University of Chicago Press.

46

Object Relations Disturbance in the First Two Years of Life: A Preliminary Report

Fiffi Piene, Ph.D. and Harriet Simonsen, M.D.

In recent years we have been seeing with increasing frequency a kind of developmental disturbance in children, usually leading to restlessness and learning difficulties. The development of concept formation and thinking ability in these children is retarded when compared to the development of their motor activity and their abilities to cope with practical tasks. Psychotherapy demonstrates a special pathology, and long-term treatment is necessary, for the foundation of the developmental disturbance seems to have been laid down in the first years of life.

A pilot study of a number of mother/child pairs gave us some clues regarding the connection between the child's uneven development and the emotional disturbance in the mother-child relationship during the child's second year of life. On the basis of this information we have instituted a special program for the treatment of such children in a day-care setting, and we have begun an investigation of the early development of object relations in these children. Currently, ten children from one to two years of age are in treatment. We have followed them from their initial evaluation, through the course of their psychotherapy and

in the day-care program, which they attend simultaneously, using direct observation and videotape recording as the major methodological tools.

The theoretical basis for the project is provided by the theories and studies of Margaret Mahler (Mahler et al., 1975), the main hypothesis being that these children do not negotiate the rapprochement phase in the usual way. As the work has progressed, our studies of the pathology evident in the rapprochement phase have led us to focus more closely on the preceding practicing period.

According to Mahler, a special link has been established between the mother and the child during the practicing period. We have come to look at that link as an elastic cord that can become longer and shorter as necessary. Children of that age (roughly nine to eighteen months) are occupied with the investigation of the world and the things they see. At the same time, they need the mother as a source of the reinforcement they must have in order to go out into the world again.

In the children we have been observing, the elastic cord seems to function very poorly between mother and child, or even to be nonexistent. For example, when one mother takes her little son off her lap and puts him on the floor, she seems no longer to exist for him, as if out of sight were out of mind. He does not do anything to diminish the distance between them. He uses neither his eyes to check where she is, nor his voice to make her notice him, nor does he react to her voice. He does not even react when she leaves the room or when she re-enters it.

The normal reaction of a child this age to the mother's leaving the room has been termed *low-keyedness* (Mahler and McDevitt, 1968). The child's mood becomes more subdued, there is diminished interest in the surroundings, as the child is apparently preoccupied with intra-psychic images, presumably those of the mother. One may view these developments as the beginning of concept formation, of imagination and speculation. Children who do not react in this way do not have this developmental possibility.

The patients in our project do not seem to use their mother as a "home base." Their mothers are not the center of gravity around whom their whole world circles. The mother does not become the stable safety factor with whom feelings and experiences are shared. As a consequence of this lack of interest in the mother, the child receives considerably less emotional feed-back from the mother. The mirroring between child and mother is missing. This appears to result in a defective development of the sense of self, or the mental self-representation. We believe this defect interferes with the child's abilities to retain new experiences and may result in learning difficulties, among other things. When the center of orientation is missing, the child's world becomes disorganized.

According to our observations, the child seems to be looking for something to fill a mental emptiness. The child constantly seeks out new types of stimuli, leading to a particularly intense development of curiosity. However, these children are often very restless. It is as if inanimate objects take the place of the mother in the child's inner world. Consequently, important emotions are linked with experiences with such objects and provide a kind of learning that these children can retain. Coping becomes important and seems to be a major source of joy and satisfaction to them. Thus they often become very skilled in handling things and in making them work: motor activity and body mastery often seems to be relatively advanced. Interest in these inanimate objects is maximal when the objects are in motion, and moving persons also attract their attention.

In summary, it seems that from an early age, these children strive to be self-contained. In the practicing period they withdraw from the mother to such a degree that they are unable to return to her in the subsequent rapprochement period. They try to develop without interaction with the mother. In general the process of differentiation seems to be less affected than the process of individuation, which may be defective. Although the ego capacities needed for skillful handling of objects and for action seem to develop well, our surmise is that the child's inner world is not inhabited sufficiently by human introjects. We conjecture that this kind of development will probably result in individuals who are dependent on and occupied with inanimate objects and actions, while the ability to elaborate deep and close human relationships will be faulty.

REFERENCES

Mahler, M. S., Pine, F., and Bergman, A. (1975). *The Psychological Birth of the Human Infant.* New York: Basic Books.
Mahler, M. S. and McDevitt, J. B. (1968). Observations on adaptation and defense *in statu nascendi:* Developmental precursors in the first two years of life. *Psychoanalytic Quarterly,* 37:1–21.

47

Infantile Origins of Disturbances in Sexual Identity

Herman Roiphe, M.D. and Eleanor Galenson, M.D.

Sexual perversions, which are often accompanied by a florid and frequently bizarre distortion of sexual identity, have attracted the attention of psychoanalytic and psychiatric investigators for the better part of this century. Many psychoanalysts agree with Freud and Bak that the dramatized or ritualized denial of castration is the central core of all perversions and that this denial is acted out through the regressive revival of the fantasy of the maternal phallus (Freud, 1905, 1923, 1927, 1938; Bak, 1968). The psychoanalytic study of the perversions, particularly that of fetishism, has increasingly implicated preoedipal factors as being responsible for the perversions. Abraham, as early as 1910, stressed the importance of the sadomasochistic elements. Gillespie (1940) pointed to important oral factors in his patients. Bak (1953) described disturbances in the early mother-child relationships and unusually strong separation anxiety in his cases.

In a series of papers on fetishism, Greenacre, (1953, 1955, 1960) pointed to disturbances in the first eighteen months of life which interfered with the child's ability to form a stable image of the body and, by bringing about complementary disturbances in the phallic phase, resulted in an exaggeration of the castration complex. According to Greenacre, the very young have more trouble in establishing an image of their genitals than of most other parts of the body. "Normally" she states,

the child's concept of the genital area becomes consolidated during the phallic phase, due to an increase in spontaneous endogenous sensations arising at that time. But when disturbances occur in the pregenital phase, such as a mother who is not good enough or an infant so impaired by injury, illness, or congenital defect that no mother can be good enough, the body-disintegration anxiety from these earlier phases combines with the overly strong castration anxiety of the phallic phase and depletes rather than reinforces the child's sense of sexual identity. (pp. 191–192)

The contributions we have mentioned have come almost exclusively from reconstructions of infantile development gained from the analysis of adult patients. Over the last several years there have been efforts to integrate clinical experience with the findings of psychoanalytically informed longitudinal studies of early development gained from direct child observations (Mahler et al, 1975; Roiphe and Galenson, 1981). In this paper we attempt to trace the possible effects of severe preoedipal castration reactions on the subsequent drive organization and on the development of self and object relatedness, ego organization, and their implications for later perverse development.

Every infant in the second half of the first year has the developmental task of psychologically containing the consequences of the recognition of its own separateness. This differentiation process (Mahler et al., 1975) results in a whole new organization of not only object relatedness but of the sexual and aggressive drives as well. The differentiation process is such that the infant now directs hostile aggressive impulses toward the very same object who is loved out of need. The stage has been set for the emergence of the infant's primary ambivalence to the external object world. According to Freud (1920), this state of affairs is complicated by the tendency of the aggressive drive at this point in development to annihilate the self- and object representation and to shatter the cohesiveness of the ego. The whole thrust of development from this point on must be to contain the disruptive aggressive force while preserving the basic attachment to the external object world. It has seemed useful to us to suggest that the optimal developmental strategy is to establish discrete channels for discharging aggressive and libidinal impulses and ultimately to develop ego structures which serve to transform the very nature and aims of the sexual and aggressive drive so that there can be a synthesis of the hostile, aggressive self and the loving self as well as the complementary integration of the bad, hated object and the good, loved object, that is, the consolidation of self and object constancy which normally takes place during the third year (*Roiphe,* 1979).

In this general dynamic context we regularly see in rapid sequence in the course of normal development, the emergence of the anal and early genital zone arousal. In the second year the two parallel zonal vectors, anal and early genital, become increasingly important in the normal temporary splitting of the primary ambivalence. The anal zone by virtue of its functional characteristics, fullness and loss, is ideally suited in some circumstances to channel certain feelings and experience having to do with the mother of separation. Consequently the anal zone may provide a means by which anger at the object may be expressed. The early genital zone may serve preponderantly as a channel for the more purely libidinal attachment to the object in that the child actively produces warm, good feelings which were earlier only passively experienced through the nurturing maternal care. These two zones then serve as body nuclei around which coherent islands of mental, ideal schemata of the good and bad object gradually consolidate. Combinations, of course, occur as development proceeds, as in the appearance of anal erotism.

In the beginning the early genital sexual development is the same for boys and girls. In the first months of the second year, generally between fifteen and nineteen months, there is normally an upsurge in genital self-manipulation as a consequence of the specific endogenous responsiveness of the genital zone. The masturbation seems at the outset to be object directed; the child often engages the mother visually as he or she smiles with pleasure. As the masturbatory pattern becomes more organized the child seems to become more withdrawn during self-manipulation. The gaze turns inward and the child appears to be engaged in a feeling-fantasy of closeness to the mother. This latter inference seems particularly fitting because the child is not uncommonly observed to use either bottle or transitional objects with which to masturbate.

An important and almost ubiquitous concomitant of the early genital zone arousal is the emergence of a distinct pattern of sexual curiosity; the child will show a decided visual and tactile curiosity about his or her own genitals, those of the parents, other children, animals, and dolls. It is at just this point that we are able to discern significant divergences in male and female development, organized around the reaction to the observation of the anatomical differences between the sexes. It is not simply the cognitive event that accounts for the powerful dynamic impact of the observation of the anatomic difference. At this juncture in development the infant has to contain the at times overwhelming object-loss and body-dissolution anxieties consequent to the separation-individuation process. The observation of the sexual difference—something is missing—exaggerates these anxieties. The genitals attain this importance in the body schema because the genital zone has become eroticized.

Although the little boys undoubtedly perceive the difference between male and female, they generally react with a profound and unusually thoroughgoing denial of the difference. This denial is reflected in action by their avoidance in looking at the female genitals and is undoubtedly supported by the fact that they can constantly reassure themselves by reference to their own bodies through visual and tactile means. The denial is further and crucially supported by the boy's increasingly turning to the father when he is actually and emotionally available in a significant identification with him. In the thirty-five little boys that we intensively studied (Roiphe and Galenson, 1981), only four, who had experienced severe traumatization in the first two years of life, developed significant preoedipal castration reactions in the latter part of the second year. These castration reactions were severe in nature, and follow-up study suggested that they had decided pathological implications for further development.

By contrast almost all of the thirty-five little girls in the study developed distinctly recognizable castration reactions, which ranged from mild, transitory patterns to severe, far-reaching, and relatively fixed reactions. The severe castration reactions developed in those children, boys and girls, whose earlier experiences had resulted in an unstable object schematization. This occurred, for example, where there had been an accompanying maternal depression (Roiphe and Galenson, 1983), an absent parent, or in general not good enough mothering. Another set of precursors of these severe castration reactions were an uncertain and fluctuating sense of body outline as a consequence of birth defect, severe body illness, or surgical intervention—developmental experiences in which no mother can be good enough.

A significant set of reactions seemed to reflect an intensification of object-loss concerns evoked by the child's observation of the anatomical differences between the sexes, evidenced in the emergence of sleep disturbances sometimes of intense proportions. Both boys and girls showed a sharp upsurge of anxiety about being left by mother as well as an increased anxious anticipation about being left, with a resultant shadowing of the mother. We often saw a greater use of the transitional object with the implied restitutive effort to blur the sharp sense of separateness. In the severe cases, use of the transitional object was not sufficient to contain this upsurge in object-loss anxiety, and we believe this is the source for Socarides's observation (1979) of the perverse individual's desire for merging with the mother in order to reinstate the primitive mother-child unity.

The awareness of the genital difference with its underlying resonance of threatened object loss seemed to produce an additional burden of disappointment and anger in these children. This occurs at the same time that they have to deal with an intense burden of object-directed hostility toward the mother as a consequence of the less than good enough nurturing experience during the first year of life. Of course their already compromised object relatedness is further impaired. The problem of bodily organization is made worse, too. The very anal and early genital zone arousal that opened important body channels utilized by the temporary splitting of ambivalence, serves also to intensify the ambivalence that results from severe preoedipal castration reactions.

Accompanying this profound intensification of ambivalence is a consequent weakening in the cohesiveness of the emerging ego and in the developing self and object representations. A common result is the mobilization of a pathological defensive splitting of the maternal image, reflected in an explosive expansion in object-loss anxiety and a recrudescence of the fear of the stranger who becomes the feared external personification of the child's potentially destructive rage directed at the mother. In extreme cases (Roiphe and Galenson, 1983), the aggression is projected onto the father, or, in the context of stranger reactions, onto others who are then similarly feared. Such an outcome may interfere with the normal crucial role of the father at this juncture in development, not only as a support in the whole separation-individuation process but as a figure for identification for the little boy.

Instead of an expansion of independence supported by a reliable and coherent mental representation of the maternal object which we normally see, these children demonstrate a heightened hostile dependence on the actual mother, almost literally clinging to her and showing a sullen mistrust of other adults and children, which does not augur well for the age-appropriate individuation thrust toward object constancy. As a consequence some of our children have shown a heightened and persistent separation anxiety well on to the fifth and sixth year of life. Some of the boys faced with this considerable expansion of object-loss anxiety developed a profound identification with the mother expressed in the emergence of a persistent cross-dressing which suggests later transvestite development. It seems to us that the preoedipal nurturing experiences and the negotiation of the separation-individuation and early genital phases have a crucial impact on the very form, nature, and outcome of the later phallic-oedipal phase. The intense hostile dependence on the mother seems to foster the relative preponderance in these children of a negative oedipal position in the later phallic-oedipal phase.

Simultaneous with this major interference in the normal consolidation of the object representation is a decided weakening of the sense of the body-self and in particular the genitals. We saw in these children a spreading castration hypochondria in which they reacted to minor cuts and bruises with panic and not uncommonly anxiously pointed to imaginary hurts of body and limb. Perhaps one of the most dramatic reflections of the castration reactions of this period is the emergence of sharply organized penis-envy syndromes in little girls. They were frequently observed to hold sticks or toys in the genital area, and the more verbal girls insisted that they were boys and had a penis.

Just what our position is on causality may seem confusing. Earlier we stated that experiences that rendered the body image and object schema uncertain and unstable dispose children to severe preoedipal castration reactions. In the last several pages we suggest that the severe preoedipal castration reactions bring about a weakening in the object and the general body-self schema as well as an uncertainty of the genital outline of the body. Indeed we mean both. The severe preoedipal castration reactions mobilize an increment in object-directed aggression, object loss, and castration anxieties, which serve to compromise further the stability of the self and object schema. The self and object schema were already uncertain and unstable as a consequence of the earlier experiences.

In many of the children who develop moderate to severe preoedipal castration reactions we find the emergence of an infantile fetish (Greenacre, 1969, 1971; Roiphe and Galenson, 1981) as the heightened aggressivation of the child's functioning interferes with the basic attachment to the transitional object. Although the infantile fetish is not necessary for sexual performance, as by definition is the case with the fetish in adulthood, our observations have suggested that the infantile fetish is necessary for the sense of the child's male sexual body integrity. Furthermore, we believe that in at least some instances there is a developmental and dynamic continuity between the infantile fetish and the fetishistic perversions of later life. This reparative construct is precipitated and split off as a result of the undermining of the sense of body integrity that follows from the observation of the anatomical difference between the sexes at a time in life when the genitals have already assumed a distinct narcissistic importance. Case material from one of the children we have studied serves to demonstrate many of the issues involved in the development of the infantile fetish (see Roiphe and Galenson, 1975, 1981).

At one extreme of the perversions is that variant in the development of sexual identity, the transsexual. In order to preserve a sense of psychological balance and integrity, that is, to contain psychologically the basic instability in the body image, the wavering primary tie to the maternal object, the anxious body narcissism, and the exaggeration of the aggressive drive, the transsexual maintains, no, insists on, a cross-gender identity even in the face of the discordant evidence of his genital anatomy.

We are sceptical of Stoller's (1975) reconstruction of an "excessively intimate and blissful symbiosis." Everything we know about the chronically depressed and bisexual mothers of transsexuals suggests that there is a highly compromised and disturbed symbiosis with significant distortions in subsequent separation-individuation and early-genital-phase developments. As a consequence of just these disturbed and less-than-satisfying nurturing experiences during the first year of life, the transsexual child must develop severe castration reactions with a consequent depletion in the body-self image and uncertainty in the genital outline of the body. We are reminded of the little boy in the throes of a severe pre-oedipal castration reaction (Sachs 1962) who cried that he wanted to have a tushy just like mama; that is, only through identification with mother could he find relief from the overwhelming fears of object loss and castration.

The heightened aggression characteristic of these children also serves to make serious inroads into the cohesiveness of the emerging ego organization, which compromises the developing sense of reality and the integrative function of the ego. The common resort to a defensive splitting of the object representation in the service of supporting the primary tie to the object world also interferes with the developing reality sense and integrative function of the ego. Finally, we frequently see a significant constriction in the developing symbolic thought and fantasy function as well as a complementary enhancement of acting-out trends.

In the extensive literature of the broad spectrum of perversions, virtually all investigators have emphasized the inability of these individuals to accept the anatomic difference between the sexes and still maintain satisfying sexual functioning because this observation evokes overwhelming castration anxiety. What is equally impressive to us is that the perverse individual has a significantly compromised capacity to deny in symbolic fantasy the anatomic distinction between the sexes. The homosexual, in the face of the underlying, overwhelming castration- body-dissolution anxiety, can only function sexually when he is visually confronted with a partner who has a sexual organ that is actually like his or her own. This is perhaps even more vividly demonstrated in our analytic work with several fetishists. These patients reported that they were able to function sexually for a while by invoking in thought the stereotyped fetishistic fantasy. After several days of sexually

functioning in this manner, they said that they were no longer able to evoke the fetishistic fantasy in thought and that they required a concrete fetish and fetishistic ritual in order to be sexually functional.

These inroads in ego functioning can be observed in statu nascendi in those of our children who develop severe castration reactions. In the beginning, faced with the overwhelming complex of castration-body dissolution anxiety, object-loss anxiety, and hostile destructive rage, they show a precociously but narrowly defensive-based emergence and florid elaboration of symbolic fantasy-thought in denying the anatomic difference between the sexes. This denial is in the service of supporting the basic general integrity of the body image, the genital outline of the body, and the fundamental object representation. In general such defensive efforts are unsuccessful and break down, and in time we see a growing constriction in symbolic fantasy-thought. These children can only ensure the basic tie to the maternal object by a shadowing and hostile clinging to the mother in the flesh, in contrast to their more normal brothers and sisters who at this time show an increased independence of the actual mother supported by a growingly secure mental representation of her. Children with these severe preoedipal castration reactions have to rely on the concrete fetish and the actual paraphernalia of cross-dressing. Some of these children ultimately attain a level of stabilization through a psychological identification with the cross-sexed parent. The transsexual is perhaps, or at least has a great deal in common with, the acting-out character; the central reparative identificatory fantasy of the transsexual, "I am a female trapped in a male body" or "I am male in a female body," cannot be maintained in wishful thinking but ultimately must be acted out through the various sex-change operations.

Unfortunately we do not have a sufficient body of prospective, longitudinally followed cases to decide some of the crucial questions of perverse development. Why does one of these children grow into a homosexual, another a fetishist, transvestite, or a transsexual? Our discussion thus far has only succeeded in suggesting a common matrix of disturbed early development for all the perversions. Finally, there are a number of children whose early development is seriously enough disturbed so that they have an obligatory attachment to an infantile fetish but who do not go on to develop adult perversions. It would be crucial to understand what alternatative resolutions there may be to these disturbed conditions of infancy and what their adult sequelae may be.

REFERENCES

Abraham, K. (1910). Remarks on the psychoanalysis of foot and corset fetishism, in *Selected Papers on Psychoanalysis.* New York: Brunner/Mazel, 1979.

Bak, R. C. (1953). Fetishism. *Journal of the American Psychoanalytic Association,* 1:285–298.

Bak, R. C. (1968). The plallic woman: The ubiquitous fantasy in perversions. *The Psychoanalytic Study of the Child,* 23:15–36. New York; International Universities Press.

Freud, S. (1905). Three essays on the theory of sexuality. *Standard Edition,* vol. 7, ed. J. Strachey. London: Hogarth Press, 1953.

Freud, S. (1920). Beyond the pleasure principle. *Standard Edition,* vol. 18, ed. J. Strachey. London: Hogarth Press, 1955.

Freud, S. (1923). The infantile genital organization. *Standard Edition,* vol. 19, ed. J. Strachey. London: Hogarth Press, 1961.

Freud, S. (1927). Fetishism. *Standard Edition,* vol. 21, pp. 125–243, ed. J. Strachey. London: Hogarth Press, 1953.

Freud, S. (1938). Splitting of the ego in the process of defence. *Standard Edition,* vol. 23, pp. 271–278, ed. J. Strachey. London: Hogarth Press, 1964.

Gillespie, W. H. (1940). A contribution to the study of fetishism. *International Journal of Psycho-analysis,* 21:401–415.

Greenacre, P. (1953). Certain relationships between fetishism and the faulty development of the body image. In *Emotional Growth.* New York: International Universities Press. 1971.

Greenacre, P. (1955). Further considerations regarding fetishism. In *Emotional Growth.* New York: International Universities Press, 1971

Greenacre, P. (1960). Further notes on fetishism. In: *Emotional Growth.* New York: International Universities Press, 1971.

Greenacre, P. (1969). The fetish and the transitional object. In *Emotional Growth.* New York: International Universities Press, 1971.

Greenacre, P. (1970). The transitional object and the fetish. In *Emotional Growth.* New York: International Universities Press, 1971.

Mahler, M., Pine, F., and Bergman, A. (1975). *The Psychological Birth of the Human Infant.* New York: Basic Books.

Roiphe, H. (1979). A theoretical overview of preoedipal development. In *Basic Handbook of Child Psychiatry.* ed. J. Noshpitz. New York: Basic Books.

Roiphe, H. and Galenson, E. (1981). *Infantile Origins of Sexual Identity.* New York: International Universities Press.

Roiphe, H. and Galenson, E. (1983). Maternal depression, separation, and a failure in object constancy. Unpublished.

Sachs, L. J. (1962). A case of castration anxiety beginning at 18 months. *Journal of the American Psychoanalytic Association,* 10:329–337.

Socarides, C. (1979). A unitary theory of sexual perversions. In *On Sexuality,* ed. T. Karasu and C. Socarides. New York: International Universities Press.

Stoller, R. (1975). *Sex and Gender,* vol. 2, *The Transsexual experiment.* New York: Jason Aronson.

48

Responses of Very Young Girls to Paternal Sexual Abuse

Shirley R. Rashkis, M.D. and Olivia Capers, M.D.

Relatively few contemporary studies of the immediate or long-term effects of childhood sexual experience with an adult have focused upon the question of how such experiences might influence the normal course of development. Observations by Greenacre (1952) of the psychological consequences of overstimulation in early life provided a basic conception of the potentially profound impact of excessive excitation upon the child's future self-regulatory capacities. Ferenczi (1949) noted that young children sexually stimulated by an adult feel great anxiety, lack the personality consolidation to protest effectively against the force and authority of the seducer, and hence may lose confidence in their senses and even in the reality of the event. Rosenfeld and colleagues (1979) have considered the child's report of incest a function of the stage of congnitive and psychosexual development and subject to the influence of fantasy, memory changes, and defensive alterations. Peters (1976) pointed out that the use of overt behavioral or psychological changes as indicators of the young child's response to sexual abuse may fail to detect early problems in the aftermath of sexual abuse, whereas changes in the child's fantasy life might provide a more sensitive reflection of the experience.

Utilizing their own clinical findings, Lewis and Sarrell (1969) discussed the relationship of seduction, rape, and incest to psychological outcomes. They reported that such experiences during infancy not only result in nonspecific signs of anxiety, but that there might also be later effects upon the resolution of such developmental tasks as establishing trust and self-pride and later modulation of response to stressful events. In the phallic-oedipal period of the children they studied, reactions occurred that related to the concerns of that phase, apparently reflecting the disparity between intensified fantasy and ego controls. The authors concluded that seduction, incest, and rape could be important contributing factors to subsequent symptom formation and character disorder. Drawing upon her analyses of adult patients who had been raped before the age of six years, Katan (1973) described a disturbance of drive fusion with a resultant escalation of primitive libidinal development and regression in the development of aggression.

In the present study, the responses of girls whose sexual abuse had taken place before they were three years old were compared to

From the Joseph J. Peters Institute, Philadelphia, Pennsylvania, a treatment center for victims of rape and incest, their families, and sexual offenders.

those of girls between three and six years of age when the abuse occurred. The girls' perception of sexual involvement with an adult was considered a function of the difference in their stage of language and other cognitive achievements, as well as of their social development. The data are based upon parents' reports, initial evaluations, and psychotherapeutic sessions, including play and verbal interviews which lasted from six months to two and a half years, and occurred at weekly to monthly intervals. The following representative cases illustrate both the common and distinctive features of the responses to sexual encounter in the two age groups, and whether the experience was perceived as an external event and/or a psychologic experience, depending upon the particular developmental stage at which it occurred.

CASE 1

A, just under two years of age when evaluated for suspected sexual abuse by her father, had reported to family members while bathing that father had hurt her with his penis; also she had numerous sore areas on her lower trunk, which she did not want touched. A had had a very warm relationship with her father, who took much responsibility for her care. Because the treating agency felt that the abuse ceased with A's entry into therapy, she remained in the home with both parents.

Despite her limited verbal ability, A could indicate that her father had hurt her in the genital area. She spanked her own backside saying, "Bad girl!" several times. In her therapeutic sessions, A was very alert to things going on about her, particularly of an interpersonal nature. She repeatedly ran out to check with her father in the waiting room, and although indignant that her father had hurt her, her fondness for him was unmistakable. Her relationship with her mother did not seem significantly affected. In their daily interaction around A's needs and household events, A was communicative and affectionate.

During the first three months of therapy, A appeared highly excited in the office. While exploring the anatomy of the dolls, she questioned whether the female therapist had a penis. In an important interview after these first three months, A's excitement increased in a rhythmic crescendo and then diminished, in a pattern resembling orgasm. Subsequently, she was noticeably calmer both in the office and at home, and, as if attempting to be a "big girl," her learning progressed more rapidly; she learned to write letters and her name, and began to draw pictures. At age two-and-a-half years she repeatedly drew phallic shapes, calling them fire engines. She pretended to smoke cigarettes, wanted to paint her fingernails, and drew a picture of herself in a bra. Her struggle with perception of anatomical differences was evident as she paid special attention to any protuberances, whether on herself, on others, or on the dolls. Her doll play was extremely tender, and the relationship with both mother and father, as depicted in play, was a positive one and essentially dyadic in nature with each of them. Her comments revealed that she was acutely aware of their intermittent marital discord.

As A's third birthday approached, A announced that girls have a penis inside, and a change occurred in her play. The father and mother dolls hugged and kissed, and the mother doll became more critical, scolding, and punishing of the children, constantly telling them to keep their clothes on, particularly their pants, and not to sit on each other. At age three years, three months, A reminded the therapist that she no longer talked about penises. She pretended to be tough, talked like a boy, then sadly acknowledged that only boys have a penis and that her father no longer put his penis on her. She mourned her own anatomical state and the lost ability to obtain her father's phallus. In play, she made clear distinctions between the possessions of boys and girls, and the mother doll began to treat the children more harshly, suggesting A's projected anger at her mother. Phallic interests seemed to become dispersed into learning. As A approached her fourth year, she became competitive with the therapist in the games they played, wanting tokens belonging to the therapist. Shortly afterward, A tried to engage her father's interest in a doll's genitals during her therapeutic session.

CASE 2

B's parents separated when she was one year old. When B was two years old, she began objecting to visits with her father, with whom she had previously had a good relationship. Her mother noted that B had a vaginal discharge and some genital bruises, but continued to have B visit her father for several months, despite B's protest.

At age three, B was able to say that her father "pinched" her in the genital area. Her reaction was openly fearful, and she did not want to see her father, labeling him "bad." However, she showed interest in him through her veiled curiosity about his visits with her older sister. B's overall behavior had changed when she was two: she began to cling to her mother, was sensitive to any angry exchange around the home, and shied away from men. Although B's manifest behavior did not reveal an increase in aggression, there were periodic guttural, angry-sounding outbursts during her play sessions. Her learning proceeded at what appeared to be a normal pace from age three to four years.

In therapy at age three years, her interest in her father quickly emerged. In a play episode with the doll house she put the little girl and father together briefly in the chimney, where the tight space required them to be very close together. She then took them down and enacted the father coming to visit and the girl fleeing to her mother's side. In another scene father was thrown down and discarded, but shortly afterward she wanted to see her father once again.

CASE 3

C was four years old when she first began to question her mother repeatedly at bath time about her own vaginal area, but she was told the vagina had to do with urination. After several months C's mother began to notice that C drew back whenever she washed C's pubic area, and on one occasion C vaguely mentioned her father. At this time C's parents had been separated for one year following physical abuse of C's mother by the father, episodes

that C had witnessed. C's father had continued to visit and baby-sit and often took the children to his home. When C's mother discussed C's reaction with C's father, he became furious but continued to visit the children. When C was five years old she specifically inquired, "What do little girls' daddies do with them?" and was told they go to the park and watch TV together. When C asked about the white stuff her daddy had put on her, C's mother vigorously confronted her husband, learned there had been at least five episodes of sexual abuse over the previous year involving penile-vaginal contact and fellatio. She immediately brought C for evaluation.

During the first interview C, a shy and reserved child, initially mentioned her father with annoyance in that he failed to pay the fee and she hadn't been able to stay in day camp. C quickly went on to recall happy experiences with her father, including driving together, sitting together, and celebrating her birthday with him. Then C related there had also been problems with her father. "My father undressed me, put his 'tee-tee' inside and between my legs and I saw white stuff on me." In the next two weekly sessions C spoke of her father frequently but in ambivalent terms. She said she had no interest in seeing him, yet kept wondering where he was and what he was doing. C remembered that when her father first began touching her genital area she was "scared of him for the first time ever" but that she did not cry. She condensed the cluster of authorities involved and the events that had occurred by saying her father had told her not to tell her mother but that she had told her mother because her mother said she would have to talk to the policewoman. C mentioned she wasn't thinking of her father much but added that she was thinking about what he had done. She began to yawn drowsily and slowly moved her hands and pigtails in front of her eyes. When asked about her thoughts, she promptly became fully attentive and acknowledged that although she didn't cry she did worry about what her father had done. She then recalled a dream that had occurred before her troubles began: her father was driving far away with some people, and she wasn't with him. C added she was unhappy with her father now and felt, as she had in the dream, that he was far away from her. In another session two months later, while reviewing her father's acts, C said resignedly, "I did nothing. I felt bad."

C's mother, an involved and caring woman had commented initially that C had become interested in any aggressive behavior she happened to observe. A few months later, C's mother reported that C had changed from a timid, quiet child into a fighter. She had hit a girl at school over a minor disagreement; she now vigorously complained that she hated her siblings and kept shouting "get off me" when her younger sister took one of her toys. C had also begun worrying about how her mother felt about her. C would snuggle up to her mother in bed at night, hugging her, wrapping her legs about her mother, and wanting to sleep with her. When mother refused, C would cry, protest that mother no longer loved her, and begin to suck her thumb.

During this time, C expressed in three weekly sessions an intense fascination with males and their dealings with females. She closely tracked each fight in the school yard and in the neighborhood, blaming males for both aggression and passivity but mostly for their inattention or indifference to her. C talked of a boy who sometimes hit her but always wanted to play with her. Upon thinking of her father, C said she had decided her father was not mean but that he had made her "feel bad and sad and mad ever since. . . . "

CASE 4

D's father left for a job away from home when she was four years old. Upon his return one year later he had engaged her in penile-vaginal contact, cunnilingus, and fellatio over a period of several months until D told her mother and was promptly brought for evaluation. D, a tall, mature, and outgoing child spoke freely and with dramatic intensity of her experiences. "I had to suck my father's private . . . he can't remember. I had to lay on top of him; sometimes he lay on top of me. At times mother was home—that's why it's a secret. He told me 'don't tell anybody'—that's a secret. I felt Mommy should know about it because she

needs to know. She told me, 'no more secrets,' that she'd stop daddy from doing it—she did. It hurt but it didn't. I can't make up my mind —like somebody pushes you down, sometimes it hurts, sometimes not." Then D turned away abruptly, became distracted by the cover on the phone book and was briefly distant and quiet. She then said that her father had been nice at other times; he had surprised her by taking her to the movies on her birthday. D emphasized that her mother was very upset that she had not told her sooner, and had repeatedly asked if she was lying. "Father lied; he said no private in my mouth. I don't feel so good. I thought grown-ups didn't lie. Hey, a little piece is missing from the puzzle." (There was a tiny cleft between the correctly placed piece and the frame of the puzzle.) We do not know whether D's perception of a piece missing related to the lie, the secret, and/or to anatomical sex differences.

In an interview with the mother a month later, during a temporary separation from her husband, she related that he had finally acknowledged his acts. D's mother also said D was complaining of feeling sick and was reluctant to go to school, where she was preoccupied, sang to herself, and took off her shoes. D herself described how her mind wandered at school: she thought about the doctor delivering her cousin's new baby, about eating pie, and about her father. She recalled playing with her father and beating him up and sitting on him. Soon after, the school reported that D scribbled on other children's drawings, sat with her legs widely spread, and ignored her teacher's responses. Although D's mother was concerned over D's developing defiance, she was ineffective in dealing with the problem.

D reviewed the revelation of the secret in two monthly sessions following the initial evaluation and again three months later when her parents reconciled. She was pleased she had told her mother and had been relieved of the secret. D said indignantly that her father would have covered her mouth had she told her mother in his presence. D said her father had lied to her mother in saying that she would come and lie under the covers. Rather, he had called her, and he had put the covers on her, and it was "nice" when he lay still. D felt certain her mother could tell if he lied. She said she would care about her father even if he hurt her again, but now she would try to tell someone about it. When her father returned home, D. spoke of her earlier reluctance to tell anyone for fear of hurting her father's feelings.

When her parents reconciled, D monitored their interaction closely, carefully observing her mother's moods and her father's activities. D's mother reported that D was alert to every argument at home and among her peers. D described fantasies that her mother became ill and that she and father caught the disease. Although she claimed she did not want to be liked more than her mother, D did express her profound feeling of isolation at times when her parents were together. D now further explained her resentment of her father's secret; it had made her feel she was "going across" her mother and that she had to do what her father said. "He almost made me swallow it. He'd not have it anymore. I might have chewed it up and be in the hospital." D recalled again that once her father "had to go to the bathroom" in her mouth and that as a result, "when I eat something good it tastes stale." D's comment suggests a contamination of her orality by strong affect and the continuing effect of sexual abuse upon the organization of her perceptual experience at this time. However, we cannot be sure of all the components of the affect or of the underlying unconscious processes.

Discussion

In all of the cases, the girl's response to sexual abuse reflected the nature of her earlier experience with her parents. The girls seemed generally less secure in their interaction with their parents following the experience of sexual abuse. They showed overexictement and hypervigilance, expressed in heightened attention and in surveillance of the environment, as well as increased alertness to aggression.

Both age groups also showed behavior indicating ambivalence toward the father-offender. In the younger girls, ambivalence was primarily conveyed in terse verbal comments, in play, and in bids for father's attention. The ambivalence of the older girls was not only conveyed through such behavior but also expressed in both pleasant and unpleasant reminiscences about father, interest in his present life, and thoughts concerning future trust in him or control by him.

Although all the girls appeared less secure, the younger group continued to relate to their mothers with no apparent loss of spontaneity. In contrast, the older girls became more self-conscious about their relationship with their mothers. In five other clinic cases of girls who had been sexually abused in early childhood (two girls close to three years of age, two girls four years old, and one girl five years old), overexcitement, hypervigilance, alertness to aggression and ambivalance toward the father-offender were also noted, and the relationship to mother had become of increased concern for two of the older girls.

Although the girls had attained different developmental levels, which affected their understanding and interpretation of their sexual experiences, the girls of both age groups were equally overexcited and hypervigilant. The hyperalertness to aggression as one manifestation of the increased vigilance of the younger girls is suggested by the clinical material, although this cannot be verified in view of their limited capacity for verbalization and the expanding interest in aggression characteristic of this age group under normal circumstances. In the older girls, alertness to aggression was clearly evident in their play and verbalization, from the reports of their mothers, and in their general behavior. Whereas the younger girls showed some aggressive play, no definite conclusions could be drawn.

Katan (1973) pointed out a result of severe sexual stimulation in early childhood: " . . . a 3-year-old who is so tremendously overstimulated simply does not have adequate discharge channels available, with the result that the mounting excitement, which at first is pleasurable, leads to frantic efforts to get rid of it. The lack of discharge would thus be experienced as painful and stimulate aggression" (p. 223n). Katan's observation is confirmed by the alertness to aggression and aggressive stance of the older girls in this study, which appeared to follow sexual overstimulation.

However, it may also be that the hypervigilance, alertness to aggression, and aggressive stance of the older girls represent an externalization of their anxiety and fear.

Certain aspects of the ambivalent relationship to the father-offender varied in the two groups. The younger girls seemed more comfortable in telling about their sexual experiences but were frustrated in doing so by the adults' difficulty in understanding them. Some would temporarily cease their efforts to recount these experiences and then attempt to be understood at a later time. Also, these younger girls struggled with their dual feelings toward father at a simple level of good and bad as they continued to be interested in him. In contrast, the girls in the three-to six-year age group seemed certain of the external reality of the sexual contact and apparently had even reviewed the events mentally. They knew what was meant by a secret and were thrown into conflict because they were supposed to tell the truth to mother as well as to obey father. The older girls also were aware that their fathers lied about their actions and responded to the father with distrust. In the older girls, the father-offender's indifference to, withdrawal from, or rejection of her after sexual abuse tended to evoke her derision. Yet in both age groups, the girls' sustained interest in their father seemed to be anchored to earlier feelings about him as well as to strong current motivation to be involved with him again, whether this was due to their excitement, anger, need to master the experience, or a combination of these.

The difference in the relationship to mother in the two age groups, following the sexual encounter, is of particular interest inasmuch as both groups showed a similar degree of insecurity and hypervigilance. As stated earlier, the relationship to mother in the younger group appeared to be unthreatened, possibly a reflection of the comparatively stronger valence of the early mother-daughter unit. Greater physical closeness and physical care from mother and a continuation of a dyadic relationship with the parents may shield the present relationship to mother against inroads of disappointment, conflict, and anxiety. In the three-to six-year age group a change in the relationship to mother following their sexual encounter was indicated by the children's statements and by their mothers' reports. These older girls, who were approaching or had actually attained oedipal stage development, were concerned about their mother's function as a needed or disappointing protector, were upset that they had failed to protect mother from worry, sadness, or anger, and also anxious about their separateness from their mother.

REFERENCES

Ferenczi, S. (1949). Confusion of tongues between the adult and the child. *International Journal of Psycho-Analysis,* 30:225–230.

Greenacre, P. (1952). Pregenital patterning. *International Journal of Psycho-Analysis,* 33:410–415.

Katan, A. (1973). Children who were raped. *The Psychoanalytic Study of the Child,* 28:208–224. New Haven: Yale University Press.

Lewis, M. and Sarrell, P. M. (1969). Some psychological aspects of seduction, incest, and rape in childhood. *Journal of the American Academy of Child Psychiatry,* 8:606–619.

Peters, J. J. (1976). Children who are victims of sexual assault and the psychology of offenders. *American Journal of Psychotherapy,* 30:398–421.

Rosenfeld, A. A., Nadelson, C. C., and Krieger, M. (1979). Fantasy and reality in patients' reports of incest. *Journal of Clinical Psychiatry,* 40:159–164.

49

Pediatric to Psychosomatic Economy: Fundamentals for a Psychosomatic Pathology of Infants

Léon Kreisler, M.D.

Clinical psychosomatics is a vast field where so many disciplines intermingle that it is important to define one's position. My position is essentially clinical, outside of neuro- and psychophysiology, although I take into account basic research that can help interpret clinical data as in sleep endocrinological and immunological disturbances (one finds, for example, correlations between mourning and a lowering of immunological resistance). Developmental biology brings much to the understanding of childhood psychosomatics.

The object of study is the sick infant, both from a psychiatric and pediatric point of view and practice. The method is based on the study of clinical case material without reference to statistical analysis (with one exception: a qualitative and quantitative study of the evolution of newborns that had spent time in an intensive care unit [Kreisler et al., 1978]). The theoretical background is based on concepts developed at the Paris Institute of Psychosomatics, where psychoanalysis is considered a necessary tool for the understanding of psychosomatic phenomena. Here are some of the essential concepts we use.

Basic Postulates

We assume that there are defenses at any age that protect the infant or child against psychosomatic disorganization. These defenses are supported by a full affective life and balanced psychic functioning. However, these two processes do not function in cases of psychosomatic disorganization, particularly when certain forms of depression are part of the clinical picture. French authors who have specifically studied psychosomatics (Fain, David, de M'Uzan, Marty) have described factors that predispose the individual to somatization: such patients are unable to cope with psychic trauma on a psychological level because they suffer from disturbances in symbolic functioning. Unconscious drive derivatives cannot be represented psychologically (or expressed psychologically); instead they find expression through somatic channels.

Historically these authors first described conditions known as *pensée opératoire* (Marty and de M'Uzan, 1962) as characterized by certain clinical modalities of expression: character neurosis and other types of neuroses that expressed themselves primarily in behavior. Marty (1958) described "an essential allergic structure" in these patients, whose affects are not expressed symbolically via their bodies (as in hysteria) but directly in bodily experiences; they have physical pain and their affects and drive derivatives are repressed.

This theory considers that the preconscious plays the important role of regulating exchanges between the conscious and the unconscious. A well-functioning preconscious structure provides defenses against traumas. Well-structured preconscious functioning is determined by its rich affective and representational content and by its capacity to remain supple. The characteristic pathological process in these "behavioral neuroses" is a permanent defect in the functioning of the preconscious: this leads to the *pensée opératoire*, characterized by a poverty of fantasy expression, expressed clinically by a lack of dreams and an absence of free associations. Stereotyped behaviors, shallow interpersonal relationships, and a poverty in expressing fantasies characterize behavioral neuroses.

In character neuroses, the preconscious is fragile and remains permeable. Fantasy formation is inhibited, and although these descriptions apply to adults, they can be applied to the child by taking into account differences in level of development.

In the child, the main psychological malformations connected with psychosomatic disorders are the following (Kreisler, 1981, 1983): (1) behavioral structure analogous to the behavioral neuroses in adults (psychic functioning in these children is monotonous and empty, showing a lack of imagination and of dreams; drawings, projective tests, and speech show little creative fantasies); (2) atypical neurotic structures which are characterized by a lack of mental elaboration (character neuroses do not form until adolescence); (3) global affective stunting, as I have described (1981) in a case of psychosocial dwarfism; and (4) the allergic structure that can be formed from latency on (Kreisler, 1982).

This list does not exhaust all possibilities. I wish to stress that the term *structure* does not refer to a permanent immobile organization but to the *present* mode of psychic functioning. Nothing is permanently settled before adolescence. Unlike what we see in adults, psychosomatic organization in children is characterized by its potential for reversibility.

Psychosomatics in infants derives information from both pediatric and psychoanalytic sources. French pediatric research first involved anorexias and sleep disturbances (Debre and Doumic, 1950, 1959) because of their obvious correlation with psychological factors.

Studies of infant psychosomatics were originally based on reconstructive data from adult patients. Spitz initiated direct observation of somatic pathology in infants. Recently, direct observation has focused on the ontogeny of infant psychosomatic disorders. My own work was based on Spitz's and Winnicott's earlier studies but utilized another methodology.

Together with Fain and Soulé, I have contributed the pediatric viewpoint in the study of early "functional" disorders, including colic, insomnia, vomiting, rumination, anorexia, encopresis, psychogenic megacolon, breath-holding spells, and infant asthma (Kreisler et al., 1981). This work drew upon the viewpoints of two disciplines: pediatrics and psychoanalysis. For the pediatrician, psychoanalytic thinking gives meaning to observations rather than drawing classifications based upon mere description of symptoms. For the analyst, pediatric observations provide the organization of the development of a real, rather than mythical, baby. Analytic propositions have to be correlated with the baby's psychological and bodily realities appropriate to its developmental status at that time.

The Psychiatric Nosology of Infancy

Psychosomatic pathology describes those disorders of organic function or those with actual visible organic changes whose genesis and evolution are determined by an important psychological contribution. Organic change from accidents, battering by the caregiver, and autoaggressive factors are excluded. In addition to these psychosomatic disorders, there are other disturbances in infants: developmental disturbances and disturbances that manifest themselves by motor expression. Beginning with the second half of the first year, psychopathology may take the form of neurotic expression, "depression," psychosis, and mental deficits (see table 49–1).

FORMS OF SOMATIC EXPRESSION

Psychosomatic disorders of infants take on a great variety of forms. They very in degree of severity, they are rarely lethal and often benign, since every child reacts through somatic channels.

The level of the infant's biological and psychological development determines the forms the pathology takes; there is little similarity between anorexia in infants and in adolescence. Insomnia is totally different according to the child's age. These age-related differences are more marked in early years, and therapeutic approaches should be based upon considerations of the child's developmental stage.

We consider infancy to extend from birth until age thirty-six months, a period that can be divided into three phases chronologically. The pathology of infancy can be classified as follows, similarly to Call's (1980) classification of disorders of attachment. This division into phases is based on stages of development in regard to interaction, ego development, and biological maturation.

First Phase (one to fourteen months)—Psy-

TABLE 49–1

Psychopathology of Infants: Nosological Groupings (Kreisler)

1. Disorders with a somatic expression
2. Developmental disorders
   Delays and unevenness in acquisition of motor skills, in language, and in relatedness to inanimate objects and to people
3. Disorders in the motor sphere
   Global disorders: inertia, agitation
   Specific disorders: rocking, nervous habits of autoerotic and autoaggressive nature
4. Disorders in the psychological sphere
   Intellectual deficit: mental retardation
   Mood disorders: depression, excitement, apathy
   Fears: of food, of inanimate objects and people
   Psychosis

chosomatic defenses are maintained by the "maternal function"; the mother-child interaction regulates the psychosomatic equilibrium.

Second Phase (from the second semester [six months] to fifteen to eighteen months [anaclitic phase])—This phase is characterized by the newly developing capacity for object relatedness, functioning which organizes the psychosomatic economy. From six months on, while the mother-child interactional system still predominates, the psychological functioning of the baby plays a role in the elaboration of psychosomatic defenses.

Third Phase (from the middle of the second year to the middle of the third year)—During this phase, autonomous mental defenses are created which protect the infant against psychosomatic disorganization. These defenses will be influenced later during the oedipal phase, latency, and adolescence.

The Psychological Side

In psychosomatics, a fundamental principle is the nature of relations between somatic homeostasis and the quality of affective functioning. In the primary phase—before six months—defenses are maintained by the mother's interaction with the baby. From six months on, true psychological functioning begins and psychosomatic disorders can develop while interactional functioning between mother and child still continues.

Infant psychosomatic disorders are best assessed by the study of mother-child interaction, the stages of the infant's development and his behavior. Observation of mother-child interaction reveals two aspects of the mother-child relationship: the concrete, observable interaction and the invisible interaction of their fantasies. The fantasy interaction (Cramer, 1982) consists of an unconscious investment of each one in the other; these remain as a background to the observable clinical behavior.

Resistance against psychosomatic regression rests upon both the psychological functioning of the child and the interaction with the mother. Sound maternal interaction is characterized by affective richness, stability, and accurate responsiveness. These three dimensions allow an assessment of the quality of mother-infant interactions. Affective richness can be observed in the mother's manipulations, her vocalizations, and the quality of her gaze. Stability results from continuity of care and of correspondence between the rhythms in the child and his environment. The mother's ability to respond specifically to the individual needs of the child makes for accurate responsiveness. Psychosomatic disorders can result from one of three categories of interaction: those characterized by an insufficient response, an excessive response, or a chaotic response.

PATHOLOGICAL INTERACTIONS

Chronic insufficiency of attachment is characterized by lack of the mother's emotional investment in the child. This is the most serious form of psychosomatic pathology. The seriousness of the syndrome is due either to the intensity of the functional disorder (severe anorexia, rumination, vomiting) or to organic lesions (asthma with infections and respiratory complications, ulcerative colitis, psychosocial growth retardation, repetitive infections in various localizations). This type of pathology is analogous to what Spitz (1945) described in hospitalism and other deprivation syndromes, where he mentioned somatic disorders. Conditions linked to institutionalization no longer exist for the most part. Instead, we see deprivations due to repeated separations, unjustified hospitalizations, or even what could be called "intrafamilial hospitalization"—that is, cases where mothers are incapable of emotionally investing their baby.

At the opposite pole from these deprivation syndromes are disorders linked to hyperstimulation and excessive excitation. Functional pathology such as colic, sleep disturbances, and breath-holding characterize these syndromes. The overloading with excitement leads to immediate discharge through a somatic channel and may be due to a defect in the child's stimulus barrier. Primary insomnia and colic during the first three months are the earliest somatic responses to a conflictual situation. In infants and older children, sleep disturbances are the most frequent evidence of excessive excitation. This excessive excitation may be global or selective. The excitement may be continuous and connected with a specific functional sphere (feeding, intestinal voiding), leading to disorders such as anorexia or psychogenic megacolon. Or certain symbiotic attachments, with maternal overprotection and exclusion of the father, can lead to stunting of emotional growth or, for example, asthma.

In our culture, psychosomatic pathology linked to inconsistent mothering is frequent. Both qualitative and quantitative irregularities in attachment hamper the building of defenses against psychosomatic disorders. The most frequent causes for this type of inconsistency are: multiple caregivers, uneven maternal behavior, with oscillation between pampering and impatient, rough handling and situations where both deprivation and inconsistency are present. This is seen in multirisk families, leading to such disorders as psychosocial dwarfism.

The second aspect of symptoms is the child's developmental dimension or stage of development. Especially with very young children, before language has developed, analysis of their behavior is essential. Excitement or apathy, autonomy or clinging, interest in inanimate objects rather than people, repetitiveness or stereotype of activities, interest in or excessive familiarity with the physician, the quality of the relation to mother and other persons are all important.

The main psychological mechanisms in psychosomatic disorganization are regression and depression. Spitz (1946) introduced the concept of anaclitic depression, a mood change with concomitant somatic disturbance and delayed development. In infants, as in adults, depression is a major psychological mechanism in psychosomatic disorganization (Kreisler, 1981; Marty, 1958). Depression in infants is an acute or subacute disturbance, the major psychological aspect of which is atonia. This presupposes that a relation of sufficiently good quality with the mother had existed, followed by sudden deprivation. There are less dramatic forms of depression which are nevertheless serious. These forms have been recognized recently in infants in severe functional disorders and various forms of organic pathology. This depression is based on a *basic affective atonia* and *not* on anxiety; it is a kind of "cold" depression or "white" depression. Symptoms are seen principally in changes in behavior: the infant becomes indifferent, without tears or complaints, turns away from people, preferring inanimate objects, and activities become repetitive and monotonous. The mechanical, monotonous quality of behavior reveals the prevalence of repetitive automatisms.

Spitz's babies had been separated from their mothers. Damage could be mended only if reunion was achieved within three to five months. While these conditions are now rare, separations remain an important factor in precipitating depression. But separation is not the only source of deprivation: in many cases, mothers are physically present but psychically absent because of their own mourning or depression. The child passes then from a full, alive relationship to one that is "white" and empty.

Where there has not been separation, psychological development varies. One form is characterized by affective shallowness, which later becomes a behavioral neurosis. There is a permanent vulnerability to psychosomatic disorganization in this disorder. These syndromes can be reversed if intervention is carried out quickly. It has been stated that depression in infancy is the prototype of later depression. This may be true if the loss of the primary object is the factor. However, the immaturity of the infant's psychic structure does not provide for the psychological characteristics of depression found in adults.

"Emotional depression" is part of a heterogeneous group of "masked depressions" where there is no moral suffering, self-deprecation, or guilt. It resembles mourning rather than melancholia, with a blunting of affects, no fantasy representations, no dream production, and little symbolization.

Psychosomatic Investigation

The goals of clinical investigation of infants are to recognize the medical and psychosomatic aspects of the physical syndrome; to understand the qualities of mother-infant interaction; to describe the modes of psychic functioning of the child; to assess the caregiver's personality, her mental structure, her capacities for reorganization, and her maternal functioning, and the relationship to father and cultural context; and to trace triggering events.

Information about the nature of the pregnancy and delivery and psychosomatic disturbances, such as anorexia and sleep disturbances, should be elicited for they are often cues to the quality of the primary maternal investment. The clinical evaluation should include the study of interaction between the infant, the mother, and the examiner.

Nosological Groupings

We propose a triaxial classification.

Axis I—Medical Basis. Included here are the illnesses and syndromes classified according to the usual medical nomenclature.

Axis II—Structural Basis. This refers to the forms of functioning vulnerable to psychosomatic disorganization. It is based first on the quality of the mother-child interaction and later on the psychological functioning of the infant. Here would be noted pathological interactions—chronically deficient mother-child relationship or excessive excitation; distortions of the mother-child interaction; poor quality, poorly timed or coordinated, and inappropriate arousal of an erogenous or functional zone; and inhibition of the individuation or separation process. After the sixth month of life, functioning of the "behavioral" type—neurotic functioning, depression, and disorganized functioning should be included.

Axis III—Etiological Basis. The influences may be (1) organic; (2) environmental, including prenatal factors, neonatal factors, prematurity, perinatal risk factors, later events such as physical illness, surgery, hospitalization, placement, separation, mourning, battering, and deprivation; (3) familial, including pathological family structure, parental psychopathology, or deviant familial attitudes; or (4) socioeconomic and sociocultural.

Examples of Disorders

Here are some examples of medical syndromes understood from the point of view of the modes of interaction and their psychosomatic organization. Many varied forms exist within the same classification.

INFANT ANOREXIA

There are benign and severe forms, with complex mechanisms which require psychiatric intervention. These complex forms have different structures: phobic, depressive with chronic disturbance in object relations, psychotic, and finally, neonatal anorexia.

Anorexia is frequent in pediatric practice, occurring mostly in the second semester when object relations are developing and other alimentary disorders appear (vomiting, rumination). It is often called "oppositional anorexia." It is an active form of food refusal and is not due to lack of appetite. Each meal is a struggle in which the baby resists with astonishing force the mother's attempts at forced feeding. This oppositional behavior may be related to a "drive for mastery" (Kreisler, 1981) and may become the core of a general negativism. These disorders can be resolved once the mother's pathogenic attitude is understood.

Anorexia based on phobia can be acute or subacute. It occurs in the second or third year.

In anorexias with depression or prolonged deprivation in object relations, passivity is the central characteristic. There is an "empty relationship" with the mother. The baby behaves as if he or she had no hunger sensations and did not know how to use the breast or the bottle. Meals are sad and stereotyped, and end in vomiting. There seems to be no drive for life. These anorexias occur in a framework of depression and insufficient attachment. In anaclitic depression, anorexia is not rare.

Chronic insufficiency of attachment is often associated with child battering and forced feeding. In one of our cases, the mother beat her child at four months to force him to eat; between meals he was practically abandoned. The mother resented the child, as if he persecuted and attacked her. In these severe cases one often also finds rumination and vomiting.

Anorexia in personality disturbances occurs in early stages of psychotic development, with a predominance of fears of devouring and of bodily disintegration. Primary anorexia in the neonatal period is still difficult to understand because we lack knowledge about influences affecting the fetus.

SLEEP DISTURBANCES

Sleep is a basic manifestation of the infant's psychosomatic organization, but at the same time it plays an essential regulating role in this organization. Waking and falling asleep are regulated by two antagonistic neurophysiological mechanisms. Most of the usual insomnias are due to hyperstimulation of the waking system, excitation which may be external or internal (intrapsychic). In early infancy, the mother plays the role of protector of sleep, later taken over by dreaming. Two periods are particularly prone to sleep disturbances: the first months and the second year.

The main pathological mechanism is excessive stimulation and irregularity of maternal involvement in the baby. External factors can interfere with sleep: in the first months it may be the interruption of the midnight meal or a schedule not respecting the baby's rhythms; later, sharing the room with the parents may activate primal-scene fantasies; premature toilet-training or a traumatic environment may interfere. Many insomnias are linked to the mother's anxiety, leading to overprotection or ambivalent behaviors.

In the second semester, one can detect degrees of excessive emotional vulnerability in the child: agitation and intense reactions to new situations or people. In the second year, there are two forms (Debre and Doumic, 1959): either the child is overly excited and plays for hours after waking or has nightmares and fears based on separation anxiety. Severe forms are rare and show intense symptoms (some babies sleep for only two or three hours). Two clinical forms predominate: a silent form, where infants remain immobile with open eyes during the entire night, and an agitated insomnia where the child might have to be restrained (as in the case of a four-month-old who hit his own head with his fists). These cases show chaotic interactions between mother and child and failure to develop a sound narcissistic core. Some cases become psychotic (Lebovici, 1983).

LACK OF ORGANIZATION

Severe affective deprivation coupled with child abuse often leads to states characterized by lack of organization involving several aspects of development: developmental distortions, disorders of communication and behavior, cognitive defects, deviant identification and individuation processes. In these mixed pictures there is considerable vulnerability to psychosomatic disorders. Failure to thrive (psychological dwarfism) is an example. The dramatic return to normal growth after the child has been withdrawn from pathogenic familial influences is most impressive. When the child goes back to his family, growth stops again. A relationship between the secretion of growth hormone and an anomaly of EEG sleep patterns has been demonstrated (Wolff and Money, 1973). Growth-hormone secretion and a return to a normal EEG pattern occur simultaneously (Guilhaume et al., 1981). The main characteristics are: (1) a highly pathogenic familial influence; these families share characteristics of child-abuse families, the parents showing severe narcissistic disturbances and repeating with their children the rejection they experienced in their own infancy and the mothers oscillating between wishes to fuse with the children and tendencies to reject them; and (2) mother-child interactions characterized by irregularity, discontinuity, violence, and unpredictable rhythms. These children are left alone in their beds for hours and are alternatively handled roughly or highly stimulated by body contact.

The form of pathology is determined by the age of the child: in the first year the attachment deficit leading to sleep disturbances predominates. Later, behavioral manifestations are marked by automatisms, and these children go through lengthy periods of waking during the night. These disorders are reversible if external conditions can be mended.

EMPTY BEHAVIOR IN THE YOUNG CHILD (KREISLER, 1981)

This syndrome was found in seven cases of children aged eighteen months to three years and suffering from severe psychosomatic disorders, including severe insomnia, repeated infection, failure to thrive, chest deformity, chronic polyarthritis. They showed the characteristic "empty behavior" with global affective atonia resembling depressive atonia. There was an absence of evidence of internal fantasy, and their behavior seemed to be determined by factual, practical issues, without a link to mental representation. This gives the impression of mechanical functioning, like robots (Loriod, 1981). The poverty of affects is remarkable to the point of total lack of responsiveness. Two of these children had never cried, so that an anomaly of lachrymal function was suspected. They seemed indifferent to pain and showed no anxiety. Their undifferentiated object relationships were evident in that they approached people indiscriminately and followed anyone. No autoerotic oral behavior or transitional object attachment was noted.

One finds in these cases a history of repeated separation. The evolution of this syndrome is remarkable: it is reversible if the relationships are altered, often through psychotherapy. The reversibility testifies to the child's resilient "life instincts." This is what differentiates this syndrome from psychosis. What threatens these children if no therapeutic interaction is provided is what we call *behavioral neurosis,* with a high psychosomatic vulnerability.

The predeterminants of behavioral neurosis can be illustrated in a case of rumination in a eight-and-a-half-month-old child. While on the mother's knees, her gaze engaged all the people present in the room except her mother. On the floor, she moved quickly from one object to another, from a toy to a person in rapid, changing attachments to what seemed to be interchangeable objects. This child had had five different caregivers between the third and the ninth month. There was no difference between her attachment to inanimate objects and to people and no evidence of anxiety. The "empty behavior" revealed a failure to establish object relations in a child with rumination.

LIFE TONUS

It is unusual to refer to life instincts when we define mental health. Yet the pediatrician takes this into account implicitly when faced with the problem of resistance to diseases. Psychoanalysis says little about this. The "instinct for life" strikes the observer from the infant's birth on. It is illustrated by the infant's appetite for food, for perception, for knowledge, and for communication through all sensory

modalities. It is also shown in the baby's need for attachment, for drive expression, and pleasure in functioning. All this is missing in babies with "depressive atonia."

The assessment of psychosomatic equilibrium is based on that of the life instinct in dialectical interplay with tendencies toward death. Gauthier (1982) describes the astonishing capacities of infants for recovery if intervention occurs in time. One must acknowledge the crucial role of early interventions in development, but this should not overshadow unpredictable and astonishing capacities for spontaneous recovery of the human psyche. The wish for life that is in the child and is also transmitted to him by his human surroundings constitutes perhaps the most decisive factor in his development and in his psychosomatic equilibrium.

REFERENCES

Call, J. D. (1980). Attachment disorders in infancy. In *Comprehensive Textbook of Psychiatry,* vol. 3. Baltimore: Williams & Wilkins.

Cramer, B. (1982). La psychiatrie du bébé. In *La Dynamique du Nourrisson,* ed. T. B. Brazelton et al. Paris: Les Editions ESF.

Debre, R. and Doumic, A. (1950). L'anorexie nerveuse de l'enfant. *Seminaires Hôpital Paris,* 11.

Debre, R. and Doumic, A. (1959). *Le Sommeil de l'Enfant.* Paris: Presses Universitaires de France.

Gauthier, Y. (1982). Traumatismes précoces et leur devenir. *Neuropsychiatrie de l'Enfant,* 80:175–191.

Guilhaume, A., Brenoit, O., and Richardet, J. M. (1981). Deficit en sommeil lent profond et nanisme de frustration. *Archives Française Pediatriques,* 38:25–27.

Kreisler, L. (1981). *L'Enfant du Désordre Psychosomatique.* Toulouse: Privat.

Kreisler, L. (1983). *La Psychosomatique de l'Enfant.* Paris: Presses Universitaires de France.

Kreisler, L., Bouchard, F., Lalande, J., and Le Loch, H. (1978). Devenir psychologique des nouveau-nés traités en unité de soins intensifs. *Annales Pédiatriques,* 25:509–518.

Kreisler, L., Fain, M., and Soulé, M. (1981). *L'Enfant et Son Corps—Etudes sur la Clinique Psychosomatique du Premier Age,* 3rd ed. Paris: Presses Universitaires de France.

Lebovici, S. (1983). *Le Bébé, la Mére, le Psychanalyste: Interactions Précoces.* Paris: Le Centurion.

Loriod, J. (1981). Variations de l'inquiétante étrangeté. *Revue Française Psychiatrie,* 45:487–500.

Marty, P. (1958). La relation objectale allergique. *Revue Française Psychiatrie,* 22:5–29.

Marty, P. (1968). La dépression essentielle. *Revue Française Psychiatrie,* 32:595–609.

Marty, P. and de M'Uzan M. (1983). La pensée opératoire. *Revue Française Psychiatrie,* 27:345–355.

Spitz, R. (1945). Hospitalism. *The Psychoanalytic Study of the Child,* 1:53–74. New York: International Universities Press.

Spitz, R. (1946). Anaclitic depression. *The Psychoanalytic Study of the Child,* 2:313–342. New York: International Universities Press.

Wolff, G. and Money, J. (1973). Relationship between sleep and growth in patients with reversible somatotropin deficiency (psychosocial dwarfism). *Psychological Medicine,* 3:18–21.

50

Infants Having to Face Early Failure of Parenting: A Workshop Report

Myriam David, M.D. (chairperson), Marthe Barracco, Catherine D. Isserlis,
Françoise Jardin, M.D., Eve-Marie Léger, Emanuella Malaguzzi-Valeri, M.D.,
Anne-Marie Merlet, Marie-Françoise Pain, and Hano Rottman, M.D.

This workshop assembled three teams working for two years in three different settings with mothers who showed serious early failure in their infant's parenting. The teams agreed that both mother and infant suffer and that it is essential to protect both the infant's integrity and potential development as well as the mother's capacities for mothering. This double aim is crucial, though hard to achieve. The main problem is to protect mother and infant against outbursts of violence which the infant's archaic needs may provoke in the mother, and to secure complementary care for the baby when needed, at the same time treating the pathological tie. We attempt either to maintain the continuity and help the maturation of this tie or, if this proves to be impossible, to achieve separation by helping mother with the mourning process and the baby with its archaic feelings of loss and with the development of its attachment to a stable mother substitute. According to the degree and type of the psychopathology of the mother-infant tie, appropriate settings are needed in order to offer the optimal physical distancing between the mother and infant at the onset of the pathological process; such settings should also provide a possibility for modifying the process according to its evolution.

We have been flexible in using these settings, moving the infants and mothers from one to another as circumstances required. The three settings are (1) psychotherapeutic foster-home care provided by the Centre Familial d'Action Therapeutique at Soisy sur Seine (referred to here as C.F.A.T.); (2) joint hospitalization of mother and infant provided by the mother-infant unit of the Mental Health District Department of Creteil; and (3) home and day care provided by the Unité de Soins Spécialisés à Domicile pour Jeunes Enfants of the thirteenth district of Paris. Each of these settings is described by a representative of each of the teams.

Psychotherapeutic Foster-Home Care (C.F.A.T. team)

Foster-home care is used for infants of isolated psychotic mothers who are unable to take care of their babies and may endanger their lives. However, in such cases, separation is a difficult decision. Emanuella Malaguzzi-Valeri explains why the decision can only be made in a crisis situation that is dangerous to both mother and child. Moreover, fostering the child is not enough. A therapeutic team located in a separate building follows mother and infant and gives support to the foster parents while the infant remains in the foster home and after reunion with the mother, which occurs in 60 percent of the cases. The aim is to help the mother with her overwhelming feelings of attachment and intolerance toward the baby during visits and to evaluate whether contacts should be pursued, how they should be dealt with, and the like.

It is also necessary to watch for subtle signs of suffering in the infant and to understand how the infant's feelings interfere in establishing a relationship with the foster parents. By monitoring the many facets of this complex situation, we hope to guide the infant to the proper place between the two families, and to help the foster parents overcome the attendant stress.

Using as examples three infants, Pierre, Cécile, and Viviane, all now seven years old, who had to be separated from their psychotic mothers in the first few weeks of life, the C.F.A.T. team reviews the main problems connected with such early separation.

The prenatal histories of these children have common features; abortion was endlessly discussed by the psychiatric team, pregnancy was accompanied by severe somatic disturbances, and the mothers were heavily medicated on account of their psychiatric illness. Delivery was normal, but for various reasons (baby underweight, skin infection, and the like, which may have convinced the staff of the mother's inadequacy), the three infants were separated from their mothers at birth and kept in the pediatric ward a few days or weeks before being given to their mothers.

The short postnatal histories of Pierre and Cécile are similar: each mother claimed that she wanted to keep her baby at all costs, but starved and neglected the baby, had aggressive outbursts, and could not bear for anyone else to care for it. Both mothers finally ran away with their babies—Pierre's mother with her naked infant, and Cécile's mother rolling on the ground. The infants were six and ten weeks old respectively when placed in foster homes. After three weeks in the pediatric ward, Vi-

viane was able to stay with her mother at home until she was four months old. Despite regular home visits, the social worker was unaware of the concealed silent stress that Viviane was arousing in her mother. With the mother supposedly at work, and Viviane in a day nursery, a neighbor reported that the flat had been shut and strangely silent for several days. The mother was found lying in bed, catatonic and delirious, convinced that the Devil, not Viviane was in the next room. Viviane was lying alone, in the dark unheated room, seriously dehydrated. She was taken for a few days to the pediatric ward and then placed with a foster family.

ATTITUDES DISPLAYED TOWARD PSYCHOTIC MOTHERS AND THEIR BABIES (EMANUELLA MALAGUZZI-VALERI, PSYCHOTHERAPIST)

When dealing with failing mothers and their "at-loss" infants, the members of a team or different teams often disagree on many aspects of management: whether the infant should be aborted, separated immediately after birth or later, and whether or how often the child in foster care should meet the mother. Team members often argue, as if protecting either the mother or the infant would necessarily damage the other. These attitudes lead to a harmful buildup of stress, and decisions made in emergencies are often equally traumatic for infant and mother. Anxiety can also impede early preventive and therapeutic care, arousing frustrating feelings of inefficiency, usually projected indiscriminately on "the other" team members. Understanding the psychodynamics of this phenomenon helps us to deal with it.

Our three cases demonstrate how problems commonly related to infant birth are unmanagable for psychotic mothers. The baby's preverbal and pregenital mode of functioning and the unavoidable violence of affects amplify and are reinforced by mother's psychosis. The strength of these feelings, transmitted by the mother-infant couple, has a heavy impact on all concerned, including the therapeutic team.

The mother-infant dyad from which the mother forcefully excludes any third party is so closely knit that the mother feels the slightest interference is tearing her apart. We also often consider mother and infant as a split object, the good part usually being the child who will heal the mother; the bad part being the mother who is felt to be destroying the child. The baby may also be considered all good or all bad, in terms of "all or nothing."

When reviewing the records, one finds that this splitting disturbs the team's functioning, leading to contradictory and uncompromising viewpoints, which break the team apart. Hence no decision can be taken until the baby's life is in such danger that no further discussion is possible. In an emergency, the team tends to be induced by the psychotic mother's intolerance of closeness to enact a kidnapping; thus they become unable to introduce a therapeutic distance and use it in time. Such distancing, moreover, is made difficult by the mother's compulsive need for refusion with the object as soon as she feels that her need to reject the threatening object is acknowledged by the team or whenever the need for distancing is mentioned.

These problems also arise concerning the visits of mother and infant. Though the teams consider visiting important, many misunderstandings and mishaps occurred in our three cases, even when decisions had been taken jointly: forgotten appointments, unsatisfactory conditions of meeting, and changes of plan without consultation. The needs of one party are often overlooked. In two of three cases, the first encounter was arranged for a moment suitable for the mother but not for the child, who was at the peak of separation and stranger anxiety. Regular visits between Cécile and her mother were arranged immediately after her placement. Despite the many signs of her suffering and her mother's uneasiness, reported by the child's worker and foster mother, the mother's team was unable to accept the observations of others, insisting on maintaining visiting until the mother broke down. It could not give up its own therapeutic aspiration to see the mother take care of her child.

The "all or nothing" system also seems to be responsible for some team members denying or minimizing the infant's symptoms, while others regard them as a hereditary illness. Equally often the team absorbs the mother's rejection

of the father, and itself rejects or ignores him, even when he has shown some interest in the child before allowing the mother to exclude him. Indeed, it seems almost impossible to resist acting upon the mother's psychotic fantasies: that is, the baby is "really" part of her, and complementary or substitute care for it would "really" be cutting off her good part and leaving the bad part in the hospital. It is understandable that these powerful feelings make a team's decision impossible. At the same time, mother and child desperately need unambivalent support from both teams in order to overcome their anxiety-producing fantasies.

THE MOTHER'S FAILURE IN PARENTING (HANO ROTTMAN, PSYCHIATRIST)

These mothers all have histories of early trauma, violence, and deprivation, which lead them to repetition of their own history, to transgressions, and sometimes to death. Their relation to the child is narcissistic, strongly ambivalent, and expressed in violence. Their explicit need of their infants is surprisingly strong, they cling to them as if they were a part of themselves, and they have tremendous anxiety about loss. At the same time, they act out in clearly dangerous ways their intolerance for the child, as if it might destroy them. Both trends are equally strong.

Both sides of the ambivalence can be worked on therapeutically. The two sides of ambivalence, symbiosis and rejection, can alternate very quickly. Often, the uppermost affect excludes, even represses, the memory of the other, not only in the patient, but also in the therapeutic team (evoking the psychotic avoidance of conflict described in psychotics by P. Racamier [1980]).

The suffering felt by the mothers of these three babies is well illustrated by one of them. We note the variety of her affects and her ability to express in various ways what the others could only express in a stereotyped way through acting out or delusional activity.

Mrs. B., a young, depressive, and drug-addicted woman whose baby entered the C.F.A.T. at the age of one year, was hospitalized for attempting suicide. Before that, the therapists in charge of her had seen little but her rejection of her child. They were uneasy about her incapacity, her aggressiveness, and her dangerous impulses toward the child. She said, "Don't you see I can't take care of him?" or "I don't have the maternal instinct." She threw the baby to the floor to resist the compulsion to throw him out of the window, and thrust her lighted cigarette in her pocket to avoid burning him.

When the child was removed, the symbiotic aspect came to the surface. She expressed her loss and suffering and her longing to make reparation by reunion with him; she persistently asked for frequent encounters with her child, behaved tenderly toward him, bought him sweets, clothes, and toys, and always acted appropriately.

What had happened to the aggressiveness of the first phase? One can hardly find in this delicate and considerate young woman, the dangerous mother previously described. Yet she sometimes misses her appointment with her son because of a fugue or a suicide attempt, or after a disappointing encounter or even an oversatisfying one. She may withdraw suddenly while interacting with her son and explain later that something was bothering her and she could not react otherwise. She also tries to provide substitute objects. She fantasies about pregnancy, saying, "This next one will be mine, no one will take him away from me." It seems to us that the disappearance of the open aggressiveness—now mainly expressed by manifestations of unconscious origin (somatic symptoms, acting out)—is an effect of the separation which, on the one hand, allows the revival of the fantasy child (more acceptable to her narcissism than the real child) and on the other hand, arouses guilt which causes her to repress her aggressiveness and allows her to feel her attachment to the child.

So we see that the complexity of the object relation between this type of mother and her child can be partly understood thanks to the concepts of ambivalence and splitting. Foster placement can be used as a therapeutic lever, which allows the mother to become aware of her attachement to the child and to work through the integration of symbiosis and rejection with the help of the therapeutic team.

BABIES AT "LOSS" (ANNE-MARIE MERLET, EDUCATOR)

Turning to the infants, we were struck by the number of their pre- and postnatal cumulative traumatic experiences. Although one would expect these to produce signs of suffering in the babies, none were mentioned by the maternity staff, pediatricians, nurses, or family. However, as soon as they entered the C.F.A.T., the infants displayed many signs of disturbance, causing a silent uneasiness in those who took care of them.

Three main types of disturbances are described: sleep, tonus, and feeding disturbances. Pierre had an early severe insomnia, day and night, which the foster mother could not remedy for many weeks. This was accompanied by screaming and a hypertonic state that could not be relieved by the foster mother's "holding." Cécile is strikingly hypotonic; she has little appetite, sucks feebly. Viviane is a rather stiff baby who never cries and seems to sleep interminably with half closed eyes, but opens her eyes at once when approached. She has little appetite and holds the food in her mouth without swallowing it.

These symptoms are not uncommon but they have more significance in the light of the concommitent early disturbances of the contact observed in these infants with regard to "looking" and "holding."

At one and a half months of age, Pierre does not yet establish visual contact and turns his head away when picked up. This avoidance of "looking at" or "being looked at" is still present at three months. If he is picked up in the hope of soothing him, he stiffens and screams louder. At two and a half months old, Cécile stares intently when approached. She seems to use this as a powerful controlling device to maintain distance and avoid intrusion. She dislikes being touched when naked and when her position is changed. At four months, Viviane has a strange way of stiffening and throwing herself backward, which makes it difficult to cuddle her.

This kind of behavior seems to consist of early defensive devices directed against human contact, which is felt to be dangerous. It is essential not to overlook these early symptoms because they do not fade out as the years pass; the uneasiness remains and progressively induces pathological features in the infant's relationship with its foster mother and disturbance in the process of individuation and the development of object relationships.

In Pierre's case, the individuation process is seriously impaired. On the one hand, he requires the constant attention and "holding" of his foster parents, and on the other he cannot let them sooth him. His anxiety becomes overwhelming and leads to overt symptoms, chief of which are insomnia and screaming. He has developed a close symbiotic tie to his foster mother whom he controls compulsively. Intensive therapeutic work with Pierre, his foster parents, and his family was needed to keep him from becoming completely psychotic. He remains borderline, with learning difficulties and a tyrannical character.

Cécile's maturation has been very slow; during her first four years, she remained fragile, hypotonic, and rather backward in motor and speech development. Like Pierre, she showed a need to control and possess her foster mother, but the latter tolerated and contained Cécile's anxieties. Both Cécile and her foster mother avoided establishing a symbiotic tie and were able to grow, though slowly, toward building an object relationship. Cécile, now age seven, is a slow learner, with writing and drawing difficulties. She easily falls into depressive moods. Viviane is subdued; she does not cry and is not demanding. Her early symptoms have developed into passive opposition, with conflicts about food and cleanliness, which make her foster mother very angry.

All three children are deeply attached to their foster families, though at different levels. All have found it difficult to relate to their sick mothers. Viviane was able to overcome her initial anxiety when her mother got better; she then developed an affectionate relationship with her "two mothers." The mothers of Pierre and Cécile remained sick (and intolerant of their growing infant); contact produced great anxiety in both children and remained destructive for both mother and child.

In conclusion, our data show how vulnerable these three babies are even after separation from their mothers. We need not seek a single responsible factor. Rather, we believe that many factors always coexist and interact, leaving the baby to face primary anxieties with its own elementary defensive and adaptive abilities. It is important not to minimize these disturbances; they must be regarded as symptoms of suffering in an infant at "loss," a characterization which is often denied. This suffering brings about deep modifications in the infant's drive and ability to relate to the mother substitute. The baby's early traumatic experience with a psychotic or otherwise disturbed mother penetrates deeply into its relationship with the foster mother.

RAISING A DISABLED MOTHER'S INFANT (EVE-MARIE LEGER, PSYCHOLOGIST)

Most foster parents bring up someone else's baby as a result of their own needs to complete themselves, to prolong their procreativity, to demonstrate and re-experience their motherly "goodness," their power to comfort, repair, undo "evil," and to produce a "good" baby. It is a shocking experience for them to be faced with the behavior of infants at "loss." They must deal with their guilt toward the mother deprived of her child and with the fear of losing the baby if the mother recovers. At the same time, this new baby, which is the foster mother's and not her husband's, seems to have a seductive influence and induces in the foster parents responses they did not allow themselves with their own children.

Mr. and Mrs. R. have brought up ten children. For Mrs. R. to be a "wife-mother" is an important part of the couple's equilibrium. This balance had been seriously upset as a result of their age and a recent abortion. So they took in Pierre. The interminable crying and sleeplessness of this three-week-old baby and the impossibility of soothing him affects them both. Mr. and Mrs. R. are not only deeply shaken by Pierre's anxiety and their inability to comfort him, but also by his mother's "folly" and by his grandparents, who keep greedily claiming him. They also know that Pierre's absence throws his mother back into psychotic spells. All this makes them, too, very possessive, and both foster parents are trapped into excessive attendance on Pierre in an effort to contain his anxiety. For Pierre, torn between his two families, the therapeutic team plays the role of a third party who mediates the omnipotence that Pierre exerts on his foster parents. It also helps him to emerge from this pathological symbiotic tie and to engage in the very first steps of individuation.

For Mr. and Mrs. L., Cécile's foster parents, she too is the last baby they allow themselves. They have already raised their own four children and a foster child who has just left. At first Mrs. L. can tolerate Cécile's fragility, oversensivity, watchfulness, distrust of intruders, and feeding problems; her previous experience with a depressed one-year-old girl helps her to do this. This helps to reduce Cécile's need for distance; she comes closer and closer, displaying a kind of eroticism which makes Mrs. L. feel uneasy. At the same time, Cécile becomes very demanding, if not tyrannical. Mrs. L. is worried, uncertain whether to resist or give in. Her desire to protect this frail child and her fear of damaging her, coupled with her allowance of a proximity that was strictly controlled with her own children, make it difficult for her to find the "right" answer. She is secure enough, however, to use the help of the therapeutic team to protect Cécile and herself from excessive closeness, a closeness that her children and husband would also willingly share in. She also uses the team to discuss her complex feelings toward Cécile's very sick mother, her fears that the mother will hurt the child during the visits, her fear that the father or other relatives will reappear and claim the child. She uses the consultation to question her own possessiveness, to discuss adoption, and to prepare for the disturbing necessity of giving helpful answers later when Cécile asks questions about her first mother and father.

For Mrs. A., who feels enslaved by an early marriage, foster care is her way to achieve independence. Viviane enables her to be a valuable foster mother recognized by society. She loves the baby deeply and warmly. Viviane is a source of pride and a narcissistic gratification. However, Viviane's tendency to withdraw, expressed through stiffening and slow eating, is a threat to Mrs. A. who tries to master the child

by overstimulating her forcefully, thus reinforcing her passive obstinacy. Viviane provokes in her outbursts of frightening anger; both partners are trapped in a vicious circle. The team has to help them escape. Mrs. A. accepts help readily as long as she can feel the reliable trust of the worker. She leaves the entire responsibility of the monthly meetings between mother and child, which began when Viviane was eleven months old, to the team. She does not interfere, prepares the child well, and talks to her about her mother, not feeling rivalry as long as she does not see mother and child together. Under these conditions, Viviane can gradually overcome her fear of her mother and grow closer to her. At first her mother reacts to the closeness by a psychotic episode which necessitates several months of hospitalization and interruption of the visits. However, as Viviane grows bigger, she is less of a threat to her mother and when she is about four years old, with the constant help of the team, she develops without too much conflict a warm and affectionate relationship with her "two mothers."

Joint Mother-Child Hospitalization (Françoise Isserlis, Psychiatrist-Assistant)

Within a general hospital, the Mental Health District Department possesses a unit of a few rooms for mother-infant hospitalization. This unit is distinguished by its easy links with other services—gynecology, obstetrics, neonatalogy, pediatrics. Its second characteristic is its very small size, allowing an organization of daily life as close to family life as possible and most unlike the usual hospital life.

Having used this service for all sorts of problems concerning babies and mothers, we gradually began to use it in overcoming early difficulties involved in the primary maternal relationship. During a crisis, joint mother-infant hospitalization is a very efficient means of protecting the child's interest: emergencies can be dealt with, and the child can be protected while the mother is treated. This temporary solution allows for direct observation of the mother-child couple in their daily interactions; intensive and immediate care of pathological mothering and disturbances appearing in the child; and psychological study as to whether the child should remain in its family or be removed. Decisions can thus be made in the interest of both parents, the child, and the rest of the family, on the basis of factual observations of the many difficulties of everyday life.

The disadvantage of this method is the exposure of a newborn child to all the hazards of the mother's pathology, with no certainty that even if there is an improvement the method can be maintained in a less well protected environment after discharge. In any case this form of help can only last for a few months at most.

Because we often feel that we are not authorized or are unable to make a decision in an emergency, we propose this type of treatment when we are concerned about the mother's disturbed behavior or delusions, regardless of whether the mother was psychotic before the pregnancy or became so subsequently.

In these difficult and distressing cases, admission is not based on clear therapeutic aims but on the negative perspective that all other possible solutions appear equally unsatisfactory. In some of the families whose problems are already well known to us, a psychological and social approach is possible from pregnancy onward. However, we are often obliged to intervene with hospitalization in a crisis.

Hospitalization may mean different things according to the person who requests it; the first step is to obtain a request from the mother herself. Although she may express herself too paradoxically to be understood, she sometimes wants a temporary physical separation from the child, and only one of them will be hospitalized to begin with.

Discussion of joint-hospitalization or immediate and presumably definitive removal of the child leads, as Dr. Malaguzzi has shown, to violent differences of opinion among the teams concerned. Staff accustomed to these problems may play a mediating role.

In a team consisting of nurses, social worker, pediatrician, child psychiatrist, psychoanalyst, everyone has a different role. Some are more concerned with the realities of daily life, others

with the patient's inner world. This diversity of roles is necessary if the affects, against which the entire staff must defend themselves, are to be bearable.

Studying all the various elements involved casts new light on a situation whose many aspects are not always apparent to everyone (staff member or outside participants) and do not seem capable of being assimilated into a coherent whole. On the staff, the child psychiatrist is coordinator with a role intermediate between the nurse's holding care and psychotherapy in the usual sense. By focusing on the child's development and the implications of the speech and behavior of the mother and the family, he can help the nurses to intervene flexibly in response to the changing reality situation. He tries to prevent the fantasies, interpretations, and changing identifications and projections of one member from taking over the entire team. He also tries to differentiate between intervention in the mother-infant dyad and the specific therapy of the mother: hospitalization is not intended to interfere with the mother's psychotherapy or psychoanalysis in other contexts.

We must emphasize the complexity of the nurse's work which ensures the double "holding" of the mother and the child. When these two are hospitalized together, it is by observing the baby that all staff members are able to respond appropriately. Their responses enable the child to participate in what is being played out around him according to his own abilities, that is, no longer according to the mother's behavior and fantasies and his reactions to them.

This requires analysis and evaluation of the daily care that the child receives from his mother—who authentically remains the mother—and the substitute care that supplements this. By "care" we mean, of course, not only the necessary physical care but also the atmosphere of feeding, changing, play, and sleep situations.

The guidelines for attempting to understand the baby's perceptions come from detailed observation of the interchanges between mother and child, or between a third person and the child. After observing the baby's responses, we then attempt to see whether he reacts positively to manipulations that may appear incoherent or exaggerated, or whether he seems to find them intolerable, as if reflecting his mother's intolerable situation.

We pay particular attention to the child's common expressions: looks, smiles, and gestures are studied qualitatively rather than quantitatively (even a charming smile may seem to us to be inappropriate in a given situation). No isolated fact can explain the meaning of distress. Only the baby's reactions as a whole, observed daily by all members of staff, each in his own capacity, allow early detection of dysfunction before it is visible as a health problem.

We try to establish a significant link between the necessity of maintaining the infant's bodily and affective comfort and limiting the violence of the mother's affects before she can effectively transfer her distress to the child.

The nurses' role is not so much to normalize maternal behavior as to shelter mother and child from the extreme emotions of self-destruction and disintegration that the mother experiences and communicates to her child. At this time, the danger is mutual, the needs of the mother and child are not in conflict. To this end, we try to put into words behaviors and affects; we help the child to understand his mother's reasons for behaving this way; and we help the mother to understand the alarming reactions that she can see in her infant.

The question of the different speeds of the mother's progress and of the child's development is sometimes particularly acute, despite the support of the institution. We have to try to make more bearable for the mother the psychotherapy that is helping the child in his individuation process.

We must reflect as soon as possible on how to create appropriate distance between mother and child: Does the mother accept the baby's presence near her? Can she take care of him completely or partially? With what help? Will she allow a third person to take care of him in her presence? Does she want a physical separation? If need be, who is best able to give substitute care? Should it be within or outside the family? (This last question refers only to non-adoptable children.)

Intervention during the neonatal period,

whatever solution may be chosen on leaving hospital, commits us to lengthier treatment in order to preserve continuity in the child's history and development. Follow-up continues throughout early childhood until the child has structured his personality and can establish relationships with others, including his own parents. The risks that these children continue to run by the very circumstances of their birth and the sometimes uneven progress of their development often necessitate additional therapy.

Therapeutic Home and Day Care (F. Jardin, Psychiatrist)

The Home and Day Care Unit, created in 1976 in Paris is part of the mental health program of the 13th district. This unit is open to thirty infants, between birth and six years of age. It works closely with the maternal and child-care centers, the adult and child psychiatric services, and the various social services of the district that refer the cases. The Unit's aim is to treat pathogenic parent-infant ties as early as possible (50 percent of the infants are now admitted during the first year of life), when the symbiotic tie and the processes of individuation are being impaired and before the infant's and mother's suffering reaches a point where hospitalization or placement is needed.

Early pathology occurs in various circumstances. The first kind of case referred to the unit concerned psychotic isolated mothers as well as couples who had undergone deprivation and ill treatment during their own infancy and childhood.[1] But many other circumstances may cause severe failure of mothering during the first months of the infant's life. The baby may arouse its parents' vulnerability through a symptom (feeding, sleeping, tonicity disturbances), thus starting a vicious circle of mutually destructive, alarming interactions. Some organic neonatal abnormality, whether slight or severe, may also arouse in each parent

---

[1]The therapeutic work with those cases was presented by Myriam David at the Congress of Lisbon and is published in the first volume of *Frontiers of Infant Psychiatry*.

strong feelings about his or her own inadequacy as genitor and parent to an extent that impedes the emotional investment of the infant. Such cases as these are both severe and unusual and require treatment. They constitute not only a psychological but even a vital danger for the child; it also seems, though this is less obvious, that the infant is very active in creating and prolonging the parents' disfunctioning. Indeed, all these mothers seem to have lost their ego ability to counterinvest, which normally helps to contain the infant's archaic anxieties. It also seems that the infant's deviance deprives the mothers of normal empathy toward the infant's primary manifestations and of their "holding" ability. Thus they are defenseless and seem to be contaminated by the infant's primary modes of functioning, merging with him into confusion and unspeakable primary anxieties described by Winnicott and the Kleinian school. These latter feelings are expressed in interaction with the child, through spells of violence, or more subtly, for example, by leaving him isolated in a closed room.

We understand why it so difficult for all these parents to seek help. They tend to conceal their stress, isolate themselves, hide the child more or less, as if any therapeutic intrusion were a threat. This reluctance makes it difficult for a pediatrician to refer the case or for the psychiatric team to approach it. On the other hand, without further intervention infants deprived of the maternal ego function produce harmful primary modes of defense, such as withdrawal, inertia, excessive sleep, overwatchfulness, spells of hypertonicity, or flabbiness. But these defense modes are usually overlooked by the foster-care team. They can be detected only if one is allowed to observe and know the baby in interaction with both his mother and with a therapeutic caregiver.

Our aim then is to create a therapeutic space for both the parents and the infant, without being too intrusive; to give equal attention to both, remaining at their side, and sharing their living experience. Usually two workers are involved, one closer to the infant (caregiver or child therapist), one closer to the parents (psychiatric nurse or psychologist). This can make a group of four, together with the mother and infant. Sometimes when mother and child are apart, one worker remains with the mother, the other with the baby. Sometimes either worker may be alone with the baby-mother dyad. Thus the infant's functioning and developmental needs are constantly kept in focus, as well as the mother's hardships, the mutual intolerance, the consequent interactions. Both workers experience personally the violent feelings of the party they represent. In order to be able to cope with these feelings without being torn apart, they tell each other their daily experiences and discuss them at regular intervals with the consultant psychiatrist. The latter also meets parents and child in a monthly consultation. This eventually enables him to interpret, to express in words the ongoing relation that connects the tumultuous interactions of parents, infant, and worker as they relate to underlying feelings of the present and past. Thus the three team members work as a therapeutic unit, accompanying the mother-infant dyad physically and psychologically along the strenuous path of individuation.

This work goes on in three different "spaces," each having its specific function: the parent's home, the Center, where the reception room is used mainly by the mother, and the playroom used mostly by the infants. In each of these spaces, mother and infant may be together or apart, and at the Center the different spaces may be open or closed to one or the other.

HOME VISITS (MARIE FRANÇOISE PAIN, PSYCHIATRIC NURSE)

Home visits are a good way for the worker to approach the mother and baby in their own environment, to observe their interactions, to view what the infant induces in the mother and why and how their relationship is interrupted. Insight into what is going on "inside" and outside may be achieved by noting what is said, and what is shown or hidden. Although parents do not always allow home visits, they sometimes welcome them as if they want us to see for ourselves what is going on. However, the worker is not there to observe and detect what goes wrong but rather to get to know each member of the family. The worker may become the object of displaced aggresiveness and become exposed to a high level of anxiety that she cannot avoid sharing; indeed, this is incumbent upon her. The worker is assaulted by manifold impressions to which she should remain open and receptive; analyzing and understanding may come later. Physical care may be part of the job when it lies in the realm of a shared experience between mother and nurse.

Home visits also extend beyond the home. One may accompany the mother and infant to the pediatrician, the day-care nursery, social services, or to the Center. This "accompanying" is a way of maintaining continuity and unity between fragments played out between the internal and the external world, between fantasy and reality. In this process, the worker is the one onto whom the overflow of anxiety and affect is projected and who is there to "contain" it, avoiding its destructive real or fantasied effects. It is therefore difficult for the home visitor to keep the right distance. In order to metabolize and to give meaning to what she is able to take in, she needs to "give it back," at a distance, to the rest of the team at the Center.

RECEPTION AT THE CENTER (MARTHE BARRACCO, PSYCHOLOGIST)

This is an open place where families know they can come without an appointment, where they are sure to find a "house mother" who is linked with one or another team member, especially the psychiatric nurse. For many parents, this is the only chance to go out, a difficult step toward escaping from isolation. It helps to know about the certainty of a welcome. Often parents arrive reticently; later they may noisily invade the place; eventually they use the opportunity more coherently. They are able to meet other mothers and fathers and to share their problems and their experiences. This space also becomes very significant for the child, especially when he learns to talk. It is a place where he can explore, move away from his parents without losing sight of them, and

come back to them when he feels like it. He rediscovers the caregivers he knew at home. The little distance that has been created between the small child and his parents enables the mothers, relieved of their responsibility, to see their children as separate people, and often to see the connection between the events of the present and their own early experiences with their own parents. Separation is experienced over and over again when the child caregivers invite the children to go to the playroom with them. There, too, at certain moments the child uses the mother's nurse to express the negative side of the ambivalence, thereby protecting the mother. The child views the nurse as a kind of extension of the mother, enabling an improvement in object relations.

CHILDREN'S PLAY GROUPS (MARTHE BARRACCO)

Whereas the frequency of the meetings at home and of the mother's visits at the Center varies according to the needs of the moment, the play groups of children are stable events for the children. They are held twice a week at the same time on the same day of the week. There are three to five children with two caregivers and a psychologist as observer. The membership of each group is constant, except for children who arrive or leave in the course of the year. Children of six to fifteen months of age attend with their mothers and sometimes their fathers, observing and being observed, getting to know a strange place and strange people, taking an interest in them or not, being active or aloof, either clung to or ignored by their mothers. The caregivers can now and then draw attention to what is happening or to what the baby seems to be saying in his or her own way.

The toddlers, aged from about fifteen to thirty months, meet in the playroom, while their mothers are in reception; the door between the rooms is sometimes open, sometimes closed, according to the request of the children, the parents, or one of the staff. One of this group's main activities, at least at first, is to go from one room to the other, as if to confirm the presence or absence of the parents and the staff; they play at going away and coming back, followed some way off by the caregiver. When they reach the age of two to five years, the children have a room of their own; the caregiver fetches the child from the home and the parents may or may not call to take it home. The journey to the Center is an important transition. The caregiver witnesses the significant moments of separation and reunion. These moments, both before and after, produce interactions loaded with affect; it is often on the journey that the child reveals part of an experience that can be taken up on the spot.

It is also a time when the child has its caregiver to itself, which helps it to join the group and become part of it. The groups are not used to stimulate the children's activity or to provide them with a better environment, but give the children a chance to try out their autonomous functions where the team is able to appreciate them. It is also a place where the child can use what we call behavioral language with very few restrictions, this being the sole means of expression in the early months. The team tries to understand this form of communication, finding the links between his emotional expression, the present situation, and what is going on at home. The group puts this into words, bearing in mind the transferential aspects of the child's relationships with the special caregiver. This worker remains close to the child, and by watching and listening, by participating in his play and by her words, she supports his moves, which are only vaguely indicated at first but then become more decisive as the child joins or leaves his mother, approaches a coveted object, explores, climbs, and so forth. The observer and the caregivers work in close cooperation, meeting after each group to decipher what has been happening. They elucidate the pattern of several sessions and discuss them with the other team members, the nurse and the doctor, who share their experiences during the same period. In this way the child is followed, together with his parents, and supported in its development and in his gradual individuation. This basic treatment is sometimes complemented or followed by psychotherapy for the child, or for the mother and child together, or possibly by referring the mother for therapy elsewhere.

REFERENCE

Racamier, P. (1980). *Les Schizophrenes.* Paris: Payot.

51

Children with Congenital Hypothyroidism

Marijke Uleman-Vleeschdrager, Ph.D., Janile A.R. Sanders-Woudstra, M.D.,
Ph.D., and Hedy Westerborg-van Loon, M.D.

In 1979 a screening program aimed at the early recognition and treatment of congenital hypothyroidism (CHT) by means of substitution therapy (Derksen-Lubson et al., 1980) was started in the Netherlands in a defined trial area. Because the anomaly may lead to severe mental retardation (Klein et al., 1972; Money et al., 1978; Raiti et al., 1971; Steinhausen et al., 1978; Wolter et al., 1979; Zabransky et al., 1975), developmental index (D.I.) measurements were made from the time substitution therapy was initiated, and these measurements constituted an important datum in evaluating the results. Such evaluation has been undertaken by the Child Psychiatry Department of Sophia Children's Hospital, which has been engaged in the psychological examination of babies in the Rotterdam area who were identified as suffering from CHT and who were given immediate treatment. A total of twenty infants have been tested; no selection other than their somatic anomaly combined with early treatment was made. These twenty infants were detected via the screening program to be described. We also offer data on the follow-up and the psychological results.

Screening

Laboratory tests are required for early detection of CHT, inasmuch as clinical manifestations are seldom obvious during the neonatal period. Screening was combined with the existing phenylketonuria (PKU) screening that was instituted nationwide in 1974. The screening protocol for CHT was drawn up by members of the National Steering Committee and the Rotterdam Working Party (Health Council, 1980; Werkgroep, 1978, 1979, 1980).

Thyroxine (T4) and thyroid stimulating hormone (TSH) were measured by microradioimmunoassay in heel-puncture blood spotted on filter paper. The heel puncture was to be performed at the age of six, seven, or eight days. If this proved to be impossible, it was performed before the end of the second week of life. In this way more than 99 percent of the newborns were screened.

Follow-up

If the heel puncture (or second heel puncture, depending on the screening result of the first heel puncture) revealed abnormal values, the infant was referred to a pediatrician, usually within twenty-four hours. The pediatrician examined the referred infants according to a protocol for history-taking and physical examination and for laboratory examinations, which were: T4, TBG-test, T3, and TSH.[1] Indi-

---

[1] The circulating thyroid hormones T4 and T3 are firmly bound to thyroxine-binding globuline (TBG).

cations for repeat serum measurements were T4 $\leq$ 60 nmol/1 (60–70 dubious), TBG-test < 80 percent, FTI $\leq$ 60 (60–70 dubious) and T3 $\leq$ 1.0 nmol/1 and TSH $\leq$ 20 nIU/1 (10–20 dubious). In case of CHT, additional investigations, such as a thyroid scan and radiological examination of the left foot and knee, were made to assess the skeletal age.

A protocol for therapy was drawn up by the Staff of the Division of Pediatric Endocrinology of the Sophia Children's Hospital (Derksen-Lubsen, 1981):

1. Combined T3 and T4—that is, initiation with 3 ug L-T3/day up to a dose of 15 ug/day. When this dose is reached, T3 is gradually decreased and eventually stopped. L-T4 treatment is started when a T3-dose of 15 ug/day is reached. Initial dose of 15 ug/day up to an eventual dose of 75 ug/day.
2. T4—initiation with a dose of 25 ug/day and increased to an eventual dose of 75 ug/day.

Table 51–1 gives the clinical data for each of the twenty infants.* These data show that the median age at diagnosis was sixteen days and the median age at initiation of treatment eighteen days. At the time of psychological examination all the babies were in a euthyreotic status. The infants came regularly for a medical examination, laboratory measurements (Tr, TSH), and subsequent substitution therapy (mean dose of T4 was 50 ug/day). Compliance with therapy was good.

Psychological Examination

The infants were tested using the Bayley Scales of Infant Development, consisting of a mental and a motor scale (Bayley, 1969). The scales have a mean of 100 and a standard deviation of 16. These tests were chosen because we had experience with them in earlier research programs involving another category of infants with perinatal problems, namely, low-birthweight infants (Sanders-Woudstra et al., 1983). In our view, the scales also provided a good framework for evaluating the results obtained in the CHT group. The group is heterogenous in composition. Ages range from seven to twenty-seven months.

Though no hypotheses were formulated beforehand, the pediatricians expected, partly on the basis of publications from Canada and the United States (Dussault et al., 1980), that the D.I.'s would not deviate from those of the normal population. Figure 51–1 shows, however, that the form of distribution has a slight bimodal tendency. A similar tendency was also found by Dussault and colleagues (1983) reporting on the retesting results of fifty-nine CHT children at thirty-six months.

Table 51–2 shows that the mean of the mental scale is slightly above the lower limit of the normal; the mean of the motor scale is slightly below it. Of the total of 40 test scores, 50 percent were below the lower limit of the normal (84). The lowest scores occurred in the lowest age group, for which, as far as we are aware, no other research results are known.

As regards behavior, one is struck by the fact that these children experience very great difficulty in acquiring the finer manipulatory skills, and the form this takes seems to be specific to CHT children. The children in the lowest age group cannot get their fingers to cooperate in grasping and releasing. Of the six youngest (seven to nine months), four had difficulty bending their fingers in grasping and holding onto objects, five in releasing them. Three of the six had not yet developed a pincer grip (norm: seven months). This means that an obstruction occurs in the developmental process at precisely the moment when these young children are about to take their first step in the exploration of the world, no longer exclusively via the mouth but through seeing, grasping, and handling—that is, eye-hand coordination. If this proceeds smoothly it gives the baby a sense of familiarity with its own body and its environment, creating self-confidence, which in turn stimulates the child to take further developmental steps, including social-interaction processes such as imitation (word formation) and functioning in free space (standing and walking alone).

In practice—and also in the test—lack of smooth progress means that simple acts such as fixating, grasping, and releasing are not sufficiently automated. Consequently, when

TABLE 51-1
Clinical Data Concerning Children with CHT

Child nr. (sex)	Birth-Weight/Gestation	Heelpuncture Day	Heelpuncture T4/s.d. TSH (mTII/1)	Age at Diagnosis (days)	T4 (nmol/1)	TSH (mU/1)	TBG (%)	FTI	T3 (nmol/1)	Sceletal Age (wk)	Scan*	Age at Treatment (days)	Treatment (nr. 1 or 2) of Protocol
1. (f)	3400/41	6	−1.2 / 282.5	16	67	310	124	54	2.8	p.n.	—	22	—
2.† (f)	2065/37	7	−3.5 / 165.0	19	48	240	106	—	2.0	p.n.	—	38	2
3.† (f)	1995/37	7	−3.5 / 155.0	16	65	240	113	58	2.0	p.n.	—	24	2
4. (f)	2800/39	7	−4.4 / 397.5	9	12	245	119	10	1.1	p.n.	—	11	—
5. (m)	3700/41	6	−4.6 / 620.0	9	12	230	121	11	—	p.n.	n.t.	11	1
6. (m)	3680/41	12	−4.1 / 482.5	18	6	950	136	4	—	p.n.	—	21	—
7. (m)	3890/41	7	−4.3 / 550.0	16	<10	1200	117	<8	1.3	32‡	n.t.	18	1
8. (m)	3180/43	6	−4.4 / 285.0	12	14	500	113	12	—	34	n.t.	12	1
9. (f)	2840/40	8	−3.5 / 540.0	16	53	1200	124	43	—	p.n.	ectopia	16	1
10. (f)	1695/37	10	−4.5 / 500.0	14	10	1100	116	10	1.0	37	n.t.	21	—
11. (f)	3500/42	9	−4.3 / 380.0	15	10	350	127	10	1.1	p.n.	n.t.	17	—
12.** (f)	—/—	—	— / —	—	—	—	—	—	—	—	—	18	—
13. (m)	3560/39	9	−5.3 / 400.0	12	17	500	112	15	1.5	38	n.t.	13	—
14. (m)	2770/37	11	−4.7 / 392.5	17	10	500	104	10	1.2	37	n.t.	24	—
15. (f)	3255/42	13	−4.1 / 367.5	16	10	50	114	10	1.0	36	n.t.	17	—
16. (f)	3810/42	11		13	<10	>400	120	<10	3.9	p.n.	—	12	1
17. (f)	3500/40	23 (nd)		44	54	600	134	37	2.4	—	—	55	2
18. (m)	3580/42	12		17	<10	700	115	<9	—	—	—	19	2
19. (f)	4010/40	14		14	22	950	121	18	—	—	—	16	2
20. (f)	3250/43	9		35	<10	>300	128	<8	0.7	—	—	35	2

—: not done   *n.t. = no thyroid   †twins   ‡skeletal age conform gestational age of 32 weeks p.n. = post-natal   **this child went to another hospital for treatment

NOTE: Data, courtesy of the Department of Endocrinology, Sophia Children's Hospital, Rotterdam, Netherlands and from G. Derksen-Lubsen, M.D., Ph.D. (1981).

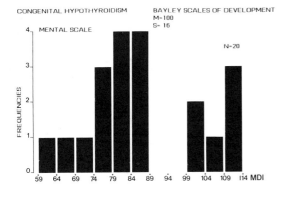

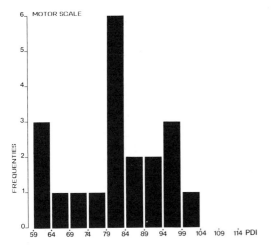

Figure 51-1

TABLE 51-2

Congenital Hypothyroidism Early Detected

Age Group	Child nr.	Mental Score	Motor Score
6–12 months			
7	16	79	87
8	20	81	64
8	14	81	77
9	12	83	80
9	15	111	80
12	19	112	86
13–18 months			
13	11	112	99
14	10	103	97
15	18	82	90
15	13	109	95
16	9	86	80
16	17	78	80
16	8	62	65
16	7	102	81
18	6	73	62
19–24 months			
21	2	85	100
21	3	85	92
21	5	77	62
22	4	87	84
> 24 months			
27	1	68	73

$N = 20$ ($♀ = 13$, $♂ = 7$)
$\overline{X}$ mental 88
$\overline{X}$ motor 82
Bayley Scales: $M = 100$; $SD = 16$

these acts have to serve as components of more complex acts (sensorimotor patterns) such as building, stagnation occurs. The continuity of the act as a whole is disrupted and it loses its gestalt character. The development of the "task" concept is thereby thwarted. The attention span remains limited, with the result that the act is performed in a slow and fragmented way and often abandoned before completion. Hence, in the literature one finds these children typified as "slow" and "having difficulties with gestalt formation," even when they are older.

In the test, those tasks which call for an ability to perform more complex acts demanding an integration of sensorimotor skills occur chiefly in the age group thirteen to eighteen months. Dussault's group (1980) reported on a study of thirty-five CHT children and found that the D.I. results at eighteen months were significantly lower than those at twelve months. A statistical analysis showed the difference was attributable to deficiencies in the CHT children in the areas of eye-hand coordination and language. The researchers assumed that a change in the mother-child relationship brought about by the first examination at twelve months had played a part in the decline. Our observations of the parent-child relationships in this group tend to support that hypothesis.

Because of his inability to master certain muscle mechanisms, the CHT infant starts later than his contemporaries on the expansion and coordination of exploratory skills. He continues for a longer period to be deeply occupied with small-scale activities such as looking around, putting things in the mouth, manipulating bits of cloth or rattles, and crumpling paper—a favorite activity in which these children can be engaged exclusively for long stretches, exercising their fingers, as it were.

CHT babies react in a less oriented and alert way to stimuli from the outside world, including stimuli from the mother. As a result, the parents feel that it is difficult to have contact with their child, which gives rise to disappointment. These babies do indeed give the impression in social contact of being unresponsive and little oriented to the person. Faced with their inability, for example, to take hold of things that attract them, the children have a tendency to become angry and upset and are not easily comforted. It is natural that children who still have so little control of themselves, and whose experience is so fragmented and discontinuous, lose control more quickly and are more difficult to calm down again (to reintegrate).

In general, then, these fairly passive babies are busy with activities that seem rather stereotyped; they are little oriented to the outside world, subject to fits of dysphoria, and sparing in sound production and imitation. Statements such as "The baby is fond of his ease" or "He'll make a good council worker" are heard more than once. The parents' fears that something is wrong, despite the reassurance given by the doctor, are thus reinforced by their child.

There are parents who, because of their need to see their fears proved unfounded, provoke so-called liveliness in their child by means of overstimulating behavior (startling the child, wild games), to which the child reacts with uncontrolled and hence dysfunctional behavior. There are also parents who react with resignation. They say they accept the fact that their child is backward and do not want to hurry him or her. They try to cover up their disappointment by assumed indifference (withdrawal of libido) and are thus in danger of offering too few stimuli. They give up games such as clap-your-hands because the child fails to react. The learning situation in which CHT children find themselves is greatly influenced, therefore, by the way in which the parents cope with their anxiety, confusion, and disappointment. The climate in which these babies are brought up is often less child-oriented than

is thought to be optimal, which means that these youngsters, vulnerable to begin with, find it even more difficult to build up a consistent world and body image.

Reports on studies of older CHT children show that they catch up to a degree in the course of time as regards their problems with eye-hand coordination. Our own findings point in the same direction. However, such behaviors as unresponsiveness in contact, slowness, fits of temper, short attention span, and difficulties in gestalt formation persist and continue to exert a disruptive influence at least until school age. The results (reported by Dussault et al., 1983) at thirty-six months still show a statistically significant difference from the control group. The children who were retested by us, all of whom showed some gain in D.I., were found to have a disharmonious intelligence distribution: a wide variance over the age-columns. Our aim therefore is to improve right from the start the climate in which these children are brought up. The steps being taken to achieve this are as follows:

1. The physician in charge must cooperate with regard to his statements to the parents. Excessive optimism causes confusion in the parents because they see that their child nonetheless has more difficulty with development than his or her contemporaries.

2. A psychological examination should be performed in the presence of the parent or parents at an early stage. The age of seven to eight months seems best. The examination is followed by a discussion concerned particularly with the specific difficulties associated with the anomaly. In general, this comes as a relief to parents, because the things which have been worrying them so much are put into words.

3. Practical advice should be offered and the opportunity to make a further appointment provided if desired. Most parents take this up eagerly.

We believe that in this way we can make a contribution to the parent-child relationship and hence to the learning and growing environment of this group of children whom we consider to be at risk despite their favorable medical prognosis.

REFERENCES

Bayley, N. (1969). *Scales of Infant Development.* New York: Psychological Corporation.

Derksen-Lubsen, G. (1981). Screening for congenital hypothyroidism in the Netherlands. Thesis, Erasmus University, Rotterdam.

Derksen-Lubsen, G., de Jonge, G. A., and Schopman, W. (1980). Bevolkingsonderzoek naar cogenitale hypothyreoidie bij pasgeborenen in een proefrigio. *Nederlands Tijdschrift voor Geneesekunde,* 124:260–263.

Dussault, J. H. et al. (1980). Psychological development of hypothyroid infants at age 12 and 18 months: Experience after neonatal screening. In *Neonatal Thyroid Screening.* New York: Raven Press.

Dussault, J. H. et al. (1983). Preliminary results on the mental development of hypothyroid infants detected by the Quebec Screening Program. *Journal of Pediatrics,* 102: 19–22.

Health Council (1980). *Recommendations for Screening for Inborn Errors of Metabolism.* The Hague: Staatsuitgeverij.

Klein, A. H., Meltzer, S., and Kenny, F. M. (1972). Improved prognosis in congenital hypothyroidism treated before age three months. *Journal of Pediatrics,* 71:912–915.

Money, J., Clarke, F. C., and Beck, J. (1978). Congenital hypothyroidism and IQ-increase: A quarter-century follow-up. *Journal of Pediatrics,* 93:432–434.

Raiti, S. and Newns, G. H. (1971). Cretinism: Early diagnosis and its relation to mental prognosis. *Archives of Diseases in Childhood,* 46:692–694.

Sanders-Woudstra, J. A. R. et al. (1983). Low-birth-weight children in their first two years of life and their difficulties. In *Frontiers of Infant Psychiatry,* ed. J. D. Call, E. Galenson, and R. L. Tyson. New York: Basic Books.

Steinhausen, H. C., Gluck, M., and Wiebel, J. (1978). Die psychische entwicklung von kindern mit hypothyroese. *Monatschriften Kinderheilkunde,* 126:90–99.

Werkgroep (1978, 1979, 1980). *Results of the Screening for Congenital Hypothyroidism in the Trial Area.* Leiden, The Netherlands: Institute for Preventive Health Care.

Wolter, R. et al. (1979). Neuropsychological study in treated thyroid dysgenesis. *Acta Paediatrica Scandinavica,* Supplement 277:41–46.

Zabransky, S. et al. (1975). Zur prognose der angeborenen hypothyreose: Psychopathologische befunde bei 30 langzeitbehandelten kindern.

52

The Offspring of Epileptic Mothers: A High-Risk Population?

Hans-Christoph Steinhausen, M.D., Ph.D., Helga Huth, Ph.D., and Sabine Koch, M.D.

From a theoretical point of view, children of epileptic parents may be regarded as being exposed to a threefold risk. First is the risk of genetic transmission, at least for some types of epilepsy. Next, teratogenic effects resulting from intrauterine exposure to antiepileptic drugs may be manifested in disorders of physical and mental development. Finally, the parental illness may be accompanied by psychopathological disturbances which can influence the child's development.

The model of children at risk via genetic inheritance, *in utero* effects, and parental psychopathology has already been utilized in the study of various psychiatric disorders; for example, parental schizophrenia (cf. the reviews of Anthony, 1978; Erlenmeyer-Kimling et al., 1980; Garmezy, 1977; Mednick et al., 1979; Sameroff and Seifer, 1981), parental depression (Conners et al., 1979; Cytryn et al., 1982; McKnew et al., 1979; Welner et al., 1977; Winters et al., 1981), and children of alcoholic parents (Steinhausen et al., 1982a, 1982b, 1983).

However, there have been only a few reports on the effects of antiepileptic medications. Among these studies of drug effects on early psychomotor and intellectual development, some have observed an unusually high rate of mentally subnormal children (Hanson et al., 1976; Hanson and Smith, 1975; Hill et al., 1974, 1982; Majewski et al., 1980; Shapiro et al., 1976; Speidel and Meadow, 1972; Vert et al., 1979), results which were not, however, confirmed by others (Dietrich, 1980; Granström, 1979, 1982; Sobczyk et al., 1977). In a retrospective pilot study we have been able to ascertain that preschool-age children of epileptic mothers do not show any increased number of psychiatric symptoms (Huth et al., 1982; Steinhausen et al., 1982a). The limited assessment and the well-known disadvantages of retrospective studies prompted us recently to start a prospectively oriented longitudinal study, of which this is a preliminary report.

Samples

We are currently endeavoring to evaluate possible genetic, teratogenic, and environmental effects on the offspring of epileptic parents. Several control groups are used in order to

This study derives from a multidisciplinary project on the effects of intrauterine exposure to anticonvulsant drugs. It was supported by a grant from Deutsche Forschungsgemeinschaft (principal investigator: Professor H. Helge, M.D.). The authors gratefully acknowledge the cooperation of Peter Eickhoff who scored the video material.

differentiate between these various effects. The target group is made up of children of mothers with epilepsy who have taken anticonvulsants during pregnancy. In addition, the children of the following subjects are examined: mothers with epilepsy who have not taken anticonvulsants, fathers with epilepsy married to healthy women, and controls where both parents are healthy. The sample characteristics and assessment procedures used at various ages are summarized in table 52–1. The match criteria of age, sex, and socioeconomic status are included, the latter based on the most widely used German system of classification (Kleining and Moore, 1968). Further match criteria not documented are birthweight, gestational age, and head circumference.

Method

The examination procedures used are multidimensional and take account of aspects of infant and early childhood development. Infant behavior is observed in the first, second, and fourth week after birth using the Brazelton Neonatal Behavior Assessment Scale (BNBAS, Brazelton, 1973). In view of the large number of variables, data reduction and analysis utilized the clusters suggested by Lester (1979). Six scores were calculated: habituation, orientation, motor performance, range of state, regulation of state, and autonomic regulation.

At six months, a video recording of mother and child in a laboratory play situation is made. At present we have completed the first analyses of ten-minute video samples following the categories developed by Ramey and colleagues (1979) for such a situation. These categories were revised by eliminating those with only inferential significance. The total duration of each behavior within the ten-minute video sample was obtained for the eight units of behavior as follows: mother vocalizes, child vocalizes, mother touches child, child touches mother, mother shows toy, child manipulates toy, mother holds child, and motor activity of the child.

At the beginning of the second year of life,

the Home System (Caldwell and Bradley 1980) is used to record mother-child interaction in natural (home) surroundings. The quality and quantity of social, emotional, and cognitive support given to the infant are recorded for forty-five items. These characteristics can be combined for a total score and can also be grouped according to five scales as follows: emotional and verbal responsivity of the mother, acceptance of child's behavior, provision of appropriate play materials, parent involvement with child, opportunities for variety in daily stimulation.

Mental development is first measured at fifteen months using the Bayley Scales (Bayley, 1969). At four years, the Columbia Mental Maturity Scale, the Illinois Test of Psycholinguistic Abilities, and the Caldwell preschool version of the Home System are administered. At the same time, behavioral abnormalities and psychiatric symptoms are assessed by means of a structured interview with the mother according to the procedure of Richman and Graham (1971). Here all symptoms are rated on a three-point scale (0 = not present, 1 = mild, 2 = severe) and a total score is obtained. Finally, at sixty months, visual perception is tested by means of the Frosting Test of Visual Perception, and the study is completed after a final examination.

Findings

The data presented here do not yet include data from all control groups, and sample sizes vary according to the test procedure and are still not complete. A few children of mothers with epilepsy who had taken anticonvulsants during pregnancy (the target group) can be compared with the children from the control group of unafflicted mothers. Even with such limited data, however, some questions relating to the following factors can be answered: the general impact of maternal epilepsy on the offspring, the significance of the type of epilepsy, the significance of seizures during pregnancy, and the effects of various drugs.

In table 52–2 the available data relating to the infant's behavior during the first and sec-

TABLE 52-1

Sample Characteristics and Assessment Procedures Utilized from Birth to 72 Months On

| | Children of Epileptic Mothers | | | | | | | | | Controls | | | | | | | | |
| | | Age of Infants (months) | | Sex of Infants (N) | | SES of Family (N) | | | Age of Infants (months) | | Sex of Infants (N) | | SES of Family (N) | |
	N	Mean	SD	Male	Female	LC	MC	N	Mean	SD	Male	Female	LC	MC
Brazelton Newborn Behavior Scales	28	4.3*	1.7	9	19	19	9	12	4.5*	1.3	6	6	7	5
Mother-Child Play Interaction in Laboratory	6	6.9	0.8	4	2	3	3	6	6.9	0.8	3	3	3	3
Home-System (CALDWELL)	12	15.3	1.1	4	8	9	3	12	15.4	.8	6	6	8	4
BAYLEY Mental Index	40	16.1	1.7	20	20	20	20	36	15.8	1.1	18	18	15	21
Intelligence and Psycholinguistic Abilities	14	52.6	5.7	5	9	7	7							
Psychiatric Status†	19	66.1	19.8	10	9	13	6	19	68.8	20.0	10	9	13	6

SES = Socioeconomic status, LC = Lower Class, MC = Middle Class
* = days
† = Determined retrospectively by interviewing mothers

ond week after birth are compared. Nonparametric analyses using the Wilcoxon Test and the Mann-Whitney Test have shown that the six scores of the infants of epileptic mothers did not change significantly from the first to the second week of life, or from the scores recorded at weeks one and two for the control group.

The analyses of mother-child play interaction carried out at six months for six target pairs and six carefully matched control pairs demonstrate significant differences between these two groups, as shown in table 52–3. Given a considerably greater variation in the control groups, it was evident that epileptic mothers hold their children significantly less and tend to touch them less. The children of these mothers also tend to show less motor activity.

The data collected in the third phase of the study at the age of twelve months by means of the Caldwell Home System are presented in table 52–4. Since the individual subtests did not deviate from the total score, only the latter is presented here. In addition to the comparison of the target group with the control group, some further factors have been analyzed, namely, type of epilepsy and the occurrence of various types of seizures during pregnancy. It can be seen that the children of epileptic mothers do not experience any difference from the control children in the social, emotional, or cognitive support in their home environments. Nor do the subgroups, defined in terms of the type of epilepsy and in terms of the presence or absence of seizures during pregnancy, differ significantly from their respective control groups.

Because of the larger sample, more extensive analyses were possible with the data collected at the time of the fourth phase of the study. Table 52–5 contains the comparison of the mental index of the Bayley Scales for the total group, as well as for a few subgroups and the respective controls, thus allowing for the analyses of possibly significant determinants. One may conclude from this table that the mental index of the Bayley test for the children of epileptic mothers does not differ significantly from the control group. The subgroups formed according to the type of seizure—containing children with mothers who suffer either from grand mal or from focal epilepsy—similarly do not differ from the controls. Also, the average Bayley scores of both subgroups with different types of seizure do not significantly differ from one another.

However, what is significant at this stage is whether the mother actually suffered seizures during pregnancy. Children of mothers with seizures during pregnancy have significantly lower test scores than the controls, lower also than the children of mothers without seizures during pregnancy ($p = .02$). It can further be seen that there is no significant difference in the Bayley Mental Index Scores at age sixteen months between the groups of children born (1) to mothers treated with anticonvulsants, (2) to mothers not so treated, (3) to mothers treated with monotherapy, (4) to mothers treated with combined therapy, and (5) to mothers in the control group. However, it is possible to show that the children of mothers treated with primidone during pregnancy have a significantly lower mental index than the controls, This was also the case when the effects of the three drugs primidone, DPH and valproic acid were compared ($F = 3.17$, $df = 2.18$, $p = 0.07$).

At four years of age, it was possible to collect data for some of the children of epileptic mothers concerning the development of cognitive functioning and to carry out a child psychiatric assessment. We compared this small series of subjects with our retrospective series (Steinhausen et al., 1982a), as well as with a control group matched to the retrospective series. Table 52–6 represents the test scores for intelligence and psycholinguistic abilities, as well as a total score for psychopathology derived from the psychiatric assessment. As can be seen from the data, a comparison of the three groups revealed no significant differences between them.

Discussion

Because of the early stage of the research project, the data presented here permit only limited conclusions. A final assessment of the extent to which children of epileptic mothers

TABLE 52–2

Neonatal Behaviour of Target Group and Controls During the First and Second Week of Life*

| | Target Group | | | | Controls | | | |
| | First Week | | Second Week | | First Week | | Second Week | |
	Mean	SD	Mean	SD	Mean	SD	Mean	SD
Habituation	7.2	1.8	6.8	1.5	7.6	0.8	7.4	1.2
Orientation	5.6	1.9	6.0	2.0	5.7	1.8	6.2	1.2
Motor performance	4.7	1.0	4.9	1.0	5.0	0.8	5.1	0.9
Range of state	3.7	0.7	3.4	0.9	3.5	0.7	3.6	1.0
Regulation of state	5.2	1.6	5.1	1.9	5.7	1.3	5.6	1.1
Autonomic regulation	5.6	1.5	6.1	1.0	6.3	1.1	6.4	1.4

*BNBAS = clusters according to Lester (1979).

TABLE 52–3

Comparison of Mother-Child Play Interaction Scores from 6 Mother-Infant Pairs at Six Months of Life

| | Target | | Controls | | |
Behavior	Mean	SD	Mean	SD	p*
Mother vocalizes	1.64	0.40	1.90	0.61	n.s.
Child vocalizes	1.12	0.46	1.43	0.31	n.s.
Mother touches child	4.43	2.69	24.75	21.14	0.08
Child touches mother	2.23	2.72	3.62	3.73	n.s.
Mother shows toy	15.82	9.72	15.36	11.16	n.s.
Child manipulates toy	8.67	2.28	16.44	11.48	n.s.
Mother holds child	10.86	7.90	32.27	19.31	0.04
Motor activity of the child	5.51	11.86	8.10	11.41	0.10

*Mann-Whitney Test

TABLE 52–4

Comparison of Total Home Scores at 15 Months of Life for Various Samples

| | | Total Home Score | | | | |
| | | Target Group | | Controls* | | |
Sample	N†	Mean	SD	Mean	SD	p‡
Entire group	12	34.9	3.9	33.1	5.4	n.s.
Children of mothers with grand mal epilepsy	5	35.6	0.9	29.0	7.2	n.s.
Children of mothers with focal epilepsy	4	34.3	7.1	37.3	2.1	n.s.
Children of mothers with seizures during pregnancy	4	31.5	5.2	32.6	6.7	n.s.
Children of mothers without seizures during pregnancy	6	36.8	1.8	33.3	5.9	n.s.

*matched pairs
†in each of the two groups
‡Mann-Whitney Test

TABLE 52–5

Comparison of Bayley Mental Index at 16 Months of Life for Various Samples

Sample	N†	Bayley Scores				Analysis of Variance		
		Target Group		Controls*				
		Mean	SD	Mean	SD	F	df	p
Entire group	40	104.6	13.3	108.9	10.3	−1.58	74	n.s.
Children of mothers with grand mal epilepsy	20	104.6	14.3	108.2	10.5	− .92	38	n.s.
Children of mothers with focal epilepsy	11	106.3	12.7	111.2	9.6	−1.02	20	n.s.
Children of mothers with seizures during pregnancy	14	99.8	14.7	111.7	13.0	−2.26	26	.03
Children of mothers without seizures during pregnancy	15	107.1	12.1	108.7	6.7	− .45	21.6	n.s.
Children of treated mothers	28	104.8	14.0	103.3	10.6	−1.30	54	n.s.
Children of untreated mothers	7	107.7	9.6	106.4	9.8	.11	12	n.s.
Children of mothers with monotherapy	22	104.2	14.7	109.6	11.7	−1.35	42	n.s.
Children of mothers with combined therapy	6	106.7	11.7	108.2	5.2	− .29	10	n.s.
Children of mothers with primidone treatment	7	93.8	11.2	110.4	9.1	−3.03	12	.01
Children of mothers with DPH treatment	7	110.7	12.4	107.1	8.3	.63	12	n.s.
Children of mothers with valproic acid treatment	7	102.7	13.9	103.7	11.1	− .15	12	n.s.

*matched pairs
†in each of the two groups

TABLE 52–6

Comparison of Intelligence, Psycholinguistic Development, and Psychopathology Among Two Target Groups and Controls

	Target Groups						Controls			Analysis of Variance		
	Prospective Series			Retrospective* Series								
	N	Mean	SD	N	Mean	SD	N	Mean	SD	F	df	p
Intelligence (T-values)†	16	54.8	10.5	19	55.4	10.5				.03	1;33	n.s.
Psycholinguistic abilities (T-values)‡	4	53.8	4.0	18	51.2	5.4				.80	1;20	n.s.
Psychopathology (total score)**	25	.24	.15	19	.16	.18	19	.18	.13	1.52	2;60	n.s.

*Data from Steinhausen et al. 1982a
†Columbia Mental Maturity Scale
‡Illinois Test of Psycholinguistic Ability
**Based on structured interview (adapted from Richman and Graham, 1971)

are children at risk must be reserved for a later date. In particular, the data collected so far do not enable us to differentiate between genetic, teratogenic, and environmental factors as potential determinants of these children's development, especially since it has not yet been possible to examine all the necessary control groups. Furthermore, it is important to stress that the findings presented here are based on cross-sectional data and that it will only be possible at a later date to link the various levels longitudinally.

Despite these limitations, however, the preliminary findings are of interest. To date, observations using the Brazelton Neonatal Behavior Assessment Scales do not support the hypothesis that the intake of anticonvulsants during pregnancy affects the behavior of the baby. This assertion is based on twelve target children and twelve control children, and it can be seen only as a general conclusion which might undergo modification in the future. It remains unresolved, for example, whether only certain types of drugs lead to detectable effects on the infant. Nor is it clear to what extent the mother's type of epilepsy or the frequency of seizures are themselves significant parameters affecting the behavior of the infant.

The initial analyses of mother-child interaction at six months have already proven to be a fruitful research strategy and have provided some support for the hypothesis that the behavior of an infant is influenced above all by its interaction with the person to whom it relates most closely. Indeed, epileptic mothers appeared to be less active in terms of holding and touching the child, and the children themselves tended in turn to be less active. However, our provisional and ongoing analyses have not as yet established the essential part of interaction between mother and child.

It should be noted that the data collected in the middle of the second year, using the Home System, are based on observations of behavior in the child's natural environment and on interviews. While these data do not incorporate sufficient detail to delineate crucial aspects of mother-child interaction, they do permit an interpretation of meaningful dimensions of support given to the child. The data analyzed so far in this study suggest that epileptic mothers give their children no less social, emotional, or cognitive support than control-group mothers. Also, examination of other possibly influential factors, such as the type of epilepsy and the frequency of seizures during pregnancy, results in no significant differences with the control group.

The largest subsample to date was measured using the Bayley Test. It was thus possible to analyze the impact of some potential predictors for the outcome of the test. At present we are not yet in a position to control for a potential cross-correlation on mental performance with IQ of the mother. Our preliminary analyses indicate that one cannot in general presume an impairment of development in the offspring of epileptic mothers, which a number of studies mentioned earlier have ascertained. However, two conditions can be cited unequivocally as factors of risk, namely, seizures during pregnancy and the treatment of the mother with primidone. Both factors are correlated with a significant reduction in mental performance as measured on the Bayley test.

The conclusions to be drawn from these findings are in one respect indisputable: It is not only in the short-term interest of the mother and child during pregnancy but also in the longerterm interest of the child's early development that seizures during pregnancy must, as far as possible, be avoided through competent treatment and with the cooperation of the mother. If the negative effect of primidone on the development of intelligence is confirmed in future studies, then, given viable alternatives, treatment using primidone should be avoided. The longitudinal nature of this work will make it possible to under take such cross-validation at a later stage. In the study of a sample taken in the fourth year of life, there was no impairment of intelligence for the total group of target children as compared with the control group. This was also the case for the development of psycholinguistic abilities. Finally, a comparison of psychiatric symptoms in groups of children studied prospectively, retrospectively, and as controls revealed no significant incidence of psychiatrically relevant symptoms.

REFERENCES

Anthony, E. J. (1978). From birth to breakdown: A prospective study of vulnerability. In *The Child in His Family: Vulnerable Children*, vol. 4, ed. E. J. Anthony et al. New York: John Wiley.

Bayley, N. (1969). *Bayley Scales of Infant Development.* New York: Psychological Corporation.

Brazelton, T. B. (1973). *Neonatal Behavioral Assessment Scale.* Philadelphia: J. B. Lippincott.

Caldwell, B. M. and Bradley, R. H. (1980). *Home Observation of the Environment.* Center for Child Development and Education, University of Arkansas (unpublished).

Conners, C. K. et al. (1979). Children of parents with affective illness. *Journal of the American Academy of Child Psychiatry,* 18:600–608.

Cytryn, L. et al. (1982). Offspring of patients with affective disorders II. *Journal of the American Academy of Child Psychiatry,* 21:389–391.

Dietrich, E. (1980). Antiepileptikaembryopathien. *Ergebnisse der Inneren Medizin und Kinderheilkunde,* 43:93–102.

Erlenmeyer-Kimling, L. et al. (1980). A prospective study of children of schizophrenic parents. *International Journal of Rehabilitation Research,* 3:90–91.

Garmezy, N. (1977). Observations on research with children at risk for child and adult psychopathology. In *Child Psychiatry: Treatment and Research,* ed. M. F. McMillan and S. Henao. New York: Brunner/Mazel.

Granström, M. L. (1982). Development of the children of epileptic mothers: Preliminary results from the prospective Helsinki study. In *Epilepsy, Pregnancy and the Child,* ed. D. Janz et al. New York: Raven Press.

Granström, M. L. (1979). Development of the children of epileptic mothers. *Neuropädietrie,* 10:423–427.

Hanson, J. W., Myrianthopoulos, N. C., Sedgwick, H., and Smith, D. W. (1976). Risks to the offspring of women treated with hydantoin anticonvulsants, with emphasis on the fetal hydantoin syndrome. *Journal of Pediatrics,* 89:662–668.

Hanson, J. W. and Smith, D. W. (1978). The fetal hydantoin syndrome. *Journal of Pediatrics,* 87:285–290.

Hill, R. H. et al. (1974). Infants exposed *in utero* to antiepileptic drugs—A prospective study. *American Journal of Diseases of the Child,* 127:645–653.

Hill, R. H. et al. (1982). Relationship between antiepileptic drug exposure of the infant and developmental potential. In *Epilepsy, Pregnancy and the Child,* ed. D. Janz et al. New York: Raven Press.

Huth, H. G., Steinhausen, H. C., and Helge, H. (1982). Mental development in children of epileptic parents. In *Epilepsy, Pregnancy and the Child,* ed. D. Janz et al. New York: Raven Press.

Kleining, G. and Moore, H. (1968). Soziable Selbsteinstufung. *Koelner Zeitschrift für Soziologie und Sozialpsychologie,* 20:502–552.

Lester, B. M. (1979). Assessment of the behavioral organization of the neonate: Research and clinical perspectives. Paper presented at the University of Michigan, (unpublished).

Majewski, F. et al. (1980). Zur Teratogenität von Antikonvulsiva. *Deutsche Medizinische Wochenschrift,* 105:719–723.

McKnew, D. H. et al. (1979). Offspring of patients with affective disorders. *British Journal of Psychiatry,* 134:148–152.

Mednick, S. A., Schulsinger, F., and Venables, P. H. (1979). Risk research and primary prevention of mental illness. *International Journal of Mental Health,* 7:150–164.

Ramey, C. T., Farran, D. C., and Campbell, F. A. (1979). Predicting IQ from mother-infant interactions. *Child Development,* 50:804–814.

Richman, N. and Graham, P. J. (1971). A behavioral screening questionnaire for use with three-year-old children—preliminary findings. *Journal of Child Psychology and Psychiatry,* 12:5–33.

Sameroff, A. J. and Seifer, R. (1981). The transmission of incompetence: The offspring of mentally ill women. In *Genesis of Behavior: The Uncommon Child,* vol. 3, ed. M. Lewis and L. A. Rosenblum. New York: Plenum Press.

Shapiro, S. et al. (1976). Anticonvulsants and parental epilepsy in the development of birth defects. *Lancet,* 1:272–275.

Sobczyk, W., Dowzenko, A., and Krasicka, J. (1977). Study of children of mothers treated with anticonvulsants during pregnancy. *Neurologia i Neurochirurgia Polska,* 11:59–63.

Speidel, B. D. and Meadow, S. R. (1972). Maternal epilepsy and abnormalities of the fetus and newborn. *Lancet,* 2:839–843.

Steinhausen, H. C., Gobel, D., and Nestler, V. (1983). Psychopathology in the offspring of alcoholic parents. *Journal of the American Academy of Child Psychiatry,* in press.

Steinhausen, H. C., Nestler, V., and Huth, H. (1982a). Psychopathology and mental functions in the offspring of alcoholic and epileptic mothers. *Journal of the American Academy of Child Psychiatry,* 21:268–273.

Steinhausen, H. C., Nestler, V., and Spohr, H. L. (1982b). Development and psychopathology of children with the fetal alcohol syndrome. *Journal of Developmental and Behavioral Pediatrics,* 3:49–54.

Vert, P., Andre, M., and Deblay, M. F. (1979). Infants of epileptic mothers. In *Intensive Care in the Newborn II,* ed. L. Stern et al. Paris/New York: Masson.

Welner, Z., Welner, A., McCrary, M. D., and Leonhard, M. A. (1977). Psychopathology in children of inpatients with depression: A controlled study. *Journal of Nervous and Mental Disease,* 164:408–413.

Winters, K. C., Stone, A. A., Weintraub, S., and Neale, J. M. (1981). Cognitive and attentional deficits in children vulnerable to psychopathology. *Journal of Abnormal Child Psychology,* 9:435–453.

53

The Origins and Fates of Psychopathology in Infancy: A Panel Discussion

Robert L. Tyson, M.D. (Chairman and Reporter), Robert N. Emde, M.D., Eleanor Galenson, M.D., and Joy D. Osofsky, Ph.D.

The purposes of the panel were defined by the Chairman in his introduction as follows: (1) to ask more precise questions about the origins of emotional disturbances in infancy; (2) to assess the adequacy of the currently available answers to these questions; and (3) to evaluate the capacity of our present theories of development to describe and to predict the origins and fates of psychopathology in the earliest months and years of life.

The ambiguities in these areas—for example, in the use of the term *psychopathology*—derive from different underlying assumptions, from different interpretations of observational data, and from different conceptual frameworks. Because there can be no such thing as psychopathology without a psyche (to paraphrase Winnicott, 1960), some would prefer the term *deviancy* to *psychopathology,* or even *behavior,* so as to by-pass the question of pathology. But the study of the beginnings of mental life can no longer be so easily restricted simply to observable behavior, any more than behavior can be ignored by those who study mental processes.

Winnicott's (1960) dictum—that there is no such thing as a baby because of the vital reciprocity between mother and infant—has been widely accepted. But as we learn more about the fluctuating and ever-evolving dynamic interaction between mother and infant, we find many more points of developmental vulnerability than were originally considered. We are forced to re-evaluate our criteria for disturbance and to reassess the implications of observed disturbance at various points of development. We want to know if what seems to be a disturbance now means that a continuing disruption of development will result, or whether subsequent development will be skewed so as to amplify vulnerability, or whether developmental plasticity will be sufficiently supple to allow an average expectable development.

The quality of plasticity in development was recognized by psychoanalysts quite early, exemplified by the principle of multiple function (Waelder, 1936), followed by the concepts of secondary autonomy (Hartmann, 1939) and persistence (Sandler and Joffe, 1967). The characteristics, dimensions, and limits of this plasticity are now very much the subjects of investigation. Somewhat parallel changes have taken place in the thinking of psychologists, so that today, more than ever before, psychologists and psychoanalysts think about development in many of the same ways. The similarities in ways of thinking may in turn serve as a basis for further distinctions to be made in our understanding. For example, to what extent does the apparently successful dissolution of an inimical mother-infant relationship come about because of a change in the caregiver or in the caregiver's response, or because of the child's skill in eliciting such a change, or because of the child's capacity to adapt on the basis of an ability to extract from other environmental sources, or because of the child's aptitude for making inner adaptations?

It is important to remember that not all psychopathology has its origins in the first three years of life. On the basis of later manifestations, we are limited in our ability to establish with certainty even the developmental level from which emotional disturbances begin. Issues of regression to earlier levels as against persistence of early modes of defense and adaptation to later periods complicate the situation. As already mentioned, not all manifestations of disturbance in infancy result in definable psychopathology in later life. Not only developmental plasticity but also the discontinuities inherent in the progress of development obscure our observation of developmental pathways to an extent not paralleled in embryology or biochemistry, for example, where markers can be followed in tracing maturational or metabolic routes. A characteristic of our contemporary theories is that we are much better at explaining deviant development and psychopathology than we are at explaining health.

In concluding his introduction, the Chairman offered a clinical illustration of his last point. A boy of four and a half was brought for help by his stepmother. She was concerned about Johnny's academic and social difficulties in school, worried about his temper tantrums, and afraid he would become a homosexual because he said he wished he was a girl and because of his intense attachment to his father, whose body he liked to fondle. Johnny was the first child of eagerly expectant parents, but their happiness was destroyed in the sixth month of pregnancy when the mother was discovered to have a rapidly growing brain tumor. She wanted an abortion, the father did not, and his wish prevailed. The mother required brain surgery which left her a relatively impassive character when Johnny was born. With some

household help she took care of him as well as she could the first six to seven months. But then she gradually became more ill, and she died when Johnny was just over two years old. This chaotic period was marked by several changes of caregivers, the very attached father providing increasing care himself. Finally, just before his wife's death, the now depressed father sustained an injury that required hospitalization; Johnny had a two-month period of foster care. Following this, a practical nurse who had helped care for the dying mother was employed to care for Johnny, but she was neglectful in every way imaginable, and punitive as well. When Johnny was about two and a half, the stepmother-to-be appeared on the scene. She immediately responded to the needs of the almost mute boy, finally managed to get rid of the practical nurse, tried to end Johnny's sleeping with his father—at least while she was there—and when Johnny was three, married his father. His subsequent development was rapid, but the stepmother remained concerned.

With such a history we are prepared to explain practically any disorder, from retardation to precocity, from infantile psychosis to atypical development. However, our theories do not prepare us to explain Johnny's ability to make meaningful and trusting relationships with adults, to understand his capacity for progression as far as the oedipal phase, or to define the origins of the elements that have allowed him to make such constructive use of psychoanalysis. Johnny's further development is certainly not free from the threat of disturbance, but we are not well equipped to predict the nature of this disturbance. To say that he is at risk for becoming homosexual is simply to make a statistical statement. And so we come back to the opening questions about the nature of psychopathology in infancy, its various origins and fates, and the questions about the theories we have to work with.

Dr. Emde presented another case for discussion, referring to previously published studies on this child (Emde et al., 1965; Harmon et al., 1982), material which in many ways offers unique opportunities to study the early infantile origins of psychopathology.

George came under observation in a residential nursery at eight days of age; he appeared fussy and alternately shy and demanding of attention for his first three months of life. By three months George had distinguished himself as a "ham" in a study of early smiling. He succeeded in getting more than the usual amount of attention in a setting where one caregiver was responsible for twelve to sixteen infants. A series of moves was dictated by nursery regimen. At age one month George entered the one- to two-month-old room, then a crib dormitory for infants up to six months of age, and then a room with children from six months to two and a half years. One week after this last transfer, George was found to have a 21 percent drop in performance on tests of infant development; four and one half weeks after transfer, the well-established smiling response to the human face had disappeared. Nine weeks after transfer, at eight months of age, stranger anxiety was noted. This was thought to be unusual for infants at the time in this nursery, in which staff limitations precluded the easy development of individual relationships. At nine months George demonstrated all the criteria for anaclitic depression, although there was no mother from whom the child was separated to account for the appearance of this syndrome. The depression lasted approximately seven and one half months and then progressively remitted, contrary to Spitz's expectation (1950) that a duration of anaclitic depression greater than three months is irreversible.

Detailed examination of the factors surrounding the onset and remission of George's disturbance (Emde et al., 1965) yielded strongly suggestive circumstantial evidence that he had made early and strong attachments to a variety of caregivers, including teen-age volunteers from whom he had been successful in eliciting special attention, and that these attachments had been disrupted for a variety of reasons. About two weeks before the resolution of his depression, the nursery staff was heavily reinforced by a number of enthusiastic teen-age volunteeers who persisted in picking George up and giving him a great deal of attention; an imporovement in peer relations was also thought to contribute to his recovery.

George was followed trom infancy to puberty (Harmon et al., 1982), the last published data being when he was age twelve. In infancy, his recovery from anaclitic depression seemed rapid and complete, and he was adopted at age twenty months. Although his original adjustment at that age was satisfactory, his adoptive mother soon required a hysterectomy and returned home depressed. George's behavior was provocative. There was considerable marital disharmony, and his adoptive parents later divorced after he was relinquished, at age two years, one month, to an orphanage (not the original residential nursery). George became ill and depressed, suffering from gastrointestinal bleeding, food allergies, and atopic dermatitis. In the succeeding months he was almost continually ill with childhood diseases. During this period he was nursed chiefly by one devoted staff member; she gradually reintroduced previously allergenic foods so that within six months he was restored to his regular diet and free of dermatitis. Not surprisingly he became strongly attached to this person and clung to her outside the orphanage.

George reacted to a second adoption at age three and one half with hyperactivity, fecal smearing, and disobedience the first week, soon followed by sitting alone and immobile, staring into space, repetitive rocking, and stereotypic, writhing finger movements. Over several months, virtually all these symptoms disappeared, though George now showed hyperphagia and hoarding of food, clothes, and toys. He was fearful of exploration outside the house, and he developed temporary animal phobias. As these symptoms were diminishing, George's adoptive mother suddenly decided to work full time and also started to attend night school. His response was sufficiently provocative and negativistic that his adoptive mother initiated steps for relinquishing him. George reverted to the staring and other symptoms, and his food allergies reappeared.

On his return to the orphanage at four years, three months, George was returned to his previous caregiver, and his recovery was completed in several weeks. As he became more lively, he was discovered to be athletically talented. His caregiver's natural abilities to nurture George were amplified by her increasing awareness that his current difficulties in the orphanage could be related to his separations from her. A transitory school phobia on beginning kindergarten was successfully handled by the caregiver, who interpreted his anxiety about his leaving her, and when the following year his food-hoarding returned, it was learned that a "routine rotation" of staff threatened another separation. Trial visits to potential adoptive families resulted in outbreaks of atopic dermatitis, and at age six and one half a separation in summer camp was accompanied by a return of his food allergies, resolved at the end of camp with his return to the orphanage and his beloved caregiver.

Concern about George's ability ever to have a successful adoption resulted in his being given psychoanalytically oriented psychotherapy once a week for three years, starting at age seven years, three months. After some months in which George's object hunger and use of the therapist as a real object were prominent, transference developments emerged, in which fantasies about his and the therapist's origins were played out and interpreted in the context of a durable treatment alliance, and with clear oedipal themes and anxieties about abandonment. Eventually an adoptive family was found and treatment continued for another five months, with termination initiated by the adoptive family. Although George spoke about his sadness and other feelings on termination and about leaving the orphanage, it seemed not to be expressed as a deeply felt emotional experience. His atopic dermatitis appeared, continued through termination, and resolved several months after treatment ended.

When seen again in a follow-up interview at age twelve, George was quiet and seemed embarrassed to see the therapist, but denied any problems. He seemed not to recall many things about his treatment and conveyed the feeling he wanted to avoid this part of his past. The family reported that George was doing well in school, was active in sports, had good peer relationships, and was free of allergies.

In summarizing, Dr. Emde said that George was now in college and reportedly doing quite well. Dr. Emde pointed out that our knowledge of George's history and development raised a number of questions, such as the role of the repetition compulsion, the factors that determine the capacity to recover, and the extent to which the individual's resiliency can be stretched. In his infancy George had no family in the usual sense, but his capacity to extract attention and care from the environment was unusual. Although this initially protected him from the vulnerability of the loss of one object, it made him vulnerable to the loss of several at a time, as can happen with staff scheduling in institutions. It appeared that his initial depression was ushered in by the appearance of multiple environmental deficits. George's psychotherapy in latency seems to have been effective in helping him to surmount the compulsion to repeat the cluster of symptoms surrounding significant separations.

Dr. Galenson next presented two vignettes chosen to illustrate two major areas of preoedipal psychopathology. In the first case, psychopathology resulted from developmental arrest; the second case was of intrapsychic conflict as the result of a traumatic incident.

Elaine, age fourteen months, was the only child born to an obese (300-pound), twenty-six-year-old mother who, at the time, had custody of four other children not her own. The mother had herself been an abused child who had repeatedly run away from foster-care homes between the ages of fifteen and eighteen, when she returned to live with her mother. Elaine had had over twelve hospitalizations; a subdural hematoma was found in x rays during the first one. The mother's provocation and abuse resulted in a poor relationship between her and the hospital staff. She was finally referred to the infant diagnostic unit within the Pediatric Outpatient Department. She and Elaine attended a special nursery three mornings weekly, and the mother had additional sessions with a social worker with whom she gradually came to express her own longing to be cared for and her fury at her mother and at herself. As this material emerged, the child became more lethargic, ate and slept poorly, and suffered from small seizures. Anticonvulsant medication was prescribed, but it was not known whether it was being administered. By age sixteen months, however, evidence of Elaine's improved development could be seen on several fronts. Whereas her inital preference for her mother remained, she seemed no longer bound to her in terror and was able to ask other female adults in the nursery for help. She now cried on separation from her mother and she initiated "separation" peek-a-boo games. Often, when regressive episodes appeared, she put up her arms indicating her wish to be held and cuddled. When this was provided, Elaine lay quietly, moulding into the recipient's arms, enjoying the tender contact previously denied. Early severe oral deprivation and fixation were inferred from her constant sucking on her pacifier or bottle, and in her chewing food minimally and without pleasure. Elaine's anal development was also delayed in that there was no awareness of bowel functioning, an awareness that ordinarily emerges between twelve and fourteen months. Physical growth and fine motor development were delayed by several months, and the basic organization of her sleep-wake cyle, eating patterns, and distress-quieting patterns had not yet been achieved. She displayed little joyfulness, and there was a marked lack of play and reciprocity between mother and child. In fact, at first Elaine did not play at all: it took several weeks for her to manifest interest in dolls or any other nursery play material.

Psychoanalytic theory can explain to some extent the source of Elaine's mother's severely damaged self-image, her projection of this self-image onto her own infant, and then her severe depression which ensued when theraputic interventions began to interfere with this projection and with the abnormal relationship that had been established between mother and child. But, in agreement with Fraiberg's (1982) findings, this mother was unexpectedly open to influence in regard to her infant. Changes took place only so long as it could be kept in view that the primary patient was the *baby*. And so the work was carried out with both mother and infant.

Predictions about the eventual outcome of such interventions as are made with infant-mother couples like Elaine and her mother must be cautious. Such a relative instability in both biological and early psychological organization usually result in the child's extreme vulnerability to the impact of normal develop-

mental crises during the oedipal phase and particularly during adolescence. Optimistically, one anticipates that continued treatment will cushion the impact of developmental crises in this child's still fragile blooming, resulting in a more benign and improved quality in her object relations.

Most problematic is the dilemma faced by children of such one-parent families where there is no steady, dependable male figure. The early genital phase, occurring sometime between sixteen and nineteen months (Roiphe and Galenson, 1982) will soon confront Elaine with the discovery of the genital differences and with the preoedipal castration reactions that are universal in girls during the latter months of the second year. It is then that the father's presence is so important if the girl is to proceed toward a heterosexual object relationship which will come to more definite structuralization during the oedipal period. It was found (Roiphe and Galenson, 1982) that when such a male figure is unavailable at this critical juncture, the girl may remain ambivalently tied to her mother, her advance to the oedipal-genital level seriously impeded.

The situation with boys differs in its dynamic structure but is certainly no less problematic. The disidentification with the preoedipal mother is a major obstacle to be negotiated by the boy, and failure to do so leads to serious psychopathology in sexual identity. One would expect to find either marked exaggerations and distortions of masculine behavior in an effort to avoid the homosexual fixation or regression from the masculine position.

Finally, with regard to the type of psychopathology in the group represented by Elaine and her mother, the vicissitudes of aggressive development, still not completely understood, will undoubtedly help to clarify the clinical picture. There is an impressive prevalence of somatic illness among infants from this poverty-level population, linked to some extent to their disturbance in early object relations and its consequent distortion of physiological organization. The health records of these infants suggest that as their psychological status improves, there is a decrease in some of the somatic disturbances, particularly respiratory and gastrointestinal. Somatization may indeed have provided these children a pathway for the discharge of early excessive aggression.

The second illustration dates back almost twenty years. Jennie was two and a half when her parents sought psychiatric help following the appearance of uncharacteristic behavior. Jennie had lost her previously good disposition, had become irritable, and had had trouble sleeping. Once she pointed at the mother's genitals while watching her undress and announced that a neighbor's boy Sam had "a toy in his tush." The parents recalled that Jennie's odd behavior dated from a few weeks ago, when she spent the night, at her own request, at the neighbor's house; her sitter for the evening was Sam, the neighbor's fifteen-year-old son. Other aspects of her behavior change included shying away from other children in the street, avoiding her formerly beloved puzzles and blocks, and a sudden upsurge in playing with dolls. She constantly demanded water to drink whenever upset and washed her hands frequently. While formerly on very good terms with her mother, Jennie was now clearly angry, biting and kicking at her. She had used her bottle for bedtime comforting all along, but now she frequently demanded her bottle during the day. Clearly there were regressions in every area of this little girl's life.

The parents concluded that Sam had engaged Jennie in sexual activity, and they soon learned that he had exposed his penis to her. Although he denied any other form of sexual advance, the material subsequently obtained during play sessions suggested otherwise. A detailed diary of Jennie's play and behavior was written by her mother during the treatment the mother carried out under Dr. Galenson's direction. Jennie gradually improved, although certain symptoms and traits remained.

Dr. Galenson pointed out that now, more than twenty years later, she could have a different view. Today she could attempt a much more intense exploration of Jennie's fantasy life through the medium of play as well as verbalization, that is, with the techniques of child psychoanalysis. It is now understood that what might have been a mildly traumatic event had it taken place during a different phase in Jennie's development, occurred at a particularly vulnerable time in the wake of Jennie's

discovery of the genital difference and the pre-oedipal castration reactions that follow. This is a time of marked interest in, as well as vulnerability to, sexual experiences of all sorts. It is now known that preoedipal children are indeed capable of experiencing sexual arousal, that this is accompanied by object-directed affect, and that prepoedipal castration anxiety can be readily re-evoked along with the accompanying anxieties and fears of bodily dissolution and of object loss (Roiphe and Galenson, 1982).

In the twenty years since Jennie was first seen, there has been a marked change in our views of the treatability of infants. Although we cannot be certain of the outcome of treatment of such children as Elaine, there is no doubt that she and her mother require, are entitled to, and can benefit from early intervention, just as Jennie's situation should have been much more extensively explored and treated at the time of her traumatic experience. Psychoanalytically oriented infant observational research has resulted in this far greater understanding of the normal progression of psychosexual development, of object relations development, and of the effect of both of these areas upon many aspects of ego functioning. We can no longer be content to wait until the young child is verbal before treatment is initiated both with the child and his parents.

Dr. Osofsky presented two case vignettes to illustrate primary prevention efforts and their usefulness for both infant and mother and the effects of early diagnostic work and follow-up.

The first case, D.J., was referred to the Child Development Center at Topeka State Hospital at age twenty-eight months because his mother could not deal with his behavior or her own difficulties. There, D.J. was observed to ignore people, to concentrate on toys, and to show no spontaneous verbalization. His mother, however, described him as swearing, throwing tantrums, and behaving uncontrollably. The hospital staff observed no signs of anxiety when separating from mother, although the mother reported that he was extremely possessive of her. She described him as being destructive with toys, though when observed during evaluation he played quietly and made no attempt to interact with mother or other adults. D.J.'s mother had been diagnosed as schizophrenic and was herself a product of a disturbed family. Her mother had given her up to her maternal grandparents who reared her to age ten, when both of them died. She was then cared for by a foster "aunt" until, at age fourteen, she was admitted to a state hospital for "rebelliousness, suicidal preoccupation, confusion and delusional thinking, extreme anxiety, and sexual confusion." Four years later she was discharged against medical advice, but just before leaving, she met a thirty-four-year-old male patient and soon married him. He had also experienced considerable early deprivation and neglect. Not unexpectedly, the marriage was chaotic with much quarreling and use of drugs and alcohol. During the pregnancy, the mother had no prenatal care, was severely malnourished, and abused alcohol. D.J.'s birth, delivery, and first year were described as normal and without problems, though the mother's accuracy is in question inasmuch as she was on drugs or alcohol much of the time. She recalled opening a can of food and placing it on his highchair table, assuming it was up to him to feed himself. It seemed likely she was able to hold and rock D.J., and to give reasonable care and attention while he was very little and dependent. During his first two years, he was abused by his father, who came home drunk, pounded the crib, and beat the child with a belt when he cried. As he became more mobile, the mother found it more difficult to meet D.J.'s needs and experienced him as a possessive adult rather than a needy child. She felt he was crazy when he had tantrums, described him as being extremely destructive, and as beating his own head on the concrete floor. The parents divorced shortly before D.J. was referred to the Center.

At the Center D.J. was placed in the toddlers' group; the mother participated in the mother's group and in individual treatment. A supportive network developed through the mother's participation in both groups. In spite of his initial distrust, within three months D.J. began to relate more to adults and to laugh, smile, play, and have fewer temper tantrums at home. During this period one of the aides often went home with D.J. and his mother to help her through the lunch hour before he went to a baby-sitter; this intervention was necessary because of the mother's extreme anger and destructive impulses toward her son. While D.J. continued to progress, there were also episodes of regression, and after a series of "accidents," it was decided to place him in foster care. The "accidents" included falling on a hot radiator, the resulting laceration requiring stitches, taking a bottle of baby aspirin, swallowing some mouthwash, and finally, falling out of a second-story window. Because of their attachment in spite of their difficulties, the separation was not easy for either mother or child. Once separated, however, the mother was better able to control her hostility and to see positive aspects of D.J., which she was not able to see while they were living together. Currently they are being seen periodically because they are still in need of help, but D.J.'s mother has become much more responsive to suggestions and guidance and has been better able to cope with raising a young child.

Dr. Osofsky's second illustration was of Susan, an adolescent mother. On the basis of prenatal history and previous background, she was identified early in pregnancy as being at high risk for problems with her baby and with parenting. She was enrolled in a special program for young mothers (the Mother and Infant Project, Topeka, Kansas) and was followed by a team including a social worker, nurse, and home visitor, for the first six months of her infant's life. Her weight-gain during pregnancy was only ten pounds—she had anemia, a kidney infection, and, probably, nutritional deficiency. Susan felt forced by her grandmother with whom she lived to go through this unwanted pregnancy. Conception occurred during a visit to her mother who lived in another state. She had had a miscarriage one year before, and now wanted to have an abortion or to relinquish the baby. She herself had been given up by her own mother at three days of age.

Although an apparently healthy infant was delivered without complications, a question arose about the integrity of the child's central nervous system because of difficulty in controlling eye movements and in focusing. These difficulties resolved, however, and a neurological evaluation revealed no abnormalities. From the beginning, Susan was noted to focus primarily on herself rather than on her infant. At home she became preoccupied with worries about the baby being ill; a month later, she phoned the nurse to report her concern that the baby's eyes were rolling back again. The nurse suggested that Susan take the infant to the hospital emergency room and call back to tell her the outcome. The nurse later phoned the hospital to find out what happened and was told the child had been left unattended on a cart with a note describing what the infant needed to eat, and the comment "Call me when you find out what is wrong." The nurse could not find Susan, so the child was taken into protective custody and a hearing held the next day. Susan found out about it and appeared, and the judge decided to return the baby to the mother under Program supervision.

In the six months that this couple has now been followed, the staff has become increasingly concerned about Susan's ability to parent her child adequately, especially in view of her clear ambivalence about becoming and acting like a parent. Although the baby's progress so far seems adequate, she has had frequent illnesses in this period, and Susan has been inconsistent in keeping her appointments with the follow-up team. She has also moved several times since delivery, and she seems socially isolated.

Dr. Osofsky pointed out that the outcome in relation to the development of psychopathology might differ in such a case, depending on the relative vulnerability of the infant. However, it is important to recognize the value of an early preventive approach to potential problems in high-risk mother-infant pairs.

Following these presentations, the discussion among the panelists and the audience repeatedly referred to the resiliency or invulnerability of some children. In the first case presented, that of Johnny, and also with George, good intelligence seems to have been an asset to their adaptation and further development. In addition to factors of endowment or of plasticity in the children, similar factors in the mothers can be important. For instance,

Johnny's stepmother came for help when he was four and one half, suggesting that something in the family situation was influential in bringing her at that time. Also, her anxiety about his homosexuality played a role that might have been different with another mother, although her concern about proving her competency in raising a healthy child is apparent.

That George was in psychotherapy should mean that some information about his resiliency will be forthcoming, and Dr. Emde confirmed that the boy's ability to use treatment was itself an indication of this resiliency. Of additional interest is the fact that George was brought up in an environment of females, but his male gender-role or identity was never in question. In his case there were relatively clear indications for intervention in latency, but in infancy the issue is less often so clear. For example, one should ask before offering preventive interventions, exactly what is to be prevented. Also, our present knowledge about risk is not always so precise that we can unquestionably decide in every case that intervention is justified. In the cases described by Dr. Osofsky and Dr. Galenson, the circumstances were certainly worrying, but the interventions seemed more on the order of management than precisely guided assistance, with the possible exception of the treatment of Elaine's mother provided by a social worker. Dr. Emde said that, in making an assessment of the need for assistance, one of the things he looks for in both mother and child is emotional availability and evidence of a diminished range of emotional expression. He agreed that what is needed is a list of items of concern, that can be used as valid criteria for intervention. Dr. Osofsky described that, in addition to emotional availability, dampening, or withdrawal, and the qualities of the particular affects being expressed, she also looked for the presence and quality of play, reciprocity, consistencies or inconsistencies in mothering activities, and the degree of support available from the family or outside it. Among many helpful contributions from the audience, one participant added that she had found it useful to look for what might be called vitality, indicated by some flexibility in object choice. It is a clinical truism that a too exclusive concentration on either inner conflict or the environment can obscure important aspects of the other.

Another area in need of more precise definition is what is meant by treatment. Often enough quite basic needs have to be supplied, and Dr. Galenson pointed out that we have to take it for granted that seriously damaged children will need ongoing help, special schools, and other services. It is true that the rate and severity of physical illness can be diminished, for example, as in the case of George. But even though the capacity for forming affective ties to others remains and can even be intense, it is distorted in these children, and they rarely achieve a true, stable oedipal-level attachment. Dr. Osofsky added that a redefinition of "prevention" should be part of this effort, as already mentioned, both in terms of what activities are involved and required and in regard to just what is being prevented. For example, an assessment of the family situation may be needed before proper support can be provided to a mother who would be otherwise unable to parent her child.

It was universally agreed that until the current controversy about diagnostic categories is settled, difficulties in understanding and describing the origins and fates of psychopathology in infancy will persist. Fecal smearing, for example, is often taken as an indication of a psychotic disorder, but in George's case the limitations of descriptive terms become evident. The category of "attachment disorders" may or may not be useful (Call, 1983).

In summary, six cases have been presented. Each one represents disturbances that are of interest not so much because of their manifestations as because of their sources. Each disturbance is clearly rooted in the nature of the infant-caregiver relationship, except perhaps Jennie's whose troubles are ascribed to trauma of external origin. Even here one could argue that her exposure was occasioned by a disturbed parent-child relationship, and certainly it became overtly disrupted after the traumatic event. But while each case was presented within a framework of psychoanalytic theory common to all, different levels of theory appear to lie behind each. Theories of early object loss and object choice are central to Johnny's case; early attachment processes and concepts of infantile depression figure in George's material. Elaine and Jenny require more complex considerations of the infant's and child's involvements in their caregivers' psychopathology, whereas D.J. and Susan refer to deficiencies in mothering, which are important to assess in order to provide needed services.

In spite of these differences, or perhaps partly because of them, our need for greater precision and clarity in framing questions about diagnosis, about the nature and aims of treatment or other interventions, and about the risks and results of preventive mediation become obvious. Our current theories are not adequate to encompass our current empirical information or to describe the origins and to predict the fates of psychopathology in the earliest months and years of life. Some of our theories are too global, others too concrete. Further study of development in theories of development is clearly necessary. There seemed to be a consensus that the scope and urgency of the questions about psychopathology in infancy were sufficient to warrant to itself the focus of a separate congress.

REFERENCES

Call, J. D. (1983). Toward a nosology of psychiatric disorders in infancy. In *Frontiers of Infant Psychiatry*. ed. J. D. Call, E. Galenson, and R. L. Tyson. New York: Basic Books.

Emde, R. N., Polak, P. R., and Spitz, R. A. (1965). Anaclitic depression in an infant raised in an institution. *Journal of the American Academy of Child Psychiatry*, 4:545–553.

Fraiberg, S. (1982). Pathological defenses in infancy. *Psychoanalytic Quarterly*, 51:612–635.

Harmon, R. J., Wagonfeld, S., and Emde, R. N. (1982). Anaclitic depression: A follow-up from infancy to puberty. *The Psychoanalytic Study of the Child*, 37:67–94. New Haven: Yale University Press.

Hartmann, H. (1939). *Ego Psychology and the Problem of Ad-*

aptation. New York: International Universities Press, 1958.

Roiphe, H. and Galenson, E. (1982). *Infantile Origins of Sexual Identity*. New York: International Universities Press.

Sandler, J. and Joffe, W. G. (1967). The tendency to persistence in psychological function and development. *Bulletin of the Menninger Clinic*, 31:257–271.

Spitz, R. A. (1950). Psychiatric therapy in infancy. *American Journal of Orthopsychiatry*, 20:623–633.

Waelder, R. (1936). The principle of multiple function. *Psychoanalytic Quarterly*, 5:45–62.

Winnicott, D. W. (1960). Ego distortion in terms of true and false self. In *The Maturational Processes and the Facilitating Environment*. New York: International Universities Press, 1965.

54

The Baby in Court

Lenore C. Terr, M.D.

Almost one hundred years ago, the United States Supreme Court offered an opinion regarding the appropriateness of bringing very young children to court as witnesses. In *Wheeler v. United States* (1897) the Court stated, "no one would think of calling as a witness an infant only two or three years old." This opinion has guided American rulings on the appearances of infants in courts of law since the turn of the century. Although the Court suggested considerable flexibility in qualifying older children as witnesses, the Supreme Court of 1897 could not predict then that within fifty years, Anna Freud, Piaget, Spitz, and others would develop an entirely new discipline dedicated to the understanding and treatment of babies—infant psychiatry.

Over the past ten years I have studied how children function as witnesses in trials, particularly following psychic trauma (Terr, 1980a, 1980b). Recently, I have been observing the effects of traumatic experiences on nonverbal or preverbal children. From these observations I am constructing an explanation (mostly theoretical) of how babies may serve as witnesses. Several cases are offered as examples to describe how these cases could have been presented in court. It is my contention that infant psychiatry is now able to bring out reliable words from the mouths of infants even younger than "two or three years old" and that infant specialists may present babies today as acceptable and reliable witnesses before magistrates, judges, administrators, and juries.

Before I discuss how babies can bear witness, I wish briefly to consider what they witness and whether they should be brought forward at all. Infants, more than older youngsters, experience abuse, neglect, abandonment, relinquishment, adoption, and argument regarding their parentage. An instant of adult ire or parental despair may leave permanent physical or emotional scars upon the baby. Furthermore, during those few moments of conception, an irreversible genetic destiny is set for the infant. The baby thus has far more at stake in legal processes involving custody and protection than does any other individual who appears in such hearings—and as the party most directly affected, the infant must be granted a voice in the decision-making process.

Should courts intervene in matters involving infants? Selma Fraiberg, to whom this current volume is dedicated, took a vigorously interventionist approach in her work with blind children (1968). The efficacy of these vigorous interventions was eventually demonstrated in her studies of abused and neglected infants (1975) and in her group's ongoing ability to change dramatically the outlook for many of these infants-at-risk (Fraiberg, 1980). Courts have the potential, when called upon, to ensure that the type of active and humane interventions on behalf of infants that Fraiberg advocated will take place.

When court interventions are required to force reluctant parents into treatment or to protect babies already harmed, infant mental health specialists must aid the legal system to understand the infant's point of view. The infant psychiatrist should, early in the case evaluation process, enter into a close working relationship with the law. The psychiatrist must collect "evidence" directly from the baby, parents, neighbors, baby-sitters, and from the hospital or community nursing and social work staffs. These data must be recorded permanently and early in the form of photographs, videotapes, audiorecordings, and legible notes, so that when the infant recovers and the still potentially abusive parents want him or her back, that recovery itself will not work against the baby. Parents who voluntarily relinquish their rights and parents who serve time in prison often change their minds or plead fervently to judges that they have been punished enough. Even the most expertly handled battering parent may break loose again. Without solid indestructable evidence from the infant "witness," the psychiatric expert may stand in the courtroom as a lone and ineffective spokesperson for a very vulnerable unheeded baby.

Direct Evidence from the Baby

There are several ways in which infants may directly serve as witnesses on their own behalf. Of course, rules of evidence, such as the very restrictive rules that apply in the United States criminal courts, may have to be loosened to allow into the courtroom some of these types of evidence.

Products from the baby's own body can be used as evidence. An infant well recovered from a subdural hematoma might never illustrate to the court how affected he or she previously was without the aid of his or her own bloody spinal fluid, or at least CAT scans and x rays of the lesion.

CASE 1

Franklin was a severely retarded baby whose arm was amputated because his neglecting mother could not admit to herself or to Franklin's visiting nurse that gangrene was developing while the little boy's limb remained caught in the rungs of his crib. Franklin's mother had already gone to jail for dropping her newborn on his head shortly after his birth. She pleaded in court that she had been punished enough by being imprisoned and that her baby should not now be taken from her. A photograph of Franklin's armless body could have been a most convincing piece of evidence in the courtroom. Rather than identifying with a highly unfortunate adult, the judge could then have perceived the child's plight most graphically. In Franklin's case no such dramatic demonstration was necessary. Testimony from the visiting nurse and surgeons was sufficient to convince the Court to remove Franklin permanently from his mother.

To ensure that the Court grasps the real condition of the infant, medical and psychological witnesses should provide—at the very least—photographs of the baby's condition. All baby products saved for courtroom use must be notarized or witnessed and signed by two medical witnesses.

CASE 2

A supposed "father" recently asked for help to claim his paternal rights to an unborn fetus. The expectant mother, upon discovering herself pregnant, had talked a previous lover into marrying her. The putative father who sought my help indicated that he was willing to pay child support and that he wanted to visit with his baby as soon as birth took place. The "father's" lawyer heard from the mother's attorney that proper tissue-typing tests could not be accomplished until the infant was six months old. By the time the baby would be "testable," its psychological bonding would be well under way. Upon investigating, I learned from an immunologist that simpler blood-typing tests could be completed at the time of birth. Both "fathers" and mother could be immediately tested, along with baby, solving in most instances the question of paternity. But the mother's attorney insisted that no testing would be allowed until the baby was six months old. Not being permitted to see his new son, the putative father lost interest. By the time testing would have been accurate beyond a doubt, he had sought work in another state and had permanently left the area.

In addition to products from the baby's own body, pictures of the infant, and audiotapes of its screams of pain, fury, or fright can serve as telling pieces of baby-generated evidence in the courtroom. It is often very difficult for a layman—such as the judge—to picture how miserably unhappy or sick a now smiling, well-nourished infant previously has been.

Videotapes of the infant and parent(s) may be brought into court for another purpose—to demonstrate emotional connectedness or the lack of it.

CASE 3

In 1968, on the infant-research ward of Babies and Children's Hospital, Case Western Reserve University, Scott Dowling and I made a 16-mm. film of a mother who was emotionally disconnected from her baby. Standing only three feet away from the mother, who was attempting to feed her malnourished five-month-old, Dowling filmed the mother's eyes wandering repeatedly to the ceiling as the nipple fell from the baby's seeking mouth and the youngster's gaze drifted away from his mother's face.

Parenting films are much easier to make today than they were fifteen years ago. The camera—complete with a close-up lens—may be installed as a permanent and relatively inexpensive fixture in the infant center. Of course videotapes must be produced only with parental consent or by order of the court. But court orders for such necessary documentation are relatively easy to obtain in the United States. I would suppose that other countries, too, would smoothly order such documentations where infants at serious risk were concerned. Films and tapes must be obtained early in the course of the infant's treatment and saved in the event that the medical and psychiatric treatment of the case does not work out as successfully as hoped. By the time court intervention is needed, the baby's condition may be more subtly distrubed than it was originally. Early documentations are the ones that will

most thoroughly convince the laymen who sit in judgment inside the courtroom.

Evidence from Bystanders

Even though child mental health workers have the professional expertise in matters before courts involving babies, lay witnesses may offer crucial evidence for both the legal and the medical-social understandings of such cases. The statements of bystanders occasionally become particularly important fragments in piecing together the puzzle that the infant presents. Police reports, depositions, and on-the-spot observations of bystanders, therefore, must not be ignored by the infant psychiatrist. Furthermore, the names and addresses of lay witnesses should be retained by the infant specialist, so that further questions—if they come up—can be posed and answered.

CASE 4

William, a four-year-old boy with relatively poor verbal skills, was stuck in his frequently malfunctioning apartment elevator for twenty hours, during which time his parents and the city police were searching for him "all over town." On Monday morning when the elevator repairmen came to the building to fix the faulty lift, they apparently did not notice that William was cowering in one corner.

About ninety minutes after the elevator was fixed, a neighbor noticed the terrified little boy and brought him back to his frantic family. The neighbor reported to William's parents that she literally had had to pull the silent and immobile preschooler by the arm in order to remove him from the place where he had originally become so frightened. The child was so fearful of further fear that he could not leave the elevator on his own.

The observations of the neighbor would be particularly useful ones for the child psychiatrist evaluating William. Fear of fear occurs immediately in cases of childhood trauma; here the neighbor herself had seen striking evidence of this phenomenon. Provided that the neighbor was an objective, reliable, and reasonably intelligent witness, she also would be able to provide meaninful testimony in any civil negligence action on William's behalf against the landlord.

Expert Testimony from the Infant Psychiatrist

By American rules of evidence, the expert medical witness—because of training and experience—is allowed to give the court an opinion and to explain the reasons for reaching this opinion. Of course, the medical witness is allowed to use direct observations, but heresay rules are also put aside because psychiatrists often rely upon communications from others in order to reach their opinions (Diamond and Louisell, 1970). Infant psychiatrists, more than other psychiatric specialists, use many of these outside "hearsay" communications—from mothers, nurses, social workers, for instance—in order to reach their conclusions. They employ these indirect sources because of course the baby patient cannot speak for her- or himself.

It is up to the infant psychiatrist to put words to the infant's behaviors so that the lay finders of fact will understand the baby's perspective. For example, reenactments, specific fears, post-traumatic play, and nightmares can all be explained by the infant psychiatrist to the judge or jury so that, in effect, his or her expert testimony will by-pass that of the traumatized youngster.

CASE 5

Nicky, at age twenty-one months, experienced a plane crash in Central America. The plane had plunged straight down like an elevator, and little Nicky had become limp as if dead in his mother's lap. With the toddler in her arms, the mother jumped out of the plane and landed knee deep in the mud of a coffee plantation. A fellow passenger offered to hold Nicky while his mother struggled to extricate herself from the muck. As she transferred the inert child into the hands of a stranger, Nicky suddenly became alert and began to scream loudly.

Months afterward, Nicky came to my office exhibiting compulsive airplane play in which planes crashed again and again. He assiduously avoided the color aqua, which for him identified the particular airline company with the "bad airplane." Nicky had nightmares following which he jumped into his mother's bed, expressed anger at the relatives who had originally put him on the ill-fated plane, and was panic-stricken whenever he was separated from his mother. These nonverbal signs were so specific to Nicky's traumatic experience that it was possible in my medical-legal report to demonstrate the full extent of the child's suffering so vividly that the little boy himself did not have to appear in the courtroom.

In such dramatic cases, the expert may by-pass the child's court appearance with ease. The nondramatic infant-parent bonding issues in adoption, infant-custody, and infant-visitation disputes are far more subtle and thus far more difficult for the professional witness to explain to the court without other supporting data.

The Baby Himself Comes to Court

Let us now consider that rare instance in which neither body products, eye-witness reports, or expert evaluations alone can serve as convincing evidence before the judge or magistrate. These cases usually have to do with infant-parent emotional connectedness and/or the lack of it: a biological mother who relinquished her infant eight months ago appears in court to claim her rights from the adoptive parent(s); a divorced or separated father wishes to spend visitation time with his infant, but mother has consistently locked him out; a baby, abandoned on a doorstep, but well fed and smiling after hospital care, regains appeal for the mother, who demands to take her or him "home." These cases are most difficult for courts to settle, and the judge's personal prejudices may determine the outcome. It is here that bringing the baby to court or, better yet, to the judge's chambers, might settle many controversies. The infant psychiatrist must be there, too, to interpret puzzling infantile behaviors. But if the baby's actions occur in a strikingly self-explanatory way, "expert" interpretations could better be kept muted or absent so that the judge may come to an independent conclusion.

Any infant beyond six or seven months—often even younger—makes special preferential distinctions toward the primary emotional caregiver(s), reaching out, smiling at her or him, but struggling or tensing when placed with others. This baby preference can be demonstrated directly to the court. Furthermore, the consistent caregiver(s) is usually more relaxed with the infant than are those with whom the child has no emotional tie. If a parent-claimant were to feed, diaper, or hold the infant in the presence of the judge, many controversies might automatically rectify themselves. Videotapes might be helpful in the same way, but some times the personal demonstration of the infant is preferable.

One takes a chance, of course. A cold awkward mother might perform marvelously well one day before the court. A baby might fuss and squirm miserably in a "psychological par-

ent's" (Goldstein et al., 1973) arms. An unscrupulous lawyer could trick the court by having the client pinch the baby, causing the infant to scream as he or she is transferred into the opposite parent's arms (this *did* occur once).

I like to think, however, that repetition is one of those psychological phenomena that we can truly count on. We can bank more on the baby's and parent's tendency to repeat than on the attorney's intellectualizations or the judge's desire to be "fair" to everyone. The baby—more than anyone else in the judge's chambers—can show us to whom he or she is psychologically bonded. If the baby behaves indiscriminately, this, too, can be explained by the infant psychiatrist.

I began with the 1897 United States Supreme Court, but end with a much earlier authority—King Solomon (Kings, I, 3:16–28). Solomon, wanting to know which of two women claiming to be the mother of a baby was the true mother, found out quickly enough by posing to them a threat to the baby's life. Solomon knew something that American's highest court did not take into account at the turn of today's century: A mute witness may plainly point the way to the truth.

REFERENCES

Diamond, B. and Louisell, D. (1970). The psychiatrist as an expert witness: Some ruminations and speculations. In *Effective Utilization of Psychiatric Evidence.* New York, Practicing Law Institute.

Fraiberg, S. (1968). Parallel and divergent patterns in blind and sighted infants. *The Psychoanalytic Study of the Child,* 23:264–300. New York; International Universities Press.

Fraiberg, S. (1975) Ghosts in the nursery: A psychoanalytic approach to the problems of impaired infant-mother relationships. *Journal of the American Academy of Child Psychiatry,* 14:387–422.

Fraiberg, S., ed. (1980). *Clinical Studies in Infant Mental Health: The First Year of Life.* New York: Basic Books.

Goldstein, J., Freud, A., and Solnit, A. (1973) *Beyond the Best Interests of the Child.* New York: The Free Press.

McCormick, C. (1980). *Evidence.* St. Paul, Minnesota: West Publishing Co.

Terr, L.C. (1980). The child as a witness. In *Child Psychiatry and the Law,* ed. D. Shetky and E. Benedek. New York: Brunner/Mazel.

Terr, L.C. (1980). Personal injury to children: The court suit claiming psychic trauma. In *Child Psychiatry and the Law,* ed. D. Shetky and E. Benedek. New York: Brunner/Mazel.

Wheeler v. United States (1980). 159 U.S. 523, 40 LEd 244, 16 Sct 93, 1897.

55

Psychiatric Aspects of Placement and Visitation of Children Under Three Years of Age

Margaret P. Gean, M.D.

While working in our infant psychiatry program, I am frequently asked to evaluate children with regard to their bonding and attachment, developmental status, and the designation of a permanent primary caregiver. This last issue is especially complex because the best interests of the child, in addition to the fitness of the parents, must be considered by the courts in making a determination. In this article I examine the issue of visitation with biologic relatives who are not providing a child's primary care. Data were gathered by retrospective chart review. The response of young children to visitation and its impact on the attachment process are discussed.

My initial hypothesis was that children under three years of age were too young cognitively and affectively to tolerate frequent visits away from the primary caregiver, and that the attachment to the psychological parent (primary caregiver) was affected by disruptions occasioned by visits to other relatives. I postulated that symptoms during and after visits appeared initially as a reactive disturbance (Adjustment Disorder, DSM-III, see American Psychiatric Association [1980]) and that severe disturbances reflected the onset of an attachment disorder.

A prevalent symptom following visits was increased attachment behavior to the primary caregiver. Sleep disturbances for several days, aggressive behavior, withdrawal, eating disturbances, and fussiness were reported. The severest problems included regressive behaviors, failure-to-thrive, chronic attachment disturbances, and developmental delays. The verbal child frequently expressed reluctance to go on the visit and had questions about the permanence of care in the foster home. In the initial phases of visitation, the children usually had several days of being symptom-free prior to the next visit. Ongoing regular visitation frequently resulted in symptoms being sustained for the entire period between visits.

Most visits were carried out to meet legal or parental needs. They were not matched to the young child's limited evocative memory or to the need for the presence of a primary caregiver in stressful circumstances. The effects of this emotional disruption on the overall attachment process and its consequences on the child's later psychosocial development were of concern.

Literature Review

A search for studies that clearly delineate the ages of children when placed and whether visitation occurred was undertaken. A shift from institutions to foster homes for the placement of infants introduced limitations in extrapolating earlier work to the present circumstances of foster care (Beres and Obers, 1950; Freud and Burlingham, 1944; Goldfarb, 1945; Tizard, 1978). As many young children are presently in day care and separated from the primary caregiver the day-care literature was reviewed. Similarities with foster children with visitation were looked for but not found. (Belsky, 1978; Caldwell, 1972; Farron et al., 1977; Moore, 1969a; Rubenstein and Howe, 1981).

Four references discussed visitation of children in placement. Solnit and his group (1973) indicated that visitation may be disruptive for a child, depending on circumstance and age. Solnit's group later (1979) elaborated on the legal complications that might arise if a parent fails to comply with the visitation schedule. A basic emphasis in both works was the need for primacy of the child's interests. Fanshel (1976) identified the extent of visitation as a predictor of a child's reunion with a biologic parent. Weinstein's study (1960) addressed the self-esteem of foster children and discussed visitation in the context of a child's identification with parent figures. Neither Fanshel nor Weinstein described the child's response to visitation or its impact on the attachment process of children under the age of three years. Numerous articles detail the judicial process and the advances in juvenile and family law, but none addresses the child's needs regarding visitation (Derdeyn et al., 1977; Foster, 1973; Gardner, 1982; Mnookin, 1975; Polier, 1975; Schetky et al., 1979).

Few studies could be found of the foster parent's role in the emotional life of the foster child. Yarrow (1965) looked at the interaction of foster mothers with several different infants and the ability of the infant to mold the caregivers' behavior and vice versa. Walker (1973) discussed the need for maturity in the foster mother to allow the child to grieve the loss of the previous caregiver. Comments on the issue of the foster parent's role regarding the child's response to visits were not found. Specific studies on the impact of visitation on the attachment process, symptom formation, and outcome appear to be lacking.

The Study

SAMPLE

Two hundred and ninety-two children under three years of age were referred to our infant-toddler clinic for evaluation between July 1979 and September 1982. Of these, sixty-seven were involved in some form of visitation with a nonprimary caregiving biologic relative. Sixty-three children were in foster placements and four children had never been placed away from their mothers. Three of the sixty-three children in placement had never been cared for by their mothers and had gone to the foster home at birth.

There were twenty-seven boys and forty girls in the group. All of their mothers had been supported by public assistance. Forty-seven of the children were white, fifteen were black, and five were racially mixed.

REFERRAL AND EVALUATION

In the majority of cases, evaluations were initiated by an agency or attorney. A telephone interview determined the reason for referral, the legal status of the case, the current placement of the child, and status of visitation. The time of day when the infant was most likely to be in an optimal state was considered in scheduling the appointment. In addition, who would be present and the tasks to be accomplished were carefully delineated.

The appointments included at least the child, the primary caregiver(s), and the representative of the referring agency. Additionally, biologic parents, grandparents, aunts and uncles, siblings (both biologic and foster), attorneys, court investigators, psychotherapists, and companions of the biologic parents were seen.

Data and observations included complete medical, developmental, psychiatric, and social histories of the child. Further information about the adults was obtained from direct psychiatric interview or from medical, psychiatric, and agency records when questions arose regarding fitness of the biologic relatives or foster parents for permanent caregiving.

Interviews with the child present included unstructured play with adult(s) and the examiner. The Bayley (1969) Scales of Infant Development were administered in their entirety, and separation and reunion events were observed between the child and the various adults. When possible, a comparison of the child's separation-reunion response to the primary caregiver and the biologic parent(s) was carried out during the same appointment. The primary caregiver was interviewed regarding her knowledge of the child's background, age at placement, prior placements, and the type and duration of response that the child exhibited upon arriving in her home. The primary caregiver's affective connection with the child, her long-term wishes regarding the optimal plan for herself and the child, as well as the legal status of the child were discussed.

Detailed information about the circumstances of the visitation was requested. How the child responded before, during, and after the visit was recorded. Feelings that the primary caregiver had about the visits and about the child's visiting biologic family were pursued in the semistructured interview. Agency personnel who participated in these visits were also asked about these details.

INTERVENTIONS

With these data in mind, interventions were aimed at resolving symptoms and preventing damage to the attachment process. An immediate designation of a permanent caregiver was usually considered of utmost importance and required extensive discussion with the legal staff, expert testimony in the court room, and work with the agency personnel. Given the general lack of specific training in infant psychiatry, many guidelines appropriate for older children but often incorrect for a child under three were available to agencies and attorneys. Lengthy legal proceedings were beyond the child's cognitive capacity and frequently exceeded the age range in which the primary attachment process can occur.

For children with symptoms in response to visitation, it was recommended that the visits be stopped and that consultation with the adults be focused on keeping the needs of the child primary. If visits had to continue for legal purposes, a hierarchy of stress-reducing plans was initiated. Least stressful would be having the visits in the home of the primary caregiver, followed by having the caregiver present during visits in an unfamiliar setting. More stressful would be having the caregiver readily available and providing transportation to and from the visit. Only as a last resort would the child be transported by a familiar agency representative to an unfamiliar setting. Decreasing the length and frequency of the visits was helpful for some children, as was a suspension of visits to allow the child to move on to a more mature developmental phase. Because there is limited opportunity to have the child's needs be primary when a change in caregiver is to occur, a brief (one-week) series of visits to familiarize the child with the next home and caregiver was used to prevent the confusion seen in children with ongoing visits.

Several examples will convey the complexity of the clinical circumstances and the results of intervention.

BOBBY

Bobby lived with his retarded and emotionally impaired mother until his only placement at ten months of age. His initial parenting was considered insufficient, for he had autistic symptoms and was failing to thrive. He improved with foster parents who wanted to adopt him, and the infrequent visits with his biologic mother were discontinued due to the several-week pervasive regressions that resulted every time he was taken for a visit.

YVONNE

Yvonne sustained physical abuse by her biologic parents prior to placement at eighteen months. She was referred for evaluation when visits to her biologic parents had progressed to five full days per week. During this time her behavior and sleep disturbance had deteriorated beyond her foster parents' tolerance. Yvonne requested not to leave the foster home. At thirty months, and against the advice of the evaluator, she was returned to her biologic parents. Her symptoms continued, with increased anxiety and aggression at home. A trial therapy for the child and her biologic mother was felt to be prolonging the agency's illusion that this child could be successfully kept in her biologic home. After five months she was returned to her original foster home. Though she gradually improved, she continued to ask questions about her permanent caregiving, masturbated excessively, and suffered from increased clinging and sleep disturbance whenever she was evaluated. Additionally, Yvonne asked to be alternately called by the name given to her by her biologic parents and the name used by her foster parents. She asks her foster parents if she can stay with them until she is married.

CYNTHIA

Cynthia was placed at one month because of risk factors associated with her single teenage mother's drug use and unstable lifestyle. Weekly visits were discontinued because the child's failure-to-thrive, which began at seven months of age, did not respond to medical management. She regained an age-appropriate weight and her foster parents continued to express a desire to adopt her.

SANDY

Sandy was placed at two months when her mother entered a drug-abuse program. As her mother repeatedly entered and left the program, this child and her older half-sister moved into five different foster homes over an eight-month period. From ten months until twenty-eight months of age, she remained with one foster family, which was both willing to adopt her and desirous of maintaining contact with her biologic family. Biannual visits without the foster parents present have occurred without symptoms. Sandy, who was premature and drug-exposed *in utero*, was recently noted to have progressed into her chronologic age range in all areas of development and to be appropriately attached to her primary caregivers.

TERESA

Teresa has never been in placement away from her mother, but has never lived with her father. Weekly visits to the paternal grandparents, without the mother present, occurred until age twenty-four months when it was thought that her general emotional immaturity, excessive fears, sleep disturbance, and clinging behavior might be in response to this visitation. Teresa's mother maintained an antagonistic, silent relationship with her husband and in-laws. With cessation of the visits, Teresa's symptoms resolved, and she appeared to be a happy three-year-old. Legal efforts to re-establish visitation are being considered although the mother does not desire this.

Findings

Sixty-seven children were involved in some form of visitation with a nonprimary caregiving biologic relative. Of these, sixty experienced at least one disruption in the attachment process prior to visitation by placement in foster care of at least two months duration. The range of placement without designation of a permanent primary caregiver was two months to fifty-two months. The mean placement was 25.9 months. Three of the children with undisrupted attachments had medical problems, were placed at birth, and had visitation with biologic relatives. The other four children were never placed away from the biologic mother but visited with the biologic fathers or grandparents. Interchanges about the visits between the caregiver and relative were absent or hostile.

The range in the number of changes in caregivers for the sixty-seven children was from 0 to 6 with a mean of 2.0 changes. Some children moved many times between two caregivers, while others had multiple changes with one of the alternating caregivers constant, the other varying with each placement, and others never returned to a previous caregiver. The distribution of the number of different caregivers ranged from 1 to 6 with a mean of 2.5. Only eleven of the sixty-seven were placed prior to three months of age, and an additional eight prior to six months of age, leaving forty-eight children (72 percent) placed after the optimal upper age of six months.

The categories suggested by Ainsworth (1962) and Yarrow (1961) of insufficient, distorted, and discontinuous parenting were used to separate issues of maternal deprivation from symptoms due to other factors in this sample. Insufficient parenting was considered to consist of a lack of stimulation by and interaction with a primary caregiver, resulting in developmental delays, deviations, and attachment disorders. Distorted parenting included physical abuse, rigidity, and extremes of parenting style. Disruptions were separations from the primary caregiver of greater than two months without contact of frequency and quality appropriate to the child's age and capacity to maintain a bond.

Eleven of the sixty-seven children (16 percent) were known to have had insufficient parenting, ten (15 percent) had distorted parenting, and 60 (90 percent) had disrupted parenting, that is, foster placement. Only five of the sixty-seven children (7 percent) had medical problems that contributed to their placement. Three were placed at birth and one each at twenty-six months and eleven months of age. Overall, twenty-three of the sixty-three placed children (37 percent) were in foster care secondary to insufficient and/or distorted parenting and/or medical problems.

It was postulated that visitation for these twenty-three children would be an inordinate stress on developing trusting relationships (Moore, 1969b; Rutter, 1981). The development of an anxious attachment (Bowlby, 1973)

seemed likely if the visits and symptoms continued. Similarly, multiple sequential caregivers would diminish the short-term ability to continue to form primary attachments (Bowlby, 1973; Yarrow, 1964). In addition to visitation-related symptoms, children with multiple sequential caregivers were often noted to have limited affective range and modulation, indiscriminate attachment behavior, poor self-protective skills, and significant discrepancies between their mental and motor development on the Bayley Scales of Infant Development.

Forty of the sixty-three placed children (63 percent) were in placements for reasons other than maternal deprivation or medical illness. Forty children came from families with unstable living arrangements that involved frequent moves or marginal housing, poor follow-up of routine medical care, a lack of cooperation with social service agencies, or drug use by the parent. These circumstances presented a marginally neglectful situation that often catapulted the children into placements with out a clear determination of parental unfitness. This was a particularly difficult type of placement to terminate quickly and usually resulted in greater acute and long-term disturbances than the child had before placement. It was a general impression that these children, while at risk, were not seriously disturbed prior to placement as a result of these less than optimal circumstances (Fanshel, 1975).

When visitation for the group of sixty-seven was investigated, eighteen children (27 percent) did not have any symptoms in response to visitation. If these eighteen children, thirteen were distinguished by great infrequency of visits (one to three per year), four by having the visits occur in the foster home, and one child was only four to six months of age during the placement. Some children did have symptoms even under these circumstances and were included in the group of forty-nine symptomatic children (73 percent). Most children had visits for one hour per week for at least a one-month period. Some had three day-overnight visits, four-hour multiple-times-per-week visits, and once or twice weekly visits for six- to nine-month periods. These schedules continued even in the face of persistent and worsening symptoms. All four children who had never been placed had symptoms.

The primary caregivers' feelings about the visits seemed to have had an impact on the children. Some children had symptoms of greater severity than might have been predicted. Discussion with foster parents revealed intense feelings on the caregiver's part about the needs of the child, the biologic mother, the visits, and their wishes to provide a permanent home if the child were freed for adoption. Most foster parents felt that their own apprehension or disagreement about the occurrence of visits should not be acted on, and they attempted to prevent the child from knowing of their feelings. Some caregivers identified periodic disturbances in the children as coinciding with their own knowledge of court dates, requests for visits by the biologic parents, and changes and complications in the permanent plans for the child.

In thirty of the sixty-seven children (45 percent) who had symptoms associated with visitation, visits were either deliberately stopped because of the distress and symptoms or because the biologic relative was not available to visit. In all children the acute symptoms noted after visits resolved within days to a month. The developmental delays and deviations gradually resolved over a longer period. Attachment disorders began improving, and the six children with nonorganic failure to thrive (none of whom were in the group with medical reasons for placement) showed improvement in their growth parameters. Children who had previous insufficient or distorted parenting often had residual pathology, even though the reactive visitation disturbance was resolved. After the visits were stopped, these children were noted to show a greater rate of improvement in these symptoms than in their other disturbances.

In brief, then, almost three quarters of the children under three years of age who were visiting biologic relatives who were not providing primary caregiving had symptoms following visitation. All those whose visits were discontinued had a resolution of the reactive symptoms and an overall improvement in other disorders. These findings suggest that many young children are being placed after the initial process of attachment has solidly begun and increased in complexity. When subjected to visitation without consideration of the child's attachment to the primary caregiver, reactive symptoms occurred that resolved with cessation of the visits. Given the prolonged length of placement, many children had undertaken, and some had completed, the primary attachment process prior to a determination of permanent custody.

Further prospective studies are necessary to determine the long-term consequences of the stress of visitation and prolonged lack of a permanent caregiver during the phase of primary attachment. Correlations should be looked for among the various symptoms, predisposing disorders, and types of maternal deprivation. Limitations of this data are their retrospective nature, the lack of standardized measures of the symptoms, the risk factors, and the caregivers' impact on the child's functioning.

REFERENCES

Ainsworth, M. D. S. (1962). The effects of maternal deprivation: A review of findings and controversy in the context of research strategy. In *Deprivation of Maternal Care: A Reassessment of Its Effects* Public Health Papers, No. 14. Geneva: World Health Organization.

American Psychiatric Association (1980). *Diagnostic and Statistical Manual of Mental Disorders*, (DSM-III) 3rd edition. Washington, D. C.: American Psychiatric Association.

Bayley, N. (1969). *Manual for the Bayley Scales of Infant Development.* New York: The Psychological Corporation.

Belsky, J. (1978). The effects of daycare: A critical review. *Child Development,* 49:929–949.

Beres, D. and Obers, S. (1950). The effects of extreme deprivation in infancy on psychic structure in adolescence: A study of ego development. *The Psychoanalytic Study of the Child,* 5:212–235. New York: International Universities Press.

Bowlby, J. (1973). *Attachment and Loss,* vol. 2, *Separation: Anxiety and Anger.* New York: Basic Books.

Caldwell, B. (1972). What does research teach us about daycare: For children under 3. *Children Today,* 1:6–11.

Derdeyn, A. and Wadlington, W. (1977). Adoption: The rights of parents versus the best interests of their children. *Journal of the American Academy of Child Psychiatry*, 16:238–255.

Fanshel, D. (1975). Parental failure and consequences for children. *American Journal of Public Health*, 65:604–612.

Fanshel, D. (1976). Status change of children in foster care: Final results of the Columbia University Longitudinal Study. *Child Welfare*, 55:143–171.

Farron, D. and Romey, C. (1977). Infant daycare and attachment behaviors toward mothers and teachers. *Child Development*, 48:1112–1116.

Foster, H. (1973). Adoption and child custody: Best interests of the child? *Buffalo Law Review*, 22:1–26.

Freud, A. and Burlingham, D. (1944). *Infants Without Families*. New York; International Universities Press.

Gardner, R. (1982). *Family Evaluation in Child Custody Litigation*. New Jersey: Creative Therapeutics

Goldfarb, W. (1945). Psychological privation in infancy and subsequent adjustment. *American Journal of Orthopsychiatry*, 15:247–255.

Moore, T. (1969a). Effects on the children. In *Working Mothers and Their Children*, ed. S. Yudkin and A. Holme. London: Sphere Books.

Moore, T. (1969b). Stress in normal childhood. *Human Relations*, 22:235–250.

Mnookin, R. (1973). Foster care: In whose best interest? *Harvard Educational Review*, 43:599–638.

Polier, J. (1975). Professional abuse of children: Responsibility for the delivery of services. *American Journal of Orthopsychiatry*, 45:357–362.

Rubenstein, J. and Howe, C. (1981). A two-year follow-up of infants in community-based daycare. *Journal of Child Psychology and Psychiatry*, 22:209–218.

Rutter, M. (1981). Stress coping and development: Some issues and some questions. *Journal of Child Psychology and Psychiatry*, 22:323–356.

Schetky, D., Angell, R., Morrison, C., and Sack, W. (1979). Parents who fail. *Journal of the American Academy of Child Psychiatry*, 18:366–383.

Solnit, A., Goldstein, J., and Freud, A. (1973). *Beyond the Best Interests of the Child*. New York: The Free Press.

Solnit, A., Goldstein, J., and Freud, A. (1979). *Before the Best Interests of the Child*. New York: The Free Press.

Tizard, B. (1978). The effect of early institutional rearing on the development of eight-year-old children. *Journal of Child Psychology and Psychiatry*, 19:99–118.

Walker, W. (1973). Persistence of mourning in the foster child as related to the foster mother's level of maturity. *Smith College Studies in Social Work*, 41:173–246.

Weinstein, E. (1960). *The Self-Image of the Foster Child*. New York: Russell Sage Foundation.

Yarrow, L. (1961). Maternal deprivation: Toward an empirical and conceptual re-evaluation. *Psychological Bulletin*. 58:459–490.

Yarrow, L. (1961). Separation from parents during early childhood. *Review of Child Development Research*, vol. 1, ed. M. Hoffman and L. Hoffman. New York: Russell Sage Foundation.

Yarrow, L. (1965). An approach to the study of reciprocal interactions in infancy: Infant-caretaker pairs in foster care and adoption. Paper presented at Biennial Meeting of Society for Research in Child Development, Minneapolis, Minnesota.

56

Holding Interactions in a Clinical Family

Elisabeth Fivaz, Ph.D., Daniel Martin, Ph.D., and Barbro Cornut-Zimmer, Ph.D.

Introduction
Tiffany Field, Ph.D.

Body position is a critical feature of social intercourse, yet one that has received little attention by nonverbal-interaction researchers. Some exceptions are the research on adult interaction positions by Adam Kendon (1970) and rhythmicity of position changes by William Condon (1976). In this presentation, Fivaz, Martin, and Cornut-Zimmer introduce a methodology for analyzing body positioning and holding of infants during their face-to-face interactions with adults.

A series of classical case studies on early pathological interactions have highlighted the importance of appropriately holding the infant during interactions (Benjamin and Tennes, 1958; Call, 1963; Spitz and Cobliner, 1965; Stern, 1971). Several of Massie's (1980) film analyses of infants who later developed psychopathology featured aberrant holding patterns by parents, cases that he appropriately called "interference with body contact and holding," and "interference with affective reciprocity, touching, gazing, and holding."

If the infant is not held in a comfortable position, he or she clearly lacks the support necessary for body relaxation, the contact comfort, and the physical freedom to engage in face-to-face behaviors. Yet the critical "context" behavior of holding has been virtually ignored. Why? Perhaps because face-to-face gaze patterns, facial expressions, and vocalizations have been highlighted by early-interaction researchers in their attempt to identify precursors to language development, or perhaps because infants are almost invariably placed in infant seats for this kind of research, or perhaps, as in adult research, touching and holding have been more difficult to study in the laboratory. They require intimate pairs, and, except in clinical situations, intimate dyads are rarely studied. The parent-infant dyad provides an exceptional opportunity for studying holding because it constitutes an intimate pair and because holding is a critical context for face-to-face interactions of infants.

Fivaz and her colleagues are presenting their methodology as applied to an infant interacting with its "postpartum decompensated family" members and with a stranger. Their film illustrations feature the mother and father holding the infant with limited support in a fairly upright, distal lap position. These holding patterns were presumed to interfere with face-to-face interaction, in contrast to the holding behavior of the stranger, which reputedly facilitated interaction. However, in the absence of normative data on holding patterns of "normal" parents and holding-pattern preferences of the average ten-week-old infant, data on one case may be misleading. We look forward to the results from a broader subject base to provide the proper context for such comparisons. In our own experience, infants of this age prefer to be held in an almost erect position (including standing on the adult's lap) with under-the-arm support for freedom of arm movements, as opposed to lying in the adult's lap with full torso and head support. The illustrations Fivaz presents show the infant's parents, not the stranger, holding the infant in these "preferred" positions. Thus, these data came as a surprise.

A related problem in analyzing parental holding patterns is identifying and coding the infant's body-movement signals. If the infant squirms, arches its back, stretches its neck, and signals discomfort by more subtle changes in muscle tonus, a parent will probably read this as a cue to reposition the infant from supine to sitting or standing. It is conceivable that the infant in this study was discomforted by parental behaviors in other channels (face, voice, and so forth), then squirmed, and the parent sensitively responded by shifting the infant to a more distal upright position. Not knowing the infant's position preferences and its behaviors prior to the parent's positioning makes it difficult to evaluate the parent's holding patterns. Still another potential confound in data on a single case is infant state-change. Without ensuring an equivalent state (for instance, alertness) across interaction partners or counterbalancing the order of interaction partner (in a larger sample), state alone could be contributing to differences in infant behavior with different partners. The simple process of habituation/dishabituation, or novelty of the stranger and the stranger's holding patterns might explain the aborted interaction with father followed by renewed responsivity of the infant to the stranger.

There is a need for broader sampling of holding behavior in both normal and clinical dyads and the antecedent and consequent behaviors, as well as position preferences of the infant. Such research might well utilize the methodology described by Fivaz and her colleagues, stimulating further investigation on holding and other context behaviors that are so critical to understanding early interactions.

REFERENCES

Benjamin, J. and Tennes, K. (1958). A case of pathological head-nodding. Paper presented at the Los Angeles Society for Child Psychiatry and at the American Psychoanalytic Association, Los Angeles, California.

Call, J. (1963). Interlocking affective freeze between an autistic child and his "as-if" mother. *Journal of the American Academy of Child Psychiatry*, 2:319–344.

Condon, W. S. (1976). An analysis of behavioral organization. *Sign Language Studies*, 13:285–318.

Kendon, A. (1970). Movement coordination in social interaction: Some examples described. *Acta Psychologica*, 32: 100–125.

Massie, H. N. (1980). Pathological interactions in infancy. In *High-Risk Infants and Children: Adult and Peer Interactions*, ed. T. M. Field et al. New York: Academic Press.

Spitz, R. and Cobliner, W. E. (1965). *The First Year of Life*. New York: International Universities Press.

Stern, D. A. (1971). A microanalysis of mother-infant interaction. *Journal of the American Academy of Child Psychiatry*, 10:501–517.

The description presented in this paper is part of a larger study which addresses the issue of the contexts for communication between parent and infant, that is, postural and face-to-face interactions. We propose that, together with communication per se, these exchanges form a hierarchical organization of three distinct and connected levels. We refer to these in descending order as *holding* (postural exchanges), *face-to-face* (head and gaze orientations, gaze distance), and *dialogue* (discrete messages via mimic, vocal-verbal, and tactile-kinesthesic channels). These three levels have been widely recognized as essential for the development of social exchanges. However, although communication and face-to-face ex-

This research is supported by the Swiss National Fund for Research and the Centre d'Étude de la Famille (Dir. Prof. L. Kaufmann), Hôpital de Cery (Dir. Prof. C. Müller). We thank Prof. H. Papoušek and Dr. M. Papoušek for their support and Dr. N. Durez for his careful reading.

changes have been scrutinized for their microspatial and temporal organization, such a study of postural exchanges—which shape what Winnicott (1960) described as holding—have hardly been studied at all. Likewise, while optimal exchanges have been the focus of much attention, there are few microanalyses of pathological exchanges.

The organization of these exchanges is admittedly a highly complex one in which individual behaviors and dyadic exchanges combine the three levels separately and together. In the present paper, we focus on the description of a single aspect of this organization, the context-to-content link that is assumed to exist between holding and face-to-face levels of exchange. Dialogue level is not to be studied here. Analysis is carried out on dyadic exchanges in order to differentiate contributions of individual behaviors at holding and face-to-face levels. Exchanges reported are infant-adult (mother, father, stranger) dyadic interactions in a postpartum decompensated family. This family, the G. family is one of a population of twelve families (nonclinical and clinical) whose data are currently being microanalyzed with the same methodology. Furthermore a number of clinical observations on a nonselected population has provided preliminary results on the way parent-infant dyads usually organize the dialogue situation in response to our instructions. Using a time-series notation method, we analyze behaviors at the holding level (H) in terms of a "basic holding context," that is, the postural norms maintained by partners as they attempt to engage in dialogue. Then some of the face-to-face (F) behaviors that actually occurred within this context are described, in order to evaluate face-to-face outcome in relation to basic holding context.

It was our work with families of infants born at risk for psychosis that prompted our exploration of these communication contexts, particularly of holding. We were perplexed by the undecipherable features of the interactions we were witnessing. Our assumption was that, prior to verbal communication, patterns of interaction might appear in early nonverbal exchanges that are similar in form to the ones described (Singer et al., 1978) in families with a psychotic member. Indeed, these investigators have demonstrated that deviations in processes of shared focal attention, as expressed in verbal communications, are highly significant features for discriminating families with a psychotic member.

Exploring early exchanges in some families at risk—wherein one of the parents was diagnosed psychotic or borderline—we were led to a more detailed analysis of gaze interactions between mother and infant in the feeding situation (Fivaz, 1980; Fivaz and Cornut-Zimmer, 1982a, 1982b; Fivaz et al., 1981). During the first twelve months, we did observe the developmental sequence one might expect (Perry and Stern, 1975): starting with reciprocal interactions, partners differentiate their interaction—mother gazing at infant while infant alternates between long orientations toward environment and short returns to mother's face —and finally they proceed to coorientations.

But these interactions were far from optimal. In one case, gaze orientations were so disorderly that hardly any pattern of exchange was recognizable. In another case, reciprocal gaze failed to stabilize. Early systematic gaze avoidance and head aversion on the infant's part were observed, while the mother's associations between head and gaze orientations were quite ambiguous: it was not possible to infer her gaze orientation from the orientation of her head. Later, in both cases, a high proportion of "external coorientations" was observed, a strategy of attention deviation that was initiated and-/or reinforced by the mother at times of conflictual negotiations. Trying to understand these phenomena, we were impressed by the paradoxical features of the parents' behaviors, which often seemed to send simultaneous signals of rejection and acceptance. Though at the time we did not analyze their postural contexts in detail, it appeared that holding was not favorable to *en face* orientations and consequently to dialogue. Thus the observed interactions were similar in several ways to the descriptions by Massie and Campbell (1983).

Our therapeutic practice also emphasized the importance of holding exchanges: it appeared that interventions aimed at modifying mother's holding of her infant were most conducive to mutual exchanges at face, gaze, and even at dialogue levels. And these interventions had the characteristic of actual or symbolic "holding of mother holding her infant" by a therapist. The microanalysis of a sequence of such a three-level exchange (observer, mother, infant) was most revealing of this aspect (Fivaz et al., in press). Incidentally, it was necessary to maintain this "holding" on a long-term basis in view of these mothers' difficulties with internalization and of their husbands' and families of origin's failure to support them.

Clinical Setting

Our observation setting has evolved into a consultation offered by the Centre d'Étude de la Famille to psychiatrists in charge of conjoint mother-infant hospitalizations in cases of postpartum decompensation. The psychiatrist brings the infant, along with its parents, for a psychological evaluation of its well-being during its hospital stay. We observe and videotape feeding and dialogue situations between the infant and three adult partners: mother, father, and a stranger. In the dialogue situation, the instruction to the parents is to "hold the baby facing you and try to have him or her do whatever he or she does habitually—smile, talk, and so on."

The dialogue situation we have observed in a nonselected population of infants up to about twelve weeks is represented in figure 56-1. The adult locates the infant in the middle of his or her lap, often on elevated thighs to compensate for size difference. The adult leans forward while holding the infant backward and supporting its head. We go through several trials in an attempt to get the best possible result—indeed, a very important issue in the consultation. We may also invite other significant persons, such as grandparents or other offspring to participate. Immediately after observation, the consultant reviews the videotape with the psychiatrist. The parents are present, and their opinions and impressions are solicited. In many cases critical issues may thus be approached, such as damage to the child and need for therapeutic support (Fivaz, 1983).

Hypotheses

Our hypotheses may be briefly stated as follows.

INTERLEVEL HIERARCHY

Optimal exchange behaviors are considered as a *three-level organization* wherein each level is distinct and connected with the other levels in a succession of context versus content relationships. Thus holding level (H) exchanges form a context for a content constituted by face-to-face level (F) exchanges; in turn, face-to-face exchanges form a context for a content formed by dialogue level (D) exchanges. Therefore, superior levels are *determinants* for lower levels: their modifications directly affect lower levels, while lower-level modifications do not necessarily affect them. As the context level is expected to adjust itself to the states manifested at content level, the content-level exchanges have a *modulating* influence on the context level exchanges. For instance a modification of location of infant on adult's lap is bound to affect face orientation, whereas a shift in face orientation would hardly be sufficient to affect location of the infant, though it might modulate it. This organization is assumed to hold for dyadic exchanges as well as for individual behaviors.

INTERPARTNER HIERARCHY

In dyadic exchanges, the hierarchy of levels is combined with an *interpersonal hierarchy*, wherein behaviors of the parent—the "framing" system—form a context for the behaviors of the infant—the developing system. In turn, the developing system's behaviors modulate the framing system's behaviors. This view is in accordance with many of the proposed models of the development of social interaction, starting with Winnicott and following with contemporary studies (Brazelton, 1974; Papoušek and Papoušek, 1979a; Stern et al., 1977; Thoman, 1979; Wertheim, 1978). Optimal exchanges are viewed as reciprocal influences where the adult behaviors are sufficiently pre-

Holding Level (H):   locations
                      postural variables (trunk, limbs)
Face-to-face level (F): head orientations
                      gaze orientations
                      gaze distance
Dialogue level (D):   vocal-verbal
                      mimics
                      tactilokinesthesic

Figure 56–1   Levels of exchange in the dialogue situation.

dictable and adjusted for the infant's developmental level. This enables the infant to treat the incoming information and to build representations of its own influence on environment; the adult behavior should also be sufficiently variable to allow for new input. In turn, the infant's behaviors, as determined by behavioral states, elicit and modulate the adult's stimulations.

PATHOLOGY

In accordance with this hypotheses, pathology might evolve when *hierarchy of levels and/or of partners is failing.* The assumed superior system (context level or "framing" partner) fails to form a sufficiently stable and adjusted context for the inferior system (content level or developing partner). According to the well-known model of Bateson and his colleagues (1963), pathology evolves from *logical typing errors,* as when mutual exchanges are attempted at a content level while being denied at a context level. This type of paradoxical exchange has been exemplified in several studies (Birdwhistell, 1976; Tronick et al., 1978; Fivaz, 1980, 1981).

Operational Criteria

Operational criteria are based on spatial and temporal fitness for dialogue. More specifically, holding exchanges are evaluated on their adjustment to mutual face-to-face exchanges (F-appropriate or not F-appropriate) and face-to-face exchanges are evaluated on their adjustment to mutual dialogue exchanges (D-appropriate or not D-appropriate). A set of criteria has been defined for appropriateness of dyadic states of each level. If the appropriateness of each individual contribution at each level is also to be evaluated, specific additional criteria are needed that take into account the distribution of postural control (Wertheim, 1978) within the dyad relative to infant's stage.

DYADIC LEVELS OF EXCHANGE

Dyadic H spatio-temporal configurations are F-appropriate only when the following criteria are fulfilled: they make provision for compensation of difference in size and control between adult and infant through adequate locations of infant relative to adult; trunks are oriented vis-a-vis; and periods of trunk "holds" (episodes of stability, (Beebe and Stern 1977), are longest relative to lower levels. In addition, trunk holds are sufficiently long to allow for episodes of engagement to occur at lower levels and sufficiently variable to allow for new input. In the absence of reference data on the durations of H holds, we assume that they are longer than the episodes known to exist at lower levels.

Dyadic F configurations are D-appropriate only when the following criteria are fulfilled: spatial configurations of F holds are simultaneously characterized by mutual gaze and *en face* orientations and by dialogue gaze distance; periods of F holds are briefer than periods of H holds and sufficiently long to allow for the development of episodes of engagement at D level according to criteria available in literature (Als et al., 1979; Fogel, 1977; Stern, 1976; Stern et al., 1977) and sufficiently variable to allow for new input.

INDIVIDUAL LEVELS OF EXCHANGE

As mentioned earlier, individual levels of exchange are evaluated according to the same general criteria as dyadic levels (appropriate or not appropriate), but they take into account the infant's level of postural control. Moreover, in addition to criteria for dyadic periods, individual periods of adult behaviors should be longer than those of the infant, at each level of exchange.

The specific operational criteria used in the evaluation of the G family exchanges, where the infant is ten weeks old, are as follows: in addition to his or her own behavior, the adult controls the infant's location and trunk postures at H level; at F level, adult controls infant's head postures in the forward/backward plane (directly through head support or indirectly through trunk support). Consequently, the adult also controls gaze distance. At H level, the infant may modulate the adult's control behaviors through movements. At F level, the infant controls the rotational and lateral planes of its head—sideways turns and tilts (see section on method) and its move-

ments, and he may modulate adult's control behaviors directly through movements in the forward/backward plane; finally, the infant controls its gaze orientation.

Subjects

We have gathered observations on a population whose common feature is mother's—and/or sometimes also father's—postpartum decompensation and conjoint mother-infant psychiatric hospitalization. From this population we have selected for our study a group of eight families with infants aged from five to thirteen weeks. Patients' diagnoses range between postpartum psychotic, borderline, to depressive decompensations with or without prior psychiatric records. As the access to these families is very difficult, we have not been able to control other important variables, such as sex of infant, age, rank order, and sociocultural background of parents. Similarly, we have not yet been in aposition to collect longitudinal evaluations. Concurrently we analyzed data from eight families with no psychiatric postpartum decompensation and no prior psychiatric treatment of either parent.

Method

Because no systematic notation existed for postural exchanges—as of now we know of two studies pertaining to postural exchanges with infant actually held by adult (Kubicek, 1980, Massie, 1983; Widmer, 1981)—we adapted the Bernese time-series notation system for nonverbal interaction (Frey et al., 1981) to the adult-infant interaction feeding and dialogue situations. Because time-series notation defines movement as a succession of positions, it has the advantage of transcribing movement and posture equally well. Frey's system is known to be reliable, and its adaptation to our study's special needs was also tested for reliability. Resolution was selected at half-second intervals.

Table 56–1 displays the list of all coded body

TABLE 56-1

Summary of Coding Scheme for the Time Series Notation of Nonverbal Behavior in Holding and Face-to-Face Adult-Infant Interaction (adult)

Categories/Coding	Body Part (variables' number)	Number of Coded Dimensions	Dimensions	Type of Scale & Number of Units	Units' Code Numbers	Columns	Type of Movement Defined by Dimension
A. Location	(16) Position on chair	1	Horizontal/Depth	Ordinal	(1–9)	68	(Left, middle, right)X(front middle, back)
B. Postures	(2) Trunk	3	Sagittal Rotational Lateral	Ordinal / 9 Ordinal / 9 Ordinal / 9	(1–9) (1–9) (1–9)	14 15 16	Forward / backward tilt of trunk Left / right rotation of trunk Left / right tilt of trunk
	(3) Shoulder	2	Vertical Depth	Ordinal / 3 Ordinal / 3	(1–3) (1–3)	17/19 18/20	Up / down shift of shoulder Forward / backward shift of shoulder
	(5 V 6) Upper arm	3	Vertical Depth Touch	Ordinal / 9 Ordinal / 9 Nominal / 9	(1–9) (1–9) (1–9)	21/24 22/25 23/26	Up / down lift of upper arm Forward / backward shift of upper arm Upper arm contact with chair / body areas / partner's body
	(7 V 8) Hand	5	Vertical Horizontal Depth Closure Touch	Ordinal / 15 Ordinal / 9 Ordinal / 8 Ordinal / 9 Nominal / 89	(01–15) (1–9) (1–8) (1–9) (01–79) (90–99)	27,28/37,38 29/39 30/40 34/44 35,36/45,46	Up / down shift of hand Left / right shift of hand Forward / backward shift of hand Opening / closing of fist Hand contact with chair / body areas / partner's body

Category	Subcategory	N	Dimension	Scale / Levels	Range	Code	Description
			Horizontal	Ordinal / 9	(1–9)	48/51	Left / right shift of **upper leg**
			Touch	Ordinal / 3	(1–3)	49	Contact between knees
C. Head	(1) Head	3	Sagittal	Ordinal / 9	(1–9)	11	Up / down tilt of head
			Rotational	Ordinal / 9	(1–9)	12	Left / right rotation of head
			Lateral	Ordinal / 9	(1–9)	13	Left / right tilt of head
D. Gaze Orientation	(15)	1	Individual states	Nominal / 4	(1–4)	64	Gazing at, not gazing at, gaze coorientation, undetermined
E. Gaze Distance	(15)	1	Type of distance	Ordinal / 5	(1–5)	65	Under dialogue distance, dialogue distance, between dialogue distance and functional distance, function distance, over function distance.
(infant)							
A. Location	(15) Height of pelvis	1	Vertical	Ordinal / 4	(1–4)	63	Up / down displacement of pelvis
	(16) Position on adult	1	Horizontal/depth	Ordinal / 9	(1–9)	68	(Left, middle, right)X(front, middle, back)
	(16) Point of support of infant	1	Point of support	Nominal / 4	(1–4)	69	Independent, in adult's hands, on adult's upper arms on adult's upper legs
B. Postures	(2) Trunk	3	Sagittal	Ordinal / 9	(1–9)	14	Forward / backward tilt of trunk
			Rotational	Ordinal / 9	(1–9)	15	Left / right rotation of trunk
			Lateral	Ordinal / 9	(1–9)	16	Left / right tilt of trunk

TABLE 56–1 *(Continued)*

Categories/Coding	Body Part (variables' number)	Number of Coded Dimensions	Dimensions	Type of Scale & Number of Units	Units' Code Numbers	Columns	Type of Movement Defined by Dimension
	(3) Shoulder	2	Vertical	Ordinal / 3	(1–3)	17/19	Up / down shift of shoulder
			Depth	Ordinal / 3	(1–3)	18/20	Forward / backward shift of shoulder
	(5) Upper arm	3	Vertical	Ordinal / 9	(1–9)	21/24	Up / down lift of upper arm
			Depth	Ordinal / 9	(1–9)	22/25	Forward / backward shift of upper arm
			Touch	Nominal / 9	(1–9)	23/26	Upperarm contact with chair / body arear / partner's body
	(7) Hand	5	Vertical	Ordinal / 15	(1–15)	27,28/37,38	Up / down shift of hand
			Horizontal	Ordinal / 9	(1–9)	29/39	Left / right shift of hand
			Depth	Ordinal / 8	(1–8)	30/40	Forward / backward shift of hand
			Closure	Ordinal / 6	(1–6)	34/44	Opening / closing of fist
			Touch	Nominal / 69	(01–59) (80–89)	35,36/45,46	Hand contact with chair / body areas / partner's body
C. Head	(1) Head	3	Sagittal	Ordinal / 9	(1–9)	11	Up / down tilt of head
			Rotational	Ordinal / 9	(1–9)	12	Left / right rotation of head
			Lateral	Ordinal / 9	(1–9)	13	Left / right tilt of head
D. Gaze Orientation	(15)	1	Individual states	Nominal / 4	(1–4)	64	Gazing at, not gazing at, gaze coorientation, undetermined

segments, the numbers and types of coded dimensions and types of scales (ordinal or nominal), and the number of positions for each segment; it also provides a brief description of the movements as defined by dimensions.

In this paper, we use the following variables for our analysis: *locations,* that is, definition of each partner's place in the space that we allocate for feeding and dialogue; *trunk* and *head positions; gaze orientations;* and *gaze distance.* Procedures used to define trunk positions will be described in detail as an example of the general procedures used for the notation of each body segment.

Figure 56–2 depicts the three dimensions used to define trunk positions: sagittal: vertical forward/backward plane (leaning); rotational: horizontal right/left plane (turning sideways); lateral: oblique right/left plane (tilting side-

ways). Each of these dimensions is scaled on nine positions (starting from upright position, slight, strong, very strong, extremely strong leaning, turning, or tilting).

On figure 56–3 are displayed graphically-processed raw data which correspond to trunk positions in the three dimensions (S, R, L) for an adult and an infant as a function of time (240 half-second intervals).

Some of the advantages of this method now become visible. As Frey has demonstrated, it allows for precise reconstruction of segment positions as well as movements, thanks to the successive definitions of positions within a given movement phase. It is also apparent that these data may be readily inspected for patterns of stability and change within single or combined and within individual or dyadic dimensions. For instance, rotational and lateral

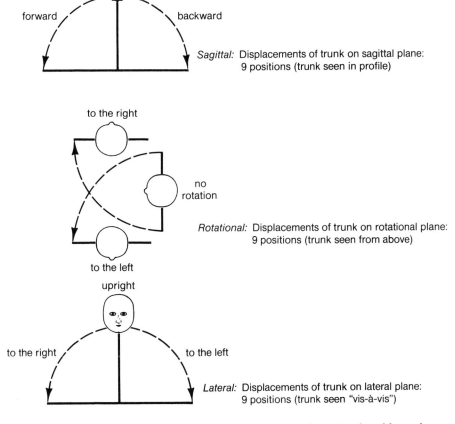

Figure 56–2   Planes of trunk displacements: sagittal, rotational, and laternal.

A

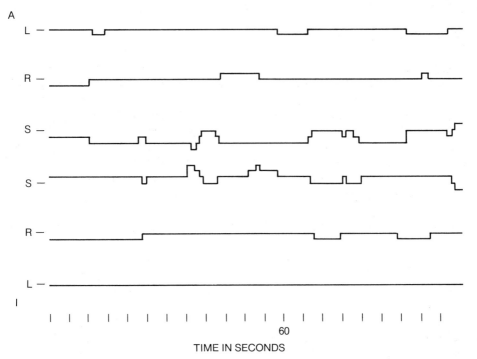

L —

R —

S —

S —

R —

L —

I

TIME IN SECONDS

60

Figure 56–3 Example of rax data graphs of trunk positions in three planes (laternal [L], rotational [R], and sagittal [S]) in a two-minute sequence of adult-infant (A-I) dialogue interaction. Adult's data are represented in the upper half and infant's data in the lower half of the graph. Middle mark of scales = upright position. Mark upward and downward from the middle = from slight to extremely strong tilting, turning, and leaning.

planes in both partners' behaviors can be seen to vary neither often nor widely, while sagittal planes are modified more often and more widely and tend to covary between partners. It is also true that the sequence may be divided into "holds," episodes of stability, and "shifts," episodes of movement, provided that some cut-off criterion is chosen.

Data: The G Family

To illustrate the method, data of the G family, a family decompensated at postpartum, are presented. The infant is a ten-week-old boy, the first child born to his parents. He was delivered without difficulty, was in good health, and was admitted to the hospital two days after his mother and a week before the present observation. The parents are middle class, in their early thirties, in good health; neither one had a psychiatric record before this crisis. At the time of the observation, the consultant was blind regarding the diagnosis and the clinical data on mother and family.

The data used for the present analysis in-

clude the first two minutes of the dialogue sequence (fifteen seconds shorter for father-infant sequence) of the three dyads: mother-infant (Mo-I), father-infant (Fa-I), stranger (the woman consultant)-infant (St-I).

Holding Exchanges

The analysis of holding exchanges is focused on Basic Holding context, which describes the postural norms and their associated periods maintained by the dyads as they attempt to engage in dialogue. Basic Holding context is evaluated on the basis of two sets of variables: locations and trunk positons. Location variables define each partner's place in the setting— place of adult on seat, place of infant on adult's lap, and its points of support as offered by adult; trunk position variables define the orientation of each partner's trunk, within these locations, in the S (sagittal), R (rotational), and L (lateral) planes. After visual inspection of all data we concluded that these are key variables for this level of exchange.

Detailed analysis of the dialogue situation

and study of data reveal that we are faced with a two-level internal organization of Basic Holding context: locations and trunk positions. Indeed, locations delimit a given space in which body positions may evolve (Stern, 1981) and are thus determinants of trunk positions. In turn, trunk positions (vis-a-vis or not vis-a-vis) are determinants of F orientations. Therefore, to evaluate Basic Holding context, we need to analyze the two levels separately and in combination for both dyadic and individual contributions.

LOCATIONS

Location variables are illustrated by sketches drawn directly from the TV screen (figure 56–4) and by graphs of the temporal distributions of holds and shifts (figure 56–5). Inspection of these data indicates that the three dyads differ in terms of types of infant locations on adult and of degree of variability. Infant locations observed in these particular data are of three types, two of which are not appropriate and one of which is appropriate for dialogue function. Those that are not appropriate are: "at distance" locations (infant seated low, on the very edge of adult's knees, supported at armpits, see figure 56–4a,c,d) which do not provide for compensation of infant's smaller size and lesser postural control and is thus assumed to be inappropriate for dialogue function; and "in fusion" locations (infant held upright in direct contact with adult's body; see figure 56–4b), which do not provide enough space between the partners for dialogue function.

Considered appropriate are the "compensation" locations (infant elevated on adult's crossed thighs, placed in the middle of lap, its head supported; see figure 56–4e) that make the necessary provisions and thus are assumed to be an appropriate context for dialogue function.

RESULTS

In Mo-I sequence (see figure 56–4a,b), alternation of "at distance" and "in fusion" locations is observed in a proportion of roughly

three to one and with a trend toward decreasing periods of "at distance" locations in favor of "in fusion" ones. Periods of shifts also tend to increase with time. In Fa-I sequence (see figure 56–4c,d), "at distance" locations are observed throughout with only one shift episode. In St-I sequence (see figure 56–4e), "compensation" locations are stabilized after an initial adjustment episode. Variability, as evaluated on the basis of time spent in shifts and of mean duration of holds (see figure 56–5) appears to be much higher in Mo-I sequence than in Fa-I and St-I sequences.

Trunk Positions

The notation of trunk positions has been described in the earlier section on method. Vis-à-vis trunk positions are defined as oblique (adult forward and infant backward) alignment of partners' trunks, without rotation. Types of trunk positions are illustrated by pictographs (figure 56–6) and by graphs of the distributions of trunk holds and shifts (figure 56–7).

Inspection of data shows that the three dyads differ as to the types of trunk positions they adopt and in degree of variability. Four categories of trunk holds are observed in this case, two of which are appropriate and two not appropriate for dialogue function. Appropriate trunk positions include "full vis-à-vis". As defined earlier, it is assumed to be an appropriate context for dialogue function (see figure 56–6c2). They also include "partial vis-à-vis": the forward/backward sagittal alignment is achieved, but one or both trunks deviate by tilting sideways; this may correspond to a signal of turning off (pause) or, when it mirrors the partner's trunk position, to a strategy for meeting the partner (see figure 56–6c1).

Not appropriate trunk positions are "non-vis-à-vis, in fusion": trunk alignment is achieved along with direct contact, clearly an inappropriate context for dialogue function (see figure 56–6a5,6); and "non–vis-à-vis, over": adult's forward deviation from upright position is wider than infant's backward deviation; in other words, adult is leaning forward more than infant is leaning backward; thus

Mo-I
(a) "at distance"

Mo-I
(b) "in fusion"

Fa-I
(c) "at distance"

Fa-I
(d) "at distance"

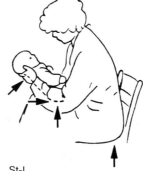

St-I
(e) "compensation"

↑ Position of adult on chair and of infant on adult's lap

→ Height of infant's pelvis

↗ Point of support of infant

--- Supposed position of infant's trunk

Figure 56–4 Types of location holds in mother-infant (Mo-I), father-infant (Fa-I), and stranger-infant (St-I) dialogue interaction.

Location holds	F(%)	Mean duration	Range
Mo-I	88	17,5	4,5-37
(-loc.hD)	(64)	(25,5)	(20,5-37)
(-loc.hF)	(24)	(9,5)	(4,5-16,5)
Fa-I	97	51	14,5-87,5
St-I	96	114,5	114,5
Location shifts			
Mo-I	12	3	1-5,5
Fa-I	3	3	3
St-I	4	5	5

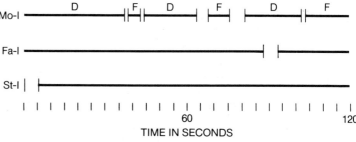

├──┤ = Location holds; at distance: D; in fusion: F

|| = Location shifts

Location Holds	F(%)	Mean Duration	Range
Mo-I	88	17,5	4,5-37
(-loc.hD)	(64)	(25,5)	(20,5-37)
(-loc.hF)	(24)	(9,5)	(4,5-16,5)
Fa-I	97	51	14,5-87,5
St-I	96	114,5	114,5
Location Shifts			
Mo-I	12	3	1-5,5
Fa-I	3	3	3
St-I	4	5	5

Figure 56–5 Partition of location holds and shifts in each dyadic sequence: Mo-I: Mother-infant interaction (120 seconds); Fa-I: Father-infant interaction (105 seconds); St-I: Stranger-infant interaction (120 seconds)

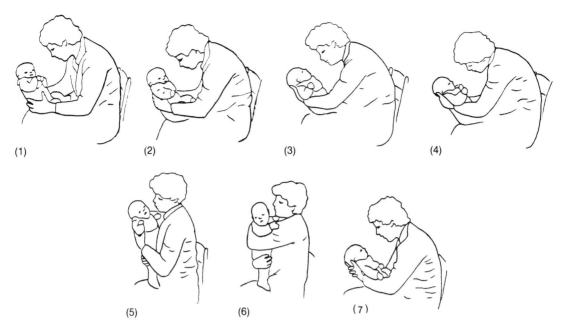

Figure 56–6a Main mother-infant trunk holds: "non vis-à-vis over" (1-4); "non vis-à-vis in fusion" (5,6); and a "full vis-à-vis" trunk hold (7) (see Final Comments section)

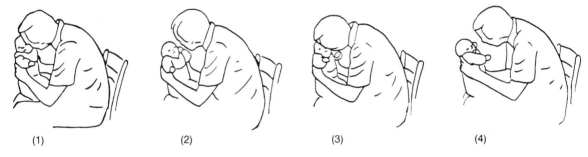

Figure 56–6b Main father-infant trunk holds: all "non vis-à-vis over"

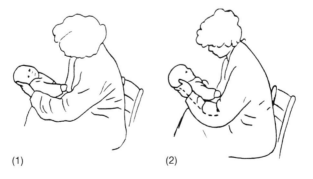

Figure 56–6c Stranger-infant trunk holds: "partial vis-à-vis" (1); "full vis-à-vis" (2)

Trunk holds	F(%)	Mean duration	Range
Mo-I	76	7	3-12,5
Fa-I	88	15	4-30,5
St-I	92	27,5	3-55,5
Trunk shifts			
Mo-I	23	2,5	0,5-5,5
Fa-I	12	2,5	0,5-4,5
St-I	8	2	0,5-4

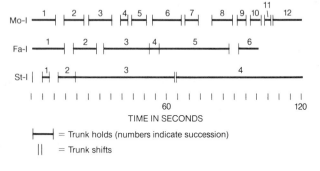

= Trunk holds (numbers indicate succession)

= Trunk shifts

Trunk Holds	F(%)	Mean Duration	Range
Mo-I	76	7	3–12,5
Fa-I	88	15	4–30,5
St-I	92	27,5	3–55,5
Trunk Shifts			
Mo-I	23	2,5	0,5–5,5
Fa-I	12	2,5	0,5–4,5
St-I	8	2	0,5–4

Figure 56–7 Partition of trunk holds and shifts in each dyadic sequence: Mo-I: Mother-infant interaction (120 seconds); Fa-I: Father-infant interaction (105 seconds); St-I: Stranger-infant interaction (120 seconds)

upper trunks come close together. This may be associated with rotations or tilts of trunks (see figure 56–6a1,2,5,6, 56–6b1,2,3,4). This type of trunk hold is assumed to be inappropriate for dialogue function; *"en face"* orientation becomes physically awkward or even impossible, gaze distance is short, and the posture in itself is tiring (incidentally, one may wonder about the existence of an optimal distance between trunks).

RESULTS

Measures of the different states are expressed in percentage of total time (%) and in mean duration in seconds of holds and shifts. In Mo-I data, only one "vis-à-vis" trunk hold out of the total ($n = 13$) is observed. The other holds are variations of the "non–vis-à-vis over" type, associated with "at distance" location holds, and "non–vis-à-vis fused" type, associated with "in fusion" location holds. Time spent in shifts (23 percent) and mean duration of trunk holds (7 sec.) indicate that variability is high.

In Fa-I data, no "vis-à-vis" trunk hold is observed. All trunk holds are of the "non–vis-à-vis over" type; they all include rotations of the infant's trunk, and most include rotations of the adult's trunk. Variability is moderate (time spent in shifts: 12 percent; mean duration of trunk holds: 15 sec.).

In St-I data, trunk holds modifications show an evolution from "partial vis-à-vis" type to "full vis-à-vis" type: forward/backward positions of trunks are stable throughout the sequence; in the beginning, the infant's trunk is rotated and tilted to the right; meanwhile, the adult's trunk shifts from no turn and no tilt to a strong tilt to the left, which mirrors the infant's trunk tilt (figure 56–6c1); but in the middle of the sequence both partners simultaneously shift to vis-à-vis trunk alignment and maintain it to the end.

Evaluation of Basic Holding Context

MO-I SEQUENCE

Analysis shows that Basic Holding context is not appropriate for face-to-face exchanges: variability is too high to make provision for episodes of engagement to occur at lower levels; types of locations are inappropriate for "vis-à-vis" trunk positions, and trunk positons are inappropriate for *en face* orientations.

Closer inspection suggests that this failure is related to the adult's repeatedly unsuccessful attempts to compensate at trunk level for the inadequate preparation at location level. Thus a *discrepancy* appears in this awkward association between location context and trunk content: the definition of locations conveys a disengagement offer, while the definition of trunk positions conveys simultaneously an (over)engagement offer. There seems to be an evolution through acceleration of unsuccessful trials toward a stabilization of "in fusion" episodes, which tend to replace "at distance" episodes.

In terms of communication theory, the injunction received by the infant at context level is: "Do not engage"; and at content level: "Do get engaged." It is difficult to read the infant's contribution in these exchanges, first because behaviors are still much under adult's control at these levels, and second, because of the confusion of these exchanges. We expect, however, that more detailed inspection of short episodes may facilitate this reading. Thus it is evaluated that the probability of occurence of episodes of engagement at Face-to-face level in this Mo-I exchange is very low.

FA–I SEQUENCE

Analysis shows that Basic Holding context is not appropriate for Face-to-face exchanges; the types of location are consistently not appropriate for "vis-à-vis" trunk positions, and trunk positions are consistently widely deviating from "vis-à-vis" alignment. Despite the observed differences between Mo-I and Fa-I data, the hypothesis of *discrepancy* (simultaneous disengagement offer at context level and overengagement offer at content level) applies here as well as its version of paradoxical communication. The remarks on Mo-I data also apply here to the infant's contribution. Thus it is demonstrated that the probability of occurrence of Face-to-face episodes of engagement in this Fa-I exchange is very low.

ST–I SEQUENCE

Analysis shows that Basic Holding context is appropriate for Face-to-face exchanges. Types of location are appropriate for "vis-à-vis" trunk orientations. In this context, trunk orientations evolve from "partial vis-à-vis" to "full vis-à-vis." In contrast to Mo-I and Fa-I exchanges, structures of locations and of trunk positions are *congruent* and the contribution of both partners in this system is much more visi-

ble: initially the infant accepts the location offer while refusing the "vis-à-vis" at trunk level (rotation and tilt sideways). However he allows the adult to meet him (through a mirroring tilt) and thereafter joins in the "full vis-à-vis" trunk orientation, which is then stabilized for a long period.

Thus it is evaluated that the probability of occurrence of episodes of engagement at Face-to-face level in this St-I exchange is initially higher than in Mo-I and Fa-I sequences and becomes high after the shift to "vis-à-vis" trunk orientation.

Face-to-Face Exchanges

Results are summarized here in order to complement the evaluation of Basic Holding context by an evaluation of its outcome at content level. As mentioned in the section on operational criteria, the analysis of F exchanges is based on three variables (gaze orientation, face presentation, and gaze distance) the values of which (expressed in percentage of time spent) are dichotomized into Dialogue-appropriate ("gaze toward," *"en face,"* and "dialogue gaze distance") and not Dialogue-appropriate ("gaze away," "not *en face,"* "not dialogue, that is; short or long gaze distance").

Individual contributions are indicated by co-occurences between each partner's D-appropriate behaviors, that is, the adult's "F offer" and the infant's "modulation." When these co-occurrences between D-appropriate behaviors are furthermore simultaneously observed in both partner's behaviors, we obtain the proportion of mutual F interactions achieved in the dyad.

RESULTS

In the Mo-I sequence, mutual F exchanges are quasi-nonexistent (1 percent). Adult's "F offer" combines: (1) quasi-constant "gaze toward" (94 percent); (2) highly variable face presentations (*"en face"*: 49 percent; mean duration of holds: 3.8 sec. "not *en face"*: 49 percent, mean duration of holds: 3.7sec.); and (3) wide variations around "short gaze distance" (66 percent, mean duration of holds: 4.6 sec.). Co-occurrence of the three D-appropriate behaviors is quasi-nonexistent (1 percent).

Thus we observe a very unstable system in which numerous oscillations (possibly attempts to achieve and stabilize mutual F interactions) invariably result in a not–D-appropriate offer; this offer is characterized by *discrepancy* between gaze and face orientation and inappropriate regulation of gaze distance. The infant's contribution is mostly not D-appropriate: "gaze toward (6 percent) and *"en face"* (20 percent) almost never co-occur (4 percent). The Infant tends to move his face between left and right sides. It appears that he actively and consistently refuses to orient toward the adult. In summary, Mo-I fail to achieve mutual F interactions. Therefore F exchanges are evaluated as not D-appropriate.

In *Fa-I sequence,* mutual F exchanges are nonexistent. The adult's "F offer" combines "gaze toward" (99 percent) "not *en face*" (96 percent), and "short gaze distance" (98 percent). Therefore co-occurrence of D-appropriate behaviors is quasi-nonexistent. (1 percent) and the behavior is both *static* and *discrepant* in terms of orientation toward the partner.

The infant's contribution is mostly not D-appropriate: the proportion of infant's "gaze toward" (2 percent) and *"en face"* (3 percent) is very low, and these two behaviors never co-occur. The most averted head positions are predominant, and their periods are longer than the less ample ones. Global variability is moderate and tends to decrease with time. The amplitude and increasing stability of head aversions indicate that infant actively orients away from the adult. In summary, Fa-I partners fail to achieve mutual F interactions. Therefore these F exchanges are evaluated as D not-appropriate.

In St-I sequence, mutual F exchanges (12 percent) do not occur during the first part of the sequence, but they *appear gradually* in the second part. The adult's "F offer" combines "gaze toward" (99 percent) and *"en face"* (87 percent) with continuous "long gaze distance" (82 percent); "dialogue distance" (18 percent) appears toward the end of the sequence. Along with "dialogue distance", small deviations are observed around *"en face"* presentation, which

correspond to "greeting responses" (Papoušek and Papoušek, 1979b).

The *infant's contribution* becomes D-appropriate during the second part (during the last 55 seconds), in which "gaze toward" and *"en face"* co-occur continuously. The infant's transition from not–D-appropriate to D-appropriate behaviors occurs in three steps: in the beginning, "gaze away" and wide head aversions; then oscillations between "gaze away" and "gaze toward" and between slight and ample head aversions; finally "gaze toward" and *"en face."* Thus the infant modifies his behavior stepwise from aversion to orientation toward partner.

In this sequence, *reciprocal influences* of partners on each other do appear clearly: modifications of the infant's orientation develop in the context offered by the adult, which is D-appropriate except for regulation of gaze distance. This may be a way of respecting the infant's refusal of contact. It is when the infant is oriented toward his partner that gaze distance, which is controled by the adult, is modified in turn and that greeting responses are activated. Thus the infant's behaviors modulate the adult's behaviors. In summary, it is shown that these exchanges are an increasingly appropriate context for D-level exchanges.

H Context Versus F Content Evaluation

Combined analysis of H and F results indicates the three following correspondences. First, F dyadic exchanges conform to the expected outcome of Basic Holding context in the three sequences: in Mo-I and Fa-I exchanges, Basic Holding context was evaluated as not appropriate for F mutual exchanges and the observed F interactions were indeed not mutual. In St-I exchanges, Basic Holding context was evaluated as increasingly appropriate for F mutual exchanges and the observed F interactions progressed stepwise toward mutuality. Second, in the three sequences, the observed H and F spatio-temporal patterns are isomorphic: degree of variability within and between states, on one hand, discrepancy versus congruence, on the other hand, were found to be consistent between H and F levels. Third, types of regulation between levels and between partners differ with type of organization: interconnections that allow tracing mutual influences between H and F levels or between adult and infant partners are visible in St-I exchanges. For instance, results show that the transition from not mutual to mutual interactions at both levels is triggered by fluctuations of the infant's behaviors at F level (between orientation away and orientation toward). In Mo-I and Fa-I sequences, analysis fails to demonstrate systematic effects: confusion associated with discrepancy, that is, paradoxical transactions, are omnipresent and no evolutive process is traced.

In conclusion, Mo-I and Fa-I interactionnal failures are associated with confusion of hierarchic levels. In contrast, the transition from nonmutual to mutual interactions in St-I is associated with a clear hierarchic organization between levels and between partners. Therefore the three observed correspondences confirm the hypothesis of a hierarchic link between H and F levels of exchange.

Final Comments

We want to comment on the importance of location variables. In this situation—and in others as well, such as feeding—locations define the "upper" context level, and as such they may prove crucial as indicators of the adult's stance: on one hand, in regards to the instruction to try to engage in mutual exchanges with the infant; on the other hand, in regard to the adult's own engagement toward the infant. Thus location variables would correspond to the "metacommunication" level in Bateson's model (Bateson et al., 1963).

Returning to our results, we see in St-I sequence that the adult clearly showed that she accepted the instruction by defining her stance through a consistent H and F offer of engagement, an offer that, however, allowed the infant to respond or not. In this context the infant was observed to orient progressively toward his partner. Incidentally, this information is also pertinent to the interpretation of the interactional failure in Mo-I and Fa-I sequences: this infant behaves differently in these different contexts.

However, in Mo-I and Fa-I sequences, both adults indicated at context level their disagreement with the instruction, while simultaneously denying it at content level. This was the paradoxical message received by the consultant. And this was the paradoxical instruction that was received by the infant. In this context the infant was observed to avert actively from adult through his own control behaviors. The observer may well be perplexed by this paradoxical message, but he has to go beyond this confusion if he is going to test the system's response to therapeutic input—the objective of consultation. Here the following anecdote illustrates how this was attempted by the consultant by means of input at the level of context definition, that is, modification of location.

The event occurred late in the Mo-I sequence, as the consultant attempted to help the mother and the infant, apparently caught up in their pattern of "more of the same failure." Perplexed at the failure of this utterly affectionate mother, the consultant, as she was relocating the infant on the middle of his mother's lap, advised her to try once more. This location (corresponding to the "compensation" type) and the ensuing reorganization of H and F levels of exchange are illustrated in figure 56–6a, b. During the following 60 seconds, partners were oriented toward each other (trunks in full vis-à-vis, mutual gaze and *en face* positioning). Dialogue was initiated, the infant smiled and vocalized, the mother gave greeting responses, smiles, and baby talk. But then the infant's stance progressively froze, and within about ten seconds he was staring at his mother's face with a cry face and then broke into tears and cried. His behavior looked very much like a reaction to a stranger.

It appears that location of infant in this situation was indeed a key context variable, but that it was far from sufficient at long term. Closer inspection of these data revealed only that gaze distance had remained regulated at "short" distance throughout this second part of the sequence. This observation demonstrates the complexity of these exchanges. Though we are far from grasping the details of their intercon-nections, we feel that careful descriptions will help to develop valuable insights for therapeu-tic and preventive early actions.

One final comment is in order. It is note-worthy that both parents fail in achieving mu-tual exchanges with their son. And although only one of them, the mother, is a psychiatric patient, inspection of results would neverthe-less indicate that the father's behaviors are more markedly inappropriate and as paradoxi-cal as the mother's. A number of clinical obser-vations and experimental results have demon-strated that members of families with a psychotic patient do share pardoxical transac-tions (Bateson et al, 1963; Singer et al., 1978). The present results are consistent with these findings.

REFERENCES

Als, H., Tronick, E., and Brazelton, T. B. (1979). Analy-sis of face-to-face interaction in infant-adult dyads. In *Social Interaction Analysis*, ed. M. E. Lamb et al. Madison: University of Wisconsin Press.

Bateson, G., Jackson, D. D., Haley, J., and Weakland, J. H. (1963). A note on the double bind. *Family Process*, 2: 154–161.

Beebe, B. and Stern, D. N. (1977). Engagement-disen-gagement and early object experiences. In *Communicative Structures and Psychic Structures—A Psycho-Analytic Interpretation of Communication*, ed. N. Freedman and S. Grand. New York: Plenum.

Birdwhistell, R. L. (1976). The age of a baby. In *Conduct and Communication—Kinesics and Context*, ed. E. Goffman, and D. Hymes. Philadelphia: University of Pennsylvania Press.

Brazelton, T. B., Kolowski, B., and Main, M. (1974). The origins of reciprocity: The early mother-infant interaction. In *The Origins of Behavior: The Effect of the Infant on its Caregiver*, ed. M. Lewis and L. Rosenblum. New York: John Wiley.

Fivaz, E. (1980). Analyse systèmique d'une famille à haut risque. *Thérapie Familiale*, 1:165–180.

Fivaz, E. (1983). Interactions parent-nourrisson et fa-milles à transactions psychotiques. In *La Thérapie Familiale Telle Quelle de la Théorie à la Pratique*, ed. J. C. Benoit. Paris: Ecole Scientifique de France.

Fivaz, E. and Cornut-Zimmer, B. (1982a). Étude ex-ploratoire du développement précoce de l'attention focale partagée dans le système mère-nourrisson, I—Méthode de micro-analyse. *Neuropsychiatrie de l'Enfance*, 30:95–101.

Fivaz, E. and Cornut-Zimmer, B. (1982b). Etude ex-ploratoire du développement précoce de l'attention focale partagée dans le système mère-nourrisson, II—Investiga-tion dans deux familles à transaction psychotique. *Neuroposychiatrie de l'Enfance*, 30:351–357.

Fivaz, E. et al. (1981a). Thérapie et institutions: Dimen-sion et communications internes du système d'encadre-ment thérapeutique. *Annales Medico-Psychologiques*, 139:853–868.

Fivaz, E., Fivaz, R., and Kaufmann, L. (1981b). Dysfunc-tional transactions and therapeutic functions: An evolutive model. *Journal of Marital and Family Therapy*, 7:309–320.

Fivaz, E., Guillemin, J., Cornut-Zimmer, B., and Martin, D. (in press). Objectivation d'une hiérarchie d'encadre-ment par la microanalyse d'échanges entre une observa-trice, une mère et son nourrisson. *Psychologie Médicale*.

Fogel, A. (1977). Temporal organization in mother-infant face-to-face interaction. In *Studies in Mother-Infant In-teraction*, ed. H. R. Schaffer. London: Academic Press.

Frey, S. et al. (1981). A unified approach to the investi-gation of nonverbal and verbal behavior in communication research. In *Current Issues in European Social Psychology*, ed. S. Moscovici and W. Doise. Cambridge, England: Cambridge University Press.

Kubicek, L. (1980). Organization in two mother-infant interactions involving a normal infant and his fraternal twin brother who was later diagnosed as autistic. In *High-Risk Infants and Children*, ed. T. M. Field. New York: Aca-demic Press.

Massie, H. and Campbell, B. K. (1983). The Massie-Campbell Scale of Mother-Infant Attachment Indicators During Stress (AIDS Scale). In *Frontiers of Infant Psychiatry*, ed. J. D. Call, E. Galenson, and R. L. Tyson. New York: Basic Books.

Papoušek, H. and Papoušek, M. (1979). Early ontogeny of human social interaction: Its biological roots and social dimensions. In *Human Ethology: Claims and Limits of a New Discipline*, ed. M. von Cranach et al. Cambridge, England: Cambridge University Press.

Papoušek, H. and Papoušek, M. (1980). Care of the normal and high-risk newborn. Psychobiological view of parental behavior. In *The At-Risk Infant*, ed. H. Papoušek and M. Papoušek New York: Elsevier.

Perry, C. H. and Stern, D. N. (1975). Mother-infant gazing during play, bottle feeding and spoon feeding. *Jour-nal of Psychology*, 91:207–213.

Singer, M. T., Wynne, L. C., and Toohey, M. L. (1978). Communication disorders and the families of schizo-phrenics. In *The Nature of Schizophrenia—New Approaches to Research and Treatment*, ed. L. C. Wynne et al. New York: John Wiley.

Stern, D. (1976). A microanalysis of mother-infant in-teraction—Behavior regulating social contact between a mother and her three-and-a-half-month old twins. In *In-fant Psychiatry*, ed. E. N. Rexford et al., New Haven: Yale University Press.

Stern, D. N., Beebe, B., Jaffe, J., and Bennett, S. L. (1977). The infant's stimulus world during social interac-tion: A study of caregiver behaviours with particular refer-ence to repetition and timing. In *Studies in Mother-Infant In-teraction*, ed. H. R. Schaffer. New York/London: Academic Press.

Stern, D. N. (1981). The development of biologically

determined signals of readiness to communicate which are language "resistant." In *Language Behavior in Infancy and Early Childhood,* ed. R. L. Stark. New York: Elsevier.

Thoman, E. and Freese, M. (1979). Individuality in the interactive process. In *The Origins of the Infant's Social Responsiveness,* ed. E. Thoman. Hillsdale, New Jersey: Lawrence Erlbaum Associates.

Tronick, E. et al. (1978). The infant's response to entrapment between contradictory messages in face-to-face interaction. *Journal of the American Academy of Child Psychiatry,* 17:1–13.

Wertheim, E. S. (1978). Developmental genesis of human vulnerability—Conceptual reevaluation. In *The Child in his Family,* vol. 4, *The Psychologically Vulnerable Child,* ed. E. J. Anthony et al. New York: John Wiley.

Widmer, R. T. C. (1981). *Les Modes de Communication du Bébé: Postures, Mouvements et Vocalises.* Neuchâtel: Delachaux et Niestlé.

57

The Pittsburgh Firstborns at Age Nineteen Years

Elsie R. Broussard, M.D., Dr. P.H.

In our clinical practice, we are accustomed to having patients bring a presenting complaint of a current situation. We are then faced with assessing this situation and obtaining a retrospective history of what went wrong, attempting to formulate our hypotheses as to how best to achieve a "cure." It was my privilege in 1963 to begin a prospective longitudinal epidemiologic study of firstborns and their families. The opportunity to study developmental outcome in a prospective fashion provides rich data. These data have the potential for answering many questions about processes that can result either in children moving into young adulthood joyfully contemplating the future, welcoming challenges, and working at them or in young adults already showing ominous signals of constricted development and a vulnerability to psychosocial disorder.

In this paper I describe the psychosocial development at age nineteen of ninety-four firstborns who were at birth healthy, full-term singletons, summarize the findings of previous clinical evaluations of firstborns at ages four and one-half, ten and one-half, and

This research was supported by the Staunton Farm Foundation, Pittsburgh, PA, NIH General Research Support Grant FR5451, and the University of Pittsburgh.

fifteen, and discuss the implications of the findings.

Background Information

Although a detailed report of the study population and methodology have previously been reported (Broussard, 1970, 1971, 1976, 1979, 1983), some summary background information is indicated.

During clinical practice, I had noted that mothers of healthy newborns varied in their responses to their newborns and their needs. Some mothers made a smooth transition from pregnancy to motherhood, took pride and pleasure in raising their infants, and their infants thrived. Others lacked pride in their infants and evidenced little pleasure in motherhood, although their infants were found upon pediatric examination to be clinically healthy and appealing. It became apparent to me, as it had to others, that the way a mother relates to her baby is influenced by her perception of the baby, and that the baby's behavior is affected by her handling. These observations led me to develop an instrument to measure the mother's perception of her neonate and to conduct longitudinal studies of healthy neonates. This instrument made it possible to assess further the relation between maternal perception of the neonate and the child's subsequent development.

INSTRUMENT OF MEASURE

The Broussard *Neonatal Perception Inventories* (NPI) were devised to measure the mother's perception of her newborn as compared to her concept of the average infant. The NPI consist of two forms, the Average Baby form and Your Baby form. Each form consists of six single-item scales: crying, spitting, feeding, elimination, sleeping, and predictability. These items were selected because past clinical experience indicated them to be concerns mothers expressed about their babies as well as areas that reflect the state of functioning of the mother-infant system during the neonatal period.

The six scales are rated from 1 (signifying none) to 5 (signifying a great deal) for each of the inventories. The lower values on the scale represent the more desirable behavior. The scores are totaled for each of the forms separately with no attempt at weighting the scales. Thus a total score is obtained for the Average Baby form and a total score is obtained for the Your Baby form. The total score of the Your Baby Perception form is then subtracted from the Average Baby Perception form. The discrepancy constitutes the NPI score. For example: given a total Average Baby score of 17 and a total Your Baby score of 19, the NPI score is −2; given a total Average Baby Score of 15 and a total Your Baby score of 14, the NPI score is +1. One-month-old infants rated by their mothers as better than average (+ score) are considered at low risk. Those infants *not* rated better than average (− or 0 score) are considered at high risk for subsequent development of emotional difficulty.

The NPI may be viewed as a projective measure because the mother is presented with a set of ambiguous stimuli which provide a gestalt upon which she projects her concept of what most little babies are like and her expectations of what her newborn will be like. Understandably, this will vary from mother to mother and is dependent upon her past experiences.

The NPI provide a measure of the *adaptive potential* of the mother-infant system. The NPI do not predict the precise nature of the psychosocial disorder. The complexity of human development makes such predictive specificity impossible. The NPI can serve to screen for potential failures in psychosocial adaptation stemming from disorders in the earliest mother-infant relationship, disorders that may exist undetected at an early state.

THE STUDY POPULATION

The study population consisted of 318 primiparae all delivering single, live, full-term healthy infants weighing 5.5 pounds or more during a specified two and one-half-month time period in 1963. Mothers were visited on the first or second postpartum day and asked if they would be willing to share their experiences in raising their firstborns. They were told that the findings from the study of their experiences in raising firstborns and how the children grew might aid professionals in helping other families in the future.

Infants were examined in the delivery room, upon admission to the newborn nursery, and again at time of discharge. If any complication occurred during the hospital stay, the infant was excluded from the study. Selection of healthy neonates weighing 5.5 pounds or more was an attempt to ensure that infants were within the range of normal endowment so that the infant was biologically equipped to elicit response from the mother and not handicapped in the ability to respond to maternal care.

The educational background of the parents ranged from grammar school to post-graduate training. Occupations included skilled and unskilled industrial work, white collar, and professional. On the Hollingshead Index of Social Position (Education and Occupation of Father), the population distribution was as follows: Class I = 1.9 percent; Class II = 13.5 percent; Class III = 29.8 percent; Class IV = 48.1 percent; Class V = 6.7 percent.

At the time of delivery, one mother was single and one widowed.[1] All others were married and living with their husbands. White respondents composed 93.6 percent of the study population. The ages of the mothers at the time of delivery ranged from 14 to 41 years, with the median of 21.8 years.[2]

Based upon the NPI score, infants were categorized as being at high risk or low risk for possible development of psychosocial disorders. One hundred and ninety-five (61 percent) infants were rated better than average and were considered to be at low risk; the 123 (39 percent) who were not rated as better than average constituted a group at high risk.

ESTABLISHING PREDICTIVE VALIDITY

In order to test the hypothesis that the maternal perception of her one-month-old infant as measured by the NPI was predictive of later psychosocial developmental outcome, follow-up studies were done at four and one-half, ten to eleven, and fifteen years of age.[3] At each of these ages, the firstborns were clinically evaluated during a single office interview by a psychiatrist who had no knowledge of the predictive risk rating on the NPI. At each age a

statistically significant association was present between the NPI rating and the psychosocial developmental rating. (At four and one-half years, $p < .0002$; at ten to eleven years, $p < .017$; at fifteen years, $p < .007$.) These findings are summarized in table 57–3.

Evaluations of the Firstborns at Age Nineteen

When the firstborns were nineteen years of age, ninety-four (fifty-four males and forty females) were evaluated clinically during a single office interview by one of three clinicians, all of whom had psychoanalytic training.[4] None had prior knowledge of the child's predictive risk rating at one month. The evaluators were free to use their own style in conducting the interview. Following the interview, each organized the data according to the following guidelines: I. Self-Esteem and Emotional Balance; II. Affective Balance; III. Rational Control of Body and Functions; IV. Ability to Discharge Emotion Through Thought and Speech When Indicated; V. Ability to Reduce Panic in Face of Dangers to Signal Anxiety Which Initiates Effective Defense; VI. Evidence of Some Future Goals; VII. Relations to Nuclear Family, Peers, Mate; VIII. Balance of Egocentricity with Concern for Others; IX. Reality Testing; X. Sexual Identity; XI. Predominant Mechanisms of Defense; XII. General Statement of Personality Functioning, Symptom Formation, Achievement, and Overall Adaptation.

Based on a summary of hospital birth records, developmental data previously gathered

---

[1]Women placing their babies for adoption were excluded from study.

[2]The 20 black subjects in the original population have been lost to follow-up study. The findings reported are on Caucasian subjects.

[3]Attrition is always a factor in longitudinal research. Following the one-month postpartum home visit, we had no contact with subjects until children were four and one-half years old. At that time, 155 were located and asked to participate in another home-visit interview. Twelve refused, and one child had died. Home interviews were conducted with 142 mothers. Of these, 121 brought the children for office evaluations (the one black subject was omitted from data analysis). We subsequently located children who had previously moved, thus increasing our available pool of subjects. *A total of 164 different firstborns* came in for one or more evaluations of their psychosocial development. The number of subjects seen for office evaluation at each time point varied. Parents often willingly participated with home interviews or permitted us to interview school personnel about their firstborn, yet were not able to bring the child to the office. At age nine, we completed 150 home visits, 127 school visits at age nine and one-half, and 104 office evaluations at ten to eleven years. At age thirteen, we completed 141 home visits, at thirteen to fourteen years, 135 school visits, and 99 office visits at age fifteen.

[4]Because evaluators were only available on a part-time basis and research subjects were unpaid volunteers with many other commitments, it was not possible to arrange a fixed assignment of a specific case number to a specific clinician. To maximize the opportunity for subjects to participate in the continued study, office appointments were scheduled on a six-day-a-week basis and with whichever evaluator was available for the clinicial interview. This, of course, meant that the ultimate number of cases seen by a given evaluator and the distribution of high-risk cases were left entirely to chance. (Thirty-nine children were evaluated by rater 1, twenty-six by rater 2, and twenty-nine by rater 3. There was no evidence of rater bias.)

by parent interviews, history of school performance obtained by teacher interview, and on the office interview with the child, the clinician formulated a diagnosis using the schema proposed by Anna Freud (1965). Thus in assessing the psychosocial functioning of the firstborns, the clinicians studied the intrapsychic functioning and adaptive capacity of the firstborns functioning in their respective environments, considered their coping mechanisms, and looked at their tendencies toward progressive development as well as any regressive tendencies operant. In addition, the clinician rated each firstborn according to a 4-point Probability of Mental Disorder Scale adapted from Leighton's Stirling County Study (Leighton et al., 1963). The categories were A = High Confidence Mental Disorder; B—Probable but Less Certain; C—Doubtful but Suspicious; D —High Confidence No Disorder.[5]

For statistical analysis, the A, B, and C categories, pooled into one group representing Gradations of Disorder, were compared with the D category representing No Disorder. The distribution of these ratings according to sex is shown in table 57–1. The distribution was similar for males and females.

Analysis of data for the ninety-four

firstborns shows that there is still a statistically significant relationship between the one-month NPI risk rating and the Psychosocial Developmental rating at age nineteen. The distribution is similar for males and females. The odds ratio indicates that those one-month-old infants viewed negatively by their mothers were 5.62 times more likely to have a psychosocial developmental disorder at age nineteen than those infants who had been positively viewed by their mothers. These data are shown in table 57–2.

COMPARISONS BETWEEN EVALUATIONS AT
AGES FOUR AND ONE-HALF, TEN TO ELEVEN,
FIFTEEN, AND NINETEEN YEARS

The NPI rating at one month of age was significantly related to the psychosocial developmental rating at each of the four later ages (four and one-half, ten to eleven, fifteen, and nineteen). To study further the effect of the NPI rating over time, the psychosocial developmental rating was also dichotomized at ages four and one-half, ten to eleven, and fifteen. For completeness, table 57–3 contains the four 2 by 2 cross tabulations.

A significant relationship is evident at each of the four time points. In each case, a positive relationship exists between the mother's rating at one month of age and the child's subsequent psychosocial development. However, as the child becomes older, more life variables evidently come to play an important part in his

---

[5]A DSM-III (American Psychiatric Association, 1980) classification was also assigned to fifty-five firstborns. The diagnoses included a wide variety—such as Simple Phobia, Substance Abuse, Narcissistic Personality Disorder, Dysthymic Disorder, Schizotypal Personality Disorder.

TABLE 57–1

Percentage Distribution of Psychosocial Disorder Among 94 19-Year-Old Firstborns According to Sex

Psychosocial Developmental Ratings	Total		Males		Females	
	N	%	N	%	N	%
A	34	36.17	22	40.74 (64.70)	12	30.00 (35.30)
B	21	22.34	9	16.67 (42.86)	12	30.00 (57.14)
C	17	18.09	9	16.67 (52.94)	8	20.00 (47.06)
D	22	23.40	14	25.93 (63.64)	8	20.00 (36.36)
TOTAL	94		54		40	

( ) represents row percentages

TABLE 57–2

The Relation between NPI and Subsequent Psychosocial Developmental Ratings at Age 19 for Males, Females, and Total

NPI Rating	Males			Females			Total		
	Disorder	No Disorder	Total	Disorder	No Disorder	Total	Disorder	No Disorder	Total
Negative	21	2	23	19	2	21	40	4	44
Positive	19	12	31	13	6	19	32	18	50
Total	40	14	54	32	8	40	72	22	94

$$\chi^2 = 6.194 \qquad\qquad \chi^2 = 3.033 \qquad\qquad \chi^2 = 9.45$$
$$p < .0128 \qquad\qquad p < .0816 \qquad\qquad p < .0021$$
$$\emptyset = .3387 \qquad\qquad \emptyset = .2754 \qquad\qquad \emptyset = .3171$$
$$\text{Odds Ratio} = 6.63/1 \qquad \text{Odds Ratio} = 4.38/1 \qquad \text{Odds Ratio} = 5.62/1$$

development. Needless to say, there is no possible way to account for the diversity of uncontrollable life experiences these children encounter as they grow. The closest relationship does exist at age four and one-half.

The number of children evaluated clinically at each age varied. This phenomenon is not unusual in longitudinal research studies. Additional insight can be gained by examining the data pertaining to those children ($N = 40$) evaluated at all four of the time points. The relationship between the NPI and psychosocial developmental ratings can be determined, and the idea of transitivity can be considered. That is, can one account for the correlations between the NPI and psychosocial developmental evaluations at age ten to eleven, at age fifteen, and at nineteen in terms of the correlations between the psychosocial developmental evaluations at ages four and one-half and ten to eleven, and at ages ten to eleven and fifteen, and fifteen and nineteen? This can be restated in the following way. Transitivity for the ten to eleven age data would mean that the correlation between the NPI and age ten to eleven evaluation is equal to the product of the correlation between the NPI with the four and one-half-year evaluation and the correlation of age four and one-half and ten to eleven. Similarly, the correlation between the NPI and the age-fifteen evaluation would equal the product of the three earlier correlations, that is, NPI with four and one-half, four and one-half with ten to eleven, and ten to eleven with fifteen. At age nineteen the correlation between the NPI and the age-nineteen evaluation would equal the product of the four earlier correlations.

Forty children (twenty-one males and nineteen females) were evaluated at all four of the time points. Table 57–4 contains the correlation matrix for the five measures.

The correlations between the NPI rating and each of the four psychosocial developmental ratings vary somewhat for the subpopulation of forty children from that for the total population evaluated at each age. Data contained in Tables 57–3 and 57–4 show the comparisons.

To check for transitivity for age ten to eleven data, the correlation between NPI and ten to eleven ($r_{1.3}$) is compared with the product of the correlation between NPI with four and one-half ($r_{1.2}$) and four and one-half with ten to eleven ($r_{2.3}$). It can be seen that $r_{1.3} = .35$ which is greater than ($r_{1.2}$) $\times$ ($r_{2.3}$) $= .1260$. Similarly, for the age-fifteen data $r_{1.4}$ is compared with the product of $r_{1.2}$, $r_{2.3}$, and $r_{3.4}$. This indicates that $r_{1.4} = .45$ which is greater than $(.36) \times (.35) \times (.23) = .0289$.

At age 19, $r_{1.5}$ is compared with the product of $r_{1.2}$, $r_{2.3}$, $r_{3.4}$, $r_{4.5}$. This shows that $r_{1.5} = .29$ which is greater than $(.36) \times (.35) \times (.23) \times (.30) = .0086$. This implies that the relationship between NPI and the psychosocial developmental ratings at ages ten to eleven, fifteen, and nineteen is more than can be accounted for by the explanation that the mother's perception of her infant at one month affected development only during the early years. The correlation of the NPI with the psychosocial developmental rating at age nineteen is over thirty-three times as large as would be expected if there were no carry-over effect beyond age four and one-half.

Another way to look at the relationship between NPI and subsequent development is as follows. Among the forty children for whom a

TABLE 57–3

Relation between NPI and Subsequent Psychosocial Developmental Ratings at Ages 4½, 10/11, 15, and 19

NPI Ratings	Age 4½			Age 10/11			Age 15			Age 19		
	Disorder	No Disorder	Total	Disorder	No Disorder	Total	Disorder	No Disorder	Total	Disorder	No Disorder	Total
Negative	24	12	36	37	5	42	30	3	33	40	4	44
Positive	10	39	49	42	20	62	31	17	48	32	18	50
Total	34	51	85	79	25	104	61	20	81	72	22	94

Age 4½: $\chi^2 = 18.50$, $p < .00002$, $\emptyset = .47$, Odds Ratio = 7.8/1

Age 10/11: $\chi^2 = 5.68$, $p < .017$, $\emptyset = .23$, Odds Ratio = 3.5/1

Age 15: $\chi^2 = 7.29$, $p < .007$, $\emptyset = .30$, Odds Ratio = 5.48/1

Age 19: $\chi^2 = 9.454$, $p < .0021$, $\emptyset = .3171$, Odds Ratio = 5.62/1 psychosocial developmental rating was available at each time point, twenty-two (55 percent) had been rated positively on the NPI and eighteen (45 percent) rated negatively. Examination of the frequency distribution of the number of psychosocial developmental ratings of disorder at ages four and one-half, ten to eleven, fifteen, and nineteen revealed that four of the children had been diagnosed as free of disorder at all four of the evaluations. All of these children had positive NPI scores. Table 57–5 summarizes this data. As noted in table 57–5, only positively rated NPI children were diagnosed as free of disorder at all four of the evaluations. None of the negatively rated NPI children were found to be free of disorder at all four of the evaluations. Since the categories can be considered as ordered, the gamma coefficient can be calculated. In this instance the

gamma is .76, which again indicates a positive relationship between the variables. Children rated positively on the NPI are more likely to be rated free of disorder over the four evaluations than are children rated negatively. Those children rated negatively on the NPI are more likely to have had a diagnosis of disorder at all four of the evaluations than those who had been rated positively on the NPI at one month of age (50 percent vs. 9.09 percent). The distribution was similar for males and females.

THE RELATIONSHIP OF OTHER SELECTED VARIABLES TO THE PSYCHOSOCIAL DEVELOPMENTAL AND THE NPI RISK RATINGS

A statistically significant association was not found between either the NPI Risk Rating or

TABLE 57–4

Correlation Matrix for NPI and Psychosocial Developmental Rating at Ages 4½, 10/11, 15 and 19 Among 40 Firstborns

		Psychosocial Developmental Ratings			
	NPI	4½	10/11	15	19
NPI	1.0	.36	.35	.45	.29
		$(p < .0239)$	$(p < .0279)$	$(p < .0042)$	$(p < .0665)$
4½		1.0	.35	.14	.38
			$(p < .0262)$	$(p < .3702)$	$(p < .0175)$
10/11			1.0	.23	.42
				$(p < .1444)$	$p < .0074)$
15				1.0	.30
					$(p < .0056)$
19					1.0

TABLE 57–5

Cross Classification of NPI Rating and Subsequent Psychosocial Developmental Ratings at Ages 4½, 10/11, 15, and 19 Years Among 40 Firstborns

NPI Rating	Number of Times Classified as Free of Disorder					
	Four	Three	Two	One	None	Total
Positive	4	5	3	8	2	22
	18.18%	22.72%	13.63%	36.36%	9.09%	
Negative	0	1	1	7	9	18
		5.55%	5.55%	38.88%	50%	
Total	4	6	4	15	11	40
	10%	15%	10%	37.5%	27.5%	100%

gamma = .76

the Psychosocial Developmental Ratings and the following variables: the type of delivery, religious preference, maternal age at delivery, educational level of the parents, the Hollingshead Index of Social Position, prenatal or postpartum complications, moves or deaths of significant others during the year prior to pregnancy or after delivery, the frequency of hospitalization of the child, illness within the nuclear family, changes in income since delivery, or the sex of the child.[6]

Discussion

I have provided evidence that the mother's perception of her one-month-old firstborn is associated with the psychosocial developmental ratings at age nineteen.

Each of the three evaluators was asked to provide a summary statement regarding general characteristics of the group of firstborns considered to be functioning in a optimal fashion as young adults (that is, "D"—Free of Disorder). A synthesis of their clinical statements follows.

Maneuverability of defensive systems in these firstborns led to flexibility and resilience in the way in which they were adjusting. These were nineteen-year-olds who could, for example, change course with ease. If this meant that a chosen career goal appeared inappropriate,

[6]On the Hollingshead Index of Social Position (Education and Occupation of Father), the population distribution was as follows: Class I = 1.9 percent; Class II = 13.5 percent; Class III = 29.8 percent; Class IV = 48.1 percent; Class V = 6.7 percent. The distribution for the ninety-four firstborns seen at age nineteen was similar: Class I = 2.1 percent; Class II = 15.9 percent; Class III = 24.5 percent; Class IV = 46.8 percent; Class V = 10.6 percent. Except for racial distribution due to the loss of the twenty black subjects in the original population, the demographic data for the original population were comparable with the data for the subpopulation evaluated at each age. The proportion of children rated at high risk was comparable between the original and follow-up groups. Nor was there a statistically significant difference between the groups with regard to other descriptive data (for example, health of mother, type of delivery). With respect to these data, the children evaluated at four and one-half, ten to eleven, fifteen, and at nineteen years were judged representative of the original 318.

they could alter it. If it meant that a view of themselves was inappropriate, they changed it. The protocols are redolent of this kind of sturdy yet elastic network of adaptive mechanisms, permitting a kind of psychic freedom to test themselves out academically and socially. They seemed to have a healthy mixture of narcissism accompanied by the ability to distance themselves and evaluate their capacities realistically.

These firstborns were characterized by the ability to experience and discuss a wide range of affects. In an interview situation where structure was kept as minimal as comfort would allow, they responded well, spontaneously chronicling their development, and were capable of humor, and, in many cases, of empathy not only with key figures in their lives but with the interviewer as well.

Firstborns classified in the "D" category were capable of exposing for their own consideration as well as that of the interviewer past and present personal events of moment. For example, they could talk about humiliations, deep sadness, hurt feelings, developing genital sexuality, and turning points in their own growth.

All of these firstborns seemed to have experienced family cohesiveness. The fact that all of these families were described as loving was not distinguishing; some of the families of firstborns categorized in the remaining three groups were also described as loving. What constituted the hallmark of the families of "D" firstborns was a consistency of ties between firstborn and family, especially parents, which enabled them to negotiate the turbulent periods and to describe them, as well as to express tenderness and gratitude toward family members. By and large these firstborns had established constructive identifications with both parents.

There was confidence about these firstborns that enabled them to tolerate uncertainty. The most frequent evidence of this were statements about future issues, for example, career choice or development of genital sexual identity. The underlying message seemed to be that these issues were being forged but were not complete; but there was a sureness about the firstborns that the problem could and would be settled in time to their satisfaction and a lack of urgency or even of any uneasiness about the speed or rigidity with which this needed to be done.

All of these "D"-classified firstborns gave ample evidence that they had a substantial repertoire of ways in which to tolerate frustration. In most cases, there were evidences of a duality: these young people could, by self-observation, find within themselves the capacity to deal with a difficult situation, or they could view, keenly and astutely, their surroundings and manipulate them so as to make the frustration bearable.

All of these factors are, quite obviously, related. Many firstborns categorized in the other three groups also display to some extent some of these abilities. The "D" firstborns seem to have the full panoply, and to have them in ample and smooth working order as they launch themselves into a future that seems to hold promise in the area of love and work.

Now we must look at the abundance of accumulated data and attempt to chart in greater depth the paths taken by these firstborns and search out the patterns of development to see if we can discern threads that span the generations. To the extent that we are successful in this undertaking, we may be aided in developing programs for fostering more optimal development.

The magnitude of psychosocial disorder is impressive—with only 23.4 percent of firstborns considered free of disorder at age nineteen. The overall results of this study show that the mother's perception of her one-month-old infant, as measured by the NPI, is related to the child's psychosocial development. From the point of view of promoting optimal infant development, this seems worthy of attention. The Neonatal Perception Inventories provide an easily administered screening measure that can identify a population of infants at high risk for subsequent psychosocial difficulty and predict the adaptive potential of a given infant-mother pair.

Many factors may interfere with the smooth functioning of the infant-mother system. Each is unique, and there can be no simplistic intervention. When the system is judged in distress, a careful clinical appraisal is needed to determine the specific nature and etiology of the dysfunction. Only then can appropriate intervention be planned and implemented.

I wish to express appreciation to Ching Chun Li, Ph.D., University Professor of Biometry and Human Genetics, Department of Biostatistics, Graduate School of Public Health, and Charles Stegman, Ph.D., Associate Professor of Education, Department of Educational Research Methodology, for their consultation regarding statistical analysis of the data.

REFERENCES

American Psychiatric Association (1980). *Diagnostic and Statistical Manual of Mental Disorders (DSM–III)*, 3rd ed. Washington, D.C.: American Psychiatric Association.

Broussard, E. R. and Hartner, M. S. S. (1970). Maternal perception of the neonate as related to development. *Child Psychiatry and Human Development*, 1:16–25.

Broussard, E. R., and Hartner, M. S. S. (1971). Further considerations regarding maternal perception of the firstborn. *Exceptional Infant: Studies in Abnormalities*, vol. 2. ed. J. Hellmuth. New York: Brunner/Mazel.

Broussard, E. R. (1976). Neonatal prediction and outcome at 10/11 years. *Child Psychiatry and Human Development*, 7:85–93.

Broussard, E. R. (1979). Assessment of the adaptive potential of the mother-infant system: the Neonatal Perception Inventories. *Seminars in Perinatology*, 3:91–100. New York: Grune & Stratton.

Broussard, E. R. (1982). Primary prevention of psychosocial disorders: Assessment of outcome. *Primary Prevention of Psychopathology: Facilitating Infant and Early Childhood Development*, ed. L. A. Bond and J. M. Joffee. Hanover, New Hampshire: University Press of New England.

Freud A. (1965). *Normality and Pathology in Childhood*. New York: International Universities Press.

Leighton, D. C. et al. (1963). Psychiatric findings of the Stirling County Study. *American Journal of Psychiatry*, 119: 1021–1026.

58

Epidemiological Survey of Functional Symptomatology in Preschool-Age Children

Françoise Davidson, M.D. and Marie Choquet, Ph.D.

The epidemiologist has two types of overall approach to functional pathology in the infant. The first and most common method consists of defining a group of children with various clinical symptoms within a sufficiently large infant population. In such a case the epidemiologist draws on the experience of physicians to determine significant symptoms and to define a high-risk group on the basis of these criteria. Comparison of this group with a control group composed of children who do not have these characteristics enables the epidemiologist to isolate differences from various possible points of view (family history, type of upbringing, type of day care, and so forth).

The other method, described here, consists of using appropriate statistical methods to establish "classes" of subjects within an unselected population of children. The classes or groups established in this manner should be as uniform as possible with respect to the overall data under study and should be established without recourse to any prior assumptions. At the same time, these groups must be as different as possible from one another. This system of classification will reveal both the most significant factors and their relationships, thereby providing a profile for each group.

By comparing the various groups established on this basis, the epidemiologist can describe them from various points of view (socioeconomic level, parents' state of health, and the like), follow them up, and validate the methods used.

Documentation and Method

FIRST PHASE OF THE SURVEY: THREE-YEAR LONGITUDINAL STUDY OF SAMPLE

The sample studied was composed of 415 children from the 14th District of Paris. They were studied from age three months to three years at four important moments in their lives (three months, nine months, eighteen months, and three years).

At each step, a questionnaire concerning the child (physical, psychological, and emotional development, type of day care, parents, and living conditions) was filled out by an experienced psychologist during an interview with the mother. Each interview lasted approximately one hour. No systematic observa-

We offer our thanks to Doctors M. Soulé, J. Noel, and L. Kreisler for their theoretical and practical support.

tion was made of the child. In order to avoid excessive subjectivity in the responses, the questions basically concerned the child's behavior at various precise moments during the day (for example, at meals, sleep, and play) and the parent's attitudes in the same situations.

The result was an epidemiological survey involving a representative population of a Paris city district (a demographic study showed that the characteristics of the initial population corresponded very well with those of the control group). The survey is longitudinal and nonretrospective. In fact, the parents were interviewed at each stage of their child's development on a precise date. In this manner, we avoid the bias of selective memories. Finally, the use of a directive questionnaire maintains a large measure of unity in the subsequent analysis.

Most of the parameters (sleep, appetite, and temperament) could be studied on a longitudinal basis, even though the questions were often formulated slightly differently at different stages in order to correspond to survey imperatives and the child's own development.

The typological analysis as described by Chandon and Pinson (1980, p. 4) appeared well suited for our purpose: "This is a method of data analysis that enables us to establish groups of objects characterized by a set of attributes or variables into classes that are not necessarily separated in a mutually exclusive manner. The classes should be both as few in number and as uniform as possible." The method ultimately selected was more specifically derived from the "dynamic cluster analysis" developed by Govaert (1977) of the Diday group.

The statistical data were organized into two sets of qualitative variables describing the subjects.

On one hand, twenty-three *"active"* variables were used to classify the subjects. These variables summarize the physical, psychological, and emotional situation, as described in the interview with the mother of the child at age three years. There are several means of responding to each of the variables used, depending on the presence or absence of stated pathologies (asthma, disorders, and accidents),

functional disorders to various degrees (sleep, appetite, and the like) behavior problems, and the parents' conduct (use of sedatives or placements in hospitals). Motor development was eliminated as being insufficiently discriminating (in the preliminary analyses, this factor was shown to be satisfactory for nearly all of the sample), the same was true of weight and height (only seven plethoric children and five significantly underweight, including three premature births out of a group of 415 children). A decision was made to eliminate the acquisition of language skills and toilet training from the group of "active" variables because of their high correlation, shown in previous analyses, with the family's sociocultural level. Utilization of an active variable classification method made it possible to establish uniform classes of children as well as to determine the combinations of parameters that characterize these classes.

On the other hand, *"illustrative"* variables were used to characterize the classes of subjects obtained on the basis of active variables. These are essentially the demographic, cultural, and psychological characteristics of the parents, as well as any history of previous problems affecting the parents. This additional information provides a clearer picture of the risk level of the groups and its significance.

SECOND PHASE OF THE SURVEY: VERIFICATION OF THE RISK FACTORS

In order to validate the method used and to verify the predictive value of the classification obtained, "high-risk" subjects and their controls (selected from the "no apparent risk" group and matched on the basis of sex, father's socioeconomic category, and mother's level of education) were located and seen again during the child's first year at primary school.

Three complementary methods were used for each child: (1) A survey questionnaire was filled out by a psychologist during a long interview with the mother (method identical to that described in the preceding stages). (2) Each of the child's teachers was interviewed about the child's behavior in school. (3) In addition, child psychiatrists and psychologists from Dr. M. Soule's service examined the children. The examiners had no knowledge of the preceding phases of the research or whether the children had been considered high risk during the three-year period of study.

This particularly interesting final stage is currently in progress. The first phase has been completed, and we present a brief run-down on the major results.

The questionnaire used for the children, age six, included the same variables as the preceding questionnaires (twelve variables: state of health, hospitalizations, accidents, serious illnesses, taking of psychotropic drugs, difficult sleep, wakes often, nightmares, bedtime difficulties, mealtime difficulties, tantrums, no playing alone). In addition, some new variables were introduced, particularly regarding reading and writing skills and functional pathology on the basis of age, pronunciation difficulties, and defects in laterality.

The survey plan is shown in figure 58–1.

Results

FIRST PHASE OF THE SURVEY

Longitudinal Study of a Sample During Three Years: Profiles of Three Groups of Children at Age Three Years. The typological analysis shows that the three groups of children are clearly differentiated. A profile can be established for each group on the basis of combinations of representative variables for each group (table 58–1).

Group III (table 58–1), which consists of 10 percent of the total sample, can be clearly distinguished from the other two groups. More than two-thirds of the total sample are boys, a highly significant difference in respect to the whole sample (one boy per two subjects). The following characteristics enable us to consider it a "high-risk" group:

Wakes often at night
Sleeping difficulties

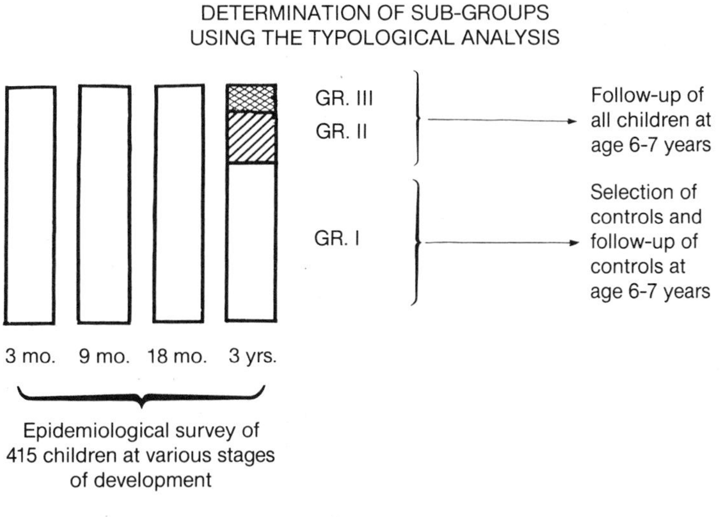

DETERMINATION OF SUB-GROUPS
USING THE TYPOLOGICAL ANALYSIS

Figure 58–1 Epidemiological survey of 415 children at various stages of development

TABLE 58–1

Characteristics of Children as Demonstrated by Typological Analysis
(in percentages)

Children	Groups			
	Total Sample N = 415	Group I N = 287	Group II N = 85	Group III N = 43
Poor health, according to mother	4	1	9	16
Asthma	2	0	5	7
Hospitalization of more than 3 days	6	2	///	23
Frequent bronchitis	9	7	12	19
Frequent ear infections	13	7	18	///
Frequent colds	17	6	25	///
Frequent ENT disorders	16	12	///	37
Two or more accidents between 18 months and 3 years	14	10	24	23
Takes prescription drugs for nervousness or insomnia	7	3	///	37
Bedtime difficulties	23	16	36	47
Sleeping difficulties	21	9	28	76
Nightmares	31	21	49	67
Wakes often at night	11	5	///	51
Erratic appetite	6	4	///	19
Lack of appetite	27	23	36	36
Frequent tantrums	18	8	28	70
Often discontent	33	18	59	84
Never plays alone	16	14	///	21
No transitional object	34	30	///	51
Rhythmies	14	9	21	28

/// This variable is not significantly linked to the class.

Bedtime difficulties
Nightmares
Poor health according to mother
Asthma
Frequent ENT disorders
Frequent bronchitis
At least one hospitalization between 18 months and 3 years
Frequent tantrums
Often discontent
Erratic appetite
No transitional object
Never plays alone
Receives sedatives
Two or more accidents between 18 months and 3 years

Eight out of ten children in this group have at least six of these characteristics (table 58–2). Eighty-four percent have sleep and behavior problems.

Group I (table 58–1) represents 69 percent of the sample. It contrasts with the preceding group and is distinguished by its lower occurrence of the characteristics just mentioned.

Most of the children have less than three combinations of factors and none has six or more (table 58–2). The several children in group I that have a number of correlations with group III are those that have had various repeated respiratory disorders and present bedtime difficulties.

Group II is located halfway between these two extremes for most of the variables. This is shown in table 58–1. However, on the basis of certain characteristics, it sometimes approaches group III (frequency of ENT disorders, lack of appetite, asthma) but is closer to group I for certain highly discriminatory variables such as sleeping or behavior problems. Nine percent of these children have a cumulative total of six variables or more (table 58–2).

With no recourse to any previous assumptions, mathematical methods have been used to identify a group of children presenting the medical and psychological characteristics of high-risk subjects as clinically defined by child psychiatrists. In addition, these methods were

TABLE 58–2

Correlations of Subjects in the Three Groups with the Profile of Cumulative Difficulties Observed in the High-Risk Group (in percentages)

	Group I	Group II	Group III
Less than 4 correlations	93	42	—
4 to 5 correlations	7	49	21
6 to 7 correlations	—	9 } 9	42 } 79
8 correlations or more	—	—	37

Group I: Group without apparent risk
Group II: Low-risk group
Group III: High-risk group

used in an epidemiological context, making it possible to quantify this high-risk group within an unselected population, as well as specifying the most significant combinations of factors and their rate of occurrence. We shall also see that these methods validate the epidemiological hypothesis based on the existence of correlations between the child's functional disorders and parental pathology.

Parental Characteristics of Extreme Groups: Demographic Characteristics of the Parents. The parents of high-risk children often have relatively low levels of education, whereas more than one out of every three children in group I has a father with a higher education. This difference may explain the correlation found between father's age and membership in this group (in fact, fathers who continue their studies have children later in life). There are no differences in terms of the mother's professional activity or her level of education. On the other hand, 59 percent of the children in group III have a mother who works more than eight hours a day, as opposed to 36 percent of the children in group I. Other working conditions (rigid schedule, amount and type of travel to work) do not account for any significant differences between the two groups.

Parents' nationalities, housing conditions, and family size do not produce any statistically significant differences between the groups considered.

Parents' Psychological Characteristics (Especially the Mother's). Parents' health problems before the birth of the child, as well as their family experiences, have been recorded, along with serious psychological disorders. However, only specific facts, such as psychological disorders with hospitalization or depression resulting in protracted psychiatric treatment were accepted in this analysis.

We observe that parents of "high-risk" children have, on a statistically significant basis, been "institutionalized" during their childhood. They appear to have a more fragile psychological equilibrium. Table 58–3 clearly demonstrates the correlations between the state of the child at age three years and the state of the mother during the prenatal period and during the birth of the same child. More often than others, these mothers subsequently describe themselves as having insomnia, being exhausted, nervous, depressed. Relations with the child are not as relaxed (table 58–4).

History of High-Risk Children. Would it have been possible to detect the pathological characteristics of group III at an earlier stage in our survey ? Table 58–5 gives an overview of significant correlations of variables throughout each stage of the survey (eighteen months, nine months, and three months). In the previous stages we observe a significantly higher level of sleeping difficulties in the risk group. In addition, an examination of the development of these problems shows the accumulation and persistence of problems in thirty-five out of forty-three cases and the relative infrequency of multiple problems appearing after eighteen months: only eight children out of forty-three presented problems after three years of age after having no earlier history.

TABLE 58–3

Relations Between Parental History and Groups of Children with Contrasting Risk Levels
(in percentages)

Parental History	High-Risk Group	Control Group	Difference
Before conception			
Parents institutionalized during early childhood	28	16	*
Psychopathological disorders of one parent before conception of the child	19	5	†
Gestation—birth			
Late detection of pregnancy (after 3 months)	No significant difference		
4 or more problems during pregnancy	35	17	†
Depressive tendencies during pregnancy	26	14	*
One or more illnesses during pregnancy	47	32	†
Difficult delivery	19	9	†
Mother extremely tired after return from the hospital	28	17	*
Breast feeding	No significant difference.		

*p < 0.05
†p < 0.01

TABLE 58–4

Mother's Health and Her Relations with the Child at Age Three Comparison of Groups with Contrasting Risk Levels
(in percentages)

	High-Risk Group	Control Group	Difference
Mother says she is:			
nervous	79	51	†
exhausted	23	9	‡
depressed	49	20	†
sleeping poorly	40	15	‡
Takes sedatives or sleeping pills	51	16	*
With respect to child, mother declares she is:			
worried	42	20	†
easily upset	63	40	†
strict	40	25	*
playful	No significant difference		
Finds that the child's meals a difficult time	49	19	‡

*p < 0.05
†p < 0.01
‡p < 0.001

TABLE 58–5

The High-Risk Group and its Previous Problems Characteristics at three, nine, and eighteen months for the forty-three Children Considered High-Risk*

3 Years	18 Months		9 Months		3 Months	
Risk Group (N = 43)	Health problems	•	Health problems	•	Health problems	
	Takes sedatives	•	Takes sedatives	•	Takes sedatives	
	Hospitalization	•	Hospitalization		Hospitalization	
	Wakes often	•	Disturbed sleep	•	Disturbed sleep	•
	Cries at night	•	Cries at night	•	Bedtime difficulties	•
	Bedtime difficulties	•	Bedtime difficulties	•	Rabid appetite	•
	Erratic appetite	•	Erratic appetite	•	Diarrhea	
	Often discontent	•	Often discontent		Vomiting	
	Frequent tantrums	•	Frequent tantrums		Skin disorders	
					Prematurity	
					Weight at birth	

*Statistically significant variables followed by •. Other variables were shown not to be significant.

THE FUTURE OF HIGH-RISK CHILDREN AND
THEIR CONTROLS

Table 58–6 shows a significantly higher persistence of pathological characteristics from the third year to the seventh year in the high-risk group (these are the health, sleeping, appetite, and behavior variables).

Table 58–7 shows a very significant difference between the two groups on the basis of new variables, which are manifestly highly discriminant for children age six to seven (acquisition of reading and writing skills, headaches, respiratory disorders, diarrhea, mood changes, pronunciation defects, and laterality).

Table 58–8 presents a detailed description of the most interesting comparisons between the groups, including certain factors that are not statistically significant but nevertheless indicate certain tendencies (example: skin disorders, lower rate in the high-risk group). The same holds true for the lack of appetite or erratic appetite.

More specifically in terms of educational progress, we observe that half of the high-risk subjects have learned to read and write without noteworthy difficulties (47 percent) and 39 percent had major difficulties. In the control group, 72 percent had no difficulty and 10 percent had major difficulties.

Finally, if we look at the cumulative totals of discriminant pathological characteristics (old and new) between the two groups, we see that 53 percent of the high-risk subjects have a total of more than four variables, as opposed to only 11 percent for the controls. As a result, the difference is significant.

Discussion

In spite of individual fluctuations, we observe that in most cases it is possible to detect children in difficulty before age three years. However, the fact cannot be overlooked that it is the persistence and the total number of problems that constitute an alarm signal, not the existence of one or even two factors at a single stage.

The test population was representative of the majority of children age three years who have not left the 14th district of Paris since

TABLE 58–6

Comparison of High-Risk and Control Groups for Particular Variables
(in percentages)

Number of Variables per Subject	High-Risk Group	Control Group	Difference
0 or 2	56	78	
3 or 4	33	19	*
5 or more	11	3	

*Statistically significant difference.

TABLE 58–7

Comparison of High-Risk and Control Groups According to New Characteristics
(in percentages)

Number of Variables	High-Risk Group	Control Group	Difference
0 or 1	33	81	
2 or 3	42 }	19 }	*
4 or more	25 }	— }	

*Highly significant difference.

TABLE 58–8

Systematic Differences Between High-Risk and Control-Group Children
(in percentages)

Signs Observed	High-Risk Group	Control Group	Difference
Serious diseases between 3 and 6 years	31	6	†
Hospitalization more than twice	19	—	*
Headaches	31	11	*
Asthma	14	—	*
Suffocation attacks	29	—	*
Diarrhea	14	—	*
Vomiting	14	5	NS
Abdominal pains	31	22	NS
Skin disorders	8	19	NS
Allergies	22	31	NS
Disturbed sleep—wakes	19	1	*
Frequent nightmares	11	—	*
Continuing enuresis	8	—	*
Left-handed	28	8	†
Pronunciation defects	31	11	*
Tics	8	8	NS
Difficult acquisition of reading skills	36	8	‡

*$p < .05$
†$p < .01$
‡$p < .001$

birth. At this age, 10 percent already had major problems and half of those, or 5 percent of the total sample, already had a number of problems by age eighteen months.

The observed proportions of three-year-olds in the high-risk group (group III—10 percent) and the low-risk group (group II—21 percent) are clearly very close to the 7 percent and 15 percent respectively, observed by Richman (1977; Richman and Graham, 1971; Richman et al., 1975) in a preschool population in a London suburb. These similarities exist in spite of important differences in data-gathering methods (semidirective questionnaire, point system).

Various clinical data observed in the child's third year are confirmed by this study in which data gathered were processed entirely by mathematicians, especially the value of sleep problems as a risk indicator (Kreisler et al., 1974); the discriminant value of behavior problems (Richman et al., 1975); asthma as a distress signal (Gauthier et al., 1976; Kreisler et al., 1974); and the importance of maternal problems in the development of the child's problems (Chawla and Gupt, 1977; Kreisler et al., 1974; Richman, 1977).

Nearly all contributors have brought to light differences between the sexes (Casadebaid and Chevalier, 1976; Robins, 1980), even though they are often observed somewhat later (starting at ten years). It appears that boys are more "fragile" than girls. This is borne out more emphatically by the fact that our sample of the general population is free of the normal bias introduced by studying a population undergoing consultation (parents' overinvestment in boys is, according to Chawla and Gupt [1977], responsible for their overrepresentation in consultations with specialists).

A number of contributors (Chiland, 1976, 1980; Lebovici and Diatkine, 1980) have pointed out the difficulties of basing a prognosis on early problems of childhood and the precautions that must be taken in terms of their significance for the future. This is confirmed by a small part of our high-risk sample that presents no important pathological signs at age seven, and especially for part of the control group (and the intermediary group) whose condition, on the other hand, has deteriorated. The influence of economic conditions often seems to be overestimated, although, as Chiland (1976, 1980) and Lebovici and Diatkine (1980) have shown, social and cultural factors weigh particularly heavily on school-age children and influence school progress, aggravating the risk of psychopathology.

Our survey was continued up to the end of the first year of compulsory education. In matching case by case on the basis of the father's socioeconomic category and the mother's level of education, we see that social and cultural factors cannot by themselves explain the child's difficulties, not even those difficulties encountered in acquiring reading and writing skills.

All of these results obtained by using mathematical methods therefore confirm the prognostic value of symptoms that have long been described by child psychiatrists. They also lead us to emphasize the significance of the cumulative total of all symptoms, none of which in itself has a pathognomonic value but in combination correspond to a high probability of risk.

We therefore hope that members of the medical and social services working in early prevention will use the concepts reported here to improve the conceptual basis of their activities with children, and possibly also to establish—on the basis of their resources—the extent to which they can intervene (whether to concentrate on high risk or to include moderate risk).

REFERENCES

Casadebaid, F. and Chevalier, A. (1976). Etude comparative entre les caractéristiques familiales et sociales des enfants pris en charge au Centre Alfred-Binet en 1972, 1973, 1974 et celles d'un groupe d'enfants des écoles du XIIIè arrondissment (année scolaire 1972–1973). *Psychiatrie de l'Enfant,* 19:304–324.

Chandon, J. L. and Pinson, S. (1980). *Analyse Typologique—Théories et Application,* First Edition. Paris: Masson.

Chawla, P. L. and Gupt, K. (1977). A comparative study of parents of emotionally disturbed and normal children. *British Journal of Psychiatry,* 134:406–411.

Chiland, C. (1980). De quelques paradoxes concernant le risque et la vulnérabilité. In *The Infant at High Psychiatric Risk,* ed. E. J. Anthony et al. Paris: Presses Universitaires de France.

Chiland, C. (1976). *L'Enfant de Six Ans et Son Avenir,* 3rd Edition. Paris: Presses Universitaires de France.

Diday, E. (1979). Optimisation en classification automatique. Rocquencourt: Institut National de Récherche en Informatique et en Automatique.

Gauthier, Y. et al. (1976). L'asthme chez le très jeune enfant (14–30 mois): Caractéristiques allergiques et psychologiques. *Psychiatrie de l'Enfant,* 19:3–146.

Govaert, G. (1977). Algorithme de classification d'un tableau de contingence. Colloques Institut National de Récherche en Informatique et en Automatique, Rocquencourt (Le Chesnay).

Kreisler, L., Fain, M., and Soule, M. (1974). *L'Enfant et son Corps.* Paris: Presses Universitaires de France.

Lebovici, S. and Diatkine, R. (1980). Le concept de normalité et son utilité dans la definition du risque psychiatrique. In *The Infant at High Psychiatric Risk,* ed. E. J. Anthony et al. Paris: Presses Universitaires de France.

Richman, N. (1977). Behavior problems in preschool children: Family and social factors. *British Journal of Psychiatry,* 131:523–527.

Richman, N. and Graham, P. J. (1971). A behavioral screening questionnaire for use with three-year-old children—Preliminary findings. *Journal of Child Psychology and Psychiatry,* 12:5–33.

Richman, N., Stevenson, J. E., and Graham, P. J. (1975). Prevalence of behavior problems in three-year-old children: An epidemiological study in a London borough. *Journal of Child Psychology and Psychiatry,* 16:277–287.

Robins, L. (1980). Conduites antisociales dans l'enfance: Frequence, pronostic et perspectives. In *The Infant at High Psychiatric Risk,* ed. E. J. Anthony et al. Paris: Presses Universitaires de France.

59

Hospital Treatment for Infants at High Psychiatric Risk

Philippe Mazet, M.D., Françoise Gerstle, M.D., Yannick Buffet, M.D.,
Didier Rabain, M.D., and Didier-Jacques Duche, M.D.

As practitioners of child psychiatry in a large Parisian general hospital, we have sometimes been called upon to intervene in situations where there is an acute incompatibility between mother and child. Confronted with the deep distress of a very young child whose somatic symptoms are life-endangering, faced with the suffering of a mother and her child where the relationship has become very unfavorable to both, or faced with the exhaustion of a mother who rejects her child, the child psychiatrist may be led to introduce an ongoing solution, to open up a space between the protagonists, to opt for a pause in order to protect them from an interaction that has become destructive and sometimes even deadly.

It was thus that we elected, in the framework of the Child and Adolescent Psychiatry Center of La Salpêtrière, to hospitalize a small number (twenty-five) of under-three-year-olds as a result of an initial experiment in 1975, when a tiny eight-month-old girl who was severely anorectic and was "letting herself die," was admitted. The outcome was very beneficial to both the child and her family. This case marked a turning point in our understanding of how to cope with certain aspects of infant psychopathology, and it prompted us to deepen the interest and the specifity of this type of

therapy, which, ever since, has never ceased to give us an opportunity for self-questioning, reflection, and the working out of new procedures and attitudes in respect to severely disturbed infant-mother (parent) interaction. Of course, such hospitalization only occupies a very restricted place among the different sorts of possible therapy for this age group. Interventions within the pediatric or maternity units, ongoing contact with the doctors, nursery nurses, and others in direct contact with the child constitute the greatest part of our care for infants.

Three main types of situation that have called for treatment in our psychiatric unit stand out. The first type is not the most common, but it is the most serious on a short-term basis; it involves infants suffering from severe somatic disorders which can endanger their lives. The life of the child suffering from physical marasmus, severe malnutrition, serious failure to thrive, massive anorexia, or severe merycism is in danger. It is obviously necessary to make an initial therapeutic intervention which takes this dimension into account, as well as to understand the family dynamics and the mother-child interactions implicit in the situation.

The case of *Karim* illustrates the kinds of

problem raised by this sort of situation. This little thirteen-month-old Algerian boy was transferred into our unit after two weeks of reanimation and realimentation in the pediatric center with the following diagnosis: nanism as a result of severe affective lack. The medicosocial team wished to place him in a therapeutic foster family center. His mother seemed to them to be "incompetent and uncaring."

Karim presented a very serious staturoponderal hypotrophy, considerable hypotonia of the corporal axis and of the members, and delay in acquiring functions. He weighed 13.2 pounds and measured 69 cms (27 inches). He was listless and anorectic, his muscles were startlingly flabby, and nothing seemed to interest him. His mother seemed to us to be lost, unarmed, and fleeing both from us and her child. It took a long time to establish contact with her.

Karim was the third child of a disputatious Algerian couple. He was nevertheless very much looked forward to by this mother who had raised her two older boys very correctly, and he was born without any problems. A beautiful baby, he was breast-fed for three and a half months and pleased his mother. Suddenly, on the advice of the *service de Protection Maternelle et Infantile,* he was hospitalized (and weaned) for the treatment of an inguinal hernia.

Then began a series of more and more precipitously repeated hospitalizations which engraved in his mind the image his mother has of him, and which she has of herself as a mother. "I've never been lucky . . . he's never been lucky . . . I've never seen a kid like this," she told us at one point.

After surgery, Karim was transferred to the medical unit where he was treated for three months for the onset of rickets. Although he recovered from rickets, a state of sadness, apathy, and a stagnation of the ponderal curve appeared. He then underwent intensive digestive explorations. Diets, first without gluten and then without milk, were tried. The results were not very conclusive, but, as he began to thrive again, he was returned to his mother, though she was warned, under threat of a new hospitalization, to follow the prescribed diets strictly.

Mrs. B. became quite worried, fearing that her child was very fragile and in constant danger. At the slightest alarm she panicked and even went so far as to have him preventively hospitalized when her other children had the measles for fear that he might catch them. After a month Karim did not come down with measles, but he bore this new separation very badly. He turned in upon himself, grew increasingly sad, and became anorectic and hypotonic. First, he could no longer sit up; then he could not hold his head up. He stopped smiling. A muscular biopsy showed normal results. His parents, despite the warning given them, took Karim for a two-month trip to Algeria. There, he twice became dehydrated through diarrhea, and he suffered from severe nutritional lack. It was in a condition of physical marasmus that he was brought back to the hospital, where he was looked after for two weeks before being transferred to our unit.

In order to heal Karim, it was necessary to take into account both the relational needs and the narcissistic wound of his mother, who, depressive and guilt-ridden, could not find the right way of dealing with her child, but desperately refused the foster-home solution proposed by her pediatrician. Several months of support, of companionship, and of mediation were needed before the two partners could find each other again and could be discharged together, for although Karim, after a long period of remaining immobile, recovered quickly, he nonetheless retained certain symptoms which his mother felt were directed at her: asthmatic-type bronchitis and a severe hypotonia which appeared only when he felt unsatisfied or frustrated and with which he showed his opposition.

In the second type of situation the clinical typology is dominated by a "cry for help" or suffering symptomatology on the baby's part (nonstop crying, sleep disturbances, eating problems, relationship disorders, and the like) which reveal crisis situations in the family or ongoing disturbances in the mother(parent)-child relationship and where the child appears to be at psychological risk.

This was the case for one-year-old Marie-Agnès, hospitalized in the pediatric center at almost the last moment in April 1980, on the recommendation of a doctor and neighbor who took it upon himself to intervene and point out to the parents that their daughter's pitiful crying, which had gone on for several months, had something pathological about it. Once Marie-Agnès was hospitalized, she stopped crying almost immediately, but upon losing her stenic behavior, she became sad, distant, apathetic, altogether more troubling than her previous crying.

We soon received her in our unit, and made contact with her parents, who at thirty years of age seemed to us like two immature and narcissistic adolescents without roots or models, ill prepared and ill at ease in their role as parents, although they also had an older son of five. We very quickly realized that they were incapable of assuming such a role and that they were constantly preoccupied with their own personal difficulties.

Marie-Agnès was a premature baby, and premature birth is a well-known factor for high psychiatric risk. Thirty percent of the children in our unit were premature. Born under such difficult conditions, Marie-Agnès was placed from the very beginning in a considerable state of parental ambivalence, and, in fact, seemed very much left to herself; she always had to initiate an action and lead her parents. Mrs. V's pregnancy had not gone well. She had had to undergo uterine cerclage at six months because her cervix was open. A period of depression combined with persecution complex elements followed, and she rejected the treatment so much that the cerclage had to be removed; and her daughter was born immediately afterward. A very premature baby, Marie-Agnès was put in an incubator and seemed mute, apathetic, and completely passive in feeding, but her parents recall that she began to cry after a blood transfusion which she had before being released from the hospital.

Marie-Agnès is a difficult-to-reach little girl, who refused for a long time any suggestion of active participation, any novelty; she disconcerted the staff of the unit who looked after her and who felt excluded and rejected by her—as had her mother.

Mrs. V. seems caught up in a repetition of her own personal history, for she herself was cut off from birth from her own tubercular mother who "never taught her anything . . . and accused her of having caused her illness" and whom she has begun to rediscover since having her own daughter. Mrs. V. sees herself as a nearly worthless person; she feels as if she bothers and disturbs others. She does not like to impose on anyone, least of all on her own daughter, who terrifies her, makes her ill, and, she claims, persecutes her.

The team's work centered, on the one hand, on Marie-Agnès's communicative difficulties, because despite her refusal to interact and her attempts to revert into herself, she expects a great deal from others, which is a good sign. On the other hand, the team worked with Mrs. V. on the possible persecution complex link between a baby and its mother. Mrs. V.'s verbalization of her difficulties with her own mother led her to gradually resolve this type of tie with Marie-Agnès and enabled her to consider with her husband a specialized short-term foster home "with an older person" for their child.

Finally, the third and last type of situation leading to an infant's hospitalization in our unit concerns preventive hospitalization when a very young child may be in immediate danger from a deeply disturbed mother who has recently given birth. There have been three cases of this type.

Eric was fifteen days old when he came to our unit. He was a superb newborn baby, very alert and healthy, who clearly showed his will to live. He was referred to us via the maternity ward where he was born. Mrs. M., his mother, had been treated for years for long-standing psychotic problems. During her rehospitalization it was discovered that she was in her fifth month of pregnancy. The psychiatric team on the maternity ward, recognizing the impossibility of considering the immediate discharge of this mother and her return home with her baby, proposed a breathing-space in which we could evaluate the competence of Mrs. M. with regard to Eric. It was thus that we received Eric in our small unit. His mother was hospitalized in the adult psychiatric ward in close proximity to ours, for we have no beds for mothers.

Mrs. M. is a thirty-nine-year-old woman who already has four daughters, three born during her marriage to an Asian whom she divorced and one whose father is unknown. Eric is the first boy, and his father is also unknown. Mrs. M. came to our unit every day to breast-feed Eric. She seemed to have a very precarious, almost dreamlike sense of reality. Her contacts, both in her unit and in ours, were fleeting; her extremely banal and superficially rational utterances attempted to hide her psychological and material difficulties in taking care of her baby.

At first Eric appeared to be little loved by his mother. She was never hostile or aggressive toward him, but rather extremely changeable, and she gave the impression that she might easily forget to come to our unit (and forget about him) for an entire day. She breast-fed at odd hours; she cleaned her brassiere before offering him her breast. She did not like to hold the child properly, seeming unable to realize his size and limitations. She did not respond when he looked at her; during the feeding, she did crossword puzzles or played electronic games. Personal hygiene also caused her to behave strangely: she might use the same piece of cotton to clean both the baby's bottom and his mouth or dress him again in soiled clothes. When he cried, she said that it upset her and she would go away.

However, it was striking to see, whenever another person was present, how well she took care of Eric, how she became "a good mother." She was very ambivalent with regard to her desire to take care of him, to support him, and she showed her own need to be mothered by saying how much she disliked being alone and by asking a nurse for a glass of warm milk for herself. Gradually she began to lean more and more on us and to become warmer and more adapted in respect to basic caregiving. She showed her attachment to the baby more clearly, and he was obviously very present in her thoughts. The situation was still precarious, but improving.

As for Eric, he is a very alert and healthy infant and a voracious eater. He is very aware of voices and awaits them. He was quickly able to recognize his mother, and he showed great pleasure when he saw her. He gazes at her intensely when suckled. On the other hand, if a nurse gives him his bottle, he looks away. He sleeps well and began smiling at six weeks; he

rapidly started gurgling happily and found his thumb.

Mrs. M. soon left the psychiatric ward and went home. She continued to come regularly to breast-feed in our unit and asked us to give her her child. We had in fact decided that she was doing fairly well, and we planned to let her have him at home for short periods. But before we could put this plan into action, the situation grew steadily worse. Mrs. M. would wander about Paris for hours in a state of anxiety and began showing impulsive phobias regarding Eric. She was afraid of hurting him, of dropping him, and said he had "a funny forehead." She came to the unit one morning at 6:30 AM drenched, having spent the entire night out in the rain. She wanted to discharge her son, "who is in danger in the hospital . . . they are going to come back . . . they're coming out of the pipes in the bathtub." She hid under Eric's bed to protect him from laser beams because "he has holes in his head." Suffering from an acute crisis of hallucinations and delerium, she had to be hospitalized once again. A foster home was found for Eric under the condition of maintaining the ties between Eric and his mother.

It is now possible for us to separate and analyze certain general points concerning interventions when faced with certain critical or serious situations. It seems to us that the unit's role is a dual one: The hospital provides a neutral meeting place for the child and the parents, a place of rediscovery for a mother and a child who have been cut off from one another, as well as a step in the process of distancing which allows the child to (re)take a more favorable road toward achieving individuation. This means that the unit must be a place of temporary support and companionship, not only for the child but also for the parents whose incapacity is often of much shorter duration and more susceptible to change than may have originally been thought.

Moreover, hospitalization has proven to represent a rest period, an opportunity for tension to subside, for reflection and for planning the future. Fourteen of our children were able to return home; eleven of them were placed in a specialized foster home, maintaining ties with the real parents so that the child might be able to rejoin them. The hospital serves to restore to the parents their parental roles on several levels; the concreteness of ordinary "mothering" skills, the conscious imaginary plane, and the fantasmic unconscious level of their relationship with the child. In this respect, it is interesting to note that in a certain number of cases, especially those where the child was suffering from severe psychosomatic problems, the failure of the mothering function, dealing with mothering skills taken altogether, seemed to be related to a dramatic incapacity on the (frequently depressed) mother's part to conceptualize her baby, to think about it in its absence; whereas, in other cases, particularly the development of very early psychosis, mothering inadequacies (indeed, quite serious but highly focused ones) seemed to be situated at the level of communicating with the child and of being in contact with the presence of an overwhelming, invading fantastic and imaginary child. In all these cases we have been able to see that a real change in the mother's (and in the father's) relationship with the child seemed to require the prior restoration of their narcissism.

This leads us to raise the second point: the role that the institution seems to have had for certain children, that is, its "grandparent" role vis-à-vis the child. This is because it functions as a tolerant, reassuring guide (by its ability to wait, to put up with aggressivity, parental failures, and so forth) and a companions hip-filled place for the parents. It never seemed to us that the parents felt competitive with us nor did they seem to view our team as all-powerful "good-parents" and themselves as "bad ones".

Of course this presupposes a carefully prepared hospitalization, carried out under the best conditions for the child and for the parents. The conditions, which are at the same time medical (we have already seen the serious and difficult somatic problems that sometimes appear) and relational, are, it must be said, difficult to achieve. They demand from the educative and nursing team[1] much delicate and difficult work which can only be carried out by someone who is very interested in and aware of the relational dimension of the work. Such a person must be always available, capable of real and accurate observation, and able to be self-questioning about his or her relations with the child and other members of the team, as far as concerns the organization and internal functioning of the unit. We know, in fact, all the dangers of relational lack inside institutions for young children (during a hospitalization, in day-care centers, and the like).

Truly, many difficulties are encountered in trying to create valid institutional therapeutic surroundings for young children and families with serious problems. It seems to us that when occasionally we manage to overcome these difficulties, we find a very useful and interesting form of therapeutic intervention.

[1]We take this opportunity to thank Mrs. Ch. Droniou and Ch. L'Heur, nurses, Mrs. M. Therond, educator, Mrs. M. Th. Ravier, social worker, and the whole team.

NAME INDEX

SUBJECT INDEX